Contents

CRAFT WISDOM & KNOW-HOW

Beadwork

BEAD AND WIRE BASICS

Nathalie Mornu & Suzanne J. E. Tourtillot

For an artist, it's no stretch to conceive of wire as a linear element, and beads as dots or points. The beauty of the projects in this book is that each transforms these simple building blocks into chic pieces to wear as ornament.

This chapter contains all the information you need to enter a world of creative expression making bead and wire jewelry.

Shopping for the materials to create the projects in this book is a little like taking a trip around the globe: you'll find African trade beads, lampworked glass crafted in India, cloisonné treasures made in China, shimmering Austrian crystal, and wire from, well, all over.

Beads

If you've never worked in this medium before, you're in for some pleasant hours of bead browsing—the hardest part is stopping! You'll find a fabulous range of beads in glass, semiprecious stone, ceramic, and polymer clay; you can buy lampworked one-of-a-kinds, silver- and rhinestone-studded spheres, and cloudy moonstone orbs. Sift through bins of carved wooden beads; pick up some bits of dichroic or tumbled glass. Build a collection and store it in stacks of beaders' boxes with little compartments.

Most beads are organized in the stores by their material, shape, and diameter. (Tiny seed beads are sized using a special scale, in which the smallest ones have the highest numbers.) Be prepared to verify that your wire fits through your beads' holes: some very large beads can have surprisingly small holes, and vice versa. Unfortunately, there's no standard relationship between the size of a bead's hole and its diameter.

If you can't find beads to replicate the projects in this book, by all means purchase different styles; bear in mind that in doing so, you may achieve a completely different look, and you'll need to make certain that your selections match the bead sizes specified in the instructions.

You can keep your beads organized by storing them in small boxes with clear lids.

Wire

Traditionally, wire made from sterling silver or gold has been a popular choice for bead and wire jewelry, but many other wire products may be used, too. Metal craft wire is now available in a wide variety of colors; relative newcomers include anodized and dyed metals such as aluminum, or niobium, which you can use alone or combined in the same piece of jewelry. Still other kinds of wire include brass, nickel, copper, and even platinum. Unlike these more malleable metals, super-springy *memory wire*, made from base metal or sometimes stainless steel, can be stretched and permanently bent, but it will always retain its initial coiled silhouette.

Whatever the metal, most wire comes in a large range of sizes and shapes, or *profiles*. Gauge is a scale of measurement that indicates a wire's diameter: the higher the numeral, the finer the wire. (Memory wire is the exception; it's sold in sizes to fit the neck, wrist, or finger.)…

The projects in this book suggest that you use a specific size of wire, generally from 14 to 26 gauge. Using gauges other than those specified in the instructions is fine, but keep in mind that very thin wire, though easier to shape, isn't strong enough for a lot of heavy beads, and very thick wire isn't suitable for small-scale designs—not to mention the limitation of the size of a bead's hole. Wires of the same gauge will all feel a bit different to manipulate, because some metals are softer than others. However, wire stiffens a bit as you work with it, adding more support to your work. This process is called *work hardening*; if wire gets handled too much, it becomes brittle and breaks.

Continued →

Silver and gold wires are made and sold in different hardnesses: *dead soft*, *soft*, and *half hard*. In most cases, our designers have recommended the appropriate silver or gold wire hardness for their projects; when in doubt, use half-hard wire. Avoid dead-soft wire; it's difficult to work with and won't retain shaping or angles.

Many of the projects use sterling silver wire, but wire made from an *alloy* (a blend of less expensive metals) is an acceptable substitute, especially for jewelry for everyday wear or for working an unfamiliar design or technique. It's a great idea to use practice wire (of a similar gauge and hardness) if you plan to make a piece of jewelry from very expensive wire. Any inexpensive alloy wire will do.

Depending on the metal, wire is sold many different ways: on spools, in prepackaged coils, by weight, and by length. Look for various types in jewelry supply shops, craft retailers, and in certain areas of hardware stores (including the electrical supply and framing departments). The Internet is also a vast resource for wire of every kind.

In addition to the plain round variety, wire is made with different cross-section profiles, such as square, half round, and triangular. Some wire companies sell lengths of pretwisted single-strand wire, or you can make your own with the pin vise tool, as explained later on. Twisted wire is also created when two lengths of nonround wire are twisted together for a beaded or rippled effect…It's possible to alternate links of round, flat, and twisted wire with stunning results.

Clasps, Pins, and Such

Findings are prefabricated, basic jewelry pieces; they are made from many of the same kinds of metals that are available in unformed wire, and there are popular silver and gold options, too. Necklaces may not need them, but bracelets almost always require clasps. To make an earring design wearable, use ear wires or posts; brooches sometimes need *pin backings*. Beads are often linked with *head pins* or *eye pins*. The head pin is simply a short, straight piece of wire with one flattened end to stop the bead, whereas an eye pin has an open loop at one end of the wire section. For either type, you form another loop at the other end after a bead has been strung onto it. Choose extra-long pins if you plan to add more than one bead.

It's easy to trim off excess wire, but there's nothing to be done when there's not enough. Just like wire, head pins and eye pins are available in different gauges. Be sure they'll fit through the beads' holes.

You can use commercial clasps or closures on any of the projects in this book, but in some cases our designers give you instructions on how to fashion them yourself, such as in the Sassy Pin. Making your own closures gives a piece of jewelry a more integrated look. Findings often become important elements to the overall design, so you'll want to take care that even purchased ones are made of materials of a quality and style that complement it.

Jump rings are another popular finding. These simple rings, usually made from plain silver or gold, or from base metal, are great for connecting links. They can be found in a variety of sizes (by diameter and by wire gauge), or you can make your own (see the Handmade Jump Rings sidebar).

For the bead-and-wire jeweler, a commercially made chain can be a foundation to which beads are attached with head pins, or else with jump rings. You can buy various styles of chain—from very delicate to quite chunky—prepackaged. Some beading shops stock commercial chain on large spools and will cut it to the length you specify. In any case, for certain projects you might need to be able to open the chain's links. If the links have been soldered closed, you'll have to use jump rings or bead loops to attach anything to them.

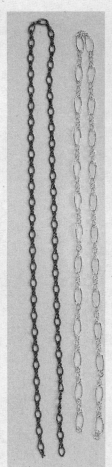

Machine-made chain and jump rings are sometimes used as important design elements in their own right.

BEADWISE

Wondering where to start when you look for beads? You could fill an entire dictionary with the evocative names of just the bead shapes that are available: rondelle, briolette, facet, montée, baroque drop, teardrop. What a whirlwind of choices!

Then there are the names that indicate a bead's function. A focal bead is one that stands out from all the rest, either due to its size or some other exceptional feature. Some have a strong, graphic quality; others use a carved or figurative motif. Spacers are generally smaller, plainer elements that are used to set off more exciting beads, but they too can be pretty interesting. Intricate little Bali beads typically come from the Indonesian island and are made from semioxidized silver; plainer-style heishi beads, originally made from seashells, are now available in stone and metals. Tube and bugle beads are long, slender cylinders, sometimes made of twisted metal. Finally, metal bead caps (and cones), placed at the ends of a round bead, can set it off and make it delightfully different.

Focal beads

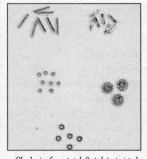

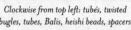

Clockwise from top left: tubes, twisted bugles, tubes, Balis, heishi beads, spacers

Bead caps

The Basic Tool Kit

In your tool kit you should have certain items that are indispensable for creating the jewelry in this book: wire cutters, needle files, pliers, crosslocking tweezers, protective eyewear, a pin vise or clamp, a permanent marker, and a ruler with both U.S. and metric measurements. Jewelry wipes, which are soft papers impregnated with polish, keep your work bright and clean. Each project's instructions presume that you have this basic tool kit, so only specialized tools needed to make a project are listed.

Wire Cutters

A good pair of wire cutters is essential for making all of the jewelry in this book. There are several different styles, but whichever ones you use, make sure they cut absolutely flush, since the shape of the cut's end, or *burr*, will need to be filed. The smaller the burr, the less filing will be needed. Since you will often need to cut wire in very small spaces, bigger is definitely not better. Pointed tips give you the most control.

Needle Files

Use a metal file with a fine tooth to smooth out the rough edges of cut wire ends and any other marring that may occur during the forming stages. Unfiled ends scratch and catch on fabric, so resist the temptation to ignore this crucial step. (And remember, too, that good wire cutters help ensure that you won't have to do a lot of filing.) Follow these rules: softer wire need be filed only with the finest of your files; start with a slightly coarser file for harder wire.

Pliers

Pliers are a bead and wire jewelry maker's best friend. Round-nose, chain-nose, and flat-nose pliers are the most-used types, although other, more specialized pliers can be found. To prevent damage to your wire as you work, select a type with smooth jaws rather than serrated ones. Inexpensive pliers are fine for beginners. If wire jewelry ever becomes your life's passion, you can easily trade up to a better brand.

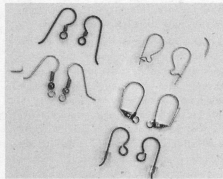
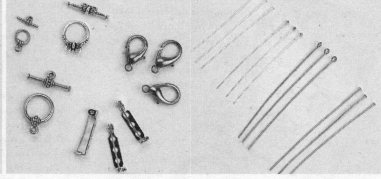

From far left, ear wires, toggles, clasps, pin backings, ball-end pins, eye pins, head pins

Round-nose pliers are essential for making loops. Because the jaws are wide at the base and tapered at the tip, you can vary the size of your loops depending on where along the jaw you place the wire to start.

Chain-nose pliers get this name because they're ideal for opening and closing chain links. They're also useful for opening and closing loops and jump rings, working in tight spots, and, if you don't have special crimping pliers (read more about them in the Additional Tools section), for crimping the ends of wire wraps. Chain-nose pliers are sometimes confused with needle-nose pliers, the electrician's tool that has serrated teeth in its jaws (though these can be used to add texture to wire). Flat-nose pliers resemble chain-nose pliers, but their jaws, instead of tapering, remain wide all the way to the tips. They're perfect for making sharp bends and for holding wire. Here's a tip: when working with colored wire, always wrap your pliers' tips with plastic tape to prevent marring the colored finish. For extra-gentle wire handling, you can sometimes find pliers with plastic-coated jaws.

The basic tool kit contains (from top): wire cutters, a set of needle files, a permanent marker, crosslocking tweezers, protective eyewear, jewelry wipes, and a ruler.

A basic array of wire-working pliers includes (from top): chain nose, round nose, and flat nose.

Pin Vise

This simple tool allows you to create lengths of twisted wire in just minutes. You can work with a pair of pin vises, or use just one pin vise and some sort of clamp (or use pliers instead, if you have only a short quantity of wire to twist)....

This fancy pin vise uses interchangeable tips, to hold wires of different sizes.

Tool Kit Additions

These tools, while not essential for every jewelry project, will be needed for some. Check the projects' tool lists before you begin.

Jig

A wire jig is a lifesaver when you're making a piece that uses multiple links made in the same shape, although lots of wire jewelry can be made without ever using one. Essentially, the tool is a base with a grid of holes that hold tiny, moveable pegs, around which you wrap the wire. The result: near-perfect consistency for each link.

Jigs are also a good design tool; just play around with some inexpensive wire and different peg placements to create your own wire patterns. Your local jewelry shop probably has books that contain a nice variety of jig patterns. You can purchase commercial jigs in craft stores or make your own with a block of wood and some finishing nails.

Mandrel

A mandrel is any straight or tapered rod around which you can wrap wire to shape it into coils. It's an essential tool for making jump rings, the loops in closures, or uniformly sized units for links. Metal knitting needles make ideal mandrels, but you can use a nail, a dowel, one of the metal rods of various diameters sold in hobby shops, or even a pen. Mandrels don't have to be round. For jewelry with a completely different look, try using a square, oval, or rectangular mandrel. For certain applications—for instance, when making long coils for jump rings—you might even try a coiling tool, but it isn't necessary for any of the projects in this book.

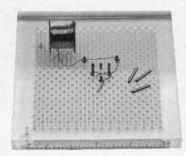

A wire jig

Hammers and Anvil

A few of the projects were hammered, or forged, to change the shape of the wire a bit. You can employ a common carpentry hammer and work on a smooth, very hard surface, such as a steel block or an anvil. To shape or flatten wire without marring it or changing the wire's profile in any way, use a rawhide or plastic hammer.

Crimping Pliers

A few projects use crimping beads, which are tiny tube-like beads made of metal soft enough to allow them to be compressed against wire or cord with a pair of crimping pliers.

Eggbeater Drill

This tool will enable you to rapidly coil long quantities of wire around a small mandrel and is particularly helpful for making a lot of jump rings. See the Handmade Jump Rings sidebar to learn about using an eggbeater drill.

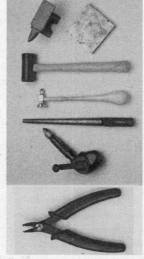

More specialty tools (from top left): steel block, anvil, rawhide and chasing hammers, eggbeater drill, and crimping pliers D

Wire Techniques

Now for the fun: learning how to wrangle the wire into a great jewelry design using basic wire techniques. Unless you're already familiar with them, you'll probably want to practice these techniques with a low-cost wire first—it's not easy to straighten wire once it's bent the wrong way. You might want to use the fun colored-wire products to make your learning curve more enjoyable. The results might be good enough to use for a later project.

Sometimes it may seem as if your wire has a mind of its own. To keep spooled wire under control, put it in a small plastic storage bag. Pull out a length of wire as needed. If you're working with a coil of wire rather than a spool, wrap a piece of masking tape around it so it can't spring open in all directions. Good-looking jewelry pieces are those with smooth and confident swoops, angles, and curves, made from kink-free wire.

Straightening

To keep it in good condition, wire is stored and sold in coils. Coiling wire saves space, but it's best to straighten out its curve before you begin working with it. To straighten a short length of wire, hold one end of it with chain-nose pliers. Just above the pliers, grasp the wire with a cloth or paper towel to keep your hands clean and to prevent friction burn. Squeezing your fingers slightly, pull the length of wire through them.

If the wire bends or crimps at any time, gently run your finger along it to smooth the kink, or rub the wire over the edge of a table padded with newspaper. Don't smooth a crimp too vigorously, or the wire could break. (Shaping wire, remember, hardens it. The more it's worked, the more brittle it becomes.)

Wrapping

No matter what you're wrapping the wire around, always pull it tightly against the pliers, mandrel, bead, or wire. When you're making jump rings, keep each pass of the wire as even and as close to the last one as possible.

Using Jump Rings

Always open and close jump rings by holding each end with pliers and twisting one ring's end toward you and the other end away, as shown in figure 1; pulling the ends straight apart, laterally, will distort the ring's shape and can undermine the strength of the wire and cause it to break.

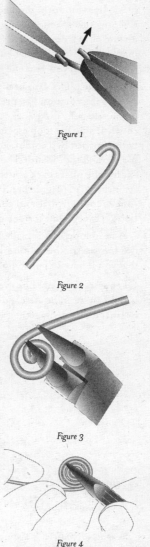

Figure 1

Figure 2

Spirals

To create flat spirals, use the tip of a pair of round-nose pliers to curve one end of the wire into a half circle or hook shape about 1/8 inch (0.3 cm) in diameter (see figure 2). Use the very tips of the pliers to curve the end of the wire tightly into itself, as shown in figure 3, aiming to keep the shape round rather than oval. Hold the spiral in flat- or chain-nose pliers and push the loose end of the wire against the already-coiled form (see figure 4); as you continue, reposition the wire in the pliers as needed.

Figure 3

Figure 4

Links and Loops

A link is simply one unit in a piece of jewelry. A link can be formed either by hand or with a jig. It can be an elaborate wire shape full of curls and curlicues or be based on a simple form, such as an S shape or a figure eight.

A loop is an important part of a link. The perfect loop should be precisely circular, centered over the straight part of the wire from which it's formed, and it should close tightly. Perfect your technique by making loops from different gauges of scrap wire.

Start with 6 inches (15.2 cm) of wire and work with a pair of round-nose pliers. Make a sharp 90-degree bend about 1/2 inch (1.3 cm) from one end of the wire, as shown in figure 5. This measurement will vary, depending on how large a loop you want to make; with practice, you'll get to know how much wire to allow for it.

Continued →

Hold the wire so that the longer portion points to the floor and the short, bent end is pointing at you. Grasp the short end with the round-nose pliers, holding the pliers so that the back of your hand faces you. The closer to the tips you work, the smaller the loops you can make. Keeping the tips themselves stationary, rotate the pliers up and away from you (see figure 6). Be careful not to pull out the right-angle bend you made earlier. Stop rotating when you've made half the loop.

Slide the pliers' tips back along the wire a bit and resume the rotation. To prevent the loop from becoming misshapen, make sure to keep one of the pliers' tips snugly inside the loop as you make it, so that the loop is being formed by a combination of rotation and shaping around the "mandrel" of the pliers. Keep working, sliding the pliers back as needed, until the loop is closed against the 90-degree bend (see figure 7). To make all your loops look nice and consistent, see the Same-Sized Loops (Every Time!) sidebar.

A bead loop link is made by enclosing a bead between two loops. Another option is to start with an eye pin, so that you'll have to fashion only one closing loop.

Of course, there are hundreds of variations of these basic links. Links can be attached to each other with jump rings or linked directly together as you make them.

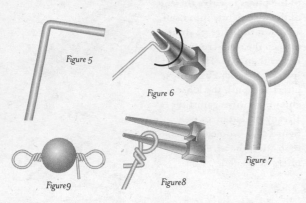

Figure 5

Figure 6

Figure 7

Figure 9

Figure 8

A *wrapped bead loop* is a simple variation of the bead loop link just described. Use an extra length of wire for the 90-degree bend. Once you've made the loop, reposition the pliers so that the lower jaw is inside it. Use your other hand to wrap the wire's tail around the base of the loop several times, as shown in figure 8. Slide on one or more beads and, if the design calls for it, repeat the loop-forming process at the other end to make a *wrapped bead loop* link (see figure 9). Trim off any excess wire.

Opening and Closing Loops

Just as with jump rings, use two pair of pliers to open and close loops. Twist the cut end sideways while keeping the other side of the loop stationary. Pulling it open any other way will distort the loop's shape. Be sure to tighten any gaps in loops after you've attached your links.

Twisting

Only square wire can be twisted. Round wire won't show the twisting properly, and the process will just work-harden it.

To create twisted wire in no time at all, work with a pair of pin vises. Insert each end of a piece of wire into a pin vise, tighten the chucks, and twist them in opposite directions until you like the look you've achieved. If you have only one pin vise, secure the other end of the wire in a clamp or table vise (or in a pair of pliers if you have just a short quantity to twist). You can also use this tool to twist two lengths of the same wire together, creating a heavier look, or to twist together two different colors of wire.

Jig-Formed Links

A jig tool helps you make the same wire shape (usually a link) consistently, over and over. To keep your links identical, always follow the same circuit on the jig and try to work in the same manner each time. Using flat-nose pliers, hold a piece of wire tightly at one end, or place its tail in an empty hole in the jig that's near the first peg (or nail). Wrap the wire tightly around the pegs, following the pattern indicated in the instructions. Once you've made one unit, remove it from the jig and repeat to make all the units that you need. It's that easy.

Polishing

You can polish your jewelry with a jewelry buffing cloth (sometimes called a *rouge cloth*) or papers, which are available from most jewelry suppliers. Before using any cleaning solution, test it on a scrap piece of wire first. A tumbler is an option for some pieces, but make sure you're familiar with its operation and consider that many beads aren't suitable for the process.

Needle Arts

Crocheting and knitting with wire aren't all that different from the yarn variety—and you needn't worry about your project shrinking in the wash later. Because wire is thinner and more slippery than yarn, the techniques may feel a little awkward at first. Even if you already have experience, you'll find that when using wire, you'll need to use a light hand in establishing the tension (i.e., how tightly or loosely the material is woven together), because this material has no elasticity whatsoever.

Creating a slipknot requires a different approach than with yarn, since wire doesn't actually slip. Instead of pulling on one end to tighten it, tug on both. The wire loop should still be able to move easily up and down the needle or hook. As you work, resist the temptation to wrap the wire around your finger, as is typical when working with yarn, because it will create even more kinks and crimps. And although you can smooth the kinks somewhat, don't worry too much about them, because for the most part they won't be noticeable in the finished piece.

Often, all the beads in a project are threaded onto the wire before you cast on, and then each one slipped into place as needed (usually after each stitch). As you cast on, be prepared to leave a tail long enough to finish the piece and hold the clasp.

Colored craft wire is popular for knitting and crocheting. If you'd like to try working with silver wire, consider using gold or fine silver wire, which is softer and lighter (though more expensive) than sterling.

Knitting

The projects in this book use only the knit or purl stitches, and they employ the standard knitting abbreviations you're used to seeing for yarn projects. Pull your knitting down and away from the needle as you go, flattening it slightly with your fingers, so as to make it easier to work the next row. Knitting needles come in different diameters and materials. Aluminum needles are more practical than wood or bamboo, simply because the wire will slip better on them, but what's most important is to use the size listed in the instructions in order to reproduce the project closely. Short, double-pointed needles are sometimes recommended for smaller-size pieces.

Crocheting

Crochet hooks also come in different sizes and may be aluminum, wood, or plastic; you can use a hook made from any material you like. Hook size affects how tightly or loosely the woven the fabric appears between stitches, so if you want to duplicate the project, make sure to use the size specified in the instructions.

The only two crochet stitches used to create the projects in this book are the simplest ones—chain stitch and single crochet. Crocheted chain has a tendency to twist, so be prepared to do some smoothing as you work. Hold the loop you're working on with the thumb and finger of your nondominant hand so you can control its size and shape.

Time for lots of beady, loopy fun! You have a basic tool kit, some wire, and an exciting array of handpicked beads; you've practiced the techniques and know a wrapped loop from a bead link. You're ready for the rewarding handicraft of making bead and wire jewelry...

The tools you can use to weave beads strung on fine wire are (from left) a crochet hook, double-pointed aluminum knitting needles, or bamboo knitting needles.

—From *Contemporary Bead-Wire Jewelry*

Key to Wire Gauges

Nathalie Mornu & Suzanne J. E. Tourtillott

The projects in this book were made using wire manufactured in the United States, whose standards for wire diameters differ from those in the British system. AWG is the acronym for American, or Brown & Sharpe, wire gauge sizes and their equivalent rounded metric measurements. SWG is the acronym for the British Standard, or Imperial, system in the UK. Refer to the chart below if you use SWG wire. Only part of the full range of wire gauges that are available from jewelry suppliers is included here.

AWG in.	AWG mm	Gauge	SWG in.	SWG mm
0.204	5.18	4	0.232	5.89
0.182	4.62	5	0.212	5.38
0.162	4.12	6	0.192	4.88
0.144	3.66	7	0.176	4.47
0.129	3.28	8	0.160	4.06
0.114	2.90	9	0.144	3.66
0.102	2.59	10	0.128	3.25
0.091	2.31	11	0.116	2.95
0.081	2.06	12	0.104	2.64
0.072	1.83	13	0.092	2.34
0.064	1.63	14	0.080	2.03
0.057	1.45	15	0.072	1.83
0.051	1.30	16	0.064	1.63
0.045	1.14	17	0.056	1.42
0.040	1.02	18	0.048	1.22
0.036	0.914	19	0.040	1.02
0.032	0.813	20	0.036	0.914
0.029	0.737	21	0.032	0.813
0.025	0.635	22	0.028	0.711
0.023	0.584	23	0.024	0.610
0.020	0.508	24	0.022	0.559
0.018	0.457	25	0.020	0.508
0.016	0.406	26	0.018	0.457

—From *Contemporary Bead & Wire Products*

Tools

Chasing hammer

Steel bench block

Dowel, ½ inch (1.3 cm) diameter

Finished Length

8¼ inches (21 cm)

Instructions

1. Cut the 16-gauge silver wire into six pieces, each 2½ inches (6.4 cm) long; set aside the 2-inch (5 cm) piece that's left. File the ends smooth. Using the chasing hammer and working on a steel bench block, flatten the last ⅛ inch (3 mm) of the wire ends slightly.

2. With round-nose pliers, form side loops, facing in opposite directions, on the wire ends (see figure 1). Form each piece of wire into an S to create a link (see figure 2).

3. To give the links some variety, gently hammer the outermost parts of the loops on the bench block. If the hammering distorts their shapes, reshape them with round-nose pliers. Set the links aside.

4. Using the dowel and the 18-gauge brass wire, make 15 jump rings. Hammer them slightly, but if their ends spread apart a bit as a result, reshape them as needed.

5. To assemble the bracelet, connect the links with two jump rings between each. Add a single jump ring to one of the outer links to serve as part of the closing clasp. Set aside the remaining two jump rings.

6. Create the hook for closing the bracelet with the leftover piece of 16-gauge wire from step 1. File both ends smooth. Gently hammer the last ⅛ inch (0.3 cm) of the ends flat. Using round-nose pliers, create a small side loop on one end. Shape this side of the wire into a hook, then flatten all but the loops. On the other end of the wire, create a large side loop, bending it perpendicular to the hook. Use two jump rings to attach this loop to the last link.

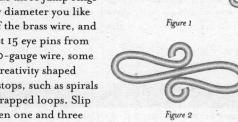

Figure 1

Figure 2

7. Make three jump rings of any diameter you like out of the brass wire, and at least 15 eye pins from the 20-gauge wire, some with creativity shaped bead stops, such as spirals and wrapped loops. Slip between one and three beads on each of these, as well as on the purchased head pins. Trim and file the eye and head pins as needed. Attach beads to all of the links and the jump rings between them.

Sassy Pin

Connie Fox, Designer

Make this eye-catching piece with beads that complement a favorite jacket, a knitted muffler, or anything that's big and bold enough to stand up to such sassiness.

Materials

2 small beads* (the project uses a striped glass bead and a square hematite one)

1 resin focal bead,* 1½ inches (3.8 cm) long

1 plastic disk bead,* ¾ inch (1.9 cm) diameter

1 dotted resin bead,* ¾ inch (1.9 cm) diameter

18-gauge dead-soft sterling silver wire, 20 inches (50.8 cm) long, for the coiled element

14-gauge dead-soft sterling silver wire, 8 inches (20.3 cm) long, for wrapping around the focal bead

16-gauge half-hard or dead-soft sterling silver wire, 15 inches (38.1 cm) long, for the body of the brooch

*The hole must be large enough to accommodate 16-gauge wire.

Finished Length

3¾ inches (9.5 cm)

Instructions

1. To make the coiled element, place the 18-gauge wire across the 14-gauge wire. Coil the lighter gauge wire around the heavier one. Remove the 14-gauge wire. To form a loop that will allow you to attach the coiled component to the brooch later, use pliers to flip the last round on one end of the coil away from the rest of them. Do the same on the other end.

2. Mark the midpoint of the 14-gauge wire with a permanent marker. Use small round-nose pliers to make a spiral that ends at the midpoint mark. Repeat the same process with the other end of the wire, making a spiral oriented in the opposite direction from the first one.

3. With the tips of the pliers, push out the central section of both spirals (see figure 1). Hold the component by its midsection, in the tips of chain-nose pliers. With your thumb and index finger, pinch the bases of the coned spirals together (see figure 2).

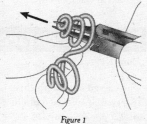

Figure 1

4. Use flat-nose pliers to stretch out the spiral to the length of the focal bead. Open the spiral slightly in the middle, insert the focal bead in one end, and stretch the wire over the other end of the bead (see figure 3). Twist the wire so that it fits snugly around the bead, then use flat-nose pliers to adjust the coil's spacing so that the rounds look even.

Figure 2

5. To form the spiral clasp, grasp the 16-gauge wire with flat-nose pliers, 1½ inches (3.8 cm) from one end, and make a right-

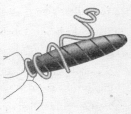

Figure 3

Continued ➡

angle bend. Grasp the long wire at the right-angle bend. Grasp the long wire at the joint with round-nose pliers, holding them parallel to the bent wire (see figure 4). Start the spiral by using your thumb to push the long wire away from you, partway around

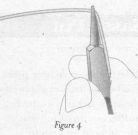

Figure 4

one of the pliers' tips. Reorient the pliers as necessary to make a spiral with five revolutions, with the short tail of wire sticking out from the center of it. Grasp the long wire with flat-nose pliers where the spiral straightens out and make a right angle. Later you'll place the beads along this wire.

6. To make a hook to hold the pin stem, hold the center of the spiral with flat-nose pliers, with the long wire extending to the right, and bend the short tail up so that it almost rests against the spiral. Now grasp the short wire with round-nose pliers, close to the bend you just made; shape the wire back over the pliers into a hook. Cut the tail so that it extends ¼ inch (6 mm) below the spiral. Using small round-nose pliers, make a small loop in the end of it. Ideally, when you look at the front of the spiral, the clasp should not show at all.

7. Place the beads on the long wire, starting with the striped one; slide it close to the right angle to serve as a stop. Next, slide on a loop end of the coiled element you made in step 1. Add the caged focal bead, the other end of the coil, the hematite cube, the plastic disk, and finally the dotted bead. To withstand the rigors of opening and closing the brooch, this last bead should be a sturdy one.

8. Form the spring by holding the brooch so the front of the spiral faces you, with the opening of the clasp pointing up. With long round-nose pliers, grasp the wire 1 to 1½ inches (2.5 to 3.8 cm) away from the dotted bead. Make one and three-quarters revolutions perpendicular to the spiral, meanwhile making sure the end of the wire rotates under the spring.

9. To make the pin stem, put the working wire into the clasp. Cut the end of the wire so that it's just slightly longer than the clasp. File it to a point sharp enough to penetrate loosely woven clothing, but not so sharp that the tip can be bent.

Lucky Necklace

Mami Laher, Designer

The carved charm on this spectacular necklace might attract good fortune. Though the bead links look ornate, they consist of just a few simple elements.

MATERIALS

25 assorted honey-colored glass beads, 5 mm

4 dichroic glass cube beads, 9 mm

12 faceted beads, 1 cm

4 rondelles, 1 cm

2 flat stone beads, 1 inch (2.5 cm) diameter

1 round carved charm, 1¾ inches (4.4 cm) diameter

20-gauge gold-filled square wire, 49 inches (1.2 m) long, for the caged bead links

22-gauge gold-filled square wire, 48 inches (1.2 m) long, for the caged bead links

18-gauge gold-filled wire, 27 inches (68.6 cm) long, for making bead loop links

16-gauge gold-filled wire, 4¼ inches (10.8 cm) long, for the clasp and a connection element

28 jump rings, 18-gauge gold filled, 5 mm diameter

2 jump rings, 18-gauge gold filled, 9 mm diameter

1 jump ring, 18-gauge gold filled, 3 mm diameter

TOOLS

Tabletop vise

Hammer and block

FINISHED LENGTH

27 inches (68.6 cm)

INSTRUCTIONS

1. Cut and twist four pieces of 20-gauge square wire, each 8 inches (20.3 cm) long.

2. Cut two pieces of twisted wire, each 3½ inches (8.9 cm) long. Cut one piece of untwisted 20-gauge square wire 4¼ inches (10.8 cm) long. Slip two 5 mm beads on each twisted wire and one glass cube on the untwisted wire and place them side by side, as shown in figure 1, shaking the wires into bundles at the ends.

3. Cut two pieces of 22-gauge square wire, each 6 inches (15.2 cm) long. Clamp the end of one in the vise and wrap the other end four times around one of the bundled wire ends; repeat for the other end. Make spirals out of all six wire ends. Repeat the process to make a total of four caged-bead links.

4. Using the 18-gauge wire, make bead loop links out of each faceted bead, rondelle, stone bead, and the remaining 5-mm beads.

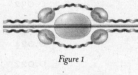

Figure 1

5. To make the clasp, use a piece of 16-gauge wire 2¼ inches (5.7 cm) long. Shape it as shown in figure 2, then forge the large outside curves. Adjust the clasp's form if the hammer's blows distort it.

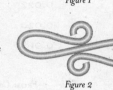

Figure 2

6. To assemble one side of the chain, attach the links with 5 mm jump rings. For the caged bead links, pass the jump ring through the spiral of the center wire. The parts are assembled with faceted beads alternating a caged bead, a stone, a caged bead, and ending with two rondelles and two 5 mm beads. On the end with a 5 mm bead, attach the clasp with a jump ring.

7. Make a second chain, as described in the previous step, but on the end with the 5 mm bead, use a 5 mm jump ring to attach a 9 mm jump ring.

8. An extra length of chain will be added to the 9 mm jump ring. To make it, link together the five remaining bead loops by their loops. Use the 3 mm jump ring to hang one of the chain to the 5 mm jump ring.

9. Cut a piece of 16-gauge wire 2 inches (5.1 cm) long and shape it to look like figure 3. Use the remaining 9 mm jump ring to hang the charm from the central loop of this element. Attach a chain through the center of each spiral with a 5 mm jump ring.

Beaded tendrils dangle from a larger bead that's framed by an unusual herringbone weave. The result is an airy design—daringly long yet light as a feather.

MATERIALS

2 deep-red faceted flat pears,* ½ inch (1.3 cm) diameter

2 deep-red faceted rondelles, 9 mm diameter

4 deep-red flat pears,* ⅜ inch (9.5 mm) diameter

8 deep-red round beads, 5 mm diameter

2 deep-red faceted rondelles, 10 mm diameter

26-gauge sterling dead-soft silver wire, 6 feet (1.8 m) long

24-gauge sterling dead-soft silver wire, 8 inches (20.3 cm) long

2 sterling silver lever-back ear wires

*Flat pears are sometimes called briolettes.

INSTRUCTIONS

1. Make the central dangles. Cut two pieces of 26-gauge wire 3 inches (7.6 cm) long each. Slip a ½-inch (1.3 cm) flat pear on each of them and use a 1-inch (2.5 cm) tail to make wrapped bead loops, trimming the tails' excess.

2. With the remaining wire and round-nose pliers, form small wrapped loops as close as possible to the ones you just made. Wind the wire on top of the previous wrapping; this gives the fine wire a more substantial appearance. Trim the wires closely.

3. Cut two pieces of 26-gauge wire 3 inches (7.6 cm) long. Make two wrapped loop bead links with a 9-mm rondelle on each, catching a ½-inch (1.3 cm) flat pear dangle at one end of each of the links. Trim off any extra wire.

4. Make the four side dangles, as you did in steps 1 and 2, using ⅜-inch (9.5 mm) flat pears instead.

5. Fabricate four smaller dangles from 4-inch (10.2 cm) lengths of 26-gauge wire. Make four wrapped bead loop links with two 5 mm beads each, catching a dangle from step 4 in one end of each. Trim away any extra wire.

6. Cut a piece of 24-gauge wire 4 inches (10.2 cm) long. Make a wrapped loop near one end of it, wrapping as many times as it takes to create a shank ¼ inch (6 mm) long. (Counting the number of times you wrap will help you replicate the shank on the opposite side of the bead.)

Figure 3

7. Slip a 10 mm rondelle onto the working end of the wire and make another ¼-inch (6 mm) shank with a wrapped loop on the other end of the wire, attaching the dangle you made in step 1 into the loop before you wrap it closed (see figure 1). Trim the ends of the wires with a flush cutter.

8. To craft a herringbone weave around the 10 mm rondelle, cut a piece of 26-gauge wire 2½ feet (76.2 cm) long. Secure the wire by wrapping it twice around one of the shanks, near the bead. Trim the tail. Bring the working wire down one side of the bead, and clockwise around the shank, from front to back, positioning the wire as close to the bead as possible; do the same on the other side of the bead. This completes one entire herringbone weave around the bead.

9. Repeat to complete five full weaves around the bead. As you progress, snug the wire against the bead's sides.

10. Weave the top of a sixth herringbone, but before wrapping the wire on the lower shank, slip one of the smaller-bead dangles onto the wire. Twist a small loop at the 4 o'clock position. After weaving the wire around the lower shank, make another small loop at the 8 o'clock position for another dangle. Bring the wire

to the top shank, wrap it tightly twice around it, and trim any extra wire.

11. Repeat steps 5 through 9 for the other earring.

12. Attach the ear wires to the empty loops at the ends of the shanks.

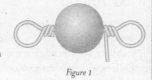

Figure 1

—From *Contemporary Bead & Wire Jewelry*

BEADING VINTAGE-STYLE JEWELRY

Marty Stevens-Heebner & Christine Calla

Bead Sizes

Regardless of their shape or type, beads are measured in millimeters, not inches (see figure 1). The millimeter measurement refers to the diameter of the bead, so that you know how much space it will occupy when it's strung (see figure 2). There are a couple of exceptions to this rule. *Drop beads*—the kind that have holes through the top—are measured in millimeters according to their length. *Seed beads*—the kind that look like tiny kernels—are sized according to number. The higher the number, the tinier the seed bead. Size 6 seed beads are the most typical type. You may see them listed in catalogues as 6/0 or 6°. They're also known as "E" beads.

Threading Materials

There are three basic kinds of stringing material: tigertail wire, nylon line, and beading thread. Each has a different level of flexibility and strength, factors you should consider when planning your project.

Tigertail wire is a thin, pliable cable composed of woven wire strands. It comes in various diameters and strengths and can be used in just about any kind of beading project. The smaller the diameter (i.e., the lower the number), the thinner the cable. Thin cable tends to be very flexible, while thicker cable is stronger and better suited for heavy beads and gemstones. Experiment with different diameters of wire (.012, .018, and .024, for example) to see what works best for you. One of the benefits of working with tigertail wire is that it's stiff enough to go through a bead on its own. You won't need a beading needle if you're using this kind of wire.

Metal wire. Whether it's sterling silver or gold-filled, metal wire adds a unique shimmer to any piece of jewelry.

Metal wire is measured in gauges: the higher the number, the thinner the wire. For example, 16-gauge wire is substantially thicker than 28-gauge wire, which is quite thin. (Note that tigertail wire is measured in the opposite way.) Metal wire also comes in different densities: dead soft (the most malleable), half-hard, and full hard (the hardest to bend). Try experimenting with different gauges and densities to see what works best for you.

Nylon line is an excellent material for beading because it's clear and durable. Make sure you buy nylon line that's specifically made for jewelry design. Don't use clear fishing line—it stretches easily and can break unexpectedly. Nylon line designated for jewelry making, however, is strong and produces a clean look, particularly with translucent beads.

Decorative cords. Unlike other types of stringing material, decorative cords are meant to be shown off and are included as part of the jewelry design. We use romantic elements like organza ribbon and velvet in many of our designs. Chain is also featured, in gold or silver.

Nylon or silk beading thread comes in different colors and thicknesses. Nylon thread is easy to work with and doesn't fray, although it may stretch over time. When choosing a thread, make sure you pick one that's thin enough to easily fit through the smallest bead you'll be stringing. Keep in mind that—depending on the type of project you're doing—you may need to run the thread through the bead a few times. Whenever possible, choose thread in a color that matches the beads you'll be using. Otherwise, select a color that's lighter than the beads in your design.

Beading needles are essential if you're going to use **beading thread**. Thread is simply so slack that a needle is required for sliding it through a bead. Some brands of thread come with a short needle already woven onto one end. Big-eyed needles are wonderful to work with—and not just because they're easy to thread. They're pliable and can handle multiple strands of thread at the same time. The needle's large eye closes up as soon as it's pushed through a bead, and you can easily reopen it with a pin or awl for rethreading.

When working with tiny seed beads or creating intricate stitches, more conventional needles are required. For these types of projects, beading needles that resemble standard sewing "sharps" and are numbered according to size—10, 13, 15, and so on—will do the trick. Remember that the larger the number of the needle, the thinner it will be.

To ease the frustration of threading, pick the largest needle (it will have the largest eye) that will fit through the smallest bead hole in your design.

Bear in mind that seed beads are numbered the same way beading needles are numbered. Therefore, a size 11 needle should fit through a size 11 seed bead. Remember that if your design calls for you to make more than one pass through a bead, you should use thinner thread and a smaller needle.

Tip

To prevent tangles from occurring, slide the thread along some beeswax before you begin to string the beads.

Wire Stringing Basics

To make a simple, single strand bracelet or necklace using tigertail wire, do the following:

1. Use the craft scissors to cut a piece of tigertail wire that's the intended length of your necklace plus a minimum of 4 inches (10 cm).

2. String the beads for your bracelet or necklace onto the wire.

3. String a crimp bead onto each end of the piece. Thread a clasp onto one end, then wind the wire around and back through the crimp bead and the first couple of beads (see figure 10). Pull the end of the wire until the crimp bead butts up against the clasp. Now crimp the bead using the needle-nose or crimping pliers, and trim away any excess wire with the scissors.

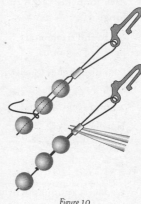

Figure 10

4. Repeat step 3 with the other end, but this time use a jump ring or split ring instead of the clasp. Make sure to pull the wire until it's tight, so that no gaps remain between the beads.

Stringing Beads with Thread

Unlike most bead wire, beading threads are usually easy to knot. You can then hide the knots by using various findings or techniques.

Using a Bead Tip

To use a simple bead tip, slide your needle and thread through the bead tip, making sure that the hook on the bead tip faces outward, toward the end of your bracelet or necklace (see figure 11). Knot the thread, tuck it into the cup of the bead tip, then knot it again. Add a bit of bead cement to the knots, then trim the thread close to the knots. Attach the bead tip's hook to the end of your clasp and close the hook with a pair of needle-nose pliers.

Figure 11

Using a Jump Ring to Finish a Threaded Piece

If you like, you can finish a piece of jewelry using a jump ring and beading thread. At one end of your string of beads, slip your threaded needle through a closed jump ring. Wrap the thread around the ring twice, and then slide the needle back through several beads. Knot the thread (see figure 12). Slide the needle back through a few more beads and knot the thread again. Add a dab of bead glue to the knots and trim away any excess thread. Carefully open the jump ring and attach the clasp to it to complete the piece.

Figure 12

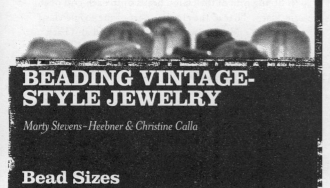

| 2 mm | 3 mm | 4 mm | 5 mm | 6 mm | 7 mm |

| 8 mm | 9 mm | 10 mm | 12 mm | 14 mm |

| 16 mm | 18 mm | 20 mm | 22 mm |

Figure 1

Inches

1   2

Millimeters

10   20   30   40   50

Figure 2

Pearl Cluster Necklace and Earrings

Groups of freshwater pearls and blue seed beads give this set an air of classic elegance.

To make the necklace: What You Need

Basic tool kit

Nylon beading thread, 72 inches (183 cm)

Beading needle

2 strands of seed beads in various shades of blue, each 16 inches (40.5 cm) long

80 round freshwater pearls, 4 x 3 mm

Chain, 2 inches (5 cm) long

2 jump rings, 8 mm

Headpin

Clasp

What You Do

1. Make a knot in the nylon beading thread about four inches from one end (this will keep the beads from sliding off the thread). Then string the opposite end of the thread through the beading needle and string 10 seed beads onto the thread, randomly mixing different shades of blue. Stitch through the beads a second time with the needle so that they form a loop. Add three more seed beads, a freshwater pearl, and another seed bead, making sure to slide the beads up against the beaded loop. Then stitch through the first two of these seed beads a second time.

2. Add a seed bead, a pearl, and another seed bead, then stitch through the same two beads a third time, and let this group settle next to the previous group of beads. Repeat this combination of beads until you've formed a cluster with five pearls around the center (see figure 1).

3. String 13 more seed beads onto the strand, followed by a pearl and another seed bead. Stitch through the 11th and 12th seed beads in this group a second time. Repeat step 2 to create a full cluster. Then repeat steps 2 and 3 fourteen more times.

4. Thread 10 seed beads onto the nylon thread, then stitch through the beads a second time so that they form a loop. Tie a double knot in the thread to secure the strand, and trim any excess thread.

5. Open one of the jump rings with the needle-nose pliers, and slide the ring through the first beaded loop and one of the end links of the piece of chain. Then close the jump ring.

6. Slide a pearl onto the headpin, and use the round-nose pliers to make a loop in the end of the pin. Then slide this loop through the remaining end link of the chain. Wrap the wire two or three times between the loop and the pearl, and trim any excess wire.

7. Repeat step 5 with the other jump ring and the opposite end of the strand, this time attaching the bottom loop of the clasp instead of the chain.

To make the earrings: What You Need

Basic tool kit

Nylon beading thread, 12 inches (30.5 cm)

Beading needle

24 seed beads in various shades of blue

2 earring wires

10 round freshwater pearls, 4 x 3 mm

All-purpose glue or jewelry cement

What You Do

1. Make a knot in the piece of nylon beading thread approximately 4 inches (10 cm) from one end. String the opposite end of the thread through the beading needle, then string 10 seed beads onto the thread, randomly mixing different hues of blue.

2. Slip the nylon thread through the bottom loop of an earring wire, then stitch through the 10 seed beads a second time. Tie a knot at the end of the thread to secure the beads. String three seed beads, a freshwater pearl, and another seed bead onto the strand, then stitch through the first two beads from this step a second time.

3. Add a seed bead, a pearl, and another seed bead, then stitch through the same two beads, letting this group settle next to the previous one. Repeat this combination of beads until you've formed a cluster with five pearls around the center.

4. Tie the nylon thread and the 4-inch (10 cm) tail from step 1 together to secure the earring, then trim any excess thread. Apply a drop of all-purpose glue or jewelry cement to the knot, and let the earring dry according to the manufacturer's directions. Repeat the process to make the second earring.

Sparkling Briolette Necklace

When it comes to vintage jewelry design, nothing can match the ageless elegance of briolette beads. In this sparkling strand, they're paired with copper-colored seed beads.

What You Need

Basic tool kit

Tigertail wire, 21 inches (53.5 cm)

Seed beads

17 round beads, 6 mm diameter

16 briolette beads, 14 x 14 mm

2 crimp beads

Toggle clasp

What You Do

1. String 32 seed beads (2½ inches [6.5 cm]) onto the strand of tigertail wire. Add one of the round beads, another seed bead, then one of the briolette beads. Follow with another round bead, a seed bead, then a briolette bead.

2. Continue with the combination of seed bead, round bead, seed bead, and briolette bead, until all of the briolettes and round beads have been strung. Then add 32 seed beads.

3. String one of the crimp beads onto each end of the necklace. Thread the circular part of the toggle clasp onto one end, then wind the wire around and back through the crimp bead and the first seed bead or two. Pull the end of the wire until the crimp bead butts up against the toggle; then crimp the bead, and trim away any excess wire.

4. Repeat step 3 with the bar part of the toggle clasp on the opposite end of the strand. Make sure that the wire is pulled tightly enough so that no gaps remain between the beads.

Tip

Gentle contrast plays an important part in the color scheme of this necklace. For an antique feel, stick to subtler hues of blue, brown, or red. For a more modern approach, try experimenting with magenta or metallic tones.

Tidbit:

A necklace belonging to Christine's grandmother inspired this design. Why not look at your mother's or grandmother's jewelry for ideas?

Fit-for-a-Queen Chandelier Necklace and Earrings

Bringing to mind the French court of the 18th century, this ornate chandelier design is a symbol of sophistication. Accented with green beads and freshwater pearls, these pieces sparkle with timeless elegance.

To make the necklace: What You Need

Basic tool kit

8 headpins (One should be 2 inches [5 cm] long.)

1 strand of freshwater pearls, 16 inches (40.5 cm) long, 2 mm diameter

20 clear crystal bicone beads, 4 mm diameter

1 oval purple bead, 18 x 13 mm (We used quartz beads.)

Chandelier finding

9 oval green beads, 8 mm (We used green aventurine beads.)

Tigertail wire

2 crimp beads

Clasp

Jump ring (optional)

Chain for necklace extender (optional)

WHAT YOU DO

1. To make the chandelier pendant, slide a freshwater pearl onto the 2-inch (5 cm) headpin, then add a clear crystal bicone bead, the oval purple bead, a clear crystal bicone bead, and a pearl. Use the round-nose pliers to form a small loop in the end of the headpin, then slide the pin through the center bottom loop of the chandelier finding. Wrap the remaining wire two to three times between the loop and the pearl, then trim any excess wire.

2. Slide a freshwater pearl onto another headpin, then add a clear crystal bicone bead and another pearl. Make a loop in the end of the headpin with the round-nose pliers, and slide the pin through the loop adjacent to the beaded wire from step 1. Wrap the remaining wire two to three times between the loop and the pearl, then trim any excess wire. Repeat this step, then attach the headpin to the other side of the beaded wire from step 1.

3. Slide a freshwater pearl onto another headpin, then add a clear crystal bicone bead, an oval green bead, a clear crystal bicone bead, and another pearl. Make a loop in the headpin with the pliers, then slide the pin through the loop adjacent to one of the beaded wires from step 2. Wrap the remaining wire two or three times between the loop and the pearl, and trim any excess wire. Repeat this step until the bottom loops of the chandelier finding are all filled.

4. To make the pearl strand, cut a 21-inch (53.5 cm) piece of the tigertail wire, then thread 3½ inches (9 cm) of freshwater pearls onto the wire. Add a clear crystal bicone bead, an oval green bead, and a clear crystal bicone bead. Then thread another 3½ inches (9 cm) of pearls onto the strand, followed by a crystal bicone bead, an oval green bead, and another bicone bead. Add the beaded chandelier finding, followed by a bicone bead, a green bead, and another bicone bead on the opposite side of the strand. Then thread on 3½ inches (9 cm) of pearls, followed by a bicone bead, a green bead, and another bicone bead. Finish out the strand with another 3½ inches (9 cm) of pearls.

5. Add a crimp bead to each end of the strand, then take one end of the strand and thread it through the clasp's loop. Thread the wire back through the crimp bead and the first few pearls, and pull the end of the wire until the crimp bead butts up against the clasp. Then crimp the bead and trim away any excess wire. Repeat this step with the opposite end of the strand, using the jump ring or, if you decide to make the necklace extender below, the end link of the chain.

6. To make the necklace extender, cut a 2½-inch (6.5 cm) piece of the chain and follow step 5 to attach it to the necklace. Then slide a crystal bicone bead, a green bead, and a bicone bead onto a headpin. Form a loop in the end of the pin with the round-nose pliers, and

slide the pin through the remaining end of the chain. Wrap any remaining wire around the pin between the bottom of the loop and the top of the bead using the needle-nose pliers. Trim any excess wire.

TO MAKE THE EARRINGS: WHAT YOU NEED

Basic tool kit

14 headpins (Two of them should be 2 inches [5 cm] long.)

28 freshwater pearls, 2 mm diameter

30 clear crystal bicone beads, 4 mm diameter

2 violet round beads, 6 mm diameter. (We used amethyst beads.)

14 oval green beads, 8 mm diameter. (We used green aventurine beads.)

2 chandelier findings

2 earring wires

WHAT YOU DO

1. Slide a freshwater pearl onto one of the 2-inch (5 cm) headpins, then add beads in the following order: one clear crystal bicone bead, one violet bead, one clear crystal bicone bead, one oval green bead, one clear crystal bicone bead, and one freshwater pearl. Then use the round-nose pliers to make a small loop in the headpin. Slide this loop through the center bottom loop of one of the chandelier findings and wrap the remaining wire two or three times between the loop and the pearl. Trim any excess wire.

2. Slide a freshwater pearl onto a headpin (not the other 2-inch [5 cm] headpin), then add beads in the following order: one clear crystal bicone bead, one oval green bead, one clear crystal bicone bead, and one freshwater pearl. Then make a loop in the headpin with the pliers, and slide it through the loop adjacent to the beaded wire from step 1. Wrap the remaining wire two to three times between the loop and the pearl, and trim any excess wire. Repeat this step five additional times until the bottom loops of the chandelier finding are all filled.

3. Use the pliers to open the bottom loop of an earring wire. Slip the earring wire through the top loop of the chandelier finding, then close it with the pliers. Repeat all of the steps to make the matching earring.

Tip

Chandelier findings can have anywhere from two to 10 loops (or any number in between) for attaching beads. Adding just a few beads hearkens back to the Victorian era. Adding lots of beads will give the piece a bohemian feel. Add as many or as few beads as you like—it all depends on your personal vision, and on what era appeals to you.

Tidbit:

Earring styles are strongly affected by hairstyles. When enormous powdered wigs were worn by the French court in the 18th century, earrings such as these needed to be large and elaborate just to be seen. Conversely, earrings all but disappeared a century later when women wore their hair severely parted in the center and pulled to the back in a tight knot, completely obscuring the ears.

Playful Pearls and Iolite Necklace

Colorful pearls pair up with bright blue iolite beads for a fun, loose, flapper-inspired necklace.

WHAT YOU NEED

Basic tool kit

Tigertail wire

94 crystal bicone beads, 4 mm diameter

47 dyed freshwater pearls (can be irregularly shaped), 8 mm diameter

47 rectangular iolite beads, 8 x 4 mm

Crimp bead

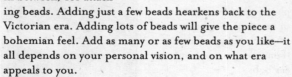

WHAT YOU DO

1. Cut a 40-inch (101.5 cm) piece of the tigertail wire, then string on a crystal bead and a freshwater pearl. Add another crystal bead, then an iolite bead. Repeat this pattern 46 more times until the necklace is 36 inches (91 cm) long.

2. Slide a crimp bead onto one end of the wire, then thread the other end of the wire through the crimp bead, going in the opposite direction. Using the needle-nose pliers, crimp the bead. Trim away any excess wire.

—From *Beading Vintage-Style Jewelry*

BEADING WITH CHARMS

Getting Started

Katherine Duncan Amione

Before You Begin

One of the joys of making jewelry is choosing your supplies from the tremendous variety of beads, charms, findings, pearls, and types of wire that are on the market. Yet the pleasurable pursuit of supplies can also be a source of frustration, particularly if you are new to this craft. Visiting a bead shop, looking through a catalog, or shopping on a Web Site makes it immediately clear that there are many decisions to make.

The Materials entries for each project in this section ease this process. You'll learn the wire gauge; size and shape of beads, crystals, and pearls; type and size of findings; recommended metal; link size for chains; and many other details that will help you achieve a look similar to the piece that is featured in the accompanying photograph. The Materials entries do, however, make some assumptions, which follow:

- All wire is round, unless specified otherwise.

- Jump ring measurements are the outer diameter.

- Charm measurements are length only.

- Beads, crystals, and pearls are length-drilled unless specified otherwise.

- A charm already has a loop attached at the top; beads, stones, or any other object not called a charm in the materials list will need to be wrapped or threaded in order to attach to a bracelet or necklace chain, or ear wire.

Continued ➡

Keep in mind that you might not be able to find an exact match for a vintage chain, finding, or piece of jewelry. In these situations, trust your sense of design and color, as well as your taste, to find a substitution. The same approach can also be applied to any of the beads.

Charms

Seasoned jewelry makers use the term *charm* rather loosely. They can be referring to a single object or a collection of objects that are treated as a single item. A charm can be beads on a head pin or attached to a small length of chain, a shape cast in metal, or even an interesting item that was never intended to be jewelry, called a *found* object.

Regardless of what a designer considers a charm, all have one thing in common: a charm is attached, usually by only one spot, so it dangles on the finished piece of jewelry.

In this book, however, a charm entry in a materials list refers to an object that already has a loop at the top. This narrow definition is just for clarity—do not let it limit your imagination about what can become a charm on a bracelet, earring, or necklace.

Attaching Charms

Position loops and jump rings so that dangles (bead stacks on head pin, or charms) will face front when attached to the chain.

On a link chain bracelet, this means that the dangles should be attached to the lower portion of a link, or to the front of link (figure 1).

As you connect your charms, the chain can twist. To ensure that the charms face the same direction, reposition the bracelet after you connect each charm.

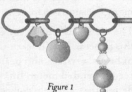

Figure 1

Reaming Beads

When the hole in a bead is too small to fit onto a wire, head pin, or finding, you can make it larger. It is not worth the effort to ream a seed bead, or any other inexpensive bead. Semiprecious stones or artisan beads, on the other hand, are ideal candidates for this process.

You can use a manual or electric bead reamer.

1. Stick the bead to a small piece of poster putty.

2. Begin reaming. Tips are diamond-coated, so using the reamer dry too often will wear off this surface. Instead, try to keep the tip wet. If using a manual tool, you can work with the reamer submerged in a shallow

bowl of water or held under running water. Never do this with an electric reamer. Instead, dip the drill bit in a small cup of water whenever it feels like the bead is sticking. Stop when you are midway through the bead's hole. Work slowly for maximum control, and do not push too hard.

3. Remove the putty, flip the bead over and stick the putty on the opposite side. Finish reaming the hole from the newly exposed opening.

Designer's Tip

Do not ream crystals. They shatter easily. Instead, choose a jump ring or wire to fit the hole. The jump ring size that fits in the crystal's hole will be sufficient to support the crystal, and will be strong enough to last with regular, everyday wear.

Using Crimp Beads and Tubes

Crimping creates a loop with beading wire, for attaching a clasp. But you can adapt crimps for other uses...

The process starts with either a crimp tube or bead. As you do more crimping, you will find that you prefer one shape over another.

1. Slide the crimp bead or tube onto the beading wire.

2. Turn the wire and insert it back through the crimp bead or tube, starting at the same end from which it just emerged. Leave a small loop of beading wire.

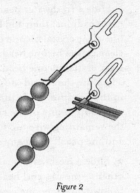

3. Place the crimp bead or tube in the crimp tool and close it (figure 2). When the crimp bead or tool curls slightly, remove it from the crimp tool.

Figure 2

4. Cut the end of the wire at the bottom of the crimp bead or tube. If desired, you can cut it long enough to thread through the closest few beads on the strand.

5. If desired, place the crimp cover around the crimp bead or tube. Grasp the cover with the end of the crimp tool and gently squeeze to secure it.

Personalizing Fit

Do you have slim—or strong—wrists? You might want to tweak the length of your bracelets so that they look just right on your body.

1. Measure your wrist, and allow a bit of slack for a comfortable fit.

2. Subtract the length of the clasp. This gives you the length of chain that you need.

Trinkets

Designer: Terry Taylor

Every child lusts for these plastic geegaws at one time or another. Celebrate your inner child by fashioning them into a pair of amusing ear bobs.

Finished Size

Elephants or whistle and ball drops, 1½ inches (3.8 cm); leaf dangles, 3 inches (7.6 cm)

Materials

4 plastic charms, 19 mm

10 matching plastic charms, 6 mm

12 sterling silver jump rings, 6 mm

4 gold-filled French ear wires with bead

2 sterling silver ear studs (ball with drop), 6 mm

2½-inch (6.4 cm) length of 1.5 mm sterling silver chain

Tools

Chain-nose pliers, 2 pair

Round-nose pliers

Wire cutters

Techniques

Using jump rings

Instructions

INSTRUCTIONS FOR DROPS

Make two for each set.

1. Open the loop at the bottom of the ear wires.

2. Slide a charm onto each loop, and then securely close the loops (figure 1).

INSTRUCTIONS FOR DANGLES

Make two.

1. Cut the chain in half. Set one piece aside for the second earring.

2. Open all of the jump rings, and slide a charm onto each one. Slip the last link of the chain onto one of the jump rings, and close it. Attach four more charms with jump rings, evenly spaced, along the length of the chain. Place the uppermost charm just a link or two from the top of the chain.

3. Slip another jump ring onto the top link of the embellished chain, and then through the loop at the bottom of the ear stud (figure 2).

Figure 1

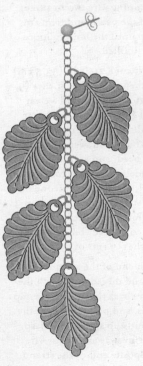

Figure 2

Outrageous

Designer: Linda Larsen

Extravagant…over-the-top…Use the largest crystals and craziest charms you can find to give this eye-catching piece its extreme personality.

FINISHED SIZE

7 inches (17.8 cm)

MATERIALS

10 sterling silver rondelle spacers, 4 mm

5 faceted round crystals, 18 mm

3 vintage round sterling silver balls with set crystals, 18 mm

5 freshwater pearls (rice), 18 mm

7 sterling silver charms, 25 to 51 mm

10 sterling silver bead caps, 10 mm

22 sterling silver jump rings, 10 mm

Sterling silver toggle clasp

8 ball-end sterling silver head pins, 2½ inches (6.4 cm) long

16-inch (40.6 cm) length of 16-gauge sterling silver wire

6½-inch (16.5 cm) length of 13 mm sterling silver chain

Scraps of 2 mm chain to total 15 inches (38.1 cm)

TOOLS

Chain-nose pliers, 2 pair

Round-nose pliers

Flush wire cutters

Pencil

TECHNIQUES

Using jump rings

Rolling simple loops

Making wrapped loops

Reaming beads

INSTRUCTIONS

1. Connect all of the charms, evenly distributed, to links on the oversize chain, using a jump ring for each one.

2. Slide a rondelle spacer, crystal, and rondelle spacer onto a ball-end head pin. Make a wrapped loop above the upper rondelle spacer. Open a jump ring and slip the loop onto it, attach the crystal on the first link of the oversize chain, and close the jump ring. Assemble and attach the remaining crystal dangles in the same manner, evenly spacing them along the chain.

3. Thread each of the silver balls with set crystals onto a ball-end head pin, and make a simple loop at the top (wrapping the wire twice around the tip of the round-nose pliers). Attach these dangles to the oversize chain using jump rings.

4. Cut three lengths of tiny chain: 1¼, 1, and ¾ inch (3.2, 2.5, and 1.9 cm). Cut a 3-inch (7.6 cm) length of wire. Make a simple loop at one end, using the round-nose pliers. Open it with the chain-nose pliers, add the end link of each piece of small chain, and then close the loop. Add a bead cap, a freshwater pearl, and another bead cap to the wire. Finish the top of the dangle with a wrapped loop. (You may have to ream out the pearl to get the wire through.) Make four more pearl dangles in the same manner.

5. Attach all of the pearl dangles to the oversize chain with jump rings, as shown in figure 1.

6. Attach the parts of the toggle clasp to the ends of the oversize chain, using jump rings.

Figure 1

Droplets

Designer: Marilyn McNutt

Delicate charms and crystals command attention when grouped along dainty chains.

FINISHED SIZE:

2¾ inches (7 cm)

MATERIALS

14 light rose bicone crystals, 4 mm

8 mauve freshwater pearls (potato), 8 mm

2 sterling silver Celtic filigree charms, 6 mm

8 sterling silver flat heart charms, 5 mm

4 sterling silver puff heart charms, 8 mm

2 sterling silver decorative heart charms, 11 mm

2 sterling silver smooth, flat heart drops, 10 mm

22 sterling silver head pins, 2 inches (5 cm) long

2 sterling silver ear hoops with 3 loops, 15 mm

24 sterling silver jump rings, 3 mm

7-inch (17.8 cm) length of 2 mm sterling silver rolo chain

TOOLS

Chain-nose pliers, 2 pair

Round-nose pliers

Flush wire cutters

TECHNIQUES

Rolling simple loops

INSTRUCTIONS

Make two.

1. Cut four pieces of chain 1 inch (2.5 cm) long and two pieces of chain 1⅜ inches (3.5 cm) long.

2. Run a head pin through a bicone, and finish with a simple loop. Add a head pin with a simple loop to the remaining bicones and pearls in the same manner.

3. Open the jump rings. Use one to attach each 1-inch (2.5 cm) length of chain to the left outside loop on the ear hoop. In the following steps, use a jump ring to attach each sterling silver charm or drop to a chain link. Attach each bicone and pearl by opening the loop at the top of the head pin.

4. Attach one of the Celtic filigree charms to the left (outside) loop of the ear hoop.

5. From top to bottom along the chain, attach a bicone, pearl, small flat heart, bicone, and small puff heart in the last link (figure 1).

6. Attach a 1-inch (2.5 cm) length of chain to the right (outside) loop of the ear hoop. Also attach a decorative heart to the right loop of the ear hoop. Add the same bicones, charms, drops, and pearls—in the same order and positions—to this chain.

7. Attach the 1⅜-inch (3.5 cm) length of chain to the center loop of the ear hoop. Attach a pearl to this same loop. From top to bottom along this chain, attach a bicone, 3 small flat heart drops, bicone, bicone, pearl, and large heart to the last link (figure 2).

Figure 2

Northern Lights

Designer: Stacey Neilson

Create dangles to showcase the favorite beads in your stash, and then layer a fine chain swag on top.

FINISHED SIZE:

3¼ inches (8.3 cm)

MATERIALS

20 base metal beads, 2.5 mm

Venetian glass bead (round, flat), 20 mm

Dark green bicone crystal, 6 mm

2 yellow bicone crystals, 4 mm

12 lead-free pewter rondelle spacers with fine silver electroplating, 4 mm

Turquoise miracle bead, 8 mm

2 aqua bicone crystals, 6 mm

3 turquoise miracle beads, 4 mm

Continued ➜

Venetian glass bead (round, 8 mm

2 aqua bicone crystals, 4 mm

Venetian glass bead (square, flat), 10 mm

2 yellow bicone crystals, 8 mm

Gray miracle bead, 4 mm

Cloisonné tube, 10 mm

Cloisonné drop bead, 17 mm

Crystal teardrop, 12 mm

AB crystal (cushion), 5 mm

Gray round bead, 6 mm

Charm with three holes: one on top, two at the bottom, 15 mm

3 lead-free pewter charms with fine silver electroplating, 6 to 8 mm

6 head pins, 2 inches (5 cm) long

6 base metal bead caps, 4 mm

7-hole safety pin brooch, 2¼ inches (5.7 cm)

7 sterling silver jump rings, 4 mm

7 sterling silver crimp tubes, 2 mm

Side-opening sterling silver calotte, 4 mm

Sterling silver jump ring (triangles), 5 mm

5¼ inch (13.3 cm) length of 3 mm link chain

6-inch (15.2 cm) length of 0.8 mm beading chain

TOOLS

Chain-nose pliers, 2 pair

Round-nose pliers

Wire cutters

Crimp tool

TECHNIQUES

Using jump rings

Rolling simple loops

Using crimp beads and tubes

INSTRUCTIONS

1. Thread a head pin with a base metal bead, cap, the large Venetian bead, cap, base metal bead, the dark green bicone, base metal bead, small yellow bicone, and base metal bead. Roll a simple loop at the top. Join this to the end link of a ½-inch (1.3 cm) piece of link chain. Attach this dangle to the first loop on the pin with a jump ring.

2. Thread a head pin with a base metal bead, rondelle spacer, turquoise miracle bead, rondelle spacer, 6 mm aqua bicone, rondelle spacer, small turquoise miracle bead, and a base metal bead. Roll a simple loop at the top. Use the simple loop to attach the dangle to the pin's second loop.

3. Make another dangle on a head pin, using a base metal bead, rondelle spacer, Venetian glass round, four rondelle spacers, small aqua bicone, rondelle spacer, and base metal bead. Roll a simple loop and then attach this dangle to the fifth loop on the pin.

4. The last head-pin dangle, which is attached to the pin's sixth loop, is stacked with a base metal bead, cap, square Venetian glass bead, cap, base metal bead, cap, large yellow bicone, cap, base metal bead, small turquoise miracle bead, base metal bead, small yellow bicone, and base metal bead.

5. Cut two lengths of beading chain, each 2½ inches (6.4 cm) long. Pinch a crimp to the end of both of the pieces. Drop a gray miracle bead and small aqua bicone down to meet one of the crimps. A quarter of the way up the length, secure another crimp and then a large yellow bicone. The bead will rest on top of the crimp. Pinch another crimp just above the midpoint,

drop on the cloisonné tube. Set aside this chain. On the other length of beading chain, drop on a cloisonné drop bead, pinch a crimp below the midpoint, add a medium-size aqua bicone, then another crimp slightly higher, followed by a small turquoise miracle bead. Place the upper end of both lengths of beading chain into a crimp, and pinch it to secure them. Put the crimp joining these two lengths into the open calotte (figure 1). Pinch the calotte closed with the chain-nose pliers. Add the calotte to a jump ring, and secure this to the fourth loop of the pin.

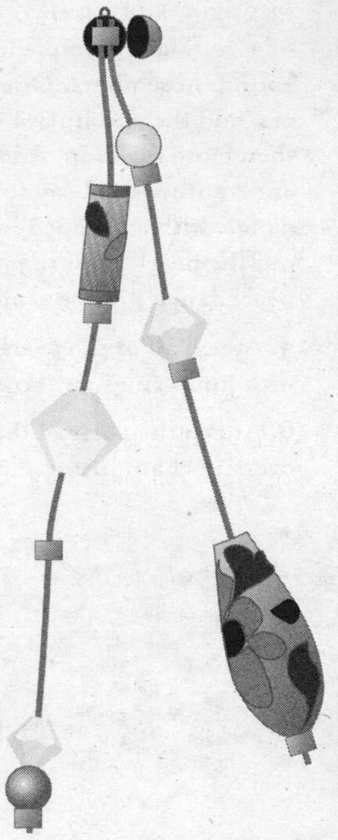

6. Put the triangular jump ring through the crystal teardrop, and pinch it closed with the chain-nose pliers. Open a jump ring and slip the triangle onto it. Temporarily close the jump ring around the last loop of the pin.

7. The last charm is made by adding two miniature earring-style drops into the lower holes of the three-hole charm. Cut four links from the link chain. Open the link at one end to join this piece to the top hole of this charm. Attach the last link to the remaining available loop on the pin. Make two more dangles that you can attach to the bottom loops of the charm. On one head pin, string a base metal bead, rondelle spacer, cushion crystal, rondelle spacer, and base metal bead. On the other head pin, string a base metal bead, rondelle spacer, large gray round bead, rondelle spacer, and the base metal bead. Close both head pins with simple loops, and then use these loops to attach the dangles to the bottom of the charm (figure 2).

8. Cut a 2½-inch (6.4 cm) piece of chain. Open the triangular jump ring that is attached to loop 7 of the pin. Slip the last link of the chain onto the jump ring.

9. Attach the center of this piece of chain to the fourth loop of the pin, using the jump ring already on that loop. Attach a link near the loose end of the chain to the existing jump ring on the first pin loop, in order to complete the swag. Let the end of the chain dangle below the pin's first loop.

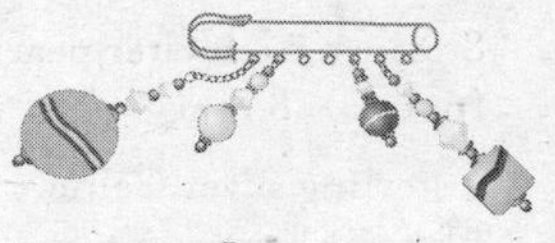

10. Use jump rings to attach a charm to the last link of the dangling end of the chain, and the center of both swags (figure 3).

—FROM *Beading with Charms*

Figure 1

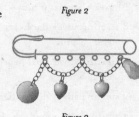

Figure 2

Figure 3

BEADING WITH CRYSTALS

Katherine Duncan Almone & Jean Campbell

Basics

The glistening beads featured in *Beading with Crystals* differ from ordinary glass beads. They're made of leaded glass, a material that's composed of the same ingredients as regular glass (silica, soda, lime, and other compounds), but with an extra kick—a fairly high concentration of lead oxide. The result is a heavier-weight glass with exceptional sparkle. When light hits this type of glass, the lead oxide particles refract in an utterly dazzling way.

The history of leaded crystal beads is an interesting one. The story begins in the 1670s, when Englishman George Ravenscroft discovered a way to outdo the crystal glass being made in Murano, Italy. The Italians were making their crystal using quartz sand and potash, but Ravenscroft added lead oxide to the mix, giving his glass an unequaled brilliance. This new type of glass was relatively easy to cut and engrave, which made it a perfect material for creating exquisite tableware, sculptures, chandeliers, and jewelry.

Up until the late 1800s, crystal items were hand-faceted by skilled artisans. In 1892, Bohemian Daniel Swarovski invented a crystal-cutting machine that made it possible to mass-produce crystal objects. He established his company in the Austrian Tyrol region, where it remains today. As time has passed, Swarovski's methods for cutting crystal have become so refined and high-tech that the facets are especially crisp, and shapes unthinkable of achieving before are common today. Although leaded crystal beads have their origin in and primarily come from Austria, they are also made in other parts of the world, including Egypt.

Crystal beads are available in a wide range of colors. It's quite possible to find just the perfect color and finish for any beaded project. There are bright, jewel-tone colors such as sapphire, ruby, and topaz, as well as subtle, sophisticated hues that resemble denim blue, khaki, deep crimson, and delicate peach. Crystal beads aren't surface dyed, like some beads, but gain their color through chemical elements added during the glass-making stage. Surface treatments are sometimes also added, one of the most popular being aurora borealis (AB), which gives beads a rainbow sheen. When a bead is labeled with a color followed by AB, it will have the treatment on one side of the bead. If it is labeled AB2X, the bead will have been coated on both sides.

Crystal beads also come in a wide variety of shapes. The round and diamond (bicone) shapes familiar to most beaders are just the beginning! Cubes, ovals, rondelles, saucers, drops, and hearts are only some of the shapes waiting to be incorporated into jewelry masterpieces.

When purchasing crystal beads, choose high quality over low price. To qualify as full-leaded crystal, beads need to be composed of at least 24% of lead oxide. The finest crystal beads have 32%. Look for finely cut facets, distinct hues, and high-quality surface treatments. Paying just a bit more per bead will improve the look of a piece tenfold, giving it a truly defined and professional look.

Violets

Designer: Vel Hirata

This simple-to-assemble set shows off the multi-faceted appeal of crystals.

Making the Bracelet

MATERIALS FOR BRACELET

33 lilac AB 4 mm bicone beads

34 violet AB 4 mm bicone beads

21 amethyst 3.5 mm crystal montées

2 sterling silver 1 x 2 mm crimp tubes

1 sterling silver 6 mm soldered jump ring

9 mm sterling silver lobster clasp

34 inches (86.5 cm) of .010 flexible beading wire

Tape

TOOLS

Wire cutters

Chain-nose or crimping pliers

TECHNIQUES

Stringing

Crimping

INSTRUCTIONS

1. Cut the beading wire into one 14-inch (35.5 cm) piece and one 20-inch (51 cm) piece. Set aside.

2. Tape the two pieces of wire to the work surface, about 2 inches from the ends and about ½ inch (1.3 cm) apart.

3. On the short wire, string a sequence of 1 lilac bead, 1 montée, 1 violet bead, and 1 montée 10 times. String 1 lilac bead, 1 montée, and 2 violet beads. Tape the wire ends to the work surface.

4. On the long wire, string 2 lilac beads and pass through the first montée added to the short wire. The wires should cross through the montée. String 2 violet beads and pass through the next montée added to the short wire. String 2 lilac beads and pass through the next montée added to the short wire (figure 1). Repeat down the length of the short wire until you've passed through all the montées. Exit from the last bead strung on the short wire.

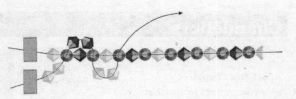

Figure 1

5. Pair the wire ends and, holding the wires tight to maintain the tension, string 1 crimp tube and the soldered jump ring. Pass back through the crimp tube and the last lilac bead from the short wire (figure 2). Squeeze it tight with chain-nose pliers, or crimp it with crimping pliers. Trim the excess wire close to the bead.

6. Undo the tape at the other end of the bracelet and repeat step 5 with the lobster clasp.

Figure 2

Making the Necklace

MATERIALS FOR NECKLACE

2 lilac 6 mm crystal bicone beads

68 violet AB 4 mm crystal bicone beads

180 lilac AB 4 mm crystal bicone beads

42 amethyst 3.5 mm crystal rose montées

2 lilac AB 4 mm crystal round beads

8 sterling silver 1 x 2 mm crimp tubes

2 sterling silver 7 mm soldered jump rings

2 sterling silver 7 mm open jump rings

2 sterling silver 1-inch (2.5 cm) head pins

2 sterling silver one-to-three loop connectors

9 mm sterling silver lobster clasp

80 inches (204 cm) of .010 flexible beading wire

48 inches (122 cm) of .014 flexible beading wire

TOOLS

Wire cutters

Chain-nose or crimping pliers

TECHNIQUES

Stringing

Crimping

INSTRUCTIONS

MAKING THE CENTERPIECE

1. Follow the instructions...to make 2 bracelets, but don't finish the ends.

2. Lay the bracelets next to each other on the work surface with the remaining 12-inch (30.5 cm) piece of .010 beading wire between them. Use a piece of tape to secure the ends of all the wires to the table. String 1 lilac 4 mm bead and pass through the first bicone bead between the montées on one of the bracelets. String 1 lilac bead and pass through the next bicone bead between the montées on the opposite bracelet. Repeat down the bracelet, lacing the two bracelets together (figure 1). When you reach the end, pull the wires tight to create a subtle ruffle.

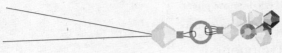

Figure 1

3. Gather the ends of all 5 wires and string 1 crimp tube and 1 soldered jump ring. Pass back through the crimp tube and pull tight. Use chain-nose pliers to squeeze the tube flat or use crimping pliers to crimp the tube. Repeat for the other wire ends.

ADDING THE STRAPS

1. Cut a 24-inch (61 cm) piece of the .014 beading wire and pass it through the soldered jump ring you last added. Slide the jump ring to the center of the wire. Pair the wire ends and string 1 crimp tube and 1 lilac 6 mm bead. Snug the crimp against the ring and squeeze the tube flat or crimp it (figure 2).

Figure 2

2. Separate the wire ends and string 28 violet beads, 1 crimp tube, and the first loop on the 3-loop side of one of the connectors. Pass back through the tube, snug the beads, and squeeze the tube flat or crimp it. Repeat for the other wire end, this time connecting to the third loop on the connector.

3. Use 1 head pin to string 1 round bead. Make a simple loop to secure the bead. Connect the bead dangle to the second loop on the connector (figure 3).

4. Repeat steps 1 through 3 to create a strap on the other side of the necklace.

5. Attach 1 jump ring to the remaining loop on each connector. Attach the lobster clasp to one of the jump rings.

5-7 Wrong Image?????

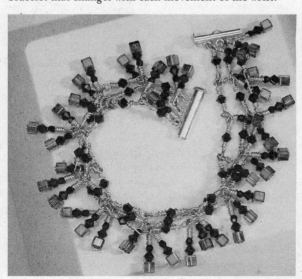

Dangling Bangles

Designer: Mary Hettmansperger

A simple wire technique is used to create this elegant bracelet that changes with each movement of the wrist.

Continued →

MATERIALS

39 to 42 light amber 4 mm crystal cube beads

75 to 81 dark charcoal brown 4 mm crystal bicone beads

39 to 42 black 3 mm crystal round beads

7 to 8 feet of 20-gauge half-hard sterling silver wire

39 to 42 sterling silver 2-inch (5 cm) head pins

Three-strand sterling silver slide-lock clasp

TOOLS

Wire cutters

Chain-nose pliers

Round-nose pliers

TECHNIQUES

Wrapped loop

Note

The bracelet shown is approximately 8 inches (20.5 cm) long and fits an average wrist. Keep in mind that for a larger or smaller bracelet you may need to add or subtract links and bead dangles to get the proper fit.

INSTRUCTIONS

1. Cut 36 pieces of wire, each 2½ inches (6.5 cm) long. Set aside.

2. Use 1 head pin to string 1 cube bead, 1 bicone bead, and 1 round bead. Make a wrapped loop to secure the beads. Repeat to make 39 bead dangles. Set aside.

3. Begin a wrapped loop about one-third of the way down a piece of the cut wire. Before making the wrap, attach the loop to one of the bead dangles and to one of the holes on half of the clasp (figure 1). Complete the wrap.

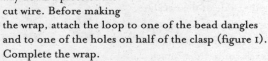

Figure 1

4. String 1 bicone bead and make a wrapped loop on the other end of the wire to complete the link. The link should be about ¾ inch (2 cm) long.

5. As in step 3, begin a wrapped loop about one-third of the way down a piece of the cut wire. Before making the wrap, attach the loop to one of the bead dangles and to the open loop of the last link you made (figure 2).

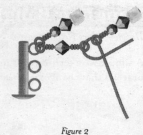

Figure 2

6. String 1 bicone bead and make a wrapped loop on the other end of the wire to complete the link.

7. Repeat steps 5 and 6 to make 9 or 10 more 2-part links.

8. Repeat steps 3 to 7 to add strands to the second and third clasp loops. Work to keep all 3 strands the same length. Test for fit, keeping in mind that you will be adding 1 more link length to connect to the other half of the clasp. Adjust the strands as needed.

9. Slide the clasp halves together.

10. Add the last link to the end of the first strand, but this time work the second wrapped loop of the link so it attaches to a bead dangle and the coordinating loop on the other half of the clasp. Repeat for each strand.

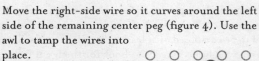

Chandeliers

Designer: Sandra Lupo

Attach bead dangles to a wire component to create an elegant chandelier effect.

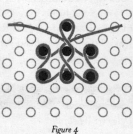

MATERIALS

2 smoky topaz 12 x 8 mm crystal polygon beads

4 opaque aqua 8 mm crystal round beads

12 opaque aqua 4 mm crystal bicone beads

6 denim blue 6 mm crystal bicone beads

4 denim blue 3 mm crystal bicone beads

10 golden champagne 3 mm crystal bicone beads

18 gold-plated 4 mm daisy spacer beads

10 gold-filled 2-inch (5 cm) head pins

2 feet (61 cm) of 22-gauge round dead-soft gold-filled wire or gold-plated wire

INSTRUCTIONS

MAKING THE WIRE FORM

1. Make a homemade jig (see bottom, left) using peg pattern 3, or set up your commercially made jig with pattern 1, shown below.

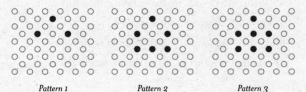

Pattern 1   Pattern 2   Pattern 3

2. Cut a 9-inch (23 cm) piece of wire. Working with peg pattern 1, center the wire above the top peg and crisscross the wire underneath the peg. Curve the left-side wire under, around, and down the inside of the bottom left peg. Curve the right-side wire under, around, and down the inside of the bottom right peg (figure 2). Use the awl to gently tamp down the wire flat to the jig.

Figure 2

3. If you're using a commercially made jig, add pegs as needed to make pattern 2. Curve the left-side wire counterclockwise around the left peg on the bottom row of pegs. Use chain-nose pliers to tighten the wrap. Curve the right-side wire clockwise around the right peg on the bottom row of pegs. Tighten the wrap.

4. Curve the left-side wire clockwise around the center peg on the bottom row of pegs and tighten (figure 3). Curve the right-side wire counterclockwise around the same peg and tighten.

Figure 3

5. If you're using a commercially made jig, add a peg to make pattern 3. Move the left-side wire so it curves around the right side of the remaining center peg.

Move the right-side wire so it curves around the left side of the remaining center peg (figure 4). Use the awl to tamp the wires into place.

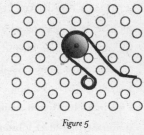

Figure 4

6. Carefully lift the wire form from the pegs. If you've firmly tamped the wires down while forming the component, you should be able to lift it off in one piece. On the commercially made jig, you may remove a few pegs to remove the wire form.

7. Use nylon-jaw pliers to firmly grasp the form so only the top loop shows. Use chain-nose pliers to wrap one wire end tightly around the crossed wire beneath the loop. Repeat with the remaining wire end, wrapping in the opposite direction. Use the wire cutters to flush cut any excess wire close to the wrap. Use bent chain-nose pliers to gently squeeze the wrap, tucking the wire ends in.

8. Adjust the form as needed, flattening wraps with the nylon-jaw pliers and reshaping loops with the single jaw of round-nose pliers.

Repeat steps 1 to 8 to make a second wire form.

Creating Your Own Ear Wires

1. If you're using a commercially made jig, position 1 regular peg and 1 large peg one peg hole diagonally away from each other on the board.

2. Cut a 2½-inch (6.5 cm) piece of wire. Use round-nose pliers to form a loop at one end of the wire that will fit onto a regular peg.

3. Place the loop on the regular peg on the board, and wrap the extra wire around the large peg (figure 5).

4. Cut any excess wire and file the wire end smooth. Use chain-nose pliers to make a slight bend in the wire away from the loop, about ¼ inch (6 mm) from the end.

Figure 5

5. Repeat steps 1 to 4 to make a second ear wire.

6. If you aren't using a commercially made jig, start with step 2. Hold the dowel in one hand and the wire loop in the other so it's perpendicular to the dowel. Wrap the straight end of the wire around the dowel to get a nice curve. Finish as in step 4. Repeat to make a second ear wire.

TOOLS

Homemade wire jig (6 x 6-inch [15 x 15 cm] wooden board and steel nails that are 2 to 3 mm in diameter) or commercial wire jig with removable stainless steel pegs (including a ¼-inch [6 mm] -wide peg)

Hammer (optional)

Heavy-duty wire cutters (optional)

¼-inch (6 mm) -diameter dowel (optional)

Wire cutters

Awl or other thin steel rod

Chain-nose pliers

Nylon-jaw pliers

Bent chain-nose pliers

Round-nose pliers

Metal needle file or emery papers (medium and fine grits)

TECHNIQUES

Using a jig

Simple loop

Opening and closing loops

Note

Each peg of the commercial jig should be 2 to 3 mm in diameter and spaced 3 to 4 mm apart.

MAKING THE DANGLES

1. Use 1 head pin to string 1 polygon bead, 2 spacers, 2 opaque aqua 4 mm bicone beads, 1 spacer, 1 denim blue 6 mm bicone bead, and 1 golden champagne 3 mm bicone bead. Make a simple loop to secure the beads and set aside. Repeat to make a second long dangle.

2. Use 1 head pin to string 1 opaque aqua 8 mm round bead, 2 spacers, 1 denim blue 6 mm bicone bead, 1 opaque aqua 4 mm bicone bead, and 1 golden champagne 3 mm bicone bead. Make a simple loop to secure the beads and set aside. Repeat to make 3 more medium dangles.

3. Use 1 head pin to string 1 opaque aqua 4 mm bicone bead, 1 spacer, 1 denim blue 3 mm bicone bead, and 1 golden champagne 3 mm bicone bead. Make a simple loop to secure the beads and set aside. Repeat to make 3 more short dangles.

ASSEMBLING THE EARRINGS

1. Attach the long dangle to the center bottom loop of one of the wire forms. Attach 1 medium dangle to each of the outside bottom loops of the form. Attach 1 short dangle to each of the outside bottom loops so they sit toward the outside of the form, away from the medium dangles.

2. Attach the ear wire to the top loop of the wire form.

3. Repeat steps 1 and 2 to assemble the second earring.

Briolette Glam

Designer: Laura Shea

Exploit the beauty of clear crystals, showing off diamond-like briolettes.

MATERIALS

1 clear 18 mm crystal briolette pendant

2 clear 15 mm crystal briolette pendants

2 clear 13 mm crystal briolette pendants

179 clear 4 mm crystal bicone beads

2 clear 3 mm crystal bicone beads

1 sterling silver 13 mm lobster clasp with jump ring

1 sterling silver 5 x 8 mm double-loop connecting ring for lobster clasp

1 sterling silver 4 mm soldered jump ring

2 sterling silver 2 x 2 mm crimp beads

Monofilament, 6-pound (2.7 kg) test, or 6 to 8-pound (2.7 to 3.6 kg) test clear braided fishing line

20 inches of flexible beading wire

TOOLS

Scissors

Size 12 beading needles

Chain-nose pliers (optional)

TECHNIQUES

Angle stitching (see instructions)

Stringing (page 00)

Crimping (page 00)

Note

The materials listed are for a 16-inch (40.5 cm) necklace. Add or subtract size 4 mm bicone beads for a longer or shorter version.

INSTRUCTIONS

Note

If you are having trouble threading your needle with the monofilament, pinch the end with chain-nose pliers, and then trim it to a point with sharp scissors. You can also work without a needle. Be sure to pull the line securely through the beads, because these types of line can kink inside the holes of the crystal beads.

STITCHING THE CENTERPIECE

Follow figure 1 for thread path.

Figure 1

1. String 12 clear 4 mm bicone beads (beads 1 through 12). Pass through bead 1 to make a circle. Leave a 6-inch (15 cm) tail.

2. String 3 clear 4 mm bicone beads (beads 13, 14, and 15). Pass through beads 1 and 2.

3. String 4 clear 4 mm bicone beads (beads 16, 17, 18, and 19). Pass through beads 13, 2, and 3.

4. String 2 clear 4 mm bicone beads (beads 20 and 21). Pass through beads 16, 3, and 4.

5. String 1 clear 4 mm bicone bead, a 15 mm pendant, and 2 clear 4 mm bicone beads (beads 22, 23 [15 mm pendant], 24, and 25). Pass through beads 20, 4, and 5.

6. String 2 clear 4 mm bicone beads (beads 26 and 27). Pass through beads 22, 5, and 6.

7. String 4 clear 4 mm bicone beads (beads 28, 29, 20, and 31). Pass through beads, 26, 6, and 7.

8. String 1 clear 4 mm bicone bead, 1 clear 3 mm bicone bead, the 18 mm pendant, and 1 clear 3 mm bicone bead (beads 32, 33 [3 mm bead], 34 [18 mm pendant], 35 [3 mm bead]). Pass through beads 28, 7, and 8.

9. String 4 clear 4 mm bicone beads (beads 36, 37, 38, and 39). Pass through beads 32, 8, and 9.

10. String 2 clear 4 mm bicone beads (beads 40 and 41). Pass through beads 36, 9, and 10.

11. String 3 clear 4 mm bicone beads and a 15 mm pendant (beads 42, 43, 44, and 45 [15 mm pendant]). Pass through beads 40, 10, and 11.

12. String 2 clear 4 mm bicone beads (beads 46 and 47). Pass through beads 42, 11, 12, and 15.

13. String 3 clear 4 mm bicone beads (beads 48, 49, and 50). Pass through beads 46, 12, 15, 48, 49, 50, 47, and 43.

14. String 9 clear 4 mm bicone beads (beads 51 through 59). Pass through beads 50, 47, 43, and 51.

15. String 2 clear 4 mm bicone beads (beads 60 and 61). Pass through beads 44, 51, and 52.

16. String 4 clear 4 mm bicone beads (beads 62, 63, 64, and 65). Pass through beads 60, 52, and 53.

17. String 1 clear 4 mm bicone bead and a 13 mm pendant (beads 66 and 67) [13 mm pendant]). Pass through beads 62, 53, and 54.

18. String 4 clear 4 mm bicone beads (beads 68, 69, 70, and 71). Pass through beads 66, 54, and 55.

19. String 2 clear 4 mm bicone beads (beads 72 and 73). Pass through beads 68, 55, 56, 57, 58, 59, 49, 48, 14, 19, 18, 17, 21, and 25.

20. String 9 clear 4 mm bicone beads (beads 74 to 82). Pass through beads 17, 21, 25, 74, 75, 76, 77, and 78.

21. String 3 clear 4 mm bicone beads (beads 83, 84, and 85). Pass through beads 78, 83, 84, 85, and 77.

22. String 4 clear 4 mm bicone beads (beads 86, 87, 88, and 89). Pass through beads 85, 77, and 76.

23. String 1 clear 4 mm bicone bead and a 13 mm pendant (beads 90 and 91 [13 mm pendant]). Pass through beads 86, 76, and 75.

24. String 4 clear 4 mm bicone beads (beads 92, 93, 94, and 95). Pass through beads 90, 75, 74, and 24.

25. String 1 clear 4 mm bicone bead (bead 96). Pass through beads 92 and 74.

FINISHING THE NECKLACE

1. Weave through all the beads again to reinforce the beadwork. Secure the working and tail threads and trim close to the beads. Set the centerpiece aside.

2. Use the beading wire to string 1 crimp bead and the soldered ring. Pass back through the crimp bead, leaving a 1-inch (2.5 cm) tail.

3. String 45 clear 4 mm bicone beads. Slide the first few beads over both wires to cover the tail. Pass through beads 83, 79, 80, 81, 82, 18, 19, 14, 48, 49, 59, 58, 57, 56, and 72.

4. String 45 clear 4 mm bicone beads, 1 crimp tube, and the clasp connecting ring. Pass back through the crimp tube, snug all the beads tight, and crimp.

5. Attach the lobster clasp to the soldered ring.

—From *Beading With Crytals*

Continued ➜

Identifying Gemstones
Valérie MacCarthy

Agate

Color: All colors

Several well-known types of agate include fire agate, moss agate, eye agate, and tree agate. It's famous for its colorful banding, which is caused by the presence of various impurities. It is often found in geode form with crystals of quartz. Agate is a type of chalcedony.

Hardness: 7

Healing values: Agate is considered to have grounding and calming qualities, balancing yin and yang as well as the physical and the emotional.

Amber

Color: Mostly golden yellow and brown but can also be green, red, violet, and black

Amber is an organic mineral created when pine-tree resin fossilized 50 million years ago. It may contain insects, moss, pine needles, and sometimes larger things, such as frogs, toads, and lizards that were trapped in the resin when it was still sticky. Amber is very light; it can float in water. When burned, it gives off the smell of incense. Be careful of imitations, because plastic or glass is often used to replicate amber.

Hardness: 2.5

Healing values: Amber is believed to release stress, clear the body of disease, and dissolve negative energy, bringing about patience, wisdom, and balance.

Amethyst

Colors: Purple, lilac, and mauve

Amethyst is a crystalline variety of quartz found inside geodes of volcanic rock. The purple color is caused by trace amounts of ferric iron.

Hardness: 7

Healing values: Amethyst is considered to be the stone of spirituality and contentment, opening up the throat chakra and channels to one's higher self, with calming qualities for meditation.

Apatite

Colors: Colorless, pink, yellow, green, blue, violet, and brown

The colors of apatite vary extensively, but they are usually very bright and strong. They can also be transparent or opaque. The name comes from the Greek word for *cheat*, because apatite has often been confused with other stones. It is a common stone, appearing in many different types of rock.

Hardness: 5

Healing values: Apatite is believed to be a healing stone, helping with communication and teaching, balancing energy, stimulating intellect, and dissolving negativity.

Aventurine

Colors: Green, reddish brown, and golden brown

The color found in this quartz variety is caused by inclusions of green fuchsite mica, pyrite, goethite, or hematite. Aventurine has often been confused with aventurine feldspar, amazonite, and jade.

Hardness: 7

Healing values: Aventurine is believed to assist with balancing the male-female energies, boosting creativity, and providing joy and clarity.

Carnelian

Colors: Shades of red, orange, and brown

Carnelian is part of the chalcedony variety of quartz. The color, which can be translucent or opaque, is due to trace values of iron oxide.

Hardness: 7

Healing values: Carnelian is believed to help ground oneself in the present, bring about good choices in business, and aid fertility.

Chalcedony

Colors: Bluish gray to whitish gray

Chalcedony is the name for all of the microcrystalline quartzes, such as agate, chrysoprase, jasper, and carnelian, but it is also used specifically to refer to the bluish white, gray variety. It is a very porous stone, a quality that makes it suitable for dyes.

Hardness: 7

Healing values: Chalcedony is believed to remove hostility and bring about benevolence and the maternal instinct.

Chrysoprase

Color: Apple green

Chrysoprase, its color due to the presence of nickel, is considered the most valuable kind of chalcedony.

Hardness: 7

Healing values: This stone is thought to relax the body and mind, energize the heart chakra, remove ego, and help with creativity and talent.

Citrine

Colors: Light yellow, dark yellow, and golden brown

Citrine, aptly named after the word *citrus*, is the yellow variety of crystal quartz. Its color is due to the presence of iron.

Hardness: 7

Healing values: Citrine is considered to be the stone of prosperity, bringing happiness, energy, and creativity.

Coral

Colors: Red, pink, orange, white, black, blue, and gold

Coral is the secreted skeleton from the marine organism called coral polyps. In its natural state, coral is dull, but it had a glassy luster when polished.

Hardness: 3

Healing values: Coral symbolizes life and energy, and it is often used as an aid in meditation and visualization.

Fluorite

Colors: Colorless as well as a wide range of colors, including yellow, blue, pink, purple, and green

Fluorite often forms in a cubic formation and can be fluorescent under ultraviolet light. Its name is derived from the Latin word for *flow*.

Hardness: 4

Healing values: Fluorite is believed to help bring order to chaos, as well as protect and sustain health, intellect, and emotional well-being.

Garnet

Colors: Various forms of garnet range from colorless, green, and yellow to shades of red and orange

The rich red color associated with garnet is due to the presence of iron and chromium. The name *garnet* comes from the Latin word for *pomegranate*.

Hardness: 6.5 to 7.5

Healing values: The varieties of garnet are believed to have a number of healing qualities, including bringing about creativity and fostering love.

Hematite

Colors: Blackish gray, brownish red, and metallic

Hematite's metallic luster can give it the appearance of metal. It has been called bloodstone because the saw coolant becomes blood-red during the cutting process. Hematite is also used to make red ocher for painting. It is found in fossils, where it filled in the spaces as the organic material disintegrated.

Hardness: 5.5 to 6.5

Healing values: Hematite is considered to have grounding and balancing qualities, aiding concentration and removing negativity.

Jade

Colors: Usually green, but also all colors

The two varieties of jade (jadeite and nephrite) are so similar that they were thought to be variations of the same stone until 1863, when they were defined as two different varieties. Jade is a very rough stone, making it excellent for carving.

Hardness: 6 to 7

Healing values: A symbol of serenity and purity, jade is believed to bring harmony to relationships, calming the emotions while bringing passion.

Jasper

Colors: Shades of brown, gray, blue, red, yellow, orange, and green

Jasper is part of the chalcedony family of quartz. It is opaque and comes in a variety of looks; orbicular and ocean jasper have white or gray eye-shaped patterns surrounded with red, while the ribbon or riband variety is striped.

Hardness: 7

Healing values: Jasper is believed to be the supreme nurturer, helping with grounding and organization, and it is the patron stone of counselors and healers.

Kyanite

Colors: Shades of blue, white, gray, and green

Kyanite is easily identified by its streaks. It can be transparent or translucent and has a glassy or pearly luster.

Hardness: 5 to 7

Healing values: Kyanite is believed to align all the chakras, bringing tranquility and calming; it does not accumulate or retain negative energy.

Labradorite

Colors: Dark gray or black, with multicolored iridescence

Labradorite is named after Labrador, the Canadian peninsula where it was discovered. It is part of the feldspar (rock) group. Due to its unique iridescence resembling an oil slick, also known as labradorescence, it is often fashioned as a gem.

Hardness: 6

Healing values: Labradorite is considered a protective stone, deflecting unwanted energies and relieving stress.

Lapis lazuli

Colors: Blue, greenish blue, and violet

Lapis lazuli is a rock, while most other gemstones are minerals. The color agent is sulfur, and it is usually found with white marble.

Hardness: 5.5

Healing values: Known as a stone of protection and enlightenment, lapis lazuli is believed to release stress, focus thoughts, and promote creativity.

Malachite

Colors: Banded, light and dark green

The green color of malachite is caused by the presence of copper. Malachite, which is often attached to copper in its natural state, grows in shell-like formation, creating rings, lines, and other shapes.

Hardness: 4

Healing values: Often considered to be the stone of transformation, malachite is thought to clear a path for desired goals, bringing fidelity in love and clarifying emotions.

Moonstone

Colors: White, light yellow, and light blue

Moonstone is a rock (not a mineral), a member of the feldspar group. As with labradorite, moonstone is fashioned for jewelry because of its beauty. It has an opalescence, similar to a soap bubble, which is caused by light reflecting off its internal structure.

Hardness: 6

Healing values: Moonstone is considered to be the stone of feminine intuition, also helping to find fulfillment of one's destiny.

Onyx

Colors: Usually black with white bands

Onyx is part of the chalcedony family of minerals. The sardonyx variety has brownish red bands; marble onyx, not a true onyx, contains colors including yellow and green. Onyx is similar to agate, with the difference that onyx bands are straight, and agate bands are curved. These straight bands have made onyx a favorite stone for carving cameos.

Hardness: 7

Healing values: Onyx is considered to be a stone of strength, bringing about stamina as well as self-confidence, and helping to focus the mind and absorb sorrow.

Pearl

Colors: White, silver, cream, golden, pink, green, blue, and black

Pearls are formed inside mollusks as a defense against irritants such as sand. The color of a natural pearl depends on the type of mollusk that formed it. Because of the porous quality of pearls, they are often found in a variety of other colors artificially created through the use of dyes. Cultured pearls are formed when humans replicate this natural process, creating pearls that are available in interesting variations of color and shape, even though they lack the innate beauty of natural pearls. The quality of cultured pearls varies, but they are much less expensive than natural pearls. I've used a lot of disk-shaped cultured pearls for pieces in this book. Shell pearls are manufactured from the seashells, then coated and polished to produce pearl-like beads. Because shell pearls are man-made, you'll find a wide range of quality, shape, size, and color.

Hardness: 3

Healing values: Pearls symbolize purity, spiritual transformation, charity, honesty, wisdom, and all the best within us. They are believed to reduce oversensitivity, bringing about peacefulness.

Peridot

Colors: Green and olive green

Peridot is the name given to the gem-quality version of the olivine mineral. Its green color is caused by the presence of iron.

Hardness: 6.5

Healing values: Peridot is considered to be a cleansing stone, bringing about clarity and well-being, aiding in understanding the purpose of life, and opening and clarifying the heart and solar plexus chakras.

Quartz

Colors: Various (see five common varieties below)

Quartz is the name for not only the clear crystal variety of this mineral, but also many colored crystal varieties, as well as the massive microcrystalline varieties such as chalcedony, agate, and carnelian. Amethyst, citrine, and other gemstones are also in the quartz family, but you'll find them listed separately here because they are more commonly known by their unique names.

Hardness: 7

• Clear quartz

Color: Colorless

Clear quartz, also known as rock crystal, is one of the most common minerals on the Earth's crust.

Healing values: This is believed to be one of the most powerful stones for healing, and it is used widely for meditation and cleansing the soul.

• Fire (harlequin) quartz

Colors: Colorless with red inclusions

The redness of fire quartz, also known as harlequin quartz, is caused by filaments of hematite or lepidocrocite in the stone.

Healing values: Fire quartz is believed to balance the polarity in the body, helping with expression of love, opening the heart chakra and connecting it to the base and crown chakras.

• Rose quartz

Colors: Bright to pale pink

The pink color in rose quartz is caused by the presence of manganese or titanium. The stone is almost always cloudy and very brittle.

Healing values: Rose quartz is considered to be the stone of love, opening the heart charka by releasing blocked emotions, with the further benefit of aiding fertility.

• Rutile quartz

Color: Clear with needle-like crystal inclusions, which can be red, black, and gold

The hair or needle-like inclusions in rutile quartz are caused by strands of the mineral rutile. Tourmaline can cause a similar effect as rutile and is called tourmalinated quartz.

Healing values: Rutile quartz is believed to help in solving problems and to increase sexual desire.

• Smoky quartz

Color: Smoky brown to black

Sometimes smoky quartz appears clear when first excavated, but it changes to a smoky color when exposed to the air.

Healing values: Smoky quartz is believed to aid in detoxification, cleansing and grounding the base chakra, while its calming qualities replace depression and fear with calm and positive thoughts.

Shells (including abalone)

Colors: Pink, peach, white, and black; abalone: iridescent blue-green

Shells are not only lovely in shape, but their inner nacreous layer is also beautiful in an entirely different style. This inner layer is commonly known as mother-of-pearl, aptly named because it plays a significant role in making a pearl.

Hardness: 2.5

Healing values: Shells represent the tides of emotion, bringing about the easy flow of feelings and sensitivities to others.

Topaz

Colors: Colorless, yellow, orange, pink, red, brown, green, blue, and violet

The name of this stone is derived from the island in the Red Sea originally named Topazius, now known as Zabargad.

Hardness: 8

Healing values: Topaz is believed to sooth, heal, and stimulate, opening the throat chakra and helping with verbalization.

Tourmaline

Colors: Varieties include colorless, pink/red, blue, yellow/brown, green/pink, green, and black

Tourmaline has a complex chemistry, which not only brings about its variety of colors but also other fascinating qualities. For example, when a tourmaline crystal is warmed, one end becomes positively charged and the other negatively charged, attracting dust!

Hardness: 7.5

Healing values: Tourmaline is considered a super activator of the heart chakra, converting dense energy into lighter energy, releasing tension, balancing the right and left brain, and bringing about inspiration and prosperity.

Turquoise

Colors: Light blue, blue-green, and green

The color of turquoise, whether primarily blue or green, is determined by the amount of iron or copper in it. The name comes from "Turkish stone," because the early trade routes bringing the stones to Europe from the Middle East and China passed through Turkey.

Hardness: 6

Healing values: Turquoise is believed to be a healing and purifying stone, helping with spiritual alignment and creativity.

—From *Beading With Gemstones*

Continued ➔

Beading Techniques

There's a wide variety of skills you'll need to know to make all the projects in this book. But don't fret. Just study the how-to information below and you'll be beading like a pro.

Stringing

Stringing beads is a simple act—simply pass the thread or wire through a bead, and you've got it! It's how you arrange beads on the stringing material that creates masterpieces—that's what takes practice.

Crimping wire is a technique used to attach wire to a finding (like a clasp). Start by stringing 1 crimp bead and the finding. Pass the wire end back through the crimp bead in the opposite direction. Next, slide the crimp bead against the finding so it's snug, but not so tight that the wire can't move freely. Squeeze the crimp bead with the back U-shaped notch in a pair of crimping pliers (photo 1). Turn the crimp bead at a 90° angle and nestle it into the front notch. Gently squeeze the bead so it collapses on itself into a nicely-shaped tube (photo 2).

Photo 1   *Photo 2*

—From *Beading with Crystals*

BEADING WITH FILIGREE

Cynthia Deis

Filigree Primer

Think of your favorite lace, maybe the cuff of a blouse or the trim on a wedding dress. Now imagine those delicate twists and intricate swirls translated into wire. The appeal of filigree lies in that contrast—the juxtaposition of dainty lace shapes wrought in tough, durable metal.

What Is Filigree?

Filigree is as old as metalworking itself. In the hot deserts of ancient Egypt and Mesopotamia, for example, artisans worked with simple tools and fires stoked to tremendous heat by slaves to create filigree pieces of amazing intricacy. Drawing a thin, even wire down from a strip of hand-wrought metal took days, as the craftsmen carefully pulled and heated the metal repeatedly. Each pull stretched the length and thinned the metal, and hammering rounded the wire until the artisan was rewarded with a fine metallic filament. The wire could then be braided, twisted, or looped to form a sort of lace, one far more durable than any made of linen or cotton fiber. (In later forms of filigree, the wires were fused with silver dust, making them even stronger.) This work decorated the heads and necks of just the ruling classes, since only the wealthy could afford to wear an item that took weeks of skilled labor to produce.

Filigree exists in some form in all human civilizations that have worked metal. Most often made of silver (although some cultures used gold), the artifacts of Asia, the Middle East, South America, Africa, and Europe include diverse items decorated with filigree: figurines, belts, reliquaries, tiny purses, spoon handles—and of course, all sorts of adornments, from clasps and buttons to headpieces and jewelry. The tradition persists to this day around the world. Hand-wrought pieces continue to be intensely laborious, requiring days to make even with machine-made wire, gas torches, and electric tools for coiling and looping.

Stamped Filigree

So how did we get from the handmade to machine-stamped filigree? We can thank the wives of Parisian doctors and London stockbrokers. In the bustling days of the early industrial revolution, the emerging merchant and middle classes clamored for the finer things once reserved for nobility. The introduction of mechanized means of production made this possible. Fine adornments, once reserved for the residents of the palace and the chateau, were copied and produced by stamping out lacy bits of filigree from solid sheets of metal.

The process was relatively simple. A block of iron, called a die, was carved with a pattern of curves and arabesques; placed in a press, the die punched out the negative shapes of the filigree from a thin sheet of metal. Today's powerful, mechanized presses make a loud thunk and whoosh as they stamp out the metal, but in the French workshop of the late 1700s, the machine would have been hand cranked by a young apprentice or two, grunting and exerting themselves mightily.

Since its invention, stamped filigree has been used widely in costume and production jewelry. Look carefully at Victorian portraits and you'll spot stamped filigree beaded with complex patterns of jet beads. Under their bobbed hair, flappers sported dangly earrings with sparkling filigree bead caps. Pearl-accented filigree adorned the necks of the torch singers of the 1930s and 1940s, and the beaded button-style earrings favored by housewives in post-war suburbia were based on filigree rosettes. Because it's pretty in and of itself but readily accepts beads or accents, filigree was and is still a popular feature in jewelry.

Metal filigree continues to be produced using steel dies, in many cases the same ones that first stamped out their metal lace more than a century ago. The production is highly mechanized so that a single machine can produce thousands of pieces in a day. Factories in the United States and France manufacture most of the stampings sold worldwide.

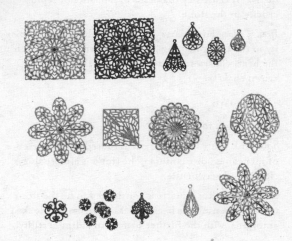

Types of Metal

Stamped filigree pieces are available in a variety of metals, but they're most often made from brass, a highly malleable alloy of copper and zinc with trace amounts of nickel. In its natural state, brass has an appealing golden finish, but when left unsealed, the air gives it a rich bronze patina. Brass can also be plated easily to resemble sterling silver, gold, or copper.

Raw or *natural brass* filigree is unplated and will range in color from bright gold to a deep bronze. If you like the color of raw brass, seal it to maintain the color. If you wish to darken or antique the brass you can apply heat with a torch, gas stove, or kiln to darken the metal.

In *antiqued brass* filigree, the metal is darkened with heat or chemicals, and then the finish is sealed with a skin-safe lacquer. It has a warm patina and is often my first choice when using brass findings. Antiquing does not cause the metal to stiffen and the lacquer can easily be burned off if you desire a raw metal surface.

Plated brass filigree is available in a variety of finishes. Because plating of any metal increases the hardness of the core metal and adds an additional, stiff layer—the plating—these components will be slightly more brittle than their unplated brass counterparts. Care must be taken if bending or forming plated filigree so that the finish doesn't crack or flake off. Keep in mind that bending this type of filigree too much can result in breakage.

Like other brass filigree, plated finishes can be heat-treated and painted.

Solid sterling silver or *gold* stamped filigree is very rarely available, but it can be used in many of the same ways as brass filigree. Pure metals like sterling silver or gold are more flexible than alloys such as brass, so these elements will bend quite easily. Do note that twisted wire filigree should not be bent, because pressure applied to soldered joints and wire twists can cause breakage.

Filigree Shapes

Filigree components come in an assortment of shapes, ranging from tiny teardrops to large flowers to beads. From item to item, you'll frequently see the same shapes replicated and repeated. For instance, a small, filigreed teardrop might also appear as the petal of a large flower, or three of the teardrops might be grouped together as a fan. Filigree forms are often symmetrical, drawing from decorative motifs seen in textiles and architecture as well as stylized natural forms. The symmetry of filigree is also an expression of manufacturing limits and functional uses. Creating a design takes time and it's more efficient to tweak an existing shape and die than to come up with an entirely new one. Producing a shape in a variety of sizes also makes it versatile; a design of filigree pieces stacked and attached to make earrings translates well into a set by using larger identical elements, also stacked and attached, for a necklace pendant.

Not only does a wide array of flat shapes exist, but filigree is also available in three-dimensional shapes. Some are bowed, some are cupped, and others still are completely spherical to form beads. The shaping, when accomplished by a machine, is called *dapping*, and it generally takes place before any plating or surface finish is applied. Machine dapping creates elements that are slightly stiffer than flat filigree, but the trade-off is smooth, complex curves or sharp folds. Bead caps, for example, begin life as flat rosettes, and curved fans start out as flat triangles of filigree.

Dapped pieces can be mixed and combined with flat pieces to produce layered effects....You can also hand-bend flat components to give them simple curves, as I did on the links for Pavlova. I explain how to make these types of bends...

Sewing Beads to Filigree

I like to attach beads to filigree by sewing them on with flexible beading wire. The wire knots so nicely and doesn't hurt my fingers. Always try to match the color of the wire to the filigree. This will ensure that any exposed sewing blends in and isn't noticed, much like matching your thread when sewing on a button! This technique can create a mess on the back of the filigree with the knots and tail strands everywhere, so I always try to cover my knotting with another piece of filigree as in the Blossoms hair pins project...

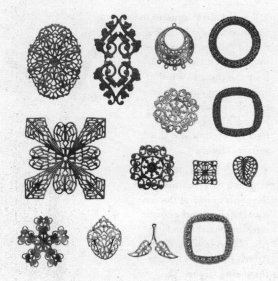

1. Cut the required amount of beading wire.

2. String on one bead, leaving a 4-inch (10.2 cm) tail. Working from the front of the filigree, push both ends of the wire through the filigree holes where specified in the instructions (photo 1).

3. Tie a secure square knot on the back of the filigree (photo 2).

4. Pass the long end of the wire up through the filigree to exit where specified (photo 3). Slip on a bead and pass the wire down through the filigree to the back of the filigree.

5. Repeat this sewing action until the filigree is beaded as required (photo 4). Tie the wire ends together in a tight square knot and trim. If you are worried about your knots holding, you can add a drop of glue, but I rarely do this.

Photo 1

Photo 2

Photo 3

Photo 4

Designing Your Own Bead-sewing Patterns

Most filigree pieces are created with even patterns that make them ideal for beading. For instance, the repeated shapes in a filigreed flower or star suggest their own beading patterns because the design naturally repeats. So, when I make my own filigree jewelry designs, the filigree patterns make bead placement easy because I just look for those repetitive filigree lines. They show where I can bead an individual section, and then repeat the beaded pattern across the filigree. And, because the stiff metal supports even rather heavy or ornate beading, I know I can bead to my heart's delight.

While I have used some very common filigree pieces in the projects in this book, you may want to need to make substitutes from time to time. The beading counts in this book are for the styles of filigree specified, but you can easily alter them for the filigree you have available. Don't be afraid to experiment with the styles you have available and mix up the techniques to create your own.

Knotting

You'll need to know how to knot stringing material and ribbon when working on the projects in this book.

An **overhand knot** (figure 1) is made by forming a loop in a single strand and passing the end of the stringing material back through the loop. Pull on the end to tighten.

A **square knot** (figure 2) is made by forming an overhand knot with both ends of the stringing material, right end over left end. Repeat this, passing the left end over the right end to make the knot tight and secure.

A **surgeon's knot** (figure 3) is formed much like a square knot, but when tying the first overhand knot you make an additional wrap with the stringing material to secure the knot. Make a second overhand knot and pull to secure. This knot it very useful when you're trying to keep a tight tension on a difficult piece of beadwork.

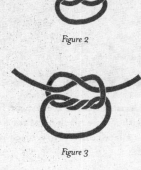

Figure 1

Figure 2

Figure 3

Forming Filigree

Just about any flat filigree can be bent to a curve or folded shape. You'll find many examples in this book of how those beautiful flat pieces can become even lovelier with a bit of a bend. Bending filigree pieces allows you to create new shapes—you can curve a large, flat piece to create a cuff bracelet, or curl the points of a filigree flower into a setting for a stone. The metal will happily hold the shape you bend, so you can create forms that can be further adorned with beads, crystals or stones.

Curves

Many flat filigree pieces are available that would make perfect bracelets if they weren't so well, flat. For a bracelet, a gentle curve enhances the comfort. I have bent large filigree pieces around just about anything that seems to have the right curve: a rolling pin, a table leg, a dowel rod or even a wooden spoon.

1. Hold the filigree against a rounded object.

2. Use your hands to press the filigrees piece into the shape as shown in photo 5. Check the shape periodically to make sure you don't over-bend the metal.

3. If you're curving several pieces of the same style filigree and each need to have identical bends, check the pieces against each other several times as you work. Try spooning, or stacking the pieces to test the shape.

Photo 5

Sharp bends

Making sharp bends in a piece of filigree completely changes the shape. You'll need to know how to make these bends when you create bezels…

1. Determine the place you want to make the bends, possibly working from a sketch or photocopy of the piece of filigree. Place the filigree flat within the jaws of chain-nose pliers at the bend point.

Photo 6

2. Slowly and carefully make the bend (photo 6). Make many small adjustments rather than a few large ones, and take care to make any bend away from the front of the filigree. For multiple bends, work the filigree from side to side, not clockwise.

Changing Metal Finishes

While metal filigree is available in a variety of finishes, there are often times when you want to change the finish. Whether you want to mix various finishes in one piece of jewelry, subtly alter a plated finish, or dramatically change a plain finish, there are a variety of methods you can use to do this.

It's important to note that all heat-treating, sealing, or painting should take place before any beads are added to the filigree. Some treatments can harm the beads and the beads can get in the way of creating the desired finishes. Heat treatments especially can affect many types of beads causing them to crack, change color, or melt.

Before you change the finish on the filigree, determine if the metal is raw brass or plated. Raw brass will range in color from a bright and shiny yellow gold color to a dark, antique-looking patina. There will usually be some variation in the finish of raw brass and a darker color will rub off with a bit of baking soda and water. Plated finished can be sterling silver, copper, or any other metal color, but will generally not rub off with baking soda. The easiest way to identify the finish is to ask about it when purchasing. When you return home, label the filigree before you store it.

Heat Treatments

Heat can be used to transform the finish on both raw and plated metals. Heat will darken bright yellow raw brass. It can remove the sealant coating on plated metal so you can paint it. Heat may darken the color, but will generally not remove a plated finish from metal.

You can apply heat to the filigree pieces in several ways. By using flame, either with a torch or your gas stove, you can remove the finish coating and do some subtle patinas. You can also use a heat gun designed for embossing or other paper arts. This method is ideal when you want to naturally darken or age raw brass filigree. Generally, heat guns will not burn off any surface coating or plating, but they will darken the metal. Filigree can also be heated using a butane torch. These torches get very hot (around 1300° F) [704.4° C]) but with care you can use one safely in your home. The torch allows you to direct the heat to specific areas of the filigree to soften the metal or to create dark, aged areas. The directed flame is more efficient than a gas stove.

When creating a patina with flame, be careful when holding the filigree over a store or other flame. Your tools will get quite hot! I use metal kitchen tongs for holding my filigree. To avoid contaminating food with any paints or patinas from the filigree I don't use the same tongs to cook my dinner. If you are heating sealed filigree to burn off a coating, please make sure you are working in a well ventilated area. Heating raw brass to patina the metal naturally, however, does not produce fumes.

To darken the metal with a heat gun:

1. Lay all the pieces you wish to darken on a heat-proof work surface. Make sure no pieces are touching.

2. Use the heat gun to gently warm the filigree pieces. As the color begins to change (within two to five minutes), watch the metal surface and pull the gun away as soon as the desired color is reached. If the surface is heating unevenly, move the gun around or rotate the piece with a pair of pliers or tongs. Be very careful as the metal will be quite hot.

3. After the pieces are cool, seal them with acrylic spray paint or allow the finish to wear naturally.

Continued ➜

To darken the metal with a gas stove or torch:

1. Hold the filigree piece with tongs or pliers just over the flame. Make sure you move the metal around to create an even color and remove the metal from the flame as soon as the desired color is achieved.

2. After the pieces are cool, seal them with acrylic spray paint or allow the finish to wear naturally.

Sealants

Once you have heat-treated the surface of the metal you can allow it to continue to darken and age naturally or you can choose to seal it. A thin coating of *clear enamel spray paint* will seal the surface and keep the finish as-is for years. Another way to seal the finish is with *beeswax*. The coating traditionally used to seal a natural brass patina was beeswax, and it still works well. Beeswax is often sold at bead and sewing shops or you can try a local farmer's market or natural foods store. Rub a very small amount of beeswax onto a soft cloth and then rub the cloth onto the filigree. The metal finish will be a bit darker with the beeswax on the surface, and the soft patina will remain tarnish-free for a long time.

Paints

For a bit of whimsy, or just a different look, I love painted filigree. The color can make the lacy metal take on a whole new look, bright and cheery in primary colors, or dramatic and graphic in black or white. You can also use it to give an aged 'whitewashed' look…

My favorite paint for use on filigree is enamel spray paint. It comes in a wide variety of colors and is readily available at most paint or hardware stores. While you can't mix your own colors in the cans, layering different colors is possible. The thin coats you can make with spray paint create a durable finish that resists wear. Avoid spray paints that are latex or advertised as "easy to clean up" or "water washable." They generally don't stick to the metal for very long. Painting filigree is easy to do, but because you're painting on metal it's important to stick to these steps.

1. Clean the filigree by heat-treating it. The heat helps remove any lacquer or burn off any processing oils, and ensures that the paint remains on the metal for years to come. After the cleaned filigree is cooled, handle it with gloves or tweezers so the oils from your hands don't cause the paint to flake later.

2. Choose a well-ventilated painting space, like a porch or garage, where the paint won't drift onto rugs or furniture.

3. Lay down a sheet or two of newsprint or scrap cardboard on the work surface. **Note**: I spray my pieces in a large shallow box about 6 inches (15.2 cm) deep. Use tweezers or wear gloves to place the filigree pieces on the paper.

4. Spray the front of the filigree with three light coats, allowing 60 to 90 minutes between coats. Flip the filigree over and paint the back in the same manner. Once the two sides have been painted, allow to dry overnight. Finish the piece with a single, thin coat of clear spray paint on each side and allow to dry for 24 hours.

You can also create a whitewashed or antiqued effect on filigree using just spray paint.

1. Clean the filigree by heat-treating it.

2. Apply a thin coat of clear spray paint.

3. While the clear coat is still quite wet, apply a thin coat of either white (for whitewash) or dark (for antique) paint. Use a smooth cotton rag to immediately wipe the surface of the filigree. This will remove the paint on the highest parts of the filigree design and leave paint in the open, lacy parts. **Note**: This is a tricky technique and you may want to practice it a few times until you get it right. You can repeat the painting and the wiping steps to make the effect more pronounced. This finish also works well on chain if you stick to working with short sections.

4. When you are pleased with the final look, allow the paint to dry overnight. Finish with a coat of clear spray paint and let dry.

Pavlova

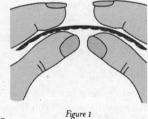

Crystals sparkle against the filigree of this cuff. Pair it with a little black dress for a night on the town, or wear it as a lacy contrast to a black sweater and jeans during the day.

Finished size:

Adjustable, up to 7 inches (17.8 cm)

Materials

3 gunmetal flat filigree squares, 42 mm

1 gunmetal teardrop filigree, 15 x 20 mm

32 light topaz crystal bicone beads, 4 mm

32 smoke metallic AB crystal round beads, 3 mm

48 gunmetal head pins, 1 inch (2.5 cm)

48 antiqued brass 20-gauge head pins, 1 inch (2.5 cm)

36 antiqued brass 20-gauge oval jump rings, or sturdy chain links, 5 x 7 mm

1 antiqued brass fish hook clasp, 19 mm

Tools

Rolling pin or wooden bracelet mandrel

Round-nose pliers

Chain-nose pliers

Wire cutters

Techniques

Metal bending

Opening and closing rings

Simple loop

Adding beads to filigree

Instructions

1. Grasp a filigreed square so it sits right side up between the thumb and forefingers of each hand. Carefully bend an even, smooth curve (figure 1). Use a rolling pin or bracelet mandrel to refine the curve. Repeat for each square. Stack the squares to make sure their curves match and make adjustments as necessary. Set the squares aside.

Figure 1

2. Look at the front of one of the squares. Note a circle made up of 16 filigree holes around the rosette pattern. Pass a brass head pin through one of the holes and trim the head pin to ⅜ inch (9 mm) (figure 2). Form a simple loop to secure the pin. Repeat around the circle to add 16 looped head pins in all. Repeat this step for each square.

3. Lay the three squares in a row, side by side. Use a round jump ring to connect the first two squares near the top and another round jump ring to connect the squares near the bottom. Repeat to connect the second and third squares (figure 3).

4. Attach an oval jump ring to a filigree hole at the center edge of the first square. Use another jump ring to connect the ring just placed to a third ring. Attach the clasp to the third ring (figure 4).

5. Attach an oval jump ring to a filigree hole at the center edge loop of the third square. Attach another jump ring to the one just placed. Continue to link oval jump rings to make a chain 14 rings long. Attach the filigreed teardrop to the last ring.

Figure 2

Figure 3

6. Slip a bead onto a gunmetal head pin. Form a simple loop to secure the bead. Repeat with all the beads to make 64 dangles in all.

7. Attach one topaz dangle to each brass loop on the first and third squares. Connect two smoke dangles to each brass loop on the second center square.

Lisbon

The tiny crystals on these shimmery earrings capture and refract the light. Wear these accent pieces with a white shirt and jeans and let them draw all eyes to you.

Finished size:

2½ inches (6.7 cm)

Materials

9 gold-plated filigree teardrops, 15 x 20 mm

36 clear AB crystal bicone beads, 2 mm

22 gold-filled head pins, 1 inch (2.5 cm)

1 pair of gold-filled 24-gauge ear wires

Gold-filled 24-gauge wire, 6 inches (15.2 cm)

TOOLS

Chain-nose pliers

Round-nose pliers

Wire cutters

TECHNIQUES

Simple loop

Opening and closing rings

INSTRUCTIONS

1. Slide one bead onto a head pin and form a simple loop to secure it. **Note**: It may help to very gently grasp the crystal with chain-nose pliers while turning the loop with round-nose pliers. Repeat to make 11 dangles in all. Set aside.

2. Cut a 1-inch (2.5 cm) length of wire. Form a simple loop at one end. Slide on one bead and form a simple loop to secure it. Repeat to make six bead links in all. Set aside.

3. Use your fingers to shape one of the ear wires until it's a smooth curve. Slide on one bead and use your fingers to reshape the ear wire.

4. Lay the teardrops, face up, in three rows: one in row 1, three in row 2, and three in row 3.

5. Attach the ear wire to the top of the row 1 teardrop. Use a bead link to connect the top of the first row 2 teardrop to the bottom left hole of the row 1 teardrop; a link to connect the top of the second row 2 teardrop to the bottom center hole of the row 1 teardrop; and a third link to connect the top of the third row 2 teardrop to the bottom right hole of the row 1 teardrop. Use bead links to connect the top of each row 3 teardrop to the bottom center hole of each row 2 teardrop (figure 1).

Figure 1

6. Add one dangle to each of the three holes at the bottom of the row 3 teardrops. Connect one dangle to the bottom left hole of the first row 1 teardrop, and one to the bottom right hole of the third row 1 tear drop (figure 2).

Figure 2

7. Repeat all steps to make a second earring.

Blossoms

These flower hair pins will take care of any bad hair day. Make a trio with beads in complementary colors, and you'll hear nothing but compliments.

FINISHED SIZE:

2½ inches (6.4 cm)

MATERIALS (FOR A SET OF THREE)

3 antiqued brass dapped six-point filigree flowers, 20 mm

3 antiqued brass flat six-point filigree flowers, 20 mm

3 faceted or smooth round glass beads, 6 to 8 mm

18 faceted or smooth round glass beads, 4 mm

12 antiqued brass oval jump rings, 4 x 5 mm

3 brown bobby pins

Medium-width flexible beading wire, 3 feet (91.4 cm)

Clear jeweler's adhesive cement (optional)

TOOLS

Wire cutters

Chain-nose pliers

TECHNIQUES

Knotting

Sewing beads to filigree

Opening and closing rings

INSTRUCTIONS

1. Cut a 12-inch (30.5 cm) length of wire and string on an 8-mm bead, leaving a 4-inch (10.2 cm) tail. Sew the bead to the center of one of the dapped flowers. Tie a square knot on the back of the flower to firmly seat the bead (figure 1). Don't trim the wire.

2. Pass the long end to the front of the flower, exiting from a petal. String on one 4 mm bead and sew it to the petal (figure 2). Repeat around to add six 4-mm beads in all. Tie a square knot on the back of the flower and trim the excess wire. Set the beaded flower aside.

Figure 1   *Figure 2*

3. Slide one flat flower into a bobby pin so the pin hooks in the dip between petals. Place a beaded flower on top of the flat flower so the petals line up. Use jump rings to attach the top two and bottom two petal points (figure 3). **Note**: Though the flower may move slightly on the bobby pin, it should be secure. To reduce the movement, place a small drop of adhesive cement on the center back of the beaded flower before attaching it to the flat one.

Figure 3

4. Repeat all steps to make two more hair pins.

Golden Shimmer

This necklace glints in the lovely space just below your collarbone, and it would be perfect to wear to a summer cocktail party. The crystals along the bottom add a row of sparkle to this easy-to-make necklace and a beaded dangle in the back is an extra that will make heads turn.

FINISHED SIZE:

Adjustable, up to 18 inches (45.7 cm)

MATERIALS

13 gold-filled filigree leaves, 12 mm x 26 mm

24 clear AB crystal round beads, 6 mm

28 clear AB crystal bicone beads, 4 mm

28 gold-filled head pins, 2 inches (5.1 cm)

20 gold-filled oval jump rings, 4 x 5 mm

1 gold-filled S clasp, 12 mm

Gold-filled 20-gauge wire, 36 inches (91.4 cm)

TOOLS

Chain-nose pliers

Round-nose pliers

Wire cutters

TECHNIQUES

Opening and closing rings

INSTRUCTIONS

1. Cut a 1-inch (2.5 cm) length of wire. Form a simple loop at one end. Slide on one 6 mm bead and form a simple loop to secure it. Repeat to make 24 bead links in all. Attach nine bead links together, end to end, to make one bead chain, and 15 links together to make a second chain. Set the short and long chains aside.

2. Slip a 4 mm bead onto a head pin. Form a simple loop to secure the bead. Repeat to create 28 dangles in all. Set aside.

3. Lay the filigree leaves in four rows: six leaves in row 1, three leaves in row 2, two leaves in row 3, and one leaf in row 4. Orient the leaves so their tips point down.

4. Make sure the leaves face forward as you connect the first lead of row 1 to the second leaf using one jump ring. Attach the second leaf to the third using two jump rings. Connect the third to the fourth and the fourth to the fifth using two jump rings, and the fifth to the sixth using one jump ring.

5. Use a jump ring to connect the right bottom of the second leaf in row 1 to the left top of the first leaf in row 2. Use another jump ring to connect the right top of the first leaf in row 2 to the bottom left of the third leaf in row 1. Continue across, attaching the top of the row 2 leaves to the bottom of the row 1 leaves. In the same manner, attach row 3 to row 2 and row 4 to row 3 (figure 1).

6. Connect dangles to the holes at the bottom of the leaves, five to the first and last leaves in row 1; two dangles each to the holes at the bottom of the first and last leaves in rows 2 and 3; and five to the leaf in row 4 (figure 2). Periodically life the necklace to your neck to see how the beads hang when the design is worn.

7. Attach five dangles to the remaining filigree leaf.

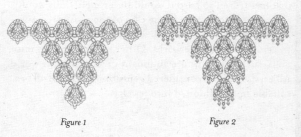

Figure 1   *Figure 2*

Continued →

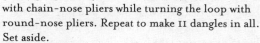

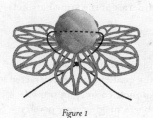

8. Connect the short chain to the left side of the first leaf in row 1 and the long chain to the right side of the last leaf in row 1. Attach the clasp to the end of the short chain and the remaining leaf to the end of the long chain. **Note**: If you'd rather not use the extender chain to fit the necklace, you may adjust for perfect fit by removing or adding bead links to the chains.

—From *Beading With Filigree*

BEADING WITH GEMSTONES

Valérie MacCarthy

Learning About Gemstones

What Is a Gemstone?

There's no exact definition to describe gems or gemstones—some have described them simply as "ornamental stones." But there are a number of specific characteristics that we ascribe to gemstones; color may be the most important to you, but some others include their atomic structure, hardness, gravity, and cleavage, or fracture. Since you'll be purchasing stones that will have already been cut and identified for you, you won't need to know much about the scientific techniques used to identify the raw material. But you're probably interested in some general information about the stones you'll use to make your jewelry.

Gemstones are most often minerals (such as topaz), but they can be organic (like coral), or, in rare cases, rock (such as lapis lazuli). All of these can be referred to as gemstones.

Minerals

A mineral is an inorganic solid crystalline structure that's found in the Earth's crust. Depending on the mineral, its crystalline formation can be clearly evident, as in this clear quartz, or too small for the naked eye to see. Sometimes minerals are referred to as crystals, which have been studied for centuries. In fact, the word crystal comes from the Greek word *krystallos*, or *kryos*, meaning "icy cold." It was once believed that rock crystal was ice that had frozen so hard it would never melt! This would almost seem to be true in the case of the most precious mineral of all, the diamond, which is rare and only exists in certain parts of the world. Other more common minerals, such as quartz, are abundant throughout the world. All crystals can be considered gemstones, but not all are suitable to be fashioned into jewelry.

Organic Stones

Organic gems are derived from living things, such as animals and plants, and they come in the form of amber, fossils, coral, and pearls. Although all of them are classified as organic gems, each has been formed in a unique manner. For instance, amber is pine-tree resin that fossilized 50 million years ago, coral is the secreted skeleton from the marine organisms called coral polyps, and fossils originate from shells and bones of animals that were trapped in layers of rock.

Pearls are formed naturally inside mollusks such as oysters to counteract the irritating effects of sand inside the shell. The mollusk covers the grain of sand with layers of nacre and, over time, the little grain of sand turns into a pearl. Cultured pearls, which are also considered gemstones, are formed when humans help along this natural process by placing the irritant in the jaws of the mollusk.

Rocks

A rock is a combination, or aggregate, of two or more minerals. We've all called a diamond a rock, but don't be fooled, because a diamond is no rock! Stones that are a combination of one or more minerals, such as lapis lazuli, labradorite, and moonstone, are designated as rocks.

Gemstones Qualities

Each type of gemstone has its own distinctive characteristics. As you become familiar with these qualities, you'll find that you can correctly identify most gemstones, and at the same time you'll be making good decisions about which stones to use for specific pieces.

Hardness

One way to identify a gemstone is by its specific hardness. All minerals can be placed on Mohs' scale of relative hardness, which was devised by German mineralogist Friedrich Mohs in 1812. As an aid in classifying the hardness of minerals, he selected 10 readily available minerals and placed them in order on the scale so that a specific mineral could scratch only the minerals listed above it, but none of those below it. Minerals of the same hardness can also scratch each other.

Color

A crystal's color is often its most striking and attractive feature, and this is probably the quality that first attracted you to a particular stone. No doubt, color is an important consideration when you begin making your jewelry pieces.

Some minerals, known as allochromatic, occur in a variety of colors. Examples of these are quartz, diamond, tourmaline, apatite, and fluorite. Other minerals referred to as idiochromatic always occur as the same

---

MOHS' HARDNESS SCALE

Following are Mohs' 10 minerals, with 1 (talc) being the softest mineral and 10 (diamond) being the hardest.

1 Talc	6 Orthoclase feldspar
2 Gypsum	7 Quartz
3 Calcite	8 Topaz
4 Fluorite	9 Corundum
5 Apatite	10 Diamond

Most semiprecious stones that you'll be using to make the jewelry pieces in this book are in the 5 to 7 range on the scale. Organic stones are much softer, in the range of 2 and 3. Be especially careful when working with these softer stones, which include pearls, coral, and amber, because they can become scratched or chipped more easily than the harder stones.

---

color. For example, peridot is an idiochromatic mineral, always appearing green.

Some stones may resemble each other to the naked eye (for instance, yellow topaz and citrine are commonly confused), but due to their specific chemical properties and ordered atomic structure, a gemologist can discern the difference. The opposite also holds true. For example, there are many different quartz varieties that look nothing like pure clear quartz. They've even been given completely different names, such as chalcedony, agate, and chrysoprase, but in fact these all belong to the same quartz family as clear quartz, amethyst, and citrine. It's important to be aware of these aspects of gemstone colors when selecting stones for your jewelry projects.

Light

The play of light and its effect on color is one of the intriguing factors concerning gemstones, and you'll probably want to design your pieces with this characteristic in mind. The particular color of a stone is primarily due to dispersion, the breaking up of white light into a spectrum (rainbow). When light passes through a gemstone, some spectral colors are absorbed while others are reflected back. Those that are reflected back give the gem its color. With colorless stones, you may see flashes of color, often referred to as fire, which is also due to this dispersion of light.

The appearance of certain colors can be due to impurities in the stone, ironically enough. For example, amethyst is rock quartz containing trace amounts of ferric iron, and the rose colors in rose quartz are created by traces of manganese or titanium.

Some crystals can make you think you're seeing double! This effect is called refraction, which occurs when light passing through a crystal is split into two rays. Because gems have more density than air, light slows down and bends, causing the double image.

Certain stones, such as moonstone and labradorite, play with light to cause effects that look similar to a soap bubble or an oil slick. This effect, which is caused by light reflecting off structures within the stone, is called interference, or sometimes opalescence or schiller.

Enhanced and Altered Stones

The appearance of some gemstones can be altered by heat, irradiation, staining, and oiling, and this may influence how you feel about using a certain stone in your jewelry pieces.

Heat treatment is used either to enhance or to change a gem's color. In the case of amethyst, heating it will turn it to crime. Irradiation also causes a stone to change color, and this can happen naturally from radioactive elements within the Earth's crust, or artificially, through human methods.

Staining can be done using stains, dyes, or chemicals. Some techniques coat the surface, while others change the entire stone. Staining can only be done on porous stones, which allow the color to enter into them. This technique is used to enhance a stone's color or to imitate another stone. For example, howlite, which is naturally white, is often dyed to imitate turquoise.

Oiling is used to enhance a stone by hiding the cracks and fissures. Emeralds and opals are often oiled to fill in their blemishes.

Know Your Gemstones

Creating gemstone jewelry is exciting and inspiring. The gemstones have a beauty of their own, even before being combined with other stones and precious metals to make rings, earrings, bracelets, and necklaces. Before you begin shopping for stones, I recommend that you get to know a little about them, especially the range of colors, characteristics, and identifying factors that make them unique....

Birthstones

Certain stones have traditionally been associated with months of the year. This came about after the breastplate of a high priest was discovered in Egypt containing these 12 stones. According to tradition, Hebrews took the 12 stones and assigned each one to represent their 12 tribes of Israel. But it was in the 18th century in Poland that wearing birthstones came into fashion. It was believed that the cosmic energy transmitted by the stones would resonate back to the wearer, creating positive energy that, in turn, would bring good luck and happiness.

Following is a list of traditional birthstones:

January: garnet, rose quartz

February: amethyst, onyx

March: aquamarine, tourmaline

April: diamond, zircon, crystal quartz

May: emerald, chrysoprase

June: pearl, moonstone

July: ruby, carnelian

August: peridot, onyx

September: sapphire, chrysolite

October: opal, pink tourmaline

November: topaz, citrine, smoky quartz

December: turquoise, zircon

Gemstone and Accent Beads

To make the gemstone jewelry designs in this book, you'll need a variety of fine gemstone beads. All of the designs use gemstones that have holes drilled into them, so they are technically called beads. I also use less-precious seed beads for accents. The process of selecting and shopping for just the right ones is one of the most exciting aspects of making your own jewelry.

I've used many different stones for these designs, but feel free to mix and match other stones in place of the ones you see. The best way to find your inner artist is by taking a risk and trying something new, even if it's only using another color or a different type of stone.

Some of the gemstones I've used are fairly common; others are rare. As you can imagine, the rarer the stone, the more valuable it is, and the more costly it is. Before you begin any project, check on the price and availability of the stones you plan to use.

Keep in mind that you can substitute many of the stones shown in the projects. For instance, where I may have used tourmaline, which is a pricey stone, you can substitute quartz or chalcedony, which are much more common and cost a fraction of the price of tourmaline. You'll have a beautiful piece of jewelry with either selection.

Do you already have a collection of gemstones and beads? Before shopping for new ones, take a fresh look at what you have on hand. You may discover that some of the projects in this book are perfect for stones you've stashed away, just waiting for you to find the perfect designs to show off their qualities.

After you've checked your own collection, visit several bead stores in your area to explore their resources and shop their inventory. What better way to become familiar with all that's involved in making gemstone jewelry? You'll be able to see firsthand the myriad beads and stones and learn more about their colors, shapes, and qualities. Many bead shops also offer how-to classes and workshops, an excellent means of discovering and learning new techniques. Be sure to check out coming shows and exhibits that you may want to attend. We all benefit from inspiration, and we all like to show off our latest work, especially to others who love to work with gemstones!

The Internet has become a valuable source for locating and purchasing beautiful stones and supplies directly from the manufacturers at affordable prices. Make use of online search resources and auction sites to find exactly the stones and supplies you're looking for.

Bead Sizes

All of the designs in this book require specified sizes of stones. Stones and beads are sized according to metric units of measure, with a stone's size usually determined by its diameter. If you're not familiar with metric measurements, you'll soon get to know the measurements that are most commonly used in making jewelry.

A slide caliper is a handy tool for measuring stones and beads, allowing you to measure their exact size. You'll want to have a caliper with you when you go shopping for stones so you can buy exactly the right size....

Bead Shapes

Stones come in all sorts of different shapes and sizes. You'll want to become familiar with the most common shapes. A visit to a bead shop or online research will provide answers to many of your specific questions about which stones are available in which specific shapes. I've included most of these shapes in the jewelry designs in this book.

Bicone: Diamond-shaped

Briolette: Teardrop-shaped bead with faceted sides or round with no flat sides

Disk or Coin: Round, flattened shape

Drop or Teardrop: Round with a soft point, pendant-shaped; the hole can be either horizontally through the top or vertically through the center

Nugget: Irregular

Oval: Egg-shaped, elliptical

Rondelle: Doughnut-shaped

Round: Ball-shaped

All of these different shapes can be faceted, smooth, or even rough. A faceted stone has flat surfaces cut into the stone. A diamond, for example, is almost always faceted. These facets throw off light, giving stones a sparkling effect. A smooth stone has no facets and is smooth to the touch. It is usually curved to give it a shape, and it has no sharp edges. A rough stone will often be in its unpolished state, but it can also be shaped this way to give it a more organic, natural look.

Making Twisted Wire Loop Links

This type of link is my favorite way of attaching any component to any other component, whether it's a bead to a chain, a bead to another bead, or a chain to a clasp.

You'll be using it frequently when making the gemstone designs in this book. Practice with inexpensive wire until you've mastered it, then cut the beads loose. I've found this linking technique to be more secure and durable than using a jump ring because it involves twisting and locking the wire into place.

To make a twisted wire loop link, use round-nose pliers to grip a piece of wire ¾ inch (1.9 cm) from the end. Bend the wire around the tip of the pliers to form a loop (photo 1).

Remove the pliers and grip the loop itself with chain-nose pliers. Twist the two wire ends around each other one and one-half times to secure. Make sure the longer wire is facing straight up from the loop. Now use wire cutters to cut off the shorter wire end close to the twist (photo 2). You've now made the first half of the loop link. Select the stone or bead that you are using for the design and slide it onto the wire.

To make the second part of the loop link, bend the wire at a 45° angle and repeat the process of looping on this end of the wire (photo 3). Wrap the wire end around to secure it, and then cut off the wire close to the twist (photo 4). For some of my jewelry designs, I use this link without a stone. To make this type of link, follow the technique described...but don't place a stone on the wire after you've completed the first loop. Make the second loop, and then wrap the wire end around the twist you just completed to secure the piece.

If you need to join links, you can build the next one by attaching it to the link you've just created. If you're attaching the link to a chain, be sure to place the chain link on the loop before closing it.

You'll be using a similar technique to attach briolette-shaped stones, as well as pearls and stones with holes drilled at the top instead of through the center. To attach these stones, slide the wire through the hole, allowing ¾ inch (1.9 cm) to pass through to the other side. Bend both wire ends up until they cross tightly. Twist the wires around to secure and cut off the shorter wire end. Bend the remaining wire at a 45° angle, and use round-nose pliers to make a loop. Hold the loop with chain-nose pliers and wrap the wire around the twist you just completed to secure the piece.

When attaching these stones, make sure the direction of the loop brings attention to the stone instead of the wire. If you've already completed your loop and it is not facing the direction you prefer, simply grip the loop with round-nose pliers and give it a small, additional twist to make the loop either forward-facing or side-facing, whichever is needed for your piece. Following up with this small but important detail will allow the stone to be the focus of your design.

You'll notice that I often say to bend the wire 45°. Bending the wire in this manner keeps the loop centered above the bead (photo 5). If you don't bend the wire, you'll find your loop will tend to veer to one side. This simple 45° bend will prevent this from happening.

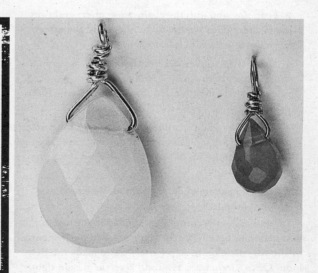

Continued →

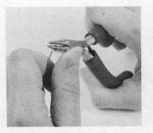

Photo 1

Photo 2

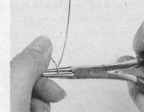

Photo 3

Photo 4

Photo 5

Photo 6

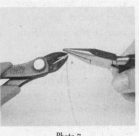

Photo 7

Photo 8

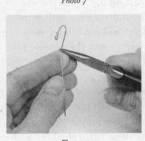

Photo 9

Photo 10

Making Earring Loops

I like to make my own ear wires, which I'll call earring loops.

1. To make an earring hoop, use wire cutters to cut a 2½-inch (6.4 cm) length of 22-gauge wire. Use round-nose pliers to grip the wire ¾ inch (1.9 cm) from the end. Wrap the wire around the pliers to form a circle (photo 6).

2. Grip the loop with the chain-nose pliers and twist the two wire ends around each other. Cut the excess from the shorter wire (photo 7).

3. Using large rubberized round-nose pliers, wrap the wire, starting at the twisted end, around one jaw of the pliers to create the rounded shape of an earring loop (photo 8).

4. I also like to add a little flip at the end of the wire as a finishing detail. To create this effect, use large pliers to grip the tip of the wire and bend it up very slightly (photo 9).

5. Use wire cutters to cut the wire to the length you desire (photo 10).

In most cases, the components added to my earring loops (stones, bead links, etc.) are attached permanently, by slipping them on in step 1 after you've made the first loop. Once a loop is made, it will keep the design tightly

---

fastened, but it also means that it can't be changed unless you cut through the twisted loop. See the project instructions for specific assembly directions for each set of earrings.

Working with Purchased Earring Findings

Rather than make your own ear wires, you can also use various types of prefabricated findings with rings or loops, such as ball-post earrings, level-back earrings, traditional French ear wires, and more. You can also use ear clips, if your ears aren't pierced. Attaching stones to these findings is very simple. With chain-nose pliers, grasp the loop on the finding and twist very slightly to one side. Never pull the loop open; instead, gently twist it to one side. Then place the chain or a stone on the open loop and close, again using the chain-nose pliers. You can see how easy it is to substitute the findings as you wish when you make your own pieces of jewelry.

Simplicity

Lemon quartz and amethyst is a perfect combination for simple earrings that you can make in a jiffy.

Finished size:

3¾ inches (9.5 cm)

Materials

2 lemon quartz nuggets, 15 mm

4 amethyst briolettes, 8 mm

7-inch (17.8 cm) length of 1 mm gold-filled chain

5-inch (12.7 cm) length of 22-gauge gold-filled wire

10-inch (25.4 cm) length of 26-gauge gold-filled wire

Tools

Chain-nose pliers

Round-nose pliers

Wire cutters

Large rubberized round-nose pliers

Ruler

Techniques

Making Twisted Wire Loop

Making Earring Loops

Instructions

Make two

1. Cut the chain, making the following four segments: two 2-inch (5.1 cm) segments and two 1½-inch (3.8 cm) segments. Count the links to be sure the chain segments are the same length.

2. Slide one 8 mm amethyst briolette onto the 26-gauge wire, with one end extending ¾ inch (1.9 cm) from the hole. Bend both wires upward until they cross. Tightly twist the wires around once. Cut off the shorter wire end.

3. Hold the remaining wire with the round-nose pliers and loop around.

4. Slide the wire through the last link in one of the chain segments. Holding onto the loop with the chain-nose pliers, wrap the wire around the twist you made in step 2. Cut off the excess wire.

---

5. Repeat steps 2 through 4 three more times, until all four briolettes are attached to a length of chain.

6. Make another loop in the 26-gauge wire, ¾ inch (1.9 cm) from the end. Place two of the chain segments (one of each length) onto the wire so they hang from the loop. Hold the loop with the chain-nose pliers and twist the wires around to secure the chains in place. Cut off the shorter wire end and bend the longer wire up so it is centered over the loop (figure 1).

7. Slide one 15 mm quartz nugget onto the wire and bend the wire 45°. Using the round-nose pliers, loop the wire around. Hold the loop with the chain-nose pliers and wrap the wire around to secure.

8. To make the earring loops, cut the 22-gauge wire into two pieces, each 2½ inches (6.4 cm) long. With the round-nose pliers, grip one piece of wire ¾ inch (1.9 cm) from the end and wrap to make a loop.

9. Slide this wire through the loop on top of the quartz nugget. Hold this new loop with the chain-nose pliers and wrap it around two times. Cut off the shorter wire end.

10. Using the rubberized round-nose pliers, clamp down on the wire right above the twist and bend the wire around the jaw of the pliers. Cut the wire to the desired length.

11. Using the chain-nose pliers, grasp the tip of the wire and bend it slightly upward to give the earring a finishing touch.

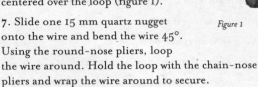
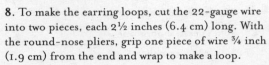
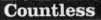

Figure 1

Countless

Create this easily adaptable bracelet using purple and green gemstones, or select other color and stone combinations to match your mood.

Finished size:

7¼ inches (18.4 cm)

Materials

18 amethyst beads (round), 8 mm

12 peridot beads (round), 6 mm

13 peridot beads (oval), 8 mm

16 gold-filled beads, 3 mm

1 gold-filled four-strand slide clasp

55-inch (139.7 cm) length of 3.5 mm gold-filled chain

88-inch (223.5 cm) length of 24-gauge gold-filled wire

Tools

Chain-nose pliers

Round-nose pliers

Wire cutters

Ruler

Techniques

Making twisted wire loop links

Working with catches and clasps

Instructions

1. Separate the two slide clasp pieces while making the bracelet, always being careful to attach each strand to the correct loop. Begin by making wire loop links to attach the chain to the slide clasp. Loop the 24-gauge wire around the round-nose pliers about ¾ inch (1.9 cm) from the end of the wire. To make the loop larger, wrap the wire around the pliers at a thicker part of the jaws. After you've made the first loop, thread the slide clasp onto it. Also place the chain on this loop before wrapping the wire around to secure it. Hold this loop with the chain-nose pliers and twist the wire around to secure. Cut off the shorter wire end. **Note:** When placing the chain on the other three wire loops that will be connected to the slide clasp, always be sure to place the chain on the same side of the loop to maintain consistency (figure 1).

2. Hold the remaining wire with the round-nose pliers and loop it again. Cut the attached chain to about ½ inch (1.3 cm) in length so that you can attach a new piece. Slip a new chain length onto the other wire loop. Hold the loop with the chain-nose pliers and wrap the wire around the twist you made in step 1. Cut off the excess wire.

3. Now for the fun part! This bracelet requires you to experiment. The stones are randomly placed throughout, which means the length of the chain between each stone is completely up to you. For the bracelet shown, I varied the length of chain between the stones from a single link to about 1 inch (2.5 cm).

4. Attach a stone or stones (I don't recommend more than two) to the end of the first chain by making a loop in the wire about ¾ inch (1.9 cm) from the end. Attach this loop to the end of the chain. Hold this loop with the chain-nose pliers and twist the wires around to secure. Place a stone or stones onto the wire, bend the wire 45, and loop it again using the round-nose pliers. Attach a new length of chain onto this loop and hold the loop with the chain-nose pliers. Wrap the wire around to secure and cut off the excess wire.

5. Repeat steps 3 and 4 on both chains until you reach the length you need and are ready to attach it to the other half of the slide clasp. **Note:** The top chain on the first end should remain the top chain on this end, too. Therefore, the top chain will need to be slightly longer because it needs to reach the first loop of the wire link (figure 2).

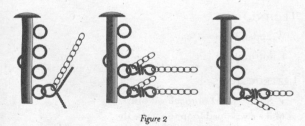

Figure 2

6. Repeat step 1 but in reverse, attaching the bottom (shorter) end to the looped wire first. Twist it to secure. Using the round-nose pliers, bend the wire a second time and slide it through the slide clasp. Place the second chain on this same loop. Hold the loop with the chain-nose pliers. Wrap the wire around the twist you just made and cut off the excess wire. You've finished the first length of the bracelet.

7. Repeat steps 1 through 6 three more times to complete the bracelet. As you work, study your completed sections to make sure you're not placing similar stones too close together. Plan the length of the chain segments so the stones are interspersed throughout.

Duet

A rich cluster of gemstones is attached to both ends of a long chain, creating this luxe lariat necklace.

Finished size:

36⅞ inches (93.6 cm)

Materials

2 moss quartz drops, 25 mm

7 jade beads, 5 mm

9 gray pearls (oval), 7 mm

8 green seed beads

9 sterling silver beads, 3 mm

6 sterling silver beads, 2 mm

2 sterling silver ball-end head pins, 1½ inches (3.8 cm) long

34-inch (86.4 cm) length of 2 mm sterling silver chain

40-inch (101.6 cm) length of 26-gauge sterling silver wire

Image missing???

Tools

Chain-nose pliers

Round-nose pliers

Wire cutters

Techniques

Making twisted wire loop links

Working with head pins

Instructions

1. Select the head pins, two 25 mm quartz drops, two 3-mm sterling silver beads, and the chain.

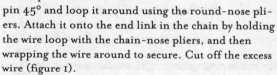

2. Slide one 3 mm bead and one quartz drop onto a head pin. Bend the head pin 45° and loop it around using the round-nose pliers. Attach it onto the end link in the chain by holding the wire loop with the chain-nose pliers, and then wrapping the wire around to secure. Cut off the excess wire (figure 1).

3. Repeat step 2 for the other end of the chain.

4. Separate the remaining beads and pearls to make two similar groups to attach to the two ends of the necklace. For this design, I've balanced the number of stones on the two ends, but the groups are not identical. I placed four 5 mm jade beads on one side and three on the other, and four 7 mm gray pearls on one side and five on the other, and so forth. In assembling the necklace, you can follow this example for bead placement or choose your own.

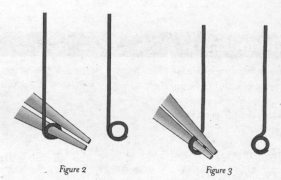

Figure 1

5. Use the 26-gauge wire to make eye pins for the detailed bead extensions. With the round-nose pliers, hold the tip of the wire. Twirl the wire around one and one-half times to make a loop (figure 2). Keep the pliers placed through the hole, but rotate them so the outer jaw is now on the straight wire. Bend the straight wire 45° to center the loop (figure 3).

Figure 2   Figure 3

6. Slide one or two beads onto the wire. **Note:** Switch the bead combinations on every head pin to create variety. For example, make one head pin with one jade bead only, a second head pin with one 3 mm silver bead and one jade bead, and a third head pin with one jade bead, one seed bead, and one 2 mm silver bead.

7. After the beads on the head pin are in place, bend the wire 45°, loop it around using the round-nose pliers, and slide this loop onto a link in the chain immediately above the 25 mm quartz drop.

8. Hold this loop with the chain-nose pliers and wrap the wire around to secure. Cut off the excess wire.

9. To attach the oval pearls, you won't need to make a head pin. Instead, slide the wire through the pearl with ¾ (1.9 cm) extending out the other side. Bend both wire ends up until they cross tightly. Twist the two wires together one and one-half times. Cut off the shorter wire end. If desired, slide a seed bead or a sterling silver bead onto this wire.

10. To attach to the chain, bend the wire 45° and wrap it around using the round-nose pliers. Slide the loop onto the chain immediately above the 25 mm quartz drop, in the same link where you attached the head pin in steps 7 and 8. Hold the loop with the chain-nose pliers and wrap the wire around to secure. Cut off the excess wire.

11. Attach a total of 10 head pins or twisted wire loop links above the large quartz drop. Use the first four links in the chain as well as the wire loop above the 25 mm quartz drop for attaching these small head pins and wire links (figure 4). To give the gemstone cluster a lush, full effect, attach a detailed head pin or wire link to both sides of these four chain links, as well as the wire loop.

Figure 4

12. After completing one end of the chain, work the other end, repeating steps 5 through 11 to complete the necklace.

13. To wear this necklace, hold both beaded ends in one hand and the loop of the chain in the other hand. Place it around your neck and slip the two beaded ends through the loop in the chain (figure 5).

Figure 5

Continued ➤

Cleopatra

The intriguing qualities of green onyx and chrysoprase are displayed to perfection in this simple yet stylish earring design.

FINISHED SIZE:

1½ inches (3.8 cm)

MATERIALS

2 green onyx briolettes, 12 mm

2 chrysoprase briolettes, 6 mm

2 gold-filled ball-post earrings with open rings

12-inch (30.5 cm) length of 24-gauge gold-filled wire

4-inch (10.2 cm) length of 26-gauge gold-filled wire

TOOLS

Chain-nose pliers

Round-nose pliers

Wire cutters

Large rubberized round-nose pliers

Ruler

TECHNIQUES

Making twisted wire loop links

Working with purchased earring findings

INSTRUCTIONS

Make two

1. With wire cutters, cut the 12-inch (30.5 cm) length of 24-gauge wire into two 6-inch (15.2 cm) segments.

2. Select one of the wires and slide a 12 mm green onyx briolette onto the middle of it. Bend the wires on both sides of the bead until they cross, and then twist them around once to secure the briolette in place.

3. Using the large rubberized round-nose pliers, bend both wires into a curve (figure 1). Before continuing, make sure the wires are curved to a pleasing size to accommodate the 6 mm chrysoprase briolette; hold it in the middle of the curve to check. Adjust the size of the curve as necessary.

4. Keeping the wires crossed and using the round-nose pliers, grasp one wire on the inside of the cross and loop it around (figure 2).

5. With the chain-nose pliers, hold both the loop you've just made and the opposite wire and twist them around just above the loop (figure 3). Cut off one wire above the twist.

6. Loop the remaining wire around and slide the ring of the ball-post earring onto the wire.

7. Hold this loop with the chain-nose pliers and wrap the wire around the twist you made in step 5. Cut off the excess wire.

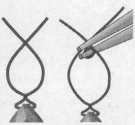

Figure 1   Figure 2   Figure 3

---

8. Cut the 4-inch (10.2 cm) length of 26-gauge wire in half, two 2-inch (5.1 cm) lengths. Slide a 6 mm chrysoprase briolette onto one wire about ¾ inch (1.9 cm) from the end. Bend both ends up until the wires are crossing.

9. Twist the wires around one and one-half times and cut off the shorter wire end. Adjust the remaining wire so that it is facing forward (not to the side).

10. Using the round-nose pliers, loop this wire and slide it through the bottom loop you created on the earring.

11. After one loop is hanging from the other, use the chain-nose pliers to hold this new loop and wrap the wire around the twist you made in step 9. Cut off the excess wire.

—FROM *Beading with Gemstones*

BEADING WITH PEARLS

ane Campbell, Editor

Pearl Primer

All natural pearls are produced by mollusks. A *naturally occurring pearl* is created when a piece of sand or other irritant gets inside the mollusk's body and the creature slowly builds layers of smooth *nacre*, a natural secretion also called "mother-of-pearl," around the irritant to make itself more comfortable.

Cultured pearls remove the chance factor in finding consistently-sized pearls. They are created by a pearl farmer who inserts a round shell bead inside a mollusk. As in nature, the mollusk builds nacre around the irritant, creating a fairly uniform pearl. Culturing pearls not only garners consistent round sizes, but offers the opportunity to produce other shapes as well. To do so, a pearl farmer plants a shaped shell within a mollusk, and the result is a pearl in that specific shape. Popular pearl shapes include coins, sticks, flat teardrops, squares, and diamonds.

Other types of pearl shapes include *keishi*, which have no nucleus—they are simply the extra nacre that may be produced by a mollusk. *Mabe pearls*, also know as *blister pearls*, are produced by inserting a half bead into a specific place in the mollusk's shell. The mollusk produces a hollow pearl that is removed, filled with glue, and then backed with mother-of-pearl to create a pearl cabochon.

PEARL PURCHASING TIPS

If you design primarily features pearls or size and shape consistency is crucial, buy the best quality you can find. If your design means that the pearls will be mixed in with dozens of other beads and consistency isn't an issue, you can get away with a less expensive option.

Natural pearls have very small holes, so if your design requires thicker stringing material than the pearl can handle, consider using a pearl reamer to make the holes larger, or buy the larger-holed glass or crystal pearls.

Pearls come in fully-drilled, half-drilled, and undrilled versions. Make sure to check that you're purchasing the proper type for the project you're making.

Find out how the pearl was colored before you buy it, especially if you plan on using it for a piece of jewelry like a bracelet, which will suffer lots of wear and tear. Most pearls are naturally colored, but some pearls are surface-dyed and the dye will rub off if they're worn frequently.

Each species of mollusk creates a slightly different type and color of pearl nacre, but the most noticeable difference is between *freshwater* and *ocean pearls*. Freshwater mollusks produce pearls that have a characteristic uneven surface. They are relatively inexpensive and easy to find at bead shops. Ocean mollusks make pearls that have a very smooth, even surface, but they're harder to come by and are often much more expensive.

Historically, the highest-quality natural pearls have come from southern India and the countries surrounding the Persian Gulf. Japan reigned in overall production for scores of years, but over the last several, China has become the largest producer, offering larger quantities and lower prices.

Other beads made to look like pearls have always been a fashion option, especially for costume jewelry. *Fine glass pearls*, also referred to as *Majorca pearls* in reference to the Mediterranean island where they were first produced in mass quantities, are made of a glass base covered with crushed shells or fish scales. *Crystal pearls* are relative newcomers to beaders' stashes—they consist of a smooth, fine crystal core covered with a pearly coating. *Plastic pearls* are beads covered with opalescent paint and are the least-desirable option for beaders as a seam is often evident, and the finish can ship off during wear.

Lasso

Designer: Diana Light

Versatile to wear, this easy-to-make piece can be worn as a necklace, bracelet, lariat, or belt. Because the knots and pearls "lock" into one another, the piece is surprisingly secure when worn.

FINISHED SIZE

4 feet (1.2 m)

MATERIALS

11 white freshwater pearls, 6.5 to 7 mm round

19 white freshwater pearls, 5 mm round

30 sterling silver 24-gauge head pins, 1½ inches (3.8 cm) long

67-inch (1.7 m) length of 1.5 mm dark brown, Greek-style leather cord

TOOLS

Chain-nose pliers

Round-nose pliers

Wire cutters

Ruler

TECHNIQUES

Wrapped loop

Knotting

INSTRUCTIONS

1. Slide a pearl onto a head pin. Make a wrapped loop to secure the pearl, but instead of trimming the wire end, keep wrapping the wire around the top of the pearl to make a small, spiral bead cap (figure 1). **Note:** Be sure to make the loop on each dangle large enough to string onto the leather cord.

Figure 1

2. Repeat step 1, using all of the pearls and head pins, so you end up with 30 pearl dangles. Set aside.

3. At the end of the leather cord, tie an overhand knot that incorporates one of the dangles in it (figure 2).

4. String one or two dangles onto the cord. Measure 1¾ to 2 inches (4.5 to 5.1 cm) down the cord and tie an overhand knot.

5. Repeat step 4 down the length of the cord, sometimes randomly stringing on dangles between knots and other times incorporating the dangles into the knots as in step 3. Be sure to tie all the knots in the same direction.

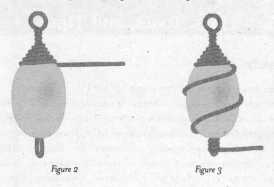

Figure 2

Twist

Designer: Jean Power

A thin, spiraling wire cages a large pearl, creating the perfect earring dangle. Experiment with wire and pearl types and the number of spiral rotations used—you'll find an array of looks at your fingertips.

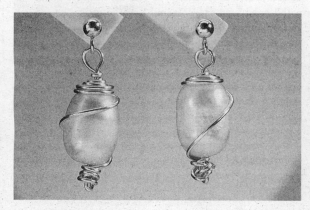

FINISHED SIZE

1³⁄₁₆ inch (20 mm)

MATERIALS

2 cream freshwater pearls, ½-inch (1.3 cm) long oval

2 sterling silver earring findings

12-inch (30.5 cm) length of 22-gauge, sterling silver wire

TOOLS

Wire cutters

Ruler or measuring tape

Round-nose pliers

Chain- or flat-nose pliers

TECHNIQUES

Wrapped loop

Coiling wire

Opening and closing rings

INSTRUCTIONS

1. Cut the wire into two 6-inch (15.2 cm) pieces. Set aside.

2. Take one of the pieces of wire and use round-nose pliers to form a ³⁄₁₆-inch (4 mm) U-shaped bend at one end. Use chain-nose pliers to squish the shape together (figure 1).

Figure 1

3. String a pearl onto the bent wire. Make a wrapped loop to secure the pearl.

---

4. Continue wrapping the wire around the top of the pearl until you have four to five coils (figure 2).

5. Make two loose spirals around the pearl to reach the bottom. Coil the remainder of the wire down the bend you made in step 2, leaving the tip of the bend exposed (figure 3). If desired, wrap the wire over itself to give the coil a heftier look. Trim any excess wire and use chain-nose pliers to tighten the wrap.

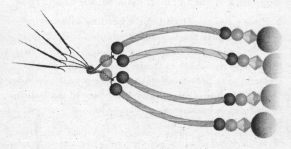

Figure 2   Figure 3

6. Attach an earring finding to the wrapped loop.

7. Repeat steps 2 through 6 to make a second earring.

Siren's Song

Designer: Ellen Gerritse

A mixture of pearls, crystals, and sterling silver evokes an underwater symphony. This necklace uses simple stringing techniques. End cones hide the knots that keep the strands together.

FINISHED SIZE

19¾ inches (50.2 cm)

MATERIALS

49 silver freshwater pearls, 8 mm potato

99 black freshwater pearls, 6 mm potato

90 black freshwater pearls, 3 mm potato

98 opal crystals in bicone and round shapes, 4 mm

49 sterling silver-plated curved and twisted tubes, 2 x 24 mm

204 sterling silver-plated seamless rounds, 2 mm and 3 mm

2 sterling silver seamless cones, 15 mm

1 sterling silver round box clasp with ivory pearl inlay, 10 mm

Dark gray silk beading thread

Clear glue

TOOLS

Scissors

7 English beading needles, size 12 or 13

TECHNIQUES

Knotting

INSTRUCTIONS

1. Cut a 28-inch (71.1 cm) length of thread. Make a square knot about 4 inches (10.2 cm) from one end. Thread it on a needle. String on beads in the following sequence to make the first strand: One 3 mm pearl, one tube, one 3-mm pearl, one seamless round, one crystal, one 6-mm pearl, one seamless round, one 8-mm pearl, one seamless round, one 6 mm pearl, one crystal, one seamless round, and one 3 mm pearl. Repeat this sequence six more times. Snug the beads against the knot and set the strand aside with the needle still attached.

2. Repeat step 1 six more times to make a total of seven strands.

3. Place two of the strands together and make an overhand knot at the top of the last beads strung. Pair the needles together and pass both needles through one seamless round. Repeat with two more strands. Knot the four strands together (figure 1).

4. Knot the remaining three strands together as you did in step 3. Gather the needles together and string on two seamless rounds. Place this set of three strands next to the set of four strands on the work surface. Arrange the strands so the first beads strung on the four-strand set are next to the last beads strung on the three-strand set. Weave the set of three strands loosely through the set of four to create a twisted effect. Group the ends of the three strands together and make a knot. Gather the needles together and string on one seamless round. Remove the needles from one end of the three-strand set and thread them on the other end.

Figure 1

5. Gather all seven strands and knot them together at each end, taking care to avoid leaving any slack in the thread. Pass the strands with the needles on them through one cone and one half of the clasp. Pass back through the cone, pull tight, and make two knots (figure 2). Glue the knots to secure. After they dry completely, trim any excess thread.

Figure 2

6. Thread the needles on the other end of the strands. Repeat step 5 on the other end of the necklace, being careful to hide the knots inside the cone.

Simple Pleasures

Designer: Debra Saldivar

A chunky button is the star of this understated bracelet. Besides being a focal element, it serves as half of the closure.

FINISHED SIZE

10¼ inches (26 cm)

Continued ➜

MATERIALS

11 blue iris freshwater pearls, 7 mm potato

10 ivory freshwater pearls, 8 mm top-drilled potato

Approximately 82 midnight blue cylinder beads, regular (comparable to size 11° seed beads)

4 sterling silver Bali-style barrels, 12 x 16 mm

1 sterling silver seamless round, 3 mm

1 sterling silver 24-gauge head pin, 2 inches (5.1 cm)

2 sterling silver crimp tubes, 2 x 2 mm

1 horn two-holed button, 3.2 cm

20-inch (50.8 cm) length of fine, flexible beading wire

TOOLS

Round-nose pliers

Chain-nose pliers

Wire cutters

Clip or bead stopper

Crimping pliers

TECHNIQUES

Wrapped loop

Crimping

INSTRUCTIONS

Note: If you require a smaller bracelet size, simply reduce the number or size of beads for the final design.

1. Slide a blue pearl onto the head pin. Make a wrapped loop with a ⅛-inch (3 mm) loop. Set the dangle aside.

2. Place a clip at one end of the beading wire. String on four cylinder beads, one crimp tube, and 20 cylinder beads. Pass the wire up through one hole of the button from back to front. String on the dangle created in the previous step so it slides over the cylinder beads. Pass down through the other hole of the button from front to back. Pass back through the crimp tube and the first four cylinder beads strung in this step so you have a ½-inch (1.3 cm) wire tail exiting the last bead (figure 1). Snug the beads and crimp the tube. Trim the excess tail wire. Remove the clip.

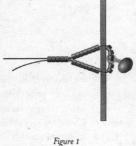

Figure 1

3. String on a sequence of one blue pearl and one cylinder bead four times. String on one blue pearl and one silver barrel. String on five ivory pearls and one silver barrel. Repeat this step.

4. String on one seamless round, one crimp tube, and approximately 58 cylinder beads, or enough that when made into a loop the beads fit snugly over the button. Pass back through the crimp tube, seamless round, and barrel bead to make a loop (figure 2). Snug the beads and crimp the tube. Trim any excess wire close to the beads.

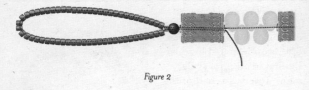

Figure 2

—FROM *Beading with Pearls*

BEADWEAVING

Carol Wilcox Wells

Materials, Tools, and Tips

Beads

Can one person have too many beads? I don't think so! The selection of beads today is ever expanding, as is their use. Beads can be found on clothing, lamp shades, coasters, shoes, tassels, purses, napkins, belts, hats, pillows, cards, and jewelry—and this is the short list. Every month a new catalog arrives with something else made from beads or using beads as embellishment. Of course I want one of each! Beads are popular—it's a fact—and we're living in a time when our choices are many.

The beads used throughout this book are mainly seed beads of different sizes, shapes, and color. A few of the projects do use larger trim beads, but usually as embellishment only. When you're buying seed beads, you'll find the larger the number the smaller the bead. For example, a size 15/0 bead is much smaller than a size 6/0 bead. However, if you think that an 11/0 bead is always the same size you'll be mistaken. There are slight differences in size when comparing an 11/0 bead from one manufacturer to an 11/0 from another manufacturer. The shape may be slightly different as well; one may be very round while another is a squared round. Seed beads come in a variety of shapes as well, but round is the most popular. Other shapes include cylinders, triangles, cubes, hexagons, and charlottes, to name a few. The more you use beads, the more you'll understand what you need to buy for a specific project.

Colors? Well, there are lots of colors, but let's start at the beginning. Seed beads are made from glass. They start out either transparent or opaque, then either the outside or the inside surface can be treated to change the look of the bead. Some of these treatments are gilt- or silver-lined, color-lined, gold- or copper-plated, galvanized, dyed, luster, gold luster, frosted or matte, rainbow/iris, metallic, and pearl, to name a few. Many of the surface treatments are then combined to produce beads such as transparent matte iris, semi-matte silver-lined, or matte metallic. The list goes on and on. Some of these surface treatments won't hold up over time due to friction, body chemistry, light, or chemicals.

Learning all of the nuances can seem overwhelming, so just take it one bead at a time. Know what you're buying. The best way to do this is to buy from someone who knows what they're selling. Support your local bead store, join a bead society, and talk to others who bead.

Threads

Choices and still more decisions to make! What should I use? Well, as in all things, being the individuals we are, we all have favorites and I, too, have mine when it comes to the threads that I use. I also know that many of the

artists who have projects in this book use a different style of thread than my usual one; it's their favorite and that's okay. I suggest that you try many different styles of thread, to find the one that suits you and the work that you do. Each project in this book recommends a style, size, and color of thread. Use these if you're a beginner; if not, use the thread of your choice.

What I need, for my current work, is a strong thread and what I need for my current age and eyes is one that's easy to thread. A nylon multifilament linear (untwisted) thread works well for me. This thread comes on bobbins, spools, and cones. Now here's something interesting: the size of the thread on a cone is heavier than the thread on a bobbin (in other words, its denier is higher). This thread comes in many sizes, from the finest OO, to O, B, D, and F, the heaviest. There are more color choices in bobbin sizes than in cones or spools. Choose a color of thread that matches the main bead color in the project or one that is slightly darker. Do keep in mind that if you're using transparent beads the thread will affect their color. Beading thread doesn't need to be treated with wax; however, you can do so if you prefer working with a waxed thread.

Pre-waxed twisted nylon threads are also available, on cards or spools. There's one size, A, and many beautiful colors. It's fairly fine, and can be used doubled for extra strength.

Silk thread, on small cones, is used to crochet with beads. Seed beads, from size 15/0 up to 8/0, can be used on size E silk. What I like about the silk is how it lets the beads move, but it's also slippery in your hands and can get away from you very quickly. Some of my students prefer a #8 pearl cotton, saying that it's easier to manipulate.

Needles

Beading needles come in many sizes 10, 12, 13, 15, and 16. The larger the needle's number, the smaller its diameter; they're about two inches long and are flexible. The size 12 needle is the most universal, fitting through some 15/0's, all 11/0's, and larger seed beads. Keep a package of each size at your work station so you can change needles quickly. Don't force the needle through a bead or it will break; instead, switch to a smaller needle.

Another needle used for beading is known as a sharp or sharps; this short, fine needle has a small eye. Because of its length it's not very flexible, which can be very handy in certain situations.

Crochet Hooks

While teaching my first crocheted-rope class, I found out that not all steel hooks are created equal. The hook size might read *US 9/1.15 mm* on a hook from one manufacturer, but another US 9 hook might read *US 9/1.40 mm*. That's quite a difference! Lydia Borin explained to me that this is because in the United States, crochet hook numbers don't refer precisely to a single size, so all metric-sized hooks that fall within a certain range of diameters are stamped with a single U.S. hook number.

Now, we all crochet with a different tension on the thread, and if we were crocheting with a stretchy fiber and had a pattern to follow, a gauge would be given to achieve consistent results. In such a case, the hook size would have to be determined by the person doing the work. The best thing to do is to experiment with the thread of your choice and different-sized hooks until you get the look you desire. The projects in this book tell you the hook size and type of thread that I used. Begin there, and if that doesn't work for you try something else.

For those of you who don't already know, a crochet hook's design has several parts: the *head* hooks the thread and pulls it through the stitch. The *throat* is tapered, and allows the thread to slide up to the shank. The *shank* section determines the hook size and the stitch size. The *grip* is where you hold the hook, and the *handle* extends beyond it (see figure 1).

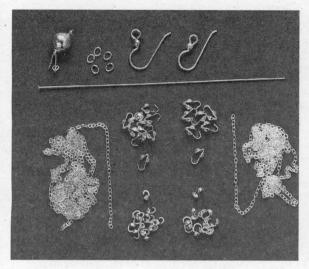

Findings

Findings are metal components used as attachments and fasteners for jewelry. They can be purchased at your local bead store, or craft shop, or from mail order catalogs, and they come in a variety of metals. The least expensive are made of base metals, but they're available in sterling silver and karat golds, too. Use the best that you can afford.

Keep an assortment of findings on hand. You'll want French ear wires, bead tips in various sizes, head pins, jump rings, crimp beads, a variety of clasps and fine chains. Try to have a supply made from sterling silver, gold-filled, and some karat golds, for that special piece.

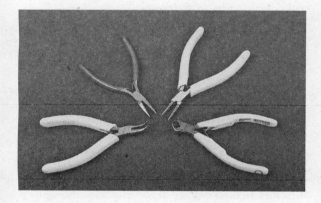

Scissors and Tweezers

Owning a small pair of very sharp scissors is one of the nicest things that you can do for yourself. Don't cut paper with them, save them for thread only. Hide the scissors from family members, if you have to—they're always a temptation to others! You'll want these sharp scissors to make clean, close cuts; it's the beads we want to see, not thread ends.

Small tweezers are also handy to have because they can help you untangle knots, pick up individual beads, and grab a dropped crochet stitch.

Larger Tools

A good set of jeweler's pliers is needed if you're going to make anything that involves metal findings. (Remember when buying them that you get what you pay for.) The basic tools needed are:

Chain-nose pliers (available as straight or bent-nose) are rounded on the outside and have a flat smooth surface on the inside. They can be used to open and close jump rings, help pull the needle through a tight spot, squeeze chain links down to a smaller size, break beads, and attach findings.

Round-nose pliers are just that, round. The tips are shaped like small cones, and are used to form a loop on the end of a wire.

Flat-nose pliers (optional) have a rectangular jaw and the edges are square. There are times when you'll want to bend a wire at a right angle, and these are the pliers to do it.

Flush cutters are useful for cutting wire; a file may be needed to smooth the rough ends.

Miscellaneous Work Station Items

There are many times when the amount of beads for a certain project needs to be known; using a calculator makes this so much easier.

When ideas strike, take the time to write them down, or draw a picture of what is in your mind. It doesn't have to be beautiful, it just has to get the idea across to you at a later date. Feel like doodling? Do it on one of the many graph papers made for specific off-loom stitches; you'll be amazed at your own creativity.

Finally, if you like charted designs than you'll have to have a metal board with magnetic strips. Your beading life becomes simpler as you slide the magnetic strip down the graph row by row.

Knots

There are three knots that I use on a regular basis: the slip knot, the square knot, and the weaver's knot. Each one handles a specific job and is easily tied. Once you learn them they'll become second nature.

Slip Knot. To start any crochet project you must use a slip knot. Hold the tail thread in your left hand, leaving about 6 inches (15.2 cm) hanging free. Make a loop with the working thread that lays over the tail thread. Now use the hook to reach through the loop, and pull up the working thread (see figure 2). Tighten the knot and you're ready to work.

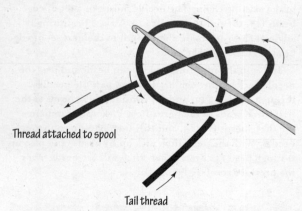

Thread attached to spool

Tail thread

Figure 2. Slip knot

Square Knot. The square knot is one of the easiest knots to tie, because it's simply two overhand knots. Be careful when doing the second half of the knot, or it can go wrong and turn into a granny knot.

An easy-to-remember rule is if you make the first knot with an overhand loop, the second knot should also use an overhand loop. This creates a loop that goes over both threads on one side and a loop that goes under both threads on the other side.

With thread A in the right hand and thread B in the left, lay A over and then under B (see figure 3). Thread A is now on the left and thread B on the right. Lay thread A over and under thread B, and pull to tighten.

Weaver's Knot. The weaver's knot is used for joining a new thread to an old thread, making a continuous strand throughout the project. This is very handy when work-

ing with a tight tension, as for a basket, when ending and adding a thread by weaving out of and into the work is prohibited. When tying this knot, try to position it as close to the work as possible, to reduce the number of times it has to pass through a bead that already is full of thread.

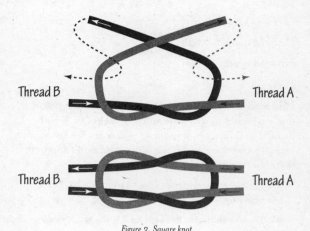

Thread B   Thread A

Thread B   Thread A

Figure 3. Square knot

Place the tail end of the new thread under the tail end of the old thread (see figure 4a). Using the long portion of the new thread, wrap it around and behind the short end of the new thread, forming a loop around the old thread (see figure 4b). Place the new thread over the old one.

Referring to figure 4c, pass the old thread end over the new and down into the loop. Close the loop by pulling on the new thread end, then pull the two old threads away from the two new threads. If the knot has been tied correctly it won't slip. Don't cut the ends; let them be woven in as you stitch. Later, if any ends are sticking out, clip them very close to the work.

How Many Beads?

Over the years people have asked me to figure out how many beads they'll need for a project. This becomes a math problem, so here's a little bit of information to help you figure out how many beads to buy. Most bead sellers sell their beads by the gram, so knowing how many beads are in a gram is important. It's also good to know how many beads of a certain size will fit in an inch (or centimeter), and in a square inch (or square centimeter), so that you can do the math.

Now, to qualify this list I must say that all beads don't weigh the same; a metallic 11/0 seed bead will weigh more than a transparent 11/0 seed bead. Each manufacturer's 11/0 seed beads are of a different size, so this is approximate. All of the beads weighed in this list were from one manufacturer, and they were all opaque black.

How Many Beads Per Gram?

Type of Bead	How Many Per Gram
15/0 seed beads	290
Cylinder seed beads	190
11/0 seed beads	110
8/0 seed beads	38
6/0 seed beads	15

How Many Beads Strung Per Linear Measurement?

Type of Bead	How Many Per Inch	How Many Per CM
15/0 seed beads	24	9
Cylinder seed beads	20	7
11/0 seed beads	18	7
8/0 seed beads	13	5
6/0 seed beads	10	4

Continued ➜

How Many Beads Per Square Area Measurement?

Type of Bead	How Many Per Sq. Inch	How Many Per Sq. CM
15/0 seed beads	330	54
Cylinder seed beads	285	42
11/0 seed beads	216	35
8/0 seed beads	108	20
6/0 seed beads	70	12

Example

How many beads will I need to make an amulet purse that's 2 inches (5 cm) wide and 2½ inches (6.4 cm) deep? First, find out how many square inches (or square centimeters) there are in the piece, and don't forget that there's a front and a back.

2 x 2½ = 5 square inches (5 x 6.4 cm = 32.5 cm²) for one side

5 x 2 = 10 square inches (12.7 x 5 cm = 63.5 cm²) for both sides

Look at the list for beads per square area measured, decide which type of bead you'll be using (cylinder beads for our example), and multiply the number of square inches (or square centimeters) by the number of beads in the square area: 10 in² x 285 (63.5 cm² x 285) = 2850 beads. Now see how many beads per gram there are for the beads you're using, and divide that into the total number of beads: 2830 ÷ 190 = 15 grams of cylinder beads that will be needed to stitch the body of the purse.

Chevron Chain

Chevron chain has so many possibilities. The stitch can be tightly woven with beads right next to each other, or it can be stitched to have an open look like a netting. You can increase the stitch in width and depth. Flat chains are the normal use of chevron chain but I like to do it dimensionally, with a tight tension, forming really strong structures. Other techniques can be worked directly off the chevron chain, expanding the possibilities even more.

Basic Stitch

Note: The illustrations are done using two colors of beads. If this stitch is new to you, follow the color placement in each drawing. If you're feeling adventuresome use colors of your choice in any bead position.

To make a sample, pick up one bead, and slide it to within 6 inches (15 cm) of the tail, then loop back through it. String on nine more beads, following the color pattern in figure 1. Now pass the needle back up through bead 1, forming a triangle (see figure 2).

Pick up six more beads, and pass back down through bead 8, then pick up six beads again and pass up through bead 14. Continue this sequence for the desired length (see figure 3).

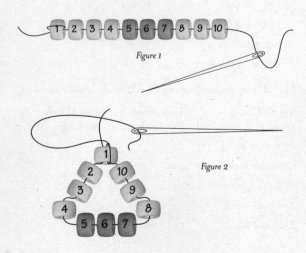

Figure 1

Figure 2

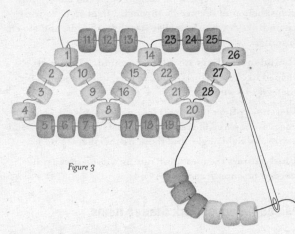

Figure 3

Joining the Chevron Chain

Before joining the ends of a chevron chain make sure that there are an equal number of sets on each side of the chain. A set is a group of beads that makes up the outside edge of an individual triangle within the chevron chain (see figure 4).

To join the two ends together pick up three of the six beads of a stitch (A, B, C), pass up through bead 4, and pick up two more beads (D, E); finish the stitch. Now pick up beads F, G, and H and pass the needle down through beads 1, 10, 9, and 8 (see figure 4).

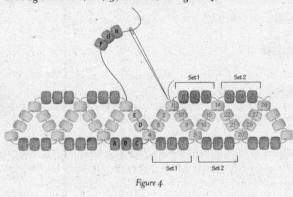

Figure 4

Adding Rows to Joined Chain

Add width to any chevron chain by adding another row to the existing chain. The needle must exit a set of edge beads (17, 18, and 19 in figure 4). Make a beginning triangle of chevron chain, then join it to the next set of edge beads in the original chain.

To begin the next row, pick up ten beads and pass the needle back up through bead 1. Now pass the needle through beads 11, 12, and 13; consider these beads as the first three beads of the next stitch. Pick up the remaining three beads (14, 15, and 16), then pass down through bead 8. With the next stitch pick up six beads, and pass up through bead 14. Every other stitch will use beads from the previous row (see figure 5).

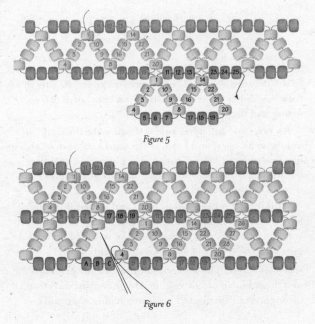

Figure 5

Figure 6

Turning and Adding Rows to Unjoined Chevron Chain

Figure 6 shows you how to close the second row of chevron chain. Pick up beads A, B, and C, and pass up through bead 4. Pick up beads D and E, and pass up through the bead at the top of the triangle. Weave through beads 17, 18, and 19 to finish the stitch.

Turning and Adding Rows to Unjoined Chevron Chain

Add another row of chevron chain by turning and stitching back the other way. Figure 7 shows how this is done, For the sample, stitch three sets of chevron chain; the needle exits bead 32 when this is completed. To make the turn, weave through beads to reposition the needle so that it exits from a set of beads on the outer edge. The diagram shows the thread path. To start the next row, string on ten beads, pass the needle back through bead 1 and beads 31, 30, and 29, and continue stitching across the row. When you reach the end you'll have to weave through beads to make the turn as you did before; follow the thread path shown in the diagram. Stitch row 3, then position the needle as if you were going to stitch another row.

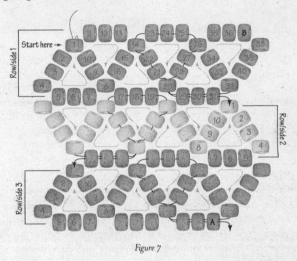

Figure 7

Dimensional Chevron Chain

Using chevron chain in a dimensional manner produces a structure that's strong yet open, one you can add to with more chevron chain or with other stitches. Make it open ended, as in this sample, or with the ends joined to form a circle. Please keep a very tight tension.

Making a Four-Sided Tube

After completing figure 7, fold the sample so that rows 1 and 3 are perpendicular to row 2. With the needle coming out of bead A in row 3 (see figure 8), string on four beads and pass the needle into bead B in row 1, heading left. Pick up three beads, and pass back down through bead 1. Now pass back through bead A and its two neighbors, pick up beads 8, 9, and 10, and weave up through bead 5. Continue across the row in this manner, closing the tube.

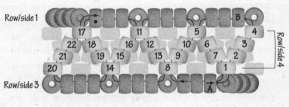

Figure 8

Adding Another Row

When adding another row of dimensional chevron chain, you'll stitch three sides. The fourth side is part of the previous chain.

Continuing to work from the completed sample tube (figure 9), make the turn and have the needle exit the bead marked with a black dot, heading to the left. Weave three sets of chevron chain to make row (see figure 9). Turn and add row 6. Make the turn and pick up four

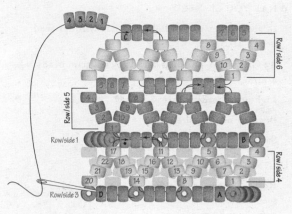

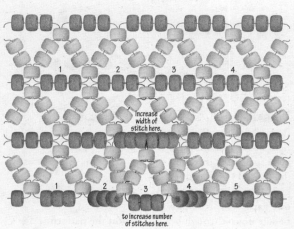

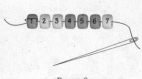

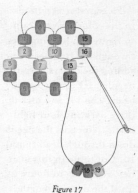

Figure 9

Figure 12

Figure 16

Figure 17

beads; the needle should be exiting bead C. Fold the work so that row 6 is over and parallel to row/side 4. Pass the needle through bead D and its two neighbors. Stitch the second tube closed in this way, weaving from the edge beads of rows 3 and 6 (refer to figure 8).

Making a Three-Sided Tube

Looking at figure 10, make two attached rows of chevron chain. Make the turn and pick up four beads, then pass the needle into bead B and close the chain, working from side to side. The process is the same as for closing the four-sided tube....

You can add more three-sided tubes to form a structure that looks like rows of pyramids on one side and is flat on the other.

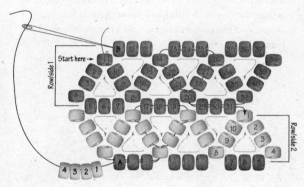

Figure 10

Increasing the Width of a Stitch

Each stitch may be increased by adding more beads to the outside edges, as shown in the second row of figure 11, or you can increase the stitch at random. If the ends are joined, increasing causes the work to flare out toward you. If they're not joined, the increased edges will be curved.

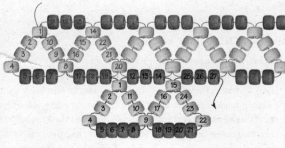

Figure 11

Increasing the Number of Stitches

Planning is important when increasing the number of stitches per row. First the width of a stitch must be doubled on one row, then that stitch is split and a new stitch is added between that group of beads when doing the next row. Figure 12 shows the process.

Adding Beads to the Surface

Add beads to the surface of the chevron chain to fill in the gaps between edge bead sets. Adding these beads helps to tighten and strengthen the weave, and it also provides the beginning step to adding peyote stitch to a piece.

Figure 13 shows how this is done. A row of dark surface beads has been added to the top row of chevron chain. Bead A is the last bead to be added to that row. Follow the thread path shown to add surface beads to the next row (bead B is the first surface bead added to the second row).

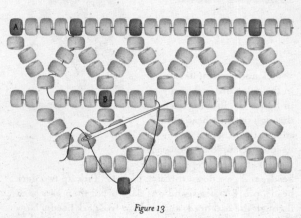

Figure 13

Variations of Chevron Chain (optional)

Variation 1. This chain is compact, with only one outside edge bead.

Pick up six beads in the color order shown in figure 14, looping back through the first bead before adding the others. Pass back up through bead 1, and pick up one light and two dark beads. Weave down through bead 5 (see figure 15), and continue in this manner for the length of the piece.

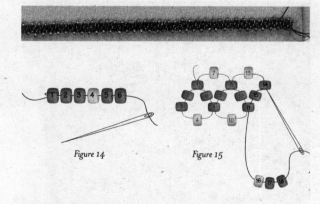

Figure 14

Figure 15

Variation 2. This narrow version is so tight that you can't see the telltale V of the chevron. Here, two beads are stitched through in every interior position, and the outside edge bead stays at one.

Pick up seven beads in the color order shown in figure 16, looping back through the first bead before adding the others. Pass the needle back up through beads 2 and 1, and pick up two dark and one light bead. Now pass the needle back down through beads 7 and 6. Continue adding three beads, passing through two for each subsequent stitch (see figure 17).

Variation 3. Here, the length of each leg of the V has been extended, and there are two outside edge beads, giving the chain an open and wider format.

Pick up nine beads in the color order shown in figure 18, looping back through the first bead before adding the others. Pass the needle back up through bead 1 and pick up two light and three dark beads. Now pass the needle down through bead 7, figure 19. Continue in this manner until the desired length is reached.

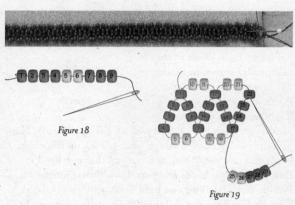

Figure 18

Figure 19

Variation 4. This very symmetrical variation is the one that I used in the basic instructions and the one that I seem to use the most when making dimensional chevron chain vessels. The outside edge beads have increased to three, pushing the V open.

Pick up ten beads in the color order shown in figure 20, looping back through the first bead before adding the others.

Weave back up through bead 1 and pick up three dark and three light beads. Now pass the needle down through bead 8. Continue in this manner, referring to figure 21, until the desired length is reached.

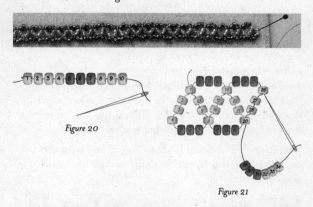

Figure 20

Figure 21

Variation 5. In this version, the chain widens and the shape of the V changes somewhat because two beads are used to join each stitch instead of one.

Continued ➜

Pick up thirteen beads in the color order shown in figure 22, looping back through the first bead before adding the others. Pass the needle back up through beads 2 and 1, and pick up three dark and four light beads. Now pass the needle down through bead 11 and 10. Continue in this manner, referring to figure 23, until the desired length is reached.

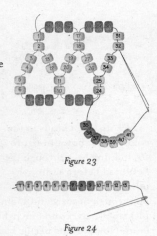

Figure 23

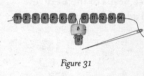

Figure 24

Variation 6. This chain is similar to Variation 1, but with a count of three edge beads and a different color placement, which gives it a braided look.

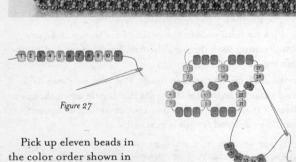

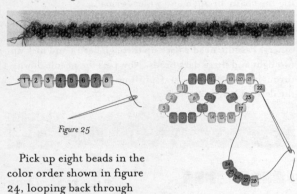

Figure 25

Figure 26

Pick up eight beads in the color order shown in figure 24, looping back through the first bead before adding the others. Pass the needle back up through bead 1. and pick up five dark beads. Now pass the needle down through bead 7. Pick up four light beads and one dark bead, and pass up through bead 12. Pick up five light beads and pass down through bead 17. Pick up four dark and one light bead, and pass through bead 22 (see figure 25). Repeat the pattern from bead 9.

Variation 7. This variation changes the color of its center bead for a different look.

Figure 27

Figure 28

Pick up eleven beads in the color order shown in figure 26, looping back through the first bead before adding the others. Pass the needle back up through beads 2 and 1. Pick up three dark beads, two light, and one dark. Now pass the needle down through beads 10 and 9. Repeat the pattern for the desired length, referring to figure 27 as you work.

Variation 8. Instead of having a row of beads on the outside edges, tiny fringes were formed at the turns for a very different look.

Pick up nine beads in the color order shown in figure 28, looping back through the first bead before adding the others.

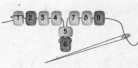

Figure 29

Pass the needle back up through bead 1. Pick up two light beads and one dark bead, pass back through the second light bead, and pick up two light beads and one dark bead. Now pass the needle down through bead 8. Repeat the pattern, referring to figure 29 as you work.

Variation 9. It seems that the variations are endless. This one has the tiny fringes on one side only, using an 8/0 bead at the drop point. The count has increased in the interior section, and the needle passes through two beads on the up stitch and one bead on the down stitch.

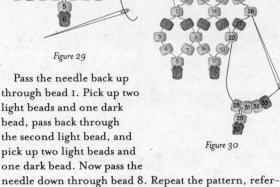

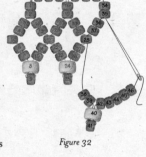

Figure 31

Pick up fourteen beads in the color order shown in figure 30, looping back through the first bead before adding the others. Pass the needle back up through beads 2 and 1. Pick up seven dark beads, and pass down through bead 12. Pick up two dark beads, one 8/0 bead, and one dark bead, then pass back through the 8/0 bead, and pick up five dark beads. Now pass the needle up through beads 19 and 18. Repeat the pattern, referring to figure 31 as you work.

Ribbon Choker

Designed by Dawn Dalto

This beautiful choker can be made with one color of base bead, some fancy trim beads, and a piece of ribbon. It's very simple and very wearable; the beads that you choose will determine its look, whether dressy or casual.

FINISHED SIZE

13½ inches (34.3 cm)

WHAT YOU'LL NEED

15 grams transparent light gray iris cylinder seed beads, 11/0

83 Czech fire-polished dark ruby iris trim beads, 4 mm

Light gray beading thread, size D

Beading needle, size 12

Satin or velvet ribbon

INSTRUCTIONS

Row 1. Using the cylinder seed beads, stitch a chevron chain 83 sets long; follow figure 1 for bead placement. The size of the chevron chain is the same for the first three rows.

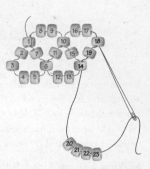

Figure 1

Row 2. Turn (see the basic instructions for chevron chain), then stitch back across the length of the initial chain.

Row 3. Turn again, and stitch the third row. The thread path is shown in figure 2 in black.

Row 4. The size of the chevron and the addition of a trim bead make row 4 a little different. After you make the weaving turn, string on five cylinder seed beads, one trim bead, and four more cylinder seed beads. Pass back up through the first cylinder bead, and continue across the row with this bead count (see figure 2). When you're finished, weave and knot the thread back into the main body of the work.

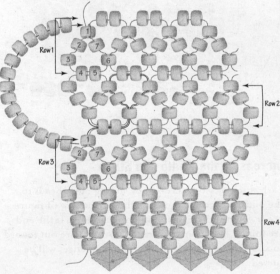

Figure 2

ADDING THE CLASP LOOPS

If the thread is long enough, weave up to bead 1 of row 3, and string on 15 cylinder seed beads. Attach this loop of beads to bead 1 of row 1. Reinforce the loop by passing back through all of the loop beads and each of the #1 beads several times. Weave and knot the thread into the main body of the work. Repeat the process of adding a loop to the other side of the choker. To wear the choker, pass the ribbon through one loop, position the choker on your neck, and thread the other loop with the ribbon; tie the ribbons into a bow.

Crocheted Ropes

Over the years I've seen beautifully crocheted ropes and I've wanted to know how to make them. While teaching a workshop in Boston—a mecca for those who crochet rope bracelets—the opportunity finally arrived when two of my students shared the basics of crocheting with beads during our afternoon break.

Early the next morning I sat down with a string of beads and a crochet hook, and tried to remember the slip stitch that I'd learned as a teen. Gradually the light dawned and I was able to chain and slip stitch with beads. I could join the chain together and stitch a row and a half and then I was lost; what I had in my hands looked like a bunch of grapes, and I didn't know where to go next!

I went back to my students for some answers. They told me that the first couple of rows are the hardest, but if I strung the beads in a simple pattern (such as A B C A B C), the pattern would help me to stitch in the correct order. With this pattern, whatever color bead the hook goes under will also be the color of bead that you'll bring down. You should be able to see the center of the crocheted tube at all times, and however many beads you chained at the start of the rope, that's how many should always be standing vertically as you work the piece. The most important tip is to roll the bead in the stitch to the back of the hook, and make sure that both the working thread and the bead that is brought down stay in front of this bead.

There are times when that ring of chained beads just won't stay where it belongs; instead it becomes a mass of beads and thread and you won't know where to go next. When this happens, try putting a supporting form (such as a straw, a dowel, or whatever fits) in the center of the joined ring of beads. Tape the tail thread to the form to hold the ring in place, and stitch the next couple of rows on the form to keep the beads in their proper positions. The stitching will be a little awkward, but well worth the effort.

Holding the Hook

There are two ways of holding a crochet hook. You can hold it like a pencil, with the hook sitting in front of the forefinger, or hold it like a knife, with the hook under the hand, and held by the thumb and middle finger. The second method is preferred for bead crochet, as it leaves the forefinger free to pull down beads or hold a stitch on the shank of the hook.

Holding the Thread

Any comfortable position of the thread in your other hand is fine, however, it must feed over the index finger. Push 1½ inches (3.8 cm) of beads up bear the crochet hook. Lay the working thread in the palm of your hand with the spool in your lap, then wrap it down and around the back of the hand and up between the middle and forefingers. If the tension is still too loose, wrap the excess around the forefinger. The beads can wrap around the forefinger and feed from there. Your pinky will naturally curl into the palm and can hold the thread there as well for a little extra security.

The Stitching

With every stitch you must do a yarn over, so let's begin there. Referring to figure 1, put a slip knot on the shank of the hook, wrap the working thread behind and over the hook, and catch the thread by the head of the crochet hook. Use the hook to pull the thread through the loop on the shank, forming a chain stitch. Now try the yarn over with a bead, and pull the thread (not the bead) through the loop, for a bead chain stitch. It's important that the chains are the same size as the shank on the hook. They can tighten up as they move down the throat, making it difficult to insert the hook into that stitch. Practice making a chain with beads.

1. To make a sample, string on 12 inches (30.5 cm) of beads in this order A B C A B C (each letter is a different color). Make the slip knot, and chain six beads. Notice that you're chaining them in reverse order; the chained beads will curl into a comma shape. Bring the first chained bead up to the hook, and put the hook into the stitch between the bead and the thread (see figure 2). It's very important that you roll the bead in that stitch over the hook, keeping it in back, and that the working thread is positioned in front of that bead.

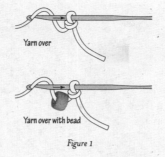

Yarn over

Yarn over with bead

Figure 1

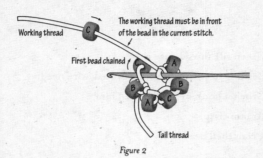

The working thread must be in front of the bead in the current stitch.

Working thread

First bead chained

Tail thread

Figure 2

2. With your forefinger, bring a bead down the working thread and put it in front of the bead that's pushed to the back. Do a yarn over, and pull the thread through the stitch and the loop on the hook; this is a beaded slip stitch. Put the hook in the next stitch (under bead B), roll the bead over the hook to the back, bring the working thread to the front, pull a bead down, yarn over, and pull through the stitch and the loop on the hook. Continue making slip stitches counterclockwise around the circle of beads. If the work starts to look like a bunch of grapes, use a support until you've made ½ inch (1.3 cm) of crocheted rope.

Your work is correct when the stitched beads lie in a horizontal position and the unstitched beads stand up in a vertical position (see figure 3). If you started with six chained beads, there will always be six beads standing as you work. If not, you dropped a stitch. To find it, pull out stitches until you have six beads standing again.

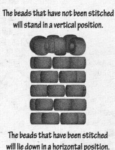

The beads that have not been stitched will stand in a vertical position.

The beads that have been stitched will lie down in a horizontal position.

Figure 3

Tips

- If you want to stop crocheting for a while, put a safety pin in the loop that's on the hook to hold your place.

- If you left a bead out of the pattern and it's time to crochet that bead, make the stitch without a bead. When you get back to that stitch, use it as if there was a bead there. Later you can sew a bead in place—just remember to do it.

- If you've strung an extra bead, put a needle in the unwanted bead, and break the bead with a pair of pliers. The needle should keep the broken bead from cutting the thread.

- A pair of small bent nose tweezers are very helpful in grabbing a stitch that has come off the hook.

- To end the rope, do slip stitches without beads until all beads are lying down. Cut the thread 6 inches (15.2 cm) from the work, then yarn-over, and pull the thread through the loop on the hook.

Adding Thread

There will be times when you'll run out of thread and need to add more to finish the project, or you've strung the pattern incorrectly and need to fix the error. Perhaps you have a very large project and you won't want to string all the beads at one time (because they become too cumbersome and it's hard to feed down the thread when you have yards of beads). At these times you'll need to know how to add a new thread.

Pat Iverson, from Massachusetts, shared this technique with me so that I could share it with all of you. It really is the easiest way to add a new thread.

1. Make sure that your last stitches on the old thread are snug and firm. To bind off, chain 1 without a bead, pull the loop until it's 4 inches (10.2 cm) tall, and cut the loop in half, leaving a small tail; pull the tail to secure the thread. Never cut the tail right next to the knot, because it will come undone.

2. When adding the new thread (to which you've already strung your beads), insert the hook, from the inside of the piece to the outside, into either the last bead you crocheted onto the piece or the last bead you crocheted into the piece.

Hold a loop of the new thread in your left hand while you grab it with the hook in the right hand, pulling the loop into the piece. While still holding onto the two tail ends of the new thread, make a chain stitch without a bead by grabbing both tails of the new thread, and pulling them through the loop on the hook.

3. Pull the chain stitch up until the short tail of the new thread comes through the old loop. Pull this short thread to tighten the knot. Now you have a loop on the hook with a tail sticking out next to it, or a knot with a sliding loop. To shorten the loop to a workable size, gently pull on the long end of the new thread (this is the piece that goes back to the spool). Gently pull on the short end of the new thread to tighten the knot. Now you can continue to crochet into the next place.

What to do with the tail threads? Let them hang outside of the piece, and weave them in later with a needle, or work them down into the center of the crocheted rope away from where you're working.

Working with Patterns and Graphs

A pattern changes when you change the number of beads chained in the initial ring. The examples here were all made from the pattern 9A (light blue) 1B (dark blue). The first three samples (see photo 1) show five, six, and seven beads chained around, respectively. Notice that in the first example the pattern spirals upward and by the third sample the pattern of dots is almost straight.

Photo 1

Photo 2 shows how bead size affects the look of a crochet rope. All were stitched with the same pattern—seven beads around—using 15/0 seed beads, 11/0 cylinder seed beads, 11/0 seed beads, and 8/0 seed beads, respectively.

Photo 2

Make samples of a pattern (you may want to later check the color, size, or gauge), and attach a small jewelry tag with the pertinent information (see figure 4).

Continued ➔

Charting your own patterns can be both fun and frustrating! It's hard to visualize from a flat graph how something will look in the round. Here I've made up three blank graphs for you to try your hand at charting, one each for stitching five, six, and seven beads around. The numbers in each block show the stringing order, but you can write a letter over each number to represent the colors you'd like to use. Look at the patterns and their graphs in the Patterns section...to get a better feel for how they work. Stitch a few of the charted ones, then try one of your own. Remember that the beads on the right-hand side of the graph meet the beads on the left side in a spiral fashion.

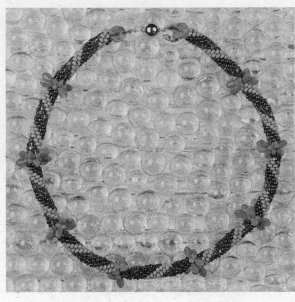

Pattern sample tags

Pattern: 9A1B
Color Key:
A=Light blue
B=Dark blue
Chain 5 around

Hook: US7/1.15mm
11/0 seed beads
Gauge = 100 beads per inch

Figure 4

31	32	33	34	35
26	27	28	29	30
21	22	23	24	25
16	17	18	19	20
11	12	13	14	15
6	7	8	9	10

Start the graph here → 1 2 3 4 5

Graph for crocheted rope 5 beads around

Graph 1

37	38	39	40	41	42
31	32	33	34	35	36
25	26	27	28	29	30
19	20	21	22	23	24
13	14	15	16	17	18
7	8	9	10	11	12

Start the graph here → 1 2 3 4 5 6

Graph for crocheted rope 6 beads around

Graph 2

43	44	45	46	47	48	49
36	37	38	39	40	41	42
29	30	31	32	33	34	35
22	23	24	25	26	27	28
15	16	17	18	19	20	21
8	9	10	11	12	13	14

Start the graph here → 1 2 3 4 5 6 7

Graph for crocheted rope 7 beads around

Graph 3

Whirligig Choker
Designed by Carol Wilcox Wells

This is a great beginner's project! The pattern is easy to follow, the beads are large, and with the addition of decorative beads, you'll have a little fun along the way.

Finished Size
17½ inches (44.5 cm) long

What You'll Need
8/0 seed beads
  10 grams opaque light green
  10 grams dark green iris
7 grams plum lined with green triangle beads, 10/0
Trim beads
  56 opaque turquoise daggers, 8 x 5 mm
  48 matte transparent pale blue iris drops, 3.4 mm
  2 turquoise faceted crystals, 10 mm

Green silk thread, size E

Beading needle, size 10, or twisted-wire needles

Crochet hook, size US 8/1.25 mm

10 mm clasp

2 clamshell bead tips

Instructions
Note: The graph shows one full repeat of the pattern.

CROCHETED ROPE SECTION

1. Thread the needle with the silk, and string on eight repeats plus one without the DE sequence. Don't cut the thread. Leaving an 8-inch (20.3 cm) tail, make a slip knot; do six chain stitches, with one bead in each stitch. The chain needs to be loose enough to produce a comma-shaped section of beads and thread. Join the ends with a beaded slip stitch. Crochet all beads.

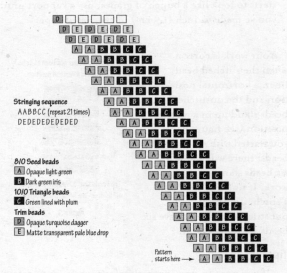

Stringing sequence
AABBCC (repeat 21 times)
DEDEDEDEDEDED

8/0 Seed beads
A Opaque light green
B Dark green iris
10/0 Triangle beads
C Green lined with plum
Trim beads
D Opaque turquoise dagger
E Matte transparent pale blue drop

Pattern starts here →

Graph 1

2. With this pattern, whichever bead color you bring down is the bead color you should crochet into. For example: if the bead on the thread nearest the work is light green, then you'll stitch under a light green bead. Use this tip to build your confidence; it will also alert you if you've made a mistake. If you'd like the choker to be longer, increase it to the desired length by adding another repeat or two of beads.

3. Do six more stitches without beads. Cut the thread 8 inches (20.3 cm) from the work, and pull the thread through the loop on the crochet hook. This closes the end and secures the beads.

THE CLASP

4. Put a beading needle on one of the tail threads. String on a 10 mm crystal bead, a bead tip, and a bead that's small enough to fit inside the bead tip. Pass the

---

needle back through the bead tip, the 10 mm bead, and into the crocheted rope. Turn and go back through all the beads again, and weave back down to the rope, securing the group to the end of the necklace.

5. Attach one end of the clasp to the bead tip. Bend the hook so that the tip is inside the walls of the clamshell, and close the two sides over the small bead and the tip of the hook. Repeat on the other side of the necklace.

Herringbone Stitch

This weave has been used for over 200 years by the Nde-bele (en-de-BEL-ay) women of South Africa. The stitch produces a pattern that resembled herringbone. Before you look at the variety of ways to start this stitch, first study a flat piece of the weave, in order to better understand how it works.

Figure 3 shows four horizontal rows stitched and the location of the spines. Notice that there are full spines and half spines marked along the working edge. A full spine is made when the thread exits one bead, two beads are picked up, and the thread is passed down through the neighboring bead.

A half spine (found only on the outside edges) results from the number of beads used to begin the stitch, or when increasing and decreasing vertical rows. The type of turn that you'll make when doing a flat herringbone piece depends on whether the beads on the outside edges are part of a half spine or a full spine.

When a half spine is on the outside edge, you'll add a bead when you're turning (as in figure 3), but when a full spine is on the outside edge, you don't need to add a bead; just pass the needle back through the last bead added (see figure 4).

The eight vertical rows on the bottom edge of figure 3 are grouped differently than on the working edge, thus creating four full spines and no half spines.

The herringbone stitch has many idiosyncrasies. I haven't been able to put my finger on all of them yet, but I'll share what I know.

Flat Herringbone Stitch

The beginning row of beads must be an even number of beads—either a multiple of four or two. A multiple of four results in an even number of vertical rows, with full spines along the beginning edge, and full and half spines along the working edge. A multiple of two produces an odd number of vertical rows, with full spines and one half spine, along both the beginning edge and the working edge. To determine which stitching method to use, first divide any even number of beads by 4. The result should be a whole number, indicating the number of full spines you'll have along the bottom edge. For example, divide 16 beads by 4; there will be four full spines in the piece.

If, however, your number of beads is not evenly divisible by 4, then divide the number by 2 instead. Now divide that number by 2 again, to find the number of full and half spines along the bottom edge. For example, divide 10 beads by 2; divide the result of 5 by 2. The final answer of 2.5 indicates that there will be two full spines and one half spine along the bottom edge.

Starting from a Multiple of Four

This is the traditional method I learned from Virginia Blakelock more than a decade ago. It's the method of starting that I prefer because it leaves the beginning edge a true herringbone.

Rows 1 and 2. Begin with a multiple of four beads. The sample has four sets of four, or 16 heads. Loop on a stop bead (which isn't necessary, but it's easier to unloop when the time comes to weave that tail thread in) and 16 beads (see figure 1). These 16 beads will make up horizontal rows 1 and 2.

Figure 1

Row 3. To make the first turn, string on one dark bead (17), then push it to the others, passing back down through bead 16 and up through bead 13, bypassing beads 15 and 14. Pick up two dark beads (18 and 19), and weave through beads 12 and 9 (see figure 2). Continue across the row, ending with the needle exiting bead 1, and heading left. Don't pass through the stop bead. Try not to pull the thread too tightly at this point. The bottom edge of the sample should be scalloped.

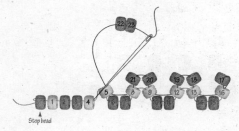

Figure 2

Row 4. Because there are half spines on the outside edges, the turns are made by adding a bead. For the sample, string on one dark bead, (which is #24, to finish row 3), and one light bead (#25, to begin row 4), then pass the needle back down through bead 24 and up through bead 23. Pick up beads 26 and 27, pass down through bead 22, and up through bead 21 (see figure 3). Continue adding beads in this manner, weaving back and forth, until you have the desired length.

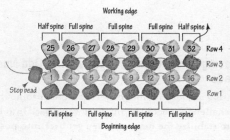

Figure 3

Starting from a Multiple of Two

After experimenting with the stitch, I found that you could start using a multiple of two, which opens your options.

Rows 1 and 2. Begin with a multiple of two beads. Make this sample with five sets of two, or 10 beads. String on one bead, loop back through it, then add nine more beads, for a total of ten (see figure 4). I did not use a stop bead in this illustration, to show you that you can use the first bead as a stop bead. These 10 beads will make up horizontal rows 1 and 2 when they're stitched.

Row 3. To make the first turn (a half spine) string on one dark bead (11), push it down to the others, then pass back down through bead 10, and up through bead 7, bypassing beads 9 and 8. Continue the row by picking up two dark beads (12 and 13), and weave through beads 6 and 3. Pick up two beads (14 and 15), and pass down through bead 2.

Row 4. To make the turn from a full spine, pass the needle up through bead 15 (see figure 4). You're now in position to start row 4. Figure 5 shows row 4 completed.

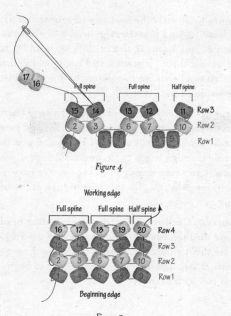

Figure 4

Figure 5

Rainbow Necklace

Designed by Carole Horn

Herringbone weave, sometimes called Ndebele, is a little tricky to get started, but once a few rows are established it's really quite easy to follow. While experimenting with the stitch, Carole discovered that if the beads were of slightly different sizes the piece would curve, forming an elegant collar.

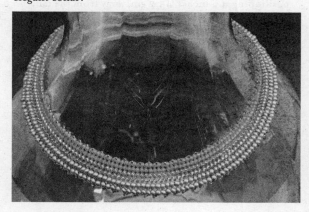

Finished Size

18 inches (45.7 cm) long

What You'll Need

9 grams matte light copper seed beads, 6/0

8/0 seed beads

    4 grams lined lavender iris

    4 grams matte transparent light eggplant

2 grams silver-lined amber cylinder seed beads, 11/0

Decorative button with shank, ½ inch (1.3 cm) diameter

Beading thread, size D, in a color to match beads

Beading needles, size 10

Instructions

Note: Seed beads make up most of this necklace; the cylinder beads are used merely to cover the thread (which would otherwise show on the edge), and they add an interesting finishing detail.

The Necklace

1. Thread a number 10 needle with 2 yards (1.8 m) of thread. Slide on a stop bead, and position it 6 inches (15.2 cm) from the tail. Loop back through the bead to secure it; it will be removed later. Pick up four 6/0 beads and four of each of the two colors of 8/0 beads (see figure 1). The twelve beads on the thread should graduate in size, from largest to smallest.

Figure 1

2. To make the turn, pick up one 8/0 bead (the same color as bead 12) and one cylinder seed bead. Following figure 2, sew back through bead 12, skip two beads, and sew through bead 9. Following the color pattern, add two 8/0 beads (14 and 15 are different colors) and sew down through bead 8. Skip two beads, and sew up through bead 5. Add two beads (16 is an 8/0 and 17 is a 6/0), sew down through bead 4, and up through bead 1. Remove the stop bead. Pull both the tail end and needle end of the thread, so that the beads form a pattern of three V's.

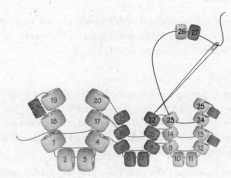

Figure 2

3. Pick up beads 18 and 19 (both are 6/0's) and two cylinder seed beads, and slide them down against the beadwork; pass the needle into bead 18. The tail end of thread and the working thread meet at this point; tie them together. This is the base row.

4. Sew up through bead 17. Following the color pattern, add beads 20 and 21, sew down through bead 16, and up through bead 15. Add two more beads (22 and 23), pass the needle down through bead 14, and up through bead 13. You're now at the inner edge; add two 8/0 beads (24 and 25), and one cylinder bead. Slide them to the work, sew down through bead 24, and up through bead 23. Continue stitching in this manner until you have the desired length. As you work, allow the necklace to curve; don't try to keep it straight.

Helpful Hints

Once the pattern is established it's really very easy. You'll always pick up two beads and sew through two beads. On the edge, pick up beads that are the same color. In the body of the necklace pick up a bead of each color (one of the color you're coming out of and the other of the color you're going into). The cylinder beads are there to hide the thread, and they're always picked up when you're making a turn.

Tension is very important to the success of this project. The necklace should form a gentle, flexible curve. You'll see some thread between the beads, but not a lot. Make sure after you add beads that you pull up the thread very snugly.

THE CLASP

5. Make the closure with a decorative button attached to a loop of beads on one end of the necklace, and make a larger loop of beads for the other end of the necklace. Weave a new thread through four beads of the second horizontal row, exiting the bead on the end. Pick up 16 cylinder seed beads and the button, and position them next to the body of the necklace, with the button shank fitting over the cylinder seed beads. Pass the needle into two beads of the third horizontal row of the necklace. Weave over to row 2, out the end, and through the beads in the loop, reinforcing the button loop; do this several times. Tie off the thread ends into the body of the work, being careful to hide the knots.

Continued ➜

6. Add a thread to the other end of the necklace in the same position, and string on approximately 25 cylinder seed beads, (the count may vary, depending on the button used). Weave into the third horizontal row, and check the fit over the button before reinforcing the loop. Tie off the thread ends, and enjoy.

Peyote Stitch

Peyote stitch produces a vertical brick pattern. Each stitch, containing one or more beads, is connected to the neighboring beads with thread. The tension you put on the thread while you're stitching controls the flexibility of the finished work. The sizes of beads you use can alter the look of a piece, making a simple project look more complex. The variations of its use continue to amaze me…

Flat Peyote

Flat peyote can be stitched with an even or odd number of vertical rows. It is easily increased and decreased, and makes a beautiful fabric of beads.

Even Count

Figure 1. String a bead onto the thread, then loop back through the bead. Position this bead 6 inches (15.2 cm) away from the end of the thread. Add beads until you have the width you need, making sure that the total number of beads is an even number.

Figure 2. To start the next row, pick up bead 9, and pass through bead 7. Continue across in this manner, picking up bead 10, skipping bead 6, and passing through bead 5. Keep the tension tight enough to form peyote's vertical brick pattern. If you're making a basket, or something that needs to be stiff, pull tightly; if you want the feel of supple material, pull with a gentler hand, but tight enough to form the vertical brick pattern.

Figure 3. To turn and go back across in the opposite direction, pick up a bead, 13, and pass through the last bead (12) that was added in the previous row. Continue adding beads until the desired length is reached.

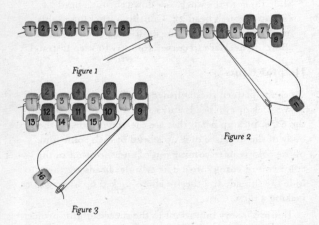

Figure 1

Figure 2

Figure 3

Odd Count

For a pattern with a center point you must use an odd number of beads. The stitch is the same as even count flat peyote, except for the way that turns are made. On one side, there's an easy turn (Turn A in the illustrations), and on the other side a more complex turn (Turn B). If any increasing (adding rows) takes place, the easy and more complex turns will change sides; however, if the piece remains the same width, the more complex turn will remain on the side of the first bead strung.

Figure 4. String a bead onto the thread, and loop back through the bead. Position this bead 6 inches (15.2 cm) away from the end of the thread. Add beads until you reach the width you need, making sure that the total number of beads is an odd number.

Figure 5. To start the next row (diagonal row 3), pick up bead 10, and pass through bead 8. This is the easy Turn A. Add beads 11 and 12. Pick up bead 13, and pass the needle through beads 2 and 1. By passing through the last two beads, you're setting up for the addition of the last bead in that row.

Figure 6. This is a more challenging turn. The needle and thread exit bead 1; pick up bead 14, and pass the needle through beads 2 and 3. Turn, and pass the needle through beads 13, 2, and 1. Change direction again, and weave through bead 14; you're now ready to begin the next row. Do this type of turn at the beginning of a piece.

Figure 7. Continue to stitch. When adding bead 22, weave through beads 15 and 14, pick up bead 23, and weave through bead 15. Turn, and weave through beads, 2, 14, and 23. You're now ready to begin the next row with bead 24.

When doing the Turn B at the beginning of a piece, you'll weave through three vertical rows (rows A, B, and C in figure 7). For each of these turns thereafter, use only two vertical rows (A and B). The more that you work with this turn, the easier it will become.

Sometimes you'll need to make a narrow strip of odd count flat peyote. At these times there's another way of stitching Turn B. Weave across the entire piece on the diagonal, then through the bead below. This creates figure-eight thread patterns.

Figure 8. Pick up a bead, and loop back through it, positioning it 6 inches (15.2 cm) away from the tail. String on beads 2, 3, and 4, then pass through beads 2 and 1. Pick up bead 5, and pass through beads, 2, 3, and 4. You're now ready to add bead 6.

Figure 9. Add bead 7 by passing through beads 6 and 4. Add bead 8 by passing through beads 6 and 5. Weave through bead 7 to set up for the next stitch.

This technique goes a little faster for narrow strips and puts the excess thread at the outside edges. I wouldn't recommended it for wide pieces, however, as it would slow down the beading process if you had to weave all the way across a large piece.

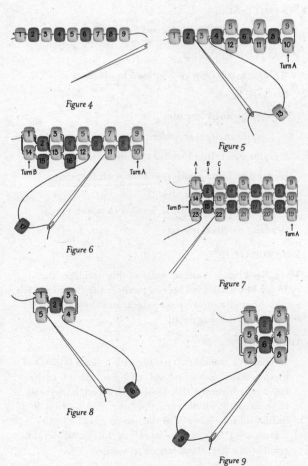

Figure 4

Figure 5

Figure 6

Figure 7

Figure 8

Figure 9

Increasing

There are a variety of ways to increase peyote stitch. You can increase the number of stitches either within the piece or on the outside edges, or you can increase the width of the stitch, either within the piece or on the outside edges.

Increasing on the Outside Edges with an Even Number of Beads

Figures 16 and 17. Pick up the quantity of beads desired. The illustrations show increasing by two rows for a total of ten vertical rows. Slide these beads to the work, and pick up another bead (19). Change direction, and pass through bead 17, making sure that all new beads are snug to the base work. Continue across with peyote stitch.

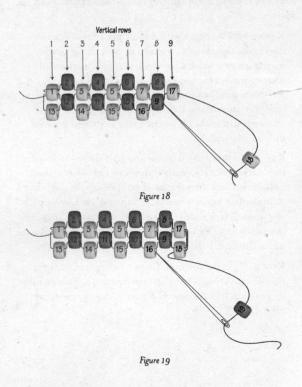

Figure 16

Figure 17

Increasing on the Outside Edges with an Odd Number of Beads

Increasing an odd number of vertical rows is somewhat more challenging because you must weave back into the piece to stabilize the new row, then get back into position to begin again.

Figure 18. To increase by one vertical row, pick up beads 17 and 18, and go back into bead 9.

Figure 19. Continue weaving through beads 8, 17, and 18. You're now ready to begin the next row with bead 19.

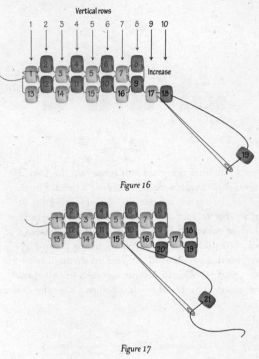

Figure 18

Figure 19

Increasing the Number of Vertical Rows Within a Piece

Increasing the number of vertical rows within a piece will cause the piece to flare out.

Figure 20. At the point of increase, pick up two beads instead of one (beads 19).

Figure 21. When stitching the next row, add a bead between the two beads that were added in the single space. Note that the vertical rows have increased by two, making the piece ten vertical rows wide instead of eight.

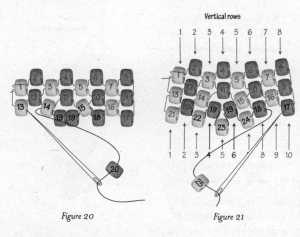

Figure 20   *Figure 21*

Increasing the Width of a Stitch

Increasing the width of a stitch is a simple way of adding texture and volume to your work. Increase as often or as little as necessary to achieve the look you need.

Figure 22. Add two beads in the space of one (these are both numbered 19 in figure 20), and continue adding two beads in that space (both numbered 27 in figure 22) as you come to it. You've increased the width of the piece, but not the number of vertical rows. You can do this on the outside edges as well.

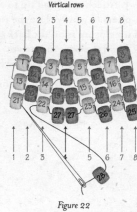

Figure 22

Decreasing

You can decrease peyote stitch—adding fewer beads to make the piece narrower—in a variety of ways.

Decreasing on the Outside Edge

Simply omitting beads at the end of the row leaves you no place to go. You must weave back into the body of the work to get into position to continue stitching.

Figure 23. After adding bead 24, start weaving from bead 17 (with the needle heading left) and pass through beads 9 and 16; then head right through beads 7 and 9; heading left again, pass through beads 17 and 24.

Figure 24. This illustration shows an odd number of beads being decreased into a point. The process is the same as in figure 23, except that the decreasing is applied to both sides.

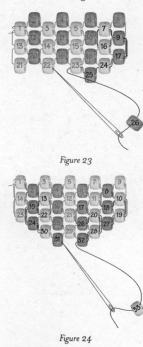

Figure 23

Figure 24

Decreasing Within a Piece

Decreasing within a piece means dropping a stitch. You'll drop one bead, but lose two vertical rows.

Figure 25. To decrease, simply don't add a bead in the stitch. Pull tightly to close the gap between the beads. On the next row, add one bead in the decreased space, then continue with peyote stitch.

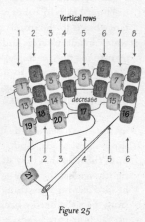

Figure 25

Two-Drop Peyote Stitch

Two-drop peyote stitch is similar to peyote, except that you'll use two beads in each stitch instead of one. (Three-drop has three beads in each stitch, and everything else is the same.) The number of beads used in each stitch is your choice. You can also combine peyote with two-drop, or a two-drop with three-drop. The combinations seem to be endless. Experiment on your own; try something different; create a look like no other!

Figure 26. For two-drop peyote, use two beads in each stitch instead of one.

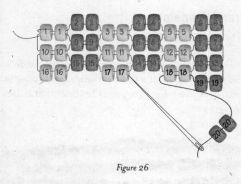

Figure 26

Kaua'i Ring Magic

Designed by NanC Meinhardt

This ring is so versatile! Dress it up or down, depending on your mood and the beads that you have on hand. Start stitching in the morning, and dazzle your friends that evening.

Finished Size

1⅜ x ⅞ x ¾ inches (3.4 x 2.2 x 1.9 cm)

What You'll Need

11/0 seed beads or cylinder seed beads

Focal point bead (larger bead for the center top)

Trim beads (embellishing the surface) 15/0's, crystals, drops, or anything that you like

Beading thread, size B or D

Beading needle, size 12

Instructions

Helpful Hint: To avoid losing your place, check off the rows as you work them.

Rows 1–10. Using a single thread, string on a stop bead, and loop back through it, leaving a 6-inch (15.2-cm) tail. Put three beads on your thread, and do odd count flat peyote stitch for a total of ten rows.

Row 11. Now you'll increase the outside vertical rows (1 and 3) to three-drop peyote by putting three beads in the space of one (see figure 1).

With the thread exiting bead A, pick up three beads, and pass through the center bead and bead B, heading right. Pick up three more beads (4, 5, and 6), and go back through the center bead and bead A, heading left. To set up for the next row, pass through beads 2 and 3, bypassing bead 1.

Row 12. Do a single peyote stitch, but pass the needle through beads 6 and 5, bypassing bead 4.

Row 13. Now you'll add four beads in vertical rows 3 and 1 (see figure 2).

Coming out of bead 5, pick up four beads (7–10), pass through the center bead (heading left) and beads 3 and 2 in row 11. Pick up four more beads (11–14), and pass through the center bead and beads 6 and 5 in row 11 (heading right). To set up for the next row, bypass bead 7, and weave through beads 8, 9, and 10.

Row 14–17. Continue doing flat peyote, using a regular three-drop in vertical rows 1 and 3 and single peyote in vertical row 2.

Row 18. Increase the center vertical row to two-drop peyote.

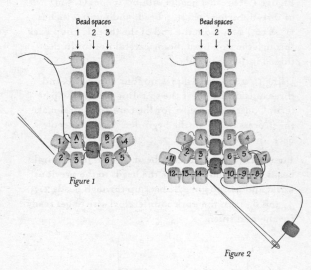

Figure 1

Figure 2

Rows 19–21. Continue doing flat peyote, using a regular three-drop in vertical rows 1 and 3 and two-drop peyote in vertical row 2.

Row 22. Continue peyote, using three-drop in vertical rows 1 and 3 and single peyote in the center.

Rows 23–27. Continue peyote, using three-drop in vertical rows 1 and 3 and single peyote in the center.

Row 28. Add the bead in the center vertical row as usual, then begin to decrease by passing the needle through two of the three beads on the outside edge.

Row 29. Pick up two beads, and go through the center bead. Pass the needle through the first two beads in the outer vertical row. Pick up two beads, and finish the odd count turn through two beads on the outside edge.

Row 30. Add one bead in the center vertical row, and pass the needle through one bead in the outer vertical row.

Row 31. Now you'll decrease so that all vertical rows are single peyote.

Pick up a bead, and pass through the center bead and one of the beads in the outer vertical row. Turn, add one bead, and finish the odd count turn.

Rows 32–38. Continue doing single peyote.

Continued ➔

Weave a new thread through a few rows on the top of the ring; don't knot the thread. Place and attach the focal point embellishment bead. Add beads to the surface around the focal point bead and all over the top. Embellish the edges with tiny beads—at this point anything goes; be creative and have fun.

FINISHING THE RING

After the ring is encrusted, finish the band on the underside to fit your finger. Add a second layer to the band by adding beads over the center vertical row.

Spiral Rope

One year at Bead Retreat, I was admiring a necklace that one of the students had made. The beads were joined in such a fashion that they spiraled around each other into this wonderful, soft rope. I was intrigued and had to ask, "What stitch is this?" My friend replied, "It's spiral rope, and I found it on the Internet." Her information led me to Hillsinger Fine Hand Beadwork, where I learned the basics for the stitch. My experimentation over the years has led me a bit further and I hope that you'll try these variations.

Spiral rope is one of those instant gratification stitches that everyone can do. The results, even for the beginner, are beautiful, and the combinations are endless.

Note: You can use any size of bead. I recommend 11/0 seed beads here because of their availability to most beaders.

Figure 1. Thread a needle with 60 inches (1.5 m) of thread. String on a stop bead, and put it 7 inches (17.8 cm) away from the end of the thread. Loop back through the stop bead, being careful not to slit the thread inside the bead.

Using 11/0 seed beads, pick up four core beads and three outside beads for the spiraling part of the pattern. Contrasting colors for the core and spiral make the process easier for the beginner. Pass the needle back up through beads 1, 2, 3, and 4.

Figure 2. Pick up one core bead (8) and three spiral beads (9, 10, and 11). Slide the beads to the previous work, and pass the needle back up through beads 2, 3, 4, and 8. Turn the work counterclockwise to get ready for the next stitch.

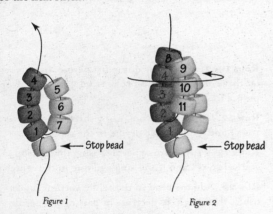

Figure 1   *Figure 2*

Figure 3. After the initial set of beads, all stitches consist of one core bead and three spiral beads. When passing back up core beads, use the previous three core beads and the new one being added. Referring to figure 3, string on bead 12 (the core bead) and beads, 13, 14, and 15 (the spiral beads), and push them to the work. Pass the needle back through core beads 3, 4, 8, and 12. Continue stitching in this manner, rotating the spiraling beads counterclockwise until you have the desired length.

Figure 4. The addition of larger beads or other fancy beads to the spiral rope can add interest and texture to your piece. Work the spiral rope to the length desired, string on the large bead; and push to the work. Pick up four core beads and three spiral beads. And push those so that they sit tightly against the large bead. Keeping everything snug, pass the needle back up the four core beads, creating the first spiral of the new segment.

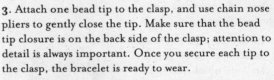

Figure 3

To reinforce and strengthen the stitching, pass the needle back down through the spiral beads 5, 6, and 7, the large bead, and into the last spiral beads (A, B, and C) of the previous segment. Now go back up the four core beads, the large bead, and the four core beads of the new segment. If the large bead is very heavy and you've enough room in all of the beads, repeat the process of weaving back into the previous segment, then back up to the new segment.

Six Strand Bracelet

Designed by Carol Wilcox Wells

Take an elegant clasp, six strands of spiral rope made with seed beads, the sparkle of a few charlottes, and some button pearls, and you have a gorgeous bracelet that belies its simple origins.

FINISHED SIZE

7⅜ x 1 inch (18.7 x 2.5 cm)

WHAT YOU'LL NEED

18 grams matte blue iris seed beads, 15/0

3 grams metallic blue iris charlottes, 15/0

22 white button pearls, for trim beads

Dark blue beading thread, size B

Beading needles, sizes 12 and 13

Large (21 x 26 mm) silver 3-strand box clasp with pearl

6 sterling silver bead caps, 4 mm

6 sterling silver bead tips

INSTRUCTIONS

Note: This spiral rope is made up of four core beads and three outside spiral beads.

THE SPIRALS

1. Thread the needle, string on a stop bead, and loop back through it 8 inches (20.3 cm) away from the tail. Do the 6 inches (15.2 cm) of basic spiral rope, using matte blue iris for the core, and one matte, one charlotte, and one matte for the spiral. Make a total of three plain spiral strips, leaving 8 to 12 inches (20.3 to 30.5 cm) of working thread at each end.

2. Stitch three more sections in the same manner, but use the pearls in place of some of the charlottes (use seven pearls on two of the strips and eight on the other one). Remove all the stop beads.

THE CAPS, TIPS, AND CLASP

1. Pair up the sections of spiral rope; putting a plain strip with a strip that has pearls. Working with one pair of ropes, put a needle on one end of each section of spiral rope. Use these two needles as you would one needle. String on a bead cap, a bead tip, and a 15/0 bead (the bead inside the tip looks nicer than a knot of thread). Pass these needles back through the tip, the cap, and into the spiral ropes. Do this again, to reinforce the connection, then tie off the threads. Repeat the process of adding the caps and tips to each end of each pair of spiral rope segments.

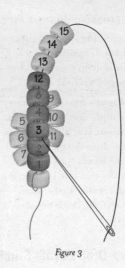

Figure 4

2. Taking one pair at a time, twist the sections around each other, and put a small stitch between the ropes where they cross over one another, to hold the twisted look in place.

3. Attach one bead tip to the clasp, and use chain nose pliers to gently close the tip. Make sure that the bead tip closure is on the back side of the clasp; attention to detail is always important. Once you secure each tip to the clasp, the bracelet is ready to wear.

—FROM *The Art & Elegance of Beadweaving*

Candle-making

BASIC CANDLEMAKING

Rebecca Ittner

Getting Started

Candlemaking can be a wonderfully satisfying craft. With the waxes, colors, and fragrances available today, you can create votives, pillars, container candles, and recycled candles in all shapes, sizes, and colors. But candles are fickle. Know that even though you follow a recipe, no two candles will ever be identical. Fluctuations in temperature, wax type, wick sizes, or even the manufacturers of your ingredients will all affect the results.

Many times these differences are happy accidents; other times they are frustrating. One of the most important things you can do is keep a detailed diary of your candlemaking journey. Use it to record things like the type, manufacturer, and amount of wax, wicks, fragrance, and colorants used; melting and pouring temperatures; and cooling times.

In this chapter you will learn the basic differences between paraffin and natural waxes, the tools and materials needed to make the candles in this book, and basic safety tips. Once you familiarize yourself with these and learn the simple techniques in the following chapter, you will be ready to start candle crafting.

Natural vs. Synthetic

For many years, paraffin has been the wax of choice for both commercial and home-based candle crafters. For those who wanted to make natural candles, beeswax was the only answer. In recent years, however, soy wax and palm wax have come to market, and with them a whole new realm of candlemaking possibilities.

But why choose natural? Natural waxes are biodegradable and come from renewable resources. There are additional benefits to using natural waxes and these are discussed in the following chapter openers in this book. Paraffin, on the other hand, is a petroleum byproduct.

Choosing natural waxes is a personal decision, one most often driven by a desire to avoid synthetic, petroleum-based products and to use waxes that are eco-friendly.

Materials and Tools

Much of what is needed to make candles can be found in your kitchen. Everything else is readily available at craft and cookware stores. Once you use an item for candle-making, it should not be used for cooking; wax, fragrance, and colorants can be transferred back into food. Consider storing your candlemaking supplies in marked boxes to prevent any cross-contamination.

The Basics

- **Candle or candy thermometer**: Used to measure wax temperature.
- **Chisel or flathead screwdriver**: Used to break up blocks of wax.

PLAYING IT SAFE

There are a few simple rules to ensure that candle crafting is a safe activity. Some basics include:

Never melt wax over direct heat. Wax is flammable and will catch fire. Never try to extinguish a wax fire with water; it will fuel the flame. Use baking soda, a saucepan lid, or fire blanket to contain a wax fire. Consider having a fire extinguisher on hand.

Never leave melting wax unattended. Also, to avoid a fire hazard make sure there is water in the bottom pan of your double boiler at all times.

Use pot holders or wear oven mitts or silicone gloves when pouring wax to prevent burns.

Never leave burning candles unattended or burn candles near things that are flammable, such as curtains, plants, or paper décor.

- **Craft knife**: Used to cut beeswax sheets.
- **Cutting board**: Plastic or wood; used to chop or break up blocks of wax.
- **Double boiler or melting pot**: Used to melt wax.
- **Glass measuring cup**: Used to measure and pour wax.
- **Kitchen scale**: Used to weigh wax.
- **Kitchen towels**: Used to wipe condensation off the bottom of the double boiler or melting pot.

Continued →

- **Knives**: Large and paring; used to cut wax into chunks and trim excess wax from molded candles.
- **Measuring spoons**: Used to measure additives.
- **Metal spoon**: Used for stirring additives into wax.
- **Mold sealer**: Used to seal the wick hole in a mold and prevent wax from leaking.
- **Molds**: Used to create shaped candles.
- **Newspaper**: Used to cover the work surface and protect it from wax.
- **Oven gloves**: Used to prevent burns from hot wax.
- **Paper towels**: Used to clean up spills and other messes.
- **Parchment paper or wax paper**: Used to collect wax so it can be reused.
- **Pouring container**: Used for pouring wax.
- **Rubber mallet**: Used with chisel or flathead screwdriver to break up blocks of wax.
- **Scissors or nail clippers**: Used to trim wicks.
- **Self-healing cutting mat**: Used with craft knife to cut beeswax sheets.

CONTAINERS AND MOLDS

The vessel you choose for a container candle should be based on the type of candle. If you are making a layered candle, you will need a clear container. If you are reusing old wax, then a pretty china container would work well. Make sure your containers are heatproof so they do not crack or break when the wax is poured.

Candles can be made from a variety of molds, from pre-made metal molds to silicone baking pans. Here are some common types of molds:

Baking molds: Metal cake molds, cookie cutters, and silicone baking items such as cupcake and muffin molds.

Metal candle molds: Available in a wide range of sizes and shapes. Long-wearing.

Plastic candle molds: Typically two-piece molds. Some require use of mold clamps and mold stands.

Soft candle molds: Made from latex or silicone, candles are easily removed from these flexible molds.

NATURAL WAX

Currently, three types of natural wax are widely available: beeswax, soy wax, and palm wax. Each type has distinct properties, so making candles is slightly different with each one.

Beeswax

Beeswax is a natural byproduct of honey production. It is filtered and purified before being packaged for use in candlemaking. Beeswax is heavy and sticky, so it can be hard to remove from some intricate molds. Molds that work well with beeswax include flexible silicone molds, two-piece molds that are easy to separate, and small metal molds.

Beeswax is readily available in three forms: pellets (also called pastilles), pre-made sheets, and 1- and 2-lb. (454 and 908 g) blocks; larger quantities can be found online. Pellets are used to make tapers, votives, pillars, and molded candles, and are easy to weigh and work with in comparison to the blocks. Beeswax sheets are commonly sold in 8 x 16-inch (20.3 x 40.6 cm) sheets and are used to make rolled and stacked candles. Beeswax blocks are the easiest to find, but must be broken up prior to use. I have the best luck using a rubber mallet and chisel or straight-edged screwdriver to break up blocks of beeswax.

Palm Wax

Palm wax is sold in flake form. Though not widely available in craft stores, many online sellers offer palm wax. There are different formulations of palm wax depending on the type of candle you want to make. The most common formulations are: crystallizing container wax, crystallizing votive/pillar wax, feathering pillar wax, and palm stearin. Palm stearin is a wax additive that increases burn time and firmness, and aids in mold release.

Soy Wax

Soy wax is also sold in flake form. For the casual crafter, 1- and 4-lb. (454 and 1816 g) packages are sold in craft stores. Larger quantities can be purchased from online sellers. In its most natural state, soy wax is a very soft wax that's best used only for container candles. Other formulations contain additives, such as palm stearin, that harden the wax and make it suitable for use in making votives, tapers, pillars, and molded candles. These formulations are referred to as either container formula or votive/pillar formula.

WAX FRAGRANCES

Scent has the ability to influence a person's mood, a room's ambiance, and even the taste of food. For instance, lavender and vanilla are calming, jasmine and clary sage are uplifting, and mandarin orange is invigorating. If you plan to use a candle as a centerpiece for a dinner table, consider leaving it unscented so it won't compete with the aromas of the food being served. Unscented candles are also a great option for people with allergies to fragrance.

There are a couple of choices when it comes to scenting your candles: essential oils and fragrance oils. Essential oils are extracted from plants, shrubs, roots, bark, flowers, peelings, and resins, and are the only truly natural way to scent candles. You can use one oil or create a blend of oils to scent your candle; there are no rules.

Creating essential oil blends is a personal journey. Essential oils can be broken down two ways: by scent family and by notes. Understanding what scent family a particular essential oil belongs to will help you build a fragrance recipe. For instance, if you want to add a woodsy note to an herbal blend, refer to the list of scent families (see Scent Families). Understanding what note category an essential oil belongs to will help you create balanced essential oil blends (see Fragrance Notes). Top notes are the main scent of the blend. Information about essential oil blending abounds in books and on the Internet. The only way to know how a blend will make a candle smell is by experimenting. Taking notes as you blend and again when you burn the candle will allow you to recreate the fragrance or let you know what doesn't work.

Fragrance oils can be a blend of essential and synthetic oils or purely synthetic. The advantage of fragrance oils is the wide range of scents available including things like pumpkin pie and chocolate. It is important to use only fragrance oils made specifically for scenting candles. These fragrance oils are designed to be fully absorbed by the wax and won't adversely affect how the candle burns. The projects in this book were scented using both natural essential oils and synthetic fragrance oils.

WAX DYES

Though natural waxes are widely available, there are no truly natural dyes. Recently, a few eco-friendly liquid dyes have become available on the market. Because of the limited availability of these dyes, the projects in this book are made using a variety of dyes, both traditional and eco-friendly.

<table>
<tr><th colspan="3">SCENT FAMILIES</th></tr>
<tr><th>FLORAL</th><th>EARTHY</th><th>CITRUS</th></tr>
<tr><td>jasmine</td><td>frankincense</td><td>bergamot</td></tr>
<tr><td>lavender</td><td>myrrh</td><td>grapefruit</td></tr>
<tr><td>neroli</td><td>patchouli</td><td>lemon</td></tr>
<tr><td>rose</td><td>vetiver</td><td>lime</td></tr>
<tr><td>ylang-ylang</td><td></td><td>orange (sweet)</td></tr>
<tr><td></td><td></td><td>tangerine</td></tr>
<tr><th>SPICE</th><th>HERBAL</th><th>WOODSY</th></tr>
<tr><td>black pepper</td><td>chamomile</td><td>cedarwood</td></tr>
<tr><td>cinnamon</td><td>clary sage</td><td>sandalwood</td></tr>
<tr><td>coriander</td><td>eucalyptus</td><td></td></tr>
<tr><td>ginger</td><td>peppermint</td><td></td></tr>
<tr><td>nutmeg</td><td>rosemary</td><td></td></tr>
<tr><td>vanilla</td><td></td><td></td></tr>
</table>

To ensure that your candles burn safely and well, use only dyes designated for candlemaking. Food coloring should not be used; they are water-based colors and will not mix with the wax. Crayons also should not be used. Though they are made using paraffin wax, other elements of the crayon can clog a wick and cause the candle to burn incorrectly. Types of candle dyes available:

Dye blocks and chips: Made of heavily dyed wax.

Liquid dye: More concentrated than dye blocks or chips.

Powder dye: The most concentrated of candle dyes. (The amount of powder that would fit in the tip of a toothpick would color a large candle.)

WICKS, WICK ACCESSORIES, AND WICK TOOLS

Choosing the correct wick size and type is key to creating successful candles. It can be a time-consuming process, but your effort will be rewarded each time you light a candle that burns correctly. There is no sure-fire method to choosing wicks; there is a lot of trial and error and testing, testing, testing. Keeping a detailed journal about your wicking experimentation will help you determine what works and what does not.

The most common types of wicks include:

Cored wicks: Braided or knitted wicks with a core that helps keep the wick upright while burning. Common core ingredients are cotton, paper, tin, or zinc. Used in floating candles, jar candles, pillars, and votives.

Flat wicks: Braided, plaited, or knitted wicks that curl in the candle flame for a self-trimming benefit. Flat, braided wicks are the most common type of wick for taper and pillar candles.

Square wicks: Braided or knitted wicks that are also self-trimming, square wicks are more rounded and a bit thicker than flat wicks. Great for all types of candles as they can help prevent clogging of the wick.

There are also specialty wicks for use with certain types of wax, including palm and soy wax. Though not widely available, you may wish to try these in your candles. An Internet search for "soy candle wicks" or "palm candle wicks" will yield information on companies that provide them.

In addition to choosing the correct type of wick, it is important to select the proper size wick for your candle. Choose the wrong size and the wick may be snuffed out by a pool of wax (caused by using too small of a wick), or the candle will smoke and wax may run down the sides (caused by using too large of a wick). Wick is sized by its ply, or number of threads that are braided or spun together. The size or ply you choose is determined by the size of the

candle you will be pouring; the larger the diameter of the candle, the larger ply of wick you will need.

Wick ply is different for each type of wick and may vary by manufacturer. Follow manufacturer recommendations to start, then adjust the size and type as needed according to your candle-testing results.

ADDITIONAL TOOLS

In addition to the wick, you will need the following:

- **Adhesive wax:** Used to hold wick tabs in place.

- **Mold sealer:** Used to seal the wick hole and hold wicks in place.

- **Pliers:** Used to clamp wick tabs closed.

- **Votive wick pin:** Used to create a wick hole in votive candles and to pierce holes in beeswax shapes.

- **Wick holders:** Include wick sticks, wooden chopsticks or skewers, toothpicks, and cocktail stirrers used to hold the wick off the surface of the candle while the wax dries.

- **Wick tabs:** Used to secure wicks in container and molded candles.

Techniques

In this section you will learn the basic techniques needed to complete the projects in this book—from melting wax and adding color and fragrance to preparing molds and pouring candles. Candlemaking is not difficult, but it can be time consuming.

If you are new to the craft, consider practicing these general guidelines on test candles before attempting the candle projects. As you become more experienced, you may choose to alter the techniques to suit your candle-making preferences…

Melting Wax

Wax can be melted a number of ways, including in an electric slow cooker, double boiler, melting pot, or commercial wax melter. The most popular are the stove-top methods—using a double boiler or melting pot.

To begin, weigh the wax using a kitchen scale, then place the wax into the melting container. (If you are using a melting pot, place the pot in a pan of water.) Melt the wax over low-to-medium heat until it reaches the recommended melting temperature (see Melting and Pouring

Temperatures chart below), also known as the melting point. The melting point is the minimum temperature that will keep wax in a liquid state. Add color and fragrance if desired.

Once the wax cools to the recommended pouring temperature (see Melting and Pouring Temperatures chart below), pour it into the mold. Pouring temperatures are important because they affect the finished look of candles. If poured too cool, candles may mottle (a snowflake effect); if poured too hot, they may get cracks (also called jump lines). As discussed in some of the following recipes, pouring temperatures can be adjusted to achieve certain effects in finished candles.

If using a melting pot, you can pour the wax directly into the mold. If using a double boiler or electric slow cooker, you will need to transfer the wax into a pouring vessel, such as a pouring pot or heat-safe glass measuring cup. Note: Wipe the bottom of the melting pot or top pan of a double boiler with a kitchen towel. Doing so will prevent any water from dripping into the wax. Wear an oven glove or mitt when you do this. The wax can now be poured into a prepared container or mold.

MELTING AND POURING TEMPERATURES

Note: These are approximate temperatures; because they can vary depending on the company that makes the wax, be sure to check the manufacturer or supplier's website for specific information.

	Melting temperatures	Pouring temperatures
Beeswax =	144° to 149° F	170°F
	(62° to 65° C)	(76° C)
Palm wax =	138° to 144° F	199° to 203° F
	(58° to 62° C)	(92° to 95° C)
Soy container wax =	115° to 130° F	110° to 130° F
	(46° to 54° C)	(43° to 54° C)
Soy pillar wax =	142° to 148° F	150° to 165° F
	(61° to 64° C)	(65° to 73° C)

Coloring and Scenting Candles

If you are adding color and fragrance to your candles, you will need to heat the wax approximately 20° F (7° C) above the melting point. Check the manufacturer

Continued ➡

instructions or website for the exact temperature range for adding color and fragrance. If using liquid dye, add it to the melted wax one drop at a time; if using wax blocks, shave a small bit of the colored wax into the melted wax; if using powder dye, first mix it into a small amount of the melted wax in a separate container, then add that wax to the larger pot of wax. The most important thing you can do to ensure even distribution of color throughout your candles is to stir, stir, stir.

After adding dye, test the color by placing a small puddle of the wax on a piece of parchment paper or wax paper and let it dry. Though it won't be the exact hue of your candle, you will get a good idea of the color.

If you are adding stearin to your candle, now is the time to do it. The typical amount of stearin used is 1 to 3 tablespoons (15 to 45 ml) per pound (454 g) of wax. Be careful not to add too much; overuse of stearin can cause your candles to flake. If you are adding both stearin and dye, melt the stearin in a separate container the same way you melt wax, then add the color to the stearin and stir thoroughly. Add the colored stearin to the melted wax and stir thoroughly to incorporate the color into the wax.

After your wax is colored, add fragrance, if desired. The recommended amount of fragrance oil is 3 tablespoons (45 ml) per pound (454 g) of wax. Use more or less, depending on how strongly scented you want your candles. If you are using essential oils, add the oil drop by drop. The recommended amount of essential oil is 1 tablespoon (15 ml) per pound (454 g) of wax. Stir thoroughly to incorporate the scent into the wax. After adding color and fragrance, remove the wax from the heat.

Working with Wicks

Though it is not essential, conditioning the wick before using it in a candle is advantageous. Doing so will help match the color of the wick to the finished candle and will encourage the wick to stand up straight. Conditioning the wick also makes the candle light easier and burn slower. Condition the wick by dipping it into the melted pot of wax, pull the wick taut, then lay the wick on a piece of parchment paper or wax paper to dry.

When making a container candle, or pushing a wick into a shaped candle, you will need to attach a wick tab to the wick. Thread the wick through the hole in the wick tab, then use pliers to squeeze the hole closed. Add a dab of adhesive wax to the bottom of the wick tab, then place the tab in the center of the bottom of a candle container and gently press in place, or push the wick into the pre-made hole of a candle.

When making a molded candle, you will need to wick the mold prior to pouring the wax. Cut a length of wick 4 inches (10.2 cm) longer than the height of the candle. If desired, condition the wick. Thread the wick through the wick hole in the mold, leaving a ½-inch (1.3 cm) tail of wick at the bottom of the mold. Secure this tail and seal the wick hole using mold sealer. Turn the mold upside down so the wick drops out of the mold. Tie the wick around a wick stick and center it on the rim of the mold. Make sure the wick is taut and straight.

After wicking the container or mold, set it on a flat surface such as a baking sheet or covered work surface. Your mold is now ready for the wax.

To ensure that your candles burn evenly and to prevent soot, trim your wick to ¼ inch (.6 cm) before and after each use.

CANDLE SUCCESS

Before starting any candle project, cover your work surface with newspaper. This makes cleanup easier even if you're not concerned about stains. You should also lay newspaper on the floor closest to your counter—scraping up wax drips is pure drudgery.

Making Container Candles

PREPARE THE MOLD

Using a pencil, make a light mark ¼ inch (.6 cm) below the rim of the container; this is the fill mark. Wick the container, then place it on a covered work surface or baking sheet.

MELT THE WAX

Following the Melting and Pouring Temperatures chart or manufacturer's instructions, melt the wax, then add color and fragrance. Always melt more wax than you think you'll need. You will use this wax later in the pouring process, and it is nearly impossible to create the same wax color twice.

POUR THE WAX

Following the Melting and Pouring Temperatures chart or manufacturer's instructions, pour the wax into the container up to the fill mark. As the wax dries, a well will form around the wick. Poke the wax around the wick with a straight pin or toothpick; this will help keep the wick centered in the mold. Re-melt the unused wax to the same temperature as you poured the candle and pour it into the well, just below the line where you poured before; this is called topping up the candle. Large candles may need to be topped up more than once.

Pour any unused wax into a heat-proof glass jar. The wax can be re-melted and used in another project. Another option for saving wax is to line a bowl with parchment paper or wax paper, then pour the wax into the bowl. Once the wax has cooled, place it in a plastic bag and store for later use.

FINISH THE CANDLE

Once the candle has cooled completely, remove the wick holder and trim the wick to ¼ inch (.6 cm).

Making Molded Candles

Prepare the Mold

Wick the mold, then place the mold on a covered work surface or baking sheet.

MELT THE WAX

Following the Melting and Pouring Temperatures chart (see page 47) or manufacturer's directions, melt the wax, then add color and fragrance. Always melt more wax than you think you will need. You will use this wax later in the pouring process, and it is nearly impossible to create the same wax color twice. If using a melting pot, you can pour the wax directly into the mold. If using a double boiler or electric slow cooker, you will need to transfer the wax into a pouring vessel, such as a pouring pot or heat-safe glass measuring cup. Note: Wipe the bottom of the pouring pot or top pan of double boiler with a kitchen towel. Doing so will prevent any water from dripping into the wax. Wear an oven glove or mitt when you do this.

POUR THE WAX

Following the Melting and Pouring Temperatures chart (see page 47) or manufacturer's directions, pour the wax into the mold. As the wax dries, a well will form around the wick. Poke the wax around the wick with a straight pin or toothpick; this will help keep the wick centered in the mold. Re-melt the unused wax to the same temperature as you poured the candle and pour it into the well to just below the line where you poured before; this is called topping up the candle. Large candles may need to be topped up more than once.

Pour any unused wax into a heat-proof glass jar. The wax can be re-melted and used in another project. Another option for saving wax is to line a bowl with parchment paper or wax paper, then pour the wax into the bowl. Once the wax has cooled, place it in a plastic bag and store for later use.

CANDLE SUCCESS

If you don't have a double boiler you can easily create your own. Simply fill a large saucepan with water and place the melting pots inside the pan. The object is to avoid direct heat to the melting pot.

REMOVE THE CANDLE FROM THE MOLD

To get started, remove the mold seal. If using a metal mold, turn it upside down and tap lightly on the bottom of the mold; the candle should slide right out. If it doesn't, place the candle in the refrigerator up to 30 minutes, then try again. If you are using a two-piece plastic mold, remove the mold clips or base if necessary, then separate the pieces. Some plastic two-piece molds require that the wick be held in the mold with tape or mold sealer, for these molds, the well side will come off easily. You will need to remove the tape or mold sealer before removing the wick side of the mold.

Once the candle is out of the mold, remove the wick holder and trip the top of the wick to ¼ inch (.6 cm). Trim the bottom of the wick even with the candle. Use a paring knife to smooth any extra wax at the seams or on the bottom of the candle.

Cleaning Candle Molds

Always clean your candle mold after completing any candle project. Leftover bits of wax or dye will mar the surface of any future candle made using the mold. Be careful not to scratch or dent the mold as you clean it as these marks will also show on the surface of future candles.

To clean plastic molds, put them in the freezer for 20 minutes or so to allow the wax to contract. Gently remove the frozen wax using a toothpick (fingernails work well in a pinch), then wash the mold in a bucket of hot, soapy water. Don't wash your molds in a household sink; the wax can build up in the pipes and cause plumbing problems later on.

To clean metal molds, line a baking sheet with aluminum foil, then place the mold upside down on the sheet. Heat your oven to 200° F (93° C) then place the sheet in the oven. Leave the mold in the oven until the wax melts and runs down onto the foil. Wearing an oven mitt, remove the molds from the oven, then immediately wipe the inside of the mold using a paper towel. Wash the mold in a bucket of hot, soapy water to get out the last traces of wax.

Making Dye-Painted Molded Candles

Another technique used to create molded candles requires that the dye be painted onto the mold instead of added to the wax. This process results in candles that have interesting dye patterns on the outside of the candle. Rebekah Ashley provided the following instructions:

PREPARE THE MOLD

Note: Metal or acrylic molds can be used with this technique.

While the wax is melting, select your color and scent (if using). To create the effect of dye on the outside of the candle, neatly apply liquid dye to the inside of the mold, either before or after wicking. You can use the blunt end of a bamboo skewer, cotton swab, or small paintbrush. Whatever applicator you choose will get stained beyond repair (unless it's metal), so you may want to avoid using expensive sable artist brushes. Wipe spills quickly with a soapy rag.

A little dye goes a long way. In a metal mold, nearly all of the wax will transfer to the candle, while in an acrylic mold, some dye is left in the mold. Also, candle dye strength varies by manufacturer. It is wise to do a test candle with plain wax and dye to play with the technique, and also to see how your chosen wick size will burn.

For the clearest results, dip the applicator, tap off the

excess, and scribble or paint a design inside. It doesn't need to be too delicate—the dye is likely to drip slightly, and a blurring effect occurs as the hot wax melts the dye off the mold. The design will be clearer if the dye can dry for 30 minutes or so before pouring the wax into the mold. Note: Remember, most candle molds form the candle upside down, so keep this in mind when deciding where you want the design to appear on the candle.

WICK THE MOLD

Condition the wick by dipping it into the melted pot of wax, pull it taut, then lay the wick on parchment paper or wax paper to dry, then wick the mold.

POUR THE WAX

To get the best results with this technique, watch the wax as it is melting and pour it into the mold as soon as the last little bit has melted, if not a little before (a small piece of soft solid wax poured into the mold will melt anyway). Pouring the wax this cool will often cause the wax to set a little on the sides as it fills the mold, giving an interesting texture to the candle surface. If the wax gets too hot, remove it from the heat and wait until it becomes cloudy or thick looking and leaves solid wax trails in the double boiler or melting pot as you tip it from side to side.

FINISH THE CANDLE

Remove the candle from the mold. Trim the wick close to the base with scissors or nail clippers. Then, using a sharp knife, trim the base if necessary. Trim the wick at the top to ¼ to ⅓ inch (.6 to .8 cm). If you have trouble getting the candle out of the mold, make sure it has cooled completely, then place in the refrigerator for about 30 minutes. After that, a quick rinse under a warm tap will expand the mold away from the cold candle. Then tap the mold on a counter top.

Making Rolled Beeswax Candles

Lay a sheet of beeswax on a self-healing cutting mat. Using a craft knife and metal-edge ruler, cut the sheet to the height of candle you wish to make. Cut a length of wick 2 inches (5.1 cm) longer than the height of the candle. Lay the wick along one end of the sheet, with 1 inch (2.5 cm) of wick past each end, then gently press the wick into the wax (see Photo A). Carefully roll over the wick end tightly once around to secure the wick (see Photo B). Continue rolling the wax until you reach the end of the sheet, then gently press the end of the sheet into the rolled candle (see Photo C). Note: The tighter you roll the sheet, the neater looking the finished candle. Take your time rolling the candle; you will be a pro in no time.

Photo A

Photo B

Photo C

—FROM *Candlemaking the Natural Way*

BEESWAX CANDLES
Rebecca Ittner

Beeswax is one of the oldest materials used to make candles, dating back to the Middle Ages when candlemakers preferred its superior qualities. Candles made with beeswax have a longer burn life than common paraffin wax, and offer a slow, nearly smokeless flame that gives off more light than other waxes.

Not only is beeswax all natural, with its own subtle honey-like scent, it's easy to mold into pillar candles or form into interesting shapes using everyday items such as cookie cutters or silicone trays. You can also roll beeswax sheets, which are available in a spectrum of colors, into beautiful candles. But don't stop there. Layer your colors and get creative with your shapes as we've done with the Mini Hearts & Stars.

Favors with Heart
Cheryl Murakami

Making candles by rolling sheets of beeswax is one of the simplest forms of candlemaking. All you need is a clean work surface, a ruler, and a craft knife. These two-tone heart candles can be personalized for any occasion with the colors you choose.

Materials

- 1 sheet each of honeycomb beeswax: red and white or contrasting colors of your choice
- Cotton square braided wick: size 1/0, 6 inches (15.2 cm) long

Tools

- Craft knife
- Metal-edge ruler
- Pencil
- Self-healing cutting mat
- Wax paper

Instructions

1. Cut each beeswax sheet into 1 x 16-inch (2.5 x 40.6 cm) strips using the ruler, craft knife, and cutting mat.

2. For each candle you will need three strips of wax trimmed to size: one red 1 x 16 inches (2.5 x 40.6 cm); one red 1 x 8 inches (2.5 x 20.3 cm); and a contrasting color strip of white 1 x 12 inches (2.5 x 30.5 cm).

3. Cut the wick to measure 6 inches (15.2 cm) long.

4. On the cutting mat, lay the wick close to the edge of the red 1 x 16-inch (2.5 x 40.6 cm) strip with approximately ¼ inch (.6 cm) sticking out of one side (this will be the bottom of the candle). Fold the edge of the wax over the wick and press down securely. Roll the wax around the wick once tightly and evenly.

5. Lay the white contrasting color strip over the first strip starting 1 inch (2.5 cm) away from the beginning of the wick roll. Lay the last red strip over the contrasting strip starting 2 inches (5.1 cm) from the bottom strip's wick roll.

6. Carefully and slowly continue rolling the candle, incorporating the second and third strip. Note: Aim for an even tension roll; if it's too tight the beeswax sheet will break, and if it's too loose the roll will come apart. To finish the roll, press the seam gently into the side of the candle.

7. You can leave the round swirl design candle at this stage or continue to add another design. To make a heart shape, wrap a 2-inch (5.1 cm) length of wax paper around the pencil. Hold the candle in one hand with the seam edge toward you and, with your other hand, press the pencil into the seam to make an indentation.

8. Lay the candle on the cutting mat with the long wick side up (top of candle) and the indentation facing directly away from you. Using both hands, hold the top of the candle with your forefingers and begin pressing the bottom of the candle inward to form a "V" shape, which will be the point of the heart shape directly across the top indentation. Turn the candle over and continue shaping in the same way.

Mini Hearts & Stars
Paoling Che

Silicone ice trays make great tools when it comes to pouring your own beeswax candles. While the beeswax stubbornly sticks to other types of molds, with silicone the candle pops right out. These little heart- and star-shaped candles are perfect for gift giving.

Materials

- 1 sheet of natural-colored honeycomb textured beeswax 8 x 16 inches (20.3 x 40.6 cm)
- 4 primed wicks: for candles 1 to 2 inches (2.5 to 5.1 cm) in diameter, 1½ inches (3.8 cm) tall

Tools

- Double boiler
- Heart-shaped silicone ice tray
- Metal spoon
- Scissors
- Star-shaped silicone ice trays
- Wicking needle or votive wick pin

Instructions

1. Heat the beeswax sheet in the double boiler until completely melted.

2. Pour the beeswax slowly to the top of each silicone ice tray cavity, reserving about 2 oz. (60 ml) of the beeswax; set aside.

3. While the wax is still warm, insert a wicking needle

Continued ➜

or votive wick pin at the center of the wax, creating a space for the wick to be placed when the candle is cooled.

4. Once the wax has completely cooled, remove the candles from the molds by popping out the wax.

5. Poke the wax through the center again with the wicking needle to ensure there's enough room for sliding the primed wick into the candle.

6. Insert a wick into each candle, making sure the wick and candle are flush at the bottom.

7. To fill the bottom of the candles and secure the wicks in place, set the candles face down on the ice trays. Reheat the remaining beeswax in the double boiler. Using a metal spoon, scoop enough molten beeswax to fill the indent on the bottom of the candles. Let cool completely, then trim the wicks to ¼ inch (.6 cm).

Everyday Pillars

Paoling Che

These square pillars are perfect for the beginner candlemaker. Beeswax sheets are available in many colors, including white and honey-colored as pictured in this project.

Materials

I sheet of natural or light-colored honeycomb textured beeswax: 8 x 16 inches (20.3 x 40.6 cm)

Primed wick: for candles I to 2 inches (2.5 to 5.1 cm) in diameter, 4 inches (10.2 cm) long

Tools

Baking sheet

Craft knife

Double boiler

Metal-edge ruler

Plastic wrap

Pliers

Self-healing cutting mat

Instructions

I. Measure the short end of the natural beeswax sheet and mark into thirds. Using the craft knife and ruler, cut the beeswax into three long strips.

2. Lay the primed wick along the short edge of one of the natural beeswax strips.

3. Start rolling the candle by curling the edge of the beeswax over the wick. Continue rolling tightly until the wax is about ½ inch (1.3 cm) in diameter.

4. Begin to press down instead of rolling. Turn the candle 90 degrees, pressing down again. Repeat for all four sides. You should begin forming the general shape of a square.

5. Continue the turn-and-press pattern, attaching the additional two strips of beeswax sheets to where the one before left off.

6. When all three strips have been used, press the end firmly into the candle to secure in place.

7. Heat the baking sheet in the oven until hot. Remove from the oven and place on a heat-resistant surface. Press the top of the candle down onto the baking sheet to create an even top. Lift the wick up, as it probably has been pressed into the candle. Trim the wick to ¼ inch (.6 cm).

—From *Candlemaking the Natural Way*

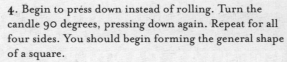

PALM WAX CANDLES

Rebecca Ittner

Relatively new in the candlemaking arena, palm wax is an all-natural, renewable resource distilled from palm trees found in Southeast Asia, Latin America, and Africa. Palm wax makes a hard, smooth candle that is soft to the touch, and can withstand warm temperatures, absorb color easily, and retain fragrance. It is also clean burning and burns with a bright flame.

The wax also molds well, giving the candlemaker countless designs and patterns to dream up, from the crystallized hue of the Simple Molded Pillar to coordinating colors found in the Layered Pillar.

The naturally creamy color of the wax appeals to many, but if you decide to color the wax, be sure to use candle colorants. Palm wax blends well with other waxes to further expand your recipe library.

Painted Wax Pillars

Rebekah Ashley

You can utilize the technique featured in this project with any pillar candle, from 6-inch (15.2 cm), three-wick candles to votives and tapers. I like to turn layered candles into winter landscapes using silhouettes of trees.

Materials

2 lbs. (909 g) palm wax container blend

Fragrance or essential oils (optional)

Oil-based candle dye: 2 to 6 drops

Square braided cotton wick: no. 3

Tools

Baking tray with sides

Bamboo skewers or chopsticks

Candy thermometer

Melting pot or double boiler

Metal candle mold

Metal spoon for stirring, scraping, testing, etc.

Mold sealer

Paring knife

Scissors

Soapy cloth

White bowl: for testing the color of dyed wax

Instructions

I. Clip the thermometer onto the melting pot or double boiler. Melt the wax in the pot until it reaches between 199° and 203° F (92° and 95° C); remove from heat.

2. Add the fragrance oil if desired at this time and stir for 2 minutes to ensure the fragrance bonds with the wax.

3. While the wax is melting, prepare the mold by applying the dye to the inside of the mold using the blunt end of a bamboo skewer or chopstick. Wipe counter spills quickly with a soapy cloth.

4. Cut the wick 4 inches (10.2 cm) longer than the mold. Condition the wick by dipping it into the melted wax. Wick the mold and seal the wick hole with mold sealer.

5. Remove the wax from the heat; let cool to lukewarm temperature. Carefully pour the melted wax into the mold. Allow the candle to cool and fully harden.

6. Remove the candle from the mold. Trim the wick close to the base using the paring knife. Trim the wick at the top to ⅓ inch (.8 cm).

7. If you have trouble getting the candle out of the mold, make sure it's fully cooled, then place it in the refrigerator until it pulls away from the mold. Pass the mold under warm tap water to expand the mold away from the cold candle, then tap the mold on the counter.

Layered Pillar

Melissa Kotz

My inspiration for this candle came from a beautiful pottery pitcher. When I happened upon the glass beads used in this project, they reminded me of the pitcher and I decided to incorporate them into the candle.

Materials

½ oz. (15 ml) fragrance oil (optional)

16 oz. (454 g) pillar blend palm wax

Beads: for the wick

Candle dye chips or liquid candle dye: brown and turquoise or desired colors

Cotton wick and wick clip

Tools

Candy thermometer

Melting pot or double boiler

Mold sealer (optional)

Paring knife

Pillar mold (preferably without a wick hole; if yours does have a hole, cover it with mold sealer)

Pouring pots (2)

Scissors

Wick bar or wooden skewer

Wooden spoon

Instructions

1. Clip the thermometer onto the melting pot or double boiler. Melt the wax in the pot until it reaches about 200° F (93° C); remove from heat.

2. Add the fragrance oil if desired at this time, and stir for 2 minutes to ensure the fragrance bonds with the wax.

3. Pour 6 oz. (180 ml) of wax into each of the pouring pots. Add dye chips or liquid dye to each pouring pot (I used brown and turquoise) and mix for at least 1 minute; repeat until the desired color is achieved.

4. Pour 1 oz. (30 ml) of the brown wax in the mold. Wait until the wax forms a thick shell but doesn't cool completely. Place the prepared wick on top of the skin, centering it with a wick bar or wooden skewer. Place the bar or skewer on top of the mold.

5. Add 1 oz. (30 ml) of the turquoise wax and wait until it forms a thick skin but doesn't cool completely. Add a thin layer of the brown wax and wait until a thick skin forms. Repeat this process, layering the two colors.

6. Carefully cut a 1-inch-deep (2.5 cm) round circle at the top of the candle with the knife, leaving about ¼ to ½-inch (.6 to 1.3 cm) sides. Gently remove the circle.

7. Pour the center with turquoise wax to refill the hole. Let candle cool completely.

8. Remove the candle from the mold. Add beads to the wick and tie a knot at the end to secure them in place. Trim the excess wick.

CANDLE SUCCESS

When you add the last layer of wax, wait until the top of the candle forms a thick shell. You'll want the shell to measure about 1 inch (2.5 cm) thick (the candle will still be warm). This can be a difficult thing to judge; you may want to gently poke the top of the wax with a skewer or toothpick to see how thick the shell is (kind of like checking to see if a cake is done). If liquid wax oozes out right away, wait a little longer. If very little liquid comes out, you're ready to proceed.

Simple Molded Pillar

Sara Werzel

All-natural palm wax retains and releases great aroma using smaller amounts of fragrance oil than other waxes. The surface of a palm wax candle is uniquely patterned simply due to the nature of the wax, giving the appearance of crystalline feathers.

CANDLE SUCCESS

On some occasions it is obvious there is air trapped beneath the surface layer of the candle. If after about an hour of cooling you notice this, simply take a skewer and carefully poke holes in the surface of the candle. The thin surface layer can be pushed into the molten wax in the mold. This releases the air, preventing air pockets in your finished candle.

Materials

¼ to ¾ oz. (15 to 22.5 ml) clove fragrance oil

12 oz. (340 g) palm wax

Liquid candle dye: red, 7 drops (do not use food coloring or crayons)

Wick: RRD 50, 8 inches (20.3 cm) long

Tools

Candy thermometer

Heat gun or blow dryer

Long-handled metal spoon

Metal pillar mold: 3 x 3½ inches (7.6 x 8.9 cm)

Mold sealer

Pan (large enough to hold pouring pot)

Pouring pot

Scissors

Wick rod or thick wooden skewer

Instructions

MELT THE WAX

1. Add 1 or 2 inches (2.5 to 5.1 cm) of water to the pan; bring the water to a boil.

2. Place the wax into the pouring pot and place the pot directly into the boiling water. Lower the heat to a simmer.

3. Periodically add water to the old pot to replace water lost to evaporation. Note: To avoid a fire hazard, never let the double boiler run dry, and avoid splashing water into the pouring pot.

4. Melt the wax until the temperature reaches between 200° and 210° F (93° and 98° C).

PREPARE THE MOLD

1. Thread the wick through the wick hole at the bottom of the mold, leaving a ¼-inch (.6 cm) tail of wick at the wick hole. Secure the wick and seal the wick hole with mold sealer.

2. Tie the opposite end of the wick to the wick rod or skewer, making sure the wick is centered and straight.

Fresh Outdoors Pillar

Angie Rodriguez

This candle captures the distinctive crystallization effect of palm pillar wax. The royal blue selected for the candle adds contrast and complements the crystallized look.

Materials

½ to 3 oz. (15 to 90 ml) Fresh Outdoors fragrance oil

3 to 4 cups (720 to 960 ml) palm pillar granule wax

Color block: royal blue

Square braided cotton wick: no. 4, 6 to 8 inches (15.2 to 20.3 cm) long

Tools

Cake pan: 9-inch (22.9 cm) round

Candy thermometer

Melting pot or double boiler

Mold sealer

Nail clippers

Paring knife

Spiral octagon pillar mold: 4 x 6 inches (10.2 x 15.2 cm)

Straight pin

Wick stick

INSTRUCTIONS

Melt the wax

1. Clip the thermometer onto the melting pot or double boiler. Melt 1 cup (240 ml) of granule wax until the temperature reaches about 160° F (71° C); remove from heat.

2. Using the paring knife, trim thin shavings of royal blue wax coloring and mix them into the granule wax until desired shade is reached (use more for deeper shades, less for paler shades). Stir thoroughly to blend coloring evenly.

3. Add 1 to 1½ oz. (30 to 45 ml) of fragrance oil and stir constantly to distribute evenly. When the temperature reaches about 150° F (65° C), pour the wax into the cake pan; let set.

PREPARE THE MOLD

1. Thread the wick (still attached to the spool or roll; don't premeasure or cut from it yet) through the wick hole of the mold and securely tie the end at the bottom of the mold (opposite the wick hole, open end) to the wick stick.

2. Wrap the other end around the stick pin 2 to 3 times and, while holding the pin against the mold, pull tightly on the remaining wick slack to ensure the wick is taut in the mold. Once all the slack is taken up, secure with mold sealer and clip the end of the wick about ¼ inch (.6 cm) from the pin.

3. Evenly spread mold sealer to cover the exposed wick to prevent leakage when pouring.

POUR THE CANDLE

1. Clip the thermometer onto the melting pot or double boiler. Melt 3 cups (720 ml) of granule wax until the temperature reaches about 160° to 170° F (71° to 76° C); remove from heat.

2. Once the wax reaches about 165° F (73° C), add remaining fragrance oil, stirring thoroughly to blend evenly. Note: Monitor your wax temperature; you will want to pour this candle at no more than 160° F (71° C) to create the crystallized look.

3. Arrange the wax chunks in the prepared mold. Pack the chunks fully for more contrast between the wax textures and colors, or sparingly for a more solid look.

4. Place the chunk-filled mold into the cake pan to trap any wax in case of leakage when pouring. Pour the wax quickly to about ¼ inch (.6 cm) from the top of the mold, reserving at least ⅛ to ¼ cup (30 to 60 ml) of wax for refilling; let set.

5. Once the candle has hardened, poke holes in various places around the wick with a straight pin; let set thoroughly before refilling.

6. Once the candle has fully solidified, reheat the reserved refill wax to 170° F (76° C). Refill the holes to

Continued →

cover the candle evenly. Note: Reheating to this temperature ensures a fairly smooth candle bottom.

7. Once the wax pulls away from the edges of the mold, remove the mold sealer and the candle should release smoothly. If you have trouble getting the candle out, make sure it's fully cooled, then place in the refrigerator until it pulls away from the mold.

8. Using the nail clippers, trim the excess wick at the bottom of the candle. Using the paring knife, level out the bottom of the candle, if necessary.

—From *Candlemaking the Natural Way*

CANDLE SUCCESS

Keep a watchful eye on the chunk wax as it solidifies. Allow it to cool long enough to harden, but not so long that it becomes fully solid. You'll want the consistency to allow cutting into strip chunks. When working with palm wax, it can be a bit tricky to judge when to cut. Palm wax tends to become brittle when cutting, so you may end up with a combination of clearly cut chunks and crumbled pieces. This is perfectly fine; each adds to the unique characteristics of the candle.

SOY WAX CANDLES

Rebecca Ittner

In addition to palm and beeswax, soy is a popular choice with candlemakers seeking environmentally friendly materials. Soy wax is made from hydrogenated soybean oil, and it burns clean with so little smoke that it often goes unnoticed. Soy candles also emit a cleaner, stronger small that lasts longer than paraffin, whether you're using soy wax in its natural state or adding fragrance to your candle.

Soy wax is easy to clean up with soap and water, which means you can reuse your utensils for more candlemaking and also save your work surfaces and tablecloths from wax drips and other damage.

Rebecca Ittner

Cupcakes are a great way to celebrate any occasion. These candles are gently scented with vanilla essential oil, but feel free to use any scent you desire or leave them unscented. Yields 6 cupcakes.

Materials

2 teaspoons (10 ml) vanilla essential oil

2 lbs. (909 g) soy pillar wax flakes

Color blocks: ivory and peach

Flat braided cotton wick: medium

Wick tabs: small or medium (6)

Tools

Adhesive wax

Candle thermometer

Double boiler

Glass measuring cups: 4-cup (960 ml) (2)

Kitchen towel

Metal cupcake pan

Paper towel

Paring knife

Pliers

Scissors

Silicone baking cups (6)

Wooden toothpicks or plastic cocktail stirrers (6)

Instructions

PREPARE THE MOLD

1. Thread a piece of wick through the wick tab and clamp the tab closed with the pliers. Note: Make sure the wick is long enough to wrap around the toothpick or stirrer at the top of the baking cup.

2. Place a dab of adhesive wax on the bottom of the wick tab, then press the tab in place in the center of the baking cup.

3. Wrap the top of the wick around the toothpick or cocktail stirrer and set it across the top of the baking cup, centering the wick in the baking cup. Place the baking cup into the cupcake pan. Repeat with the remaining baking cups. Note: Placing the baking cups into the cupcake pan will help hold the shape of the candles.

MELT THE WAX FLAKES

1. Clip the thermometer onto the double boiler. Melt the wax flakes until the temperature reaches about 160° F (71° C); remove from heat. Stir in the essential oil, then pour a quarter of the wax into a glass measuring cup and set it aside. Note: Carefully wipe the bottom of the pan with a kitchen towel before pouring the wax into the glass to prevent any water from dripping into the wax.

2. Pour the remaining wax into the second measuring cup. Using the paring knife, trim thin shavings of peach wax coloring and mix them into the remaining glass of wax until the desired shade is reached (use more for a deeper shade, less for a paler shade). Stir thoroughly to blend the coloring evenly.

POUR AND FINISH THE CANDLES

1. Pour the wax into the baking cups, filling them about three-quarters full. Allow the wax to completely cool.

2. Once the wax has cooled, reheat the uncolored wax. You can do this by placing the measuring cup in a pan of water, then heating the water until the wax is melted. Remove the measuring glass from the pan of water. Note: Add water to the pan as needed.

3. Stir the wax occasionally as it cools. Once the wax begins to thicken, pour it on top of the wax in the baking cups, leaving at least ¼ inch (.6 cm) between the top of the wax and the edge of the baking cups.

4. Once the candles have completely cooled, remove the toothpicks or cocktail stirrers and, using the scissors, trim the excess wick at the top of the candles. Remove the baking cups from the cupcake pan, then remove the baking cups from the candles.

Spheres

Rebecca Ittner

Clean, simple lines give these candles the versatility to blend in anywhere. They look great on their own or in containers. Unbuffed, the candles have a matte finish. Buffed, they have a gorgeous sheen.

Materials

1 lb. (454 g) soy pillar wax flakes

Color block: desired color

Flat braided cotton wick: large

Tools

Adhesive wax

Baking sheet

Candle thermometer

Craft knife

Double boiler

Glass measuring cup: 4-cup (960 ml)

Kitchen towel

Mold sealer

Nylon stocking

Paring knife

Polycarbonate two-piece mold: round

Scissors

Wooden skewer

Instructions

PREPARE THE MOLD

Note: There are two sides to this mold that twist together in the middle.

1. Put the two pieces of the mold together and twist to secure.

2. Cut a length of wick to fit your mold, leaving a ¼-inch (.6 cm) tail of wick at the bottom of the mold and enough length of wick at the top to wrap around the wooden skewer.

3. Using the mold sealer, cover the bottom hole and wick tail, making sure to smooth the sealer on the surface of the mold to prevent leakage.

4. Wrap the top of the wick around the wooden skewer and set in place at the top of the mold. Use a dab of adhesive wax to hold the wooden skewer in place, if necessary.

MELT THE WAX FLAKES

1. Clip the thermometer onto the double boiler. Melt the wax flakes until the temperature reaches about 160° F (71°C); remove from heat.

2. Using the paring knife, trim thin shavings of wax coloring and mix them into the wax until the desired shade is reached (use more for a deeper shade, less for a paler shade). Stir thoroughly to blend coloring evenly.

POUR THE CANDLE

1. When the temperature reaches 150° F (65° C), pour the wax into the measuring cup. Note: Carefully wipe the bottom of the pan with a kitchen towel before pouring the wax into the glass to prevent any water from dripping into the wax.

CANDLE SUCCESS

Candle dye is very staining and difficult to remove, especially from plastics because of the molecular similarity. It comes off wood floors well with a little bleach, linoleum with a lot (soak for hours). Sealed tiles aren't a problem but your grout could get stained beyond repair; better to put down newspaper and pick up sheets that get spilled on before they can soak through.

2. Pour the wax quickly to about ¼ inch (.6 cm) from the top of the mold, reserving at least ⅛ to ¼ cup (30 to 60 ml) of wax for refilling; let set.

3. Allow the candle to cool. As it cools, the wax may shrink away from the wick. Carefully poke holes in the wax near the wick using a toothpick. Repeat this 2 to 3 times as the candle cools. Note: Cooling times will vary depending on the size of your candle.

4. Once the candle has completely cooled, reheat the reserved refill wax to 160° F (71°C). Refill the holes to cover the candle evenly.

REMOVE THE CANDLE FROM THE MOLD

1. When the candle is fully hardened, remove it from the mold. First, remove the mold sealer, then gently pry the two pieces of the mold apart.

2. Using the paring knife, trim the excess wax from the poured end of the candle. This is now the candle bottom.

3. Using the scissors, trim the ends of the wick. Buff the seams and surface of the candle smooth with a nylon stocking.

Bright Votives

Patrick Troxell

The materials needed for this project are basic and easily found at any candle-making supply store or online source. The votives are fairly easy to make; however, it may take some trial and error before you achieve perfection.

Materials

6 tablespoons (90 ml) fragrance oil: desired scent

3 lbs. (1364 g) soy pillar wax

Liquid dye: 3 colors, 1 to 7 drops each

Wick: small

Wick tabs

Tools

Candy thermometers (3)

Large pan

Melting pots (3)

Metal spoon

Votive molds

Votive wick pins (optional)

Instructions

1. Clip a thermometer onto each melting pot and place the pots into a large pan of water. Place 1 lb. (454 g) of soy pillar wax in each melting pot.

2. Melt the wax until the temperature reaches about 165° to 170° F (73° to 76° C). Adjust the heat to a medium-low setting. Note: The water needs to be boiling, but it does not have to come to a rolling boil. Check the temperature of the wax occasionally to make certain it is not getting too hot. Adjust the temperature as needed.

3. While you are waiting for the wax to melt, prepare approximately 24 votive molds; add wick pins, if desired. Note: Ensure the molds and pins are clean by using mold cleaner or cooking spray.

4. Once the wax reaches between 165° and 170° F (73° and 76° C), add 2 tablespoons (30 ml) of fragrance oil

to each 1 lb. (454 g) of wax. Add between 1 and 3 drops of dye to one of the pots and stir 3 to 5 minutes.

5. After stirring, pour the first color of wax into the molds, filling them about ¾ inch (1.9 cm), or about a third of the mold.

6. Allow the first pour to dry approximately 20 minutes at room temperature. You want the wax to harden but not dry completely or it will not fuse properly with the second and third pours. While you are waiting for the first pour to dry, maintain the second pot at about 170° to 175° F (76° to 79° C) and begin melting a third pot of wax.

7. After the first pour has dried to the desired state, ensure the second pot is at 170° to 175° F (76° to 79° C). Add 1 to 3 drops of dye and stir 3 to 5 minutes. Pour the second color of wax into the molds about another ¾ inch (1.9 cm) on top of the first pour. Allow to dry approximately 20 to 25 minutes.

8. Heat the third color of wax to between 180° and 185° F (82° and 85° C), add 1 to 3 drops of dye, and stir 3 to 5 minutes.

9. Pour the wax in the third pot to the top of the molds. Note: The candles will have a much better appearance if you fill the mold completely to the top.

10. Allow the candles to cool for approximately 2 hours. I do not recommend refrigerating or freezing as this could cause cracking. When the candles are completely cool they will fall right out of the molds when turned upside down. Note: If you are using votive wick pins, after taking the candle out of the mold, turn it upside down and lightly tap the wick pin on a flat surface. After the pin starts to come out, pull the pin completely out from the bottom of the candle.

—From *Candlemaking the Natural Way*

UPCYCLED NATURAL CANDLES

Rebecca Ittner

Whether you have a stash of nearly spent candles, or a couple of candle projects that didn't turn out so well, there's no reason to waste the unwanted. The beauty of candle wax is that it can be reheated and melted at any state, combined with other waxes, and recolored and remade into a beautiful new candle.

You can also upcycle candles that are faded, stained, or simply outdated in color or style.

Natural Beauty

Rebecca Ittner

Quickly transform plain, ho-hum pillars using this simple dipping method. Thin objects such as reeds, dried flowers, or photographs work best. Uncolored wax provides the clearest view of the embedded items, but colored wax would also work.

Materials

• 1½ to 2 lbs. (685 to 908 g) soy container wax flakes

• Dried reeds

• Small pillar or votive candle

• Stearin: 5 tablespoons (75 ml)

Tools

• Candle thermometers (2)

• Double boilers (2)

• Newspaper

• Parchment paper

• Pouring pot or tail, thin jar

• Scissors

Instructions

PREPARE THE REEDS

Measure the height of the candle and cut the desired amount of reeds the same height or a bit shorter than the candle. Set aside.

MELT THE WAX

Note: Melt the palm stearin and soy wax flakes in separate containers at the same time. You will need to add the palm stearin to the wax once both reach their melting points.

1. Clip a thermometer onto a double boiler. Melt the palm stearin until the temperature reaches about 135° F (57° C).

2. Clip a thermometer onto the remaining double boiler. Melt the soy wax flakes until the temperature reaches about 125° F (52° C); remove from heat, then stir in the palm stearin. Let the wax cool to about 110° F (43° C), then pour it into the pouring pot or jar.

DIP THE CANDLE

1. Pick up the candle by the wick and carefully dip the candle into the melted wax. Lift the candle out of the wax, then let the excess wax drip back into the melted wax. Set the candle onto the parchment.

2. Working quickly, carefully press the cut pieces of reed into the wax. Allow the wax to cool.

3. Once the candle has cooled, reheat the wax, then let it cool to about 110° F (43° C). Repeat Step 1.

4. Once the candle has completely cooled, use the paring knife to trim any excess wax from the bottom edge of the candle, if desired.

Cookie Cutter Shapes

Rebecca Ittner

These layered candles are the result of a damaged beeswax pillar. I remelted the failed candle, then poured the wax into a cake pan and used cookie cutters to cut shapes in the warm wax.

Materials

• 2 lbs. (909 g) flat beeswax: 2 coordinating colors

• Flat braided cotton wicks: large (3)

• Vegetable spray

• Wick tabs: small (3)

Tools

• Cake pans: 9-inch (22.9 cm) round (2)

• Candle thermometer

• Cookie cutters: various shapes and sizes

• Double boiler

• Kitchen towel

Continued ➜

- Parchment paper
- Pliers
- Scissors
- Tongs
- Votive wick pin

Instructions

1. Cover your work surface with parchment paper. Spray the cake pans with vegetable spray; set aside.

2. Clip the thermometer onto the double boiler. Melt one color of the wax until the temperature reaches about 160° F (71° C).

3. Cut a 12-inch (30.5 cm) length of wick. Using the tongs, dip the wick into the melted wax twice. Pull the wick taut, then set the dipped wick on the parchment paper to dry.

4. When the temperature reaches 160° F (71° C), pour the wax into one of the cake pans. Note: Carefully wipe the bottom of the double boiler with a kitchen towel before pouring the wax into the cake pan to prevent any water from dripping into the wax.

5. Repeat steps 1 to 4 with the second color of wax.

6. Let the wax cool to the point where it is rubbery. Using the cookie cutters, cut shapes from the wax and place the shapes on the flat, parchment paper-covered surface; let cool. Note: You may need to use pliers to remove the cookie cutter from the wax.

7. Stack the shapes in alternating colors, then push the votive wick pin through the center of the stacked shapes.

8. Cut a length of wick 2 inches (5.1 cm) longer than the height of the stacked shapes, thread the wick through a wick pin, and close the wick pin with the pliers. Thread the wick up through the stack of shapes. Note: If the wick gets too soft to thread through the shapes, put it in the freezer for a few minutes and try again.

Wax Rejects

Rebecca Ittner

Every candle maker has a stash of leftover wax in various colors. When there's not enough wax in any one color or coordinating colors to create a pretty candle, consider melting them all together and pouring them in an interesting porcelain or metal container to conceal the mottles color.

Materials

- 1 to 1½ lbs. (454 to 681 g) leftover colored soy container wax
- Flat braided cotton wick: large

CANDLE SUCCESS

Keep an eye on the cake pans as the wax is cooling. You will need to use the cookie cutters when the wax is warm and rubbery, not liquid. If the wax cools too much, the cookie cutters will not go through the wax.

Tools

- Adhesive wax
- Candle thermometer
- Container: porcelain or metal
- Double boiler
- Glass measuring cup: 4-cup (960 ml)
- Kitchen towel
- Paper towel

- Pliers
- Scissors
- Wick tab: medium
- Wooden skewer

Instructions

PREPARE THE MOLD

1. Thread a piece of wick through the wick tab and clamp the tab closed with the pliers. Note: Make sure the wick is long enough to wrap around the wooden skewer at the top of the container.

2. Place a dab of adhesive wax on the bottom of the wick tab, then press the tab in place in the center of the container. Wrap the top of the wick around the wooden skewer and set it across the top of the container, centering the wick in the container. If necessary, use a dab of adhesive wax to hold the wooden skewer in place.

MELT AND POUR THE CANDLE

1. Clip the thermometer onto the double boiler. Melt the colored wax until the temperature reaches about 160° F (71° C); remove from heat.

2. When the temperature reaches 150° F (65° C), pour the wax into the measuring cup. Note: Carefully wipe the bottom of the pan with a kitchen towel before pouring the wax into the glass. This will prevent any water from dripping into the wax.

3. Pour the wax into the container, leaving about ¼ to ½ inch (.6 cm to 1.3 cm) between the wax and the top edge of the container.

FINISH THE CANDLE

1. Once the candle has completely cooled, remove the wooden skewer and trim the excess wick at the top of the candle.

2. Clean the adhesive wax from the edge of the container with a paper towel, if necessary.

—FROM *Candlemaking the Natural Way*

PARAFFIN CANDLE-MAKING

Norma Coney

Candlemaking Equipment

This section includes information on the basic equipment the home-based candlemaker needs.

For the beginner, there are many questions to consider before buying equipment. Your budget, what types of candles you want to make, what equipment you have on hand that may be converted permanently to candlemaking, and how serious you are about candlemaking as a continuing hobby, will all affect the decisions you make about purchasing equipment.

I have tried to sort out what equipment is most important for you to have and not cut corners on. When I began candlemaking, I did so on a shoe-string budget. I improvised as much equipment as I could and bought some basics to fill in the gaps. Eventually, I became frustrated with my improvised equipment. In candlemaking, there is much to be said for the old adage "the right equipment for the right job." The essential items you absolutely need to purchase are a wax melter, mold weights, mold sealer, and a mold holder for working with metal molds.

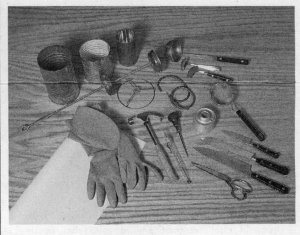

Clockwise from back center: commercial ladle, spoon ladles, mold weights, end former, kitchen knives in various sizes, scissors, awl, thermometer, hammer, rubber gloves, freezer paper, dipping frame, wick-centering spider, assorted cans.

A complete list of required equipment is provided at the beginning of each of the following sections: Hand-Dipped Tapers, Candles from Molds, and Container Candles. I suggest you review these lists before you purchase any equipment so that you will have a better idea of what you need to make the candles that interest you.

Wax Melter. A good, durable wax melter is essential to the home candlemaker and is not the place to skimp. Wax melters are usually seamless aluminum; this prevents wax from being caught in the seam. The flat bottom allows the wax melter to sit right on the heat source, eliminating large, clumsy double-boiler setups. The sturdy handle allows a firm, steady grip for pouring hot, molten wax. I consider this to be the most important feature; a tenuous grip on a can of hot wax is not safe! If you can find an old stove-top coffee pot, it may serve you as well as a melting pot.

Candy or Wax Thermometers. A durable candy or wax thermometer is a necessity if you are to pour your wax at the proper temperature. When purchasing a thermometer, look for a long probe, a clip for hanging it on the side of a pot, and a scale that is large and easy to read. Crucial temperatures to be read for candlemaking range from 150° to 300° F (66° to 149° C).

Dipping Vat. A dipping vat for tapers is an important piece of equipment. Galvanized vats are available at a depth of 15 inches (38 cm) and measure about 6 inches (15 cm) across. If you wish to dip long tapers, a dipping vat is a wise investment. If you will not be making many tapers and do not care about having long, perfect tapers, a dipping vat can be improvised. Juice cans, coffee cans, and various household items can be substituted. You will need a container 2 to 3 inches (5 to 7.5 cm) deeper than the length of taper you wish to make. Also, make certain that the vat you choose is going to be wide enough to accommodate the width of your dipping frame, should you choose to use one.

Double-Boiler Bottom. When a double-boiler bottom is called for, do not take it literally! In fact, it would be a shame to damage a nice piece of kitchen equipment. A double-boiler bottom needs to accommodate cans of wax set in the container to melt. Expect the inside of the double boiler to get scraped up and—eventually—lined with wax. Essentially what you need is a pot—not too high and fairly wide (it has to fit on a large burner on your heat source). An old, seldom-used pot or a find at the thrift store will work nicely. I have had to resort to a 5-gallon (22.5 l) can to use as a double-boiler bottom for my large dipping vat, but this is necessary only when I am making long tapers on my dipping ring.

Dipping Frame. A dipping frame for tapers is a necessity if you want to make many perfectly straight tapers. Wick is threaded on the frame, which keeps the wick absolutely taut and helps avoid the sag that can occur when you dip tapers by hand. Dipping frames are available commercially or you can improvise by constructing the one detailed in Hand-Dipped Tapers.

Several sizes of double-boiler bottoms are shown here, as well as a wax melter (center left) and a dipping vat (back left).

Wick Holder. A wick holder is a simple alternative to a dipping frame. A wick holder made of wood, fitted with hooks to hold the wick, can dip two or three pairs of tapers at a time. Instructions for making a simple wick holder are found in the section on hand-dipped tapers.

Wick Rod. Wick rods are useful for holding the wick in place while the wax hardens. Often, wick rods come with metal molds; you can certainly use these with other molds or container candles. A length of coat hanger wire or a pencil work just as well.

End Former. This is a useful tool the professional candlemakers use to make a cleanly crimped end on tapers; this makes the tapers fit snugly in candle holders. Not a necessity, but nice to have.

Cool-Water Bath. A cool-water bath is a vessel in which cool water (not cold water) is placed in order to speed up the wax-cooling process. Cool-water baths must be scaled to the size of the candle you are making. They should be able to accommodate the entire length of the candle. If you are dipping tapers and are using a cool-water bath, it will need to be about the same size as the dipping vat you are using. If you are making molded candles, your cool-water bath must accommodate your mold.

Cool-water baths do not incur damage, and are best chosen when you choose your mold or taper length. Any pot, pan, or container (a bucket works for large molds) that is the correct size can be used. Never use your sink or bathtub directly as a cool-water bath.

Mold Sealer. Mold sealer is a pliable putty made specifically for sealing the wick holes in molds. Mold sealer works well, even if it must stick to wax or has some wax incorporated into it, making it worth its weight in gold to a candlemaker. Many manufacturers of molds include with the purchase of a mold enough mold sealer to seal one mold. It is always a good idea to have an extra stash of this invaluable material on hand.

Mold Weights. Mold weights are long, flexible ropes of lead. Because they are flexible, they wrap around a mold easily. Mold weights are intended mainly for use with open-end molds, which would most likely tip—spilling the wax—when placed in a water bath. Two or three weights are sometimes required for a large mold.

Mold Holder. Mold holders are a good safety device that are used to pick up a large mold filled with hot wax and move it into a cool-water bath. Springs help keep the mold in place, and this lessens the danger of burning your hand or spilling hot wax on yourself. I have found this device to be especially useful when working with large molds especially metal ones.

Piercing Device. A piercing device is needed to relieve the surface tension of the wax and to expose any hidden air pockets near the wick. A very thin, long knitting needle works well, as does a length of stiff wire or an awl. Your piercing device needs to be about as long as the wick on the candle you are making.

Wick Centering Spiders. You will often need a device to center the wick in the wax while the candle hardens. Some candlemakers choose to improvise and make these by hand, but I've found the top ring for a lamp shade (the washer-top style) works wonderfully. You can purchase these in a variety of sizes from a lamp shade supply company or take one from an old lamp shade you have around the house. If you get lucky, you might find exactly what you need at your local thrift store.

Assorted Odd Containers. This assortment can include cake pans, old ice-cube trays, bread pans, and any other similar items. They should be made of metal or tempered glass. You can accumulate these items as you need them. They are very useful to have on hand to pour wax into when you are finished working for the day. The wax then hardens, can be removed, wrapped, labeled, and stored so that it stays clean.

Old Frying Pan. This pan need not be large. It is used mainly to hold small containers of wax or dye safely on a burner when you are making some of the specialty candles.

Cans of Various Sizes. It is helpful to assemble several cans of different sizes. These are useful to melt wax in (double-boiler style) when you do not have to pour the wax—for example, when making rolled appliqués. Any cans you set aside for this purpose should have sturdy seams and be clean and free of debris on the inside.

Small Tea Strainer. This need not be in mint condition but should be rust free. It is useful in helping clean debris out of wax (it happens to us all sometimes!) so that it can be used again.

Awl. A useful tool for punching holes in found molds, for widening holes, and for performing other useful procedures.

Mold-Release Spray. This silicone-based spray is used to coat the inside of molds to help the wax release from them.

Scale. A small scale is handy to have around your work station. It is especially helpful when you need to estimate the overall weight of your wax and to calculate additives by percentage. (These tasks are difficult to do otherwise.)

Freezer Paper. Freezer paper helps keep your work surface clean or, as in my case, it keeps the wax clean if it is spilled. Having paper under the molds can save a lot of work later.

Old Towels. A small stack of old towels is good to have on hand. They can be used to insulate your work surface from a hot wax melter, hot molds, and so forth.

Rubber Gloves. Rubber gloves are used mainly for picking up hot items such as cans and molds. They have decent gripping ability and allow your hands some freedom of movement.

Solvent. A wax-removing solvent comes in handy at times because wax is so difficult to clean up. Look for one with chlorothene as its active ingredient from your supplier of candle equipment.

Spoon Ladles. Formed by simply bending a spoon to form a ladle, these are extremely useful when working with odd-sized and small molds, particularly votive molds. Bear in mind that some spoons will break when you try to bend them, so do not be discouraged when this happens.

Wicks, Waxes, and Additives

This section is devoted to the physical ingredients that constitute a candle—the wick, the wax, and the additives that give candles special properties. Additives can affect the rate at which a candle burns. The size and type of wick also affect the burning rate. The quality and condition of the wax and its specific melting point play important roles, too. It is important for you to understand the properties of these essential candlemaking materials and how each impacts the final product. This knowledge can help you figure out what went wrong if a particular candle burns poorly or does not

live up to your expectations. However, it is important to keep in mind that candlemaking can be unpredictable. If you are a beginner, expect a period of trial and error.

Wicks

In days gone by, country folk (and sometimes city people) made their own wick. Today most people are not interested in making wicks—with good reason. Professional-quality wicks are readily available at very reasonable prices. Homemade wicks do not measure up to the tightly braided or wound wicks commonly found in today's marketplace.

Most candlemakers use three standard types of wick: flat-braided wick, square-braided wick, and wire- or lead-core wick. Each type of wick comes in several different sizes and each is used for a different type of candle. The size of the wick directly corresponds to the diameter of the candle you are making.

In most cases, you should put the wick in before you pour the wax, although sometimes (such as when making floating candles) the wick can be added after the candle sets up.

FLAT-BRAIDED WICK

Flat-braided wick is used mostly for tapers. It can also be used for small pillar candles. Flat-braided wick looks like a flattened piece of string. It comes in sizes that indicate the number of plies or strands in the wick: 24 ply, 30 ply, 36 ply, and so on. The smaller the number, the smaller the wick, and the smaller the candle it is appropriate for.

SQUARE-BRAIDED WICK

Square-braided wick is used primarily for block candles. The term block candle refers to a candle (either round or square) that is not a taper, but a large block of wax. The metal molds shown in the section on candle molds are made to cast block candles.

In spite of its name, square-braided wick appears to be more round than square. It comes in numbered sizes: #1, #2, #6, and so on. The larger the number, the larger the wick. The smaller the wick, the smaller the diameter of the candle it is appropriate for.

WIRE-CORE WICK

Wire-core wick is used for container candles and votives. As its name indicates, wire-cork wick has a metal wire center. This allows the wick to stand upright under conditions that might make other wicks bend and drown in liquid wax. The available sizes that concern the home candlemaker are small, medium, and large. These sizes also correspond to the size of the candle.

PRIMING THE WICK

Priming the wick for the candles you make is a good practice. Simply dip the wick into melted wax and coat it completely. Allow the wax to harden. Dip the wick into the melted wax again, and set it aside until you need it. This step accomplishes several things: 1) It ensures that the candle will light more easily. 2) Professionals will tell you that primed wicks burn more reliably. 3) Priming the wick prevents water or moisture from being absorbed by the wick…Please note that in an effort to streamline the individual projects…I do not include the step of priming the wick. However, it is a good habit and I recommend that you build it into your work routine.

Waxes

The discovery of paraffin wax in the 1850s brought this wax to the forefront of candlemaking by the late 1800s. Until the discovery of paraffin, natural waxes and fats were used for candles. In North America, bayberry wax and beeswax were most commonly used. In other parts of the world, people exploited available natural resources for other natural waxes, such as the wax derived from the tallow tree in China.

Continued ➔

All these waxes have different characteristics. Some burn slowly, others burn quickly, some are mildly fragrant, others are not.

Paraffin

Paraffin wax is a by-product of the petroleum industry. It is a white semi-transparent hard wax that is suitable for a wide range of uses in candlemaking. It is odorless and burns faster than beeswax. When you purchase paraffin wax, always be sure of its melting point. As shown in chart 1, the different melting points of paraffin determine what types of candles you should make from the wax. Usually the paraffin will be listed with a melting-point range; for example 140° to 145° F (60° to 63° C).

When you buy paraffin wax, make sure you consider the quality of the wax. Many inferior waxes are sold today. Get to know the going rate for the waxes you purchase and be wary of very low prices. Generally you get what you pay for, and wax is no exception to this rule.

Chart 1

Melting Point	Type of Candle	Flash Point
126°–131° F (52°–55° C)	container, hand-rolled tapers	approx. 410° F (210° C)
140°–145° F (60°–63° C)	tapers, block candles, sand candles	approx. 450° F (232° C)
154°–156° F (68°–69° C)	hurricanes, sand candles, over-dipping	approx. 480° F (249° C)

Note: The melting point of a wax indicates the temperature at which the wax liquefies. The flash point of a wax indicates the temperature at which the wax ignites!

Additives

Over the years, there have been many materials added to wax to give it certain characteristics. Workability, slow rate of burning, added hardness, and opacity are a few desirable traits that additives can give wax.

A list of additives follows. If adding to the burning time of the candle is your only objective, then some of the additives listed will be interchangeable. Before doing much experimentation with candles, it is imperative that you understand what each of these additives is used for and how it is likely to affect the candles you make.

Stearic Acid. Discovered in the early 1800s, stearic acid is derived from tallow. It is a fatty acid that brings to wax the most desirable attribute of tallow—it adds to the hardness of the wax, giving it the ability to burn longer. Stearic acid also aids the ability of the wax to release from the mold by causing the wax to shrink slightly. Add stearic acid at a rate of 2 to 5 tablespoons (30 to 74 ml) per 1 pound (454 g) of wax.

Luster Crystals. Luster crystals have many useful qualities. This compound hardens the wax, adds to the burning time of the candle by raising the melting point, improves gloss or sheen, and brightens colors. It can replace stearic acid in any candle. Luster crystals should be used at 1 tablespoon (14.8 ml) per 1 pound (454 g) of wax.

Clear Crystals. Clear crystals also raise the melting point of the wax, thus adding to the hardness and the burning time of the candle. They also brighten colors and eliminate bubbles on the surface of the wax. Clear crystals are more translucent than most additives. All these attributes make them very useful when making hurricane candles. Use clear crystals at a rate of 1 tablespoon (14.8 ml) per 1 pound (454 g) of wax. One cup (200 g) of clear crystals per 1 pound (454 g) of wax can be used as an overdip to make your tapers absolutely dripless.

Microcrystalline Waxes. Microcrystalline waxes have become important in candlemaking. Their fine crystalline structure and opaqueness set them apart from paraffin waxes. They are powerful additives when used properly and each brings a particular quality to the wax.

You will find many varieties of micro waxes on the market, make sure you buy the one that will produce the results you desire. Different candle supply sources use different names for these waxes. Chart 2 should help you purchase a micro wax according to the particular properties you want.

Chart 2

Wax Type	Tendencies	Type of Candle
Micro 170	Makes wax harder and less brittle	Hurricane
Micro 180	Eliminates internal bubbles	Hurricane, sand candles
Workable Micro (Sometimes called white beads)	Makes wax workable	Water candles, hand rolled, cut-and-curl
Micro Tacky (May be called sculpture wax)	Builds layers of wax quickly, useful in appliqué, because of tacky quality, "glues" wax to wax	Cut-and-curl, appliqué overdipped
Micro Opalescent	Increases the interior glow, Helps deter mottling	Container candles

Care and Storage of Your Supplies

To keep your materials in good condition, they should be properly stored and handled. Though wax seems to be indestructible (unless you heat it), it can develop problems in storage. Below are some guidelines for storing your waxes and wicks.

- Keep wicks packaged in plastic bags to prevent them from absorbing moisture. Always keep the manufacturer's label intact or make your own label that indicates the type and size of the wick stored in each package.

- Keep paraffin wax labeled to indicate the melting point of the wax. Wrap wax blocks in labeled plastic bags and store in a box. Keep away from light and moisture. Sure in a cool location.

- Label all wax additives and store in plastic bags, snap-top containers, or similar airtight containers. Keep away from light and in a cool location.

- Be wary of rodent damage when you are storing wax—especially from mice, who can worm their way into even the nicest homes! Mice will eat wax, given the opportunity.

Safety, Time Savers, and Handy Things to Know

Working with wax can be challenging. We all want to do our best to come up with a beautiful candle. Sometimes it is easy to become so caught up in the mechanics of what you are doing that you lose sight of what should always be in the back of your mind—safety.

Wax is flammable. A key to safety in any craft is knowing the limitations of what you are working with and what the consequences are if you go beyond those limitations. I have taught enough craft classes to say with confidence that you need to be cautious with—not afraid of—the materials you work with. With fear comes doubt, and when you doubt yourself, you are accident prone. By the same token, you should have a healthy respect for your materials.

Another key to safety is organization. To stay organized, you must be familiar with what you will be doing next, and you must establish a clear and sensible working order. To work efficiently, you need to concentrate on the task you are doing and also think ahead to the next steps you will be undertaking. It is a good idea to read through the instructions provided for each type of candle before you start to follow the steps. That way, you will stay organized, efficient, and safe.

Last, it is vital that you build safe habits into your working order. Learn what the risks are, then learn ways to avoid them. Build these avoidance techniques into your routine from the beginning, and they will always be your shutoff valve to problems.

Safety aside, there are always things to know about any craft that can save you time and energy. Short cuts, measurements, and sometimes things that seem obvious can save you a lot of trial and error. Read this section carefully before you make your first candle, and refer to it whenever you arrive at a roadblock.

Safe Work Habits

Listed below are some rules to follow when you work with wax. Some of them may be obvious, but it pays to read them anyway. An ounce of prevention is worth a pound of cure!

- Working with wax is time consuming. Set aside time or choose a time when you will not feel rushed. Many accidents can happen when you start cutting corners.

- Work in a large, well-ventilated space.

- Work in clothes you do not mind spattering with wax.

- Do not skimp on equipment. Working with makeshift items can create situations that put you and your loved ones at risk. In the equipment section I list the equipment I consider absolutely necessary.

- Cover your worktable with clean freezer paper. This protects your work surface and helps keep the spilled wax free of debris so that it can be recycled.

- Never leave wax unattended on any heat source.

- When you are melting wax, it is essential to be able to put out a fire quickly should one occur. Always keep close at hand a lid that snugly fits your wax melting pot. If the wax catches on fire, put the lid on the pot and immediately turn off the heat source. This should extinguish the fire. Pay particular attention to this safety practice if you are new to candlemaking and are using a wax-melting pot; the temperature of wax melted in this fashion can rise faster than you might imagine and accelerate to dangerous levels.

- When you are melting wax, keep a thermometer in it at all times. With a glance, you can check the temperature of the wax and know if you are in danger of reaching the flash point. The flash point varies for paraffin wax, but if you are over 300° F (149° C), you are in danger. Turn off the heat source and immediately remove the wax from it as safely as possible.

- Never try to put out a wax fire with water; this will just scatter the flames! Wax fires should be smothered with a lid from a sturdy pan or with a wet, heavy cloth or towel. Always keep these items handy—just in case.

- Clean up all wax spills as soon as they happen. This is especially true for wax spills on your heat source, particularly if it is your kitchen stove.

Chances are the burners have drip pans, and when the wax spills repeatedly in the catchalls, a dangerous situation is created; the next time you turn that burner on a high setting, you will have a full-fledged kitchen fire. Wax spills on the stove can be cleaned up more easily if the stove surface is warm.

When using a wax melter it is easy for small amounts of wax to drip down the outside of the pot as you pour and build up on the bottom of the wax melter. As a result, wax can accumulate under the burner and create excessive amounts of paraffin fumes in the air. To prevent this, wipe the bottom of the wax melter with paper towels after each time you pour.

Keep pot handles turned in toward the rear of the stove to reduce the risk of you or someone else catching a sleeve on the handle and getting burned.

Keep pets, children, and other potential distractions out of the work room while you are working.

Never pour wax down a drain or create a situation in which it might accidentally go down the drain. Never place a candle directly into a sink or bath tub for a cool-water bath. The following true story will make you think twice before doing so.

A candlemaker was making a hurricane candle. It was poured and the mold was supposedly sealed with mold sealer. The candlemaker filled the sink with cool water and put the mold directly into the sink. The phone rang and a conversation ensued—away from the sink. When the candle was checked, there was no water in the sink—it had drained out—and there was no wax in the mold; the sealer was not tight or possibly had failed! The wax had run down the drain and into the septic system and leach field, clogging the works when it hardened. The bill came to about $1,500!

Time Savers

Time savings is a crafter's dream. It is not always possible, but once in a while we can do it. Here are some ways I have developed that save me time in my workshop.

Generally wax is sold in large, heavy blocks which are difficult to break into useable pieces. To make the job go faster, simply place the block in a clean, sturdy cardboard box and give it a few good whacks with a good hammer. This is very effective (and also feels great if you are in a bad mood!). Store these smaller chunks in bags, being sure to label them so that you know exactly what kind of wax it is.

Accurately calculating how much wax you need to pour to make a candle in a particular mold can be a time and wax saver. The following method is an easy way to estimate wax amounts. Plug the hole in the mold with mold sealer and fill it with water. Pour the water out, measuring as you go. For each 9 ounces (250 ml) of water in the mold, you will need approximately ½ pound (227 g) of wax. Dry the mold thoroughly.

When you are finished for the day, there is always extra wax left over. Do not leave this wax in your wax-melting pot! Have handy some secondhand (but clean) pans and pour the leftover wax into one of the appropriate size. Make a tag, detailing what fragrance the wax is, what melting point, and what additives have been used in it. These notations will come in handy when you need wax for a project down the road and will ensure that you do not use the wrong wax for the job. When the wax hardens, wrap it in plastic and position the label so that it can be easily read.

Making wax chunks for chunk candles requires pouring the wax into an old, clean baking pan. Sometimes the wax can be a bit tough to remove. To prevent this, oil the pan first with a spray of vegetable oil that you would use in the kitchen. The wax should then lift right out of the pan.

Handy Things to Know

This is a collection of tips and reminders for you to use as a reference. It includes some things that have been included elsewhere and some that never found a place in other sections.

Removing Seams on a Candle. Some molds will leave a noticeable seam line on the candle. These lines are easily removed. Hold a paring knife almost at a right angle to the candle on the seam. Turn the candle or use a smooth motion with the knife until all the extra wax has been removed. The remaining marks can be buffed off with a nylon stocking.

Cleaning Soiled Wax. If you work with wax long enough, it will happen—you will end up with dirty wax or sediment in the wax. Your wax can probably be saved. Melt the wax over water in a small can. Cut a couple of thicknesses of clean muslin cloth and place them in a small tea strainer. When the wax is hot, pour it slowly through the tea strainer into an old baking pan or similar item. Allow to harden, checking the bottom of the wax. If there is any sediment left, repeat this process or simply scrape it off the bottom.

Cleaning Soiled Candles. Soiled candles can often be cleaned with a soft nylon cloth and a little elbow grease. Buff the candle lightly with the cloth. If the dirt is stubborn, try putting a tiny drop of mineral oil on the cloth and buff again. Candles with dull surfaces can sometimes be buffed to a better surface using this process.

Making Molds Go Further. Metal molds in particular can be used to make several different sizes of candles. I always buy the tallest mold offered of a particular diameter. Using the same mold, I can make shorter candles by filling the mold less full. For efficiency, wick as usual, tying the wick to the rod, but do not cut off the wick—leave it attached. This leaves all the extra wick intact for another candle.

When you pour the wax, try not to drip any wax on the inside walls of the mold above the candle's height because this extra wax makes it harder for the candle to release from the mold. Keeping the wax off the walls of the mold is easier to accomplish when you work with larger diameter candle molds. To remove this wax, simply trim the drips at the height of the candle right after the drips harden, then peel off the rest of the wax with a knife.

Distorted Color. Working with candle dyes is a lot of fun, but sometimes the color becomes distorted. Why does this happen? Colors become distorted when the temperature of the wax rises too high. Temperatures over 225° F (107° C) can damage some colors, so, for best results, keep the wax at recommended pouring temperatures.

Stubborn Wicks. Sometimes a wick is just a bit too limp or stubborn to go through a wick hole. To make the job easier, dip the end in melted wax, let cool just a bit, and roll it between your fingertips. The wick should go through the hole with room to spare. Another way to solve this problem is to prime the wick.

Wax on the Inside of Pots and Pans. When you use double-boiler setups for some of the procedures in this book, wax is sure to find its way into your pans. This really bugs me, because the next time the pan is heated, the wax will melt and coat everything in the pan with a film of wax. To get wax off my pans (and sometimes other things), I boil some water in my tea kettle and take the kettle and the pan outside. Pour the water over the wax and it will come off nicely. (The wax doesn't do much for the grass, so this is better done where grass is not important.)

Wax Removed from Other Surfaces. Solvents are available to help remove wax from some items, but you need to read the directions because they can not be used on all surfaces. Look for a solvent with the active ingredient chlorothene. Some wax can be removed from fabrics by applying ice until the wax becomes brittle enough to fleck off.

Warped Candles. It happens all the time—candles become warped in storage or possibly your hand-rolled candles do not set up as straight as an arrow. There is a simple solution that works most of the time for me. Place the candles on freezer paper, then on a heat source that is not hot, but warm. For example, I put them on top of my 30-cup coffee pot for several hours. There is no danger of them melting there, because it is not that hot. After a few hours, the candle has been warmed sufficiently. Remove it and the paper from the heat and roll on a flat surface until the warp rolls out. Flared candles can be straightened by suspending them from the wick end. **Caution:** Do not place the candle on heat unless you are sure it will not melt.

Stuck Wax. Stuck wax in your candle molds can prevent the candles from coming out! Stuck wax can be removed easily from molds. For help with this problem, refer to the section on candle molds for details on how to clean each type of mold.

How to Glue Wax to Wax. Whether you are applying appliqués or constructing a unique candle from scratch, being able to affix wax to wax surfaces can be a real benefit. It is easy to do with a fine microcrystalline wax that is tacky when melted, then dries to a hard surface. Just melt a little of this wax in a can and apply to both surfaces with an old, small paintbrush.

Candle Dripping Problems. Do your candles drip, no matter what you do? The solution is at hand, melt 1 cup (200 g) of clear crystals in 1 pound (454 g) of wax and dip the entire surface of your candle in this mixture. No more dripping!

Make Your Candles Burn Longer. It is easy to make your candles last longer. Stearic acid, luster crystals, and clear crystals will all do the trick. There is no need to use more than one of these additives, but one can be substituted for the other. For the rate at which you add them and other information, see the section on additives.

Making a Mold. You can improvise to create a mold for a candle shape you like even if no mold exists. To do this create a sand pit in a dishpan, as described for sand candles in the section on specialty candles. Sculpt your mold out of the sand by hand or by using an object similar in shape to your desired mold. Melt wax and pour it into the impression in the sand to 150° to 160° F (66° to 71° C). When the wax has hardened a little, place a thick wire in the wax where the wick will be inserted later.

When the wax is completely cool and removed from the sand, little or no sand will cling to the wax, because the pouring temperature was so low. Any excess sand can be brushed away. Insert the wick, and you have a candle of your own design.

Container Candles

Container candles have enjoyed enormous popularity in recent years, perhaps because they are extremely versatile, attractive, and functional. When not in use, they can become decorative accents in your home or can be easily covered and stored. Container candles are particularly appealing to collectors and recyclers, because they transform some of your household clutter into beautiful and functional candles.

When searching for candle containers, use your imagination. Many discarded household items cry out for a second life as a container. In order for a container to successfully accommodate a candle, however, a few requirements need to be satisfied. The container's opening must

Continued ➤

not be too small (anything smaller than 2 inches [5 cm] in diameter would be too hard to light), the material from which it is made must be able to withstand the pouring temperature of the wax and be nonflammable, and the container must be able to stop the flow of the wax.

Examples of candle containers are countless: attractive perfume vessels, old, rustic-looking tins, small decorative bowls, crockery, terra-cotta pots, mason jars, candy jars, and even shells may be used to house candles. The key to making good container candles is using the proper wax formulation. In addition, wick tabs and wire-core wicking replace regular wicking techniques and allow the wick to stand erect in the container.

Wax Formulations

A paraffin wax with a low melting point is best for container candles. The ideal melting point for the wax or combination of waxes is 128° F (53° C).

· 50 percent paraffin, 131° F (55° C) melting point

· 50 percent paraffin, 126° F (52° C) melting point

· ½ ounce (14 g) of micro opalescent wax for each pound (454 g) of wax.

Wicks and Wick Tabs

Wire-core or lead-core wicking is a special type of wick that has a stiff wire as its center. The stiffness of these wicks allows them to stand upright in situations in which another wick might fall over and extinguish itself. Wick size will vary with the diameter of the container you use for each candle.

Wick tabs hold the wick to the bottom of the container while the wax is poured and help to keep the wick upright. Tabs are available in several sizes. Choose them based on the size of your container. Use small wire-core wick for containers under 2 inches (5 m) in diameter, use medium wire-core wick for containers 2 to 4 inches (5 to 10 cm) in diameter, and use large wire-core wick for containers 4 inches (10 cm) in diameter and up.

Pouring Temperature

Container candles should be poured at 160° to 180° F (71° to 82° C). Warm the container just before you pour the wax. To be safe, test glass containers ahead of time by placing them in a sink, warming them with hot tap water first, and then filling them with near-boiling water. If the container holds up to this, it should be safe to use as a container. Wax poured into glass containers should be poured at 160° F (71° C).

MATERIALS

Paraffin wax, 130° F (54° C) melting point

Paraffin wax, 126° F (52° C) melting point

Micro opalescent wax

Candle dye and fragrance*

Wire-core wick

Wick tabs

Container of your choice

Small tin can

EQUIPMENT

wax melter

candy thermometer

mold sealer

wooden spoon

coat-hanger wire or wick rod

coat-hanger wire as long as your container

newspaper or an old towel

rubber gloves

*optional

INSTRUCTIONS

When pouring container candles, avoid spilling was on the outside of the container, as it can be difficult to remove from some surfaces.

1. Melting the wax: Place wax or waxes in the wax melter with the microcrystalline wax (if you are using it), then put the melter on your heat source on a medium setting.

2. Making final adjustments to the wax: Stir waxes together thoroughly. Bring the temperature of the wax to 160° to 180° F (71° to 82° C). Melt dye in a separate can and add to the wax. Add fragrance, if desired, and stir both dye and fragrance in completely.

3. Preparing the wick and tab: If your container has a hole in the end, such as a terra-cotta pot, secure it with mold sealer. Cut a sufficient length of wick for the container—with some extra to wrap around the coat-hanger wire or wick rod. Prime the wick. Secure one end of the wick in a wick tab. As soon as the wax has melted, pour a small amount into the bottom of the container.

Using the longer coat-hanger wire, press the wick tab firmly into the wax (photo 1). Pour enough wax into the bottom of the container to securely cover the wick tab and allow it to harden into place. This will keep the tab secure while you are making any adjust-

Photo 1

ments with the wick after pouring the wax. Position the wick rod across the top of the container, then wrap the other end of the wick around the support.

4. Pouring the candle: Put a rubber glove on the hand that will be holding the container; this will insulate your hand from the hot container when the wax is poured. Warm the outside of the container by holding it under warm tap water. Make sure that you have an old towel or newspaper on which to place the container once it has been filled.

Pick up the container in one hand, tipping it slightly. Pour the melted wax into the container, filling it to the neck of the container (photo 2).

Adjust the wick to be certain it is centered.

5. Topping off the candle: As the candle cools, a well will form just as in a molded

Photo 2

candle. (How long this takes depends on the size of the container, so check the candle every few minutes.) When the well forms, pierce the wax around the wick with the longer coat-hanger wire, piercing all the way to the bottom. Bring the wax back up to the pouring temperature and fill the well. Repeat this until a well no longer forms. Allow the candle to harden. Trim the wick to ½ to ¾ inch (1.5 to 2 cm).

Molded Candles

Advances in mold making now allow us to make intricately detailed candles that, at one time, crafters could only dream of. Candle molds come in many shapes and sizes and are made from a variety of materials. Metal, plastic, and flexible pop-out molds are readily available from candle supply companies.

With a little imagination, you can turn any number of household items into candle molds. Orange juice containers, cleanser cans, and dairy cartons work well. A small selection of purchased molds and found molds should offer enough options to satisfy the most discrimi-

nating crafter. To ensure the longevity of your molds, however, proper care is essential.

Making molded candles is perhaps the easiest form of candlemaking to learn, and it is a good starting point for children and beginners. Your results can be spectacular, the time investment is minimal, and you will reap hours of enjoyment from your labors. Also, molded candles are less demanding than fine tapers, in respect to both time and equipment.

Whether you are using a found mold or a commercial mold, the basic techniques for molded candles are the same. Most of the time commitment in making molded candles is in the initial melting of the wax and waiting for it to harden in the mold. One step you can take to reduce the time is to use a cool-water bath. Cool-water baths also improve the finish of candles by making them smoother. You can also save time by planning ahead to make several molded candles from the same wax once it is melted.

Wax Formulations

Molded candles may be made from a large number of wax formulations, many of which contain additives for special effects. Because it is easy to get carried away when using additives, try experimenting with one additive at a time so that you can be certain of its effect on the finished candle. Paraffin wax is the easiest wax to use for molded candles. If you use 100 percent beeswax, it will easily release from pop-out molds but not metal molds. If you plan to use beeswax in traditional molds, you must mix the beeswax with paraffin.

Here are several reliable formulations:

1. 100 percent paraffin, 140° to 145° F (60° to 63° C) melting point

2. 100 percent paraffin, 140° to 145° F (60° to 63° C) melting point, with 5 tablespoons (74 ml) stearic acid and 1 teaspoon (5 ml) luster crystals added per pound (454 g) of wax

3. 50 percent paraffin, 140° to 145° F (60° to 63° C) melting point, 50 percent beeswax

4. 100 percent beeswax

Estimating in advance the amount of wax you need to fill a certain mold has obvious advantages. Many manufacturers include this information with individual molds. If this information is not available, you can estimate the amount of wax you will need using the following method. Fill the mold with water. Pour the water out and measure how much it took to fill the mold. Each 9 ounces (252 g) of water equals approximately 8 ounces or ½ pound (227 g) of solid wax. Be sure to thoroughly dry the inside of the mold.

Wicks

It is important that you choose the right wick for molded candles. The wick must be appropriate for the wax formulation and the size of the candle.

Wax formulations can affect wick performance. Additives such as stearin and luster crystals extend the burning time of the candle. This, in turn, influences how the wick performs. Therefore, you may need to adjust the wick size as necessary. The quality of the wax used in the candle will also have a significant effect on how the wick burns.

Chart 3 suggests wick sizes for various molded candle diameters, including both flat-braided (F.B.) and square-braided (S.B.) wicks. The recommendations are based on wax formulations and candle diameters. If your candle does not burn properly, you will need to consult the troubleshooting guide.

Pouring Temperatures

These recommendations for the pouring temperature of wax are general. Many times manufacturers include instructions that include pouring temperatures with specialty molds. Manufacturer's recommendations should always be followed.

For metal molds: pour wax at 200° F (93° C)

For plastic and acrylic molds: pour wax at 180° to 190° F (82° to 88° C)

For rubber molds: pour wax at 190° F (88° C)

For 100 percent beeswax candles: pour wax at 170° F (77° C)

For cardboard found molds: pour wax at 190° F (88° C)

CHART 3

Candle Size	Wick Size
1–2 inches (2.5–5 cm)	F.B. 15 or 24 ply, S.B. #5/0
2–3 inches (5–7.5 cm)	F.B. 30 ply, S.B. #2
3–4 inches (7.5–10 cm)	F.B. 30 ply, S.B. #3
4–5 inches (10–12.5 cm)	F.B. 30 or 36 ply, S.B. #3 or #4
5–6 inches (12.5–15 cm)	F.B. 45 ply, S.B. #5
6–9 inches (15–23 cm)	S.B. #6
Beeswax/paraffin candles	S.B. #1 or #2
Beeswax candles over 2 inches (5 cm) in diameter	S.B. #4 or #5

Making Molded Candles

The following lists specify the materials and equipment you need to make molded candles.

MATERIALS

Paraffin wax, 140° to 145° F (60° to 63° C) melting point

Stearic acid (do not use for rubber molds)*

Luster crystals*

Wick, enough for the candle plus a few extra inches (5 cm)

Candle dye*

EQUIPMENT

Wax melter

Candy thermometer

Wooden spoon

Rubber gloves

Cool-water bath*

Mold of your choice

Mold stand, purchased or improvised (to hold flexible molds during pouring)

Mold sealer

Mold weights

Mold holder (makes it easier to move large metal molds to the water bath)*

Wick-centering spiders*

Coat-hanger wire as long as the mold or a long, thin knitting needle

Coat-hanger wire or wick rod

Old metal pie pan

optional

INSTRUCTIONS

Establish the following working order when you set up to make molded candles. If you are a beginner, make sure you read the safety precautions and time-saving tips in the section on safety before you begin.

1. Setting up to melt the wax: Place the wax (in the formulation you have chosen) in the wax melter. Put any additives in other containers and melt them separately. Place the melter on your heat source and heat it on a moderate setting. Position a thermometer in the melter.

2. Preparing the wick and mold(s): Prime enough wick for the mold(s) you want to pour. Primed wicks will light much easier than those that have not been primed. To prime the wick, see the section on wicks, waxes, and additives.

Wick the mold. Make certain that the wick hole is completely sealed with mold sealer (photo 1). Metal molds should be warmed by running warm water over the outside of the mold before the wax is poured. If you are using a metal mold, attach the mold holder at this point. If you will be placing the mold in a cool-water bath, be sure to attach mold weights to the bottom of the mold at this point.

Photo 1

3. Set up a cool-water bath. If you are using a cool-water bath, it should be deep enough to accommodate the entire length of the candle. It is a good idea to set the cool-water bath in a sink for ease of emptying it when you are finished, but never use your sink or tub directly as a cool-water bath. You should not use a cool-water bath for beeswax candles.

4. Final adjustment of the wax and additives: Check the temperature of the wax as soon as it has melted and bring it to the correct pouring temperature. When the wax reaches the correct pouring temperature, add the additives, fragrance, and dye, stirring them into the wax thoroughly.

5. Pouring the candle: You might want to wear rubber gloves to insulate your hands from the heat when you pour the wax. With one hand, tip the mold slightly. Slowly pour the liquid wax into the mold until the mold is filled to the desired depth (photo 2). Reserve a small amount of the wax for the topping-off process. Adjust the wick to make sure that it is correctly centered in the mold. Allow the filled mold to sit for two or three minutes, then tap all around the sides gently, but firmly, with a wooden spoon. This removes air pockets or bubbles that can sometimes form on the sides of the molds.

Photo 2

6. Carefully place the mold in the cool-water bath (photo 3). Make sure that the mold is properly weighted and that it will not tip. If you have made a beeswax candle, skip the cool-water bath and move on to step 7.

7. Special instructions for beeswax molded candles: This step is only for candles made from 30 percent or more beeswax. Beeswax needs to cool very slowly, and so cannot be placed in a cool-water bath. If they cool too quickly, these candles will have a tendency to develop large cracks as they harden. To slow down the cooling process, place the mold in a container that can be covered. A crock, glass mixing bowl, dutch oven, cardboard box, or plastic container will work as long as it can be covered. The idea is to keep the heat from escaping quickly. If you do not have a container large enough, place the mold in an out-of-the-way location and carefully cover it with a heavy towel.

Photo 3

8. Topping off the candle: Paraffin wax candles need to be topped off because the wax shrinks significantly as it cools. This shrinkage forms a deep well and submerged air pockets in the center of the candle. These need to be refilled with liquid wax. The time it takes for the well to form depends on the size of the candle, so it is best to check it every ten minutes or so. Candles with a larger diameter may take up to 45 minutes before the well is evident.

When a well has formed in the center of the candle, it can be topped off. First, heat the reserved wax to the correct pouring temperature. Using a wire or knitting needle, pierce the wax directly around and down the entire length of the wick several times (photo 4). (This allows any submerged air pockets to be filled.) Fill in the candle with the reheated wax (photo 5). Be sure that you do not pour the wax any higher than the original wax in the mold, as this will make the candle harder to remove. Large paraffin candles may need to be topped off two or three times. When a well no longer forms, allow the candle to harden overnight.

Photo 4

Photo 5

9. Removing the candle and finishing the base: Untie the wick from the open end of the mold and remove the mold sealer and/or screw from the other end. Candles made from metal molds may be placed in the refrigerator for an hour to help make them easier to remove. Gently tap the mold against your hand until the candle emerges (photo 6). Trim the wick on the top of the candle to ½ inch (1.5 cm). Trim the wick on the base of the candle as close to the wax as possible. If the candle base is not level, put it, with its base down, on an old pie plate, then place the plate on a warm burner (photo 7). The offending wax will melt away and your candle will be perfect!

Photo 6

Photo 7

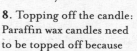

Hand-Dipped Tapers

Dipping tapers by hand is perhaps the most ancient form of candlemaking still practiced on a regular basis. Tapers appeal to crafters because the process has an age-old rhythm and because tapers have a wonderful simplicity, both in the finished form and in the materials.

Continued ➡

Hand-dipped tapers are made by repeatedly dipping a wick into melted wax. Dipping tapers can take an hour or so; if you are making very long tapers, it can take all afternoon. Longer tapers not only need more time to cool between dips, but the amount of wax needed can take more than an hour to

melt. Leave yourself plenty of extra time, especially if you have never dipped tapers before. Usually 30 to 45 dips in the wax are necessary, but the simple elegance of the final product makes hand-dipped tapers well worth the effort.

The most efficient way to dip tapers is to use a cool-water bath or multiple dipping rings. With multiple rings, the first tapers dipped have cooled by the time their next turn comes around.

Choosing a Wicking Method

There are several ways to arrange the wick for dipped tapers. The method that you choose will depend on your budget, the ease of acquiring supplies, the time you choose to put into the craft, and the items you have on hand.

Using a naked wick is the simplest way to make one pair of tapers. To make more than one pair at a time, you may want to use either a wick holder or a dipping frame; instructions for making both are found in this section.

Naked wicks. Tapers are always dipped in pairs. The easiest way to make one pair of tapers is to dip a primed naked wick into the wax repeatedly. An extra length of wick loops over your fingers and separates the tapers so they do not rub together and mar the candle surface during the dipping process.

The obvious advantage to this method of wicking is simplicity. However, despite your best efforts, there will still be a tendency for your candles to develop sags or ridges. There are several methods to prevent this from happening. One approach is to weight the wick with a lead sinker or heavy metal washer. Another method is to dip the taper in as hot a wax as possible. Using luster crystals in your wax formula will also minimize sagging (see Wax Formulations). Placing your dipping vat in a double boiler can also minimize sags and ridges because that set up helps to keep the temperature of the wax more constant. If all else fails and you wind up with lumpy tapers, let the final dips harden slightly and then roll the candles on a clean sheet of freezer paper to smooth the edges. Having said all this, if you desire or are satisfied with a more rustic-looking candle that is not perfectly tapered, you will probably want to dip a naked wick.

Wick holders. Using a wick holder is an easy way to dip more than one pair of tapers at a time. The actual size and shape of your wick holder should be determined by the shape of your dipping vat. A wick holder uses pairs of hooks screwed into a piece of wood to accommodate the wicks and to keep the tapers from rubbing together. Wick holders are easy to use, but tapers made with them may also exhibit a somewhat rough, rustic finish. See the instructions for making a simple wick holder on this page.

Dipping frames. A dipping frame will help you make perfect tapers with smooth sides. A professional dipping frame can accommodate four pairs of tapers. The dipping frame shown is a simplification of the dipping ring used by professional candlemakers. It makes two pairs of tapers at a time, is easy to make, and is inexpensive.

It is well worth the effort to make a couple of these frames if you plan to dip a lot of tapers. This dipping frame is adjustable and will make tapers 3 inches (7.5 cm) to 1 foot (.3 m) long. It is narrow and can be used with narrow dipping vats.

Making a Wick Holder

A wick holder that can accommodate more than one pair of tapers is practical and easy to use. The wick holder pictured can accommodate three pairs of tapers (photo 1). It is made from the simplest of materials and is easy enough for a child to make. It can be used to dip tapers in a 3-pound (1.3 kg) coffee can, or you can modify the plans to size the wick holder to your dipping vat.

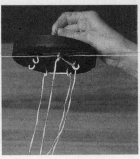

Photo 1

MATERIALS

1 4½-inch (11.5 cm) round piece of wood, ¾ inch (2 cm) thick

Pencil

1 Small nail

1 Large screw eye

6 ¾-inch (2 cm) screw hooks

INSTRUCTIONS

1. Measure ½ inch (1.5 cm) in from the outside edge of the wood and mark it with a pencil all around the perimeter of the wood. Connect these points to create a circle.

2. Choose a starting point on this circle and mark it. From this point, measure 1¾ inches (4.5 cm) and mark it. Continue measuring 1¾ inches (4.5 cm) all around the circle, marking each point as you go. When you are finished, there should be six marks on the circle.

3. Mark each of the hash marks you have made with a dot where the mark and the circle intersect. On each dot, use a nail to start a hole for the screw hooks. Screw a hook into each location.

4. Find and mark the center on top of the wood. Using a nail, start a hole for the screw eye. Attach the screw eye to the wood.

Making a Dipping Frame

This dipping frame, made from materials that can be found in any good hardware store, can help you make perfect tapers. Another advantage is that is it adjustable; it will dip tapers from 3 to 12 inches (7.5 to 30.5 cm) in length, but is particularly useful for making tapers over 6 inches (15 cm) long.

MATERIALS

1 3-foot (.9 m) threaded steel rod, ¼ inch (.5 cm) diameter

4 Nuts to fit the steel rod

4 Lock washers to fit the steel rod

1 Screw-eye bolt, ¼ inch (.5 cm) diameter

1 1½-inch (4 cm) coupling nut to fit the steel rod

2 Stainless-steel sink baskets with drainage holes, with all the hardware removed; these can be new or, better yet, recycled! Check to be sure that the opening in the center is large enough to slip over the steel rod.

EQUIPMENT

Hacksaw

Metal file

INSTRUCTIONS

1. Using the hacksaw, cut the steel rod in half. File the rough edges with the metal file until smooth.

2. Screw or thread on the following items 2 inches (5 cm) from the end of the rod (in this order): one nut, one lock washer, one sink basket with the open end down (open end facing away from the longer section of rod), one lock washer, one nut. Tighten the nuts to hold the sink basket firm. This will be the bottom of your dipping frame.

3. Screw or thread on the following items on the opposite end of the rod (in this order): one nut, one lock washer, one sink basket with the open end up, one lock washer, one nut. Tighten the nuts to hold the basket firm. This is the top of the dipping frame. By adjusting the location of the top basket on the rod, you can vary the length of the tapers you make.

4. Screw on the coupling nut partially and tighten it down. Thread on the screw eye as far as it will go. This will be the hanger.

Wicking the Dipping Frame

Instructions

1. Thread the wick through one of the holes on the bottom basket and tie securely.

2. Thread the wick through the corresponding hole on the top basket. Be sure that the wick is straight. There should be enough play in the baskets to turn them slightly if the holes are not identically aligned. The wick should be as tight as you can manage without straining it. You will have to adjust this tension again before tying and cutting the wick.

3. Count three holes over and thread the wick through the fourth hole.

4. Thread the wick through the corresponding hole on the bottom basket. Tie the wick securely, making sure that both wicks stay taut. Cut off the extra wick.

Photo 2

5. Thread the other side of the dipping frame in the same fashion. Before dipping, double check to be sure that the wick is taut and as straight as possible (photo 2).

Wax Formulations

Tapers can be made from several different formulations of wax. The melting point of the paraffin you use is the most important variant; tapers made from wax with an inappropriate melting point will dip excessively and burn poorly. Below are some wax combinations you may wish to try for dipping tapers.

- 100 percent paraffin wax with a 140° to 145° F (60° to 63° C) melting point

- 90 percent paraffin wax with a 140° to 145° F (60° to 63° C) melting point, and 10 percent beeswax

- 100 percent paraffin with a 140° to 145° F (60° to 63° C) melting point, with 5 tablespoons (74 ml) stearic acid and 1 tablespoon (14.8 ml) luster crystals added per pound (454 g) of wax (especially good for dipping with a naked wick)

- 100 percent beeswax

Wick

Flat-braided wicks work best for tapers. For tapers under 1 inch (2.5 cm) in diameter, use 15-ply flat-braided wick. For tapers over 1 inch (2.5 cm) in diameter, use 24-ply flat-braided wick. For tapers made of 100 percent beeswax, use 24-ply flat-braided wick for all sizes.

Temperature

Tapers can be dipped at temperatures from 160° to 180° F (71° to 82° C). The dipping temperature will affect the finish on the candle. Dipped at 160° F (71° C), the tapers will have a grainy finish and may be lumpy. Dipped at 180° F (82° C), the tapers will have a smooth, glossy finish. Dipping at 170° F (77° C) is prudent and gives a nice finish. If you want a glossy finish, you can raise the temperature of the wax to 180° F (82° C) for the final dip.

A note on dipping long tapers. If the temperature in your dipping vat is 170° F (77° C) near the top of the vat, it is likely to be higher than that at the bottom. Because of the length of the tapers, each dip takes substantially more time than with shorter tapers. If the temperature at the bottom of the vat is over 180° F (82° C), the tapers may lose some wax on each dip and become slightly narrower at the bottom than they should be. To head off this problem, take the temperature of the wax as close to the bottom of the vat as possible and be aware that the problem may develop. Tapers that are narrower at the bottom can be overdipped a few times after they are taken off the dipping ring to correct the problem.

Making Dipped Tapers

The following lists detail the items you will need for dipping tapers.

Materials

Paraffin wax, melting point of 140° to 145° F (60° to 63° C)

Beeswax*

Stearic acid*

Luster crystals*

Flat-braided wick, 15- or 24-ply

Candle dye and fragrance*

Equipment

Large pan for the bottom of the double boiler

Dipping vat

Candy thermometer

Cool-water bath*

Wick holder*

Dipping frame*

Hooks or place to hang the candles between dips*

*optional

Instructions

Having the working order of dipping candles firmly established in your mind can keep you from doing quite a bit of fumbling on candlemaking day! The setup and technique listed below have worked well for me.

1. Setting up your dipping vat: Choose the pot you will be using as a bottom for your double-boiler setup. If your tapers are short enough, it is easier (as we have done here) to use a wax melter as the dipping vat. Place the dipping vat in the pan and put it on the stove top. Place wax chunks in the dipping vat about as deep as the tapers you are making are long. Keep track of the weight of the wax if you are using a wax formula that uses additives.

Note: Under certain circumstances, tapers dipped in a wax melter without a double-boiler pot underneath it can develop sags or ridges. This occurs because of uneven temperatures of the wax in the melter or because the temperature of the wax fluctuates too quickly. If you experience this, you may want to use a double-boiler setup.

2. Melting the wax: Slowly add water to the pan, making sure not to tip the dipping vat. Ideally the water should come up at least one-half the height of the dip-ping vat, more if you can do so without tipping it over or causing it to float. Place the vat on a burner over medium heat; you do not want the water to boil wildly, but want it just hot enough to melt the wax and bring it to the right temperature. When some of the wax begins to melt, place a candy thermometer in the liquid wax.

3. Preparing the wicks: This will vary, depending on the method you are using. If you are dipping naked wicks or are using a wick holder, the wicks will be much easier to work with if they are primed at this point. If you are using a dipping frame, priming is not necessary, so follow the directions for threading the dipping frame.

4. Adjusting the level of the wax. Check on the melting wax. It is likely that you will need to add more wax to the dipping vat at this point. The main factor in the depth of the wax is the length of the tapers you are making, so gently add more wax if necessary. NOTE: Wax expands slightly as it is heated, so you are better off adding it a little at a time.

5. Set up a cool-water bath. If you are using a cool-water bath to speed up the dipping process, set it up now. Be certain that the cool-water bath is able to accommodate the entire length of the taper. Place the cool-water bath in a nearby location, perhaps on an empty burner on the stove top.

6. Final adjustment of the additives and wax temperature: If you are using additives in your tapers, they should be stirred in now. Remember that additives with high melting points such as luster crystals should be melted separately first, then added to the wax. To do this, use a small tin can, add the correct amount of additives in proportion to the number of pounds of wax you have melted and

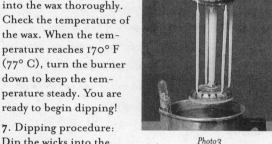

melt them over hot water on a spare burner. Stir into the wax thoroughly. Check the temperature of the wax. When the temperature reaches 170° F (77° C), turn the burner down to keep the temperature steady. You are ready to begin dipping!

7. Dipping procedure: Dip the wicks into the liquid wax for three or four seconds, then remove the wicks from the wax. If you are using the dipping ring, allow the excess wax to drain off (photo 3). You can give the ring a shake, but do not tip it. Wait until the excess wax has drained off, then hang the wicks or dip them momentarily into the cool-water bath.

Photo 3

If you are using the cool-water bath, you must be sure to allow all the water to drain off the taper before dipping again or bubbles will form on the surface. If you are using the wick holder or naked wicks, take care that the tapers do not swing back and forth and touch each other during the dipping and hanging process.

If you are not using the cool-water bath, let the wax harden on the wicks for two minutes or so before dipping again. Continue dipping the wicks into the liquid wax. It usually takes 30 to 40 dips to achieve complete tapers. Check the temperature periodically to be sure that it does not deviate too much.

After you have dipped awhile, you may need to replace some of the wax, especially if you are making long tapers. Always replace the wax slowly. Take into account that when you dip the tapers again, they will displace some of the wax. If you add too much wax in the dipping vat, liquid wax will spill over the edge and seep into the water bath. Continue dipping until the tapers are the desired size (photo 4).

8. Final step: To give the tapers a smooth, glossy finish, heat the wax to 180° F (82° C) and give them a final dip (photo 5). Hang the tapers up to cool for about 10 minutes. Trim the ends with a sharp knife or a pair of sharp scissors (photo 6).

Photo 4

Photo 5 | *Photo 6*

Finishing Touches

Making Perfect Ends

If you plan to use the tapers in candlesticks or other holders, the ends can be finished with a base former. Place the base former in an old frying pan and heat it on a moderate setting on the stove. When thoroughly heated, place the end of each taper in the base former for just a few seconds, then remove them (photo 7). The excess wax will be caught in the frying pan, and you will have perfectly made taper ends!

Photo 7

Color

The best way to give color to tapers is through a process called overdipping. Overdipped candles are made from uncolored wax first, then dipped several times in colored wax. By overdipping, you eliminate the need to color the large amount of wax in which you dip; this wax can then be used for other purposes. Tapers can also be given a marbleized look by overdipping them in a certain fashion.

Overdipped Candles

Overdipping is a widely used technique that some candle artisans swear by to give their candles an extra glow when they burn. The process is a simple one: white candles are dipped several times in colored wax as a finishing technique. Overdipping can also be used to give unique color patterns to candles, such as shaded colors and marbled candles.

Overdipping Solid Colors

Materials

Paraffin was, 140° F (60° C) melting point

Colored wax

White tapers

Continued ➡

EQUIPMENT

Large pot

Wooden spoon

INSTRUCTIONS

1. Melt the uncolored wax in a vessel deep enough to dip your candle. Melt the dye and add it to the melted wax until the desired shade is achieved.

2. Holding the candle by the wick, dip the candle into the wax for just a few seconds. Allow extra wax to drip back into the heated wax. Repeat this process until the candle has taken on enough color. It will usually take ten or so dips to give an even, vibrant color.

Color-Graded Candles

Color-graded candles have a very old-fashioned look and work best when a strong color is used.

MATERIALS

Paraffin wax, 140° F (60° C) melting point

Colored wax

White tapers

EQUIPMENT

Large pot

Wooden spoon

INSTRUCTIONS

1. Melt the wax in a vessel deep enough to dip the desired candle. Melt dye in the color you want to work with and stir it into the melted wax.

2. Dip the candle, submerging the entire length in the colored wax (photo 1). Allow any excess wax to drip off (photo 2). Dip the candle again, this time submerging it only

Photo 1

75 percent of the way into the wax and again allowing excess wax to drip off (photo 3). Submerge the candle again, this time only 50 percent of the way into the wax and allow excess wax to drip off. Then give the candle a final dip, submerging it only 25 percent of the way into the wax.

Photo 2

Photo 3

Marbelized Candles

MATERIALS

Melted paraffin wax—white or colored

Colored wax

White or colored candle

EQUIPMENT

Large pot

Toothpick or thin stick

INSTRUCTIONS

1. Fill a vessel with water—deep enough to accommodate the desired candle—and heat the water to just under a boil. If the candle is white: Place a small amount of wax that has been dyed white on the surface of the water. Next, place a small amount of wax that has been dyed a color on the surface of the water. With a toothpick or similar object, gently swirl the waxes to form a swirled pattern on the top of the water. Avoid stirring the two colors together. If the candle is colored, follow the instructions above, omitting the white wax.

2. Hold the candle by the wick, and dip it into the colored wax, swirling it as you submerge it. Remove the candle in the same fashion. Repeat if necessary until you achieve the desired effect.

Troubleshooting

When learning a new craft, we all make mistakes, and candlemaking is no exception. It requires considerable practice and patience to successfully make some of the candles in this book. Over time you will develop a "touch" when working with the wax that will enable you to be a good candlemaker and a good troubleshooter.

However, standard types of candles develop more predictable problems and most of these are easily overcome after experiencing them one or two times. This section is designed to help the beginner sort out the problem when something does go wrong.

Problem #1:

The candle will not release from the mold.

Causes:

- Wax built up on the insides of the mold above the height of the poured candle.
- The mold type does not permit easy release.
- The well was overfilled when the candle was topped off.
- If the mold is metal, it may be dented.
- Poor-quality wax was used or the wax was too soft.
- The candle cooled too slowly.

Solutions:

- Use only beeswax in pop-out molds or in combination with paraffin wax for molded candles.
- Do not fill melted wax beyond the hardened wax in your molds.
- Store molds in original packaging; purchase a new mold.
- Buy quality waxes from a reputable source; beware of extremely inexpensive wax and additives.
- Use a cool-water bath for most molded candles (see individual instructions).

Problem #2:

There are cracks or fractures inside the candle.

Causes:

- The candle cooled too quickly after pouring
- The well in the candle was topped off after the wax in the mold hardened.

Solutions:

- Do not use a cool-water bath for beeswax candles; cool the candle in a covered container.
- Watch for a well to develop as the candle cools, and fill it immediately.

Problem #3:

There is mottling on the outside of the candle.

Causes:

- Old wax that had been reheated too many times was used.
- There is high oil content in the wax.
- Candle allowed to cool too slowly.

Solutions:

- Use fresh wax; buy high-quality ingredients and waxes.
- Use a cool-water bath to cool candles more quickly.

Problem #4:

There are air bubbles on the surface of the candle.

Causes:

- The mold was not tapped to rid it of air pockets.
- There was dust in the mold.
- The candle was poured too quickly.
- There was water in the mold.

Solutions:

- Tap the mold with a wooden spoon to rid it of air pockets before placing it in a cool-water bath.
- Keep molds stored in the original packaging when not in use.
- Pour the candle slowly and evenly.
- Make sure that the inside of the mold is dry before pouring the candle.

Problem #5:

There are frost marks on the candle.

Causes:

- The mold was too cold when the candle was poured.
- The wax was not hot enough when the candle was poured.
- The candle was removed from the mold too early.

Solutions:

- Warm the outside of the mold with hot tap water before pouring the candle.
- Measure the temperature of the wax with a reliable thermometer; bring the wax to the proper pouring temperature.
- Be certain that the candle is completely cooled before trying to remove it from the mold.

Problem #6:

The candle caved in on the side.

Causes:

- The surface tension around the wick was not released by piercing (until the wax hardened too much).

Solutions:

- Pierce the wax on the well as it forms, before it hardens completely; make sure that you pierce the wax all along the length of the wick.

Problem #7:

There are bubbled lines around the circumference of the candle.

Causes:

- The water level in the cool-water bath was not at the level of the wax in the mold.

Solutions:

- Make sure that the water bath can accommodate the entire length of the candle.

Problem #8:

The flame burns a hole down through the candle, leaving a rim of unmelted wax around the outside.

Causes:

- The wick is too small for the diameter of the candle.
- Wax additives are slowing the burning of the candle so much that the wick selected is too small for the wax formulation.
- Too much stearin or additive to slow the burning was used.

Solutions:

- Do not overuse additives that lengthen the burning time of the candle.
- Use the proper wick for the diameter candle you are making.

Problem #9:

There is excessive smoking.

Causes:

- The wick is too large for the candle.
- There is a draft in the room.
- Trim the wick to a maximum of 1 inch (2.5 cm).

Solutions:

- Use the proper size wick for the candle's diameter.
- Do not burn candles in a strong draft.

Problem #10:

The wick snuffs itself out in the melted wax.

Causes:

- The wick is too small to take up the molten wax.
- The wrong wick type was used.

Solutions:

- Use the proper size wick for the diameter candle you are making.
- Use the proper wick for the type of candle you are making.

Problem #11:

The candle drips excessively.

Causes:

- The wick is not properly centered in the candle.
- The wax is too soft.
- There is a draft in the room.
- The wick is too small for the diameter of the candle.
- The wick is too small for the wax formulation of the candle.

Solutions:

- Use wick-centering spiders or be sure to center the wick properly.
- Buy high-quality waxes.
- Do not burn candles in drafty room.
- Use the proper size wick for the candle diameter you are making.

Problem #12:

The candle sputters.

Causes:

- There are impurities on the wick.
- There is water on the wick.

- There is water in the wax around the wick (common in ice candles).

Solutions:

- Do not use crayons to color candles; use clean wax free of debris.
- Prime all wicks before making the candle; keep wicks sealed in plastic to keep out moisture when not in use.
- Allow water candles to dry thoroughly before burning them.

Problem #13:

The wick lights poorly.

Causes:

- The wick is wet (common in water and ice candles).
- There is mold sealer on the wick.
- The wick was not primed.

Solutions:

- Use clean, dry wick; prime all wicks.
- Clean all mold sealer off the wick before lighting the candle.

Problem #14:

Container candles smoke excessively.

Causes:

- The wick is too large for the candle diameter.

Solutions:

- Use proper size wick for the diameter of the container used.

Problem #15:

There is wax left on the sides of the container.

Causes:

- The candle burned for short periods of time.
- The melting point of the wax was not low enough.

Solutions:

- Burn container candles for several hours at a time.
- Use the correct wax formulation for all container candles.

—From *The Complete Candlemaker*

GEL CANDLEMAKING

Marchianne Miller

There are four key elements to a successful gel candle: the gel itself and what you can do to it; the containers that hold the gel; the embeds and other objects you put into the gel; and the wick that transforms the combination of the other elements into a candle you can light and enjoy.

All About Gel

Gel candle wax is a specialized mineral oil (a by-product of the distillation of petroleum) that has been mixed with a chemical agent to thicken it to a gelatin-like consistency.

Gel is no more dangerous than the oil you rub on a baby's skin. Of course, you shouldn't eat gel (you don't eat baby oil, do you?), but if you did accidentally swallow

some, it wouldn't kill you. The oil is not digestible; it would just go right through your system.

Knowing that the gel is oil tells you other things. If you get gel on a silk shirt, it will probably leave a permanent stain. But most porous materials that come into contact with the gel—work clothes, dishtowels, and tablecloths, for example—can be laundered safely with a grease-eating detergent. Removing gel from nonporous surfaces is easy once you learn the secret—wait until the gel has cooled. If you try to wipe gel spills from glass containers when the gel is hot, for example, you'll just smear the gel and make a bigger cleanup chore. You can peel off cooled gel easily. Ammonia, adhesive-tape removers, mineral spirits, and other grease-cutting cleansers work best.

Big globs of spilled gel are better than little globs. You can see big globs of gel, after all. But little globs—oh dear!—they can get in, on, under, and around just about anything! Although you don't have to be a precision-nut in most aspects of gel candlemaking, it does help to be very neat and careful with the gel so you don't drive yourself crazy trying to clean up later.

Keep the gel—even tiny bits of it—off your stove-top burners. Gel on burners is hard to see, but you'll know it's there the next time you use the burner and the stinky burned gel sets off your smoke alarm! As you pour gel, it can run down the sides of the pan, and end up on the burner when you return the pan to the stove. To help you avoid gel spills, we recommend using certain types of pans and utensils. (See Gel Candlemaking Tools.)

Gel is wonderfully recyclable. Don't like the way a candle turned out? Just re-melt the gel and try again. Tired of the royal blue candles you made for the holidays? Re-melt the gel, add some green dye, and create a beautiful, sea-goddess-green candle to inspire dreams of summer at the beach. Fun, huh?

Gel oil should never go down the drain. If you want to discard it, do the same thing you would with bacon grease—let it solidify in a covered metal container, and throw it out with your trash.

Making Gel Candles—Safety First

Because gel is made with oil, it's flammable—that's why it's used to make candles. Unless you're using beeswax or coconut oil-based candles, most of the candles you've burned in your life—paraffin wax candles—are also refined from petroleum.

Oil and water don't mix, so if you should overheat the gel and it catches fire—water won't put the fire out. Think of a gel fire as a grease fire and you'll already know how to handle it—smother the fire with a pan lid to starve it of oxygen. Keep a big lid set out and ready to use—you don't want to have to scramble for it in a panic. You can also smother a small fire with baking soda—which now comes in a shaker-top container that is much easier to handle in a hurry than opening up the old-fashioned box. Of course, you should have a fire extinguisher in the kitchen at all times. Know how to use it and keep it within easy reach.

Liquid gel is hot enough to melt a plastic ladle, but not hot enough to ignite newspaper if you dropped hot gel on it. But if you spill liquid gel on yourself, it will hurt! Hot gel will stick to your skin and hold its high temperature on you long enough to cause a significant burn. In other words, be careful! And use those kitchen mitts and potholders. If you should suffer a hot gel burn, treat the burned area immediately by applying ice, and follow up with medical care, if necessary.

Your gel candlemaking work area should be well-ventilated, well-lit, and efficiently laid out so you don't have to fumble for knives, skewers, and other sharp utensils.

If you're new to gel candlemaking, you'll be amazed by how quickly the gel liquefies. Don't try to speed up an already speedy process by turning up the heat—the gel can reach its flash point more quickly than you expect. And don't even think about heating gel in the microwave.

Continued ➜

It doesn't work, it may injure you, and it will ruin your microwave.

You might think that large batches of gel will melt quickly too, but the truth is it can take a surprisingly long time to melt large batches. Be patient! You can speed things up—safely—if you crumble the gel into small pieces with your hands before putting it into the pan. Especially when you work with large batches of gel, wear protective eyewear to prevent injury from hot gel splatters.

When you're heating gel, stay with the gel. Never leave it unattended. No matter how multi-tasked you may be in the rest of your life, you can not be in two places at one time when heating gel.

Respect gel's potential for danger—and you'll be safe.

Burning Gel Candles—Safety First

Many people prefer candles made from gel because they burn so long—at least twice as long as candles made from paraffin. An 8-ounce (.2 L) gel candle (about the size of a coffee mug) can burn for 100 hours or longer!

Gel candles also burn hotter than paraffin candles. Gel candles have pool temperatures (the pool is the circle of melted gel around the wick) ranging from 245° F to 280° F (118° C to 137° C)—compared to paraffin wax pool temperatures of 180° F (82° C) or higher.

Although they burn longer and hotter, gel candles have smaller flames, which means it's easy to forget you've got a gel candle burning. Not a good idea!! If a gel candle is allowed to burn for too long, it can get very hot, and may burst into a flame so big you don't even want to think about how dangerous it could be!

If you make gel candles as gifts (and what gel candlemaker doesn't?), it would be an excellent idea to print the safety tips on a card and include it with your candles. (See How to Burn Your Gel Candle Safely. You have our permission to reproduce these tips.)

Where to Find Gel

Gel comes in different grades. The medium polymer (MP) grade is the most popular among candlemakers and is the one we used in the projects in the book. Craft stores usually sell MP candle gel wax in solid form in small tubs. You can order larger amounts through the stores or contact the distributors directly. In North America, most distributors of gel wax and accessories have toll-free telephone numbers, and many have Web sites on the Internet, where you can place orders and keep up with the latest news in gel candlemaking. Just type in "gel candles" on your search engine; you'll find an amazing

number of resources, including newsletters for virtual neighborhoods of gel candlemakers!

How Much Gel?

Pour water into your candle container until the water reaches the level that you'd like the gel to reach. Then measure the water by pouring it into a measuring cup—that's the amount of liquefied gel you'll need. After the first few times of measuring precisely, you'll get pretty good at eyeballing how much gel you need.

Getting Started

There are two ways to get the gel out of the container. Do your Miss Manners imitation and try to remove it with a large spoon—but it's not easy to push the spoon through the hard gel, and you may end up in a most unladylike snit! Or dig right into it with your bare hands—hey, gel candlemaking is supposed to bring out the creative child in you! Once you get out those first few clumps with your hands, the rest of the gel will come out easily with a spoon. In no time at all, you'll get used to gel's rubbery texture.

Gel Candlemaking Tools

Those who make paraffin candles may wonder why gel candlemakers don't use double boilers to liquefy the gel. The reason is simple: You can't achieve temperatures in a double boiler that are high enough to liquefy gel. An ordinary stove-top saucepan that is light enough for you to handle is fine for heating the solid gel. The ideal pan has two features: a pour spout on the rim that makes it easy to pour the gel into the containers without spilling the gel, and a heat-resistant handle. Just scrub the pan well with a grease-dissolving dish detergent after each use.

The small tools for gel candlemaking are inexpensive and easy to find.

A clip-on pan thermometer is essential—using it is the only way to measure the gel temperature accurately. You don't want to make the beginner's foolish mistake—testing the temperature of the hot gel by sticking your finger into it!

Even better than the pan-and-thermometer combination is an electric slow cooker with an adjustable temperature control. This handy appliance can be set to a specific temperature and will maintain it, making the process of liquefying the gel safe and easy.

Ladles help you control the pour of the gel. We recommend two—a large one and a small one—for containers of different sizes and for a variety of pouring jobs.

Metal spoons and metal skewers are the only ones you should use when stirring gel or inserting embeds. Don't use wood utensils; wood can react chemically with the gel and cause it to bubble excessively.

Cookie sheets are extremely handy. Use them to help you safely carry candles to the oven for slow cooling or reheating, and to make large sheets of colored gel.

A pizza cutter, which has a circular, rotating blade, is an excellent tool for slicing layers of gel. In fact, we found that it was the only tool that did the job easily.

A bubble stick is a long flat plastic stirrer that helps reduce the number of bubbles after you've poured the gel into the container. You can find bubble sticks in stores that sell food-canning supplies.

Utility knives, hot-glue guns, tweezers, pliers, wire cutters, scissors, a tape measure, and felt-tip markers—as you make gel candles, you'll probably use one or more of these tools at one time or another.

Gathering all your tools and reserving them just for candlemaking—including several pans—is more efficient in the long run; you won't have to interrupt your creative urges by rummaging through the junk drawer looking for that tool you must have now.

Heating Gel

Although the term "melt" is commonly used among gel candlemakers, the truth is gel doesn't really melt. It simply decreases in viscosity—or liquefies—as it is heated. Conversely, as the liquid gel is cooled, it increases in viscosity—or solidifies to its hardened, gel, state. Unlike paraffin, which has a definite point at which it melts, gel's liquefy/solidify process takes place gradually, over a range of temperatures.

Heating gel is a process of achieving the right temperature range for what you want the gel to do. For example, you must first heat gel at a high enough temperature to liquefy it. But if you add items such as dye or fragrance—which require time to stir thoroughly—the gel loses some heat. So you may need to re-heat the gel. Depending on how much gel you are heating, what you put into it, and how high you want the pouring temperature to be (which relates to how many bubbles you want), the time it takes to reach a temperature range can take anywhere from a few seconds to many minutes.

Gels produced by different manufacturers can vary. That's why, in all the instructions for the projects in this book, we refer you to the manufacturer's recommendations, which are included on the gel package, or available from the manufacturer.

On the other hand, we realize that, for any number of unforeseen reasons, a very small minority of our readers might not have the manufacturer's recommendations. Rather than having a reader guess—and guess wrong—about gel's temperature ranges, we offer the following ranges of temperatures as guidelines to help if you're in a pinch. Be aware that temperatures in your particular candlemaking situation can vary considerably from these ranges.

• The "melting" or liquefying range, when solid gel becomes liquid (the consistency of corn syrup) is 180° F to 220° F (82° C to 104° C).

• The pouring range is 190° F to 205° F (88° C to 96° C).

- If you want a lot of bubbles, pour at a temperature at the lower end of the range.
- If you want fewer bubbles, pour at a temperature at the higher end of the range.
- The baking or reheating range is 170° F to 175° F (77° C to 79° C).
- The cooling range, when the liquid gel becomes solid, is 140° F to 167° F (60° C to 75° C).

Warning: Never heat gel as high as 230° F (110° C). It's unsafe—gel can start burning at this temperature. And it's wasteful—if you scorch the gel, it's ruined and there's no way to save it. You'll have to discard it.

Remember—you can't tell what the temperature of gel is just by looking at it. Always use a clip-on thermometer—or the adjustable temperature control on the electric slow cooker—to ensure the safe and beautiful production of your gel candles.

Some candlemakers experiment with different temperature ranges to suit their specific situations—but what works for them may not work for you. Our advice is to stay on the side of extreme caution, following manufacturer's recommendations and your good common sense.

Conquering Bubbles

Gel candlemakers tend to fall into two camps: Bubble Haters and Bubble Lovers. We admit we are tiptoeing toward the Bubble-Lover camp. After all, bubbles are a part of gel, and these are gel candles we're making. And even if we didn't like bubbles, we know that, no matter what we do, sometimes bubbles appear!

The six causes of bubbles are: 1) the temperature of the container; 2) the temperature of the gel when you pour it; 3) the pouring method you use; 4) the reaction of the gel to items you put into it, such as spoons, fragrances and embeds; 5) the method you use to cool the gel; and 6) who knows?

How successfully you deal with these causes depends on your experience, skill—and luck!

PREHEAT YOUR CONTAINER

Warm up your container before you pour the gel into it by putting the container in a 175° F (80° C) oven for about 10 minutes. After a while, it's easy to remember to do this. Just put the container in the oven right after you put the gel in the pan or slow cooker. (It's easy to forget an empty container is hot. Remember to use protection on your hands when you remove the empty container from the oven.)

CHECK YOUR POURING TEMPERATURE

Generally, the higher the pouring temperature, the fewer the bubbles. That means for each candle. When you're making more than one candle at a time, double check the temperature before you pour each candle. Melted gel cools quickly. You might have a temperature at the high end of the pouring range when you pour your first candle, but in just a few minutes between pours, the gel temperature could drop low enough to produce twice as many bubbles in the later candles.

PERFECT YOUR POURING METHOD

The way you pour the gel affects how much air gets into it, thus affecting how many bubbles will form. To minimize bubbles, pour the gel as you would pour a beer to get less suds—by holding the container at an angle and pouring slowly.

ADD ONLY BUBBLE-FRIENDLY ITEMS

Anything you put into the gel should be compatible with it. Fragrances and embeds that are not compatible with gel, for example, cause excessive bubbling. See the section on Fragrances. Also see the section on Embeds, which goes into detail about what kinds of embeds are compatible.

Even the perfect embed will cause bubbles if it has impurities, including water, on it. Wash and dry thoroughly any object that you want to embed.

Pretreat embeds to test them and give them a protective seal. Pour a small amount of hot gel into a bowl, and coat the items in the gel. Watch for bubbles. If none appear, use tweezers to remove the items, holding them over the gel to let the excess gel drip back into the bowl. If bubbles do appear, stir occasionally, leaving the embeds in the gel until the bubbling stops. If, after a few minutes, the bubbling continues, either decide not to use those embeds, or live with the bubbles. Don't make candles with the gel that you've used to pretreat embeds.

Right after you pour the gel, if you gently stir it with a bubble stick, you can decrease the bubbling. If bubbles appear on the surface, just prick them with a pin.

EXPERIMENT WITH GEL COOLING METHODS

Bubble Conquerors are divided into two opposing camps: the Fast Coolers and the Slow Coolers. On the theory that quick cooling arrests the formation of bubbles, the Fast Coolers place their gel candles into the refrigerator immediately after pouring. (Rest the candle on a bed of dishtowels or other heat resistant cushion so the hot container doesn't break a cold glass refrigerator shelf.)

The Slow Coolers attempt to decrease bubbles by slow cooling, such as leaving the candles undisturbed in a secure place—even outdoors on a sunny day—for several hours. You can actively slow down the cooling process by wrapping the candles in towels or baking them in a warm (175° F or 80° C) oven for several hours, even overnight.

Which method works? They all do. Since each candlemaker's environment, technique, additives, equipment, and patience level differs, our advice is to experiment with both fast and slow methods of cooling and find out what works best for you. A notebook with a record of your findings can be invaluable.

RE-HEAT SOME CANDLES

If a candle develops bubbles (it's amazing how they do reappear!), you can reheat many kinds of gel candles in the oven. Usually, but not always, the reheating process will reduce the bubbling. Remember the obvious, though: you can't reheat layered candles (the layers will melt into one another), or candles with floating embeds (the embeds will sink), or candles with meltable embeds, such as wax embeds.

When you want to reheat a candle, place it on a cookie sheet before setting it in the oven. In a worst-case scenario, the candle container might shatter and the gel spill. Make sure the oven rack is level so your gel surface doesn't harden lopsided.

Enhancing Gel with Color

You can create fantastic candles by playing with gel's capacity to accept color easily. The techniques are simple, fun to learn, and forgiving—if you don't like the results, you can liquefy the gel and start over. In Fantastic Gel Candles, we played with color in four basic ways: by tinting the whole candle, making layers of different colors, making appliqués, and making molds.

USING DYE

There are excellent dyes made specifically for gel candles and you can also use dyes made for traditional paraffin candles. You can't use food coloring—it's water-soluble and doesn't mix with oil.

Dye comes in two forms—liquid and solid—and a little bit of either goes a long way. To color gel, heat the gel until it's completely liquefied (see Heating Gel), then gently stir in small amounts of dye, with a metal spoon, until you have the color you want. With liquid dyes, add a few drops at a time. For solid dyes, use a food grater to scrape the dye into small pieces.

Keep a handful of small gel candle containers near your work area. If you end up with too much dyed gel,

just pour it into the stand-bys (Lots of Little Squares). Or remove hardened gel from the pan and store it in a sealable plastic bag or a glass container with a lid.

TESTING THE COLOR

Dyed gel looks darker in the pan than it will in the candle, so test the color before pouring. Place a small amount of the tinted gel in a glass or place a few drops on a sheet of heavy, white paper.

Allow the gel to solidify, and then see how you like the color. If the color appears too dark, simply dilute it by adding more clear gel to the pan. If the color appears too light, just add more dye.

MAKING LAYERS OF COLOR

Making candles with different colored layers of gel is as easy as dying gel for an entire candle—it just takes longer to make more colors. Successful layering depends on your choice of colors and how you arrange them. Use your own good color sense to guide you. Red and green, for example, will eventually blend into a muddy brown color where the layers meet, but red and blue will blend to form a nice purplish color.

Layers in gel candles tend to be less distinct because the transparent nature of the gel seems to blend the colors. To create layers that are as distinct as possible, allow each layer to cool and harden completely before you pour the next layer. Be patient. A candle with several layers can take many hours to complete.

MAKING APPLIQUES OF COLOR

Experienced gel candlemakers have learned the wisdom of preparing sheets of gel ahead of time, so that they're handy when the inspiration for a new gel applique candle hits them. Line a cookie sheet with aluminum foil, placing the shiny side of the foil face up, (The shiny side is smoother; so the gel won't stick to it,) Spray any cooking oil-or lubricating oil, such as the oil you use to fix a squeaky door-onto the foil.

Pour dyed gel onto the foil-covered cookie sheet to make layers. For thin appliques for small candles, make ⅙ to ⅛-inch-thick (1.6 mm to 3 mm) layers. For thicker appliques and strips of gel make each layer ¼-inch (6mm) thick, When the gel is cool, cut out shapes with cookie cutters; use a pizza cutter to slice out strips of gel.

If you don't need a whole cookie sheet of gel, make smaller "trays" of foil on the cookie sheet: cut a doubled layer of foil to the size tray you want, fold up the sides, and fold and pinch the corners together:

To keep dyed gel sheets for future use, cut them into convenient sizes and place them between pieces of waxed paper: Put the wrapped gel into sealable bags or containers, and store them in the refrigerator.

MAKING MOLDS

Using muffin tins or soapmaking molds to create gel candles easily expands your candlemaking possibilities. Just dye the gel, pour it into the mold, and let it cool, Because they're tiny, small gel mold candles are more for show than for practical use; they melt quickly once their wicks are lit, (But oh, how impressive they are while they last!)

If you use plastic molds... pout the gel at the lower temperature range to avoid melting the mold. The key to success with molds is twofold. First, the mold needs to rest flat. Fill the mold with water. If the water fills the mold completely, the mold is flat. If the mold isn't flat, make it so by securely propping the mold up with towels or scrap aluminum foil. Secondly, use a ladle to control pouring the gel into the small molds.

Enhancing Gel with Fragrance

Fragrances add a delightful, second sensory pleasure to the visual beauty of gel candles. Many—but not all—of the fragrances used in paraffin candles can also be used in gel candles. Fragrances can contain chemicals—sometimes,

Continued ➜

as many as 50 different aroma chemicals can go into the composition of a fragrance. When chemicals mix, they don't always react positively with one another.

That's what can happen with gel and fragrances that aren't compatible. And that's why the addition of fragrances to gel is a major safety issue for candlemakers.

A compatible fragrance is often referred to as nonpolar, which means that it is compatible with the hydrocarbons that make up the material oil gel. When you see the term non-polar on the label of a candle fragrance, you know that fragrance is fine for use in gel candles.

Our advice is to use a fragrance only if you know it's compatible with the gel. The easiest way to be sure is to buy fragrances with labels that indicate they are gel compatible. If there's no label on the fragrance, here's a test to determine if it's compatible. Mix one part fragrance with three parts mineral oil. If the fragrance mixes in completely, with no cloudiness, it's fine for gel. If it separates out or makes the oil cloudy, don't use it in your gel candles. Don't use perfume. It contains alcohol and won't mix well with the oil-based gel.

Adding scents requires a delicate touch. Experts suggest that the fragrance load for the MP grade of gel (the one that is most commonly used) should be only 3 to 5 percent. Add the scent just before you pour the gel into the container so that the heat doesn't evaporate it immediately. Mix the fragrance gently but thoroughly into the gel. If the fragrance is not mixed throughout, it can cause the flame to burn unevenly or make the gel cloudy.

Enhancing Gel with Glitter

Gel glitter is a finely grained, gel-compatible additive that gives a lovely sheen to gel. Follow the manufacturer's directions on the package. Add the glitter to the gel after you've added the dye and just before pouring. As with fragrance, a little bit of glitter goes a long way, so experiment with a light touch first.

All About Containers

Unlike traditional candles, in which the container is just something that holds the candles, gel candle containers share equal billing with the gel. Often, it's the container itself that inspires a candle. Containers range from practical and homey to sophisticated and spectacular—with a lot of creative space in between.

In general, choose glassware that is designed to be stable so it won't tip over easily. Thick glass containers are sturdy, and because they slow down the cooling process, often help prevent bubbling. Very thin glass may not handle the heat of the gel. For proper heat dissemi-

nation, the top of a gel candle container should not be narrower than the bottom, and the top should be at least 2 to 3 inches (5 to 7.6 cm) wide.

Glass is the preferred material for gel candle containers because it shows off the gel's beauty, but you can also use porcelain and pottery containers.

Everyday Glass

Start your search for gel candle containers in your own home. Drinking glasses, glass mugs, orphaned or outdated goblets, and vases that no longer hold their appeal make wonderful gel candle containers. Colored glass containers are great for timid beginners—just add the gel and the wick, and get the applause! Empty glass food jars are excellent containers, especially if they have lids, which give the candles a finished look when they're not in use, and which also make it easy and safe to pack the candles for shipping.

Decorated Containers

Glass containers come in two basic categories: glass that is already decorated beautifully in itself, such as etched glass, glass with decals, and pressed glass; or glass that is quite ordinary until the gel candlemaker transforms it. For many gel candlemakers, creating beautiful containers, especially painting or decorating glass, is as important as mastering the techniques of working with the gel.

Collectible Glass

Many of us have vintage glass that's been handed down through the family but doesn't suit our contemporary decorating style. When you take those old glasses out of hiding and turn them into gel candles, they look terrific in any décor.

Show-Off Containers

Deep, wide bowls are ideal when an expanse of clear gel is a key element in your design (Zen Rock Garden), or when you have lots of pretty objects.

Tall cylinders make spectacular gel candles. Reality check: Most of the gel in tall candles never gets burned because you can't reach down far enough inside to cut the wick. If you love tall candles the way we do—just for the pure pleasure of looking at them—go for it. Gel burns so slowly that you'll get many hours of enjoyment, no matter how much of the gel you eventually melt and reuse. Remember that in a narrow candle, the hottest part of the candle—the pool around the wick—has no space to spread and dissipate the heat. Two things could happen. The high heat could shatter the glass. Or the gel could get so hot it could ignite. Our advice: avoid very narrow containers.

All About Embeds

Embeds are the objects placed into the gel that can be seen through the glass container. For some gel candlemakers, finding and placing embeds is their favorite part of the craft. Embeds are everywhere—in drawers of old jewelry, children's toy boxes, antique shop bargain bins—anywhere small treasures are kept.

Besides deciding how attractive an embed will be in a candle, you'll have three other considerations: safety, gel compatibility, and placement of the embed in the candle.

Safety and Compatibility Concerns

The safety of an embed in a gel candle relates to its flammability. There are non-flammable embeds, meltable embeds, and flammable embeds.

Non-Flammable Embeds

The good news is most non-flammable embeds are also compatible with gel, meaning they are less likely to cause cloudiness or excessive bubbling.

Gloss embeds accentuate gel's 3-D effect, especially when several are used in the same candle and placed at various levels.

Ceramic and pottery embeds come in a variety of shapes and sizes. Even broken pieces of pottery can look terrific in a candle.

Metal embeds are wonderful in gel candles, particularly since metal can range from thin wire shapes to solid forms such as coins and bells.

Natural ingredients, such as rocks, pebbles, and seashells, are both sturdy and elegant in candles.

Meltable Embeds

You can mold paraffin wax embeds yourself or purchase them readymade at craft stores or on the Internet. The trick with wax embeds is to avoid melting them with hot gel. Just heat the gel to the point where it's pourable but not completely liquid. Pour at least 1 inch (2.5 cm) of this gel over the embed, which will seal it. Fill the rest of the container with hotter gel.

Flammable Embeds

Objects such as photographs, paper, wood items, silk flowers, and fabric swatches should not be used as embeds. Even though you may not think of plastic and rubber as flammable, they certainly are at high temperatures, and they should not be used either. There are so many wonderful—and safe—things to use as embeds, why risk using materials that aren't safe or about which you have doubts? If you don't know whether an item is flammable or not, don't use it as a gel candle embed. If you insist on using it, then keep it at least 1 inch (2.5 cm) away from the wick.

Placing Embeds

Tweezers and metal cooking skewers are helpful tools when you're working with embeds. Use them to place embeds in the container before you pour the gel and to reposition them, if necessary, after the gel has been poured.

If you want to position your embeds at specific heights in the container, suspend them with sewing thread that's tied to a skewer placed across the rim of the container, before you pour the gel, if your embed doesn't have a hook or hole for the thread, then use two or three lengths of thread to create a "hammock," and hang them that way. After the gel has been poured and has cooled, gently tug on the threads to remove them.

All About Wicks

Wicks are the unsung heroines of gel candles. Their type, size, preparation, positioning, and maintenance are crucial to both the appearance and safety of gel candles.

Select the Proper Wick Type

Zinc-cored wicks are stiff and thus stay straight when they're inserted into the gel; they're the wicks of choice for most gel candlemakers. These wicks come in several styles—with or without anchor tabs and with or without waxing. An anchor tab is a good safety feature because it helps prevent the wick from burning to the very bottom of the candle. Do not use cotton or paper-cored wicks.

Select the Proper Wick Size

Wicks come in an assortment of sizes. Select a size that's appropriate for the size of your container. Refer to the wick manufacturer's instructions for guidance, but this is a general rule of thumb for zinc-cored wicks: small for containers with diameters of 2 to 3 inches (5.1 to 7.6 cm), medium for 3 to 4 inches (7.6 to 10.2 cm), and large for 4 to 5 inches (10.2 to 12.7 cm).

You can burn a candle only as far down as you can trim the wick—so there's no point in using a wick that goes all the way down to the bottom of the candle, unless the container is wide enough to allow you to reach in and trim the wick. A short wick is fine in a tall candle, especially a tall narrow candle.

Don't be tempted to use a wider wick just because gel candles burn twice as slowly as paraffin candles. A wick that is too wide can cause the flame to burn too hot—and ignite the gel.

Prepare the Wick for Gel

To reduce bubbling, pretreat your wicks, especially wax-coated wicks. Coat the wicks in hot melted gel and leave them in the gel until the bubbling stops. Remove the wicks, wait at least 30 seconds, and then run your fingers down them to remove the excess gel.

Position the Wick Properly

Attach an anchor wick to the bottom of the container before you pour the gel. Dip the end of the wick into hot gel and press it against the bottom of the container with a metal skewer. Or use a hot-glue gun to fasten it to the bottom. (The glue may react with the gel and cause some bubbling but the wick will be very secure.)

Loop the other end of the wick around a skewer or pencil and position it over the top of the container. After you pour the gel and it is almost cool, give the wick a gentle tug to remove any slack. When the gel is cool, remove the wick from the skewer or pencil and trim it to ¼ inch (6 mm). Save the rest of the wick to use as short wicks for other candles.

Another way to insert a wick is to pour the gel first, and when the gel is almost cool, insert the wick from the top. If you want the wick to go into the gel more than a few inches, first insert a length of thin, sturdy wire through the gel to make a narrow hole. Remove the wire and, using the tunnel it left in the gel as a guide, insert the wick, keeping it at least 1 inch (2.5 cm) from the bottom of the container.

If the wick goes askew, you can just leave it alone and enjoy its wayward ways, or reheat the candle in a 175° F (80° C) oven until the gel melts. If the wick is an anchor wick, position it properly in the cooling gel and tug it taut to remove any slack that has developed. If you want a wick at the top, remove the wick before you reheat the candle. After the gel has melted and started to cool, re-insert the wick.

Maintain the Wick

Trimming the wick is not an option. You have to do it. A tall, exposed wick is a potential safety hazard because its large flame can generate enough heat to ignite the gel. Trim the wick to ¼ inch (6 mm) the first time you burn the candle. Then, every time you light the candle, make sure the wick is no taller than ⅙ inch (1.6 mm). Keep it

short; keep it safe. To trim the wick, wait until the gel has cooled completely. Then turn the candle upside down, so no blackened bits of the wick will fall into the gel, and trim the wick with a pair of small scissors or nail clippers. Don't try to trim the wick while it's burning the result will be a big mess.

The Projects

Our projects were designed to accentuate the gel itself, emphasizing its unique beauty and adaptability as an artistic medium. We wanted the projects to be easy enough for beginners to make—and provide a wide variety of techniques to inspire experienced candlemakers. We hope Fantastic Gel Candles encourages you to have as much fun as we did!

Lots of Little Squares

Designer: Terry Taylor

It couldn't be easier to create this eye-catching display of simple square glass containers filled with gels of brilliant colors. The short, sturdy shapes make safe candles for use outdoors.

WHAT YOU NEED

Small glass containers

Pan

Clip-on pan thermometer

Candle gel wax

Gel dyes in bright colors

Metal spoon

Ladle

Wicks

INSTRUCTIONS

1. In a pan placed over low heat, melt enough gel to fill one of the containers, heating the gel to the highest temperature recommended by the manufacturer. Use the thermometer to make sure the gel doesn't get too hot. Gradually add a few chips or drops of dye, and stir gently with the metal spoon until you get the intense color you want.

2. When the temperature of the gel is as high as it should be, ladle the gel into the container.

3. Repeat steps 1 and 2 to prepare and pour the other colors.

4. When the gel is almost cool, insert the wicks.

DESIGN TIP

Keep small glass containers handy in your candlemaking area, so you'll always have some ready to be filled with leftover colored gel.

Mini Tree Lights

Designer: Terry Taylor

Charming, colorful, and clever—this candle is so appealing you'll never grow tired of looking at it! The tiny lightbulbs spiral through the clear gel, as if they were dancing.

WHAT YOU NEED

Clear glass container

Scrap wire

Measuring tape or ruler

Package of tiny colored lightbulbs

18- or 20-gauge (1.00 or .75 mm) colored craft wire

Wire cutters

Pan

Clip-on thermometer

Candle gel wax

Metal skewer

Wick

INSTRUCTIONS

1. Shape a piece of scrap wire into a spiral to fit the container. Remove it, measure it, and double its length to determine how much wire you'll need to make the finished double-strand spiral.

2. Thread one of the bulbs onto one of the strands. Twist both strands to secure it in place. Continue twisting the wire for about 1 inch (2.5 cm) and slide another bulb onto one of the strands. Repeat until the strand is filled with bulbs. Fit the spiral inside the container, using wire cutters to trim the wires, if necessary.

3. In a pan placed over low heat, melt enough clear gel to fill the container, heating the gel to the highest temperature recommended by the manufacturer. Use the thermometer to make sure the gel doesn't get too hot. Let the gel cool slightly and then pour it gently into the container, being careful not to disturb the lights.

4. Make sure the wire is placed away from the wick. Use the metal skewer to adjust it, if necessary. When the gel is almost cool, insert a wick.

DESIGN TIP

Make other candles for use any time of year—with beads, bells, charms, medals—any intriguing objects you can string on wire.

Zen Rock Garden

Designer: Terry Taylor

The utter simplicity of this candle is a pleasure to the eye, a subtle invitation to be still and look inward. The clear gel accentuates the natural beauty of the river pebbles. Four wicks emphasize balance.

WHAT YOU NEED

Wide square glass container with thick walls

Oven

Cookie sheet

Aluminum foil

Continued ➜

Pan

Clip-on pan thermometer

River pebbles

Candle gel wax

Wicks

INSTRUCTIONS

1. Choose a wide square container with thick glass walls that can bear the weight of the pebbles.

2. Make sure that your oven rack is level. Pour water into the container, set it on the rack, and observe it at eye level. If the layer is not level, adjust the container with supports of folded aluminum foil. Remove the container from the oven and dry it thoroughly.

3. Pre-heat the oven to 175° F (80° C).

4. Wash the pebbles and let them dry completely to remove all traces of water or residue that could make the gel cloudy. Arrange the pebbles in a layer on the bottom of the container.

5. In a pan placed over low heat, melt enough gel to fill the container to the highest temperature recommended by the manufacturer. Use the thermometer to make sure the gel doesn't get too hot. Pour the gel over the pebbles.

6. Place the candle in the pre-heated oven for several hours to cool slowly and to remove as many bubbles as possible. Be careful to hold the container level when you carry it, so the gel layer will be perfectly straight.

7. When the gel is almost cool, insert the four wicks.

DESIGN TIP

Other objects that make stunning bottom layers are glass pebbles, marbles, tumbled glass, and coins.

Tower with Hoops of Beads

Designer: Allison Smith

Layers of brilliantly colored gel and hoops of tumbled glass beads turn an easy-to-make candle into a breath-taking work of art. By the time you reach the top layer of this tower candle, your feelings of accomplishment will have soared as high as your imagination. Go for it!

WHAT YOU NEED

Tall, glass container

Measuring cup

Assortment of tumbled glass beads

18- or 20-gauge copper wire

Wire cutters

Pliers

Tape measure or ruler

Felt-tip marker

Pan

Clip-on pan thermometer

Candle gel wax

Gel dyes in compatible colors

Ladle

Metal skewer

Wick

INSTRUCTIONS

1. Fill your container with water and measure the amount with a measuring cup to determine how much gel you'll need. Then divide the total by the number of layers to determine how much you'll need for each layer. (This project took 2 quarts [1.9 L] of gel for all six layers.) Dry the container thoroughly.

2. Choose enough pretty beads to make the number of hoops you want in your design. (This design has five hoops.) Tumbled glass beads look lovely through the gel, but any pretty, gel-compatible beads will do. When using dark gel colors, you can't see the details of the beads, so choose beads with distinctive shapes.

3. String the beads onto the copper wire and bend the wire into hoops. Fit each of the hoops inside the glass container to make sure it rests flat and fits snugly against the glass walls. Using the pliers, make a hook at each end of each wire and crimp the ends with the pliers to make a secure circle.

4. With the felt-tip marker, measure and mark off equidistant lines on one outside wall of the container to indicate the top of each layer. Use these marks to help you pour the gel and position the beaded hoops.

5. In a pan placed over low heat, melt enough gel for one layer, heating the gel to the highest temperature recommended by the manufacturer. Use the thermometer to make sure the gel doesn't get too hot. Gradually add a few chips or drops of dye until you get the color you want.

6. When the temperature of the gel is as high as it should be, ladle the gel into the container to the level indicated by the mark. To create distinctive lines between the layers, let the gel cool completely before adding the next layer.

7. When the gel is completely cool, place a beaded hoop on top of it. If necessary, use the metal skewers, to press it flat.

8. Repeat steps 5 to 7 with each of the different colored gel layers and beaded hoops. After you position the last hoop, pour in the final layer of colored gel.

9. When the last layer is almost cool, insert a wick about two layers in length.

10. When the candle has burned down too far to trim the wick easily, pull out the wick and add fresh layers of gel and a new wick.

DESIGN TIP

Glass beads look translucent in the gel, so use a pretty wire that will show through them. If you use opaque beads, you won't see the wire, so any wire is fine.

SAFETY TIP

Don't be tempted to create a tall flame to match the tall container! Keep the wick trimmed to no more than 1/16 inch (1.6 mm) after its first burn.

—FROM *Fantastic Gel Candles*

Polymer Clay Crafts

WORKING WITH POLYMER CLAY

Dawn Cusick & Megan Kirby, Editors

Polymer clay continues to increase in popularity as crafters realize its potential for stunning jewelry, home décor items, and even small sculptures. Polymer clay can be found in an incredible array of colors, and it can be stamped, sculpted, embedded, painted, sanded, and even drilled!

Materials and Tools

Polymer Clay

Each brand has its own unique prebaking malleability and postbaking strength and flexibility. Experiment with different types to discover your favorite.

Pasta Machine

Pasta machines allow you to form even layers of clay with little effort. For safety's sake, do not use the same pasta machine for cooking and crafting.

Acrylic Rod, Brayer, and Rolling Pin

Use instead of or in addition to pasta machine. Acrylic is best, rubber second. Avoid wood products—they leave grain marks and can be difficult to clean.

Cutting Blade

Many craft stores have cutting blades sold specifically for polymer clay crafters. Look for a blade that's 4 to 5 inches (10 to 12 cm) long. Wallpaper scraper blades will work, but razor blades are too short.

Craft Knife

Best for cutting tight curves and angles or intricate detail.

Work Surface

Ceramic tiles are handy and can be used as a baking surface, too.

Baking Tray or Tile

Put a piece of paper on the baking surface to prevent a shiny spot on the clay where it touches the tile.

Oven

A dedicated oven is best; if not possible, make a "tent" of aluminum foil to go over the baking tray.

Oven Thermometer

Oven thermometers are often inaccurate, so purchase one in a kitchen store.

Shape Cutters

Small cookie cutters or canapé cutters can be used to cut fun shapes for a variety of projects.

Needle Tool or Knitting Needle

For piercing holes in beads.

Sculpting Tools

Specialty tools are available, or you can use found objects such as a golf tee, a chair caning peg, cuticle pusher, crochet hook, etc. Or make your own from polymer clay.

Texture

Commercially made texture sheets are available, but you can use window screen, lace, plastic embroidery canvas, textured wallpaper, etc. Always use a mold release to prevent sticking.

Mold Release

Water, nonaerosol auto interior vinyl protectant, or cornstarch.

Wet/dry Sandpaper

Find this in the auto supply store. Never skip grits, and keep it wet to avoid breathing polymer dust and to prevent scratching.

Buffing Wheel

Use a jeweler's buffing wheel or a bench grinder to add shine.

Basic Techniques

Making the Clay Workable

Conditioning or kneading makes hard clay more malleable. Even soft-from-the-package clay should be conditioned to mix the plasticizer throughout the polymer clay. Unconditioned clay may break easily after baking.

Continued ➜

1. Condition clay by hand by squeezing a one-ounce (28 g) block into a ball. Roll it into a snake shape, fold it back on itself, and roll it out again. Repeat until the clay stretches when it's pulled apart. Try not to incorporate air bubbles. Alternatively, clay can be conditioned with a pasta machine by cutting slabs just a little thicker than the thickest pasta machine setting, and rolling them through the machine. Fold in half and repeat, as many times as needed for the clay to stretch instead of break when pulled. Never feed clay into the machine fold-side-up, or you'll trap air and create bubbles.

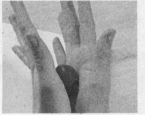 

2. If your clay is very soft and sticky, it will need to be leached to remove some of the plasticizers. To do this, roll it into a sheet and place it between two sheets of paper. Some of the plasticizer will leach onto the paper after a couple of hours. Repeat until the clay loses its stickiness, then condition it as described in Step 1.

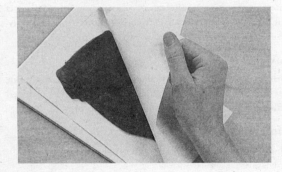

Designer Tip

Colored sand, rubber stamp embossing powders, dried spices, even potting soil can be physically mixed into polymer clay to create many interesting effects. They're especially useful in creating certain faux stones. Mix in enough of the inclusion to show, but not so much that it affects the integrity of the clay body. Be aware that cutting clay with inclusions in it will dull your blade faster, so you may want to dedicate one blade specifically to this technique.

Baking

Polymer clay is picky! No matter how long you bake it, it won't fuse properly at too low a temperature, and the resulting pieces may be weak and easily broken. Too high a temperature and it burns. Learn your oven and its idiosyncrasies.

Although toaster oven temperatures are frequently inaccurate and their heating elements can easily burn the clay, they can still do a good job of baking polymer clay. Place a small ceramic tile in the toaster oven as a heat sink to help maintain an even temperature, and make a "tent" of aluminum foil to protect your projects from the heating elements. Be sure to ventilate well, especially if you burn the clay!

If a dedicated oven is not possible, you should clean your oven after baking polymer clay. Wipe with a little baking soda on a damp sponge, then wipe clean with a wet rag.

Polymer clay can be baked as many times as you want with no adverse effects. It doesn't shrink when baked, but it may be necessary to support some objects during baking to prevent sagging. Use polyester fiberfill or a wadded-up cotton cloth.

Do not microwave polymer clay!

Making Molds

Molds can be made from seashells, buttons, beads, charms, and any number of other items.

1. To make a mold, wad up a piece of polymer clay that is larger than the object you want to make a mold of. Use strong clay; if you're using scrap, mix it thoroughly until it's all one color.

2. Set the clay on a piece of waxed paper on your work surface and cover with another piece of waxed paper. Flatten slightly and evenly by pressing with a flat object such as a jar lid. Remove the top piece of waxed paper and apply mold release generously directly to the clay.

3. Press the object into the clay using a straight downward motion. Don't twist or turn the object. Then pull the object straight out.

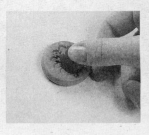

4. Peel the waxed paper from the back of the mold and place the mold on your baking sheet. Bake at the manufacturer's recommended temperature for an hour. The longer baking time ensures a stronger mold.

5. To use the mold, apply a mold release directly to the mold and tamp out the excess. Roll polymer clay into a cone shape, place the point of the cone into the center of the mold, and press.

6. While the polymer is still in the mold, cut excess clay from the back side with a polymer clay cutting blade.

Adding Texture

Texturing creates visual interest and hides fingerprints. Window screen, fabric, rubber stamps, textured wallpaper, textured leather, lace, plastic needlepoint canvas, and many other items are great for adding texture.

1. Apply a spritz of water from a spray bottle directly to the clay, or use a soft brush to apply cornstarch to serve as a mold release. Mica powders will act as their own mold release as well as add color to the texture.

2. If the clay and texture together aren't too thick, roll them through the pasta machine for deep, even texturing.

Blending Clay

This technique, known as a Skinner Blend, lets you create subtle blends of color.

1. Roll two colors of polymer clay into sheets at the thickest setting of your pasta machine. Cut each diagonally, and set half of each aside. Fit the two remaining triangles next to each other.

2. Fold this sheet in half, bottom to top, and run it through the pasta machine. Repeat this many times, always folding from bottom to top.

3. After 20 or so passes through the pasta machine, the colors will have subtly blended from one to the other. You can experiment with more than two colors of triangle shapes. Just be sure to fold the clay and insert it into the pasta machine rollers in the same direction each time.

Sanding and Buffing

A deep, lustrous shine can be created on your polymer pieces with elbow grease instead of varnish.

1. Use wet/dry sandpaper in the very fine grits that are available at auto parts stores. You can go as low as 320 grit to smooth lumps, but it's usually sufficient to start at 400 grit.

2. Keep the paper and the object wet, but constant immersion is not necessary. Use a bowl of water and frequently dip the paper and polymer to rinse them.

3. Don't skip grits, and sand each grit perpendicular to the previous one. For a soft sheen, buff by hand on a piece of soft denim or other cloth.

4. For a shine, use a cotton buffing wheel. A jeweler's buffing wheel is ideal, but a bench grinder with a cotton wheel attached will work well, too. For small objects, you can use an electric handheld rotary tool but use caution since the small wheel can easily gouge the clay.

Caneworking

A glass-working technique that has been adapted to polymer clay, caneworking is sometimes referred to as millefiori, which translates to "a thousand flowers." A cane is a tube or log of polymer clay that has an image or pattern running through the length of it, and as slices are removed from the cane, the image is revealed. Caned patterns can be very complex, but even simple ones can be very effective elements of a project. Thick cane slices can be pierced to create beads, and thin slices can be used in a variety of ways for decoration.

Jelly-roll Cane. Roll out rectangular sheets of two colors of polymer clay and place one on top of the other, being careful not to trap air bubbles between the sheets. Starting at one of the shorter ends, roll the polymer clay into a tube.

Try varying the look of this simple cane by using more than two colors or by using sheets of differing thicknesses.

Bull's-eye Cane. Roll one color of polymer clay into a short log. Roll out a sheet of a contrasting color and trim the edges neatly. Place the log onto the sheet and roll it up. Trim the sheet so that the edges butt against each other when the log is completely wrapped. Add as many rings of color as you'd like. Vary the thicknesses for added interest.

Striped Cane. Roll two or more contrasting colors of polymer clay into sheets and stack them. Cut the stack in half and place one half on top of the other. Repeat until you have the number of stripes you want. Roll your brayer or acrylic rod over the stack as you layer it, to press out air bubbles and to compress the layers. Again, varying the thicknesses of the sheets can result in interesting effects.

Checkerboard Cane. Roll two thick sheets of contrasting colors of polymer clay. Stack one on the other and trim the edges. Use your cutting blade to cut the stack into strips, then flip over every other strip. Cut the resulting stack in half and place one half on top of the other.

Slicing Canes. Remove slices from your cane with a polymer clay cutting blade. If the cane squishes or smears, the clay may be warm from working with it, and you'll get better results if you allow it to rest for a few hours or even overnight.

Wipe the blade on an alcohol-dampened paper towel to keep it clean between slices. Rotate the cane a quarter turn between each slice to keep it even.

Reducing Canes. Reducing canes refers to making the diameter of the cane smaller. You can reduce the entire cane you've made, or cut off portions and reduce each to a different diameter.

Roll a circular cane on your work surface, applying even pressure with your hands over the entire length of the cane. Roll it slowly and carefully to minimize distortion. To reduce a square or rectangular cane, roll over it with your brayer or acrylic rod, flipping the cane over occasionally to make sure the pressure is applied evenly. Allow canes to rest and cool after reducing them.

Getting to Know Your Polymer Clay
Irene Semanchuk Dean

Brands

Several brands of polymer clay are available from which to choose. In general, different brands of clay have varying qualities, and each works well for certain types of projects. I'll point out a few observations below, but use your own judgment and develop your own preferences as you experiment with clays. There are a lot of great products on the market, and new ones are being developed all the time!

Most brands of polymer clay are sold in two-ounce (56 g) packages as well as larger, one-pound (0.45 kg) bricks that can be special-ordered. Polyform Products creates several polymer clays including Sculpey III, which is a popular brand. Characteristically very soft and workable, it works well for children and beginners. After baking, it tends to be fragile, so I don't recommend it for projects that use thin sheets of clay. However, it works fine for solid shapes, and has a nice, slightly matte finish after it is baked.

Premo! Sculpey by Polyform Products was developed by Marie and Howard Segal of the Clay Factory of Escondido in response to a need for a polymer clay that combined the workability of Sculpey III with the strength and durability of Fimo polymer clay (see below). Premo is very easy to condition and work with, while being firm enough for creating distinct design elements. It is very strong and considerably flexible after baking.

Fimo, perhaps the best-known brand among polymer clay users, is a product of Eberhard-Faber in Germany. Its firmness makes it an excellent clay for canework because it ensures that intricate designs will remain distinct with little distortion. Fimo can be difficult to condition, which is often frustrating for beginners. Because of this a polymer clay called Fimo Soft has been developed. Like Premo! Sculpey, Fimo Soft is easily conditioned, yet strong after baking.

Cernit polymer clay, a favorite of dollmakers because of its wide range of skin tone colors, is produced by the T+F GmbH Company in Germany. It has a medium-range texture that can be described as somewhere between the softness of Sculpey III and the firmness of Fimo. It will respond quickly to the heat of your hands, and, because of this, can be overworked easily. Cernit is strong and slightly flexible after it has been cured, and has a lovely, porcelain-like quality.

Other brands of polymer clay include Modelene (made in Australia) and Du-Kit (made in New Zealand). These clays are easily workable, without being too soft, and are extremely strong when baked. Jonco (a Dutch clay) and Formello (also called Modello) are both easily worked and are slightly less fragile than Sculpey III.

You can mix together any of the brands of polymer clay to create new colors or degrees of workability. If you do this, mix them thoroughly to achieve color consistency and strength. If they're not completely mixed, there may be weak areas in the resulting clay, especially if two dissimilar clays (such as Sculpey III and Fimo) are combined.

Color

Although polymer clay is available in a wide variety of colors, sometimes the package color is not quite the right shade for your design. Fortunately, you can mix polymer clays to create nearly any color. Many people mix colors randomly, adding a pinch of this and a smidgen of that until it's just right.

When creating your own color recipes, you should know some of the basics of mixing color that apply to paint and polymer clay. To darken a color, add small amounts of black. To lighten it, add some white. From the primary colors—red, yellow, and blue—you can make all other colors. Combine yellow and blue to get green, red and blue to get purple, and yellow and red to get orange. If you mix together complementary colors (red and green, yellow and purple, or orange and blue), you'll probably end up with brown, but a small pinch of each complementary color can create a nice effect.

In an overall design, choose colors that contrast in value as well as hue. If the colors are similar in value, you can separate them with "outlines" created by thin lines of black or another dark color, especially when working with canes that will be reduced to a smaller size.

If you think you may want to repeat a color that you've blended, write down the proportions of each of the colors that you combine. To make it simple to record proportions, use any size or shape of cutter to cut equal-sized pieces from sheets of various colors that you can then cut in half, quarters, or other parts of the whole before mixing. Using cutters enables you to create combinations on a small scale before you mix a larger batch of clay. Once you've established the color that you like and recorded the proportions, you can simply increase the quantities in the same proportion to one another to make a bigger batch.

After mixing the color, roll out a small, flat piece of it, and cut out a sample piece of it with a cutter. Punch a hole in the top with a drinking straw or other tool. Bake it, and after it cools, write the recipe directly on the clay with a permanent marker to create a color chip for future reference. As chips accumulate, string them on a cord or ball chain so that you'll always be able to find a color recipe for future projects.

—From *Polymer Clay*

Continued ➜

Shaping Canes. You can reshape a cane by squeezing carefully with your fingers. For instance, turn a round bull's eye cane into a triangle by pinching the top slightly and pressing down at the same time. Flip it onto its side and repeat on ends of the other sides. Smooth the sides with your fingertips or with your brayer.

Storage

Properly stored polymer clay will last indefinitely. Store your leftover clay away from heat and direct sunlight. Cover with waxed paper or keep it in a covered container to keep out dust and dog hair. Conditioned polymer clay may require brief kneading to get it to a workable state if it's been stored a while. Old canes can usually be brought back to a workable condition with careful warming and slight pressure.

—FROM *The Michaels Book of Arts & Crafts*

POLYMER CLAY PROJECTS

Dawn Cusick & Megan Kirby, Editors

Molded Knobs

Designer: Irene Semanchuk Dean

Does your kitchen need a splash of color and originality? Personalize your cabinets and drawers with these great handmade polymer-clay knobs. And there's no end to the found objects you can use to create design motifs.

MATERIALS AND TOOLS

Wooden cabinet knobs

Heat-resistant PVA glue

Polymer clay in color of your choice, ½ ounce (15 g) for each knob

Craft knife

Pasta machine, brayer, or acrylic roller

Waxed paper

Sandpaper

1½-inch (4 cm) circle cutter

Mold made with a found object

Baking sheet or tile

Acrylic paint in color of your choice

Cyanoacrylate glue (optional)

WHAT TO DO

1. Use your fingers to coat the cabinet knob with a thin, even layer of PVA glue. Allow to dry completely.

2. Roll out a sheet of polymer clay that is long enough to wrap around the base of the knob. (The clay should not cover the top of the knob, but should be just wide enough to extent over the top edge.) Cut one end of the clay straight across with a craft knife, then press the clay end into the base of the knob.

3. Wrap the clay around base of the knob, pressing firmly against the base as you wrap. Trim the clay with a craft knife where it overlaps and smooth the seam with your fingertips. Smooth clay against the top of the knob and slightly over edge, then trim away any excess clay. Set knob aside.

4. Roll a sheet of polymer clay on a pasta machine, brayer, or acrylic roller and position on a piece of waxed paper.

5. Spray or wipe water (this serves as a mold release) onto the clay, then texture the clay sheet by pressing sandpaper into the clay until an impression is made. Use the cutter to make a circle from the clay.

6. Center the circle on top of the knob and press clay firmly in the center to adhere. (Don't worry about marring the texture, as the molded object will cover any marks.) Press the rest of the circle of clay onto the knob, then texture with the sandpaper to cover any fingerprints (see Step 5). The circle should overlap the clay that has been wrapped around the base of the knob (see Step 3).

7. Create a molded object. Center the molded object on the textured area of the knob. Press as firmly as possible without marring the surface of the molded object. Bake knob for 30 minutes at the manufacturer's recommended temperature. Allow to cool completely.

8. When knob is cool, apply acrylic paint with your fingertips, pushing the paint into every crevice. Wipe thoroughly with a paper towel to remove most of paint, leaving paint only in the recessed areas. When paint has dried, bake knob for 10 minutes at 200° F (93° C) to set paint. If the molded objects do not attach to the knob properly, secure with cyanoacrylate glue.

Designer Tip

When gluing onto baked polymer clay, always wipe the clay and the piece you're gluing to it with an alcohol-dampened paper towel or cotton ball. This will remove any oils or residue that would interfere with the glue bond.

Three-Legged Bowl

This little bowl—perfect for a ledge or small nook—is adorned with an assortment of decorations that speak to the carefree attitude of the artist.

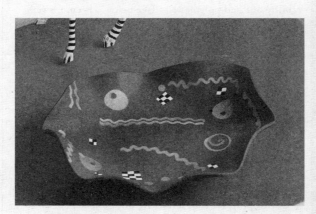

MATERIALS AND TOOLS

Polymer clay, 1 ounce (28 g) each blue and purple, ½ ounce (14 g) black, and small amounts of other contrasting colors

Pasta machine

Waxed paper

Small shape cutters (optional)

Ripple blade or handheld crinkle French fry cutter (optional)

Cane slices (optional)

Acrylic rod or brayer

Texturing material (such as plastic embroidery canvas, lace, or window screen)

Craft knife

Oven-safe bowl

Cyanoacrylate glue (optional)

WHAT TO DO

1. Create a Skinner blend from the blue and purple clay. Roll clay out, using the thickest setting on a pasta machine. Place the clay on a piece of waxed paper.

2. Create one or more Skinner blends from the other contrasting colors and roll them on a very thin setting on the pasta machine. Place these pieces on a separate piece of waxed paper.

3. From the smaller blended sheets, cut a variety of shapes and stripes, using shape cutters and the ripple blade cutter, if desired. Position these randomly over the surface of the blue/purple blended piece of clay. Add thin cane slices as well, if desired.

4. When you're happy with the design, lay a piece of waxed paper over the clay and roll gently with a rod or brayer to press the embellishments into the background clay. Flip the sheet of clay to the other side, decorate, and roll, just as you did with the first side.

5. Position the clay sheet, with the top facing down, on a piece of waxed paper. Spray or wipe water (this serves as a mold release) onto the polymer clay sheet, then position the textured material on top. Roll over the textured material to create an impression in the clay. Gently dab away excess water with a paper towel.

6. Cut a large circular shape from the clay, using a craft knife. Smooth the cut edges of the bowl gently with your fingertips. (Don't worry about cutting the shape exactly round.) Set the excess clay aside and peel off the waxed paper.

7. Turn an oven-safe bowl upside down, and center the clay bowl (textured side up) in the oven-safe bowl. Use your fingers to work with the clay bowl until the curves along the outside rim are somewhat evenly shaped. Bake for 30 minutes, following the manufacturer's instructions, then allow to cool.

8. When the clay bowl is completely cooled (but still on the oven-safe bowl), add the feet. To make the feet, roll three equal-sized balls from black polymer clay and decorate with small pieces of colored clay. Position the balls so that they are evenly spaced on the underside of the clay bowl, then press them onto the clay.

9. Lay a piece of waxed paper on the balls (now the feet of the bowl) and turn the clay bowl right side up on the work surface. If the bowl does not sit evenly, gently press down where necessary to level.

10. Turn the clay bowl back onto the oven-safe bowl, remove the waxed paper, and bake again for 20 minutes. After the bowl has cooled, the feet can be secured with cyanoacrylic glue.

Safety Note: Do not put anything edible on or inside of polymer clay.

Caneworked Beads

Designer: Irene Semanchuk Dean

The variety you get from one cane is truly amazing! Once you create your canes, you can use them in almost limitless ways. They make wonderful beads, and can be worked into different shapes and sizes.

MATERIALS AND TOOLS

Polymer clay, in colors to coordinate with your canes

Polymer clay canes

Needle tool

Steel weaving needle, knitting needle, or bamboo skewer

Polymer clay cutting blade

Shape cutters

Waxed paper

WHAT TO DO

CANE-SLICE BEADS

For sliced beads, cut thick slices (³⁄₁₆ to ⅛ inch [4.5 to 3 mm]) from your canes. Hold a slice between the finger and thumb of one hand, and insert the needle tool into the side of the slice. Press gently but firmly, rotating the needle tool in your fingers as you press it through the clay. When you see the tip of the tool appearing on the other side of the slide, withdraw the needle tool and repierce from the other side, which will ensure that the holes are neat.

SHAPED BEADS

1. To create beads of exactly the same size, roll a piece of polymer clay into a sheet. Cut numerous shapes from the sheet, and roll each into a bead in the palms of your hands. Using the same shape cut from the same sheet will result in uniformly-sized beads. By combining two or more shapes, you can also use this technique to make beads of graduated sizes.

2. Cut thin slices from your polymer clay canes and arrange them on the solid color bead shapes. Depending on your cane patterns and your desired outcome, the cane slices can overlap, or they might look better butter against each other. Roll gently in the palms of your hands to smooth the cane slices into the clay. Keep an eye on what you're doing, so you don't roll too much and distort the pattern.

3. Pierce as described in Step 1. Bake the beads on a nest of fiberfill or on wires suspended across a box or frame.

TUBE BEADS

1. Roll a sheet of polymer clay to a medium thickness on your pasta machine. Cut many slices from your canes and apply them to the surface of the clay sheet. When the sheet is covered, place a piece of waxed paper on top and gently roll over the sheet to adhere all the slices.

2. Roll the sheet though the pasta machine on a setting one notch thicker than the sheet (the cane slices have made the sheet thicker!). Set the pasta machine one notch thinner, turn the sheer 90°, and roll it through the pasta machine again, then set aside.

3. Roll a piece of scrap clay the size of a walnut in the palms of your hands. Pierce it with a long weaving needle, knitting needle, or bamboo skewer and leave the piercing tool in place. Roll this with the palm of your hand on your work surface to elongate the scrap clay. Roll slowly and gently so the hole doesn't become too enlarged. If it does, squeeze it together around the skewer. Roll until the scrap clay has formed a long tube of even thickness.

4. Cut a straight edge on your sheet of cane-decorated clay and turn the sheet right side down. Set the tube of scrap clay, still on the skewer, on the sheet of clay at the edge. Roll the sheet of clay around the pen, and trim the sheet so the edges meet but don't overlap. Roll the tube on your work surface to smooth it.

5. Fold a piece of paper into an accordion shape, place the tube in one of the folds, and bake for 30 minutes at manufacturer's recommended temperature. Alternatively, you could suspend the skewer across a box or frame.

6. When the clay has finished baking, remove the skewer from the tube of clay. Do this while the clay is still warm, but not so hot that you burn yourself. Use your cutting blade to cut the tube into bead lengths, using quick, straight, downward motions. You can allow the clay to cool completely, but it's more difficult to achieve clean, straight cuts.

Designer Tip:

Make buttons to match your jewelry! The stronger brands of polymer clay will withstand machine washing. Poke holes through the buttons for thread or use cyanoacrylate glue to attach plastic shanks to the polymer clay after baking. Turn the garment inside out and air-dry. Do not dry clean.

—FROM *The Michaels Book of Arts & Crafts*

MORE POLYMER CLAY PROJECTS

Irene Semanchuk Dean

Faux Bronze Light Switch Plate

Designer: Debbie Kreuger

This elegant light switch plate elevates the use of the rubber stamp to an art!

YOU WILL NEED

1 ounce (28 g) dark green polymer clay

½ ounce (14 g) translucent clay

Rolling pin or pasta machine

One sheet of variegated gold leaf

Plastic or metal light switch plate

Craft knife

Pencil or golf tee

Rubber stamp of your choice (bold lines are better than tiny details)

Small sponge

Sheets of 400- and 800-grit wet/dry sandpaper

Bronze acrylic paint

Paper towel

Soft cloth

1. Use the rolling pin or pasta machine to roll out the conditioned dark green clay to a ⅛-inch-thick (3 mm) sheet that measures about 4 inches (10 cm) square. Carefully press the clay onto the sheet of gold leaf before flipping it over.

2. Roll out a paper-thin sheet of the conditioned translucent clay (#6 or thinner setting on an Atlas machine). Lay the sheet on top of the gold-leafed sheet of green clay. To crackle the gold leaf, run the layered clay through the pasta machine at the thickest setting, or roll it in one direction with the rolling pin to about a ⅛-inch (3 mm) thickness. Turn the clay a quarter turn. Run it back through the pasta machine to form a ¹⁄₁₆-inch-thick (1.5 mm) sheet, or roll it to this thickness with a rolling pin turned to a position perpendicular to the original rolling direction.

3. Lay the clay on top of the light switch plate, smoothing out any air bubbles by pressing gently from the center out towards the edges. Trim away the excess clay from the edges and the switch holes with a craft knife. Use a pencil or golf tee to poke the clay out of the screw holes.

4. Dampen the rubber stamp with a wet sponge, and press the stamp into the clay. Repeat this process to emboss the surface with a pleasing pattern. Bake the plate for 30 minutes according to the clay manufacturer's instructions. After it cools, wet-sand the surface of the switch plate with 400-grit wet/dry sandpaper.

5. Dry it off thoroughly with a paper towel, and apply bronze acrylic paint to the surface with your fingers, making sure to get paint into every groove created by the rubber stamp. Wipe away the excess paint with a paper towel, and allow it to dry completely. Wet-sand the surface with 800-grit paper, then dry it off. To set the paint, bake the plate for 10 minutes at 250° F (121° C). Buff the surface with a soft cloth.

Continued ➡

Multi-Patterned Kite Magnet

Designer: Diane Villano

Use readymade canes or create your own to make into this whimsical, colorful kite that flies safely out of harm's way on your refrigerator door.

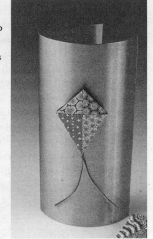

YOU WILL NEED

Photocopy of kite template (below)

1 ounce (28 g) of dark purple polymer clay

4 small canes in coordinating colors

Rolling pin or pasta machine

Waxed paper

Brayer or rolling pin

Cutting blade

Wire nippers or cutters

Eye pin

Cyanoacrylate glue

6-inch-long (15 cm) piece of ⅛-inch (3 mm) ribbon in color of your choice

Small, flat magnet

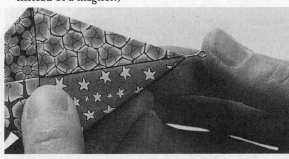

1. Use the rolling pin or pasta machine to roll out half of the purple clay out to a ¹⁄₁₆-inch (1.5 mm) thickness. Cut very thin slices from one of the canes, and place them onto the sheet of clay, covering an area the size of one triangular section of the kite template.

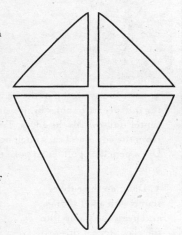

2. Place a piece of waxed paper over the cane slices, and roll over the clay with the brayer or rolling pin until the seams between the slices disappear. Lay the triangle on top of the cane-covered section, and cut around it with the cutting blade. (To create a clean clay edge, hold the blade perpendicularly as you push it down, rather than dragging it.) Repeat this process by using the other three canes and triangular sections to create the remaining sections of the kite.

3. Position the four triangles together as shown in the photo, and gently press them into place to form a kite. Bake the sections for 20 minutes

at the clay manufacturer's recommended temperature. Allow the clay to cool.

4. Roll the other half of the purple clay out to a ⅛-inch (3 mm) thickness. Lay it out on your work surface, and place the clay kite on top of it. Press the kite gently with your fingertips to adhere it to the clay. Use your cutting blade to trim around the edges of the kite, and remove the excess purple clay.

5. Use the nippers or wire cutters to cut an eye pin to a total length of ¾ inch (1.9 cm), and insert it into the clay backing at the bottom point of the kite. Bake the kite for 20 minutes according to the clay manufacturer's instructions, and allow it to cool. Remove the eye pin, apply a drop of cyanoacrylate glue to it, and reinsert it into the hole in the kite. Insert one end of the ribbon through the eye pin, and knot it close to the edge of the kite. Glue the magnet to the back of the kite. (For a variation, glue a pin back onto the kite instead of a magnet.)

Mosaic Face Clock

Designer: Irene Semanchuk Dean

This clever timepiece makes the phrase "face of the clock" take on new meaning! See you at half past an eyelash!

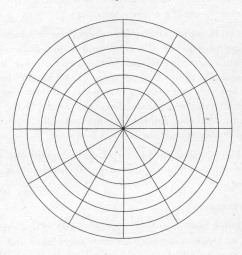

YOU WILL NEED

Photocopies of clock template and numbers template

4 ounces (112 g) of black polymer clay

4 ounces (112 g) of white polymer clay

½ ounce (14 g) gold polymer clay

Gessoed hardboard (such as Masonite), cut to 5½ inches (13.8 cm) square, with hole drilled in center to accommodate shart of clock mechanism

Small paintbrush

Heat-resistant PVA glue

Straightedge or ruler

Pencil

Scissors

Rolling pin or pasta machine

Cutting blade

Craft knife

Plain white paper

Drinking sraw

Brayer or rolling pin

Cyanoacrylate glue

Small V-shaped printmaking gouge made for cutting lineoleum block (found at art supply stores)

Sculpting tool or spoon used only for polymer clay

Small square of stiff plastic (such as a credit card)

Brayer or rolling pin

Baby wipe cloths

Masking tape

400-, 600-, and 800-grit wet/dry sandpaper

Soft buffing cloth or buffing wheel, optional

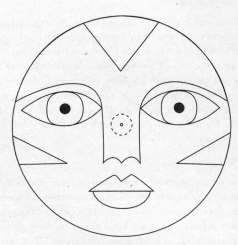

Enlarge 200%

1. Use the paintbrush or your fingertips to coat the Masonite with a light, even coat of glue, and allow it to dry overnight. Use the pencil and straightedge to draw lines that form a cross on the hardboard square. (You'll use these lines to guide you in placing the clay pieces later.) Cut out the circular clock template.

2. Use the rolling pin or pasta machine to roll out the white polymer clay to just under ⅛-inch (3 mm) thickness. The piece should measure at least 6 by 3 inches (15 x 7.5 cm). Repeat this process with the black polymer clay. Place the two sheets on your work surface. Use the straightedge and the cutting blade to trim one 6-inch-long (15 cm) side on each sheet. Butt the two sheets together on white paper. Center the circle template over the seam joining

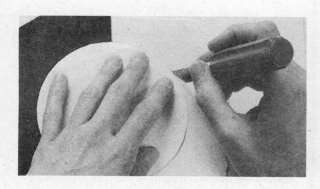

the two pieces of clay. Trace around the template with a craft knife, and mark the center of the circle on the clay. Carefully remove the outer ring of clay, and set it aside intact.

3. Cut apart the clock template along the lines dividing the parts of the face. Position the nose/forehead template on the circular piece of clay, and cut out around it with the craft knife. Remove the template, and leave the clay intact. Repeat this process with the templates for the lips, eyes, and cheek and forehead triangles.

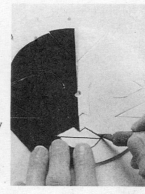

4. Peel off the pieces for the nose/forehead, lips, and cheek triangles. (To do this with minimal distortion, lift and bend the paper slightly as you do it.) Flip and reposition these pieces as shown. (Note that the forehead triangles at the very top of the face remain in the same position.) Cut out a hole in the center of the face with a drinking straw.

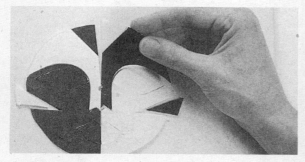

5. Remove the eyes, and position them on your work surface. With the end of your pencil, trace the irises onto the eyes, using the template as a guide. Cut each out with the craft knife, and then reverse the irises in the eye. Use the drinking straw to cut out the pupil from each eye, then swap them. Position each eye in the face.

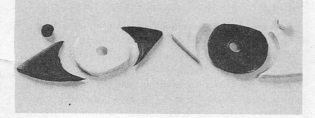

6. When all the parts of the face are in place on the paper, position the piece of Masonite beside it. Move each piece carefully onto the Masonite by bending the paper slightly and peeling it off. Use the center hole and the guidelines you drew in step one to assist in repositioning the face. Retrieve the clay that you removed in step 2, and cut it in half from side to side to form two corners of white clay and two of black clay. Frame the face with the clay by placing it

on the Masonite backing as shown. Gently smooth out any air bubbles.

7. Lay the clock number template on top of the face. Use the drinking straw to remove small circles of clay to represent each number. Reposition the circular pieces in the holes so that black is against white and white is against black. Lay a piece of clean white paper over the clock face, and use a rolling pin or brayer to gently rub over the entire face to ensure good adhesion to the Masonite and remove air bubbles. Clean away excess clay from the center hole with the craft knife so that it matches the one in the Masonite. Run your cutting blade along the edges of the Masonite to remove excess clay from the sides. Bake for 15 minutes at the clay manufacturer's recommended temperature. Allow the clay to cool.

8. Roll out a ⅛-inch-thick (3 mm) sheet of black clay, and cut two strips from it that measure 5½ inches (13.8 cm) by ⅜ inch (9 mm). Repeat this process with white clay. Place a couple of drops of cyanoacrylate glue along the edge of one of the facial quadrants, and push each segment into place to form a frame, as shown. (Note that each strip wraps around a corner.) Bake the piece again for 15 minutes. When the clock has cooled, use the V-shaped gouge to define the lines between the black and white pieces of clay. (See page 71 for tips.) To make smooth lines, hold the lino block cutter in one place on the clock, and use the other hand to carefully move it under the cutter. Brush away the bits of shaved off clay.

9. Roll the gold clay into long, 1/16-inch-wide (1.5 mm) pieces. Press these strands into the spaces between the black and white clay. Use a sculpting tool or the back of a spoon to force the gold clay into the spaces. Scrape away the excess gold clay from the surface with a small piece of stiff plastic. When you have grouted all spaces, use a baby wipe cloth to clean all excess grout from the surface. Bake the clock again for 15 minutes. Allow it to cool. Protect the exposed Masonite at the center hole with a piece of masking tape, and sand the surface with wet/dry sandpaper. (Wet the sandpaper, not

the clock.) Buff the surface if desired, and assemble the clock mechanism in the clock's hole according to the instructions.

—From *Polymer Clay*

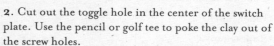

KIDS' POLYMER CLAY PROJECTS

Irene Semanchuk Dean

Makin' Faces Switch Plates

Here are some funny faces you can make without getting in any trouble.

What You Need

Polymer clay:

    1 ounce (28 g) purple

    ½ ounce (19 g) light green

    Small amounts of white, red, green, and turquoise

    Slices from a simple cane (optional)

Rolling tool

Plastic or metal light switch plate

Texturing tools

Craft knife

Pencil or golf tee

Brightly colored craft wire

What You Do

1. Roll out a thin sheet of purple clay. Lay it onto the front of the switch plate, and smooth from the center to the edges to work out any air bubbles. Add some texture to the clay if you want (photo 1). Flip the plate over, and trim the excess clay from the back.

2. Cut out the toggle hole in the center of the switch plate. Use the pencil or golf tee to poke the clay out of the screw holes.

3. Now's the fun—adding the face parts! (When decorating, make sure not to cover the holes you just cut.) Cut two almond shapes from a sheet of white clay for eyes. Place these just above the toggle hole. Flatten two small balls of turquoise clay for the irises. Use a very thin strip of purple along the top edge of the eyes for eyelids (photo 2).

4. For lips, roll two marble-sized balls of red clay into short, thick logs, about 1½ inches (4 cm) long. Taper the ends of the logs so that each lip is much wider in the middle. Roll the edge of a pencil along the center of one lip to create the indentation in the middle of the upper lip. Place the lips together as shown (photo 3), then place them onto the switch plate.

5. Coil the wire around the pencil. Slide it off, and spread the coils out by pulling on each end slightly. Cut this into three or more pieces. Straighten ½ inch (1.3 cm) of one end of each coil, and press this end into the switch plate on the upper edge (see photo 4).

6. Roll a sheet of green clay, and cut it into a lopsided rectangle for a hat (see photo 5). Place this at the top of the switch plate, covering where the wire is inserted. Decorate along the edge with the tip of the golf tee or needle tool. Trim the edges of the hat.

7. Add some hat decoration by cutting some leaf shapes from green polymer clay. Use some cane slices to represent dangling earrings, too (photo 5). Bake for 20 minutes.

Pushpinzzzzzzzzz

People are sure to buzz around your bulletin board if you make and use these bee-utiful pushpins.

What You Need

Polymer clay:

 ¼ ounce (7 g) each of fluorescent, black, and glow-in-the-dark*

Pushpin

Rubbing alcohol

Paper towel

Rolling tool

Craft knife

Polyester batting or paper towel

Amounts indicated here are for one bee.

What You Do

1. Clean one pushpin with a little bit of rubbing alcohol on a paper towel. Roll the fluorescent clay into a ¼-inch-thick (6 mm) sheet. Cut a strip from this sheet wide enough to fill in the middle area of the pushpin. Place the clay around the middle of the pin, and press it into place (photo 1). Trim with the craft knife so that the clay doesn't overlap. Set this aside.

2. Roll some thin spaghetti-sized snakes, some in the same fluorescent color you used to cover the pushpin, and some in black. Cut them into pieces about as long as your index finger.

3. Line the snakes up, alternating black and fluorescent, until you have a strip about ½ inch (1.3 cm) wide. Gently flatten them slightly with the rolling tool until they stick to each other (photo 2).

4. Trim the strip until it's as wide as the body of the pushpin. Cut one edge straight. Place it onto the body of the pushpin, and roll it so the stripes go around the body all the way without overlapping. Press the stripes in place (photo 3).

 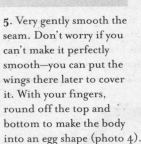

5. Very gently smooth the seam. Don't worry if you can't make it perfectly smooth—you can put the wings there later to cover it. With your fingers, round off the top and bottom to make the body into an egg shape (photo 4).

6. To finish the body, roll a piece of black clay into a ball the size of a pea. Cut it in half. Insert the point of the stinger, I mean the pin, into the flat side of one piece of the black clay, and push the clay up the pin until it touches the striped body (see photo 5). Press it to adhere, and smooth where you need to.

7. Use the other half of the pea-sized ball you made in step 6, and roll it into a ball for the head. Stick it to the body (photo 6). Use glow-in-the-dark and black clay to make eyes, a mouth, and antennae.

8. Roll two pea-sized, glow-in-the-dark teardrop shapes for the wings. Flatten them slightly, and press them onto the body. Bake the bee on a piece of polyester batting or wadded paper towel for 30 minutes. For more bees, simply use different colors of clay.

Big Fat Pen

The only thing better than a beautiful pen is a beautiful *fat* pen. If this pen is too fat for you, use a thinner sheet of clay in step 1.

What You Need

Polymer clay:

 4 ounces (113.4 g) of any color

 Your choice of a handmade or purchased cane

Pen with a white plastic or gray rubber barrel*

Rolling tool

Polymer clay cutting blade

Piece of paper

Cornstarch or talcum powder

Clear plastic pens will melt!

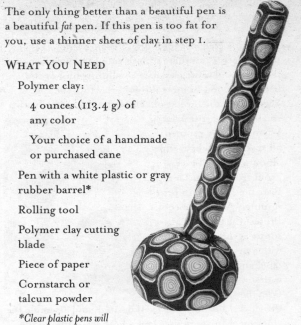

What You Do

1. Remove the ink cartridge from the pen, and set aside. Roll the clay into a thick ¼-inch (6 mm) sheet. Cut one edge straight, and place the pen barrel along

---

this edge. Cut the clay as long as the pen, leaving a little extra at the top end. Roll the sheet of clay around the pen, and trim the sheet so that it covers the pen but doesn't overlap (photo 1).

2. Pinch the top closed. Gently and slowly roll the pen on your work surface to make sure the clay is smooth and sticking to the pen really well (photo 2). If any air bubbles show up, slice them open with the cutting tool and reseal the clay.

3. Place cane slices on the pen (photo 3). When you've covered the pen, roll it again to press the slices in and even them out. Trim away any clay that has been pushed beyond the edge of the barrel on the end of the pen where you'll need to reinsert the ink cartridge later.

4. Fold a piece of paper into an accordion shape, place the pen on one of the folds, and bake for 30 minutes (photo 4).

 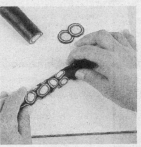

5. Roll the rest of your solid color of polymer clay into a ball for the holder. Cover it with cane slices to match the pen, and roll it in the palms of your hands until the slices are all well-adhered to the clay.

6. Press down from the top to flatten the bottom of the ball, but leave the top rounded (photo 5).

7. When the pen has cooled off, put the ink cartridge back in. Then lightly dust some cornstarch or talcum powder onto the pen tip. Decide where you want the pen to stick into the holder—at a slight angle just to the side of the center works nicely—and press the pen in at this point. Push it in as deeply as you can without going all the way through to the bottom (photo 6). Twist the pen in your fingers a bit so the hole is nice and round, but don't move it around so much that you make the hole wider than the pen.

8. Remove the pen from the holder, clean off any excess cornstarch on the pen with a paper towel, and bake the holder for 40 minutes.

Locker Mirror

Yes, yes, you're the fairest one of all. Now get to class.

WHAT YOU NEED

Polymer clay:

4 ounces (113.4 g) dark blue (depends on the size of your mirror)

Rolling tool

Small mirror (from a craft store)

Waxed paper

Talcum powder or cornstarch

Rubber stamps

Craft knife

White acrylic paint

Paper towels

Rubbing alcohol

2 to 4 strong magnets

Cyanoacrylate glue

WHAT YOU DO

1. Roll a sheet of clay that's larger than the mirror by at least an inch (2.5 cm) in every direction, and that's as thick as the mirror. Place it on a piece of waxed paper.

2. With a fingertip, lightly dust the clay with powder or cornstarch. Press the rubber stamps into the clay. Use a variety of images if you want a collage. You'll be removing the center of the clay for the mirror and trimming the outer edges, so concentrate your artistic efforts accordingly.

3. When you're finished decorating, place the mirror in the middle of the sheet. Use the craft knife to cut the clay around the mirror (photo 1). Remove the mirror and the piece of clay under it. Set the clay aside, and put the mirror in the hole you just made.

4. To create the back of the mirror frame, cover the mirror and clay frame with another piece of waxed paper, and flip the whole thing over. Remove the waxed paper.

5. Roll the extra clay into another slab as thick as the first one. Place this over the back of the mirror and frame. Press it into place, but don't distort the stamped images on the other side by pressing too hard.

6. Cover with a sheet of waxed paper, and flip the whole thing over once again. Remove the top piece of waxed paper, and use the craft knife to trim the frame to the size and shape you want (photo 2).

7. If you'd like to add some embellishments, now's the time. The frame in the photograph has some thin pieces of a striped cane just under the bottom of the mirror.

8. Peel the waxed paper from the back of the frame, and bake for 30 minutes. When the frame has cooled completely, remove the mirror by flexing the frame very gently until they separate (photo 3). Set the mirror aside.

Halloween Party Picks

Bethany Lowe

Two 1920s German lapel pins from my vintage Halloween collection were the inspiration for these party picks. Hand-sculpted paper clay heads adorn skewers and make a delightful addition to dessert or hors d'oeuvre trays.

[insert CLAY SB2-1. No caption]

MATERIALS

Acrylic paint: black, orange, red

Crepe paper: black, orange

Polymer clay

Wooden skewers

TOOLS

Craft scissors

Hot glue gun and glue sticks

Oven

Paintbrush: size 000

Ruler

INSTRUCTIONS

Shape the desired party pick head from polymer clay using your fingers. Using a wooden skewer, form the ridges, mouth shape, and eyes. The circumference of the head should be approximately 2½ inches (6.4 cm).

Cut the skewers to measure 4½ inches (11.4 cm) long. Insert one wooden skewer into the base of the sculpted head. Bake the clay pieces according to manufacturer's directions.

Allow the clay pieces to cool then paint them as desired using acrylic paints.

From both colors of crepe paper, cut one ½ x 6-inch (1.3 x 15.2 cm) strip. Cut ⅛-inch (3 mm) long strips along one 6-inch (15.2 cm) side to form a fringe.

Hot glue the uncut edge of the fringed strip to the base of the party pick head with the fringe pointing toward the head; let dry. Fold the fringe down to form the collar.

[insert CLAY SB2-2 (optional). No caption]

Baking Is Optional

The party picks can be made with paper clay. Paper clay doesn't require any baking time as it air dries, and it can be painted and embellished as desired.

—FROM *Bethany Lowe's Folk Art Halloween*

Continued ➡

9. To highlight the stamped images, rub some acrylic paint into the clay with your finger. Make sure to push it into all the indentations you made with the stamps (photo 4). As soon as you rub the paint on, immediately wipe it off with a paper towel. You can add more paint if you need to or remove some more with a damp paper towel (photo 5).

10. Wipe the back of the mirror and frame with a bit of rubbing alcohol on a paper towel or cotton ball. Also wipe out the recess where the mirror will be glued in. The alcohol removes any oils that might keep the glue from doing its thing. Glue the mirror into place, and then glue the magnets onto the back. Use at least two magnets.

Flower Power Vase

The flowers on the outside of this vase will stick around a lot longer than the ones inside.

What You Need

Polymer clay:

   1 ounce (28 g) each of 2 shades of green

   1 ounce (28 g) each of 2 shades of blue

   ½ ounce (14 g) yellow

Clean glass vase of jar

Polymer clay cutting blade

Gold tee

Toothpick

What You Do

1. Roll the green clays into two long snakes, not quite as thick around as your pinky. Press down along one side of each green snake to create a teardrop shape (photo 1).

2. Use the cutting blade to cut a bajillion slices from these snakes. Okay, not a bajillion, but a lot. Each slice is a leaf, so of course the more leaves you want, the more slices you need. If the clay starts to squish too much to one side, flip over the snakes and cut from the other side.

3. Place a clay leaf on the lower portion of the vase. If you touch a clay leaf with your fingertip, it will stick to your finger. Then you can place it on the vase and kind of roll your finger off, the leaf should stick to the glass (photo 2).

4. Repeat step 3 a bajillion times. (That's one for each leaf). Place each leaf on the glass, pointing upward or slightly to one side. Make sure each leaf is touching other leaves, but also make sure to leave some blank spaces between the leaves for the flowers (photo 3).

5. Cover the lower part of the vase with leaves, mixing the different shades of green randomly. Your fingerprints add interesting texture to the leaves, and you can poke some of them a little with the end of the golf tee to add detail. Set the leafy vase aside.

6. Now for the flowers. Roll the blue clays into snakes thinner than your pinky. Each round slice from these snakes will be a flower petal. The flowers on the vase in the photo each have five petals, but you can make yours with three, four, six—whatever you want.

7. Slice a whole lotta slices from the blue snakes. Pick up a slice with your finger and set it onto the vase where there's a blank spot but where the petal will touch a leaf or two. Release the petal onto the vase. Use the golf tee to make an indentation in the petal, near the center of the flower. Apply all the petals for the flower, and then continue making blue flowers all over the vase (photo 4).

8. Roll the yellow clay into a skinny snake, and cut one slice for each flower. Pick up each slice with the toothpick, and set it into the dent in the center of each flower. Poke the toothpick into the yellow clay in several places to give it some texture and to make sure that the centers are stuck to the flowers (photo 5).

9. When you've created a floral masterpiece, set the vase in a cold oven and bring the temperature up to the temperature recommended for that brand of clay. Bake for 30 to 40 minutes.

—From *Kids' Crafts—Polymer Clay*

TEXTURED POLYMER CLAY BEADS

Grant Diffendaffer

Using Texture Plates

I could write a whole book on texture plates, which you can use to texture your beads by rolling the beads across them, pressing the beads between them, or stretching them to conform to a mold. A texture plate can be used either to create replicas of one texture, or as a basis to improvise on variations of a texture. It can be used with mica clays to create a "ghost image," or the illusion of texture where there is only a smooth surface. You can produce a whole range of effects from using just one texture sheet on a mokume gane sheet or block of clay. Using recursive molding, you can transform a texture into a vast array of fascinating three-dimensional forms.

There are numerous types of texture plates, each with their own special characteristics and unique ways of affecting the clay. While most texture sheets serve multiple purposes, nothing beats the right texture sheet for the job.

Polymer Clay Texture Plates

The simplest way to create a texture plate is with polymer clay itself. Such a plate is suitable for making ghost images but will not provide the precise, even impression necessary for a perfectly smooth, uniformly high-contrast ghost image with fine detail. Impressions can, however, be made very deep, resulting in bold contrasts in the ghost image. They can be used for mokume gane, as the foundation of the patterning process in the Textured Beads section. The beauty of these plates is that they are low-tech, easy to make, and immediately gratifying. They can be sculpted and embellished in detail. Beginning with a photopolymer plate, rubber stamp, or other commercial texture sheet, while not necessary, will allow you to quickly build a library of patterns.

To make a texture plate, you need a 10-inch (25 cm) sheet of scrap clay; texture plates; rubber stamps, etc. (optional); small objects to press into the clay such as a ball stylus, twine, string, and straws; and a linoleum carving tool.

Step by Step

1. Condition scrap clay and roll out a sheet on your thickest pasta machine setting. Double it over to form a sheet approximately 5 x 5 inches (13 cm square).

Photo A

2. Use your favorite texture implements to pattern approximately half the sheet. Try starting with a photopolymer plate, rubber stamp, or commercial texture sheet, and then embellish the texture with your ball stylus, pieces of twine that you impress into the surface to create curving lines, straw ends for tiny ring shapes, and other objects (photo A). You can also cut small holes with clay cutters that will make bold impressions

?Image 6-1a? Photo B

excellent for ghost imaging. And you can use the clay cutters to make impressions in the texture sheet. Creating stripes of texture across the texture sheet will make patterns wrap around the bead in bands. Leave spaces that you can come back to and carve with your linoleum tool after you cure the sheet (photo B).

3. Cure the sheet per the clay manufacturer's instructions.

Photo C

4. Using your linoleum-carving tool (I like the small V-gouge), carve your texture sheet until it is densely textured (photo C).

Photopolymer Texture Plates

Photopolymer texture plates allow you to efficiently turn a two-dimensional drawing, computer graphic, or photo into three-dimensional polymer art. These plates can be both relatively deep and precisely detailed—an excellent combination for ghost imaging, mokume gane, and texturing applications. Because they are clear, you can see when you have made an effective impression. They are an excellent foundation for making a number of different texture sheets.

Although I usually prefer to make them myself because it is less expensive and I have full control of the process, it can be messy and frustrating. It takes some experimentation to get the exposure correct and the exposure unit

requires special training to build and operate. If you want to use texture plates to make beads, you will probably want to have a rubber stamp or flexographic plate maker make the actual photopolymer plates from artwork that you have created. (Photopolymer resin suppliers are good sources for plate makers.)

So you understand the entire process, photopolymer is an ultraviolet light-sensitive liquid resin, with a consistency of honey. During manufacture, the resin is sandwiched between sheets of glass, with a "negative" image on a transparency, and exposed to UV light. Where the light passes through the transparent areas of the image (the negative space), the resin hardens. Where blocked by the ink of the image, the resin stays liquid. After washing away the liquid resin, you are left with a plate bearing a three-dimensional relief of the original image. The resulting product can serve as a texture sheet, a flexographic printing plate, or a rubber stamp. So while you may choose to turn to a professional to create the actual plate, you can exercise your creativity when creating the design for the plates.

Preparing the Artwork

Your design must be composed entirely of black-and-white elements (no gray). The black elements become the etched-away portion of the texture plate, yielding raised elements in the clay. This surface texture is cut away to reveal a ghost image in mica clay. The white elements print clear on the transparency and harden into ridges on the plate, which in turn yield impressions in the clay.

The wider the mark on the transparency, the deeper the impression on the plate. Deeper impressions translate to bolder and more impressive ghost-image effects as well as the potential for more dramatic texturing applications.

Fine black line elements make shallow impressions on the plate, translating into shallow impressions in clay, which aren't much use for ghost imaging, mokume gane, or texturing applications, but which may work well for inking and other printing techniques. Creating a design with thin elements of negative space, or "white," in a sea of ink can lead to the washing away of the delicate exposed pieces with the still-liquid resin. Designs with many fine elements are generally more successful with a thinner and more shallowly etched stamp.

Despite not being able to complete the entire process yourself, it is an almost magical way to transform your own complex line art into three dimensions. There is nothing better I you want to make a detailed ghost image with high contrast and a perfectly smooth surface. It is also an excellent starting point for creating the polymer clay texture sheets described earlier.

Flexible Texture Sheets

Flexible texture sheets can be bent and stretched to follow the contours of a curved bead, or even to create the contours of a curved bead....

Room-temperature vulcanizing silicone, or "RTV silicone" is a two-part mold-making material which comes in both liquid and putty forms. Putty is easier to work with, and once mixed, it is pressed around an object to create a mold, or into another texture sheet (such as photopolymer or polymer clay) to create a flexible texture sheet. The putty sets in just a few minutes. These sheets are great for rolling textures onto beads with curved profiles, such as those turned on a lathe. RTV silicone is available from jewelry and sculpture supply shops.

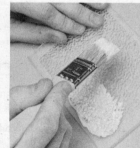
Photo D

Liquid latex rubber, available from art and sculpture supply shops, makes flexible, strong texture sheets ideal for recursive mold-making techniques. To create sheets,

paint latex on a textured surface, such as a texture plate, and allow it to dry (photo D). Then add another coat. It takes several coats to make a thick-enough sheet with suitable strength. Latex takes longer to set up than RTV—approximately 48 hours. Because it is not as dense, latex creates sheets that won't make impressions as crisp or as deep as RTV. They are, however, very stretchy and can conform closely to complex surfaces.

Creating Tube Beads

I make a big batch of plain tube beads at once, as a core for all my textured and many of my lathe-turned beads. This process can be varied to create tube beads with a beauty all their own. Try playing with colors. Try layering them with canes, swirling different colors together, using translucent clays, foils, or other inclusions.

Step by Step

1. Condition and roll out a sheet of clay on the thickest setting of your pasta machine. The sheet should be as wide as your machine and about 8 to 12 inches (20 to 31 cm) long. The core will be covered with clay later but may be exposed again in the process, so use a color that will match your finished bead. This process will make a lot of tube beads. (There is no such thing as too many, and they are much easier to make in bulk!)

2. Trim one end so that you have a straight edge.

3. Lay a 12-inch (31 cm) steel mandrel (⅛-inch, or 3 mm, mild steel welding rod) across the end of the sheet, pinching up the leading edge to wrap it around the mandrel.

4. Roll the clay and mandrel forward, wrapping the whole sheet of clay around the mandrel (photo E). Take care not to trap any air bubbles as you roll. Trim off the outer end of the sheet at the point where the sheet began in the middle. This helps you roll tube beads of even thickness.

Photo E

5. Roll the tube back and forth, applying even pressure from all sides, and gently pulling as you roll from the middle to the ends to stretch the tube to the length of the mandrel. You can also grasp the tube with your fingertips and pull and twist it back and forth. Do not push down on the ends of the mandrel as you roll, as this will widen the hole through the bead (photo F).

6. When the tube reaches the length of the mandrel, cut it in half around the middle. Remove half of the tube to roll later. Continue rolling the tube and repeating the process until you have a tube about ⅜ inch (1 cm) thick (photo G). Roll the tube with a piece of 36-grit sandpaper to texture the raw clay. This allows the clay to adhere to the surface when you later turn the bead into its finished form. Leaving the final tube on the mandrel, cut it into individual bead lengths (approx 1¼ inches, or 3 cm). The length of the core tube bead will determine the length of your finished bead.

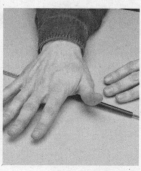
Photo F

Photo G

7. Cure the tubes on the mandrel in the oven, per the clay manufacturer's instructions.

8. Remove the tubes from the mandrels while they are still warm (photo H).

Photo H

Adhering Beads to Mandrels

I have tried many different ways of adhering beads to mandrels, which must be done to turn a bead with a mandrel on the lathe. The best way I have found is to essentially create a friction fit with the mandrel, by spraying the mandrel with a rubberizing solution designed to create a coating on tool handles.

Step by Step

1. Spray an even coat over 3 to 4 inches (8 to 10 cm) in the middle of your mandrels.

2. After it dries, spray another coat, focusing more toward the middle of the mandrel.

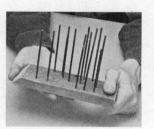
Photo I

3. Repeat this process once or twice more for as many times as necessary to achieve a friction bond with your bead) (photo I). After the rubber has dried, slide your bead into the middle of the mandrel. You may have to push on the bead with the end of the mandrel braced against another surface, such as your work surface. Be careful not to bend the mandrel as you push the bead on (photo J). Your bead

Photo J

Continued ➡

should fit snugly enough that it won't spin on the mandrel when you turn it on the lathe, yet not so snugly that you have to struggle to get it on the mandrel.

Finishing Techniques

After you've created your beads, there is still finishing work to be done.

Sanding Beads by Hand

I use wet/dry sandpaper in the following grits: 220, 320, 400, 600, 800, 1000, 1200, and 1500. If you can't find these at your local hardware store, try an auto paint shop or jewelry supply store.

If you need to do a lot of shaping, you may want to start with a lapidary belt sander, a rasp, or drywall screen. If you only need to put a polish on a relatively refined surface, start with 400-grit sandpaper.

There are several effective ways to sand a bead by hand. To sand perfectly flat surfaces, place your sandpaper on a smooth work surface and move your bead against it (photo A). To sand curves, try placing a ½-inch-thick (1 cm) (or thicker) sponge under your sandpaper (photo B). Also try holding your bead in your dominant hand and cut the sandpaper in the other. Sand the bead by moving it against the curved sandpaper surface (photo C).

For more delicate work, you may want to brace your bead against the table with one hand and use a small piece of sandpaper in your other hand (photo D). However you sand the bead, rinse it frequently in a bucket of water to remove buildup. Rinse your sandpaper regularly.

Photo A

Photo C

Photo B

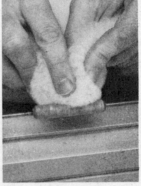

Photo D

Finishing Beads on a Lathe

Using a lathe is a speedy way to give lathe-turned or textured beads a perfect finish. If your beads are rough, or require a lot of shaping, you may start with 80-grit (and then 120-grit) drywall screen. From there, move on to 220-grit wet/dry sandpaper. Holding a 2 x 2-inch (5 cm square) piece of sandpaper in your hand, press it gently against the turning bead (photo E). Wet the sandpaper and rinse it frequently to prevent buildup. You can also use a toothbrush or a sponge. Move through successive grits, as high as you like. Don't skip grits, and be sure to thoroughly sand the bead with each grit to remove scratches from the previous one. You can stop as early as 600 grit, or go as high as 1500 for a glossier finish.

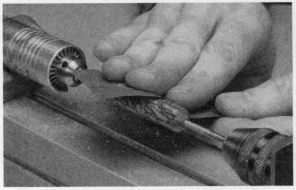

Photo E

Tumbling Beads

Beads can also be finished by using a vibratory tumbler. This update on the old-fashioned rock tumbler is used by rockhounds and jewelers alike, and can quickly put a nice shine on your beads. Vibratory tumblers are especially effective at polishing irregular surfaces. I have had success using plastic pellets as a tumbling media with successive tumbles of 220-, 400-, and 600-grit powders. Try experimenting with different tumbling media. You will find more information on media where you buy your tumbler.

Buffing

Always finish your sanded beads by washing them with a little dish detergent and water, and drying and buffing them. Buffing removes any dust or other coatings remaining after sanding and gives your beads a beautiful luster. You can give them a soft sheen by buffing them on your jeans, or on a soft cloth. For more shine, try using a piece of lamb's wool while they are turning on the lathe (photo F). Take care with buffing wheels. Muslin wheels can easily "burn" the surface of a polymer bead, requiring you to sand it again. Use unsown wheels on lower speeds. I use a lamb's-wool wheel that I bought at an auto paint store and mounted on a drill press.

Photo F

Drilling and Piercing

Part of the beauty of polymer clay is that you can do much of the finishing in the raw state. Drilling the cured clay can be more precise, but it can stress the clay. If you can pierce your raw bead without damaging the surface and shape, then do it, as it will make a stronger hole. In some instances, you will build around a bead mandrel, thus eliminating the need to drill at all. Whether you pierce the raw clay with toothpicks, skewers, metal pins, or mandrels; or drill it cured, start with a small tool for each, creating a hole from each side and having them meet them in the middle. Increase tool size gradually until the hole is the size you need (photo G).

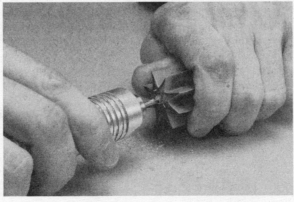

Photo G

The strength of the hole varies depending on how you string the bead. Thicker, softer, and more flexible cord puts fewer demands on the hole. Thin stringing material with great tensile strength is more likely to cut into the edge of the bead hole. The strongest holes are formed when the clay is raw and the surface outside the hole is approximately perpendicular (at a 90° angle) to the hole for about ⅛ inch (3 mm) before it curves back towards the other end of the bead. Avoid tapering away from the edge of the hole at more than a 45° angle.

> ### TIPS FOR FINISHING
>
> - Dry off your bead between sandings. You won't see any scratches or other surface details when the bead is wet. Learn what the surface looks like after being properly sanded with each grit. This is important to minimize the time resanding with lower grits to remove scratches.
>
> - Use only wet/dry sandpaper from one manufacturer.
>
> - Used sandpaper essentially acts at a higher grit than it did when it was new.
>
> - Wear a dust mask when you use drywall screen, especially on the lathe. Ventilate your work area and clean up dust after work.

Textured Tube Beads

To create the first set of beads. I put a cured core bead on a mandrel and covered it with a thin layer of raw clay. This allowed me to roll the bead across the texture sheet without distorting the form or touching the raw clay with my hands. The result was a slender tube bead with lush, interlocking texture.

TOOLS & MATERIALS

Tube beads

Use these as bead cores. I assume you know all about these.

Polymer clay in your choice of color

I prefer pearlized clays because of the mica-shift effect. Choose one color for the raised portions of the bead and one color for the impressed texture. It takes just a little bit of each to make a bead.

¹/₁₆-inch (3 mm) bead mandrels

Polymer clay or RTV silicone texture sheets

Ideal texture sheets will be densely patterned with textures about ¹/₁₆ inch (2 mm) deep.

Spray bottle of water

Dome molds for shaping the ends of the beadsd (see below).

Wet/dry sandpaper in the following grits: 220, 320, 400, 600, 800, 1000, and 1200.

Before You Begin

To make a dome mold, find a domed shape slightly larger than the end of your bead. Try pressing the end of a tool handle, a marble, or a dapping tool into a small lump of clay and poke a hole through the middle of the impression with a ¹⁄₈-inch (3 mm) mandrel. Wiggle the mandrel a bit to stretch the hole. (If you skip this last step, the hole will shrink in the oven and your mandrel will no longer fit through.) Create two end molds (photo A) and cure them in the oven.

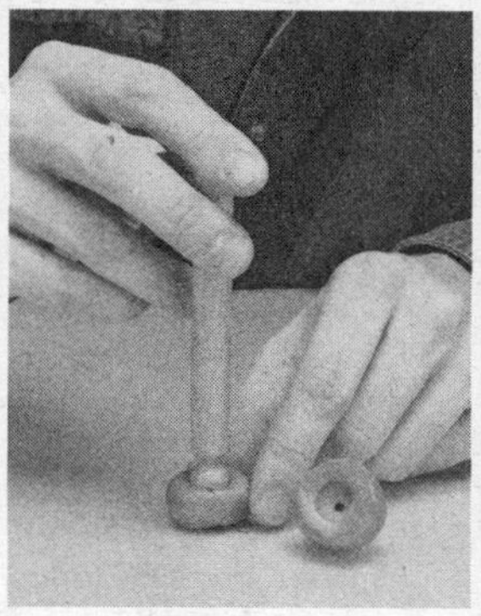

Photo A

Step by Step

1. Center a tube bead on a 6-inch (15 cm) mandrel. The bead should be about ¼ to ⅜ inch (6 to 10 mm) in diameter. If you didn't texturize the bead before baking, scrape it up with some low-grit sandpaper.

2. Decide on the color for your finished bead, and smear a thin layer of clay into the sandpapered texture on the bead to ensure that the clay will stick (photo B).

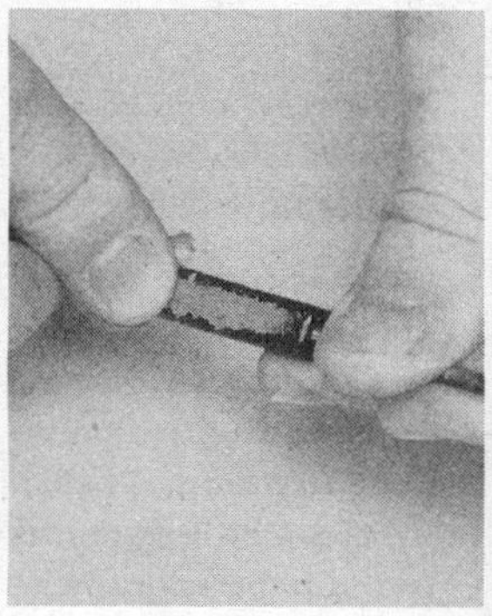

Photo B

3. Layer the core with enough clay to fill the texture on your texture sheet, but not so much that the bead shape is greatly distorted when you roll it. This works out to a medium setting on my machine.

4. Prepare the clay to cover the bead with. Choose a color for the raised portions of the texture and roll out a 3-inch (8 cm) sheet on your thickest pasta-machine setting. Roll out a 3-inch (8 cm) sheet of the other color on your thinnest setting. Layer these two sheets together and run them through on a medium setting (photo C).

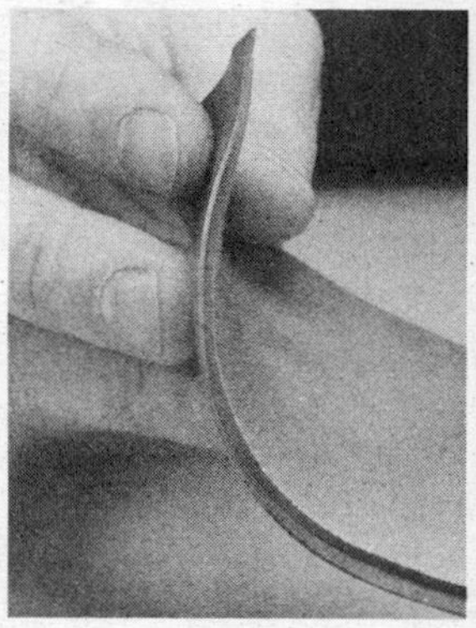

Photo C

5. Cut a strip of the layered clay about ¹⁄₈ inch (3 mm) longer than the core bead, and lay it on your work surface, thin layer down. Lay the bead across it so that it overlaps by ¹⁄₁₆ inch (2 mm) on each end. Wrap the clay once around the core bead, and trim it where it overlaps (photo D). Butt the ends together and try to hide the bottom layer of clay at the seams by making a clean joint. Roll the bead on your work surface, pressing the clay with your fingers to seal the seam and make the clay adhere to the core bead. Wrap the clay around the ends to cover the core up to the mandrel (photo E). Use a needle tool to pop any air bubbles.

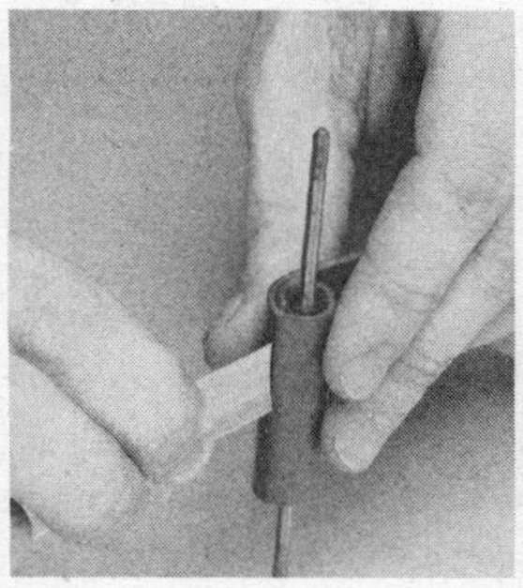

Photo D

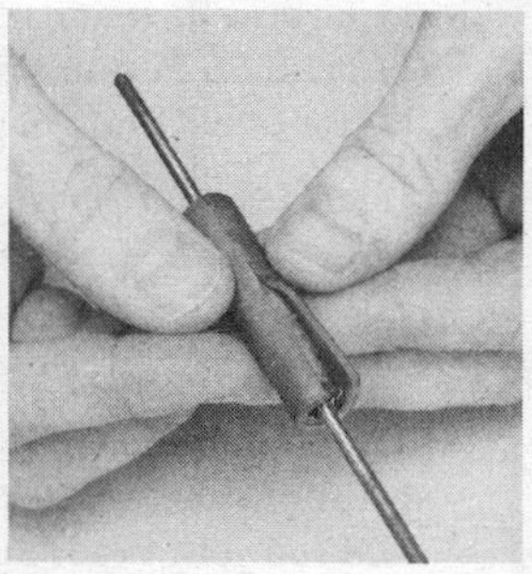

Photo E

6. Thoroughly spray the texture sheet with water to act as a release. (RTV silicone sheets will not require any release.) **Note**: Some clays become gummy as they come into contact with water. If you have this problem, use cornstarch as a release. Take care to keep the cornstarch out of your raw clay supply, as it will weaken it.

7. Place the bead on the texture sheet and gently but firmly press on the mandrel to impart texture to the bead. Lightly rocking the bead from one end to the other will help ensure that it is fully and deeply textured (photo F).

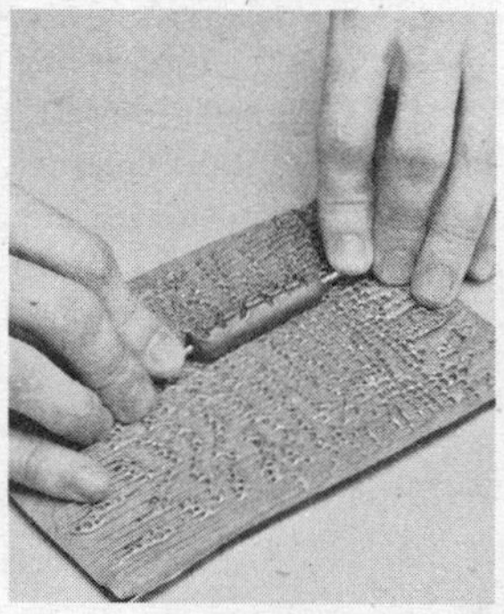

Photo F

8. Release pressure and roll the bead slightly forward without lifting it from the texture sheet. Repeat the pressing process. Continue until the whole bead is textured, overlapping the texture slightly at the end.

9. Spray the domed end molds with water and slide them onto the ends of your bead mandrel, pressing the bead between them (photo G).

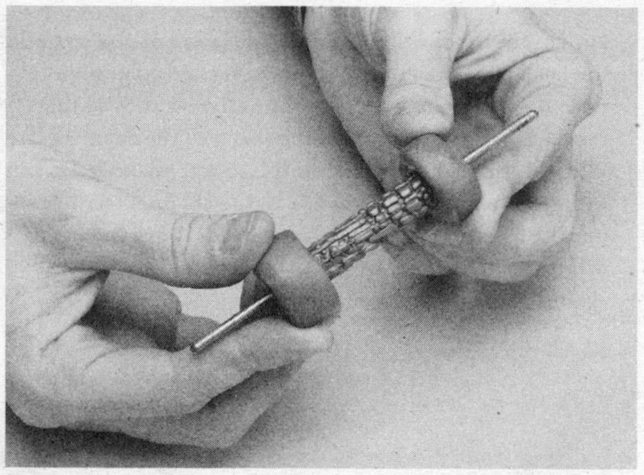

Photo G

10. Use your ball stylus, sandpaper, or needle tool to further sculpt and texture your bead. This is a great way to quickly and easily add variation to beads.

11. Bake the bead to the clay manufacturer's recommended specifications.

12. Sand and buff to finish. If you are sanding by hand, I suggest starting with 400-grit. If sanding on a lathe, begin with 220. (The lathe is efficient at getting out the scratches from the lower grits, which can be difficult to do my hand.) Sand with the initial grit until the second layer of clay is revealed and the bead is shaped to your satisfaction.

Variations

A simpler version of this bead: Create contrast between the raised and etched portions of the design by antiquing the bead with acrylic paint. Cover the bead with paint and wipe off the excess, leaving paint in the crevices and highlighting the texture. It is easier to control the contrast of the paint with the clay than with clay alone. You may enjoy applying several layers of paints for varied effects. The disadvantages to the acrylic paint method are the extra steps to finish the bead, the mess, and the fact that the color is not an integral part of the bead.

To antique a bead, coat the whole bead with acrylic paint in a contrasting color. Wipe off the excess with a paper towel. Bake the bead again at 250°F (121°C) for 20 minutes to dry and bond the paint.

Textured Discs and Spheres

Textured discs and spheres take the texturing process to the next level—essentially the same process as the tube beads, but rather than layering raw clay over a baked tube, you layer it over a rounded form. You'll need to make a curved texture plate, or texture channel. This is a bit tricky and time-consuming, but the rewards are well worth it.

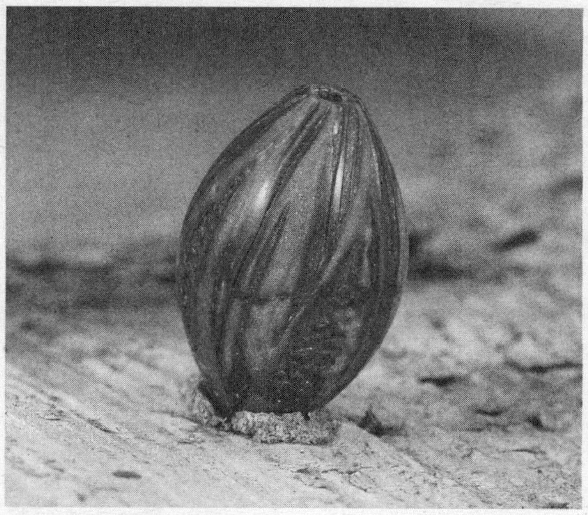

Tools & Materials

Tube beads

¹⁄₈ (3 mm) bead mandrels

8-inch (20 cm) sheet of scrap clay

Use this to create a texture channel.

Texture tools, such as ball stylus and sharp pebbles

Spray bottle of water

Polymer clay in your choice of color

I prefer pearlized clays for their mica-shift effect.

A wooden dowel, 8 inches (20 cm) long and ¼ inch to 1 inch (1 to 3 cm) in diameter

The larger the dowel, the larger the bead.

Wet/dry sandpaper in the following grits: 220, 320, 400, 600, 800, 1000, and 1200

Step by Step

1. To create the texture channel, condition your scrap clay so that it is soft—the softer, the better.

2. Roll your cheet of scrap clay into a tube.

3. Lay your dowel lengthwise on top of the tube of clay (photo A).

4. Press down on the dowel so that it sinks into the clay halfway up the diameter of the dowel. So not press more than halfway because you will be texturing the sides of the channel, which will in turn be used to texture your bead (photo B).

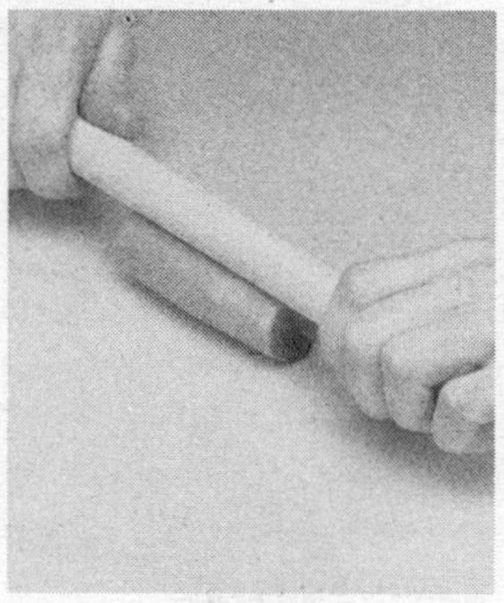

Photo A

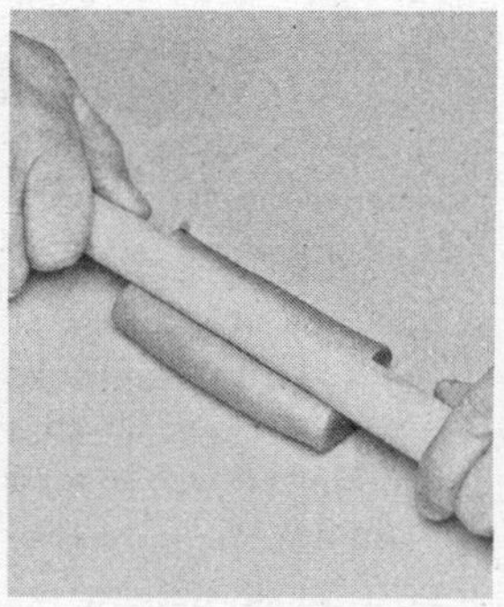

Photo B

Continued ➜

5. The height of the clay will vary somewhat along the length of the dowel. Using a board, hardback book, or a similarly rigid, flat surface, press the clay to create an even surface (photo C).

6. Remove the dowel. You should have a smooth channel with walls of equal height on each side (photo D).

Photo C   Photo D

7. Texture the channel with your texture tools. Press straight down toward your work surface. Make the texture densely detailed. Spending time on your texture channel will really pay off (photo E).

8. Cure the channel in the oven to the clay manufacturer's specifications.

9. To create a core bead, build up layers of raw clay on a cured tube bead, until the bead fits the channel. Using a tissue blade, cut the tube bead short enough so that when you put it on a mandrel and lay the mandrel across the channel, the bead fits entirely inside the channel. The length of the tube bead will vary depending on the width of the channel and the thickness of the original bead (photo F).

Photo E

10. If you didn't texturize your tube bead before baking, scrape it up with low-grit sandpaper.

11. Smear the tube bead with a thin layer of raw clay, as an adhesive for the next layer of clay (photo G).

12. Build up a core bead that perfectly fits the channel by rolling a sheet of clay (the color of your finished bead) on your thickest setting.

13. Cut a strip of clay about 1/8 inch (3 mm) wider than your tube bead and long enough to wrap around it.

14. Lay your bead on the strip of clay so the clay overlaps by about 1/16 inch (2 mm) on either end of the bead (photo H).

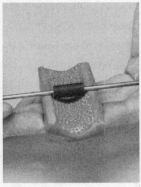

Photo F

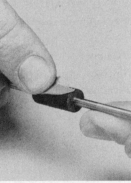

Photo G

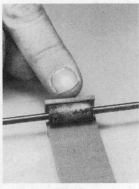

Photo H

15. Wrap the clay around the bead once and trim off the excess. Press the clay onto the bead.

16. Roll the bead against your work surface, pressing it with your fingers so that the raw clay adheres securely to the core bead.

17. Spray the texture channel with water.

18. Place the bead in the texture channel. For a small bead (a quarter-dowel), the raw clay should make contact with the channel. For larger beads, the raw clay should connect with the channel at least on the ends of the bead. Roll the bead gently back and forth to shape the raw clay to the channel (photo I).

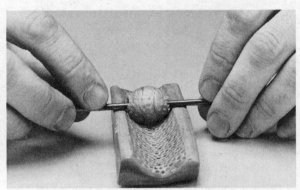

Photo I

19. Larger beads will need multiple layers of clay to build the bead to sufficient size. Cut the second strip slightly narrower, and succeeding strips narrower still, so that the core bead approximates the shape of the channel. When there is enough clay on the core to make contact with the channel, roll it gently in the channel to round out the bead. With the ideal core bead, the mandrel will rest on the edges of the channel with the core bead against the inner surface (photo J).

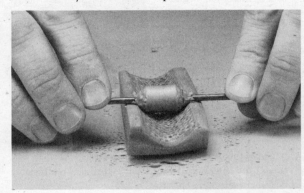

Photo J

20. Roll your core bead the length of the channel. Any low spots on the bead won't make contact with the channel. Add more clay to the bead in these spots.

21. Cure your bead in the oven, per the clay manufacturer's instructions.

22. After the bead is cured, rough it up with low-grit sandpaper.

23. Smear the surface of the bead with a thin layer of clay.

24. Prepare the clay to cover the bead. Choose a color for the raised portions of the texture, and roll out a 3-inch (8 mm) sheet on your thickest pasta-machine setting. Roll out a 3-inch (8 cm) sheet of the other color on your thinnest pasta machine setting. Layer these two sheets together and run them through your pasta machine on a medium setting. You may need to experiment. If the clay is too thick, your bead will distort and you will not get a deep impression. IF it is too thin, you will not get a deep impression either.

25. Cover the bead with the layered clay, applying the thick layer against the bead and the thin layer on top. Use a circle cutter to cut a circle large enough to cover half the bead, pierce it with the mandrel, slide it on, and

wrap it over the bead. Do the same on the other side of the bead, and make the seam match up as well as possible to hide the bottom layer of clay. Press the clay firmly into place and pop any air bubbles with a needle tool (photo K).

26. Spray the texture channel thoroughly with water.

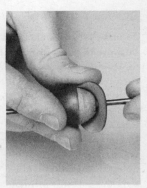

Photo K

27. Place the bead in the channel and press down firmly on the mandrel, rocking it lightly from side to side (photo L).

28. Lift up slightly on the mandrel and roll the bead lightly along the channel (photo M).

29. Press down firmly again and repeat the rocking motion.

30. Repeat steps 28 and 29 until the whole bead is textured.

31. If desired, embellish the bead using your texture tools. I find the ends of the beads often need some attention. A ball stylus can be used to make round impressions in a sculptural fashion. Sometimes I texture the ends lightly with sandpaper.

32. Finish the ends of the bead by pressing the clay into place with a rubber clay shaper (photo N).

33. Cure the bead for 30 minutes, at the manufacturer's recommended temperature.

34. Sand and buff to finish. If you are sanding by hand, start with the 400-grit. On a lathe, begin with the 220-grit. The lathe is efficient at getting out scratches from the lower grits, which can be very

Photo L

Photo M

Photo N

difficult to do by hand. Sand with the initial grit until the top layer of clay has been removed from the high points of texture. Continue sanding as much as you like, to shape the bead.

Variations

As with the tube bead, you can choose to antique this bead for contrast rather than using two contrasting colors of clay.

- For larger texture channels, try wrapping the dowel with twine or string when you make the original impression in your scrap clay (see step 4). This will create raised lines on your beads.

- If you leave untextured space when you bake your texture channel, you can carve it with a linoleum-carving tool later. I use a small V-gouge. Carving works better with larger channels.

- Try using flexible RTV silicone texture sheets with a blank channel. Place the texture sheet in the channel and roll your beads on it. One channel will yield a variety of textures.

- To bring in more color, try back-filling. Make impressions with your stylus (or other tool) in the raw clay of your bead. Cure it and then fill these impressions with colored clay.

—From *Polymer Clay Beads*

Play Clay Box

Nicole Steiman

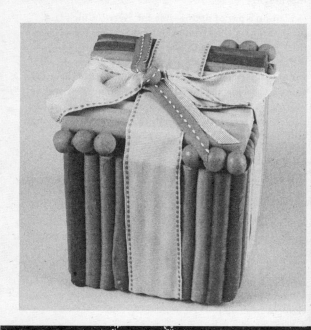

MATERIALS

Modeling clay: blue, pink (1 strip each)

Modeling clay: 5" (12.5 cm) square (5)

Plastic box: 5" (12.5 cm) square

Ribbon: ¼" blue, pink (5" [12.5 cm]), 2" green (24" [61 cm])

Scissors

INSTRUCTIONS

1. Place one square of modeling clay on each side of box, and one square on top. **Note:** Modeling clay is usually purchased in multicolor blocks as shown in this project. If you prefer a different color combination, simply purchase individual colors and form coils to fit your box.

2. Tie green ribbon around box on all four sides; knot ribbon at top. Trim ends at an angle.

3. Tie blue and pink ribbons around knot of green ribbon. Trim ends at an angle.

4. Roll small balls of pink and blue clay. Place along top edge of box on opposite sides; press in place to secure.

5. Roll two long coils of pink and blue clay. Twist two colors together. Place along top edge opposite clay balls.

—From *Make It in Minutes: Quick & Clever Gift Wraps*

BREAD DOUGH

Dawn Cusick & Megan Kirby, Editors

Dough craft is an ancient domestic art. On record since the beginnings of Western civilization, bread dough ornaments and devotional tributes decorate households around the world. Wherever there is grain and salt, people have used their hands and hearths to create fairy-tale figures, religious subjects, and seasonal symbols. Crafting with bread dough (or "saltdough")—flour, salt, and water—provides both handsome ornaments and the joy of participating in a craft has lasted for generations.

Materials and Tools

Flour

Choose all-purpose flour, not self-rising. Best results are obtained with flour that requires as little water as possible to make a strong, flexible dough.

Salt

A fine-textured salt blends well and forms the smoothest surface. Many experts recommend noniodized, non-flouridated table salt.

Additives and Enhancements

Wallpaper paste can increase salt dough firmness, and is important if you plan to air dry your pieces. Cornstarch or a small amount of vegetable oil or glycerin can improve flexibility.

Tools and Crafting Supplies

Scissors, modeling tools, paintbrushes, polyurethane varnish, a plastic ruler, paper clips, floral wire, wire cutters, pliers, household glue, and a pocket comb are all helpful.

Kitchen Supplies

Your kitchen probably already contains many of the supplies you'll need: mixing bowls, measuring cups, a container for clear water, cookie sheets, cooking oil, cake decorating tips, cookie or biscuit cutters, a small sieve or strainer, small knife, rolling pin, a cheese grater with several options for fineness, a garlic press, a potato ricer, and table forks. Aluminum foil, drinking straws, black peppercorns, cloves, and toothpicks are also helpful.

Optional Inspirations

Dried flowers, nuts and seeds, shells, pebbles, glass forms, ribbons, raffia, and moss are just a few possibilities.

Basic Techniques

Salt dough behaves best in a cool room, i.e., 70° F (21° C), or below. Rinse your hands with cool water frequently to prevent over-warming of the dough. Keep dough covered when you are not using it.

Preparing the Dough

Salt dough must be kneaded until it is perfectly smooth and flexible. A sturdy hand mixer, or a food processor fitted with a dough attachment saves time and effort. Be sure not to overheat your equipment with large batches.

Try to make only as much dough as you can work with at one time; fresh dough handles easily and stays moist longer. If you want to store it, however, seal out air and keep it in a cool place (not the refrigerator).

Recipes

Basic proportions for your dough:

4 cups (500 g) all-purpose flour

1 cup (273 g) salt

1½ cups (355 ml) water

Different flours add variety in color and weight. Adjust the basic recipe for the browning tones of rye flour by preparing a large batch in combination:

3 cups (375 g) all-purpose flour

1 cup (102 g) rye flour

2 cups (546 g) salt

1½ cups (355 ml) water

Having more dough on hand will help you adjust to rye flour's heavier weight in your models.

For more elasticity, or if you prefer to air dry your pieces, add 2 tablespoons (30 g) of premixed wallpaper paste to a regular recipe. Reduce water to ½ cup (120 ml).

To make a finer salt dough for delicate modeling, combine:

2 cups (250 g) flour

1 cup (273 g) salt

⅔ cup (100 g) cornstarch

¾ cup (175 g) water

Make a firm salt dough for textured models:

2 cups (250 g) flour

2 cups (546 g) salt

½ cup (120 g) water

For even more firmness, as when you are making tiles or other flat pieces, add 2 tablespoons (30 g) of wallpaper paste to this mixture.

Modeling

Begin modeling on a layer of aluminum foil or a cookie sheet that you have oiled and brushed lightly with water. This smoothes the back of the model, eliminates air bubbles, and, as you will place the foil or pan directly in the oven, you won't risk distorting the piece by moving it. Avoid nonstick pans that have a slightly textured surface; cover them with aluminum foil if necessary.

Many projects have multiple parts to be attached after modeling. Join the freshest parts of a piece by brushing the surfaces with water, taking care not to spread moisture farther as it will stain the dough. If one part is dry, or if you are repairing a break in an unvarnished, dry piece, use a bread dough adhesive to connect them: add water to scraps of fresh dough and stir it until it forms a paste. Dried bits of dough can be powdered in a mortar and then mixed with water. Once pieces are dry, smooth with sandpaper as necessary. Painted and varnished pieces must be connected or repaired with wood glue, epoxy or fast-drying household glue.

Continued ➜

Air-Dry Clay Alternative

If you are in a modern hurry, air-dry clay will produce similar results in less time. There's no dough to make, and there's no baking; completed projects air-dry in about 24 hours.

These pliable, ready-made clays come in a variety of colors. For additional hues, you can knead two or more colors together or mix acrylic paint into the clay. After it has dried, it can be sanded and painted with acrylic paints.

Essentially the same tools and techniques are used to work saltdough and air-dry clay. While the family cooking utensils are often used for saltdough, it's probably wise to dedicate a separate set of those tools for clay. Since clay is somewhat denser than dough, an inexpensive plastic extruder works better than the garlic presses and cake-icing bags beloved by dough-crafters.

Foundations

To build basic models, practice the following steps until you feel confident enough to proceed to more complicated forms.

Frames and plaques: Add wallpaper paste or cornstarch, if you need to, to increase firmness. Roll dough at least ½-inch (12 mm) thick on the baking surface. Cut edges straight or use a modeling tool, such as a crimper. For a frame effect on a round or oval base roll a rope, moisten it, and nestle it to the base, smoothing out points of connection. For squared edges, lightly define the rope as it turns the corners, and smooth the connection. Alternatively, cut the rope into four appropriate lengths (bevel the ends if you wish) and connect them at the corners.

Braids and wreaths: Roll oblongs of dough with closed fingers and flat hands into ropes of equal length. Begin braids by crossing ropes at their centers and twisting them away toward the ends. Place the ropes under each other as you braid to the left; place them over each other as you work toward the right. Bring the braids together before you, and cut the ends diagonally to match (undercut one, and overcut the other to fit). Press them together and blend carefully to eliminate "seams."

Three-dimensional objects: Save energy and time by removing weight and moisture from certain kinds of models. For hollow forms, bake pieces for two hours, or until the outer layer is dried through about the thickness of an onion layer. Core out the interior, leaving about ½ inch (1.3 cm) of the outer wall. Or create support forms with coated cardboard or aluminum foil. Aluminum foil also makes excellent "upholstery" for thick models. Simply wad it into

the shape you want, coat it with ½ inch (1.3 cm) of bread dough, and proceed to ornament or baking. The foil can be removed from open forms or left inside, as you wish.

Reproduction: Layer saltdough around your own vases and bowls, lightly coated with oil, or line the inside of a favorite pot or bowl if that is easier.

Patterns and Textures

Toothpicks, tweezers, fork times, and patterned buttons are just the beginning; nearly anything with points or a pattern can be used to add texture and dimension to saltdough creations. A basket may sport plaits or a herringbone weave, repeated florals can trip out a plaque, picture frames gain depth from leaf-and-twig patterns, and fanciful figures can be enhanced by randomly stamped stars, moons, and clouds. Clove stalks become stems for cherries or apples; press stem in and star out and they are the blossom end of a pear or a kumquat. Black peppercorns are very effective as eyes for small people and animals.

Two tools in particular are extremely handy for producing special effects; create fine lengths of "hair" by pressing dough through a strainer; thicker, curlier strands are possible with a garlic press. Form a halo of waving locks around a face, or pass a knife over the plate of the garlic press to cut pelts of sheep's wool.

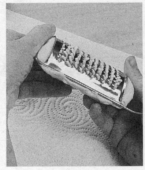

Drying and Baking

You can dry your models in the open air, bake them in electric, gas, or convection ovens, or heat them through in a microwave unit. Consider whether you want most to save time or heating expertise as you plan. Air-drying costs nothing and can take days to weeks to complete. Baking saltdough involves simple adjustments to take into account the rate and amount of water loss as your models dry. Electric ovens do the job in hours, depending upon the temperature setting; gas stoves provide natural

evaporation and take half the time. Convection speeds surface drying; extra time is required to finish baking the interior. A microwave oven can be most efficient if the heating process is carefully monitored.

Air-Drying

Air drying is a convenient option to baking. This is the best method for very thin, flat creations since it reduces cracking. Adding wallpaper paste to your recipe will firm the dough.

Plan on a day of drying time for every ¹⁄₁₆ inch (1.5 mm) of dough thickness. A practical choice for a large, thick model might be to place it near—not on—a radiator or heating element for a day, or in a very warm, dry room. An air-dried project can be finished in the oven if you start at a low temperature setting, to prevent overheating of a still-moist interior. Watch for a pocked or curved undersurface, caused by moisture loss; dampen it and "spackle" with salt sough paste to smooth.

Oven Baking

Electric: Set temperature at 300° F (150° C) and allow one hour per ¼-inch (6 mm) thickness of the model. Thus, a 1½-inch (4 cm) piece will bake in about six hours. Tap on the surface; if it returns a thick, dull sound, raise the temperature every 20 minutes to 200° F (95° C), then 250°F (120° C), then 300°F (150° C), or until the model sounds like hardened clay when tapped. Note: Begin baking colored dough at 150° F (66° C), and limit temperatures to 250° F (120° C), to avoid changes in shade.

Convection: Set temperature at 170° F (75° C). Bread dough models may require 12 hours to heat through. If further baking is needed, raise the temperature 25° F (4° C) every half hour, up to 250° F (120° C). Watch for browning; cover with aluminum foil to preserve color.

Gas: The natural moisture content in gas results in an even evaporation of water, reducing drying time substantially. Set temperature at 225° F (110° C) and leave the oven door open for an hour (taking precautions, of course, for the safety of children and pets). Prick any bubbles in the dough, and leave the door halfway open for the second hour. Then close the door until the project is finished.

Microwave: This method is great for impatient bakers, including eager children. Position your bread dough piece on an ungreased plate and use the "defrost," or lowest, setting, for five minutes at a time. Open the door after each session for several minutes to allow steam to escape. As the model dries, reduce cooking time and monitor carefully, watching for bubbles. Experiment to learn how various dough and model weights affect cooking time in your oven.

If you don't plan to paint or varnish your work right away, store it in a dry, airtight container.

Color

Dough may be colored in batches or in small quantities, if you don't want to paint later. Use food coloring if lightfastness is not a concern. Gouache (thick watercolor in tubes) or other liquid paints may be kneaded into dough by adding color to the center of

a small section, folding it over, and working it through. Try dissolved coffee, cocoa, paprika, and other spices for natural hues.

Painting, while requiring practice, can add wonderful dimension to bread dough pieces. Use good-quality artist's brushes in a range of sizes and shapes, from very fine to broad. Remove rough edges from a baked piece to be painted with a knife or sandpaper. Polish it with a smooth, dry brush. For bright, clean color, apply a primer coat first, and allow it to dry.

Acrylics, watercolors, gouaches, and inks all take well to baked saltdough. Acrylic craft paint is glue based, so brushed must be kept wet during use and then washed out carefully. Watercolors lend a translucence that can be as light or deep as you desire. Gouaches are dense and cover surfaces well. Gold and silver paint in gouache or acrylic form can be applied before baking. Poster paints may be affected by the salt in the dough, taking on a greenish cast. Enamel paints are solvent based and therefore unsuitable for use by children and in unventilated rooms. They must be thinned with solvent and spray varnished to avoid ruining the color. Gold and silver enamels, applied after baking, are bright and lustrous and may be worth the extra effort required.

Simple, rustic effects can be achieved with natural glazes. To create a salt glaze, brush them lightly with salt-water several times in the last half hour of baking, if the temperature is above 250° F (121° C), to make a tawny surface with a soft shine. A salt glaze can look deeper with a final application, during high-heat baking, of milk and water or egg yolk and water. Create a high-gloss look at the same heat with a mixture of corn syrup and water.

It takes practice to achieve the fetching beauty of painted models in a manual. Make a few extra decorations—an apple, shoes, leaves, a rosebud, a moon—each time you mold and bake. Practice using different paints and inks, experiment with shading, and try low- and high-gloss varnishes to view their effects. Always keep notes on techniques that work for you.

Natural Materials

Grasses, pods, seeds, and flowers that dry well add texture and dimension to your work. Try incorporating yarrow, statice, or thistle in graceful groups or as single stems, Gild them with paint spray before gluing into place, or leave the natural color. A spritz of hair spray will intensify colors; spray varnish is enduring. Clean models with a hair dryer on a low, cool setting.

Varnish

This step brightens and illuminates colors and preserves models from settling dust. Varnish also protects against moisture, which is drawn in and held by salt. Choose from wood varnish, which will add a yellow cast, or marine varnishes or polyurethane, which are transparent and bright. Both matte and glossy formulas are available.

If possible, select a varnish from the line of paints you are using. Place your completely dry creation facedown on a pillow covered with plain plastic or parchment paper, to protect delicate work. Varnish the back of the model first, in two or three coats, allowing four hours' drying time for each coat. Apply them carefully; keep the liquid from trickling underneath and spoiling the front. Clean the brush with mineral spirits between each application.

Mounting and Hanging Models

Press coated paper clips, hairpins, or stub wire into dough before baking to serve as hangers for small pieces. Larger models can be safely mounted if you core out holes with a drinking straw before baking, and then use ribbon or wire to hang the piece after baking.

Holiday Ornaments

The accessories—hats and beards—are the fun feature in these ornaments. Think of favorite hats from sports, a wedding, a garden party, or an equestrian event, then make them in bread dough, adding as much detail as you wish.

MATERIALS AND TOOLS

Ingredients for 2 batches of bread dough (see page 83)

Rolling pin

Liquid cake icing dye in red, royal blue, and green

Cutting board

Garlic press

Round toothpick or needle sculpting tool

Glass pony beads for eyes

Mini star cutter

Paper clips cut into U-shaped thirds with wire cutter

Foil-lined cookie sheet

Sealant

CLAY ALTERNATIVE
Replace the bread dough and liquid cake icing with air-dry clay in red, blue, green, white, and brown. (The white and brown are for flesh tones; mix the two in whatever proportions you like.) Replace the garlic press with a craft extruder. After forming the ornaments, allow them to air-dry for 24 hours.

WHAT TO DO

1. Mix together one batch of bread dough, referring to the recipe on page 00, and color it with bright white liquid icing.

2. Mix together a second batch of bread dough. Divide it into four equal portions. Using the liquid icing dye, tint one portion red, one blue, and one green; leave the fourth portion untinted to serve as flesh-tone dough.

3. To make a face, form a 2-inch (5 cm) ball of flesh-tone dough. Place it on cutting board and use the palm of your hand to flatten it to a 1/3-inch (8 mm) thickness.

4. Place the pony beads about a third of the way down the face, using the toothpick or needle tool to pick them up and push them firmly into dough. Use the toothpick or needle tool to "draw" a smile. Repeat to make as many faces as you like.

TO MAKE THE HATS

For a Santa hat, make a 2-inch ball of red dough and shape it into a cone. Place it above the face and fold top of cone to the side.

For a cowboy hat, use red dough to make a 1¼-inch (32 cm) ball. Form a "peanut" shape with the ball, then place sideways above head.

For an Uncle Sam hat, roll a 6-inch (15 cm) cylinder of red and of white dough, just a little larger than 1/8 inch (3 mm) wide. Cut each cylinder into 1½-inch (4 cm) lengths. Press the cylinders together to form a red-and-white-striped cylinder 1½ inches (4 cm) long. Cut off uneven edges, then position it vertically on head.

5. Load your garlic press with white dough and squeeze out 2-inch (5 cm) lengths. For each length, use the needle tool to scrape the strings off and curl around the tool. Place one length at a time around your Santa's face, in desired way, to make his beard.

6. Form two long, thin teardrop shapes from the white dough to form the mustache. Place the fat sides together in middle of face, and curl the ends up on top of his beard. Use a small ball of flesh-colored dough to form a nose.

TO MAKE THE HAT RIMS

For the Santa hat, use a strip of white dough 3 inches (7.5 cm) long, ½ inch (13 cm) wide, and 1/16-inch (1.5 mm) thick. Make a 1/3-inch (8 mm) tassel from the white dough, then form tiny leaves from the green dough for a holly decoration.

For the cowboy hat brim, roll a 4-inch (10 cm) cylinder. Flatten with finger to 1/8 inch (3 mm) thick and ¾ inch (2 cm) wide. Place around head and curl up ends on each side. Use green dough to form tiny holly leaves on hat.

For Uncle Sam's hat brim, roll out a 3-inch (7.5) strip of blue dough, flatten to 1/16-inch (1.5 mm) thick, and place over hat. Cut out three stars from the white dough and press them onto the brim.

7. Press U-shaped paperclip pieces into the top of each hat for a hanger, then place them on a foil-lined cookie sheet and bake for approximately 2 to 3 hours. To test for doneness, remove from sheet and press very hard in thickest part of ornament. If it is still soft, put it back in the oven; continue testing every half hour until it is completely hard, then allow it to completely cool.

8. Glaze with your favorite sealant.

Continued ➔

Holiday Wreath

Designer: Bonnie Bone

Richly textured and gleaming with color, this wreath has heirloom potential. Experiment with new surfaces, and handle the pressed dough tufts carefully to avoid clumping.

MATERIALS AND TOOLS

Ingredients for 2 batches of bread dough (see page 83)

Liquid cake icing dye in green, red, brown, yellow, and blue

Rolling pin

Mini Christmas cookie cutters, one a gingerbread man

Garlic press

Needle sculpting tool

Paper clip

Foil-lined cookie sheet

Nonserrated knife

Sealant

WHAT TO DO

1. Mix together one batch of bread dough, referring to the recipe on page 00. Tint the dough with green liquid icing dye.

2. Mix together a second batch of bread dough. Divide it in two equal portions. Tint one of portions with red liquid icing dye. Next, divide the second half of the dough into three equal portions. Tint one portion brown, one yellow, and one royal blue.

3. Roll a green rope of about 18 to 20 inches (45 to 50 cm) long and ¾ inch (2 cm) wide. Arrange it in a circle in the middle of your cookie sheet. Allow at least 2 inches (5 cm) of room on all sides of sheet.

4. Load garlic press with green dough. Squeeze out tufts of dough about 2 inches (5 cm) long. Scrape off each tuft and casually place it in a random arrangement on the circle until the entire circle is covered and the wreath is of uniform width.

5. Flatten out a 4-inch (10 cm) ball of brown dough with a small roller or the back of a spatula to a thickness of ¼ inch (6 mm). Cut two gingerbread men out of the brown and decorate them with dough to resemble traditional gingerbread men cookies. Place one on each side of wreath.

6. To make the bow, roll two 2½-inch (6 cm) balls of red dough. Shape one into a cylinder and flatten it to a thickness of ⅛ inch (3 mm), 1 inch (2.5 cm) wide, and 6 inches (15 cm) long. Place the rolled dough at the top of the wreath, gently overlapping the ends to form a graceful ribbon.

7. To continue forming the bow, shape the second ball into a cylinder about 5 inches (13 cm) long, and flatten to a thickness of ⅛ inch (3 mm). Fold the ends over onto the center and pinch center to form a bow tie. Transfer the bow to the top of the ribbons, and gently press to stick. Roll out a ½-inch-long (1.3 cm) cylinder, flatten, and cover the pinched center of bow tie, using the needle tool to tuck the ends under the tie.

8. Make two to four small candy canes by rolling red and white ropes together (⅛ inch [3 mm] thick and 1½ inches [4 cm] long). Gently press the two lengths together, then twist them together. Press them onto the desired areas on the wreath and bend them into candy-cane shapes.

9. Cut mini stars or other Christmas shapes from the dough and place them randomly on the wreath. If you don't have mini cutters, you can hand-form various shapes.

10. Roll tiny colored balls and place them randomly around the wreath to resemble lights.

11. Cut a large paper clip into thirds, pressing the largest piece into top of wreath as a hanger.

12. Bake wreath for 2 to 3 hours at 250° F (120° C). Cool completely. Test for doneness by pressing hard on the thickest part of the cooled wreath. If it is not completely hard, return to oven for another 30 minutes. Repeat until the piece is completely done. After it cools, glaze with a coat of sealant.

—FROM *The Michaels Book of Arts & Crafts*

CLAY ALTERNATIVE

Replace the bread dough and liquid cake icing with air-dry clay in green, red, brown, yellow, and blue. After forming the wreath, allow it to air-dry for at least 24 hours.

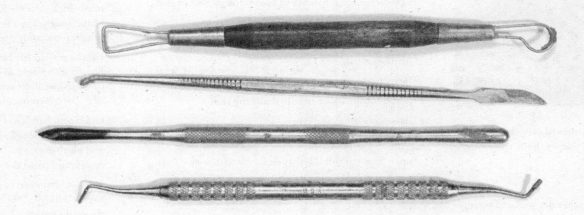

Floral Crafts

FAUX FLOWER ARRANGEMENTS

Melody Thompson

Introduction

Flowers add luxury to our lives. They bring softness and color to living spaces. They introduce a textural design element, whether in an entire room or a wall thought out vignette in a small space. From a single bud to a lavish seasonal display, flowers complement any décor.

Faux flowers such as silk, dried, or paper are found in a wide variety of colors, sizes, and shapes, and they vary in quality and price points.

Containers are not limited to standard vases. Pots, boxes, jars, and baskets, along with many everyday items, all lend themselves to serving as a vase for floral displays. Gather your favorites and simply apply some of the basic techniques outlined on the following pages.

Use these projects as inspiration and change the colors or materials as you desire. In no time at all, your "pink thumb" will blossom.

Getting Started

When making a floral arrangement or accessory, consider where it will be placed when finished or how it will enhance the space. Is there a theme or style of décor to be considered? The flowers and container should harmonize both with each other and the area where they are placed.

Consider the design elements of color, form, line, space, and texture. Study nature, period history, and art to develop your own ideas. This chapter will show simple techniques that will allow you the freedom of expression while learning good mechanics and some new trends in design.

Basic tools and supplies are available at local hobby and craft stores. When working with faux flowers, a few items from the trade are necessary to create a project. Following is a list of supplies you will want to add to your design table.

Supplies

Anchor Pins

Four-prong plastic "frogs" used to hold floral foam. Anchor pins are usually attached to container base with glue or clay. Useful for containers with low or no sides.

Candle Stakes

Green plastic holder with prongs that are pushed into foam to hold taper or pillar candles in an arrangement.

Container

Choose containers to complement the setting, décor, or theme. Traditional vases or baskets are fine; however, anything is possible, including decorative boxes, candlesticks, frames, terra-cotta urns, kitchen ware, tin cans and coffee pots, toy trucks, shoes, and teapots, to name a few.

Dried Floral Foam

Used to hold floral stems in place. Available in blocks and bricks. Use a serrated knife for cutting. This product has a finer texture than polystyrene foam and is a good choice for most design work.

Floral Spray Paint

Spray paints created specially for use in the floral industry. Paint dries quickly while providing good coverage to design material. Use to change the color of containers or add color to natural floral materials such as branches, pods, and foliage.

Gentle-Grip Floral Foam

Available in blocks and bricks and has a very fine texture for delicate stems and dried materials.

Moss

Used to cover floral foam and arrangement mechanics. Popular varieties include Spanish moss in natural or green, sheet moss, and reindeer moss. All achieve coverage; choice depends on personal preference and design style.

Continued ➡

Polystyrene Foam

Available in green or white and has a very coarse texture. It comes in sheets and preformed shapes such as spheres, cones, and wreaths. Sheets can be scored lightly with a serrated knife and then broken cleanly with a snap. Perfect for thicker wired stems of faux flowers.

"S" pins

Also known as floral pins, these hairpin-shaped pins are used to secure moss to foam bases or to pin materials to floral foams.

Wire

Wire is very important for sturdy design. It is available in a variety of gauges ranging from #16 to #28; the smaller the number of wire, the larger gauge thickness of the wire. Use heavier wire for floral stems, thinner wire when delicate support is needed. Wire can be purchased in precut lengths of 12" (30.5 cm) or on a roll. Rolled wire is called paddle or reel wire. It is used in garlands and wreath-making when one continuous strand is needed for stability.

Wired Wooden Floral Picks

The wooden picks come in 2½"-6" (6.5–15 cm) lengths and have an attached wire. Primarily used to add extra length or provide stability to thin-stemmed faux flowers.

Wooden dowel

Round wood dowels come in a range of sizes from ¼"-3" (6 mm–7.5 cm) in diameter. Use for creating stems in topiary forms or to provide support on large plant materials.

Adhesives

Floral Adhesive

Floral adhesive comes in a gel form in a tube and looks similar to heavy-duty rubber cement yet it provides a lasting hold. This glue is used primarily on polystyrene floral foams and bonds well to plastics.

Floral Clay

This sticky clay is found in roll or block form and is used to attach foam to the container, providing a semipermanent hold.

Floral Stem Tape

This waxy tape is the professional way to cover wires and floral stems. Tapes come in a variety of colors to match your project.

Heavy Adhesive Tape

Sometimes called bowl or anchor tape. Used to secure foam in container liners and to wrap stems in hand-tied bouquets. Can also be used in a crisscross pattern/grid on container opening to facilitate free stem arranging.

Hot Glue

Available in sticks for a glue gun, or pillows for an electric skillet. Pillows are melted in a pan and typically used for large jobs or extended use, as it can take longer to melt. Hot glue sticks are melted with a hot-glue gun and

provide a secure hold for attaching foam to containers and design materials to their base.

Spray Adhesive

Comes in a spray can and is used to quickly cover surfaces with a light misting of glue. Use when covering a polystyrene form with potpourri, berries, or petals. This product dries very quickly, so work fast.

Tools

Floral Snips

Hand-held clippers used to cut natural floral materials and fresh flowers. Perfect for use on dried flowers or lightweight silk floral stems.

Hot-Glue Gun

This appliance heats glue sticks to liquid form. The glue sticks are available in both hot and cool melt varieties and dry quickly. Use with care when working using hot glue; always keep a bowl of water nearby in case of accidents.

Scissors

Used for trimming ribbons or fraying silk petals.

Serrated Knife

Small knife with a jagged edge used for cutting floral foams.

Stapler/Staples

A stapler provides a handy quick fix for silk leaves or petals that may come apart.

Wire Cutters

A heavy-duty cutter makes your task easier and more efficient when cutting faux floral stems and craft and floral wire.

Techniques

Taping Wire

Begin covering wire by wrapping floral tape around top of wire, stretching tape slightly and using your thumb and index finger to twist tape around the wire. Work down the wire, gently stretching tape with one hand as you twist tape down wire with your thumb and index finger of your other hand. Pinch off tape at end of wire.

Shaping Hairpin Wires

Hairpins are used to pin moss and foliage into foam. They are easily made if "S" pins are not available or a smaller discreet pin is needed in the design. Using wire cutters, cut 20- or 22-gauge wire into 2" (5 cm) segments. Bend at center and fold wire into equal parts to create hairpin.

Preparing Floral Foam

Cut foam using a serrated knife so it fits the container snugly and is ½" (1.3 cm) below container rim. If arrangement will drape or have horizontal elements, allow foam to extend about 1" (2.5 cm) above empty container. Hot glue foam to container at bottom. Cover foam with moss, securing in place with 2-3 floral pins, depending on area to be covered.

Using a Clear Container

Cut block of foam to fit in center of container, leaving about ½" free on all sides. Using anchor pin and floral clay, secure foam. Fill in area surrounding foam with moss, marbles, seeds, potpourri, or similar material to hide the mechanics.

Hand Tying a Bouquet

As the name implies, this bouquet is made while holding flowers in your hand. In addition to an abundance of flowers and foliage, you will need anchor tape and ribbon or raffia to complete this design. Start by stripping leaves from the lower half of all stems. Pick up one flower and one foliage stem. Begin by placing one stem directly on top of the other at about a 45-degree angle. Throughout the process, always hold flowers and foliage midway up the stems between your thumb and fingers. Continue adding stems of flowers and foliage at an angle, building your bouquet in a clockwise fashion. Keep your hand relaxed—don't choke your flowers. When you have a handful of flowers, bind with anchor tape where your hand is holding the flowers. Trim stems evenly at bottom and finish with ribbon or raffia bow.

Making a bow

Bow making can be mastered easily with a little practice. For ease in learning, choose a ribbon that is medium width and pliable. Wired ribbon is easy to work with and very forgiving.

Make a loop, allowing a "tail" of ribbon. "Tail" length is approximately same size as loop. Gather ribbon and hold between thumb and fingers (Fig. 1).

Bring the ribbon over to form another loop, holding both loops in the center "pinch." Make two more loops in this figure-8 style. Make a smaller center

Figure 1

Figure 2

loop if desired by looping the ribbon in a small, full circular motion and then pinching at center gather point (Fig. 2).

While holding the center gather point with your thumb and forefinger, use a floral tape–covered wire to fold over the pinched center and twist to secure (Fig. 3).

Pull loops into position to create bow (Fig. 4).

Figure 3

Figure 4

Single Blooms

The simplistic design of a single bloom is vastly under-rated. Full, lush floral arrangements have their place in interiors; however, sometimes less is more. Contemporary, modern spaces call for clean design lines and simple shapes. The lowly bud vase is no longer a floral stem in water, but an art form. Containers are now integral parts of the design.

Consider unusual ceramics and wrought iron containers for inspired works. Take the clear glass containers to new levels by wrapping with polished wire, moss-covered twine, or even large leaves. Use wire grids, braided raffia, or rattan balls to create support for a stem or two in a larger container. Space defines and accents the shape of the flowers so that they may be fully appreciated for themselves.

Iris

MATERIALS

    Anchor pin
    Art glass bowl
    Floral clay
    Floral foam (½ round sphere)
    Hot glue
    Iris stem (1)
    Polished river rock (1 bag)
    Reed stems (3)
    Ruler
    Serrated knife
    Wire cutters

INSTRUCTIONS

1. Prepare art glass bowl by securing anchor pin to inside bowl base with a bit of floral clay. Cut foam sphere in half using serrated knife and press onto anchor pin.

2. Using wire cutters, cut iris stem to about 12"–15" (30.5–38 cm); insert into center of floral foam. Secure with hot glue.

3. Cut reeds to 8" (20.5 cm) and cluster together at base of iris.

4. Add river rocks to the bowl to cover floral foam.

TIME-SAVING TIP
FROM ASHTRAY TO FLORAL CONTAINER
Murano art glass is very beautiful and quite collectible. Iris project uses a vintage art glass ashtray as its container. Look for unusual shapes and sizes for your project.

Stargazer Lily

MATERIALS

    Braided raffia ball (4" diameter [10 cm])
    Floral snips
    Hot glue
    Pussy willow fan (1 stem)
    Reindeer moss
    Ruler
    Stargazer lily
    Wire cutters
    Wrought-iron basket

INSTRUCTIONS

1. Prepare wrought iron basket container by adding about a 2" (5 cm) thickness of moss at bottom. Place braided raffia ball inside container and fill around ball with more moss, allowing top of ball to show.

2. Using wire cutters, cut stargazer stem into two blooms and insert the stems into top of exposed raffia ball. Slightly stagger stem placement at center of ball. Secure stems with hot glue.

3. Using floral snips, clip pussy willow fan stem to about 12" (30.5 cm). Insert into raffia ball at a complementary angle; secure with hot glue.

TIME-SAVING TIP
CUT OUT THE RAFFIA BALL
Lily can also be completed by using floral foam instead of the braided raffia ball. Simply layer the moss, cut the floral foam slightly smaller than the interior of the container, and secure from underneath with several "S" pins and hot glue (if needed). Then cover the foam with moss.

Centerpieces

A centerpiece is an arrangement designed to be the focal point of a particular space, usually a table. Centerpieces are typically symmetrical in shape and meant to be viewed from all sides. The height and size depends on the setting; low, long arrangements are perfect for dinner conversation, while taller, more dramatic centerpieces are reserved for buffets or pedestals. A grouping of smaller floral arrangements and/or accessories can combine to provide a center focal point.

Try an unusual container or use a container out of context to help reiterate the focal point. Combine fruit or vegetables with flowers for an organic feel. From traditional to the unexpected, flowers finish the table-scape and provide unity for the tabletop elements.

Tabletop Wreath

MATERIALS

    Artichokes (3)
    Candle stakes (4)
    Dendrobium orchids (2 stems)
    Floral snips
    Galax leaves (12)
    Hot glue
    Hydrangea (1 stem)
    Moss wreath
    Peppergrass (1 bunch)
    Reindeer moss
    Statice (3 stems)
    Taper candles (3)

INSTRUCTIONS

1. Insert four candle stakes into wreath, grouping as desired; secure using hot glue. Cover stake sides with moss. Add candles to establish height and balance for remaining materials.

2. Separate floral stems using floral snips as needed. Accent candles with sprigs of orchids; secure using hot glue. Insert artichokes using two as a grouping and one in the candle stake. **Note:** This is done to add height to the artichokes.

3. Add statice and hydrangea blooms to fill voids and add texture; secure using hot glue. Add reindeer moss to the base for visual texture; hot glue in place.

4. Insert sprigs of peppergrass and hot glue galax leaves to underside of wreath, fanning outward.

TIME-SAVING TIP
KEEP IT SIMPLE
Decorate your tabletop wreath using large silk blooms. Bold design materials require less products to make a design statement. Center large pillar candles within the wreath for a different look.

Bubble Bowl

MATERIALS

    Curly willow branches (4)
    Fig branches (3)
    Floral snips
    Glass bowl (12" [30.5 cm] diameter)
    Ming Aralia branches (3)
    Rhododendron branches (3)
    Wire cutters

INSTRUCTIONS

1. Wrap and twist three willow branches in a circular fashion and insert into bowl (they will fan out to fill the

Continued →

space). Reserve one willow stem to be used later.

2. Clip each rhododendron branch using floral snips into two separate stems and insert in a free-form fashion.

3. Fill empty space with Ming Aralia branches as needed. Cut remaining willow branch into two or three pieces using wire cutters, depending on twists and curls of branch. Insert for added dimension.

4. Group fig branches and add among flowers and branches.

Note: Shorten flowers and branches with floral snips or wire cutters if needed.

TIME-SAVING TIP
THINK NATURAL

Bubble Bowl should have a very casual feel. Do not get too caught up in "arranging" the flowers. Just keep balance and scale design elements in mind. The willow branches add an unusual interior vase accent and can be utilized in fresh floral arrangements too.

Topiaries

From simple stems to multi-head forms, topiaries are creations of royalty dating back to Julius Caesar. Artful and dimensional, these whimsical-style designs provide a breath of fresh air to traditional floral arrangements. The basic construction can be produced as a single, double, or triple ball topiary. Purchase a preformed shape or create your own structure. Topiaries can also be created by tying several flower heads together to create the "ball-on-a-stem" look. Create interesting variations by using leaves or berries to cover the foam base. Use matching topiaries on a mantel for a traditional look or mini individual pots as place cards on a party table. Topiaries can be as diverse as the setting so be creative when selecting materials for your design.

Orchid Trellis

MATERIALS

Corsage pins (15)

Floral snips

Hot glue

Orchid stem

Pepperomia stem

Premade moss ball topiary wire form

Reindeer moss

Ruler

Wire cutters

Wired twine

INSTRUCTIONS

Note: Begin this project with a premade wire topiary form with moss-covered balls.

1. Using wired twine, wrap form loosely, allowing the wire to curl and twist around the form. Cut short segments (about 8" [20.5 cm] long) using wire cutters and create abstract curly cues twisted around the existing wire form.

2. Clip orchid stem into individual blossoms and place randomly spaced on the form. Secure blooms using hot glue. Following lines of the flowers, insert the clipped pepperomia stems into foam, hot gluing into place.

---

3. Press corsage pins into the foam moss balls in small groupings for added visual interest. Randomly add reindeer moss in small clumps, securing in place with hot glue.

TIME-SAVING TIP
MAKING TOPIARY FORMS

For the industrious types, create your own topiary form using a tomato plant cage. Simply invert the form and tie off the top with wire. Paint the wire form green and add your own moss-covered foam balls in graduated sizes. Crisscross paddle wire over the bottom of the cage to hold the balls in place. Then, decorate as desired.

Berry Beautiful

MATERIALS

Faux berry multi-stem branches (3)

Floral adhesive

Floral snips

Foam cone (10" [25.5 cm])

Garden-style pot (4" [10 cm])

Hot glue

Mini faux pears (3)

Ostrich feather tips (2)

Satin ribbon (½ yard [45.5 cm])

Scissors

Silk foliage leaves (6)

INSTRUCTIONS

1. Separate individual berries using floral snips. Dip underside of each berry in floral adhesive and place on foam cone, covering form completely. **Note:** Be sure to place berries closely together.

2. Wedge cone into container; secure sides using hot glue.

3. Tie ribbon into a shoe-string bow and hot glue to base of cone; trim ends of ribbon. Insert feathers behind bow. Tuck in silk leaves and mini pears. Secure all in place using hot glue.

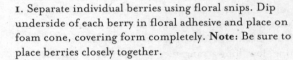

TIME-SAVING TIP
LAYER & ROLL

You may also cover the Berry Beautiful foam form with craft glue using a foam brush and then roll the cone into a layer of berries if using smaller pieces. Potpourri or dried petals are also quick and easy embellishments.

Wall Décor

Artwork is not just paint on canvas. You can create original, dimensional art with faux flowers for your walls. Enhance wrought iron with flowers, pods, and moss…

Half baskets or wall pockets can be created to fit any décor. Use dried naturals or soft spring blossoms to fit the season. Can't afford a Monet or Picasso original? The artisan in you can turn your blank wall into art.

English Garden Basket

MATERIALS

Blooming vine (2 strands)

English ivy bush

Floral foam

Floral snips

Hot glue

Jasmine bush

Petunia bush

"S" pins

Serrated knife

Spanish moss

Spray roses (6 stems)

Strand of pearls

Wire cutters

Wire half basket

INSTRUCTIONS

1. Line wire basket with Spanish moss. Using serrated knife, cut foam to fit basket. Nestle foam into moss and secure with several "S" pins inserted directly through back of basket into foam; hot glue pins into place.

2. Cut bushes and spray roses into individual stems using wire cutters. Insert stems in foam, arranging tallest stems toward back and shorter stems in front. **Note:** In a garden-style arrangement, insert some stems in between the wire spaces like natural plants and flowers would grow.

3. Weave snippets of ivy through wire and up handle; secure using hot glue as needed. Insert loops of strand of pearls and blooming vine. **Note:** Shorten flowers and branches with floral snips if needed.

TIME-SAVING TIP
CREATE A HALF BASKET

Woven willow baskets can be cut in half to create the English Garden Basket look. Simply use your floral snips to cut the basket in half behind the handle. Hot glue floral foam inside the handle half and cover with moss.

Arrangements

An empty vase and an imagination are the beginnings of floral art. In the past, flower arrangements were often staid and unimaginative, but new concepts and techniques have emerged. Emphasis is placed on the flowers and the way they grow naturally.

Flowers are arranged freely with inspiration taken from nature. Never have there been more faux design materials to choose from and containers to put them in. Try tropical florals in bamboo, spring bulbs in moss, or lilies in small rocks. Allow color to enthuse, and shape and form to guide. Dramatic purple tulips, soft pink geraniums, or sweet daisies will inspire you.

Whether a few stems or a profusion of blooms, faux floral design materials await your creative endeavors.

French Wire Garden

MATERIALS

Calla lilies (3)

Floral foam

Floral snips

Horsetail reed (2)

Hot glue

Iris (3)

Ranunculus (3)

"S" pins

Serrated knife

Sheet moss

Statice (2)

Swedish ivy (1 bunch)

Thistles (3)

Wire basket

INSTRUCTIONS

1. Line wire basket with sheet moss. Cut foam to fit container using serrated knife. Nestle foam inside moss; secure with "S" pins and hot glue.

2. Insert horsetail reeds to establish height. Working downward from reeds, insert calla lilies and then iris and thistles. **Note:** Group same flowers together to achieve maximum visual impact.

3. Fill lower portion of arrangement with ranunculus and statice to create depth. Add ivy to fill around base. **Note:** Shorten flowers and branches with floral cnips if needed.

TIME SAVING TIP:

TAKING CUES FROM NATURE

Think of the French Wire Garden arrangement as "a little clump of nature." Place flowers as they would grow in the garden. Use flowers that would naturally be found growing together and in the same growth season (e.g., bulb flowers in the spring, pansies and kale in the winter, etc.).

Café Time Canister

MATERIALS

Coffee-themed canister with lid

Daisies (1 bunch)

Floral foam

Floral snips

Floral wire

Hot glue

Raspberries (1 stem)

"S" pins

Scissors

Serrated knife

Silver teaspoon

Spanish moss

Wired ribbon (1 yard [91.5 cm])

Wooden floral pick

INSTRUCTIONS

1. Cut foam with serrated knife to fit snugly in coffee-themed canister. Insert in canister and cover with moss, securing with "S" pins.

2. Hot glue small piece of foam to back side of lid and insert wooden floral pick. Place lid into canister foam with pick toward back of arrangement.

3. Using floral snips, clip daisy bunch into individual stems. Fill container with flowers in a natural, gathered look.

4. Snip raspberry stem into three pieces and tuck berries in among daisies.

5. Tie multiple-loop bow and place in arrangement; trim ends of bow. Tuck silver spoon in center of bow, wiring to secure in place.

—FROM *Make It in Minutes: Faux Flower Arrangements*

TIME-SAVING TIP

USING HOUSEHOLD ITEMS AS CONTAINERS

Household items make perfect containers for your designs. Try vintage kitchenalia for your cottage décor or pot some silk daffodils in an old pail. Use your chipped china pieces to create a matching arrangement on your table.

SILK FLOWERS

Dawn Cusick & Megan Kirby, Editors

Colorful and natural-looking artificial flowers, fruits, vegetables, grasses, and foliage are readily available, often in abundant supply, at craft- and art-supply stores. Though rarely made of real silk, all artificial plants are referred to as "silks." Silks are a joy to work with, because silk arrangements are long-lasting, can be re-created at the designer's whim, and the finished arrangements require very little care.

Materials and Tools

Floral Foam/Polystyrene

Use porous, green floral foam (soaked in water) as a stabilizing base when combining silks with fresh flowers. Use only dry, gray or green floral foam when working exclusively with silks. Polystyrene is a less-expensive option and works very well with materials attached to floral picks; it is not a good choice for dried or delicate stems.

Floral Picks

Floral picks are used to give support to delicate stems, to lengthen stems, and to connect several stems. That said, picks may not be necessary for all silks, since many silk flowers are sold already wired.

Floral Pins

These U-shaped pins (also called U pins or moss pins) are indispensable in securing moss and ribbon to the base material as well as in attaching silks to straw or foam bases.

Floral Tape

Floral tape, also called stem wrap, is handy for securing floral foam to containers, binding together several pieces of foam, and, when used with floral wire (see below), extending stems. The key to working with floral tape is pulling the tape taut as you wrap it; this makes the tape sticky, and thus allows for a secure hold.

Floral Wire

Floral wire comes in a variety of gauges and colors, and is used chiefly to extend and strengthen stems, though it is also useful in attaching flowers and foliage to wreaths, swags, and topiaries.

Flower Frogs/Stabilizers

Flower frogs, which come in a variety of shapes and sizes, stabilize flowers at the bottom of an arrangement when floral foam is not being used. Use adhesive clay to secure the frog at the base. For a translucent container or vase, consider using marbles, pieces of glass, stones, or another filler that will both stabilize stems and add character to the design. To create the illusion of water, acrylic water is available in craft and floral supply stores and also serves as a stabilizer.

Hot-Glue Gun

This crafter's mainstay is essential to the silk-flower designer. Use hot glue to affix flowers to bases and to make repairs to individual silks. A slow-drying gun works well for silk-flower design, since it allows the designer time to reposition flowers as needed.

Wire Cutters

Because most silk flowers have a wire running the length of the stem (for stability and to aid in manipulating the blooms), you will need a sturdy pair of wire cutters to make necessary adjustments. (Scissors can be used to cut very thin or unwired stems.)

Bases

Commercially prepared bases or forms are useful when creating topiaries, swags, and wreaths, and are usually made of straw, grapevine, floral foam, or polystyrene. Of course you can make your own, though most designers find purchased bases are worth the minimal expense.

Containers

Just about any container can be used for silk-flower arrangements, from ceramic vases to terra-cotta pots to baskets. Choose a container that best suits the style of the particular arrangement. Use your imagination—since a silk-flower arrangement doesn't need to hold water, the possibilities are limitless.

Basic Techniques

Preparing Materials

Sometimes the best designs begin with an interesting container; on the other hand, a selection of gorgeous silks is also a grand start. Whatever your inspiration, a little preparation will help a great deal.

1. Use a serrated knife to cut floral foam or polystyrene to fit inside the container. For vertical arrangements, the foam should fall just below the rim of the container. For arrangements with cascading elements, the foam should extend several inches above the container. Floral foam can often be wedged securely in place, though floral tape or hot glue may also be used, if necessary.

2. If the foam and/or floral tape will be visible in the finished piece, secure moss to the foam with floral pins or hot glue. (These components can be disguised later with well-positioned flowers.) Spray the moss slightly with water and press down with fingers, if desired, to achieve a snug fit.

3. Choose the flowers and other elements for the design and position materials on the work surface. For a more pleasing arrangement, use materials with a variety of textures, colors, and shapes. Experimenting with combinations of silk materials is the fun part!

4. Make sure the stems will fit securely into the floral foam or polystyrene. Delicate flowers, as well as large, top-heavy flowers, most likely will require additional support. For double-wired stems, separate the wires with scissors to form a fork. If necessary, affix wire with floral tape or use floral picks to create additional support for single-wired stems.

Container Arrangements

Having an infinite number of container possibilities is one of the biggest advantages to working with silks. This may also save you time and money, since you probably already have the perfect vessel in your house or garden!

Continued ➡

1. Establish the approximate dimensions of the arrangement—the height, width, and shape—by inserting several larger stems to form a framework. In general, flowers should be about 1½ times as tall as the container, though this is certainly not written in stone. Dip stems in craft glue before inserting them into base. If you are using very thick branches or stems, use an awl or other sharp tool to make a hole in the foam, then insert the stem.

2. Beginning with the central elements and focal flowers, and ending with filler materials, gradually fill in the arrangement with the remaining flowers and foliage. Turn the base as you work to make sure the piece looks good from every side. Position plants on different planes and manipulate the flower heads so that they face a variety of angles.

3. Stand back from the arrangement and see where adjustments or additions need to be made. Turn any visible wire spines away from the front side, or wrap stems with floral tape for a more authentic look. (Nothing gives away an artificial flower like an exposed wire.) If necessary, hot-glue individual flowers to the arrangement to conceal empty spaces.

Spring Arrangement

Designer: Cynthia Gillooly

Have a touch of spring fever in January? Here's a cure for even the most severe case: bright blooms in a darling spring arrangement. Instant gratification!

MATERIALS AND TOOLS

Basket

Moss

Floral foam

Floral pins

Hot-glue gun

Assorted spring silks

Floral tape

Craft glue

WHAT TO DO

1. Use a serrated knife to cut floral foam to fit inside and extend 2 inches (5 cm) above the top of the basket. Use hot blue or floral tape to secure the foam. Disguise the top of the foam with moss and secure with floral pins.

2. Plan the design and gather silk materials. Here we've used irises, lilies, daffodils, narcissus blooms, roses, and a variety of smaller blooms and filler materials. Look for spring flowers with a variety of shapes, colors, and textures. Attach floral picks to flowers, if necessary. Wrap wire stems with floral tape for a more authentic look.

3. Begin the design. Remembering that the arrangement should be about 1½ times the height of your basket, establish the dimensions of the design by inserting the central and focal flowers. Use floral picks, floral pins, or hot glue (whichever method is most suitable for each piece) to secure flowers to the foam. Position the flowers on a variety of planes. Dip floral picks in craft glue before inserting into floral foam.

4. Turning the basket as you work and beginning with the largest elements, fill in with the rest of the flowers. Position some flowers and leaves so that they spill over the edge of the basket. Continue to position silk materials until you are pleased with the arrangements from every side.

Silk-Flower Gift Decorations

Designer: Megan Kirby

Use leftover silk flowers and individual leaves to fashion super-easy, super-impressive gift decorations. Even the simplest designs have amazing impact when they feature a strong floral element. Covering the entire top surface of the package with smaller blooms can also make for a lovely presentation.

MATERIALS AND TOOLS

Paper or gift wrap

Raffia, ribbon, or twine

Assorted silks

Scissors

Hot-glue gun

WHAT TO DO

1. Wrap the gift. Here we've used white paper to provide a nice contrast to the silk flowers. Craft paper or any gift wrap will work, though do try to choose a color or design that coordinates with your silks.

2. Tie raffia, twine, or ribbon around the present. Center the raffia (or other material) across the top of the package, wind around to the back side and twist, then bring around to the front again and knot. For the sunflower package here, we tied an additional length of raffia around the knot and fluffed the material for a more dramatic effect.

3. Remove the stem of the silk flower and hot-glue the flower to the center of the package.

4. If desired, position and hot-glue leaves to the design as well. If you are using ivy or any other trailing silk material, wrap stem around the tied material, hot-gluing in spots to secure, and allow ends to spill over edge of package.

—FROM *The Michaels Book of Arts & Crafts*

DRIED FLOWERS

Dawn Cusick & Megan Kirby, Editors

The natural beauty of fresh flowers is retained in many types of dried flowers and greenery. Dried flowers are a remarkably versatile crafting material. You can create large, expansive arrangements, small nosegays, garlands, and much more. They can be used in traditional ways—as a centerpiece on a dining room table, for example—or in much more novel ways—as curtain tiebacks, for example.

Dried Flowers

Dried flowers offer a wonderfully complex array of textures and colors, and can serve as focal or accent flowers as well as background or filler material. Because of their versatility, dried flowers work well when combined with silks and fresh flowers, and can be used in all sorts of craft projects.

Floral Foam

Used as a stabilizer for floral arrangements, floral foam comes in a variety of shapes and sizes. Delicate dried flowers will need to be attached to floral picks or floral wire to add extra support; more sturdy dried material can be inserted directly into the floral foam.

Floral Wire

This wire comes in a variety of thicknesses, or gauges, and is used to attach dried flowers as well as other materials to a base. Try to position wire where it will not show in the finished design.

Floral Tape

Floral tape, also called stem wrap, comes in an array of widths and colors. It's handy for securing floral foam to containers, binding together several stems or pieces of foam, and lending extra support to delicate materials. For best results, pull the tape taut as you wrap; this makes the tape sticky, and thus allows for a secure hold.

Floral Pins

These U-shaped pins (also called U pins or nose pins) are curved pieces of wire used to secure moss and ribbon to the base material as well as to attach plant materials to straw or foam bases.

Floral Picks

These are wooden picks with an attached wire that are used to give extra support to delicate stems, to bundle several stems together, or to serve as a stem lengthener.

Bases

Straw, grapevine, foam, polystyrene, and wire forms make creating wreaths, topiaries, and swags easy. Visit your local craft store and you'll be amazed by the assortment. Although each type of base has its own benefits and drawbacks, when working with delicate, wispy dried flowers, a wire base is ideal.

Hot-Glue Gun

Crafters swear by this trusty tool, and dried-flower designers in particular can find many uses for a glue gun. A dab of hot glue is the perfect (and invisible) way to attach delicate dried flowers to a base without damaging the flower.

Basic Techniques

Using Floral Picks

Floral picks prevent damage to delicate stems and can save you a significant amount of time.

1. To attach materials to a floral pick, arrange several stems of dried flowers together in a mint bouquet. Place the stems next to the pick about midpoint down the pick with the pick's pointed side facing down.

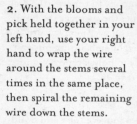

2. With the blooms and pick held together in your left hand, use your right hand to wrap the wire around the stems several times in the same place, then spiral the remaining wire down the stems.

3. To use a picked mini bouquet, simply insert it by the tip into floral foam (for a low-based arrangement) or into a wreath base. When inserting bouquets into wreath bases, be sure to insert them at an angle. You may need to add a small amount of hot glue at the tip of the pick to help it stay in place.

Using Floral Tape

Floral tape comes in hues of green and brown. You will need to use floral tape only when there's a chance that your picked mini bouquet will show in your finished project, so be sure to choose the color that will be the least conspicuous in your finished project.

1. To use floral tape, hold it against your picked bouquet. Stretch it slightly, then spiral it down the picked stems.

2. To use a taped floral bouquet, insert or glue it into a base material.

Working with Single Blooms

Single blooms are easy to work with and can create a wide array of projects. If you have a lot of blooms, you can cover an entire surface area, such as a topiary ball or a wreath base, with blooms. Otherwise, simply follow the instructions below.

1. Cover the surface you plan to decorate with moss using floral pins or hot glue.

2. Remove the stems from the blooms and add a dab of hot glue to their backs, then press them into the moss.

3. For maximum effect, vary the size and color of the blooms you use.

Note: See the Silk Flowers section for information on creating arrangements.

Dried Rose Topiary

Designer: Heidi Tyline King & Nancy Worrell

Simply elegant or sweetly simple? You choose. By using florals—rosebuds or rose petals—or herbals—lavender or potpourri, you can make this topiary a delight to look at or an aromatic centerpiece. Mix and match the florals with the herbals for a bedroom delight, or use only rosebuds to create captivating table adornments for a bridal shower. Your choice of ribbon will dress it up or down—grosgrain, satin, or raffia. While the hint of Spanish moss adds a texture that takes you to remembrances of gentle and gracious summer evenings.

Materials and Tools

4-inch-diameter (10 cm) polystyrene ball

Loose rosebuds, lavender, rose petals, or potpourri

Floral foam

6-inch-diameter (15 cm) terra-cotta pot

½-inch-diameter (1.5 cm) twig, 15 inches (38 cm) long

Spanish moss

Ribbon (optional)

Hot-glue gun and glue sticks

What to Do

1. Cover a small portion of the polystyrene ball with hot glue, then stick rosebuds onto ball one at a time until the entire ball is covered.

2. Cut a piece of floral foam to fit snugly inside the terra-cotta pot and wedge into place.

3. Stick the end of the twig into the bottom of the ball and the other end into the floral foam.

4. Cover the top of the floral foam with Spanish moss.

5. If desired, tie a bow around the center of the twig or around the top of the pot.

DESIGNER TIP

Pressing has been a popular method of drying and preserving flowers for centuries, and it is still a lot of fun. And though flower presses are widely available, a simple press is easy and inexpensive to improvise at home. Just remove the blooms and leaves from their stems, then arrange the plant material on a sheet of porous paper. Make sure you allow an adequate amount of space between plants. Cover the plants with another sheet of paper, then position the pages inside a heavy book. Open the book every few weeks to check the drying process.

Raffia Garland

Designer: Cynthia Gillooly

Bunches of raffia are knotted together to create an appealing swag that can be as thick or as long as you want it to be. This garland measures 10 feet (9 m)—a great length for draping around doors or large windows.

Materials and Tools

Package of raffia

4 yards (3.6 m) sheer organza ribbon, 2 inches (5 cm) wide

Bunch of dried German statice

Bunch of dried purple annual statice

16 dried roses

1½ yard (1.4 m) wired satin ribbon, 1 inch (2.5 cm) wide

Hot-glue gun

Floral tape

Continued ➡

What to Do

1. Measure the length of the area where you would like to hang the swag. Separate the raffia and gather strands together into the desired thickness, then tie the lengths together in knots until the desired length is achieved.

2. Thread organza ribbon through the raffia; tie to the raffia at intervals to secure.

3. You will need to make a bouquet for every raffia knot in your swag. Here, we've alternated large and small bouquets. Make the large bouquets by arranging the dried flowers into three bouquets of seven to nine stems and securing the stems with floral tape. Secure the large bouquets at the raffia knots by inserting the stem into the knots, then tying at the base of bouquet with loose strands of raffia. Finish off by tying each large bouquet with a knotted bow made with ½ yard (0.45 m) of the 1-inch (2.5 cm) ribbon.

4. Make the small bouquets by hot-gluing five to seven stems of flowers in a pleasing arrangement directly to every other knot.

—From *The Michaels Book of Arts & Crafts*

MAKING WREATHS WITH FAUX FLOWERS, FRUITS & GREENS

Taylor Hagerty

Getting Started

Every craft has tools, materials, and techniques that make projects come together quickly and easily, allowing you to showcase your creative flair. The first thing to do when designing a wreath is to determine its theme. That decision will guide you in choosing the type of base and embellishments. When it comes to bases, you can always choose from traditional shapes and materials; however, using something unique, such as flip-flop sandals or a wooden frame, ratchets up the uniqueness quotient from the everyday to truly spectacular. Learn how to tie an impressive bow or make your own wreath bases using grapevine, foam, or a simple wire hanger. Once you've mastered these techniques, you're well on your way to designing distinctive wreaths for any occasion.

Embellishments

Buttons

Buttons have come a long way from the basic round shape. They are available at craft and fabric stores in themed novelty sets and large-quantity assortment bags. Adhere with glue dots, hot glue, strong-hold glue, or craft glue.

Fabric

With a nearly unlimited variety of textures, weights, and colors, fabric is a multipurpose element in wreath design. Use airy tulle to tie an ethereal bow or wrap the base in denim for a casual, masculine touch.

Flowers, Plants, and Herbs

Traditionally, some sort of plant material is used when making a wreath. Everything from evergreen branches to herbs to flowers and even lowly weeds has graced the curve of a wreath.

Found Items

Practically everyone has a stockpile of everyday items such as costume jewelry, stray game pieces, unused keys, and mismatched spoons. They can be an untapped resource for unique wreaths.

Glitter

Glitter is available in a rainbow of colors with sheer and opaque qualities. Textures range from ultra fine to chunky grains to snowflake-like drifts of mice. A solid bond is ensured by using double-sided tape, glitter glue, or adhesive paper. A fine tip for glitter glue is essential for detailed work.

Memorabilia

Anything that reminds you of a special occasion, whether it is photos, souvenirs, ticket stubs, or coins from a foreign country, can make a sentimental wreath project. Create a wreath using greeting cards for a milestone birthday or favorite holiday.

Natural Items

Creating an organic wreath is easy to do using natural elements such as bamboo pieces, a bird's nest, birdseed, realistic plastic or foam eggs, feathers, moss, or pinecones. When using these materials it's a good idea to display the wreath in a protected spot, because it won't withstand buffeting by the elements.

Raffia

Raffia is a natural material made of strips from a large palm tree that are cut and dried. The resulting fibers are a natural creamy brown that can be dyed different colors. It can withstand some moisture but if it's been dyed, it will likely bleed on the surrounding area.

Ribbon

Available in a mind-boggling variety of widths, colors, and materials, there is surely a perfect ribbon for every type of wreath. It is important to choose good-quality ribbon for your projects—nothing can ruin a wreath more quickly than sub-par ribbon.

Seashells

Seashells make wonderful embellishments on any nautical-themed wreath. Shells can be used as subtle accents or clustered with ornaments, ideal for holiday décor.

Twine

Twine is composed of two or more strands of yarn, cotton, sisal, jute, or hemp twisted together to create a strong string. It's usually a neutral tan color but is also available in many colors. Twine is a great substitute for ribbon in natural or country-style designs.

Yarn

In addition to its use as wrapping for a wreath base, yarn is a textural choice for both the eyes and the fingers. It is found in a wide variety of colors, thicknesses, styles, and materials. Tied into a bow or gathered into bunches, yarn is an uncommon accent on a wreath.

Adhesives

Craft Glue

This thick, versatile adhesive can be applied with a foam brush and will hold heavy embellishments securely in place. It does take some time to dry and form a bond, so take that into account as you are choosing adhesive for a wreath project.

Double-Sided Tape

This convenient tape works best for paper-to-paper adhesion. It is simple to use and creates a quick, permanent bond.

Floral tape

This tape is a strong, stretchy, non-sticky material that is ideal for securing floral wire to the stems of silk or fresh flowers, reinforcing weak stems while simultaneously hiding the wire.

Hot Glue Gun and Glue Sticks

This adhesive is used for most projects in this book. It works quickly and is quite strong on most surfaces. It is available in two forms: high-temp (hot) glue and low-temp glue. High-temperature glue melts at a high temperature and is best for bonding ceramics, metal, plastics, wood, or other nonporous materials or heavy items. In general, the higher the melt temperature of the glue, the stronger the bond created. Low-temp glue melts at a lower temperature and cools quickly. Use it on lightweight embellishments and when applying adhesive directly to polystyrene foam forms. (High-temp glue will melt most foam.)

Permanent Adhesive

Permanent adhesive is sold in a squeeze tube and bonds a wide variety of surfaces, including glass, metal, and plastic.

Spray Adhesive

Spray adhesive comes in a spray can and is used to quickly cover surfaces with a light misting of glue. Use it when covering a polystyrene form with potpourri, berries, or petals. This product dries very quickly, so work fast.

Materials

Floral Pins

These pins work well to secure materials to foam shapes. Pins are available in a variety of shapes and sizes. The most common sizes are the longer corsage pins that range between 2" and 2½" (5 and 6.5 cm). The shorter boutonniere pins are usually between 1¼" and 2" (3 and 5 cm) long.

Floral Spray Paint

An easy way to integrate a wreath base into your color scheme is to use spray paint. Available in a wide range of colors and finishes, spray paint is fast and dries fairly quickly. Choose an interior-exterior paint for durability. Use multiple light coats instead of one or two heavy ones to avoid a runny, drippy mess.

Foam Core Board

This useful, lightweight board is made by adhering heavy paper to both sides of a thin foam core. Available at most craft stores in many colors, thicknesses, and sizes, foam core board is great for making unusually shaped bases and for reinforcing paper elements such as signs and photos.

Moss

Used to cover floral foam and arrangement mechanics. Popular varieties include Spanish moss in natural or green, sheet moss, and reindeer moss. All achieve coverage; choice depends on personal preference and design style.

Polystyrene Foam

Available in green or white and has a very coarse texture. Polystyrene foam comes in sheets and preformed shapes such as spheres, cones and wreaths.

Wire

Wire is very important for sturdy design. It is available in a variety of gauges ranging from #16 to #28; the smaller the number of wire, the larger the gauge thickness. Wire can be purchased in precut lengths of 12" (30.5 cm) or on a roll. Rolled wire is called paddle or reel wire. It is used in wreath-making when one continuous strand is needed for stability.

Tools

Craft knife

Craft scissors

Floral snips or shears

Foam brushes

Measuring tape

Needle-nose pliers

Polyurethane spray

Ruler

Sandpaper

Serrated knife

Wire cutters

Wired floral picks

Wreath Bases

The foundation of a wreath supports both the elements of the wreath and the theme of the design. It can be made using traditional bases, which range from polystyrene foam to twigs, vines, or wire and are available in most craft stores. For a more unusual base, consider using flip-flop sandals, a lariat, or jump rope.

Foam

Foam wreath bases are best used with floral or other lightweight embellishments and are available in green injection-molded and white polystyrene as well as floral foam. The injection-molded foam base is difficult to insert materials into without first piercing a hole in the foam. White polystyrene foam is easy to work with and works best if embellishments are hot glued to the form. Floral foam is specifically designed for use with fresh flowers and greens. It is usually soaked in water until it is thoroughly saturated and then decorated.

Natural Materials

Bases made from flexible vines, willow, twig, straw, and grains such as broomcorn are wonderful bases for nature-inspired wreaths. Grapevine and willow-type bases tend to be sturdier and will withstand the elements in a sheltered location. They can also support heavier embellishments. Straw, twig, and grains generally require the additional support of a wire base.

Wire

These preformed bases made of several rows of wire provide a uniform shape. Wire bases are good for delicate dried flowers but can also handle heavyweight embellishments. A basic wire base formed using a coat hanger is a simple, inexpensive alternative, but it doesn't offer a lot of support, so you'll need to use lightweight materials for embellishment.

Wood

A wooden frame with wide edges makes for an unusual wreath. Decoupage paper onto the frame or wrap it with strips of fabric. To add bulky softness, first wrap strips of batting around the frame and then cover with strips of fabric. Another unusual type of wooden form is a large embroidery hoop. These are made from balsa wood and are available in a variety of sizes.

TIME-SAVING TIP

MAKING INTERESTING WREATHS

Unconventional shapes such as rectangles, ovals, squares, or even giant monograms are an interesting twist. Consider making very small or very large wreaths for different effects. Use three smaller embellished wreaths strung together to form a wreath garland.

Hanging a Wreath

When you're ready to display your creation, you can always use a nail; however, this creates a hole in your door or wall. Instead, there are a wide variety of hangers on the market. Some use a plastic hook and removable adhesive, others feature a molded over-the-door arm with a hook, and some employ magnets.

Each product will have a recommended weight limit to help you choose the correct type for your wreath. You can make your own wreath hanger using a plain wire coat hanger. Straighten the hanger and then bend it to fit over your door so you can hang the wreath on the hook.

Making a Foam Core Base

Create your own foam base by drawing the desired shape on a piece of foam core board and then cutting it out with a craft knife. To add bulk, simply adhere polystyrene foam blocks to the foam core shape using a low-temp glue gun. Use a paring or serrated knife to shape the blocks if necessary. You can also use heavy-duty cardboard in place of foam core board.

Making a Grapevine Wreath

To make a grapevine wreath, soak several long vines in a large tub of water until they are flexible. Remove the vines from the water and trim leaves and unnecessary twigs with floral shears as desired. **Note**: Use fresh vines to skip the soaking.

Coil the vine into approximately the finished size you want, weaving any excess vine into the coil. Continue to weave additional vines, starting in a different spot on the wreath, until you've reached the thickness you want. **Note**: Secure the vines in spots with twists of floral wire to maintain the shape of the wreath.

Because the wreath was soaked, or if you used fresh-cut vines, you'll need to allow the wreath to dry. Leave it outside in the sun for a few days or bring it inside and hang it. If you hang the wreath, you'll need to rotate it periodically to maintain its shape. To accelerate the drying time, place the wreath in an oven set at 170 degrees F (76.6 C) or lower and watch it carefully for approximately 30–40 minutes. If the wreath begins to warp out of shape, place it between two oven racks to flatten.

Making a Simple Wire Base

You can make a simple wire base using a wire coat hanger. Form the hanger into the shape you want—a circle or heart shape is your best bet. Leave the hook attached to use as a hanger or cut it off in the middle of the twist using wire cutters. Bend the cut ends down the wreath shape.

Shaping Hairpin Wires

Hairpins are used to pin moss and foliage into foam. They are easily made if "S" pins are not available or a smaller discreet pin is needed in the design. Using wire cutters, cut 20- or 22-gauge wire into 2" (5 cm) segments. Bend at center and fold wire into equal parts to create hairpin.

Storing a Wreath

There comes a time, particularly with seasonal wreaths, when you'll want to store your wreaths. Proper packaging will ensure that the wreath emerges next season in flawless condition, ready to be displayed. There are plastic and fabric wreath bags available for purchase that will protect their contents from dust, insects, and facing, but you can also use inexpensive large black plastic drawstring bags. Place the wreath in the bag so the drawstring is at the bottom and then pierce a hole in the seam of the bag and thread a large hook through to hang it. Pull the drawstring tight and knot. Other options include specially made cardboard wreath boxes that will allow you to store the wreath lying down instead of hanging it. Of course, a regular cardboard packing box in the appropriate size will work just as well.

Taping Wire

Begin covering wire by wrapping floral tape around the top of the wire, stretching tape slightly and using your thumb and index finger to twist the tape around the wire. Work down the wire, gently stretching the tape with one hand as you twist the tape down with wire with your thumb and index finger of your other hand. Pinch off tape at the end of the wire.

Tying a Simple Bow

Make one loop at each end of a ribbon length, being careful not to twist or bunch the ribbon. Cross the right loop over the left, wrapping the right loop behind the left, then under, and up through the hole. Pull the loops into a smooth knot. Adjust the loops and trim the tails so they are slightly longer than the loops.

The bow may be attached directly to the project with hot glue or attached with floral wire.

Making a Florist Bow

Pinch the ribbon and form a loop, leaving desired length of ribbon for one bow tail (Fig. 1). Make same-size loop in the opposite direction (Fig. 2).

Continue adding loops on each side, securing them under thumb and forefinger, decreasing loop lengths for each layer (Fig. 3).

Figure 1   *Figure 2*

Once you have desired number of loops, twist one last small loop around your thumb to make center loop (Fig. 4). Insert floral wire through center loop and twist tightly on bow back, securing all loops. Fluff out bow, starting with bottom two loops.

Figure 3   *Figure 4*

Continued ➡

Pull loops tightly in opposite directions. Continue with remaining loops until you have desired bow shape (Fig. 5). Trim tails to desired length using an angled cut. To create a forked cut, fold end of ribbon in half lengthwise and cut at an angle toward folded edge.

Figure 4

Using a Bow-Making Tool

Bow-making tools were invented to hold looped ribbon in place, leaving your hands free to secure the bow with wire. They also make it easy to get creative with your floral bows by adding a variety of different ribbons and even strings of pearls, greenery, feathers, and flowers. They are fairly inexpensive, but if you love to use ribbon, consider creating your own.

MATERIALS

Craft knife

Foam core board (2Ð square)

Pencil

Ruler

Wire

INSTRUCTIONS

1. Measure, mark, and cut 4" (10 cm) line in one side of foam core board using craft knife (Fig. 1). Make slit wide enough to hold several folds of ribbon.

2. Follow directions for making a Florist Bow, but instead of holding loops with fingers, simply slide ribbon loops into cut (Fig. 2).

3. When you are done, carefully pull out layered bow and twist wire around middle of loops to secure.

Flowers, Fruits, & Greens

A wreath embellished with flowers, herbs, or fruits will tantalize the senses both visually and by its aroma. The following projects are perfect housewarming gifts and are a wonderful way to use the bounty of your garden to decorate your home. They recall the renewal of spring, the warm days of summer, and an abundant fall harvest deep in the heart of winter when all that is green and growing lies dormant....Let go of any preconceived notions of what "must" be on a wreath and allow your imagination to discover new ways to use everyday plants.

Organic Succulent

MATERIALS

15" (38 cm) moss-covered wreath

Chicken and hen plant

Dusty Miller plants (2)

Faux bamboo

Glass stones (5)

Hot glue gun and glue sticks

Jade plants (2)

Lambs' ears (5)

Moss-covered stones (3)

Ruler

Sedum plants (2)

Wire cutters

Wired wooden picks (12)

INSTRUCTIONS

1. Ready wreath form by securing any loose moss in place with hot glue.

2. Using wired wooden picks, lengthen stems of succulent plants as needed. **Note:** This will help ease the plants' insertion into the wreath.

3. Insert largest plants first, opposite one another for balance, hot glue in place.

4. Using smaller plants, create clusters and fill in wreath; hot glue in place. Add moss-covered stones to fill in empty spaces; hot glue in place.

5. Cut faux bamboo into two 15" (38 cm) segments using wire cutters. Adhere on top of wreath and hot glue in place.

6. Hot glue glass stones as accents among clustered plants, grouping stones for impact.

Rosemary

MATERIALS

12" (30.5 cm) wire wreath form

Cheesecloth

Craft scissors

Dried cooking herbs

Floral snips

Fresh rosemary

Paddle wire

Raffia: green, orange

Ruler

Twine

Wire cutters

INSTRUCTIONS

1. Snip rosemary into 5" (12.5 cm) segments and then gather 8-10 pieces into small bundles. Using short pieces of wire, wrap one end to secure. **Note:** You will need about 16-18 bundles to cover the 12" (30.5 cm) wreath.

2. Lay one bundle on wreath and secure by wrapping with wire twine.

3. Continue layering bundles to cover stem ends and wrapping each with wire to completely cover wreath.

4. Tie raffia in bow and wire to wreath form.

5. Create bouquet garni with 5" (12.5 cm) square pieces of cheesecloth filled with dried cooking herbs. Tie closed tightly with twine.

6. Tie bouquet garni onto wreath form and then the raffia bow at center. **Note:** The bouquet garni can be snipped from the wreath as needed for cooking.

Dried Hydrangea

MATERIALS

15" (38 cm) foam wreath: green

Craft scissors

Craft wire

Dried hydrangea (20–33 heads)

Floral snips

Hot glue gun and glue sticks: low-temp

Pearl tassel

Pearls

Polyurethane spray

Ribbon: 2" (5 cm) green wire-edge

Ruler

Sheet moss: green

Wire cutters

Wired wooden picks

INSTRUCTIONS

1. Cover edges of foam wreath with green sheet moss; secure in place with hot glue.

2. Snip hydrangea heads into small clusters using floral snips, following natural stem breaks. Add wooden pick to each stem.

3. Insert hydrangea clusters into foam, snuggling one bundle against the next. Continue to fill and cover wreath.

4. Spray wreath with polyurethane to preserve hydrangea; let dry.

5. Hot glue pearls randomly into wreath to accent.

6. Tie 1 yard (91.5 cm) of ribbon into bow and trim ends; add pearl tassel at center with wire. Using wire, tie bow onto wreath base.

TIME-SAVING TIP

TRY A DIFFERENT SHAPE

It's easy to create the look of the Dried Hydrangea wreath using other foam shapes such as an open heart, solid heart, or cross for a special holiday design.

Fragrant Lavender

MATERIALS

12" x 15" (30.5 x 38 cm) wooden frame

Craft scissors

Dried lavender (1 bunch)

Floral snips

Hot glue gun and glue sticks

Paddle wire

Pepper grass (1 bunch)

Ribbon: 1½" (4 cm) purple silk wired

Ruler

Silk wax flowers (4 stems)

Wire cutters

INSTRUCTIONS

1. Divide lavender into small bundles of 15–16 stems. Gather stems and bind with short length of wire. Snip stems to about 4" (10 cm) in length. Continue creating bundles until you have about 16. Repeat with wax flowers and pepper grass.

2. Using wire, wrap free end around wooden frame twice at top corner. Lay one small bundle on top corner of frame and wrap wire twice around stems and frame.

3. Lay second lavender bundle on frame covering stems of first bundle; wrap stems twice with wire. **Note:** Do not cut the wire; use the continuous strand to complete this project.

4. Continue with remaining bundles to complete frame, alternating wax flowers and pepper grass between lavender bundles.

5. Cut ribbon into four 18" (45.5 cm) segments; tie each into a simple bow end and trim ends.

6. Place one bow in each corner of wreath, securing in place with hot glue.

TIME-SAVING TIP

MAKING SCENTS

To keep the Fragrant Lavender scent heady, add a small drop of lavender oil as needed to freshen.

Mini Pumpkins

MATERIALS

3" (7.5 cm) miniature faux pumpkins (8)

18" (45.5 cm) twig wreath

Clear polyurethane spray

Hot glue gun and glue sticks

INSTRUCTIONS

1. Arrange pumpkins evenly around inside edge of twig wreath.

2. Adhere pumpkins in place with hot glue gun.

3. Spray entire wreath with polyurethane spray; let dry.

TIME-SAVING TIP

EYE ON THE BASE

A good preassembled wreath base can be found in a discount store, hidden under unattractive decorations. It's easy to remove poor-quality silks and plastic decorations and create your own wreath using the base.

Monogram Letter

MATERIALS

12" (30.5 cm) wooden letter form

Floral snips

Hot glue gun and glue sticks

Jeweled butterfly

Polyurethane spray

Silk hydrangea bush

INSTRUCTIONS

1. Using floral snips, cut individual flower blossoms from silk hydrangea bush.

2. Hot glue individual flower blossoms to letter, clustering closely to cover completely. Use any remaining blooms to fill in open gaps.

3. Spray wreath with polyurethane to preserve hydrangea; let dry.

4. Hot glue jeweled butterfly at top of wreath to accent.

TIME-SAVING TIP

GET INTO SHAPE

You can also use corrugated paper or polystyrene foam to form the Monogram Letter base. Simply trace a letter template of your choice and cut to shape with a serrated knife. The form can be covered with ribbon or moss before adding flowers or greenery.

—FROM *Make It in Minutes: Wreaths*

FLORAL HOME ACCESSORIES

Melody Thompson

A good design is not complete without accessories. They are the finishing touch that lends personality and style to a room. What better way to accessorize than with flowers—flowers add warmth and a natural, organic element to hard surfaces.

Fill a box or bowl with blossoms for softness and color. Enhance picture frames, a small wooden clock, or a napkin ring with a few blooms. Use a candlestick to fashion a mini floral arrangement. Don't forget items that are easily embellished inside and out with faux flowers such as baskets or glass bowls or jars.

Personalizing traditional accessories with faux flowers brings a fresh appeal with an exclusive feel that maximizes visual impact.

Continued ➜

Basket Organizer

MATERIALS

Basket with handles

Dried lotus pod

Gerbera daisies (3)

Hot glue

Scissors

Silk leaves: large (3)

Wire cutters

Wired ribbon (1 yard)

INSTRUCTIONS

1. Remove stems from daisies and lotus pod at blossom head using wire cutters.

2. Tie ribbon in a small loopy bow and hot glue to basket corner.

3. Nestle two gerberas and lotus pod near bow and hot glue in place.

4. Hot glue remaining daisy to opposite corner of basket. Hot glue silk leaves to clusters.

TIME-SAVING TIP

MAKING ORGANIZATION PRETTY

Add some sunshine to your desk space with faux flowers. Use a variety of basket sizes, decorating each a little differently for a delightfully organized grouping. Try color-coded blossoms on containers for specific tasks with your favorite flower.

Mosaic Floral Frame

MATERIALS

Assorted flower heads with texture (4-5 of 6 varieties)

Floral foam

Floral snips

Hot glue

Picture frame

Serrated knife

Sheet moss

INSTRUCTIONS

1. Prepare frame by removing back easel and lay flat. Cut foam to fit within frame opening using serrated knife; hot glue to secure.

2. Cover foam with sheet moss; secure in place using hot glue.

3. Remove flower heads from stems with floral snips. Arrange in vertical rows on moss-covered foam in pleasing color placement. Hot glue each bloom in place.

TIME-SAVING TIP

CREATE COORDINATING PIECES

Use any leftover flowers from the Mosaic Floral Frame project to coordinate with another frame by gluing clusters to the top and corner of the frame for a colorful accent.

Seashell Napkin Ring

MATERIALS

Amaranthus stem (1)

Berry stem (1)

Cardboard roll

Floral snips

Hot glue

Natural varita sticks (12 per napkin)

Ruler

Scissors

Seashells

INSTRUCTIONS

1. Cut cardboard roll into 2" (5 cm) segments using scissors to create napkin rings.

2. Cut amaranthus into two 5" (12.5 cm) segments using floral snips. Wrap flower around each ring's edge and secure using hot glue.

3. Hot glue assorted seashells and individual berries to fill in open space.

4. Bundle varita sticks and slide into ring along with napkin.

—FROM *Make It in Minutes: Faux Flower Arrangements*

TIME-SAVING TIP

CONTINUE THE THEME

Shells are a very versatile accent. Their natural beauty provides an ethereal setting. Combine them with candles for a romantic feel or buckets and shovels for a casual look. Pile extra seashells in individual bowls at each place setting to continue your theme.

SACHETS & POTPOURRIS

Dawn Cusick & Megan Kirby, Editors

Just as your garden provides beauty, color, and fragrance to your home in the warmer months, potpourri can offer these qualities year-round. Indeed, your summer garden can live on in gorgeous bowls of potpourri, in sachets, and in a variety of other fragrance-based crafts. What better gift than a lovely, fragrant sachet?

Materials and Tools

Purchased Potpourri

Commercially made potpourris are available in dozens of colors and fragrances.

Flowers and Herbs

Dried plants of all kinds, with or without natural color or fragrance, can make terrific materials for potpourri. Whether you grow your own plant materials or purchase them, experiment with a variety of flowers, herbs, and spices to find the ones that best suit your tastes.

Filler Material

Wood shavings are popular filler material for homemade potpourris since they are inexpensive, readily absorb fragrance, and provide a nice texture to potpourris. Clean straw and moss are also good choices. Depending on the potpourri you choose, a filler material may not be necessary.

Fragrance

Fragrance oils, also called essential oils, are becoming less expensive and more widely available, and make it practical to use nonfragrant plant material just for the sake of color or texture. Add these oils in small amounts until the desired fragrance level is achieved, then as needed to refresh potpourris. (Be careful: these oils can leave stains on wood, fabric, and walls.) There are many ways to impart fragrance, so be creative; for example, scented wax or even shavings from a scented bar of soap can lend fragrance.

Fabric

Because most sachets are quite small, and thus require very little fabric, you can treat yourself to high-quality fabrics. Though any fabric will work as a sachet, natural fibers (such as cotton, silk, or linen) are more effective at releasing scent. Wedding netting, tulle, and lace are also good choices.

Embellishments

Think of your sachet as a blank canvas just waiting for your own creative touch. Buttons, ribbons, lace, dried or silk flowers, beads, stamps, and fabric paint can turn a simple sachet into a special item—and you will need only a few embellishments to make a big impact.

Hot-Glue Gun

This is a great tool for securing ribbons, buttons, and other embellishments to sachets, as well as for attaching pieces of floral material. If you don't have a sewing machine or the time to hand stitch, hot glue can be used to make simple sachets.

Fabric Glue

If you don't have a sewing machine or the inclination to sew, fabric glue can be used to make a variety of simple sachets. Look for it in sewing departments.

Basic Techniques

Making Potpourri

Though potpourri is widely available, crafters have long understood the benefits of making one's own special potpourri blend. Remember that everyone (yes, everyone) has fragrance preferences. Before you begin a potpourri project, take a moment to consider your preferences or those of the recipient.

1. Create a fragrant base by combining an assortment of scented, fully dried plant materials in a large, nonmetal bowl. At this point, you should focus on scent, so continue to add ingredients until you are pleased with the fragrance.

2. Now, make your potpourri look pretty by adding dried blooms, leaves, seed pods, berries, or other plant material. Add any filler material at this time, as well. Choose materials with complementary colors and textures. Mix everything together loosely with your hands or a wooden spoon. **Note:** If your potpourri will be used for a sachet, this step may be unnecessary.

3. Add the fixative of your choice. For every cup of potpourri, add 1 tablespoon (15 g) of fixative. (Fixatives are natural materials such as orrisroot, gum benzoin resin, tonka beans, sandalwood bark, and patchouli leaves.)

4. To intensify the fragrance, add a few drops of essential oil, if desired. (Choose a fragrance that is the same as or complementary to the scented materials you've used in Step 1.) Use a wooden spoon to carefully combine all the ingredients.

5. Place potpourri in a paper bag, and roll the top of the bag several times to close tightly. Store bag in a dark location and shake it once a day for a week to distribute and blend the scents. For the following five weeks, shake the bag once a week. In six weeks, your potpourri is ready to display and enjoy.

Sewing a Sachet

These simple sachets require only small pieces of fabric and simple sewing skills. Go ahead, splurge on fancy cottons and rich silks!

1. Cut a piece of fabric 12 inches wide x 10 inches high (30 x 25 cm). Turn down a narrow hem across one long edge. Press and stitch.

2. Press down a second, larger hem (about an inch, 2.5 cm), then fold the fabric in half with right sides facing. Pin the side and bottom seams, then stitch.

3. Turn right sides out and press. Fill with potpourri and tie with a pretty ribbon.

Note: Interesting variations can be made when using cotton eyelet fabrics. Just arrange the embroidered openings at the top and thread the ribbon through them to tie.

Two-Minute Sachets

Need a quick gift? Give a handkerchief sachet as a gift by itself or tie one into a bow on a wrapped package.

1. Place the handkerchief face down on a flat surface, then add several large spoonfuls of potpourri to the center.

2. Gather the sides of the handkerchief up and over the potpourri. Twist several times just above the potpourri, then tie with a pretty ribbon.

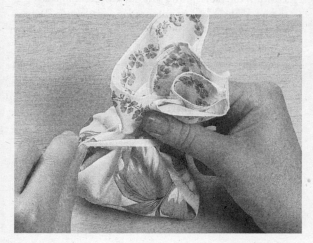

DESIGNER TIP

Have the perfect container but not enough potpourri to fill it? Just fill the bottom with a piece of floral foam or some newspaper or tissue paper. Just make sure the potpourri covers the filler material below completely.

Quick No-Sew Sachets

A few simple supplies—fabric glue, pinking shears, and a small piece of pretty fabric—are all you need to create great sachets.

1. Cut out two 5-inch (12.5 cm) squares of fabric. Pink the edges to prevent the fabric from unraveling.

2. Place one square face down on a flat surface, then place a large spoonful of potpourri in the center of it.

3. Outline the fabric square about ¼ inch (6 mm) in from each edge with fabric glue.

4. Place the second square on top of the first, right side facing up, and press it gently into the glue. Allow it to completely dry before handling.

The ancient Greeks placed a muslin sachet beside each guest at banquets; surely you can find many uses for sachets in your home as well. Though a sachet can also be secured with a hot-glue gun, a sewn sachet will be more secure and long lasting. The sachet described is finished on all sides, but you can also leave one side open, finish the open end with a simple stitch, then tie with a ribbon.

Perfectly Simple Potpourris

Simple potpourris radiate both beauty and fragrance. You can purchase special bowls to display your potpourris, or simply use something pretty from your china cabinet.

MATERIALS AND TOOLS

Potpourri of your choice (store bought or homemade)

Display bowls

Fragrant oils

WHAT TO DO

1. Place your potpourri in a bowl and add a drop or two of fragrant oil if needed.

2. Choose a display location away from direct sunlight and high moisture. (Sunlight quickly fades the bright colors of potpourri, while moist areas cause the dried blooms to reabsorb moisture.)

Continued ➜

DESIGNER TIP

Another easy sachet: Purchase a muslin tea bag at any health food store, fill with your favorite potpourri blend, then pull string tight to secure. These little bags are inexpensive and easy to embellish and are great for tucking all around the house.

DESIGNER TIP

Making your own potpourri is a fun alternative to store-bought varieties. Here are some fragrant plant materials that work well in potpourri: roses, lemon verbena, scented geraniums, honeysuckle, eucalyptus, lemon balm, lemon thyme, lemon basil, lemon grass, lavender, mint, sassafras, dried citrus peel, rosemary, allspice, nutmeg, cloves, bay, sage, star anise, or cinnamon sticks.

No-Sew Hankie Sachets

Perhaps you're lucky enough to have a box filled with your grandmother's cherished handkerchiefs. If not, check out flea markets and vintage shops for old-fashioned handkerchiefs made of fine linen and embellished with hand embroidery or tatting. Here's a great way to make great use of them without causing the hankie itself any harm.

Materials and Tools

    Assorted handkerchiefs

    Potpourri of your choice

    Ribbon

    Beads (optional)

What to Do

RIBBON-TIED HANKIE SACHET

1. Launder and press the handkerchief and position the fabric, with the decorative side facing down, on a clean, flat surface.

2. Place a small amount of potpourri in the center of the handkerchief. (Several small spoonfuls should be plenty). Optional: If you want to use less potpourri, then add a few drops of essential oil to a couple cotton balls, and put those on the hankie with the potpourri.

3. Draw up all four sides of the handkerchief, then tie ribbon to secure. Thread beads on the ends of the ribbons, if desired.

FOLDED HANKIE SACHET

Sew or glue the decorative edges together to form an envelope, leaving one side open to insert potpourri. Fill sachet, then glue remaining edge closed.

Dream Pillows

These dream pillows are the ultimate pamper-yourself gift and are charming when presented as sets tied with ribbons and adorned with beads—try a stack of different-colored sachets all in the same size, a set of pillows in graduated sizes, as we've done here, or perhaps an array of interesting shapes (hearts, circles, and diamonds, for example). In no time you can make dozens of these scented treasures and have a handy stash of inexpensive, one-of-a-kind gifts.

Materials and Tools

    Fabric of your choice

    Needle and thread or sewing machine

    Potpourri (or other fragrant filling of your choice)

What To Do

1. Determine what sizes you would like for your pillows to be. These are 4 x 6 inches (10 x 15 cm), 5 x 7 inches (12.5 x 17.5 cm), and 6 x 8 inches (15 x 20 cm).

2. Cut two pieces of fabric to the chosen dimensions. Position the fabric with right sides together and sew them together, leaving an opening for turning. Trim seams and turn right sides out.

3. Fill the pillow. It works well to fill small pillows with potpourri. For larger pillows, it may be overwhelmingly fragrant or too expensive to fill them with potpourri alone; you may want to use a combination of potpourri and cotton balls, adding a few drops of fragrance oil, if desired. Slip stitch the opening closed.

—From The Michaels Book of Arts & Crafts

DESIGNER TIP

Look in unexpected places for materials to make sachets. An old pair of lace or crocheted gloves—perhaps you own a pair or can find one at a thrift store—makes a terrific sachet when stuffed with potpourri and tied with a pretty ribbon. Antique linens that are too damaged or stained to use as a tablecloth or bed sheet surely have a corner or section that can be salvaged to make a darling sachet for your lingerie drawer. A loose-tea strainer is a marvelous container for fragrant potpourris.

Glass Crafts

PAINTING GLASS

Dawn Cusick & Megan Kirby, Editors

Take a quick glance around and you'll discover glass objects everywhere, just waiting to be transformed into dazzling works of art. Goblets, plates, bowls, bottles, pitchers, vases, and even light fixtures can be embellished with rich translucent colors and eye-catching designs. Perfect for beginners, the new glass paints are so easy to use that you'll soon find yourself squeezing, sponging, and brushing them onto every available glass surface, with spectacular results!

Materials and Tools

Glass Objects

Collect old and new glass of all kinds. Don't forget what's in the recycling bin!

Isopropyl Alcohol and Cotton Balls

These are used to condition glass surfaces before painting.

Paint

Glass paints come in bottles, tubes, pens, and spray cans. Sample different types (and brands) before purchasing an entire collection of colors. The boxed text has more on paints.

Artist's Brushes and Stencil Brushes

You'll want a variety of shapes and sizes. If you can, spend a bit more for a higher quality brush.

Sponges

Kitchen sponges (cut into various shapes) or dishcloths, precut sponges in fun designs, or even crumpled paper can all be used to press, rather than brush, paint onto glass.

Mixing Palette

Inexpensive plastic palettes are handy for holding and mixing paints while you work. You can also make your own from a flat plastic lid or use a saucer covered with plastic wrap.

Plastic Applicator Bottles

Pour glass paint into these and you'll be able to squeeze, rather than brush, it onto your glass surface.

Changeable Paint Tips

Used with tube paints or applicator bottles, these plastic or metal tips create special effects when you squeeze paint through them. Be sure the tips will fit your tubes or bottles.

Stencils

A large variety of stencils can be purchased precut, or you can make your own from heavy paper or acetate.

Painter's Tape or Masking Tape

Use tape to mask areas of glass you want to keep free from paint. You can also paint between strips of tape to create straight lines.

Peel-off Leading

These adhesive circles and lines of "leading" press onto glass for a stained glass effect.

Combing Tool

Drag this tool through paint to create wavy lines or other special effects. You can also use toothpicks, knitting needles, or dry ballpoint pens to "etch" patterns into paint.

Carbon Paper

Carbon paper is used to transfer patterns onto the glass surfaces.

Rubber Bands

Rubber bands serve to secure patterns and stencils to curved surfaces. They're also useful to mask areas to paint straight lines.

Spray Adhesive

Spray adhesive is used to temporarily attach a stencil to a glass surface.

Continued →

The variety of glass paints is enough to make you dizzy! New products pop up every day, so read the package to find out if that brand will work with your plans to decorate, use, and clean your glassware. Keep the following distinctions in mind when shopping for paint.

Air-drying or Thermohardening?

Glass paints are either air-drying or thermohardening. Air-drying paints (also called "no-bake") simply sit and dry for a few days after application. Because the finish is less durable than that of thermohardening paints, use these for decorative items that won't be handled or washed often and for objects that won't fit in your oven. Thermohardening paints are baked in a standard oven after they've completely air-dried. This baking makes them wear better than air-drying paints so they can be used on items that will be handled or washed. (Most brands still require hand-washing rather than the dishwasher.) Because the type of paint will determine the finishing process needed, you should not use both thermohardening and air-dry paints on the same object.

Water- or Solvent-Based?

Glass paints are also either water- or solvent-based. Water-based paints are easy. You can squeeze, brush, dab, or spray them on. Mistakes and cleanup are taken care of with water. Simple to mix, water-based glass paints dry to opaque, transparent, translucent, and even textured finishes. A colorless acrylic medium can be added to make water-based glass paint more transparent without thinning its consistency. Solvent-based paints are usually no more durable than water-based paints, but they do require a bit more time for both preparation and cleanup. Brushes and spills need to be cleaned with mineral spirits, and the flammability of solvent-based paints makes proper ventilation a must.

Basic Techniques

The Basic Process

As you'll soon discover, the various techniques for applying paint to glass are almost endless, but the essential process can be broken down into three simple steps.

1. To clean and prepare the glass, first remove all stickers and labels, then wash the glass well in warm, soapy water. Rinse the glass with warm water. Once the glass has dried thoroughly, wipe the surface that will be painted with a cotton ball

dipped in isopropyl alcohol (this conditions the glass for painting).

2. Prepare your design as described in the following sections.

3. Paint the glass. The simplest way to do this is with glass paint and an artist's brush or with squeeze-type outliner tubes and bottles.

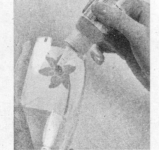

4. Seal your design. Air-dry paints can simply be left to dry for a few days, but you may want to apply a glaze or gloss to your design to give it a more polished appearance. Thermohardening paints will require baking in an oven following the paint manufacturer's instructions.

Transferring Patterns

You don't have to be an accomplished artist to paint intricate designs on glass. Just photocopy your pattern, enlarging or reducing as needed. Then use one of the following three simple methods to transfer patterns onto glass, and painting will be as easy as tracing.

Tracing Simply place a copied pattern on the back or inside of your object so it shows through to the correct position on the side you'll be painting. If the surface is curved, cut small vertical slits into the paper to help it fit the contours of the glass. Tape the pattern in place, and then trace the pattern as

you paint. Containers, such as drinking glasses and vases, can be filled with beans or another substances to help hold the paper tight against the glass.

Silhouetting To transfer simple shapes—such as hearts, circles, and stars— create a template by cutting carefully around the edges of a copied pattern. Tape or hold the shape in position on the glass, and then trace around its edges with a water-based marker.

Carbon paper Place carbon paper (carbonside down) on the glass surface and place the copied pattern on top. Hold these in place with tape or rubber bands. Trace the pattern lines with a ballpoint pen.

Stenciling

Here's an easy way to get professional-looking results quickly. Stencils allow you to repeat a pattern and decorate glass quickly, making them perfect for decorating an entire set of dinnerware.

1. Either buy precut stencils or cut your own from heavy weight paper or acetate (acetate will cling to curved surfaces better and can be used over and over). To make your own, first photocopy a template (resizing it if necessary), then use spray adhesive to mount the photocopy to your paper or acetate and allow it to dry for about ten minutes. Once the adhesive has dried, use a craft knife to carefully cut out the stencil.

2. Spray the back of the stencil lightly with spray adhesive and position it onto your glass surface (rubber bands may be used to secure stencils to cylindrical objects).

3. Pour a few drops of glass paint onto a palette, plastic lid, or saucer covered with plastic wrap. Dip the tip of a stencil brush into the paint and then blot it on a paper towel to remove any excess paint—an overloaded brush will cause paint to seep under the stencil. Dab paint into the hole of the stencil with a light, circular movement. (You can use a sponge instead of a stencil brush; just make certain the sponge isn't overloaded with paint.) Allow the paint to dry before removing the stencil.

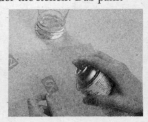

Sponging

For quick, easy coverage, try sponging glass paint. This low-tech technique creates a soft, luminous effect in minutes.

1. Pour paint onto your palette, a plastic lid, or a saucer covered with plastic wrap for easy cleanup. Dampen your sponge; then squeeze out any excess water.

2. Holding the sponge level, dip it into the paint. Try a test press against an old jar or a piece of plastic wrap. Apply more paint if the pattern is too faint, blot the sponge against an absorbent paper towel if the paint is too heavy.

3. Now simply press the sponge against your glass surface, keeping in mind that heavier pressure will result in more contact with the glass and more uniform coverage, while a lighter touch will create a softer finish. You can use the sponge to "stamp" simple shapes onto the glass or to cover the entire surface. For a graduated effect, use one color and start dabbing paint onto the bottom of your object, then lighten the pressure as you work your way up. For a graduated effect with multiple colors, use several colors, blending one color into the next as you progress.

Masking

Wondering how to get crisp, straight lines when you lack the steady hand of a neurosurgeon? Learn the simple trick of masking (using tape to keep a section of your glass paint-free), and decorating your glass with parallel stripes and geometric grids will be a snap.

1. Apply painter's tape or masking tape onto glass, remembering that the areas covered with tape will remain free of paint. For instance, to paint a stripe around a drinking glass, place two parallel horizontal strips of tape around the glass, keeping in mind that the distance between the two pieces will determine the width of the stripe.

2. Paint around and over the tape. To make the stripe, paint between and on the lines of tape. Leave the tape in place while the paint dries according to the manufacturer's directions. When the paint has completely dried, remove the tape.

OUTLINING

Outlining paint (also called "relief outliner," "contour paint," or "liquid lead") can enhance your designs with bold lines and borders. This paint comes in tubes or bottles with narrow tips, so applying it is similar to decorating a cake with icing. Make sure your outliner paint is compatible with any other glass paint used on your project. Use thermohardening outliner with thermohardening paint, air-drying outliner with air-drying paint.

Learning to outline can be a bit tricky, so practice first on an old jar, keeping in mind that outliner paint flows best in a warm, dry room. Start off making dots to get a feel for how little pressure is required when using outliner. To make a line, touch the applicator tip against the glass. Then, applying light, consistent pressure, lift the tip just slightly above the glass while moving the tube or bottle. Finish the line by gently pressing the tip back against the glass surface while releasing pressure on the tube or bottle. Wipe the tip with a paper towel and replace the cap after each use.

Projects

Citrus Splash Lemonade Set

Designer: Diana Light

As sunny as a summer afternoon, this cheerful lemonade set practically shouts "party time!" The cool design will have your guests chillin' before they even take their first sip.

MATERIALS AND TOOLS

Clear glass pitcher and 4 clear glasses

Air-drying or thermohardening glass paints in 2 yellows (one light, one darker) and 2 greens (one light, one darker)

Paper

Pen or pencil

Scissors

Clear tape

Painter's tape

Medium round artist's brush

Small round or flat artist's brush

WHAT TO DO

1. Clean and prepare the glass surfaces.

2. Cut large, medium, and small circles out of the paper (use the project photo as a guide to the size and number of circles).

3. Tape the circles to the inside of the pitcher and glasses in a random pattern. (Use the project photo as a guide for placement, keeping in mind that the circles on the glasses should be placed below where your lips will touch when drinking.)

4. Use the medium brush to fill in the large- and medium-size circles, some with the light yellow paint and some with the darker yellow paint. Don't worry about making perfect circles.

5. Use the medium brush and the lighter green paint to fill in the smaller circles.

6. When the large light yellow circles are dry, use the small artist's brush and the dark yellow paint to paint the fruit segment shapes onto only about one-third of the large light yellow circles.

7. When the large dark yellow circles are dry, use the medium brush and the light yellow paint to paint the fruit segment shapes onto only about one-third of the large dark yellow circles.

8. Once all the circles are dry, use the small brush and the darker green paint to connect some of the yellow and green circles with straight lines and some with wavy lines. (Notice that not every circle is connected by a line.) Use the painter's tape, if needed, to paint the straight lines.

9. Once the paint is completely dry, bake or glaze it according to the paint manufacturer's instructions.

Fanciful Bottle Set

Designer: Diana Light

This winsome trio shows the pleasing effect of decorating colored glass with darker shades of the same color. What goes into these playful vessels is entirely up to you.

MATERIALS AND TOOLS

3 glass bottles in solid colors

Air-drying or thermo-hardening glass paints in shades darker than or in contrast to the bottle colors

Carbon paper and pen

Medium round artist's brush

Fine detail artist's brush

WHAT TO DO

1. Wash and prepare the glass surfaces.

2. Photocopy the templates, reducing or enlarging as needed. Use the carbon paper and pen to transfer the designs to the bottles, using the photo as a guide for placement. Transfer the leaves, seeds, and berry patterns to one bottle, placing larger leaves toward the bottom of the bottle. Transfer the spiral and star burst patterns to another bottle, varying the direction and size of the spirals. Transfer the star pattern to the last bottle, making the stars a bit larger toward the bottom of the bottle.

3. Paint over the carbon lines in desired colors. (For our bottle with stars, we used silver paint to fill in some stars and to outline others with a shadow effect.)

4. Once the paint is completely dry, bake or glaze it according to the paint manufacturer's instructions.

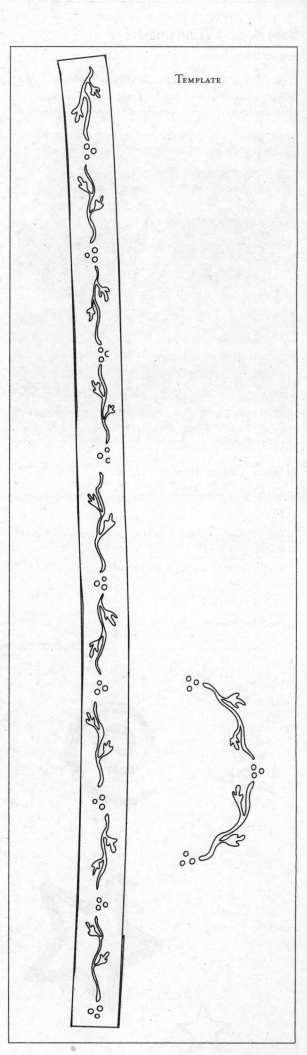

TEMPLATE

Continued →

Ruby-&-Gold Wine Goblets

Designer: Diana Light

Here's an easy way to add old-world charm to hand-painted stemware. Just a touch of gold transforms everyday glassware into an elegant set perfect for special occasions.

MATERIALS AND TOOLS

2 clear glass wineglass

8 rubber bands

Water-based, thermohardening transparent glass paint in ruby and gold

Medium flat or round artist's brushes with natural bristles

Fine detail brush

Craft knife

WHAT TO DO

1. Wash and prepare the wine glasses.

2. To mask off areas for the ruby and gold bands of paint, place two rubber bands on each wineglass. Position the higher rubber band just below where your lips will touch the glass when drinking and the lower one about ⅜ inch (1 cm) below that. Adjust the rubber bands so they are parallel and level with the rim of the glass.

3. Use the medium brush to fill in the area between the rubber bands with the transparent ruby paint, being careful not to allow the paint to pool in one spot. This will be easiest if you rotate the glass slowly with one hand while holding the brush and painting with the other. Allow the paint to dry thoroughly before going on to the next step.

4. Hold your craft knife against the inside edge of the top rubber band and slowly rotate the glass in your left hand to loosen the rubber band. Repeat with the lower rubber band. Gently pull the rubber bands away from the glass. Use the tip of your craft knife to remove any paint that went under the rubber bands.

5. To create an even gold border, place a rubber band above and below the ruby border, spacing it a pleasing distance. Paint the marked area gold with the detail brush. Allow to completely dry, then repeat Step 4 to remove the rubber bands.

6. Photocopy the two leaf and tendril patterns, reducing or enlarging if needed. Tape the straight leaf and tendril pattern onto the inside of the wineglass, positioned carefully behind the band of ruby paint, so that the photocopied image shows through the ruby paint and can be traced in the next step.

7. Use the detail brush and gold paint to paint the leaf and tendril design following the photocopied image showing through the glass.

8. Tape the curved leaf and tendril pattern onto the bottom of the glass's base so it shows through to the top of the base, then use the detail brush and the gold paint to paint the design.

9. Bake the wineglasses in your oven following the paint manufacturer's instructions.

—FROM *The Michaels Book of Arts and Crafts*

TEMPLATES

PAINTED RECYCLED GLASS PROJECTS

Susan Wasinger

Painted Bottle Vases

Vase Lift: Wine and spirit bottles come in graceful, iconographic shapes, many too beautiful to throw away. Unadorned, the bottles look like someone forgot to take out the recycling. But, enrobed simple in a graphic paint treatment, the shapes come alive and strike an unusual balance between the primitive and the refined. The humble white matte paint brings out an obsidian sheen in the bottle-green glass and, suddenly, ordinary trash makes a leap to extraordinary treasure.

Materials

green glass wine and beer bottles

masking tape

round stickers (or other appealing shapes)

white or cream-colored tempera or low-VOC interior latex paint

Tools

scissors

paintbrush

rubber gloves

Make it

1. Collect glass beverage bottles of interesting shapes and colors. Remove the labels by soaking them for an hour or two in soapy water, then dry the bottles thoroughly inside and out.

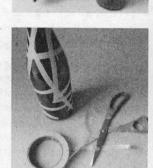

2. Simple yet striking patterns can be applied to the bottles with masking tape. Create alternating bands of light and dark by wrapping tape around the bottle. This bold design was made by wrapping narrow strips of masking tape in random directions around the bottle. Wider tape will not adhere smoothly to the contours of the shape, so use scissors to cut the tape in half along its length. Remember that this project works in relief, so the areas you cover now will be the areas of exposed glass later.

3. You can also sprinkle round paper stickers on a bottle. Whether tape or stickers are used, they must be applied firmly with no corners sticking up to allow paint to get under them and obscure the pattern.

4. So far, this project has been a breeze. Here comes the messy part: Use acrylic, tempera, or low-VOC wall paint in a white or cream color. Do not thin the paint. Apply it with a small brush, being sure to cover the entire surface of the bottle. You may need to go over some areas twice to ensure even coverage. Next, holding the bottle by the top of the neck, pull the tape off slowly and discard it. The tape must be removed before the paint dries or it will pull off in large sheets and ruin the relief pattern. Be sure to have a trash bag handy for discarding the strips of unwieldy tape covered in wet paint. Rubber gloves are useful for this step, as you are bound to get some paint on your fingers. A craft blade may help loosen the edges of the tape or stickers to make removal easier. Once all of the tape is removed, set the bottles on a piece of newspaper to dry completely.

Message on a Bottle

Write on: The surplus of glass bottles in need of recycling seems almost endless. Here's a practical way to reuse them a little closer to home. A swipe or two of blackboard paint turns old bottles and jars into stylish storage. More practical than store-bought canisters or jugs, these are containers you can write on to keep track of what you have and when you need to use it.

Materials

empty glass jars and bottles

black chalkboard paint

low-VOC wall paint in eggshell, satin, or gloss finish

masking tape

The energy saved when you recycle one glass bottle can run a 100-watt light bulb for four hours. But a bottle relegated to the landfill will take one million years to degrade.

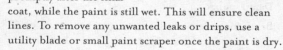

All kinds of jars and bottles can find a second life as practical storage in your kitchen or bath. Our favorite candidates include jars for baby food, salsa, and jam. Fancy beverage bottles can be reused for bulk coils and flavored vinegars.

Tools

paintbrush

utility blade or paint scraper

Make it

1. Use the masking tape to define the area of the jar that will be your chalkboard "label." Press the edge of the tape securely to the glass to ensure that no paint will leak out and smear the line.

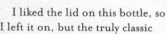

2. With a small paintbrush, apply black chalkboard paint to the jar or bottle. You will need to do two or three coats to get a solid black area to write on. Wait about five minutes or so between each coat. Remove the tape promptly after the final coat, while the paint is still wet. This will ensure clean lines. To remove any unwanted leaks or drips, use a utility blade or small paint scraper once the paint is dry.

3. Low-VOC wall paint in an eggshell, satin, or gloss finish will cover the old printing on the lids and ensure the containers fit with your kitchen décor. A variety of shades of the same color will make your jars spunky but tasteful (I used several greens like olive, lime, and sage). Paint the outside of the lid only. Don't put these jars in the dishwasher; they should be hand-washed gently when needed.

—From *Eco Craft*

RETRO GLASS CRAFTS
Suzie Millions

As an avid reuser, I'm delighted by the broad range of glass containers you can get for free at the grocery store, if you just buy what comes in them. Sadly, more and more glass containers are disappearing from the shelves, replaced by plastics that are neither very reusable not very attractive. When the elegant amber glass Mrs. Butterworth stepped down off the shelf for her flimsy plastic replacement, it was a dark day for retro crafters everywhere. Fortunately, some manufacturers still offer food in interesting glass jars, which means there will be crafters like me scrubbing out jars, peeling off labels, and storing them for future projects.

Masking Tape Pleather Jar

Materials

Clean bottle (interesting shape is a plus)

Masking tape

Shoe polish in a can

Soft rag

This was a hippie-era dorm room fixture, right up there with the macramé plant holder and the Chianti bottle with candle drips. The method is frequently referred to in vintage publications as the "Leather Look." I'm not so easily fooled, hence the "Pleather."

I liked the lid on this bottle, so I left it on, but the truly classic "Leather Look" was a soda pop bottle transformed into a vase for dried flowers. It's an excellent watching-a-movie, talking-on-the-phone, I-wanna-be-sedated craft. It's as mindless as mindless can be, but the end result fetches plenty of compliments.

1. Round up every odd remnant of masking tape you can find; different tapes absorb the shoe polish differently, adding a fun "wild card" element to the finished piece.

2. Rip the tape into small pieces and put them on the bottle. Overlap them. Vary the size and orientation.

3. Keep ripping.

4. Keep ripping. It takes a while.

5. Cover the entire bottle. If you're making a vase, push some of the tape over the lip into the neck.

6. Rub shoe polish over the tape-covered bottle with the rag. It's like magic.

7. Polish it gently. The bottle pictured had one coat of brown polish. Mix it up by using more coats or other colors of polish.

8. Far out. Slip on a mood ring, light some patchouli incense, and dig out your copy of *Déjà vu*. (If you're a youngster, Google "*Déjà vu*" with the initials "CSNY.")

Continued ➡

It Looks Like a Priceless Heirloom, But It's Just a Memento

Materials

Plate

Convex glass that fits comfortably into the plate

Photograph

Cardboard

Masking tape

Antique gold paint (acrylic will keep things speedy)

Epoxy (epoxy will keep things speedy as well)

Plastic table knife

Trims: ribbon, flowers, buttons, etc.

Tools

Pencil

Scissors

Small paintbrush

Choose a plate that matches the era and the attitude of the photo you're using. Select a piece of convex glass that fits well inside the plate, leaving plenty of rim still showing. You can buy convex glass new from places that sell clock supplies. Old clocks are a great source of domed glass. Keep an eye out for them when you're junking. All the better if they're not working, but sometimes even when the clock still works, the junk dealer may sell you the clock and all for less than the price of the glass. Religious icons and dried flower arrangements from the 1970s are also good sources for domed glass.

Take the plate with you to the store to find exactly the right piece. Prices can vary wildly so do your homework first by calling ahead, or checking prices online.

1. Use the glass as a template to trim the photo and the cardboard to size.

2. Put the photo, facing up, on top of the cardboard, and put the glass over them both.

3. Tear off a piece of masking tape about a quarter of the circumference of the glass. Run it around the edge of the assembled photo and glass, with about 1/16" overlapping onto the glass.

4. Press the tape down against the glass, allowing it to pleat to maintain an even curve. Flip the photo dome over. Smooth the tape out on the back of the cardboard. Continue placing and smoothing tape till the entire edge of the glass is sealed to the cardboard and photo.

5. Paint the top and side edges of the tape antique gold.

6. Use the plastic knife to mix epoxy directly on the center of the plate, keeping well within the area that will be covered by the photo dome.

7. Apply a thin, even coat of epoxy to the back of the cardboard, and immediately press down in the center of the plate.

8. Use epoxy to add trims.

These make great gifts because they're so easy to customize, and endlessly adaptable for all sorts of occasions. Include a plate stand or hanger.

Recipe for a Sweet Sweet Plate

Materials

Vintage magazines, cookbooks, and old recipe cards

Paper doilies

Clear plate

Paper towels

Decoupage medium

Backing (use felt for a decorative plate, or tissue paper and sealer for a plate you want to be able to hand wash)

Tools

Scissors

Craft knife

Cookie sheet

Pencil

Drop cloth

Rag

Bowl of water

Brush for medium

Damp sponge

Brush for sealer

Snip, snip, snip

1. Cut out gooey, gorgeous pictures of sugar-sprinkled delights. Clip some recipes, too. I'm especially fond of hand-scrawled notes next to recipes. Extinct advertising icons, dainty details clipped from paper doilies, and era-revealing recipe names ("Lady Bird Johnsons Pecan Pie") will give your plate the retro touch.

2. Plan your design. (Working on a cookie sheet will give you the luxury of moving the clippings easily if you need to.) Lay the clippings out and put the plate over them, upside down, to see how you're doing. Adjust until it's just so. Trace around the plate with pencil, and trim the clippings to size.

Set up & get messed up

3. Being organized going into this will reduce the stress of being up to your elbows in glue. Put a drop cloth down on your work surface. Set the bowl of water someplace above your elbow space so you don't tump it over. Lay a stack of paper towels to the side of that, and have the roll at the ready. Have a damp rag handy, too, to wipe your hands on when the need arises.

4. Pick up a clipping and drop it in the bowl of water. It will curl up at first and then flatten out. (This process of relaxing the paper will minimize wrinkling.)

5. Gently take the clipping out of the water when it flattens, and lay it on the pad of paper towels. Brush the entire front surface with the medium, and put it in place on the backside of the plate. Gently dab the back of it with the dampened sponge to push out any air bubbles and to set it firmly against the plate. The clippings are fragile when they're soggy, so handle them with care.

6. Repeat with the remaining clippings. Work with the front of the plate facing you, making sure there are no air bubbles or wrinkles showing on the face of the plate, and that the clippings are positioned how you want them to be. Turn it over now and then to check that things are flat and smooth on the back. You can overlap images all you like using this method.

7. When you're finished gluing on the images, brush an even coat of medium over the entire back of the plate, and leave it facedown to dry overnight.

Backing & finishing

If you plan to use the plate with food, it will need to be covered with tissue paper and then sealed. Felt is okay if you plan to hang the plate on the wall or only use it decoratively.

8. Put the plate upside down on the backing material, and trace around the outside edge. If there's a lot of paper overhanging the edge of the plate, trim it first with a craft knife.

9. Brush medium on the back of the plate. Smooth the backing over the medium, pressing out any wrinkles or air bubbles. Don't worry if the backing overlaps the plate edge at this point. Set the plate facedown to dry again overnight.

10. When it's completely dry, trim the excess backing from the rim with a craft knife. If you backed it with felt, skip ahead to step 12.

11. Apply a couple of coats of clear sealer to the back, allowing it to dry between coats per the directions for your sealer. Even with the sealer on it, hand wash only.

12. Clean up any errant glue or smudges on the surface of the plate. You're done! Go show it to somebody. Take them cookies on it for extra credit.

Whimsical Whimsey Bottle

Materials

1950s home and garden magazine

Black cardstock (light enough to roll)

White glue

1/8" x 1/8" (3 x 3 mm) balsa stick

1/32" x 4" x 36" (.75 mm x 10.2 cm x 91.4 cm) balsa plank

Brown acrylic paint

Disposable cup for paint

1/4 cup of sand

Grass green hobby moss (reindeer moss, or lichen; it should be soft and flexible, not crispy or dusty)

2 very small artificial flowers

Hot glue

Game die

1½" (4 cm) length of ¼" x ⅜"
(6 x 9.5 mm) balsa wood stick

Green acrylic paint to match the moss

Alphabet pasta

Scrap of cardstock

Toothpicks

½" (1.3 cm) glue dots

Bottle

Tools

Brush for glue

Pencil

Craft knife

Straightedge

Brush

Rag

Scissors

Hot glue gun

Small bowl

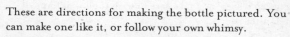

These are directions for making the bottle pictured. You can make one like it, or follow your own whimsy.

It looks daunting, but it's not very hard to make. Set aside a couple of hours, or if you plan on coming up with your own design, better set aside a day. The hardest part for me was convincing myself I could do it.

Special Prep Materials

Something to elevate the bottle on the work area

Materials to build special tools:

Four 18" lengths of Balsa sticks, ¼" x ⅜"

Flexi-straw

Masking tape

2 paintbrushes

Tissue

Cardstock

Funnel with a long nose (or a homemade paper funnel)

A plastic container approximately the same size as the bottle

Craft saw

Prepare to be whimsical

1. It's nice to be able to see in the bottle at eye level while you work on it. Elevate it. I put a blender jar on my work desk, with a plate on top of that to set the bottle on.

2. This project requires some long-handled tools. To make extended handles for some of them, I used gigantically long (18"!) vintage barbecue skewers. Balsa sticks work well, too. They should be thick enough to be sturdy, but small enough to navigate the narrow space.

Flexible brush—Cut the elbow section out of a flexi-straw. Cut most of the handle off a cheap paintbrush, and push it into the elbow. Attach it to the elbow with masking tape, then tape the other end of the elbow to the extended handle.

Brush and buff—(Used to clean off any specks on the glass inside the bottle.) Pick a soft-bristled paintbrush that will fit through the bottleneck. Strap it onto an extension with masking tape. Wrap a couple of layers of

tissue around the other end to make a soft pad. Tape them in place.

Paddle—(The paddle helped me to arrange all the details inside the bottle.) Cut a small piece of cardstock, around ⅝" x 2". Fold it down to ⅝" x 1", and attach it to the extension with a couple of drops of hot glue.

Funnel—(If you plan on using any sort of substrata, like the sand in this bottle, you'll need a funnel to get it down into the bottle without making a mess. The funnel could also be used to direct small accessories to a specific place.) You can buy a cheap, long-nosed funnel at an auto store. I rolled up a piece of cardstock and hot glued it together.

Poker—I used unembellished barbecue skewers and Balsa sticks to jab at stuff once it was inside the bottle.

3. Browse the grocery shelves for a clear plastic container that's close in size to your bottle. (I found mine in the produce section, full of delicious juice.) Clean it and cut it open with a craft saw. Use it to test your design ideas, and to adjust the size and quantity of what you plan on putting in the bottle.

Ready, set, go

4. Copy a happy mower and a ranch house from a vintage magazine. Mount them on black cardstock with white glue.

5. Put the ⅛" x ⅛" balsa stick in the bottle. Mark it at the place where it meets the lip. Take it out and trim it down to the mark.

6. Cut four strips, each 3" x ½", from the 1/32" balsa wood plank.

7. Water down a little brown acrylic paint in the disposable cup. Brush it on the balsa strips, front, back, and edges. Wipe off the excess with a rag. Brush and wipe the balsa stick you just trimmed, too. These will make your sign post.

Work in the test container

…until every piece of the design is made and put in place, and until these directions tell you to start working in the bottle.

8. Pour sand into the bottom of the test container.

9. Lay about 1" of moss on the sand. Hot glue a couple of tiny artificial flowers to it, along the front edge.

10. Add another piece of moss, about the size of an egg, on top of the moss already in the container.

11. Cut out the happy mower and the house.

12. Hot glue the die to the back of the mower, in the center of the bottom edge (see photo above). Stand the mower up in the foreground of the test container, with the egg-shaped clump of moss behind her.

13. Hot glue the ¼" edge of the 1½" length of ¼" x ⅜" balsa to the center back of the ranch house. Paint the top, front, and sides of the balsa strip green. Hot glue the house to the mound of moss in the back of the test container (apply the glue to the bottom of the balsa strip.)

14. Pour the alphabet pasta into a bowl. Pull out the letters to spell "With God as My Witness I'll Never Mow Again." Break a tiny curved piece off of a letter to make the apostrophe. Lay the letter out on the balsa planks as follows:

Plank 1—With God As

Plank 2—My Witness

Plank 3—I'll Never

Plank 4—Mow Again

15. Pour a little white glue on a scrap of cardstock, and apply it to the backs of the letters with toothpicks. Put them in place.

16. Put the balsa post for the signs in the center of the test container. Push down until it goes in as far as it can. Make a mark a little bit above the spot where the post meets the moss.

17. Press a glue dot in the center back of each of the four sign planks. With the bottom edge even with the mark you just made, press the bottom plank to the post. Add the other planks, about ½" apart. Tip them at different angles.

Assess your layout, and make any adjustments now.

You're ready to hit the bottle

Have your long-handled tools and whatever you plan on using to lift your bottle to eye level in place in your work space.

18. Lift the signpost, the happy mower, the ranch house, and then the moss out of the test container. (I like to keep things together on a tray so nothing gets lost.)

19. Give the bottle a last minute look-see to make sure it is absolutely spotless before you begin. Use your long-handled brush and buff tool to eliminate any specks or smudges.

20. Put the long funnel into the bottom of the bottle. Pour in the sand from the test container. Give the bottle a tiny wiggle to level it out.

21. Stuff the bottom layer of moss through the neck of the bottle, poking it in with your finger, saving the portion with the flowers till last. It's okay if it breaks off. Keep stuffing. Arrange it with one of the long-handled pokers so that the flowers are in the front of the bottle. Roll up the bump of moss with the house glued to it, and push it into the bottle. Use the long-handled poker to push down on the anchor strip behind the house to arrange it. It should be on top of the mound in the back of the bottle.

22. Gently roll the edges of the mower back until she's narrow enough to fit through the neck of the bottle. Do not crease her. You want her to relax and unroll after she clears the neck. Push her in. Arrange her with the long-handled paddle and a poker. Use a poker to push down firmly on the die mounted on her back to help place her. She should be front and center, and her lawn mower should appear to be chewing into that unruly lawn.

23. Gently push up on the ends of the signs so that they rotate on the post, staying attached, but lining up almost parallel to it. Guide the post through the bottle into the center of the bottle. Push down till it feels like it can't go any farther. Use the paddle to gently push the signs back into position.

24. Make like Edward Scissorhands, and use the long-handled brushes and tools to arrange things inside the bottle, and to clean up anything that needs tidying. Put a lid on it.

—From *The Complete Book of Retro Crafts*

Continued →

ETCHING GLASS

Dawn Cusick & Megan Kirby, Editors

It can be your little secret: how easy it is to make unique and functional etched glass items. Though etched glass may conjure images of dangerous, complicated tools and tedious design work, creating fabulous designs on glass is as simple as applying a cream or liquid, then rinsing. The bonus: the results are not only beautiful (think great gifts) but permanent and food- and dishwasher-safe.

Materials and Tools

Etching Cream and Liquid

These are the magic potions in glass etching. Ammonium bifluoride, the active ingredient in etching cream and liquid, changes the glass surface to a permanent frosty, matte surface in approximately 15 minutes.

Glass

Just about any glass surface can be etched. Flat glass or glass with simple curves will prove the easiest surfaces on which to apply the stencil. Glass with many curves or textured glass works best when dipped in etching liquid or when a freehand design is applied with etching cream or resist gel. Colored glass can be etched, as long as the glass is truly colored and not color-coated.

Resists

Anything that covers a portion of the glass to prevent etching is called a resist. Stencils are the most commonly used resists, though shapes cut from self-adhesive vinyl, resist gel, and found objects also work very well. Some stencils are sold with adhesive backing, though you can also use spray adhesive to apply to glass surface.

Resist Gel

Resist gel can be applied with an applicator bottle, usually in a freehand manner. Once the gel dries, etching cream or liquid is applied over the gel. Resist gel can also be brushed on to cover a larger area.

Squeegee

Plastic, T-shaped squeezes are the perfect tools for smoothing on adhesive stencils, applying etching cream evenly to the surface of the glass, and scraping excess reusable cream back into the bottle.

Paintbrush

Sometimes you may find it easiest to use a paintbrush to apply etching cream; this technique is particularly useful when etching a freehand design.

Applicator Bottle

An applicator bottle makes it possible to apply etching cream or resist gel in a freehand manner. Use an assortment of tips to create lines in a variety of widths.

Craft Knife/Scissors

A craft knife is the best tool for cutting out some stencils; scissors work best for others. A swivel blade works well for rounded shapes.

Sand Etcher

This technique etches the glass by sandblasting the surface. The materials to do this safely at home are now available in a kit that you can purchase at craft supply stores. A nozzle attached to a bottle of abrasive grit and a can of propellant delivers the sand exactly where you want it.

Making Stencils

The design and style of the resist are probably the most important decisions you will make in glass etching, and your options are unlimited. Although stencils are widely available in craft stores, it is simple and fun to make your own.

1. You can create a stencil from just about any design, though it's a good idea to choose images with simple lines and shapes, at least at first. Enlarge or reduce images to the desired size.

2. Position a sheet of self-adhesive vinyl on a flat work surface with the adhesive side facing down. Lay a sheet of carbon paper on top of the vinyl, then lay the design on top of the paper. Applying a few strips of double-sided tape between layers is a good idea.

3. Use a ballpoint pen to trace around the design; the carbon will transfer the design on top of the vinyl. Remove the design and the carbon paper.

4. Determine whether you want to cut out the stencil before or after applying it to the glass. This will vary according to the design. For simple designs in which you would like to save the inner portion of the stencil, cut out the design before applying the stencil. For larger or more intricate designs, apply the stencil to the glass first. Use a craft knife to cut out the stencil. Remove the inner pieces of the stencil by lifting them out from the center of the piece with the tip of the craft knife.

Applying the Resist

Regardless of which type of resist you choose, it is essential that the resist be applied properly to achieve a clean etching. Don't rush through this step.

1. Thoroughly clean and dry the glass surface to be etched. Gather materials and place them on your work surface.

2. Press or apply the resist onto the glass surface. If you are applying the stencil to a curved surface, it helps to use scissors to cut darts or wedges around the edges of the stencil so the stencil will adhere smoothly. If the stencil has an adhesive backing, slowly begin to peel off the backing, then lay the stencil down gradually, smoothing it down as you work from one side to the other. If using an object without backing as a resist, apply spray adhesive to the resist.

3. Rub the resist with a squeegee or your fingers to make sure all areas of the resist are firmly adhered to the glass (using a scrap of vinyl on top of the stencil can provide a buffer that helps keep the stencil from shifting). Pay particular attention to the edges of the resist, making sure there are no wrinkles or air bubbles where etching cream or liquid can seep in.

4. Use a slightly moistened cotton swab or clean rag to wipe off any residual adhesive that may have smeared from the vinyl onto the glass.

Applying Etching Cream

When applying etching cream or liquid, work in a well-ventilated area, and take care to wash tools well immediately after use.

1. If you are etching on a curved surface, cut strips of self-adhesive vinyl and apply strips around the outer edges of the stencil to build up an area where the cream can settle; this will allow you to apply enough etching cream to the glass surface without worrying about seepage.

2. Pour or spoon etching cream onto the unexposed area of the resist. If you are etching a drinking glass or other curved surface, steady the glass by nestling it into a towel. Use a squeegee to pull a thick, even layer of etching cream across the exposed area of the glass—or apply cream with a paintbrush for a less even, more textured look. You may also apply cream directly to the glass with an applicator bottle at this point. Work slowly and carefully, as any spilled cream will leave a permanent mark.

3. Let stand 15 minutes or according to manufacturer's instructions. Scrape cream off surface of the glass with a squeegee. (Cream can be scraped back into the original bottle for later reuse.) Rinse off the cream thoroughly with warm water, then remove the resist. Once the glass is completely dry, the etched design will be visible!

Dipping with Etching Liquid

Perhaps the simplest approach to glass etching, dipping is great when you want the entire surface of the glass to be etched or if you're using reverse resists.

1. Determine how much of the glass item you would like to be etched and fill a plastic container with etching liquid to the desired level. Place the container on a flat, level surface.

2. Carefully place the glass item into the liquid, taking care to avoid any splashing. For small items that are to be completely etched, simply submerge the item in the etching liquid.

3. Let glass sit in liquid for the period of time recommended by the manufacturer. Lift glass out of container, rinse thoroughly, then dry.

Projects

Oil and Vinegar Decanters

Designer: Megan Kirby

Inexpensive decanter tops are widely available and can turn any ordinary glass bottle into a functional dispenser. Add stickers and etching cream and you'll have bottles that are unique and handsome additions to any dinner table.

Materials and Tools

Glass bottles (with decanter tops)

Glass cleaner

Paper towels

Electrical tape or masking tape

Stickers or decals (paper or plastic)

Paintbrush or squeegee

Etching cream

Rubber gloves and goggles (optional)

Ruler (optional)

What To Do

1. Gather materials together on a flat surface in a well-ventilated, warm workspace (above 70° F or 21° C). Etching creams and liquids will not work properly in cold temperatures. It's a good idea to wear goggles and rubber gloves to protect your eyes and skin. Read and follow all manufacturer instructions.

2. Clean and dry bottles thoroughly with glass cleaner and paper towels.

3. Define the borders of the design by wrapping strips of electrical or masking tape above and below the design area. If necessary, use a ruler to make sure the strips of tape are even. Smooth out any wrinkles or air pockets in the tape.

4. Apply stickers or decals to the surface of the glass in a pleasing design. Use your fingers, a squeegee, or a clean, dry cloth to remove wrinkles or air pockets.

5. Use a paintbrush or a squeegee to carefully apply a thick coat of etching cream to the area of the glass to be etched.

6. Allow the etching cream to set for several minutes, then remove cream by running glass under warm water.

7. Peel off stickers and tape. Clean the glass bottles thoroughly with glass cleaner and paper towels.

Etched Tumblers

Colored glassware is widely available at antique markets. Don't worry about looking for sets; collect glasses in an assortment of shapes and sizes and etch each glass with a different design.

Materials and Tools

Glasses

Glass cleaner

Paper towels

Car detailing tape (available at auto supply stores)

Etching cream

Paintbrush or squeegee

Rubber gloves and goggles (optional)

Measuring tape and grease paint pen (optional)

What To Do

1. Gather materials together on a flat surface in a well-ventilated, warm workspace (above 70° F or 21° C). Etching creams and liquids will not work properly in cold temperatures. It's a good idea to wear goggles and rubber gloves to protect your eyes and skin. Read and follow all manufacturer instructions.

2. Clean and dry glasses thoroughly with glass cleaner and paper towels.

3. Create a pattern on each glass by applying car detailing tape to the outside of the glass surface. You may want to use a measuring tape and a paint pen to mark off sections of the glass. (Make sure you mark the inside of the glass; do not mark areas where you will apply the etching cream.) Smooth out any wrinkles or air pockets in the tape.

4. Use a paintbrush or a squeegee to carefully apply a thick coat of etching cream to the area of the glass to be etched.

5. Allow the etching cream to set for several minutes, then remove cream by running glass under warm water.

6. Remove tape. Clean the glass thoroughly with glass cleaner and paper towels.

Sunburst Table

Designer: Megan Kirby

This project features a glass tabletop with an appealing etched design reminiscent of the sun's rays. Folding a craft-paper template in half repeatedly is a simple way to create a tabletop with pleasing, elegant symmetry.

Materials and Tools

Table with glass top

Craft paper

Pencil

Scissors

Spray adhesive

Glass cleaner

Paper towels

Masking tape

Paintbrush or a squeegee

Etching cream

Rubber gloves and goggles (optional)

What To Do

1. Gather materials together on a flat surface in a well-ventilated, warm workspace (above 70° F or 21° C). Etching creams and liquids will not work properly in cold temperatures. It's a good idea to wear goggles and rubber gloves to protect your eyes and skin. Read and follow all manufacturer instructions.

2. Create a template of the tabletop by carefully laying the glass top on a sheet of craft paper and tracing around the edge with a pencil. Remove the tabletop and cut out the template.

Continued →

3. Fold the template circle in half, then fold in half twice more to create 16 even sections. Unfold the paper and trace over the folds with the pencil.

4. Trace around the cap of the spray adhesive or any other similarly sized circular item (a juice glass works well) on a separate piece of craft paper, then cut out the template.

5. Position the glass tabletop on top of the large template. Clean the surface thoroughly with glass cleaner and paper towels. Spray the back of the small circular template with adhesive spray then apply to the center of the glass top. Smooth out any wrinkles or air pockets and make sure the edges of the template are firmly adhered to the glass.

6. Carefully following the pattern on the template, make alternate sections of the design with masking tape, pressing tape firmly as you work. (You may want to clean the glass again once tape is applied to remove any fingerprints or adhesive from the exposed sections.)

7. Use a paintbrush or a squeegee to carefully apply a thick coat of etching cream to alternate sections of the tabletop.

8. Allow the etching cream to set for several minutes, then remove cream with warm water.

9. Peel off tape and remove small circular template. Clean the glass thoroughly with glass cleaner and paper towels, then place the tabletop back on table base.

—From *The Michaels Book of Arts & Crafts*

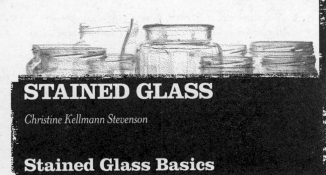

STAINED GLASS

Christine Kellmann Stevenson

Stained Glass Basics

The following sections will give you a thorough overview of the glass, materials, supplies, tools, and equipment that you'll be working with as you create stained glass pieces. Read through them to familiarize yourself with each item, and then use them as a reference for purchasing items from a stained glass supplier.

Types of Stained Glass

Even before being cut and pieced together into a project, the sheer beauty of stained glass is magical. So many colors, textures, and types are available that you may feel thrilled and overwhelmed at the same time! But don't fear, the following section will help you sort through the main types and give you a working knowledge.

At the beginning of each project, you'll find a list of the types of glass used to create the particular piece. Even though we suggest glass combinations, you may want to come up with your own color schemes.

In general, stained glass falls into two main categories: cathedral and opalescent (or opals). Cathedral glass is the category of all clear and transparent colored glass. By contrast, opalescent glass is made with a material that causes the glass to crystallize during the cooling process, resulting in glass with varying degrees of opaqueness that reflects light rather than transmitting it.

There are many variations within the categories of cathedral and opalescent. Some of the more common types are described below. Keep in mind that terminology varies from region to region, and even from studio to studio. So don't be alarmed if your local retailer or a glass catalogue refers to what you're looking for by another name. Based on the photos of the projects in this book, you should still be able to find something very close to what we've used.

Many of the glass types that you'll discover are combinations of various types, such as hammered iridescent cathedral glass or glue-chip bevels. Glass manufacturers are constantly developing new and exciting combinations to keep the ever-evolving field of stained glass alive.

In addition, found objects such as geodes, seashells, marbles, glass tiles, or any object that can be copper-foiled or leaded can be used to enhance and complement the different kinds of glass in your project.

ANTIQUE GLASS

Made to look like it's old, the machine-made version of this glass has a slightly distorted texture while being even in color and thickness. Mouth-blown antique glass is made using a technique that results in distortions, some bubbles, and variations in color intensity within individual sheets.

BEVELS

These thick, flat, precut glass shapes have been machine-beveled to an angle. Bevels act as prisms, refracting the light that passes through them into a rainbow of colors. They are available in a number of geometric shapes as well as groupings, called clusters. They are usually clear (cathedral) or may be glue-chipped (see below).

GLUE-CHIP GLASS

This textured cathedral glass has been treated so that it resembles a frost-covered window. The name refers to the technique used to create the effect: Hot glue is applied to sandblasted glass, and, as it dries, the glue peels away flakes of glass, resulting in the pattern. Double glue-chipped glass has been treated twice to create a tighter texture.

IRIDESCENT GLASS

This glass, which can be either cathedral or opalescent, has been thinly coated with metallic oxides to produce a colorful rainbow-like shimmer. The rainbow effect is more pronounced on darker colors of glass.

HAMMERED TEXTURE GLASS

This glass, which comes in both cathedral and opalescent, has a texture similar to that of hammered copper.

GLASS NUGGETS

These small globs of glass are made by dropping hot glass on a flat surface. They are flat on the bottom and rounded on the top. Nuggets come in both cathedral and opalescent.

RING-MOTTLED GLASS

This opalescent glass is mottled with small, roughly circular patterns that are more opaque than the surrounding glass.

RIPPLE GLASS

This glass, which is either cathedral or opalescent, has a rippled texture. The effect varies from manufacturer to manufacturer, and various colors are available.

RONDELS

These are mouth-blown glass pieces, spun into a flat circular shape much like the bottom of a bottle. They vary in size and shape and are usually transparent (cathedral).

SEEDY GLASS

Usually of the cathedral variety, this glass derives its name from the seed-like bubbles trapped below the surface. (Note: When cutting this glass, you'll learn to "roll" over the bubbles as you score over them.)

WISPY GLASS

This glass is made by mixing cathedral glass with another more transparent color. However, the cathedral glass usually dominates.

STREAKY GLASS

Glass made up of one or more cathedral colors mixed together with a white opalescent color to create a thinly streaked, multi-colored glass. In this glass, the opalescent glass usually dominates.

WAVY GLASS

This popular glass has the appearance of a gently rippled lake. Combinations of both cathedral and opalescent are available.

Tools of the Trade

The following list, divided by usage, gives you an overview of tools and supplies used in this book. A well-stocked stained glass shop will carry most of the things that are made particularly for this craft. Detailed descriptions and how to use them follow in this chapter.

Don't be intimidated by the number of items. You can pick and choose from them as you learn and when you decide which projects you want to undertake. (Each project has a separate list of supplies you'll need to make it). Some of these things are so simple that they need no explanation—it's just a good idea to have them around. In fact, you may already have them in your house or garage.

PATTERNS & GLASS CUTTING

MATERIALS & SUPPLIES

- Permanent markers in black and white
- Carbon paper
- Heavyweight kraft paper
- Glass in various colors and patterns

TOOLS

- Pattern shears
- Scissors
- Glass cutter and cutting fluid
- Straightedge, triangle, and other tools for drawing lines
- Breaking pliers
- Running pliers
- Grozing pliers
- Glass grinder, face shield, coolant
- Carbide grinding stone
- Light table (optional)

SOLDERING

MATERIALS & SUPPLIES

- Solid-core 50/50 and 60/40 solder
- Flux (liquid, paste, or gel), flux brush, flux remover
- Sponge

TOOLS

- Soldering iron (900-1000° F [500-537° C]) and holder

LEAD WORK

MATERIALS & SUPPLIES

(specific to projects in this book)

- Lead came, H-channel: 7/32" inch (5 mm) and 1/4 inch (6 mm)
- Brass came, U-channel, 3/8 inch (9.5 mm)
- Brass-capped lead came, H-channel: 7/32 inch (5 mm)
- Zinc came, U-channel: 1/4 (6 mm) and 3/8 (9.5 mm)

TOOLS

- Lead vise
- Lead nippers (dykes)
- Hacksaw (handsaw) with metal cutting blade or small electric cutting saw (optional)
- Metal files
- Horseshoe nails (50 mm)
- Glazing hammer
- Wire brush
- Channel-lock pliers

COPPER FOIL WORK

MATERIALS & SUPPLIES

(specific to projects in this book)

- Copper foil: 3/16 inch (4 mm) and 7/32 inch (5 mm) in regular, black, and silver-backed
- Copper reinforcing strip

TOOLS

- Crimper or burnisher
- Single-blade razorblade cutter

FINISHING

MATERIALS & SUPPLIES

- Patinas
- Stained glass cement
- Whiting
- Cotton balls, lint-free paper towels or cotton rags, cotton-tipped swabs

TOOLS

- Natural-bristle hand brush

DISPLAY

MATERIALS & SUPPLIES

(specific to projects in this book):

- 18-gauge tinned wire
- 21-gauge copper wire
- Brass hangers
- Brass shim (1/16 inch [1.6 mm])
- Brass pin-back clips
- Jack chain

TOOLS

- Wire cutters
- Needle-nose pliers

SAFETY

MATERIALS & SUPPLIES

- Safety glasses
- Rubber gloves
- Shop apron
- Kitchen hot pad or oven glove
- "Thumb savers" and face shield for grinder

GENERAL CLEANING

MATERIALS & SUPPLIES

- Non-ammonia glass cleaner
- Lint-free towels

TOOLS

- Table brush
- Dustpan

Materials & Supplies

The following descriptions cover many items. You won't need all of them to begin working in stained glass, so you might want to purchase just what you need for a project. Later, as your interest and skill grows, you'll want to keep certain items stocked in your workspace.

CAME

Came is grooved metal stripping that holds glass pieces together. It can be made from lead, brass-capped lead, zinc, brass, or copper. Solder is used to tack the joints together where the pieces meet.

The most commonly used and durable came is made of lead. For this reason, all projects assembled with came are referred to as leaded, even if they're held together with other types of came.

Lead makes sense for stained glass, particularly outdoor pieces, because it resists corrosion by water and chemicals. It's also a wonderfully malleable metal, making it relatively easy to bend and shape around pieces of glass. Lead came is easy to cut with special lead nippers. On the other hand, this material's relative softness and malleability make it prone to sagging. To increase the rigidity of lead came, you have to stretch it before using it.

Zinc, brass, or copper came is much harder than lead and has to be cut with a bladed hacksaw. Because these cames don't bend easily, they're used primarily for straight lines, such as panel-borders or geometric designs without curves. Because it's strong and lightweight, zinc came is specified for the borders on most of the projects in this book.

BUMPERS

These are scrap pieces of came left over from assembling a panel that you can use to hold the glass pieces in place while you construct a panel with came of the same size. Because they're the same height and width, they show you how far the final pieces of came will

overlap the glass. This will allow you to accurately measure and cut the came pieces so that you can replace them as you assemble.

COPPER FOIL

When making projects from smaller, intricate pieces, it's better to join them using copper foil and solder. Adhesive-backed copper foil, sold in 36-yard (32.4 m) rolls, is wrapped around the smooth, ground edges of each piece of glass. The foil serves as a base for the solder to hold the glass together.

Copper foil comes in several sizes, but 3/16- and 7/32-inch (5 and 5.5 cm) widths are the most common. Since it will show through the glass, the adhesive backing is

---

made in copper, silver, or black. For instance, if you plan to apply a black patina to your finished project, be sure to use black-backed foil on clear or light-colored glass. Likewise, if you plan to leave the solder its natural silver color, you'll probably want to use a silver-backed foil.

You can buy a dispenser for your copper foil that makes it easier to handle. Regardless, always store your foil in an airtight bag or container when not in use to prevent oxidation.

COPPER REINFORCING STRIP (RE-STRIP)

A thicker, sturdier strip of copper can be inserted between copper-foiled pieces of glass before the seams of the project are soldered to strengthen the panel. In our projects, we use it to reinforce the horizontal axis. In larger stained glass pieces, it can be used in several places for more reinforcement.

SOLDER

In the world of stained glass, solder is the glue that holds it all together. The solder used in stained glass work has a solid core and is an alloy made of lead, zinc, and tin. Solder is heated until molten with a soldering iron before it's applied to either foil or lead projects. On copper-foiled projects, you'll solder along the entire length of each seam. On leaded projects, you'll apply about a 1/4-inch-wide (6 mm) solder seam to each came joint.

Solder is also used to attach the hardware for hanging your finished work. Tinning refers to a light coat of solder applied to metal wire, brass shim, or brass lamp caps—just enough to turn the metal silver.

Alloys made from combinations of silver, tin, and copper in various proportions are available as lead-free alternatives, but with varying results. A silver solder is also manufactured to reduce the amount of lead in pieces that will be handled regularly, such as jewelry and boxes. If you're concerned about lead content in your work, you can try these alternatives.

FLUX, FLUX REMOVER

Flux, a chemical agent available in liquid, paste, or gel, plays a crucial role in soldering. It assists in dispersing the heat from the iron, cleans the metal, and allows the solder to flow smoothly and stick to foil and lead.

Flux is applied with a special brush. All types of flux should be removed as soon as possible after the completion of soldering to avoid oxidation on solder or lead. Liquid and gel flux are often water-based so that they clean off easily with water-based flux remover. In most cases, liquid fluxes can also be removed with a bit of liquid detergent and water. To remove paste flux, use a cotton ball moistened with acetone.

Continued ➜

I have a preference for the old-fashioned paste flux. I find liquid flux more difficult to work with, since it's easy to spill and evaporates quickly.

STAINED GLASS CEMENT/GLAZING COMPOUNDS

Stained glass cement, a thick, turpentine-based product, glazing compounds, and glass putty are all used for finishing glass panels. However, stained glass cement is your best choice, since its performance surpasses that of old-fashioned glazing compounds and putty. Cement breathes best in the changing temperatures of outdoor weather and also serves to darken leaded came lines, lending panels a finished look.

Cement or glaze must be applied to larger leaded panels that will be exposed to outdoor weather in order to strengthen and weather-proof them. You should also cement or glaze larger indoor projects to give them strength and prevent pieces from shifting or rattling. In either case, always apply the compound to both sides of a panel.

I prefer the black-tinted, premixed cementing compounds. This cement must be turned in the can several times for a few days to keep it from settling, making the mixing process easier. It has the consistency of a thick mud when stirred.

Before applying cement or glaze, protect your work surface with several layers of paper. Spread the compound on a completed panel with a natural-bristle hand brush, pushing it under each piece of came. Some of it will naturally flow to the back side of the piece (photo 1).

Photo 1

Collect any excess cement or glaze on the brush, and return it to the can. Clean the brush with a nail, between the rows of bristles. After this step, apply powdered whiting (see next section), and brush the entire panel and came with a clean brush.

Turn the panel over, and cement the other side using the same process. Clean up the excess cement or glaze compound with whiting, and use another nail to clean out corners and tight points. Soak the cement brush in mineral spirits. Setting time varies with humidity and temperature conditions, but some setting up will occur in a few hours. However, you should allow the project to sit and harden for 24 to 48 hours.

WHITING

Whiting is used to seal the cement or glaze, remove any residue on the glass, and clean the came. Sprinkle a little bit of this powder over the completed panel once the excess compound is removed, then scrub the glass and came with a natural-bristle hand brush (photo 2).

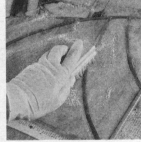

Photo 2

To avoid a cloud of dust, use a fine-haired table brush to carefully sweep the whiting into a dustpan (photo 3). Sweep around the table edges as well. Repeat on the other side.

Whiting is also used, in small quantities, to polish stained glass panels. Use an old toothbrush to polish small items. For larger panels of glass, clean them with lint-free paper towels or cotton rags.

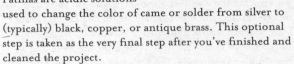

Photo 3

PATINAS

Patinas are acidic solutions used to change the color of came or solder from silver to (typically) black, copper, or antique brass. This optional step is taken as the very final step after you've finished and cleaned the project.

Before using a patina on lines of came, scrub them with a wire brush to remove any oxidation. If solder lines aren't completely clean and fresh or no longer a shiny silver, wipe them lightly with fine steel wool or an abrasive cloth before applying the patina. This might be the case if the project's been sitting around for more than a few days.

To apply patinas, follow the manufacturer's instructions carefully. You can shake and pour a small amount of the solution into the cap of the container, or weigh down the bottle so that it doesn't tip over. Use cotton-tipped swabs to brush the patina onto the panel's came and/or solder lines (photos 4 and 5). Change swabs as they get dirty.

Photo 4   *Photo 5*

Repeat this process until you're satisfied with the results. As the patina dries, use a clean rag or paper towel to skim around each glass edge to remove any excess solution.

As you work, not only should you avoid getting the solution on your skin, but you should be careful not to spill it on the glass. If a patina solution dries too long, it may leave an iridized-looking stain. If you goof, stain removers made specifically for stained glass can be used to remedy this problem.

KRAFT PAPER, CARBON PAPER

For making templates and patterns needed to cut glass pieces accurately, use heavyweight kraft paper (available at craft supply stores). A few sheets of carbon paper can be used to trace your enlarged patterns onto this paper.

WATERPROOF MARKERS

To avoid confusion when working with pattern pieces, use markers and a numbering system to label all the parts of your pattern before you cut them apart. Then, transfer this number to each piece of glass as you cut it. Use a white or gold waterproof marker/pen on dark-colored glass and a black pen on light-colored glass.

These markers also come in handy when you need to mark off an edge that doesn't quite fit the pattern after

you've cut the glass. The line will provide you with a guide for grinding away excess glass.

LINT-FREE COTTON RAGS OR PAPER TOWELS, COTTON BALLS, COTTON-TIPPED SWABS

Keep all of these supplies in your workspace for wiping glass clean, applying patinas, lubricating glass cutters, removing flux, polishing projects after they've been brushed with whiting, and general cleaning.

AMMONIA-FREE GLASS CLEANER, RUBBING (ISOPROPYL) ALCOHOL

Clean glass cuts more easily than dirty or filmy glass. To clean stained glass, use a glass cleaner that doesn't contain ammonia, since it can interfere with the application of patinas. Instead, use a vinegar-based cleaner or rubbing alcohol.

DISPLAY HARDWARE

The most common method of displaying a stained glass panel is to suspend it by one or two lengths of chain attached to a hanger soldered directly into the panel's outer came. For the hanger, you can use a preformed brass hanger, if available, or heavy-gauge wire (often already tinned, or coated with a thin film of solder) that can be twisted into shape before soldering it to the came. If you use regular copper or brass wire, it must be tinned first. You can also cut apart brass-pin backings, and use the center portion, as shown above.

Although many types of chain can be used, I prefer jack chain with links that can be opened and closed with needle-nose pliers. This allows you to attach the chain to hangers, and shorten or lengthen it as needed when hanging the panel.

Tools & Equipment

Many of the tools in the following section are made specifically for stained glass and can be purchased through a stained glass supplier. Once you learn how to make these clever helpers work to your advantage, you'll be able to concentrate on the real joy of being creative with glass.

PATTERN SHEARS

Pattern shears are designed specifically to cut out the interior lines of the template for stained glass panels. As they cut, they leave a thin strip of paper representing the distance between the pieces of glass to be occupied by the heart of the came or the copper foil.

These shears are available in two sizes, one tailored to the needs of copper foil projects ($\frac{1}{32}$ inch [.75 mm]) and the other made for leaded projects ($\frac{1}{16}$ inch [1.6 mm]). This slight difference in width can make or break your project when you're working with these two different assembly methods, so make sure to use the right shears for the technique you're using!

When cutting with pattern shears, hold them with the blades perpendicular to the paper and take short strokes, discarding the paper strings as you work.

GLASS CUTTERS, LUBRICANT

Despite the name, glass cutters don't actually cut glass; rather, they score it by means of a small beveled wheel that rolls across the surface. Almost invisible to the eye, these score lines weaken the glass enough that it can be broken into very specific shapes.

There are lots of styles and shapes of glass cutters. If you're a beginner, a straight, steel-wheel cutter will work well. Other options include comfort grips with long-lasting carbide wheels, self-lubricating cutters, and pistol-grip cutters.

To hold a standard straight cutter, hold it between your first and second finger, with the cutting wheel facing you. Grasp your thumb on the front of the flat hold, and place your first and second fingerprints on the back of the thumb rest (photo 6). This will keep the wheel perpendicular to the glass, helping you to maintain control over its movement. Cup your other hand over the cutter with your thumb resting on the top part of the cutter, allowing you to apply downward pressure without straining your wrists (photo 7).

Photo 6

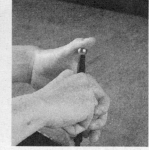

Photo 7

Now, stand with your feet apart. With the line to be scored directly in front of you, pull (don't push!) the cutter along it. Begin at the edge of the glass farthest from you. Use the weight of your shoulders to apply pressure, and avoid twisting your elbows or wrists, even when scoring curves. By using your body and shoulder weight, you can avoid straining your arms and hands. Keep your eye on the front of the cutting wheel to follow the line.

Tips: Keep the cutting wheel perpendicular to the glass; it must never tilt to the left or right. Scores made with a tilted cutter can break at an angle or fail to break along the whole score. Glass will only break properly if you begin the score on one edge of a piece of glass and continue through to the other. Try to apply even pressure to your cutter as you pull it across the glass, or the score will be uneven in depth, and the glass may not break evenly. Also, keep the speed of your movement even as you pull the cutter along the score line. When you score a line correctly, you should see a barely visible line, not a white, powdery line. If this happens, ease up on the pressure.

Pistol-grip cutters will be more comfortable for you if you have poor wrist or hand strength, but the cutting method is different. To use these cutters, cut away from yourself along a score line, rather than towards you. Consequently, you may find that you have less visibility.

As you're working, you'll need to keep the glass cutter's wheel well-lubricated with oil. Stained glass cutting lubricants are available in oil-based, water-based, and eco-friendly formulas. They all provide ease in cutting and protection for your glass-cutting wheel. For convenience, place several cotton balls in the bottom of an old coffee cup and saturate them with oil. After a few scores, return the cutter to the cup to keep the wheel clean. As the cotton balls get soiled, replace them with new ones. Even if the cup rolls over, the liquid won't spill.

You can learn to cut glass shapes on clear, inexpensive window glass. It's readily available, thin, and cuts easily. Place the cutter at the top edge of the glass and press down vertically—just enough to create a visible scratch on the glass in the direction you wish. Continue smoothly to the other end of the glass sheet. Repeat this process, breaking each score as you go and using multiple cuts to extract the shape you want. With practice, it will begin to feel like a natural process.

BREAKING PLIERS

Use breaking pliers to remove smaller pieces of glass that you're not able to break comfortably with your hands. These smooth-jawed pliers act as an extension of your hand, allowing you to grasp the glass firmly without scratching it.

Breaking pliers

RUNNING PLIERS

Designed to exert equal amounts of pressure on each side of the score line, running pliers are used to break long scores (whether straight or curved) on large glass pieces.

These pliers have two cushioned jaws—one concave and one convex—that serve to exert firm pressure on either side of the score, running the break along its entire length.

Running pliers

Some models have a screw adjustment on the top, allowing you to adjust them according to the glass's thickness. Place the top center of these adjustable pliers over the end of the score line, tighten the screw on top lightly, and release the screw back three-quarters of a turn. Then squeeze them until the glass breaks.

GROZING PLIERS

Grozing pliers have grooved jaws with little teeth that can nibble and chip away excess glass, allowing you to smooth sharp edges and round corners. They're particularly helpful for trimming away more glass than a grinder is designed to remove (see next section). You should always use them over a trashcan or some other container, since glass chips tend to fly and scatter during this process.

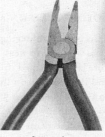

Grozing pliers

GLASS GRINDER, FACE SHIELD

A glass grinder is used to grind the edges of glass until they're smoothly sanded and perpendicular. Equipped with interchangeable bits, this electric-powered tool allows you to create more intricate shapes and curves than with a glass cutter and grozing pliers. An array of grinding bits are available with varying circumferences.

This piece of equipment has a water reservoir and a rotating, diamond-coated head. Soft water is recommended. To provide longer lift to your grinder, add coolant to the water reservoir, which decreases friction and prevents the diamond bits from rubbing off. To extend its life, move the height of the bit as it wears down.

Grinding the edges of glass is imperative for copper foiling. The degree of perfection can be less for leaded work, but it's still important to even up the glass edges for insertion into the came.

To use a grinder, place the cut glass flat on the grinder's work surface, and push the edge of it gently but firmly against the spinning bit (photo 8).

Photo 8

The water should wash away any glass dust, so if you see dry dust on the grinding bit, add more water to the reservoir. Avoid overfilling it to prevent the water from spraying on you.

To check your progress, dry the glass piece thoroughly, then compare it to its pattern (photo 9). If glass shows around the pattern, continue grinding those areas until

the piece matches perfectly. (You can use a marker to draw lines, if needed.) The smaller-diameter grinding bits allow you to grind out tiny grooves and small areas.

Photo 9

GRINDING STONE

A simple alternative to a grinder is a grinding stone. After wetting it, you simply file down the glass edges by rubbing the stone against it. This can be a very laborious process, however, and may leave you running to the nearest supplier to buy a grinder instead!

LEAD VISE

Before lead came can be used in a project, it must be stretched, both to straighten it and increase its strength. For this purpose, you can use a small, grooved vise that is spring-loaded. The vise mounts to your workbench or table with a nail or screw.

Lead vise

To stretch the came, begin by cutting a manageable length for your workbench. Insert one end of it into the vise's jaws with the channel facing up. Give the top of the vise a firm tap with a hammer or pliers to make sure its teeth get a good grip on the lead. Untwist the came so that it's straight, then grip the other free end with slip-joint pliers, standing at the opposite end of your workbench.

Hold the pliers in front of you, bracing yourself against the table, since lead can snap or pull from your grasp (photo 10). You can place a folded towel beneath the pliers in case the lead pulls out, saving your knuckles from smacking the tabletop if the came happens to break. Larger came sizes typically don't stretch as far, or break as easily, as smaller sizes do.

Pull firmly with the strength of your arms until the lead is straight and taut, so that it adds about 1 to 3 inches (2.5 to 7.6 cm), to the length of the came, depending on the size of the lead.

Photo 10

HACKSAW, ELECTRIC CUTTING SAW

Brass, zinc, and copper are all much harder than lead, so you can't cut them with nippers. To cut an occasional piece of came made from any of these metals, you can use a hand-held hacksaw with a fine-toothed blade.

After marking the angle you need to cut on the top face of the came, hold it in place with your hand and begin sawing on the mark until the blade catches on the metal. Continue sawing from the front to back until you complete the cut.

If you intend to do a lot of work with brass, zinc, or copper came, you'll probably want to go ahead and purchase a more efficient alternative—a small electric, metal-cutting saw.

Continued ➜

Lead nippers (dykes)

Lead nipper

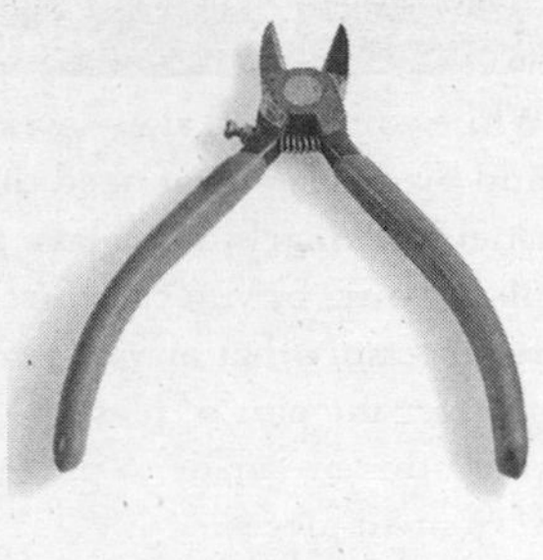

You'll need a pair of lead nippers to cut lead came. These special pliers have a flat jaw and an angled one, resulting in a flush (or straight) cut on the portion of the came toward which the flat jaw is aimed, and a V-shaped cut on the other piece (photos 11 to 13). You can use leftover V-shaped pieces for bumpers to temporarily hold glass pieces in place as you measure and fit your permanent pieces of came.

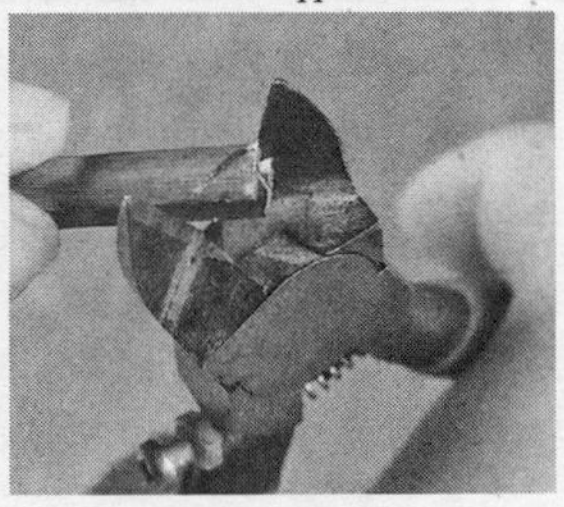

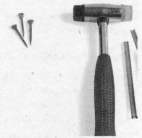

Photo 11

Metal files

These files, which come in a variety of styles, are used to smooth the corner edges of came after you assemble a piece.

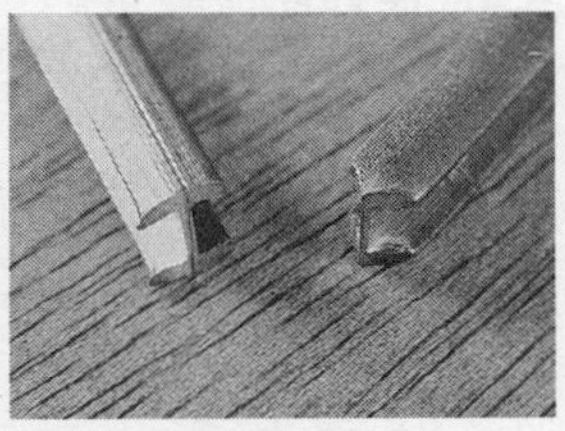

Photo 13

Crimper or burnisher

When you're assembling with copper foil, it's applied and folded over the edges of each cut piece of glass. Then it has to be flattened, burnished, and crimped around the glass edges to remove air bubbles and ensure a tight, even seal.

Photo 12

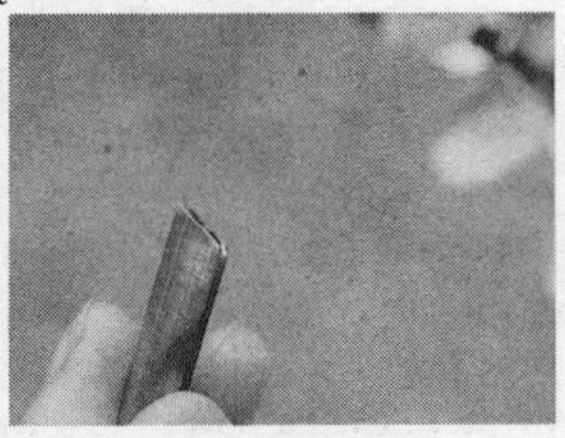

To make this job as simple as possible, you'll need a commercial crimper, a tool that will perform all these jobs in one step. There are many styles available from which to choose.

However, you can also use a wood fid, dowel, chopstick, or any found tool that works for you to rub or burnish the foil. When you're using highly irregular-shaped pieces, such as geodes and nuggets, you'll use this simpler tool because of the uneven textures.

Horseshoe nails

Pounded directly into the wooden top of your work surface with a hammer, horseshoe nails are used to hold came and glass pieces in place as you assemble your project.

These nails are sold by weight, and a #5 nail (50 mm) works well for most jobs. Make sure the nails are placed so that their flat sides abut the came or bumpers. Remove them by rocking them side to side, taking care not to bend their tips. With proper care, you should be able to use the same ones for many years.

Glazing hammer

You can use a small household hammer for pounding horseshoe nails, but a glazing hammer is more versatile. This tool has a dual-faced head; one side is plastic, the other rubber. The plastic side works well for hammering horseshoe nails, and the rubber side can be used to tap wide-edged glass into lengths of came.

Horseshoe nails and glazing hammer

Wire brushes

To clean lead came prior to fluxing and soldering, you'll need to scrub each joint with a wire brush (photo 14). Prior to applying patina, use the brush to scrub the entire length of came before wiping it off with a clean rag or paper towel.

Photo 14

Flux brushes

To apply flux, you'll also use a special brush. Because flux is corrosive, you should store your flux brushes away from other tools. A jar works well for this purpose.

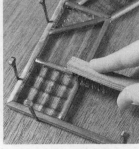

Natural-bristle hand brushes

These small brushed have traditionally been made for scrubbing hands and nails, but now they're a staple item for stained glass. This wooden brush with straight bristles is used for cementing and applying whiting after cementing.

Soldering iron and holder

This type of soldering iron, made specifically for stained glass work, has a heat-resistant handle fitted with replaceable chisel-shaped tips. For the projects in this book, you'll need an iron that heats to a temperature of 900° to 1,000° (482° to 538°C), and a ¼-inch (6 mm) tip to accompany it. Typically, these irons are either lightweight and slim, made to be held like a pencil, or slightly heavier, made to be held with an overhand grip. Purchase this piece of equipment from a glass studio or supplier.

Soldering iron and holder

Keep a damp, chemical-free sponge available to periodically clean off the tip while you're soldering. Doing this eliminates contaminant from the solder line, which is especially important when you're using copper foil.

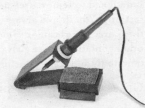

Table brush

This standard brush has soft bristles, perfect for catching the smallest bit of glass and removing them from harm's way. Don't ever use your bare hands to try to whisk away glass particles. Use this brush after each work session.

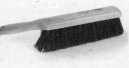

Table brush

SAFETY

Buy a stand/holder for your iron. There are several styles available. The safest version has a ceramic collar and rubber grips on the bottom to prevent it from skidding.

A soldering iron controller or rheostat can be used to control the amount of heat produced and turn the iron's power on and off. Don't leave your iron unattended or idle for more than a few minutes.

Light box/table

A light box or table may give you more workspace while allowing you to see pieces of glass lighted as they'll appear once they're displayed. The box also can be used for lighting and tracing patterns, and for cutting glass by the English method.

You can purchase a light box, or you can make one by using ¼-inch-thick (6 mm) frosted glass inlaid in a wooden frame/box with a fluorescent light mounted inside. If you wish, you can add legs to the box to make it freestanding.

Workspace & Safety

Stained glass is a rewarding hobby, but not one that's without risks. You'll be working with sharp glass pieces, high temperatures, lead, and various chemicals. Protect yourself, your family, and your pets by following the safety tips mentioned throughout this book. Please read these guidelines carefully, and keep them in mind as you set up your workspace.

Even though it's an enviable luxury, a separate studio is not necessary to begin working with stained glass. You simply need an area with good lighting and ventilation, at least one electrical outlet with a grounded circuit, and easy access to running water. Choose a location that isn't close to your kitchen or any other area where food is prepared. Never allow children or animals to enter your workspace unless you'll be able to keep your eyes on them at all times.

You'll also need a steady, level table or workbench with a surface that's above your standing waist height. You can use an existing table or have one made to suit your needs, which is really the ideal thing to do. Choose a height that's comfortable for you to prevent back strain when working. Since you'll be standing to do most glass cutting, give your feet some comfort and relief by placing a sturdy, non-slip floor mat cushion beside your workbench.

In addition to a number of other tasks, you'll use this table for cutting and assembling stained glass panels, which means it's going to get hammered full of nail holes and burned by soldering. For this reason, any tabletop surface that you use should be at least 5/8-inch (1.6 cm) thick. You can replace this top as it gets too full of holes with years of use.

Keep your workspace clean, well organized, and free of clutter. If you have a glass grinder, place it on a tray in one corner. Protect the surrounding area from spraying water and glass dust by using a plastic-covered backsplash around the sides and back of the grinder or a backshield made for the grinder.

Most grinders come equipped with a face shield that is installed horizontally above the grinder. This shield is a must to keep the water and particles out of your eyes, hair, and clothes. Keep a small towel handy to dry glass as you grind.

Wear safety glasses when you're scoring and breaking glass. Use a fine, soft table brush and dustpan to sweep off your workbench as you cut and assemble.

In addition, store your tools together after each session, away from flux and chemicals and within easy reach of your workbench. Sheets of glass should be stored vertically and can be sorted by size and color. Never lift them above your head!

When working with lead came, wash your hands frequently between steps and use disposable towels to dry them. Wear gloves when working with acid patinas.

When you're fluxing or soldering, run a small fan to draw away any fumes, especially if you don't have good ventilation in your work area.

In general, use common sense about caring for your workspace as well as your health. Always read the labels of any products that you use. Proceed slowly as you learn how to best utilize tools and supplies.

Techniques

At first glance, stained glass might seem as if it's a very complex art. After all, given the gorgeous end results, you might think that it can't be easy.

Although some of the specific techniques might take some time to master, none of them are inherently difficult. With practice, you'll be able to master this art, and the learning process can be very exciting.

This chapter describes, in sequence, various techniques you'll use to create stained glass projects. The sections that follow show, among other things, how to work with a pattern and cut glass. You'll also learn the secrets of assembling glass with both copper foil and came. How-to photos and steps will guide you smoothly through the process.

If you're just beginning, take time to read all the way through this chapter before beginning one of the projects. You'll save a lot of frustration if you familiarize yourself with the techniques first. As you work on various projects, thumb back to sections as needed for reference.

Making & Using Patterns

All stained glass pieces begin with a full-sized template, similar to a large map. Each project in this book is accompanied by a small black-and-white template that you can enlarge to the finished size indicated or vary to accommodate your specific needs. Without it, you won't be able to precisely fit together all the pieces of your glass puzzle.

If you're using the first method described below, you'll make a traced and numbered pattern on heavyweight kraft paper from the original template. The second method, called the English method, allows you to work directly from the pattern, and only works with clear and light-colored glass.

WORKING WITH A CUT-APART PATTERN

The most popular and accurate way of cutting out the interlocking pieces of a stained glass panel is to trace the pattern onto heavyweight kraft paper before cutting it into individual pieces. Use the directions that follow to guide you.

I. Begin by making an enlarged copy of the pattern with a photocopy machine or enlarger (small overhead projector). To transfer the template, spread out sturdy kraft paper on your work surface. Place a sheet or two of carbon paper facedown on top of it before placing the full-size template over the carbon paper. To keep them in place as you work, tack down all three layers to the work surface with horseshoe nails.

2. Use a pencil or pen to firmly trace over all the pattern lines. Assign a number to each piece of the design. If you're using glass with a pattern or grain, draw arrows indicating the direction you need in the project. For instance, if your piece includes sky and backgrounds, you may want the grain to be horizontal, contributing to the effect of the design.

3. Take out a few nails so that you can lift up one end of the pattern and carbon paper to make sure you traced all the pattern lines, numbers, and arrows (photo I). Then remove the rest of the nails, and lay the original template aside.

4. With regular scissors, cut around the outer edge of the enlarged pattern. Then, cut out the individual pieces using the appropriate pattern shears. For copper-foiled projects, you'll need 1/32-inch (.75 mm) shears. For leaded projects, you'll need 1/16-inch (1.6 mm) shears.

Photo 1

5. Center the shears directly over the pattern line, perpendicular to the paper. Cut in short strokes, primarily at the top of the blades, discarding the paper strips as you go (photo 2).

6. Use the pattern pieces you've cut to trace the designs on the appropriate pieces of glass, leaving enough space around each piece to cut and break them out comfortable, at least 1/4 to 1/2 inch (.6 to 1.3 cm). If you'll be cutting more than one piece from one sheet of glass, minimize waste by spending some time arranging your pattern pieces economically to fit the sheet, but leave at least one inch (2.5 cm) of space around each. To trace, use a black

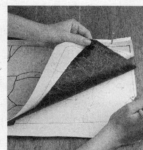
Photo 2

permanent marker on lighter-colored glass, and a white or gold marker on darker glass (photo 3). Don't forget to copy the number from each pattern piece to its matching shape on the glass.

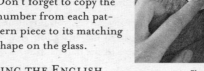

Photo 3

USING THE ENGLISH METHOD OF CUTTING

This method is a less laborious way to cut out a design. The full-sized template is used as your guide for cutting, skipping the use of individual, puzzle-like pattern pieces. This method works well only if you're using very transparent or light-colored glass. Several of the projects included in this book require clear textured glass and bevels, and these types of glass work well with this method.

If your project includes even a couple of opaque pieces, you can't use this method. Instead, use the former method of cutting all the pattern pieces apart. The following steps describe the specifics of this method.

I. Instead of making a pattern and tracing each individual pattern piece onto each piece of glass to be used, place each sheet on top of the full-size pattern where it belongs. The pattern line beneath the glass serves as your guide for scoring, just as the traced marks on the glass did in the first method we introduced. For better visibility, work on a light table or over white paper (photo 4).

Photo 4

2. Turn the piece of glass and template as needed to position the score line in front of you (photo 5). Score on the middle to the inside of the pattern line to allow room for foil or came. Number the pieces as you go.

3. Score and break pieces as described in the next section.

Photo 5

4. When they're all laid out on the full-size template, your glass pieces should still have a bit of space between each piece to accommodate foil or lead.

Scoring & Breaking the Glass

Even though it's referred to as "cutting the glass," you'll really be scoring and breaking it into specific shapes. This process often takes more than one or two cuts; for instance, you can't cut out circular pieces all at once. Instead, you'll make a series of scores and breaks, gradually "carving" away excess glass to reveal the desired shape (photo 6).

Photo 6

Before you begin, review the description of how to hold and use a glass cutter on page 19, and remember to practice your cutting technique on plain window glass before risking more expensive stained glass.

One note before you get started: Don't be discouraged if glass breaks the wrong way, or if you cut a piece too small, too large, or just plain wrong. It happens to the most experienced artists! Chalk it up to the learning process, and move on. However, if you find yourself making the same mistake on a shape after a couple of

tries, try doing the cutting sequence in a different order (see the troubleshooting section). If you get frustrated with anything come back to it at another time.

The following steps will guide you in this process of scoring and breaking glass.

I. If you're cutting several pieces from a single sheet of glass, your first step will be to cut the sheet apart into more manageable pieces (photos 7 and 8). Begin by placing the wheel of your cutter near the top edge of the glass. Press down vertically, pulling in the direction you wish, using just enough pressure to make a visible scratch. When you're cutting along a line, score along the middle to the inside of the line to allow room for the copper foil or came.

Photo 7   *Photo 8*

2. As you pull the cutter, maintain its vertical position to ensure a nice, perpendicular edge on your glass. Whether you're cutting a straight or a curved line, you should score glass from one edge of the sheet to another, using a single, smooth, continuous motion (photo 9). Avoid lifting the cutter from the glass in the middle of a score or making more than a subtle change in direction. Never go back over a score line once it's been made, since this might ruin the sharp edge of the cutting wheel. Remember to keep the wheel of your cutter clean and lubricated with oil.

Photo 9

3. As you make each score, break the glass along the score line while the surface tension if fresh. (A line made 24 hours prior seldom breaks correctly!) When working with a piece of glass that's comfortable to hold in your hands, use your thumbs and knuckles to make the break. To do this, grip the glass with a hand on either side of the score with your thumbs close to the bottom of it on the upper face. In addition, bend the first knuckle of each hand directly underneath the glass (photo 10). Apply equal pressure from both hands, while pulling the glass down and apart. If the piece doesn't break easily, you can try using your pliers for more leverage (see step 4).

Photo 10

4. If you're working with a piece of glass that has a side too small to break comfortably with your hands, you can use breaking pliers. Grip the glass near the bottom of the score on the small edge with the ends of the jaws of the pliers parallel to the score (photo 11).

Photo 11

Continued →

5. Grasping the glass on the opposite side of the score (photo 11) with your other hand, gently pull the pliers downward and apart to break the glass. For very small pieces, you can use two pairs of pliers, as shown in photos 12 and 13.

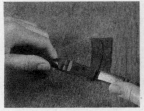
Photo 12

Photo 13

6. To break out a long score on a larger piece of glass, use running pliers. Grasp the edge of the glass in the full width of the pliers' jaws, centering them over the score line about ½-inch (1.3 cm) from the edge (photo 14). (Many models of these pliers have a line scribed on the outside of the upper, concave jaw that can be used to accurately align them with the score line.) Squeeze the handles gently to run the break up the score line.

7. After you've cut the sheet into smaller, more manageable pieces, you can begin to score and trim away the excess glass from around each pattern shape.

Photo 14

Grozing & Grinding

Even if you've scored and broken your glass with expert care and precision, the edges of your pieces will probably still have uneven areas that don't quite match your pattern. But, fortunately, there's a simple solution. You can groze and grind the edges until they match, as described below.

1. To check the cutting job on each piece, match the cut glass piece up with its pattern piece by number. Then hold the two up to compare them (photo 15). If edges of glass extend beyond the pattern piece, hold the glass with the pattern on top of it over a trashcan or other container. Then nibble away the areas with your grozing pliers until the outline matches the pattern (photo 16).

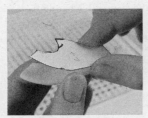
Photo 15

Photo 16

2. If you're preparing pieces for a copper-foiled project, you'll need to use your grinder after grozing to make the edges as smooth and exact as possible. Be careful not to grind away too much glass during this process, so take things slowly. If you've never used a glass grinder before, take the time to read the manufacturer's operating and care instructions carefully. For leaded projects, you can skip the grinding process unless the glass doesn't fit correctly into the came during assembly. Dry each piece thoroughly after grinding.

Tips:

- When cutting a piece with a sharp point, cut away from the point, and make the break at the larger end. Doing this gives you room to hold on with your pliers, and decreases your chances of breaking off the slimmer, sharper point.

- When scoring and breaking curves, always break the convex (inside) curves first to save glass. This way, if you break off too much of a curve, you can retrace the pattern piece as needed and try again. Score and break the concave (outside) curves next.

- To handle very deep or long curves, you might need to make several, progressively larger scallop-shaped scores to deepen the curve to the pattern line.

- Score and break the straight lines last, they're the easiest.

Methods of Assembly for Glass Pieces

The stained glass projects in this book are assembled with channeled came, copper foil, or a combination of the two methods. Leading is the traditional way of assembling panels, lending strength to combined glass pieces. Copper foil involves more soldering, and works well for assembling more intricate panels.

COPPER FOIL ASSEMBLY

If you want to attach pieces of glass together without using channeled came, you can use the copper foil method of assembly. This technique was first adapted during the late 1800s to make Art Nouveau lamp shades and other pieces. Since lead wasn't pliable enough to be shaped into the curvy, intricate shapes of the patterns, flexible copper or brass channeling was used instead as a base for soldering.

This method results in finer line quality than lead does, and works well for smaller, more detailed pieces. With copper foiling, you don't have the advantage of being able to hide imperfect edges under came, but some beginners find this to be an easier method to learn. The following steps will tell you how to apply copper foil.

1. After you've finished cutting all of your glass pieces, assemble them on top of the full-size template with which you began your project. Place them in their proper spots as if you're piecing together a puzzle. If your pieces matched their patterns exactly after grinding and grozing, they should fit perfectly, with just a slight bit of space between each shape. If they don't fit exactly here and there, use the individual patterns and spend a little more time grinding them to fit where they don't.

2. Choose a width of copper foil that will adequately cover the edge of the glass you're using, with room to fold it slightly over both faces of the piece. Thick or heavily textured glass, for instance, will require wider foil than thin or non-textured glass. If you plan to apply a patina to the finished panel, remember to use foil with a backing that will match.

3. Choose a piece to begin copper foiling. Peel away the paper backing from the foil, and center the adhesive side of it along the edge of the glass. For pieces that don't form part of the outside edges of the finished panel (interior pieces), you can start and end (overlap) foiling at any point. You'll eventually foil the exterior edges of your piece, or use a came border. If you're making a panel that you plan to frame with came, you won't need to foil the exterior edges.

4. Center the adhesive side of the foil on the edge of the glass piece, and begin pressing the strip into place. Make sure that it's even and centered as you work your way around the glass. At this point in the process, it's easy to peel back some of the foil and readjust it before folding it down over the edges (photo 17). End by overlapping the foil by about ¼ inch (6 mm) over the starting point.

Photo 17

Note: There are now gadgets on the market that are made specifically to help you center foil, if you find this process too tedious.

5. Press down the outer edges of the foil over the front and back faces of the glass, folding the corners down neatly with your fingers. (Now you'll see why it as so important to center the foil along the edges!) While doing this, resist sliding your fingers along the sides of the foil, or you may get a nasty cut. Use a crimper or burnisher to seal the edges, smoothing out any air bubbles and forming a tight seal (photo 18).

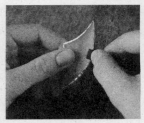
Photo 18

6. Inspect your foiled piece to make sure you've applied the foil evenly. You can use a razor-blade cutter to trim away any obvious areas that are too lopsided, or peel the foil off and start again if the visual problem can't be fixed with a slight trimming. With some practice, applying the foil evenly can become second nature.

SOLDERING OF COPPER FOIL PANELS

If you've foiled and trimmed your glass pieces carefully, the assembly of your copper foil panel should go smoothly. The following steps will tell you how to do this.

TACK-SOLDERING

Once you position the pieces of your panel, you'll need to tack them together at a few joints with bits of solder to hold them in place before you begin doing the real work of creating solder beads. The following section will warm you up for the job ahead.

1. Assemble all the foiled pieces on your work surface on top of the full-size template, using the numbers as a guide. The pieces should butt up lightly against each other (photo 19). Don't worry if you notice some small spaces between edges because the solder will fill these.

2. Pay attention to the exterior lines of the pattern, using them to line up the outer edges of the piece. They must be straight.

Photo 19

3. Once the borders of the panel are even and square, you'll tack-solder a few joints together to hold them in place.

4. Turn on your soldering iron, and allow it to heat up for a minute or two. Meanwhile, apply a bit of flux at several seams where the glass joins along the outside edges of the panel.

5. Unwind about 6 to 8 inches (15.2 to 20.3 cm) of 50/50 solder from the spool. Hold the spool in one hand, and position the end of the solder just above one of the freshly fluxed joints.

6. Holding your soldering iron in your other hand, touch the hot tip of the iron to the top of the solder wire, and press the molten solder down onto the foil seam, just long enough for the solder to adhere to the foil. It shouldn't take more than a second or two. Repeat this process to tack down more outer edge joints until the panel is stable around the edges.

7. Flux and tack-solder some of the interior seams together on the panel until the seams feel as though they're tightly held in place.

FLAT-FILLING

The subsequent part of soldering in the copper foil method is called flat-filling. This means that you'll run just enough solder into the seams between glass pieces to fill them. Read through this section carefully before you begin.

1. When you're ready, begin by applying flux to the seam you plan to flat-fill first. You can do the seams in any order. Hold the tip of the solder wire over the seam, and heat a bit of it until melted, then drop it onto the seam and drag it along an inch (2.5 cm) or so.

2. Keep moving the iron along the seam, adding solder as you go. Continue melting solder in this fashion, pulling it along the seam to fill in the spaces between the pieces and make the copper foil turn silver (photo 20).

3. If you plan to use came around the border, begin flat-filling about ¼ inch (6 mm) from the panel's outer edges; otherwise the soldered edge won't fit into the came's channel.

Photo 20

HIGH-BEADING THE SEAMS

Once the seams are flat-filled, you'll go back over the seams to make them attractively finished. To do this, you'll smooth out the solder line and run a high bead of 60/40 solder on top of them—a slightly raised, rounded line of solder. Due to a higher tin content, the 60/40 solder cools more slowly than the 50/50 version, so you'll be able to manipulate it more effectively into a smooth finish.

1. As in the process of flat-filling, you'll begin to make a bead by holding the iron's hot tip against the end of the solder wire. This time, however, touch the top side of the iron with the solder wire, and allow gravity to pull the molten solder to the underside of the tip so that it forms a bubble.

2. Drag the bubble along the seam, adding more solder as needed.

3. When you're working with molten solder, you'll notice that it flows and levels out to form a smooth bead. This can take some practice, so be prepared to learn your timing on this maneuver (photo 21).

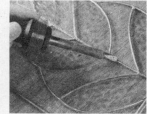

Photo 21

4. To smoothly join lines of solder at a joint where they meet, move up the joint just enough to re-melt the adjoining line of solder, then smooth out the seam as much as possible. You can smooth out any bumps in the solder by holding the iron in the same position that you've been using and gently moving it up and down.

5. As soon as you've finished soldering one side of a panel, clean the flux off of the seams. If you used paste flux, wipe the seams with a cotton ball moistened with acetone. To clean liquid or gel flux, use a commercial flux remover, following the manufacturer's instructions. The panel doesn't have to be perfectly clean yet, but you should take the time to remove the flux.

5. Carefully turn the panel over, and finish the seams with a high bead as you did on the reverse.

6. Add outer came as required using bumpers of the same size and insert hangers where required. Attach outer came to any outer foil seams that extend to the panel's edge with tack-soldering. Remove all flux residue

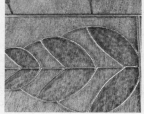

Photo 22

(photo 22). (Flip ahead to page 00 for instructions on how to do these final things.)

SPECIAL-EFFECT SOLDERING

- Intentional large holes between pieces of glass, created for the purposes of your design, may be filled in with scraps of lead and soldered over (photo 23). Textures in these areas can be created by lightly dragging the iron and lifting it up, purposely leaving a rough surface (photo 24). Fill in the spaces slowly, allowing the solder to solidify. Then add a little flux to put a high smooth finish on the area.

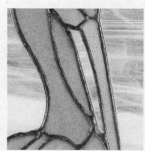

Photo 23   *Photo 24*

- To add solder details, such as dots or "eyes," use 60/40 solder. On a finished, clean panel drop a spot of solder onto the seamline to create the appearance of a raised eye (photo 25).

Photo 25

ASSEMBLING LEADED PANELS WITH CAME

The traditional method of assembling glass panels uses a metal framework composed of came pieces soldered at each joint. Leaded panels can be assembled with lead, zinc, brass, and/or copper came. The came not only holds the glass together, but defines the lines in the panel's design. The edge of each glass piece abuts the heart of the came, which is surrounded by the leaves (figure 1). In most instances, the heart is approximately ¹⁄₁₆-inch (1.5 mm) thick, no matter how wide the came. For this reason, the pattern lines in leaded glass patterns are assumed to be this size.

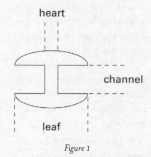

Figure 1

If you've done your homework, and cut all the pieces according to your pattern, you won't have much trouble fitting the pieces together like a jigsaw puzzle. But, if some of them don't fit exactly, you may be able to fix the problem with a bit of shaping (see grozing and grinding). Keep in mind that the glass edges will be hidden underneath the came, and they don't have to be shaped as they do for copper foiling.

Depending on the panel design, it may make sense to begin assembling in a corner, on an edge, or even in the middle of the pattern. For this reason, each leaded project in this book has numbered pieces indicating a logical sequence for assembling them.

In most of the projects in this book, lead is used for the interior pieces, while the outside is assembled with lighter-weight zinc came. Zinc is a good choice for square or rectangular panels because it provides excellent support without unnecessary weight.

The following illustrated steps take you through the process of assembling a particular panel. In this case, notice that we begin assembling at the top of the piece. Although the order of assembly varies in the projects, these steps will show you how to use bumpers, cut the lead, and shape it as needed.

1. Brush off your work surface before you begin, then place the template flat on your table, positioning it so that you're starting at the point closest to you. (In this case, we're assembling with the template positioned upside down—in other words, from the panel's top across to the bottom. This position makes it easier to negotiate the curves.)

2. Place the matching glass pieces on the template, using the numbers as a guide (photo 26). There will be a bit of space between the pieces.

Photo 26

3. You'll need horseshoe nails and bumpers (scrap lead pieces the same size as the final came) to hold each piece in place while you're adding it to the panel. Keep in mind that you're building the panel one piece at a time. In this case, we're starting at one end of the panel with a glass piece that will be held in place on one side by the frame. To secure your first piece of glass, use a hacksaw to cut a scrap of border zinc to fit along the outside edge.

(You must cut zinc with a saw, in contrast to lead that is stretched and then cut with lead nippers.) Use several lead came scraps to shore up the rest of the glass edges. Hammer horseshoe nails with their flat edges against the came to hold the pieces in place (photos 27 and 28).

Photo 27   *Photo 28*

4. Now you'll cut the first piece of interior lead came that will become a part of the final panel. Cut a foot (30.5 cm) or more of lead with a flat cut on the left end. Position this cut end along the left edge of the glass and across the whole length, on top of the bumpers. Use a nail to mark the other end (photo 29), and cut it flat with your nippers. Replace the bumpers with this length of lead.

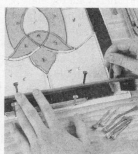

Photo 29

5. Continue by adding another piece of glass next to the first, following the numbered sequence. Remove nails as needed in order to slide in adjacent glass pieces, using bumpers to hold each new piece in place (photo 30). (Notice that we're working upwards and filling the center of the design. The vertical border lines lend strength to the panel, so always use an unbroken length of came for long lines such as these.)

Photo 30

6. When you lead curved pieces, you'll need to mark and cut the came at angles where the lines meet (photo

Continued ➞

31). Since gaps will be covered with solder later, cut the came so that it fits comfortably. Don't force it into place, or it will throw things out of alignment.

Photo 31

7. After the central piece is fitted into the Y-shaped joint, you'll cut the longest curved line next. To do this, bend a length of came slightly longer than the line, using the bumpers as a guide (photo 32). This extra length gives you room for error.

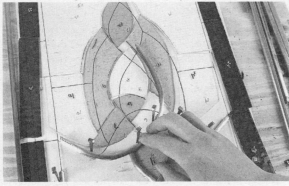

Photo 32

8. As you continue adding glass pieces, wrap the edges of came smoothly around them, cutting pieces as needed with the flat side of the nippers. Then, fit them together snugly (photo 33). (Never try to bend lead around corners or sharp points. Use two pieces of lead instead.)

Photo 33

9. Continue to build your panel by adding more pieces and nailing them in place (photo 34). Once the inner part of the panel is fitted and nailed, you'll be ready to add the glass border pieces. As a part of this process, measure and cut a long length of came to fit along the left side (photo 35).

Photo 34

10. Add more pieces until the glass border is in place and the outside edges are all secured with zinc bumpers in preparation for adding the zinc frame (photo 36).

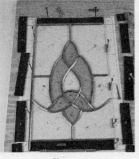

Photo 35

Photo 36

11. To add the frame, position the first piece of came along the right side, on top of the bumpers. Use a saw to miter the edge where it meets the corner of the panel. Then, position the second piece that goes along the bottom edge, and mark the next angle to cut (photo 37).

Note: When all the pieces are nailed down, the lead lines should be straight and any curves should be smooth and flowing. Keep in mind that the solder joints will hide the cuts.

12. When everything is in place, and nails are fitted around the edges, you can add the hangers to the frame. To do this, remove the nails from one side of the outer edge, lift up the piece of came, and insert a tinned hanger into the came channel. Reposition the came with the hanger out. Repeat this process on the other side.

Photo 37    *Photo 38*

13. Before soldering, use the wire brush to clean each came joint, and then flux the joints before soldering them. Strive to make a smooth, clean, overlapping joint, as shown (photos 38 and 39).

Photo 39

14. When all the joints are soldered, clean off the flux, carefully turn the panel over. Repeat the soldering process on the back side.

15. Do a final check of your finished panel to make sure that you didn't miss any joints that need soldering. Clean the piece, and add chain to the hangers.

Assembling Panels that Combine Lead and Copper Foil

In stained glass, you have the option of combining copper foil and lead in one panel. These projects can be challenging to assemble, but the results are beautiful.

If a project contains a group of copper-foiled pieces that touch one another, grind, foil, and solder these pieces together as if they're a separate unit, leaving the edges exposed (no foil) where they'll be leaded. After this, high-bead both sides of the copper-foiled unit up to the edges, allowing room for the lead to overlap.

If you're placing foiled pieces whose edges pass underneath lead lines, insert the edges into each came channel on either side. Such pieces are soldered later as a part of the final construction (photo 40). When a small foiled piece cuts through a lead line (photo 41), cut the lead pieces on either side of it before dropping in the piece.

Photo 40

Photo 41

After all the pieces are in place, wire-brush the lead joints and spots where the foiled pieces meet the lead. Flux these areas and solder them, using a very small amount of solder for the foiled joints. After the front is soldered, turn the panel over and solder the exposed copper-foil seams.

Overlays

An overlay is a piece added to the front of the panel once it is finished. An overlay can be composed of a foiled, tinned, and cleaned piece of glass, shaped pieces of wire, or shapes cut from sheets of metal. The overlay is tack-soldered onto the piece as a final step.

To add an overlay, position it on the panel, and apply a small amount of flux on either side of the piece where it joins the lead or foil line. Tack-solder the piece in place. Don't allow the flux or solder to seep underneath the overlay.

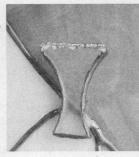

Photo 42

When using a patina, it's recommended that you apply it to the overlay before attaching it, then reapply it to any solder joints (photos 42 and 43).

Photo 43

Turning Over Panels During Construction

Until it has been soldered on both sides, a stained glass panel is a somewhat fragile thing. After soldering the first side, you'll need to carefully turn the panel over, in its fragile state, to solder the other side. Use the following technique to avoid damaging your panel.

To do this properly, slide about half of the panel over the edge of your work table, toward yourself, supporting the bottom edge with one hand.

With the other hand, grasp the edge of the panel's top edge and allow it to drop into an upright position in your lower hand, balancing the center on the table's edge (photo 44). Lift up the panel so that its lower edge is positioned toward the back of the workbench, leaving a space behind it that is at least half the panel's width. Move your hands around to the sides to grasp them at the panel's top. In a quick, even motion, allow the panel to descend to the table with gravity guiding you (photo 45). Slide the panel backward onto the worktable. Now you're ready to work on the backside of the panel. Once soldered, the panel will have much more strength, making it easier to clean and handle.

Photo 44   *Photo 45*

Attachments for Hanging Panels

A popular and attractive way of hanging stained glass panels is inserting pre-made brass hangers into the tops of the two side pieces of the came frame. You'll do this once you've assembled your panel, and all pieces, including the frame, are nailed into place (to make sure that everything fits).

To add these hangers, you must lift out the side pieces to access the top ends. Next, tin or lightly coat the hangers with 50/50 solder on both sides (photo 46). Brush and flux the came pieces at the top before inserting the hangers into their cavities (photo 47). Let the hangers cool longer than usual since brass takes longer to cool and solidify than some metals. Test the solder joints by pulling on each hanger with needle-nose pliers. If it feels firm and doesn't move, it will hold your panel. If not, solder it again, and let it cool.

Photo 46

Photo 47

You can also hang panels with heavy-gauge, tinned wire formed into a loop with twisted ends. These can be attached inside the came, as described above, or on the outside of the frame. Test your solder joint for strength after it cools.

The Projects

The following section presents a wide range of stained glass designs. As you thumb through, you'll find that the most complex pieces are placed at the end of this section. You may want to take these projects on as you become more accomplished.

If you find a project that you like, and want to begin there, you will have complete instructions. But keep in mind that you must learn the basics in the front of the book before beginning any project. Thumb back to a particular section when you need help during the process.

Each project is accompanied by a detailed template showing you how to cut the pieces apart. Enlarge it to the suggested finished size or to another size of your choice. If it is assembled with came or combines came and copper foil, the pieces are numbered to tell you the most practical order of assembly. If a project is constructed only of copper-foiled pieces, they are not numbered because you can assemble them in any order of your choice. Add your own numbering system to these pieces.

Each project also references two or more toolboxes under the heading of "tools and equipment." You'll find these lists on the following page. The basic toolbox contains all items (both tools and supplies) that you will routinely use to make the projects.

The glass colors that we used are listed, but keep in mind that you can change the palette of your pieces in any way that you like. You can also vary other factors such as the patina, the came that you use for your frame, or how you hang the piece. Again, we have merely suggested those things for your convenience.

Remember that learning stained glass takes some patience, especially when you're assembling, and this book will make the process as smooth as possible for you. For troubleshooting tips, refer to the end of the section. Most important, relax and have fun!

Basic Toolbox & Supplies

- Heavy kraft paper
- Carbon paper
- Glass cutter and cutting fluid
- Breaking pliers
- Grozing pliers
- Running pliers
- Glass grinder with face shield and coolant
- Light table (optional)
- Flux, flux brush, and flux remover
- Soldering iron, holder, and tip
- Cleaning sponge
- Wire brush
- Glazing hammer and horseshoe nails
- Waterproof marking pens in black, white and/or gold
- Natural-bristle hand brush
- Table brush and dust pan
- Needle-nose pliers
- Scissors
- Wire cutters
- Safety glasses
- Safety gloves
- Kitchen hot pad or oven glove

- Non-ammonia based glass cleaner
- Lint-free towels
- Cotton-tipped swabs

Lead Toolbox

- Lead pattern shears
- Lead vise and channel-lock pliers
- Hacksaw (handsaw) with metal cutting blade or electric came saw
- Lead nippers (dykes)
- Metal files

Copper Foil Toolbox

- Foil pattern shears
- Foil crimper or burnisher
- Single-blade razor or craft knife

Blue Rondel Design

Use rondels and bevels as accent pieces on a leaded panel to create interesting visual contrasts.

GLASS

- Clear/textured
- Cobalt blue/cathedral
- 2 blue rondels, each about 3 inches (7.6 cm) in diameter
- Clear, oval-shaped bevel, 3 x 6 inches (7.6 x 15.3 cm)

TOOLS & EQUIPMENT

- Basic toolbox and supplies
- Lead toolbox

SUPPLIES

- 6 feet (1.8 m) of ⁷/₃₂-inch (.55 cm) H-channel lead came
- 6 feet (1.8 m) of ¼-inch (.64 cm) U-channel zinc came
- 50/50 solder
- 2 brass hangers
- Silver-colored or black chain

Suggested finished size: 26 x 12 inches (66 x 30.5 cm)

INSTRUCTIONS

1. Enlarge the project template to the suggested finished size. Because the rondels and bevels can vary in shape, trace them onto the enlarged template where they belong, and mark the top center of each glass piece for later reference.

2. If all of your glass is fairly transparent, use the English cutting method to cut out the pieces. If the blue rondels are fairly dark, use the cut-apart pattern method (with lead pattern shears) instead. Be sure to number your pieces as you cut them.

3. Turn the template 90° so that the first five pattern pieces are closest to you. Position the glass pieces on the template. Use lead bumpers to assist you as you begin leading in the bottom right corner. Pay attention to the pattern, making sure to keep the long vertical came pieces whole. (Don't be tempted to break them up with pieces that cross them as you assemble.) Groze or grind the glass pieces to fit as you work.

4. Wrap the bevel and rondels with came as described in the project on page 00. Use the marks made in step 1 as your beginning point for wrapping. After these

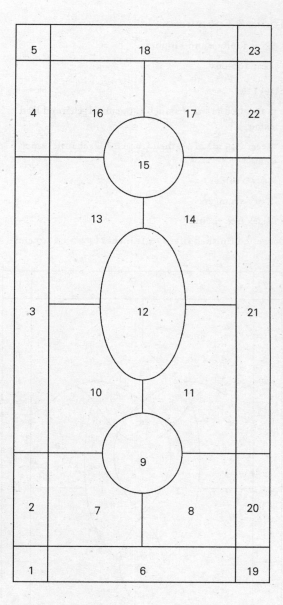

pieces are wrapped, position them during assembly without soldering them. Simply nail them in place. Align any cut in the surrounding came with a lead seam that crosses it. When you solder later, you'll be able to hide the seam.

5. Use a saw to cut and miter the zinc came to fit around the piece as a frame/border. Hold the entire configuration (glass pieces and frame) in place with nails, making sure that everything fits. After this step, lift out each of the side pieces of the frame to add a hanger to the top. Tin the hangers, and solder them.

6. Clean all the lead joints before you flux and solder them. After soldering, remove all the nails. Clean off the flux residue. Carefully turn the panel over. Solder and clean the other side.

7. Polish the panel, cleaning the glass thoroughly.

8. Measure out a length of chain for hanging your piece. Open the link on one end, and attach it to one of the hangers. Close the link and secure it, then repeat this process on the other hanger.

Victorian Tulip

This small piece shows you how to negotiate curves on a leaded panel.

GLASS

- Clear/hammered
- Dark wine/cathedral
- Medium wine/glue-chip/cathedral
- Light wine/wispy

Continued ➔

TOOLS & EQUIPMENT

Basic toolbox and supplies

Lead toolbox

SUPPLIES

6 feet (1.8 m) of 7/32-inch (.55 cm) H-channel lead came

5 feet (1.5 m) of 1/2-inch (.64 cm) U-channel zinc came

50/50 solder

2 brass hangers

Black jack chain

Suggested finished size: 17 x 11 inches (43.2 x 27.9 cm)

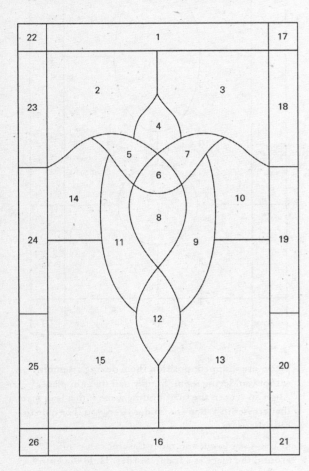

INSTRUCTIONS

1. Enlarge the project template to the suggested finished size. Depending on the opacity of your glass, use the English cutting method or cut-apart pattern method (with lead pattern shears) to cut out and number each piece of glass.

2. Turn the template upside down on your work surface so that you begin working at the top of the piece. Position the glass pieces on the template. Use lead bumpers to assist you as you begin assembling the pieces with lead. Groze and grind the glass to fit the pattern.

3. Follow the instructions on pages 116 to 118 for specifics about assembling this piece.

4. Use a saw to cut and miter the zinc came to fit around the piece as a frame/border. Hold the entire configuration (glass pieces and frame) in place with nails, making sure that everything fits. After this step, lift out each side of the frame to add a hanger to the top of the came. Tin the hangers, and solder them.

5. Clean all the lead joints before you flux and solder them. After soldering, remove all the nails. Clean off the flux residue. Carefully turn over the panel. Solder and clean the other side.

6. Polish the panel, cleaning the glass thoroughly.

7. Measure out a length of chain for hanging your piece. Open the link on one end, and attach it to one

of the hangers. Close the link and secure it, then repeat this process on the other side.

Classic Geometric Design with Bevels

This design combines subtle green glass with clear bevels for an elegant look.

GLASS

Light green/opalescent

Clear/textured

2 bevels, each 2 inches square (5.1 x 5.1 cm)

2 bevels, each 1½ inches square (3.8 x 3.8 cm)

TOOLS & EQUIPMENT

Basic toolbox and supplies

Lead toolbox

SUPPLIES

6 feet (1.8 m) of 7/32-inch (.55 cm) H-channel lead came

5 feet (1.5 m) of ¼-inch (.64 cm) U-channel zinc came

50/50 solder

2 brass hangers

Silver-colored chain

Suggested finished size: 20 x 8 inches (50.8 x 20.3 cm)

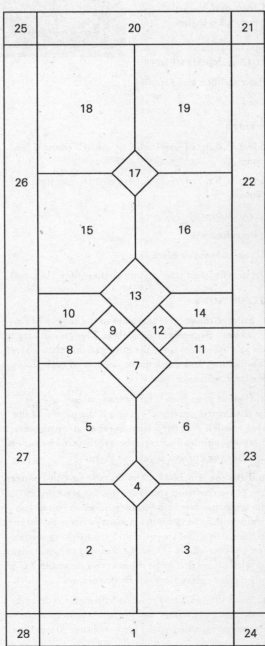

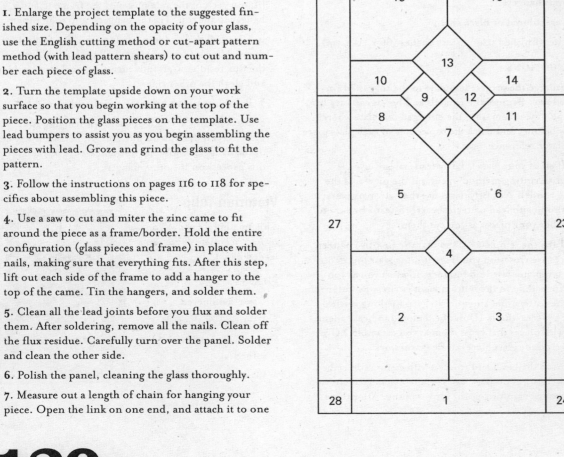

INSTRUCTIONS

1. Enlarge the project template to the suggested finished size. Trace it on to kraft paper, and cut the pieces apart with lead pattern shears. Cut out and number the glass pieces.

2. Begin by leading the bottom central piece, grozing and grinding pieces as needed to make them fit. Work up and through the center before adding the side pieces. Keep vertical lines in whole came lengths.

3. Use a saw to cut and miter the zinc came to fit around the piece as a frame/border. Hold the entire configuration (glass pieces and frame) in place with nails, making sure that everything fits. After this is determined, lift out each of the side pieces of the frame to add a hanger to the top. Tin the hangers, and solder them.

4. Clean all the lead joints before you flux and solder them. After soldering, remove all the nails. Clean off the flux residue. Carefully turn the panel over. Solder and clean the other side.

5. Polish the panel, cleaning the glass thoroughly.

6. Measure out a length of chain for hanging your piece. Open the link on one end, and attach it to one of the hangers. Close the link and secure it, then repeat this process on the other side.

Falling Leaves Panel

The length of this copper-foiled panel accentuates the gentle, downward movement of the leaves.

GLASS

Clear/textured

Gold seedy/cathedral

Green with gold seedy/cathedral

Green seedy/cathedral

Red and gold seedy/cathedral

TOOLS & EQUIPMENT

Basic toolbox and supplies

Copper foil toolbox

SUPPLIES

2 lengths of ¼-inch (.64 cm) U-channel zinc came, each 6 feet (1.8 m) long

3/16-inch (.48 cm) and 2⅓-inch (.55 cm) black-backed copper foil

50/50 and 60/40 solder

2 brass hangers

Black patina made for solder

Black patina made for zinc

Black jack chain

Suggested finished size: 36 x 8 inches (91.4 x 20.3 cm)

INSTRUCTIONS

1. Enlarge the template to the suggested finished size. Trace the pieces onto kraft paper, and cut them out with copper foil pattern shears. Cut out and number the glass pieces. Groze and grind them to fit the pattern in preparation for foiling.

2. Apply copper foil to the pieces, and position them on the template.

3. Apply flux close to the outer edges, then tack-solder the pieces together with 50/50 solder. Leave a small margin around the edges to allow for the zinc came

frame as you solder. Flux, tack-solder, and flat-fill the inner seams with 50/50 solder, then high-bead with 60/40 solder. Clean off the flux residue.

4. Use a saw to cut and miter the zinc came to fit around the piece as frame/border. Hold the entire configuration (glass pieces and frame) in place with nails, making sure that everything fits and is square. After this step, lift out each side of the frame to add a hanger to the top of the came. Tin the hangers, and solder them.

5. Clean the zinc at the corners and where the foiled seams meet it. Flux and solder the corner seams, and tack-solder the foiled pieces to the zinc frame along the border. Clean off the flux residue. Turn over the panel.

6. Solder the panel's reverse side. Clean off the flux residue.

7. Apply the black patina made for solder to the solder seams. Use the wire brush to clean the zinc came, then apply the black patina made for zinc to both sides.

8. Polish the panel, cleaning the glass thoroughly.

9. Measure out a length of chain for hanging your piece. Open the link on one end, and attach it to one of the hangers. Close the link and secure it, then repeat this process on the other side.

Street Address Sign

Begin with the basic template shown, then add your own street numbers. You'll cement the border pieces to prepare the piece for hanging outside, and frame it with wood.

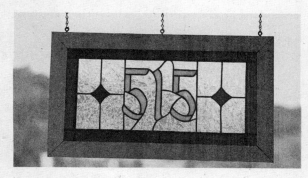

Glass

Clear/glue-chipped

Blue streaky/opaque

White/opaque

Tools & Equipment

Basic toolbox and supplies

Lead toolbox

Copper foil toolbox

SUPPLIES

6 feet (1.8 m) of ¼-inch (.64 cm) H-channel lead came

6 feet (1.8 m) of ⅜-inch (.95 cm) U-channel zinc came

7/32-inch (.55 cm) black-backed copper foil

50/50 and 60/40 solder

Black patina for solder

Cement or glazing compound (for edges)

Whiting (for edges)

Painted wooden frame made to fit around piece

Several screw eyes

Silver-colored jack chain

Suggested finished size: 12 x 24 inches (30.5 x 61 cm)

INSTRUCTIONS

1. Enlarge the template to the suggested finished size. In the center area, we've indicated how we drew and cut the numbers "515." Study these numbers, as well as the other examples, to see how surrounding cut lines are used to fit the pieces together. Emulate this method for your numbers, making small thumbnail sketches to work out the best design. If you wish, you can draw the design small and enlarge it to fit on top of the template before tracing it along with the surrounding pieces.

2. After you've created the template, trace the pattern pieces on kraft paper and cut them out with copper foil pattern shears. Cut out and number the glass pieces.

3. Apply black-backed copper foil to all the pieces of the inner section (numbers and rectangular designs on either side), leaving the outer edges free so that they can be fitted into lead came.

4. Position the foiled pieces on the template. Flux and tack-solder the outer edges with 50/50 colder. Flat-fill the inner seams with 50/50 solder, then high-bead them with 60/40 solder. When you solder, remember to leave an allowance for the came to overlap around the outer edges.

5. Lead the border pieces in the order shown on the template. The two vertical border lines on either end are formed by unbroken pieces of came. This means that you'll be working with two short pieces of came on either end to complete the long horizontal lines that cross these vertical lines.

6. Use a saw to cut and miter the zinc came to fit around the piece as a border. Hold the entire configuration (glass pieces and frame) in place with nails, making sure that everything fits.

7. Clean the lead and zinc came joints, then flux and solder them. Tack-solder the areas where the foiled pieces touch the came. Clean off the flux residue.

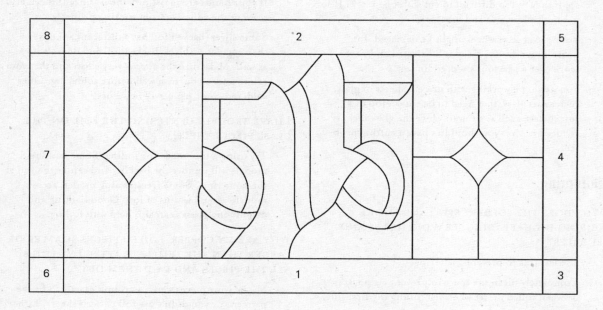

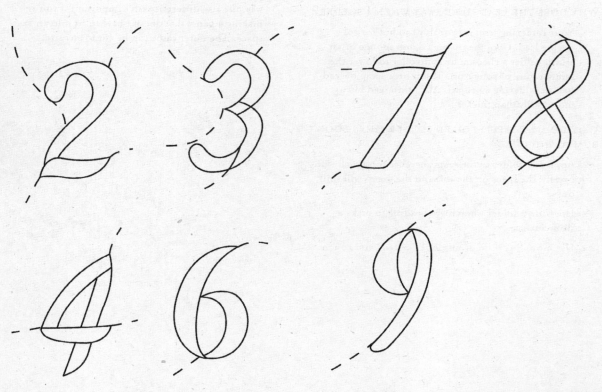

Continued →

8. Turn the piece over and solder the back. Clean off the flux residue.

9. Apply cement or glazing compound and whiting to the leaded border pieces. Repeat on the front side and allow to cure.

10. Apply black patina to the soldered seams.

11. Position the piece in the wooden frame, and use small nails or other hardware to secure it.

12. Add screw eyes to the top of the frame.

13. Measure a length of chain for hanging, and open the link at one end. Attach it to the screw eye by closing the link. Repeat on the other side.

Troubleshooting Tips for Stained Glass

The following tips offer you answers to frequently asked questions.

Glass Cutting

Why does my glass keep breaking in the wrong places?

- Make sure you're applying enough pressure on the glass cutter to make a proper score line.
- Look at the shapes you're cutting out of the glass to see if they're too difficult to cut with one score. If so, use multiple scores and breaks.
- Your glass cutter wheel might be damaged if it doesn't turn freely. Keep it lubricated and never score over a previously scored line.
- You might be working with uneven sheets of glass, such as art glass, that need to be cut on top of a soft surface such as a towel. Once the glass sheet is reduced in size, you shouldn't have a cutting problem.

Soldering

WHY DOES THE SOLDER "SPIT" AND SMOKE DURING HIGH-BEADING, LEAVING HOLES AND BUBBLES?

- Use less flux to prevent spattering.
- Completely fill in the space to prevent air pockets between foiled pieces when flat-filling the first side.

WHY DOES THE LEAD MELT AWAY WHEN I SOLDER?

- Your soldering iron is probably too hot for soldering lead. Cool the tip on a damp sponge often and consider a rheostat or controller to lower the temperature of your iron. Test it on a scrap of lead before soldering a project. Also, thin lead burns more easily than thicker lead.

WHY DO MY COPPER-FOILED SOLDER LINES LOOK BUMPY AND DULL?

- Apply less solder to the seams because too much will overfill the space on the foil and the excess will spill out.
- Use 60/40 solder when high-beading to make a shiny surface.
- Use more flux if the seams look "pitted" and rough.

WHY DID A PIECE OF MY GLASS CRACK DURING SOLDERING?

- Glass isn't heat resistant, so if an area is heated long enough, the glass can fracture, especially on smaller pieces. The solder lines remain hot during soldering, so it's best not to overwork one area. After a couple minutes move to another area, and allow the glass and solder to cool, then go back and make any corrections. This is especially true for intricate, small pieces of a pattern and large open gaps that are filled with solder.

WHY DOES MY ZINC CAME RESIST SOLDERING, EVEN AFTER I'VE BRUSHED AND FLUXED IT?

- Metal came that has been allowed to oxidize won't be shiny, and wire brushing alone might not clean it enough. Use fine steel wool or another abrasive before fluxing it.
- Zinc takes more heat to solder than lead. Be sure you leave the iron on the joint long enough for the solder to melt to the zinc. A properly soldered joint won't pop apart when pulled.

Copper Foiling

WHY DOESN'T MY FOIL STICK WELL TO MY GLASS?

- Be sure your hands and the glass are clean and dry. Remove any powder that may remain from grinding. If your hands are moist, dry them, since this can also prevent the adhesive from sticking properly.
- Some silver-backed foil has a different adhesive than regular or black-backed foil and doesn't stick as well. Make sure the glass is very clean and that you crimp and/or burnish well before soldering. Once soldered, your panel will be secure.

I HAVE TROUBLE CENTERING THE FOIL ON THE GLASS PIECES—HELP!

- Try using a tool made for foiling. Some handheld models will remove the backing and center the foil at the same time. Some freestanding models accommodate several widths of foil. Good lighting and magnifying glasses can also help with foiling.

WHY ARE MY COPPER-FOILED PIECES SMALLER OR LARGER THAN THE TEMPLATE AFTER I'VE FOILED ALL THE PIECES AND LAID THEM OUT?

- Maybe your pieces weren't ground exactly to fit the pattern, or you didn't use foil pattern shears. Either way, the size difference isn't important if you're making a panel that doesn't have to fit into an exact space. The outer came can be cut to any size.

Leading

WHY DO MY LEAD PANELS GROW IN SIZE AS I ASSEMBLE THE PIECES OF MY PROJECT?

- The glass may not be tightly placed or seated in the grooves of the lead.
- The glass might be wider than the came channel. You can widen lead came with a plastic foil burnisher, or tap the glass into the came with the rubber side of your glazing hammer. If the glass is deeply textured, reduce the thickest part by grinding it at about a 45° angle to the bit, flattening out the peaks so that it fits better. Grinding prevents the glass from chipping if it is forced into hard came such as zinc and brass. Most came is 5/32 inch (.48 cm), made to accommodate 1/8-inch thick (3 mm) glass.
- If a lead piece is cut too long, it bumps the piece that follows it too far, creating loose-fitting pieces and a design larger than intended. All the cames should be cut short enough to allow abutting cames to seat completely.
- If a piece of glass just won't fit, remove the came so you can see the relationship between it and the edges of glass. You might need to groze or grind the edges again.
- When leading curvilinear glass pieces, make sure to hold the glass in one hand and shape the lead around it.

—FROM *Creative Stained Glass*

Knitting & Crochet

BASIC KNITTING TECHNIQUES

Nathalie Mornu

Slipknot

Slipknots are used in knitting and crochet to cast on the first stitch of a project. Start by leaving a tail, then make a loop with the yarn that looks like a cursive e (figure 1). Holding the area where the yarn crosses with one hand, push a new loop through the existing loop with your other hand (figure 2). Place the new loop on the needle or hook and lighten both yarn ends to create the slipknot (figure 3).

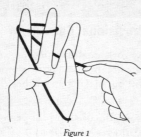

Figure 1

Figure 2

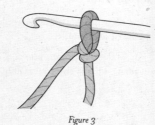

Figure 3

Figure 5

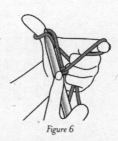

Figure 6

Longtail (Double) Cast-On

Calculate about 1 inch (2.5 cm) of yarn per stitch that you'll be casting on; this will be your tail.

Letting the tail hang, tie a slipknot around one of your knitting needles. You'll now have two strands of yarn hanging down from your needle—the tail and the strand connected to the ball (figure 4). Placing the needle in your right hand, separate the two strands of yarn with your left thumb and index finger. Secure both loose ends under your ring finger and pinky (figure 5).

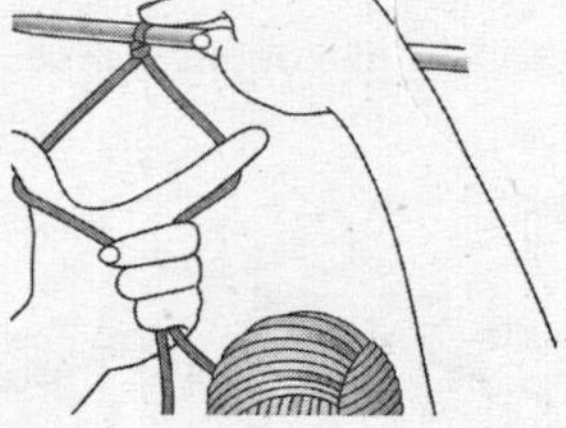

Use your needle to scoop under the outer strand of the thumb loop (figure 6) then over the inner strand of the index finger loop (figure 7). Let the loop fall off your thumb (figure 8) and pull the tail so that the stitch fits loosely onto your needle. Repeat until you've cast on the desired number of stitches.

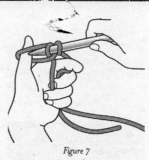

Figure 4

Figure 7

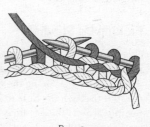

Figure 8

Knit Stitch

For the knit stitch, hold the needle with stitches on it in your left hand; the working yarn is held in your right hand and in the back of the work. Insert the right-hand needle, from bottom to top, into the stitch as shown in figure 9. The tips of the needles will form an x. Use your right index finger to wrap the strand of yarn, counterclockwise, around the right-hand needle (figure 10).

Figure 9

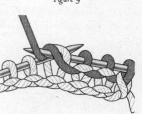

Figure 10

Continued →

Bring the yarn through the stitch with the right-hand needle and pull the loop off the left-hand needle (figure 11). You now have one complete knit stitch on your right-hand needle.

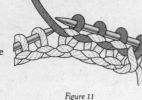

Figure 11

Continue until the end of the row, or as the pattern directs.

Purl Stitch

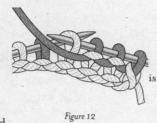

For the purl stitch, hold the needle with the stitches on it in your left hand, the working yarn held in the right hand and in front of your work. Insert the right-hand needle, from top to bottom, into the stitch (figure 12). Using your right index finger, wrap the strand of yarn counterclockwise around the right-hand needle (figure 13). Bring the yarn through the stitch with the right-hand needle and pull the loop off the left-hand needle (figure 14). Continue until the end of the row, or as the pattern directs.

is

Figure 12

Figure 13

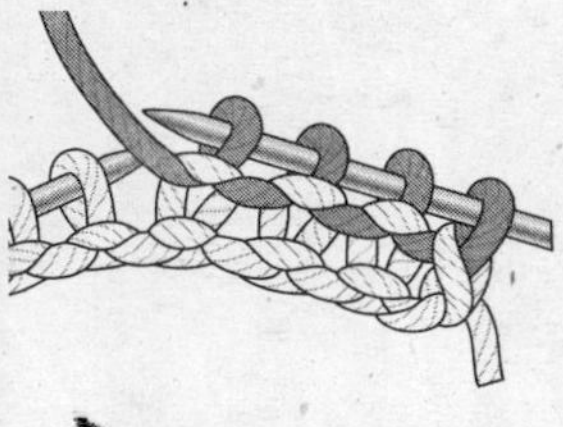

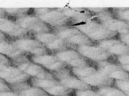

Figure 14

Stockinette Stitch

This is probably what you think of when you hear "knitted." To do stockinette, you alternate knit and purl rows, or, if you're working on circular needles, knit every row. Both sides of the stitch are shown here—what's generally considered the right side at top, with the wrong side (also called reverse stockinette) beneath it. Reverse stockinette is so pretty that it's frequently chosen to show on the exterior of a garment.

Garter Stitch

This attractive stitch consists of nothing more than doing knit stitch every row.

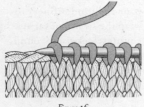

Picking Up Stitches

To pick up stitches along a bound-off edge, insert your needle into the space under both loops of the existing stitch (figure 15). Bring the yarn under the needle and scoop it through the hole to create one stitch on the needle. *Insert the needle into the next space, wrap the yarn counterclockwise, and scoop the loop through the space. Repeat from* until you've picked up the desired number of stitches (figure 16).

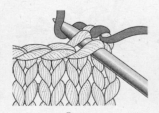

Figure 15

Figure 16

Yarn Over

Bring the working yarn to the front and knit the stitch normally. This wraps the yarn around the needle, creating a yarn over.

Inc 1 (Make 1 Increase)

With the right-hand needle, pick up the loop at the base of the next stitch on the left-hand needle. Place the loop on the left-hand needle. Treat the loop as a new stitch and knit into it normally.

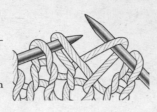

Slip, Slip, Knit

Slip your next two stitches, one at a time, to the right-hand needle. Insert the tip of the left-hand needle into the fronts of these stitches, from left to right, and knit them together (= two stitches decreased).

Slip Stitch Purlwise

Slipping a stitch means you pass a stitch from one needle to another without working it. A slipstitch purlwise won't twist like it does knitwise. To slip one stitch purlwise, insert your right needle into the next stitch on your left needle as though purling the stitch. Pull the stitch off your left needle, the stitch will now be on the right needle.

Bind Off

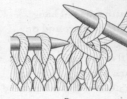

Knit two stitches. *With the tip of your left-hand needle, pull the second stitch on the right-hand needle over the first (figure 17) and let it drop off. You'll now have one stitch left on the needle (figure 18). Knit another stitch and repeat from * (figure 19).

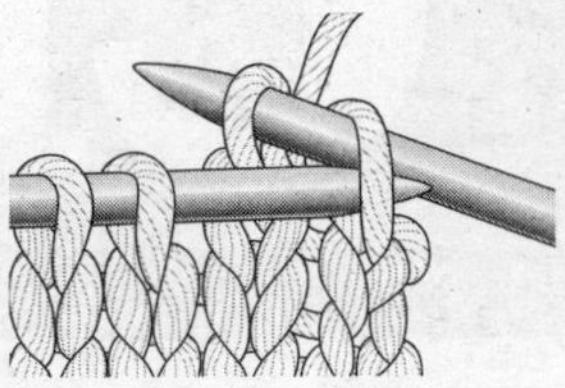

Figure 17

Continue in this manner, or as the pattern directs.

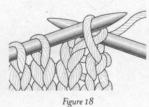

Figure 18

Figure 19

Sewn Bind-Off

Break off a length of yarn about three times as long as the knitting, and thread it onto a yarn needle. *Insert the needle into the first 2 stitches on the knitting needle as if to purl and draw the yarn through (figure 20). Reinsert the needle into the first stitch on the knitting needle as if to knit, draw yarn through, then slip the stitch off. (figure 21)* Repeat from * to *.

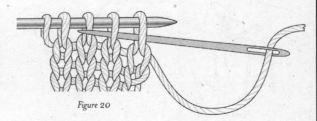

Figure 20

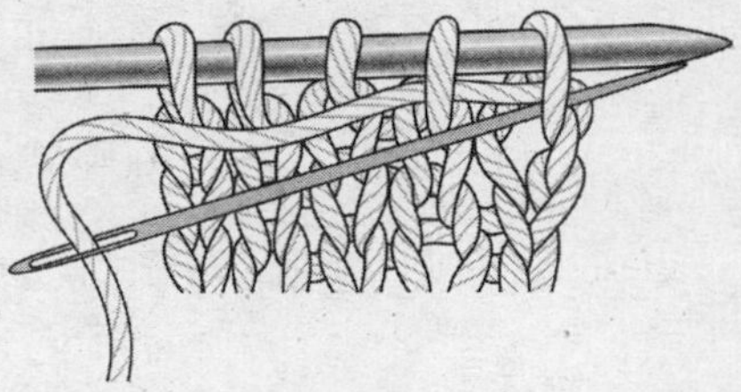

Weave in Ends

Using a tapestry needle, weave the loose ends of yarn in and out of the stitches on the wrong side of the work. Whenever possible, weave the ends into seam lines.

Figure 22

Single Crochet

Insert the hook into both loops of the stitch from the row below, as shown in figure 22. Wrap the yarn counterclockwise around the hook and draw it through the first loop (figure 23). Wrap the yarn counterclockwise once more, and draw it through both loops (figure 24). Insert the hook into the next stitch (figure 25). Wrap the yarn and draw it through the first loop, then wrap the yarn again and draw it through both loops. Continue in this manner.

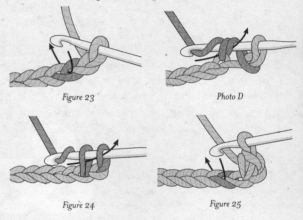

Figure 23

Photo D

Figure 24

Figure 25

—From *Knit & Wrap*

MORE BASIC KNITTING TECHNIQUES

Suzanne J. E. Tourtillott

Provisional Cast On

A provisional cast on can be removed from the knitting, so you can work a border or another part of the garment without picking up stitches. To work a provisional cast on:

1. Using a crochet hook slightly larger than the knitting needles used in your project, make a chain about ten stitches longer than the number of stitches you need to cast on.

2. Pick up one stitch (st) through each bump on the wrong side of the chain, as shown in figure 1.

Cable Cast On

This technique uses two needles and is similar to creating a row of knitting.

1. Make a slip knot about 4"/10cm from the end of the yarn. This is the first stitch.

2. Knit one stitch. Leave the slip knot on the left needle, and place the new stitch back on the left needle as well. You now have two stitches on the left needle and the right needle is empty.

3. Insert the right needle between the last two stitches on the left needle and wrap the yarn as if to knit (see figure 2). Pull the yarn through.

4. Place the new stitch back on the left needle, as shown in figure 3.

Repeat steps 3 and 4 for the required number of stitches.

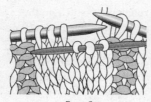

Figure 1

Figure 2   *Figure 3*

Short Row Shaping

A short row is simply a row that has fewer stitches than the full piece of knitting. By knitting short rows along one side of a narrow knitted piece, you can make the piece curve. Turning in the middle of the row leaves a small hole. The hole can be eliminated by wrapping the stitch at the turning point. When instructions tell you to wrap and turn (W&T):

1. Work to the turning point.

2. Wrap: Slip the next stitch onto the right needle. Bring the yarn to the front; then slip the same stitch back to the left needle (see figure 4).

3. Turn: Turn the work so the opposite side is facing you and work the next row as instructed.

This wrap-and-turn technique creates a "float" (an extra loop of yarn) on the right side of the work. On the next complete row, you'll work back over the wrapped stitch. Knit the wrap together with the corresponding stitch on the left-hand needle to close up the holes created by the short row shaping (see figure 5).

Figure 4   *Figure 5*

Cables

Cables are made when stitches in the knitted fabric cross over each other. Cable needles are short, double-pointed needles made especially for the purpose of knitting such patterns. They usually have a notch, ridges, or a curved section to keep the stitches from falling off while you're manipulating the cable.

To make a left-crossing cable:

1. Slip 3 stitches to the cable needle.

2. Hold the needle in front of the work (see figure 6).

3. Knit the next 3 stitches from the left needle.

4. Knit 3 stitches from the cable needle.

To make a right-crossing cable:

1. Slip 3 stitches to the cable needle.

2. Hold the needle in back of the work (see figure 7).

3. Knit the next 3 stitches from the left needle.

4. Knit 3 stitches from the cable needle.

Figure 6   *Figure 7*

Circular Knitting

Knitting in the round is used to create a seamless garment or garment piece. The technique is used frequently for making socks and neckbands, and sometimes is used for entire sweaters. When you're knitting in the round, you never turn your work, so the right side of the knitting is always facing you. To join your work:

1. Spread the stitches out on a circular needle or divide them evenly on three or four double-pointed needles, and check to make sure the cast-on edge is not twisted.

2. Join as shown in figure 8.

Figure 8

Lace

Lace is made by combining yarn overs with decreases. The yarn overs make holes in the knitting that are arranged to create an openwork pattern. Each yarn over adds one stitch to the knitting, so decreases are used to eliminate the extra stitches. To work a yarn over (yo):

1. Bring the yarn between the needles to the front, and then over the needle again to the back of the work to begin the next knit stitch as shown in figure 9.

2. On the next row, work the yarn over as a regular knit or purl stitch.

Figure 9

Finishing

The way you finish your knitting makes the difference between handmade and homemade results. These techniques will help you finesse your finishing so you're proud to wear your handknits.

TUBULAR BIND OFF

The tubular bind off creates a very stretchy edge. Unlike more conventional bind off techniques, it's worked with a tapestry needle instead of knitting needles. To work a tubular bind off:

1. Cut the yarn, leaving a tail at least twice as long as the width of the knitting you want to bind off. Thread the tail onto a tapestry needle.

2. Insert the tapestry needle into the 1st stitch as if to knit and slip the stitch off the knitting needle (see figure 10).

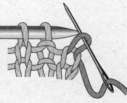

Figure 10

3. Insert the tapestry needle into the 3rd stitch as if to purl and pull the yarn through (see figure 11).

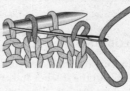

Figure 11

4. Insert the tapestry needle into the 2nd stitch as if to purl and slip the stitch off the knitting needle (see figure 12).

Figure 12

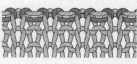

Figure 13   *Figure 14*

5. Insert the tapestry needle into the 4th stitch, as shown in figure 13, and pull the yarn through.

6. The 2 stitches on the needle now count as stitches 1 and 2. Repeat steps 2–5 until all stitches are bound off (see figure 14).

SEWING SEAMS

There are many different ways to sew seams on knitted garments. These are some of the techniques used in this book.

Mattress Stitch

A mattress stitch seam, sewn on the right side, appears nearly invisible. It joins two pieces of knitting together, and the finished garment appears as if it were knit as one large piece. Mattress stitch is used to sew the side seams and sleeve seams on a sweater. To sew a mattress stitch seam:

1. With the right sides facing up, place the 2 pieces to be seamed on a flat surface.

2. With a tapestry needle and matching yarn, go under the bar between the 1st and 2nd stitches near the edge of one piece of knitting. Make your stitches ½ stitch (for very bulky yarn) or 1 stitch (for lighter yarn) in from the edge.

3. Repeat step 2 on the other piece.

Tip: For a quicker seam, catch two bars from each side as you make each stitch.

Figure 15

4. Continue to work from side to side, pulling gently on the yarn to close the seam after every few stitches (see figure 15).

End-to-End Seams

End-to-end seams are used to join the cast-on and bound-off edges of knit pieces. End-to-end seams are used to sew shoulder seams on a sweater.

1. With the right sides of the fabric facing up, place the 2 pieces to be seamed on a flat surface.

2. With a tapestry needle and matching yarn, catch the knit V just inside the edge of one piece of knitting.

3. Repeat step 2 on the other piece.

4. Continue to work from side to side, pulling gently on the yarn to close the seam after each stitch (see figure 16).

Figure 16

Tip: The seam should be at the same tension as your knitting and look like a row of stockinette stitches.

Armhole Seam

To sew a sleeve into an armhole, use a combination of mattress stitch and end-to-end seaming as shown in figure 17.

Figure 17

Backstitch

A backstitch seam is often used to sew knitted pieces together, especially sewing sleeves into armholes. To work a backstitch seam:

Continued ➜

1. With right sides together, place the pieces to be joined on a flat surface.

2. To begin the seam, take the needle around the edge stitch twice, from back to front.

3. Insert the needle into the same spot where the yarn came out from the previous stitch and back up ¼"/.5cm to the left, and pull through, as shown in figure 18.

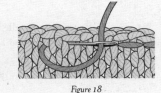

Figure 18

4. Repeat step 3 until the entire seam is sewn.

Overcast Seam

An overcast seam can be used to join pieces knit in different directions and to create a decorative seam. To sew an overcast seam:

1. With the right or wrong sides of the fabric facing up (as indicated in the project instructions), place the 2 pieces to be seamed on a flat surface.

2. With a tapestry needle and matching or contrasting yarn, use one smooth motion to catch the stitch on the edge of one piece of knitting and then catch a stitch on the other piece.

3. Continue along the seam, pulling gently on the yarn to close the seam after every few stitches (see figure 19).

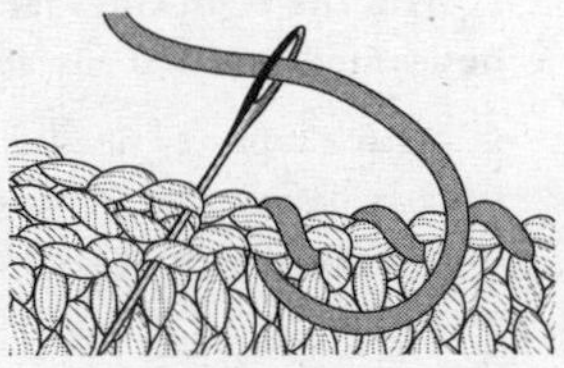

Figure 19

Three-Needle Bind Off

The three-needle bind off is used to join two pieces of knitting without sewing. It's often used to join shoulder seams on a sweater. Both pieces of knitting must have exactly the same number of stitches. To work three-needle bind off:

1. Holding the 2 pieces together on 2 needles, insert a 3rd needle as if to knit into the first stitch on the front needle and into the first stitch on the back needle. Knit these 2 stitches together, making 1 stitch (see figure 20).

2. Knit another stitch as in step 1. You not have 2 stitches on the right needle.

3. Insert the left needle into the 2nd stitch from the tip of the right needle and pass it over the first, dropping it off the needles. One stitch remains on the right needle (see figure 21).

Repeat steps 2 and 3 until 1 stitch remains. Fasten off.

Figure 20 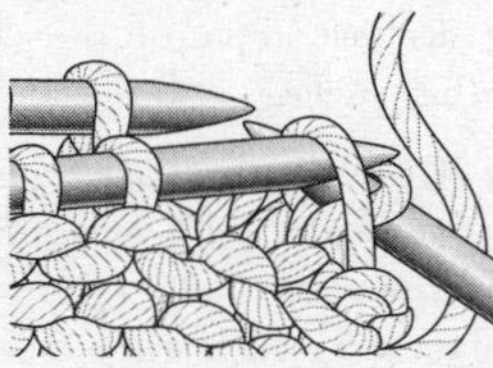   *Figure 21*

Grafting (Kitchener Stitch)

Grafting two pieces of knitting together creates an invisible join similar in appearance to the Mattress stitch. It's used to close the toes of socks and, sometimes, to join the shoulder seams on sweaters.

To join a seam with the Kitchener stitch, first arrange the stitches over two needles with half of the stitches on each needle, and the beginning and end of the needles lining up with the sides of the knitting. Cut the yarn, leaving a tail at least twice as long as the width of the knitting to bind off. Thread the tail onto a tapestry needle.

To prepare the 1st stitches, draw the yarn through the first stitch on the front needle as if to purl, and leave the stitch on the knitting needle. Then draw the tapestry needle through the first stitch on the back needle as if to knit, and leave the stitch on the knitting needle.

1. Draw the working yarn through the 1st stitch on the front needle as if to knit, and then slip this stitch off the knitting needle.

2. Draw the yarn through the next stitch on the front needle as if to purl, and leave this stitch on the knitting needle.

3. Draw the yarn through the 1st stitch on the back needle as if to purl, and then slip that stitch off the knitting needle.

4. Draw the yarn through the next stitch on the back needle as if to knit, and leave this stitch on the knitting needle (see figure 22).

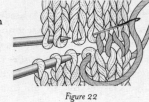

Figure 22

Repeat steps 1-4 until one stitch remains. Thread the yarn through the last stitch and pull tight.

Slip Stitch Crochet Seams

Slip stitch crochet can be worked through two layers of knitting at once to create a seam that works up quickly and is easy to rip out if you make a mistake. To work a crochet seam:

1. Place the 2 pieces of knitting together with right sides facing in.

2. Insert a crochet hook into a stitch on the edge of the knitting, making sure to go through both pieces, and draw up a loop of yarn. Wrap the yarn around the hook and draw a 2nd loop through the 1st loop to secure.

3. Working from right to left, insert the crochet hook into the next stitch on the edge of the garment.

4. Pull the working yarn through to the front and through the loop of yarn on the hook. One stitch has been created and one loop remains on the hook (see figure 23).

Figure 23

Repeat steps 3 and 4 until the entire seam is joined. Fasten off.

Herringbone Stitch

Herringbone stitch is used to sew hems because it creates a flat seam that is invisible on the right side of the work. It's also used to sew elastic into casings. To use the Herringbone stitch to encase elastic, working from left to right, sew the Herringbone stitch as shown in figures 24 and 25. To use the Herringbone stitch for a hem, working from left to right, sew the Herringbone stitch as shown in figure 26.

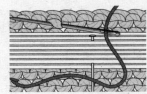

Figure 24

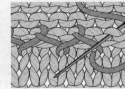

Figure 25   *Figure 26*

Blocking

Blocking, either by washing or steaming knitted pieces, evens out the stitches and creates a flat, smooth texture. Blocking also allows you to gently stretch the knitted pieces into shape to match the specified measurements in the project instructions.

The bands on most knitting yarns include blocking recommendations. Check these instructions before treating any yarn. Wash and block your swatch in the way you intend to treat the finished garment to make sure you like the results.

Washing a garment to relax the knitted fabric works especially well on cables and other knit-and-purl stitch patterns where pressing the item would flatten out the texture. To wash and block a garment:

1. Soak the item in cool water until the fiber is completely saturated.

2. Roll the item in a towel and squeeze (don't wring or twist) it to remove the excess water.

3. Spread the item out on a flat surface, stretching it slightly to the correct finished measurements. If desired, used rust-proof pins to hold the item in place until it's thoroughly dry.

Steaming works well to even out the stitches on colorwork and plain knitting, which may seem uneven or even sloppy before blocking. To steam a garment:

1. Wet and wring out an old towel.

2. Place the garment on a flat, padded surface and lay the towel over it.

3. Lightly press the piece through the towel, letting the steam penetrate the fibers.

4. Leave the item in place until it's thoroughly dry.

Embellishment

Embellishments add flair and style to plain garments. Most embellishment techniques can be learned with a small amount of practice. If one of these techniques is new to you, try it out on a swatch before attempting it on a large project.

Beads

Working beads into your knitting requires no special techniques. You simply string the beads onto a yarn-threaded needle as shown below, and then push a bead up to the knitting needles whenever the project instructions tell you to. To string beads onto yarn:

1. Cut a piece of thread 3 or 4 inches (7.6 to 10.2 cm) long, fold it over a piece of yarn, and thread it onto a sewing needle as shown in figure 27.

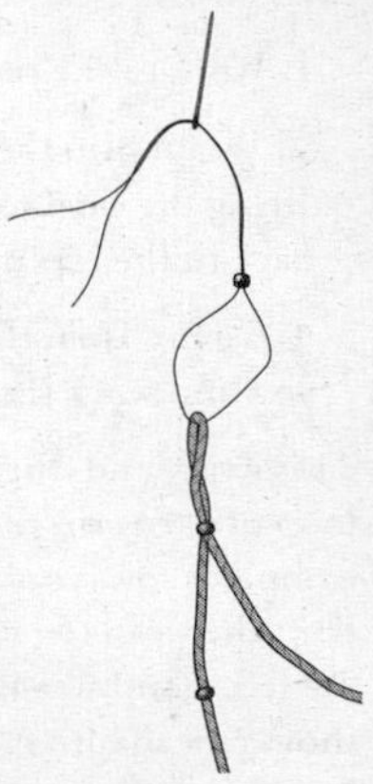

Figure 27

2. Push the thread through the bead; then pull the yarn through.

If you have trouble stringing your beads onto the yarn with a regular sewing needle, you may prefer using a flexible beading needle with a large eye, as shown in figure 28.

Crochet Stitches

Crochet stitches are often used to embellish knitting, because they work up quickly and are easy to rip out should you make a mistake.

Figure 28

Single Crochet

Single crochet (sc) is often used to create a flat edging on a piece of knitting. To work a row of single crochet on a piece of knitted fabric:

1. Insert a crochet hook into a stitch on the edge of the knitting and draw up a loop of yarn. Wrap the yarn around the hook and draw a 2nd loop through the 1st to secure.

2. Working from right to left, insert the crochet hook into the next stitch on the edge of the garment.

3. Pull the working yarn through to the front. Two loops are now on the hook.

4. Pull the working yarn through both loops on the hook. One stitch has been created and one loop remains on the hook (see figure 29).

Repeat steps 2–4 until the entire edge is covered. Fasten off.

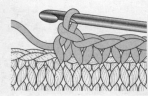

Figure 29

Crab Stitch

Crab stitch, also known as reverse single crochet, creates a decorative beaded edge. To work a row of crab stitches:

1. Insert a crochet hook into a stitch on the edge of the knitting, and draw up a loop of yarn. Wrap the yarn around the hook and draw a 2nd loop through the 1st to secure.

2. Working from left to right, insert the crochet hook into the next stitch on the edge of the knitting.

3. Pull the working yarn through to the front. Two loops are now on the hook.

4. Pull the working yarn through both loops on the hook (see figure 30). One stitch is now complete and one loop remains on the hook.

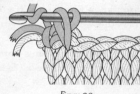

Repeat steps 2–4 until the entire edge is covered. Fasten off.

Figure 30

Twisted Cord

Twisted cords make decorative belts, and they are very easy to create. To make a twisted cord:

1. Cut 2 lengths of yarn about 5 times the length of the finished cord, or the length indicated in the project instructions, and knot both ends. Attach one end over a hook or doorknob.

2. Insert a knitting needle through the other end and twist clockwise, keeping a slight tension on the cord, until the strands of yarn begin to kink if the tension is released.

3. Hold the center of the cord and place both ends together, keeping the cord taut to prevent tangling.

4. Release the center so the two halves can twist around each other, smooth out the twists so they are uniform, and then re-knot both ends, leaving an inch or two of fringe, and trim the fringe so it's even (see figure 31).

2-31 Figure 31

I-cord

I-cord is a long, thin tube of knitting, usually made on three or four stitches. It's often used for belts and ties.

1. With a double-pointed needle, cast on 3 or 4 stitches as directed in the project instructions.

2. Knit all stitches. Do not turn.

3. Slide the stitches to the opposite end of the needle (see figure 32).

Repeat steps 2 and 3 for desired length. Bind off.

Figure 32

—From *Expectant Little Knits*

KNITTING MATERIALS AND TOOLS

Suzanne J. E. Tourtillott

One of the most fun parts of knitting is shopping for the materials and tools that are used to create original and stylish garments. The following sections will give you some ideas on stocking your yarn stash and your toolkit.

Yarn, Fabulous Yarn

Who can resist a shop full of gorgeous yarns in rainbow colors? The yarns available today are both beautiful and functional. There are many types of yarn on the market, and each has different properties, benefits, and drawbacks. A little thought will help you make selections that are best for your personal lifestyle.

Protein Fibers—such as wool, alpaca, and mohair—are easy to knit because they have natural stretch. These yarns knit up into springy fabrics that are warm in winter and cool in spring and fall. Most are too hot for summer wear.

Plant Fibers—such as cotton, linen, and bamboo—are less stretchy and often make stronger yarns. These fibers are a little more challenging to knit with than wool because they can be quite slippery.

Synthetics—such as nylon, polyester, and acrylic—are man-made fibers. These fibers can be machine-washed and dried, and make very practical, hard-wearing items.

Novelty Yarns are usually made from man-made fibers or several different fibers blended or plied together in unusual textures and color combinations. They can be difficult to knit with because of their unusual textures, but these textures also help hide mistakes.

Knitting Needles

Knitting needles are the tools you'll use most often, so take the time to try different kinds and see what's most comfortable for you. Needles come in many shapes, sizes, and materials. Each type behaves differently. Here are some options to consider:

Straight Needles are used for knitting garments that are made in separate pieces and sewn together. **Circular Needles** are used for projects that are knitted in the round with no seams. These types of needles come in various lengths, so check the requirements in the pattern to be sure you purchase needles of the correct size and length. **Double-Pointed Needles** are used for knitting small circular sections of garments, such as the cuffs on sweater sleeves that are knitted in the round. Double-pointed needles are also used for some special techniques such as I-cord.

For beginning knitters, **Wooden** or **Bamboo Needles** are good choices because they aren't slippery, or "fast." The extra texture of these needles makes dropping stitches less frequent. After you've finished a few projects, you may want to try **Plastic** or **Metal** needles. These are "faster" than wood, but give slightly less control. Wood and plastic are warmer than metal needles, and you may find them more comfortable to the touch, especially in colder weather or if you have arthritis.

Building a Knitter's Toolkit

After you've decided what types of knitting needles you like to work with, it's time to fill up the rest of your knitting toolkit. Here are some common notions and supplies that you'll find useful.

ABBREVIATIONS

approx	approximately
b	back
beg	begin/beginning
bet	between
BO	bind off
ch	chain
cm	centimeter(s)
cn	cable needle
CO	cast on
cont	continue
dc	double crochet
dec	decrease
dpn(s)	double pointed needle(s)
est	established
f	front
foll	follow(s)/following
g	gram
G st	Garter stitch
inc	increase/increases/increasing
k or K	knit
k1 tbl	knit 1 through back loop
kwise	knitwise
k2tog	knit 2 stitches together
LH	left hand
m	meter(s)
mm	millimeter(s)
M1	make 1 stitch
oz	ounce(s)
patt	pattern
p or P	purl
PM	place marker
p2tog	purl 2 stitches together
p1 tbl	purl 1 through back loop
pwise	purlwise
rem	remain/remaining
rep	repeat(s)
RH	right hand
RS	right side
sc	single crochet
sl	slip
SM	slip marker
ssk	slip, slip, knit these 2 stitches together
st(s)	stitch(es)
St st	Stockinette stitch
tbl	through back loop
tog	together
wyib	with yarn in back
wyif	with yarn in front
WS	wrong side
yd(s)	yard(s)
yf	yarn forward (an increase)
yo	yarn over

Continued ➡

A small **tape measure** that fits in your knitting bag is essential for measuring gauge and making sure your garments are working up to the desired size.

A blunt **tapestry needle** is used for weaving in ends and sewing seams.

Small scissors or a yarn cutter are used to trim ends. If you travel a lot with your knitting, make sure to check with the airline to find out what types of cutting tools are allowed.

An **emery board** and **hand cream** will help keep your fingers from catching on your knitting.

Crochet hooks are useful for picking up dropped stitches. Buy an inexpensive set with multiple sizes so you have the right size on hand when you need to add a crochet edging or accent to your project.

Row counters will help you keep your place in patterns and charts.

Stitch markers are essential for keeping track of your work, and they also help stop you from losing your place when you're knitting a complicated lace or cable pattern.

Needlepoint protectors and plastic pins are also handy additions to your toolkit.

You should always make a **photocopy of your pattern** and keep it, along with a **pencil**, in your knitting bag so you can make notes as you go. To build a useful reference guide after you finish your project, put the pattern into a journal, along with a yarn label, your gauge swatch, and a photo of the finished project. You'll find this handy in the future if you want to remake a garment from the same pattern, see what yarn or needles you used, or give help to a friend in designing something for her wardrobe.

Keeping It All Together

A knitting bag large enough to hold your project—and with a pocket to hold small tools—is one of the most fun things to shop for. From a basic, recycled shopping bag to gorgeous tapestry totes, there are bags available for every taste and budget. Make sure the one you select is large enough to hold your project as it grows. When you start, you'll have just one ball of yarn, your needles, and your pattern. But when you're getting close to the finish line, you'll have an entire garment in your bag.

Zipper-locking freezer bags and plastic pencil pouches help organize your tools and keep everything dry should a disaster happen. These can be slipped inside a large knitting bag for easy knitting bag for easy access.

—From *Expectant Little Knits*

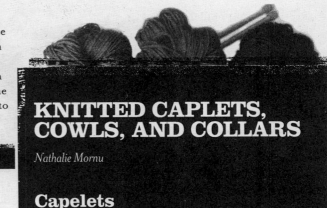

KNITTED CAPLETS, COWLS, AND COLLARS

Nathalie Mornu

Capelets

Capelets float and flutter about the shoulders. They exude sophistication. Wear one, and you'll want to shrug or flounce to accentuate every point you make. Capelets say, yes, I'm modern, but I know when the tailors of yore had a great thing going, and I'm getting some of it for myself.

Most ponchos, they just don't have the same panache. Don't know why. Maybe it's their shape and length, which draws the eye away from a gorgeous face? Maybe it's the childish fringe. At any rate, it raises a question: What's the difference between a poncho and a capelet? Simple: Capes fasten at the neck (creating the opportunity to

---

Needle Conversion Chart

Metric (mm)	U.S.
2	0
2.25	1
2.5	1
2.75	2
3	3
3.25	3
3.5	4
3.75	5
4	6
4.25	6
4.5	7
5	8
5.5	9
6	10
6.5	10½
7	10½
8	11
9	13
10	15
12	17
15	19
19	35
20	36
25	50

Types of Yarns

Linda Kopp

Yarns are made from animal, plant, and vegetable fibers as well as synthetic fibers, which are from man-made materials. Each fiber has its own strengths and weaknesses, so it stands to reason that a yarn's fiber content is a combination of various fibers in order to capitalize on a fiber's best attributes, and lessen its weaknesses. Following is a brief description of some of the more common yarns you might encounter when making a hat.

Wool has been a popular favorite used throughout the years—and with good cause. Spun from sheep's fleece, it is extremely elastic and durable, and so garments made of wool will hold their shape well and last a good long while. Long appreciated for its warmth, wool is a natural choice for winter wear. An outstanding characteristic of wool is that it can absorb up to one-third of its weight before it actually feels wet, allowing for the gradual absorption and release of perspiration. Wash wool in a woolwash and lay flat to dry. If you like to toss everything in the washer, select a "superwash" wool where the fiber's surface has been coated with a microfine resin. Be mindful not to wash wool in hot water as it may shrink or felt—unless that is your intention.

Alpaca is a member of the camelid family. Yarns spun from alpaca sheerings are soft, lightweight, and extremely strong. The inner core of alpaca fiber is hollow, resulting in a high insulation value for lightweight, yet warm garments. Its incredible softness is often compared to that of the much costlier cashmere yarn, which is made from fiber combed annually from bellies of cashmere goats. Garments made from alpaca yarns should be washed in cool water on the delicate cycle of your washer, or gently hand-washed.

Silk. The silkworm produces long, fine filaments that it uses to spin its cocoon. The filaments are unwound and used to produce a wondrous fiber that absorbs moisture well, and acts as an insulator, keeping you warm in the winter and cool in the summer. Silk fiber is light, yet very strong, and exudes a luxurious luster, making it ideal for creating elegant garments. It is normally combined with other fibers such as wool or cotton, due to its tendency to stretch.

Mohair is spun from the fleece of angora goats and produces a yarn that is valued for its soft, fuzzy appearance. Due to its "hairy" nature, mohair should be used in projects with simple stitches, so as to not obscure more intricate patterns. Many people find mohair to be itchy, so it is wise to combine it with other fibers like alpaca or wool.

Angora fiber is made from the fur of Angora rabbits when they naturally shed their coats or are shorn. The shorn method results in some shorter hairs, and so some shedding may occur. Angora fiber is slippery and so is often blended with wool to increase its workability. Similar to alpaca, the core of angora fibers is hollow, giving the resulting yarn outstanding breathing and wicking capabilities. To clean, machine wash and then dry on a cool cycle.

Cotton yarn is made with the fiber that surrounds the seeds in a cotton pad. We're all familiar with products made from cotton—they absorb moisture, but dry slowly once wet. Items made with cotton are easy to wash, and will hold their shape after washing, although they will start stretching out over time.

Acrylic is a synthetic yarn that boasts several advantages—it's strong, elastic, inexpensive, and is very easy to maintain. Toss it in your washer, pull it out of the dryer, and it's ready to wear again. Acrylic yarns tend to pill (little fuzzy balls that result from fibers rubbing and tangling together), and they don't breathe—meaning they don't wick moisture away from the body. That means if acrylic gets wet, it won't keep you very warm (something you should consider if your intention is to crochet a hat for that purpose).

—From *Cool Crocheted Hats*

use gorgeous buttons or sinfully lavish ribbons), while ponchos don't. And capelets are merely shorter versions of capes.

Everyone knows that with the rules under your belt, you're free to break them.

Impulse

design by Ella Averbukh

You just can't help it—you hug people you hardly know, kiss on the first date, and get lost in the excitement of your crushes.

SKILL LEVEL

Easy

FINISHED MEASUREMENTS

12"/30cm wide; 42"/107cm in circumference

MATERIALS + TOOLS

- Lion Brand Fettuc-cini (45% wool, 45% acrylic, 10% wool; 1.75oz/50g=33yd/30m): (A) 2 skeins, color Twi-light—approx 66yds/60m of bulky-weight yarn

- Patons Up Coun-try (100% wool; 3.5oz/100g=78yds/71m): (B) 1 skein, color Deep Steel Blue—approx 78yds/71m of bulky-weight yarn

- Knitting needles: 25mm (size 50 U.S.) or size needed to obtain gauge

- Cable needle

- Tapestry needle

Back

Front

GAUGE

3½ sts = 4"/10cm worked on 25mm (size 50 U.S.) needles in St st

Always take time to check your gauge.

SPECIAL ABBREVIATIONS

C6F Place 3 sts onto cn and hold in front, k3, then k3 from cn.

INSTRUCTIONS

With one strand each of A and B held tog. CO 10 sts.

Row 1 (WS) P1, k1, p6, k1, p1.

Row 2 (RS) K1, p1, k6, p1, k1.

Row 3 (WS) P1, k1, p6, k1, p1.

Rows 4–9 Red Rows 2 and 3 for 6 rows.

Row 10 (RS) K1, p1, C6F, p1, k1

Row 11 P1, k1, p6, k1, p1

Row 12 K1, p1, k6, p1, k1.

Rows 13–20 Red Row 11 and 12 for 8 rows. BO.

FINISH

Use last loop (st) rem from closing last row of Front of Wrap as first st when casting on connecting sts on both sides (A and B) of Front Piece.

Connect top corners (of A and B) of Front Piece with loop.

CO 1 st on 2nd row st of Side B—2 sts on needle

K1, p1, then connect 1 st on 3rd row side A—3 sts on needle

P1, k1, p1, then connect 1 st on 4th row side B—4 sts on needle

---

Cont in this manner until 10 rows of Sides A and B are connected.

BO. Weave in yarn ends.

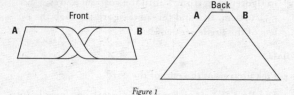

Figure 1

Charm

design by Tanya Wade

Proper Victorian capelet? Depends on how you rock it. Wear it with jeans, stilet-tos, and a décolleté down to here, and people will be calling the fire department.

Front

SKILL LEVEL

Intermediate

FINISHED MEASUREMENTS

19"/48cm wide at collar; 50"/127cm wide at base; 15"/38cm from top to bottom

MATERIALS + TOOLS

- Debbie Bliss Como (50% merino wool, 50% cash-mere; 1.75oz/49g=46yds/42m) 9 balls, color Gray #2—approx 414yds/379m of super bulky-weight yarn

- Knitting needles: 10mm (size 15 U.S.) 36"/91cm circular needles or size needed to obtain gauge

- Cable needle

- 2 removable markers

- Tapestry needle

- Link chain, 35"/89cm long

- 1 brooch

GAUGE

8 sts/14 rows = 4"/10cm worked on 10mm (size 15 U.S.) needles in pattern

Always take time to check your gauge.

SPECIAL ABBREVIATIONS

C6F Place 3 sts onto cn and hold to front of work, k3, then k3 from cn.

SM Slip marker

C6B Place 3 sts onto cn and hold to back of work, k3, then k3 from cn.

INSTRUCTIONS

Using 10 mm (size 15 U.S.) needles, CO 154 sts. Work 5 rows in Garter st.

Row 1 (RS): K5, PM, k144. PM, k5.

Note Keep first 5 and last 5 sts in Garter st until decs.

> ### VARIATION
>
> Use any brooch you like to fasten the capelet—from antique gemstone set in filigree to vintage rhinestone bling, or just a simple and elegant gold circlet. Just be sure to match the color of the chain to the base color of the brooch. You'll look as good coming as you do going.

Row 2 and all WS rows K5, SM, p144, SM, k5

Row 3 K5, SM. *k6, C6F; rep from *, SM, k5.

Row 4 Rep Row 2.

Row 5 Knit all sts.

Row 6 Rep Row 2.

Row 7 K5, SM, *C6F, k6; rep from *, SM, k5.

Row 8 Rep Row 2.

Row 9 Knit all sts.

Row 10 Rep Row 2.

Row 11 K5, SM, *k2tog, k4, C6F; rep from *, SM. K5—142 sts.

Row 12 Rep Row 2.

Row 13 K5, SM, k132, SM, k5.

Row 14 Rep Row 2

Row 15 K5, SM, *C6B, k5; rep from *, SM, k5.

Row 16 Rep Row 2.

Row 17 Knit all sts.

Row 18 Rep Row 2.

Row 19 K5, SM, *k2tog, k3, C6F; rep from *, SM, k5—130 sts.

Row 20 Rep Row 2

Row 21 Knit all sets.

Row 22 Rep Row 2

Row 23 K5, SM, *C6B, k4; rep from *, SM k5.

Row 24 Rep Row 2.

Row 25 Knit all sts.

Row 26 Rep Row 2.

Row 27 K5, SM, *k2tog, k2, C6F; rep from *, SM, k5—118 sts.

Row 28 Rep Row 2.

Row 29 Knit all sts.

Row 30 Rep Row 2.

Row 31 K5, SM, *C6B, k3; rep from *, SM, k5.

Row 32 Rep Row 2.

Row 33 Knit all sts.

Row 34 Rep Row 2.

Row 35 K5, SM, *k2tog, k1, C6F; rep from *, SM, k5—106 sts.

Row 36 Rep Row 2.

Row 37 Knit all sts.

Row 38 Rep Row 2.

Row 39 K5, SM, C6F, k2; rep from, FM, k5.

Row 40 Rep Row 2.

COLLAR DECS BEG

Row 41 K4tog, *k2, k2tog; rep from * last 6 sts, k2, k4tog tbl—76 sts.

Row 42 P2, p2tog tbl, p2, p2tog tbl, p to last 8 sts, p2tog, p2, p2tog, p2—72 sts.

COLLAR

Row 43 K3, *C6F; rep from * to last 3 sts, k3.

Row 44 Purl all sts.

Row 45 Knit all sts.

Row 46 Purl all sts.

Row 47 *C6B; rep to end.

Row 48 Purl all sts.

Row 49 Knit all sts.

Row 50 Purl all sts.

Row 51 K3, *C6F; rep from * to last 3 sts, k3.

Continued ➜

Row 52 Purl all sts.

Row 53 Knit all sts.

Row 54 BO all sts pwise.

FINISH

Weave in yarn ends.

Thread the chain through the openings in 1st row made from Basketweave Cable. To wear the capelet closed, open the brooch and slide the pin through both end links of the chain, then close the brooch. Alternately, you can eliminate the chain closure and simply close the capelet with a brooch.

Cowls

Cowls nestle below the chin when they're small, and they're just adorable. But the voluminous ones sprawl out with a command: Look at me! You have to work these, baby, make 'em yours—drape them around the shoulders like you're a socialite; let them dangle, all relaxed like, from the neck; hide from view, snuggled deep inside; or play the diva by pulling an edge over your head like a hood.

Sugar

design by Lana O'Neill

Think those are pom-poms? Look closer: those little puffballs are actually knitted and stuffed.

SKILL LEVEL

Easy

FINISHED MEASUREMENT

10 x 23"/25 x 58cm in circumference

MATERIALS + TOOLS

- Cascade 220 (100% wool; 3.5oz/100g=220 yds/201m); 2 skeins, color White #8505—approx 440yds/402m medium-weight yarn
- Knitting needles: 3.75mm (size 5 U.S.) circular needle, 16"/41cm long; 3.5mm (size 4 U.S.) double-pointed needles or size to obtain gauge
- Stitch markers
- Fiberfill
- Tapestry needle

GAUGE

16 sts = 4"/10cm worked on 3.75mm (size 5 U.S.) circular needle in rib

Always take time to check your gauge.

INSTRUCTIONS

COWL

Using circular needle, CO 92 sts. Mark the last st with a st marker, then join and work in rnds as foll: Work around in k2, p2 rib until piece measures 3"/8cm from beg.

Next Rnd *K1, k2tog twice, k1, (p2, k2) for next 18 sts; rep from * 2 more times, k1, k2tog twice, k1, (p2, k2) rib to end of rnd—84 sts.

Next Rnd *K2tog twice, work in est rib on next 18 sts; rep from * 2 more times, k2tog twice, (p2, k2) rib to end of rnd—76 sts.

Cont around in k2, p2 rib until cowl measures 10"/26cm from beg.

Eyelet patt *K2, yo, p2tog; rep from * around.

Cont in k2, p2 rib for 3 more rnds. BO.

I-CORD

Using dpn, CO 3 sts. *K3 sts. Do not turn the work. Slide sts to right end of the needle, pull yarn to tighten; rep from * until the cord measures 55"/140cm. BO and thread the cord through the eyelets of the turtleneck cowl.

BALLS

Pick up 6 sts at the end of the cord.

Inc Rnd *K1 st, pick up 1 st by inserting a needle into the loop of the st 1 rnd below and k through it, rep from * until you have 12 sts.

Divide 12 sts evenly on 3 dpns. Join and knit around for 9 rnds.

Insert fiberfill stuffing inside the knitted ball piece.

Dec Rnd *K2tog; rep from * around—6 sts rem.

Cut off the yarn, leaving enough to sew rem sts together. Thread the yarn through the tapestry needle and draw the yarn through the rem sts. Fasten off.

Rep the same process at the other end of the cord.

To make 2 extra balls, pick up 3 sts from the I-cord, approximately 3–4"/8–10cm from the edge. Work the I-cord approximately 3–4"/8–10cm or to the desired length, then pick up 6 sts at the end of the cord and work the ball as above.

Rep the same process at the other end of the cord.

FINISH

Weave in yarn ends.

Glances

design by Rosario Thury Cornejo

Wear it loose around the neck, wear it up over your head, but wear it often. Make it in a pretty color that makes your skin glow.

SKILL LEVEL

Easy

FINISHED MEASUREMENTS

9½ x 26"/24 x 66cm before sewing

MATERIALS + TOOLS

- Lion Brand Wool-Ease Thick & Quick (80% wool, 20% acrylic; 6oz/170g=106yds/97m): 1 skein, color #640-112 Raspberry—approx 106yds/97m of super bulky-weight yarn
- Knitting needles: 9mm (size 13 U.S.) or size needed to obtain gauge
- Small amount of waste yarn in contrasting color
- Tapestry needle

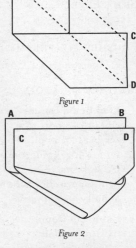

Back

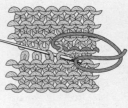

Back

GAUGE

9 sts/16 rows = 4"/10cm worked on 9mm (size 13 U.S.) needles in Garter st

Always take time to check your gauge.

INSTRUCTIONS

CO 24 sts using the waste yarn.

Change to main color yarn, leaving a short tail. Work in Garter st (k every row) for 112 rows.

Lay out and fold as shown in the illustration, then

bring C and D onto A and B, respectively (figure 1). The result should look like figure 2.

Work grafting st as follows: Remove the waste yarn on the top part and replace the loops on a needle. Insert the threaded tapestry needle into the first st at the RH edge of the upper piece. Put the needle down through the 1st st on the lower piece and bring it up through the next st. Bring the needle up through the 1st st on the upper piece and put it down through the next st. The needle's path is up-down on the upper piece, down-up on the lower piece, inserting the needle knitwise with up meaning purlwise; you p the upper row of sts and k the lower row (figure 3). Rep until all the sts are joined.

FINISH

Weave in yarn ends.

Figure 1

Figure 2

Figure 3

> ### VARIATIONS
>
> Make the I-cord different lengths so the balls are at different heights; when the ties are tied at the neck, they'll appear to cascade down. You can also stick to making only 2 balls, instead of 4.

Collars

Collars, those dapper little accessories—think of them as trims and garnishes that fit snugly at the neck. The projects in this section fasten on with buttons. You'll find a focus on texture and pattern.

Flirt

Design by Brenda Lavell

Meeting that special someone for drinks after work? Get pretty in a wide cabled collar.

SKILL LEVEL

Intermediate

FINISHED MEASUREMENTS

8¼ x 34"/21cm x 86cm

MATERIALS + TOOLS

- Lion Brand Wool-Ease Thick & Quick (80% wool, 20% acrylic; 6oz/170g = 106yds/97m): 2 skeins, color Citron #640-134—approx 212yds/194m of super bulky-weight yarn
- Knitting needles: 12mm (size 17 U.S.) or size to obtain gauge
- 1 large cable or double-pointed needle
- 1 button, 1½"/4cm in diameter
- 2 buttons, 1"/2.5cm in diameter
- Thread in color matching yarn
- 2 small pieces of wool or felt to stabilize the button (optional)

- Sewing needle
- Tapestry needle

GAUGE

8 sts/12 rows = 4"/10cm worked on 12mm (size 17 U.S.) needles in St st, after blocking

Cable Panel = 6"/15cm worked on 12mm (size 17 U.S.) needles in St st, after blocking, measured from the widest part of the large cable edge

Always take time to check your gauge.

Back

SPECIAL ABBREVIATIONS

ICR (RS I-cord edge) First 3 and last 3 sts of every RS row: K1, sl 1 pwise wyif, k1.

ICW (WS I-cord edge) First 3 and last 3 sts of every WS row: Sl 1 pwise wyif, k1, sl 1 pwise wyif, k1, sl 1 pwise wyif.

Note: For longer length, add one Body repeat for each 6"/15cm of desired length (additional ⅓ skein or 57yds/52m of yarn for each additional 6"/15cm).

INSTRUCTIONS

FRONT/TOP FLAP

CO 30 sts.

Row 1 (RS) ICR, p2, k3, p4, k6, p4, k3, p2, ICR.

Row 2 and all even numbered rows (WS) ICW, k the k sts and p the p sts to within last 3 sts, ICW.

Rows 3–6 Rep Rows 1-2 twice.

Row 7 ICR, p2, (sl 3 to cn or dpn and hold in front, p2, k3 from cn), p2, k6, p2, (sl 2 to cn and hold in back, k3, p2, from cn), p2, ICR.

Row 9 ICR, p4, (sl 3 to cn and hold in front, p2, k3 from cn), (sl 3 to cn and hold in front, k3, k3 from cn), (sl 2 to cn and hold in back, k3, p2 from cn), p4, ICR.

Row 11 ICR, p6, *(sl 3 to cn and hold in back, k3, k3 from cn)*, rep from * to *, p6, ICR.

Row 13 ICR, p6, k3, (sl 3 to cn and hold in front, k3, k3 from cn), k3, p6, ICR.

Row 15 ICR, p4, (sl 2 to cn and hold in back, k3, p2 from cn), k6, (sl 3 to sn and hold in front, p2, k3 from cn), p4, ICR.

Row 17 ICR, p2, (sl 2 to sn and hold in back, k3, p2 from cn), p2, k6, p2, (sl 3 to sn and hold in front, p2, k3 from cn), p2, ICR.

Row 18 Rep Row 2.

BODY

Row 19 Rep Row 1.

Row 21 Rep Row 7.

Row 23 Rep Row 9.

Row 25 Rep Row 11.

Row 27 Rep Row 13.

Row 29 ICR, p6, *(sl 3 to cn and hold in back, k3, k3 from cn)*, rep from * to *, p6, ICR.

Row 31 ICR, p4, (sl 2 to cn and hold in back, k3, p2 from cn), (sl 3 to cn and hold in front, p3, k3 from cn), (sl 3 to hold in front, k3, p2 from cn), p4, ICR.

Row 33 Rep Row 17.

Row 34 Rep Row 18.

Rep Rows 19–34 three more times (4 total cable patt reps).

BOTTOM FLAP

Rep Rows 1–2 for 12 total rows, ending WS.

Purl, BO in patt.

Weave in ends (utilize the I-cord edge and cables to hide and secure ends).

FINISH

Block to measurements. Weave in yarn ends.

Note: Before attaching the buttons, read these directions carefully and check your own finished cowl to mark the best attachment spots.

Securely attach the large button to the center end of the bottom flap. First attach the felt pieces to the flap, bottom and top, then sew the button through all 3 layers (felt, knitted cowl, felt) to provide stability and strength during buttoning. The button will slip through the small opening in the very first cable cross on the top flap.

Attach each smaller button underneath the top flap, approximately 2 I-cord sts from the end and one I-cord st from the side, securely sewing through the I-cord sts while avoiding showing the stitching through the front of the flap. The buttons will slip through a st (no buttonholes needed) on the under flap.

Breathless

design by Linda Lunn

Elegant but softly shaped, this collar has crossed ends that echo the intersecting cables in its motif.

SKILL LEVEL

Intermediate

FINISHED MEASUREMENTS

10 x 30"/25 x 76cm

MATERIALS + TOOLS

- Rowan Big Wool (100% merino wool; 3.5oz/99g=87yds/80m): 2 balls, color Latte #018—approx 174yds/159m of bulky-weight yarn
- Knitting needles: 10mm (size 15 U.S.) or size needed to obtain gauge
- Row counter
- 2 large wooden buttons, 2 x 1½"/5cm x 4cm
- Tapestry needle

Back

GAUGE

7½ sts and 9 rows = 4"/10cm worked on 10mm (size 15 U.S.) in St st

Always take time to check your gauge.

INSTRUCTIONS

CO 22 sts.

Use a row counter to keep count of all rows. Purl 3 rows.

**Next Row (RS) K6, k2tog, k2, yf, k5, yf, k2, k2tog, k3.

Row (WS) K2, purl to last 2 sts, k2.

Next Row K5, k2tog, k2, yf, k1, yf, k2, k2tog, k8.

Next Row K2, p to last 2 sts, k2.

Next Row K4, k2tog, k2, yf, k3, yf, k2, k2tog, k7.

Next Row K2, p to last 2 sts, k2.*

Next Row K3, k2tog, k2, yf, k5, yf, k2, k2tog, k6.

Next Row K2, p to last 2 sts, k2.

Next Row K8, k2tog, k2, yf, k1, yf, k2, k2tog, k5.

Next Row K2, p to last 2 sts, k2.

Next Row K7, k2tog, k2, yf, k3, yf, k2, k2tog, k4.

Next Row K2, p to last 2 sts, k2.**

Rep from ** to ** 5 more times

Rep from ** to * once. There should be 81 rows completed from CO.

Purl 2 rows.

BO all sts pwise.

FINISH

Weave in ends. Soak in cool water for 20 minutes. Roll in towel to squeeze out the excess water, and lay flat to dry.

Sew buttons at desired position. Eyelets in the pattern will serve as buttonholes.

—FROM *Knit & Wrap*

KNITTED CLOTHES FOR MOMS-TO-BE

Suzanne J. E. Tourtillott

Comfy Camo Top

Design by Lara Ruth Warren

Go commando with this babydoll-style top—a first-ever camouflage maternity piece! The ingenious design, comprised of rectangles, tubes, and trapezoids, make it a low-stress knitting adventure.

[insert KC 5-1 and 5-2. No captions.]

EXPERIENCE LEVEL

Easy

SIZE

S (M, L, XL)

FINISHED MEASUREMENTS

Bust: 27 (29, 31, 33)"/69 (74, 79, 84)cm, unstretched

Skirt width: 39¼ (40½, 41¾, 43)"/100 (103, 106, 109)cm, ungathered

Skirt length: 18 (18, 20, 22)"/46 (46, 51, 56)cm

Note: Bust has negative ease and stretches to fit; skirt is gathered with extra room built in.

MATERIALS

- **Approx total:** 1140yd/1042m of worsted weight acrylic yarn:
  Color A: 896yd/819m in black

Continued ➡

Color B: 244yd/223m in camouflage

- **Knitting needles**: 4.5mm (size 7 U.S.) needles, *or size to obtain gauge for tube top* 6mm (size 10 U.S.) circular needle 29"/74cm long, *or size to obtain gauge for skirt*
- 8mm (size 11 U.S.) needles for sleeves
- 10yd/9m black elastic thread
- 4yd/3.6m black grosgrain ribbon ½"/13mm wide
- Tapestry needle

GAUGE

Top: 14 sts and 28 rows = 4"/10cm over Garter st using smallest needles

Skirt: 14 sts and 20 rows = 4"/10cm over St st using medium needles

Always take time to check your gauge.

PATTERN STITCHES

Stockinette stitch (circular)

All rnds: Knit.

Garter stitch (back and forth)

All rows: Knit.

INSTRUCTIONS

TUBE TOP

Using smallest needles and B, CO 33 (35, 37, 39) sts.

Work Garter st until piece meas 27 (29, 31, 33)"/69 (74, 79, 84)cm.

BO. Sew short ends together to form a tube.

SKIRT

Using circular needles and color A, CO 157 (162, 167, 172) sts. Join to knit in the round, being careful not to twist sts.

Knit every rnd until piece meas approx 18 (18, 20, 22)"/46 (46, 51, 56)cm.

BO rem sts.

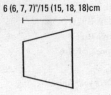

6 (6, 7, 7)"/15 (15, 18, 18)cm

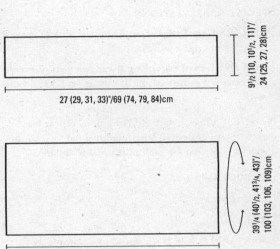

9½ (10, 10½, 11)"/
24 (25, 27, 28)cm

27 (29, 31, 33)"/69 (74, 79, 84)cm

39¼ (40½, 41¾, 43)"/
100 (103, 106, 109)cm

18 (18, 20, 22)"/46 (46, 51, 56)cm

ABBREVIATIONS

Knitting patterns are often full of abbreviations intended to save space. This list will help you identify any abbreviations with which you're unfamiliar.

TERM	DEFINITION
"	inch(es)
*^	repeat instructions between * symbols as indicated
()	repeat instruction in parentheses as indicated
beg	begin(ning)
BO	bind off
cm	centimeter(s)
cn	cable needle
CO	cast on
circ	circular
dec	decrease
dpn(s)	double-pointed needle(s)
est	established
foll	follows
g	gram(s)
inc	increase
k or K	knit
k2tog	knit two stitches together as one
k3tog	knit three stitches together as one
kf/b	knit into the front and back of the same stitch, increasing one stitch
m	meter(s)
LH	left hand
m1 or M1L	make one left slanting: With the left needle inserted from front to back, pick up the bar between the stitches
on	the left and right needles. Knit into the back to twist the stitch.
M1R	make one right slanting: With the left needle inserted from back to front, pick up the bar between the stitches on the left and right needles. Knit into the front to twist the stitch.
meas	measures
oz	ounce
p or P	purl
p2tog	purl two stitches together as one

TERM	DEFINITION
p2tog-tbl	purl two together through the back loops: Keeping the yarn in front, slip two stitches as if to knit, then place them back on the left needle. Purl these same two stitches together through the back loops.
patt	pattern
pm	place marker
psso	pass slip stitch over
rem	remain(ing)
rep	repeat(ing)
Rev St st	reverse stockinette stitch, reverse stocking stitch
RH	right hand
RS	right side
rnd(s)	round(s)
s2kp	slip two, knit one, pass slipped stitches over: Slip next two stitches as if to knit them together, knit next stitch, pass slipped stitches together over the stitch just knit.
sc	single crochet
sm	slip marker
ssk	slip, slip, knit: Slip the next two stitches one at a time to the right needle as if to knit. Insert the left needle into the front of the stitches and knit the two stitches together through the back loops.
sssk	slip, slip, slip, knit. Work as ssk but with three stitches.
sl	slip
st(s)	stitch(es)
St st	stockinette stitch, stocking stitch
tbl	through the back loop
tog	together
W&T	wrap and turn
wyif	with yarn in front
wyib	with yarn in back
WS	wrong side
yd	yard(s)
yo	yarn over

SLEEVES (MAKE 2)

Using largest needles and color B, CO 14 sts.

Row 1 (RS): *Sl 1, k1, yo, k2tog; rep from * to last 2 sts, sl 1, k1.

Rows 2 and 4 (WS): Sl 1, p across row to last st, yo, k1—16 sts after row 4.

Row 3: *Sl 1, ssk, yo; rep from *, to last 3 sts, sl 1, k2.

Note: The row end will change on each repeat as the number of sts increases. When you do not have enough sts to work the full pat rep at the end of the row, knit the rem sts.

Repeat rows 1–4 another 8 (8, 10, 10) times—32 (32, 36, 36) sts.

Knit 1 row. BO.

FINISHING

Using two strands of black elastic thread held together, thread the elastic through the top of the Skirt. Gather the Skirt in until it is the same size as the Tube Top, then tie the elastic in a knot to secure. Bury the ends of the elastic in the knitting.

Sew Skirt to Tube Top: Using two strands of black elastic thread held together, thread the elastic through the BO edge of each Sleeve. Sew the short ends of each Sleeve to the front and back of the Tube Top. Cut two strands of color A approx 6"/15cm longer than the curved edge of the Sleeve. Use the tapestry needle to weave a strand through the curved edge of the Sleeve to gather it in a little. Weave in the ends.

Weave the black grosgrain ribbon through the bottom of the Tube Top approx ½–1"/1–2.5cm from the waist, and tie the ends of the ribbon in a bow.

This dress was made with:

(A) 2 skeins of Red Heart's *Supersaver Solids*, 100% acrylic; 10oz/282g = 488yd/446m, Black

(B) 1 skein Red Heart's *Supersaver Prints*, 100% acrylic; 5oz/141g = 244yd/223m, Camouflage

Deauville Car Coat

design by A. L. de Sauveterre

This car coat is designed to be worn both during and after pregnancy, open or closed with a pretty brooch. Slim sleeves fall to ribbed bell cuffs, and the ribbed border forms both a shawl collar and a cutaway hem.

EXPERIENCE LEVEL
Easy

SIZE
S (M, L, XL)

FINISHED MEASUREMENTS

Bust: 34 (38, 42, 46)"/86 (97, 107, 117)cm

Length: 40 (41, 41, 41)"/102 (104, 104, 104)cm

MATERIALS

- 1800 (1900, 2000, 2100)yd/1646 (1737, 1829, 1920)m hand-painted, Aran-weight cashmere yarn in dark brown
- Knitting needles: 5.5 mm (size 9 U.S.) *or size to obtain gauge*
- 5.5mm (size 9 U.S.) circular needles 60"/152cm long
- Tapestry needle for sewing seams
- 2 stitch markers or safety pins
- Jeweled brooch

GAUGE

18 sts and 24 rows = 4"/10cm over St st
Always take time to check your gauge.

PATTERN STITCHES

Slip Stitch Rib Pattern

Row 1 (RS): P2, *K1, sl1 purlwise, K1, p2; rep from * to end.

Row 2: K2, *P3, K2; rep from * to end.

Rep rows 1 and 2 for pat.

Stockinette Stitch

Row 1 (RS): Knit.

Row 2: Purl.

Rep rows 1 and 2 for pat.

INSTRUCTIONS

Tip: When using hand-painted yarn, for more even distribution of color, knit with two balls at a time, alternating between each ball every other row.

Back

Bottom Edge:

CO 34 (44, 52, 62) sts.

Work in St st, shaping as foll:

Row 1 (RS): Knit.

Row 2: CO 3 sts, work these 3 sts, then work the next st through the back loop, work to end.

Rows 3–9: Rep row 2.

Row 10: Purl.

Row 11: Knit.

Row 12 and 13: Rep row 2.

Rep rows 10 through 13 twice more—76 (86, 94, 104) sts.

Pm at each end of the piece. When joining seams, the bottom edges of the two front pieces will line up from these markers.

Main Body

Work even in St st until piece meas 6"/15cm from bottom. End after completing a WS row.

Dec 1 st on each side, every 22 (16, 22, 22) rows 2 (3, 2, 2) times, then inc 1 st on each side, every 22 (16, 22, 22) rows 2 (3, 2, 2) times.

Work even until piece meas 18 (18½, 18½, 18½)"/46 (47, 47, 47)cm from markers. End after completing a WS row.

Armhole Shaping

BO 2 (4, 5, 6) sts at beg of next 2 rows, then dec 1 st on each side, every other row 2 (3, 4, 6) times—68 (72, 76, 80) sts rem.

Work even until armhole meas 8 (8½, 8½, 9)"/20 (22, 22, 23)cm. End after completing a WS row.

Shoulder Shaping

BO 5 (6, 6, 7) sts at beg of next 4 (6, 2, 4) rows, then BO 6 (0, 7, 8) sts at beg of next 2 (0, 4, 2) rows.

BO rem 36 sts.

Right Front

CO 3 sts.

Row 1 (RS): Inc 1, knit to end—4 sts.

Row 2: Purl.

Working in St st, continue to inc 1 st at center front edge every other row 34 (39, 43, 48) more times. AT THE SAME TIME, when piece meas 6"/15cm from CO edge, dec 1 st on side edge every 22 (16, 22, 22) rows 2 (3, 2, 2) times, then inc 1 st on side edge, every 22 (16, 22, 22) rows 2 (3, 2, 2) times—38 (43, 47, 52) sts.

Work even until piece meas 15 (16, 16, 16½)"/38 (41, 41, 42)cm from markers. End after completing a WS row.

(RS) Beg with next row, dec 1 st at neck edge every other row until 16 (18, 20, 22) sts rem. AT THE SAME TIME, when piece meas same as back to armhole, beg armhole shaping on a WS row.

Armhole Shaping

Next row (WS): BO 2 (4, 5, 6) sts at beg of row.

Dec 1 st at beg of row, every other row 2 (3, 4, 6) times.

Work even until armhole meas 8 (8½, 8½, 9)"/20 (22, 22, 23)cm. End after completing a RS row.

Shoulder Shaping:

BO 5 (6, 6, 7) sts at beg of next 2 (3, 1, 2) WS rows, then BO 6 (0, 7, 8) sts at beg of next 1 (0, 2, 1) WS rows.

Left Front

CO 3 sts.

Row 1 (RS): Knit to last st, inc 1—4 sts.

Row 2: Purl.

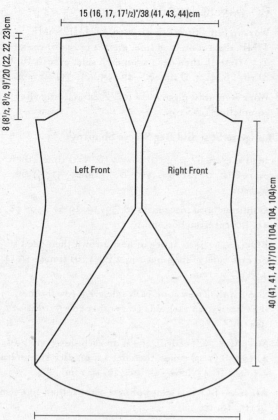

Working in St st, continue to inc 1 st at center front edge every other row 34 (39, 43, 48) more times. AT THE SAME TIME, when piece meas 6"/15cm from cast on, dec 1 st on side edge every 22 (16, 22, 22) rows 2 (3, 2, 2) times, then inc 1 st on side edge, every 22 (16, 22, 22) rows 2 (3, 2, 2) times—38 (43, 47, 52) sts.

Work even until piece meas 15 (16, 16, 16½)"/38 (41, 41, 42)cm from markers. End after completing a WS row.

(RS) Beg with next row, dec 1 st at neck edge every other row until 16 (18, 20, 22) sts rem. AT THE SAME TIME, when piece meas same as back to armhole, beg armhole shaping on a RS row.

Armhole Shaping

Next row (RS): BO 2 (4, 5, 6) sts at beg of row.

Dec 1 st at beg of row, every other row 2 (3, 4, 6) times.

Work even until armhole meas 8 (8½, 8½, 9)"/20 (22, 22, 23)cm. End after working a WS row.

Shoulder Shaping

BO 5 (6, 6, 7) sts at beg of next 2 (3, 1, 2) RS rows, then BO 6 (0, 7, 8) sts at beg of next 1 (0, 2, 1) RS rows.

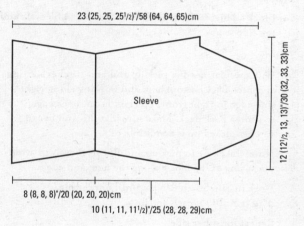

15 (16, 17, 17½)"/38 (41, 43, 44)cm

8 (8½, 8½, 9½)"/20 (22, 22, 23)cm

Left Front   Right Front

40 (41, 41, 41)"/101 (104, 104, 104)cm

17 (19, 21, 23)"/43 (48, 53, 58)cm

23 (25, 25, 25½)"/58 (64, 64, 65)cm

Sleeve

12 (12½, 13, 13)"/30 (32, 33, 33)cm

8 (8, 8, 8)"/20 (20, 20)cm

10 (11, 11, 11½)"/25 (28, 28, 29)cm

Continued →

SLEEVES (MAKE 2)

CO 57 (57, 62, 62) sts.

Work in Slip Stitch Rib pat, and AT THE SAME TIME, dec 1 st on each side, every 2 (4, 4, 6) rows 1 (2, 2, 3) time(s), then dec 1 st on each side, every 4 (6, 6, 8) rows 6 (4, 3, 1) time(s)—43 (45, 52, 54) sts rem.

Work even until piece meas 10"/25cm, ending after completing a WS row.

Change to St st and Beg Sleeve Shaping:

Inc 1 st every 6 (9, 9, 10) rows 4 (6, 5, 1) times, then every 8 (0, 0, 12) rows 3 (0, 0, 3) times—57 (57 62, 62) sts.

Continue until piece meas 18 (19, 19, 19½)"/46 (48, 48, 50)cm from bottom.

BO 2 (4, 5, 6) sts at beg of next 2 rows, then dec 1 st on each side, every other row 2 (3, 4, 6) times—49 (43, 44, 38) sts rem.

Size S only: Dec 1 st on each side every row 6 times, then dec 1 st on each side every other row 5 times—27 sts rem.

Sizes M, L, XL only: Dec 1 st on each side every 2 (2, 4) rows 8 (7, 4) times, then dec 1 st on each side every 4 rows 1 (1, 4) times—25 (28, 22) sts rem.

All sizes: BO 3 sts at beg of next 4 rows, then BO rem 15 (13, 16, 10) sts.

FINISHING

Block all pieces. Sew shoulder seams, set in Sleeves, and sew side seams.

Band

With circular needle, pick up and knit stitches starting at center Back bottom hem and working along right side edge to right front, up right Front neck edge to center Back neck. Make sure that the number of stitches picked up is a multiple of 5 + 2.

Note: Take case to pick up and BO sts loosely to avoid puckering of the fabric along the hem and edges.

Work in Slip Stitch Rib pat until border meas 9"/23cm. BO loosely in rib.

Repeat for other side.

Sew ribbed border at center Back neck and center Bottom hem. Weave in ends. Block or steam press garment again as necessary. Secure sweater with brooch as desired.

This Project was Made with:

18 (19, 20, 21) balls of A.L. de Sauveterre's *Pippin*, 100% cashmere, 1.75oz/50g = approx 100yd/91m per ball, color Chocolate

Anjou Sleeveless Top

design by Angela Hahn

Put a positive spin on "pear-shaped" with this empire-waist top, perfect for before, during, and after pregnancy. The fabric is gently gathered with decreases below the bust and with increases in the bust area for a flattering shape.

EXPERIENCE LEVEL

Intermediate

SIZE

S (M, L, XL)

FINISHED MEASUREMENTS

Bust: 33 (36, 41, 45)"/84 (91, 104, 114)cm

Under Bust (measured at bra band): 28 (32, 36, 40)"/71 (81, 91, 102)cm

Length: 23 (24, 25, 25½)"/58 (61, 64, 65)cm

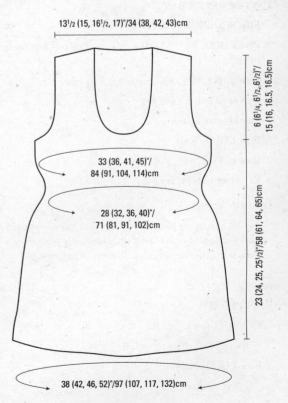

Note: This top was designed to have minimal to slightly negative ease at and just under the bust.

MATERIALS

- 850 (925, 1025, 1125) yd/777 (846, 937, 1029) m of cotton or cotton blend light worsted weight yarn in light green

- **Knitting needles:** 4mm (size 6 U.S.) straight needles and circular needle 36–42"/91–107CM long *or size to obtain gauge*

- 3.5mm (size 4 U.S.) circular needle 36–42"/91–107CM long or size to obtain gauge

- 3.5mm (size 4 U.S.) circular needle 16–20"/41–51cm or set of double-pointed needles

Note: Long circular needles should be slightly shorter than finished bust measurement.

Third needle of similar size for three-needle bind off

Stitch markers

Stitch holders or waste yarn (optional)

Tapestry needle

GAUGES

23 sts and 29 rows = 4"/10cm over Twist Stitch pat on larger needles, blocked

20 sts and 26 rows = 4"/10cm over Baby Cable Rib on smaller needles, blocked

Always take time to check your gauge.

PATTERN STITCHES

Right Twist (RT)
(Worked over 2 sts)

Skip first st on LH needle and knit 2nd st, then k first st and drop both sts from LH needle.

Twist Stitch Pattern (Circular)
(Worked over a multiple of 4 sts)

Rnd 1 (Twist Rnd): *K1, RT, k1. Rep from * to end of rnd.

Rnds 2–4: Knit.

Rnd 5 (Twist Rnd): K1, *k2, RT. Rep from * to last stitch, RT (working twist using last st of this rnd and first st of next rnd).

Rnds 6–8: Knit.

Rep rnds 1–8 for pattern.

Twist Stitch Pattern (back and forth)
(Worked over a multiple of 4 sts)

Row 1 (Twist Rnd, RS): *K1, RT, k1. Rep from * to end of rnd.

Row 2 (and all WS rows): Purl.

Row 3: Knit.

Row 5 (Twist Rnd): K1, *k2, RT. Rep from * to last stitch, RT (working twist using last st of this rnd and first st of next rnd).

Row 7: Knit

Rep. rows 1–8 for pat.

Baby Cable Rib Pattern
(Worked over a multiple of 3 sts)

Rnd 1: *K2, p1; rep from * to end of rnd.

Rnd 2: *RT, p1; rep from * to end of rnd.

Rnds 3–5: *K2, p1; rep from * to end of rnd.

Rnds 6–9: Rep rnds 2–5.

Rnd 10: *RT, k1; rep from * to end of rnd.

Rep rnds 1–10 for pat.

INSTRUCTIONS

BODY

With larger, long circular needle, CO 216 (240, 264, 300) sts.

Set Up Rnd: Join, place right side marker, k108 (120, 132, 150) sts for Back, place left side marker, k108 (120, 132, 150) sts for front.

Work even in Twist Stitch pat until 23 (24, 25, 26) twist rnds have been completed; body should meas approx 13 (13½, 14, 14½)"/33 (34, 36, 37)cm from CO edge.

Work 1 more rnd.

Dec Rnd: Change to smaller, long circular needle. *K2tog, k1; rep from * to end of rnd—144 (160, 176, 200) sts.

Work rnd 1 of Baby Cable Rib pat, and AT THE SAME TIME, inc 0 (1, 1, 1) st immediately after right side marker and inc 0 (1, 0, 0) st immediately after left side marker, working incs into rib pat—144 (162, 177, 201) sts.

Work rnds 2–10 of Baby Cable Rib pat.

Knit one rnd.

Increase Rnd: Inc 12 (15, 19, 19) sts evenly spaced across 72 (81, 89, 101) Back sts—84 (96, 108, 120) sts in Back, then:

For Size S only: K3, (inc 1, k2) 15 times, inc 1, k6, (inc 1, k2) 16 times, k3—104 sts in Front.

For Size M only: K2, inc 1, k6, (inc 1, k2) 13 times, inc 1, k6, inc 1, k6, (inc, k2) 13 times, inc 1, k6, inc 1, k3—112 sts in Front.

For Size L only: K3, (inc 1, k2) 19 times, inc 1, k6, (inc 1, k2) 20 times, k3—128 sts in Front.

For Size XL only: K14, (inc 1, k3) 3 times, (inc 1, k2) 14 times, (inc 1, k3) 2 times, inc 1, k6, (inc 1, k3) 2 times, (inc 1, k2) 14 times, (inc 1, k3) 3 times, inc 1, k4—140 sts in Front.

After inc rnd, you should have 188 (208, 236, 260) sts total.

13½ (15, 16½, 17)"/34 (38, 42, 43)cm

6 (6¼, 6½, 6½)"/15 (16, 16.5, 16.5)cm

33 (36, 41, 45)"/84 (91, 104, 114)cm

28 (32, 36, 40)"/71 (81, 91, 102)cm

23 (24, 25, 25½)"/58 (61, 64, 65)cm

38 (42, 46, 52)"/97 (107, 117, 132)cm

Knit 1 rnd then change to Twist Stitch pat. Work until 5 (5, 6, 6) twist rnds have been completed.

For a proper fit, the Baby Cable Rib band must sit comfortably below the bust. Try on the sweater. When the top edge of the garment is held up to slightly below the underarm level, the top edge should just cover the top of the bust, and the band should rest below the bust. If the band is riding too high, work additional rnds, ending after working a twist rnd.

Knit 1 more rnd, stopping 5 (6, 7, 8) sts before end of rnd.

Divide for Front and Back:

Continue in Twist Stitch pat as est (if RT falls within 2 sts of edge, knot those sts instead). AT THE SAME TIME, bind off next 10 (12, 14, 16) sts, work across Back sts until 5 (6, 7, 8) sts before left side marker, BO next 10 (12, 14, 16) sts.

Left Front

Work across the next 39 (41, 46, 50) sts, turn.

Note: Leave the rest of the body sts on the needle while working only the Left Front sts, or place rem sts on hold.

Next Row (WS): BO 3 sts, p to end.

Next Row (RS Twist Row): K1, k2tog, work to end.

Next Row: BO 2 (2, 3, 3) sts, p to end.

Cont to dec 1 st at armhole edge every RS row 4 (5, 6, 7) more times, and AT THE SAME TIME, dec 1 st at neck edge every row 6 (6, 8, 8) times, then every RS row 5 (5, 4, 6) times, then every 4 rows 5 (5, 5, 4) times—13 (14, 16, 18) sts rem in left shoulder.

Note: For neck edge, decs on RS rows, work to last 2 sts, ssk; on WS rows, p2tog-tbl, work to end.

Work even until 12 (13, 14, 14) twist rows have been completed above underarm bind off and top meas approx 22 (23, 24, 24½)"/56 (58, 61, 62)cm.

Shape Shoulder using Short Rows:

On 2nd WS row after twist st row, p6 (7, 8, 9), W&T, on RS work to end.

Next Row (WS): Work across all sts, picking up wrap.

Place sts on holder.

Right Front

Place center 16 (18, 22, 24) Front sts on holder. Join yarn to RS of rem 39 (41, 46, 50) Front sts.

Next Row (RS): BO 3 sts, work to last 3 sts, ssk, k1.

Next Row (WS): Purl

Next Row (Twist Row): BO 2 (2, 3, 3) sts, work to 2 sts before end, dec 1 as above.

Next Row: Purl.

Cont to dec 1 st at armhole edge every RS row 4 (5, 6, 7) more times, and AT THE SAME TIME, dec 1 st at neck edge every row 6 (6, 8, 8) times, then every RS row 5 (5, 4, 6) times, then every 4 rows 5 (5, 5, 4) times—13 (14, 16, 18) sts rem in left shoulder.

Note: For neck edge decs, on RS rows, k2tog, work to end; on WS rows, work to last 2 sts, p2tog.

Work even until 12 (13, 14, 14) twist rows have been completed above underarm and pieces meas the same as Left Front to shoulder shaping.

Shape Shoulder using Short Rows:

On first RS row after twist row, k7 (7, 8, 9), W&T, on WS work to end.

Next Row (RS): Work across all sts, picking up wrap, and working RT only on longer side of shoulder.

Work 1 more row, then place sts on holder.

Back

Join yarn to WS of Back; work 1 row.

Next Row (RS): K1, k2tog, work to last 3 sts, ssk, k1.

Dec every RS row 4 (5, 6, 7) more times, then work even until 12 (13, 14, 14) twist rows have been completed above underarm bind off.

Shape Shoulders using Short Rows:

*On next RS row, work to 6 (7, 8, 9) sts before end, W&T; repeat from * once more.

Next Row (RS): Work across all sts, working RT as directed above.

Work 1 more row, working across all sts and picking up wraps—13 (14, 16, 18) sts on each end will be used to seam shoulders; the center 38 (44, 48, 52) sts will form the Back neck.

FINISHING

Turn garment inside out so RS of Front and Back are facing each other. Using 13 (14, 16, 18) sts held from Front for left shoulder and the facing sts from Back, seam shoulder using the three-needle BO. Place the 38 (44, 48, 52) center Back sts on holder and seam 2nd shoulder using rem Back sts.

NECKBAND

With RS facing, using short circular or dpns and starting at RS, knit across held Back sts, dec 10 (11, 11, 13) sts evenly spaced; pick up and knit 45 (45, 46, 46) sts between Back neck and center Front sts; k across center Front sts, dec 5 (6, 7, 8) sts evenly spaced; pick up and knit 45 (45, 46, 46) sts between center Front and Back neck—129 (135, 144, 147) sts.

Rnds 1–4: Work Baby Cable Rib pat.

BO in twist st pat as follows:

P1, *k 2nd st on left-hand needle. Without allowing first st to fall off left-hand needle, rotate needle tips to bring tip of left-hand needle in front of right-hand needle, and use tip of left-hand needle to slip first st on right-hand needle over 2nd and off the needle—one st bound off.

Knit 1st st on left-hand needle and allow 2nd st on that needle (already knit) to drop off needle. Use tip of left-hand needle to slip 1st st on right-hand needle over 2nd and off the needle—2 sts bound off.

Purl 1 st; use tip of left-hand needle to slip 1st st on right-hand needle over 2nd and off the needle—3 sts bound off.

Rep from * until all sts are bound off.

Armhole Bands

With RS facing, using short circular or dpns and starting at center of 10 (12, 14, 16) BO underarm sts, pick up and knit 3 (4, 4, 5) sts along 5 (6, 7, 8) bound off sts; pick up 69 (73, 76, 80) sts evenly spaced along armhole; pick up and k3 (4, 4, 5) sts along last 5 (6, 7, 8) bound off sts—75 (81, 84, 90) sts.

Work as for neckband. Repeat on 2nd armhole.

Weave in ends and block to measurements.

Twisted-Cord Belt

Cut three lengths of yarn, each approx 12'/3.6m long, and make a twisted cord for a belt. To wear, tie the belt comfortably under the bust, at the midpoint of the Baby Cable Band.

This project was made with:

5 (5, 6, 6) skeins of Classic Elite's *Provence*, 100% mercerized cotton, 3.5oz/100g = 205yd/186m per skein, color #2639

—From *Expectant Little Knits*

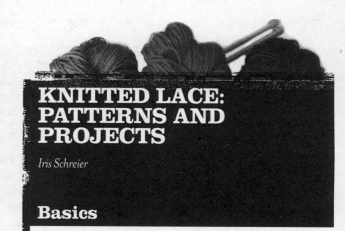

KNITTED LACE: PATTERNS AND PROJECTS

Iris Schreier

Basics

There are a variety of patterns in this section ranging from very easy to more advanced designs. Some use common stitches; others require more complex and unusual ones. Some pieces have little or no shaping, while others are shaped and formed with lace.

My goal is for you to be able to understand the construction of the garment you're knitting to the point of being able to knit it without having to follow line-by-line instructions. This makes the knitting more fun and even addictive.

That's why I recommend that, regardless of what level knitter you are, you read through this section, paying particular attention to the information on stitch patterns and following your lace.

Stitch Patterns

LONG STITCH AND DOUBLE LONG STITCH

This is usually a double long stitch. It is formed over 2 rows. In this book elongated stitches are used as decorative elements to enhance and open the knitted fabric.

Directions: Insert the needle into the next stitch as though to knit. Normally, you would wrap the working yarn around the needle one time in order to pull a new stitch from the old stitch, and after pulling the loop through you would drop the old stitch from the needle. To create the elongated stitch, wrap the working yarn

Long stitches form a lacy effect.

twice (instead of the usual one time) around the needle, and draw both loops through to form two stitches on the right needle. After you have pulled the double loop through, drop the old stitch from the needle. On the return row, only knit into the first loop of the double wrap, dropping the second loop to form a long stitch.

In some projects you'll be instructed to make a Double Long stitch; this is formed by wrapping the yarn around the needle three times when knitting. On the return row, only knit into the first loop of the triple wrap.

OPENWORK STITCH

This is an easy 2-stitch pattern that is used extensively in this book. This stitch forms the openings or eyelets in the knitting to make the lace pattern.

Directions: First row: *yo, SKP; repeat from * to end.

Usually a knit stitch is added at the beginning and end of each row.

Following row: Always slip the previous row's SKP stitch and knit the previous row's yo stitch.

Following your lace is important for you to keep track of any inadvertently dropped or missing yo stitches—a very common mistake. This will maintain a consistent and even fabric.

Continued ➜

Traveling Lace

Reading your knitting is the most important thing you can learn to do as you work on projects. It will free you from having to carry around and refer to cumbersome patterns and charts, and will allow you to concentrate on your piece and how it is constructed. You will catch errors before you have taken them too far and prevent much frustration.

It may not look like it, but creating the lace in this section is really quite simple—the eyelets and lace ridges patterns being clear to follow. One project that will require you to "read" your lace and follow the pattern are Diagonals in Flight. You will notice that the eyelets (openings) run on the diagonal. That means that the knitting shifts over on every other row (the lace is only knitted on every other row, with the alternate rows knitted or purled across). The pattern will be spelled out in order to establish the pattern. From that point on, you will follow it in sequence by reading your lace.

It is also important to note that new lace panels start when there are enough stitches available. On the Right Front, for example, when working the right side rows, you are instructed to knit across all extra sts at the end when there are fewer than five stitches and a full lace pattern repeat cannot be completed. You will need to add a new lace panel in sequence at the beginning of the row whenever there are five knit stitches.

Exercise One

Here is a good practice exercise for learning how to follow your lace.

Lace Pattern

Row 1: *yo, slip 2 sts together as if to knit, k1, then pass both slipped sts over k st, yo, k3; repeat from * to last 3 sts, yo, sl 2tog, k1, p2sso, yo.

Row 2: Purl across.

Note: Whenever there are not enough stitches to knit a complete lace stitch pattern, simple knit across those remaining stitches. Line up all lace ridges at all times.

Cast on 17 sts.

Row 1: K1, work Row 1 of Lace Pattern to last st, k1.

Row 2 and all even-numbered rows: K1, work Row 2 of Lace Pattern to last st, k1.

Rows 3 through 8: Repeat Rows 1 and 2 three times more.

Row 9: K2tog, work Lace Pattern in established pattern to last st, k1—16 sts.

In other words: K2tog, k5, work Lace Pattern once (yo, sl 2tog, k1, p2sso, yo, k3), to the last 4 sts, yo, sl 2tog, k1, p2sso, yo, k1.

Row 11: K1, work Lace Pattern in established pattern to last st, k1—16 sts.

In other words: K1, k5, work Lace Pattern once (yo, sl 2tog, k1, p2sso, yo, k3), to the last 4 sts, yo, sl 2tog, k1, p2sso, yo, k1.

Row 13: Inc 1, work Lace Pattern in established pattern to last st, k1—17 sts.

In other words: Inc 1, k5, work Lace Pattern once (yo, sl 2tog, k1, p2sso, yo, k3) to last 4 sts, yo, sl 2tog, k1, p2sso, yo, k1.

Row 15: K1, work Lace Pattern in established pattern to last st, k1—17 sts.

In other words: K1, work Lace St (yo, sl 2tog, k1, p2sso, yo, k3) twice, to last 4 sts, yo, sl 2tog, k1, p2sso, yo, k1.

As you can see from this example, a decrease at the beginning of Row 9 prevented you from knitting the first Lace Pat panel, as established in Rows 1 through 8. So instead, you k5 across the 5 remaining stitches. But after Row 13, when there are once again enough stitches to reinstate the Lace Pat panel, it is knitted again. Always use the lace ridges and eyelets as a guide as to where the new row's lace panel must be inserted. And if there are not enough stitches (in this case fewer than 6), knit across them instead of working the Lace Pat.

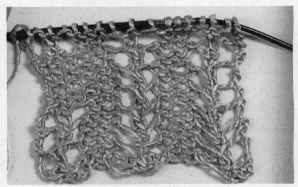

On the left side one lace pattern repeat is removed when there are insufficient stitches to complete it (after a decrease at the edge)—instead the remaining stitches are knitted. The lace pattern repeat is added again when there are sufficient stitches (after an increase at the edge).

As you can see, the eyelets will line up from previous rows.

Here is a second exercise that will help you work on multidirectional traveling.

Exercise Two

Lace Pattern

Row 1: Edge stitch (as specified in pattern), *yo, sl 1, k2tog, psso, yo, k3; repeat from * to last 4 sts, yo, sl 1, k2tog, psso, yo, edge stitch (as specified).

Row 2: K across.

Cast on 3 sts.

Step 1: Build width of Center-Increase Triangle

Row 1: K1, inc 1, p1—4 sts.

Row 2: Inc 1, inc 1, k1, p1—6 sts.

Row 3: Inc 1, k1, inc 1, PM, k2, p1—8 sts.

Row 4: Inc 1, k to marker, RM, inc 1, PM, k to last st, p1—10 sts.

Row 5: Inc 1, yo, sl 1, k2tog, psso, yo, RM, inc 1, PM, yo, sl 1, k2tog, psso, yo, k1, p1—12 sts.

Cast On—When no special cast on is specified in this book, a long tail case on is assumed. Make a slip knot in your working yarn, leaving sufficient yarn for the number of cast on stitches specified by the pattern and work your way back toward the end as you form the stitches—the extra tail used in this method is the "long tail."

Cast Off—(also referred to as Bind Off). Bind off by knitting a stitch, then knitting the next stitch and passing the first knitted stitch over the second knitted stitch (a decrease of 1 stitch).

Double Long St—Knit stitch wrapping yarn three times around needle to form 3 loops. On following row, knit into first loop of triple wrap and drop second and third loops to form double elongated stitch.

Garter stitch—knit every row

inc—increase

Inc 1—Knit into front loop, then into back loop of same stitch (1 st increased)

K1tbl—Knit 1 stitch through back loop of stitch

K1tfl—Knit 1 stitch through front loop of stitch

K2tog—Knit two stitches together as if they were one (1 st decreased)

K3tog—Knit 3 stitches together as one (2 sts decreased)

LP—lace panel, Yo, sl 1, k2tog, psso, yo (3 sts worked over 3 sts)

Long st—Knit a stitch by wrapping yarn around needle twice (instead of once). On following row, knit just the first of the two wraps, letting the second one drop from needle to create a stitch twice as long as a regular stitch.

M1—Make one. With left needle tip, lift, connecting strand between last knit stitch on right needle and next stitch on left needle to form loop on left needle. Knit into back of this loop (1 st increased).

P2sso—Pass the 2 slipped stitches over the knitted stitch (2 sts decreased).

P2tog—Purl 2 stitches together as one (1 st decreased)

P3tog—Purl 3 stitches together as 1 (decrease of 2 sts)

PM—Place marker on needle

Psso—Pass slipped stitch over last worked stitch (decrease of 1 st)

Repeat from *—Repeat instructions following asterisk as many times as indicated, in addition to the first time.

RM—Remove marker

Round—Continuous row worked around on circular or double-pointed needles

RS—Right side of work

Short rows—Partial row is worked, then piece is turned and worked back to original edge; used for adding fullness to one section of piece.

SKP—Slip, knit, pass—Slip 1 stitch knitwise, knit next stitch, pass slipped stitch over knitted stitch (1 st decreased).

Sl 1—Slip 1 stitch knitwise (as though to knit)

Sl 1 wyib—Slip 1 stitch with yarn in back of work (on right-side rows).

Sl 1 wyif—Slip 1 stitch with yarn in front of work (on wrong-side rows)

Sl 2tog—Slip 2 stitches together with yarn in back as though to knit

SSK—Slip, slip, knit (decrease of 1 st)—Slip each of next 2 stitches knitwise to right needle, insert left needle into fronts of these stitches from left to right. Knit them together (1 st decreased).

SSP—Slip, slip, pass (decrease of 1 st). Slip first stitch knitwise, slip second stitch knitwise, pass first slipped stitch over second slipped stitch without knitting either stitch.

Stockinette st—Knit on right side rows, purl on wrong side rows.

st, sts—Stitch(es)

tbl—Through back loop

tfl—Through front loop

tog—Together

Turn—Transfer the left needle to the right hand and the right needle to the left hand, bringing the yarn up and over to the back between the tops of the two needles.

WS—Wrong side of work

wyib—With yarn in back of work

wyif—With yarn in front of work

yo—Yarn over. Bring yarn forward under right needle tip and wrap it front to back over needle to form loop over needle, adding 1 stitch. On following row, work this added loop as a stitch.

yo twice—Yarn over twice (2 wraps). On following row, knit into front loop, then into back loop of double wrap (2 sts increased).

Row 6 and all even-numbered rows: Inc 1, k to marker, RM, inc 1, PM, k to last st, p1—2 sts increased.

Row 7 and all odd-numbered rows: Inc 1, work Lace Pat as established to marker, RM, inc 1, PM, work Lace Pat as established to last st, p1—2 sts increased.

This means that you work the even-numbered rows as for Row 6 and all odd-numbered rows as follows:

Row 7: Inc 1, k1, yo, sl 1, k2tog, psso, yo, k1, RM, inc 1, PM, k1, yo, sl 1, k2tog, psso, yo, k2, p1—16 sts.

Row 9: Inc 1, k2, yo, sl 1, k2tog, psso, yo, k2, RM, inc 1, PM, k2, yo, sl 1, k2tog, psso, yo, k3, p1—20 sts.

Row 11: Inc 1, k3, yo, sl 1, k2tog, psso, yo, k3, RM, inc 1, PM, k3, yo, sl 1, k2tog, psso, yo, k4, p1—24 sts.

Row 13: Inc 1, k4, yo, sl 1, k2tog, psso, yo, k4, RM, inc 1, PM, k4, yo, sl 1, k2tog, psso, yo, k5, p1—28 sts.

Row 15: Inc 1, k5, yo, sl 1, k2tog, psso, yo, k5, RM, inc 1, PM, k5, yo, sl 1, k2tog, psso, yo, k6, p1—32 sts.

Row 17: Inc 1, add new lace panel as follows: (yo, sl 1, k2tog, psso, yo); then, k3, continue existing lace panel: (yo, sl 1, k2tog, psso, yo); k3, add new lace panel: (yo, s1, k2tog, psso, yo); RM, inc 1, PM, add new lace panel: (yo, sl 1, k2tog, psso, yo); k3, continue existing lace panel: (yo, sl 1, k2tog, psso, yo); k3, add new lace panel: (yo, sl 1, k2tog, psso, yo); k1, p1—36 sts.

Note that because you increased twice on each row, after 12 rows you have added 24 stitches, and at this point you have enough sts to insert 4 new lace panels, 1 before and 1 after the previous lace panel on each side of the center increase, ending with a total of 6 lace panels. **Important**: Always add lace panels on both sides of the center increase on the same row for symmetry.

For example, if you were to continue working an additional 12 rows, at the end of Row 29 there would be 10 lace panels (5 on each side of center increase), with one panel added at each outer edge (beyond the previous panel) and one added on each side of the center increase. For this exercise, end the piece at Row 18: Inc 1, k16, inc 1, k16, k1, p1—38 sts.

Step 2: Square off the sides maintaining 38 sts every row

Row 1: K1, work Lace St as established to marker, RM, inc 1, PM, work Lace St as established to last 2 sts, p2tog.

Row 2: K to marker, RM, inc 1, PM, k to last 2 sts, p2tog.

Repeat Rows 1 and 2 until piece is at desired length.

In other words, to repeat these 2 rows, you will be working as follows:

Row 1: K2, (yo, sl 1, k2tog, psso, yo), k3, (yo, sl 1, k2tog, psso, yo), k3, (yo, sl 1, k2tog, psso, yo), k1, RM, inc 1, PM, k1, (yo, sl 1, k2tog, psso, yo), k3, (yo, sl 1, k2tog, psso, yo), k3, (yo, sl 1, k2tog, psso, yo), k1, p2tog—38 sts.

Row 2: K18, RM, inc 1, PM, k17, p2tog—38 sts.

Row 3: K1, (yo, sl 1, k2tog, psso, yo), k3, (yo, sl 1, k2tog, psso, yo), k3, (yo, sl 1, k2tog, psso, yo), k2, RM, inc 1, PM, k2, (yo, sl 1, k2tog, psso, yo), k3, (yo, sl 1, k2tog, psso, yo), k3, (yo, sl 1, k2tog, psso, yo), p2tog—38 sts.

Row 4: Repeat Row 2.

Row 5: K6 (you have just knitted across the previous row's lace panel because you no longer have enough stitches to maintain it—k1 needed to maintain selvage-st edge and k5 for pattern is insufficient), (yo, sl 1, k2tog, psso, yo), k3, (yo, sl 1, k2tog, psso, yo), k3, RM, inc 1, PM, k3, (yo, sl 1, k2tog, psso, yo), k3, (yo, sl 1, k2tog, psso, yo), k5, p2tog (you have now omitted the last lace panel from the previous row)—38 sts.

Row 6: Repeat Row 2.

Row 7: K5, (yo, sl 1, k2tog, psso, yo), k3, (yo, sl 1, k2tog, psso, yo), k4, RM, inc 1, PM, k4, (yo, sl 1, k2tog, psso, yo), k3, (yo, sl 1, k2tog, psso, yo), k4, p2tog—38sts.

Row 8: Repeat Row 2.

Although the stitch count remains the same once you square off the sides of the triangle, you will find that when you add lace panels they will always be at the center (on either side of the center increase); when you discontinue lace panels by knitting across them, they will always be at the edges (see row 5 on previous page). This is because you are increasing the number of stitches at the center and decreasing the number of stitches at the edge.

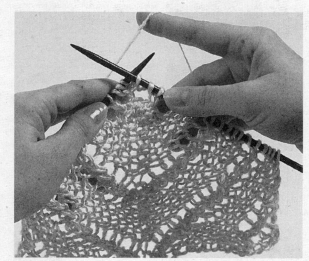

Squared-off Sides with lace panels running diagonally away from the center. As you can see, they are discontinued (knitted across) when they reach the edge. But new lace panels will be added as stitches are increased in the center (top).

Important: Continue working an additional 16 rows by repeating original Rows 1 and 2. Then compare your swatch to photo 4. This will be the real test of whether you have learned to follow your lace, since row-by-row instructions are not provided in this last repeat....

TIPS FOR SUCCESS

Some of the patterns are unusual in their construction. Even experienced knitters (and especially experienced knitters who are used to standard techniques) may misunderstand the instructions and become frustrated if they presuppose that they understand what to do without reading through this section. Please approach these projects with an open mind as though you are knitting these types of patterns for the first time. Following are some specific suggestions for a successful outcome.

READ YOUR WORK

It is a common mistake to assume that there is something wrong with your knitting because it does not resemble the specified shape. To check the shape and measurements of your piece, remove the stitches from the knitting needles as follows: Thread a tapestry needle with a length of yarn (at least 1 yd or 1 m long). Draw the threaded needle through the stitches and slide them off the knitting needle. Lay the fabric completely flat and unstretched to determine the shape and measurements.

To continue on the piece, return the stitches to the knitting needle, being careful to keep them in the proper order, with markers in place, and without twisting the stitches.

Here are some other pointers that are helpful in case you drop your marker or lose your place. In order to assure success, you must learn to read your work.

Increases in the center-increase triangles take place at the beginning and center of each row. You can tell which stitch requires the increase by tracking the pair of stitches from the previous row that represent the very centermost point of your row; they are closely joined because that was the position of increase in the previous row, and both loops emerged from one stitch. You can feel that by tugging on them, and if you flip your work over, you'll notice that one of the stitches is actually a ½ stitch in that it does not have any "roots" in other stitches, but hangs suspended since it was just added. This is the stitch where you'll always work the center increase.

Squaring off the sides of triangles is done in a way that balances the number of increases to the decreases in each row, so the stitch count remains the same on each row.

Squaring off the top of the center-increase triangle (or binding off) is generally done in two parts. The row is divided in half and each half is worked separately. Decrease on both ends of each half, until there are 2 or 3 stitches left. Bind off these remaining stitches. Cut yarn. Repeat on the other side, making sure to attach yarn and start knitting at the centermost point.

Stitches are left behind (1 stitch per ridge) while the right side is being worked to create V.

Leaving Unworked Stitches in the center-increase triangle creates a V neckline. This technique is used in the Perfect Choice Sweater when the right and left sides of these pullovers are worked separately. Stitches are left behind in order to form the "V" neckline, which is later knitted in the opposite direction connecting the 2 sides.

MEASURE YOUR WORK

Probably the most important thing you can do to ensure proper fit is to ensure that you are on gauge with your knitting. Here are some special tips for doing this:

If you're working with silk, note that it is a fiber with very little 'give," meaning that it barely stretches or springs back when you knit. It is ideal for lace because it requires little blocking to open up the eyelets. However, knitted fabric with silk becomes very stretchy, and this additional ease must be taken into account when you swatch, measure, and knit the garments. Often, silk garments look small but fit well when worn.

Be very careful trying to substitute rayon or cotton in fitted multidirectional garments. Check not only the gauge, but the weight of the yarn. If your yarn is heavier than the one used in the garment, the knitted fabric will weigh more and may not fit properly.

So choose your substitute yarn based on the yards/meters per ounces/grams.

There are a number of projects that start with center-increase triangles. These projects require that your work be on flexible needles in order to see the shape forming. In addition, you will generally be instructed to measure the width of the piece at the base of the triangle.

To check the measurements of your triangle, remove the stitches from the knitting needles as follows: Thread a tapestry needle with a length of yarn (at least 1 yd or 1 m long). Draw threaded needle through the stitches and slide them off the knitting needle. Lay the fabric completely flat and unstretched to determine the measurements.

Measuring your work.

To continue working on the piece, return the stitches to the knitting needle, being careful to keep them in the proper order, with markers in place, and without twisting the stitches.

RECOMMENDED TOOLS

Good needles can make all the difference in your knitting experience. For silk, cashmere, and mohair, Rosewood needles work especially well. Rosewood is softer than bamboo, smooth, and extremely lightweight. These needles have become popular now and are available through most yarn shops and online re-sellers. You will find that your hands do not get tired with these needles, and the yarn stays put without slipping. Because most of the lace

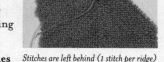

Rosewood needles—double pointed, circular, and straight versions (left to right)

Continued →

patterns here require yarn-over stitches, and because this type of stitch tends to get hung up on the joints of circular needles, be very careful about the circular needles that you select. Make sure to find circular needles that have smooth joins and plastic cords that do not fight you.

Use markers that can be easily clipped on and will stay put with a locking device, and are just as easily removed. They will give you the most flexibility in these patterns.

Techniques Used

This section includes a review of standard techniques that are used. Most of the techniques described are commonly used in many knitting patterns on the market today.

LOOSE CAST OFF METHOD AND CROCHET BIND OFF

The easiest way to cast off loosely is by using larger needles. If these are not available, merely knit every other stitch twice before binding it off. Work as follows:

Knit one stitch. Transfer it back to the other needle. Knit it again. Bind it off by pulling the second stitch on the needle over the first on the needle.

Another method of loosely binding off is with a crochet bind off.

Insert a crochet hook through first stitch to be cast off as if you were knitting it, catch yarn on hook and draw it through the stitch on the needle (new stitch is now on crochet hook), drop original stitch from needle. Continue working as follows: *Insert hook into next st on needle knitwise, catch yarn on hook, drawing it through the st on the needle and in one continuous motion, draw it through the previous stitch on the hook. One stitch is now bound off, the new stitch is on the hook; drop the original worked st from the needle. Repeat from * across until all stitches are bound off. Cut yarn and fasten off last st on crochet hook.

SHORT ROWS WITH AND WITHOUT WRAPS

Short rows are used throughout the book, and in most cases on the diagonal.

Diagonal short rows require no wraps, so there is not much to say about them here, except that it is important to follow the instructions exactly and NEVER stop to take a break in the middle of a row. Always take a break only after you have knitted back and all your stitches are on one needle. Sometimes that is hard in the setup phase of knitting where there are quite a few cast-on stitches that must be worked, so make sure to dedicate a nice amount of time without a break for starting a new project.

Slip stitch from left needle to right needle as if to purl with yarn in back.

Wrap short rows as follows: If purling in the pattern, when instructions say "wrap and turn," slip the next stitch purlwise, bring the yarn between the needles from the front to the back, slip the same stitch back to the left needle, and turn the work, bringing yarn to the knit side between the needles. If knitting in the pattern, when instructions say "wrap and turn," slip the next stitch purlwise, bring the yarn between the needles from the back to the front,

Bring yarn from back to front between both needles.

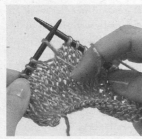
Slip wrapped stitch back to left needle.

Slip stitch from left needle to right needle as if to purl with yarn in front.

Slip wrapped stitch back to left needle.

When all short rows are worked, knit as usual to the wrapped stitch. Insert the needle knit wise into the wrap and the stitch that was wrapped. Then knit the wrapped stitch together with the wrap as shown in order to hide the wrap. This technique will prevent holes from forming where you turned your work

slip the same stitch back to the left needle, and turn the work, bringing yarn to the purl side between the needles.

Then on the way back you will pick up the wrap along with the stitch that has been wrapped in order to close up any holes. This helps to make a smooth transition between the extra row and the preceding and following ones.

Bring yarn from front to back between both needles.

When all short rows are worked, purl as usual to the wrapped stitch. Then insert the needle from behind into the back loop of the wrap as shown and place it on the needle. Purl the wrap along with the stitch that was wrapped in order to hide the wrap. This technique will prevent holes from forming where you turned your work.

I-CORDS, TWISTED CORDS, AND FRINGE

I-cords are formed with special 3-pronged gadgets, or simply by knitting a few stitches in the round with two double-pointed needles as follows:

Cast 3 sts onto one double-pointed needle. *Slide the sts to the opposite end of the needle and now hold the needle with sts in your left hand, with right side of work facing you. Draw the working yarn to the right behind the cast-on sts, and using the second needle, knit the 3 sts again. Repeat from * until the I-cord is the desired length, and as you work, be sure to draw the working yarn somewhat tightly across the back of the stitches so that an evenly rounded cord is formed.

Twisted cord is formed by cutting the number of suggested lengths of yarn indicated in the pattern and tying one end of the lengths together to a doorknob. Twist the other end of the strands tightly, and when the twist feels sufficient fold the cord in half, letting it twist onto itself. Knot each end of cord to fasten, and trim ends.

Fringe is made by using the number and length of strands specified in the project. Holding the strands together evenly, fold them in half to make a loop. Insert a crochet

Draw the loop through making it large enough for catching all the strands

Pull down on the ends so the loops tighten snugly around the stitch.

hook into the garment where you plan to apply the fringe, and catch all the strands in the center. Draw the loop end through, making it large enough so you can pull the ends of the yarn through the loop. Pull down on the ends so the loops tighten snugly around the stitch.

KNITTED CAST ON

This method allows you to add new stitches to existing stitches on the left-hand needle. If you do not already have any stitches on your needles, cast on 1 stitch by making a slip knot, or any way you wish, and hold the needle with the stitch in the left hand. Continue process as follows.

Insert the right-hand needle into the first stitch on the left-hand needle, as if to knit it. Knit the stitch, but do not drop the stitch from the left needle. Place the newly knitted stitch back on the left-hand needle. Continue adding new stitches in this manner, until you have added as many stitches as the pattern calls for.

Draw the loop through making it large enough for catching all the strands

THREE-NEEDLE BIND-OFF

Three-needle bind-off is used to join two pieces together while binding off. This eliminates the need to sew seams. With wrong sides of the knitted fabric facing outward, hold two needles together. With a third needle, knit two stitches together, working one stitch from the front needle and one stitch from the back needle. *Knit next two stitches together as before, taking one stitch from the front and one from the back. Pass the previous stitch worked over the latest stitch worked to bind off. Repeat from * until all stitches have been bound off.

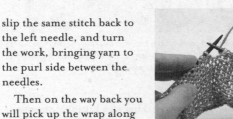
Pull down on the ends so the loops tighten snugly around the stitch.

Finishing

TIPS ON ASSEMBLING GARMENTS

Block all pieces before sewing them together. When working with soft and stretchy knitted garments, use the finest yarn used in the project to seam the pieces so it does not show. Make sure to sew side seams of garments before inserting sleeves.

CARE OF LUXURY FIBERS

It is best to hand-wash these garments carefully with a very mild soap specifically meant for fine washables. Do not wring them, but after soaking in a cool, mild soap bath and rinsing, roll them in a towel to absorb the excessive moisture, and carefully lay them on a flat surface to dry completely without being moved.

To block these yarns, use a hand steamer. If you do use an iron, make sure to place a protective cloth, such as a dish towel, between the hot iron and the knitted fabric.

After Five Lace Shrug

EXPERIENCE LEVEL
Easy

SIZES
Small/medium, (large/extra large)

This lightweight short- or long-sleeved shrug will add elegance and romance to any outfit. Wear it over any sleeveless garment and feel bathed in the soft silkiness of the knitted fabric.

Photo D

FINISHED MEASUREMENTS

About 43"/109cm (50"/127cm) long (sleeve edge to sleeve edge) and 16"/40.5cm (20½"/52cm) wide (from top edge to lower edge at center back), lying flat and unstretched. Because of lace pattern, piece can be stretched in length or in width.

MATERIALS

- Approx total: 489yd/447m (652yd/596m) silk light-weight yarn
- Knitting needles: 5mm (size 8 U.S.) *or size to obtain gauge*
- Tapestry needle for finishing

GAUGE

16 sts and 22 rows = 4"/10cm in Trellis Lace pattern

Always take time to check your gauge.

PATTERN SWITCH

TRELLIS LACE

(pattern from *The Harmony Guides, 450 Knitting Stitches*, Volume 2, page 51)

(*Multiple of 6 sts, plus 5*)

Row 1 (RS): K4, *yo, sl 1, k2tog, psso, yo, k3; repeat from * across to last st, k1.

Row 2: K1, p to last st, k1.

Row 3: K1, *yo, sl 1, k2tog, psso, yo, k3: repeat from * across to last 4 sts, yo, sl 1, k2tog, psso, yo, k1.

Row 4: K1, p to last st, k1.

Repeat these 4 rows for lace pattern.

INSTRUCTIONS

SHRUG

Starting at one sleeve edge, cast on 65 (83) sts. Work in Trellis Lace pattern, working 10 (13) pattern, working 10 (13) pattern repeats across, until piece measures 43"/109cm (50"/127cm) from beginning.

Bind off all sts. Cut yarn. Weave in ends.

FINISHING

At each end of piece, fold side edges in to meet at center to form sleeve. With right sides together, seam these edges together, starting at sleeve edge, for about 9½"/24cm adjusting length of seam as needed to accommodate various sizes.

This project was knit with:

3 (4) skeins of Artyarns Regal Silk, 100% silk lightweight yarn, 1.8oz/50g = 163yd/149m per skein, color #137, variegated beige.

Four Rectangle Sweater

EXPERIENCE LEVEL

Easy

SIZES

X-Small (Small, Medium, Large)

It's hard to believe that this form-fitting sweater is made with just four simple rectangles. The vertical panels running down each side are not only attractive design elements, but serve to make the top visually slimming.

FINISHED GARMENT MEASUREMENTS

Bust: 31 (35, 39, 43)"/79 (89, 99, 109)cm

Standard Fit

MATERIALS

- Approx total: 624 (728, 832, 938)yd/571 (666, 761, 858)m Merino wool medium-weight yarn (yarn A), and

- Approx total: 414 (552, 690, 690)yd/379 (505, 631, 631)m ⅛"/3mm-wide silk ribbon (yarn B)
- Knitting needles: 4.5mm (size 7 U.S.) *or size to obtain gauge*
- Extra needle, same size, for 3-needle bind off
- Tapestry needle for finishing

GAUGE

18½ sts and 29 rows = 4"/10cm in Daisy Pattern Stitch

Always take time to check your gauge.

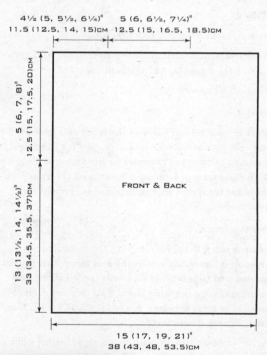

4½ (5, 5½, 6¼)" 11.5 (12.5, 14, 15)cm   5 (6, 6½, 7¼)" 12.5 (15, 16.5, 18.5)cm

5 (6, 7, 8)" 12.5 (15, 17.5, 20)cm

13 (13½, 14, 14½)" 33 (34.5, 35.5, 37)cm

FRONT & BACK

15 (17, 19, 21)" 38 (43, 48, 53.5)cm

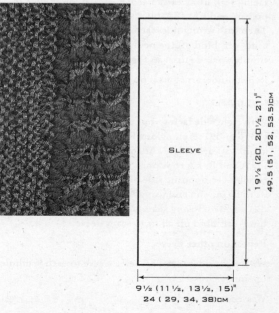

SLEEVE

19½ (20, 20½, 21)" 49.5 (51, 52, 53.5)cm

9½ (11½, 13½, 15)" 24 (29, 34, 38)cm

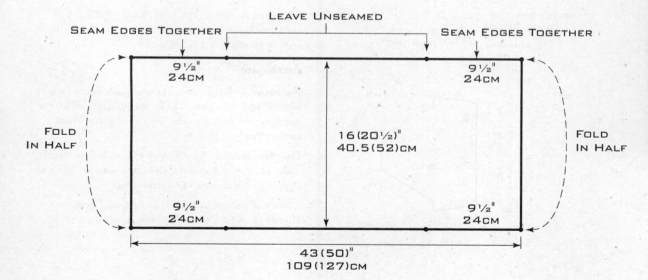

LEAVE UNSEAMED

SEAM EDGES TOGETHER   SEAM EDGES TOGETHER

9½" 24cm   9½" 24cm

FOLD IN HALF   16(20½)" 40.5(52)cm   FOLD IN HALF

9½" 24cm   9½" 24cm

43(50)" 109(127)cm

Continued ➜

PATTERN STITCH

DAISY PATTERN

Rows 1 and 2: With A, k across over both rows. Drop A; attach B. Carry yarn not in use loosely along side edge of work as you proceed.

Row 3 (RS): With B, *k1, k3tog through front loops and leave the original 3 sts on the left needle, then working on these same 3 sts, k3tog through the back loops, then k3tog through the front loops again (k3tog worked 3 times over the same 3 stitches) and then remove the original 3 sts from the left needle; rep from * across, ending k1.

Row 4: With B, k1, p to last st, k1. Drop B; pick up A.

Rows 5 and 6: With A, k across over both rows. Drop A; pick up B.

Repeat Rows 3 through 6 to continue in pattern.

INSTRUCTIONS

BACK

- With yarn A, cast on 69 (81, 89, 97) sts.

Work in Daisy Pattern until piece measures 18 (19½, 21, 22½)"/45.5 (49.5, 53.5, 57)cm. Bind off all sts with A, using Loose Cast-off Method in Techniques Used, page ???.

FRONT

Work same as for back.

SLEEVES

Make 2.

With A, cast on 45 (57, 65, 73) sts.

Work in Daisy Pattern until sleeve measures 19½ (20, 20½, 21)"/49.5 (51, 52, 53.5)cm

Bind off all sts with A.

FINISHING

Mark the bound-off edges of the front and back 22 (26, 28, 30) sts in from each arm edge for shoulders, leaving 25 (29, 33, 37) center sts for neck opening. With right sides of front and back together, seam each shoulder from arm edge to marker. Turn right side out.

UNDERARM GUSSET

Leaving top 5 (6, 7, 8)"/12.5 (15, 17.5, 20)cm unworked for armhole opening and using yarn B, pick up and k 61 (65, 69, 73) sts evenly spaced along one underarm edge (working about 2 sts in every A ridge and 1 st in every B ridge). K 12 (14, 16, 18) rows. Cut yarn, leaving sts on needle.

At the same underarm, with B and right side of work facing you, using extra needle, start at lower edge to pick up and k 61 (65, 69, 73) sts along matching edge. Then with wrong sides facing you, using 3-needle bind-off, bind off the newly picked up sts and the previously worked gusset sts together for underarm seam.

Repeat underarm gusset on other side of garment.

SLEEVE GUSSET

With right side facing you, using A, pick up and k 76 (78, 80, 82) sts along one long sleeve edge (working about 1 st each ridge). Attach B and k 2 rows. Alternating A and B, k 2 rows once more. Cut A, leaving sts on needle. On opposite side of sleeve, with right side of work facing you and using A, pick up and k 76 (78, 80, 82) sts. With wrong sides facing you, using 3-needle bind-off, bind off all sts to seam sleeve.

Repeat on other sleeve.

With right sides together, sew a sleeve to each armhole opening.

Weave in yarn ends.

This project was knit with:

6 (7, 8, 9) skeins of Artyarns Supermerino, 100% Merino Wool medium-weight yarn, 1.8oz/50g = 104yd/95m per skein, color #229 blue (yarn A,) and 3 (4, 5, 5) skeins Artyarns Silk Ribbon, ⅛"/3mm-wide 100% silk ribbon, .9oz/25g = 138yd/126m per skein, color #229 blue.

Baby's Breath Tee

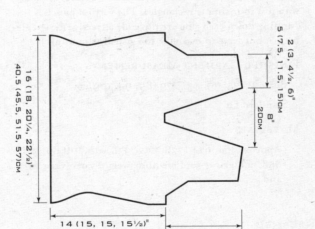

Intermediate

SIZE

X-Small (Small, Medium, Large)

You can't help but feel exceedingly feminine in this hip-skimming tee. The lace neckline is as delicate and light as a summer's breeze. Knitted in together with the front, the neckline uses a silk mohair yarn in exactly the same color as the silk yarn used for the bodice.

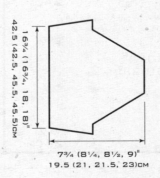

FINISHED MEASUREMENTS

Note: Measurements given below are for when this form-fitting garment is actually worn, and include several inches of stretching. The garment, lying flat and unstretched, will measure less than indicated below.

At bust: 32 (36, 40½, 45)"/81 (91.5, 103, 114.5)cm

Length to armhole: 14 (15, 15, 15½)"/35.5 (38, 38, 39.5)cm

Snug fit

MATERIALS

- Approx total: 652 (815, 978, 114)yd/546 (745, 894, 1043)m silk lightweight yarn (yarn A) and
- 230 (230, 230, 230)yd/210 (210, 210, 210)m mohair and silk blend superfine yarn (yarn B)
- Circular needle: 4mm (size 6 U.S.) or size to obtain gauge, 24"/61cm long
- Knitting needles (optional): 4mm (size 6 U.S.) or size to obtain gauge

GAUGE

19 sts and 24 rows = 4"/10cm in Lace Stitch pattern.

21 sts and 28 rows = 4"/10cm in St st

Always take time to check your gauge.

PATTERN STITCHES

St st in rounds

Knit every round.

St st in rows

Row 1 (RS): Knit.

Row 2: Purl.

Repeat these 2 rows of pattern.

LACE PATTERN IN ROUNDS

(Multiple of 6 sts)

Round 1: K1, *yo, k1, k3tog, k1, yo, k1; repeat from * to last 5 sts, yo, k1, k3tog, k1, yo.

Round 2: K1, *p5, k1; repeat from * to last 5 sts, p5.

Repeat these 2 rounds for lace pattern.

LACE PATTERN IN ROWS

(Multiple of 6 sts, plus 2)

Row 1 (RS): K1, *yo, k1, k3tog, k1, yo, k1; repeat from * to last st, k1.

Row 2: K1, *p1, k5; repeat from * to last st, k1.

Repeat these 2 rows for lace pattern.

INSTRUCTIONS

LOWER BODY

Note: This piece is worked in rounds on a circular needle starting at the bottom and working upward to armholes.

With yarn A, cast on 156 (180, 204, 228) sts. Join work and mark beginning of rounds. Work Lace Pattern in rounds for 2¼" /5.5cm.

Waist shaping

Next row: K78 (90, 102, 114) sts, place marker on needle, k78 (90, 102, 114) sts. Beginning and center markers now indicate side "seams" of piece. Work 3 more rounds of St st.

Decrease Round: K1, k2tog, k to 3 sts before marker, SSK, k2, k2tog, k to last 3 sts before marker, SSK, k1, slipping each marker (4 sts decreased).

Continue in St st in rounds and repeat Decrease Round every fifth round 3 times more.

Schematic measurements:
16 (18, 20¼, 22½)"/40.5 (45.5, 51.5, 57)cm

14 (15, 15, 15½)"/35.5 (38, 38, 39.5)cm

8 (8¼, 8¼, 8½)"/20.5 (21, 21, 21.5)cm

2 (3, 4½, 6)"/5 (7.5, 11.5, 15)cm

8"/20cm

16¾ (16¾, 18, 18)"/42.5 (42.5, 45.5, 45.5)cm

7¾ (8¼, 8½, 9)"/19.5 (21, 21.5, 23)cm

Work even in St st on remaining 140 (164, 188, 212) sts until piece measures 7½ (8, 8, 8½)"/19 (20, 20, 21.5)cm from beginning.

Increase Round: K2, M1, k to 2 sts before marker, M1, k4, M1, k to last 2 sts, M1, k2 (4 sts increased).

Continue in Stockinette St and repeat Increase Round every fifth round 3 times more.

Work even in St st on 156 (180, 204, 228) sts until piece measures 14 (15, 15, 15½)"/35.5 (38, 38, 39.5) cm from beginning.

Divide for armholes

Transfer the last completed 78 (90, 102, 114) sts between markers onto a holder for the front.

BACK

Change to straight needles if desired to work on back sts as follows:

Armhole shaping

Working St st in rows, bind off 6 sts at beginning of next 2 rows. Decrease 1 st at each end of every other row 3 times. Work even on remaining 60 (72, 84, 96) sts until armholes measure 7¼ (8, 8, 8¼)"/19.5 (20, 20, 21)cm, ending with a purl row.

Neck shaping

Next row: K12 (18, 24, 30) sts, attach another ball of yarn and with this new yarn, bind off center 36 sts. K remaining 12 (18, 24, 30) sts. Work each side separately with its own yarn and work as follows: At each neck edge decrease 1 st every row twice. At each arm edge, bind off remaining 10 (16, 22, 28) sts.

FRONT

Transfer the 78 (90, 102, 112) front stitches from holder onto needle, using straight needles if desired. With right side of work facing you, join A at beginning of row.

Armhole shaping

Working St st in rows, bind off 6 sts at beginning of next 2 rows. Decrease 1 st at each end of next row, then every other row twice more; purl 1 row after last decrease row—60 (72, 84, 96) sts remain.

Neckline trim

Note: As you change from one yarn to the next yarn for working the trim section, be sure to wrap the yarns, bringing the new yarn up from under the previously used yarn to twist them and prevent holes in your work.

Row 1 (RS): With A, k26 (32, 38, 44) sts; drop A and attach B; with B, k8; drop B and attach a new ball of A; with new A, k remaining 26 (32, 38, 44) sts.

Work each section with its own separate yarn, remembering to twist yarns as you change from one to the next.

Row 2: With A, p25 (31, 37, 43); drop A and pick up B; with B, p10; drop B and pick up A; with A, p25 (31, 37, 43).

Row 3: With A, k24 (30, 36, 42); with B, k12; with A, k24 (30, 36, 42).

Row 4: With A, p23 (29, 35, 41); with B, p14; with A, p23 (29, 35, 41).

Row 5: With A, k22 (28, 34, 40); with B, k16; with A, k22 (28, 34, 40).

Row 6: With A, p21 (27, 33, 39); with B, p18, with A, p21 (27, 33, 39).

Row 7: With A, k20 (26, 32, 38); with B, k20; with A, k20 (26, 32, 38).

Row 8: With A, p19 (25, 31, 37); with B, p22; with A, p19 (25, 31, 37).

Row 9: With A, k18 (24, 30, 36); with B, k24; with A, k18 (24, 30, 36).

Row 10: With A, p17 (23, 29, 35); with B, p26; with A, p17 (23, 29, 35).

Row 11: With A, k16 (22, 28, 34); with B, k28; with A, k16 (22, 28, 34).

Row 12: With A, p15 (21, 27, 33); with B, p30; with A, p15 (21, 27, 33).

Row 13: With A, k14 (20, 26, 32); with B, establish Lace Pattern in rows as follows:

K1, *yo, k1, k3tog, k1, yo, k1; repeat from * 4 times more, k1; with A, k14 (20, 26, 32).

Row 14: With A, p13 (19, 25, 31); with B, k2, * p1, k5; repeat from * 4 times more, p1, k1; with A, p13 (19, 25, 31).

Row 15: With A, k12 (18, 24, 30); with B, k3, *yo, k1, k3tog, k1, yo, k1; repeat from * 4 times more, k3; with A, k12 (18, 25, 30).

Row 16: With A, p11 (17, 23, 29); with B, k4, *p1, k5; repeat from * 4 times, p1, k3; with A, p11 (17, 23, 29).

Row 17: With A, k10 (16, 22, 28); with B, yo, *k3tog, k1, yo, l1, yo, k1; repeat from * 5 more times, k3tog, yo; with A, k10 (16, 22, 28).

Row 18: With A, p10 (16, 22, 28); with B, *p5, k1; repeat from * 5 more times, p4; with A, p10 (16, 22, 28).

Rows 19 through 22: Repeat Rows 17 and 18 twice more.

Row 23: With A, k10 (16, 22, 28); with B, loosely bind off all 40 sts of trim section; with A, k10 (16, 22, 28).

SHOULDERS

Work each side separately with its own ball of A, continuing in St st until armholes measure 8 (8¼, 8¼, 8½)"/20.5 (21, 21, 21.5)cm. Bind off all remaining sts on each side.

SLEEVES

Make 2.

With yarn A and straight needles if desired, cast on 80 (80, 86, 86) sts. Work in Lace Pattern in rows for 12 rows.

Cap shaping

Working in St st in rows for remainder of sleeve, bind off 6 sts at beginning of next 2 rows. Decrease 1 st at each end of every other row 3 times—62 (62, 68, 68) sts.

Work even for 4 rows. Then decrease 1 st at each end of every row 8 (2, 6, 4) times, then decrease 1 st at each end every other row 7 (12, 11, 13) times—32 (34, 34, 34) sts. Bind off 3 (4, 4, 4) sts at beginning of next 2 rows, then bind off 2 sts at beginning of next 4 rows. Bind off remaining sts.

FINISHING

With right sides together, sew front to back along shoulder seams. Sew underarm seam of each sleeve. With right sides together, pin a sleeve to one armhole, matching center top of cap to shoulder seam and sleeve seam to center of body armhole; sew sleeve in place. Repeat for other sleeve.

With crochet hook and yarn A, work a row of single crochet (sc) around neck edge, omitting neckline trim section on front and spacing sts to keep edge smooth and flat.

Weave in yarn ends.

This project was knit with:

4 (5, 6, 7) skeins of Artyarns Regal Silk, 100% silk lightweight yarn, 1.8oz/50g = 163yd/149m per skein, color #223, pale yellow (yarn A), *and*

1 skein Artyarns Silk Mohair, 70% mohair/30% silk blend superfine yarn, 9oz/25g = 230yd/210m per skein, color #223, pale yellow (yarn B).

Diagonals in Flight

EXPERIENCE LEVEL

Intermediate

SIZES

X-Small (Small, Medium, Large)

The front bands of this cardigan are knitted on the diagonal, and fall in place nicely because the diagonal garter stitch gauge is equivalent to that of the stockinette lace body stitch. It's meant to be worn loosely over garments, so the pattern allows plenty of ease.

Continued ➜

FINISHED MEASUREMENTS

Bust: About 36 (40, 44)"/92.5 (101.5, 111.5)cm

Total Length: 21½ (23, 25)"/54.5 (58.5, 63.5)cm

Loose fit (about 4"/10cm ease)

MATERIALS

- Approx total: 1040 (1040, 1300)yd/952 (952, 1190)m silk and mohair/silk blend medium weight 2-strand yarn
- Circular needles: 5mm (size 8 U.S.) *or size to obtain gauge*, at least 24"/61 cm long
- Stitch marker
- Stitch holder
- Buttons with shanks, about ½" /1.3mm in diameter and small seed beads
- Tapestry needle for finishing
- Sewing needle and matching thread

GAUGE

16 sts and 20 rows = 4"/10cm in Lace Pattern

Always take time to check your gauge.

PATTERN STITCHES

GARTER STITCH

Knit every row.

LEFT-LEANING LACE PATTERN
(multiple of 5 sts)

Note: When working odd-numbered rows, k across all extra stitches at the end of row when there are fewer than 5 sts and a full Lace Pattern repeat cannot be worked.

Row 1: *Yo, SKP, k3; repeat from * across.

Row 2 and all even-numbered rows: Purl across.

Row 3: K1, *yo, SKP, k3; repeat from * across, k any extra sts at end to last st (see note above) k1.

Row 5: K2, *yo, SKP, k3; repeat from * across k any extra sts to last st, k1.

Row 7: K3, *yo, SKP, k3; repeat from * across, k any extra sts at end to last st, k1.

Row 9: K4, *yo, SKP, k3; repeat from * across k any extra sts at end to last st, k1.

Row 10: Purl across.

Repeat Rows 1 through 10 for pattern.

RIGHT-LEANING LACE PATTERN
(multiple of 5 sts)

Note: When working odd-numbered rows, p across all extra stitches at the end of row when there are fewer than 5 sts and a full Lace Pattern repeat cannot be worked.

Row 1: *Yo, p2tog, p3; repeat from * across, p any extra sts at end to last st (see note above), k1.

Row 2 and all even-numbered rows: Knit across.

Row 3: P1, *yo, p2tog, p3; repeat from * across, p any extra sts to last st, k1.

Row 5: P2, *yo, p2tog, p3; repeat from * across, p any sts to last st, k1.

Row 7: P3, *yo, p2tog, p3; repeat from * across, p any extra sts to last st, k1.

Row 9: P4, *yo, p2tog, p3; repeat from * across, p any extra sts to last st, k1.

Row 10: Knit across.

Repeat Rows 1 through 10 for pattern.

RIGHT/LEFT LACE PATTERN
(multiple of 10 sts, plus 2 selvage sts)

Row 1: K1 (selvage), *k3, k2tog, yo; repeat from * to center marker, slip marker, **yo (working these meeting yo's, at center, by wrapping yarn twice around needle—once on each side of market), SKP, k3; repeat from ** across to last st, k1 (selvage).

Row 2: K1, purl across, working inc 1 into double wrap of center yo (placing one st on each side of marker to maintain stitch count) to last st, k1.

Row 3: K3, k2tog, yo, *k3, k2tog, yo; repeat from * to last st before center marker, k1, slip marker, k1, **yo, SKP, k3; repeat from ** across, ending yo, SKP, k3.

Row 4: K1, purl across to last st, k1.

Row 5: K2, k2tog, yo, *k3, k2tog, yo; repeat from * to last 2 sts before marker, k2, slip marker, k2, **yo, SKP, k3; repeat from ** across, ending yo, SKP, k2.

Row 6: K1, purl across to last st, k1.

Row 7: K1, k2tog, yo, *k3, k2tog, yo; repeat from * to last 3 sts before marker, k3, slip marker, k3, **yo, SKP, k3; repeat from ** across, ending yo, SKP, k1.

Row 8: K1, purl across to last st, k1.

Row 9: K2tog, yo, *k3, k2tog, yo; repeat from * to 4 sts before marker, k4, slip marker, k4, **yo, SKP, k3; repeat from ** across, ending k2tog.

Row 10: K1, purl across to last st, k1.

Repeat Rows 1 through 10 for pattern.

INSTRUCTIONS

RIGHT FRONT

Cast on 36 (41, 46) sts. Cut yarn. Slide sts to other end of circular needle and attach yarn at other end of cast-on row, ready to work. Work back and forth in rows on circular needles.

Begin by working short rows as follows to establish diagonal front band:

Row 1: Inc 1, k1, turn; sl 1, k2.

Row 2: Inc 1, k3, turn; sl 1, k4.

Row 3: Inc 1, k5, turn; sl 1, k6—39 (44, 49) sts on needle.

Now work button border across all sts on needle as follows:

Row 4 (RS): Inc 1, k5, SSK, k across to end.

Row 5 (WS): K across to end.

Repeat Rows 4 and 5 once more.

Continue front band and begin Lace Pattern as follows:

Row 1 (RS): Inc 1, k6, SSK (front band sts), work Left-leaning Lace Pattern to end.

Row 2 (WS): K1, p to last 9 sts, k9.

Repeat these 2 rows until piece measures 13 (13½, 15)"/33 (34.5, 38)cm.

Armhole shaping

Starting at arm edge and maintaining continuity of pattern as established, bind off 4 sts once, then at same edge bind off 3 sts every other row once. Decrease 1 st at same edge every other row 3 times—29 (34, 39) sts.

Work even in pattern until piece measures 18 (18½, 20)"/45.5 (47, 50.5)cm, ending with a WS row.

V-neck shaping

Row 1: Starting at front neck edge, K8, SSK, work Lace Pattern (repeating directions for previous row) to end, turn; k1, p back to last 9 sts, k9 (note that front band has moved over by one stitch).

Rows 2 and 3: Repeat row 1.

Row 4 (short row): K8, turn; sl 1, k7.

Repeat Rows 1-4 3 times more—17 (22, 27) sts.

Shoulder shaping

Work band sts and decrease as follows for shoulder shaping:

Row 1: SKP, k8, turn; sl 1, k to end.

Repeat Row 1 until 10 sts remain.

Next row: SKP, k6, SSK, turn; sl 1, k to end.

Following row: SKP, k4, SSK, turn; sl 1, k to end.

Next row: SKP, k2, SSK, turn; sl 1, k to end.

Following row: SKP, SSK, turn; SKP.

Cut yarn and fasten off.

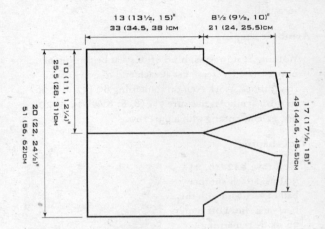

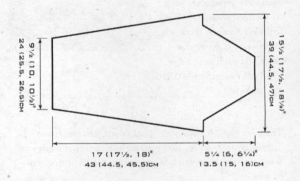

LEFT FRONT

Cast on 36 (41, 46) sts. Work back and forth in rows on circular needles.

Begin by working short rows as follows to establish diagonal front band.

Row 1: Inc 1, k1, turn; sl 1, k2.

Row 2: Inc 1, k3, turn; sl 1, k4.

Row 3: Inc 1, k5, turn; sl 1, k6—39 (44, 49) sts on needle.

Row 4 (WS): Inc 1, k5, SSK, purl across to last st, k1.

Row 5: K1, p to last 9 sts, k9 (band sts).

Repeat Rows 4 and 5 once more.

Continue front band and begin Right-leaning Lace Pattern as follows:

Row 1 (WS): Inc 1, k6, SSK (front band), work Right-leaning Lace Pattern to last st, k1.

Row 2 (RS): K across

Repeat these 2 rows until piece measures same length as Right Front to armhole.

Armhole shaping

Starting at arm edge and maintaining continuity of pattern as established, bind off 4 sts once, then at same edge bind off 3 sts every other row once. Decrease 1 st at sane edge every other row 3 times—29 (34, 39) sts.

Work even in pattern until piece measures same as Right Front to V-neck, ending with a RS row.

V-neck shaping

Row 1: K8, SSK, work Lace Pattern (repeating directions for previous row) to end, turn; k back to end (front band has moved over by one stitch).

Rows 2 and 3: Repeat Row 1.

Row 4 (short row): K8, turn; sl 1, k7.

Repeat these 4 rows 3 times more—17 (22, 27) sts.

Shoulder shaping

Work same as for Right Front shoulder.

BACK

Cast 72 (82, 92) sts onto circular needles. Work back and forth in rows on circular needles.

Knit 4 rows, placing a marker on needle at center of last row, 36 (41, 46) sts in from ends.

Work Right/Left Lace Pattern until piece measures same as fronts to armhole.

Armhole shaping

Keeping continuity of pattern as established, bind off 4 sts at beginning of next 2 rows, then bind off 3 sts at beginning of following 2 rows. Decrease 1 st at each end of every other row 3 times—52 (62, 72) sts.

Work even in Right/Left Lace Pattern, continuing to work a selvage st at each end, as before, until piece measures 20 (21½, 23½)"/51 (54.5, 59.5)cm.

Knit 8 rows. Bind off all sts for shoulders and back neck.

SLEEVES

Make 2.

Starting at wrist edge, cast on 36 (36, 42) sts.

Work back and forth on circular needles.

Knit 6 rows, placing a marker on needle at center of row, 18 (18, 21) sts in from ends.

Establish Right/Left Lace Pattern as follows:

Row 1: K1 (1,4), k2tog, yo, *k3, k2tog; repeat from * to center marker, slip marker, **yo (working these meeting yo's, at center, by wrapping yarn twice around needle—once on each side of marker), SKP, k3; repeat from ** across, ending yo, SKP, k1 (1, 4). First and last k sts are the selvage sts.

Row 2: K1, purl across, working inc 1 into double wrap of center yo (placing one st on each side of marker to maintain stitch count) to last st, k1.

Continue working pattern as established, with eyelets shifting outward and a new eyelet pattern starting after every 10 rows as for the back, and at the same time, increase 1 st at each end of every 4th row 15 (0, 0), every 5th row 0 (12, 6), and every 6th row 0 (4, 9) times, working added sts in pattern. Then work even on 66 (68, 72) sts until sleeve measures 17 (18, 18½)"/43 (45.5, 47)cm.

Cap shaping

Keeping continuity of pattern, bind off 4 sts at beginning of next 2 rows, then bind off 3 sts at beginning of next 2 rows. Decrease 1 st at each end every other row 3 times—46 (48, 52) sts. Work even in pattern for 4 rows. Then decrease 1 st each end every row 6 times, then 1 st each end every other row 5 times—24 (26, 30) sts. Work even until cap measures 5¼ (6, 6½)"/13.5 (15, 16)cm. Bind off 4 sts at beginning of next 2 rows, then bind off 2 sts at beginning of next 2 rows. Bind off remaining 12 (14, 18) sts.

FINISHING

Block all pieces to appropriate size. With right sides of fronts and back together, sew shoulder and side seams, aligning lace panels at seams. Sew underarm seam of each sleeve. Sew a sleeve to each armhole, matching center top of cap to shoulder seam and matching sleeve seam to side seam at underarm.

BUTTONED VERSION (GREEN CARDIGAN)

On top of front band on Right Front, gently push stitches aside with a knitting needle up to make a buttonhole. Repeat at corresponding position on Left Front. With sewing thread, stitch around opening to make a buttonhole. Link the two buttons together making several long stitches between them with sewing thread and stringing small seed beads so they are about 1"/2.5cm apart; to form a firm joining between the buttons. To close sweater at neckline, slip a button through each buttonhole.

This project was knit with:

4 (4, 5) skeins of Art yarns Silk Rhapsody, 100% silk and 70% mohair/30% silk medium-weight 2-strand yarn, 3½oz/100g = 260yd/238m per skein, color #145, variegated pale blue (blue version) and color #2234, variegated pale green (green version).

—From *Lacy Little Knits*

KNITTING WITH SPECIALTY YARNS

Iris Schreier & Laurie J. Kimmelstiel

Basics

Walk into any yarn shop these days and you'll be mesmerized by all the beautiful and unique fibers on display. To keep pace with the booming popularity of hand knitting, yarns are becoming more spectacular every season. But this question always arises: What can you make with these yarns? We've faced the same challenge ourselves, and we want to share some of our solutions for achieving knitting nirvana. We'll point out techniques to create one-of-a-kind knitted accessories worthy of the most luxurious fibers.

Enter our knitting heaven and explore the world of glorious fiber. We have found some of the most exotic yarns for the designs in our book. With origins from Peru to the Far East, these yarns are more accessible than ever, whether at your local yarn purveyor or through one of the many online fiber boutiques.

It never hurts to review the basic qualities of yarns, no matter how fancy or plain. Characteristics such as fiber weight, elasticity and drape, luster, hand and texture, color, and fiber type all play a role in determining what sort of pattern works best with which yarn.

Weight refers to the thickness as well as the weighted heft of the yarn. It's usually determined by calculating the yardage (or the weighed amount) per skein, ball, or hank. For example, a thin or fine yarn generally includes more yards in a standard ball than does a thick or heavy yarn. You'll want to use a fine yarn in projects that call for more detailed work, because it will show off the design better. For the quickest, easiest projects, knit heavy weight yarn with larger needles. Some of the fibers used in this book, such as lattice, ribbon, and sequin yarns, aren't categorized by their weight at all. The term can seem a bit vague, so your best indicator of a yarn's weight is in the relationship of the weighed amount to its yardage.

The stretchiness of the fiber is called *elasticity*. Pull on the strand to see if it becomes longer and, more important, whether it bounces back. Incredibly, totally inelastic yarns, such as ribbon and cotton, often knit up into fabrics that are very elastic, so stretchiness can't be determined solely by examining the unknitted fiber; the weave of the knitted piece will impart a certain degree of elasticity. If a knitted yarn has *give*, another term for elasticity, it's usually more "forgiving" and therefore easier for a beginner knitter, who might have a tendency to tense up when first learning to knit. The fibers that lack elasticity are better suited to those more experienced in the craft.

Luster is the brightness of yarn as it shines with reflected light. Yarn luster comes in all varieties ranging from bright to dull. Some fibers are so lustrous they have a kind of "wet" look, while others are matte, with a smooth finish that has limited shine, or none at all. Use matte yarn for a dressy look. The Trellis Stole was knitted both ways so you can see what a difference luster makes. Another option is to add interest to a project by mixing yarns with different lustrous qualities.

Try knitting a large swatch in your pattern stitch and check the fabric to determine the *drape* of your fiber. How does it fall? Is it stiff or limp? Does it bunch up or hang down neatly on its own? Perhaps you need to knit the piece on larger or smaller needles. Changing the needle size—or even the needle type—can make all the difference between a piece that lies properly and one that hangs stiffly or awkwardly. Maybe you can add another yarn to improve how the fabric falls.

Check the *hand*—those appealing tactile qualities of texture, fineness, and durability—of the fiber. Some stiffer or coarser fibers are better suited for accessories, such as purses or vests, that won't come in direct contact with your skin. Other, softer fibers, such as cashmere and qiviut, are perfect right next to the body.

Texture can vary dramatically from smooth to loopy and everything in between—even within similar fiber categories. Is it coarse or soft to the touch? Flat yarns, such as ribbons, and others, like the carrier-thread yarns with extra fibers that jut out from them, can enhance whatever yarn they're combined with. In general, the more texture in the fiber, the larger the needles you'll need to guarantee that the yarn's unique characteristics aren't crushed or buried in the fabric.

Color variations depend on the methods used to dye the yarn as well as on the fiber itself. The same color can appear muted in one type of yarn and vivid in another. Variations in color between dye lots are not uncommon, so be sure to purchase a sufficient quantity in one dye lot before you begin a project. It's likely that you won't be able to buy more later, because many yarns go in and out of fashion as quickly as bellbottom pants.

Fiber type refers to the source of the yarn—specifically, whether the yarn is of protein, plant, or synthetic origin. Wool, silk, rayon, and other animal fibers and plat fibers, including cotton and linen, are all considered natural fibers. Synthetics include nylon (polyamide), acrylic, and polyester.

Wool varies in texture depending largely on the breed of the sheep, and we love merino wool, primarily because of its softness. Merino also has a beautiful luster and a good amount of elasticity, and, not surprisingly, it's a wonderful yarn for a beginner knitter.

By far the warmest, lightest, and most luxurious yarns for hand knitters are cashmere and qiviut (KIV-ee-uht). While cashmere comes from the soft, fine undercoat of the goat, qiviut is taken from the undercoat of the musk ox. Due to its incredibly soft hand, this type of yarn often looks best knitted in a textured pattern or in stitch types that are found in rib, seed stitch, or basket weave patterns that use both knit and purl stitches in the same row.

Mohair also comes from goats, while angora is plucked from rabbits. Both fibers are naturally fuzzy and provide incredible warmth despite their light weight. Mohair

Continued ➡

can almost always be knitted on needles larger than you would expect to use with yarns of similar size and weight. Both mohair and angora have a unique *loft* that spreads the fiber as it's knitted, and can produce very dense garments.

Silk, a filament extruded by silkworms of certain moths, is a lustrous fiber with good drape and little elasticity. While believed to be warmer than wool, silk can also produce sheer, cool fabrics suitable for all climates. Silk lends strength and character to yarn when it's spun together with other fibers. Many of the yarns used in this book are silk blends.

Rayon, a manufactured natural fiber that is often very shiny, is strong and has a beautiful drape. It's a component of several of the specialty yarns we've used here, including faux suede, sequin, and some of the ribbon types.

Many man-made fibers offer interesting textures and colors not readily found in natural fibers, including slub, chainette, eyelash, railroad, loop, tube, polka dot, plaited ribbon, metallic, and filigree yarns. We carefully chose these exotic yarns for many of the designs created for this book. Synthetics aren't necessarily of lesser quality—even among artificial fibers you'll find a range of grades, so choose them with care. Experiment. Some of these unusual yarns produce unexpected results. Some will create softer fabrics, others might offer a lighter drape, and, of course, these fibers offer the most unique and unusual opportunities for creative knitting.

Although the designs included in this section, if followed exactly, will ensure exciting and dramatic results, we urge you to consider them as starting points. Think about using other yarns and making modifications to the patterns as needed. Here are some tips to ensure a successful outcome.

If the design doesn't look right with the substitute yarn you've chosen, experiment by making small swatches with different stitch combinations. Put together unexpected color combinations—combine two different textured yarns in related colors. You'll be amazed at how different the knitted result looks from the two yarns that went into it. We knitted some of our projects in an alternate version so you could see just how versatile and rewarding using different yarns can be. We've also shown close-up photos of the individual strands of yarn used in every project to guide you in creating your own versions.

The incredible variations and selections of yarns now available are yours to enjoy and play with. But beware...as you knit these beautiful accessories, expect to get requests from friends and relatives for knitted gifts. Strangers may even offer to buy them from you! Most important, knit something you love and cherish it for years to come. And always be on the lookout for rare, unusual, and exotic luxury fibers to create accessories that will enhance any wardrobe.

Techniques

A few special techniques are used in this section. A novice knitter may want to try some of our more advanced projects, and we encourage it. The standard knitting techniques referred to here that may be unfamiliar to a beginner can be found in any good how-to-knit book.

Transferring to Double-Pointed Needles from Circular Needles

Count your stitches and divide that number more or less equally by three or four, according to the number of double-pointed needles (dpn) called for in the pattern. (Double-pointed needles are sold in sets of either four or five, depending on the manufacturer.) Knit that number of stitches from your circular needle onto the first double-pointed one. Knit the next group of stitches onto another double-pointed needle, and so on, until you've completely transferred the row.

Placing Markers on Double-Pointed Needles

Any markers placed at the end of double-pointed needles are sure to fall off. You have two choices: you can put point protectors on the tips of each end of the needles or move your stitches on the needles so that at least one stitch is on either side of a marker. To avoid confusion and to help remember which marker indicates the end of a row, consider using a larger or smaller marker here, or another color to help you differentiate.

Double-Knit Pattern

Double knitting as it's used in this book creates a reversible fabric with knit stitches facing out on both sides of the work. You'll knit on both sides at the same time, and the result is a two-layer fabric. You will always use two different-color yarns for the double-knitted projects in this book.

Colors A and B are always used together to cast on. Whenever AB is specified in the instructions, knit or purl with both strands together. Whenever A or B are specified separately, knit or purl with the individual strands.

Our double-knit patterns have been designed in such a way that after the first row you won't need to refer to any charts or patterns. After you've turned the work to start the next row, just knit the knit stitches and purl the purl stitches, using the same color strand that was used in the previous row as it now faces you. The most important thing to remember is that when knitting you should bring both strands to the back, and when purling bring both strands to the front.

Here's how to do this: Keep color B strand above color A strand so that you can more easily knit with color A and purl with color B. Hold both strands behind the work when knitting (photo 1) and hold them both in front of the work when purling, as shown in photo 2. Try to keep the strands from twisting while you maneuver them from front to back, knitting A and purling B separately.

Photo 1

Photo 2

If you've never used this technique before, practice with two identical yarns in two contrasting colors to create a swatch. Comments follow the sample instructions given here:

CO 12 sts with AB

Hold two strands together, one of each color (A and B)

Row 1: K1 AB, (k1 A, p1 B) 5 times, k1 AB Knit 1 with both AB in the first stitch. Alternate knitting 1 with A, and purling 1 with B, for a total of 5 times. Knit 1 with both AB in the last stitch, for a total of 12 sts.

Row 2: K1 AB, (k1 B, p1 A) 5 times, K1 AB

This row is the same as row 1, except now you'll knit with B and purl with A.

Repeat rows 1 and 2, and you'll see how you've created two separate layers of fabric at the same time. If the stitches appear uneven, use smaller needles than the ones specified in the pattern.

Ribbon Wrapping

Weave the ribbon instead of knitting with it, bringing it forward and in front of all knit stitches and sending it behind all purl stitches (photos 3 and 4). Make sure to stretch out the knitted work at the completion of each row to keep the ribbon from tightening the fabric.

Photo 3

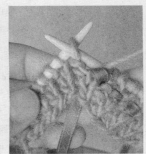
Photo 4

ABBREVIATIONS

beg—beginning

beg pat—beginning of pattern

BO—bind off

CO—cast on

cont—continue, continuing

dec—decrease

dpn—double-pointed needle(s)

dyo—drop wrap, or yarnover, that was added in previous row

foll—follow(s), following

inc—increase

k—knit

k1inc1—knit into front and back of same stitch, making two stitches out of one stitch

k2tog—knit two stitches together, making one stitch out of two stitches

p—purl

p1inc1—purl into front and back of same stitch, making two stitches out of one stitch

p2tog—purl two stitches together, making one stitch out of two stitches

pat—pattern

pm—place stitch marker

rem—remain, remaining

rep—repeat

RS—right side

s1—slip one stitch knitwise if following stitch is knit stitch, or purlwise if following stitch is purl stitch

skkp—slip one stitch knitwise, knit two stitches, pass slipped stitch over both knit stitches (decrease from three stitches to two stitches)

skp—slip one stitch knitwise, knit one stitch, pass slipped stitch over knit stitch (decreases from two stitches to one stitch)

ssk—slip one stitch knitwise, slip another stitch knitwise, knit through both slipped stitches (decreases from two stitches to one stitch)

spp—slip one stitch purlwise, purl one stitch, pass slipped stitch over purl stitch (decreases from two stitches to one stitch)

sppp—slip one stitch purlwise, purl two stitches, pass slipped stitch over both purl stitches (decreases from three stitches to two stitches)

st—stitch

sts—stitches

tog—together

WS—wrong side

yo—wrap yarn over needle, making an extra stitch, or yarnover

Winter Squares Scarf

design by Iris Schreier

SKILL LEVEL

Easy

Don't let this scarf's deep, rugged texture fool you; it's as soft and light as can be. The two yarns are subtly twisted together in the center, with both colors carried through from row to row. You won't need to cut the yarn until you've completed the scarf, saving you the work of weaving in a lot of ends. Best of all, the scarf is completely reversible.

FINISHED MEASUREMENTS

86 x 5"/218 x 13cm

MATERIALS

- **Approx total**: 260yd/238m cashmere or cashmere blend chunky weight yarn
- **Color A**: 130yd/119m in gray tweed
- **Color B**: 130yd/119m in natural
- **Knitting needles**: 8mm (size 11 U.S.) or size to obtain gauge

GAUGE

11 sts and 13 rows = 4"/10cm in Garter Stitch

Always take time to check your gauge.

INSTRUCTIONS

Note: The gray tweed squares are worked in Garter Stitch; the natural squares are worked in Seed Stitch. The two yarns are always twisted in the center of the scarf, in the same direction and on the same side. To avoid holes when switching colors, make sure to twist the yarns as specified in the instructions. For example, if A is in the front, twist it over and around B, bringing A from the front to the back. If A is in the back, twist it over and around B, bringing A from the back to the front.

With A, CO 14 sts.

FIRST PAIR OF SQUARES

Row 1: With A, k7. Do not cut; attach B, and with B, *k1, p1; work from & total of 3 times, k1.

Row 2: With B, *k1, p1; work from * total of 3 times, k1. With B in front, twist B over and around A. With A, k7.

Row 3: With A, k7. With A in back, twist A over and around B. With B, *k1, p1; work from & total of 3 times, k1.

Rows 4–9: Rep rows 2-3 three times.

Row 10: Repeat row 2.

Row 11: With A, k7. With A in back, twist A over and around B. With A, k7.

SECOND PAIR OF SQUARES

Row 12: With A, k7. With A in front, twist A over and around B. With B, *k1, p1; work from * total of 3 times, k1.

Row 13: With B, *k1, p1; work from * total of 3 times, k1. With B in back, twist B over and around A. With A, k7.

Row 14–19: Rep rows 12-13 three times.

Row 20: With A, k7. With A in front, twist A over and around B. With A, k7.

Rep 1st and 2nd pairs of squares (rows 2–20) until the scarf measures 86"/2.2m or desired length. With A, BO all sts. Cut yarn and weave ends.

This project was knit with:

2 skeins of Classic Elite's *Forbidden*, 100% cashmere, chunky weight, 1.8oz/50g = approx 65yd/59m per skein, color #60550 Marled Storm

2 skeins of Classic Elite's *Forbidden*, 100% cashmere, chunky weight, 1.8oz/50g = approx 65yd/59m per skein, color #10015 White

Black Tie Wrap

design by Laurie Kimmelstiel

SKILL LEVEL

Easy

I knitted this scarf while spending a few days at the Peters Valley Crafts Center in New Jersey, and it was a hit with potters as well as fiber artists, men and women alike. This triangular scarf looks most dramatic and interesting when worn in a way that shows off its open, wispy design. And although the yarns have very unusual textures, they rarely become knotted. Be sure to practice knitting with them before you begin the project itself.

FINISHED MEASUREMENTS

Yarn A: 43yd/39m confetti on carrier thread in black

Yarn B: 60yd/55m filigree yarn in black

Knitting needles: 12mm (size 17 U.S.), wood or bamboo recommended, *or size to obtain gauge*

GAUGE

6 sts and 7 rows = 4"/10cm in Garter Stitch

Always take time to check your gauge.

INSTRUCTIONS

Note: Yarns A and B are worked together throughout until the last 3 or 4 rows, when B is worked alone.

With A and B, CO 3 sts.

Row 1: K1inc1, k to end—4 sts.

Rep row 1, inc at beg of each row, until all of yarn A has been used. Secure A by knotting its end to B. Cont to rep row 1 with B alone for 3 or 4 rows. BO loosely and cut yarn. Weave in ends.

This project was knit with:

2 balls of Habu Textiles' *A-107 Feather Moire*, 83% polyester/17% nylon, 1oz/28g = approx 53yd/48m, color Black

1 ball of Habu Textiles' *A-28 Kasumi*, 100% polyester, 0.5oz/14g = approx 60yd/55m, color #10 Black

Trellis Stole

design by Iris Schreier

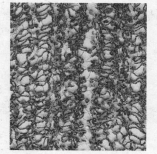

SKILL LEVEL

Easy

Can spring be far off when you're wearing a stole made to look like tiny flowers that peek through lacy latticework? You'll find that even though the finished piece looks elaborate, it's a quick and very easy project (it's knit lengthwise). The pattern is so versatile that you'll get decidedly different results depending on the yarns you choose. Combine the confetti yarn with cotton for a casual and sturdier version, or use a sparkly fiber for a positively slinky look.

FINISHED MEASUREMENTS

75 x 13½"/191 x 34.5cm

MATERIALS

Yarn A: Approx 250yd/229m multicolored confetti on carrier thread

Yarn B: Approx 250yd/229m light cotton or synthetic lightweight yarn in teal

Knitting needles: 9mm (size 13 U.S.) or size to obtain gauge; wood or bamboo circular 29"/74.5cm or longer needle recommended

GAUGE

5 sts and 14 rows = 4"/10cm with A and B tog in Pattern Stitch

Always take time to check your gauge.

INSTRUCTIONS

Note: The project is worked with both A and B together, as well as separately, throughout. Don't cut the yarns when alternating them—just carry them over from one row to the next. Rows 24 and 25 form the center of the symmetrical pattern.

With A and B tog, CO 100 sts.

Rows 1–3: With A and B tog, k.

Row 4: With B, *k1, yo; rep from & to last st, k1.

Row 5: With B, *k1, dyo; rep from * to last st, k1.

Rows 6–7: With A, k.

Rows 8–15: Rep rows 4-7 twice.

Continued ➤

Rows 16–17: With B, k.

Rows 18–19: With A, k.

Row 20: With A and B tog, *k1, yo; rep from * to last st, k1.

Row 21: With A and B tog, *k1, dyo; rep from * to last st, k1.

Rows 22–23: With B, k.

Row 24: With A, *k1, yo; rep from * to last st, k1.

Row 25: With A, *k1, dto; rep from * to last st, k1.

Rows 26–27: With B, k.

Row 28: With A and B tog, *k1, yo; rep from * to last st, k1.

Row 29: With A and B tog, *k1, dyo; rep from * to last st, k1.

Rows 30–31: With A, k.

Rows 32–33: With B, k.

Rows 34–35: With A, k.

Row 36: With B, *k1, yo; rep from * to last st, k1.

Row 37: With B, *k1, dyo; rep from * to last st, k1.

Rows 38–45: Rep rows 34–37 twice.

Rows 46–48: With A and B tog, k.

BO all sts loosely. Cut A and B and weave in ends.

This project was knit with:

4 balls Trendsetter's Flora, 76% viscose/24% polyamide confetti yarn, 1.8oz/50g = approx 70yd/64m per ball, color Fall Leaves #166

3 balls Trendsetter's Sunshine, 74% viscose/25% polyamide, lightweight yard, 1.8oz/50g = approx 95yd/86m per ball, color #51 Dark Teal

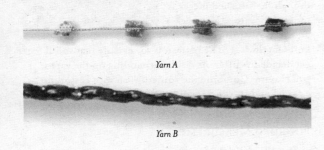

Yarn A

Yarn B

Romantic Ruffled Scarf

design by Laurie Kimmelstiel

SKILL LEVEL

Easy

Our frilly scarf is perfect for the knitter who wants to create something a bit exotic and still be able to complete a garment quickly and easily. This project has no complicated charts or confusing patterns to follow.

Simple Garter Stitch and an easy yarn-over design show off this exquisite scarf with distinctive curly ribbon trim. Try knitting it using contrasting colors or experiment with various ribbons to create your own special border. Put on this soft scarf over a suit jacket or do the unexpected—wear it with a sweater and jeans.

FINISHED MEASUREMENTS

67 x 5"/170 x 13cm, including trim

MATERIALS

- **Yarn A:** 370yd/338m mohair or mohair blend superfine weight yarn in pink

- Or 230yd/210m mohair or mohair blend lightweight yarn in pink

- **Yarn B:** 20yd/18m curly ribbon tape or ½"/1.5cm flat ribbon in gray

- Knitting needles: 5.5mm (size 9 U.S.) wood or bamboo needles *or size to obtain gauge*

GAUGE

18 sts and 20 rows = 4"/10cm in Garter Stitch
Always take time to check your gauge.

INSTRUCTIONS

Note: If you're knitting with superfine weight mohair, the project is worked with two strands throughout. For lightweight mohair, work it with a single strand.

With 1 or 2 strands of yarn A (see note), CO 24 sts.

Rows 1–2: K.

Row 4: *K1, yo; rep from * to last st, k1.

Row 5: *K1, dyo; rep from * to last st, k1.

Row 6: K.

Rep row 6 until the scraf measures 58"/147cm.

Rep rows 4–5 and then rows 1–2. Loosely BO all sts on last row. Cut A.

BOTTOM TRIM

With Yarn B pick up 21 sts evenly across one end of scarf. If using curly ribbon tape, k 3 rows, being careful that the needle doesn't pierce the ribbon.

If using flat ribbon, work as follows:

Rows 1–3: K.

Row 4: *K1, yo; rep from * to last st, k1.

Row 5: *K1, dyo; rep from & to last st, k1.

Row 6: K.

BO all sts. Rep at other end of scarf. Cut yarn and weave in ends.

This project was knit with:

2 balls of Habu Textiles' *A-32B Silk/Mohair*, 60% super kid mohair/40% silk, fingering weight, 0.5oz/14g = approx 185yd/169m per ball, color #32 Suo Pink

1 ball of Habu Textiles' *A-67 Fringe Tape*, 100% acetate, 1oz/28g = approx 20yd/18m, color $3 Gray

Mermaid's Tail Evening Bag

design by Laurie Kimmelstiel

SKILL LEVEL

Intermediate

The dangling strands of ribbon attached to the fishtail bottom of this delicate, shiny knitted purse will wriggle along as you move. We love the collaboration of stretchy knitted ribbon fabric and smooth glistening fringe. You'll find this roomy little handbag simple to make and fun to wear.

FINISHED MEASUREMENTS

7½ x 6½"/19 x 16.5cm, in Stockinette Stitch; width measured at base

MATERIALS

- 184yd/168, ¼"/6mm multicolored shiny ribbon

- *Knitting needles:* 3.5mm (size 4 U.S.) *or size to obtain gauge*

- Medium crochet hook

- Pins for fastening seams

- Tapestry needle for sewing seams

- Corder for twisting ribbon for purse strap or 2 dpns 3.5mm (size 4 U.S.) for I-cord strap method

GAUGE

19 sts and 27 rows = 4"/10cm in Stockinette Stitch
Always take time to check your gauge.

INSTRUCTIONS

Note: This purse is knitted from the top of one side down to the bottom, then back up to the top of the other side.

CO 28 sts.

Rows 1–5: K.

Row 6: K.

Row 7: P.

Rep rows 6–7 until piece measures 5¼"/15cm, ending with a p row.

INCREASE BOTTOM

Row 1: *K1inc1, k8; rep from * 2 more times, k1inc1—32 sts.

Row 2: P.

Row 3: *K1inc1, k9, k1inc1, k10, k1inc1, k9, k1inc1—36 sts.

Row 4: P.

Row 5: K1inc1, k10, *k1inc1, k11; rep from * once, k1inc1—40sts.

Rows 6–7: P.

Rows 8, 10, 12, 14: K.

Rows 9, 11, 13, 15: P.

Row 16: P.

DECREASE FOR BODY

Row 17: K2tog, k10, k2tog, k11, k2tog, k11, k2tog—36 sts

Row 18: P.

Row 19: K2tog, k9, k2tog, k9, k2tog, k10, k2tog—32 sts.

Row 20: P.

Row 21: *K2tog, k8; rep from * 2 more times, k2tog—28 sts.

Cont as foll:

Row 1: K.

Row 2: P.

Rep rows 1–2 until piece measures 13"/33cm, ending with a p row.

ENDING

Rows 1–5: K.

BO loosely. Cut yarn and weave in ends.

Gently press completed piece with a warm iron. Fold piece in half, WS tog, and pin. Thread tapestry needle with yarn; stitch piece together and turn inside out.

STRAP

The strap can be twisted with a corder or knitted into an I-cord.

If using a corder, cut 3 pieces of yarn, each approx 4½yd/4m long. Knot the 3 pieces 8"/20.5cm from each end. Follow the directions for the corder and twist the yarn until cord doubles onto itself. Cut 3 pieces of yarn, each 18"/46cm. Fold in half and slip through folded end of cord. Slip this yarn through its loop to secure to end of cord so that each end of cord now has 6 ribbons hanging from knots at each end. To secure the cord to the corners of the purse, pull the knotted end through the seamed edge of purse (strap will stay in place with knot on outside of seams). Rep with other end of strap on opposite edge of purse. Weave in all loose ends.

If making an I-cord, with dpn, leave an 8"/20.5cm tail and CO 2 sts. *K 1 row. Without turning your work, slip the sts back toward the other end of the needle. Pull the yarn snugly and begin knitting again. Repeat from * until cord is desired length. BO, making sure to leave an 8"/20.5cm tail of ribbon at end of cord. With crochet hook, slip this folded loop of yarn through end st of I-cord. Slip all ends of yarn (there will be 7 total, including tail attached to knot). Pull these down snugly to tighten and then knot once or twice to secure strap in place. With crochet hook, pull other end of I-cord through opposite side of purse and repeat from *. Trim ends to even lengths. Weave in all loose ends.

This project was knit with:

2 balls of Muench's *Venezia*, 93% rayon/7% nylon ribbon yarn, 1.8oz/50g = approx 92 yd/84m per ball, color #4 Green/brown/multi

—FROM *Exquisite Little Knits*

Ribbon Yarn

KNITTING WITH BEADS

Jane Davis

Getting Started

This section covers six basic techniques for knitting with beads and yarn, each presented with a number of projects using each technique. First, Beads Sewn to Knitwear features three ways to add embroidery and beadwork to finished garments. Then, Beads on the Yarn describes three methods of stringing beads onto the yarn and sliding them along the yarn as you knit. Finally, Pulling It All Together presents several projects that utilize the skills you have learned working through the projects in the first two sections by combining more than one technique in a single project.

I have written Knitting With Beads for the intermediate-to-advanced knitter who may or may not have experience with beads and beadwork. The knitting instructions assume knowledge of and experience with knitting, but the beadwork instructions should be understandable even if you've never worked with beads before. Even so, experienced beadworkers who knit should enjoy this book as well, since so many of the projects use large beads, a nice break from the tiny cylinder seed beads, 15s, and charlottes that are most commonly used.

Materials and Supplies

BEADS

Beads come in all sizes, shapes, and colors, and are manufactured from many materials. Those used for projects in Knitting With Beads, are made from glass, wood, clay, stone, pearl, or metal. Most projects use sizes 11, 8, 6, or 5 beads. The size 11 beads are for embroidery and beadwork, the size 8 beads can be strung onto sport weight and thinner yarn, and the size 5 and 6 beads can be strung onto worsted weight yarn. Even though beads are categorized by size, you will still find that some are larger or smaller within a size, depending on the manufacturer. Also, each bead is a little different from every other bead in its lot. (Generally speaking, Japanese beads have larger threading holes and are more uniform in size.) In bead embroidery, the size of the bead you use depends only on the look you want for the finished piece. But for the bead stringing techniques, either the size of the bead hole, or the outside diameter of the bead, will affect the finished outcome of your project. For bead netting, beaded bands, or fringes try to use the bead sizes suggested in the project's materials list. If you need to substitute, make a small swatch of the pattern first to see if the beadwork will fit nicely when added to your knitwear. For projects in Beads on the Yarn, string some beads onto the yarn first to make sure they will fit. (Some large beads can have surprisingly small holes.) It's also a good idea to knit a small swatch to see how the bead colors look worked up in the pattern, and to see if the bead is large enough to fill the space in the design.

I have listed specific bead sizes as often as possible. You may find beads like those pictured. However, in some projects you may not find nor wish to use the same beads that I used. This is your opportunity to create, and to cultivate the art of searching for that perfect bead which will express your taste.

Beads today come in many finishes, some of which are deceiving because they may appear one color, such as blue, in a bag or tube, but will look more purple or gray when placed next to other beads or with the yarn you have chosen. Many things can affect the finished appearance of a bead: the color of thread or yarn used to sew it on; the color of the beads around it; the density of beads on the fabric. It's very disappointing to spend hours on a project only to see at the end that one of the colors was too dull, or too bright, or just not right for its place in the garment. That's why it's important to make a test swatch of your project with the beads you've selected to make sure they look the way you want them to look in the finished project.

Beads are sold in many types of containers including small plastic bags (which may be reclosable), plastic tubes, loose hanks (which are usually 12 strands of beads on thin thread), or by the individual strand. If your beads don't come in reclosable containers, you can purchase reclosable bags or use empty plastic containers to store them.

When working with beads, you need a place to put them where they won't roll all over the table and get lost on the floor. A container that will corral the beads is an important tool for beadwork and there are many types available. The simplest, least expensive, and usually the most handy is a paper plate. Paper plates can be easily stacked for storage of a work (or many works) in progress. There are also plastic trays with separate compartments to keep bead colors organized and lids to make it easier to travel with a project you're working on.

The surface you choose to work on can also facilitate beading. There are several surfaces that beadworkers favor, such as a piece of suede, thin foam padding, or a velvet-lined board. Any of these will keep the beads from rolling and make nice surfaces for picking up the beads with a needle. You may want to try several, starting with what is on hand or easily obtainable, to find out which container and beading surface you like best.

The easiest way to pick up many beads is to have a pile of beads on your beading surface. Scoot the needle across the top of the pile so the beads slide onto the needle. Then, when the needle is full of beads, slide the beads onto the thread, counting them off by twos or fives. When you need to count a great number of beads, it helps to separate them on the yarn in groups of 100, keeping a 2- or 3-inch (5 or 7.6 cm) gap of yarn between each group. That way it's simple to count how many beads you've already strung.

THREAD

Several specific thread types may be used for beadwork. A nylon continuous multifilament thread is commonly used and is readily available in many colors and sizes. It is a good choice for projects in the first three sections of the book. Silk thread is also often used, though some worry about its longevity, and it tends to tangle easily. Another popular choice is two-ply, pre-waxed, synthetic thread. For large beads, I use a strong cotton crochet thread or quilting thread. Try to use thread thick enough so the beadwork is not too flimsy and the beads stay in place. If you are new to beading, I encourage you to experiment with your thread choices. If you are a quilter, try quilting thread; if you crochet with thread, try that for beadwork.

WAX

Quilters and beaders alike spend a lot of time conditioning their thread so it will tangle or knot less and be easier to use. Beeswax or a special thread conditioner are common supplies in beadwork. Some threads, such as silk and cotton, benefit greatly from conditioning. To wax thread, cut the desired length, then holding it firmly against the wax or conditioner, pull the thread between your thumb and the conditioner to the end of the thread. Repeat several times so the thread is coated on both sides; then pull the thread between your fingers several times to soften the wax and help the conditioner penetrate the thread. If you are using conditioner, this will also build up static electricity in the thread so the tail will stay away from the working thread, reducing knotting.

Continued ➜

Helpful Techniques

Many of the practices you have learned as a knitter will also be helpful in beadwork. There are also some techniques specific to knitting with beads that can make your work easier and the projects you produce more pleasing.

TENSION

Just as in knitting, tension plays a big role in beadwork. It takes practice and experimentation to achieve the proper tension. Completing some test swatches before beginning a project can be invaluable.

When embroidering on knitwear (see Bead Embroidery), you need to be careful not to pull stitches too tight or the knitting will lose its elasticity and the beads may not stay on the front of the knitting. Then again, beads sewn too loosely on knitwear are also a problem since the thread may show or the beads may move to the back of the knitting.

However, in beadwork (see Beaded Fringe and Beaded Applique) tension is relative. Sometimes you will want to pull all the stitches tight to make something that is sculptural, but most of the time you want your beadwork to be flexible, to fold and drape, like fabric. To achieve this effect, you must pull tight enough to get the beads to stay in place and to hide the thread, but maintain enough slack so the beadwork drapes. This is especially important for beadwork that will be attached to garments that need to drape. However, beadwork on an item such as the carpetbag will benefit from a tight stitch.

In all types of knitting with the beads pre-strung on the yarn, you need to find the proper tension so the beads stay on the front side of the knitting but don't hang low on loose strands of yarn. In knitting beads where the bead is brought in front of a slipped stitch (see Beads over Slip Stitch), you don't want to pull too tight or your knitting will be gathered along that row and the bead may slip through to the back. In Beaded Knitting, where groups of beads are draped between stitches, you need to knit tightly on either side of the beads, otherwise you will end up with a long draping strand of yarn not fully covered with beads. And finally, when doing the projects in Bead Knitting, you need to have very tight tension so your stitches hold the beads on the front of the work.

HANDLING THREADS IN BEADWORK

When we envision beadwork, we often see thousands of beads stitched together into glassy surfaces for purses and jewelry, or orderly beads worked in stitches such as peyote stitch or netting. In this type of beadwork, the goal is to have the beads organized in a specific pattern based on the thread's path through the beads. For maximum impact and sheer beauty, you will want as little of the thread to show as possible. Therefore, when weaving-in loose ends, beginning or ending a thread, always try to hide the thread in the beads, following the thread in the beads, following the thread path of the stitch pattern you are using. Never pass the thread over a bead, or group of beads. And never knot where the knot, or thread, will show on the finished work.

STITCHING BEADS TO KNITWEAR

When adding beads to finished knitwear, the stretch and openness of the fabric may seem to be an obstacle to getting those little beads to stay in place on the front of the garment while maintaining the fabric's elasticity. Here are two simple ways to make it easier:

1. When stitching small beads to knitted fabric, always try to stitch through a strand of yarn rather than around a knitted stitch. This way the beads are caught on the front side of the fabric and are less likely to slide around to the back of the work (see figure 1).

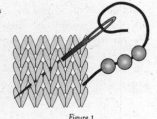

Figure 1

2. To preserve the horizontal stretch in a knitted fabric, either work up and down, stitching beads in place, or zigzag across the fabric. Don't make a straight horizontal line of stitching as this will eliminate the stretch in the fabric at that point (see figure 2).

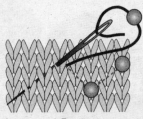

Figure 2

ADJUSTING BEADWORK

Beadwork is a very personal process which, like knitting, is affected directly by how tightly or loosely each beader works her threads. A strip of beadwork done by different beaders could end up different lengths. This is because each beader has an individual "tension" when pulling the thread. Because of this, it's important to check that your beadwork will fit the intended finished knitwear item; if it won't, adjust the beadwork by completing more or fewer rows so it will fit. The same is true for embroidery and fringes where your stitching may be further apart or closer together than mine, so you will need to make more or fewer repeats of a pattern.

WASHING KNITTED GARMENTS

Most of the projects in this book are made with hand-washable wool. I recommend spot cleaning or hand washing for most items, though a few can actually be machine washed and dried in the dryer. Treat them as you would any of your fine handmade garments.

Glossary

Backward crochet: A relatively new technique in which you work single crochet stitches toward the right, rather than the left. It creates a nice finish for knitted and crocheted garments.

Bead knitting: A technique for knitting with beads in which the beads are strung onto the yarn and then pushed into stitches as the stitches are made. Traditionally made in twisted stockinette stitch in which all stitches are twisted, though projects in this book use a form of the method of plaited stockinette stitch (developed by Alice Korach) in which only the right-side stitches are twisted.

Beaded knitting: A technique of knitting with beads in which the beads are strung onto the yarn and then slid between stitches as they are made. This technique was often used for knitted purses and bags 100 years or more ago, using small beads and thread.

Cast on: Unless otherwise stated, all projects are begun with the long tail cast on method.

Double decrease (centered): Work to 2 sts before st to be decreased around. Sl the next 2 sts knitwise as one. Knit the next st. Pass the 2 sl sts over the knit st as one.

False row: There are several ways to do this. For projects in this book, the simplest way is to make a crochet chain in a contrasting yarn and pull the number of sts needed for knitting through the back loops of the chain. Later, when you are ready to knot from the "cast on" end, you simply pull out the contrasting yarn chain while inserting the knitting needle into the loops of your knitting.

Fringe: A loose or tight grouping of dangles of beads.

Netting: A variation of peyote stitch in which a group of beads are strung, and then the needle is passed through one or more beads of the row before, creating an openwork pattern.

Peyote stitch: A beadwork stitch, also known as gourd stitch, in which beads are stitched together in an offset grid pattern, like brickwork set on end, with beads being added between beads of the previous row.

Plaited stockinette stitch: On the knit row, work as for "plk," described in Abbreviations. Purl stitches are worked in the usual manner.

Reverse stockinette stitch: Wrong side of stockinette stitch used as the right side.

Stop bead: A bead tied near the end of the thread to keep beads from sliding off the thread in the beginning stages of beadwork.

Beads Sewn to Knitwear

There are three distinct techniques in this section, bead embroidery, beaded fringe, and beadwork appliqué. Following are descriptions of each and, when applicable, some specific information that will help you as you make the projects. Each project is identified by a graphic that indicates which technique it employs.

Bead Embroidery

Embroidery is a vast field of needlework, which can vary from dots of detail across a surface, to densely beaded areas of color and texture. Using beads in place of colored thread and yarn adds a new texture to the surface design of the knitted garment.

ABBREVIATIONS

B#: Bead number. For beaded knitting, slide the specified number of beads up to the needle to be held in place between sts. For bead knitting, plk or purl the number of sts indicated, sliding a bead into each st as it is made.

beg—Begin/beginning.

Bp—Slide a bead into the p st.

Bplk—Slide a bead into the plk.

dec—Decrease.

dk—Double knitting, a size of yarn.

ea—Each.

inc—Increase I st by knitting into the back and the front of the st.

k—Knit.

k2tog—K 2 sts together as I.

M—Make/increase one st.

M1—For this increase, pick up the strand between sts and place it on the left needle. K into the back of the strand, making a new st.

M1a—Make/increase I st by knitting into the back of the strand after the current st.

M1b—Make/increase I st by knitting into the back of the strand before the current st.

M2—Make/increase 2 stitches, I on each side of stitch.

p—Purl.

p2tog—P 2 sts together as I.

plk—Plaited k st: insert the right needle into the back of the st on the left needle knitwise, and wind the yarn around the right needle clockwise. Complete the st as usual.

rem—Remaining.

rtx—Right cross. Drop 2 st off the left needle. With the left needle, pick up the first st dropped, then use the right needle to pick up the second st dropped and place it on the left needle. K each st.

SKP—Slip a st, purlwise, k a st, pass the slipped stitch over the knit stitch (to dec a st).

St(s)—Stitch(es)

st st—Stockinette st (k on the right side, p on the wrong side).

tog—Together.

WS—Wrong side.

yo—Yarn over.

Beaded Fringe

Beaded fringe is usually made up of long dangles of beads lined up in a row to swish, sway, and glitter as they move; but if you make them short or space them far apart you can achieve a different look altogether.

The fringe is made up of beaded strands called dangles. From two basic types of dangles, an amazing array of variations can be created by bead choice, by twisting strands of beads, and by varying the strand lengths and distance from each other.

One of the most common ways to make fringe is to string a length of beads, skip the last bead strung, and then pass the needle back up through the other beads. This creates one single hanging strand of beads with a bead at the end that holds them all in place. There are many ways to vary this basic technique. You can use different sizes of beads along the length of the strand. You can leave more than one bead at the bottom of the strand before you pass back up through the other beads. Or you can pass up through some beads, string some more beads and then pass back through some more beads, creating a thick and thin pattern in the strand.

The other type of fringe dangle is made with long, narrow loops of beads. This is the easiest and fastest type of fringe to make. Simply string the beads and then take a stitch in the fabric for each loop.

Making beaded fringe is easy to do, but there are a few techniques you need to know in order to make it perfectly.

1. Each dangle of beads in the fringe should be pulled tightly enough so that there aren't any gaps of bare thread showing at the top of the dangles, but not so tightly that the dangles are stiff and don't drape (unless that is the intention).

2. When pulling the thread back up through the beads, hold onto the "turn around bead(s)," (the bead, or group of beads, at the bottom of each dangle that you skip before you pass the needle back up the beads). Doing this allows you to pull the other beads snugly up to the fabric.

3. It's a good idea to make a little knot after each dangle to lock the finished beadwork in place. A simple half hitch (take a small stitch in the fabric, then pass through the loop before you pull the stitch right) is enough to hold the beads in place. Don't make a larger knot, just in case you need to correct errors.

Beadwork Applique

These projects differ from bead embroidery in that there is a large amount of beadwork to be done and then sewn to the knitwear, as opposed to simply sewing a few beads onto the garment. This technique can be used with a variety of beadwork stitches, and has the advantage that the

beadwork can, in some cases, be removable so the knitted piece can be washed separately. Be sure to review the supplies information on beads, thread, tension, and wax if you are new to beadwork.

Beads on the Yarn

The following three sections—Beads Over Slip Stitch, Beaded Knitting, and Bead Knitting—cover techniques that are most purely knitting with beads. Beads are strung onto the yarn and then slid in front of, between, or onto the stitches as they are made. The beads can be sprinkled across the surface, or slid into each stitch to form a color pattern or shape. One color of beads can be strung onto the yarn, or you can follow a color chart, carefully stringing a pattern to be knit into the fabric.

Beads Over Slip Stitch

In this technique, before beginning to knit, string beads onto the yarn you will be using. When working on the knit side, when you reach the stitch where the pattern shows a bead, bring the yarn to the front of your work, slide a bead down to the needle, slip the next stitch purlwise from the left needle to the right needle, then bring the yarn to the back of the work, and continue knitting. When working on the purl side, when you reach a stitch where the pattern shows a bead, bring the yarn to the back of the work (the knit side on this row), slide a bead down to the needle, slip the next stitch purlwise from the left needle to the right needle, then bring the yarn to the front of the work (the purl side of this row) and continue purling. This causes the bead to hang on a horizontal strand of yarn in front of the slipped stitch. You can also slide several beads in front of one slipped stitch to make a small loop of beads, or slide several beads in front of two or three slipped stitches in a row to make a horizontal stripe of beads. But with this stitch, you can't make a vertical line of beads since you would be slipping the same stitch again and again, and the garment would never get knitted. However, you can do it every other row, still affording a lot of possibilities, depending on the size of beads you use and your pattern.

Beaded Knitting

Hard to believe, but bead knitting and beaded knitting are not the same. In bead knitting you slide a bead into the stitches you knit. The beads are all on the front of the finished knitting, sitting on one strand of a specific stitch. In beaded knitting you slide one or more beads between stitches, traditionally in garter stitch, so that the beads hang at the back of the current row. Because every row of garter stitch is a knit row, you end up with beads on the front and the back of the finished knitting.

Beaded knitting is the technique used for swag purses popular in the 1920s. These bags were distinguished by vertical bands of beads tapering to points at the top of the bag. It is the easiest technique for working with pre-strung beads in knitting. Beads are strung onto the yarn before beginning, and then one or more beads are slid between stitches. To do this you simply knit to the place where the bead is indicated in the pattern, then slide a bead up to the needle and continue knitting. The bead will sit on the front of the knitting if you purl both stitches next to the bead and on the back of the knitting if you knit both stitches. You can slide one or more beads between stitches. The more beads, the wider the knitting will be at that point. As you do this, the strand of beads will hang in a graceful arc from the weight of the beads. Most antique purses were knit in garter stitch so there was a double thickness of beads throughout the purse since each row was a knit row allowing the beads to hang at the back of the current row. The Denim Tank Top, Denim Purse, and Cascading Diamonds Scarf are made using a variation of this technique.

Bead Knitting

Bead knitting is the process of pre-stringing beads onto the yarn before knitting, then pushing the beads, one at a time, into each stitch indicated on the pattern. (If you are using different colors of beads, you string them in reverse color sequence.) With this process, you can fill the whole surface (as in the knitted purses of the late 1800s and early 1900s), or you can use one color of beads, forming a pattern on the knitted fabric, which is a variation of plaited stockinette stitch.

On the charts for bead knitting using the plaited stockinette stitch variation, you may notice that some of the designs look as if the beads are in the wrong place, just a little off from where they should be. This is because the graph is in straight columns and rows, but when you create plaited knitting, the stitches (and therefore the beads) slant to the right in the knit row, and to the left in the purl row. So, when you knit your project you will see the beads fall into place as in the sample projects, rather than looking a little off as in the charts. If, when you are knitting you find that your beads are way off from where they should be, double check; you may be knitting the purl rows, and purling the knit rows!

About Beads on the Yarn

For these projects you will need a variety of different needles, including variously sized knitting needles, tapestry needles for sewing knitted seams, and beading needles to stitch beads together. Beading needles are longer and thinner than most sewing needles and come in sizes that loosely correspond to bead sizes, from size 10 to size 16. The trick is to find the largest needle possible, so it is easier to thread, but which will still fit through the smallest beads you are using for your project. (A size 16 needle is much smaller than a size 10. A size 10 needle will go through most size 11 beads and is the easiest to thread.)

When stringing beads onto yarn for pre-strung projects, you have several options. You can use a needle that has a large enough eye to thread the yarn, yet is thin enough to pass through the beads. If this is not possible, you can tie a thread over the yarn, so the yarn is folded in half, and thread a beading needle with the thread. This way you can string beads with smaller holes, carefully sliding them onto the folded yarn. Or you can use specialty needles. One such variety has points at both ends and a large collapsing opening in the middle, making it easy to thread the yarn and string beads (the points at both ends can be a hazard though).

Another specialty needle is a wire needle with a collapsible eye. These are made from wire folded in half and twisted, and come in different thickness. In the supply lists for the instructions I have indicated "needle to string the beads onto the yarn," rather than listing a specific needle, since which you choose will depend on your preference.

Working with beads strung onto the knitting yarn is a simple idea, but there are some basic techniques that make working with the beads and yarn easier.

Beads can be embroidered or sewn to a garment made of almost any kind of yarn, but there are limitations to the types of yarn that can be used for pre-strung projects with beads since the yarn must fit through the bead hole. The bead can slide loosely on the yarn, or fit snugly. Some yarns can be damaged by the friction of beads sliding along them, so it is wise to test a small piece of yarn by running the beads you want to use along it several times to see how well it stands up. Acceptable yarn will be relatively regular in diameter (no thick and thin hand-spun effects, no nubby boucle). It is difficult, but not impossible, to knit with beads on multiple strands of yarn since one strand will often lag behind, especially if the yarns vary in thickness or type. The easiest yarn to work with when knitting with beads is soft, resilient, and uniform. Beads will easily slide into place and stay where you want

Continued ➡

them. This type of yarn is also somewhat forgiving if your tension is a bit too tight or too loose.

After you have all your beads on the yarn, you need to be able to have enough bare yarn available to knit your project, yet still have enough beads close to your working area on the yarn to slide easily into the knitting as you work. Leave the number of beads needed for the first row up near the beginning of the yarn, and slide the rest of the beads about 4 feet (1 m) away. You will then need to move beads up for each row, and slide the rest of the beads further down the yarn.

To slide beads along yarn, always slide a small amount at a time, usually not more than 3 to 4 in (7 to 10 cm) of beads, so that the action of sliding the beads on the yarn abrades the yarn as little as possible. For these projects, I have placed all the beads for a specific section onto the yarn at once. Some yarns are more easily worn down by the action of sliding beads along them; if you need to substitute yarn, be sure to slide some beads along it first to see if it will hold up to the abrasion.

Since you are pulling out long amounts of yarn from your skein which are now covered with beads, you need to have a way to keep your yarn from getting into a tangled mess as you work. Many knitters wrap the bead-covered yarn back around the skein to keep it corralled. I don't like this technique since you are constantly unwrapping it again to move beads either toward your knitting to knit them into the piece, or away from your work so you have bare yarn to knit. I always place my skein of yarn in a basket and slide the beads down the yarn so the yarn and beads pile loosely there. This way all the elements are together so I can move them easily to wherever I want to work, the yarn doesn't get tangled, and I don't ever have to wind and unwind yarn to move beads.

Checking your gauge is extremely important when knitting a garment with an intended size, but less important when making something, such as a scarf, which can vary in width and length. When knitting with beads, there are times when gauge is crucial. Gauge is important in bead knitting where the goal of the technique is to fill each stitch with a bead color to create the intended design. If your gauge is too loose, the beads won't sit next to each other and the design will look scattered and sketchy, and you may have most of your beads sliding around to the back of the work. If your gauge is too tight, your stitches will change in size from where the beads are to where there are no beads in the knitting. (This is not an issue if all the stitches are filled with beads, such as in antique bead knitted purses.) The gauge is determined by a combination of your tension, the thickness of the yarn and knitting needles, and the size of the beads. It's important to make test swatches to get the proper tension and gauge so beads appropriately fill the space of the stitch. The same is true for stranding beads in front of your knitting (Beads Over Slip Stitch) where you want the bead or beads to fill the strand of yarn in front of the slipped stitch. In beaded knitting the gauge isn't as important to the bead part of the project, though it is still just as important to achieve the proper gauge for garment sizing, and to make your stitches tight enough on either side of the bead or beads so there isn't a gap of yarn.

Pulling It All Together

The creative possibilities for knitting with beads increase exponentially when you start combining techniques. For instance, you can pre-string beads and knit them into your garment, then add a fringe or embroider a pattern as well. The Black Diamond Hat has a touch of beaded knitting at its cuff and a group of fringe dangles at the tip. The Delicate Lace Scarf employs sparkly crystals and size 8 seed beads in beaded knit diamonds, and then adds a delicate pearl and crystal fringe. Finally, the Black Evening Camisole uses an all-over pattern of beaded knitting and ends with a bead netted fringe. Be sure to look back to the basic steps in the previous sections for helpful information on unfamiliar techniques.

Black-Diamond Hat

Simple and quick to make, this funky hat with its long tail is a great beginning project for knitting with beads. Make it red or green with white beads to wear during the holidays and you'll feel like one of Santa's elves.

SKILL LEVEL

Easy

SIZES

To fit 20- to 22-in (51- to 56-cm) circumference head

FINISHED KNITTED MEASUREMENTS

14 in (35.5 cm) circumference, unstretched

About 27 in (68 cm) long, from end to end

MATERIALS

- Approx. 270 yd (250 m) of worsted-weight yarn
- 108 hexagonal beads large enough to string onto the yarn
- 1 oz (28 gr) of size 11 seed beads
- ¼ oz (7 gr) of size 8 seed beads
- 1 large accent bead
- 12 size 5 or size 6 round beads
- 12 small drop beads
- Size 8 (5 mm) needles, or size to obtain gauge
- Needle to string beads onto yarn
- Size 11 beading needle
- Beading thread
- Tapestry needle for sewing seams together

GAUGE IN STOCKINETTE STITCH

18 sts = 4 in (10 cm)

26 rows = 4 in (10 cm)

INSTRUCTIONS

String the hexagonal beads onto the yarn. Cast on 98 sts. Follow the line-by-line instructions below, or the pattern in chart A, through Row 7.

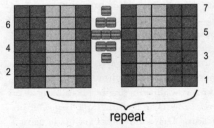

repeat

▢ Knit on the right side, purl on the wrong side

◼ Purl on the right side, knit on the wrong side

▦ Slide the number of beads indicated between stitches

Row 1: (p2, k2) repeat to the last 2 sts, p2.

Row 2: K the knit sts, and p the purl sts.

Row 3: (p2, k2, p1, B1, p1, k2) repeat to the last 2 sts, p2.

Row 4: (k2, p2, k1, B2, k1, p2) repeat to the last 2 sts, k2.

Row 5: (p2, k2, p1, B3, p1, k2) repeat to the last 2 sts, p2.

Row 6: (k2, p2, k1, B2, k1, p2) repeat to the last 2 sts, k2.

Row 7: (p2, k2, p1, B1, p1, k2) repeat to the last 2 sts, p2.

Repeat Row 2 until the hat is 7½ in (19 cm) long. Dec 1 st at each end every 4 rows, until there are 36 sts left. Cut the yarn to 24 in (61 cm) and weave through the rem sts. Sew side seam. Weave in ends.

BEADWORK TASSEL

Attach an 8-ft (2.4 m) length of beading thread to the point of the hat. String the large accent bead, then make a dangle by stringing the beads as shown in figure 1, passing back through all the beads except the last 3 beads strung. Pass the thread through the yarn at the point of the hat and then back through the large bead. Make about 12 dangles in the same way, and then anchor the thread in the tail of the hat and weave in the end.

This project was made using:

4 skeins of Berroco's Sensuwool, 80% wool/20% nylon, 1.75 oz (50g), 90 yd (83 m), color #6334 black.

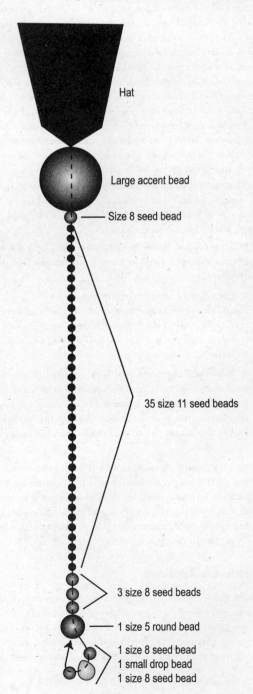

Hat

Large accent bead

Size 8 seed bead

35 size 11 seed beads

3 size 8 seed beads

1 size 5 round bead

1 size 8 seed bead
1 small drop bead
1 size 8 seed bead

Delicate Lace Scarf

Making this delicate piece is like learning to do two scarves in one lesson. The three-point beginning, with the pre-strung bead knitting and diamond pattern lace-work, switches over to a simple openwork pattern with an easy bead-embroidered fringe. Make it as shown or fashion a whole scarf with one or the other pattern.

SKILL LEVEL
Challenging

FINISHED KNITTED MEASUREMENTS
55 x 10 in (139.5 x 25.5 cm), including fringe

MATERIALS
- Approx. 250 yd (230 m) of lace weight yarn
- 175 clear Swarovski crystals, 4mm in size
- 225 pearl-toned size 8 seed beads
- Fringe beads: 4 gr size 11 clear seed beads, 4 gr size 8 white seed beads, 4 gr size 15 white seed beads, 18 Swarovski crystals, 4mm in size, 18 pearls, 6mm in size
- Size 4 (3.5 mm) needles or size to obtain gauge
- Needle to thread beads onto yarn
- Beading needle and thread for fringe

GAUGE IN STOCKINETTE STITCH
24 sts = 4 in (10 cm)

38 rows = 4 in (10 cm)

INSTRUCTIONS

Use the adjacent pre-stringing guide to string the beads onto the yarn before beginning the first half of the scarf.

Following chart A, knit the first point of the scarf. Break the yarn leaving a 4-in (10-cm) tail and leave the knitting on the needle. Repeat chart A, making another point and slide it next to the first, breaking the yarn and leaving a 4-in (10-cm) tail. Repeat once more, but don't break the yarn. You will have three points on one needle.

Follow row 10 on chart B, using the working yarn and knitting across all 3 points, joining them together.

Follow row 11 through 24 on chart C, working each

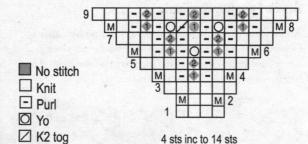

legend

- ■ No stitch
- □ Knit
- – Purl
- O Yo
- ╱ K2 tog
- ╲ SKP
- ① Slide one crystal between stitches
- ② Slide two crystals between stitches
- ① Slide one seed bead then purl the next two stitches tog
- ② Slide two seed beads between stitches
- ③ Slide three seed beads between stitches
- M Make one stitch

4 sts inc to 14 sts

side once and the center section 3 times.

Follow chart D for the lace pattern on the scarf, working rows 25 through 39, then repeating rows 26 through 39, then working rows 40 through 77, then repeating rows 64 through 77. Work row 78, then repeat rows 79 through 84 until the scarf measures approximately 52 in (132 cm) long. Work in st st for 5 rows. Bind off very loosely. Block, stretching with pins placed in edge holes to pull sides into scallops along sides of scarf.

Following the design pattern in figure 1, stitch the

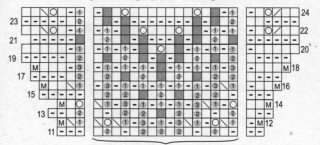

Repeat three times for each row

42 sts inc to 51 sts

DELICATE LACE SCARF PRE-STRINGING GUIDE

◇ – 4mm Swarovski Crystal
□ – Size 8 seed bead

String each column, top to bottom, beginning with the left column and working to the right.

34 ◇	4 ◇	2 ◇	1 ◇
1 □	6 □	9 □	9 □
4 ◇	4 ◇	2 ◇	6 □
1 □	5 □	10 □	6 □
4 ◇	4 ◇	2 ◇	1 □
1 □	5 □	10 □	6 □
4 ◇	4 ◇	1 ◇	4 □
1 □	3 □	8 □	4 □
4 ◇	4 ◇	2 ◇	3 □
2 □	6 □	8 □	5 ◇
4 ◇	4 ◇	2 ◇	2 □
2 □	6 □	8 □	5 ◇
4 ◇	4 ◇	2 ◇	2 □
2 □	6 □	8 □	5 ◇
	4 ◇	2 ◇	1 □
	9 □	8 □	
	3 ◇	9 □	
	9 □	1 ◇	
	3 ◇	9 □	
	9 □		
	3 ◇		
	9 □		
	2 ◇		
	8 □		
	2 ◇		
	8 □		

Individual point of scarf–string pattern three times.

2 ◇	
2 □	
3 ◇	
1 □	
10 ◇	

Chart D

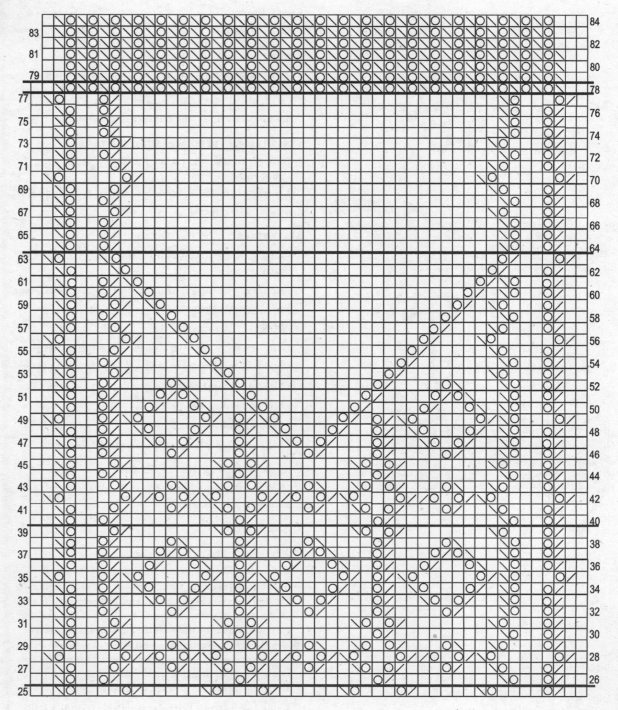

Continued ➤

fringe beads onto the ends of the scarf.

This project was made using:

I skein Crystal Palace's *Lace Yarn*, 100% wool, 3.5 oz (100 g), 848 yd (775 m), color #57 natural.

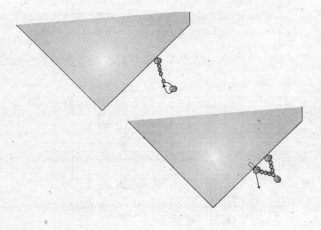

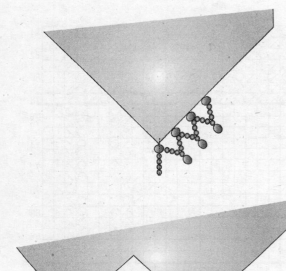

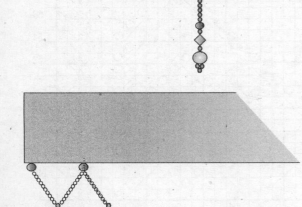

Black Evening Camisole

An opulent camisole for a fabulous evening out, this loose fitting top is embellished with scattered, smoky, silver-toned beads and a swaying fringe at the hem. The beads are easy to knit into the fabric.

SKILL LEVEL

Intermediate

SIZES

To fit chest sizes 34 in (36, 38, 40, 42 in), (86.5, 91.5, 96.5, 101.5, 106.5 cm). Instructions are for the smallest size, with larger sizes in parentheses. If there are no parentheses, the number is for all sizes.

FINISHED KNITTED MEASUREMENTS

Bust: 34 in (36, 38, 40, 42 in), (86.5, 91.5, 101.5, 106.5 cm)

Length, not including straps and fringe: 11½ in (29 cm)

Straps: 9 in (23 cm)

MATERIALS

- 4 (5, 5, 6, 6) 90 yd (83 m) skeins of worsted weight yarn
- Approx. 3 oz (85 gr) of size 6 steel-colored seed beads
- Approx. 3 oz (85 gr) of size 11 steel-colored seed beads
- Approx. 50 ½-in-long (1.3 cm) dagger drop beads
- Size 8 (5 mm) circular needle, or size to obtain gauge
- Size 7 (4.5 mm) needles
- Size 10 beading needle
- Beading thread
- Tapestry needle for sewing seams together

GAUGE IN STOCKINETTE STITCH

18 sts = 4 in (10 cm)

24 rows = 4 in (10 cm)

INSTRUCTIONS

BODY

Before beginning knitting, string 125 of the size 6 beads onto 1 skein of yarn. Use this skein for beginning the body. As you are knitting, and you get near the end of the skein of yarn, add more beads from that end, if you need them, or slide off the extra beads, if necessary. Before beginning the next skein of yarn, note how many beads you used on the first. That will be how many you need to string on the second skein before attaching it. Repeat for each skein as you work.

Using size 8 (5 mm) circular needle, cast on 154 (160, 172, 184, 190) sts. Join into a circle. Place marker. This marks the front just before the cable detail.

Row 1: (P1, B1, p1) repeat around.

Rows 2–5: Work in st st.

Row 6: P2, k2, p2, k8, p2, k2, p2, (p1, B1, p1, k4) repeat to last 2 sts in row, p1, B1, p1.

Rows 7–10: P the purl sts, k the knit sts of the first 20 sts, work in st st for the rem sts.

Row 11: P2, k2, p2, next 2 sts to holder in back, k2, k2 from holder, next 2 sts to holder in front, k2, k2 from holder, p2, k2, p2, k3, (p1, B1, p1, k4) repeat to last 5 sts, p1, B1, p1, k3.

Rows 12–15: Repeat rows 7–10.

Next 3 rows: Purl the p sts, knit the k sts.

Next row: (P1, B1, p1) repeat around. Bind off.

Front and Back

34 (36, 38, 40, 42)"

RIGHT STRAP

String 72 size 6 beads

Using size 7 (4.5 mm) needles, cast on 10 sts.

Row 1: Knit.

Row 2: K3, p4, k3.

Row 3: Knit.

Row 4: K2, B1, k1, p4, k1, B1, k2.

Row 5: K3, 2 sts to st holder in front, k2, k2 from st holder, k3.

Rows 6, 8 and 10: Repeat row 4.

Row 7 and 9: Knit.

Row 11: Repeat row 5.

Repeat row 6 through row 11 ten times (12 twisted cables)

Repeat row 4 and row 3 twice.

Repeat row 2.

Bind off.

LEFT STRAP

Work the same as for the right strap, except on row 5, move sts on st holder to the back of the work, instead of the front.

Sew straps to body, 4 in (10 cm) from center front and center back.

BEADED FRINGE

Follow the fringe pattern in figure 1, stitching the fringe to the beads knitted into the first row of the body.

The sample project was made using:

5 skeins of Sensuwool, 80% wool/20% nylon, 90 yd (83 m), 1.75 oz (50 gr) per skein, color #6334 black by Berroco.

—FROM *Knitting With Beads*

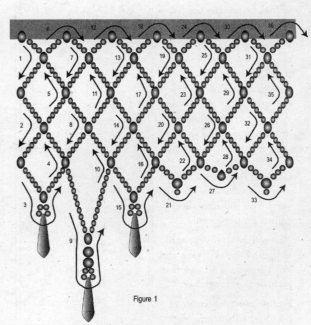

Figure 1

KNITTING SWEATERS FROM THE TOP DOWN

Getting Started

Why Knit from the Top Down?

Knitting a sweater from the top down is a logical progression: yoke follows neckline, hem follows body, and finally the sleeves and cuffs. After the neckline stitches are cast on, there's only one direction to go, and that's down to the hem.

Seams are eliminated, which leads to a better fit and more finished appearance. There's little to sew together (usually just the underarm holes), and there are no unsightly seam lines running up and down the sides of your garment.

Top-down knitting also allows for easier fitting and shaping. Because a top-down garment is made in one piece from the start, you can try it on at various stages to get the best fit possible, making adjustments along the way. Need your sleeves longer? Just keep knitting. Need them shorter? Just rip out and bind off. It's fun to see the garment evolve as you make it.

And finally, top-down knitting makes it easy to incorporate ornamentation and other details, such as stitch texture, beading, and shaping, into your design. By reducing or even eliminating fit and sizing issues, you can focus on the styling—the twists and turns of a ruffled cuff, or tapering the body to add a little zing.

This section is aimed primarily at beginners, so if you're already experienced with top-down knitting, you may want to skip ahead to the patterns. First off, the language of top-down knitting differs a little, so you'll want to get used to what might be new abbreviations for you in the list below.

The biggest difference between top-down construction and traditional piecemeal knitting is that the former is worked in one piece, whereas piecemeal sweaters are by definition completed piece by piece. Pullovers made using the top-down method are worked entirely in the round (ITR). For cardigans, the sleeves are worked (ITR) and the body is worked back and forth (B&F). Sound confusing? Read on.

Your knitting equipment will be different, too. To achieve the seamless perfection of a top-down sweater, circular needles (cn) and double-pointed needles (dpn) are the tools of the trade. Lastly, traditional (B&F) knitting is worked in rows (r), whereas top-down (ITR) knitting is worked in rounds (rnds).

Knitting (ITR) requires an ability to work with cn and dpn needles. You will also need to learn how to achieve the same stitch pattern while going from one method to the other. For example, to create a garter stitch working (B&F), you just knit every row, whereas when working (ITR), the same effect is achieved by alternating knit and purl rounds. Here are some of the more common similarities and differences:

Reading and Understanding Top-Down Patterns

Before you begin to cast on to make a top-down sweater, take a moment to read through these general pattern outlines—one for pullovers, one for cardigans. They will give you an overall idea of how a top-down sweater is formed. Pay particular attention to the round or row where you will be placing markers to denote the yoke increases. The proper placement of these markers is the key to forming the sleeve and body parts correctly. They'll eventually indicate where you divide the yoke once it's finished. For novices, I recommend starting with the simplest form: a pullover with a straight body (no shaping), long, tapered sleeves, and the neck design of your choice.

Basic Pullover Pattern

Collar (work ITR)

Start with a 16"/40cm circular needle (cn). Stitches are cast on starting at the outermost edge of the collar or neckline. Without twisting the cast-on stitches, connect the two sides and work as instructed.

Yoke (work ITR)

ABBREVIATIONS & KNITTING TERMINOLOGY

beg—beginning

B&F—back-and-forth

BO—bind off

CO—cast on

cont—continue

cn—circular needle

dec—decrease

dpn—double-pointed needle(s)

inc—increase

ITR—in-the-round

k—knit

KB—knit st with a bead

K2tog—knit two stitches together

MB—make a bobble

m1—increase by knitting into the back of a stitch and then knitting the stitch itself

p—purl

p2tog—purl two stitches together

pm—place marker

psso—pass slip st over

r—row

rnd—round

RS—right side

SH—stitch-holder

sl 1—slip a stitch

slm—slip marker

sn—straight needle

St.st.—stockinette stitch; (B&F) alternating knit and purl rows, (ITR) knit every rnd

t1—increase by pulling up a stitch from between the two stitches in the row below

WS—wrong side

YO—yarn over

To form the yoke, place markers (pm) at designated positions around the collar. These markers indicate where increases will be made to expand your yoke down and outward, creating the front and back of the sweater and the shoulders (which eventually form the sleeves). This first round is called the "set-up round." Set-up rounds (rnds) commonly read as follows.

Rnd 1: k__sts (front sts), pm,

k__sts (sleeve sts), pm,

k__sts (back sts), pm,

k__sts (sleeve sts), pm.

Recount your stitches and check marker placement.

The next row is the first increase row, where eight (8) sts will be added—2 on either side of each marker. Markers must be slipped (sl m) from one needle to the other as you work to note where increases have to be made as the yoke is worked around.

Rnd 1 (Inc rnd): m1, *k to 1 st before marker, m1, sl m, m1, repeat from ** around for each marker, end m1.

Rnd 3: Work across without any increases.

The yoke is formed by repeating Rnds 2 and 3 for as many times as the pattern specifics, until it reaches the underarm. Try on the sweater to make sure the yoke is long enough. While knitting the yoke, you'll need to switch to the longer cn's to accommodate the growing number of stitches.

Increases on either side of the markers can be accomplished in a number of ways, depending on how you want the garment to look.

Body (work ITR)

Divide up the stitches on various cn and/or stitch holders so the body can be worked separately from the two sleeves. You'll need several extra cn's for holding the sleeve stitches while you work the body stitches. A typical yoke division round reads as follows:

Using the main cn:

k__(front) sts, CO 1 st (underarm ease—the number of stitches varies by pattern), pm (to denote body side), CO 1 st (underarm ease), Slip__(left sleeve) sts on a 16"/40cm cn to be worked later, k__(back) sts, CO 1 st (underarm ease), pm (to denote body side), CO 1 st (underarm ease) place__(right sleeve) sts on 16"/40cm cn to be worked later.

The front and the back stitches should now be on the main cn needle along with the stitches and markers that you have added at the underarms. The explanations in the parentheses above are added only for your benefit—most patterns don't include them.

Now, work the body of the sweater (ITR). Try the sweater on before you join the front and back to make sure the fit is correct. Use several cns, so that you can stretch the garment over your head without dropping stitches.

The sweater body can be worked straight without further shaping. If you want to shape the body for a more form-fitting structure, you can decrease stitches along the side seams or create darts down the front and back.

Hem (work (ITR)

After you've knitted the body to the desired length, follow the pattern instructions to complete the hem or alter the design (see page 00). Try the sweater on once again to check length before you bind off (BO) loosely.

Sleeves (work ITR)

Each sleeve will be worked separately on either 16"/40cm cn or double-pointed needles (dpn). If you don't have enough stitches to make it comfortably around a cn, then use dpn (you should be able to use

Stitch Pattern	How to Achieve Basic Stitch Pattern		
	(B & F)		Top-Down (ITR)
Garter stitch	k all rows		k 1 rnd, p 1 rnd, repeat 2 rnds
Stockinette stitch	k 1 row, p 1 row—repeat those 2 rows		k all rnds

Continued →

around a cn, then use dpn (you should be able to use cn for at least 1"/2.5cm or so before switching to dpns). Most often you will end up using dpns anyway, as the number of stitches quickly diminishes when you make the underarm decreases required for a tapered sleeve. Sleeve instructions typically read as follows:

Using 16"/40cm cn, CO 1 st, pm, CO 1 st (at the underarm, for ease, but the number varies by pattern).

Slip marker as you work around: k for 1"/2.5cm, ending at underarm.

For a straight sleeve, with no shaping: work ITR to desired length.

For a tapered sleeve: dec at the underarm on either side of the marker, as follows (remembering to shift to dpn as sleeve sts diminish).

K2tog, k around, k2tog.

Repeat last rnd, every 4th rnd, ___ times.

Patterns will always indicate the intervals of dec, rnds and how many you'll have to complete. If you are designing your own sweater, you'll have to do a bit of math.

Cuff (work ITR)

Try on your sweater to check the length, then follow the pattern directions for the cuff. BO loosely.

FINISHING

Sew together seams under the arm and weave in ends.

Basic Cardigan Pattern

Unlike a pullover, in which both the body and the sleeves are worked ITR, only the sleeves of the cardigan are done this way. The cardigan yoke and body are worked B&F, but still on a cn (to accommodate the large number of sts). When knitting ITR, you are always working with the right side (RS) facing. However, with cardigans, you're turning the work from one side to the other, so you'll need to know which is the right side (RS) and which is the wrong side (WS).

Collar (work B&F)

Start at the outer edge and work toward the necklace. Cast on the specified number of stitches and work the collar B&F. You can work on straight needles until the number of stitches makes doing so unwieldy.

Yoke (work B&F)

Divide up the stitches and place markers to begin the yoke increases. You'll need at least four (4) markers to delineate the sleeves and body front and back. It's also helpful (but optional) to add two more markers to denote the beginning and end of the front band stitches. A typical set-up row reads as follows:

Row 1 (RS): —Set-up rnd and place markers

k___(front left band) sts, pm,

k___(left front) sts, pm,

k___(sleeve) sts, pm,

k___(back) sts, pm,

k___(sleeve) sts, pm,

k___(right front) sts, pm,

k___(right front band) sts.

Row 2 and all even rows (WS): sl 1, p across.

Note: Alternating k and p rows will produce a stockinette st, so if you want the front bands to be in garter st, the first and last 2 to 5 sts (depending on how wide you want the band) will always be knit sts. To achieve a smooth outer edge, slip the first stitch in each row.

The third row is the first inc row where 8 sts will be added, 2 on either side of the 4 inside markers (not the ones denoting the front bands).

Row 3 (RS): sl 1, k___ (left front band) sts, sl m, *k to next marker, m1, sl m, m1, repeat from * across for

next three markers, work across to last marker, sl m, k___ (right front band) sts.

Repeat Rows 2 and 3 the number of times designated in the pattern. End by finishing a row 2.

Body (work B&F)

Using the main cn, regroup the stitches to create the body and sleeves as follows:

Row 1 (RS): divide the yoke sts into front, back, and two sleeves, sl 1, k___(left front band) sts, sl m, k___(left front) sts, CO 1 st, pm (underarm), CO 1 st, place sleeve sts on cn holder, k___(back) sts, CO 1 st, pm (underarm), CO 1 st, place sleeve sts on holder, k___ (right front) sts, sl m, k___(right front band) sts.

Note: The number of sts CO at the underarm will varies by pattern.

Row 2: sl 1, p across (working the two front bands in garter st if specified).

Repeat Rows 1 and 2 for the desired length.

The sweater body can be worked straight without further shaping. For a more form-fitting structure, you can dec sts along the side seams or create darts down the front and back.

Hem (work ITR)

Follow the pattern instructions to complete the hem or alter it to your taste. Try on the sweater to check length before you bind off (BO) loosely.

Sleeves (work ITR)

Cardigan sleeves are worked in the same way as pullover sleeves.

Understanding Sizing and Size Charts

Sizing is an elusive concept, at least in the United States, where there is no national standard measurement for body shapes. The good news is that some trade organizations have taken the lead in establishing standards for their particular industries. Most yarn manufacturers and knitting designers follow the standards set by the Craft Yarn Council of America (www.craftyarncouncil.com). Those guidelines were used for this collection.

The easiest way to determine which size you want to make is to refer to the *actual finished garment measurement*. This is especially important, as people have different preferences for how they want to wear a garment. Some like tight-fitting garments, whereas others want a looser fit. The Craft Yarn Council has also considered this and has defined fit terminology as follows:

Type of Fit	Description
Very close fitting	Actual chest/bust measurement or less
Close fitting	1–2"/2–5cm
Standard fitting	2–4"/5–10cm
Loose fitting	4–6"/10–15cm
Oversized	6"/15cm or more

Again, the safest bet is to look at the *actual measurement* of the completed *garment*.

In this section, size and gauge options also differ from past writings on one-piece knitting. Top-down patterns used to offer myriad sizes based on chest size, measured in 1"/2.5cm increments. Here, we've distilled this approach and use only four basic sizes—S, M, L, XL—again, based on the Craft Yarn Council's standards.

On the other hand, gauge options have been expanded dramatically. Top-down patterns used to be written mainly for tried-'n'-true worsted yarn. Nowadays, however, there are many yarn options in the market, so there's a real need to have patterns that will accommodate the many choices available.

The really good news is that the basic patterns in the "Knitting Sweaters from the Top Down" section are expressed in *eight gauges* for both standard pullover and cardigan shapes. These patterns provide outlines to help you get started in designing your own styles. Once you get the hang of knitting top-down sweaters, you can begin to tailor the patterns further and hone them to your personal measurements. Refer to the Top-Down Math section to assist you in making any alterations.

The charts will also be a useful reference point when making further alterations. For example, you might observe that the average long-arm length for a Medium is 17"/43cm. But if you know that your arms are longer or shorter, you can make a note of that and add or subtract a ball or two to your final yarn purchase.

Top-Down Math

You can easily use this book without ever having to delve into the behind-the-scenes math; just follow the patterns as you would any other. However, understanding the why and wherefore of the numbers will enable you to alter the basic patterns and ultimately help you to expand your own design options.

Calculating Cast-On Stitches at the Neckline

The most important number in a top-down sweater pattern is the stitch count for the necklace—the baseline neck. This produces a garment with a neck circumference that will touch the bottom of the neck hole for that given size. If you want a tighter neckline, use the neck circumference chart below, left. Make the collar with fewer stitches (as dictated by a narrower neck), but when you get ready to start the yoke, add enough stitches in the last row of the collar equal to the baseline neck number for the garment size and yarn gauge you are using.

by the yarn gauge:

Cast-On Stitches (CO) = Baseline neck circumference (in or cm) x yarn gauge (sts/in or cm)

So for example, to make a Large sweater in a 5-gauge yarn (sts/in or cm), you will need to cast on 90 sts: 18 in x 5 st/in.

The baseline neck number also helps determine how to construct the collar. For the example, you'll cast on 90 sts.

Neck Circumference

	S	M	L	XL
Baseline neck: falls at bottom of neck hole				
in	16	17	18	19
cm	40.5	42.5	46	48
Tighter neck: hits top of neck hole				
in	15	16	17	17.5
cm	38	40.5	43	44.5
Tightest neck: neck circumference				
in	14.5	15	15.5	16
cm	37	38	39	40.5

to make a polo collar, simple round neck, etc. However, for a simple ruffle collar, you'll have to double the CO sts because you're beginning the ruffle at its outermost edge (the fluffy side). You'll cast on at least 180 sts (90 x 2). After you have worked the desired ruffle width, k2tog across arrive at the desired number of baseline neck sts, ready to begin the yoke.

Let's do a calculation for a tighter collar or neckline. For example, to make a turtleneck with a chunky yarn (3 sts/in) in size Small, refer to the chart which says that you'll require a neck circumference of 14.5"/37cm. Multiply this number by the gauge of the chunky yarn (3sts/in) to get to the number of sts that you have to cast on to work the collar. You'll come out with 43.5, but round up to get 44 sts.

14.5"/37cm x 3 sts/in gauge = 43.5, round up to 44

Work the turtleneck ITR for 6 to 7"/15 to 18cm, depending on your neck length. When it's complete, work 1 row plain, increasing to the number of sts to reach the baseline number for your side sweater and yarn gauge. So you'll need to increase the number of your stitches to reach a 16"/40.5cm neckline at a gauge of 3 sts/in.

16"/40.5cm x 3 sts/in gauge = 48

Which means, you'll have to add only 4 sts on the last row to reach the baseline (48 sts − 44 sts = 4 sts).

Again, remember that before you start the increase of the yoke, you have to return to the number of baseline sts required for your size and weight of yarn.

Establishing the Yoke

Many top-down patterns describe how to "short-row" the back section before starting the yoke increases, allowing the front to lay forward, which, the argument goes, makes for a better fitting sweater. However, if not done absolutely properly, this technique can leave holes at the turns.

Here's an easier method that works just as well. It's based on how the CO sts are divided up to create the front, back, and sleeves. In sum, allocate more stitches to the front section than to the back, so that the sweater will in effect be "front-heavy." This creates the same effect as short-rowing and provides greater room on the front of the sweater, where most women are larger.

Using the example of 90 sts (required for a large sweater in yarn gauge 5 st/in or cm), divide by 3 to get 30: one-third sts for the front, one-third for the back, and one-third for the sleeves. If you get fractions, round down for the sleeves, or round up for the back and front, but check to make sure that after rounding you still have the same total you began with (in this case, 90 sts):

Front	30
Back	30
Sleeve	30/2 = 15
Sleeve	30/2 = 15
TOTAL	90

Next, readjust the sleeve allocations so that the number of sts for each sleeve equals only 2"/5cm worth along the neckline. For this example, that means allocating 12 sts for each sleeve (2" x 5 sts/in or cm (yarn gauge). Add the leftover sleeve stitches (15 st − 10 sts) = 5 sts per sleeve, or 2 x 5 = 10 sts, to the front stitch allocation for a total of 40 sts. Your stitches will be "front-loaded."

Front	30
Back	30
Sleeve	30/2 = 10
Sleeve	30/2 = 10
TOTAL	90

For the basic patterns, I used a slightly different allocation method, with hardly a difference except for a stitch here and there. The results are essentially the same—the front gets a disproportionate amount of stitches.

Calculating the Number of Increase Rows in the Yoke

After you've established your baseline neck sts and divvied them up on the cn using markers, you'll start to work the yoke. This is done by alternating an increase rnd with a non-increase row. An increase rnd is one in which you increase one stitch on either side of each of the four markers that separate the front, back, and sleeve sts. After you have completed one inc round, you'll have added 8 sts (2 sts for every marker). After an increase rnd, work one row without increases. Alternating these two rows forms the yoke. So how many times do you repeat them?

Determining the number of increase rows starts with the chest measurement. For the large size, the chest measurement is 44"/112 cm. Multiply this measurement by your gauge, in this case, 5 sts/in.

Chest circumference (finished garment) x gauge (sts/in or cm) = number of sts for chest measurement

You get 220 sts, which represents the total number of sts on the cn, the front, back, and CO sts at the underarm that you want to arrive at once the yoke increases have been made.

To calculate the number of increase rnds needed, take the difference between the chest measurement in sts and the neckline measurement and divide by 4 (not 8) because 4 is the number of sts added to the body section—front and back—in each increase rnd.

Sweater Sizing (inches)

Sizes	S	M	L	XL
Chest				
actual chest size	32–34	36–38	40–42	44–46
finished garment *	36	40	44	48
Neckline				
slightly dropped, front starts at base of neck hole	16	17	18	19
Yoke				
top of mid-shoulder to underarm	8½–9	9½–10	10–11	11–11½
Body				
short: underarm to below bust	4	5	6	6½
mid-length: underarm to hip	11	12	13	13½
long: underarm to below hip	14	15	16	16½
Sleeve				
short: underarm to mid-bicep	4	4½	5	5½
three-quarter sleeve: underarm to lower elbow	9	10	11	11½
long: underarm to wrist	17	17½	18	18½
cuff circumference	8	9	10	10

Sweater Sizing (CM)

Sizes	S	M	L	XL
Chest				
actual chest size	81–86	92–97	102–107	112–117
finished garment	91	102	112	123
Neckline				
slightly dropped, front starts at base of neck hole	41	43	46	48
Yoke				
top of mid-shoulder to underarm	22–23	24–25	25–27	27–28
Body				
short: underarm to below bust	10	13	15	16.5
mid-length: underarm to hip	28	30.5	33	34
long: underarm to below hip	35.5	38	41	42
Sleeve				
short: underarm to mid-bicep	10	11	13	14
three-quarter sleeve: underarm to lower elbow	23	25	28	29
long: underarm to wrist	43	44	46	47
cuff circumference	20	23	25	25

Continued ➔

Garment chest measurement (expressed in sts) – (baseline neck + front sts) /4 = number of increase rows in the neck

Using the example, you'll get the following:

220 total sts for 44" chest/gauge of 5 sts/in (40 starting front sts + 30 starting backsts)/4 = 37.5 increase rnds

In this example, we get 37.5 inc rnds, which means that we need 75 total rnds (37.5 x 2), alternating an increase rnd with a non-inc rnd, to make the yoke. However (and this is where the art of knitting comes in), at a vertical gauge of 7 rnds per inch (remember each yarn has a row gauge as well), the armhole that extends longer than desired. So, at this point, I make an artistic decision to keep the most increase rows I can to get to my chest measurement while avoiding creating an extended armhole. I do this by lopping of 2 inc rows. After I finish 35 increase rows, I stop, then I add 4 sts on the body at the underarm to get as close to the 220 chest sts desired. In the end, I get a total of 218 sts, which is close enough to the 220 sts needed for a 44"/112 cm chest.

Shaping the Body

The basic idea behind shaping is to calculate the difference in body width from start to finish and express this measurement in stitches. In doing so, remember to work with finished garment measurements.

Let's take the example of tapering to the waist versus just knitting a straight body shape. Begin with the garment chest measurement (which is determined by the number of sts on the main cn needle after the yoke has been worked, after the sleeve sts have been added at the underarm on the body sides). In our example, we have 218 sts at this point. Let's decide to take the waist in by 3"/7.6cm, which means that 15 sts (3"/7.6cm x 5 sts/in gauge) need to be decreased. This can be done a number of ways, depending on how you want it to look. If you knit down a number of ways, depending on how you want it to look. If you knit down to the waist and then decrease the entire 15 sts in one rnd, the garment will take on a blouson look. A more tapered look is achieved by making two darts down the front and two down the back, and dividing the 15 sts among these four points. But by far the easiest thing to do is to take regular, incremental decreases down the sides of the body, tapering to the waist. Because we also want to make an even number of decreases (2 sts on either side of the side markers), we'll round our number up to get an even number, making 15 sts into 16 sts for the sake of ease.

Now you'll have to determine how to space the 16-st dec along the side body. First, work the body about 1"/2.5cm straight before you begin your decreases to prevent any bunching under the arms. Remember to place two markers, one at each underarm to designate the decrease locations. Divide the number of stitches you want to eliminate by the number of decrease locations (in this case, by 2 for each side) for an 8-st dec per side. Then decide how you want to decrease—by 1 st on each side for a very gradual taper or by 2 sts on each side for a more dramatic one. Next, measure from your underarm to your waist (your result should be in the range of 6 to 8"/15 to 18cm) and subtract 2"/5cm because the armhole hangs lower. You can also try on the yoke and measure the distance from its lower edge to your waist. Then, multiply that measurement by the rnds/in of your yarn (this should tell you how many rnds you need to work to reach your waist, which will indicate how to divide up the increases along the sides). Remember to deduct the 1"/2.5cm that you worked on the body from the yoke to start. For our example, you'd need to work 6"/15cm to get from the bottom of the yoke to the waist, minus 1"/2cm already worked, for 5"/13cm. This means we'll have to work 35 rnds (5 x 7 rnds/in for the yarn in the example). So you'll want to decrease 8 sts each side within these 35 rnds. Since 16 sts need to be decreased, you'll need to work 4 dec rnd where one st gets eliminated either side of the 2 dec markers. To determine the interval, at which

a dec rnd occurs, divide the rounds that must be worked from the base of the yoke to the waist (35 rnds) by the number of dec rnds (4) needed. That comes out to 8.75 (round up to 9). Now you know that once a dec rnd is worked, you'll have to complete 8 rnds before completing another dec rnd.

Calculating Tapered Sleeve Decreases

WHAT IS THE RND/ROW GAUGE FOR MY YARN?

First, check the yarn label. The row or rnd per inch should be listed there. However, don't rely on that number alone. Always make a swatch of your yarn and measure. The chart below offers approximations, as a guideline.

Approximate Rounds or Rows by Gauge

Yarn type	Sts/in or 2.5 cm	Rnds/row/in or 2.5 cm
Bulky	2	2.25
	2.5	3–3.5
Chunky	3	4–4.5
	3.5	4–5
Heavy Worsted	4	5–5.5
	4.5	5–6
DK Worsted	5	6–7
	5.5	7

This is the same principle as described for body shaping—calculate the difference in sts between your starting and end points to determine the number of sts you need to decrease.

It might help to visualize the process, so have a piece of paper and a pencil at hand to sketch out what you are doing. Start by outlining a sleeve and walk through the following calculation, noting the steps on your drawing.

As an example, calculate the taper for a three-quarter-length sleeve by first listing the data you already have. You've finished the yoke, and you know how many sleeve sts you've set aside (80 sts in our example). Divide that number by your yarn gauge—this measures the circumference of your upper arm in inches. For example, the 80 sts divided by 5 sts/in or cm (gauge) gives you 16"/40.5cm. Measure the circumference of your lower arm where you want the sleeve to end. Let's say it's 11"/28cm. Next, measure the length of your arm, starting 1"/2.5cm down from the armpit to a little beyond your elbow—say, 9"/22.5cm.

Data

sleeve sts on cn = 80

Circumference, upper arm (in/cm) = 80 sts/5sts/in or cm (gauge) = 16"/40.5cm

Lower arm circumference = 11"/28cm

Length, underarm to sleeve's lower edge = 11"/28cm

To determine the number of sts you have to end up with at the lower arm circumference multiply the lower arm circumference by the yarn gauge:

Lower edge sleeve (sts) = 11"/28cm circumference x 5 st/in or cm (gauge) = 55 sts

Calculate the number of sts to be decreased by taking the number of sts you start with and subtracting the number of sts you want to end up with:

80 sts – 55 sts = 25 sts to be decreased at underarm seam

Because sleeve decreases happen in pairs (one st is dec either side of underarm marker), you'll dec 24 sts (instead of 25) for 12 dec rnds.

24 sts/2 sts per dec per rnd = 12 dec rnds

Now, determine the interval at which these decreases will occur along the length of the sleeve. This is done by determining the number of rows it will take to achieve the 9"/22.5cm length. For our example, we use the full length. For our example, we use the full length of the sleeve, minus the initial 1"/2.5cm we worked after the yoke, which equals 8"/20cm (9" - 1" = 8"). Take this 8"/20cm length and multiply it by the row/rnd gauge of your yarn (let's say it's 6 rnds per 1"/2.5cm) to get 48 rnds. This means that the 12 dec rnds will have to be placed within these 48 rnds. To determine the interval at which the dec rnds will occur, divide the total number of rnds (48) by 12 dec rnds, to get 4. So, for every decrease rnd, you'll work 3 non-dec rnds and make the 5th rnd the dec rnd.

It really is easy—just remember that you're converting length (in/cm) into stitch equivalents to write your knitting directions.

Choosing Yarn and Determining Yardage

Your yarn will dictate what pattern to use or how to write your own (as you know, gauge is all important). Yake a look at the basic patterns. They are written by gauge, so you'll be able to do just about any top-down sweater using these templates. The following charts will help you to pick out the correct size needles as well.

Determining Yardage

Figuring out how much yarn you need is one of the more perplexing knitting decisions you'll make—you don't want to make a costly or inconvenient mistake. One way to take some of the anxiety out of the decision is to find a yarn shop which has a return policy for leftover balls. Another way is to relax and keep the extra yarn—build up a yarn stash to experiment with on a rainy day.

The following chart can help in your decision-making process. These are approximations based on averages taken from completed projects. You'll want to purchase enough yarn to complete your project using one dye-lot, to avoid making a garment with a mottled appearance or having another color line running through it.

You can also adjust the amounts using the following formulations.

For sleeveless styles, subtract 45%

For short sleeves, subtract 30%

YARN TYPE, GAUGE, AND NEEDLE SIZE

Wool Weights	Gauge sts per in	sts per 10 cm	Needle Size U.S.	(mm)
Bulky	2–2.5	8–10	11+	8+
Chunky	3–3.5	12–14	9–10	5–5.6
Heavy Worsted	4–4.5	16–18	7–8	4.5–5
DK Weight	5–5.5	20–22	6–7	4–4.5

For three-quarter-length sleeves, subtract 20%

For hip-length hem, add 20%

Note: After you've determined your needle size, make a simple swatch. Don't depend on the yarn label for the gauge—it's only a ballpark figure. Everyone knits differently and with different tension, so your results will be unique.

YARDAGE: LONG SLEEVE & JUST-ABOVE-HIP LENGTH*

Chest Size	S	M	L	XL
Actual body/in	32–34	36*38	40–42	44–46
Finished garment/in	34–36	38–40	42–44	46–48
Actual body/cm	80–85	90–95	100–105	110–115
Finished garment/cm	85–90	95–100	105–110	115–120
Gauge:				
2 sts/in	600	675	750	850
2.5	650	700	800	900
3	725	825	925	1075
3.5	875	1000	1125	1325
4	1020	1175	1300	1540
4.5	1140	1300	1475	1700
5	1275	1460	1660	1935
5.5	1400	1600	1800	2100

Basic Patterns

Basic patterns are templates from which to create your own sweaters. They are general instructions, not complete patterns, for pullover and cardigan shapes in various gauges. Stitch counts outline the basic sweater shape. Use the design ideas at the front of the book to decide what type of collar and cuffs to add, as well as how to form the body and shape the sleeves.

Note: The cardigan template does not include stitches for front bands—the instructions are for an open-front cardigan. If you want to include front bands for buttonholes, to create an overlap, add "1-inch worth" of sts on both sides, so for example, for 2 to 2½ sts/in gauge add 2 sts to each side, for 3 to 3½ sts/in gauge, add 3 sts, etc.

Basic Bulky Pullover: 8 st gauge

SIZES

Small (Medium, Large, X-Large)

FINISHED MEASUREMENTS

Bust 32–34 (36–38, 40–42, 44–46)"/81–86 (92–97, 102–107, 112–117)cm

Garment 36 (40, 44, 48)"/91 (102, 112, 122)cm

MATERIALS

- Yarn: 500 (600, 650, 750) yd/457 (549, 595, 686)m bulky weight yarn
- Needles: 9–10 mm (size 13–15 U.S.) *or size to obtain gauge*
- Circular (cn): one 29"/74cm, two 16"/40cm *or size to obtain gauge*
- Double-pointed (dpn): 10"/25cm set
- Tapestry needle

GAUGE

8 sts/10 row = 4"/10cm in

Always take time to check your gauge.

INSTRUCTIONS

COLLAR (WORK ITR)

Using 16"/40cm cn, CO 32 (34, 36, 38) sts. Work collar.

YOKE (WORK ITR)

Place markers:

Rnd 1 (RS): k13 (14, 15, 16) front sts, pm, k5 sleeve sts, pm, k9 (10, 11, 12) back sts, pm, k5 sleeve sts, pm.

Rnd 2 (Inc rnd): m1, K to 1 st before marker, m1, sl m, m1, repeat from * around 3 times more, k until 1 st remains, m1 (8 sts inc)—40 (42, 44, 46) sts.

Rnd 3: k (sl markers along the way).

Repeat Rnds 2 and 3, 11 (12, 13, 15) times more—128 (138, 148, 166) sts.

DIVIDE YOKE (WORK ITR)

Separate body and sleeve sts:

RS: k37 (40, 43, 48) front sts, CO 1 (1, 2, 1) sts, pm, CO 0 (1, 1, 1) st, place 29 (31, 33, 37) sleeve sts on 16"/40cm cn and *hold aside,* k33 (36, 39, 44) back sts, CO 0 (1, 1, 1) st, pm, CO 1 (1, 2, 1) st, place 29 (31, 33, 37) sleeve sts on 16"/40cm cn and *hold aside*—72 (80, 88, 96) body sts remain on main cn.

BODY (WORK ITR)

Join front and back portions, work for 11 (12, 13, 14)"/28 (31, 33, 36)cm or to desired length.

Hem

Work for 2"/5cm.

BO loosely.

SLEEVES (WORK ITR; WRIST-LENGTH AND TAPERED)

Work each sleeve separately, changing to dpn as necessary:

Using 29 (31, 33, 37) sts on 16"/40cm cn, CO 1 st, pm (underarm), CO 1 st—31 (33, 35, 39) sts.

Work for 1"/2.5 cm.

Beg underarm sleeve dec:

Next rnd: k2tog, work around, end k2tog (2 st dec)—29 (31, 33, 37) sts.

Work 4 (5, 4, 3) rnds, repeat last 5 (6, 5, 4) rnds, 6 (1, 5, 8) times more.

Next rnd: k2tog, work around, end k2tog (2 st dec).

Work 0 (4, 3, 2) rnds, repeat last 0 (5, 4, 3) rnds, 0 (4, 1, 0) times more—17 (19, 19, 19) sts.

Cuff

Work for 2"/5cm.

BO loosely.

Work second sleeve same as the first.

FINISHING

Sew underarms together and weave in ends.

Basic Bulky Pullover: 10 st gauge

SIZES

Small (Medium, Large, X-Large)

FINISHED MEASUREMENTS

Bust 32–34 (36–38, 40–42, 44–46)"/81–86 (92–97, 102–107, 112–117)cm

Garment 36 (40, 44, 48)"/91 (102, 112, 122)cm

MATERIALS

- Yarn: 625 (675, 750, 800)yd/572(618, 686, 732)m bulky weight yarn
- Needles: 9-10 mm (size 13-15 U.S.) *or size to obtain gauge*
- Circular (cn): one 29"/74cm, two 16"/40cm.
- Double-pointed (dpn): 10"/25cm set
- 4 stitch markers
- Tapestry needle

GAUGE

10 sts/12 rows = 4"/10cm

Always take time to check your gauge.

INSTRUCTIONS

COLLAR (WORK ITR)

Using 16"/40cm cn, CO 40 (42, 45, 48) sts. Work collar.

YOKE (WORK ITR)

Place markers:

Rnd 1 (RS): k16 (17, 19, 20) front sts, pm, k6 sleeve sts, pm, k12 (13, 14, 16) back sts, pm, k6 sleeve sts, pm.

Rnd 2 (*inc rnd*): m1, *k to 1 st before marker, m1, sl m, m1, repeat from * around 3 times more, k until 1 st remains, m1 (8 sts inc)—48 (50, 52, 56) sts.

Rnd 3: k (sl markers along the way).

Repeat Rnds 2 and 3, 13 (15, 17, 19) times more—152 (170, 189, 208) sts.

DIVIDE YOKE (WORK ITR)

Separate body and sleeve sts:

RS: k44 (49, 55, 60) front sts, CO 2 (2, 1, 1) sts, pm, CO 1 st, place 34 (38, 42, 46) sleeve sts on 16"/40cm cn and *hold aside*—k40 (45, 50, 56) back sts, CO 1 st, pm, CO 2 (2, 1, 1) sts, place 34 (38, 42, 46) sleeve sts on 16"/40cm cn and *hold aside*—90 (100, 109, 120) body sts remain on main cn.

BODY (WORK ITR)

Join front and back portions and work for 11 (12, 13, 14)"/28 (31, 33, 36)cm or desired length.

Hem

Work for 2"/5cm.

BO loosely.

SLEEVES (WORK ITR; WRIST-LENGTH AND TAPERED)

Work each sleeve separately, changing to dpn as necessary:

Using 34 (38, 42, 46) sts on 16"/40cm cn, cn, CO 1 st, pm (underarm) CO st—36 (40, 44, 48) sts.

Work for 1"/2,5cm.

Beg underarm sleeve dec:

Next rnd: k2tog, work around, end k2tog (2 st dec)—34 (38, 42, 46).

Work 5 (4, 4, 4) rnds, repeat last 6 (5, 5, 5) rnds, 1 (7, 8, 2) times more.

K2tog, work around, end k2tog (2 st dec).

Work 4 (3, 0, 3) rnds, repeat last 5 (4, 0, 4) rnds, 5 (0, 0, 7) times more—20 (22, 26, 26) sts.

Cuff

Work for 2"/5cm.

BO loosely.

Work second sleeve same as the first.

FINISHING

Sew underarms together and weave in ends.

Continued →

Basic Bulky Cardigan: 8 st gauge

Size:

Small (Medium, Large, X-Large)

Finished Measurements

Bust 32–34 (36-38, 40-42, 44-46)"/81–86 (92–97, 102–107, 112–117)cm

Garment 36 (40, 44, 48)"/91 (102, 112, 122)cm

Materials

• Yarn: 500 (600, 650, 760)yd/457 (549, 595, 686)m bulky weight yarn

• Needles: 9–10 mm (size 13–15 U.S.) *or size to obtain gauge*

• Circular (cn): one 29"/74cm, two 16"/41cm *or size to obtain gauge*

• Double-pointed (dpn): 10"/25cm

• 4 stitch markers

• Tapestry needle

Gauge

8 sts/10 rows = 4"/10cm

Always take time to check your gauge.

Instructions

COLLAR (WORK B&F)

Using 16"/40cm cn, CO 32 (34, 36, 38) sts.

Work collar.

YOKE (WORK B&F)

Place markers:

Row 1 (RS): k7 (7, 8, 8) left front sts, pm, k5 sleeve sts, pm k8 (10, 10, 12) back sts, pm, k5 sleeve sts, pm, k7 (7, 8, 8) left front sts.

Row 2 (WS): p (slip markers along the way).

Row 3 (*inc row*): *k to 1 st before next marker, m1, sl m, m1, repeat from * across 3 times more, k to end—40 (42, 44, 46) sts.

Repeat Rows 2 and 3, 11 (12, 13, 15) times more—128 (138, 148, 166) sts.

DIVIDE YOKE (WORK B&F)

Separate body and sleeve sts:

RS: k19 (20, 22, 24) left front sts, CO 1 (1, 2, 1) sts, pm, CO 0 (1, 1, 1) sts, place 29 (31, 33, 37) sleeve sts on 16"/40 cm cn and *hold aside,* k32 (36, 38, 44) back sts, CO 0 (1, 1, 1) st, pm, CO 1 (1, 2, 1) sts, place 29 (31, 33, 37) sleeve sts on 16"/40cm cn and *hold aside,* k19 (20, 22, 24) right front sts—72 (80, 88, 96) body sts remain on main cn.

BODY (WORK B&F)

Join front and back portions and work for 11 (12, 13, 14)"/28 (31, 33, 36)sm or desired length.

Hem

Work for 2"/5cm.

BO loosely.

SLEEVES (WORK ITR; WRIST LENGTH AND TAPERED)

Work each sleeve separately, changing to dpn as necessary:

Using 29 (31, 33, 37) sts on 16"/40cm cn, CO 1 sts, pm (underarm) CO 1 st—31 (33, 35, 39) sts.

Work for 1"/2.5cm.

Beg underarm sleeve dec:

Next rnd: k2tog, work around, end k2tog (2 st dec)—29 (31, 33, 37) sts.

Work 4 (5, 4, 3) rnds, repeat last 5 (6, 5, 4) rnds, 6 (1, 5, 8) times more.

Next rnd: k2tog, work around, end k2tog (2 st dec)

Work 0 (4, 3, 2) rnds, repeat last 0 (5, 4, 3) rnds 0 (4, 1, 0) times more—17 (19, 19, 19) sts.

Cuff

Work for 2"/5cm.

BO loosely.

Work second sleeve same as the first.

FINISHING

Sew underarms together and weave in ends.

Basic Bulky Cardigan: 10 st gauge

Size

Small (Medium, Large, X-Large)

Finished Measurements

Bust 32–34 (36-38, 40-42, 44-46)"/81–86 (92–97, 102–107, 112–117)cm

Garment 36 (40, 44, 48)"/91 (102, 112, 122)cm

Materials

• Yarn: 625 (675, 750, 800)yd/572 (618, 686, 732)m bulky weight yarn

• Needles: 9–10 mm (size 13–15 U.S.) *or size to obtain gauge*

• Circular (cn): one 29"/74cm, two 16"/41cm *or size to obtain gauge*

• Double-pointed (dpn): 10"/25cm set

• 4 stitch markers

• Tapestry needle

Gauge

10 sts/12 rows = 4"/10cm

Always take time to check your gauge.

Instructions

COLLAR (WORK B&F)

Using 16"/40cm cn, CO 40 (42, 45, 48) sts.

Work collar.

YOKE (WORK B&F)

Row 1 (RS): k8 (9, 10, 10) left front sts, pm, k6 sleeve sts, pm, k12 (12, 13, 16) back sts, pm, k6 sleeve sts, pm, k8 (9, 10, 10) left front sts.

Row 2 (WS): p (sl markers along the way).

Row 3 (*Inc row*): *k to 1 st before next marker, m, sl m, m1, repeat from * across 3 times more, k to end—48 (50, 52, 56) sts.

Repeat Rows 2 and 3, 13 (15, 17, 19) times more—152 (170, 189, 208) sts.

DIVIDE YOKE (WORK B&F)

Separate body and sleeve sts:

RS: k22 (25, 28, 30) left front sts, CO 2 (2, 1, 1) sts, pm, CO 1 st, place 34 (38, 42, 46) sleeve sts on 16"/40cm cn and *hold aside,* k40 (44, 49, 56) back sets, CO 0 (0, 1, 1) st, pm, CO 0 (0, 1, 1) st, place 34 (38, 42, 46) sleeve sts on 16"/40cm cn and *hold aside,* k22 (25, 28, 30) right front sts—90 (100, 109, 120) body sts remain on main cn.

BODY (WORK B&F)

Join front and back portions, work for 11 (12, 13, 14)"/28 (31, 33, 36)cm or desired length.

Hem

Work for 2"/5cm.

BO loosely.

SLEEVES (WORK ITR)

Work each sleeve separately, changing to dpn as necessary:

Using 34 (38, 42, 46) sts on 16"/40 cm cn, CO 1 st, pm (underarm) CO 1 st—36 (40, 44, 48) sts.

Work for 1"/2.5cm.

Beg underarm sleeve dec:

Next rnd: k2tog, work around, end k2tog (2 st dec)—34 (38, 42, 46) sts.

Work 5 (4, 4, 4) rnds, repeat last 6 (5, 5, 5) rnds, 1 (7, 8, 2) times more.

Next rnd: k2tog, work around, end k2tog (2 st dec).

Work 4 (3, 0, 3) rnds, repeat last 5 (4, 0, 4) rnds, 5 (0, 0, 7) times more—20 (22, 26, 26) sts.

Cuff

Work for 2"/5cm.

BO loosely.

Work second sleeve same as the first.

FINISHING

Sew underarms together and weave in ends.

Basic Chunky Pullover: 8 st gauge

Sizes

Small (Medium, Large, X-Large)

Finished Measurements

Bust 32–34 (36-38, 40-42, 44-46)"/81–86 (92–97, 102–107, 112–117)cm

Garment 36 (40, 44, 48)"/91 (102, 112, 122)cm

Materials

• Yarn: 700 (775, 875, 950)yd/640 (709, 800, 869)m chunky weight yarn

• Needles: 6–6.5 mm (10–11 US) or size to obtain gauge

• Double-pointed (dpn): 10"/25cm set

• 4 stitch markers

• Tapestry needle

Gauge

12 sts/16 rows = 4"/10cm

Always take time to check your gauge.

Instructions

COLLAR (WORK ITR)

Using 16"/40cm cn, CO 48 (51, 54, 57) sts.

Work collar.

YOKE (WORK ITR)

Place markers:

Rnd 1 (RS): k19 (21, 22, 24) front sts, pm, k8 sleeve sts, pm, k13 (14, 16, 17) back sts, pm, k8 sleeve sts, pm.

Rnd 2 (*Inc row*): m1, *k to 1 st before marker, m1, sl m, m1, repeat from * around 3 times more, k until 1 st remains, m1 (8 sts inc)—56 (59, 62, 65) sts.

Rnd 3: k (sl markers along the way).

Repeat Rnds 2 and 3, 17 (19, 21, 23) times more—192 (211, 230, 249) sts.

DIVIDE YOKE (WORK ITR)

Separate body and sleeve sts:

RS: k55 (61, 66, 72) front sts, CO 1 (1, 2, 2) sts, pm, CO 1 st, place 44 (48, 52, 56) sleeve sts on 16"/40cm cn and *hold aside,* k49 (54, 60, 65) back sts, CO 1 st, pm, CO 1 (1, 2, 2) sts, place 44 (48, 52, 56) sleeve sts on 16"/40cm cn and *hold aside*—108 (119, 132, 143) body sts remain on main cn.

BODY (WORK ITR)

Join front and back portions, work for 11 (12, 13, 14)"/28 (31, 33, 36)cm.

Hem

Work for 2"/5cm.

BO loosely.

SLEEVES (WORK ITR; WRIST-LENGTH AND TAPERED)

Work sleeves separately, changing to dpn as necessary:

Using 44 (48, 52, 56) sts on 16"/40cm cn, CO 1 st, pm (underarm), CO st. 46 (50, 54, 58) sts.

Work for 1"/2.5cm.

Beg underarm sleeve dec:

Next rnd: k2tog, work around, end k2tog (2 sts dec)—44 (48, 52, 56) sts.

Work 4 (5, 4, 4) rnds, repeat last 5 (6, 5, 5) rnds, 10 (2, 11, 5) times more.

Next rnd: k2tog, work around, end k2tog (2 sts dec).

Work 0 (4, 0, 3) rnds, repeat last 0 (5, 0, 4) rnds, 0 (7, 0, 7) times more—24 (28, 30, 30) sts.

Cuff

Work for 2"/5cm.

BO loosely.

Work second sleeve same as the first.

FINISHING

Sew underarms together and weave in ends.

Basic Chunky Pullover: 10 st gauge

SIZES

Small (Medium, Large, X-Large)

FINISHED MEASUREMENTS

Bust 32–34 (36–38, 40–42, 44–46)"/81–86 (92–97, 102–107, 112–117)cm

Garment 36 (40, 44, 48)"/91 (102, 112, 122)cm

MATERIALS

- Yarn: 775 (900, 1100, 1250)yd/709 (823, 1006, 1144)m chunky weight yarn
- Needles: 6–6.5 mm (10–11 US) *or size to obtain gauge*
- Circular (cn): one 29"/74cm, two 16"/40cm *or size to obtain gauge*
- Double-pointed (dpn): 10"/25cm set
- 4 stitch markers
- Tapestry needle

GAUGE

14 sts/18 rows = 4"/10cm
Always take time to check your gauge.

INSTRUCTIONS

COLLAR (WORK ITR)

Using 16"/40cm cn, CO 56 (59, 63, 66) sts.
Work collar.

YOKE (WORK ITR)

Place markers:

Rnd 1 (RS): k23 (25, 27, 28) front sts, pm, k8 sleeve sts, pm, k17 (18, 20, 20) back sts, pm, k8 sleeve sts, pm.

Rnd 2 (*Inc row*): m1, *k to 1 st before marker, m1, sl m, m1, repeat from * around 3 times more, k until 1 st remains, m1 (8 sts inc)—64 (67, 71, 74) sts.

Rnd 3: k (sl markers along the way).

Repeat Rnds 2 and 3, 19 (22, 25, 27) times more—216 (243, 271, 290) sts.

DIVIDE YOKE (WORK ITR)

Separate body and sleeve sts:

RS: k63 (71, 79, 84) front sts, CO 1 (1, 1, 2) sts, pm, CO 1 st, place 48 (54, 60, 64) sleeve sts on 16"/40cm cn and *hold aside*, k57 (64, 72, 78) back sts, CO 1 st, pm, CO 1 (1, 1, 2) sts, place 48 (54, 60, 64) sleeve sts on 16"/40cm cn and *hold aside*—124 (139, 155, 168) body sts remain on main cn.

BODY (WORK ITR)

Join front and back portions, work body for 11 (12, 13, 14)"/28 (31, 33, 36)cm.

Hem

Work for 2"/5cm.

BO loosely.

SLEEVES (WORL ITR)

Work sleeves separately, changing to dpn as necessary:

Using 48 (54, 60, 64) sts on 16"/40cm cn, CO 1 st, pm (underarm), CO 1 st—50 (56, 62, 66) sts.

Work for 1"/2.5cm.

Beg underarm sleeve dec:

Next rnd: k2tog, work around, end k2tog (2 sts dec)—48 (54, 60, 64) sts.

Work 5 (5, 4, 4) rnds, repeat last 6 (6, 5, 5) rnds, 7 (5, 11, 5) times more.

Next rnd: k2tog, work around, end k2tog (2 sts dec).

Work 4 (4, 3, 3) rnds, repeat last 5 (5, 4, 4) rnds, 2 (5, 1, 9) times more—28 (32, 34, 34) sts.

Cuff

Work for 2"/5cm.

BO loosely.

Work second sleeve same as the first.

FINISHING

Sew underarms together and weave in ends.

Basic Chunky Cardigan: 8 st gauge

SIZES

Small (Medium, Large, X-Large)

FINISHED MEASUREMENTS

Bust 32–34 (36–38, 40–42, 44–46)"/81–86 (92–97, 102–107, 112–117)cm

Garment 36 (40, 44, 48)"/91 (102, 112, 122)cm

MATERIALS

- Yarn: 700 (775, 875, 950)yd/640 (709, 800, 869)m chunky weight yarn
- Needles: 6–6.5 mm (10–11 US) *or size to obtain gauge*
- Circular (cn): one 29"/74 cm, two 16"/40cm or
- Double-pointed (dpn): 10"/25cm set
- 4 stitch markers
- tapestry needle

GAUGE

12 sts/16 rows = 4"/10cm
Always take time to check your gauge.

INSTRUCTIONS

COLLAR (WORK B&F)

Using 16"/40cm cn, CO 48 (51, 54, 57) sts.
Work collar.

YOKE (WORK B&F)

Place markers:

Row 1 (RS): k9 (10, 11, 12) left front sts, pm, k8 sleeve sts, pm, k14 (15, 16, 17) back sts, pm, k8 sleeve sts, pm, k9 (10, 11, 12) right front sts.

Row 2 (WS): p (sl markers along the way).

Row 3 (*Inc row*): *k to 1 st before next marker, m1, sl m, m1, repeat from * across 3 times more, k to end—56 (59, 62, 65) sts.

Repeat Rows 2 and 3, 17 (19, 21, 23) times more—192 (211, 230, 249) sts.

DIVIDE YOKE (WORK B&F)

Separate body and sleeve sts:

RS: k27 (30, 33, 36) left front sts, CO 1 (1, 2, 2) sts, pm, CO 1 sts, place 44 (48, 52, 56) sleeve sts on 16"/40cm cn and *hold aside*, k50 (55, 60, 65) back sts, CO 1 st, pm, CO 1 (1, 2, 2) st, place 44 (48, 52, 56) sleeve sts on 16"/40cm cn and *hold aside*—108 (119, 132, 143) body sts remain on main cn.

BODY (WORK B&F)

Join front and back portions, work for 11 (12, 13, 14)"/28 (31, 33, 36)cm.

Hem

Work for 2"/5cm.

BO loosely.

SLEEVES (WORK ITR)

Work sleeves separately, changing to dpn as necessary:

Using 44 (48, 52, 56) sts on 16"/40cm cn, CO 1 st, pm (underarm), CO 1 st—46 (50, 54, 58) sts.

Work for 1"/2.5cm.

Beg underarm sleeve dec:

Next rnd: k2tog, work around, end k2tog (2 sts dec)—44 (48, 52, 56) sts.

Work 4 (5, 4, 4) rnds, repeat last 5 (6, 5, 5) rnds, 10 (2, 11, 5) times more.

Next rnd: k2tog, work around, end k2tog (2 st dec).

Work 0 (4, 0, 3) rnds, repeat last 0 (5, 0, 4) rnds, 0 (7, 0, 7) times more—24 (28, 30, 30) sts.

Cuff

Work for 2"/5cm.

BO loosely.

Work second sleeve same as the first.

FINISHING

Sew underarms together and weave in ends.

Basic Chunky Cardigan: 10 st gauge

SIZES

Small (Medium, Large, X-Large)

FINISHED MEASUREMENTS

Bust 32–34 (36–38, 40–42, 44–46)"/81–86 (92–97, 102–107, 112–117)cm

Garment 36 (40, 44, 48)"/91 (102, 112, 122)cm

MATERIALS

- Approx total: 775 (900, 1100, 1250)yd/709 (823, 1006, 1144)m chunky weight yarn
- Needles: 6–6.5 mm (10–11 US) *or size to obtain gauge*
- Circular (cn): one 29"/74cm, two 16"/40cm *or size to obtain gauge*
- Double-pointed (dpn): 10"/25cm set
- 4 stitch markers
- tapestry needle

Continued ➔

GAUGE

14 sts/18 rows = 4"/10cm

Always take time to check your gauge.

INSTRUCTIONS

COLLAR (WORK B&F)

Using 16"/40cm cn, CO 56 (59, 63, 66) sts.
Work collar.

YOKE (WORK B&F)

Row 1 (RS): k11 (12, 13, 14) left front sts, pm, k8 sleeve sts, pm, k18 (19, 21, 22) back sts, pm, k8 sleeve sts, pm, k11 (12, 13, 14) right front sts.

Row 2 (WS): p (sl markers along the way).

Row 3 (*Inc row*): *k to 1 st before next marker, m1, sl m, m1, repeat from * across 3 times more, k to end—64 (67, 71, 74) sts.

Repeat Rows 2 and 3, 19 (22, 25, 27) times more—216 (243, 271, 290) sts.

DIVIDE YOKE (WORK B&F)

Separate body and sleeve sts:

RS: k31 (35, 39, 42) front sts, CO 1 (1, 1, 2) sts, pm, CO 1 st, place 48 (54, 60, 64) sleeve sts on 16"/40cm cn and *hold aside*, k58 (65, 73, 78) back sts, CO 1 st, pm, CO 1 (1, 1, 2) sts, place 31 (35, 39, 42) sleeve sts on 16"/40cm cn and *hold aside*—124 (139, 155, 168) body sts remain on main cn.

BODY (WORK B&F)

Join front and back portions, work for 11 (12, 13, 14)"/28 (31, 33, 36)cm.

HEM

Work for 2"/5cm.

BO loosely.

SLEEVES (WORK ITR; WRIST-LENGTH AND TAPERED)

Work sleeves separately, changing to dpn as necessary:

Using 48 (54, 60, 64) sts on 16"/40cm cn, CO 1 at, pm (underarm), CO 1 st—50 (56, 62, 66) sts.

Work for 1"/2.5cm.

Beg underarm sleeve dec:

Next rnd: k2tog, work around, end k2tog (2 st dec)—48 (54, 60, 64) sts.

Work 5 (5, 4, 4) rnds, repeat last 6 (6, 5, 5) rnds, 7 (5, 11, 5) times more.

Next rnd: k2tog, work around, end k2tog (2 st dec).

Work 4 (4, 3, 3) rnds, repeat last 5 (5, 4, 4) rnds, 2 (5, 1, 9) times more—28 (32, 34, 34) sts remain.

Cuff

Work for 2"/5cm.

BO loosely.

Work second sleeve same as the first.

FINISHING

Sew underarms together and weave in ends.

Basic Heavy Worsted Pullover: 8 st gauge

SIZES

Small (Medium, Large, X-Large)

FINISHED MEASUREMENTS

Bust 32–34 (36–38, 40–42, 44–46)"/81–86 (92–97, 102–107, 112–117)cm

Garment 36 (40, 44, 48)"/91 (102, 112, 122)cm

MATERIALS

- Yarn: 900 (1000, 1200, 1400)yd/823 (915, 1098, 1281)m heavy worsted yarn
- Needles: 5–5.5 mm (8–9 US) *or size to obtain gauge*
- Circular (cn): one 29"/74cm, two 16"/40cm *or size to obtain gauge*
- Double-pointed (dpn): 10"/25cm set
- 4 stitch markers
- tapestry needle

GAUGE

16 sts/20 rows = 4"/10cm in St st

Always take time to check your gauge.

INSTRUCTIONS

COLLAR (WORK ITR)

Using 16"/40cm cn, CO 64 (68, 72, 76) sts.
Work collar.

YOKE (WORK ITR)

Place markers:

Rnd 1 (RS): k27 (29, 31, 33) front sts, pm, k9 sleeve sts, pm, k19 (21, 23, 25) back sts, pm, k9 sleeve sts, pm.

Rnd 2 (*Inc row*): m1, *k to 1 st before marker, m1, sl m, m1, repeat from * around 3 times more, k until 1 st remains, m1 (8 sts inc)—72 (76, 80, 84) sts.

Rnd 3: k (sl markers along the way).

Repeat Rnds 2 and 3, 22 (25, 28, 31) times more—248 (276, 304, 332) sts.

DIVIDE YOKE (WORK ITR)

Separate body and sleeve sts:

K73 (81, 89, 97) front sts, CO 2 sts, pm, CO 1 st, place 55 (61, 67, 73) sleeve sts on 16"/40cm cn and *hold aside*, k65 (73, 81, 89) back sts, CO 1 st, pm, CO 2 sts, place 55 (61, 67, 73) sleeve sts on 16"/40cm cn and *hold aside*—144 (160, 176, 173) body sts remain on main cn.

BODY (WORK ITR)

Join front and back portions, work for 11 (12, 13, 14)"/28 (31, 33, 36)cm.

Hem

Work for 2"/5cm.

SLEEVES (WORK ITR)

Work each sleeve separately, changing to dpn as necessary:

Using 55 (61, 67, 73) sts on 16"/40cm cn, CO 1 st, pm (underarm), CO 1 st—57 (63, 69, 75) sts.

Work for 1"/2.5cm.

Beg underarm sleeve dec:

Next rnd: k2tog, work around, end k2tog (2 sts dec)—55 (61, 67, 73) sts.

Work 4 (4, 3, 3) rnds, repeat last 5 (5, 4, 4) rnds, 7 (5, 14, 7) times more.

Next rnd: k2tog, work around, end k2tog (2 sts dec).

Work 3 (3, 0, 2) rnds, repeat last 4 (4, 0, 3) rnds, 3 (6, 0, 9) times more—33 (37, 39, 39) sts.

Cuff

Work for 2"/5cm.

BO loosely. Work second sleeve same as the first.

FINISHING

Sew underarms together and weave in ends.

Basic Heavy Worsted Pullover: 10 st gauge

SIZES

Small (Medium, Large, X-Large)

FINISHED MEASUREMENTS

Bust 32–34 (36–38, 40–42, 44–46)"/81–86 (92–97, 102–107, 112–117)cm

Garment 36 (40, 44, 48)"/91 (102, 112, 122)cm

MATERIALS

- Yarn: 1000 (1200, 1300, 1500)yd/915 (1098, 1189, 1372)m heavy worsted yarn
- Needles: 5–5.5 mm (8–9 US) *or size to obtain gauge*
- Circular (cn): one 29"/74cm, two 16"/41cm *or size to obtain gauge*
- Double-pointed (dpn): 10"/25cm set
- 4 stitch markers
- Tapestry needle

GAUGE

18 sts/22 rows = 4"/10cm

Always take time to check your gauge.

INSTRUCTIONS

COLLAR (WORK ITR)

Using 16"/40cm cn, CO 72 (76, 81, 84) sts.
Work collar.

YOKE (WORK ITR)

Place markers:

Rnd 1 (RS): k31 (33, 36, 37) front sts, pm, k9 sleeve sts, pm, k23 (25, 27, 29) back sts, pm, k9 sleeve sts, pm.

Rnd 2 (*Inc row*): m1, *k to 1 st before marker, m1, sl m, m1, repeat from * around 3 times more, k until 1 st remains, m1 (8 sts inc)—80 (84, 89, 92) sts.

Rnd 3: k (sl markers along the way).

Repeat Rnds 2 and 3, 25 (27, 31, 34) times more—280 (300, 337, 364) sts.

DIVIDE YOKE (WORK ITR)

Separate body and sleeve sts:

RS: k83 (89, 100, 107) front sts, CO 1 (2, 2, 2) sts, pm, CO 1 (2, 2, 2) sts, place 61 (65, 73, 79) sleeve sts on 16"/40cm cn and *hold aside*, k75 (81, 91, 99) back sts, CO 1 (2, 2, 2) sts, pm, CO 1 (2, 2, 2) st, place 61 (65, 73, 79) sleeve sts on 16"/40cm cn and *hold aside*—162 (178, 199, 214) body sts remain on main cn.

BODY (WORK ITR)

Work for 11 (12, 13, 14)"/28 (31, 33, 36)cm.

Hem

Work for 2"/5cm.

BO loosely.

SLEEVES (WORK ITR)

Work sleeves separately, changing to dpn as necessary:

Using 61 (65, 73, 79) sts on 16"/40cm cn, CO 1 st, pm (underarm), CO 1 st—63 (67, 75, 81) sts.

Work for 1"/2.5cm.

Beg underarm sleeve dec:

Next rnd: k2tog, work around, end k2tog (2 sts dec).

Work 4 (5, 4, 3) rnds, repeat last 5 (6, 5, 4) rnds, 10 (0, 7, 15) times more.

Next rnd: k2tog, work around, end k2tog (2 sts dec)—61 (65, 73, 79) sts.

Work 3 (4, 3, 2) rnds, repeat last 4 (5, 4, 3) rnds, 1 (11, 6, 1) times more—37 (41, 45, 45) sts.

Cuff

Work for 2"/5cm.

BO loosely.

Work second sleeve same as the first.

FINISHING

Sew underarms together and weave in ends.

Basic Heavy Worsted Cardigan: 8 st gauge

SIZES

Small (Medium, Large, X-Large)

FINISHED MEASUREMENTS

Bust 32–34 (36–38, 40–42, 44–46)"/81–86 (92–97, 102–107, 112–117)cm

Garment 36 (40, 44, 48)"/91 (102, 112, 122)cm

MATERIALS

- Yarn: 900 (1000, 1200, 1400)yd/823 (915, 1098, 1281)m heavy worsted yarn
- Needles: 5–5.5 mm (8–9 US) *or size to obtain gauge*
- Circular (cn): one 29"/74cm, two 16"/41cm
- Double-pointed (dpn): 10"/25cm set
- 4 stitch markers
- Tapestry needle

GAUGE

16 sts/20 rows = 4"/10cm in St st
Always take time to check your gauge.

INSTRUCTIONS

COLLAR (WORK B&F)

Using 16"/40cm cn, CO 64 (68, 72, 76) sts.
Work collar.

YOKE (WORK B&F)

Place markers:

Row 1 (RS): k11 (12, 13, 14) left front sts, pm, k9 sleeve sts, pm, k18 (20, 22, 24) back sts, pm, k9 sleeve sts, pm, k11 (12, 13, 14) right front sts.

Row 2 (WS): p (sl markers along the way).

Row 3 (*Inc row*): *K to 1 st before next marker, m1, sl m, m1, repeat from * across 3 times more, k to end—72 (76, 80, 84) sts.

Repeat Rows 2 and 3, 22 (25, 28, 31) times more—248 (276, 304, 332) sts.

DIVIDE YOKE (WORK B&F)

Separate body and sleeve sts:

RS: k37 (41, 45, 49) left front sts, CO 2 sts, pm, CO 1 st, place 55 (61, 67, 73) sleeve sts on 16"/40cm cn and *hold aside*, k65 (73, 81, 89) back sts, CO 1 st, pm, CO 2 sts, place 55 (61, 67, 73) sleeve sts on 16"/40cm cn and *hold aside*, k37 (41, 45, 49) right front sts—144 (160, 176, 192) body sts remain on main cn.

BODY (WORK B&F)

Join front and back portions, work for 11 (12, 13, 14)"/28 (31, 33, 36)cm.

Hem

Work hem for 2"/5cm.

BO loosely.

SLEEVES (WORK ITR)

Work sleeves separately, changing to dpn as necessary:

Using 55 (61, 67, 73) sts on 16"/40cm cn: CO 1 st, pm (underarm), CO 1 st—57 (63, 69, 75) sts.

Work for 1"/2.5cm.

Beg underarm sleeve dec:

Next rnd: k2tog, work around, end k2tog (2 st dec)—55 (61, 65, 73) sts.

Work 4 (4, 3, 3) rnds, repeat last 5 (5, 4, 4) rnds, 7 (5, 14, 7) times more.

Next rnd: k2tog, work around, end k2tog (2 st dec).

Work 3 (3, 0, 2) rnds, repeat last 4 (4, 0, 3) rnds, 3 (6, 0, 9) times more—33 (37, 39, 39) sts.

Cuff

Work cuff for 2"/5cm.

BO loosely.

Work second sleeve same as the first.

FINISHING

Sew underarms together and weave in ends.

Basic Heavy Worsted Cardigan: 10 st gauge

SIZES

Small (Medium, Large, X-Large)

FINISHED MEASUREMENTS

Bust 32–34 (36–38, 40–42, 44–46)"/81–86 (92–97, 102–107, 112–117)cm

Garment 36 (40, 44, 48)"/91 (102, 112, 122)cm

MATERIALS

- Yarn: 1000 (1200, 1300, 1500)yd/915 (1098, 1189, 1372)m heavy worsted yarn
- Needles: 5–5.5 mm (8–9 US) *or size to obtain gauge*
- Circular (cn): one 29"/74cm, two 16"/41cm *or size to obtain gauge*
- Double-pointed (dpn): 10"/25cm set
- 4 stitch markers
- Tapestry needle

GAUGE

18 sts/22 rows = 4"/10cm
Always take time to check your gauge.

INSTRUCTIONS

COLLAR (WORK B&F)

Using 16"/40cm cn, CO 72 (76, 81, 84) sts.
Work collar.

YOKE (WORK B&F)

Row 1 (RS): k13 (14, 15, 16) left front sts, pm, k9 sleeve sts, pm, k22 (24, 27, 28) back sts, pm, k9 sleeve sts, pm, k13 (14, 15, 16) right front sts.

Row 2 (WS): p (sl markers along the way).

Row 3 (*Inc row*): *K to 1 st before next marker, m1, sl m, m1, repeat from * across 3 times more, k to end—80 (84, 89, 92) sts.

Repeat Rows 2 and 3, 25 (27, 31, 34) times more—280 (300, 337, 364) sts.

DIVIDE YOKE (WORK B&F)

Separate body and sleeve sts:

RS: k42 (45, 50, 54) left front sts, CO 1 (2, 2, 2) sts, pm, CO 1 (2, 2, 2) sts, place 61 (65, 73, 79) sleeve sts on 16"/40cm cn and *hold aside*, k75 (81, 91, 99) back sts, CO 1 (2, 2, 2) sts, pm, CO 1 (2, 2, 2) sts, place 61 (65, 73, 79) sleeve sts on 16"/40cm cn and *hold aside*, k42 (45, 50, 54) right front sts—162 (178, 199, 214) body sts remain on main cn.

BODY (WORK B&F)

Work body for 11 (12, 13, 14)"/28 (31, 33, 36)cm.

Hem

Work hem for 2"/5cm.

BO loosely.

SLEEVES (WORK ITR)

Work sleeves separately, changing to dpn as necessary:

Using 61 (65, 73, 79) sts on 16"/40cm cn, CO 1 st, pm (underarm):

CO 1 st—63 (67, 75, 81) sts.

Work for 1"/2.5cm.

Beg underarm sleeve dec:

Next rnd: k2tog, work around, end k2tog (2 st dec)—61 (65, 73, 79) sts.

Work 4 (5, 4, 3) rnds, repeat last 5 (6, 5, 4) rnds, 10 (0, 7, 15) times more.

Next rnd: k2tog, work around, end k2tog (2 st dec).

Work 3 (4, 3, 2) rnds, repeat last 4 (5, 4, 3) rnds, 1 (11, 6, 1) times more—37 (41, 45, 45) sts.

Cuff

Work cuff for 2"/5cm.

BO loosely.

Work second sleeve same as the first.

FINISHING

Sew underarms together and weave in ends.

Basic Dk Pullover: 8 st gauge

SIZES

Small (Medium, Large, X-Large)

FINISHED MEASUREMENTS

Bust 32–34 (36–38, 40–42, 44–46)"/81–86 (92–97, 102–107, 112–117)cm

Garment 36 (40, 44, 48)"/91 (102, 112, 122)cm

MATERIALS

- Yarn: 1300 (1500, 1700, 1800)yd/1189 (1372, 1555, 1647)m dk weight yarn
- Needles: 3.75–4.5 mm (5–7 US) *or size to obtain gauge*
- Circular (cn): one 29"/74cm, two 16"/41cm *or size to obtain gauge*
- Double-pointed (dpn): 10"/25cm set
- 4 stitch markers
- Tapestry needle

GAUGE

20 sts/24 rows = 4"/10cm
Always take time to check your gauge.

INSTRUCTIONS

COLLAR (WORK ITR)

Using 16"/40cm cn, CO 80 (85, 90, 95) sts.
Work collar.

YOKE (WORK ITR)

Place markers:

Rnd 1 (RS): k35 (38, 40, 43) front sts, pm, k10 sleeve sts, pm, k25 (27, 30, 32) back sts, pm, k10 sleeve sts, pm.

Rnd 2 (*Inc row*): m1, *k to 1 st before marker, m1, sl m, m1, repeat from * around 3 times more, k until 1 st remains, m1 (8 sts inc)—88 (93, 98, 103) sts.

Rnd 3: k (sl markers along the way).

Repeat Rnds 2 and 3, 27 (30, 34, 37) times more—304 (333, 370, 399) sts.

Continued →

DIVIDE YOKE (WORK ITR)

Separate body and sleeve sts:

RS: k91 (100, 110, 119) front sts, CO 2 (2, 2, 3) sts, pm, CO 2 (2, 2, 3) sleeve sts, place 66 (72, 80, 86) sleeve sts on 16"/40cm cn and *hold aside*, k81 (89, 100, 108) back sts, CO 2 (2, 2, 3) sts, pm, CO 2 (2, 2, 3) sts, place 66 (72, 80, 86) sleeve sts on 16"/40cm cn and *hold aside*—180 (197, 218, 239) body sts remain on main cn.

BODY (WORK ITR)

Join front and back, work for 11 (12, 13, 14)"/28 (31, 33, 36)cm.

Hem

Work for 2"/5cm.

BO loosely.

SLEEVES (WORK ITR)

Work sleeves separately, changing to dpn as necessary:

Using 66 (72, 80, 86) sts on 16"/40cm cn, CO 1 st, pm (underarm), CO 1 st—68 (74, 82, 88) sts.

Work for 1"/2.5cm.

Beg underarm sleeve dec:

Next rnd: k2tog, work around, end k2tog (2 sts dec)—66 (72, 80, 86) sts.

Work 8 (8, 8, 6) rnds, repeat last 9 (9, 9, 7) rnds, 3 (6, 1, 8) times more.

Next rnd: k2tog, work around, end k2tog (2 sts dec).

Work 7 (7, 7, 5) rnds, repeat last 8 (1, 8, 6) rnds, 5 (2, 8, 4) times—48 (54, 60, 60) sts.

Cuff

Work for 2"/5cm.

BO loosely.

Work second sleeve same as the first.

FINISHING

Sew underarms together and weave in ends.

Basic Dk pullover: 10 st gauge

SIZES

Small (Medium, Large, X-Large)

FINISHED MEASUREMENTS

Bust 32–34 (36–38, 40–42, 44–46)"/81–86 (92–97, 102–107, 112–117)cm

Garment 36 (40, 44, 48)"/91 (102, 112, 122)cm

MATERIALS

· Yarn: 1400 (1600, 1800, 2000)yd/1281 (1464, 1647, 1830)m dk weight yarn

· Needles: 3.75–4.5 mm (5–7 US) or size to obtain gauge

· Circular (cn): one 29"/74cm, two 16"/41cm *or size to obtain gauge*

· Double-pointed (dpn): 10"/25cm set

· 4 stitch markers

· Tapestry needle

GAUGE

22 sts/26 rows = 4"/10cm

Always take time to check your gauge.

INSTRUCTIONS

COLLAR (WORK ITR)

Using 16"/40cm cn, CO 88 (93, 99, 104) sts.

Work collar.

YOKE (WORK ITR)

Place markers:

Rnd 1 (RS): k39 (42, 45, 47) front sts, pm, k10 sleeve sts, pm, k29 (31, 34, 37) back sts, pm, k10 sleeve sts, pm.

Rnd 2 (*Inc row*): m1, *k to 1 st before marker, m1, sl m, m1, repeat from * around 3 times more, k until 1 st remains, m1 (8 sts inc)—96 (101, 107, 112) sts.

Rnd 3: k (sl markers along the way).

Repeat Rnds 2 and 3, 29 (33, 37, 40) times more—328 (365, 403, 432) sts.

DIVIDE YOKE (WORK ITR)

Separate body and sleeve sts:

RS: k99 (110, 121, 129) front sts, CO 2 (2, 2, 3) sts, pm, CO 2 (2, 2, 3) sts, place 70 (78, 86, 92) sleeve sts on 16"/40cm cn and *hold aside*, k89 (99, 110, 119) back sts, CO 2 (2, 2, 3) sts, pm, CO 2 (2, 2, 3) sts, place 70 (78, 86, 92) sleeve sts on 16"/40cm cn and *hold aside*—196 (217, 239, 260) body sts remain on main cn.

BODY (WORK ITR)

Join front and back portions, work for 11 (12, 13, 14)"/28 (31, 33, 35)cm.

Hem

Work for 2"/5cm.

BO loosely.

SLEEVES (WORK ITR)

Work sleeves separately, changing to dpn as necessary:

Using 70 (78, 86, 92) sts on 16"/40cm cn, CO 2 sts at underarm, pm between—72 (80, 88, 94) sts.

Work for 1"/2.5cm.

Beg underarm sleeve dec:

K2tog, work around, end k2tog (2 sts dec)—70 (78, 86, 92) sts.

Work 9 (9, 8, 7) rnds, repeat last 10 (10, 9, 8) rnds, 0 (3, 9, 2) times more.

K2tog, work around, end k2tog (2 sts dec).

Work 8 (8, 7, 6) rnds, repeat last 9 (9, 8, 7) rnds, 8 (5, 0, 10) times more—52 (60, 66, 66) sts.

Cuff

Work for 2"/5cm.

BO loosely.

Work second sleeve same as the first.

FINISHING

Sew underarms together and weave in ends.

Basic Dk Cardigan: 8 st gauge

SIZES

Small (Medium, Large, X-Large)

FINISHED MEASUREMENTS

Bust 32–34 (36–38, 40–42, 44–46)"/81–86 (92–97, 102–107, 112–117)cm

Garment 36 (40, 44, 48)"/91 (102, 112, 122)cm

MATERIALS

· Yarn: 1300 (1500, 1700, 1800)yd/1189 (1372, 1555, 1647)m dk weight yarn

· Needles: 3.75–4.5 mm (5–7 US) *or size to obtain gauge*

· Circular (cn): one 29"/74cm, two 16"/41cm *or size to obtain gauge*

· Double-pointed (dpn): 10"/25cm set

· 4 stitch markers

· Tapestry needle

GAUGE

20 sts/24 rows = 4"/10cm in St st

Always take time to check your gauge.

INSTRUCTIONS

COLLAR (WORK B&F)

Using 16"/40cm cn, CO 80 (85, 90, 95) sts.

Work collar.

YOKE (WORK B&F)

Row 1 (RS): k17 (19, 20, 21) left front sts, pm, k10 sleeve sts, pm, k24 (27, 30, 33) back sts, pm, k10 sleeve sts, pm, k17 (19, 20, 21) right front sts.

Row 2 (WS): p (sl markers along the way).

Row 3 (*Inc row*): *k to 1 st before next marker, m1, sl m, m1, repeat from * across 3 times more, k to end—88 (93, 98, 103) sts.

Repeat Rows 2 and 3, 27 (30, 34, 37) times more—304 (333, 370, 399) sts.

DIVIDE YOKE (WORK B&F)

Separate body and sleeve sts:

RS: k46 (50, 55, 59) left front sts, CO 2 (2, 2, 3) sts, pm, CO 2 (2, 2, 3) sts, place 66 (72, 80, 86) sleeve sts on 16"/40cm cn and *hold aside*, k80 (89, 100, 109) back sts, CO 2 (2, 2, 3) sts, pm, CO 2 (2, 2, 3) sts, place 66 (72, 80, 86) sleeve sts on 16"/40cm cn and *hold aside*, k46 (50, 55, 59) right front sts—180 (197, 218, 239) sts remain on main cn.

BODY (WORK B&F)

Work for 11 (12, 13, 14)"/28 (31, 33, 36)cm.

Hem

Work for 2"/5cm.

BO loosely.

SLEEVES (WORK ITR)

Work sleeves separately, changing to dpn as needed:

Using 66 (72, 80, 86) sts on 16"/40cm cn, CO 1 st, pm (underarm), CO 1 st—68 (74, 82, 88) sts.

Work for 1"/2.5cm

Beg underarm sleeve dec:

Next rnd: k2tog, work around, end k2tog (2 st dec)—66 (72, 80, 85) sts.

Work 8 (8, 8, 6) rnds, repeat last 9 (9, 9, 7) rnds, 3 (6, 1, 8) times more.

Next rnd: k2tog, work around, end k2tog (2 st dec).

Work 7 (7, 7, 5) rnds, repeat last 8 (1, 8, 6) rnds, 5 (2, 8, 4) times more—48 (54, 60, 60) sts.

Cuff

Work for 2"/5cm.

BO loosely.

Work second sleeve same as the first.

FINISHING

Sew underarms together and weave in ends.

Basic Dk Cardigan: 10 st gauge

SIZES

Small (Medium, Large, X-Large)

FINISHED MEASUREMENTS

Bust 32–34 (36–38, 40–42, 44–46)"/81–86 (92–97, 102–107, 112–117)cm

Garment 36 (40, 44, 48)"/91 (102, 112, 122)cm

MATERIALS

- Yarn: 1400 (1600, 1800, 2000)yd/1281 (1464, 1647, 1830)m dk weight yarn
- Needles: 3.75–4.5 mm (5–7 US) *or size to obtain gauge*
- Circular (cn) one 29"/74cm, two 16"/41cm *or size to obtain gauge*
- Double-pointed (dpn): 10"/25cm set
- 4 stitch markers
- Tapestry needle

GAUGE

22 sts/26 rows = 4"/10cm

Always take time to check your gauge.

INSTRUCTIONS

COLLAR (WORK B&F)

Using 16"/40cm cn, CO 88 (93, 99, 104) sts.

Work collar.

YOKE (WORK B&F)

Row 1 (RS): k19 (21, 22, 23) left front sts, pm, k10 sleeve sts, pm, k30 (31, 35, 38) back sts, pm, k10 sleeve sts, pm, k19 (19, 21, 22, 23) right front sts.

Row 2 (WS): p (sl markers along the way).

Row 3 (*Inc row*): *K to 1 st before next marker, m1, sl m, m1, repeat from * across 3 times more, k to end—96 (101, 107, 112) sts.

Repeat Rows 2 and 3, 29 (33, 37, 40) times more—328 (365, 403, 432) sts.

DIVIDE YOKE (WORK B&F)

Separate body and sleeve sts:

RS: k49 (55, 60, 64) left front sts, CO 2 (2, 2, 3) sts, pm, CO 2 (2, 2, 3) sts, place 70 (78, 86, 92) sleeve sts on 16"/40cm cn and *hold aside*, k90 (99, 111, 120) back sts, CO 2 (2, 2, 3) sts, pm, CO 2 (2, 2, 3) sts, place 70 (78, 86, 92) sleeve sts on 16"/40cm cn and *hold aside*, k49 (55, 60, 64) right front sts—196 (217, 239, 260) body sts remain on main cn.

BODY (WORK B&F)

Work body for 11 (12, 13, 14)"/28 (31, 33, 36)cm.

Hem

Work for 2"/5cm.

BO loosely.

SLEEVES (WORK ITR)

Work sleeve separately, changing to dpn as necessary:

Using 70 (78, 86, 92) sts on 16"/40cm cn, CO 1 st, pm (underarm), CO 1 st—72 (80, 88, 94) sts.

Work for 1"/2.5cm.

Beg underarm sleeve dec:

Next rnd: k2tog, work around, end k2tog (2 st dec)—70 (78, 86, 92) sts.

Work 9 (9, 8, 7) rnds, repeat last 10 (10, 9, 8) rnds, 0 (3, 9, 2) times more.

Next rnd: k2tog, work around, end k2tog (2 st dec).

Work 8 (8, 7, 6) rnds, repeat last 9 (9, 8, 7) rnds, 8 (5, 0, 10) times more—52 (60, 66, 66) sts.

Cuff

Work for 2"/5cm.

BO loosely.

Work second sleeve same as the first.

FINISHING

Sew underarms together and weave in ends.

New Leaf

An homage to k2/p2 ribbing, this design features the ribbing for the neckline, extended cuffs, and body of the sweater. The basic, chunky-weight pullover pattern was adjusted to accommodate the 4-stitch-multiple required for a 2/2 rib pattern. The result is a stylish, fitted pullover that's as easy to wear as it is to make.

EXPERIENCE LEVEL

Beginner

SIZES

Small (Medium, Large, X-Large)

FINISHED MEASUREMENTS

Bust 36 (40, 44, 48)"/91 (102, 112, 122 cm)

MATERIALS

- Approx total: 654 (709, 870, 980)yd/598 (649, 795, 897)m chunky weight yarn
- Circular knitting needles (cn): 6 mm (size 10 U.S.), one 29"/73 cm and two 16"/40cm, *or size to obtain gauge*
- Double-pointed needles (dpn): 6 mm (size 10 U.S.) *or size to obtain gauge*
- 4 stitch markers
- Tapestry needle

GAUGE

12 sts = 4"/20 cm in St st

Always take time to check your gauge.

INSTRUCTIONS

COLLAR (WORK ITR)

Using 16"/40cm cn, CO 48 (52, 56, 56) sts.

Rnds 1–5: Join sts and rib k2/p2.

Rnd 6: k, inc 0 (dec 1, dec 2, inc 1) sts evenly spaced—48 (51, 54, 57) sts.

YOKE (WORK ITR)

Rnd 1 (RS): k19 (21, 22, 24) front sts, pm, k8 sleeve sts, pm, k13 (14, 16, 17) back sts, pm, k8 sleeve sts, pm.

Rnd 2: m1, *k to 1 st before next marker, m1, slm, m1,

repeat from * around for each marker, k, end, m1 (8 sts inc)—56 (59, 62, 65) sts.

Rnd 3: k.

Repeat Rnds 2 and 3, 17 (19, 21, 23) times more—192 (211, 230, 249) sts.

DIVIDE YOKE (WORK ITR)

Separate body and sleeves:

Rnd 1 (RS): k55 (61, 66, 72) front sts, CO 1 (1, 2, 2) sts, pm, CO 1 (1, 1, 2) sts, place 44 (48, 52, 56) sleeve sts on 16"/40cm cn and hold aside, k49 (54, 60, 65) back sts, CO 1 st, pm, CO 1 (2, 2, 2) sts, place 44 (48, 52, 56) sleeve sts on 16"/40cm and *hold aside*—108 (120, 132, 144) sts on main cn.

BODY (WORK ITR)

Rnds 1–6: k.

Work k2/p2 rib for 11 (11, 12, 13)"/28 (28, 30, 33)cm from underarm.

BO loosely in rib.

SLEEVES (WORK ITR)

Using 44 (48, 52, 56) sleeve sts on 16"/40cm cn, join and work as follows, switching to dpn as necessary:

Rnd 1: k around, CO 1 st, pm, CO 1 st (2 sts inc)—46 (50, 54, 58) sts.

K 5 rnds.

Begin underarm sleeve dec, changing to dpn as needed:

Rnd 1: k2tog, k around, end k2tog (2 sts dec)—44 (48, 52, 56) sts.

Rnds 2–4: k 3 rnds.

Repeat Rnds 1–4, 4 (4, 6, 6) times more—36 (40, 40, 44) sts.

Cuff

Work k2/p2 rib until sleeve measures 17 (17½, 18, 18½)"/43 (44, 46, 47)cm from underarm or desired length.

BO loosely.

Work second sleeve same as the first.

FINISHING

Sew body and underarms together on each sleeve.

Using tapestry needle, weave in ends.

This project was made with:

6 (7, 8, 9) balls of Classic Elite's *Paintbox*, 100% wool, 1.75oz/50g = approx 109yd/100m, color #6897 (water-color green)

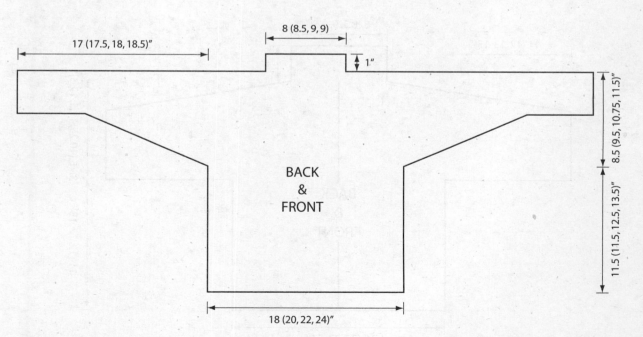

8 (8.5, 9, 9)"

17 (17.5, 18, 18.5)"

1"

BACK & FRONT

8.5 (9.5, 10.75, 11.5)"

11.5 (11.5, 12.5, 13.5)"

18 (20, 22, 24)"

Continued →

Photo D

Flora

Polo collars frame any face nicely, and they are very easy to execute. Cast on the required number of neckline stitches and knit to the desired length. To finish, three-quarter-length sleeves are versatile, practical, and universally flattering.

EXPERIENCE LEVEL

Easy

SIZES

Small (Medium, Large, X-Large)

FINISHED MEASUREMENTS

Bust 38 (40, 44, 48)"/91 (100, 110, 120)cm

MATERIALS

- Approx total: 775 (850, 925, 1000)yd/709 (778, 846, 915)m chunky weight yarn
- Circular needles (cn): 6 mm (size 10 U.S.), one 29"/73cm and two 16"/40cm, *or size to obtain gauge*
- Double-pointed needles (dpn): 6 mm (size 10 U.S.), 10"/25cm, *or size to obtain gauge*
- 4 stitch markers
- Tapestry needle

GAUGE

14 sts = 4"/20cm in garter st

Always take time to check your gauge.

PATTERN STITCH

Garter stitch (work B&F): k every row.

Garter stitch (work ITR): k 1 rnd, p 1 rnd.

INSTRUCTIONS

COLLAR (WORK B&F)

Using 29"/73cm cn, CO 56 (59, 63, 66) sts.

Work garter st for 4"/10cm, slipping the first st in each row.

YOKE (WORK B&F)

Note: sl the first st of each row.

Row 1 (RS): sl 1, k10 (11, 12, 13) left front sts, pm, k8 sleeve sts, pm, k18 (19, 21, 22) back sts, pm, k8 sleeve sts, pm, k11 (12, 13, 14) right front sts.

Row 2 (WS): sl 1, k across.

Row 3 (RS): sl 1, *k to 1 st before marker, m1, sl marker, m1, repeat from * across for each marker, k across, (8 sts inc)—64 (67, 71, 74) sts.

Repeat Rows 2 and 3, 19 (22, 25, 27) times more—216 (243, 271, 290) sts.

DIVIDE YOKE (WORK B&F)

Separate body and sleeves:

Row 1 (RS): sl 1, k30 (34, 38, 41) left front sts, CO 1 (1, 1, 2) sts, pm, CO 1 st, place 48 (54, 60, 64) sleeve sts on 16"/40cm cn and *hold aside*, k58 (65, 73, 78) back sts, CO 1 st, pm, CO 1 (1, 1, 2) sts, place 48 (54, 60, 64) sleeve sts on 16"/40cm cn and *hold aside*, k31 (35, 39, 42) right front sts—124 (139, 155, 168) sts on main cn.

BODY (WORK B&F)

K for 11 (12, 12, 13)"/27 (30, 30, 32)cm, slipping the first st in each row.

BO loosely.

SLEEVES (WORK ITR)

Using 48 (54, 60, 64) sleeve sts on 16"/40cm cn:

CO 1 st, pm, CO 1 st at underarm—50 (56, 62, 66) sts.

Join and work garter st for 1"/2.5cm (see note for how to make garter st ITR), ending completing a p rnd.

Underarm sleeve decs; change to dpn as necessary:

Rnd 1 (*Dec rnd*): k2tog, k around, end k2tog (2 sts dec)—48 (54, 60, 64) sts.

Work 4 rnds in garter st.

Repeat Rnds 1 through 5, 5 (6, 8, 8) times more—38 (42, 44, 48) sts.

Work until sleeve measures 11½ (12½, 13½, 13½)"/29 (31, 34, 34)cm or desired length.

BO loosely.

Work second sleeve same as the first.

FINISHING

Sew body and underarms together on each sleeve.

Using tapestry needle, weave in ends.

This project was made with:

11 (11, 12, 13) balls of Muench's *Oceana*, 55% viscose/30% nylon/15% cotton, 1.75oz/50g = approx 77yd/70m, color #4806 (green)

Cherry Blossom

This Asian-inspired top has a horizontal-patterned yoke that is split down the front. If you prefer, you can also shorten the split by joining the yoke together sooner. Both the cap sleeves and the bottom hem detail echo the mandarin collar, and they are hemmed for a smooth, finished look. This style hugs the body—fewer stitches are added at the top and, after the yoke, no stitches are added on the sides.

EXPERIENCE LEVEL

Intermediate

SIZES

Small (Medium, Large, X-Large)

FINISHED MEASUREMENTS

Bust 34 (38, 42, 46)"/86 (96, 105, 117)cm

MATERIALS

- Approx total: 720 (765, 810, 900)yd/659 (700, 741, 823)m heavy worsted weight yarn
- Circular needles (cn): 4 mm (size 6 U.S.), one 29"/73cm and two 16"/40cm, *or size to obtain gauge*
- 4 stitch markers
- Tapestry needle
- Six ½"/1.25cm pearl beads or buttons

GAUGE

18 sts = 4"/10cm in St st

Always take time to check your gauge.

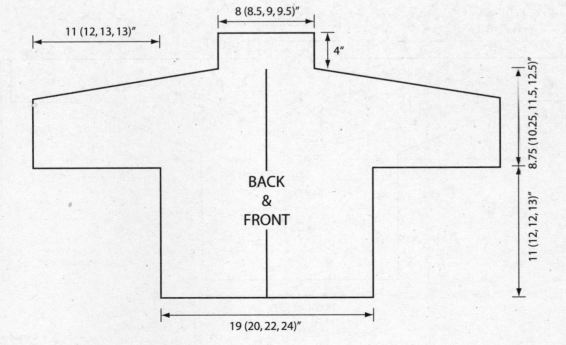

8 (8.5, 9, 9.5)"

11 (12, 13, 13)"

4"

8.75 (10.25, 11.5, 12.5)"

11 (12, 12, 13)"

BACK & FRONT

19 (20, 22, 24)"

PATTERN STITCH

YOKE ROW PAT (WORKED B&F)

Row 1 (RS): k.

Row 2: p.

Row 3: k.

Row 4: k (ridge row).

YOKE RND PAT (WORK ITR)

Rnd 1: k.

Rnd 2: k.

Rnd 3: k.

Rnd 4: p (ridge rnd).

INSTRUCTIONS

COLLAR (WORK B&F)

For a smooth front edge, sl 1st st in each row until the front yoke is connected:

Using 29"/73cm cn, CO 65 (70, 75, 75) sts.

Row 1: k.

Row 2: p.

Rows 3–8: rep Rows 2 and 3, 3 times more.

Row 9: p (turning ridge).

Row 10: k.

Row 11: p.

Rows 12–17: rep Rows 10 and 11, 3 times more.

Row 18: k, inc 7 (6, 6, 9) sts evenly spaced across—72 (76, 81, 84) sts.

Row 19: k.

YOKE (WORK B&F)

Row 1 (RS): sl 1, k14 (15, 17, 17) left front sts, pm, k9 sleeve sts, pm, k24 (26, 27, 30) back sts, pm, k9 sleeve sts, pm, k15 (16, 18, 18) right front sts.

Row 2 (WS): sl 1, k1 (front band), p across, end k2.

Row 3 (*RS, Inc rnd*): sl 1, *k to 1 st before marker, m1, sl marker, m1*, repeat between ** across for each marker around, k to end (8 sts inc)—80 (84, 89, 92) sts.

Row 4 (ridge row): sl 1, k to end.

Rep in order: Rows 3, 2, 3, 4, five times more.

Join and beg to work ITR:

Note: pm on right-hand needle denoting middle front.

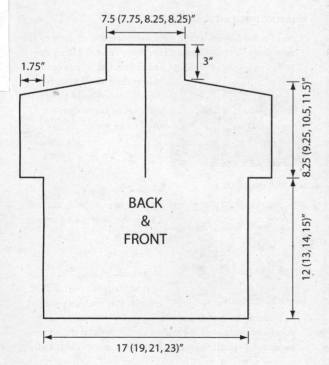

1.75"

7.5 (7.75, 8.25, 8.25)"

3"

8.25, 9.25, 10.5, 11.5"

12 (13, 14, 15)"

BACK & FRONT

17 (19, 21, 23)"

Next row (RS): *k to 1 st before marker, m1, sl marker, m1*, repeat between ** across for each marker except middle front marker, k to end (8 sts inc)—88 (92, 97, 100) sts.

K 1 row.

Cont alternating an inc row with a non-inc row, while keeping to the established yoke pat, until 25 (28, 32, 35) inc rows have been completed, ending last row at marker denoting the beg of the front sts—272 (300, 337, 364) sts.

DIVIDE YOKE (WORK B&F)

Separate body and sleeve sts:

(RS): k80 (88, 100, 106) front sts, place 59 (65, 73, 79) sleeve sts on 16"/40cm cn and *hold aside*, k74 (82, 91, 99) back sts, place 59 (65, 73, 79) sleeve sts on 16"/40cm cn and *hold aside*—154 (170, 191, 205) sts on main cn.

BODY (WORK ITR)

K for 9 (10, 11, 12)"/22.5 (25, 27.5, 30.5)cm.

Hem

Rnd 1: p.

Rnds 2–4: k.

Rnds 5–12: rep Rnds 1 to 4, 2 times more.

Rnd 13: k.

Rnd 14: p (ridge row).

Rnds 15–18: k 4 rnds.

BO loosely.

SLEEVES (WORK ITR)

Using 61 (65, 73, 79) sleeve sts on 16"/40cm cn, pm at underarm:

Rnds 1–5: k.

Rnd 6: p (ridge row).

Rnds 7–11: k.

BO loosely.

Work second sleeve same as the first.

FINISHING

Sew body and underarms together on each sleeve.

Using tapestry needle, weave in ends.

Fold mandarin collar inward and baste on the inside of collar. Sew buttons/beads on, each in one of the three bottom ridges and on either side of yoke (garment shown is sewn up the front until the point where the buttons begin, or you can leave it open for a more plunging neckline).

This project was made with:

8 (9, 9, 10) balls of Karabella's *Empire Silk*, 100% silk, 1.75oz/50g = approx 90yd/83m, color #508 (pink)

—From *Knitting Sweaters From the Top-Down*

Hat Construction and Knitting Techniques

Knitted hats can be made in myriad ways, the only limit being your imagination. They can be knitted as a whole, knitted in pieces and patched together, or knitted in pieces and patched together, or knitted sideways and seamed together. But for our purposes (making standard shapes), most of the instructions in this section call for making a hat in one piece, either from the brim upward or from the crown downward.

Many (if not most) of the hat patterns in this collection specify top-down construction, which means that you will begin making the hat starting at the very center of the crown. As you knit, regular and periodic increases are made that multiply the number of stitches and expand the crown as required to meet the head circumference for an easy fit. That means that you will need to start with a set of four double-pointed needles (dpn). As the number of stitches increases, you can switch over to a circular needle (cn) or continue to knit it entirely on double-pointed needles.

All top-down hats begin with 12 stitches, which can be cast on in a number of different ways. The Wrap Method is one that I highly recommend because it's fun to do and creates a holeless crown as well. It works especially well for felted hats, because the felting makes the starting stitches disappear into the hat entirely.

Hats knit from the bottom up are different. You start out with a large number of stitches to create the brim, then decrease to achieve the shaping of the crown. Top-down and bottom-up methods are essentially the same process in reverse. However, for sizing and shaping, the top-down method is preferable because if you make a mistake, want to customize the hat, or make its rise longer for some reason, you won't have to tear apart the entire hat to do so.

Knitting In-the-Round

The optimal way to fashion a classic knitted hat is without seams, which means knitting in-the-round. Seamless knitting provides the best appearance and fit. Except for hats with irregular tops, most of the other styles are knitted from the top down using double-pointed needles (dpn) and then circular needles (cn) as the stitches multiply.

Mastering double-pointed needles (dpn) and circular needles (cn) is the biggest challenge for any would-be hatmaker. The good news is that it's not really difficult at all. In fact, it's lots of fun once you get the hang of it. The general idea is that you're knitting stitches off one needle and onto another, repeating the process as you go around.

If you haven't knitted with double-pointed needles before, practice and do a few trial runs before you begin to make your first hat.

Knitting In-the-Round

SETTING UP

Holding the two dpn together, CO 24 sts. Holding them together allows the first row to be cast on evenly and with room to knit the next row. Once you have 24 sts, slip one needle out so that

Continued ➡

now you have a loosely cast on set of sts. Without twisting the needles or stitches, divide the 24 sts amongst 3 needles, 8 sts on each needle.

KNITTING STS ONTO THE FIRST DPN

With a dpn, knit 8 sts off the first needle.

KNITTING STS ONTO THE SECOND DPN

With the free needle, knit the next 8 sts off the first needle.

KNITTING STS ONTO THE THIRD DPN

With the free needle, knit the final 8 sts off the first needle.

PATTERN ABBREVIATIONS

b—back

beg—beginning

BO—bind off

CO—cast on

con—continue

cn—circular needle

dec—decrease

dpn—double-pointed needle(s)

f—front

inc—increase

k—knit

ktbl—knit through the back loop

k2tog—knit two stitches together

MB—make a bobble

m1—increase, make a stitch by knitting into the back of a stitch and then knitting the stitch itself

p—purl

p2tog—purl two stitches together

pm—place marker

PU—pick up

rnd—round

RS—right side

s1—slip one stitch knitwise if following stitch is knit stitch, or purlwise if following stitch is purl stitch

skp—slip 1, knit 1, pass slip stitch over

t1—increase; make a stitch by pulling up a stitch from between the two stitches in the row below

WS—wrong side

yo—yarn over

ARRANGING THE NEEDLES TO WORK IN-THE-ROUND

The 24 sts should now be evenly divided among 3 dpns. With the free needle, begin to knit the 8 sts off of the first needle, at the same time connecting the third needle with the first. So, you are now knitting "in-the-round" (rnd) instead of in rows.

Casting On: Traditional Method 1

SETUP FOR CASTING ON

Measure off 1 inch/3cm of yarn for every st that you want to cast on. For 12 sts, you want to measure off at least 12 inches/30cm of yarn plus a few extra. Make a slip knot at this junction and place on two needles being held together. Slip your thumb and index finger through the doubled-up strand of yarn created by the slip knot.

ARRANGING THE YARN ON YOUR HANDS TO BEGIN CASTING ON

Holding both sides of the yarn with your left baby finger for tension, draw your hand back to begin casting on stitches.

MAKING A STITCH

Slip a dpn under the thread farthest to the left and grab the left-side thread positioned on the index finger.

COMPLETING THE STITCH, PART I

Pull this thread under and through the first thread, then slide this st onto the right-hand needle. Repeat until you have 12 sts.

COMPLETING THE STITCH, PART II

To avoid unnecessary loops or gaps in your first row, make sure each new stitch is pulled firmly before you begin the next cast-on stitch.

SETUP FOR KNITTING IN-THE-ROUND

Once you have 12 sts, divide them among three dpn and begin to knit in-the-round.

Casting On: Traditional Method II

SETUP FOR CASTING ON

Make a simple loop stitch or slipknot.

MAKING A STITCH

Knit into the loop stitch.

TRANSFERING THE STITCH

Place that stitch on the right-hand needle. Repeat until there are 12 sts.

KNITTING IN-THE-ROUND

Divide the 12 sts among three dpn and knit 1 rnd. Continue by following the pattern instructions.

Casting On: the Wrap Method

STARTING THE WRAP, PART I

Holding the two dpns together and starting from the left, wrap the yarn around the needles as shown.

STARTING THE WRAP, PART II

You should have three "wraps" or sts, on each side.

TRANSFERING THE STITCHES

Using the third needle, knit the 3 sts on the left needle, turn the work and using another needle, knit the 3 sts on that side.

STARTING INCREASES

Next round, with a free dpn, increase 1 st in each of the next 2 sts. Using another free dpn, repeat. Using the third and last dpn, repeat. When the round is completed, you should have 4 sts on each of three dpn for a total of 12 sts.

K 1 rnd.

MAKING INCREASES

For the next round, k1, inc 1 st in the next st and repeat around.

K 1 rnd.

Next rnd, k2, inc 1 st in the next st, repeat around. K 1 round. Repeat this pattern, increasing by 1 additional st between increases, until you have increased the crown to the desired diameter or size. Once all increases have been completed, knit the sts onto a cn for medium size (16"/41cm) or large size (24"/61cm); small size hats have to be completed on dpn.

Increasing Stitches

Increasing and decreasing stitches shapes the knitted piece you're making. There's more than one way to increase the number of stitches on your needle. This section focuses on increasing, rather than decreasing because of the top-down construction of many of the patterns in this section. You'll be multiplying stitches to obtain the proper head circumference. You might ask, "Why do I need to know more than one way to increase?" The answer is that each method creates a different appearance in the finished knitted piece. For instance, a yarnover (yo) increase leaves holes, which is why the kind of increase is commonly used in lacemaking. Pulling a stitch from behind the next one to be worked on the needle has the opposite effect. You'll need to make increases exactly as specified in a pattern in order to achieve the desired effect.

Yarnovers (yo)

This method involves bringing the yarn forward and over the right-hand needle, thereby placing another stitch on the needle. The stitch immediately following is then knitted or urled, securing the yarnover in its place. Yarnovers are most often used for mesh or lacemaking, but they are also needed for picot edgings and to create spaces to run ribbon or a string through a knitted piece.

Take One (t1)

For this increase, slip the right-hand needle between the two sts in the row below, and pull up 1 st, placing it on the right-hand needle. This also creates a hole, but usually not as large as a yo.

Make One (m1)

This increase involves knitting in the back of the st on the left-hand needle, and then knitting the stitch itself, creating an almost invisible increase (i.e., no hole).

Finishing

After you have finished knitting your hat, you will have yarn ends hanging out. One at a time, thread each end onto a needle and then work it into the back of the fabric, ideally for 2 inches/5 cm.

If you have not used the Wrap Method to cast on at the beginning, but instead cast on 12 sts in one of the more traditional ways, you will also need to secure the hole that was made.

To do this, thread a darning needle with the yarn end, and take a stitch in each loop around. Once you have gone all the way around, pull firmly and push the needle through to the wrong side and secure inside, draring the thread through the fabric for 1 to 2 inches/2.4 to 5cm.

Yarn and Gauge

Knitted hats can be made with just about any yarn weight, but this collection relies primarily on heavier weight yarns that produce fewer stitches per inch. With heavier yarn, hats knit up more quickly, but more important, the weight of the yarn offers more heft and, therefore, more shape to the hat.

Using Multiple Strands of Yarns

Instead of using yarn right off the skein, try creating a yarn mix to achieve the same gauge specified in the project instructions. Using multiple strands of different colors of yarn or shades of a single color instantly creates new and unique textures that can give a hat a whole new dimension. Best of all, you get a one-of-a-kind look.

Before you buy your yarn, check your own stash of leftover skeins and balls first. Experiment and play with various combinations and mixes. You might be able to come up with a creation made completely out of scraps, but if not, don't be shy about supplementing what you have with a great new ball of something wonderful in your local yarn shop. Here are a few design tips:

- Create a "tonal" hat by using strands in the same color family—for example, cool blues and greens, hot reds and oranges, or even neutral browns and grays.

- Stretch your leftover yarn supply—if you have a substantial amount of yarn in a certain color, but not quite enough, put a stripe in the hat. The stripe can be broad (see Jesse) or the stripe can be the entire brim. Adding embellishments, such as pompoms, fringe, tassels, beadwork, or even embroidered designs made with leftovers, can provide the unique look you seek.

Whether you intend to use scraps or head out to the yarn shop, it might help to envision, sketch, or describe the hat you would love to make. On the flip side, look at the yarns first and become inspired! There are infinite ways to get the creative juices flowing.

Make Swatches to Ascertain Gauge

Establishing the proper gauge for the pattern is of the utmost importance. This is even more so for hats than for garments, because if you are 1 inch/2.5cm or so off, you'll either be wearing the hat down around your nose, or worse yet, you might not even be able to get it on. If, after making a swatch, you have too many stitches per inch using the needles specified, you will have to increase the needle size. Conversely, if there are too few stitches per inch for the needle specified, try a smaller needle.

Start the hat only when you have figured out the combination of needles and yarn that will give you the proper gauge. Use the chart as a guideline for the approximate needle size that each weight of yarn requires. The chart indicates the gauge range used for this pattern collection, but it doesn't take into account your own personal knitting style, or your tension and the resulting gauge, which in the end is why swatchmaking is a must.

Yarn Types

Just because a yarn is labeled worsted or sport doesn't necessarily make it so. Most companies try to stay within certain guidelines for categorizing a yarn, but then again there is no yarn "bureau of standards" and you are left on your own to determine the actual weight. This is especially true for novelty yarns. However, in no way should you walk away from the mystery ball that is dazzling your eyes and fingers because you're not sure of what to call it or do with it!

The only thing that should matter to you about any fiber is what gauge it will give you in the end.

If you are really unsure, try it and make a swatch, or ask the salesperson—many stores have swatches already prepared. DK weight yarns are often the most difficult to determine—some knit up like a sport yarn and others as worsteds. Again, check the gauge.

And finally, don't pass up an interesting ball of yarn because it appears too thin (i.e., it has a small gauge). Consider blending it into a mix of yarns using the chart to get the gauge your pattern requires. It's lots of fun, and often the results are unexpectedly pleasing.

Hat Patterns

Jesse

Here's a head-hugging cap for the flapper, rapper, or preppy in you! Knit it in wool, and you've got a casual accessory; knit it in metallic or silk yarn (with beads!), and it's just right for a night on the town.

Skill Level

Easy

Size

Medium: 20 to 21"/51 to 53cm

Large: 22 to 23"/56 to 58cm

Materials

- Color A: Approx 45(55)yd/41(50)m chunky weight yarn

- Color B: Approx 55(45)yd/50(41)m chunky weight yarn

- 5.75mm (size 10 U.S.) dpn and 16"/41cm on *or size to obtain gauge*

- Stitch marker

- Darning needle

Gauge

12 sts =4"/10cm
Always check gauge.

Instructions

crown

Using dpn and A, CO 12 sts and divide among 3 dpn, or do the Wrap Method.

Rnd 1 and all off rnds: K.

Rnd 2: *k1, m1,* repeat around—18 sts total.

Rnd 4: *k2, m1,* repeat around—24 sts total.

Rnd 6: *k3, m1,* repeat around—30 sts total.

Mix it Up by Blending Yarns

Yarn weight	Gauge (sts per in)	Needles	Yarn Combinations and Approximate Equivalents
Fingering	7/18 cm	#0 to #4	—
Sport	6/15 cm	#5 or #6	2 fingering
Worsted	5/13 cm	#7 or #8	2 sport OR 1 sport and 2 fingering
Heavy Worsted	4 to 4½/ 10 to 11.5 cm	#8 or #9	3 sport OR 1 sport and 1 worsted
Chunky	3 to 3½/ 7.5 to 9 cm	#10	1 heavy worsted and worsted OR 1 worsted and 2 or 3 sport
Bulky	2 to ½/ 5 to 6.5 cm	#10½ or #11 or even larger!	3 worsted OR 1 mohair and 1 chunky OR 1 chunky and 1 worsted OR 1 thick chenille

Continued ➡

Repeat rnds 1 and 2, each time adding an additional k st before each m1, until there are 8(9) sts before each m1—60(66) sts total.

Switch to cn.

K 1 rnd.

RISE

With B, k for 6½(7)"/17(18)cm from top of crown.

BRIM

Using color A, k 1 rnd.

K1/p1 rib for 3 rnds.

BO loosely in k1/p1 rib.

FINISHING

Sew in all ends.

This hat was knit with:

Classic Elite's *Two, Two*, 100% wool, 1¾oz/50g = 55yd/50m

Large (on model)

Color A: 1 ball, color #1585 (pumpkin)

Color B: 1 ball, color #1532 (zinnia)

Variation

Use bulky weight yarn for a more substantial look and greater warmth.

MATERIALS

- Color A: Approx 65(75)yd/59(69)m bulky weight yarn
- Color B: Approx 75(65)yd/69(59)m bulky weight yarn
- 8mm (size 11 U.S.) dpn and 16"/41cm on *or size to obtain gauge*
- Stitch marker
- Darning needle

GAUGE

10 sts = 4"/10cm

Always check gauge.

INSTRUCTIONS

CROWN

Using dpn and A, CO 12 sts and divide among 3 dpn, *or do the Wrap Method.*

Rnd 1 and all odd rnds: K

Rnd 2: *k1, m1,* repeat around—18 sts total.

Rnd 4: *k2, m1,* repeat around—24 sts total.

Rnd 6: *k3, m1,* repeat around—30 sts total.

Repeat rnds 1 and 2, each time adding an additional k st before each m1, until there are 6(7) sts before each m1—48(54) sts total.

Switch to cn.

K 1 rnd.

RISE

With B, k for 6½(7)"/17(18)cm from top of crown.

BRIM

Using color A, k 1 rnd.

K1/p1 rib for 2 rnds.

BO loosely in k1/p1 rib.

FINISHING

Sew in all ends.

This hat was knit with:

Brown Sheep's *Burley Spun*, 100% wool, 8oz/226g = 132yd/121m

Medium

Color A: 1 ball, color #BS115 (oatmeal)

Color B: 1 ball, color #BS07 (sable)

Large

Color A: 1 ball, color #BS115 (oatmeal)

Color B: 1 ball, color #BS120 (pine)

Skip

Nothing could be easier to knit than this ribbed skullcap. When done in a small gauge, the look is traditional. But take it up a notch and use a wider gauge, and you're there with the latest of trends.

SKILL LEVEL

Easy

SIZE

Medium 20 to 21"/51 to 53cm

Large 22 to 23"/56 to 58cm

MATERIALS

- Approx 140(150)yd/128(137)m heavy worsted weight yarn
- 5.75mm (size 10 U.S.) dpn and 16"/41cm cn *or size to obtain gauge*
- Stitch marker
- Darning needle

GAUGE

12 sts = 4"/10cm

Always check gauge.

INSTRUCTIONS

BRIM AND RISE

Using cn for Large, dpn for Medium, CO 76(84) sts.

Pm to denote bed/end of rnd.

K2/p2, rib for 12"/30cm.

CROWN

Switch to dpn.

Rnd 1: *k2tog, p2,* repeat around—27(30) sts remain.

Rnd 2: *k1, p2,* repeat around.

Rnd 3: *k1, p2tog,* repeat around—18(20) sts remain.

Rnd 4: *k1, p1,* repeat around.

Rnd 5: K2tog around—9(10) sts remain.

Rnd 6: K.

Rnd 7: K2tog around, ending k1—10(11) sts remain.

FINISHING

For the remaining stitches, cut the yarn, leaving a 5"/13cm tail, and string the stitches onto this yarn; pull the stitches tight and sew in the end on the WS.

This hat was knit with:

Classic Elite's *Montera*, 50% llama/50% wool, 3½oz/100g = 127yd/116m

Medium: 2 balls, color #3850 (Cape Breton forest)

Variation

For a much more substantial look, use bulky weight yarn and a larger needle.

Skip in bulky yarn D

MATERIALS

- Approx 85(90) yd/78(92)m bulky weight yarn
- 9mm (size 13 U.S.) dpn and 16"/41cm cn *or size to obtain gauge*
- Stitch marker
- Darning needle

GAUGE

10 sts = 4"/10cm

Always check gauge.

INSTRUCTIONS

BRIM AND RISE

Using cn, CO 36(40) sts.

Pm to denote bed/end of rnd.

K2/p2, rib for 12"/30cm.

CROWN

Switch to dpn.

Rnd 1: *k2tog, p2,* repeat around—27(30) sts remain.

Rnd 2: *k1, p2,* repeat around.

Rnd 3: *k1, p2tog,* repeat around—18(20) sts remain.

Rnd 4: *k1, p1,* repeat around.

Rnd 5: K2tog around—9(10) sts remain.

Rnd 6: K.

Rnd 7: K2tog around.

FINISHING

For the remaining stitches, cut the yarn, leaving a 5"/13cm tail, and string the stitches onto this yarn; pull the stitches tight and sew in the end on the WS.

This hat was knit with:

Blue Sky Alpacas' *Bulky Hand Dyes*, 50% wool/50% alpaca, 3½oz/100g = 45yd/41m

Medium: 2 balls, color #1013 (dark blue)

Bobbi

At first glance, making the bobbles on this charming pillbox may seem like a complicated and time-consuming process. But give it a try—you'll find that they're fun to make and the texture they add to your design is well worth the effort.

SKILL LEVEL

Intermediate

SIZE

Medium: 20 to 21"/51 to 53m

Large: 22 to 23"/56 to 58cm

MATERIALS

- Approx 120(130)yd/110(119)m heavy worsted weight yarn
- 5.25mm (size 9 U.S.) dpn and 16"/41cm cn *or size to obtain gauge*
- Stitch marker
- Darning needle

GAUGE

16 sts = 4"/10cm

Always check gauge.

SPECIAL ABBREVIATIONS

Make Bobble (MB)

To make a bobble, k into a st 6 times, pulling up the new sts starting at the back and alternating to the front. You will end up with a cluster of sts on your right-hand needle. Starting with the outmost st on the right side of the cluster, pull the st over all the others, dropping it as you go, and repeat this with every subsequent st until only 1 st remains. Sl st this last st onto the left needle and knit it. That completes the bobble.

INSTRUCTIONS

CROWN

Using dpn, CO 12 sts and divide among 3 dpn or do the Wrap Method.

Rnd 1 and all odd rnds: K.

Rnd 2: *k1, m1,* repeat around—18 sts total.

Rnd 4: *k2, m1,* repeat around—24 sts total.

Rnd 6: *k3, m1,* repeat around—30 sts total.

Repeat rnds 1 and 2, each time assign an additional k st before each m1, until there are 10(11) sts before each m1 st—72(78) sts total.

K 1 rnd.

Switch to cn; pm to denote beg/end of rnd.

TURN OF CROWN

P 3 rnds.

RISE

Rnd 1: K.

Rnd 2: k0(2)tog, k around—72(77) sts remain.

Rnd 3: k0(3), k0(2)tog, k around—72(76) sts remain.

Rnd 4: *k3, MB,* repeat around.

Rnds 5 to 7: K.

Rnd 8: k2, *MB, k3* repeat around, end MB, k1.

Rnds 9 to 11: K.

Rnd 12: k1, *MB, k3* repeat around, end MB, k2.

Rnds 13 to 15: K.

Rnd 16: *MB, k3,* repeat around.

Rnds 17 to 19: K.

Rnd 20: Repeat rnd 4.

Rnds 21 to 23: K.

BRIM

P 6 rnds.

BO loosely.

FINISHING

Sew in all ends.

This hat was knit with:

Blue Sky Alpacas' *Heavy Worsted Alpaca*, 50% alpaca/50% wool, 3½oz/100g = 100yd/91m

Medium: 2 balls, color #2005 (butter)

Valery

Architectural in form, yet sensuous and curvy, this versatile hat suits both men and women. It also complements both contemporary and traditional wardrobes.

SKILL LEVEL

Intermediate

SIZE

Medium: 20 to 21"/51 to 53cm

Large: 22 to 23"/56 to 58 cm

MATERIALS

- Color A: Approx 45(55)yd/41(40)m bulky weight yarn
- Color B: Approx 45(55)yd/41(40)m bulky weight yarn
- 8mm (size 11 U.S.) dpn and 16"/41cm and 24"/61cm cn *or size to obtain gauge*
- Stitch marker
- Darning needle

GAUGE

10 sts = 4"/10cm

Always check gauge.

INSTRUCTIONS

CROWN

Using dpn and A, CO 12 sts and divide among 3 dpn, or do the Wrap Method.

Rnd 1 and all odd rnds: K.

Rnd 2: *k1, m1,* repeat around—18 sts total.

Rnd 4: *k2, m1,* repeat around—24 sts total.

Rnd 6: *k3, m1,* repeat around—30 sts total.

Repeat rnds 1 and 2, each time adding an additional k st before each m1, until there are 6 (7) sts before each m1—48(54) sts.

K 1 rnd.

Switch to cn (16"/41cm for Medium, 24"/61cm for Large); pm to denote beg/end of rnd.

TURN OF CROWN AND RISE

With B: K 1 rnd.

P 5 rnds.

With color A: K 5 rnds.

With color B: K 1 rnd.

P 5 rnds.

With color A: K 5 rnds.

With color B: K 1 rnd.

P 5 rnds.

With WS facing, BO loosely.

FINISHING

Sew in all ends.

This hat was knit with:

Brown Sheep's *Burley Spun*, 100% wool, 8oz/226g = 132yd/121m

Large:

Color A: 1 ball, Burley Spun, #BS05 (onyx)

Color B: 1 ball, Burley Spun, #BS07 (sable)

Bret

Some things just never change, and thankfully that old adage applies to the simple beret. This pattern updates the classic version using the chunkiest yarn ever. Just slip it on, give it a slight tug to one side, and off you go!

SKILL LEVEL

Beginner

SIZE

Medium: 20 to 21"to 51 to 53cm

Large: 22 to 23"/56 to 58cm

MATERIALS

- Approx 100(110) yd/91(101)m chunky weight yarn
- 6.50mm (size 10½ U.S.) dpn and 24"/61cm cn *or size to obtain gauge*
- Stitch marker
- Darning needle

GAUGE

12 sts = 4"/10cm

Always check gauge.

INSTRUCTIONS

CROWN

Using dpn, CO 12 sts and divide among 3 dpn or do the Wrap Method.

Rnd 1 and all odd rnds: K.

Rnd 2: *k1, m1,* repeat around—18 sts total.

Rnd 4: *k2, m1,* repeat around—24 sts total.

Rnd 6: *k3, m1,* repeat around—30 sts total.

Repeat rnds 1 and 2, each time adding an additional k st before each m1; until there are 13(14) k sts before each m1—90(96) sts total.

K 3 rnds.

Switch to cn; pm to denote beg/end of rnd.

UNDERSIDE

Rnd 1: *k13(14), k2tog,* repeat around—84(90) sts remain.

Rnd 2 and all even rnds: K.

Rnd 3: *k12(13), k2tog,* repeat around—78(84) sts remain.

Rnd 5: *k11(12), k2tog,* repeat around—72(78) sts remain.

Rnd 7: *k10(11), k2tog,* repeat around—66(72) sts remain.

Rnd 9: *k9(10), k2tog,* repeat around—60(66) sts remain.

K 3 rnds.

BO loosely.

FINISHING

Sew in all ends.

This hat was knit with:

Rowan's *Chunky Print*, 100% wool, 3½oz/100g = 110yd/100m

Medium and Large: 1 ball, color #76 (blue multi)

Continued ➡

Ella

Unlike other styles in this book, this entrelac beret is probably not one that you are going to knit in the car on the way to the ski slopes. But if you're looking for a challenge, your efforts will be rewarded. Entrelac knitting creates a basket weave effect that looks as though the individual strips had been knit together, just like the latticing of a cherry pie.

CROWN

Using dpn, CO 12 sts and divide among 3 spn or do the Wrap Method described on page 00.

Rnd I and all odd rnds: K.

Rnd 2: *k1, m1,* repeat around—18 sts total.

Rnd 4: *k2, m1,* repeat around—24 sts total.

Rnd 6: *k3, m1,* repeat around—30 sts total.

Repeat rnds I and 2, each time adding an additional k st before each m1, until there are 7(8) k sts before each m1—54(60) sts total.

K I rnd, switch to cn (16"/24cm for Medium, 24"/61cm for Large); pm to denote beg/end of rnd.

TURN OF CROWN

P 2 rnds.

RISE

(The Beginning of the Entrelac Pattern)

Rnd I (this rnd makes half-squares or triangles which form the base row):

*k2, turn,

s1, p1, turn,

k3, turn,

s1, p2, turn,

k4, turn,

s1, p3, turn,

k5, turn,

s1, p4, turn,

k6,

Repeat from * to end of round.

Rnd 2: turn, p6 sts just knitted.

Using dpn, **PU 6 sts from edge of square below and p them.

*turn, k6, turn.

Note: PU is to 'pick up' sts; often a dpn is helpful in doing so; also you should not be attaching a ball of yarn, just pick the stitches up in the designated row.

P5, p2tog.

Note: The second stitch of the p2tog comes from the next group of 6 sts on the needle.

Repeat from * 5x more.

Repeat from ** 8(9)x more.

Rnd 3: Turn and k 6 sts just purled.

Using dpn, ** PU 6 sts from the edge of square below and k them

*turn, p6 sts.

K5, skp.

Repeat from * 5x more.

Repeat from ** (8, 9)x more.

Rnd 4: Turn, p6 sts just knitted.

Using dpn, *PU 6 sts from edge of square below and p them, turn,

k6, turn,

p5, p2tog, turn,

k5, turn,

p4, p2tog, turn,

k4, turn,

p3, p2tog, turn,

k3, turn,

p2, p2tog, turn,

k2, turn,

p1, p3tog,

repeat from ** around.

BRIM

With RS facing, k 7 rnds.

BO loosely.

FINISHING

Sew in all ends.

This hat was knit with:

Brown Sheep's *Lamb's Pride Bulky*, 85% wool/15% mohair, 4oz/113g = 125yd/114m

Large: I ball, color #M-16 (seafoam)

Kringle

Nothing could be easier to knit than this gathered-tube topper, it's a great pattern to use with a variety of textured and patterned yarns. What sets it off stylistically from other "easy" hats is the tie (your choice) that serves to gather the crown together.

SKILL LEVEL

Beginner

SIZE

Medium: 20 to 21"/51 to 53cm

Large: 22 to 23"/56 to 58cm

MATERIALS

- Color A: Approx 160(175)yd/146(160)m heavy worsted weight yarn
- Color B: Approx 30yd/27m heavy worsted weight yarn
- 5.25mm (size 9 U.S.) dpn and 16"/41cm cn or size to obtain gauge
- Stitch marker
- Darning needle

GAUGE

16 sts = 4"/10cm

Always check gauge

INSTRUCTIONS

BRIM AND RISE

Using cn and A, CO 72(76) sts.

Pm to denote beg/end of rnd.

K for 9½"/24cm.

K2, k2tog, yo, repeat around, end k2(0).

K for 1½"/4cm.

Using B, BO loosely.

FINISHING

Sew in all ends. Using a double strand of B, make a chain 18"/46cm long. Weave this in and out of the yo row, evening out the chain and then securing it with a square knot. Make two 1"/2.5cm pompoms (a quick pompom: wind yarn around two fingers held together and then tie in the middle) and attach to the bottom of the chain.

This hat was knit with:

Classic Elite's *Bazic*, 100% wool, 1¾oz/50g = 64yd/59m

Variations

For just a little more texture, try one of these tweed chunky weight yarns.

MATERIALS

- Color A: Approx 109(135)yd/98(123)m chunky weight yarn
- Color B: Approx 30yd/27m chunky weight yarn
- 5.75mm (size 10 U.S.) dpn and 16"/41cm cn or size to obtain gauge
- Stitch marker
- Darning needle

GAUGE

12 sts = 4"/10cm

Always check gauge.

INSTRUCTIONS

BRIM AND RISE

Using cn and color A, CO 60 (64) sts.

Pm to denote beg/end of rnd.

K for 9½"/24cm.

K2, k2tog, yo, repeat around.

K for 1½"/4cm.

Using a double strand (3yd/3m long) of color B, BO loosely.

FINISHING

Sew in all ends. Using a double strand of color B, make a chain 18"/46cm long. Weave this in and out of the yo row, evening out the chain and then securing it with a square knot. Make two 1"/2.5cm pompoms (a quick pompom: wind yarn around two fingers held together and then tie in the middle) and attach to the bottom of the chain.

This hat was knit with:

Rowan's *Yorkshire Tweed Chunky*, 100% wool, 3½oz/100g = 123yd/113m and Rowan's *Yorkshire Tweed DK*, 100% wool, 1¾oz/50g = 123yd/113m

Medium:
Color A: 2 balls, *Tweed Chunky*, color #556 (flaming)
Color B: I ball, *Tweed DK*, color #347 (skip)

Large:
Color A: 2 balls, *Tweed Chunky*, color #550 (damp)
Color B: I ball, *Tweed DK*, color #344 (scarlet)

Cosima

Featuring subtly textured stripes and luxuriously soft wool, Cosima is a versatile choice. It's whimsical enough to wear with jeans, but wouldn't look out of place with a dressy coat.

SKILL LEVEL

Intermediate

SIZE

Medium: 20 to 21"/51 to 53cm

Large: 22 to 23"/56 to 58cm

MATERIALS

- Color A: 100(110)yd/91(101)m chunky weight yarn
- Color B: 40(40)yd/37(37)m chunky weight yarn
- 5.25mm (size 9 U.S.) dpn and 16"/41cm on or size to obtain gauge
- Stitch marker
- Darning needle

GAUGE

13 sts = 4"/10cm

Always check gauge.

INSTRUCTIONS

CROWN

Using dpn and A, CO 12 sts and among between 3 dpn or do the Wrap Method.

Rnd 1 and all odd rnds: K.

Rnd 2: *k1, m1,* repeat around—18 sts total.

Rnd 4: *k2, m1,* repeat around—24 sts total.

Rnd 6: *k3, m1,* repeat around—30 sts total.

Repeat rnds 1 and 2, each time adding an additional k st before each m1, until there are 10(11) k sts before each m1—72(78) sts total.

K 1 rnd.

Switch to cn; pm to denote beg/end of rnd.

TURN OF CROWN

P 3 rnds.

RISE

K 2 rnds.

With B: P 2 rnds.

With A: K 3 rnds.

Repeat the last 5 rnds, 4x more.

With A: K 2 rnds.

P 2 rnds.

BO 7(9), p16(17) place on dpn, for earflap, BO 26(26), p16(17) place on dpn, for earflap, BO7(9).

EARFLAPS

With RS facing and working back and forth on dpn, attach A:

Row 1: k3, p10(11), k3.

Row 2: p3, k10(11), p3.

Rows 3 and 4: Repeat rows 1 and 2.

Row 5: k3, p2tog, p6(7), p2tog, k3.

Row 6: p3, k8(9), p3.

Row 7: k3, p2tog, p4(5), p2tog, k3.

Row 8: p3, k6(7), p3.

Row 9: k3, p2tog, p2(3), p2tog, k3

Row 10: p3, k4(5), p3.

Row 11: k3, p2tog, p0(1), p2tog, k3.

Row 12: p3, k2tog(k3tog), p3.

Row 13: K.

Row 14: p1, p2tog, p1, p2tog, p1.

Row 15: k2tog, k1, BO, k2tog, BO.

Draw a string through the remaining st and fasten off.

FINISHING

Sew in all ends.

With B, make two tassels and sew them to the ends of the earflaps.

This hat was knit with:

Tahki Stacy Charles' *Bunny*, 50% wool/25% alpaca/25% acrylic, 1¾oz/50g = 81yd/89m

Medium (on model):
Color A: 2 balls, color #5 (mint green)
Color B: 1 ball, color #4 (soft pink)

Large:
Color A: 2 balls, color #13 (rust)
Color B: 1 ball, color #3 (gray)

—FROM *Hip Knit Hats*

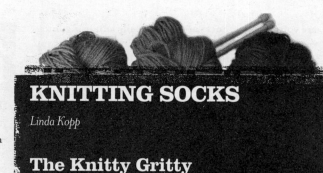

KNITTING SOCKS

Linda Kopp

The Knitty Gritty

Sock Anatomy 101

A simple sock consists of many parts, each of which has a different function and can be worked in a number of ways. Here's a little sock anatomy review: no blushing!

Not all socks emphasize or include all parts. Many of the projects don't use traditional gusset shaping; instead, a general increase of stitches (arch expansion) is worked near the heel shaping to provide the needed room for the arch.

Anatomy of a sock Missing Image???

THE WAY YOU WORK IT

Socks can be worked in several different directions. A sock knitter can begin at the cuff and work down to the heel, turn the corner (working the heel), and then work the foot and toe (called "cuff down," as in A Roll in the Hay. Alternately, in a process called "toe up," the knitter begins at the tow, works the foot, turns the corner, and then works up the leg and cuff. An explorative knitter might also work either from the cuff down or the toe up, skip the heel shaping, complete the sock, and then return to insert the skipped heel. This is a technique dubbed the "afterthought heel."

HUGGING THE CURVES

You'll get the most bang for your buck if you spend some time on heels and toes; these sock parts invite the most variety, creativity, and foot-hug-ability. The projects in *The Joy of Sox* demonstrate a number of different heel constructions, including standard, short row, Cyber Flirt, and afterthought. A standard heel consists of a heel flap that lies down the back of the heel and a heel turn that wraps under the heel. A short row heel—which most resembles a commercial sock heel—consists of a series of progressively shorter short rows followed by an equivalent number of progressively longer short rows that form a cup for the heel (and may include a heel flap). Decidedly more impressive than its name, an afterthought heel is worked, in decreasing rounds, into an opening created when initially knitting the sock.

Toe constructions include standard, star, Quickie Socks, short row, and rectangle. A standard toe is formed with paired decreases (cuff down) or increases (toe up) worked on either side of the toe. A star toe is formed with rounds of evenly spaced decreases. A short row toe is formed, like a short row heel, with a series of progressively shorter short rows followed by an equivalent number of progressively longer short rows. A rectangle toe is formed with a small rectangle of knitting, around which stitches are picked up and worked to begin the foot.

Does Size Matter?

It's an age-old question, and, when it comes to socks, the answer is yes and no. Knitted fabric stretches and is very forgiving. So, a sock of any size will fit a range of feet, within reason, of course. The most important dimensions of a sock are the leg length, foot length, foot circumference, and calf circumference (for taller socks). Your foot length is measured from the back of the heel to the tip of the longest toe. Foot circumference is measured around the widest part of the foot near the ball of the foot. The calf circumference is the distance around the widest part of the calf.

Most of the socks in this book are designed to fit women's feet, although some provide instructions for multiple sizes and others do not. In most designs, the leg length and foot length are easily altered by working fewer or more rounds. Work the leg until it measures the desired length. Work the foot until it measures 1½ to 2 inches (4 to 5 cm) less than desired foot length to allow for the tow (cuff down) or heel (toe up).

BIG SHOES? BIG FEET!

Nobody likes to be average, but it's nice to have some standard measurements to work with when you're making socks. Here's a handy chart for average foot length and circumference measurements, along with standard shoe sizes.

MAKING ADJUSTMENTS

Adjusting the foot or calf circumference of your knitted creation can be achieved in three ways. Thicker yarn or larger needles, thus a different gauge, will produce socks with a smaller circumference. Of course, you could also change both the yarn weight and the needle size. To check what circumference will be achieved by changing yarn thickness or needle size:

1. Knit a gauge swatch. Work in the round and use the appropriate pattern stitch. Measure the gauge swatch and determine the number of stitches per 4"/10cm.

Shoe Size (Euro)	Foot Length	Foot Circumference
Children's 4–6 (19–22)	4½–5½"/11.4–14cm	5½"/14cm
Children's 7–9 (23–25)	5½–6½"/14–16.5cm	6"/15.2cm
Children's 10–12 (27–30)	6½–7½"/16.5–19cm	6½"/16.5cm
Children's 13–3 (31–34)	7½–8½"/19–21.6cm	7¼"/18.4cm
Women's 3–5 (34–35)	8–9"/20.3–22.9cm	7½"/19cm
Women's 6–9 (37–40)	9–10"/22.9–25.4cm	8"/20.3cm
Women's 10–12 (41–44)	10–11"/25.4–27.9cm	8½"/21.6cm
Women's 13–14 (45–47)	11–12"/27.9–30.5cm	9¼"/23.5cm
Men's 4–7 (35–40)	9–10"/22.9–25.4cm	8"/20.3cm
Men's 8–10 (41–43)	10–11"/25.4–27.9cm	8½"/21.6cm
Men's 11–13 (44–47)	11–12"/27.9–20.5cm	8¾"/22.2cm
Men's 14–15 (11–49)	12–13"/30.5–33cm	9"/22.9cm

Continued ➔

2. Divide the number of stitches worked (at widest point of circumference) by the number of stitches of the gauge, and multiply the result by 4"/10cm.

If changing the yarn or needle size is not an option (perhaps it would result in fabric that is too floppy or too stiff):

1. Measure the circumference of your foot (or calf).
2. Divide the circumference by 4"/10cm, and multiply the result by the stitch gauge (number of stitches per 4"/10cm). Round this number to the nearest stitch (or color) pattern multiple. This is the number of stitches that will need to be worked around the circumference of the foot to achieve the desired size. If the stitch pattern multiple is large, try inserting a small column of Stockinette stitch between repeats of the pattern.

Changing the number of stitches around the widest point of the foot or calf may also require adjusting the heel shaping and other parts of the sock. The number of heel stitches worked should be proportional to the number of stitches worked around the widest part of the foot. Use a proportion to determine a reasonable number of heel stitches to work. First, divide the new number of foot stitches by the old number of foot stitches. Multiply the result by the old number of heel stitches. Round this result for the new number of heel stitches needed.

Specific instructions for working the heel over the new number of stitches depend on the type of heel being worked.

Working a Standard Heel (cuff down)

Note: There are many variations on this technique.

Heel Flap: Work back and forth in rows over all stitches until flap is as long as desired.

Turn Heel:

Row 1: Work slightly more than one-half of the heel stitches (how many depends on the desired width for the back of the heel). Note the number of stitches left unworked, turn.

Row 2: Work across, leaving the same number of stitches unworked as were left in first row, turn.

Row 3: Work to one stitch before the gap formed by the turn of the previous row, decrease over the next stitch and the stitch following the gap, work one more stitch.

Repeat the last row until all heel stitches have been worked.

Note: The last couple of repeats may not need to work an additional stitch following the decrease.

WORKING A SHORT ROW HEEL

Note: There are many variations on this technique.

Rows 1 and 2: Work to last heel st, wrap and turn.

Row 3: Work to 1 st before first wrapped st, wrap and turn.

Repeat last row until section of unwrapped stitches measures desired width for back of heel and there are an equal number of wrapped stitches on either side of the unwrapped stitches.

Next row: Work to first wrapped st, pick up the wrap and work it together with the st it wrapped.

Repeat last row until all wraps have been worked.

Sock Techniques

Whether you're a backseat-of-the-Mustang or an on-the-couch-in-front-of-the-television kind of knitter, you won't get very far in the sock world without the tools, tricks, and techniques of the trade.

USING YOUR TOOLS

No knitting kit would be complete without at least a few toys, and, thankfully, there's no shortage of sox paraphernalia out there. However, your most important tools are your needles. Socks are traditionally knit using four or five double-pointed needles. But don't feel bad if you want to explore a little, experimentation is good. Recent advances in materials have inspired new sock knitting techniques that use one or two circular needles.

DPNs, Baby!

Double-pointed needles are the physical embodiment of sock efficiency, although all those pointy ends can feel a little sadistic at times. Cast on to one needle, distribute the stitches over three or four needles, and arrange the needles in a ring. With an additional needle—the working needle—work the stitches from the first needle. The newly empty needle then becomes the working needle. Use the working needle to work the stitches from the next needle, and so on, until all stitches on all needles have been worked, and a round has been completed.

Here's how: One or two needles hold the front of the leg (or instep) stitches, and two needles hold the back of the leg (or sole or heel) stitches. The first needle to be worked is needle #1, and the remaining needles are numbered, in increasing order, clockwise. Each round of knitting instructions specifies how all the stitches on all the needles are to be worked (e.g. Round 2: Knit.) or how the stitches on each of the three or four needles are to be worked (e.g. Round: Needle #1: K to last 3 sts, ssk, k1; Needle #2: K1, k2tog, k to last 3 sts, ssk, k1; Needle #3: K1, k2tog, k to end).

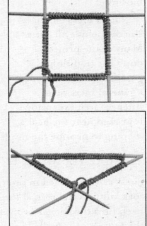

Two Circulars: Twice the Fun!

In the mood for something a little less conventional? Try working with two 24"/61cm circular needles. Cast on to one needle, and then slide one-half of the stitches onto the other needle. Hold the stitches (the set of stitches with the working yarn attached) on the cable of one needle—the holding needle—and allow the tips to dangle behind the work. Work the stitches on the other needle, called the active needle. When all the stitches on the active needle have been worked, slide them to the cable and allow the tips to dangle. Rotate the work clockwise, bringing the other needle to the front. Slide the held stitches to the tip of the needle, and work these stitches to complete a round.

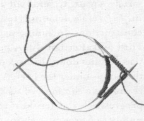

Here's how: One needle holds the front of the leg (or instep) stitches, and the other holds the back of the leg (or sole or heel) stitches. The needles may be numbered, needle #1 and needle #2 (or needles a and B). Each round

of knitting instructions specifies how all the stitches on all the needles are to be worked (e.g. Round 2: Knit) or how stitches on each of the two needles are to be worked (e.g. Round 2: Needle #1: Work in instep pattern across; Needle #2: Knit).

Rules for the Solo Circular

Are you a quick-and-dirty kind of knitter? Using a single long circular needle, the magic loop method might be for you. Cast on to the needle. Gently pull the cable out from the midpoint of the stitches, forming a large loop and leaving one-half of the stitches lying on each end of the cable. Leave one set of stitches (the set of stitches with the working yarn attached) on the cable, and slide the other set of stitches onto the tip. Draw out enough of the cable to work comfortably (forming another loop), and work the set of stitches from the tip. Slide the recently worked stitches to the cable, rotate the work (bringing the unworked stitches to the front), and slide the unworked stitches onto the tip. Draw out enough of the cable to work comfortably, and work this set of stitches to complete a round.

Here's how: One set of stitches is the front of the leg (or instep) stitches, and the other set is the back of the leg (or sole or heel stitches). Since there is only one needle, it is not numbered. Each round of knitting instructions specifies how all the stitches are to be worked (e.g. Round 2: Knit) or how each set of stitches are to be worked (e.g. Round 2: Work in instep pattern across instep sts, slide stitches, knit across heel sts) and may indicate when the sets of stitches need to be redistributed between the cable and the tip.

Mixing Things Up

A little variety can help spice up your sox life. Sometimes it's best to use a combination of needle techniques to get the best of both worlds. In either case, the project instructions specify whether double-pointed needles, two circular needles, or a single circular needle are needed. However, any of the projects can be worked using any of the needle techniques, so you can always work with what you've got.

Double-pointed needle instructions worked on one or two circular needles: Work the instructions for the heel over the stitches on one of the two circular needles or one set of stitches on the single circular needle. Work the instructions for the instep stitches over the stitches on the second of the two circular needles or the other set of stitches on the single circular needle.

Circular needle instructions worked on double-pointed needles: Work the instructions for one of the two circular needles, or one set of stitches on the single circular needle, on stitches distributed evenly over two double-pointed needles. Work the instructions for the second of the two circular needles, or the other set of stitches on the single circular needle, on stitches distributed evenly over two more double-pointed needles.

SOXPERT SECRET #14:
To stay oriented, place markers to indicate the beginning of the set of stitches associated with each double-pointed needle.

Two circular needle instructions worked on one circular needle: Work one set of stitches on the single circular needle in the same manner as stitches on one of the two circular needles. Work the other set of stitches on the single circular needle in the same manner as stitches on the second of the two circular needles.

One circular needle instructions worked on two circular needles: Work the stitches on one circular needle in the same manner as one set of stitches on the single circular needle. Work the stitches on the second circular needle in the same manner as the other set of stitches on the single circular needle.

CASTING ON/GETTING IT ON

So, you're primed, ready, and in the mood for a little sock making. Time to get started, but don't rush things with a kinky cast on. Many of these projects will work using any basic cast-on technique, including long tail, knit-on, cable, and backwards loop/e-wrap. If a particular cast-on technique is not specified in the project instructions, use the technique that you like.

PROVISIONAL CAST-ON TECHNIQUES

A provisional cast on allows a knitter to easily work into the stitches along the opposite side of the cast-on edge. This technique is useful when working a fold-over cuff or working a toe-up sock like Big Tease. There are a number of other provisional cast-on techniques, any of which may be used in projects that do not specify a particular provisional cast on. Here are two specific provisional cast-on methods that you might not have worked with before.

WASTE YARN PROVISIONAL CAST ON

Use a length of waste yarn to work the first round. Work the next round with the project yarn. When the stitches along the opposite side of the cast-on edge are needed, carefully remove the waste yarn exposing the stitches, and slip the exposed stitches onto needles.

You can also use the waste yarn technique to easily work into a section of stitches in the middle of a piece, for example, when you're working an afterthought heel. Work the waste yarn in the desired location, then resume work with the project yarn, first working across the stitches of the waste yarn. When the stitches around the waste yarn are needed, carefully remove the waste yarn to expose the stitches, and slip the exposed stitches onto needles.

CHAINED CAST ON

Use a crochet hook and waste yarn to make a length of chains. Make two more chains that the number of stitches to be cast on. Beginning in the second chain, pick up one stitch in each chain until the desired number of stitches has been placed on needles. As with the waste yarn cast on, when the stitches along the opposite side of the cast-on edge are needed, carefully remove the waste yarn chain, expose the stitches, and slip the exposed stitches onto needles.

Some knitters like the slow buildup of working from the toe up the leg. There are specific cast-on techniques particularly suited for the toe-up method. All of the following cast-on techniques can be worked with circular or double-pointed needles.

Turkish Cast On

Hold two needles in your left hand, one on top of the other. Make a slip knot with the working yarn and place it on the lower needle. Wrap the working yarn back underneath the needles, up and over the top of the needles, and back down to the bottom (this is your first stitch). Continue wrapping yarn around your set of needles until the correct number of stitches are placed; each needle holds one half of the total number of stitches (step 1). Pull the lower needle

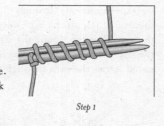
Step 1

YARN-O-RAMA

If there's a sensual part of a sock, and we're pretty sure there is, it's got to be the yarn. Socks have been made from almost every imaginable fiber—from flax to cotton, alpaca to silk, and acrylic to latex—in various degrees of tactile appeal. But, of course, it's not all about pleasing the fingers. Sock yarns are selected for durability, warmth, absorbency, elasticity, and beauty. Wool is one of the warmest fibers, while acrylic is one of the most durable. Cotton is highly absorbent, alpaca is seriously soft, and silk reflects color beautifully. And the choices continue; modern sock yarn blends combine the best qualities of several fibers to achieve every desirable characteristic. For an extra foot-hugging fit, a thin strand of elastic can be worked along with a strand of yarn to provide additional stretch and strength to the cuffs, heel, or toes of socks.

The weight (or thickness) of yarn has a profound effect on the process and result of knitted socks. The standard yarn weight system groups yarns into seven weight categories: 0-lace, 1-superfine, 2-fine, 3-light, 4-medium, 5-bulky, and 6-super bulky. The majority of socks are knit with yarn weights ranging from 0 to 4.

0-lace weight (10-count thread): Not afraid of commitment? Built for comfort—not for speed—this weight requires the use of very thin needles and a large number of stitches; you're going to have to take your sweet time. This yarn yields lightweight socks with that "barely there" feel.

1-superfine (fingering or sock weight): Tried and true. As the name "sock weight" suggests, this weight is frequently used for knitting socks. It produces a light yet sturdy fabric for a product that's, dare we say, "dependable."

2-fine (sport or baby): Wishing for socks with a little athletic prowess? Sport weight yarn allows for a little more speed and strength, allowing you to really go the distance. This slightly thicker yarn works up quickly on larger needles with a smaller number of stitches and yields a sock with a bit more "oomph."

3-light (double knit or light worsted): Want to have your cake and eat it too? Light worsted weight yarn can provide the speed and strength of sport weight yarn, but the result is a sleeker sock. Think velour track suit: sporty, yes, but who runs in velour?

4-medium (worsted): Looking for a quickie? This weight works up very quickly with large needles and few stitches. Socks made with worsted weight yarn are perfect for cushion and warmth, and you don't have to feel guilty the next morning.

---

through the stitches so they are sitting on the end of the needle (or on the cable of 1 or 2 circulars). Knit the stitches of the upper needle as written in the pattern (step 2). Flip work so that the lower and upper needles are switched. Pull the lower needle through the stitches so they are sitting on the end of the needle (or on the cable of 1 or 2 circulars). Pull the upper needle through the stitches so the stitches are ready to be knit (step 3). Remove the slip knot, and knit the stitches of the upper needle as written in the pattern.

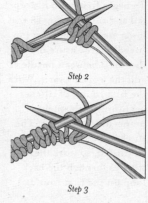
Step 2

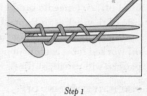
Step 3

FIGURE-8 CAST ON

Hold two needles in your left hand, one on top of the other. Hold the yarn against the lower needle, and bring the yarn between the two needles, from front to back. Wrap the yarn up and over the upper needle and back between the two needles, from front to back. Bring the yarn under and over the lower needle, from back to front, and bring the yarn between the two needles. Repeat this process until you have cast on the number of stitches desired; each needle holds one-half of the total number of stitches. The process should end with the yarn between the two needles and the lower-needle being the last needle wrapped (steps 1 and 2). Work the first round of stitches beginning with stitches on the upper needle (step 3). Flip the work when you reach the end of one needle, then work the stitches on the next needle. The stitches on the lower needle will be twisted, so work these stitches through the back loop on the first round.

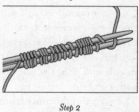
Step 1

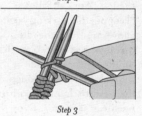
Step 2

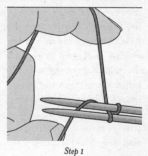
Step 3

Note: You may wish to tighten the stitches on the lower needle before working round 1 on these stitches. Tighten them, one by one, as you would your shoelaces.

Magic Cast On

Leaving a long tail (long enough to cast on one-half of the stitches), place a slip knot on one needle. Hold two needles in your right hand, one on top of the other, with the slip knot on the upper needle (the slip knot is the first stitch case on the upper needle). Hold the tail and working yarn in your left hand. Hold the tail above the needles (upper strand) and the working yarn below the needles (lower strand) (step 1). Wrap the tail of the yarn under the lower needle, from back to front, then in front of the needle and back between the two needles (one stitch cast onto lower needle). Wrap the working yarn over the upper needle, from back to front, then in front of the needle and back between the two needles (one more stitch cast onto the upper needle) (step 2). Continue alternating wrapping the lower needle with the tail (upper strand), and wrapping the upper needle with the working yarn (lower strand), until

Step 1

Continued ➜

desired number of stitches have been cast on (step 3). To begin first round, drop tail and turn needles so that lower needle is now on top (needle #1). Ensure that the tail is between needle #1 and the working yarn. Work the first round of stitches beginning with stitches on needle #1 (step 4). The stitches on needle #2 will be twisted, so work these stitches through the back loop on the first round.

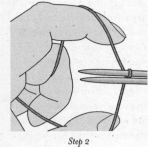

Step 2

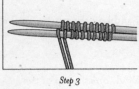

Step 3

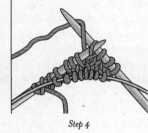

Step 4

THE GRAND FINALE: BINDING OFF

Make sure your socks end happily with the appropriate bind-off technique. When working cuff-down socks, use a sewn bind off such as Kitchener Stitch or a stretchy sewn bind off. A 3-needle bind off, worked from the wrong side of the sock as in Puppy Love, is another toe-finishing option. When working toe-up socks, any common bind off worked loosely (consider using a larger needle) and in pattern will usually suffice.

STRETCHY SEWN BIND OFF

Cut your yarn, leaving a tail that is four times longer than your bind-off edge. Thread the tail onto a yarn needle and hold the work with right side facing you. The yarn should come from the left. Work as follows: *keeping the working yarn above, insert the needle through the first two stitches on the knitting needle as if to purl, then sew through the first stitch on the knitting needle as if to knit. Drop the first stitch off the knitting needle; repeat from * until all stitches are bound off.

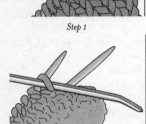

Step 1

Step 2

KITCHENER STITCH BIND OFF

Thread the long tail onto a tapestry needle. With the wrong sides together, hold both knitting needles together and even, insert the tapestry needle into the first stitch on front needle as if to purl, and draw yarn through. Leave st on needle. Hold the yarn in the back, insert the tapestry needle as if to knit into the first stitch on the back needle, and draw the yarn through. Leave the stitch on needle. Hold the yarn in front, insert the tapestry needle as if to knit through the first stitch on the front needle, and draw the yarn through. Slip the stitch off the needle. Insert the tapestry needle through the next stitch on the front needle as

Step 1

Step 2

Step 3

---

if to purl, and draw the yarn through. Leave the stitch on the needle. Insert the tapestry needle as if to purl through the first stitch on the back needle, and draw the yarn through. Slip the stitch off the needle. Insert the tapestry needle through the next stitch on the back needle as if to knit, and draw the yarn through. Leave the stitch on the needle. Repeat the last two steps until all but one stitch has been eliminated. Draw the yarn through the stitch to secure.

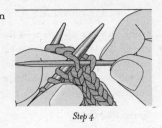

Step 4

Step 5   Step 6

KNITTING ABBREVIATIONS

CABLES

C2B: Cable 2 back—Slip 2 stitch onto cable needle and hold in back, k1, k1 from cable needle.

C2F: Cable 2 front—Slip 1 stitch onto cable needle and hold in front, k1, k1 from cable needle.

RT: Right Twist—Skip the first stitch, knit into 2nd stitch, then knit skipped stitch. Slip both stitches from needle together OR k2tog leaving stitches on left needle, then k first stitch again. Slip both stitches off needle.

C2Bp: Cable 2 back purl—Slip 1 stitch onto cable needle and hold in back, k1, p1 from cable needle.

C2Fp: Cable 2 front purl—Slip 1 stitch onto cable needle and hold in front, p1, k1 from cable needle.

C3B: Cable 3 back—Slip 2 stitches onto cable needle and hold in back, k1, k2 from cable needle.

C3F: Cable 3 front—Slip 1 stitch onto cable needle and hold in front, k2, k1 from cable needle.

C3Bp: Cable 3 back purl—Slip 1 stitch onto cable needle and hold in back, k2, p1 from cable needle.

C3Fp: Cable 3 front purl—Slip 2 stitches onto cable needle and hold in front, p1, k2 from cable needle.

C4B: Cable 4 back—Slip 2 stitches onto cable needle and hold in back, k2, k2 from cable needle.

C4F: Cable 4 front—Slip 2 stitches onto cable needle and hold in front, k2, k2 from cable needle.

C5Fp: Cable 5 front purl—Slip 3 stitches onto cable needle and hold in front, k2 (p1, k2) from cable needle.

dec: decreas(e)(ing)(s).

k: knit

k2tog: Knit 2 stitches together.

k3tog: Knit 3 stitches together.

kfb: Knit in front and back of stitch (increase).

inc: increase(e)(ing)(s)

m1: make 1

On RS (m1k): make 1 knit: Insert right needle from back to front under the strand between two stitches, lift this loop onto left needle and knit into the back of the loop.

On WS (m1p): make 1 purl: Insert right needle from back to front under the strand between two stitches, lift this loop onto left needle and purl into the front of the loop.

p: purl

pfb: Purl in front and back of stitch (increase).

---

p2tog: Purl 2 stitches together.

sl: slip

skp: Slip 1 stitch, knit, pass slipped stitch over.

sk2p: Slip 1 stitch, k2tog, pass slipped stitch over.

S2kp2: Slip 2 stitches as if to knit 2 stitches together, knit 1, pass both slipped stitches over (2 stitches decreased).

ssk: slip, slip, knot—Slip 1 stitch as if to knot, slip next stitch as if to knit. Insert left needle through the front loops of the two slipped stitches and knit them together.

ssp: slip, slip, purl—Slip 1 stitch as if to purl, slip next stitch as if to knit, slip both stitches back to left-hand needle and p2tog through back loop.

sssk: slip, slip, slip, knit 3 slipped stitches together.

st(s): stitch(es)

St st: Stockinette stitch

tbl: through back loop

w&t: wrap and turn

(RS) Move the yarn to the front of the work (between the needles), slip the next stitch, move the yarn to the back of the work (between the needles), slip the stitch back onto the left needle, turn.

(WS) Move the yarn to the back of the work, slip the next stitch, move the yarn to the front of the work, slip the stitch back onto the left needle, turn.

wyib: with yarn in back

wyif: with yarn in front

Keeping It Clean

If you want your socks to last a long time, you'll have to put in a little extra work. Many yarn labels provide washing instructions, so save the label or note the fiber content and the recommended cleaning and drying instructions. With sock cleaning, a gentle hand is best; never use harsh chemicals, extreme temperatures, or methods other than those suggested on the yarn label. Prior to washing, remove any non-washable trims and make any needed repairs, as cleaning can enlarge a hole and unravel loose hems.

> ### SOXPERT SECRET #4
> Rather than laying your socks flat to dry, place them over appropriate-sized sock blockers to make sure they retain their size and shape. Sock blockers are available for purchase or you can make your own using carefully bent wire coat hangers, plastic canvas, or other materials.

The Sox

A Roll in the Hay

by Gina House

So named for their attractive wheat sheaves stitch pattern, these socks are a joyful combination of soft, supple texture and come-hither hues.

SKILL LEVEL
Intermediate

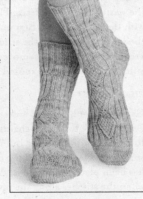

FINISHED MEASUREMENTS

Foot circumference 8½"/21.5cm

Leg length 8"/20.5cm

Foot length 7½ (9½)"/19 (24)cm

MATERIALS AND TOOLS

- Approx total: 400yd/360m of fingering weight yarn, superwash wool/bamboo/nylon blend, in gold
- Knitting needles: 2.75mm (size 2 U.S.) set of 5 double-pointed needles, *or size to obtain gauge*
- Stitch markers (optional)
- Stitch holder (optional)
- Cable needle
- Yarn needle

GAUGE

30 sts and 40 rows = 4"/10cm in Stockinette Stitch (knit every round)

Always take time to check your gauge.

MODIFIED WHEAT SHEAVES PATTERN
(MULTIPLES OF 15 ST +14)

Row 1: (P2, k2) 3 times, p2, m1, p1, m1, p2, (k2, p2) 3 times.

Row 2: (P2, k2) 3 times, p2, k1, p1, k1, p2, (k2, p2) 3 times.

Row 3: (P2, k2) 3 times, p2, m1, p1, k1, p1, m1, p2, (k2, p2) 3 times.

Row 4: (P2, k2) 3 times, p2, (k1, p1) twice, k1, p2, (k2, p2) 3 times.

Row 5: (P2, k2) 3 times, p2, m1, (p1, k1) twice, p1, m1, p2, (k2, p2) 3 times.

Row 6: (P2, k2) 3 times, p2, (k1, p1) 3 times, k1, p2, (k2, p2) 3 times.

Row 7: (P2, k2) 3 times, p2, m1, (p1, k1) 3 times, p1, m1, p2, (k2, p2) 3 times.

Row 8: (P2, k2) 3 times, p2, (k1, p1) 4 times, k1, p2, (k2, p2) 3 times.

Row 9: (P2, k2) 3 times, p2, m1, (p1, k1) 4 times, p1, m1, p2, (k2, p2) 3 times.

Row 10: P1, pfb, sl 10 sts as if to purl wyif, pass first slipped st over the other 9 slipped sts, p2, (k1, p1) 5 times, k1; end 2nd repeat with p2 instead of k1.

Row 11: (P2, k2) 3 times, p1, ssk, (p1, k1) 3 times, p1, k2tog, p2 (k2, p2) 3 times.

Row 12: (P2, k2) 3 times, p2, (k1, p1) 4 times, k1, p2, (k2, p2) 3 times.

Row 13: (P2, k2) 3 times, p2, ssk, (p1, k1) 2 times, p1, k2tog, p2, (k2, p2) 3 times.

Row 14: (P2, k2) 3 times, p2, (k1, p1) 3 times, k1, p2, (k2, p2) 3 times.

Row 15: (P2, k2) 3 times, p2, ssk, p1, k1, p1, k2tog, p2, (k2, p2) 3 times.

Row 16: (P2, k2) 3 times, p2, (k1, p1) 2 times, k1, p2, (k2, p2) 3 times.

Row 17: (P2, k2) 3 times, p2, ssk, p1, k2tog, p2, (k2, p2) 3 times.

Row 18: (P2, k2) 3 times, p2, k1, p1, k1, p2, (k2, p2) 3 times.

Row 19: (P2, k2) 3 times, p2, sk2p, p2, (k2, p2) 3 times.

Row 20: (P2, k2) 3 times, p2, k1, p2, (k2, p2) 3 times.

Repeat rows 1–20 for Modified Wheat Sheaves pattern.

CUFF

Cast on 68 sts onto one needle. Distribute the stitches evenly over four needles (17 sts per needle). Place a stitch marker for beginning of round. Taking care not to twist stitches, join to work in the round.

Work in K2, p2 Rib pattern for 2"/5cm.

LEG

Round 1 (set-up round): K2tog, p2tog, k2tog, (p2, k2) 3 times, p2, m1, p1, m1, p2tog, p1, (k2, p2) 3 times, kfb, k1 (p2, k2) 3 times, p2, m1, p1, m1, p2tog, p1, (k2, p2) 3 times—68 sts.

Round 2: *(K1, p1, k1); work row 2 of Modified Wheat Sheaves pattern; repeat from * around.

Rounds 3–40: *(K1, p1, k1); work next row of Modified Wheat Sheaves pattern; repeat from * around—64 sts.

Round 41 (transition round): P2, k1, p2, (k2, p2) 3 times, (m1, k1, m1), (p2, k2) 2 times, p2, (k2tog) twice, (p2, k1, p2), (k2, p2) 3 times, m1; continue with a different needle as follows: k1, m1, (p2, k2) twice, p2, (k2tog) twice, keep working with same needle and continue in pattern over next 19 stitches from the first needle.

You should now have 33 sts on last needle used (for instep) and 31 sts (total) on other needles (for heel).

HEEL FLAP

Work back and forth over 31 heel sts only. If desired, place instep stitches on a stitch holder or waste yarn.

Row 1 (RS): Sl 1, k2tog, *(sl 1, k1); repeat from * across—30 sts.

Row 2 (WS): Sl 1, purl across.

Row 3: *SL 1, k1; repeat from * across.

Row 4: Sl 1, purl across.

Repeat last two rows 13 more times or until heel flap measures approx 2"/5cm.

TURN HEEL

Continue to work back and forth on heel stitches only.

Row 1 (RS): Sl 1, k16, ssk, k1, turn.

Row 2 (WS): Sl 1, p5, p2tog, p1 turn.

Row 3: Sl 1, k6, ssk, k1, turn.

Row 4: Sl 1, p7, p2tog, p1, turn.

Continue working in this manner working one additional stitch before the decrease on each row, until 18 stitches remain, ending with a WS row.

Pick-up round: With RS of heel facing and spare needle, sl 1, k8 heel sts; with another needle k9 remaining heel sts, pick up and k15 sts along side of heel flap, pick up and k1 st in the corner (needle #1); work row 2 of Modified Wheat Sheaves pattern across instep stitches (needles #2 and #3); with another needle, pick up and k1 st in the corner, pick up and k15 sts along the opposite side of heel flap, k sts from spare needle (needle #4)—83 sts (25 sts each on needles #1 and #4, and 33 sts over needles #2 and #3).

SHAPE GUSSET

Round 1:

Needle #1: Knit to last 3 sts, k2tog, k1—24 sts;

Needles #2 and #3: Continue in established Modified Wheat Sheaves pattern—33 sts;

Needle #4: K1, ssk, knit to end—24 sts.

Round 2:

Needle #1: Knit;

Needles #2 and #3: Continue in established Modified Wheat Sheaves pattern;

Needle #4: Knit.

Repeat last 2 rounds until 65 stitches remain (33 instep stitches, and 32 heel stitches).

Repeat round 2 only, beginning with row 1 of Modified Wheat Sheaves pattern, until rows 1–20 of Modified Wheat Sheaves pattern have been worked once (twice) more. End ready to work stitches from needle #1.

Wheat Sheaves

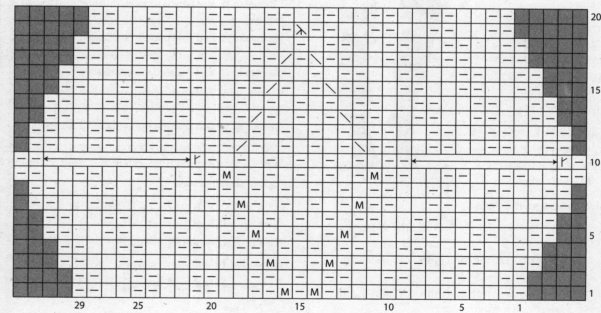

Wheat Sheaves

	k on RS, p on WS			M	make 1
	−	p on RS, k on WS		Γ	pf&b: purl in front and back of same st
	╱	k2tog			sl 10 sts as if to purl, pass first slipped st over the other 9 slipped sts
	╲	ssk			no stitch
	⋏	sk2p: sl 1 knitwise, k2tog, psso			

Continued ➡

SHAPE TOE

Round 1:

Needle #1: Knit to last 3 sts, k2tog, k1—15 sts;

Needles #2 and #3: K1, ssk, k12, k2tog, k12, k2tog, k1—30 sts;

Needle #4: K1, ssk, knit to end—15 sts (60 sts total).

Round 2:

Knit.

Round 3:

Needle #1: Knit to last 3 sts, k2tog, k1—14 sts;

Needles #2 and #3: K1, ssk, knit to last 3 sts, k2tog, k1—28 sts;

Needle #4: K1, ssk, knit to end—14 sts.

Repeat last two rounds until 20 total stitches remain (5 sts each on needles #1 and #4, 10 sts over needles #2 and #3). End with round 2.

FINISH TOE

Knit stitches of needle #1 onto needle #4, and slip stitches from needle #2 onto needle #3 (two sets of 10 stitches each on two needles). Cut yarn, leaving a 20"/51cm tail. Use Kitchener Stitch to sew the two sets of 10 stitches together.

FINISHING

Weave in ends.

This project was knit with:

Sereknity SockOptions' Shimmer Sock, 1 fingering weight, 60% superwash merino, 30% bamboo, 10% nylon, 3.75oz/106g = approx 400yd/360m per skein 1 skein, pharaohs gold colorway

Takeout for Two

by Cathy Carron

Going out or staying in, you're bound to hit it out of the park with these bold baseball-inspired socks. And after one spin on the dance floor in these babies, you may never knit socks with toes and heels again.

SKILL LEVEL

Easy

FINISHED MEASUREMENTS

Foot circumference 8 (9½)"/20.5 (24)cm

Calf circumference 12 (14½)"/30.5 (37)cm

Leg length 23 (25½)"/58 (65)cm

Foot length (toeless) 3½ (5)"/9 (12.5)cm

MATERIALS AND TOOLS

- Approx total: 675 (770)yd/608 (693)m of sport weight yarn, alpaca
- Color A: 200 (220)yd/180 (198)m of sport weight yarn, alpaca, in dark gray
- Color B: 200 (220)yd/180 (198)m of sport weight yarn, alpaca, in medium gray
- Color C: 200 (220)yd/180 (198)m of sport weight yarn, alpaca, in light gray
- Color D: 75 (110)yd/68 (99)m of sport weight yarn, alpaca, in red
- Knitting needles: 3.5mm (size 4 U.S.) set of 5 double-pointed needles, *or size to obtain gauge*
- Yarn needle

GAUGE

20 sts and 32 rows = 4"/10cm in Stockinette Stitch (knit every round)

Always take time to check your gauge.

INSTRUCTIONS

LEG #1

Beginning at the foot, with D, cast on 40 (48) sts. Distribute the sts evenly over four double-pointed needles (10 (12) sts per needle). Taking care not to twist stitches, join to work in the round.

Work in K2, p2 Rib pattern until piece measures 3½ (5)"/9 (13)cm from beginning.

Make Heel Opening

Next round: Bind off 22 (26) sts, continue in K2, p2 Rib around.

Next round: Cast on 22 (26) sts, continue in K2, p2 Rib around.

Work in K2, p2 Rib for 12 (16) more rounds.

ANKLE

Change to C.

Round 1: Knit.

Rounds 2–16: Work in K2, p2 Rib for 15 rounds.

Note: Each time the color is changed, work the indicated number of rounds by knitting the first round and working in the established rib pattern for the remaining number of rounds.

Change to A, and continue as established for 8 rounds.

Change to B, and continue as established for 8 rounds.

CALF

Change to C.

Next round: Knit.

Next round: Work in K2, p2 Rib.

Next round (increase round): *(Kfb in next st) twice, p2; repeat from * around—60 (72) sts.

Next round: *K4, p2; repeat from * around.

Repeat last round 4 more times.

Change to B, and continue as established for 12 (20) rounds.

Change to A, and continue as established for 12 rounds.

Change to C, and continue as established for 8 rounds.

Change to A, and continue as established for 12 rounds.

Change to B, and continue as established for 12 rounds.

Change to C, and continue as established for 8 rounds.

KNEE AND LOWER THIGH

Continue with C.

Next round: Knit.

Next round: Work in K2, p2 Rib.

Repeat last round 14 more times.

Change to A, and continue as established for 20 (28) rounds.

Change to C, and continue as established for 28 rounds.

Bind off loosely in K2, p2 Rib.

LEG #2

Work as for leg #1 to ankle.

ANKLE

Change to A.

Round 1: Knit.

Rounds 2–24: Work in K2, p2 Rib for 23 rounds.

Change to C, and continue as established for 8 rounds.

CALF

Change to B.

Next round: Knit.

Next round: Work in K2, p2 Rib.

Next round (increase round): *(Kfb in next st) twice, p2; repeat from * around—60 (72) sts.

Next round: *K4, p2; repeat from * around.

Repeat last round 4 (12) more times.

Change to A, and continue as established for 8 rounds.

Change to C, and continue as established for 24 rounds.

Change to B, and continue as established for 8 rounds.

Change to A, and continue as established for 8 rounds.

Change to C, and continue as established for 8 rounds.

Change to A, and continue as established for 8 rounds.

KNEE AND LOWER THIGH

Continue with C.

Next round: Knit.

Next round: Work in K2, p2 Rib.

Repeat last round 10 more times.

Change to B, and continue as established for 16 (24) rounds.

Change to C, and continue as established for 20 rounds.

Change to A, and continue as established for 16 rounds.

Bind off loosely in K2, p2 Rib.

FINISHING

Weave in ends. With D, sew a few stitches on either side of each heel opening to reinforce. Block if desired.

This project was knit with:

Blue Sky Alpaca's *Sport*, sport weight, 100% alpaca, 1.75oz/50g = approx 110yd/99m per skein
(A) 2 skeins, #509 natural dark gray
(B) 2 skeins, #508 natural medium gray
(C) 2 skeins, #507 natural light gray
(D) 1 skein, #511 red

Quickie Socks

by Susan Pierce Lawrence

Knitted socks are a labor of love, but we say less labor, more lovin'! Knit with worsted weight yarn, these socks work up quick with an easy-to-memorize offset rib pattern.

SKILL LEVEL

Intermediate

FINISHED MEASUREMENTS

Foot circumference 6"/15cm

Leg length 5½"/14cm

Foot length 8½"/21cm

Note: This sock is very stretchy and will fit a wide range of foot circumferences.

MATERIALS AND TOOLS

- Approx total: 200yd/180m of worsted weight yarn, wool, in gray
- Knitting needles: 3.75mm (size 5 U.S.) set of 5 double-pointed needles, or size to obtain gauge

- Stitch marker (optional)
- Waste yarn
- Yarn needle

GAUGE

28 sts and 28 rows = 4"/10cm in Stocjinette Stitch (knit every round)

Always take time to check your gauge.

INSTRUCTIONS

CUFF

Loosely cast on 40 sts onto one needle. Distribute the stitches evenly over four needles (10 sts per needle). Place a stitch marker for beginning of round. Taking care not to twist stitches, join to work in the round so the purl side of the case-on edge is on the RS.

Rounds 1, 3, and 5: Knit.

Rounds 2, 4, and 6: Purl.

LEG

Work Rib and Garter Stitch pattern 2 times (36 rounds total). The leg of the sock should measure approximately 5½"/14cm from the cast-on edge.

Rib & Garter Stitch (multiples of 2 sts)

Rounds 1, 8, 10, and 17: Knit.

Rounds 2–7: *K1, p1; repeat from * around.

Rounds 9 and 18: Purl.

Rounds 11–16: *P1, k1; repeat from * around.

Repeat rounds 1–18 for Rib & Garter Stitch pattern.

HEEL FLAP

Set-Up: K21, place the next 19 sts onto a piece of waste yarn. Turn work so the WS is facing you. Work back and forth over the 21 heel flap stitches only.

Rows 1, 3, and 5: Sl 1, k19, p1, turn.

Rows 2 and 4: Sl 1, k20, turn.

SHAPE HEEL

Short-Row Decreases

Row 1 (RS): Sl 1, k19, w&t.

Row 2 (WS): K19, w&t.

Row 3: K18, w&t.

Row 4: K17, w&t.

Continue working in this manner, knitting one fewer stitch before working the wrap and turn on each row, until there are 8 unwrapped stitches in the center of the heel.

Last Short-Row Decrease (RS):

K7, w&t.

Short-Row Increases

Row 1 (WS): K8, w&t.

Row 2: K9, w&t.

Row 3: K10, w&t.

Row 4: K11, w&t.

Continue working in this manner, knitting one more stitch before working the wrap and turn on each row, until the first and last heels sts have been wrapped twice.

Last Short Row Increase (RS):

K19, w&t. Now, there is one stitch on the right needle and 20 sts on the left needle.

Redistribute stitches as follows: Knit the next 10 heel stitches onto the right needle (needle #4); the left needle, holding the remaining 10 heel stitches is now needle #1; remove the 19 instep sts from the waste

yarn and divide them over two double-pointed needles (needles #2 and #3). You will now knit in the round again. The beginning of the round is at the center back of the sock.

Pick-up round:

Needle #1: K10, pick up and k3 sts along the side of the heel flap—13 sts.

Needles #2 and #3: Work in established Rib & Garter Stitch pattern beginning with round 10 (when you work round 1 of the leg, needle #2 will begin with a purl stitch), pick up and k3 sts along the opposite side of the heel flap—19 sts.

Needle #4: Pick up and k3 sts along opposite side of heel flaps, knit to end—14 sts (46 sts total).

GUSSET

Round 1:

Needle #1: Knit to last 3 sts, k2tog, k1—12 sts;

Needles #2 and #3: Continue in Rib & Garter Stitch pattern as established;

Needle #4: K1, ssk, k to end—13 sts.

Round 2:

Needles #1 and #4: Knit to end;

Needles #2 and #3: Continue in Rib & Garter Stitch pattern as established.

Repeat last 2 rounds two more times—40 sts.

Repeat round 2 only until foot measures approx 2"/5cm less than the total desired length, measured from the back of the heel.

SHAPE TOE

Rounds 1, 3–7, 9–11, and 13: Knit.

Round 2: *K3, k2tog; repeat from * around—32 sts.

Round 8: *K2, k2tog; repeat from * around—24 sts.

Round 12: *K1, k2tog; repeat from * around—16 sts.

Round 14: *K2tog; repeat from * around—8 sts.

Note: For a neater finish to the toe, work round 14 with a 2.75mm (size 2 U.S.) needle.

FINISH TOE

Cut yarn, leaving a 12"/30.5cm tail. Using the yarn needle, thread the yarn tail through the remaining stitches and pull it snug to close the opening.

FINISHING

Weave in ends.

Tip: The sock looks just as nice worn inside out.

This project was knit with:

Artyarns' *Ultramerino* 8, worsted weight, 100% hand-dyed merino wool, 3.5oz/100g = approx 188yd/169m per hank 2 hanks, UMB 117

Cyber Flirt

by Mary McCall

Who has time to date in person anymore? Next time you hop online for a bit of inter-flirting, wrap your toes in cabled splendor.

SKILL LEVEL

Experienced

FINISHED MEASUREMENTS

Foot circumference 8½"/21.5cm

Leg length 8½"/21.5cm

Foot length 9"/23cm

MATERIALS AND TOOLS

- Approx total: 440yd/396m of worsted weight yarn, superwash wool, in gray
- Knitting needles: 3.25mm (size 3 U.S.) set of 4 double-pointed needles or size to obtain gauge
- Stitch markers
- Cable needle
- Stitch holder
- Waste yarn
- Yarn needle

GAUGE

26 sts and 32 rows = 4"/10cm in Stockinette Stitch (knit every round)

Always take time to check your gauge.

SPECIAL ABBREVIATIONS

Dry Bones Cable (DBC): Slip 4 sts to cable needle and hold in front, drop the next st off the left needle, slip the 3 purl sts back onto the left needle, slip the dropped knit st back onto left needle, k1, p3 from left needle, k1 tbl from cable needle.

C8B (Cable 8 Back): Slip 4 sts onto cable needle and hold in back, k2, k2 from cable needle and bring to front, k2, k2 from cable needle.

INSTRUCTIONS

TOE

Cast on 20 stitches with waste yarn. Taking care not to twist stitches, join to work in the round.

Knit 1 round. With the "real" yarn, leave a nice long tail and knit the next round. Distribute the stitches as follows: 5 stitches each on needles #1 and #3, and 10 stitches on needle #2.

TOE INCREASES

Round 1 (increase):

Needle #1: Knit to last 2 sts, kfb, k1.

Needle #2: K1, kfb, knit to last 2 sts, kfb, k1.

Needle #3: K1, kfb, knit to end.

Round 2: Knit.

Repeat rounds 1 and 2, until there are 56 sts.

INSTEP

Redistribute stitches as follows: 14 sts on needle #1 (for first half of sole), 28 sts on needle #2 (for instep), 14 sts on needle #3 (for second half of sole). The beginning of each round is at the center of the sole.

Round 1:

Needle #1: Knit;

Needle #2: Work row 1 of Instep Chart;

Needle #3: Knit.

Round 2:

Needle #1: Knit;

Needle #2: Work next row of Instep Chart;

Needle #3: Knit.

Repeat round 2 until all 40 rows of the Instep Chart are completed, or until foot measures 2"/5cm less than desired foot length. Note: If you need more than the 40 rows of the Instep Chart, continue over the center 28 sts of the Leg Chart. Take note of where you stop (on Instep or Leg Chart). Take care to begin in the same place when beginning the leg of the sock.

Continued ➔

Leg

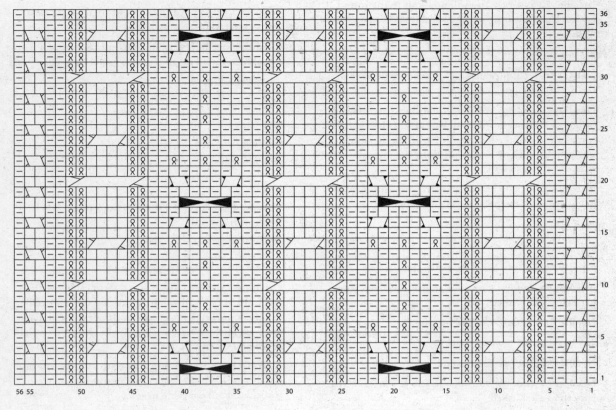

Leg

	k on RS, p on WS
	p on RS, k on WS
℞	k tbl on RS, p tbl on WS
	C2F: Cable 2 Front - sl 1 st onto cn and hold in front, k1, k1 from cn
	C2B: Cable 2 Back - sl 1 st onto cn and hold in back, k1, k1 from cn
	C2Fp tbl: Cable 2 Front purl - sl 1 st onto cn and hold in front, p1, k1 tbl from cn
	C2Bp tbl: Cable 2 Back purl - sl 1 st onto cn and hold in back, k1 tbl, p1 from cn
	C4B: Cable 4 Back - sl 2 sts onto cn and hold in back, k2, k2 from cn
	C8B (Cable 8 Back): Slip 4 stitches onto cn and hold in back, k2, k2 from cn and bring to front, k2, k2 from cn
	Dry Bones Cable (DBC): Slip 4 sts to cn and hold in front, drop the next st o the left needle, slip the 3 purl sts back onto the left needle, slip the dropped knit st back onto left needle, k1, p3 from left needle, k1 tbl from cn

Instep

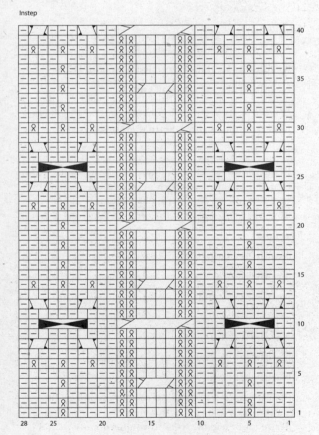

Note: The heel is worked in short rows. A short row heel is the heel that most resembles the heel of a commercial sock. It is worked on half of the leg stitches (28 in this case).

Place the 28 instep stitches on a holder. Work back and forth on heel sts only. Place a marker at the center of the heel stitches. You will be leaving the last stitch (or the last unwrapped stitch) unworked on each row. This is the stitch that gets wrapped.

Row 1 (RS): Knit to last st, w&t.

Row 2: Purl to last st, w&t.

Row 3: Knit to 1 st before wrapped st, w&t.

Row 4: Purl to 1 st before wrapped st, w&t.

Repeat rows 3 and 4 until you have 1"/2.5cm of unwrapped stitches at the center of the heel (½"/1.5cm on either side of the marker); end with a WS row.

Next row: Knit to first wrapped st, pick up the wrap and place it on the left needle, knit the stitch and wrap together, turn.

Next row: Purl to first wrapped st, pick up the wrap and place it on the left needle, purl the stitch and wrap together, turn.

Repeat the last 2 rows until all wrapped stitches have been worked. End ready to work from center of heel (needle #1).

LEG

When working the first round, pick up a stitch or two where the heel meets the instep stitches. Decrease them away on the next round (or two) with k2tog. This will help prevent the hole that sometimes forms there.

Note: Take care to start the leg pattern where you left off when working the instep pattern.

Working from Leg Chart (or Instep Chart then Leg Chart, if you worked a shorter foot) until all rounds of Leg Chart have been completed or leg measures 2"/5cm less than desired length.

RIBBING

Round 1 (decrease): P1, k2tog, p2, k2tog, k1, p2, k2tog, k1, p2, k2, p3, k2, p2, k2tog, k1, p2, k2tog, k1, p2, k2, p3, k2, p2, k2tog, k1, p2, k2tog, k1, p2, k2tog, p1—48 sts.

Round 2: P1, k1, (p2, k2) 3 times, p3, (k2, p2) 3 times, k2, p3, (k2, p2) 3 times, k1, p1.

Repeat round 2 until ribbing measures 2"/5cm or desired length of ribbing.

FINISHING

Bind off using a stretchy bind off.

FINISH TOE

Remove the waste yarn and put the "real" stitches back onto two double-pointed needles, being sure that the toe is oriented correctly. Use Kitchener Stitch to sew the two sets of stitches together.

Weave in ends.

This project was knit with:

Cascade Yarn's *Casvade* 220, worsted weight, 100% superwash wool, 3.5 oz.100g = approx 220/yd/198m per skein

2 skeins, color #900

Many thanks to Robley Brown (now deceased) for showing me that a short-row heel can fit, and for giving me permission to paraphrase her heel instructions.

—FROM *The Joy of Sox*

CROCHET: GETTING STARTED

Terry Taylor

Tools

One of the chief pleasures of crochet—aside from working with wonderful yarns—is that you need relatively few tools to accomplish the work. Aside from yarn, you simply need a hook. That's it! Of course, there are always additional tools that are handy and helpful to have, but not essential.

The Hook

Long ago, crochet hooks were made of hand-carved wood, bone, or even ivory. Today hooks are most commonly made of aluminum, plastic, or steel, although you can still readily purchase wooden hooks with decoratively turned handles or light-as-a-feather bamboo hooks in specialty yarn shops. If you're so inclined, you can even seek out bone

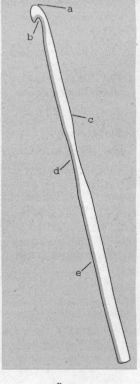

Figure 1

SHORT ROW HEEL

and ivory hooks in antique shops and online auctions. Aluminum, plastic, and wooden hooks are normally used with all types of yarns; steel hooks, with fine threads.

A crochet hook—no matter what material it's made of—has five basic parts, each with a specific function (figure 1). The point of the hook (a) is used to insert the hook into stitches. The throat (b) grabs the yarn to pull it through a stitch. The diameter of the shaft (c) helps determine the size of your stitches. It holds the loop or loops you're working with. The thumb rest (d) gives your fingers and thumb a flat area to grasp firmly as you work. The handle (e) is used for balance or leverage.

In the directions for each project in this section and for any other crochet pattern you might work on, you'll be instructed to use a specific hook size. Whether you use aluminum, plastic, or wooden hook is a matter of personal preference. What matters is the size of the hook—it determines the stitch size and, to some extent, the gauge (number of stitches per inch) that the pattern is based on.

You will encounter three different systems of hook sizes when you start to amass a working collection of hooks. The Continental (European) system uses millimeters, the U.S. (American) system uses a combination letter/number system, and the United Kingdom uses a numeric system. The hook sizes listed in the projects are of the Continental and U.S. systems.

Additional Tools

Scissors, especially small ones with sharp points, are indispensable tools. Breaking yarn is not an efficient way to cut yarn. Always use scissors.

Stitch markers are handy when you need to mark the end of a row in your work or a specific stitch within a row. If you don't wish to purchase stitch markers, use a safety pin or a short length of contrasting yarn to mark your spot.

Rulers and cloth tape measures with both standard and metric measurements are useful tools that you probably already have. You will use these tools to measure your work as you progress, to check your gauge, and to measure finished pieces as you finish and block them.

Rustproof pins of all types—straight pins, T-pins, and safety pins—all have their uses. Make absolutely sure that any type of pin you choose to use is rust-proof. T-pins are useful for blocking and safety pins can be used as stitch markers. Straight pins are great for securing crocheted pieces together as you stitch them and later as you block them.

Tapestry needles with large eyes and blunt points are necessary for finishing a completed crochet project. Using a plastic or metal needle is a matter of preference. Use them to weave loose yarn ends back into your stitches, or to sew together the seams of a garment.

Bags make it easy for you to take your crochet anywhere and everywhere you go. You may choose to tuck your current project, yarn, and a few tools in a plastic grocery bag or invest in a stylish, multipurpose needlework tote. Just be sure your bag doesn't have any tiny holes your hooks or pins might slip through.

Variety, luxury, and novelty are some of the buzzwords you encounter when reading about yarn today. The range of different types of yarn is, simply put, mind-boggling. If you've never shopped for yarn you may easily be overwhelmed as you look for material for a specific project (pleasantly so, I might add). Give in to the addictive pleasure of acquisition; don't resist it! After all, you can always find a way to use it sooner or later.

Each project in this section lists a generic, yarn type to use. In addition, each project lists the manufacturer, style, and color of the specific yarn used to create the project. Pay attention to the type of yarn specified for each project and, if you wish to use a yarn other than the one the designer used (see Substituting Yarn), look for that type of yarn.

For our purposes, yarn or thread are catchall terms for any fiber-like material we use for crochet, even if we're crocheting with ribbon, cloth, or other materials.

Yarn Types

In general, yarns—both natural and synthetic—are grouped into types classified by weight or size (yarn thickness). There is some crossover between types, but in general they are separated into six distinct groups.

Super Fine yarn is commonly referred to as fingering or sock weight yarn. It's the thinnest of yarn types. It's also referred to as baby weight and used to make delicate, lightweight garments for, you guessed it, babies.

Fine yarns are medium weight yarns used for a wide variety of projects. Sport weight and, sometimes, baby weight are used to describe this type of yarn depending on the manufacturer.

Light yarns are double knitting (DK) weight and light worsted yarns. These are slightly thicker than fine yarns. This common type of yarn can often be used in patterns that call for sport weight yarns, the end result being a slightly heavier fabric.

Medium weight yarns are usually called worsted weight yarns. These readily available yarns are used in many ways. They're the type of yarns you're certain to find in large discout chains or stores that don't offer a wide variety of yarn products.

Bulky weight yarns are also known as chunky, craft, and rug yarns. They work up quickly.

Super Bulky yarns work up even more quickly. If they haven't been spun into a recognizable form of yarn, they may also be referred to as roving.

Novelty Yarns

Novelty yarn is an all-purpose term used to describe all of those glorious, tantalizing yarns that have bumps, bouclé, nubs, or threads that wiggle and dangle. Their underlying structure—unlike strictly spun yarns—can be spun, woven, chained, or knit; their finish can be smooth or brushed. Novelty yarns are dazzling and a real temptation for those of us who are addicted to purchasing yarn. They can be worked alone, worked in tandem with standard types of yarn, or used as decorative accents.

In general, a novelty yarn is either heavier than a bulky or chunky weight yarn or is a thin, almost threadlike yarn. But that doesn't always hold true. Manufacturers have responded to consumer demand and are creating novelty yarns in a wide range of sizes.

Substituting Yarn

Let's imagine that you don't like a particular shade of green used in a scarf pattern or that you're allergic to a specific type of wool called for in a sweater pattern. What do you do? Abandon the project? Certainly not! You can substitute the yarn of your choice for the same type of yarn called for in the pattern.

However, don't imagine that you can substitute bulky yarn for a pattern that calls for fingering yarn. You won't be happy with the results at all. Simply follow the four steps that follow to substitute the yarn of your choice.

First, identify the yarn type that the pattern calls for. If needed, re-familiarize yourself with the different standard yarn types. Once you know the type of yarn you need, look for a similar type of yarn that suits your needs and desires.

Second, determine how much yarn the project requires. Jot down the total length of each ball of the original yarn in the pattern. Multiply the number of balls called for by yards/meters per ball. This will tell you how much yarn you will need. Write down the total amount of each yarn type you will need for the project.

Third—and here's the fun part—go shopping! When you have found the yarn you want to use, divide the total yardage you need by the yards/meters per ball of your new yarn. Round up to the next whole number (you don't want to find yourself running short of yarn!). This will give you the number of skeins you'll need of the substitute yarn.

Finally, crochet a gauge sample with the recommended hook and the yarn you've purchased. Don't skip this step. If the gauge is accurate, crochet away!

The Pattern: Your Road Map to Success

I hope you've thumbed through this section and thought to yourself: I'd like to make that! And that! So how do you go about making that project? It's easy; you gather the materials and follow the pattern instructions.

Written patterns give you a lot of important information *before* you actually pick up your hook and yarn. Reading a pattern from beginning to end before you crochet isn't an optional step; it's required, and simple makes sense. Even experienced crocheters do it. Think of it as if you were sitting down with a road atlas before embarking on a long road trip: It's easy to map out where you're going and how to get there before you leave the house—a whole lot easier than attempting to whip out the map and read it in eight lanes of speeding, rush hour traffic in a strange city!

Let's take a look at what you can expect to learn from crochet patterns in this book or any other book or magazine.

Experience Level

A pattern will tell you which level of experience it's designed for: beginner, easy, intermediate, or experienced. Pay attention to the level of experience needed to create a project, then read through the pattern just to be sure it's right for you.

Beginners will use basic stitches in a straightforward manner. There will be minimal shaping of the project.

Easy patterns use basic stitches, simple repetitive stitch patterns, simple color changes, and easy-to-master shaping and finishing techniques.

Intermediate patterns use a variety of stitches and more complex stitch patterns. Lace patterns and complex color changes may also be used.

Experienced level patterns will use intricate stitch patterns, work from charted stitches, use finer threads, smaller hooks, and detailed shaping and finishing.

Size or Dimensions

A pattern will give you the finished dimensions of a project or provide you with the size ranges that can be made with the pattern.

Materials and Tools

Every pattern will list the materials, the specific hook size, and other tools that you'll need. The pattern will tell you exactly which type of yarn is used and approximately how much you'll need to create the project. In most cases, the pattern will tell you the specific brand of yarn used to crochet the project.

Stitch List

The stitches used in the pattern will be listed. If advanced or specialty stitches are used, you'll be given directions for the stitches. These stitches will be listed in abbreviated form to save space. If special changes in standard stitch construction or unique working methods are used, those changes will be noted and brought to your attention before you start.

Continued ➜

Gauge

There will be a gauge specified for the design. Pay attention to the gauge. If you want your project to be the size you intend it to be, make a gauge sample. Read Gauging Success for more information on creating a gauge sample.

Instructions, Pattern Notes, and Graphs

Every pattern will be written with step-by-step instructions for each and every row you crochet. (Really.) It will begin with the number of chain stitches you need for your foundation row, then continue with a row-by-row description of the stitches or pattern stitches needed to complete the project. If the project is made with several pieces, each piece will be given separate step-by-step directions.

If there are special stitch variations or unusual working methods for the pattern, these will be noted in a separate section of pattern notes or working notes.

If there are specific color changes that make up a pattern for checks or stripes, these changes may be shown graphically with an illustration or a charted graph. Each square on a charted graph will be equal to a given number of stitches.

When a garment is made up of one or more pieces, you may be given a diagram that shows the dimensions of each piece needed to create the project.

Finishing and Assembly

Finally, if your project needs to be blocked (shaped) or assembled, the instructions will tell you what to do and, in some cases, how to do it.

In addition, if the project calls for buttonholes, fringe, pompoms, or other embellishments you'll be given instructions on how to create each one as needed.

How to Read a Pattern

Crochet directions are written in a special (but not secret!) language with abbreviations, punctuation marks, and special terms and symbols. They may look mysterious or even forbidding, but with a little practice and a bit of thinking through each direction, you'll soon catch on.

Familiarize yourself with the table of abbreviations and refer back to it as often as needed. These standardized abbreviations are commonly used in most crochet instructions around the world. In no time at all, you'll know what hdc means without thinking about it twice.

In addition to abbreviations, you'll need to pay attention to a few special symbols and punctuation marks. They serve a useful purpose when reading crochet directions.

Symbols and Punctuation

*—An asterisk is used to shorten instructions. Work all instructions following an * as many times as indicated.

:—A colon tells you to stop and pay attention. Usually a number will follow that tells you the number of stitches you should have in that row or round.

( )—Parentheses are often used to enclose a set of steps and to indicate changes for different sizes.

[ ]—Brackets will be used to indicate another block of instructions grouped within patentheses.

Speak It to Yourself

1. Read through the directions from beginning to end, row by row, translating each abbreviation into a word or phrase. Then, read the directions aloud. Yes, it sounds like a silly thing to do, but it works.

2. As you begin to work a specific stitch pattern, make a mantra of the sequence of stitches you need to work.

Repeat the mantra to yourself as you make each part of the pattern. After a while, you'll be able to execute the stitch pattern almost without thinking about it.

Gauging Success

You wouldn't want to build a door for your house without measuring the opening first, now would you? The door you build might be too large or too small to fit the opening. You wouldn't be happy putting all of that time, effort, and expense into creating a door that doesn't fit in the intended opening.

How do you ensure that what you crochet matches the size you want for the project? It's simple: Create a gauge sample each and every time, before you start any project. The gauge of any pattern is stated right after the stitches that are used in the project, right along with the hook size and yarn type (see How to Read a Pattern).

Gauge is measured by stitches or rows of stitches per inch. If your project is made solely with single crochet, you'll use single crochet stitches to make the sample. If the project has a set of several different stitches that repeat across the row, you'll need to create a sample for that set of stitches. If you're not very experienced with crochet, you may have a few questions about the process.

Why should I make a gauge sample?

It's an excellent way to practice your stitches, and it's the only way to insure your project will be the size you desire. Each and every yarn type differs slightly from manufacturer to manufacturer. In the same way, every person who crochets does so a bit differently. Stitch tension varies from person to person, and from day to day!

How large a sample do I need to make?

In general, people tend to crochet tighter at the beginning and end of rows. You'll want to measure your gauge in the sample where the stitches are most consistent—the center. Create a gauge sample that measures 4 x 4 inches (10 x 10 cm) or larger. It's imperative that you create your sample with the same yarn and hook that you plan to use to crochet the project.

What do I do with the sample?

For the most accurate measurement of your gauge, you need to treat your sample just as you would your finished project. If your pattern calls for blocking the project, you'll need to block the sample square. Lay the sample flat to measure and count both the number of individual stitches and rows per inch.

What do I do if my sample doesn't measure up?

If your sample doesn't result in the specified gauge, do not, I repeat, do not throw up your hands and quit. Simply rework a sample with a larger (or smaller) hook size or by adjusting your stitch tension as you crochet until your sample matches the required gauge. It's as simple as that.

Gauge is important. If you want that top or skirt to fit as intended, you need to work on achieving the gauge required before you start in on the project. On the other hand (there's always another side to the coin), gauge is not quite so crucial if you're crocheting a simple scarf or a rectangle shawl where fit is not critical. If gauge isn't critical many designers will simply say so at the start of the pattern.

—From *The New Crochet*

BASIC CROCHET STITCHES

by Linda P. Schapper

Introduction

Although crochet is thought to have originated as early as the Stone Age, when there were no needles available to join clothing and a rough crude hook was used, very little about early crochet has survived in the way of a written record. It is possible that we have adopted the French word for hook—*crochet*—as the name of the craft because the French did more than any other group to record crochet patterns.

Patterns were passed down through families, and new patterns were copied by examining the design with a magnifying glass. In the 19th century, written instructions became more popular as reading levels of women improved. Instructions, however, often can be long and tedious and, although perfectly clear to the writer, frequently difficult for the crocheter.

Crochet itself is based on a few simple stitches used in endless variation. It begins with a chain, and the way the stitches are formed determines the pattern. You need only a hook, your hand, and the thread. It's easy to carry with you and can be done anywhere. Unlike knitting and weaving, it is difficult to make a mistake which cannot be corrected immediately.

Crochet is versatile. It can make generous lace patterns, mimic knitting patchwork, or weaving, and it can form any number of textile patterns.

This section includes an extensive list of the symbols used in the International Crochet Symbols system. It's easy to read after you have worked out the four or five basic stitches, and it makes crocheting easier. This system allows you to see the whole pattern in proportion, and it's a nice experience to be able to pick up a crochet book in Russian and understand the crochet symbols. The symbols themselves look a great deal like the actual crochet stitches and, as you will see, are not at all difficult to follow.

NOTES FOR THOSE USING THE WRITTEN INSTRUCTIONS

· Stitch is always counted from the last stitch used.

· The abbreviations used are the American ones. British readers should keep this in mind since a few British abbreviations are different.

· The diagrams are easier once you have learned them. When in doubt, check the diagrams.

Basic Stitches

Slip Knot

Step 1: Make a loop with the end of the yarn, as shown. Pass the hook through the loop, under the working thread, and catch the thread with the hook.

Step 2: Slip knot on hook to begin.

Chain (ch)

Step 1: Yarn over hook (yo), and draw yarn through the loop on hook (ch made). Repeat as required.

Slip Stitch (sl st)

Step 1. Insert hook in designated stitch.

Step 2. Yo, draw yarn through stitch and the loop on hook (sl st made).

Single Crochet (sc)

This is a short, tight stitch.

 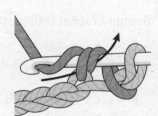

Make a chain of desired length.
Step 1: Insert hook in designated st (2nd ch from hook for first sc).

Step 2: Draw yarn through stitch.

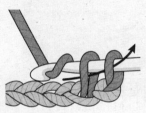 

Step 3: Yo, draw yarn through 2 loops on hook (sc made).

Step 4: Insert hook in next chain, and repeat steps to create another single crochet.

Half Double Crochet (hdc)

This stitch gives a lot of body and structure and resembles knitting.

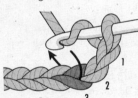 

Make a chain of desired length.
Step 1: Yo, insert hook in designated st

Step 2: Yo, draw through stitch (3 loops on hook)

Step 3: Yo, draw yarn through 3 loops on hook (hdc made).

Step 4: You will have one loop left on the hook. Yo, insert hook in next ch, and repeat sequence across row.

Double Crochet (dc)

This is perhaps the most popular and frequently use crochet stitch.

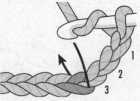 

Make a chain of desired length.
Step 1: Yo, insert hook in designated st (4th ch from hook for first dc).

Step 2: Yo, draw through stitch (3 loops on hook).

Step 3: Yo, draw yarn through first 2 loops on hook.

Step 4: Yo, draw yarn through last 2 loops on hook (dc made).

Step 5: Yo, insert hook in next st, and repeat steps to continue across row. Repeat steps 2–4 to work next dc.

Treble Crochet (tr)

Make a chain of desired length.
Step 1: Yo twice, insert hook in designated st (5th ch from hook for first tr).

Step 2: Yo, draw through stitch (4 loops on hook).

Step 3: Yo, draw yarn through 2 loops on hook (3 loops on hook).

Step 4: Yo, draw yarn through 2 loops on hook (2 loops on hook).

Step 5: Yo, draw yarn through 2 loops on hook (tr made).

Step 6: Yo twice, and repeat steps in next ch st.

Bobble (shown for 4-looped bobble)

Can be made with 2 to 6 loops. Shown for 4 loops.

Step 1: Yo, insert hook in designated st.

Step 2: Yo, draw yarn through st and up to level of work (first loop).

Double Crochet (dc) (continued, top right)

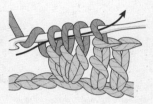

Step 3: (Yo, insert hook in same st, yo, draw yarn through st) as many times as required (3 more times for 4-looped bobble st–11 loops on hook).

Step 4: Yo, draw yarn through all loops on hook (bobble made).

Puff Stitch (shown for 3-dc puff stitch)

Can be made with 2 to 6 sts. Shown for 3 dc.

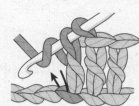

Step 1: Yo, insert hook in designated st (4th ch from hook for first puff st), yo, draw yarn through st, yo, draw yarn through 2 loops on hook (half-closed dc made–2 loops remain on hook).

Step 2: Yo, insert hook in same st, yo, draw yarn through st, yo, draw yarn through 2 loops on hook for each additional dc required (2 more times for 3-dc puff stitch–4 loops on hook).

Step 3: Yo, draw yarn through all loops on hook (puff stitch made).

Popcorn (pop)

Can be made with 2 to 6 sts. Shown with 5 dc.

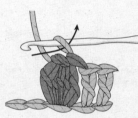

Step 2: Drop loop from hook, insert hook from front to back in top of first dc of group, pick up dropped loop, and draw through st, ch 1 lightly to secure (pop made).

Pop on RS rows:
Step 1: Work 5 dc in designated st (4th ch from hook for first pop).

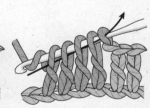

Pop on Ws rows:
Step 1: Work 5 dc in designated st (4th ch from hook for first pop).
Step 2: Drop loop from hook, insert hook from back to front in top of first dc of group, pick up dropped loop, and draw through st, ch 1 tightly to secure (pop made).

Cluster

Shown for 4-dc cluster.

Step 1: Yo, insert hook in designated st, yo, draw yarn through st, yo, draw yarn through 2 loops on hook (half-closed dc made—2 loops remain on hook).

Step 2: Yo, insert hook in next designated st, yo, draw yarn through st, yo, draw yarn through 2 loops on hook) as many times as required (3 more times for 4-dc cluster—4 half-closed dc made—5 loops on hook).

Step 3: Yo, draw yarn through all loops on hook (cluster made).

Continued ➜

Picot

Shown for ch-3 picot.

Step 1: Ch 3.

Step 2: Sl st in 3rd ch from hook (picot made).

Crossed Stitch (crossed tr shown)

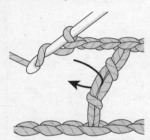

Step 1: Skip required number of sts (skip 2 sts shown), tr in next st, ch required number of sts (ch 1 shown), working behind tr just made, tr in first skipped st.

Y-Stitch (y-st)

Step 1: Work tr in designated st.

Step 2: Ch required number of sts (ch 3 shown), yo, work dc in 2 strands at center of tr just made (Y-st made).

V-Stitch (v-st), or shell

Work 4 dc in designated st (shell made).

X-Stitch (x-st)

Shown for tr X-st.

Make a chain of desired length.
Step 1: Yo twice, insert hook in designated st (6th ch from hook for first X-st), yo, draw yarn through it.

Step 2: Yo, draw yarn through 2 loops on hook (3 loops remain on hook), yo, skip designated number of sts (skip 2 ch shown), insert hook in next st, yo, draw yarn through st (5 loops on hook).

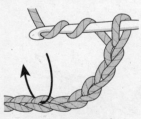

Step 3: Yo, draw yarn through 2 loops on hook (4 loops remain on hook).

Step 4: Yo, draw yarn through 2 loops on hook three times (1 loop remains on hook) (inverted Y shape made).

Step 5: Ch required number of sts (ch 2 shown), yo, insert hook in 2 strands at center of "cluster" just made, yo, draw yarn through st (3 loops on hook).

Step 6: Yo, draw yarn through 2 loops on hook (twice) (X-st made).

Front Post Double Crochet (fpdc)

Stitch is raised to front side of work.

Step 1: Yo, insert hook from front to back to front again, around the post of next designated st.

Step 2: Yo, draw yarn through st, (yo, draw yarn through 2 loops on hook) twice (FPdc made).

Back Post Double Crochet (bpdc)

Stitch is raised to back side of work.

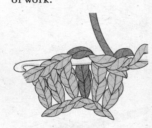

Step 1: Yo, insert hook from back to front to back again, around the post of next designated st.

Step 2: Yo, draw yarn through st, (yo, draw yarn through 2 loops on hook) twice (BPdc made).

Stitch Samples

Single Crochet

Chain any multiple plus 1.

Row 1: Sc in 2nd ch from hook, turn.

Row 2: Ch 1, sc in each sc across, turn.

Rep Row 2 for pattern.

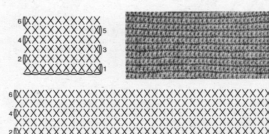

Single Crochet & Chains

Chain multiples of 4 plus 2.

Row 1: Sc in 2nd ch from hook, *ch 5, skip next 3 ch, sc in next ch; rep from * across, turn.

Row 2: Ch 5 (counts as dc, ch 2), (sc, ch 5) in each ch-5 loop across to within last ch-5 loop, sc in next ch-5 loop, ch 2, dc in last sc, turn.

Row 3: Ch 1, sc in first dc, (ch 5, sc) in each cn-5 loop across, ending with sc in 3rd ch of turning ch, turn.

Rep Rows 2–3 for pattern.

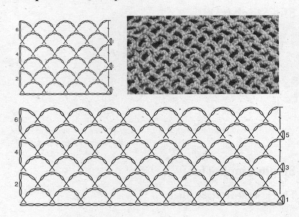

Double Crochet & Chains

Chain any multiple plus 3.

Row 1: Dc in 4th ch from hook, dc in each ch across, turn.

Row 2: Ch 3 (counts as dc), skip first dc in each dc across, ending with dc in 3rd ch of turning ch, turn.

Rep Row 2 for pattern.

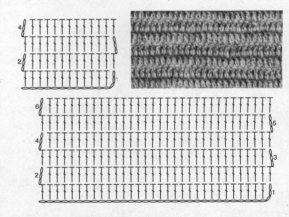

Single Crochet, Double Crochet & Chains

Chain multiples of 10 plus 6.

Row 1: Sc in 2nd ch from hook, sc in each of next 4 ch, *dc in each of next 5 sc, sc in each of next 5 ch; rep from * across, turn.

Row 2: Ch 3 (counts as dc), skip first sc, dc in each of next 4 sc, sc in each of next 5 dc, dc in each of next 5 sc; rep from * across, turn.

Row 3: Ch 1, sc in each of first 5 dc, *dc in each of next 5 sc, sc in each of next 5 dc; rep from * across, ending with last sc in 3rd ch of turning ch, turn.

Rep Rows 2–3 for pattern.

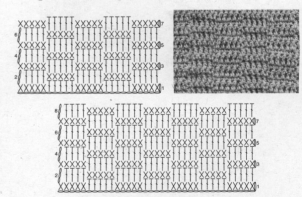

International Crochet Symbols

Symbol name			Symbol name	
2-dc cluster			chain stitch (ch)	
3-dc cluster			slip stitch (sl st)	
4-dc cluster			single crochet (sc)	
5-dc cluster			half double crochet (hdc)	
crossed dc			double crochet (dc)	
X-stitch (X-st)			treble crochet (tr)	
V-st			Front Post double crochet (FPdc)	
3-dc shell			Back Post double crochet (BPdc)	
4-dc shell			picot	
5-dc shell			3-dc popcorn (pop)	
4-dc shell with ch-2 space			4-dc popcorn (pop)	
6-dc shell with ch-2 space			5-dc popcorn (pop)	
dropped double crochet			2-looped bobble	
working over previous rows			3-looped bobble	
Y-stitches			4-looped bobble	
			5-looped bobble	
			2-dc puff st	
			3-dc puff st	
			4-dc puff st	
			5-dc puff st	

Treble Crochet, Double Crochet, Single Crochet & Chains

Chain any multiple plus 4.

Row 1: Tr in 5th ch from hook, tr in each ch across, turn.

Row 2: Ch 4 (counts as tr), skip first tr, tr in each tr across, ending with tr in 4th ch of turning ch, turn.

Rep Row 2 for pattern.

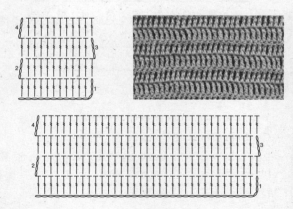

Bobble

Bobble: *(Yo, insert hook in next st, yo, draw yarn through st and up to level of work) 3 times in same st, to, draw yarn through 7 loops on hook.*

Chain multiples of 2 plus 1.

Row 1: Bobble in 4th ch from hook, *ch 1, skip next ch, bobble in next ch; rep from * across to within last ch, dc in last ch, turn.

Row 2: Ch 4 (counts as dc, ch 1), (bobble, ch 1) in each ch-1 space across to last ch-1 space, skip next bobble, dc in 3rd ch of turning ch, turn.

Row 3: Ch 3 (counts as dc), (bobble, ch 1) in each ch-1 space across to turning ch, bobble in ch-1 space of turning ch, dc in 3rd ch of turning ch, turn.

Rep Rows 2–3 for pattern.

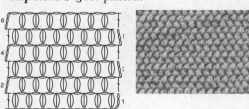

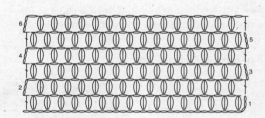

Puff Stitch

2-Dc Puff st: *(Yo, insert hook in next st, yo, draw yarn through st, yo, draw yarn through 2 loops on hook) twice in same st, yo, draw yarn through 3 loops on hook.*

Chain multiples of 10 plus 2.

Row 1: Sc in 2nd ch from hook, sc in each ch across, turn.

Row 2: Ch 1, sc in each of first 3 sc, *ch 3, skip next 2 sc, 2-dc puff st in next sc, ch 3**, skip next 2 sc, sc in each of next 5 sc, rep from * across, ending last rep at **, sc in each of last 3 sc, turn.

Continued ➡

Row 3: Ch 1, sc in each of first 3 sc, *2 sc in next ch-3 loop, sc in next puff st, 2 sc in next ch-3 loop **, sc in each of next 5 sc; rep from * across, ending last rep at **, sc in each of last 3 sc, turn.

Row 4: Ch 6 (counts as dc, ch 3), skip first 3 sc, *sc in each of next 5 sc, ch 3, skip next 2 sc**, 2-dc puff st in next sc, ch 3, skip next 2 sc; rep from * across, ending last rep at **, dc in last sc, turn.

Row 5: Ch 1, sc in first dc, *2 sc in next ch-3 loop, sc in each of next 5 sc, 2 sc in next ch-3 loop, sc in next puff st; rep from * across, ending with last sc in 3rd ch of turning ch, turn.

Rep Rows 2–5 for pattern.

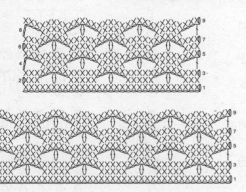

Puff Stitch Combinations

3-Dc Puff st: *(Yo, insert hook in next st, yo, draw yarn through st, yo, draw yarn through 2 loops on hook) 3 times in same st, yo, draw yarn through 4 loops on hook*

Chain multiples of 2.

Row 1: 2 dc in 5th ch from hook, *skip next ch, 2 dc in next ch; rep from * across to within last ch, dc in last ch, turn.

Row 2: Ch 3 (counts as dc), skip first 2 dc, *2 dc between last skipped and next dc**, skip next 2 dc; rep from * across, ending last rep at **, skip next dc, dc in top of turning ch, turn.

Row 3: Ch 4 (counts as dc, ch 1), skip first 2 dc, *3-dc puff st between last skipped and next dc, ch 1**, skip next 2 dc; rep from * across, ending last rep at **, skip next dc, dc in 3rd ch of turning ch, turn.

Row 4: Ch 1, sc in first dc, sc in next ch-1 space, (ch 2 sc) in each ch-1 space across, sc in 3rd ch of turning ch, turn.

Row 5: Ch 3 (counts as dc), 2 dc in each ch-2 space across to last ch-2 space, skip next sc, dc in last sc, turn.

Rep Rows 2–5 for pattern.

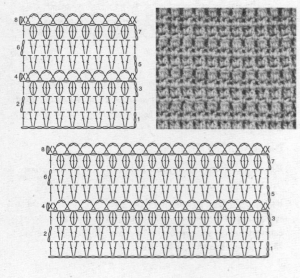

Popcorn Stitch

Popcorn (pop): 5 dc in next st, drop loop from hook, insert hook from front to back in first dc of group, pull dropped loop through st.

Chain multiples of 4 plus 1.

Row 1: Dc in 4th ch from hook, dc in next ch, *pop in next ch, dc in each of next 3 ch; rep from * across, turn.

Row 2: Ch 1, sc in each st across, ending with last sc in 3rd ch of turning ch, turn.

Row 3: Ch 3 (counts as dc), skip first sc, dc in each of next 2 sc, *pop in next sc, dc in each of next 3 sc; rep from * across, turn.

Rep Rows 2–3 for pattern.

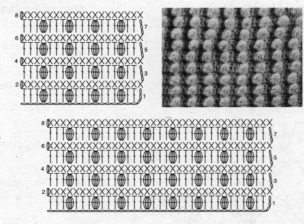

Cluster

Chain multiples of 2.

Row 1: Work 2-dc cluster working first half-closed dc in 4th ch from hook, skip next ch, work 2nd half-closed dc in next ch, yo, complete 2-dc cluster, *ch 1, work 2-dc cluster working first half-closed dc in same ch holding last dc of last cluster, skip next ch, work 2nd half-closed dc in next ch, yo, complete 2-dc cluster; rep from * across to last ch, dc in last ch already holding last dc of last cluster, turn.

Row 2: Ch 3 (counts as dc), work 2-dc cluster working first half-closed dc in first dc, skip next dc, work 2nd half-closed dc in next ch-1 space, yo, complete 2-dc cluster, *ch 1, work 2-dc cluster working first half-closed dc in same ch-1 space holding last dc of last cluster, skip next cluster, work 2nd half-closed dc in next ch-1 space, yo, complete 2-dc cluster, rep from * across to turning ch, dc in 3rd ch of turning ch already holding last dc of last cluster, turn.

Rep Row 2 for pattern.

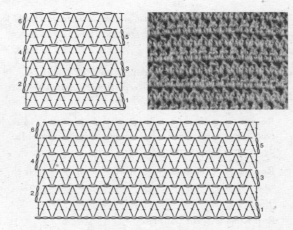

Picots

Chain multiples of 2.

Row 1: (Sc, ch 3, sc) in 5th ch from hook, *skip next ch, (sc, ch 3, sc) in next ch; rep from * across to within last ch, ch 1, hdc in last ch, turn.

Row 2: Ch 3 (counts as dc), skip next ch-1 space, dc in next ch-3 loop, (ch 1, dc) in each ch-3 loop across to last ch-3 loop, skip next ch of turning ch, dc in next ch of turning ch, turn.

Row 3: Ch 3 (counts as hdc, ch 1), sc in first dc, (sc, 3 sc) in each ch-1 space across to last ch-1 space, ch 1, hdc in 3rd ch of turning ch, turn.

Row 4: Ch 4 (counts as dc, ch 1), skip next ch-1 space, (dc, ch 1) in each ch-3 loop across to last ch-3 loop, dc in 2nd ch of turning ch, turn.

Row 5: Ch 3 (counts as hdc, ch 1), (sc, ch 3, sc) in each ch-1 space across to ch-1 space of turning ch, ch 1, hdc in 3rd ch of turning ch, turn.

Rep Rows 2–5 for pattern.

Chain multiples of 4.

Row 1: Sc in 2nd ch from hook, ch 3, sl st in 3rd ch from hook (picot), *sc in each of next 4 ch, picot; rep from * across to within last 2 ch, sc in each of last 2 ch, turn.

Row 2: Ch 4 (counts as dc, ch 1), work 2-dc cluster, working first half-closed dc in first sc, skip next 3 sc, work 2nd half-closed dc in next sc, complete 2-dc cluster, *ch 3, work 2-dc cluster, working first half-closed dc in same sc as last dc of last cluster, skip next 3 sc, work 2nd half-closed dc in next sc, complete 2-dc cluster; rep from * across to within last 2 sc, ch 3, work 2-dc cluster, working first half-closed dc in same sc as last dc of last cluster, skip next sc, work 2nd half-closed dc in last sc, complete 2-dc cluster, turn.

Row 3: Ch 1, sc in first cluster, *(2 sc, picot, sc) in next ch-3 loop, sc in next cluster; rep from & across to turning ch, sc in ch-1 space of turning ch, sc in 3rd ch of turning ch, turn.

Row 4: Ch 3 (counts as dc), skip first 2 sc, dc in next sc, *ch 3, work 2-dc cluster, working first half-closed dc in same sc as last dc worked, skip next 3 sc, work 2nd half-closed dc in next sc, complete 2-dc cluster; rep from * across to last sc, ch 1, dc in last sc, turn.

Row 5: Ch 1, sc in first dc, picot, sc in next ch-1 space, *sc in next cluster, (2 sc, picot, sc) in next ch-3 loop; rep from * across to last ch-3 loop, skip next dc, sc in 3rd ch of turning ch, turn.

Rep Rows 2–5 for pattern.

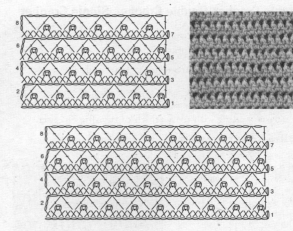

Y-Stitches

Y-st: *Tr in next st, 2 dc in center of last tr made.*

Chain multiples of 4 plus 2.

Row 1: Sc in 2nd ch from hook, *ch 3, skip next 3 ch, sc in next ch; rep from * across, turn.

Row 2: Ch 4 (counts as tr), (Y-st, ch1) in each ch-3 loop across to within last ch-3 loop, Y-st in last ch-3 loop, tr in last sc, turn.

Row 3: Ch 1, sc in first tr, (ch 3, sc) in each ch-1 space across, ending with last sc in 4th ch of turning ch, turn.

Rep Rows 2–3 for pattern.

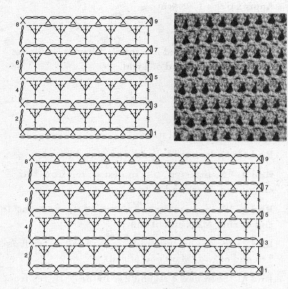

V-Stitch

Chain multiples of 2.

Row 1: 2 dc in 4th ch from hook, skip next ch, *2 dc in next ch, skip next ch; rep from * across to within last ch, dc in last ch, turn.

Row 2: Ch 3 (counts as dc), skip first 2 dc, *2 bet last skipped and next dc, skip next 2 dc; rep from * across to within last 2 sts, skip next dc, dc in 3rd ch of turning ch, turn.

Rep Row 2 for pattern.

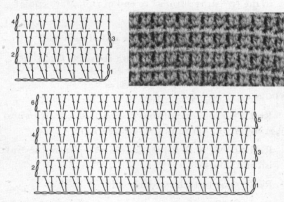

Simple Shell

Chain multiples of 3 plus 2.

Row 1: Sc in 2nd ch from hook, *ch 2, skip next 2 ch sc in next ch; rep from * across, turn.

Row 2: Ch 3 (counts as dc), dc in first sc, 3 dc in each sc across, ending with 2 dc in last sc, turn.

Row 3: Ch 1, sc in first dc, *ch 2, skip next 2 dc, sc in next dc; rep from * across, ending with last sc in 3rd ch of turning ch, turn.

Rep Rows 2–3 for pattern.

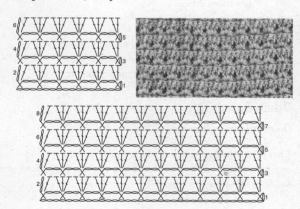

Shell—Overall Pattern

Chain multiples of 6 plus 3.

Row 1: Sc in 2nd ch from hook, sc in next ch, *ch 4, skip next 4 ch, sc in each of next 2 ch; rep from * across, turn.

Row 2: Ch 3 (counts as dc), (2 dc, ch 2, 2 dc) in each ch-4 loops across, dc in last sc, turn.

Row 3: Ch 5 (counts as dc, ch 2), (2 sc, ch 4) in each ch-2 space across to within last ch-2 space, 2 sc in last ch-2 space, ch 2, skip next 2 dc, dc in 3rd ch of turning ch, turn.

Row 4: Ch 4 (counts as dc, ch 1), 2 dc in next ch-2 space (2 dc, ch 2, 2 dc) in each ch-4 loop across to last ch-4 loop, 2 dc in ch-2 space of turning ch, ch 1, dc in 3rd ch of turning ch, turn.

Row 5: Ch 1, sc in first dc, sc in next ch-1 space, ch 4, (2 sc, ch 4) in each ch-2 space across to turning ch, sc in last ch-1 space of turning ch, sc in 3rd ch of turning ch, turn.

Rep Rows 2–5 for pattern.

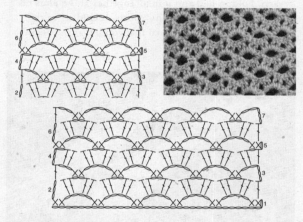

Shell—Treble Crochet

Chain multiples of 6 plus 5.

Row 1: Tr in 6th ch from hook, tr in each of next 2 ch, ch 3, tr in next ch, *skip next 2 ch, tr in each of next 3 ch, ch 3, tr in next ch; rep from * across to within last 2 ch, skip next ch, tr in last ch, turn.

Row 2: Ch 4 (counts as tr), (3 tr, ch 3, tr) in each ch-3 loop across to last ch-3 loop, skip next 3 tr, tr in top of turning ch, turn.

Rep Row 2 for pattern.

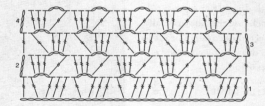

Post Stitch

Front Post Double Crochet (FPdc): *Yo, insert hook from front to back to front again around the post of designated st, yo, draw yarn through, (yo, draw yarn through 2 loops on hook) twice.*

Chain multiples of 4 plus 1.

Row 1 (WS): Dc in 4th ch from hook, dc in each ch across, turn.

Row 2: Ch 3 (counts as dc), skip first dc, dc in each of next 2 dc, *FPdc around the post of next dc**, dc in each of next 3 dc; rep from * across, ending with last dc in 3rd ch of turning ch, turn.

Row 3: Ch 3 (counts as dc), skip first dc, dc in each st across, ending with dc in 3rd ch of turning ch, turn.

Row 4: Ch 3 (counts as dc), skip first dc, *FPdc around the post of next dc**, dc in each of next 3 dc; rep from

* across, ending last rep at **, dc in 3rd ch of turning ch, turn.

Row 5: Rep Row 3.

Rep Rows 2–5 for pattern.

Front Post Double Crochet (FPdc): *Yo, insert hook from front to back to front again around the post of designated st, yo, draw yarn through, (yo, draw yarn through 2 loops on hook) twice.*

Back Post Double Crochet (BPdc): *Yo, insert hook from back to front to back again around the post of designated st, yo, draw yarn through, (yo, draw yarn through 2 loops on hook) twice.*

Chain multiples of 8 plus 1.

Row 1 (WS): Dc in 4th ch from hook, dc in each ch across, turn.

Row 2: Ch 3 (counts as dc), skip first dc, dc in each of next 2 dc. *FPdc around the post of next dc, dc in each of next 3 dc**, ch 1, skip next st, dc in each of next 3 dc; rep from * across, ending last rep at **, with last dc in 3rd ch of turning ch, turn.

Row 3: Ch 3 (counts as dc), skip first dc, dc in each of next 2 dc, *BPdc around the post of next dc, dc in each of next 3 dc**, ch 1, skip next ch-1 space, dc in each of next 3 dc; rep from * across, ending last rep at **, with last dc in 3rd ch of turning ch, turn.

Rep Rows 2–3 for pattern.

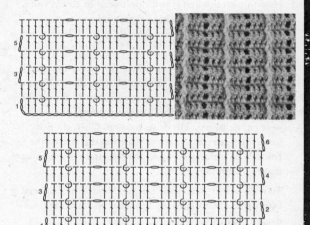

Continued →

- Approx 240yd/216m worsted weight orange yarn for a wide belt
- Hook: 6.5mm/K/10½ or size needed to obtain gauge

GAUGE

Gauge isn't critical in this pattern.

STITCHES USED

Chain stitch (ch)

Single crochet (sc)

Double crochet (dc)

Slip stitch (sl st)

Bobble Stitch (Bbl st)

Beg the Bbl st like a dc in the desired st. In other words, yo, put hk through st and draw up a loop, yo, pull through 2 lps. You have just made the post of the Bbl St.

*Yo hook and insert the hook from the front around the back and to the front of the post. Yo, pull up a loop around the post, rep from * 2 more times. Yo hook and draw through all 8 loops on hook to form the Bbl St.

PATTERN NOTES

You start working these belts in a row, then work around the row: first around the side, then the bottom, the other side, and ending on the top.

How to start the belt if you don't want to count your stitches: Make a loose chain that measures approximately as long as you want the belt to be. Chain a few more—just in case.

Then, starting with row 1, follow the directions until you get near the end of the foundation chain. Measure the belt—if it's about as long as you want it, finish the first row by making a Bbl st in the pattern, ch1, skip next ch, dc in next ch, dc in next ch. Ch 1, do not turn. The extra foundation chains at the end of the row can be unknotted up to the last stitch when you are finished with the belt.

To make a belt shorter or longer, chain a multiple of 4 (56, 60, 64, 68), plus 2 additional ch for your foundation chain.

NARROW BELT

Foundation Chain: Leave a long tail (approx 8"/20cm), ch a multiple of 4, plus 2, to measure approx 65"/165cm.

Row 1: Dc in 4th ch from hk. Ch 1, sk next ch in foundation, Bbl st in next ch. Ch 1, sk next ch in foundation, *dc in next ch, ch 1, sk next ch, Bbl st in next ch, ch 1, sk next ch. Rep from * across, ending dc in next ch, dc in last ch. Ch 1, do not turn.

EDGING

Rnd 1: 3 sc around the post of the last dc in row 1. Sc in each bottom loop of the foundation chain, 3 sc around the 3 chs at the beg of row 1, sc in each dc, Bbl st, and ch-1 sp across the top. End with Sl st in first sc. Fasten off, leaving an 8"/20 cm tail.

FRINGE

For each end of the belt, cut twenty 16"/41cm pieces of yarn. Fold in half and join all together at the ends of the belt, over the dc or ch-3 posts, including in the fringe the long tails of yarn you left at the beginning and the end.

WIDE BELT

Foundation Chain: Leaving a long tail approx 8"/20cm, ch a multiple of 4, plus 2, to measure approx 65"/165cm.

Row 1: Dc in 4th ch from hook. Ch 1, sk next ch in foundation, Bbl st in next ch. Ch 1, sk next ch in foundation, *dc in next ch, ch 1, sk next ch, Bbl st in next ch, ch 1, sk next ch. Rep from * across, ending dc in

next ch, dc in last ch. Ch 1, turn.

Row 2: Sc in each st and ch-1 sp across. Ch 3 (counts as dc), turn.

Row 3: Sk first sc, *dc in next sc, ch 1, skip 1 sc. Bbl st in next sc, ch-1, skip next sc, rep from * across, ending dc in next ch, dc in last ch. Ch 1, do not turn.

EDGING

Round 1: 2 sc around the post of the last dc in row 3, 2 sc around the post of the last dc in row 1, *sc in the next ch-1 sp, sc in the bottom lp of the same ch where there is a Bbl st, sc in the next ch-1 sp, sc in the bottom lp of the same ch where there is a dc, repeat from * across, ending sc in the bottom lp of the same ch where there is a dc, 2 sc around the ch 3 at the beginning of row 1, 2 sc around the ch 3 at the beg of row 3, sc in each dc, Bbl st, and ch-1 sp across. End with sl st in first sc. Fasten off, leaving an 8"/20cm tail.

FRINGE

For each end of the belt, cut twenty 16"/41cm pieces of yarn. Fold in half and join all together at the ends of the belt, over the dc or ch-3 posts, including in the fringe the long tails of yarn that you left at the beginning and the end.

This project was created with:

1 skein of Berroco's *Suede* in Calamity Jane (#3745) or Tonto (#3715); 2 skeins of Clementine (#3757), 100% nylon, 1.75oz/50g = approx 120yd/108m per skein.

Perfect Little Bag

Design by Barbara Zaretsky

Perfect for either evening or daytime—take your pick. This gem of a bag is worked in one simple stitch with a heavy cotton thread that's both durable and great to crochet with. Add specially selected decorative beads to the drawstring cord for a dressy look.

SKILL LEVEL

Beginner

FINISHED MEASUREMENTS

Approx 5 x 5"/13 x 13cm

MATERIALS

- Color A: Approx 108yd/97m heavy worsted weight mercerized cotton thread in green
- Color B: Approx 108yd/97m heavy worsted weight mercerized cotton thread in beige
- Hook: 5mm/H-8 or size needed to obtain gauge
- Stitch marker
- Tapestry needle
- Decorative beads

STITCHES USED

Chain st (ch)

Single crochet (sc)

GAUGE

Take time to check your gauge.

Approx 6 sc = 1"/2.5cm

PATTERN NOTES

This project is worked in a spiral. Turning chains are not needed at the end of a rnd.

INSTRUCTIONS

BODY

Ch 8 and join with sl st.

Rnd 1: 2 sc in each ch, mark end of rnd (16 st).

Rnd 2: * Sc in first st, 2 sc in next sc, rep from * to end of rnd. Mark end of rnd.

Rnd 3: *Sc in next 2 sts and 2 sc in 3rd st, rep from * to end of rnd. Mark end of rnd.

Rnd 4: *Sc in next 3 sts and 2 sc in the 4th st, rep from * to end of rnd. Mark end of rnd.

Rnd 5: *Sc in next 4 sts and 2 sc in the 5th st, rep from * to end of rnd. Mark end of rnd.

Rnd 6: *Sc in next 5 sts and 2 sc in the 6th st, rep from * to end of rnd. Mark end of rnd.

Rnd 7: *Sc in next 6 sts and 2 sc in the 7th st, rep from * to end of rnd. Mark end of rnd.

Rnd 8: *Sc in next 7 sts and 2 sc in the 8th st, rep from * to end of rnd. Mark end of rnd.

Rnd 9: Change to color B, *sc in next 8 sts and 2 sc in the 9th st, rep from * to end of rnd. Mark end of rnd.

Rnd 10: Change to color A, *sc in next 9 sts and 2 sc in the 10th st, rep from * to end of rnd. Mark end of rnd.

Rnds 11–32: Sc in ea st. Mark end of each rnd.

Change to color B for stripe on rows: 13, 17, 21, 25 and 29 or as desired.

EDGING

Rnd 33: From end of row 32, *ch 4, sk 3 sc, sc in next st, rep from * around the row. Mark end of rnd.

Rnd 34: *Sc in first 4 st, sk next st* rep from * to finish rnd. Mark.

Rnd 35: Sc in each st. Mark end.

Rnd 36: *Sc in first st and 2 sc in next st, rep from * to finish row. Fasten off.

Turn bag inside out and weave in thread ends.

DRAWSTRING CORD

Work with 2 strands ea approx 4yd/4m long. Ch st until strand is approx 1yd/1m long.

Trim end to 3"/8cm and pull yarn through last st to fasten off.

Knot end of chain, add bead and knot again.

Lace crocheted cord through holes. Knot cord approx 4"/10cm from end.

This project was created with:

1 skein each of Tahki's Cotton *Classic* in green (3763) and linen (3200), 100% mercerized cotton, 1.75oz/50g = approx 108yd/97m per skein.

Urban Beach Tote

Design by Lindsay Obermeyer

This tote is just as at home when you're trudging down city streets as it is when you're strolling on tropical white sands or down country lanes.

Skill Level

Intermediate

Finished Measurements

Approx 12 x 16 x 4½"/30 x 41 x 11cm

Materials

- Approx 810yd/729m sport weight linen or cotton yarn in green
- Approx 270yd/243m sport weight linen or cotton yarn in off-white
- Hook: 3.25mm/D-3 or size needed to obtain gauge
- 4 buttons
- Tapestry needle

Stitches Used

Chain stitch (ch)

Single crochet (sc)

Half double crochet (hdc)

Gauge

Take time to check your gauge.

5 sc and 4 rows = 1"/2.5cm

Instructions

TOTE BOTTOM

Using the green yarn, ch 82.

Sc in 2nd chain from hk and in each remaining ch until end. *Chain 1. Turn work and sc into 2nd ch from hk with hk inserted into both halves of the st. Cont until end of row.* Repeat procedure from * to * until bottom is approx 4½"/11cm wide.

TITE BODY

Work in rounds.

Make 26 hdc evenly along short side into back loop (BL) of stes until you come to the first corner. Work 3 hdc into corner st. Turn and hdc along the long side into BL of st until you come to 2nd corner. Work 3 hdc into corner st. Turn and make 26 hdc evenly along short side into BL of stes until you come to 3rd corner. Work 3 hdc into corner st. Turn and hdc along the long side into BL of st until you come to the final corner. Work 3 hdc into corner st.

Work hdc around, into both halves of the st until height of tote measures approx 12"/30 cm. Finish off with sl st, cut yarn, and fasten off. Weave in all ends.

PICOT EDGING

Using off-white yarn, fasten the yarn to the 1st st. *Ch 3, 1 sc in the first of the ch-3 sts. Sk 1 st on the crochet work. 1 sc in the next st. Rep from * around. Finish picot edge with sl st in first st. Cut yarn and fasten off. Weave in the end.

HANDLES (MAKE 2)

Using off-white yarn, ch 13. Work in rows, in sc in both halves of the st for approx 2½"/6cm. Connect using a sl st. Working in rnds, sc in both halves of the st for approx 16"/41cm. The front side does not show the opening to the tube, so with front side facing you sc across 7 st, ch 1. Turn and insert hk into 2nd st from hk, sc across 8 st, ch 1. Turn and insert hk into 2nd st from hk, sc across 9 st and increase 1, ch 1. Turn and insert hk into 2nd st from hk, sc across 10 st, ch 1 (11 sc).

Continue working in rows with sc in both halves of the st until approx 2½"/6cm long, do not chain on last row, when sc in final st, cut yarn and fasten off.

Repeat to make another handle, weave in all ends.

FINISHING

With the bag laying flat, measure in fron each side 4"/10cm and line up outer edge of handle tabs. Pin with top edge of tab before increase/decrease to top row of hdc on bag. Using green yarn, st handles to bag with a running stitch using tapestry needle. Knot and weave in ends. Sew buttons to handle tabs to finish.

This project was created with:

3 skeins Euroflax's *Linen Yarn* in willow (18-2554) and 1 skein Euroflax's *Linen Yarn* in natural (18-2304), each 3.5oz/100g = approx 270yd/243m per skein.

Spiral design water buffalo horn buttons (NPL 340-31B) from One World Button Supply Company

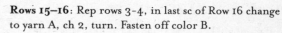

Shawls, Ponchos & Scarves

Mile Long Scarf

Design by Robyn Kelley

Well, truth be told, it's not really a mile long. But it's so much fun to make and wear that you'll be tempted to try it!

Skill Level

Easy

Finished Measurements

Approx 5 x 91"/13cm x 2.3m

Materials

Yarn A: 154yd/139m blue super bulky eyelash yarn

Yarn B: 408yd/367m green light yarn

Hook: 6.5mm/K-10½ or size needed to obtain gauge

Yarn needle

Stitches Used

Chain stitch (ch)

Half double crochet (hdc)

Double crochet (dc)

Gauge

Take time to check your gauge.

2 stitches and 8 rows = 3"/8cm

Pattern Note

Color B is to be worked in back loops (BL) only of previous row.

Pattern

Using yarn A, ch 20.

Row 1: 1 dc in 3rd ch from hook, 1 dc in ea ch across, ch 2, turn.

Row 2: 1 dc in next dc and ea dc across, at last dc change to color B, ch 1, turn. Fasten off color A.

Row 3: 1 sc in next dc and ea dc across, ch 1, turn.

Row 4: 1 sc in BL only of next sc and ea sc across, ch 2, turn.

Row 5: 1 hdc in BL only of next sc and ea sc across, ch 2, turn.

Row 6: 1 hdc in BL only of next hdc and ea hdc across, ch 1, turn.

Rows 7–8: Rep rows 3–4. Remember to work in back lps.

Rows 9–10: Rep rows 5–6.

Rows 11–12: Rep rows 3–4.

Rows 13–14: Rep rows 5–6.

Rows 15–16: Rep rows 3–4, in last sc of Row 16 change to yarn A, ch 2, turn. Fasten off color B.

Row 17: Using color A and working in both top lps now, 1 dc in next sc and ea sc across, ch 1, turn.

Row 18: 1 dc in next dc and ea dc across, in last dc change to yarn B, ch 1, turn. Fasten off yarn A.

Continue repeating rows 3–18 until scarf measures approx 91"/2.3m or desired length. You should end the scarf with the same color you started with. Weave in ends.

This project was created with:

Yarn A: 2 balls Bernat's *Eye Lash* in Hip (#35142), 100% nylon, 1.75oz/50g = approx 77yd/70m ea

Yarn B: 3 balls Patron's *Grace* in Ginger (#60027). 100% mercerized cotton, 1.75oz/50g = approx 136yd/125m ea

Orange Sorbet Wrap

Design by Katherine Lee

A wrap as light and refreshing as...you guessed it! If you've been leery of working with fancy novelty yarns, this simple shawl in an open lace stitch pattern is a great project—especially suitable for a beginner. You won't run into the difficulty of inserting your hook in hard-to-locate stitch loops: you work your double crochets into a space instead.

Skill Level

Beginner

Finished Measurements

Approx 57 x 27"/145 x 68cm (excluding fringe)

Materials

- Approx 330yd/297m of ⅜"/10mm wide ribbon yarn
- Hook: 11.5mm/P-16 *or size needed to obtain gauge*

Stitches Used

Chain stitch (ch)

Slip stitch (sl st)

Double crochet (dc)

Gauge

Take time to check your gauge.

4 sets of (1 dc, ch 1) and 4 rows = 4"/10cm over pattern stitch

Pattern

Begin work at the bottom point of the triangle.

Ch 4, join with a sl st to 1st ch to form ring.

Row 1: Ch 4 (counts as 1 dc, ch 1), 1 dc in ring, (ch 1, 1dc in ring) 2 times, turn.

Row 2: Ch 4 (counts as 1 dc, ch 1), 1 dc in 1st dc, ch 1, (1 dc in next ch-1 sp, ch 1) 2 times, (1 dc, ch 1, 1 dc) in ch-4 sp created by tch, turn.

Row 3: Ch 4 (counts as 1 dc, ch 1), 1 dc in 1st dc, ch 1, *1 dc in next ch-1 sp, ch 1; rep from * to tch, (1 dc, ch 1, 1 dc) in ch-4 sp created by tch, turn.

Rep row 3 until you have 28 rows total. Fasten off.

FINISHING

Cut 17"/43cm lengths of yarn. Using 1 folded strand for each fringe, place fringe evenly at each ch-4 sp and dc along bottom edges and at ch-4 ring at bottom corner.

Continued ➤

This project was created with:

Balls of GGH's *Celine* ribbon yarn in Orange Cream (#12), 35% cotton/65% mylon, 1oz/50g = approx 66yd/60m ea

Lacey Rainbow Scarf

Design by Katherine Lee

This scarf is a perfect introduction to using pattern stitches. It's so easy that soon you'll be crocheting away, just enjoying the silky softness and glorious hand-painted colors of the yarn as you go.

SKILL LEVEL

Beginner

FINISHED MEASUREMENTS

Approx 6 x 80"/15 x 203cm (without fringe)

MATERIALS

654yd/587m DK or light worsted weight wool/silk yarn

Hook: 5mm/H-8 *or size needed to obtain gauge*

Tapestry needle

STITCHES USED

Chain stitch (ch)

Double crochet (dc)

GAUGE

Take time to check your gauge.

5 groups of (3 dc, ch 3, 1 dc) = 6"/15cm

8 rows = 5"/13cm over lace stitch

INSTRUCTIONS

SPECIAL PATTERN STITCH

Lace Stitch (worked over a multiple of 6 stitches plus 5)

Row 1: 1 dc in 6th ch from hk, 1 dc in each of next 2 ch, ch 3, 1 dc in next ch, *sk 2 ch, 1 dc in ea of next 3 ch, ch 2, 1 dc in next ch; rep from * to last ch, sk 1 ch, 1 dc in last ch, turn.

Row 2: Ch 3 (counts as 1 dc), *(3 dc, ch 3, 1 dc) in next ch-3 sp; rep from * to last 3 dc, sk 3 dc, 1 dc in next ch, turn.

Row 3: Ch 3 (counts as 1 dc), *(3 dc, ch 3, 1 dc) in next ch-3 sp; rep from * to last 4 dc, sk 3 dc, 1 dc in 3rd ch of t-ch, turn.

Rep row 3 for pattern.

SCARF

Ch 35, turn.

Work in Lace Stitch for rows 1-3.

Rep row 3 until scarf measures approx. 80"/203cm (129 rows total). Fasten off.

FINISHING

Lightly steam scarf and block as needed.

Cut 16"/41cm lengths of yarn (you will need 72). Using 3 strands for each fringe, attach 12 fringe ends evenly along each end of scarf.

This project was created with:

Hanks Schaefer's *Helene* in Isadora Duncan, 50% Merino wool/50% cultivated silk, 3oz/84g = approx 218yd/196m ea

Soft As Moss Poncho

Design by Katherine Lee

The woodsy colors of pale lichens and moss tint this delicate poncho. It's crocheted in the round from the neck down in a delightful-to-wear silk and cashmere blend yarn. Don't worry: The lacey stitch looks intricate, but it's deceptively simple to create.

SKILL LEVEL

Intermediate

FINISHED MEASUREMENTS

Approx 14"/36cm long at center (without fringe)

Approx 30"/76cm around neck opening

MATERIALS

· Yarn A: approx 292yd/263m wool/silk blend sock, fingering, or baby weight yarn in green

· Yarn B: approx 292yd/263m wool/silk blend sock, fingering, or baby weight yarn in light green

· Yarn C: approx 146yd/121m wool/silk blend sock, fingering, or baby weight yarn in off-white

· Hook: 5mm/H-8 *or size needed to obtain gauge*

· Tapestry needle

STITCHES USED

Chain stitch (ch)

Double crochet (dc)

GAUGE

Take time to check your gauge.

5 (1 dc, ch 3, 3dc) groups = 5½"/14cm

2 rows = 11/4"/3cm over pattern stitch

PATTERN

Using yarn A, ch 168, join with a sl st to 1st ch to form ring.

Rnd 1: Ch 3 (counts as 1 dc), 1 dc in next ch, ch 2, 1 dc in ea of next 2 ch *(sk 2 ch, 1 dc in ea of next 3 ch, ch 3, 1 dc in next ch) 13 times*, sk 2 ch, 1 dc in ea of next 2 ch, ch 2, 1 dc in ea of next 2 ch, rep from * to * once, join with a sl st to top of ch-3.

Rnd 2: (Inc rnd) Sl st in next dc, sl st in next ch-2 sp, ch 3 (counts as 1 dc), (1 dc, ch 2, 2 dc) in same sp, (1 dc, ch 3, 3 dc) in sp between next 2nd and 3rd dcs, [(1 dc, ch 3, 3 dc) in next ch-3 sp] 13 times, (1 dc, ch3, 3 dc) in sp between next 1st and 2nd dc's, (2 dc, ch 2, 2 dc) in next ch-2 sp, (1 dc, ch 3, 3 dc) in sp between next 2nd and 3rd dc's, [(1 dc, ch 3, 3 dc) in next ch-3 sp] 13 times, (1 dc, ch 3, 3 dc) in sp between next 1st and 2nd dc's, join with a sl st to top of ch 3.

Rnd 3: Sl st in next dc, sl st in next ch-2 sp, ch 3 (counts as 1 dc), (1 dc, ch 2, 2 dc) in same sp, *[(3 dc, ch 3, 1 dc) in next ch-3 sp] 15 times*, (2 dc, ch 2, 2 dc) in next ch-2 sp; rep from * to * once, join with a sl st to top of ch-3. Fasten off.

Change to yarn B.

Rnd 4: Sl st in next dc, sl st in next ch-2 sp, ch 3 (counts as 1 dc), (1 dc, ch 2, 2 dc) in same sp, *[(1 dc, ch 3, 3 dc) in next ch-3 sp] 15 times*, (2 dc, ch 2, 2 dc) in next ch-2 sp; rep from * to * once, join with a sl st to top of ch-3.

Rnd 5: (inc rnd) Sl st in next dc, sl st in next ch-2 sp, ch 3 (counts as 1 dc), (1 dc, ch 2, 2 dc) in same sp, (3 dc, ch 3, 1 dc) in sp between next 2nd and 3rd dcs, [(3 dc, ch 3, 1 dc) in next ch-3 sp] 15 times, (3 dc, ch 3, 1 dc) in sp between next 3rd and 4th dcs] in sp between next 2nd and 3rd dc, (3 dc, ch 2, 2 dc) in next ch-2 sp, (3 dc, ch 3, 1 dc) in sp between next 2nd and 3rd dc's, [(3 dc, ch 3, 1 dc) in next ch-3 sp] 15 times, (3 dc, ch 3, 1 dc) in sp between next 3rd and 4th dc's, join with a sl st to top of ch-3.

Rnd 6: Sl st in next dc, sl st in next ch-2 sp, ch 3 (counts as 1 dc), (1 dc, ch 2, 2 dc) in same sp, *[(1 dc, ch 3, 3 dc) in next ch-3 sp] 17 times*, (2 dc, ch 2, 2 dc) in next ch-2 sp; rep from * to * once, join with a sl st to top of ch-3.

Rnd 7: Sl st in next dc, sl st in next ch-2 sp, ch 3 (counts as 1 dc), (1 dc, ch 2, 2 dc) in same sp, *[(3 dc, ch 3, 1 dc) in next ch-3 sp] 17 times*, (2 dc, ch 2, 2 dc) in next ch-2 sp; rep from * to * once, join with a sl st to top of ch-3. Fasten off.

Change to yarn C.

Rnd 8 (inc rnd): Rep rnd 2, but work instructions in brackets 17 times.

Rnd 9: Rep rnd 7, but work instructions in brackets 19 times. Fasten off.

Change to yarn B.

Rnd 10: Rep rnd 6, but work instructions in brackets 19 times.

Rnd 11 (inc rnd): Rep rnd 5, but work instructions in brackets 19 times. Fasten off.

Change to yarn A.

Rnd 12: Rep rnd 6, but work instructions in brackets 21 times.

Rnd 13: Rep rnd 7, but work instructions in brackets 21 times.

Rnd 14 (inc rnd): Rep rnd 2, but work instructions in brackets 21 times.

Rnd 15: Rep rnd 7, but work instructions in brackets 23 times.

Rnd 16: Rep rnd 6, but work instructions in brackets 23 times. Fasten off.

Change to yarn C.

Rnd 17 (inc rnd): Rep rnd 5, but work instructions in brackets 23 times.

Rnd 18: Rep rnd 6, but work instructions in brackets 25 times.

Rnd 19: Rep rnd 7, but work instructions in brackets 25 times. Fasten off.

Change to yarn B.

Rnd 20 (inc rnd): Rep rnd 2, but work instructions in brackets 25 times. Fasten off.

Change to yarn A.

Rnd 21: Rep rnd 7, but work instructions in brackets 27 times.

Rnd 22: Rep rnd 6, but work instructions in brackets 27 times. Fasten off.

Change to yarn B.

Rnd 23 (inc rnd): Rep rnd 5, but work instructions in brackets 27 times. Fasten off.

Fanciful Mesh Sweater

Design by Marty Miller

You'll have no trouble making a catch when you wear this stunning, asymmetrically-styled mesh sweater.

SKILL LEVEL

Intermediate

FINISHED MEASUREMENTS

This sweater is designed to fit bust sizes S (34"/86cm), M (38"/96cm), and L (42"/107cm)

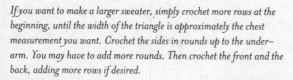

MATERIALS

726yf (968, 1089)/653m (871, 980) worsted weight cotton blend yarn in yellow-green

Hook: 6.5mm/K/10½ or size needed to obtain gauge

STITCHES USED

Chain stitch (ch)

Single crochet (sc)

Double crochet (dc)

Slip stitch (sl st)

SPECIAL STITCHES

Picot: Ch 3, sl st in 3rd ch from hk, sk 1 sc, sl st in next sc = 1 picot

Dec dc: Start a dc, yo, insert hk, yo, pull through, yo, pull through 2 lps on hk. Yo, insert hk in next st, yo, pull through, yo, pull through 2 loops on hk, yo, pull through all lps on hk = 1 dec dc

GAUGE

Take time to check your gauge.

Mesh pattern: 6 pattern repeats = 6 rows = approx 4"/10cm

PATTERN NOTES

When you are working with yarn in this particular pattern stitch you may find that the material stretches. When you measure your gauge, place the fabric on a flat surface, without pulling the edges out. Your gauge will be approximate; because of the nature of the material, it won't be exact. If your gauge is off by a lot, change your hook size.

The completed garment will drape well and stretch a bit. It is meant to be somewhat loose.

The sweater is worked in one piece, from the bottom up, in rows, starting at the point. Once the bottom triangle is worked, the rows become rounds when you join the side. The body is worked up to the armholes, then the sweater is divided into front and back.

The sleeves are added on after the shoulder seams are joined. The back of the sweater is the same as the front—and there is no right or wrong side of the fabric until you get to the neck edge. Then the right side of the sweater is the last row of the neck edge.

Be sure to join the shoulder seams with the right sides of the front and back facing each other, so the seam will be on the inside.

If you want to make a larger sweater, simply crochet more rows at the beginning, until the width of the triangle is approximately the chest measurement you want. Crochet the sides in rounds up to the underarm. You may have to add more rounds. Then crochet the front and the back, adding more rows if desired.

Finally, follow the sleeve directions, again, adding more rows at the top if needed. You might want to decrease every 3rd or 4th row, or add rows to the bottom of the sleeve.

INSTRUCTIONS

BOTTOM TRIANGLE

Ch 5: (Counts as an elongated dc, ch 1 here and throughout)

Row 1: Dc in 5th ch from hk; (2 dc). Ch 5, turn.

Row 2: Dc in first dc (beg inc made), ch 1, dc in next dc, ch 1, dc in 4th ch of tch, ch 1, dc in same ch of tch (end inc made); (4 dc). Ch 5, turn.

Row 3: Dc in first dc (beg inc), ch 1, *dc in next dc, ch 1. Rep from * across to tch, dc in 4th ch of tch, ch 1, dc in same ch of tch (end inc); (6 dc). Ch 5, turn.

Rows 4–25 (27, 31): Rep row 3; [50 (54, 62) dc]. Ch 1, join with a sl st to 4th of first ch 5 in the row. You will now be working in rounds. Ch 4, turn. (Ch 4 counts as dc, ch 1 here and throughout.)

Rnd 1: Sk the first dc, dc in the next dc, ch 1, *dc in next dc, ch 1. Rep from * around; [50 (54, 62) dc]. Join with a sl st in 3rd ch of tch. Ch 4, turn.

Rnds 2–11 (13, 15): Rep rnd 1, until side measures approx. 8"(8½, 10)/20cm (21, 25); join as above. Ch 4, turn.

FRONT

You will now be working in rows.

Row 1: Sk the first dc, dc in the next dc, *ch 1, dc in next dc. Rep from * 22(24, 28) times; [24 (26, 30) dc]. Ch 4, turn. (Remember, the ch 4 at the beginning of each row counts as the first dc, ch 1.)

Rows 2–11 (15, 15): Rep row 1. [Row 11 (15, 15) is the RS of the sweater.] Fasten off, leaving a long tail to sl st the shoulders together.

BACK

Join the yarn in the last rnd before you started crocheting the front in the next dc after the last stitch of the first row of the front. Ch 4.

Rows 1–11 (15, 15): Rep the directions for the front.

JOINING THE SHOULDERS

With RS of the sweater facing each other, sl st the shoulder seams tog, going into the top lp only on each stitch. Leave about 10" (10½, 10¾)/25cm (27, 27) open in the middle for the neckline.

EDGING

Rnd 1: From the RS, join yarn, ch 1, sc evenly along the neck edge. Join to the 1st ch with a sl st. Ch 1, do not turn.

Rnd 2: Sl st in same st as joining, *ch 3, sl st in 3rd ch from hk, skip 1 sc on neck edge, sl st in next sc. (1 picot made). Rep from * around. Join with sl st to 1st sl st.

SLEEVES

The sleeves are worked in rounds.

Rnd 1: From the RS of the sweater, join the yarn in the dc on the left side of 1 of the underarms. Working along the edges of the rows of the bodice, ch 4, dc in the ch st at the end of the 1st row, *ch 1, dc at the end of the next row. Rep from * around; [23 (31, 31) dc]. Join with a sl st to the third ch. Ch 4, turn.

Rnd 2: Sk the 1st dc, *dc in next dc, ch 1. Rep from * around. Ch 4, turn.

Rnds 3 and 4: Rep rnd 2.

Rnd 5: Sk the first dc, *dc in next dc, ch 1. Rep from * around until you get to the last two dc. Dec dc in the last two dc, ch 1, join with sl st to third ch of tch; [22 (30, 30) dc]. Join as above.

Rnds 6–8: Rep rnd 2.

Rnd 9: Rep rnd 5; [21 (29, 29) dc].

Rnds 10–12: Rep rnd 2.

Rnd 13: Rep rnd 5; [20 (28, 28) dc].

Rnd 14: Rep rnd 2.

Rnd 15: Rep rnd 5; [19 (27, 27) dc].

Rnd 16: Rep rnd 2.

Continue in this manner, dec on the next rnd and in every other rnd after that until you have 23 rnds; [15 (23, 23) dc]. Fasten off. (If you want your sleeves longer, just rep rnd 2 as needed.)

Repeat these directions on the other side of the sweater for the other sleeve.

CUFF POINT ON SLEEVE

Fold sleeve in half to find the middle dc that lines up with the shoulder seam. Follow that dc to the bottom edge of the sleeve. Place a marker there. On the RS of the sleeve, at the bottom edge, attach yarn at the 3rd dc from the left of the center dc that you found.

Row 1: Ch 3, sk 1st dc, dc in next dc, *ch 1, dc in next dc. Rep from * 2 more times. Dec dc in next 2 dcs. Ch 3, turn.

Row 2: Sk 1st dc, *dc in next dc, ch 1. Rep from * 1 more time. Dec dc in last 2 dc. Ch 3, turn.

Row 3: Skip 1st dc. Dec dc in last 2 dc. Ch 1, do not turn.

Repeat these directions on the other sleeve.

PICOT EDGE

You are working on the RS of the sleeve. Work the picot edge around the sleeve edge, keeping the stitches even and the picot edge flat. Start with a sl st in the next st, *ch 3, sl st in 3rd ch from hk, sk a distance on the sleeve edge, sl st. (1 picot made). Rep from * around. Join with sl st to 1st sl st.

Repeat for the other sleeve.

This project was created with:

6 (8, 9) skeins of Schoeller Stahl's *Portofino* in Lemon (#4712), 40% cotton/40% acrylic/20% polyamide, 1.75oz/50g = approx 121yd/110m ea

Snuggly Azure Shrug

Design by Donna May

Imagine wrapping yourself in a puffy cloud snatched from out of the blue: soft, light, yet capable of warding off the chill of an early spring day.

SKILL LEVEL

Easy

FINISHED MEASUREMENTS

Finished rectangle measures approx 30 x 55"/76 x 140cm

One size fits most

Continued ➜

MATERIALS

783yd/704m fancy worsted weight yarn*

Hook: 9mm/M/N-13 *or size needed to obtain gauge*

Tapestry needle

Elastic thread (optional)

For a thicker fabric (and even more snuggly shrug), work two strands of yarn together throughout (1566yd/1408m).

STITCHES USED

Chain stitch (ch)

Half double crochet (hdc)

GAUGE

Take time to check your gauge.

Approx 8 st = 4"/10cm

7 rows = 4"/10cm

PATTERN NOTES

Hdc is worked in first stitch at beginning of row throughout. After starting a new ball of yarn, weave in ends before continuing.

PATTERN

Ch 99 and make 1 hdc in 3rd ch from hk and in ea ch across; ch 2, turn (96 sts).

Rows 1–4: Hdc across; ch 2, turn. Tie a short piece of contrasting color yarn around a st in first row to mark RS.

Row 5: 1 hdc in first 46 hdc; 2 dec hide, 1 hdc in ea of next 46 hdc; ch 2, turn (94 sts).

Row 6: 1 hdc in first 44 hdc; 3 dec hdc, 1 hdc in ea of next 44 hdc; ch 1, turn, (91 sts)

Rows 7–58: Hdc in each hdc across; ch 2, turn, (91 sts)

Row 59: Hdc in each of first 44 hdc; 3 inc hdc; 1 hdc in ea of next 44 hdc; ch 2, turn. (94 sts)

Row 60: Hdc in each of first 46 hdc; 2 inc hdc; 1 hdc in ea of next 46 hdc; ch 2, turn. (86 sts)

Rows 61–64: Hdc in each hdc across (96 sts); fasten off. Weave in ends.

ASSEMBLY

SLEEVE SEAMS

With right sides together, fold piece in half lengthwise, bringing top edge to foundation chain edge (figure 1). Mark off 14"/36cm on each end where edges meet (long edge). Back stitch edges of one 14"/36cm section together to create sleeve seam. Fasten off. Weave in ends. Repeat with other section.

OPTIONAL SLEEVE LENGTH

To extend sleeves to wrist length attach yarn now to right side of the fabric at the cuff and crochet around cuff edge in hdc. Continue crocheting in the round until sleeve is desired length.

(Do not ch 2 at beginning of each round; simply make the first hdc of round 2 and later rounds into the first stitch of the last round.) When sleeve is desired length, join, fasten off and weave in ends.

GATHERING CUFFS

Thread about a 40"/102cm length of yarn or elastic thread in needle and fasten to WS of one sleeve seam at cuff edge. Make a running stitch near edge, around circumference of sleeve opening. Pull to gather cuff to 5½"/14cm diameter opening. Check before fastening to be sure there is enough stretch to allow the hand through the opening, as elasticity may vary in different threads. Fasten off. Weave in end. Repeat for other cuff.

FINISHING

This section is crocheted in the round. You will crochet in each stitch; however, in half the round, you will crochet into hdc stitches and the other half of the round you will crochet into the free loops of your foundation chain. No stitch count is necessary for these rounds and is not provided, as the number will vary slightly with number of stitches sewn in the sleeve sections.

With RS facing you, fasten yarn in one inner sleeve seam at armhole opening and ch 2. (Tie a contrasting color yarn in this stitch to mark the beginning of the round.)

Rnd 1: Inc hdc in ea st around. Sl st in top ch of beginning ch 2 to join; ch 2, turn.

Rnds 2–3: Hdc in 1st st and in ea st around. Sl st in top ch of ch-2 to join, ch 2, turn.

Rnd 4: Hdc in ea st around. Sl st in top ch of ch 2 to join. Fasten off. Weave in ends.

FORMING COLLAR

Lay the shrug flat with sleeve seams facing you and centered half way between top and bottom edges of sleeves. (It doesn't matter which side you use for the top of the shrug.) Create collar by folding back the middle section of the open center edge. The collar will fold back naturally due to the stitching, however, the width may adjusted as desired.

If desired, tack down collar by catching several stitches along the back of the collar and sewing to the shrug body directly underneath. Catch only bottom loops of back of collar to avoid stitches showing on top.

This project was created with:

9 balls of Online Punta Yarn *in Aqua-Mauve, 45% viscose/45% nylon/10% polyacryl, 1.75oz/50g = approx 87yd/80m ea*

Reversible Halter and Scarf

Design by Ruthie Marks

You'll need to pay a bit more attention when you crochet this top, but the result is well worth the effort. If your skill level isn't top-notch, the scarf is a delightful project.

SKILL LEVEL

Top: Experienced

Scarf: Easy

FINISHED MEASUREMENTS

Top: S (29"/74cm), M (31"/79cm), L (33"/84cm)*

Scarf: approx 8 x 54"/20 x 137cm (excluding fringe)

* *The fabric of this garment, because it is worked loosely, is very stretchy, so dimensions are smaller than standard sizing.*

MATERIALS

- Yarn A: approx 460yd (544, 628)414m (490, 565) of fine/sport weight yarn in orange
- Yarn B: 376yd (460, 544)/338m (414, 490) of fine/sport weight yarn in pale green
- Hooks: 6.5mm/K-10½, 6mm/J-10, 5.5mm/I-9, 3.5mm/E-4 or sizes needed to obtain gauge
- Tapestry needle
- 20"/51cm 3mm elastic thread

STITCHES USED

Chain stitch (ch)

Single crochet (sc)

Half double crochet (hdc)

Double crochet (dc)

GAUGE

Take time to check your gauge.

Top: 14 st = 4"/10cm

12 rows = 4"/10cm

Scarf: 6 arches = 4"/10cm

14 rows = 4"/10cm

PATTERN NOTES

This is a double-sided garment. No ends are fastened off until each section is completed.

Use an overhand knot at the end of each row to keep stitches from unraveling while you work.

If you find that the 2 stitches you're picking up are not in alignment, chances are you have picked up an extra stitch or dropped one along the way. Count your stitches often.

When you lay down your work, have both working threads at the same end; this tells you that yarn A begins the next row.

INSTRUCTIONS

BACK

Row 1: With yarn A and 6.5mm/K-10½ hk, ch 50 (54, 58), sc in 2nd ch from hk and each ch across, turn [49 (53, 57) sts].

Row 2A: Ch 1, sc in front loop of each sc across, drop A, do not turn.

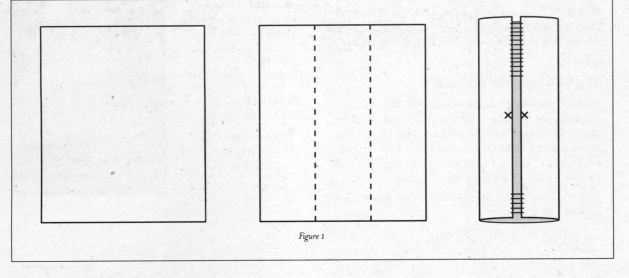

Figure 1

Row 2B: With B, go back to beg of row 2A and, *inserting the hk from the top down, sc in the back lp of the 1st stitch of row 2A and the free lp of the 1st stitch of row 1, rep in the 2nd st and each st across, drop B, pick up A.

Row 3A: With A, ch 1, turn and, *inserting the hk from the top down, sc in the back lp of B and the free lp of A, rep from * across, drop A, pick up B.

Row 3B: With B, ch 1, turn and, *inserting the hk from the bottom up, sc in the free lp of B and the free lp of A, rep from * across, drop B, pick up A.

Row 4A: With A, ch 1, turn and, *inserting the hook from the bottom up, sc in the free lp of A and the front lp of B, repeat from * across, drop B, pick up A.

Row 4B: With B, ch 1, turn and, *inserting the hk from the top down, sc in the back lp of A and the free lp of B, repeat from * across, drop B, pick up A.

The pattern is a repeat of rows 3A, 3B, 4A, 4B.

Work in pattern stitch until approx 9 (9, 10)"/23 (23, 25)cm from beginning. At the end of last 2 rows fasten off A and B.

FRONT

Work as back to 9 (9, 10)"/23 (23, 25)cm from beg.

Row 1A: (beg dec): Sk 1st 2 sts of B, with A sl st in first 2 sts of A, (sl st, ch 1, sc in A and B) in next st, work in pattern in next 45 sts, leave last 2 sts unworked [45 (49, 53) sts]

Row 1B: With B, work same as 1A.

Row 2A: Sk 1st st of B, with A sl st in first st of A, (sl st, ch 1, sc in A and B) in next st, work in pattern in next 43 sts, leave last st unworked. [43 (47, 51) sts]

Row 2B: With B, work same as 2A.

Row 3A: With A, ch 1 and work even across.

Row 3B: With B, work same as 3A.

Rows 4A and 4B: Rep row 2A and 2B [41 (45, 49) sts]

Rows 5A and 5B: Rep row 2A and 2B [39 (43, 47) sts]

Rows 6A and 6B: Rep row 3A and 3B [29 (43, 47) sts]

Repeat rows 4A–6B for approx 5"(6, 6)/13cm (15, 15) from beg to dec. [31 (27, 27) sts]. Fasten off A and B.

JOINING SIDE SEAMS (2 EACH FOR A AND B)

With side A facing, use a strand of yarn A and a tapestry needle to sew both side A edges together.

With side B facing, use a strand of yarn B and a tapestry needle to sew both side B edges together.

CASING (ACROSS TOP OF FRONT)

Row 1: With side B facing, 5.5mm/I-9 hook and 2 strands of A, attach with 1 sc in first st and sc across, turn [31 (27, 27) sts].

Row 2: Ch 3 (counts as hdc and ch 1), sk first 2 sc, hdc in next sc, *ch 1, sk 1 sc, hdc in next sc, repeat from * across, fasten off.

EDGING AROUND TOP EDGES

Starting at side seam with side B facing, 5.5mm/I-9 hook and 2 srands of A, going through both loops of both B and A, matching stitch for stitch, (sl st, ch 1) in each st across back and up side, (sl st, ch 1) in each hdc only across top, (sl st, ch 1) in each st down other side, sl st to beg sl st, fasten off.

BOTTOM EDGING

Rnd 1: With side B facing, 5.5mm/I-9 hook and 2 strands of A, join with sl st at side seam. Working in sps between sts, *sk 2 spaces, 5 dc in next sp, skip 2 sps, sl st in next sp, repeat from * around, ending sl st in beg sl st, turn.

Rnd 2: *5 dc in middle dc of dc group in rnd 1, sl st in next sl st, rep from * around, ending sl st in beg sl st, fasten off.

NECK CORD

With 5.5mm/I-9 hook and 2 strands of A, ch 170, fasten off (approx 40"/102cm). Tie a knot in end and trim ends to 1"/2.5cm. Thread through row of hdc at top of halter and tie in a bow behind the neck.

FINISHING

If desired, thread tapestry needle with elastic thread. Weave thread through edging across back of garment and adjust to customize fit. Secure ends.

SCARF

SIDE A

Row 1: With yarn A and 3.5mm/E-4 hk, ch 302, sc in 6th ch from hk, *ch 5, sk 3ch, sc in next ch, rep from * to end, turn.

Rows 2–14: Ch 5, sc in next ch-5 arch, rep from * to end, turn. Fasten off at the end of row 14.

SIDE B

Row 1 (RS): Working across the other side of the foundation row, join B with sc in the first ch, *ch 5, sc opposite the next sc, rep from * to end, turn.

Rows 2–14: Rep rows 2–14 of side A.

FRINGE

Using an 8"/20cm wide piece of cardboard, wind and cut 48 strands each of A and B. Work with groups of 6, attach in beginning ch-5 loops of 4 rows at each end of scarf. Trim ends evenly.

This project was created with:

Skeins ea of Red Heart's *Luster Sheen* in Persimmon (#257) and *Tea Leaf* (#615), 100% acrylic, 4oz/113g = approx 335 yds/306 m ea

—FROM *The New Crochet*

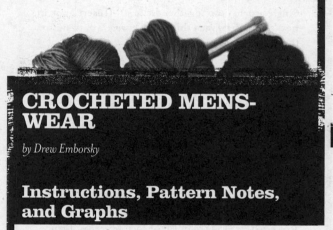

CROCHETED MENS-WEAR

by Drew Emborsky

Instructions, Pattern Notes, and Graphs

I've written every pattern with detailed step-by-step instructions, so feel free to challenge your crochet skills. Each pattern begins with the number of chain stitches you need for the foundation row, and then continues with a row-by-row description of the stitches or pattern combinations needed to complete the project. If the project has more than one piece, I've provided separate step-by-step directions for each piece, along with assembly instructions.

The patterns range from rank beginner to downright experienced, but I've taken special care to write them clearly. If you take your time and follow the instructions step by step, you can make any of the projects you want.

If a pattern requires special stitch variations or unusual working methods. I've explained them in a separate section. Look for these pattern notes at the beginning of the project instructions. If a pattern uses specific color changes for checks or stripes, I've shown these changes graphically in an illustration or a charted graph. Sometimes it's easier to follow the chart, so if you have a question about the written instructions, go ahead and cross check it with the chart to see if it clears things up for you. Each square on a charted graph equals a given number of stitches—and that number is noted each time.

Whenever a garment has multiple pieces, a diagram shows the dimensions of each piece. And if a stitch combination is a bit complex, a symbol chart shows the exact construction of the fabric.

Stitch Key

— =Worked in front loop only
— =Worked in back loop only

Symbol	Stitch	Symbol	Stitch
⌐	Chain stitch (ch)	↗	Back post dc (BPdc)
·	Slip stitch (sl st)	↗	Front post tr (FPtr)
X	Single crochet (sc)	↗	Back post tr (BPtr)
T	Half double crochet (hdc)	↗	front post dtr (FPdtr)
T	Double crochet (dc)	⋏	Front post dc two together (FPdc2tog)
T	Treble crochet (tr)	⋏	Back post dc two together (BPdc2tog)
X̃	Reverse sc	X	Crossed dc (X-st)
↗	Front post dc (FPdc)	V	V-st

Abbv. Spkn Here

As you probably know—or will find out very soon—the language of crochet instructions uses a lot of abbreviations. Or to put it another way, when I write "yo" in a project I'm really saying "yarn over," and not doing my awesome Stallone-as-Rocky impression. Abbreviations are great for keeping instructions short, but if any unfamiliar ones are making you scratch your head, just look them up in the chart.

Choosing the Right Size

Perhaps you aren't accustomed to having this many projects for guys all in one place (even though you and I both know that you have been wanting men's crochet designs for years now). Let me point out a few things to keep in mind.

It seems obvious, but choosing the correct size will help you to create a garment you (or your loved one) will love to wear over and over again. I took special care to ensure that these clothes are comfortable and good-looking, especially for the larger sizes. I included the added length right in the pattern, so the garments will be comfortable even for big guys.

If you are making one of the sweaters for yourself, a great way to choose the size that is right for you is to use your favorite shirt or sweater...you know, the one that the womenfolk in your life have been trying for years to secretly throw away, but you always find it in time, pull it out of the trash, wash it, and wear it anyway, much to their dismay? Why not just get its size? Measure across, right under the sleeves, and use that chest measurement as your rough guide to choose the right size sweater to make. It's that simple.

Remember when I said earlier that I designed the bigger sizes with extra length for maximum comfort? Now it's time to admit that I wrote all the sweater patterns so

Continued →

that the sleeves will be long. I like long sleeves. There really isn't anything more uncomfortable than sleeves that ride up when I'm working on a project or playing a sport. It's easier to roll up your sleeves when you need to. And, once you've finished making a sweater, making the sleeves longer really isn't a good option.

If you are making a sweater as a gift, here is a basic chart to use:

Men's Sweater Sizes

Size	Chest	Back to Hip Length
S	38	25" (63.5 cm)
M	40	26½" (67.3 cm)
L	42	27" (68.6 cm)
XL	44	27½" (69.9 cm)
XXL	46	28½" (72.4 cm)

I designed some sweaters to be loose and some to be form-fitting. Compare the chest size from the chart to the finished measurements in the pattern. If the pattern is about 2 to 4 inches (5 to 10 cm) bigger than the chest size in the chart, the resulting sweater should fit comfortably. So if you're making a sweater as a gift and you don't know the exact size, here's my advice: when in doubt, always go for the bigger size!

ABBREVIATIONS

alt—alternate
alt lp st—alternate loop stitch
approx—approximately
beg—begin, beginning
BL—back loop
BP—back panel
ch—chain
ch-sp—chain space
cont—continue
dc—double crochet
dec—decrease(s/ing)
dtr—double treble crochet
ea—each
FL—front loop
FP—front panel
hdc—half double crochet
hk—hook
inc—increase(s/ing)
lp(s)—loop(s)
lp st—loop stitch
oz—ounce(s)
prev—previous
puff st—puff stitch
rem—remaining
rep—repeat
reverse sc—reverse single crochet
RS—right side
rnd(s)—round(s)
sc—single crochet
sk—skip
sl st—slip stitch
sp—space(s)
st(s)—stitch(es)
tch—turning chain
tog—together
tr—treble crochet
WS—wrong side
yo—yarn over

Projects

Head Banned

Sitting in the stands one freezing November day, I was sure this would be the homecoming my ears fell off, and I would have to carry them home to stick them back on later. No more! I've made this band in my old school colors, but you can change yarns if you root for someone other than the ol' Red and White.

SKILL LEVEL

Beginner

FINISHED SIZE

21"/53.5cm circumference—one size fits most ears

YOU WILL NEED

- Color A: 38yd/35m of super bulky weight yarn
- Color B: 8yd/7.5m of super bulky weight yarn
- Hook: 6.50mm (size K-10½ U.S.) *or size to obtain gauge*
- Yarn needle
- Team spirit and snow (optional)

STITCHES USED

Chain stitch (ch)

Half double crochet (hdc)

Single crochet (sc)

Slip stitch (sl st)

SPECIAL STITCH

Single crochet two together (sc2tog): (Insert hook in next st, yo, draw yarn through st) twice, yo, draw yarn through 3 loops on hook.

GAUGE

13 sts x 11 rows = 4"/10cm in sc in BL only

Always take time to check your gauge.

INSTRUCTIONS

FIRST HALF [D]

With A, ch 17.

Row 1 (RS): Sc in 2nd ch from hook and in each ch across, turn–16 sc.

Rows 2–12: Ch 1, sc in BL of each sc across, turn.

Rows 13–17: Ch 1, working in BL of sts, sc in first sc, sc2tog in next 2 sts, sc in each sc across to within last 3 sts, sc2tog in next 2 sts, sc in last sc, turn–6 sc rem at end of row 17.

Rows 18–29: Ch 1, sc in BL of each st across, turn. Fasten off.

SECOND HALF

Row 1: With RS facing, working across opposite side of foundation ch, join A with sc in the 1st foundation ch, sc in each ch across, turn—16 sc.

Rows 2–29: Rep rows 2–29 of First Half. Fasten off.

ASSEMBLE

Fold project in half along foundation ch with RS together, whipstitch rows 29 together to form headband. Turn headband RS out.

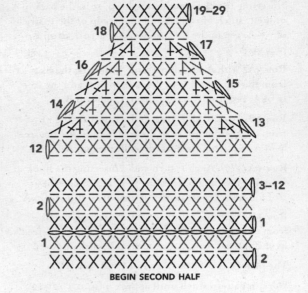

FIRST HALF

BEGIN SECOND HALF

FINISHING

First Edging

Rnd 1: With RS facing, join A with sc along one side edge, sc evenly around one side of headband, slip st to first sc to join. Fasten off.

Rnd 2: With WS facing, join B with sl st to FL of any st in rnd 1 of edging, ch 2, hdc in FL of each sc around, sl st in top of beg ch-2 to join. Fasten off.

Second Edging

Rep First Edging on other side edge of headband.

Weave in ends.

Yarn Used:

Colorway I:

Caron Simply Soft Quick, 100% acrylic, 3oz/85g = 50yd/46m

(A) 1 skein, Navy (#0005)

(B) 1 skein, Mango (#0017)

Colorway II:

Caron Simply Soft Quick, 100% acrylic, 3oz/85g = 50yd/46m per skein

(A) 1 skein, Autumn Red (#0007)

(B) 1 skein, White (#0001)

Dawg

Who knew that a hoodie would become a timeless classic? I've always had a hooded sweatshirt or two in my closet, so I wanted to design a crochet version. The soft and comfy fiber used here creates a denim look.

SKILL LEVEL

Intermediate

FINISHED SIZE

S (M, L, XL, XXL): 42 (44, 46, 48, 50)"/106.5 (112, 117, 122, 127)cm

YOU WILL NEED

- 1673 (1725, 1935, 2091, 2196)yd/1530 (1578, 1770, 1912, 2008)m of medium weight yarn
- Hook: 5.00mm (size H-8 U.S.) *or size to obtain gauge*
- Yarn needle

- Long sewing pins
- Stitch marker

STITCHES USED

Back post double crochet (BPdc)

Chain stitch (ch)

Double crochet (dc)

Front post double crochet (FPdc)

Single crochet (sc)

Slip stitch (sl st)

GAUGE

12 sts x 10 rows = 4"/10cm in pattern stitch

Always take time to check your gauge.

INSTRUCTIONS

PATTERN STITCH

Row 1: Sc in 2nd ch from hook, dc in next ch, *sc in next ch, dc in next ch; rep from * across, turn.

Row 2: Ch 3 (counts as dc) sc in next sc, *dc in next dc, sc in next sc; rep from * across, turn.

Row 3: Ch 1, sc in same first sc, dc in next dc, *sc in next sc, dc in next dc; rep from * across, turn.

Repeat rows 2–3 for pattern.

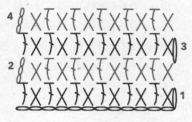

Pattern stitch

BACK

Ch 65 (67, 71, 73, 77).

Work even in pattern stitch on 64 (66, 70, 72, 76) sts until piece measures 15 (15½, 16, 16, 16½")/38 (39.5, 40.5, 40.5, 42)cm from beg.

Shape Armholes

Next row: Work in established pattern across to within last 8 sts, turn, leaving rem sts unworked—56 (58, 62, 64, 68) sts.

Next row: Rep last row—48 (50, 54, 56, 60) sts.

Work even in pattern until piece measures 24 (25, 26, 26½, 27½")/61 (63.5, 66, 67.5, 70)cm from beg. Fasten off.

FRONT

Work as for back including armhole shaping until piece measures 22 (23, 24, 24½, 25½")/56 (58.5, 61, 62, 65)cm from beg.

Shape First Shoulder

Next row: Work in pattern across first 16 (16, 16, 18, 18) sts, turn, leaving rem sts unworked—16 (16, 16, 18, 18) sts.

Work even until piece measures 24 (25, 26, 26½, 27½")/61 (63.5, 66, 67.5, 70)cm from beg. Fasten off.

Shape Second Shoulder

Next row: Sk 15 (18, 20, 22, 24) sts to the left of last st made in first row of first shoulder, join yarn in next st, work in established pattern across, turn—16 (16, 16, 18, 18) sts.

Work even in pattern until piece measures 24 (25, 26, 26½, 27½")/61 (63.5, 66, 67.5, 70)cm from beg. Fasten off.

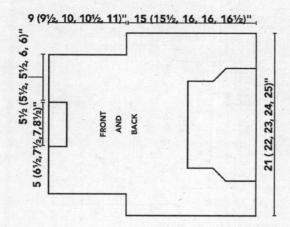

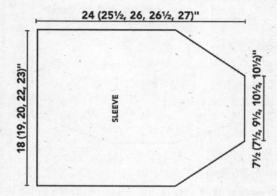

SLEEVE (MAKE 2)

Ch 23 (23, 29, 31, 31).

Work even in pattern stitch for 4 rows—22 (22, 28, 30, 30) sts. Maintaining pattern stitch, inc 1 st in pattern at end of each row until 53 (57, 59, 63, 65) sts are on work. Work even until length of sleeve measures 24 (25½, 26, 26½, 27")/61 (65, 66, 67.5, 68.5)cm from beg.

POCKET

Ch 41.

Rows 1–8: Work even in pattern stitch, turn—40 sts.

Rows 9–12: Work in pattern stitch across to within 2 sts, turn, leaving rem sts unworked—32 sts at end of last row.

Rows 13–21: Work even in pattern stitch, turn. Fasten off.

Edging

Rnd 1: Ch 1, sc evenly around entire pocket, sl st in first sc to join. Fasten off.

DRAWSTRING

Make a 60"/152.5cm long ch. Fasten off. Tie ea end of drawstring in an overhand knot.

ASSEMBLE

Sew shoulder seams. Set in sleeves. Sew sleeve and side seams. Center pocket on front of sweater, sew in place, leaving sides of rows 9–21 unattached.

FINISHING

Hood

Row 1: With RS facing, join yarn at center front of neck opening, work in row 1 of pattern stitch around entire neck opening, working a multiple of 4 sts. Do not join, turn.

Work even in pattern stitch until hood measures 12"/30.5cm from beg.

Shape First Side

Place marker at center of last row

Row 1: Work even in pattern stitch across to within 2 sts of center marker, turn, leaving rem sts unworked.

Row 2: Work even in pattern stitch across, turn.

Row 3: Work even in pattern stitch across to within last 2 sts, turn, leaving rem sts unworked.

Row 4: Work even in pattern stitch across, turn. Fasten off.

Shape Second Side

Row 1: Sk 2 sts to the left of center marker, work in pattern stitch across, turn.

Row 2: Work even in pattern stitch across, turn.

Row 3: Sl st in first 3 sts, work in pattern stitch across, turn.

Row 4: Work even in pattern stitch across turn. Fasten off.

Bottom Ribbing

Rnd 1: With RS facing, join yarn on bottom edge at one side seam, ch 3 (counts as dc), dc evenly around, working an even number of sts.

Rnd 2: Ch 2 (counts as hdc), *BPdc around the post of next dc, FPdc around the post of next dc; rep from * around, ending with BPdc around the post of last dc, sl st in 2nd ch of beg ch-2 to join.

Rnd 3: Rep rnd 2. Fasten off.

Cuffs

Rnd 1: With RS facing, join yarn on cuff edge of one sleeve, at seam, ch 3 (counts as dc), dc evenly around, working an even number of sts.

Rnds 2–3: Rep rnds 2–3 of bottom ribbing. Fasten off.

Rep cuff on other sleeve.

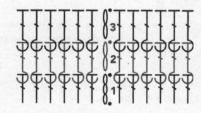

Bottom ribbing and cuffs pattern.

Hood Ribbing

Row 1: With RS facing, join yarn at lower right-hand corner of hood edge, ch 3 (counts as dc), dc evenly across to lower left-hand corner, working an even number of sts.

Row 2: Ch 2 (counts as hdc), *BPdc around the post of next dc, FPdc around the post of next dc; rep from * across, ending with hdc in top of ch-3 tch, turn.

Row 3: Rep row 2. Fasten off.

Weave in ends.

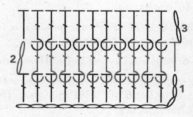

Hood ribbing pattern.

Yarn Used:

Moda Dea Fashionista, 50% acrylic/50% tencel lyocell, 3½ oz/100g = 183yd/168m per skein

10 (10, 11, 12, 12) skeins, Blue Jean (#6130)

Continued ➜

Comforolled

Some guys don't like the ribbing on most sweaters. That's why I've created this sweater that has a rolled hem instead of ribbing. The entire sweater is worked up in single crochet, so this is a great project for beginners.

SKILL LEVEL

Intermediate

FINISHED SIZE

S (M, L, XL, XXL): 38 (40, 42, 44, 46)"/96.5 (101.5, 106.5, 112, 117) cm

Sweater shown in size XL.

YOU WILL NEED

- 1404 (1538, 1680, 1800, 1976)yd/1284 (1407, 1536, 1646, 1807)m of medium weight yarn, in green
- Hook: 5.00mm (size H-8 U.S.) *or size to obtain gauge*
- Long sewing pins
- Yarn needle

STITCHES USED

Chain stitch (ch)

Single crochet (sc)

Slip stitch (sl st)

SPECIAL STITCH

Single crochet two together (sc2tog): (Insert hook in next st, yo, draw yarn through st) twice, yo, draw yarn through 3 lps on hook.

GAUGE

17 sts x 17 rows = 4"/10cm in sc

Always take time to check your gauge.

INSTRUCTIONS

ROLLED HEM

Row 1 (RS): Sc in FL of 2nd ch from hook, sc in FL of ea ch across, turn.

Row 2: Ch 1, sc in BL only of each sc across, turn.

Row 3: Ch 1, sc in FL only of each sc across, turn.

Rows 4–5: Rep rows 2–3.

Row 6: Rep row 2.

BACK

Ch 82 (86, 90, 95, 99)

Row 1 (RS): Sc in FL of 2nd ch from hook, sc in FL of ea ch across, turn—81 (85, 89, 94, 98) sc.

Rows 2–6: Work rows 2–6 of Rolled Hem pattern.

Working in both lps of sts, work even in sc until piece measures 15 (15½, 16, 16, 16½)"/38 (39.5, 40.5, 40.5, 42)cm from beg.

Shape Armholes

Next Row: Ch 1, sc in each sc across to within last 9 sts, turn, leaving rem sts unworked—72 (76, 80, 85, 89) sc.

Next row: Rep last row—63 (67, 71, 76, 80) sc.

Work even in sc until piece measures 23 (24, 25, 25½, 26½)"/58.5 (61, 63.5, 65, 67.5)cm from beg.

Shape First Shoulder

Next row: Ch 1, sc in each of next 16 (18, 20, 22, 24) sc, turn, leaving rem sts unworked—16 (18, 20, 22, 24) sc.

Work even in sc until piece measures 24 (25, 26, 26½, 27½)"/61 (63.5, 66, 67.5, 70)cm from beg. Fasten off.

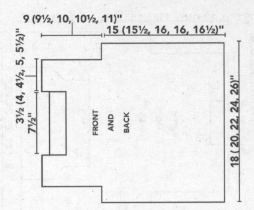

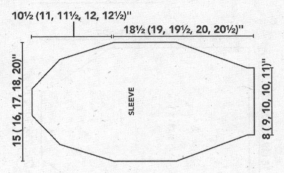

Shape Second Shoulder

Next row: Sk 31 (31, 31, 32, 32) sts to the left of last st made in first row of First Shoulder, join yarn in next sc, ch 1, sc in ea sc across—16 (18, 20, 22, 24) sc.

Work even in sc until piece measures 24 (25, 26, 26½, 27½)"/61 (63.5, 66, 67.5, 70)cm from beg. Fasten off.

FRONT

Work as for back including armhole shaping until piece measures 21 (22, 23, 23½, 24½)"/53.5 (56, 58.5, 59.5, 62)cm from beg. Shape shoulders same as back.

SLEEVES (MAKE 2)

Row 1 (RS): Sc in FL of 2nd ch from hook, sc in FL of ea ch across, turn—34 (38, 43, 43, 47) sc.

Rows 2–6: Work rows 2–6 of Rolled Hem pattern.

Working in both lps of sts, work in sc, inc 1 sc at beg and end of every 3rd row until 64 (68, 73, 77, 85) sc are on work. Work even in sc until Sleeve measures 18½ (19, 19½, 20, 20½)"/47 (48.5, 49.5, 51, 52)cm from beg.

Shape Sleeve Cap

Continue in sc, dec 1 st at end of each row 31 (31, 31, 30, 26) times. Dec 1 st at beg and end of each row 14 (16, 18, 21, 27) times. Fasten off.

ASSEMBLE

Sew shoulder seams. Set in sleeves. Sew sleeve and side seams.

FINISHING

Collar

Foundation rnd: With WS facing, join yarn at center back of neck, ch 1, sc evenly around, sl st in first sc to join, turn.

Rnd 1 (RS): Ch 1, sc in FL of ea sc around, sl st in FL of first sc to join, turn.

Rnd 2: Ch 1, sc in BL of ea sc around, sl st in BL of first sc to join, turn.

Rnd 3: Ch 1, sc in FL of ea sc around, sl st in FL of first sc to join, turn.

Rnds 4–9: Rep rnds 2–3.

Rnd 10: Rep rnd 2. Fasten off. Weave in ends.

Yarn Used:

Patons Décor, 75% acrylic/25% wool, 3½ oz/100g = 210yd/193m per skein

7 (8, 8, 9, 10) skeins, New Green (#16523)

Jock Block Hat & Scarf

It's a challenge for a dude to wear clothes from high school or college without looking foolish. This hat and scarf project will bring back fond memories of when clothes declared that you should just "Relax" and "Choose Life!" At least it did for me.

SKILL LEVEL

Beginner

FINISHED SIZE

Hat: 24"/61cm in circumference—one size fits most adult heads

Scarf: 70"/178cm long— one size fits all

YOU WILL NEED

- Color A: 124yd/114m of bulky weight yarn, in brown
- Color B: 124yd/114m of bulky weight yarn, in beige
- Color C: 124yd/114m of bulky weight yarn, in green
- Hook: 5.00mm (size H-8 U.S.) *or size to obtain gauge*
- Stitch marker
- Yarn needle

STITCHES USED

Back post double crochet (BPdc)

Chain stitch (ch)

Double crochet (dc)

Front post double crochet (FPdc)

Half double crochet (hdc)

Single crochet (sc)

Slip stitch (sl st)

SPECIAL STITCH

Single crochet two together (sc2tog): (Insert hook in next st, yo, draw yarn through st) twice, yo, draw yarn through 3 lps on hook.

GAUGE

12 sts x 13 rows = 4"/10cm in sc; 5 rows = 4"/10cm in dc

Always take time to check your gauge.

INSTRUCTIONS

SCARF PATTERN STITCH

Row 1: Ch 3 (counts as dc), dc in each dc across, turn.

Row 2: Ch 3 (counts as dc), dc in FL only of ea st across, turn.

HAT

Crown

With B, ch 75, and without twisting ch, sl st in first ch to form a ring.

Rnd 1: Sc in each ch around, do not join—75 sc. Work in a spiral. Place marker at beg of rnd and move marker up as work progresses.

Rnd 2: *Sc in next 13 sc, sc2tog in next 2 sts; rep from * around—70 sts.

Rnd 3: *Sc in next 12 sc, sc2tog in next 2 sts; rep from * around—65 sts.

Rnd 4: *Sc in next 11 sc, sc2tog in next 2 sts; rep from * around—60 sts.

Cont to dec 2 sts ea rnd as established until 5 sts remain. Fasten off, leaving a long sewing length. Use tail to weave through tops of last 5 sts. Gather and secure.

Trim

Rnd 1: With RS facing, working across opposite side of foundation ch, join Color B with sl st to any st along foundation ch, ch 1, 2 sc in first sc, sc in ea around, sl st to first sc to join—76 sc. Fasten off.

First Ribbing Half

Row 1: With RS facing, join Color A with sl st in any sc in rnd 1, ch 3 (counts as dc), dc in next 37 sts, turn—38 dc.

Row 2: Ch 2, *FPdc around the post of next dc, BPdc around the post of next dc; rep from * across, ending with hdc in last st, turn—38 sts.

Rows 3–5: Rep row 1. Fasten off.

Second Ribbing Half

Row 1: With RS facing, join C with sl st in 1st st to the left of last st made in row 1 of First Ribbing Half, ch 3 (counts as dc), dc in next 37 sts, turn—38 dc.

Row 2: Rep row 2 of First Ribbing Half. Fasten off.

Seam ribbing where Ribbing Halves meet.

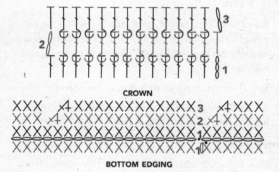

CROWN

BOTTOM EDGING

Hat ribbing and edging pattern.

SCARF

First Half

With A, ch 13.

Row 1 (RS): Dc in 4th ch from hook and in each ch across, turn—11 dc.

Row 2: Ch 3 (counts as dc), dc in FL only of ea st across, turn—11 dc.

Fasten off A, join B.

Starting with row 1 of scarf pattern stitch, work in the following color sequence: *2 rows C; 2 rows B; 2 rows A; rep from * three times; then work 2 rows C; 24 rows B. Fasten off.

Second Half

With RS facing, working across opposite side of foundation ch, join B in first ch. Starting with Row 1 of scarf pattern stitch, work in the following color sequence: 24 rows B; *2 rows A; 2 rows C; rep from * twice. Fasten off.

Edging

Rnd 1: With RS facing, join A with sc to any corner of scarf, work 2 more sc in same corner, sc evenly around, working 3 sc in ea corner and 2 sc in the end of each row, sl st to first sc to join.

Side Panel

Row 1: With scarf lengthwise and RS facing, join A to center st of top right-hand corner of scarf, ch 3

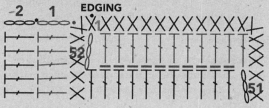

SIDE PANEL

EDGING

SCARF FIRST HALF

SCARF SECOND HALF

Scarf pattern

(counts as dc), dc in each st across long side of scarf, do not turn. Fasten off.

Row 2: With RS facing, join C in first st of last row, ch 3 (counts as dc), dc in ea dc across. Fasten off.

Weave in ends.

Yarn Used:

Moda Dea Metro, 94% acrylic/6% nylon, 3½oz/100g = 124yd/114m per skein

(A) 1 skein, Chocolate (#9340)

(B) 1 skein, Wheat (#9321)

(C) 1 skein, Wasabi (#9632)

The Sport of Crochet

The combination of cotton yarn and a mesh-like stitch pattern helped me create this jersey. It's perfect for a good workout or for a brunch at that neighborhood restaurant you've been meaning to try.

INSTRUCTIONS

PATTERN STITCH

Ch required number of sts.

Row 1 (RS): Sc in 2nd ch from hook, *ch 1, sk next ch, sc in next ch; rep from * across, turn.

Row 2: Ch 1, sc in 1st sc, sc in next ch-1 sp *ch 1, sc in next ch 1 space; rep from * across to last ch-1 sp, sc in last sc, turn.

Row 3: Ch 1, sc in 1st sc, *ch 1, sc in next ch-1 sp; rep from * across to last ch-1 sp, ch 1, sc in last sc, turn.

Rep rows 2–3 for pattern stitch.

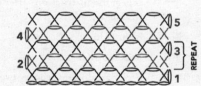

Pattern stitch

BACK

With A, ch 72 (76, 84, 86, 92).

Work in pattern stitch until piece measures 22 (23, 24, 24½, 25½)"/56 (58.5, 61, 62, 65)cm from beg—71 (75, 83, 85, 91) sts.

Shape First Shoulder

Next row: Work in pattern stitch as established across 1st 25 (25, 25, 27, 27) sts, turn, leaving rem sts unworked.

Work even in pattern stitch until piece measures 23 (24, 25, 25½, 26½)"/58.5 (61, 63.5, 65, 67.5)cm from beg. Fasten off.

Shape Second Shoulder

Next row: Sk 21 (25, 33, 31, 37) sts to the left of last st made in 1st row of first shoulder, join A in next st, starting in same st, work in pattern stitch across, turn—25 (25, 25, 27, 27) sts.

Work even in pattern stitch until piece measures 23 (24, 25, 25½, 26½)"/58.5 (61, 63.5, 65, 67.5)cm from beg. Fasten off.

Continued →

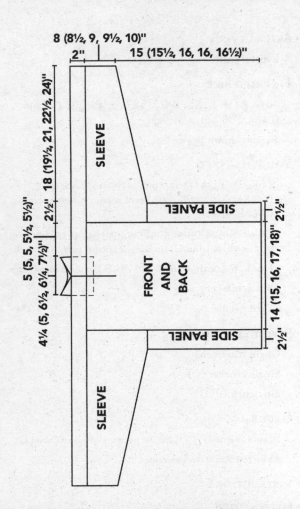

8 (8½, 9, 9½, 10)"
2"
15 (15½, 16, 16, 16½)"

SLEEVE

SIDE PANEL
2½"

FRONT AND BACK

SIDE PANEL
2½"

SLEEVE

18 (19½, 21, 22½, 24)"
2½"
5 (5, 5, 5½, 5½)"
4¼, (5, 6½, 6¼, 7½)"
14 (15, 16, 17, 18)"
2½"

FRONT

Work same as back until piece measures 18 (19, 20, 20½, 21½)"/45.5 (48.5, 51, 52, 54.5)cm from beg. Place stitch marker in center st of last row.

Shape First Shoulder

Next row: Maintaining pattern stitch as established, work across, working sc in last st before stitch marker, turn, leaving rem sts unworked—35 (37, 40, 42, 45) sts.

Maintaining pattern stitch, work even until piece measures 23 (24, 25, 25½, 26½)"/58.5 (61, 63.5, 65, 67.5)cm from beg. Fasten off.

Shape Second Shoulder

Next row: Join A in 1st to the right of stitch marker, ch 1, sc in same st, work in pattern st across, turn—35 (37, 40, 42, 45) sts.

Maintaining pattern stitch, work even until piece measures 23 (24, 25, 25½, 26½)"/58.5 (61, 63.5, 65, 67.5)cm from beg. Fasten off.

Side Edging

Row 1: With RS facing, join A with a sc to 1st st on one long edge of front, *ch 1, skip 1 row, sc in end of next row; rep from * across, ending with sc in last row. Fasten off.

Rep side edging on other long edge of front and on ea long edge of back.

SIDE PANELS

Work the following to create the side panels on each edge of both front and back (the black area under the armholes).

Place a marker 15 (15½, 16, 16, 16½)"/38 (39.5, 40.5, 40.5, 42)cm above bottom edge on both side edges of both front and back.

First Side Panel

Row 1: With WS facing, join B with a sc in 1st st on left side edge of front, work even in pattern across to marker, turn, leaving rem sts unworked.

Work even in pattern stitch until side panel measures 2½"/6.5 cm from beg. Fasten off.

With RS facing, rep first side panel across right side edge of front.

Rep side panel on 2 sides of back.

SLEEVE HALF (MAKE 4)

With A, ch 20.

Work even in pattern stitch for 4 rows.

Note: All increases will be worked on one side of sleeve half while other edge will be straight.

Inc 1 st at beg of next row and every 4th row thereafter until 41 (43, 45, 47, 49) sts are on work, then work even until piece measures 20½ (22, 23½, 25, 26½)"/52 (56, 59.5, 63.5, 67.5)cm from beg. Fasten off.

SLEEVE TRIM

Row 1: With RS facing, join A with a sc in 1st st on straight edge of one sleeve, *ch 1, skip next row, sc in end of next row; rep from * across to end of sleeve. Fasten off.

Rep sleeve trim on ea of 3 rem sleeve halves.

Set in sleeve pieces into the notch created by the side panels, and whipstitch into place.

TOP PANEL

Row 1: Join B with sc in first st in top edge of front right shoulder, work in pattern stitch across shoulder, then across top edge of sleeve, turn. Work even in pattern stitch for 4 more rows. Fasten off.

Rep top panel across top edge of left side of front and left sleeve. In same manner, rep top panel across left shoulder of back and left sleeve. Rep top panel across right shoulder of back and right sleeve.

ASSEMBLE

With RS facing, using B, sew shoulders, tops of sleeves, and sides. With A, sew bottom sleeve seams.

FINISHING

Collar

Row 1: With RS facing, join B with a sc in 1st row in top of top panel on right side of back neck, work in pattern stitch across right side of neck edge, across back neck edge, and up left side of neck edge, sc in next st on top edge of front, turn.

Row 2: Work in pattern stitch across back neck edge, sc in next st on top edge of front, turn.

Rep row 2 until all rem sts on top edge of front are worked. Fasten off.

Weave in ends.

Yarn Used:

Nashua Handknits Cilantro, 70% cotton/30% polyester, 1 ¾ oz/50g = 136yd/125m per skein

(A) 10 (12, 12, 13, 14) skeins, Lime Sorbet (#012)

(B) 4 skeins, Black (#002)

—From *The Crochet Dude's Designs for Guys*

This table lists the common crochet abbreviations used in the project instructions.

Abbreviation	Description	Abbreviation	Description
"	inch(es)	FPdtr	front post double treble crochet
( )	repeat the instructions in the parentheses the number of times specified	FPtr	front post treble crochet
*	repeat the instructions after the * as instructed	g	gram(s)
		hdc	half double crochet(s)
beg	begin(ning)	hk	hook
BL	back loops(s)	inc	increase/increasing
BPdc	back post double crochet two together	lp(s)	loop(s)
BPdc2tog	back post double crochet two together	m	meter(s)
		mm	millimeter(s)
BPdc3tog	back post double crochet three together	oz	ounce(s)
		pbdc	piggyback double crochet
Cbl-A	cable A	rem	remain(ing)
Cbl-B	cable B	rep	repeat(ing)
Cbl-C	cable C	rnd(s)	round(s)
Cbl-D	cable D	RS	right side(s)
ch(s)	chain(s)	sc	single crochet(s)
cm	centimeter(s)	sc2tog	single crochet two together
cont	continue	sk	skip
dc	double crochet(s)	sl st	slip stitch(es)
dc2tog	double crochet three together	sp	space
dec	decrease/decreasing	st(s)	stitch(es)
dtr	double treble	tr	treble crochet(s) sometimes called triple crochet
ea	each	V-st	V-stitch
FL	front loop(s)	WS	wrong side(s)
FPdc	front post double crochet	X-st	crossed double crochet
FPdc2tog	front post double crochet together	yd	yard(s)
		yo	yarn over hook

COOL CROCHETED HATS

inda Kopp

Fuzzy Kitty Hat

Designer: Emily North

Keep both your head and ears warm in a playful manner with this comfy hat. A great design for those new to crocheting, it's worked circular from the top edge down, forming an enclosed square shape.

SKILL LEVEL

Beginner

SIZE

This hat is designed to fit a woman's head. If you would like to make it larger, check the size after you've joined the foundation chain, and adjust as needed.

YOU WILL NEED

- Color A: 135yd/123m bulky weight yarn in green
- Color B: 201yd/183m worsted weight in gray (for edging and earflaps)
- Hook: 5mm/H-8 or size needed to obtain gauge
- Stitch markers

STITCHES USED

Chain stitch (ch)

Single crochet (sc)

GAUGE

Take time to check your gauge.

10 sts and 12 rows = 4" in sc

PATTERN NOTES

This hat is worked from the top down in spiraling rounds; do not join rounds unless otherwise stated. Use a stitch marker to indicate first stitch in round, move it up at beginning of each round. The earflaps will be crocheted in rows. The corners of the square create "kitty ears" when worn.

INSTRUCTIONS

HAT

With color A, ch 24.

Rnd 1 (right side): Sc in 2nd ch from hook, sc in each ch across, working across opposite side foundation ch, sc in each ch across (46 sc). Do not join, work in a spiral.

Rnds 2–23: Place marker in 1st st, sc in each sc around (46 sc). At end of last rnd, join with sl st in next sc. Fasten off A.

EDGING

Rnds 24–26: With RS facing, join color B in any st at center of back of hat. Work in a spiral as before. Place marker in 1st st, sc in each sc around (46 sc). Do not fasten off.

FIRST EARFLAP

Lay hat flat. Place a marker 7 sts to the left of center back. Sc in each st across to marker.

Row 1: Sc in marked sc, sc in each of next 8 sc. Ch 1, turn leaving remaining sts unworked (9 sc).

Rows 2–3: Ch 1, sc in each of next 9 sc. Ch 1, turn (9 sc).

Row 4: Ch 1, sk 1 st sc, sc in each sc across. Ch 1, turn (8 sc).

Rows 5–11: Ch 1, sk 1 st sc, sc in each sc across. Ch 1, turn (1 sc at end of last row). Fasten off, leaving a 3" (7.5 cm) length of yarn. Cut a 6"(15 cm) strand of color B.

FRINGE

Weave strand through st at tip of earflap. With ends of fringe even, tie 3 strands in an overhand knot, at base of fringe.

SECOND EARFLAP

Row 1: With RS facing, skip 16 sts to the left of last st made in Row 1 of first earflap, join color B in next st, ch 1, sc in same st, sc in each of next 8 sc. Ch 1, turn leaving remaining sts unworked (9 sc).

Complete same as first earflap.

Weave in all yarn ends.

This project was created with:

- 1 ball of Lion Brand's *Jiffy* in *Grass* Green (#173), 100% acrylic, 3oz/85g = 135yd/123m.
- 1 skein of Patrons *Canadiana* in Dark Grey Mix (#312), 100% Acrylic, 3.5oz/100g = 201yd/183m.

Classic Beret

Designer: Don Halstead

The beret has endured through the ages and has been embraced by both men and women in many cultures. We think the wide attraction is due to its versatility, allowing the wearer a multiplicity of fashionable looks. This design looks fabulous in blue.

SKILL LEVEL

Intermediate

SIZE

This hat is designed to fit most adult heads.

MATERIALS

- 218yd/200m sport weight wool yarn in blue
- Hook: 5mm/H-8 or size needed to obtain gauge
- Yarn needle

STITCHES USED

Chain (ch)

Single crochet (sc)

Double Crochet (dc)

Treble Crochet (tr)

Sc2tog (single crochet decrease): Insert hook in next st and draw up a loop, insert hook in next st and draw up a loop, yo, draw through all loops on hook.

Dc2tog (double crochet decrease): Yo, insert hook in next st and draw up a loop, yo and draw through 2 loops, yo, insert hook in next st and draw up a loop, yo, draw through 2 loops, yo, draw through all loops on hook.

Tr2tog (treble crochet decrease): *Yo (twice), insert hook in next st and draw up a loop, (yo and draw through 2 loops) twice; repeat from * once, yo, draw through all loops on hook.

GAUGE

Take time to check your gauge.

First 3 rnds = 2¼" in diameter

12 sts – 4"

PATTERN NOTES

This hat is worked from the top down in spiraling rounds; do not join rounds unless otherwise stated. Use a stitch marker to indicate first stitch in round, move it up at beginning of ea round.

Some rounds are worked through both loops, while some rounds are worked through the back loop only. Notations are made for each technique throughout the pattern.

INSTRUCTIONS

BERET

Starting at center top, ch 3, sl st in first ch to form ring.

Rnd 1: Ch 1, work 6 sc in ring. Do not join, work in a spiral.

Work Rnds 2–9 in back loops only of sts.

Rnd 2: Place marker in 1st st, 1 sc in next sc, 2 sc in each sc around (11 sc).

Rnd 3: Ch 3 (counts as dc), dc in same st as joining, 2 dc in each sc around. Join with sl st in top of ch 3 (22 dc).

Rnd 4: 2 tr in each of next 21 dc, (tr, dc) in next dc (44 sts).

Rnd 5: *Sc in each of next 3 sts, 2 sc in next st; repeat from * around (55 sc).

Rnd 6: *Sc in each of next 4 sts, 2 sc in next st; repeat from * around (66 sc).

Rnd 7: *Tr in next st, 2 tr in next st; repeat from * around to last st, (tr, dc) in last st (99 sts).

Rnd 8: Sc in each st around (99 sc).

Rnd 9: *Dc in next 8 sts, 2 dc in next st; repeat from * around (110 dc).

Work Rnds 10–12 in both loops of sts. Continue to work in a spiral as before.

Rnds 10–12: Sc in each st around (110 sc).

Work Rnds 13–15 in back loops only of sts. Continue to work in a spiral as before.

Rnd 13: *Dc in each of next 8 sts, dc2tog in next 2 sts; repeat from * around (99 dc).

Rnd 14: Sc in each st around (99 sc).

Rnd 15: *Tr in next st, tr2tog in next 2 sts; repeat from * around (66 tr).

Rnd 16: Working in back loops only, *dc in each of next 4 sts, dc2tog in next 2 sts; repeat from * around (55 dc).

BAND

Work rnds 17–18 in both loops of sts. Continue to work in a spiral as before.

Rnds 17–18: Sc in each st around (55 sc). At end of last rnd, sl st in next sc to join. Fasten off. Weave in all yarn ends.

This project was created with:

2 skeins Gjestal Ren NY Ull Superwash Sport Wool in blue, 100% Wool, 1.75 oz/50g = 109yd/100m.

Continued ➔

Denim Deco Ribbon Cloche

Designer: Marty Miller

Do your friends know you as a free spirit? Do you believe in good karma? Then this relaxed cloche might fit you to a T. The designer used comfortable ribbon yarn in shades of denim, and popped on an optimistic crocheted sunflower.

SKILL LEVEL
Easy

SIZE
The finished hat will fit most adult heads.

MATERIALS
- 240yd/219m of ribbon yarn in blue variegated for hat (color A)
- 10yd/9m ribbon yarn in white for flower center (color B).
- 50yd/46m of ribbon yarn in yellow for flower petals (color C).
- Hook: 5.5mm/I-9 hook *or size needed to obtain gauge*

STITCHES USED
Chain stitch (ch)

Single crochet (sc)

Slip stitch (sl st)

GAUGE
Take time to check your gauge.

First 4 rnds = 2" in diameter.

7 sts = 2"

8 rows = 2" in sc.

PATTERN NOTES
You will be working in the round from the top down.

Join ea rnd with a sl st in the 1st sc of that round.

INSTRUCTIONS
CROWN

With color A, ch 2.

Rnd 1: 6 sc in 2nd ch from the hook (6 sc). Join with sl st to first sc.

Rnd 2: Ch 1, 2 sc in ea sc around (12 sc). Join with sl st to first sc.

Rnd 3: Ch 1, *2 sc in the next sc, sc in the next sc; repeat from * around (18 sc). Join with sl st to first sc.

Rnd 4: Ch 1, *2 sc in next sc, sc in ea of next 2 sc; repeat from * around (24 sc). Join with sl st to first sc.

Rnd 5: Ch 1, *2 sc in next sc, sc in ea of next 3 sc; repeat from * around (30 sc). Join with sl st to first sc.

Rnd 6: Ch 1, *2 sc in next sc, sc in ea of next 4 sc; repeat from * around (36 sc). Join with sl st to first sc.

Rnd 7: Ch 1, *2 sc in next sc, sc in ea of next 5 sc; repeat from * around (42 sc). Join with sl st to first sc.

Rnd 8: Ch 1, *2 sc in next sc, sc in ea of next 6 sc; repeat from * around (48 sc). Join with sl st to first sc.

Rnd 9: Ch 1, *2 sc in next sc, sc in ea of next 7 sc; repeat from * around (54 sc). Join with sl st to first sc.

Rnd 10: Ch 1, *2 sc in next sc, sc in ea of next 8 sc; repeat from * around (60 sc). Join with sl st to first sc.

Rnd 11: Ch 1, *2 sc in next sc, sc in ea of next 9 sc; repeat from * around (66 sc). Join with sl st to first sc.

Rnd 12: Ch 1, *2 sc in next sc, sc in ea of next 10 sc; repeat from * around (72 sc). Join with sl st to first sc.

Rnds 13–30: Ch 1, sc in ea sc around (72 sc). Join with sl st to first sc.

BRIM

Rnd 31: Ch 1, *2 sc in next sc, sc in ea of next 11 sc; repeat from * around (78 sc). Join with sl st to first sc.

Rnd 32: Ch 1, sc in ea of next 6 sc, *2 sc in next sc, sc in ea of next 12 sc; repeat from * around, end with sc in last 6 sc (84 sc). Join with sl st to first sc.

Rnd 33: Ch 1, *2 st in next sc, sc in ea of next 13 sc; repeat from * around (90 sc). Join with sl st to first sc.

Rnd 34: Ch 1, sc in ea of next 7 sc, *2 sc in next sc, sc in ea of next 14 sc; repeat from * around, ending with sc in last 7 sc (96 sc). Join with sl st to first sc.

Rnd 35: Ch 1, *2 sc in next sc, sc in ea of next 15 sc; repeat from * around (102 sc). Join with sl st to first sc.

Rnd 36: Ch 1, sc in ea of next 8 sc, *2 sc in next sc, sc in ea of next 16 sc; repeat from * around, ending with sc in last 8 sc (108 sc). Join with sl st to first sc.

Rnd 37: Ch 1, *2 sc in next sc, sc in ea of next 17 sc; repeat from * around (114 sc). Join with sl st to first sc.

Rnd 38: Ch 1, sc in ea of next 9 sc, *2 sc in next sc, sc in ea of next 18 sc; repeat from * around, ending with sc in last 9 sc (120 sc). Join with sl st to first sc. Fasten off, weave in all yarn ends.

FLOWER CENTER

With color B, ch 2.

Rnd 1: Work 6 sc in the 2nd ch from the hook (6 sc). Join with sl st to first sc.

Rnd 2: 2 sc in ea sc around (12 sc). Join with sl st to first sc. Fasten off color B.

PETALS

Rnd 3: With RS facing, join color C in front loop of 1 st sc in rnd 2, ch 1, working in front loops only of sts, sl st in front loop of 1st sc, *ch 7, sl st in 3rd ch from hook, sl st in ea of next 4 ch sts, sl st in same sc, sl st in next sc; repeat from * around (12 petals). Join with sl st in back loop of 1st sc in rnd 2.

Rnd 4: Working in back loops only of sts in Rnd 2, *ch 9, sl st in 3rd ch from hook, sl st in ea of next 6 ch sts, sl st in same sc of Rnd 2, sl st in next sc of Rnd 2; repeat from * around (12 petals). Join with sl st in first sl st. Fasten off. Weave in all yarn ends.

This project was created with:

3 skeins of Crystal Palace's *Deco-Ribbon* in Jeans (#7237) (color A), 70% Acrylic/30% Nylon, 1.75oz/50gr = 80yd/73m.

1 skein of Crystal Palace's *Deco-Ribbon* in white (#300) (color B), 70% Acrylic/30% Nylon, 1.75oz/50gr = 80yd/73m.

1 skein of Crystal Palace's *Deco-Ribbon* in yellow (#305) (color C), 70% Acrylic.30% Nylon, 1.75oz/50gr = 80yd/73m.

Luxurious Hooded Cowl

Designer: Dot Matthews

Lend elegance to any coat or cape with the addition of this graceful wool band. The incredibly soft mohair trim adds a striking accent. Once you've reached your destination, you can push the hood back to form a cowl.

SKILL LEVEL
Easy

SIZE
This hat is designed to fit most adult heads.

MATERIALS
- Color A: 330yd/302m of worsted weight wool blend in blue-green tweed.
- Color B: 21yd/19m of worsted weight mohair blend in cream
- Hooks: 8mm/L-11 (optional for foundation ch), 6.5mm/K-10½ (for wimple) and 5.5mm/I-9 (for trim) *or sizes needed to obtain gauge*
- Yarn needle

STITCHES USED
Chain stitch (ch)

Double crochet (dc)

Single crochet (sc)

GAUGE
With 6.5mm/K-10½ hook, 6 sts = 2"

7 rows in pattern = 2"

INSTRUCTIONS
HOOD

With 8mm/L-11 hook and color A, ch 90 and without twisting ch, sl st in 1st ch to form ring.

Rnd 1 (right side): with 6.5mm/K-10½ hook, ch 1, sc in ch, ch 1, sk next ch; repeat from * around (45 ch-1 spaces). Join with sl st in 1st sc, turn.

Rnds 2–50: (Sc, ch 1) in ea ch-1 space around (45 ch-1 spaces). Join with sl st in 1st sc, turn. Fasten off color A.

TRIM

Rnd 51: With RS facing, using 5.5mm/I-9 hook, join color B in any ch-1 space at back of wimple, ch 1, *sc in ch-1 space, sc in next sc; repeat from * around (90 sc).

Rnds 52–54: Ch 1, sc in each sc around. Fasten off B. Weave in all yarn ends.

This project was created with:

3 balls of Plymouth Yarn's *Sun Merino* in blue-green (#791) (color A), 55% Suri Alpaca/45% Extra Fine Merino Wool, 1.75oz/50g = 110yd/100m.

1 ball of Louet Sales' *Mohair* in cream (#83.1302) (color B), 78% mohair/13% wool/9% nylon, 1.75oz/50gm = 105yd/96m.

Peruvian Stocking Cap

Designer: Lindsay Obermeyer

The colorful textiles of Peru inspired this warm stocking cap, worked in a bright wool blend with a downy mohair. The snug bouclé earflaps can be worn flipped up, weather permitting.

SKILL LEVEL
Intermediate

SIZE
This hat is designated to fit most adult heads.

MATERIALS

- Color A: 154yd/137m of worsted weight bouclé wool blend in multi-color.
- Color B: 90yd/82m of worsted weight mohair blend in pink
- Color C: 90yd/82m of worsted weight mohair blend in salmon
- Hook: 6mm/J-10 or size needed to obtain gauge
- Yarn needles

STITCHES USED

Chain stitch (ch)

Double crochet (dc)

Slip stitch (sl st)

Dc2tog (double crochet decrease) Yo, insert hook into st and draw up a loop, yo and draw through 2 loops, yo, insert hook in next st and draw up a loop, yo, draw through 2 loops, yo, draw through all loops on back.

GAUGE

12 stitches and 7 rows = 4"

PATTERN NOTES

This hat is worked in rounds using dc in back loops (BL) only. Hat is worked in a stripe pattern in the following color sequence: *2 rows color A, 2 rows color B, 2 rows color A, 2 rows color C; repeat from * through rnd 38.

INSTRUCTIONS

With color A, ch 60 loosely and without twisting ch, sl st in 1st ch to form ring.

Rnd 1 (right side): Ch 3 (counts as dc), sk 1st ch, dc in each ch around. Join with sl st in top of ch 3 (60 sts).

Rnd 2: Ch 3 (counts as dc), dc in each st around. Join with sl st in top of ch 3 (60 dc). Fasten off color A, join color B.

Rnds 3–11: Maintaining color sequence as established, repeat row 2.

Rnd 12: Ch 3 (counts as dc) dc in next 17 sts, dc2tog in next 2 sts, place a marker in last st, *dc in next 18 sts, dc2tog in next 2 sts, place a marker in last st; repeat from * around. Join with sl st in top of ch 3 (57 sts). Move markers up as work progresses.

Rnd 13: With next color in sequence, ch 3 (counts as dc), dc in each st around. Join with sl st in top of ch 3 (57 dc).

Rnd 14: Ch 3 (counts as dc), dc in each st around, working dc2tog at each marker. Join with sl st in top of ch 3 (54 sts).

Rnds 15–38: Maintaining color sequence, repeat rnds 13–14 (21 sts at end of last rnd). Fasten off color A at end of last rnd, join color B.

Rnds 39–41: With color B, ch 3, (dc2tog in next 2 sts) around. Join with sl st in top of ch 3 (6 sts at end of last rnd). Fasten off, leaving a sewing length. With yarn needle, weave sewing length through the sts of last rnd, gather sts and secure.

FIRST EARFLAP

Row 1: With right side facing, working across opposite side of foundation ch, join color A in any ch on bottom edge of cap, ch 3 (counts as dc), dc2tog in next 2 ch, dc in next 6 ch, dc2tog in next 2 ch (8 sts). Ch 3, turn.

Rows 2–3: Dc2tog in next 2 sts, dc in ea st across to last 2 sts, dc2tog in last 2 sts (5 sts at end of last row). Ch 3, turn.

Row 4: (Dc2tog in next 2 sts) twice (3 sts). Ch 3, turn.

Row 5: Dc2tog in next 2 sts (2 sts). Fasten off, leaving a sewing length. With yarn needle and sewing length, sew tops of sts together forming a point.

SECOND EARFLAP

Row 1: With right side facing, sk 20 sts to the left of last st made in row 1 of first ear flap, join color A in next ch, ch 3 (counts as dc), dc2tog in next 2 ch, dc in next 6 ch, dc2tog in next 2 ch (8 sts). Ch 3, turn.

Rows 2–5: Rep rows 2–5 of first earflap. Weave in all yarn ends.

This project was created with:

2 skeins of Noro's *Blossom* in multi color (#6) (color A), 30% kid mohair/40% wool/20% silk/10% nylon, 1.4 oz/40g = 77yd/70m. 1 ball each of Classic Elite's *La Gran* in Late Summer Rose (#6599) (color B) and Pomegranate (#6565) (color C), 76.5% mohair.17.5% wool/6% nylon. 1/48oz/42gm = 90yd/82m.

Peachy Waffle-Weave Shell

Designer: Kalpna Kapoor

Need a hat and need it quick? Work up this simple shell hat in a chunky yarn, and you'll be done before you know it.

SKILL LEVEL

Beginner

SIZE

This hat is designed to fit most adult heads.

MATERIALS

- 88yd/80m chunky yarn
- Hook: 5.5mm/I-9 *or size needed to obtain gauge*
- Yarn needle

STITCHES USED

Chain stitch (ch)

Double crochet (dc)

Slip stitch (sl st)

GAUGE

First 2 rnds = 2¾" in diameter

12 sts = 4"

7 rows in pattern = 4"

INSTRUCTIONS

CROWN

Starting at center top, ch 4 and sl st in 1st ch to form ring.

Rnd 1: Ch 3 (counts as dc), work 11 dc in ring. Join with sl st in top of ch 3 (12 dc).

Rnd 2: Ch 3 (counts as dc), dc in same st as join, 2 dc in ea dc around. Join with sl st in top of ch 3 (24 dc).

Rnd 3: Ch 3 (counts as dc), 1 dc in same st as join, 2 dc in each of next 2 dc, 1 dc in next dc, *2 dc in each of next 3 dc, 1 dc in next dc; repeat from * around. Join with sl st in top of ch 3 (42 dc).

Rnd 4: Ch 3 (counts as dc), 1 dc in same st as join, ch 1, sk next dc, *2 dc in next dc, ch 1, sk next dc; repeat from * around. Join with sl st in top of ch 3 (21 ch-1 spaces).

Rnd 5: Sl st in 1st ch-1 space, ch 3 (counts as dc), 1 dc in same space, ch 1, (2 dc, ch 1) in each ch-1 space around. Join with sl st in top of ch 3 (21 ch-1 spaces).

Rnds 6–12: Rep rnd 5.

Note: If longer hat is desired, continue to repeat rnd 5 until hat measures desired length. Fasten off. Weave in all yarn ends.

This project was created with:

1 ball of Lana Grossa's *Multicot Print* in tan (#513), 60% cotton, 40% acrylic, 1.75oz/50g = 88yd/80m.

Houndstooth Lidcap

Designer: Don Halstead

We like this lidcap's flat top and slightly hourglass shape. Not only is it simple to experiment with color combinations using the two-color houndstooth pattern, but the pattern can also be easily altered to fit a child.

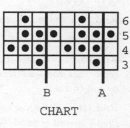

SKILL LEVEL

Advanced

SIZE

This hat is designed to fit most adult heads.

FINISHED MEASUREMENTS

Hat: 20½" circumference

MATERIALS

Version 1:

- Color A: 40yd/37m sport weight cotton yarn in black
- Color B: 40yd/37m sport weight cotton yarn in turquoise

Version 2:

- Color A: 40yd/37m sport weight cotton yarn in black
- Color B: 40yd/37m sport weight cotton yarn in white
- Hook: 4mm/G-6 *or size needed to obtain gauge*

STITCHES USED

Chain stitch (ch)

Single crochet (sc)

Slip stitch (sl st)

GAUGE

Take time to check your gauge.

9 sts and 9 rows = 2" in sc

First 3 rnds of top = 2" in diameter

PATTERN NOTES

Pattern creates an hourglass-shaped flat-topped lidcap. Because of the two-color technique involved, cap will not stretch as much as a typical crocheted piece. Hat should fit somewhat tightly to head for the hourglass shape to be created in body of the cap. You can experiment with color alternatives as this design was created to work very easily with just about any color combination you may choose. Substituting materials (for example, wool rather than cotton) should be tested for sizing and appearance.

	●				●			6
●	●	●		●	●	●		5
●	●				●	●		4
	●				●			3

B   A

CHART

CHART KEY

▣ = sc in col

▢ = sc in col

The color pattern can easily be adjusted by adding or subtracting multiples of 4 stitches. Always crochet a test swatch first to achieve gauge, and it is advised you try on Lidcap after about 4 rounds are crocheted to make sure it fits properly. If you need to increase or decrease size of cap. Increase or decrease the foundation ch in increments of 4 stitches to accommodate the charted pattern.

Continued ➔

Sides are worked in two colors following a chart for color changes. Read all rows from right to left, repeating from A to B around. To change color, work last sc of first color until 2 loops remain on hook, yo with second color, draw first color, and carry loosely across to be picked up later, work over first color with second color. Sides can be worked to any depth you would like. Directions are for a hat that is 3½" deep.

Top is worked in back loop only throughout, in spiraling rounds; do not join rounds unless otherwise stated. Use a stitch marker to indicate first stitch in round, move it up at beginning of each round.

INSTRUCTIONS

SIDES

Starting at bottom edge, with color A, ch 92 (or a multiple 4 ch sts to fit snugly around top of head) and without twisting ch, sl st in 1ˢᵗ ch to form ring.

Rnd 1 (right side): Ch 1, sc in each ch around. Join with sl st in 1ˢᵗ sc (92 sc).

Rnd 2: Ch 1, sc in each sc around. Join with sl st in 1ˢᵗ sc (92 sc).

Rnd 3: With color A, ch 1, *with a, sc in sc, drop A, join B, with B, sc in each of next 3 sc, drop B, pick up A; rep from * around (1ˢᵗ row of chart complete). Join with sl st in 1ˢᵗ sc (23 pattern repeats; 92 sc).

Rnds 4–6: Work even in sc following chart for color changes, reading all rows from right to left; repeat from A to B around. Join with sl st in 1ˢᵗ sc (23 pattern repeats; 92 sc).

Rows 7–14: Repeat rows 3–6 twice.

Rows 15–16: Repeat rows 3–4.

TOP

With color A, ch 3 and sl st in 1ˢᵗ ch to form ring.

Rnd 1 (right side): Ch 1, 2 sc in back loop of each ch around (6 sc). Do not join, work in a spiral.

Rnd 2: Place a marker in 1ˢᵗ st, 2 sc in each sc around (12 sc).

Rnd 3: 2 sc in each sc around (24 sc).

Rnd 4: *Sc in next sc, 2 sc in next sc; repeat from * around (36 sc).

Rnd 5: Sc in each sc around (36 sc).

Rnd 6: *Sc in each of next 2 sc, 2 sc in next sc; repeat from * around, ending with sc in each sc to beginning of rnd (48 sc).

Rnd 7: Sc in each sc around (48 sc).

Rnds 8–9: Rep rnds 6–7 (64 sc).

Rnd 10: *Sc in each of next 3 sc, 2 sc in next sc; repeat from * around, ending with sc in each sc to beginning of rnd (80 sc).

Rnd 11: Sc in each sc around, working 4 increases, evenly spaced around (84 sc).

Rep rnd 11, increasing 4 sc in each rnd until top measures same diameter as sides. Fasten off. Weave in all yarn ends.

FINISHING

Turn sides inside out. With RS facing down, place top over opening on top edge of sides. Tack top in four places around sides. With yarn needle and color A, working through back loops of sts, sew sides to top, easing in fullness. Optional: Sew a favorite button or tassel to center top of hat. You can even sew a row of buttons, evenly spaced, all around the sides of the hat. Or simply pin your favorite brooch to the center front of the hat.

This project was created with:

Version 1:

I skein each of Schoeller Stahl *Winter Cotton* in black (color A) and turquoise (color B), 60% cotton, 40%

---

acrylic, 1.75oz/50g = 76yd/70m

Version 2:

Skein each of Schoeller Stahl *Winter Cotton* in black (color A) and white (color B), 60% cotton, 40% acrylic, 1.75oz/50g = 76yd/70m

—From *Cool Crocheted Hats*

CROCHET PROJECTS FOR KIDS

ane Davis

Introduction

Crochet has been around for a very long time. The word "crochet" comes from the French word for hook. But more than 100 years ago, when hooks were commonly made from fish bones or old silver spoons, crochet was *sometimes* called "shepherd's knitting," because shepherds often did their crochet work as they watched their flocks of sheep out in the fields. Mittens were one of the most common items made from the basic crochet slip stitch. They were prized for their thickness because they kept hands warm and dry in the cold wet winters of Scotland, Norway, and Sweden. But wherever winters were cold, men, women, and children alike worked stitches to make warm clothing.

The Projects: Fun & Games!

These simple projects will get you started with crochet. You'll get used to holding the hook and yarn and making the stitches. When you're done, you'll have games to play and some colorful accessories to wear. As you keep practicing, you'll get faster and your stitches will get more and more even. Before you know it, you'll be moving on to make the other great projects.

Scrunchies

Tired of all your old scrunchies? Can't find the right color to wear? Personalize your look by making your own just the way you want! Shown are two versions, one plain and one with ruffles.

SKILL LEVEL
Easy

FINISHED SIZE

About 3 inches across for the plain scrunchy, and 4 inches across for the ruffled version

MATERIALS

- I skein of medium-weight yarn in your favorite color
- Size H (5mm) crochet hook
- I plain elastic hair band

GAUGE

4 double crochet (dc) = 1"

STITCHES USED

Chain (ch)

Slip stitch (sl st)

Double crochet (dc)

INSTRUCTIONS

1. Make a slip knot about 3 inches from the end of the yarn.

2. Insert the hook (hk) into the hair band.

3. Yarn over (yo), and pull the yarn through the hair band.

4. Yarn over (yo), and pull the yarn through both loops (lps) on the hook (hk).

5. Chain 3 (ch 3).

6. Double crochet (dc) in the hair band. To do this: first yarn over (yo) and insert the hook (hk) into the hair band. Then yarn over (yo) and pull through the hair band. Next, yarn over (yo), and pull the yarn through the 2 loops (lps) on the hook (hk), yarn over (yo) and pull the yarn through the last 2 loops (lps) on the hook (hk) ([yo, pull through 2 lps on the hk] twice.)

7. Repeat (rep) step 6 until you have worked the stitches (sts) all the way around the ring.

8. Slip stitch (sl st) in the top of chain 3 (ch-3) to join the stitches into a circle, as shown in figure 1.

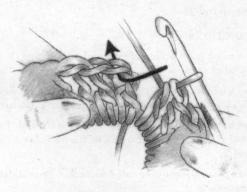

9. Cut the yarn, leaving a tail that's about 3 inches long, and pull it through the last loop (lp). Weave in the end.

Now try it a different way! To make a ruffled scrunchy, work through step 8 above, the continue as follows:

10. Chain (ch 3), and then work 3 double crochet (dc) in the next stitch (st).

11. Now work 4 double crochet (dc) in the next stitch (st), as shown in figure 2.

12. Repeat (rep) step 11 for each stitch (st) around.

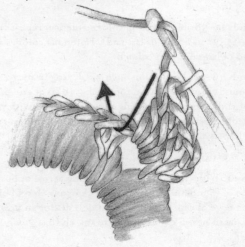

13. Slip stitch (sl st) in the top of chain 3 (ch-3) to join the stitches into a circle.

14. Cut the yarn to leave a tail about 3 inches long, and pull it through the last loop (lp) then weave in the end.

Yarn Used:

1 skein of Coats & Clark Yarn's *Red Heart Kids*, 100% acrylic, 4oz/113g, in Beach #2940.

Comfy Slippers

Even when you're chillin. You can have warm feet. The secret to shaping these slippers, made from simple crocheted rectangles, is the bottoms you sew on later. They're suede on the outside, warm and woolly on the inside, and have holes along their edges that make them easy to sew onto the crochet. (You can get the bottoms through mail order or at many specialty yarn stores.)

SKILL LEVEL

Easy

FINISHED SIZE

(according to your shoe size)

Child's 1–4, (Child's size 5–10, Child's size 11–Women's size 5, Women's size 6–10. Men's size 9–12).

(according to the length of your shoe bottom)

4–5 inches (6–7, 8–9, 9–10, 11–12 inches) [10–12.5 cm (15–17.5, 20–23, 23–25.5, 28–30.5)]

MATERIALS

- 2 skeins each in red and black lightweight sport-weight yarn, or 2 skeins of a red-and-black variegated medium worsted-weight yarn
- 1 pair of fleece-lined slipper bottoms
- Size H (5mm) crochet hook
- Tapestry needle
- Safety pins
- 2 buttons

GAUGE

14 st = 4"

15 rows = 4"

STITCHES USED

Chain (ch)

Single crochet (sc)

SPECIAL NOTE

These slippers were made by holding two strands of yarn together, one black and one red, and crocheting them as one.

INSTRUCTIONS

RECTANGLES (MAKE TWO)

Foundation: Chain 6 (8, 9, 11, 12) turn.

Row 1: Chain 1 (ch 1), single crochet (sc) in second chain (ch) from hook (hk) and in each chain (ea ch) across, turn. You will not have 6 (8, 9, 11, 12) stitches (sts) total.

Row 2: Chain 1 (ch 1), single crochet (sc) in each stitch (es st) across, turn.

Repeat row 2 until the crochet work is 9 inches (23 cm) 13, 17, 20, 23 inches (33, 43, 51, 58.5 cm) long. Weave in the ends.

SIZING IT UP

This project has different sizes in the instructions. Most clothing instructions are set up this same way. The first number is for the smallest size, and the other numbers in parentheses are for the other sizes, in order, from second smallest to largest. To follow the instructions, find your shoe size under Finished Size. You can also measure the bottom of your shoe and make your slippers according to that size. Once you know the size you're going to make, only pay attention to the numbers in that location in the instructions. Some people like to photocopy the instructions and then use a highlighter to mark the size they will be making throughout the instructions.

ASSEMBLY

As shown in figure 1, overlap the left end over the right end of one rectangle. This will become the toe of the slipper; the other end will be the heel. Use safety pins to pin a shoe bottom to the slipper. Pin it to the center of the toe (at the center of the overlapping ends) and at the center of the heel.

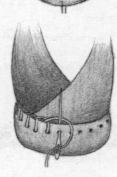

As shown in figure 2, use a 60-inch (152.5 cm) length of yarn to stitch the crocheted slipper top to the bottom. Use the simple buttonhole stitch—the drawing shows you how to make it. Begin by stitching through both layers of crochet formed by overlapping the rectangle for the toe section, and then stitch all along one side to the heel and back up the other side to the toe. Remove the safety pins.

Weave in the ends. Repeat the process for the other slipper, but this time overlap the right end over the left. Try on the slippers and pin the top two layers together where you want the button to be. Walk around a little to make sure it's up far enough to hold the slippers on your feet. Then make sure you can get them on and off easily. Sew the button in place through both layers where you placed the pin. Remove the pin.

Yarn Used

2 skeins of Dale of Norway Yarn's *Tiur*, 60% mohair, 40% pure new wool, 1¾ oz/50g, 126yd/115m, in color #4027

2 skeins of Berroco Yarns' *Sensuwool*, 80% wool, 20% nylon, 1 ¾ oz/50g, 90yd/82m, in Black #6334

Purse

Dressing up or dressing down? Taking this purse from dressy to casual all depends on the type of yarn and button you use. You could also use a thicker yarn and larger hook to make a bigger shoulder bag using the same pattern.

SKILL LEVEL

Intermediate

FINISHED SIZE

About 3½ x 6 inches (9 x 15 cm) with a 38-in-long (96.5 cm) strap

MATERIALS

- 1 skein of lightweight DK or sport-weight cotton yarn in gold
- Size G (4mm) crochet hook
- Tapestry needle
- 1-inch (2.5 cm) button
- Steam iron
- Spray starch

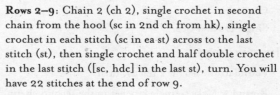

GAUGE

17 sts = 4" (10 cm)

22 rows = 4" (10 cm)

STITCHES USED

Chain (ch)

Single crochet (sc)

Half double crochet (hdc)

Double crochet (dc)

INSTRUCTIONS

BODY OF PURSE

Button loop: Chain 12 (ch 12), slip stitch in 1st chain (sl st in 1st ch), forming a circle, turn. Figure 1 shows how to do this.

Row 1: Chain 1 (ch 1), single crochet in next 6 chains (sc in next 6 ch), turn.

Rows 2–9: Chain 2 (ch 2), single crochet in second chain from the hool (sc in 2nd ch from hk), single crochet in each stitch (sc in ea st) across to the last stitch (st), then single crochet and half double crochet in the last stitch ([sc, hdc] in the last st), turn. You will have 22 stitches at the end of row 9.

Row 10: Chain 2 (ch 2), single crochet in the next stitch, double crochet in the next stitch. Repeat the pattern 11 times ([sc, dc] 11 times), turn. You will now have 22 stitches (22 sts total).

Repeat (rep) row 10 until crochet work measures 13½ inches (34 cm) long from row 1. Weave in the end.

STRAP

Foundation: Begin with an 8-inch (20 cm) end. (This will be used later to sew the strap to the bag.) Chain 160 (ch 160), turn.

Row 1: Slip stitch in the back half of each stitch (sl st in the back half of ea st), cut the yarn, leaving an 8-inch (20 cm) end, pull the end through the last stitch (st).

ASSEMBLY

As shown in figure 2, fold the straight end of the bag up 4½ inches (11.5 cm) and the top flap down just beyond the last row of single crochet.

With an adult present, use the iron with steam to go over the folds you made to set them. Once you have the fold lines, use the iron and spray starch to make the crochet stiffer to help the purse keep its shape. Sew the side seams together, and then sew the strap ends to each side of the bag with their 8-inch (20 cm) ends. Sew the button

Continued →

to the front of the bag where the point of the flat sits when closed.

Yarn Used:

1 skein of El. D. Mouzakis Yarns' *Butterfly*, DK yarn, 100% mercerized cotton, 1¾oz/50g, 108yd/100m, in Gold #3356.

Hacky Sack

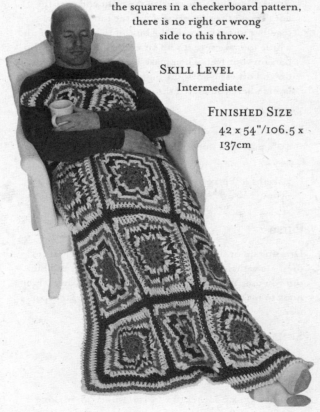

This hacky sack is just like the ones you buy in the store, only better, since you make it yourself!

SKILL LEVEL

Intermediate.

FINISHED SIZE

2½ inches (6 cm) in diameter

MATERIALS

- 1 skein each of lightweight sport-weight cotton yarn in red and burgundy
- Size C (2.75mm) crochet hook
- Tapestry needle
- 1 cup dried beans, such as pinto beans
- Stitch marker

GAUGE

6 sts = 1" (2.5 cm)

6 rows = 1" (2.5 cm)

STITCHES USED

Chain (ch)

Single crochet (sc)

INSTRUCTIONS

Foundation: Chain 2 (ch 2), turn.

Round 1: Make 6 single crochet in the second chain from the hook and place a marker, do not turn. (6 sc in 2nd ch from hk, pm, do not turn.)

Round 2: Make 2 single crochet in each stitch around. Move marker to the last stitch you made. When you're finished, you'll have 12 stitches. (2 sc in ea st around. (12 sts total).)

Round 3: Single crochet in the next stitch, then make 2 single crochet in the next stitch. Do this 6 times. Move marker to the last stitch you made. When you're finished, you'll have 18 stitches. ([Sc in next st, 2 sc in next st] 6 times (18 sts total).)

Round 4: Single crochet in the next 2 stitches, then make 2 single crochet in the next stitch. Do this 6 times. Move marker to the last stitch you made. When you're finished, you'll have 24 stitches ([Sc in next 2 sts, 2 sc in next st] 6 times, pm (24 sts total).)

Round 5: Single crochet in the next 3 stitches, then make 2 single crochet in the next stitch. Do this 6 times. Move marker to the last stitch you made. When you're finished, you'll have 30 stitches. ([Sc in next 3 sts, 2sc in next st] 6 times, pm (30 sts total).)

Round 6: Single crochet in the next 4 stitches, then make 2 single crochet in the next stitch. Do this 6 times. Move marker to the last stitch you made. When you're finished, you'll have 36 stitches. ([Sc in next 4 sts, 2 sc in next st] 6 times, pm (36 sts total).)

Round 7: Single crochet in the next 5 stitches, then make 2 single crochet in the next stitch. Do the 6 times. Move marker to the last stitch you made. When you're finished, you'll have 42 stitches. ([Sc in next 5 sts, 2 sc in next st] 6 times, pm (42 sts total).)

Rounds 8–10: Single crochet in each stitch around, place marker. (Sc in ea st around, pm.)

Round 11: Change to burgundy yarn, single crochet in each stitch around. Place marker. (Sc in ea st around, pm.)

Rounds 12–14: Change to red yarn, single crochet in each stitch around. Place marker. (Sc in ea st around, pm.)

Round 15: Skip the next stitch, and single crochet in the next 6 stitches. Do this 6 times. Place marker. When you're finished, you'll have 36 stitches. ([Sk the next st, sc in next 6 sts] 6 times, pm (36 sts total).)

Round 16: Skip the next stitch, and single crochet in the next 5 stitches. Do this 6 times. When you're finished, you'll have 30 stitches. ([Sk the nest st, sc in next 5 sts] 6 times, pm (30 sts total).)

Round 17: Skip the next stitch, single crochet in the next 4 stitches. Do this 6 times. Place marker. When you're finished, you'll have 24 stitches. ([Sk the next st, sc in next 4 sts] 6 times, pm (24 sts total).)

Round 18: Skip the next stitch, single crochet in the next 3 stitches. Do this 6 times. Place marker. When you're finished, you'll have 18 stitches. ([Sk the next st, sc in next 3 sts] 6 times, pm (18 sts total).)

Round 19: Skip the next stitch, single crochet in the next 2 stitches. Do this 6 times. When you're finished, you'll have a total of 12 stitches. ([Sk the next st, sc in next 2 sts] 6 times, pm (12 sts total).)

Stuff the sack loosely with beans.

Round 20: Skip the next stitch, single crochet in the next stitch. Do this 6 times. When you're finished, you'll have 6 stitches. ([Sk the next st, sc in next st] 6 times, pm (6 sts total).)

Weave in the end, closing the opening as you work.

Yarn Used:

2 skeins Plymouth Yarn's *Wildflower D.K.*, 51% cotton/49% acrylic, 1¾oz/50g, 137yd/125m, one skein each in Red #63 and Burgundy #62.

—From *Crochet*

Convertible Cover

Drew Emborsky

As I was designing this afghan square, I realized that the back looked just as fantastic as the front! By alternating the squares in a checkerboard pattern, there is no right or wrong side to this throw.

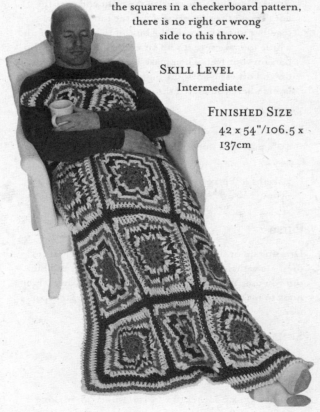

SKILL LEVEL

Intermediate

FINISHED SIZE

42 x 54"/106.5 x 137cm

YOU WILL NEED

- Color A: 450yd/411m of super bulky weight yarn
- Color B: 300yd/274m of super bulky weight yarn
- Color C: 250yd/229m of super bulky weight yarn
- Hook: 6.50mm (size K-10½ U.S.) *or size to obtain gauge*
- Yarn needle

STITCHES USED

Chain stitch (ch)

Double crochet (dc)

Front post double crochet (FPdc)

Slip stitch (sl st)

SPECIAL STITCHES

Reverse single crochet (reverse sc). Working from left to right, insert hook from front to back through next st to the right, yo, draw yarn through st, yo, draw yarn through 2 lps on hook.

V-stitch (V-st): (Dc, ch 1, dc) in same st or sp.

GAUGE

7 sts x 5 rows = 4"/10cm in dc; first 2 rnds of motif = 4½"/11.5cm in diameter; motif = 12"/30.5cm square

Always take time to check your gauge.

INSTRUCTIONS

MOTIF (MAKE 12)

With B, ch 4, join with sl st to form a ring.

Rnd 1 (RS): Ch 5 (counts as dc, ch 2), (3 dc in ring, ch 2) three times, 2 dc in ring, sl st to 3rd ch of beginning ch-5 to join.

Rnd 2: Sl st in next ch-2 sp, ch 5 (counts as dc, ch 2), 2 dc in same sp, *sk next dc, V-st in next dc, sk next dc**, (2 dc, ch 2, 2 dc) in corner ch-2 sp; rep from * around, ending last rep at **, dc in corner sp, sl st in 3rd ch of beginning ch-5 to join. Fasten off.

Rnd 3: Ch 3, (dc, ch 2, 2 dc) in same sp, *sk next dc, FPdc in next dc, V-st in next ch-1 sp, sk next dc, FPdc in next dc, sk next dc**, (2 dc, ch 2, 2 dc) in corner sp; rep from * around, ending last rep at **, sl st in top of beginning ch-3 to join. Fasten off.

With RS facing, join C with sl st in any corner ch-2 sp.

Rnd 4: Ch 3, (dc, ch 2, 2 dc) in same sp, *sk next dc, FPdc in each of next 2 sts, V-st in next ch-1 sp, sk next dc, FPdc in each of next 2 sts, sk next dc**, (2 dc, ch 2, 2 dc) in corner ch-2 sp; rep from * around, ending last rep at **, sl st in top of beginning ch-3 to join. Fasten off.

With RS facing, join A with sl st in any corner ch-2 sp.

Rnd 5: Ch 3, (dc, ch 2, 2 dc) in same sp, *sk next dc, FPdc in each of next 3 sts, V-st in next ch-1 sp, sk next dc, FPdc in each of next 3 sts, sk next dc**, (2 dc, ch 2, 2 dc) in corner ch-2 sp; rep from * around, ending last rep at **, sl st in top of beginning ch-3 to join. Fasten off.

With RS facing, join B with sl st in any corner ch-2 sp.

Rnd 6: Ch 3, (dc, ch 2, 2 dc) in same sp, *sk next dc. FPdc in each of next 4 sts, V-st in next ch-1 sp, sk next dc, FPdc in each of next 4 sts, sk next dc**, (2 dc, ch2, 2 dc) in corner ch-2 sp; rep from * around, ending last rep at **, sl st in top of beginning ch-3 to join. Fasten off.

With RS facing, join A with sl st in any corner ch-2 sp.

Rnd 7: Ch 3, (dc, ch 2, 2 dc) in same sp, *sk next dc, FPdc in each of next 5 sts, V-st in next ch-1 sp, sk next dc, FPdc in each of next 5 sts, sk next dc**, (2 dc, ch 2, 2 dc) in corner ch-2 sp; rep from * around, ending last rep at **, sl st in top of beginning ch-3 to join. Fasten off.

With RS facing, join C with sc in any corner ch-2 sp.

Rnd 8: Work 2 more sc in same sp, *sc in BL only of

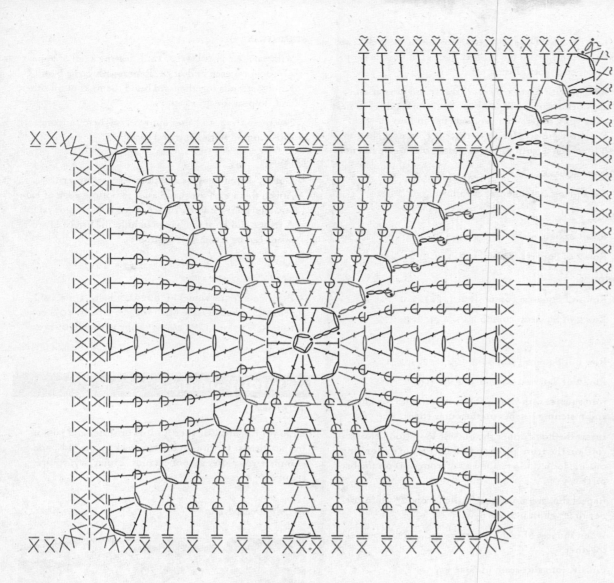

each st across to next corner**, 3 sc in corner ch-2 sp; rep from * around, ending last rep at **, sl st to first sc to join. Fasten off.

ASSEMBLE

Lay out afghan in three strips of four squares each. Alternate RS and WS facing up in a checkerboard pattern. Use C to whipstitch squares together.

FINISHING

Weave in all ends, being sure to hide them well so that they are not visible on either side of the afghan.

Afghan Border

With either side facing, join C with sl st in 2nd sc of any corner.

Rnd 1: Ch 3, (dc, ch2, 2 dc) in same st, *dc in each st across to next corner sc**, (2 dc, ch 2, 2 dc) in corner sc; rep from * around, ending last rep at **, sl st in top of beginning ch 3 to join. Fasten off.

With same side facing, join A with sl st in any corner ch-2 sp.

—From *The Crochet Dude's Designs for Guys*

Not Your Granny's Halter Top

Terry Taylor

These "Friendship Squares" start new friendships all 'round. When you step out in this fun, retro-style halter top, crocheters will want to know how-to, and others will just want to know: Who's the girl in the groovy top?

Design by Gwen Blakley Kinsler

Joining Crochet Blocks
Linda P. Schapper

Joining Blocks

Blocks such as squares, triangles, and hexagons, and even some other designs can be joined together directly without using a different shape to fill out the pattern. Other, such as circular or floral blocks, must be alternated, sometimes with a pattern of a different shape. This provides an opportunity to use your imagination in the selection of a complementary pattern. There is no right or wrong way. Whatever looks good to you can be used.

Joining Motifs Together

There are several methods for joining motifs together. Sewing and crocheting are the most popular methods. Sewn seams are the least bulky, but if you prefer to avoid sewing, I've included two methods of crocheting seams.

Joinings can be worked with right sides or wrong sides facing. Worked with the wrong-sides facing, the joining will stand out on the front of the piece. Placing the motifs with right sides of the motifs facing, the joining will be on the back and less noticeable. Use whichever method you prefer, just be consistent throughout.

Joinings can be worked through both loops of stitches for a sturdy join or through only the back loops of both pieces for a flexible seam. Illustrations show sewing and slip stitching through back loops of stitches and single crocheting through both loops of stitches. Always work joining stitches as loosely as the crocheted pieces to avoid tight seams that distort the fabric.

Sewn or Whipstitched Seams

Place motifs together with right (or wrong) sides facing. Using a yarn needle and matching yarn, insert needle through back loop only of corner stitches of both pieces, draw yarn through and secure with a knot, *insert needle from top to bottom through the back loop of the next stitch of each piece, then draw yarn through, repeat from * across side to be joined, to next corner stitch. Fasten off.

Slip Stitches Seams

Place motifs together with right (or wrong) sides facing. Using crochet hook and matching yarn, make a slip knot with yarn. Insert hook through back loop only of corner stitches of both pieces, place slip knot on hook, *insert hook through back loop of next stitch of each piece, yo, draw yarn through all three loops on hook; repeat from * across side to be joined, to next corner stitch. Fasten off.

Single Crocheted Seams

Place motifs together with right (or wrong) sides facing. Using crochet hook and matching yarn, make a slip knot with yarn. Insert hook through both loops of corner stitches of both pieces, place slip knot on hook, ch 1, insert hook through same two stitches, yo, draw yarn through stitches, yo, draw yarn through 2 loops on hook, *insert hook through both loops of next stitch of each piece, yo, draw yarn through stitches, yo, draw yarn through two loops on hook; repeat from * across side to be joined, to next corner stitch. Fasten off.

—From *300 Classic Blocks for Crochet Projects*

Continued ➡

FINISHED
MEASUREMENTS

Approx 5 x 5"/13 x 13 cm each square

The top is designed to fit bust sizes S (34"/86cm), M (38"/96cm), and L (42"/107cm)

MATERIALS

- Yarn A: 330yd/306m cotton/nylon worsted weight ribbon in green
- Yarn B: 110yd/102m cotton/nylon worsted weight ribbon in plum
- Yarn C: 220yd/204m cotton/nylon worsted weight ribbon in variegated green/blue
- Hook: 4mm/G-6 *or size needed to obtain gauge*
- Approx 80 pony beads
- Sewing needle and matching thread
- Tapestry needle

STITCHES USED

Chain stitch (ch)

Single crochet (dc)

Double crochet (dc)

Reverse single crochet (rev sc)

2 double crochet cluster (2-dc cl)

3 double crochet cluster (3-dc cl)

PATTERN NOTES

Color Combinations

Color Combo 1: 2 rnds of yarn A, 1 rnd each of yarns B, C, A

Color Combo 2: 2 rnds of yarn C, 1 rnd each of yarns A, C, A

Color Combo 3: 2 rnds of yarn B, 1 rnd each of yarns A, C, A

Squares Needed per Size

Small = 12 squares: 6 of combo 2, 3 ea of combo 3 and 1

Medium = 14 squares: 7 of combo 2, 3 of combo 3, 4 of combo 1

Large = 16 squares: 4 ea of combo 1 and 3, 8 of combo 2

INSTRUCTIONS

FRIENDSHIP SQUARE

Ch 4, sl st to form ring.

Rnd 1: Work 8 sc in ring; join with sl st to first sc. Do not turn.

Rnd 2: Ch 3, work dc in same place as sl st, ch 2, *yo hook, draw up lp in next sc, yo, draw through 2 lps on hk, yo, draw up lp in same stitch, yo, draw through 2 lps on hk, yo draw through remaining 3 lps on hk (2-dc cl made), ch 2; rep from * 6 times; join with sl st to top of ch 3 (eight 2-dc cl, counting ch 3 as 1 dc). Fasten off.

Rnd 3: With next yarn color, sl st in any ch-2 sp, ch 3, work 2-dc cl in same sp, ch 3, (yo, draw up lp in same space, yo, draw through 2 lps on hk) 3 times, yo, draw through remaining 4 lps on hk (3-dc cl made: 1st corner), * ch 2, work 3-dc cl in next ch-2 sp, ch 2, work 3-dc cl, ch 3 and 3-dc cl in next ch-2 sp (another corner complete). Rep from * twice; ch 2, 3-dc cl in next sp; join with sl st. Fasten off.

Rnd 4: With next yarn color, sl st in any corner ch-3 sp, work 1st corner in same sp, *(ch 2, work 3-dc cl in next ch-2 sp) twice; ch 2, work corner in next ch-2 sp. Rep from * twice; (ch 2, work 3-dc cl in next ch-2 sp) twice; ch 2; join. Fasten off.

Rnd 5: With next yarn color, sl st in any corner ch-3 sp; work 1st corner in same sp, * (2, work 3 dc cl in next ch-2 sp) 3 times; ch 2, work corner in next ch-3 sp. Rep from * twice; (ch 2, work 3-dc cl in next ch-2 sp) 3 times; ch 2; join with sl st. Fasten off. Weave in ends.

JOINING SQUARES

Lay squares in sequences as follows:

SMALL

Row 1 of Squares: combo 2, 3, 2, 3, 2, 3

Row 2 of Squares: combo 1, 2, 1, 2, 1, 2

MEDIUM

Row 1 of Squares: combo 1, 2, 1, 2, 1, 2, 1

Row 2 of Squares: combo 2, 3, 2, 3, 2, 3, 2

LARGE

Row 1 of Squares: combo 2, 1, 2, 1, 2, 1, 2, 1

Row 2 of Squares: combo 3, 2, 3, 2, 3, 2, 3, 2

Join squares with yarn A. Sl st, holding RS together and matching stitches on the outer edges.

Insert the hook under the outside loop (loop closest to you) on the front piece and under the corresponding outside loop (loop farthest away from you) on the back piece.

Repeat this process for each stitch from 2nd ch in corner to 2nd ch in next corner.

When squares of each row are joined, join 2 rows together.

Finally, join side seam in same way.

TOP EDGING

With front of halter facing, using yarn A, sc evenly around entire top edge; do not fasten off, ch 1, work rev sc in each sc just worked. Fasten off.

BOTTOM EDGING

With front of halter facing, sl st to join to any stitch at side. Ch 3, sk 1 stitch, hdc in next st, *ch 1, sk 1 stitch, hdc in next stitch; repeat from * around; join with sl st in 2nd ch of ch 3. With yarn A, make a chain of approx 44" (49, 54)/112cm (124, 137) and weave through ch-1 spaces at lower edge of halter.

STRAPS (MAKE 2)

With yarn A, ch 100 (110, 120), leaving a tail of approx 4"/10cm on each end of ch. Repeat with yarns B and C. Knot 3 strands together and braid them; knot on other end. Repeat for 2nd strap.

Sew these straps to halter approx 2½"/6cm in from side seam on both front and back.

FRINGE

Cut 25"/64cm lengths of all three colors of yarn. Attach them with overhand knot to bottom edge of halter, alternating colors. Attach 3 beads to ends of yarn A fringe and knot the fringe to hold the beads. More beads can be attached if desired.

This project was created with:

Berroco's Zen in Kimchi (#8222), 3 balls; Umeboshi (#8224), 1 ball; Osake Mix (#8139), 2 balls, 40% cotton/60% nylon, 1.75oz/50g = approx 110yd/102m ea

—FROM *The New Crochet*

Jammin' Jeans

Terry Taylor

Grab your board (whether it's surf or skate) and jam on in these jeans. Or hop in the van, pick up the kids, and complete your after school errands. Either way, you're stylin'.

Design by Donna Hulka

SKILL LEVEL

Intermediate

FINISHED MEASUREMENTS

Approx 5"/13cm

YOU WILL NEED

- 1 pair of Capri jeans*
- Yarn A: approx 100yd/90m variegated blue worsted weight machine washable yarn
- Yarn B: approx 60yd/54m beige worsted weight machine washable yarn
- Hk: 5.5mm/I-9 or size needed to obtain gauge
- Stitch marker

- Tape measure or ruler
- Awl or sharp-pointed scissors
- Sharp-pointed needle with eye large enough to thread your yarn

Any style jeans may be used. Simple cut hem to Capri length.

Stitches Used

Chain stitch (ch)

Slip stitch (sl st)

Single crochet (sc)

Double crochet (dc)

Gauge

Take time to check your gauge.

13 sc and 16 rows = 4"/10cm

Preparation

Mark around hem at ½"/1cm intervals, approximately ⅛"/3mm above hem edge. Use an awl or sharp-pointed scissors to pierce the fabric at the marked intervals.

Thread needle with Yarn A and whipstitch loosely around hem edge, inserting needle into each hole previously made. Tie off, leaving ends to work in later.

Pattern Note

You will not turn your work except at the ends of rounds 3 and 4.

Instructions

EDGING

Rnd 1: With yarn B, sl st into any whipstitch, ch 1, 2 sc in same whipstitch, 2 sc in next whipstitch, (1 sc in next whipstitch, 2 sc in next whipstitch) 3 times, **(2 sc in next whipstitch) twice, (1 sc in next whipstitch, 2 sc in next whipstitch) 3 times**, rep from ** to ** around entire hem. (Note: It's fine if you reach the end of the hem without fully completing the final rep.)

Count the number of sc in this rnd and make a note of it; then sl st in 1st sc to join. Do not turn.

Rnd 2: If your number of stitches on rnd 1 is a multiple of 5, you do not need to inc on this round; otherwise, calculate the next highest multiple of 5 and inc to that number of sts on this round.

Ch 1, sc in same sc as sl st and in each sc around, spacing incs (2 sc in 1 sc) evenly around (if needed, as indicated above), sl st in 1st sc to join. Do not turn.

Rnd 3: Ch 1, sc in same sc as sl st and in ea sc around, spacing 10 incs (2 sc in 1 sc) evenly around, sl st in 1st sc to join. Fasten off. Turn.

Rnd 4: Attach yarn A with a sl st in last sl st of rnd 3, sl st in next 4 sc; 1st flower: ch 7, sl st in back ridge only of 5th ch from hk (this is the flower center) (1st half of 1st petal made and 2nd petal made), *ch 4, sl st in flower center* (3rd petal made), rep from * to * once (4th petal made), ch 2, sl st in same sc in which you began this flower (2nd half of 1st petal made) (first flower made.)

sl st in next 5 sc. Next flower: ch 5, sc in center of 4th petal of previous flower (inserting hk from front to back of petal), ch 2, sl st in back loop only of 3rd ch of the ch 5 with which you began this flower (this is the flower center) (1st half of 1st petal made and 2nd petal made), *ch 4, sl st in flower center* (3rd petal made), rep from * to * once (4th petal made), ch 2, sl st in same sc in which you began this flower (2nd half of 1st petal made) (flower made), rep from ** to ** around until you have completed the 3rd petal of the last flower.

4th petal of last flower: ch 2, sc in center of 2nd petal of 1st flower (inserting hk from back to front of petal), ch 2, sl st in flower center (4th petal made), ch 2, sl st in same sc in which you began this flower (2nd half of 1st petal made), sl in 1st sl st to join. Fasten off. Turn.

Rnd 5: Attach yarn B with a sl st in center of 3rd petal of any flower, ch 4 loosely, *sl st in 3rd petal of next flower, ch 2 loosely*, rep from * to * around, sl st in 1st sc to join. Do not turn.

Rnd 6: Ch 1, sc in same sl st, sc in each of next 4 ch (inserting hk through both the front and back lps of ch), *sc in next sl st, sc in each of next 4 ch*, rep from * to * around, sl st in 1st sc to join. Do not turn.

Rnd 7: The number of stitches you worked on rnd 6 should be equal to the number worked on rnd 3: if this number is odd, work 5 incs on this rnd; if it is even, work 6 incs on this rnd.

Ch 1, sc in same sc as sl st and in each sc around, working incs (2 sc in 1 sc) evenly around (as indicated above), in last sc switch to yarn A, sl st in 1st sc to join. Do not turn.

Rnd 8: Ch 4, sk sc with sl st, *sk next sc, dc in next sc, ch 1*, rep from * to * around, sl st in 3rd ch of beg ch 4 to join. Do not turn.

Rnd 9: Sl st in 1st ch-1 sp, ch 4, *dc in next ch-1 sp, ch-1*, rep from * to * around, sl st in 3rd ch of beg ch 4 to join. Do not turn.

Rnd 10: Ch 1, sc in 1st ch-1 sp, place st marker in sc just made (to help you keep your place), ch 1, *sc in next ch-1 sp, ch 1*, rep from * to * around, remove st marker, sl st in 1st sc (where st marker was) to join. Do not turn.

Rnds 11–15: Rep rnd 10 five times. At the end of rnd 15, place st marker in the ending sl st. Do not turn.

Rnd 16: Sl st in next ch-1 sp, *sl st in next sc, sl st in next ch-1 sp*, rep from * to * around, remove st marker, sl st in 1st sl st (where st marker was) to join. Fasten off and work in ends.

Rep pattern for second leg of jeans.

This project was created with:

Yarn A: 1 skein of Plymouth's *Encore Colorspun* (#7991), 75% acrylic/25% wool, 1.75oz/50g = approx 150yd/135m.

Yarn B: 1 skein Plymouth's *Encore* (#1415), 75% acrylic/25% wool, 1oz/30g = approx 60yd/54m

—From *The New Crochet*

SHIRT EDGING

Jane Davis

Love your t-shirts, but feel like they're missing something? Add some color and texture with crochet edgings. The shirts used here already had small looped trim along the edge, making it easy to crochet into. If your shirt doesn't have this, you could add the loops using a needle and thread or the correct cotton. If the knit is loose enough, you could even crochet righ into the edge of the shirt. This pattern gives you two edgings—one uses a single crochet, and the other uses picot to make it more decorative.

Skill Level

Intermediate

Finished Size

Basic edging: About ¼ inch wide

Picot edging: About 1 inch wide

Linda P. Schapper, Illustrations © Karen Manthey

You can use crocheted borders to finish projects in weaving, knitting, sewing, and in many other handcrafts. You can utilize bands to decorate clothing, household textiles, or any type of sewing. In Switzerland, crocheted filet bands were used to piece together sheets and tablecloths before looms were large enough to make one wide piece.

Use borders to embellish blankets, place mats, towels, or sheets. Decorate handkerchiefs, altar cloths, curtains, or children's clothing with them. Enlarge the pattern, and you could use a border design as a curtain. Smaller versions could be perfect as doll clothes or collars. There is no limit to the number of ideas and uses for crocheted borders. All you have to do is vary the size of your needle, the material you use, and the way you use it.

Joining Borders to Fabric

Most borders patterns give directions for a stand-alone border, worked across a foundation chain. As written, they are designed to be sewn onto fabric after completion. Borders can also be worked directly onto the fabric. To do so, eliminate the foundation chain and work a row of single crochet with the necessary multiple of stitches, then work pattern row 1 across sc row. Alternately, work row 1 of the pattern directly onto the fabric, evenly spacing stitches and loops, as per photograph of finished border.

Crocheting Borders onto Fabric

Method 1: Work a row of single crochet on the edge of the fabric before working the border.

Method 2: Work border directly onto the fabric, spacing stitches as per photograph of the border.

Border Worked on Edge of Fabric Diagram

Method 1: Work a row of single crochet on the edge of fabric before working the border.

Method 2: Work border directly onto fabric, spacing stitches as per photograph of border.

—From *The Complete Book of Crochet Border Designs*

Continued ➡

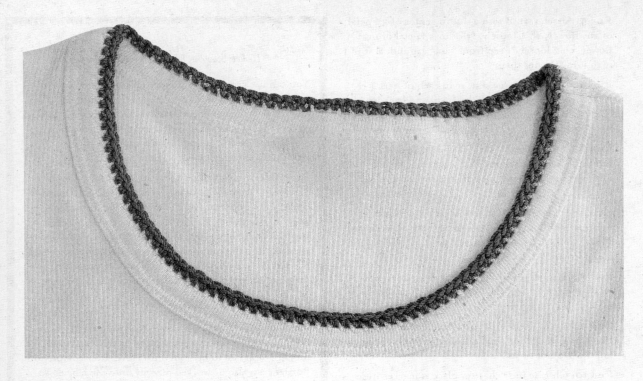

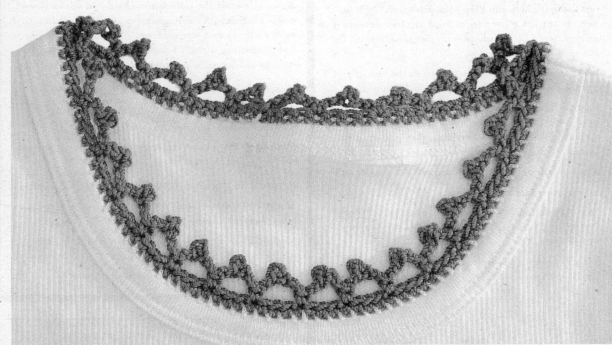

MATERIALS

- 1 ball of turquoise crochet cotton cord in size 3
- Size B (2.25mm) crochet hook
- Tapestry needle
- Shirt with looped edging

GAUGE IN SINGLE CROCHET (SC)

20 sts = 4"

STITCHES USED

Chain (ch)
Single crochet (sc)
Slip stitch (sl st)

INSTRUCTIONS

SINGLE-CROCHET EDGING

Attach the cotton cord to a loop on the neck edge at the back of the shirt, sc in ea lp around the shirt. Cut the cord to 8 inches (20 cm) and pull the tail through the last lp. Weave in the end.

PICOT EDGING

Attach the cotton cord to a loop on the neck edge at the back of the shirt.

Row 1: Sc in ea lp around the shirt, join to the first st with a sl st.

Row 2: [Ch 5, sl st in the 3rd ch from hk, ch 2, sk 3 sts, sc in the next st] repeat around.

Weave in the end.

Yarn Used:

1 ball of Coats & Clark Yarns' *J.P. Coats Royal Fashion Crochet Thread*, size 3, 100% mercerized cotton, 150yd/137m in Warm Teal #0065.

—From *Crochet*

Mosaics

MOSAIC BASICS

Connie Sheerin

Mosaic Materials

Finished mosaics can look complicated, but mosaic techniques are simple to learn and many mosaic projects are quick and easy to do. Many mosaic materials are readily available and inexpensive, and some materials—such as broken china, seashells, and beach glass—are free or cost very little.

All You Need Are:

- **Tesserae** are tiles, glass pieces, broken china or terra cotta that are pieced together on a surface to create the design

- **Surface**, such as wood, terra cotta, plaster, or metal

- **An adhesive**, such as white craft glue or a silicone adhesive, to hold the tesserae to the surface

- **Grout**, to fill the spaces between the tesserae, smooth the surface, and add strength and durability to the mosaic

- **Tools**—a few simple tools such as tile or glass nippers and a rubber mallet.

How to Estimate How Much Material You'll Need

There are several ways to estimate how much mosaic material you'll need to complete a particular project. Experience is the best teacher, and it is, of course, better to have too much than not enough. Here are some guidelines and tips.

Some artists and crafters just buy lots of tiles—more than they think they'll need—knowing they'll use what's left eventually. When you're beginning, it's good to have some extra tiles on hand, especially if your design calls for precise cutting or nipping.

Another option is to measure the project and multiply the dimensions of the mosaic area to determine the size of the mosaic in square inches or, for really large mosaics, in square feet. If you're working only with tiles, a close estimate is possible because when tiles are sold by the package or the sheet, the coverage in square feet or square inches is noted for the consumer.

If you're creating a mixed media mosaic, you can do a rough estimate based on the dimensions of the finished piece minus the amount of coverage provided by the china or terra cotta or plaster pieces. It's also possible to estimate how much material you'll need for a mixed media design by roughly laying out the design on the surface or—if you're using a pattern—on the pattern, allowing space between the pieces for grout. This is easy to do on a flat surface, but all surfaces aren't flat. If the surface isn't flat, measure the dimensions (if it's a bowl, for example, measure the height and the circumference),

draw a diagram of the surface area using those measurements on graph paper or brown kraft paper, and lay out the material on the paper diagram.

For most of the projects in this book, the mosaic area size is given in square inches. Some projects are fairly precise in what's required, for others, the final design is up to you. If a design uses whole tiles of a specific size, the size and number are noted. If broken tiles are to be used, the size of the tiles can vary, and the number needed would too.

When working in mixed media, the number of broken plates or broken tiles needed to cover a space varies, depending on many factors, including the size of the plate, how big the design area is, and how usable the broken pieces are. If you're creating a mosaic on a table or a lamp, the table or lamp you want to use may not be the same size as the one I used. Feel free to improvise.

Ceramic Tiles

Ceramic tiles are made from clay or china that has been shaped in a mold and fired. They are available in a huge array of shapes, sizes, and colors, individually and on sheets, decorated and plain, glazed and unglazed. The color of the tile may be due to the color of the clay it is made from or from a glaze that is applied before firing. Some tiles have painted designs; you can also paint or stencil your own designs on tiles with permanent enamel paints. Tiles may have a textured or smooth surface and a glossy or matte finish.

Continued ➔

Tiles can be bought at crafts and building supply stores and specialty stores that sell tile and bathroom fixtures.

Glass & Mirror

You also can create mosaics using only pieces of glass (some early mosaics were made only of small, opaque glass cubes) or with a combination of tiles, broken china, glass, and mirror.

Glass Tiles

Glass tiles are small squares of stained or clear glass. They are typically sold in packages in crafts stores and stores that sell mosaics supplies.

Stained Glass

Stained glass pieces, cut in shapes with a glass cutter or broken into irregular pieces, can be used to create mosaics. Stained glass pieces are available from crafts stores and catalogs. Because stained glass is generally not as thick as tiles, you may wish to build up the surface under the glass pieces with silicone adhesive so they will be flush on the surface with thicker tiles if you use glass and tile in the same mosaic piece. The unpolished edges of glass pieces are sharp and dangerous if not grouted.

Polished Glass

Polished glass pieces are pieces of irregular clear glass and colored textured glass that have smooth, polished edges, so they're safe to handle and use. They are typically sold in packages in crafts stores. These are great to use for ungrouted mosaics and they are also effective with grouting.

Beach Glass

Beach glass or "beaten glass" are pieces of glass you can find on the beach. They are likely pieces of broken bottles that have been pounded on the beach by the surf, resulting in a frosted appearance and smooth edges. You can also find commercially produced beach glass.

Mirror

Mirror pieces can be found as small square "tiles" or in larger sizes that can be broken into irregular shapes. Various thicknesses are available. You can buy mirror glass at crafts and department stores and from dealers who specialize in glass and mirror.

Marbles

Flatbacked marbles are available in a wide range of clear and opalescent colors. They are made by melting and cooling glass pieces—when the molten glass cools on a flat surface, it assumes a rounded shape on the top while the bottom conforms to the flat surface underneath.

Flatbacked marbles are available at crafts stores and from stores and catalogs that sell supplies for stained glass.

Mixed Media

Mixed media mosaics can be made of broken china, seashells, molded plaster pieces, or terra cotta. I have found many of the pieces I have used in my home, my friends' homes, secondhand shops, yard and tag sales—even the trash! Soon you'll have a wonderful collection. Ask your friends and neighbors to save broken china and flower pots for your mosaics. You can reward them with a mixed media mosaic piece as a gift!

China

Broken china pieces can come from plates, bowls, cups, or saucers. Plates or saucers are the best sources because they will break into flat pieces. Store the pieces in a jar until you're ready to use them.

Pottery

Terra cotta pieces come from broken clay flower pots and saucers. **Broken pottery** can also create interesting looks for your designs.

Shells

Seashells can be found at the beach for free or purchased at crafts stores. Mosaics are the solution for what to do with those leftover souvenirs of beachcombing.

Buttons

Buttons can also be used. Everyone has a jar of old buttons—mosaics are a great place to use them.

Plaster

You can make **molded plaster pieces** or buy them. To make them, you'll need plaster or candy molds and craft plaster—all available at crafts stores. Follow the package instructions for molding and drying.

Back Boards & Surfaces

Ceramics & Plaster

Terra cotta pots and planters are excellent surfaces for mosaics. An additional benefit is that the mosaic further insulates the pot, protecting the plant's soil from drying out. You can purchase **plaster** surfaces such as frames and trivets at crafts and ceramics stores or mold them yourself with craft plaster. **Cement** stepping stones, decorated with mosaics, add a personal touch to your garden or patio. You buy them at garden supply stores or mold them yourself. Buy the molds at crafts stores. **Glazed** ceramics or china can also be used as a base for your designs.

Metal

Metal trays, pitchers, and bowls also are good surfaces for mosaics. Clean before using and sand to remove rust and rough spots. Look for great deals at tag and yard sales and thrift stores.

Glass & Mirror & Plastic

You can create mosaics on trays made of glass or mirror or sturdy plexiglass. Look for sturdy pieces with smooth edges at yard sales and thrift stores. You can also have pieces of glass or mirror or hard plastic cut to shape at glass and mirror dealers. Choose material that is ¼" (.6 cm) thick and have them polish the edges smooth. Use stick-on felt pads on the bottom.

Wood

Wood surfaces such as unfinished furniture and accessories such as frames, wall shelves, and plates can be purchased at crafts, department, and furniture stores. Furniture pieces such as tables and chairs and accessories—bookends, candlesticks, bowls, and boxes, for example—can be found at yard and tag sales, auctions, and thrift stores. Flat mosaic pieces also can be built on plywood or fiberboard that has been cut to any shape. You can buy plywood and fiberboard at building supply stores.

Wood surfaces that will receive mosaics should be sealed with a clear acrylic sealer and allowed to dry before tesserae is applied.

Papier-Mâché

Sturdy papier-mâché items, available at crafts stores, are also suitable surfaces for mosaics. Seal the surface before applying the tesserae.

Adhesives

A variety of adhesives can be used to glue tesserae to surfaces. The one you choose depends on the base and the mosaic materials you are using—the adhesive should be compatible with both surfaces. The two adhesives used extensively in this section are white craft glue and silicone adhesive.

White craft glue can be used for gluing flat materials (tile, flat glass, flatbacked marbles) to flat, horizontal surfaces. It holds the pieces securely, dries clear and flattens as it dries, leaving room for grout between the tile pieces.

Silicone adhesive works best on curved surfaces or vertical surfaces. Because it is thick, it will hold pieces in place while drying. However, it does not flatten, so you must be careful that you don't use too much or that too much does not "ooze" between the tile pieces, leaving no room for grout. It's also the adhesive of choice when gluing ungrouted mosaic effects. Silicone adhesive also is useful when you're using materials of different thicknesses and you wish to build up the thinner material to be level with the others.

A craft stick is a convenient spreader for glues and adhesives. *Don't* use your finger!

Mastic is a ready-to-spread adhesive sold by the bucket or the container that is applied with a trowel. Mastic is suitable for mosaics that will be used outdoors. It is generally used on large, flat surfaces (like walls) but can be used on smaller pieces like backsplashes and stepping stones. Follow manufacturer's instructions for application. Mastic is available where tile is sold.

Always read the manufacturer's instructions on glue and adhesives packages and follow all precautions and warnings. Many glues give off fumes as they dry. Avoid inhaling them and work in a well-ventilated area or outdoors.

Grout

Grout is the material that fills the spaces between the tile, china, and glass pieces, adding to the strength and durability of a mosaic piece. Grouts are made of Portland cement; some grouts also contain polymers, which contribute additional strength and flexibility.

Tile grout is available two ways: non-sanded and sanded. **Non-sanded grout** is preferred for mosaics with crevices up to ¼" (.6 cm) wide, especially those made of material that is easily scratched. **Sanded grout** is just that—grout with sand added to it. Use it for mosaics with larger crevices (more than ¼"[.6 cm]). Grout is available by the container and by the pound at crafts, hardware, tile, and building supply stores.

Grout can be purchased in more than 30 colors, ready to mix with water. If you want a strong color, buy colored grout. Adding a colorant to white grout and getting a really strong color is nearly impossible.

White grout can be colored with **liquid or powder colorants**—you mix the colorant with the grout while you're preparing it. Mix powdered colorant with the grout powder before adding water; mix liquid colorant with the water before adding the water to the grout. Options for coloring grout include concentrated food dyes, acrylic paints, herbs, glitter, and spices.

You also can color the grout after it has dried on your mosaic with liquid fabric dyes (natural and otherwise) or strong coffee or tea. Experiment with the dye on pieces of dried grout to check the color before you apply it to your finished piece.

Mix grout in a **small plastic bucket** or a **disposable plastic container**, following the instructions on the grout package. (It should be the consistency of nut butter or fudge.) If you want to use your mixing container again, clean out the leftover grout before it dries and rinse the container thoroughly. Using a disposable container is handy—you can throw it (and your leftover grout that's in it) away when you're finished. I like to use plastic yogurt containers. Wear gloves to apply grout.

Don't pour leftover grout down the sink or flush it down the toilet—it can clog your pipes. If you are sensitive to dust, wear a mask when mixing grout.

Use a **sponge** to wipe away excess grout from the surface of the mosaic. Keep a bowl of water nearby to rinse and squeeze out the sponge often as you wipe. Wear gloves to protect your hands.

When the grout has dried, you can smooth the edges with **sandpaper**. Sandpaper can also be used to remove grout from a surface where it doesn't belong.

Sealers

Grout sealer is a clear liquid that comes in a bottle or can. Apply it with a brush to seal the grout to protect it from stains and the elements. Sealing is recommended for table tops (to protect them from stains) and for mosaics—especially flat surfaces—that will be used outdoors. Buy it where grout is sold.

Tools

Only a few simple, inexpensive tools are needed for creating mosaics. Many of these you may already have around your home.

Nippers

For cutting or breaking tiles, glass, and china, you'll need **tile nippers** or **glass nippers**. They look and are handled much like pliers—some have sharp blades and others have round disks and they have spring-action handles. To use them, grasp the material you want to cut or break with the nippers. When the blades or disks are pressed together, they will crack and break the material. Choose nippers that feel comfortable in your hand. *Caution: Always use goggles when nipping pieces of tile, ceramic, or glass.*

Mallet

I use a **rubber mallet** to break plates or large numbers of tiles into irregular pieces. Some people use a *hammer*, but I don't—with a mallet, you have more control and the pieces won't break into such tiny shards and dust.

Spreaders

Use **craft sticks** or **plastic spreaders** to spread adhesives on the surface or to apply adhesives to individual tiles. They can also be used to fill grout into tight places or used to smooth grout on edges.

To spread grout over the glued tesserae, use a **rubber spatula** or a **plastic putty knife**.

Tweezers

A pair of long-handled **tweezers** can be of help when you're placing small pieces.

Brushes

A **foam brush, bristle paint brush**, or **artist's paint brush** can be used to paint trim and backgrounds for mosaic designs. When the grout has begun to dry, use a **stiff bristle brush** to brush away the excess.

Miscellaneous

For mixing grout, you'll need a **measuring cup** to measure the water.

Use a **damp sponge** to wipe away excess grout. Have a **bowl** (stainless steel or plastic) of water nearby to rinse the sponge as you wipe.

Use a **ruler** for measuring when you want to make a precise cut.

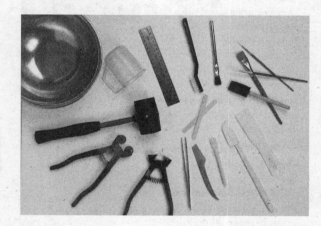

Protective Gear

Mosaic materials break into sharp pieces and have sharp edges. Until you become used to handling them, be especially cautious.

Protect your eyes when cutting and breaking tiles and china by wearing **protective goggles**. Wear **latex gloves** when grouting so you won't cut your fingers on any sharp edges and so the grout won't dry out your hands.

Tile cutters, used to score and break precise, straight cuts on flat tiles, especially ones thicker than ¼" (.6 cm).

Pattern Drawing & Other Supplies

Pattern Drawing Supplies

To draw your own designs, you'll want **graph paper** or brown kraft paper for making patterns, a **ruler**, a **circle template** for drawing round shapes and curves, and a **pencil**. You'll find them at crafts, arts supply, and office supply stores.

Use **transfer paper** to transfer your designs to surfaces. After transferring, go over the outline of the design with a **permanent black marker** so the lines will be easier to see once you have spread the glue and are filling in with the tiles.

Other Supplies for Creating Mosaics

Other supplies used for the projects in this section can be found at crafts stores.

Permanent enamel paints can be used to decorate plain tiles. The colors are painted or stenciled on, then baked in the oven.

Acrylic craft paints are used to paint trim areas and surfaces.

Stencils can be used with permanent enamel paints to create designs on plain tiles.

Metallic rub-on wax can be used to enhance molded plaster motifs, grout, and painted wood. Apply it with your always-available tool—your finger. (I find nothing works quite as well.) You can remove what's left on your finger when you're finished with nail polish remover.

The Direct Mosaic Technique for Patterned Tile Designs

The direct technique is the easy—what you see is what you get. The tile is cut to size and glued face up on the surface. When the glue dries, the piece is grouted. This colorful frame is a fun project that's easy for beginners. You'll need enough tile to cover about 40 square inches (101.6 cm).

PROJECT SUPPLIES

Wooden frame, 7" x 9" (17.8 x 22.9 cm)

Square tiles, ⅜" (9. cm) and ⅞" (2.2 cm), in 10 different colors

4 round tiles, 1" (2.5 cm), in various colors

7 round tiles, ½" (1.3 cm), in various colors

3 round tiles, ⅝" (1.6 cm), in various colors

White craft glue

Clear acrylic sealer

Non-sanded grout—white

TOOLS & OTHER SUPPLIES

Sandpaper, 220 grit

Circle template; Ruler; Pencil

Black permanent marker; Graph paper

Tile nippers; Safety goggles

Glue spreader or craft stick

Plastic container; Latex gloves

Rubber spatula; Measuring cup

Sponge; Stiff bristle brush; Soft cloth

Metal or plastic bowl

Prepare Surface & Transfer Design

1. All surfaces should be oil-free and clean. To prepare a wooden surface, sand lightly to be sure the area where the tiles will be glued is even and to smooth any part of the surface that will be painted. Wipe or brush away sanding dust.

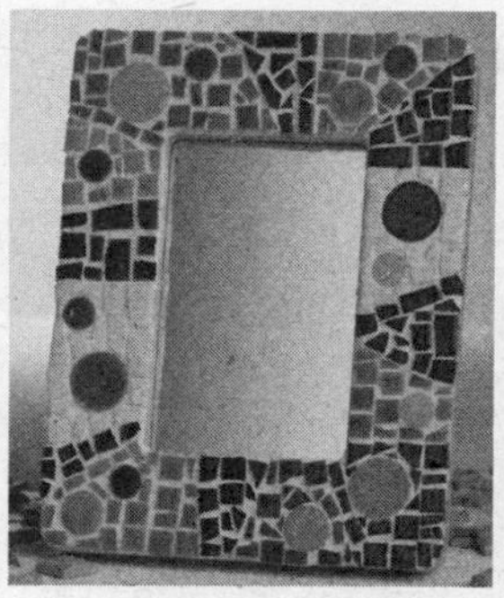

2. Seal the areas of the wood where you're planning to glue the tile with clear acrylic sealer to protect them from the moisture of the grout. Let dry.

3. Draw the design to size on graph paper (**photo 1**) or, if you're using a pattern, trace the pattern on tracing paper. Using transfer paper and a stylus, transfer the design to the surface.

Continued ➡

Prepare Tiles

4. Using tile nippers, nip square tiles into a variety of smaller shapes (**photo 2**). Just nip about ⅛" (.3 cm) and the tile will snap across. They will not always break perfectly—don't be concerned! That's part of the beauty and forgiving nature of mosaics. *To break a large number of tiles,* place the tiles between layers of newspaper, in a brown grocery bag, or inside a thick plastic bag. Use a rubber mallet to strike the tiles and break them into smaller pieces. Don't overdo it though, or you'll end up with tiny shards and dust.

Photo 1

Photo2

Attach Tiles to the Surface

5. **Spread Glue**: Working one small section at a time, spread glue on the project surface with a rubber spatula or a craft stick (**photo 3**). It's also a good idea to spread glue on the backs of the larger tile pieces for better contact and adhesion.

Photo 3

6. **Place Tiles**: Place the key design pieces (in this case, the circular tiles) first. Then position the remaining tiles, one section at a time (**photo 4**).

7. **Nip to Fit As You Go Along**: As you place the tiles, nip pieces to fit as needed (**photo 5**). This is like putting the pieces of a puzzle together. Remember they don't have to fit perfectly—that's what grout is for!

Photo 4

Grout the Design

8. **Mix**: Measure grout and water in a plastic container, following package instructions (**photo 6**). With experience, you'll learn to judge how much grout you need to mix.

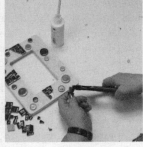

Photo 5

- How much grout you need depends on the size of the piece and how close together the pieces are. A larger mosaic, of course, requires more grout than a small one. A mosaic piece where the tiles are farther apart will require more grout than a piece of the same size where the tiles are placed closer together.

- You can buy colored grout or mix in a colorant. If you're using a colorant, mix it in as you mix the grout.

- You can't save unused grout if you mix too much, so if you're not using a colorant, mix a little at a time, use that, and mix more as needed. If you're using a colorant, you need to mix all the grout you need at once so all the grout in the piece will be the same color.

9. **Spread Grout**: Using a rubber spatula, a craft stick, or your gloves fingers, spread the grout over the design and push the grout into all areas between the tiles (**photo 7**). Personally, I prefer to use a gloved finger. There is no tool that works better for "feeling" that you've packed the grout into spaces properly.

Photo 6

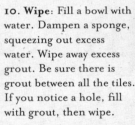

Photo 7

10. **Wipe**: Fill a bowl with water. Dampen a sponge, squeezing out excess water. Wipe away excess grout. Be sure there is grout between all the tiles. If you notice a hole, fill with grout, then wipe.

11. Rinse the sponge, squeeze out excess water, and wipe again. Do this over and over until all the tile pieces are visible through the grout (**photo 8**). Wipe gently but thoroughly. Allow 15 minutes to dry.

Photo 8

12. **Brush**: Before the grout is completely dry, brush away any "crumbs" of grout with a stiff bristle brush—you can use a throwaway bristle brush or old toothbrush (**photo 9**). Let dry completely.

13. **Polish**: As the grout dries, a haze or film will form over the tile. When the piece is completely dry, polish off the haze by rubbing with a soft cloth (**photo 10**). The tiles or glass will return to a beautiful gleam.

Photo 9

Finish the Piece

14. Sand the edges of the frame with sandpaper to smooth the edges of the grout and to remove any stray grout from the sides of the frame (**photo 11**). Wipe away dust.

15. Paint the edges of the frame with acrylic craft paint, using a foam brush (**photo 12**). You may want to use a smaller brush for this. Also, be sure to paint the inside edges where the mirror will reflect the wood.

Note: *You can also choose to paint your project surface before beginning mosaics. If you do this, you may need to touch up the paint after mosaic has dried. I do whatever method seems best for a particular project.*

Photo 10

Photo 11

Photo 12

Photo 13

Mixed Media Technique with Random Placement

Tiles, molded plaster pieces, flatbacked marbles, and the broken pieces of a floral patterned china plate are combined to make this mosaic frame. After the plaster pieces and flatbacked marbles are glued in place, the space around and between them is filled with randomly placed broken china, whole tiles, and pieces of tile. The size of the mosaic area is 33 square inches (83.8 square cm).

PROJECT SUPPLIES

Wooden frame, 6" x 8" (15.2 x 20.3 cm)

15 square pink tiles, ⅜" (1 cm)

9 flatbacked opalescent marbles, pink and white

China plate with pink floral motifs and gold border

Plaster molds:

    Right-facing angel

    Left-facing angel

    Large star

    Medium star

Craft plaster

Gold metallic rub-on wax

White craft glue

Acrylic craft paint—pink

Non-sanded grout—white

Grout colorant—pink

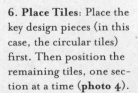

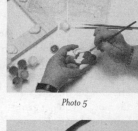

Photo 4

Tools & Other Supplies

Sandpaper, 220 grit

Newspaper

Rubber mallet

Tile nippers

Safety goggles

Glass nippers

Glue spreader or craft stick

Plastic container

Rubber spatula

Metal or plastic bowl

Sponge

Latex gloves

1" (2.5 cm) foam brush

Prepare the China

1. Place the china plate between several thicknesses of newspaper (**photo 1**).

Photo 1

2. Hold a runner mallet at a slight angle above the plate between the thicknesses of newspaper (**photo 2**). Hit the plate with the mallet. The plate will break into large pieces. *Be sure to wear safety goggles.*

3. Lift newspaper occasionally to check the size of the pieces (**photo 3**). Keep smashing away until the pieces are easy to handle and close to the size you want.

Photo 2

4. Break china into smaller pieces or pieces of specific sizes and shapes with glass nippers (**photo 4**). Be careful—the pieces can be sharp—wear gloves and safety goggles.

Prepare Plaster Pieces

5. Mold plaster pieces, following instructions on the plaster package.

Photo 3

6. When dry, molded plaster pieces can be painted with paints made specifically for painting plaster or with acrylic craft paints (**photo 5**).

Photo 5

7. For an easy metallic finish for your plaster pieces, rub on gold metallic wax for gleam and shine (**photo 6**).

Attach Pieces to Surface

8. Glue plaster pieces and flatbacked marbles in place. Spread glue on backs of larger pieces (**photo 7**). For smaller pieces, spread glue on project surface.

Photo 6

9. Fill in the space between and around the plaster pieces and marbles with broken china, whole tiles, and broken tiles. Use photo as a guide. Attach all pieces. Let dry.

Photo 7

Grout the Design

10. Mix dry grout with water in a plastic container, using proportions specified on the grout package. If you want colored grout, mix dye colorant with grout according to package instructions (**photo 8**).

11. Spread grout around the plaster pieces and over the tiles and broken china, using a rubber spatula (**photo 9**). Try to keep grout off the tops of the plaster pieces.

12. Wipe away excess grout with a damp sponge. Let dry about 15 minutes.

Photo 8

13. Brush away grout crumbs with a stiff bristle brush. Allow project to dry completely.

Photo 9

Finish the Project

14. Polish the piece with a soft cloth.

15. If, in applying the grout, some of the paint or metallic wax is removed from a plaster piece or grout gets lodged in a crevice of a plaster piece, touch up the plaster with paint or metallic wax after the grout has dried (**photo 10**).

16. Paint the edges of the frame with pink paint.

Photo 10

Mosaics on Curved Surfaces

Creating a mosaic on a curved surface is a challenge that's easily accomplished by using a full-bodied adhesive, such as a silicone adhesive, as a glue. The adhesive fills the

---

space between the curved project surface and grabs it, keeping the flat tiles from sliding while you work. Be sure to read and follow the adhesive manufacturer's instructions and cautions and work in a well-ventilated area.

Project Supplies

2 white ceramic pots, 5" and 6" (12.7 and 15.2 cm) diameter (or terra cotta pots painted white)

1 terra cotta pot, 4" (10.1 cm) diameter

125 square tiles, ⅜" (1 cm), for the 6" (15.2 cm) pot:

  Green

  Teal

  Cream

40 square tiles, ½" (1.3 cm), for the 5" (12.7 cm) pot:

  Red

  Dark Blue

  Light Blue

  Mauve

30 square tiles, ½" (1.3 cm), for the 4" (10.1 cm) pot:

  Light blue

  Turquoise

  Teal

  Green

  Peach

Clear silicone adhesive

Gold metallic rub-on wax

Dried leaves and flowers in several colors

Clear acrylic varnish

Non-sanded grout—buttercream

White craft glue

Decoupage finish

Tools & Other Supplies

1" (2.5 cm) foam brush

Toothpicks

Glue spreader, such as a craft stick

Rubber spatula

Plastic gloves

Decoupage scissors

Disposable plastic container

Craft stick

Metal or plastic bowl

Sponge

Continued →

Measuring cup

Soft cloth

Safety goggles

PREPARE SURFACE

1. Be sure pots are clean and dry. To seal terra cotta pots, apply clear varnish inside and out. Let dry.

2. Apply leaves and flowers to sides of pots, using photo as a guide for placement or creating your own designs.

- Trim the leaves and flowers with decoupage scissors as needed to complete your design.
- Apply decoupage finish to surface of pot where you wish dried flowers and leaves to be placed.
- Press the leaves and flowers firmly with a damp paper towel, being sure there are no air bubbles. Use paper towel to wipe away excess finish.
- If the flowers start to lift, use a toothpick and some white glue to glue them back down.

3. Apply two to three coats clear acrylic varnish to the sides of the pot over the leaves and flowers (**photo 1**). Let dry between coats. Let final coat dry completely.

Photo 1

Prepare Tiles

4. Measure the circumference of the pot and decide how many tiles you'll need to circle the rim by dividing the circumference in inches by the width of the tiles in inches (or cm x cm). (Approximate numbers for each pot are listed with Project Supplies.)

5. Select the tiles, choosing pleasing combinations of colors, to be glued in rows around the tops of the pots (**photo 2**).

Photo 2

Attach Tiles

6. Spread the silicone adhesive on one section of the rim of the pot (**photo 3**).

- A thick glue such as a silicone adhesive holds the pieces in place on the curved surface and dries quickly.
- Use enough glue to hold the tiles and fill the gap between the flat back of the tile and curved surface of the pot, but don't use so much that the glue fills the spaces between the tiles or squishes up between the tiles.
- Remove any excess adhesive that squishes up between the tiles with a toothpick while the adhesive is still wet.

7. Place tiles on rim over glue (**photo 4**). Add more glue, then more tiles, working around the rim. Check the spacing of the tiles as you get near the end, you may need to place the tiles just slightly closer together or just slightly farther apart to get a good fit. Let glue dry.

Photo 3   *Photo 4*

Grout

8. Mix grout in a plastic container, following package instructions.

9. Wearing a protective glove, spread the grout over the design and push the grout into all areas between the tiles (**photo 5**). Try to keep the grout on the rim and not on the sides of the pot. If you get grout on the sides of the pot, wipe away immediately.

10. Wipe away excess grout with a damp sponge. Allow to dry about 15 minutes.

11. Wipe away grout crumbs with a stiff bristle brush.

12. When the grout dries, there will be haze or film over the tile. Polish the haze off with a soft cloth.

Photo 5

Photo 6

Finishing

13. Rub gold metallic wax on the top edge of each pot.

Ungrouted Mosaic Effects

You also can create interesting mosaic effects without grout, using polished glass pieces, which are available in clear, iridescent, and a variety of colors. In the ungrouted mosaic technique, the glass pieces are arranged on a surface and attached with clear adhesive.

PROJECT SUPPLIES

2 wood photo frames, 4" x 5" (10.1 x 12.7 cm)

Gold spray paint

Clear silicone adhesive

Clear and iridescent polished glass pieces

Purple, blue, and green polished glass pieces

Sandpaper, 220 grit

Tweezers

Prepare Surface

1. Sand frames lightly. Wipe away dust.

2. Spray both frames with gold paint, being sure to achieve complete coverage. Let dry completely.

3. Apply silicone adhesive to a section of one frame (**photo 1**).

Place Glass Pieces

4. Arrange glass pieces over silicone adhesive.

5. Apply adhesive to another part of the frame and arrange glass pieces (**photo 2**). Use photo as a guide for placement. Repeat, working around the frame until the surface is covered with glass pieces. (Be sure to remove any excess adhesive before it dries—once dry, it is nearly impossible to remove.)

Photo 1

Photo 2

---

6. Add a second layer of glass pieces to partially cover the first. You will find tweezers helpful when placing smaller glass pieces. See photo for placement ideas. Let dry.

7. Use the same technique to apply glass pieces to the second frame. In these examples, the frame on the right was decorated with clear and iridescent glass pieces, and the frame on the left was decorated with colored glass pieces.

Wonderful Projects for Your Home

Each project includes step-by-step instructions and a list of tesserae and other supplies for that project. For most of the projects in this section, you'll also need the basic tools & supplies as listed below.

BASIC TOOLS & SUPPLIES FOR ALL PROJECTS

Keep the following tools and supplies on hand for each of the mosaic projects you create.

Tile nippers

Sponge

Rubber mallet

Metal or plastic bowl

Glue spreader or craft stick

Stiff bristle brush

Plastic container for mixing grout

Soft cloth

Rubber spatula

Safety goggles

Measuring cup

Latex gloves

Veggie Delight Frame

METHOD:

Mixed Media

MOSAIC AREA:

113 square inches (287 square cm)

SUPPLIES

Wooden frame, 12" x 14" (30.5 x 35.6 cm) with a 6-½" x 8-½" (16.5 x 21.6 cm) opening

Square tiles, 1" (2.5 cm):

Green

Red

Yellow

White

18 flatbacked marbles, ½" (1.3 cm), in various colors

Plaster molds—vegetable shapes and garden motifs:

Watering can

Peas

Corn

Eggplant

Bell pepper

Tomato

Carrot

Watermelon

Craft plaster

Plaster paints or acrylic craft paints:

Light green

Dark green

Orange

Bright pink

Yellow

Gray

Red

Purple

Transparent gold metallic paint

Plaster sealer—gloss finish

Sanded grout—white

Strong coffee (less than a cup)

Small sponge

Paint brushes for decorative painting

Basic tools & supplies

INSTRUCTIONS

PREPARE PLASTER PIECES:

1. Mold the plaster pieces according to package instructions. Let dry.

2. Paint with plaster paints or acrylic craft paints. Let dry.

3. Paint plaster pieces with transparent gold metallic paint. The paint will settle in the crevices and add shimmer to the plaster pieces.

4. Coat the plaster pieces with several coats of gloss finish plaster sealer to protect them from the grout. Let dry between coats.

PREPARE TILES:

5. Nip green tiles in half to create oblong pieces.

6. Nip red and yellow tiles into pieces about ½" square (1.3 cm square).

7. Break the white tiles into small rectangles in a variety of sizes.

8. Glue green tiles around inside edge of frame.

9. Glue red and yellow tiles, alternating colors, around the outer edge of the frame.

ATTACH PIECES:

10. Glue the plaster pieces to the frame, using photo as a guide for placement.

11. Glue the flatbacked marbles to the frame, using photo as a guide for placement.

12. Fill in the space between the borders and around the plaster pieces and marbles with white tiles. Nip the tiles as needed to fit. Let glue dry.

GROUT:

13. Mix grout and spread over mosaic. Spread the grout right up to **but not over** the plaster pieces—sanded grout can scratch the paint on the plaster. Wipe away excess grout. Let dry.

14. Buff with a soft cloth to remove haze.

15. Tint the grout with very strong coffee, dabbing it on with a sponge until you achieve a tint you like. Let dry.

FINISH:

16. If needed, touch up the paint on the plaster pieces. Add another coat of gloss sealer to seal the new paint.

Library Mosaic Bookends

Simple wooden bookends found at a thrift shop or yard sale become a colorful accessory when decorated with tiles. Look for bookends with nice flat surfaces. Small decorated tiles can be hand painted with permanent ceramic paints or purchased at tile stores. Build the color scheme around the colors of the decorated tiles.

METHOD:

Direct

MOSAIC AREA:

35 square inches (89 square cm) (The area of each bookend is 3-½" x 5" [8.9 x 12.7 cm].)

SUPPLIES

1 pair wooden bookends

2 square decorated tiles, 2" x 2" (5.5 x 5.5 cm) in blues and greens

Square tiles, ⅜" (.9 cm), in coordinating colors and white

Acrylic craft paint—deep blue

Non-sanded grout—deep blue

White craft glue

Sandpaper, 220 grit

Tack cloth

½" (1.3 cm) foam brush

Basic tools & supplies

INSTRUCTIONS

PREPARATION:

1. Lightly sand surfaces of bookends to prepare for painting. Wipe away dust.

2. Position the bookends on the edge of your work surface so you are working horizontally. Glue a decorated tile at center of each bookend.

ATTACH TESSERAE:

3. Glue square tiles around edges to create a border, alternating colors. See photo.

4. Fill in area between border and decorated tiles with white tiles. Nip as needed to fit. Let dry.

GROUT:

5. Mix grout and apply over tiles. Wipe away excess. Let dry.

6. Wipe away haze with a soft cloth.

FINISH:

7. Clean grout from areas to be painted with sandpaper, if needed. Wipe away dust.

8. Paint edges with deep blue paint. Let dry.

Place of Honor Bowl

This is a grand way to turn an old wooden salad bowl into a piece of art. Have fun combining scraps and snippets of china and pieces of broken tiles with various irregularly shaped tiles to create lovely colors and shapes.

METHOD:

Mixed Media

MOSAIC SIZE:

To determine, measure the circumference of your bowl. Multiply by the height of the bowl.

SUPPLIES

Wooden bowl

Variety of unusually shaped tiles, various colors

Pieces of broken tiles

Pieces of broken china

Acrylic craft paints:

Gloss white

Metallic gold

Silicone adhesive

Clear gloss spray sealer

Plastic wrap

Disposable plate or palette

Sanded grout—gray blue

Sandpaper, 220 grit

Tack cloth

Masking tape

Basic tools & supplies

INSTRUCTIONS

PREPARATION:

1. Sand bowl to smooth surface. Wipe away dust with a tack cloth.

2. Paint the bowl, inside and out, with gloss white paint. Let dry.

ATTACH TESSERAE:

3. Glue china pieces, tile pieces, and tiles randomly to sides and bottom of bowl with silicone adhesive. Let dry.

GROUT:

4. Mix grout according to package instructions. Spread over tiles and china pieces. Wipe away excess. Let dry.

5. Wipe away haze with a soft cloth.

FINISH:

6. Remove any grout from the top edge or inside of the bowl. Sand if needed. Paint the inside and the top edge of the bowl with another coat of gloss white paint. Let dry.

7. Pour a little gold metallic paint on a disposable plate or palette. Cut a piece of plastic wrap about 6" x 6" (15.2 x 15.2 cm). Wearing a disposable latex glove, crumple the plastic, dip in paint, blot on a paper towel, and press on the inside of the bowl to create a mottled look. Continue dipping, blotting, and pressing until the inside of the bowl is mottled. Let dry completely.

8. Mask off the mosaic area with tape. Spray the inside of the bowl with one to two coats gloss sealer. Let dry. Remove tape.

—FROM *Mosaics in an Afternoon*

Continued ➡

FIRST TIME MOSAICS

Alison Hepburn

This section contains simple, first-time projects for people who want to try their hand at mosaics but who have no experience. The next three projects in this section use uncut tiles of different sizes and shapes so you can get used to handling the materials without concerns about shaping the tiles or the expense of wastage.

Trivet

Direct method

A mosaic trivet for the center of a table is both decorative and functional. It is a good project to start on because of its simple shape and, if the size is planned carefully to accommodate the tiles, there is no need for cutting. This allows the freedom to play with color and pattern, and it is very easy to progress to a design of your own. I have used glass tiles because of their beauty and because, unlike some ceramic tiles, they do not stain and are heat resistant.

MATERIALS

Vitreous tiles

Fiberboard (MDF) or plywood 11 x 11 inches (30 x 30 cm)

White paper for design

Pencil

Trace down paper

Permanent marker

Sharp knife

White craft glue (EVA) and brush

Rubber gloves

Grout and squeegee

Clean cloth

Tile cleaner

Black enamel or gloss paint, primer, brush, and cleaner

INSTRUCTIONS

1. Draw the grid on white paper and then trace it down on the fiberboard, reinforcing it with the permanent marker. Score the fiberboard for added purchase.

2. By crosshatching the pattern in at this stage there is less chance of becoming confused and putting the wrong color tiles down later.

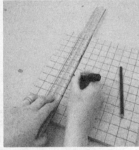

Photo 1

3. Starting with the dark red tiles for the border, use the brush to apply glue to the reverse (grooved) side of the tiles. Do not put it on too thickly or it will ooze out between the tiles, but make sure there is enough to cover the back. Continue until the border is complete.

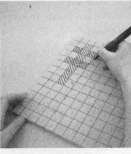

Photo 2

 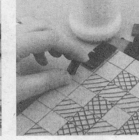

Photo 3a *Photo 3b*

4. Begin the central pattern by sticking down the first color using the crosshatching on the board to ensure that the pattern is correct.

5. Continue the design by adding the second color tiles.

Photo 4 *Photo 5*

6. Glue the third color tiles in place to complete the pattern.

7. Leave 24 hours for the glue to dry thoroughly. Be careful at this stage because, until the work is grouted, the tiles are vulnerable to damage. Grout and clean the mosaic and paint the edges.

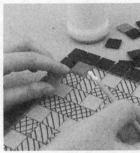 

Photo 6 *Photo 7*

Chessboard

Direct Method

Chess sets have an intrinsic beauty that is rarely matched by the board, and which is usually a piece of folded paper or board that is put away when the game has finished. By making a permanent chessboard you can create an object that will always encourage people to play, can be left out set up as part of the furniture, and which will last as long as the pieces themselves. I have chosen a glass chess set to complement the glass tiles.

MATERIALS

Vitreous tiles in two sizes

Fiberboard (MDF) or plywood 21.25 x 21.25 inches (54 x 54 cm)

White paper for the design

Pencil

Trace down paper

Permanent marker

Sharp knife

White craft glue (EVA) and brush

Rubber gloves

Grout and squeegee

Clean cloth

Tile cleaner

Black enamel or gloss paint, primer, brush, and brush cleaner

INSTRUCTIONS

1. Transfer the design from white paper to the fiberboard using the trace down paper, and reinforce with a permanent marker. Score the board for added purchase.

2. Crosshatch the squares for the border to clarify which colors are used where in the pattern.

 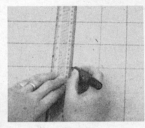

Photo 1 *Photo 2*

3. Starting with the large black and white tiles, glue each tile down.

4. Be careful to keep the space between the tiles even.

5. Start on the first color for the border, laying the tiles out carefully according to the design.

6. Continue the design by adding the second color tiles.

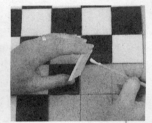 

Photo 3 *Photo 4*

Photo 5 *Photo 6*

Photo 7

7. Glue the third color tiles in place to complete the pattern.

8. Leave 24 hours for the glue to dry thoroughly. Be careful at this stage because, until the tiles are grouted, they are vulnerable to being chipped or dislodged. Grout and clean the mosaic and paint the edges of the board.

Sun Catcher

Direct method ungrouted

Mosaic has a long history and has developed over the years as new materials have been invented and discovered. The use of silicone glue enables us to stick clear glass tiles and other objects to clear glass or perspex. While this isn't a traditional mosaic method, it enables us to get the full

glory of the glass in a way that wasn't available before. Glass is such a beautiful material that it seems a pity to leave this aspect of it to the stained glass artists and therefore I have included this project.

I have used flower arrangers' beads and shapes that combine well with the transparent tiles to create the design. While feeling at liberty to use anything transparent that has caught my eye, I have retained the feel of a mosaic in the formality of my design and the use of repeated squares.

MATERIALS

Collection of transparent glass tiles and glass beads

Perspex 7.75 x 13 inches (19.7 x 33 cm), with holes drilled

White paper for the design

Pencil

Silicone glue

Sharp knife

Wire for hanging

1. Draw the design out onto a piece of white paper the same size as the perspex.

2. Place the perspex on top of the design with the holes at the top and start to stick down the tiles, beginning with the border and being careful not to cover the drilled holes. Do not add too much glue because it is difficult to remove later if it oozes out onto the perspex. (Excess glue can be cut off when dry with a sharp knife.)

Photo 1

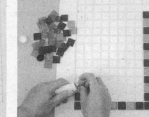
Photo 2

3. Keep the design very even and, when putting in the glass beads or other objects, place the tiles around them first—to keep the spacing correct—before gluing the irregular shapes.

Photo 3

4. There is no grouting, but regular spacing will provide continuity amid the mixture of colors and shapes.

5. Continue gluing the tiles until you reach a single line in the middle.

Photo 4a

Photo 4b

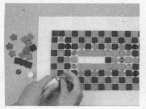
Photo 5a

Photo 5b

6. The glue takes 12 hours to dry completely, although it is touch-dry in 15 minutes. There is no need to grout or clean this piece so when it is dry, thread the wire through the holes ready to hang.

—FROM *Beginner's Guide to Mosaics*

MOSAICS WITH PRESSED FLOWERS UNDER GLASS

Connie Sheerin

You can make beautiful tiles to use in your mosaics by sandwiching arrangements of pressed flowers and leaves between two pieces of glass and securing the edges with adhesive-backed foil tape. Use decorative papers, foil, or leaf to create backgrounds for the arrangements…

Making Glass Sandwich Tiles

Supplies

- **Glass squares,** ⅛" (.3 cm) thick, 2 for each tile. The sizes I use most are 2" (5 cm) and 4" (10.2 cm) squares. In the photos that follows, 4" (10.2 cm) glass was used.

Tip: Find a glass shop in your area that is willing to cut squares of glass for you.

- **Pressed flowers, fern fronds, and leaves.** Press your own flowers or purchase packaged pressed flowers.
- **Background,** such as handmade paper, foil, or metallic leaf.
- **Adhesive,** such as a glue stick or white craft glue, to hold background paper and pressed florals in place.
- **Adhesive-backed foil tape,** to seal the edges of the glass sandwich.
- **Scissors,** for cutting the paper or trimming the flowers and leaves.
- **Tweezers,** for arranging the flowers and moving foil and metallic leaf.
- **Toothpicks,** for applying glue to flowers and leaves.

Attach Backing

Cut paper backing to size with scissors. Rub glue stick over one side of piece of glass. Press paper to glass.

Arrange Flowers

Create an arrangement with pressed flowers and greenery on the paper backing, working back to front. Hold the pressed florals with tweezers while you use a toothpick to apply tiny amounts of glue to their backs to help hold them in place.

Use the tweezers to position the pressed pieces on the paper backing.

Cover with Glass & Add Foil Tape to Edges

When your arrangement is complete, place the second piece of glass squarely on top of the first, making a sandwich. (The glass pieces are the bread, the arrangement is the filling.) Study the arrangement to be sure the result pleases you.

Wrap the edges of the glass sandwich with adhesive-backed metallic foil tape. Starting at one corner, stick the tape on and guide it all the way around the glass sandwich, making sure to smooth it as you go so as not to leave any air bubbles. Overlap the tape about ½" (1.3 cm) at the end. Go back and be sure it is tightly sealed—you don't want grout or moisture to leak in and spoil your sandwich tile when you grout the piece. **Caution:** Be careful—glass edges can be sharp!

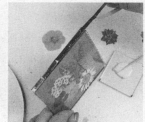

Terra Cotta Candle Holder

SUPPLIES

Terra cotta candle holder with a top that slants from 3" to 5" (7.6 to 12.7 cm)

8 tiles, ¾" (1.9 cm)—2 each in terra cotta, purple, light purple, yellow

2 pieces of ⅛" (.3 cm) thick glass, 2" (5 cm) square

Adhesive-backed foil tape, ¼" (.6 cm) wide

Mixed color faux foil leaf

Foil leaf adhesive

Pressed pansy, ferns, leaves

Tile nippers

Tweezers

Glue stick or white glue

Sanded grout—buttercream

Toothpick

Gold metallic wax

Small scissors

Soft scrubby brush

INSTRUCTIONS

PREPARE:

Nip colored tiles into pieces about ¼" to ½" (.6 to 1.3 cm).

Continued ➔

MAKE GLASS SANDWICH TILE:

1. Apply foil adhesive to one piece of the 2" (5 cm) glass squares, following package instructions.

2. Using tweezers, place different colored pieces of foil over the adhesive. Allow to dry about five minutes.

3. Wipe over the foil very gently with a soft scrubby brush.

4. Pick up pansy with tweezers. Put a dot or two of white glue on the back of the pansy, using a toothpick. Position pansy on foiled background. Allow to dry.

5. Put the second piece of glass over the pansy. Seal the edges of the glass with adhesive-backed foil tape. Press it on well—you don't want grout or moisture to leak in when you grout the piece.

ATTACH TESSERAE:

1. Glue glass sandwich tile to the front of the terra cotta candle.

2. Glue tile pieces all around the glass tile, mixing the colors. Let dry.

GROUT:

1. Mix grout. Spread over tesserae. Wipe away excess. Let dry.

2. Wipe away haze with a soft cloth.

FINISH:

Embellish the edges of the candle holder with gold metallic wax.

—FROM *Backyard Mosaics*

MOSAIC TECHNIQUE: INDIRECT METHOD

Suzan Germond

Indirect mosaic methods should be used when you want to create a mosaic with a flat surface, such as a tabletop or chair seat, using materials of varying thicknesses or when you want to create your mosaic in one location and install it elsewhere. There are several different techniques.

In the **reverse method**, you temporarily glue tesserae upside down and backwards on brown kraft paper. After the glue dries, you pre-grout the mosaic, prepare the surface with adhesive mortar, and turn the mosaic onto the mortar adhesive. When it dries, you wet the brown paper, remove it, then grout.

The **double reverse method** is simpler and less intimidating because you always see the front of your project. You create the mosaic on a low density polyethylene mounting paper. This transparent, waxy paper has a smooth side and a sticky side, much like clear self-adhesive shelf paper, but with different adhesion and release properties. (Tesserae won't remain attached to regular self-adhesive paper throughout this process.) You place your tesserae on the sticky side of the mounting paper and cover it with another piece of mounting paper with the sticky side down so the mosaic is sandwiched between the two pieces of mounting paper. To install the mosaic, you flip it over, remove the bottom piece of mounting paper, and turn it over into a bed of cement adhesive and level the surface. When it dries, peel off the top piece of mounting paper and then grout.

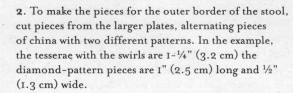

Black & White Mosaic Stool

The **Black & White Mosaic Stool** is used as an example to show the indirect mosaic technique.

Supplies for Stool

SURFACE:

Wooden stool with round seat

TESSERAE:

5 black-and-white patterned plates, 12" (30.5 cm) diameter

6 plates with black-and-white patterned rims, 6" (15.2 cm) diameter

1 plate with black-and-white patterned rim, 8" (20.3 cm) diameter

9 round mirror pieces, various sizes (¼" to 2" [or 6 to 5 cm])

4 white plastic buttons, 1-¼" (3.2 cm) diameter

3 polymer clay beads with yin-yang pattern

7 round black ceramic tiles, ½" (1.3 cm)

8 black-and-white buttons, ⅜" (1 cm) diameter

13 small black-and-white patterned millefiori

OTHER SUPPLIES

2 sheets mosaic mounting paper (sold online)

White thinset mortar

Sanded grout—White

Cement colorant—Yellow

Grout sealer

Acrylic paints—Black, cream

Paint brushes

Painter's masking tape

Sandpaper

White primer

Tile cleaner

Safety gear

TOOLS:

Wheel cutters *and/or* tile nippers

Button shank remover *optional*

Notched trowel

Level

PREPARE THE STOOL

1. Clean, sand, and prime the stool.

2. Design a pattern for your stool. Draw the design on white paper, using the photo as a guide.

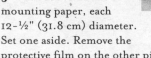

3. Cut out two circles of mounting paper, each 12-½" (31.8 cm) diameter. Set one aside. Remove the protective film on the other piece of mounting paper (Photo 1) and place it, sticky side up, on top of the pattern.

Photo 1

Prepare the Tesserae

1. Use either wheel cutters (for thinner plates) or tile nippers (for thicker plates) to break the rims from the plates. (Photos 2 & 3)

---

2. To make the pieces for the outer border of the stool, cut pieces from the larger plates, alternating pieces of china with two different patterns. In the example, the tesserae with the swirls are 1-¼" (3.2 cm) the diamond-pattern pieces are 1" (2.5 cm) long and ½" (1.3 cm) wide.

3. Cut ½" (1.3 cm) square pieces of china to make two rings inside the border. Choose four motifs for these pieces; you will alternate the two motifs on each ring.

Photo 2

Photo 3

Position the Tesserae

1. Beginning with the outer ring, select pieces of cut china one at a time and press firmly on the sticky paper that is on top of the pattern. (Photo 4)

2. When the outer border pieces are in place, position the next two rings of cut pieces. (Photo 5)

3. Fill the center area of the mosaic with buttons, beads, mirror circles, millefiori, and round black tiles.

Photo 4

4. When all the pieces are attached, take the second circle of mounting paper and remove the protective film.

5. Lay the mounting paper, sticky side down, on top of the mosaic. (Photos 6 & 7) Press to adhere so the mosaic is sandwiched between two pieces of mounting paper. Because the pieces are not uniform in height, be sure to individually burnish each piece to the mounting paper. (Photo 8)

6. Turn over the mosaic, which is sandwiched between the two pieces of mounting paper. The tesserae will not be upside down. (Photo 9) **Tip:** This is easier, particularly if your mosaic is a large one, if you place the mosaic between two pieces of board when you flip it.

7. Peel off the mounting paper from the bottom of the mosaic. (Photo 10) Your tesserae are now upside down, still adhered to the second sheet of mounting paper.

 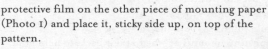

Photo 5   *Photo 6*

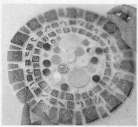

Photo 7

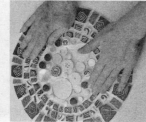

Photo 8

Photo 9

Photo 10

Apply the Mortar Base

1. Mix two to three cups of white thinset mortar. Tint it with cement colorant to achieve a pale yellow color.

2. Use your hands or a large spoon to place the thinset mortar on the seat of the stool. (Photo 11)

3. Spread the mortar with hands to evenly distribute it. (Photo 12)

4. Use a notched trowel with widely spaced teeth to level the thinset, dragging the trowel across the seat so it creates ridges and evenly distributes the adhesive mortar on the surface. (Photo 13) **Note:** This mortar bed must be slightly thicker than your thickest tesserae so the surface of the finished mosaic will be flat. Remove extra mortar from sides of stool.

5. Flip the tesserae, still attached to mounting paper, onto the seat of the stool. (Photos 14 & 15)

Photo 11

Photo 12

Photo 13

Photo 14

Photo 15

Photo 16

6. Press the mosaic in place. Do not press too hard because you don't want the thinset to ooze up too far between the tiles. (Photo 16)

7. Use a level to make sure the top of the mosaic is flat. (Photo 17)

8. Use a sponge to wipe away excess thinset from around the edge of the mosaic. (Photo 18) Let dry completely (24 hours).

9. Peel off the mounting paper. (Photo 19)

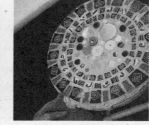

Photo 17

Photo 18

Grout the Mosaic

Photo 19

1. Mix the grout, using the same proportion of colorant to white grout powder that you used to tint the white thinset. (You only need a small amount of grout. Because the colored thinset will be exposed along the edge of the stool it is important to use a grout that matches the thinset color.)

2. Use your gloved hand or a spatula to place about a handful of grout on the surface. Press the grout into the spaces between the tesserae. Repeat until all areas of the mosaic have been grouted.

3. With a damp sponge, wipe away excess grout. Use circular strokes.

4. Use paper towels to wipe off the rest of the excess grout. Let dry.

Finish

1. Use painter's tape to mask off wide bands on the legs of the stool, using the photo as a guide. Paint the stretchers, the edge of the seat, and the bands with black paint. Remove tape and let dry completely.

2. Mask off and paint the remaining areas of the stool with cream paint. Let dry.

3. Varnish the painted portions. Let dry.

4. Seal the mosaic grout with grout sealer. Let dry.

—From *Found Art Mosaics*

MOSAIC PROJECTS FOR YOUR GARDEN

White Daisies Table

Designed by Carla D'Iorio

This table is widely available—the top is made of pressed fiberboard and is usually shown with a table skirt. The legs screw into the bottom of the tabletop. This is a good design for beginners. Be sure to seal the surface before you start your mosaic. Then let the fun begin!

Supplies

Pressed fiberboard table, 19" (48.3 cm) in diameter, 25" (63.5 cm) high

12 white tiles, 4" x 4" (10.2 x 10.2 cm)

2 red tiles, 4" x 4" (10.2 x 10.2 cm)

12 marigold yellow tiles, 4" x 4" (10.2 x 10.2 cm)

2 hunter green tiles, 4" x 4" (10.2 x 10.2 cm)

Indoor/outdoor paint—hunter green

Paint brush

Tile nippers

Sanded grout—dark green

Adhesive of your choice

Basic tools & supplies

Instructions

PREPARE:

1. Draw design on tabletop, using photo as a guide.

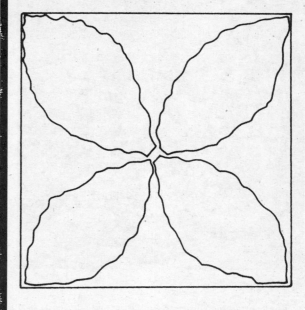

2. Nip flower petal shapes from the white tiles, using the pattern provided.

3. Nip rounded flower centers from the red tiles. Don't get stressed over making them perfect.

4. Nip the marigold tiles into different sized squares (½" to 1-¼" [or 1.3 to 3.2 cm]). (You can nip them down further later if you need some little fill-in pieces.)

5. Nip hunter green tiles ¼" to ½" (6 to 1.3 cm) to create the stems.

ATTACH TESSERAE:

1. Glue the red flower centers to the tabletop.

2. Glue the white petals around each center.

3. Glue the hunter green stems.

4. Glue marigold tile pieces around the outer edge of the table to make a frame.

5. Glue marigold tile pieces of various shapes to fill in around the flowers.

GROUT:

1. Mix grout and apply. Wipe away excess. Let dry.

2. Wipe away haze with a soft cloth.

3. Seal the grout.

FINISH:

1. Screw the legs to the table.

2. Paint the edge of the table and the legs with hunter green indoor/outdoor paint.

Continued ➡

- Make a round tabletop template. When you think of a design you like, sketch it out. These tables make great gifts.
- Buy a few of these tables when you see them on sale. You will always have a weekend project!

Grapevines Decanter & Candlestick Holders

I bought the terra cotta wine holder and the candlesticks at a thrift shop. Somehow they seemed to belong together and needed to become a set. I can see them on a deck table, where lovers have dinner with wine by candlelight on a summer evening.

SUPPLIES

Terra cotta wine cooler, 8-½" (21.6 cm) tall

2 wooden candlesticks, 5" (12.7 cm) tall

40 royal blue tiles, ¾" (1.9 cm)

4 sq. ft. (1.2 sq m) yellow stained glass

½ sq. ft. (15.2 sq m) green stained glass

1 brown and yellow speckled china bowl

19 purplish blue iridescent round marbles

Indoor/outdoor paint—navy blue

½" (1.3 cm) paint brush

Sanded grout—terra cotta

Basic tools & supplies

INSTRUCTIONS

PREPARE:

1. Sketch the placement of the grape cluster and grape leaves on the cooler.

2. Nip royal blue tiles into fourths. Make some smaller pieces.

3. Nip yellow glass into larger pieces for the cooler and smaller pieces for the candlesticks.

4. Nip green glass into medium pieces for the leaves on the cooler and smaller pieces for the candlesticks.

5. Nip pottery bowl into pieces.

ATTACH TESSERAE:

Candlesticks:

Make stripes of color, start at the top with royal blue tiles, then pottery pieces, yellow glass, green glass, yellow glass, pottery pieces, and royal blue tiles. Finish the bottom with yellow glass.

Wine Cooler:

1. Glue the marbles in place, then the leaves.

2. Trim the top edge with pieces of the speckled pottery.

3. Glue a row of the royal blue tile halves at the bottom.

4. Fill in the rest of the space with yellow glass.

GROUT:

1. Mix grout. Spread over tesserae. Wipe away excess. Let dry.

2. Wipe away haze with a soft cloth.

3. Seal grout.

FINISH:

Paint the bases of the candlesticks with navy blue paint.

Colored Glass Votive Holders

Designed by Robyn Huber

"Votives are fun and quick and so easy that kids can make them," says Robyn. "And the votives can be used right away!"

For the sun votive, Robyn used little tiny pieces of glass in red, yellow, and orange radiating out from the center, filled in the space with black glass, and finished it off with black grout. The blue star votive used star-shaped glass accent pieces and irregularly shaped blue triangles.

"Connie gave me a jelly jar," says Robyn, and the tall glass votive idea was the result. "The top was not smooth since the jar had a twist-off lid. I glued glass flowers around the top and along the sides, where I also used glass strips and glass tiles."

Sun & Moon Votives

SUPPLIES

Clear glass votive

Clear silicone glue

Stained glass pieces

Sanded grout (preferably a dark color)

Cloth rag, such as an old hand towel

Basic tools & supplies

INSTRUCTIONS

PREPARE:

1. Select the glass you want to use. Choose at least some glass that will let the fire show.

2. Cut glass shapes. The pieces should not be any bigger than ¾" (1.9 cm) on a side.

ATTACH TESSERAE:

Use a cloth rag to lay your votive on so it won't roll around while you work. Using a craft stick, apply glue to each piece of glass and place it on the votive. Place pieces no more than ½" (1.3 cm) apart. (They can be as close as you like.) Be careful not to apply too much adhesive. If the adhesive gets on the side of the glass it must be wiped off immediately. Glue all the glass on one side before moving to another side.

GROUT:

1. Mix the grout. Spread over the tesserae. Remove excess. Keep turning the votive to make sure you have grouted all sides.

2. Using a small brush, brush off any remaining grout. With a damp paper towel or cloth, wipe off the glass. Let dry 72 hours.

3. Wipe away haze with a soft cloth.

4. Seal the grout.

Tip:

- You only have to seal the grout on your votive if you are planning to leave it outside for extended periods.

Tall Glass Votive Holder

SUPPLIES

Glass jelly jar

Stained glass pieces in a variety of shapes and colors

12 glass flowers

Sanded grout—purple

Clear silicone glue

Basic tools & supplies

INSTRUCTIONS

PREPARE:

Cut glass into strips, squares, and rectangles.

ATTACH TESSERAE:

1. Glue flower shapes around top of jar, placing them so they stand up above the edge of the jar.

2. Glue remaining flower shapes on sides of the jar.

3. Glue vertical strips and rows of rectangles on sides of jar around glass flowers. Let dry.

GROUT:

1. Mix the grout. Spread over the tesserae. Remove excess. Keep turning the votive to make sure you have grouted all sides.

2. Using a small brush, brush off any remaining grout. With a damp paper towel or cloth, wipe off the glass. Let dry 72 hours.

3. Wipe away haze with a soft cloth.

4. Seal the grout if you plan to keep it out in the weather.

Mosaic Stepping Stones

Stepping stones are useful (they keep your shoes and feet clean and dry), beautiful (they add color and interest all year long), and—best of all—they are easy and quick to make. Use them in sets or as accents.

You can buy stepping stones in a variety of sizes and shapes at home improvement stores and garden centers. At crafts stores, you can buy molds and mediums for molding your own stepping stones.

Bright Flowers

At a chain plant store in our area I came across some really ugly stepping stones. Apparently they were very old stock (only three were left in the store), and the price

was very low. I am sure not even the manager thought anyone would buy them, but, of course, I did! I wish you could have seen the cashier's face when she asked me if I was sure I wanted all three. I am still chuckling! You just never know where you will find a good surface!

SUPPLIES

Stepping stone, 12" (30.5 cm)

2 lbs. (32 oz) leaf-shaped tiles in assorted sizes and colors

½ lb. (8 oz) round tiles in assorted sizes and colors

100 white tiles, ¾" (1.9 cm) or white china pieces

Indoor/outdoor paint—dark blue

1" (2.5 cm) paint brush

Sanded grout—pewter

Adhesive of your choice

Basic tools & supplies

INSTRUCTIONS

PREPARE:

1. Make a paper template of the stepping stone and lay out how many flowers you want and where you want them placed. You will need five leaf tiles for the petals for each flower and one circle for each flower center.

2. Nip lots of white tiles so once your flowers are glued down you will be able to begin filling in the background.

Patterns for flowers

ATTACH TESSERAE:

1. Glue flowers according to your paper template.

2. Glue white tile pieces to fill in around flowers. Make sure you use flat pieces along the outside edges. This frames your piece and helps keep the grout from falling off the edges.

GROUT:

1. Mix grout. Spread over tiles. Wipe away excess. Let dry.

2. Wipe away haze with a soft cloth.

3. Seal the grout.

FINISH:

Paint the outer edge with dark blue paint.

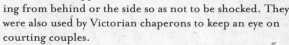
Hearts & Flowers Gazing Ball

This gazing ball idea happened a few years ago when I was asked to do something creative with an old bowling ball. Having been a disco dancing queen in my day, I immediately thought of combining the disco ball and gazing ball looks to create a conversation piece for the garden.

Victorians used gazing balls in their gardens to check who was approaching from behind or the side so as not to be shocked. They were also used by Victorian chaperons to keep an eye on courting couples.

SUPPLIES

Used bowling ball

Plastic or wood putty

1 lb. (16 oz) assorted flatbacked marbles—cat's eyes, opaque, clear, frosted, iridescent

1 lb. (16 oz) assorted color square tiles, ⅜"

½ lb. (8 oz) assorted china pieces

1 lb. (16 oz) assorted pastel ceramic tile shapes—ovals, hexagons, rectangles

1 lb. (16 oz) heart-shaped tiles in assorted colors, 1" (2.5 cm)

Mirror tiles, ½" (1.3 cm)

1 lb. (16 oz) tiles in assorted shapes

Acrylic craft paints in vibrant colors—purple, neon green, yellow, deep pink, bright yellow, turquoise, orange

Cosmetic sponges

Sanded grout—buttercream or white

Old towel

Clear silicone adhesive

Basic tools & supplies

INSTRUCTIONS

PREPARE:

1. Clean bowling ball well with soap and water. Fill the holes with plastic or wood putty. Allow a couple of days for the putty to dry thoroughly since the finger holes are fairly deep.

2. Nip some of the larger tiles into pieces so they will lie on the rounded surface.

3. Nip the china pieces to size.

4. Lay out lots of little groups of designs that you may want to incorporate all over the ball. This will make your ball very interesting to view at any angle.

ATTACH TESSERAE:

1. Set your ball on a bunched up towel to keep it from rolling as you work. Group colors and glue tiles and china pieces in sections. Let each section dry thoroughly before going onto the next one.

2. After you finish all of the sections, go back over it and fill in with bits and pieces so all the colors work together. Let dry.

GROUT:

1. Mix grout. Spread over tesserae. Wipe off excess. Let dry.

2. Wipe away haze with a soft cloth.

3. Color grout, using the multi-color technique. See "Creating Multi-Color Grout."

4. Seal with grout sealer.

Tips:

- Call your local bowling alley and ask for "damaged" and "worn-out" balls. They will be happy to recycle them to you. Although I have always offered, no one has ever asked me or my students to pay for one. (But who knows what will happen if there is a huge demand for used bowling balls!)

- This is a good place to use up bits and pieces left from other projects.

- Look for a great gazing ball stand to show off your work of art.

Sunshine Bird Bath

When I spotted this birdbath. I yelled with glee so loudly that I think I scared shoppers for several aisles. (My husband, who is getting used to these sorts of reactions, nonchalantly followed the sound. He smiled, knowing that there had to be something more wonderful than he could see.)

It was different and like none other I had ever seen, not to mention that it is lightweight and the top comes off. I had been saving that round sun tile for something very special, and this was it! You will love matching the colors and working around the colors in your centerpiece tile.

SUPPLIES

Wrought iron birdbath, 3 ft. (91.4 cm) high with a 16" (40.6 cm) wide bowl

52 royal blue tiles, ¾" (1.9 cm)

36 yellow tiles, ¾" (1.9 cm)

6 iridescent gold glass stars, ¾" (1.9 cm)

6 iridescent blue glass stars, ¾" (1.9 cm)

Round sun handpainted tile, 4-¼" (10.8 cm)

18 round tiles, various sizes and colors

8 flatbacked marbles, various colors

14 yellow tiles, ⅜" (1 cm)

14 gold ochre tiles, ⅜" (1 cm)

Broken pieces from a brown and gold patterned piece of pottery or china

Broken pieces from a goldish tan piece of pottery or china

Sanded grout—dark blue

Adhesive

Basic tools & supplies

Continued ➡

INSTRUCTIONS

PREPARATION:

1. Nip all the pottery pieces so once you start gluing you can just continue working the design.

2. Cut the yellow ¾" (1.9 cm) tiles in half.

ATTACH TESSERAE:

1. Glue the round tile in the center.

2. Glue the yellow and gold ochre ⅜" (1 cm) square tiles, alternating the two colors around the center tile.

3. Glue the royal blue tiles around the outside edge. Glue the yellow half tiles in a second row under the blue.

4. Place the stars and marbles in the open space, scattering them in an attractive way.

5. Fill in with the broken pieces of pottery. Let them dry 24 hours.

GROUT:

1. Mix grout and apply from the center out to the rim.

2. Let dry for about 15 minutes. Wipe with sponge.

3. Let dry for another 15 minutes. Wipe again and buff the tiles with a soft cloth.

FINISH:

Seal with grout sealer, following the manufacturer's instructions. Let dry 24 hours before filling with water.

Blue Triangles Birdhouse

Designed by Robyn Huber

"This birdhouse had a cute heart-shaped opening so I decided to use heart-shaped glass accents," says Robyn. Because she also loves blue glass, she created a blue roof and put blue glass and blue mirror on the walls. The mirror is very beautiful in the sunshine as the light dances off reflections of blue.

SUPPLIES

Wooden birdhouse with heart-shaped opening

Stained glass—blue, purple, aqua

Mirror squares

3 iridescent glass hearts

Sanded grout—purple

Clear silicone glue

Indoor/outdoor acrylic paint—purple

Basic tools & supplies

INSTRUCTIONS

PREPARE:

1. Cut ¾" (1.9 cm) glass and mirror squares for the roof. (They do not have to be perfect!)

2. Cut remaining blue and purple glass pieces into irregular triangle shapes.

ATTACH TESSERAE:

1. Glue heart-shaped glass pieces in a row under the opening.

2. Glue irregular triangle-shaped pieces to the sides of the house. Place pieces no more than ½" (1.3 cm) apart. (They can be as close as you want.) Fill in all space on one side before moving to another side.

3. Glue square glass and mirror tiles to roof.

GROUT:

1. Mix grout. Spread over tesserae on roof. Wipe away excess. Let dry.

2. Spread grout over tesserae on sides, working one side at a time. Wipe away excess. Let dry.

3. Wipe away haze with a soft cloth.

FINISH:

1. Paint openings and edges of roof with purple paint. Let dry 72 hours.

2. Seal grout.

Tips:

• You do not have to glue glass on every side of the house. You can paint some of the sides or maybe the roof instead of creating a mosaic.

• Be careful not to apply too much adhesive. If the adhesive gets on the top side of the glass, wipe it off immediately. Remove excess dry glue with a razor blade.

Feed the Birds Bird Feeder

Designed by Dolly Clark

Dolly wanted to make something with mosaics for her parents' shore house, and this is her first mosaic. I hope it encourages those of you who are just beginning. Choose paint colors that complement the mosaic part of the birdfeeder—it really doesn't matter what colors you choose, as anything matches the outdoors!

Be sure to hang it so you can see it through a window in your home.

SUPPLIES

Wooden bird feeder, 6" (15.2 cm) wide, 10" (25.4 cm) high, with 7" (43.2 cm) square base

1-½ lbs. (24 oz) tiles in various colors, ⅜" (1 cm)

15 flatbacked marbles in various colors

30 various shells, including mini sand dollars, a seahorse, and a starfish

Indoor/outdoor paints—mint green, pink, baby blue, yellow

½" paint brush (1.3 cm)

Sanded grout—buttercream

Brush-on laminating liquid

Optional:

Sea sponge

INSTRUCTIONS

ATTACH TESSERAE:

1. Outline the roof with ⅜" (1 cm) tiles.

2. Place flatbacked marbles and seashells in a scattered pattern on all surfaces.

3. Fill in the rest of the area with the ⅜" (1.cm) tiles.

GROUT:

1. Mix grout and apply according to general instructions.

2. Seal grout.

FINISH:

1. Paint the exposed wooden areas in pastel colors. Let dry. *Option:* Sponge the base with layers of color as shown in the photo. Let dry between layers.

2. Seal paint with brush-on laminating liquid.

3. Glue a few sea findings on the painted part of the birdfeeder to embellish.

—FROM *Backyard Mosaics*

SPECIAL MOSAIC TECHNIQUES

Reham Aarti Jacobsen

How do I mosaic a picture under glass?

In this quick and easy mosaic technique you will attach clear glass tesserae directly onto the front of your chosen print, encasing the picture under the glass.

Country Cherries

Designed by Suzy Skadburg

WHAT YOU NEED TO GET STARTED:

TESSERAE

Clear beveled glass, 16" (40.6 cm) square

ADDITIONAL SUPPLIES

Acrylic paints: dark green, light green, off-white

Acrylic crackle texture medium

Cherries print, 9" x 13" (23 x 33 cm)

Grout, cement-based, sanded: white

Masking tape

Miter saw

Paintbrushes

Picture hanger

Piece of wood, 9½" x 13½" (24 x 34.3 cm)

Silicone adhesive

Spray adhesive

Spray sealant

Tape measure

Trim molding

Wheel glass cutter/nipper

Wood glue

HERE'S HOW:

1. Spray adhesive onto back side of print, covering the entire surface. Center and adhere print onto wood, making certain to eliminate all lumps or air bubbles. If necessary, use a ruler or the back of a spoon to smooth it out.

2. Cut beveled glass into approximately 1"-square (2.5 cm square) tesserae.

3. Apply a bead of silicone adhesive across the top of the print. Press the glass squares into the adhesive. Working in rows, continue attaching the glass from the top to the bottom.

Note: If your picture has a feature, like a face or an eye, make certain to maneuver the glass so you are placing the feature in the center of the square. If you do not, you will lose it in a grout line.

4. Allow to set at least 24 hours.

5. Measure trim molding to fit around mosaic. Cut molding to measurements with miter saw.

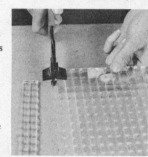

6. Apply a bead of wood glue along outside edge of mosaic. Press molding into glue to create picture frame. Allow to set 24 hours.

7. Refer to Grouting with Cement-based Sanded Grout below. Grout; allow to set.

8. Cover mosaic with masking tape to avoid getting paint on the glass or grout.

9. Paint trim with off-white. Allow to dry.

10. Paint trim with crackle texture medium. Allow to dry until tacky.

11. Mix dark green and light green paint to make an olive green color. Paint trim with olive green. The paint will begin to crackle so the off-white color shows through. Allow to dry.

Note: Make certain to only brush paint over an area once to avoid mixing it with the crackle texture medium.

GROUTING WITH CEMENT-BASED SANDED GROUT

1. Pour the determined amount of powdered grout into a dedicated mixing bowl (one cup per square foot is an average amount).

2. Following the manufacturer's directions, add water or grout additive, stirring in a little at a time until the mixture is similar to the consistency of mayonnaise or sour cream.

3. Mix well, making certain to scrape the bottom and sides of the mixing bowl.

4. Allow the grout to 'slake' before spreading it onto your piece. Slaking means allowing the grout mixture to sit for approximately 15 minutes to give all the polymers, latex, or other strengthening agents in the mixture sufficient opportunity to blend, ensuring the best possible grout finish for your piece.

5. Spoon a glob; of grout onto your mosaic. While wearing gloves, use your hands, a float, a trowel, or other tool to spread the grout. Make certain to work in a crosshatch pattern: working left to right, top to bottom, then right to left, bottom to top. The point is to fill all the spaces in your mosaic with grout, leaving no gaps.

6. Allow the grout to set for approximately 10-15 minutes.

7. With a damp, well-wrung sponge, wipe down the mosaic. The object is not necessarily to clean it, but to remove most of the excess grout from the tesserae.

8. Allow the mosaic to set again for approximately 30 minutes, then do a quick wipe-down with an old rag or paper towel. If the excess grout wipes from the tesserae easily, it is dry enough to do a first wipe-down; if it smudges all over, allow it to set for another 30 minutes and try again.

9. When the piece is thoroughly dry, wipe it down again and buff it to a shine with a clean cloth.

10. If you choose to seal the mosaic, follow the manufacture's directions on the sealant.

---

12. Spray sealant over molding. Allow to dry and remove masking tape.

13. Attach a picture hanger onto back of mosaic.

SUBSTITUTIONS

Use a different print and paint colors for trim.

How do I mosaic in a picture frame?

A picture frame provides a perfect recess for holding a mosaic design. Simply adhere the plate glass into the frame to give yourself a base onto which you can attach the tesserae.

Framed Wild Heart

WHAT YOU NEED TO GET STARTED:

TESSERAE

Plate glass, clear, 5" x 7" (12.7 x 17.8 cm) (2)

Stained glass: jade

ADDITIONAL SUPPLIES

Cork-backed metal ruler

Craft knife

Denatured alcohol

Glass cutter

Grout, cement-based, sanded: black

Marking pen

Masking tape

Patterned paper: leopard print

Picture frame with 5" x 7" (12.7 x 17.8 cm) picture opening

Silicone adhesive

Wheel glass cutter/nipper

Wooden skewer

HERE'S HOW:

1. Prep the glass surface.

2. Cut one piece of clear glass into approximately ⅜"- (1 cm-) square tesserae. Cut some of the squares into a few sharp triangular tesserae.

3. Attach tesserae onto patterned paper, leaving spaces between the pieces.

4. Allow to set at least 24 hours.

5. Cut stained glass into ⅝"- (1.6 cm-) square tesserae.

6. Apply a bead of adhesive along the recess on the inside of the frame. Adhere the remaining piece of clear glass inside the frame so grout will not seep out.

7. Allow to set at least 24 hours.

8. Center and draw a heart design on front side of glass in frame, using the marking pen.

Note: If you do not like the way the drawing turned out, use denatured alcohol to remove the marks and start over.

9. Using a craft knife, cut the paper around each clear glass tessera until paper is flush with the glass.

10. Attach the papered tesserae onto the heart drawing, paper side down. Begin by outlining the heart, then fill in the center.

11. Fill in the background with the stained glass. Trim some of the squares to fit around the heart shape.

Notes: Using a simple opus will give your piece good contrast.

If you are afraid your edges will not be uniform, you can cut a wooden skewer and lay it along the outside edge of the piece. Just remember to remove it before grouting.

12. Allow to set at least 24 hours.

13. Cover the picture frame with masking tape to keep it clean and undamaged during grouting.

14. Grout; allow to set.

15. Remove masking tape.

Continued ➜

SUBSTITUTIONS

You can substitute many simple designs for the one we used (e.g., a star, sun, crescent moon, etc.)

Be aware of how the frame you choose affects your design. Avoid choosing a frame that will take attention away from your piece. Think about where you will display your piece and how it will fit in that room.

Experiment with different patterned papers for endless design possibilities.

How do I mosaic glass on glass?

Attaching your glass tesserae onto a glass surface allows the light to shine through and show off their true beauty. Use a multipurpose adhesive and small tesserae when working on a glass surface.

Stained-glass Light Cover

WHAT YOU NEED TO GET STARTED:

TESSERAE

Transparent millefiori, ⅜" (1 cm) pieces

Transparent stained glass: dark blue, light blue, light green, lavender, teal

ADDITIONAL SUPPLIES

Cork-backed metal ruler

Glass cutter

Grout, cement-based, sanded: gray

Grout sealer

Light fixture with clear glass cover

Multipurpose adhesive

Wheel glass cutter/nipper

HERE'S HOW:

1. Cut stained glass into approximately ⅝"- (1.6 cm-) square tesserae.

2. Prep the glass surface of the cover.

3. Attach the millefiori around the bottom edge of the cover.

4. Attach each color, one row at a time, using the following pattern from the millefiori row up to the top of the light cover: one row of lavender, one row of light blue, one row of light green, one row of all colors alternating, one row of teal, one row of lavender, one row of light blue, and one row of light green.

Note: Remember to leave the top edge uncovered so it will fit into the light fixture.

5. Allow to set at least 24 hours.

6. Grout; allow to set.

7. Seal the grout.

SUBSTITUTION

Use different colors and patterns of glass in your design.

How do I use mesh to make a mosaic?

Mesh is essential when you are creating a mosaic that needs to be moved from one place to another. While in your own work space, you can attach tesserae onto the mesh. Once the design is complete, the entire piece can be moved to the final site.

Garden Sun

WHAT YOU NEED TO GET STARTED:

TESSERAE

Mirror: dark blue, light blue, medium blue, bronze, light bronze, light gold, orange, red, yellow

ADDITIONAL SUPPLIES

Cork-backed metal ruler

Glass cutter

Grout, cement-based, sanded: to match wall

Grout additive

Grout sealer

Masking tape

Marking pen, permanent

Mesh

Pencil

Plastic wrap (or other plastic sheeting)

Silicone adhesive

Wheel glass cutter/nipper

HERE'S HOW:

Note: Use this technique when you need to mosaic evenly onto an uneven or slightly curved surface. It also allows you to create the mosaic in your workshop and move it to its final location. Usually, it is also recommended that you pre-grout the piece before attaching it; however, if the final destination is not totally flat, this could cause a problem.

1. Enlarge and photocopy Garden Sun Pattern to desired size.

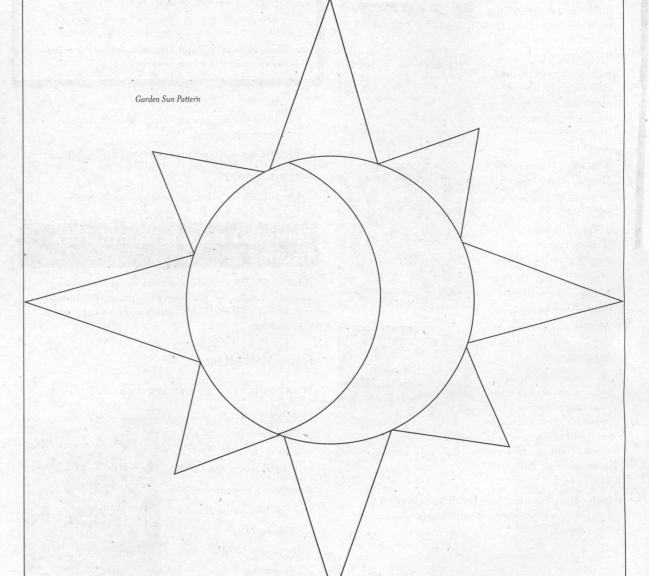

Garden Sun Pattern

2. Tape the drawing to the work surface.

3. Tape a piece of clear plastic over the drawing to protect it from adhesive.

4. Lay the mesh over the plastic tape in place.

5. Draw the design onto the mesh, using the marking pen.

6. Cut mirror pieces into approximately 1"-(2.5 cm-) square tesserae.

Note: Keep the colors separated in small containers for ease in working.

7. Using silicone, attach the tesserae onto mesh. Alternate shades of blue for crescent; red and orange for sun; and shades of bronze, gold, and yellow for rays.

8. Allow to set for 2-3 hours, then flip over and remove the clear plastic so it does not stick permanently to the piece.

9. Allow to set for at least 24 hours.

10. Trim mesh to ¼" (6 cm) around the mosaic.

11. Prep the surface.

Note: If the surface is flat, pre-grout your piece before attaching it.

12. Hold the mosaic up to the surface and draw a light outline, using the pencil on the final location.

13. Mix epoxy resin, following the manufacturer's directions.

Note: Use a quick-set (5-minute) epoxy for vertical applications.

14. Spread a thin layer of epoxy inside the outline.

Note: Be aware that it will run a little if the area is not horizontal.

15. Quickly attach the piece onto the resin. Hold in place as necessary.

16. Allow resin to set completely (usually a couple of hours).

17. Grout with additive and allow to set.

18. Seal the grout.

SUBSTITUTION

You can mosaic this pattern using the direct method if you have access to the surface during the entire process.

—FROM *Mosaics for the First Time*

CREATING MULTI-COLOR GROUT

Allow grout to dry for at least 30 minutes before dyeing. Of course, it's fine of the grout is entirely dry. This must be done before the grout is sealed. Here's how:

1. Mix a squirt of acrylic paint with water to make several color washes that complement the colors of your design. Mix each in a different container.

2. Sponge colors on sections of the ball, dying and coloring the grout. Overlap colors that go well together when blended so some of the color blends into the color next to it. Wipe paint from tiles. Let dry completely (overnight).

FOUND ART MOSAIC PROJECTS

Suzan Germond

Buttons & Pebbles

Vase

Here's a way to use and enjoy a button collection. Because this project is not grouted, use buttons that are the same color as the object you are covering. Be sure to place the buttons as close together as possible. Here, I covered an old white pitcher with a variety of white buttons and white pebbles.

SUPPLIES

SURFACE:

Vase or pitcher, 10" (25.4 cm) high (20" [50.8 cm] circumference, 5" [12.7 cm] opening)

TESSERAE:

300-400 white buttons, various sizes

16 oz. white floral or aquarium pebbles

OTHER SUPPLIES:

Silicone adhesive

Fine grit sandpaper

All-purpose cleaner and degreaser

TOOLS:

Button shank remover

Toothpicks *or* dental tools

2 cloth towels

INSTRUCTIONS

PREPARE:

1. Use the button shank tool to remove the backs of the shank buttons so they will lay flat.

2. Clean the vase or pitcher with an all-purpose cleaner and degreaser.

3. Lightly sand the exterior to give the smooth surface some texture ("tooth") to hold the adhesive.

4. Lay the vase or pitcher on its side between two rolled towels.

ATTACH THE TESSERAE:

1. Working from the bottom upward, glue the buttons, one at a time, to the surface with small dabs of silicone.

· You do not want glue oozing up between the buttons. Should this occur, use a toothpick or other thin tool to scrape away excess glue.

· Try to arrange the buttons randomly, rather than in rows. Fill in any small spaces with the smaller buttons.

· Let one side of vase dry completely before turning it over to work on the other side.

2. When the body of the vase or pitcher is covered with buttons and the adhesive is fully set, apply a thin layer of silicone with a craft stick around the base and cover

Continued ➡

the glue with white pebbles. Because the pebbles are small, it is not necessary to glue each one individually.

3. Use the same technique to apply pebbles around the neck of the vase or pitcher. Leave the very top of the rim uncovered. Let dry.

Glittering Jewels

Belt Buckle

Mosaics can decorate any size surface, from the side of a building to a small piece of jewelry. This mosaic belt buckle uses old costume jewelry—brooches, earrings, and some beads—glued on a crystal glass tile mosaic. Blank belt buckles are popular with artists who fuse glass and are available through stained glass suppliers. Look for one with a lip or rim to protect the edges. Belts with removable buckles are also readily available online. One of my customers displays her buckles on small easels when she is not wearing them.

SUPPLIES

SURFACE:

1 blank belt buckle, 3" diameter

TESSERAE:

Crystal glitter tiles, 1" (2.5 cm)—1 royal blue, 1 turquoise, 1 sage green

2 gold brooches, 1" (2.5 cm) diameter, with blue and green stones or beads

1 gold brooch of figure (Mine is a dancer.)

Fire opal cabochons, ½" (1.3 cm)

2 blue opal cabochons, ¼" (.6 cm)

3 earrings—Butterfly, star, flower

OTHER SUPPLIES:

Sanded white grout

Acrylic paint—Lime green

PVA white adhesive

Epoxy adhesive (Two-barrel epoxy may be the best choice—you only need a small amount.)

Jewelry cleaner

TOOLS:

Long nose pliers

Wheel glass cutters

Craft knife or single-edge blade

INSTRUCTIONS

PREPARE:

1. Using pliers, remove the backs of the brooches and earrings so they lay flat.

2. Clean jewelry, if necessary, so it sparkles.

ATTACH THE TESSERAE:

1. Nip the three crystal glass tiles into random shapes.

2. Glue on the belt face with white glue, arranging them randomly with even grout lines throughout. Let dry.

GROUT:

1. Mix ½ cup (4 fl oz) white grout with green acrylic paint to make a pale lime color.

2. Spread over the tesserae. Wipe away the excess. Clean with paper towels. Let dry.

FINISH:

1. Following the product instructions, mix about one teaspoon of two-part epoxy.

2. Use a craft stick to apply a small dab of epoxy to the back of each brooch and arrange on top of the crystal tile mosaic.

3. Add the earrings and beads until you have covered most, but not all, of the tiles underneath. If anything starts to slip, tape it in place, Let dry 24 hours.

4. Carefully remove any excess dried epoxy with a craft knife or blade.

Violet Textures

Picture Frame

Odds and ends of mosaic materials that don't necessarily seem to belong together can be combined to make decorative picture frames. For this frame, I decided on a purple and white color scheme and found all kinds of goodies in those two colors: tiles, earrings, buttons, charms, beads, cabochons, parts of Christmas ornaments, and millefiori. The combination of materials gives the frame a rich texture. There is no set method for arranging so many different pieces—my rule of thumb is to work in one direction and place the pieces until the frame is full. Because the piece is not grouted it is important to use a strong adhesive and place as close together as possible. You can always go back and fill blank spots.

SUPPLIES

SURFACE:

Frame, 8" (20.3 cm) square with a 3" (7.6 cm) opening and 2" (5 cm) border

TESSERAE:

Approximately 4 cups (32 fl oz) of small purple and white objects, such as:

4–5 purple glass tiles (various sizes)

14 buttons (random sizes)

16 glass beads

1 small pearl necklace, taken apart

Opaque violet glass, 2" (5 cm) square

Opaque white glass, 2" (5 cm) square

Purple mirror, 2" (5 cm) square

4 earrings

3 glass flowers

2 glass butterflies

10 plastic beads

2 plastic icicles

4 sequin flowers

Lavender seed beads

1 baby rattle charm

1 charm with Chinese character

8 cabochons

1 large painted flat-back marble

3 millefiori

OTHER SUPPLIES:

Acrylic paints—White, lavender

Silicone glue

White PVA glue or epoxy adhesive

TOOLS:

Pliers

Button shank remover *optional*

Tweezers

Wheel cutters

Craft knife or window scraper

Paint brushes

INSTRUCTIONS

PREPARE:

1. Clean the frame, if necessary. Paint with white paint. Let dry.

2. Using tools, take apart all brooches, earrings, and necklaces so individual beads and pieces can be used. Remove shanks from any buttons you might be using.

ATTACH THE TESSERAE:

1. Choose a starting point on the frame. Apply a 2" (5 cm) square of adhesive with a craft stick and begin laying the various pieces side by side, alternating colors and shapes. Repeat until the frame is covered.
Tips: For balance, place larger items on each side of frame. Awkwardly shaped pieces may require epoxy for good adhesion.

2. Using tweezers, place the smallest beads into the little spaces. Let dry for 24 hours.

FINISH:

1. Clean off any excess dried glue with a craft knife or window scraper.

2. Touch up the paint.

3. Paint lavender stripes along the edges of the frame. Let dry.

Black & White & Yellow

Domino Box

I made this as a gift for a fanatic domino player to store his game pieces. It started out with three objects: a simple wooden box with a hinged lid, a square candle holder base, and a metal flower. I wanted the box's purpose to be obvious so I covered it with game pieces that, conveniently, are the same thickness as the yummy yellow smalti. They make a nice contrast to all the black and white. This quick and easy project does not require cutting or grouting. I painted the inside of the box with fire engine red for another jolt of color.

Supplies

SURFACE:

Wooden box with hinged lid, 8" (20.3 cm) square, 6" (15.2 cm) tall

TESSERAE:

36 dominoes

54 pieces bright yellow smalti

38 white flat-back marbles, ¼" (.6 cm)

28 black flat-back marbles, ½" (1.3 cm)

1 flat metal candle holder with ball feet, 4" (10.2 cm) square

1 metal flower

Decorative center for flower (flat-back marble, bead or jewel)

OTHER SUPPLIES:

Acrylic paints—Black, red, white, yellow

Metal paints—White, yellow

White primer

Metal primer

Thinset mortar

TOOLS:

Paint brushes

Artist's paint brush or pencil

INSTRUCTIONS

PREPARE:

1. Prime the wooden box. Let dry.

2. Paint the interior with red paint.

3. Paint the exterior with black paint. Let dry.

4. Prime the candle holder and the flower with metal primer.

5. Turn the candle holder upside down. Paint it white with black feet.

6. Paint the flower yellow. Let dry.

ATTACH THE TESSERAE:

1. Lay the box on its side. Glue the dominoes and smalti in rows, starting on the bottom left. Use this sequence: 1 vertical piece of smalti, 1 horizontal domino, 1 vertical piece of smalti, 2 horizontal dominoes. Alternate the pattern by one space on each subsequent row.

2. Adhere one row of yellow smalti horizontally along the top.

3. Glue the small white marbles along the edge of the lid. Let the glue dry.

4. Turn the box and glue another side, repeating until all sides are covered. Let the glue dry before turning to the next side.

5. Glue the candle holder upside down on the center of the lid. Let dry. Glue the flower at the center of the candle holder.

6. Glue black flat-back marbles along the edge of the lid to fill in the space between the edge and the candle holder. Let dry.

FINISH:

1. Add white polka dots to the flower with the handle end of a paintbrush.

2. Touch up the paint, as necessary. Let dry.

Chandelier Mosaics

Lamp Shades

Mosaic lamp shades on a chandelier are a jazzy alternative to fabric shades or plain glass shades. To make these, cover glass shades (found inexpensively at home recycling centers or thrift shops) or hard plastic shades (available at craft stores) with glittering colored mirror, glass, and flat-back beads and finish with beaded fringe. Be sure to use silicone adhesive—it works best with mirror tesserae and will withstand the heat of light bulbs. So more light will shine through the shade, I used silver seed beads to fill the "grout" spaces for a more transparent effect. Beads can replace grout on many indoor projects (tabletops are an exception), but the process requires a little more time and patience than the usual grouting. Depending on the look you want to achieve, you can use micro glass beads (the tiny kind that don't have holes), seed beads, or tiny pearls.

Supplies (for one shade)

SURFACE:

Glass or plastic chandelier lamp shade, 5" (12.7 cm) tall

TESSERAE:

20 squares colored mirror in variety of colors, ½" (1.3 cm)

26 squares blue-purple Van Gogh glass, ½" (1.3 cm)

80 random-shaped pieces champagne gold mirror

70 (approx.) flat-back beads of various colors

OTHER SUPPLIES:

2 tubes silver glitter seed beads (for the "grout")

105 (approx.) assorted beads (for the fringe)

16 gauge wire

2 oz. plastic bottle with a fine metal tip, or syringe

Silicone adhesive

Adhesive for glass

Painter's masking tape

Acetone

2 towels

TOOLS:

Long nose pliers

Lazy susan

Empty jar or glass (to hold the shade while you work)

Toothpicks or dental tool

Craft knife or single-edge blade

Continued ➡

1. Carefully place the shade on its side between two rolled towels. Fill the 2-oz. bottle with glass glue and attach the fine metal tip.

2. Working one small area at a time, apply glue in the grout lines between the tesserae and sprinkle with silver seed beads, allowing the beads to cover the glue and fill the spaces between the tesserae. Let that part of the shade dry before turning it to apply more beads. (This may seem time-consuming but in the long run is more efficient and less messy than covering the whole grout area with glue and pushing on lots of beads at once.) *Options:* Instead of the metal tip, use a toothpick or a veterinary syringe to apply the glue.

3. Repeat until all areas between the tesserae are filled with glue and seed beads. Let dry.

FINISH:

1. Touch up any blank spots with more beads.

2. Remove excess silicone with acetone and a craft knife or blade.

—From *Found Art Mosaics*

INSTRUCTIONS

PREPARE:

1. Place the shade on the jar or glass. Place the jaw or glass on the lazy susan.

2. Divide the area of the shade to make five bands with a ½" (1.3 cm) mirror band along the center.
Tip: Use painter's tape to temporarily mark the divisions.

MAKE THE BEADED DANGLES:
The fringe is made up of beaded dangles.

1. Cut a 3" (7.6 cm) piece of wire.

2. Thread a small bead on the wire, ¼" (.6 cm) from the end. Fold the ¼" (1.6 cm) end of the wire back over the bead and twist the wire so the small bead is secured in place.

3. Add a larger bead that covers the twisted wire. Add three more beads and set aside.

4. Repeat to make 26 beaded dangles, each ¾" (2 cm) long.

ATTACH THE TESSERAE:

1. Glue a row of colored mirror squares along the center of the shade with dabs of silicone. If excess silicone oozes up between the tesserae, remove with a toothpick or dental tool. (It is important to keep the "grout" spaces clean for the beads.)

2. On the bottom edge of the shade, apply a small dab of silicone and position one beaded dangle with the end of the wire in the silicone and the top bead right at the bottom of the shade. Put a square of blue-purple glass over the wire. Repeat all the way around the shade. Let dry 24 hours. Cut off any excess wire that extends above the glass squares.

3. Glue pieces of gold mirror to form a band between the two rows of square tesserae.

4. Glue a second band of gold mirror pieces the same width as the previous band above the row of colored mirror squares.

5. Finish the top of the shade by gluing flat-back beads along the top 2" (5 cm). Let dry.

Paper Crafts

HANDMADE PAPER

Diane Flowers

Handmade Paper: Fun and Easy

Creating your own handmade paper with natural plant materials is fun, and it's much easier than you might think. Plus there is so much opportunity to use your creativity to make unique and beautiful papers. Start by pulverizing some junk mail, add in some natural plant materials, form it on a mesh mold—and the result is a truly beautiful and unique sheet of handmade paper.

Paper is made of interlocking fibers held together by cellulose, a natural plant material. Paper sheets are formed using a frame mold with a screen mesh bottom, some water, and paper pulp. The mold is placed in a vat of water and the pulp is added. As the mold is lifted out of the water a layer of interlocking fibers remains on the surface of the screen. Water, which helps the fibers to expand and bond together, is drained through the bottom of the mold. More water must be removed before the paper sheet is pressed and dried.

To make paper you need pulp, which is made of some type of cellulosic material, such as wood pulp or cotton fibers or previously made paper. The easiest way to make your own paper pulp is to recycle junk mail or any paper that you might otherwise throw away. All kinds of plant material, including grasses, vegetables, flowers, leaves, seeds, and needles, can be added to paper with beautiful results. Although commercial paper makers use large machines to beat their pulps, for making small amounts of paper an everyday food blender works just fine....

Getting Started

This section is intended for beginner papermakers. It includes the step-by-step instructions for the basic paper making process and tells how to get started making papers with natural materials that are easy to find. It also includes recipes for ... handmade papers and ... projects for creating unique gifts and decorative items with your handmade papers that you will be proud to display in your home and share with your friends and family.

Like any new endeavor, paper making may require a little practice and experimentation. If your first attempts are not successful, don't despair—just keep trying. You'll discover what works for you. Feel free to use the recipes and projects ... to develop your own paper making style.

Paper Making Supplies

This section explains and pictures the basic supplies and tools you will need to be successful at papermaking. Some items you will be able to find around your house. Other items you will find at craft or hobby stores as well as online sources. Several paper making suppliers offer kits that contain everything you need to make paper as well as additives and other materials.

Be Safe!

After using household tools for making paper, they should never be used for preparing or storing food. Keep them with your craft supplies. It is a good idea to label spoons, bowls, or other household items with a note that says "Use for Paper Making Only."

Paper Pulp

Paper pulp is the fiber source for making paper. You can make this from paper you have or you can buy pulp that is already processed and ready to use. Below are some guidelines for choosing paper pulp.

Prepared Paper Pulp

High-quality prepared fibers and pulps can be purchased from art supply stores and paper making suppliers, which usually include instructions for preparing and using them. Cotton and abaca are the most common prepared fibers. Both fibers are processed in the blender in the same way that recycled paper is processed.

Cotton linter makes an opaque, soft sheet. It is made from the seed hair fiber that is a result of the cotton ginning process. Cotton may come in sheets that are easily torn or in bags of loose pulp pieces that do not require tearing.

Continued →

Abaca is made from the leaf stalks of banana plants. Abaca is very thick and hard to tear. It should be soaked in water before adding to your blender.

Paper pulps

Recycled Paper to Use for Pulp

Pulp can also be made by recycling junk mail or any other kinds of papers you have. Sources of recycled pulp include shredded office papers, advertising circulars, postcards, greeting cards, unused credit card applications, envelopes, shipping and packing paper, wrapping paper, tissue paper, pages from books and magazines, brown paper bags, and unused napkins or paper plates. Newspaper, though readily available, will not make a strong thick paper and is not a good choice for pulp making.

The quality of your sheets will only be as good as the quality of the recycled paper you use. One way to judge paper's quality is by its source. Banks, cultural organizations, and image-conscious entities use higher-quality paper. (Think symphony programs or stationery from an elected official.) Lower-quality paper, such as magazine pages, will produce nice gray sheets, but the ink may form a film that will coat your mold, screen, and couching sheets. It's best to opt for quality papers when you recycle.

Business communication papers and envelopes, custom bags from upscale retailers, wrapping papers, plain brown bags, and tissue papers are good sources for color.

The color of the recycled paper you use will affect the resulting color of your handmade paper. However, there is no good way to predict what the resulting color might be except through experimentation. Since most colored construction papers bleed when wet, I only use them when I want that appearance in my sheets.

Papers for making recycled pulp

Molds

Molds are used to make individual sheets of paper. They are frames with wire screen attached to the bottom. You can make your own molds or purchase them from specialty paper making suppliers.

The two basic types of molds are dip molds and pour molds. With a pour mold, the paper pulp is poured into the mold after the mold is placed in a vat of water. The mold is raised up through the water, and the pulp stays on the screen at the bottom of the mold. With a dip mold, the mold is dipped into a vat of water to which paper pulp has been added. The sides of a pour mold are taller than those of the dip mold. With practice, you can use a pour mold for dipping, but the dip mold's shorter sides make the process a little easier.

Left to right: Pour mold, handmade dip mold, purchased dip mold

How to Make Your Own Mold

It is easy to make your own dip mold. Use waterproof staples or screws to attach rustproof screen to a wood frame or embroidery hoop. Support the screen from the bottom with ¼ inch (6 mm) mesh hardware cloth. To avoid cutting your hands, cover the edges of the wire with duct tape. For added protection from water damage, paint the wooden frame pieces with several coats of water-resistant polyurethane.

With use, the wire screen and mesh in homemade molds will eventually sag and need to be replaced. To prolong the life of your screen, attach a piece of plastic grid (the kind used in fluorescent light fixtures) to the frame under the screening to provide extra support.

Paper making suppliers after a polypropylene screen that can be used instead of wire screening that lasts longer than other screening materials. It is glued to the frame, and then made taut by heating with a hair dryer.

Blender

Most household food blenders work perfectly for blending water wit paper pulp. One with multiple speeds and a pulse button is handy when using fragile flowers and botanicals. Choose a blender with a larger container—one that will allow the addition of at least three cups of water to the dry paper pulp. **Caution!** Once you've used a blender for paper making, never use it again for food preparation.

Other Molding Supplies

Deckles

Deckles are forms that look like cut out stencils that are placed inside the mold to make special sizes and shapes of papers. They are made of sturdy plastic or other waterproof materials. You can buy deckles or make your own using ¼ inch (6 mm) thick plastic sheets or plastic foam. An envelope deckle is easy to make: Take apart an envelope of the desired size, trace around it on a piece of plastic or plastic foam, and cut out the traced shape, leaving the outline.

Vat

The vat is a large plastic tub. It should be deep enough to hold at least 3 inches (7.5 cm) of water and your mold. To determine the size you need, measure your mold and

add 6 inches (15 cm) to the outside dimensions. For example, if your mold is 9 x 12 inches (23 x 30.5 cm), you'll want a vat that measures at least 15 x 18 inches (38 x 45.5 cm).

Whisk

Use a whisk to mix the pulp after pouring the pulp into a mold or vat. A whisk can also be used to mix and position materials inside the mold or vat.

Additives

Available in liquid or powder form, acid free additives can be added to wet pulp before blending to ensure smooth, acid free sheets of paper. Buy them from paper making suppliers, and follow the package instructions for use.

Measuring Cups & Spoons

Glass and plastic measuring cups are indispensable for measuring water, paper pulp, and plant materials. Measuring spoons are needed for measuring additives.

Strainers & Netting Fabric

Strainers are used for straining pulp after blending. A strainer lined with netting fabric is useful for quickly removing water from wet pulp to prepare the pulp for storage. Strainers are also used to remove pulp from a tub or vat when the pulp-and-water (slurry) mixture is too thick.

Tip—Use pH test strips to determine the level of acidity in paper pulp when you want to make archival-quality papers. Anything less than 8.5 is considered acid free.

Supplies for Drying Paper

After the sheets are molded and pulled from the water vat, they then have to be couched and dried. Couching (rhymes with "pooching") is the process of removing water from wet paper sheets after they are removed from the mold. After the sheets have been couched they are then left to dry thoroughly. There are several options you can choose for the final drying of your handmade paper sheets.

Pictured: 1—Deckles, 2—Vat, 3—Whisk 4—pH strips, 5—Acid free additive, 6—Glass measuring cups, 7—Plastic measuring cups, 8—Strainers, 9—Measuring spoons

Couch Sheets

Couch sheets are highly absorbent sheets made to soak up water from the wet paper. Couch sheets should be rinsed after each use. After they are dry (this can take several hours), they can be reused. Buy them from paper making suppliers. Other types of cloth materials can be used for couching, such as felt, blankets, blotter paper, or mesh dishcloths. Mesh dishcloths are not as absorbent or efficient as the other materials.

Waterproof Tray (or Couching Tray)

Use this tray to hold the wet paper sheet and couch sheets while removing (couching) water from the paper. This

has to be perfectly flat, hard, and smooth. You could put a plastic cutting board inside a plastic lid from a tub to create a hard, smooth waterproof tray.

Heatproof Board

You will need this during the drying and pressing stage when using an iron for the drying process.

Mesh Dishcloths

Reusable, disposable mesh cleaning cloths or dishcloths, which are available at supermarkets, can be used to absorb water and protect paper sheets during the pressing and drying stage when using an iron. They are large enough to cover both sides of an 8½ x 11-inch (20.5 x 28 cm) sheet of paper, dry quickly, and can be ironed dry for quick reuse.

Sponges

Regular household sponges are used to remove (couch) water from wet paper sheets.

Pressing Block & Roller Tool

These tools help press water from the paper sheets during couching. A pressing block is a small piece of solid, flat wood; a roller tool can be made of hard rubber, plastic, or wood.

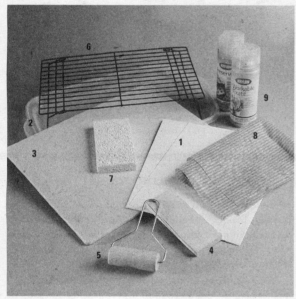

Pictured: 1—Couch sheet, 2—Lid from a plastic tub used for couching tray, 3—Plastic heatproof board, 4—Pressing block, 5—Roller tool, 6—Wire racks, 7—Sponges, 8—Mesh dishcloth, 9—Protective sprays

Tip: Protective Sprays

Fixatives, spray sealers, and acid free sprays can be used to protect dry papers from the elements. Always use sprays outdoors and allow the sprayed papers and other materials to dry completely before handling them. Spraying dried plants and flowers with a sealer before mixing them with wet pulp helps them retain color and avoid bleeding.

Paper Presses—Drying Option 1

A *homemade paper press* can be made by layering wet paper sheets between several dry couch sheets and placing them between two pieces of polyurethane-coated wood. C-clamps are used to hold and press the paper and wood.

As an option, *professional paper presses* can be purchased. They create beautiful, flat, even sheets of paper. The pressure they provide helps compress the fibers, forming a denser and stronger bond that makes a higher quality, more durable sheet of paper.

Drying Racks—Drying Option 2

Stackable wire racks that allow air to circulate around the wet sheets of paper can be used for air drying. Air drying produces a more textured paper that does not dry completely flat. The papers will curl naturally but will flatten if glued to a flat surface.

Drying Box—Drying Option 3

To speed the drying process when making several sheets of paper, you can make a drying box using a box fan, pieces of cardboard, and couch sheets or paper blotter drying sheets. For best results use bi-wall or tri-wall cardboard (two or three pieces laminated together) for making your drying box.

Paper press that you can purchase for professional results.

Here's how:

1. Cut pieces of cardboard slightly larger than your paper sheets. Position the corrugated channels running the same direction on all the pieces. You can stack the pieces as tall as your box fan.

2. Place the damp paper sheets between drying sheets and stack them between the cardboard pieces. Place the stack in front of the fan, aligning the channels in the cardboard pieces so the air can flow through them. Position two pieces of cardboard against the sides of the stack.

3. Secure the side pieces and the top with weights, blocks, or bricks so the stacked papers and cardboard pieces will not move when the fan blows air through them.

4. Turn the fan on high speed. The sheets should be dry in 24 hours.

Microwave—Drying Option 4

Your microwave oven can be used to speed the paper pressing and drying processes. A purchased microwave flower press can be used for drying small sheets of paper, or you can make a microwave paper press by layering paper towels between two pieces of cardboard and securing them with rubber bands.

Iron—Drying Option 5

When you are in a hurry to dry your paper sheets, use a medium to hot iron to speed drying after couching. Always place a dry mesh dishcloth or any other thin cloth between the iron and the paper sheet; when the cloth gets wet, swap it for a dry one. An iron with a non-stick soleplate works best.

Plant Preparation Supplies

In the Paper Making Recipes section, you'll find instructions for preparing and using different types of plant materials, including fresh leaves and flowers, dried flowers and herbs, coffee, tea, spices, seeds, and fibers. Some plant materials require cooking in an alkaline solution to break down the fibers before blending them with paper pulp or using them to make paper; others require boiling, soaking, or chopping. Some only need to be torn into small pieces.

Pots & Utensils

Cook plants you're preparing for paper making in non-reactive pots—ones that are made of stainless steel or glass

or are enamel-coated. Use stainless steel or enamel-coated utensils or wooden spoons for stirring. *Never* use pots and utensils that you've used for paper making for cooking food. *Always* cook plant materials outside on a hot plate or outdoor stovetop.

Alkalizing Agents

Soda ash, washing soda, and fireplace ashes can be added to water to make an alkaline cooking solution for plant materials. Soda ash can be purchased from paper making suppliers; washing soda can be found at most grocery stores. Some papermakers claim they achieve the same results with washing soda and soda ash; others maintain washing soda leaves a residue in the paper, while soda ash does not. Use extreme care—alkaline compounds can be caustic. Wear protective clothing, eye protection, and gloves. Avoid splashing yourself and work outdoors. For instructions for using alkalizing agents, see "Preparing Plant Materials" in the Paper Making Recipes section.

Making Your Own Fireplace Ash Solution

Follow these steps to make an alkaline solution using wood ashes from your fireplace or wood stove. Be safe! Work outdoors and wear protective gear to protect yourself from accidental splashes.

1. Fill a large stainless steel, enamel-coated, or glass pot halfway with ashes. Add cold water to the pot until it is three-quarters full.

2. Stir the ashes and water while bringing to a boil. Let boil 30 minutes.

3. Remove from heat. Allow the mixture to settle overnight.

4. Strain and save the alkaline solution. Discard the wet ashes.

Measuring Cups & Spoons

You'll need glass and plastic measuring cups and plastic measuring spoons to measure amounts of water, alkalizing solutions, plant materials, and additives.

Strainer & Netting Fabric

Use a strainer for draining, rinsing, and separating plant material from water after cooking. Line the strainer with netting fabric when straining small pieces of boiled plant material.

Crafting Supplies

These are some of the supplies you'll need for creating some of the special papers and the handmade paper projects in this book. The recipes in the Paper Making Recipes section and the individual project instructions in the Handmade Paper Projects section tell you how and when these supplies are used.

Mechanical Presses

Flower pressing kits that contain everything you need to press flowers and leaves can be purchased, or you can make your own with two pieces of wood, some papers, cardboard, and four bolts and wing nuts.

Microwave Presses

A flower press specifically made for use in the microwave is an easy way to press flowers and leaves quickly. Special microwave presses can be purchased or a homemade microwave flower press can be made with two pieces of cardboard, paper towels, and rubber bands.

Iron & Waxed Paper

Still another option for pressing flowers and leaves is to use a hot dry iron and waxed paper. Simply position the leaves or flowers between two pieces of waxed paper and slowly move the iron across them. Lift the waxed paper and allow the leaves and flowers to cool before handling them.

Pieces of waxed paper are also used to separate and protect newly glued book covers and pages before placing them in a press to dry.

Continued ➔

Tweezers

Use tweezers to handle fragile dried and pressed plant materials and flowers.

Adhesives

Most types of basic crafting glues that dry clear will work well with dried and pressed plant materials, flowers, and leaves when adding them to dried sheets of handmade papers. You may also want to try these specialty glues for your paper making projects:

- PVA (polyvinyl acetate) is a glue used by many paper-makers and bookmakers. It is strong, dries clear, and contains a preservative that protects papers and dried materials from mold.
- Methyl cellulose, an archival water-based adhesive, can be easily removed with water. Buy it from paper-making suppliers.
- Use decoupage gel to attach decorative elements to your papers and to seal and protect them.
- For making envelopes, there's a special glue you can put on the flap that is activated when moistened.

Tip—Another option for pressing and drying flowers and leaves is to use your old telephone directories and some weights. The pages of the directory are absorbent and make great drying sheets. Simply place the plants between the pages of the phone books, put weights on top, and allow the plants to dry undisturbed.

Tip—One of my favorite tools for tearing paper is a metal deckle-edge ruler—I use it for making a straight deckle edge on stationery, envelopes, and cards.

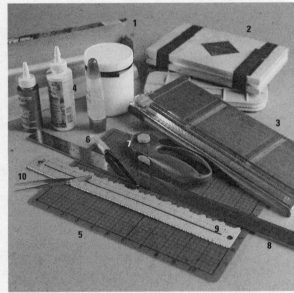

Pictured: Crafting Supplies, 1—Wax paper, 2—Flower presses, 3—Paper trimmer, 4—Adhesives, 5—Cutting mat, 6—Craft knife, 7—Rotary cutter, 8—Metal ruler, 9—Deckle edge ruler, 10—Tweezers

Cutting Tools

Use scissors, a rotary cutter with decorative blades, or a craft knife to cut your papers. A paper trimmer with a sliding blade is useful for card making and trimming larger paper sheets.

Rulers

A clear plastic ruler is useful for lining up different materials when layering papers and for making straight seams or borders while cutting or tearing. You'll want a metal ruler to use as a guide when you're cutting straight lines with a craft knife.

Cutting Mat

A self-healing cutting mat will protect your work surface and prolong the life of your blades and cutting tools.

The Paper Making Process

Now you are ready to set up your work area and start making paper. This section shows you, step by step, how

to make handmade paper. Paper making is basically a four-step process: sheet forming, couching, pressing, and drying.

Keep a Paper Making Diary

After going through the process of making a sheet of paper, you may discover that a certain sheet of recycled paper or a particular plant or flower you added to your pulp did not produce the result you hoped for. By keeping a diary to record what you did and what materials you used, you can keep track of your successes and learn from past mistakes (and avoid repeating them). The more details you record, the more you will learn as you experiment with different materials and processes. With practice, some techniques will become second nature. Each sheet you make will teach you something new.

Paper Making Overview

Before you start to make paper, it's a good idea to educate yourself about the process. Setting up your work area properly and understanding the flow of the process will help ensure fabulous results. I recommend that you read this chapter to familiarize yourself with the steps before you start. After you make your first sheet, you can make adjustments and begin to develop your own techniques. Several steps and a lot of water are involved in making a sheet of paper. The basic steps are outlined below. Details appear on the following pages.

1. **Prepare.** Select your pulp materials, plant materials, and additives and prepare them for processing in the blender.
2. **Blend your pulp.** Place your pulp in a blender and add water.
3. **Pour.** Pour the blended pulp into a vat of water (if you're using a dip mold) or into your mold in a vat of water (if you're using a pour mold).
4. **Stir.** Stir the pulp to mix it with the water in the vat so that it floats freely and loosely in the water.
5. **Lift.** Lift the mold out of the water. The sheet of paper will be formed as the water drains away from the pulp that remains on the screen at the bottom of the mold.
6. **Remove from mold.** Remove the wet pulp sheet from the mold and place it on top of a couch sheet on a waterproof tray.
7. **Begin removing water.** Cover the wet pulp sheet with a dry couch sheet. Press a sponge over the couch sheet to remove the excess water.
8. **Remove more water.** Wring the excess water from the sponge. Turn over the wet pulp sheet and the two couch sheets. Remove the top wet couch sheet.
9. **Continue removing water.** Place a dry couch sheet over the wet pulp sheet. Press it with the sponge. Repeat wringing the sponge, turning over the sheets, exchanging the wet couch sheets for dry ones, and pressing them with the sponge until the sponge cannot remove any more water.
10. **Dry.** Press and dry the sheet using a combination of ironing, placing it in a press, and/or microwaving, or simply allow it to air dry.

Work Area Setup

Because so much water is used in making paper, it is worth your time and effort to organize your work area to avoid getting everything wet.

Work Outdoors If You Can

Working outdoors eliminates the need to worry about cleaning up water that might escape from the vat or tub. Perform all cooking in a well-ventilated area. If using alkaline solutions, always cook outside.

Be Safe!

Wear a protective mask and gloves when cooking with alkaline solutions. Protect yourself from accidental splashes and spills and avoid exposure to fumes. Make

sure your work area is free of electrical hazards. Keep extension cords away from faucets and hoses.

Work Near Your Water Source

Blending is more efficient if you do not have to transport water. Position your vat or tub of water close to your water source.

Choose a Comfortable Height

Position your vat or tub of water at a comfortable height which allows you to see inside the mold and deckle when they are inside the tub or vat.

Arrange Your Work Table

Place a waterproof tray beside your tub or vat for couching. Allow space on your work table beside your waterproof couching tray for storing your wet mold and deckle. Keep extra couch sheets available beside your couching tray.

Work space set up

RECYCLING WATER

I recycle the water from our dehumidifier for paper making. During the summer I try to reuse the water that drips out of our air conditioner. (Most of the time I only need a bucketful, which can easily be collected in just a few hours.)

But do not use recycled water when making archival quality papers. As a precaution, test your water and pulp to be sure they are pH neutral before making archival quality sheets. See "About pH Levels" for more information.

Making the Paper Pulp

There are many different ways to prepare paper pulp. Different processes yield different results—thick or thin papers, smooth or rough, translucent or opaque are only a few of the variations. With experimentation and experience you will learn what works best for you.

These instructions are for making one cup of basic recycled pulp that is used in most of the recipes in this book. Approximately five sheets of recycled 8½ x 11 inches (21.5 x 28 cm) paper will make three or more cups of wet pulp or one cup of strained dry pulp that can be stored and used later. One cup of strained dry pulp will make one or two sheets of 8½ x 11 inches (21.5 x 28 cm) paper, depending on the desired thickness.

Pulverizing the Paper

1. Tear five 8½ x 11 inches (21.5 x 28 cm) sheets of recycled paper into 2" squares. (Photo 1)

2. Pour water in your blender container until it's about half full. Add the paper pieces to the water in the blender con-

Photo 1—Tearing the paper.

tainer. Some papermakers prefer to soak the torn paper for one hour or longer before blending. I recommend soaking when using thicker paper or fibers. Normally soaking is not required if using standard thickness papers. (Photo 2)

Photo 2—Putting the paper pieces in the blender.

3. Add more water until the blender container is about three-quarters full. Blend at medium speed for about 30 seconds or until at least half of the fibers are mushy and almost dissolved. (Photo 3, Photo 4)

Photo 3—Starting to blend.   Photo 4—Completing the blending.

4. To determine if the pulp is ready, put a small amount in a jar of cold water, attach the lid, and shake. If the fibers are evenly distributed in the water, the pulp is ready to use. (Photo 5) Now you're ready to strain and rinse the pulp and add your chosen plant materials. At

Photo 5—Testing to see if the pulp is ready

this point, you can also store the pulp for later use. See "Making Pulp for Storage."

Paper Blending Tips

How much paper should you use in your blender?

The basic rule is to allow enough water to provide room for the paper fibers to swell and move away from each other. When working with recycled paper, I start with multiple pieces or one piece of paper that is equal to twice the size I want my finished sheet to be. For example, to make one or two 8½ x 11 inches (21.5 x 28 cm) sheets of average thickness, I tear five 8½ x 11 inches (21.5 x 28 cm) sheets or mix several different pieces to equal this amount. I add 3 cups (710 ml) of water to the blender (and may use up to ½ cup (120 ml) more water, depending on the amount of paper.) For smaller size sheets, use less paper and less water.

Should I soak the paper before using it?

You can soak your papers before blending them for 1 hour or overnight, depending on the thickness. Some papermakers boil recycled papers before blending to remove sizing and other impurities.

How long to blend?

Because all blenders are not alike, the blending times listed are only guidelines. Keep notes when you first start making papers to learn how your blender behaves with certain fibers and pulp mixtures. Start slowly and observe your pulp as you blend it. A good rule is to blend long enough so that half of the paper fibers are liquefied.

Adding an Acid-Free Additive

If you wish to include an acid-free additive, this is the time to add it. An acid-free additive will help avoid bleeding of colors from plant materials and will help prolong the life of your papers. Be sure that you read

and follow the supplier's instructions for the correct measurements and to ensure the best results.

Adding Plant Materials

You can use a variety of plant materials or botanicals—leaves, flowers, vegetables, grass, and herbs—to give texture and interest to papers. (Here, it's rose petals.) They can be added to the pulp in the blender or when you form the sheet in the mold. Mixing them with the pulp in the blender allows you to control the density of the particles. Pulse them briefly to retain the plant's visual characteristics and to make a sheet with more texture and variation.

Many natural plant materials will need to be cooked before adding them to the pulp. You will find instructions for cooking the fibers in Paper Making Recipes. It gives numerous recipes for using plants and other materials in your sheets.

Adding Color—Optional

Using the colors in tissue and other recycled papers is the best (and easiest) way to color your pulp. You can also use natural dyes, such as coffees or teas, or vegetables such as beets. Simply brew a strong batch of coffee or tea or use the cooking water from beets and add them to your pulp. Use extra care to protect your tools and supplies. Natural dyes can permanently stain your drying sheets, other tools, and work surfaces.

To tint paper pulp with tissue paper, start by making a batch of white pulp in your blender. Tear some colored tissue paper into 2-inch (5 cm) squares. Add some of the torn tissue paper pieces to the pulp in the blender. Start with just a few pieces—you can always add more.

Blend the pulp to incorporate the tissue paper and tint the pulp. If the color is not as intense as you'd like, add more tissue until the result pleases you.

Making Pulp for Storage

You can make a large amount of pulp and store it until you are ready to make paper sheets by following these steps. Pulp stored in this way can be used within a few days or stored in the refrigerator for several months. Stored, strained pulp will need to be re-hydrated and lightly blended before using.

INGREDIENTS

Bowl

Strainer

Netting fabric (tulle), cut into 12-inch (30.5 cm) squares

Zipper-top plastic bags or airtight plastic storage container(s)

1. Place the strainer over the bowl. Place a piece of tulle inside the strainer to catch the pulp. (Photo 1)

2. Pour the pulp from the blender container into the strainer. Allow the water to drain into the bowl. (Photo 2)

Photo 1   Photo 2

3. When the pulp has drained, lift the tulle (with the pulp inside) with one hand and, with the other hand, squeeze the pulp to remove as much moisture as possible. (Photo 3)

4. Place the damp pulp in a storage container with an airtight lid. (Photo 4) **Tip**—If stored pulp starts developing an odor, mix it with a few drops of bleach and rinse thoroughly before using.

Photo 3

Photo 4

Forming Sheets

The next step is to form the pulp into sheets of paper. You can make free-form or uneven sheets on your mold frame, or you can use a deckle—which is a template that will help you to form sheets with straight edges or into various shapes.

Using a Dip Mold

A dip mold is useful when making multiple sheets of the same kind of paper and when using larger amounts of pulp. The sheets are formed by lifting the mold (and the deckle, if you're using one) out of a vat of water.

1. To get started, assemble your dip mold with the screen attached.

2. Build up your couching surface slightly so that it is almost the same thickness as the sides of your dip mold. To do this, place soft absorbent materials (couch sheets, mesh dishcloths, felt, blankets, towels, or paper towels) on a flat, waterproof tray. Place a couching sheet on materials on the couching tray.

3. Pour your blended paper pulp into the vat. There should be at least 3 inches (7.5 cm) of slurry (mixed paper and water) in the vat. (Photo 1)

Photo 1—Pouring the prepared pulp into the vat.

Continued ➡

Tip—When using a dip mold, you'll need to experiment to determine the ratio of pulp to water you'll need to obtain the sheet thickness you want. Using more pulp makes a thicker sheet; removing pulp with a strainer (leaving a higher ratio of water) makes a thinner sheet.

4. Mix the pulp vigorously with your hands to distribute the fibers, making sure they are suspended in the water, not settled near the bottom. (Photo 2)

Photo 2—Mixing the pulp to distribute the fibers.

5. Run water over your mold before using it the first time so that the pulp will not resist the mold. Dip the mold into the vat at a 45-degree angle and scoop up some of the pulp. (Photo 3)

Photo 3—Dipping the mold in the vat.

6. In one smooth movement, position the mold inside the vat as you level it so it's parallel to the bottom of the vat. Pull the mold up out of the vat without stopping. (Photo 4)

Photo 4—Pulling the mold out of the vat.

7. Holding the mold level above the vat, allow the water to drain. Shake the mold a little, moving back and forth and left and right (but not too much, or the fibers will shift) as the sheet forms on the screen. Stop shaking when the fibers start to settle on the screen.

8. Place the mold with the wet formed sheet facing the couching sheet. (Photo 5) Turn the mold with the sheet facing down on the couching sheet. (Photo 6)

Photo 5—Positioning the mold at the edge of the couching sheet.

Photo 6—The mold, sheet side down, on the couching tray.

9. Press down on all of the edges of the mold. Lift one edge of the mold carefully to see if the wet sheet has released from the screen. Carefully lift the mold from the wet sheet. (Photo 7)

Photo 7—Lifting the mold from the sheet.

Cleaning the Mold

To remove pulp from a dip mold, first remove the deckle if you are using one. Flip the mold over and smack the mold on the surface of the water. The pulp will fall into the water and your mold will be clean. This is called *kissing off*. Stir the vat and adjust your pulp mixture before making another sheet.

Using a Pour Mold

When using a pour mold you submerge the mold in a vat of water and pour the blended pulp into the mold. The sides of a pour mold are deeper than the sides of a dip mold. A pour mold is most useful when working with smaller amounts of pulp or when combining different pulps together to form a single sheet.

The pour mold I like best came in a paper making kit. It is constructed with hook-and-loop tape straps that allow the bottom screen (and the deckle, if you're using one) to be separated easily from the mold with the wet paper sheet positioned on the screen. This makes couching much easier.

1. To get started, assemble the mold, following the manufacturer's instructions. Place the mold upside down on a flat surface and pull the straps across the drain rack as tightly as you can. Turn the mold right side up.

2. Holding the mold at a slight angle, lower it into the water in the vat or tub. (Photo 1) When the mold is resting on the bottom, there should be 2 to 3 inches (5 to 7.5 cm) of water in the mold. Add more water, if needed, until the water is at the proper depth.

3. Pour the prepared pulp into the mold. (Photo 2)

Photo 1—Placing the mold in the water.

Photo 2—Adding the paper pulp.

4. Use your fingers to mix the paper pulp with the water standing inside the mold. (Photo 3)

5. Lift the mold out of the water, holding it level and allowing the water to drain. Gently shake the mold back and forth and left and right as the sheet forms on the surface of the screen. Be careful not to shake too much. Stop shaking when the fibers are starting to settle on the screen. (Photo 4)

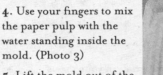

Photo 3—Mixing the pulp with the water in the mold.

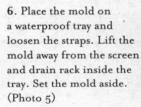

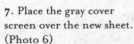

Photo 4—Lifting the mold from the water.

6. Place the mold on a waterproof tray and loosen the straps. Lift the mold away from the screen and drain rack inside the tray. Set the mold aside. (Photo 5)

7. Place the gray cover screen over the new sheet. (Photo 6)

8. Press the sponge firmly over the gray cover screen to absorb water from the paper pulp. Wring out the sponge when it gets full of water. Continue pressing the sponge over different areas of the paper sheet and wringing out the sponge until you've blotted as much water as you can (when the sponge is no longer absorbing water). (Photo 7)

9. Carefully lift one corner of the gray cover screen from the paper slowly and peel up the cover screen. Set it aside. (Photo 8)

10. Prepare a hard surface with a couch sheet on top of it. Pick up the white papermaking screen with the newly formed paper sheet on it. Turn it over and place it on top of a dry couch sheet so that the new paper sheet is between the white papermaking screen and the couch sheet. Press the sponge firmly on top of the white papermaking screen to pick up water from the paper. Wring out the sponge

Photo 5—Removing mold from formed sheet.

Photo 6—Placing cover screen on formed sheet.

Photo 7—Pressing water from sheet.

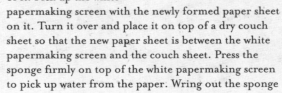

Photo 8—Lifting the screen.

as needed. Continue pressing the sponge over the screen and wringing it out until the sponge will absorb no more water. (Photo 9)

11. To remove the papermaking screen, place one hand near the middle and one hand at the corner of the screen and lift the corner. Continue lifting the screen while you slowly move the other hand back, revealing the paper sheet. (Photo 10) **Tip**—If the sheet sticks to the screen, start with another corner.

Photo 9—Pressing water from formed sheet.

Photo 10—A formed sheet ready to be couched.

Cleaning the Mold

To remove wet pulp from a pour mold, very slowly lower the mold at a slight angle back into the water in the vat. Mix the pulp with your fingers and make adjustments to the pulp mixture before making the next sheet.

Finish the process by proceeding to the instructions for Couching. You can also use a deckle in a dip mold—if you do, lay the deckle on top of the mold, put the white papermaking screen on top of the deckle, and the drain rack on top of the screen when assembling the mold. See instructions for using a deckle later in this section.

Couching

The term *couch* (which rhymes with "pooch") comes from the French verb *coucher*, which means "to lay down." Couching is the process of using a sponge and dishcloths, felts, blankets, blotter paper, or couching sheets to remove water from the formed sheet of paper. The process of wringing the sponge, flipping the sheets, and replacing wet couch sheets with dry ones is repeated until the paper sheet is damp, not wet, and all the water that can be removed by couching has been removed.

1. Put a dry couch sheet on top of the wet paper sheet. (Photo 1)

2. Press a sponge firmly over the top of the couch sheet, allowing it to soak up water. (Photo 2) Wring out the sponge. Continue pressing the sponge on all parts of the sheet to remove water and wringing out the sponge until no more water is absorbed by the sponge.

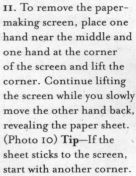

Photo 1—Placing a dry couch sheet on top.

Photo 2—Using a sponge to remove water.

3. Place one hand near the middle of the couch sheet and one hand at one corner. Lift the corner while moving the other hand back. Remove the wet couch sheet. **Tip**—If the paper sheet does not separate from the couch sheet, try another corner.

Photo 3—Using a wooden press bar to remove water.

4. Put a dry couch sheet over the paper sheet. Use a wooden press bar (Photo 3) or a roller (Photo 4) to press down on the couch sheet. Continue rolling or pressing on all parts of the couch sheet to flatten the paper sheet and press out more water.

5. Remove the top couching sheet. (Photo 5)

Photo 4—Using a roller to remove water.

Photo 5—Removing the top couching sheet.

Photo 6—Peeling away the couch sheet from the new paper sheet.

6. Pick up the bottom couch sheet with the paper sheet on top.

7. Carefully turn the paper sheet onto a dish-cloth or other absorbent cloth and gently peel away the couch sheet. (Photo 6)

You are now ready to proceed to the Pressing and Drying stage. There are a variety of options for drying the paper sheets.

Tip—Always clean your mold, deckle, and vat or tub after each use and place them on a level surface to dry. Rinse your couch sheets after each use to remove excess pulp and allow them to dry. Clean cooking pots and utensils after each use. Recycled paper materials contain a lot of ink and processing chemicals that can leave residues, which eventually build up on your tools if you don't clean them regularly.

Pressing & Drying

There are a number of options you can choose for drying your paper sheets. When allowed to dry naturally, paper sheets will curl and buckle. To make smoother, flatter sheets, use an iron or a paper press. Presses will push the wet fibers closer together, resulting in a stronger sheet of paper.

Ironing: Option 1

Ironing sheets of damp (already couched) paper will speed the drying time considerably. The iron will flatten and compress the paper; the heat will evaporate moisture. When ironing, work on a heatproof board to protect your work surface, and place a dry mesh dishcloth (or other thin cloth) under the paper sheet.

1. Cover the paper sheet with another dry dishcloth (or other thin cloth), using it like a pressing cloth.

2. Using a dry iron set medium to hot, move the iron continuously over the sheet. (Photo 1) The dishcloths will absorb moisture; swap wet ones for dry ones frequently.
Tip—An iron with a non-stick soleplate works best—

Photo 1—Pressing the paper sheet with an iron.

some paper additives might stick to the hot iron.

Using a Homemade Paper Press: Option 2

You can make a simple homemade press by layering damp paper sheets between dry couch sheets and positioning them between two pieces of polyurethane-coated wood. The sheets and wood are pressed together with c-clamps. (Photo 2)

Pressing sheets in a homemade press is done just the same as when using a professional press. Place each damp, couched sheet between two dry couch sheets. After 20 minutes, swap those couch sheets

Photo 2—A homemade drying press.

for dry ones. Replace the couch sheets again after a few hours. Leave the paper in the press overnight for best results. Thicker sheets may require additional drying after they are removed from the press.

Using a Professional Paper Press: Option 3

Professional paper presses speed drying time and create beautiful, flat, even sheets of paper. (Photo 3) The pressure they provide helps compress the fibers, creating a denser, stronger bond that produces a higher quality, more durable sheet of paper. To press sheets in a purchased press, place each damp, couched sheet between two dry couch sheets. After 20 minutes, swap those couch sheets

Photo 3—A purchased paper press.

for dry ones. Replace the couch sheets again after a few hours. Leave the paper in the press overnight for best results. Thicker sheets may require additional drying after they are removed from the press.

Air Drying: Option 4

Wire racks allow air to circulate around the wet sheets of paper (Photo 4), producing a more textured paper that won't be completely flat. (The paper will curl naturally but will flatten if glued to a flat surface.) Allow 24 hours for air drying thinner sheets, longer for thicker sheets.

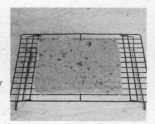

Photo 4—Drying a paper sheet on a wire rack.

Using a Microwave: Option 5

You can use a simple homemade press in your microwave to speed paper pressing and drying. (Online and mail order outlets sell microwave flower presses that can be used for drying small sheets of paper.)

1. Place sheets of damp, couched paper between four dry paper towels or dishcloths and put them between two pieces of cardboard. (Photo 5)

2. Secure the layered cardboard, papers, and paper towels with two rubber bands. (Photo 6)

3. Remove the rotating ring from your microwave (if you have one) and turn the glass platter upside down in the center of the microwave so it will elevate the cardboard press.

4. For best results, dry everything in multiple stages. After each stage, wait a few seconds to let the paper cool. Then remove the rubber bands and check the dried materials before proceeding. The first stage will be the longest, followed by multiple shorter ones. Use the high setting on your microwave and refer to the Microwave Drying Chart times for the stages.

Photo 5—Layering paper, dishcloths, and cardboard to make a microwave press.

Photo 6—The microwave press secured with rubber bands.

With practice you will discover what works best for your microwave. Other factors that affect drying times are the thickness and dampness of the papers. Either could add time to the process.

Using a Deckle

A deckle is a template or form used to make special sizes and shapes of paper. The paper pulp will settle inside the deckle, forming a specific paper shape or size. You can use a deckle with a dip mold or a pour mold. We show it here with a dip mold.

Step 1: Position the deckle on the dip mold and hold the deckle in place with your thumbs as you dip the mold into the vat.

Step 2: Lift the mold from the vat, still holding the deckle in place.

Step 3: Carefully lift the deckle off the mold.

Step 4: The shaped paper pieces are ready to be placed on couching sheets to dry. Proceed to Couching then Pressing & Drying.

Embedding Dried Flowers

Dried flowers, petals, and leaves can be easily added to wet pulp sheets before couching. These embedded materials make beautiful sheets of paper with extra depth and dimension. Simply place the materials you want to embed on a wet pulp sheet and partially cover them with more pulp. The materials will join with the paper as it dries. You can also embed other items such as different colors of pulps, threads, lace, or fibers.

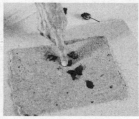

Step 1: Place individual flower petals on a wet pulp sheet.

Step 2: Add a little wet pulp around each petal, then couch the sheet, press, and dry.

Laminating

This is another creative technique to try. Couch two wet sheets of pulp together with dried, pressed materials between the sheets—called laminating. See "Layered Herb Paper" and "Laminated Lavender Paper" in the Paper Making Recipes section for instructions.

Adding Texture

You can use simple everyday items in your home to make textured imprints in your papers, including bricks, burlap, fabrics, wood, foam, wire, baskets, the soles of your shoes, doilies, rugs, bubble wrap, and leaves. Simply cover a couched paper sheet with an item that had a raised pattern to make impressions in the paper. Allow to dry

Microwave Drying Chart			
MicrowaveWattage	600 or Lower	750	950 or Higher
First cycle	45 seconds	30 seconds	20 seconds
Second cycle	23 seconds	15 seconds	10 seconds
Additional cycles	5-10 seconds	5-10 seconds	5 seconds

Continued ➤

with the item in place, then remove. Here, two straw placemats are used to create a textured paper sheet.

Step 1: Position a couched paper sheet on one placemat.

Step 2: Put the other placemat on top of the paper sheet and press with your hands. Allow to dry.

Coloring

Adding color to your sheets can be done with a variety of mediums. The color is added during the pulp making process. See Adding Color in the section entitled Making the Paper Pulp for more details.

A paper sheet with imprint of the straw placemats.

Paper Making Recipes

This section includes recipes for making … handmade papers, plus a wealth of recipe variations.… The lists of ingredients include the prepared recycled pulp from the Paper Making Process section. The amount of recycled pulp included in the recipes is based on using previously blended and strained pulp. Water is added to the blender and the pulp is rehydrated by blending. Each recipe should make one or two sheets of 8½ x 11 inches (21.5 x 28 cm) paper, depending on thickness—to make thicker sheets add more pulp; to make thinner sheets add more water. A comprehensive list of plants to use for paper making appears at the end of the recipes.

As you work, keep in mind that making paper with natural materials is not an exact science. Even if you measure carefully, it is almost impossible to get the same results twice. Sit back, take your time, relax, and enjoy the unpredictable results that appear with each new sheet. There is no single right way to make a sheet of paper.

After trying these recipes, I hope you will experiment with different materials and learn how they respond to each other. With time and practice, you will learn the best ways to incorporate your favorite plant materials in papers and develop a style of your own.

Preparing Plant Materials

Gathering and preparing plant materials takes work, ingenuity, and some experimentation. Many natural plant materials need to be cooked before adding them to your pulp. The recipes in this chapter will give specific instructions for cooking.

Materials such as grass clippings from your lawn, rhubarb stalks, lettuce leaves, onion skins, beets, kiwifruit, and carrot tops can be cooked in plain water and added to your paper recipes. The fibers in more dense plant parts, such as thick leaves or stalks, will break down faster if they are cooked in an alkaline solution. You can mix a solution with water and soda ash, washing soda, or fireplace ashes. For instructions for making a fireplace ash solution, see the Paper Making Supplies section.

Safety Tips for Cooking with Alkaline Solutions

- Cook outside, if possible.
- Wear gloves and a mask to protect yourself from accidental splashes.
- Use stainless steel, enamel-coated, or glass pots and stainless steel or wooden spoons and other utensils. Never use aluminum, tin, or iron pots or utensils—they can react chemically with the alkaline solutions and produce a toxic gas.
- Don't use the pots or utensils you use for preparing plant materials for cooking food. Store them separately, out of the kitchen.
- Add the alkaline solution to the water before it boils; add plant materials after the solution is dissolved.
- Never add more water to the boiling solution—it could cause a chemical reaction and result in uncontrolled splattering.

Cooking with Soda Ash or Washing Soda

Option #1: Add ½ ounce or I tablespoon (14 g) of either soda ash or washing soda to each quart of water.

Option #2: Measure 3½ oz (100 g). for each pound (455 g) of dry fibers and add water to cover.

Cooking with Fireplace Ash Solution

Option #1: Use I oz. or 2 tablespoons (28 g) of fireplace ash solution.

Option #2: Measure 7 oz (195 g). for each pound (455 g) of dry fibers. Add water to cover.

Flower Petal Paper

Dried flower petals make beautiful and colorful papers. For best results, use the freshest, most colorful dried flowers available to get the best color retention. You can dry the petals by pressing or using a desiccant. While almost all flowers or petals fade over time, the process can be delayed by spraying or coating them with surface sealers and avoiding exposure to direct light, heat, humidity, or extreme hot or cold temperatures. Some dried flower petals, such as marigolds and carnations, hold their color better than roses. Purchased cotton pulps will make a brighter sheet of paper than recycled pulp. More delicate petals look better when mixed with cotton pulp.

INGREDIENTS

½ cup (112 g) crushed dried rose petals or other dried flower petals

I cup prepared and strained paper pulp

Spray fixative

Sizing or acid-free additive

INSTRUCTIONS

1. To avoid bleeding, spray the petals with fixative and allow them to dry or blanch them for 5 minutes in boiling water. Drain and allow them to cool completely.

2. Add the pulp and sizing or acid-free additive to the blender container. Follow the package instructions regarding how much sizing or additive to use. Add water to the container until it is three-quarters full.

3. Blend for 30 seconds.

4. Add the petals. Here are three options:

- Add the petals to the blender and pulse for 2 to 3 seconds.
- To retain the natural look of the petals in the finished sheet (and to avoid over-blending), add the blanched petals to the pulp after you've poured it into the mold rather than adding them to the blender. Stir them into the pulp inside the mold with a whisk or your fingers.

- Add some of the blanched petals to the blender and blend; add the rest to the mold and stir.

5. Follow the steps in the Paper Making Process section to make your paper.

To Bleed or Not to Bleed?

Dried flower petals can bleed color into the surrounding paper or they may fade in color. Deep red flowers may turn blue; yellow and white flower petals may turn brown; pink will possibly lose all of its color. While no method will guarantee that dried flowers will not bleed or fade, here are some suggestions for preserving color:

- To reduce color bleeding with roses, spray them with a fixative and add an acid-free additive to your pulp mixture.
- Blanching dried flowers for about 5 minutes in boiling water will help to retain more color and avoid bleeding. However, blanching may alter the flower's color.
- Instead of stopping the bleeding process, consider encouraging it to naturally occur by mixing the pulp and flower petals with water and allowing them to steep for 5 minutes or longer before making your sheets.

Seed Paper

It is very easy to make paper with embedded seeds that can be planted. Small flat seeds like those of forget-me-not, hollyhock, lavender, chili pepper, and tomato work wonderfully. Be sure to stir the mixture in the vat or mold before making sheets to ensure even seed distribution. The sheet shown contains sunflower seeds.

Seed paper with sunflower seeds

INGREDIENTS

½ cup (120 ml) flat flower seeds or vegetable seeds

I cup (240 ml) prepared and strained recycled paper pulp

Acid-free additive

INSTRUCTIONS

1. Put the paper pulp and acid free additive in the blender container. See the package instructions regarding how much additive to use. Add water until the container is about three-quarters full.

2. Blend for 30 seconds.

3. Add the seeds to the blender and pulse for 2 to 3 seconds or add them to the pulp after pouring it in the mold and stir the seeds into the pulp with a whisk or your fingers.

4. Follow the steps in the Paper Making Process section to make your paper.

Include these instructions with your gift of plantable seed papers.

Denim Paper

Paper can be made with almost any kind of fabric, lace, or burlap using this recipe. (Now you have a use for all of those tiny little fabric swatches that you have been saving!) Fabric paper is also known as rag paper. The beautiful paper can be quickly dried with an iron. This recipe was developed from a recipe created by Patty Cox.

INGREDIENTS

1 cup (240 ml) denim fabric or other fabric

5 sheets recycled paper, each 8½ x 11 inches (21.5 x 28 cm)

TOOLS

Scissors

Bowl or bucket

Blender

INSTRUCTIONS

1. Cut the denim or other fabric into ½-inch (1.3 cm) pieces. Tear the recycled paper into 2-inch (5 cm) pieces. Put the fabric and paper pieces in a bowl or bucket.

2. Fill the bowl or bucket with enough water to cover the pieces of fabric and paper. Allow to soak overnight. (Photo 1)

Photo 1—Soaking the paper and fabric pieces.

3. Squeeze the water out of one handful of the soaked fabric and paper mixture and form it into a 2-inch (5 cm) ball.

4. Put the ball in the blender container. (Photo 2). Add water to the container until it is three-quarters full.

Photo 2—Putting a ball of pulp in the blender.

5. Blend on medium to high speed for 30 seconds or more. (Photo 3) **Note**—If you hear the blender straining, stop it immediately and check the blades to see if threads from the fabric have wrapped around them. Remove any clumps of threads and continue blending.

Photo 3—Blending the pulp with water.

PLANTING INSTRUCTIONS

Plant in the Ground

Tear off bits of paper that contain seeds and plant directly in the ground. The paper will compost naturally.

Sprouting the Seeds Before Planting

To sprout the seeds before planting, dampen the paper and put it in a plastic bag. Check periodically to be sure the paper stays moist. Keep the plastic bag at room temperature until the seeds sprout, then transplant them to pots or directly in the garden.

6. If the pulp is not evenly blended after one minute, use your fingers to remove any clumps of threads that haven't blended and add more fabric and pulp. Keep blending and removing clumps until the pulp is evenly blended and smooth.

7. Follow the steps in the Paper Making Process section to make your paper. Store leftover pulp in airtight containers in the refrigerator for later use.

Herb Paper

Dried and fresh herbs make very fragrant papers, but the scent will not last long. Try rosemary, thyme, basil, parsley, oregano, or dill. You can also add powdered spices (paprika, tumeric, curry powder, saffron, or chili powder) and seeds (sesame seeds, poppy seed, celery seeds) for texture and color.

INGREDIENTS

4 tablespoons (60 ml) dried herbs and/or ¼ to ½ cup (60 to 120 ml) fresh herbs (depending on the look you desire)

1 cup (240 ml) prepared and strained recycled paper pulp

INSTRUCTIONS

1. Place the recycled paper pulp in the blender container. Add water until the container is about three-quarters full.

2. Blend for 30 seconds.

3. Pull the leaves off the mint stems and put them in the blender.

4. Pulse for 2 to 3 seconds to distribute the leaves.

5. Follow the steps in the Paper Making Process section to make your paper. **Option**: If you want larger leaf pieces in your paper, prepare the pulp and pour it into the mold, then add leaves to the pulp in the mold. Use a whisk or your fingers to mix the leaves with the pulp before making the sheet.

VARIATION: LAYERED HERB PAPER

Herb stems and sprigs can be laminated between two couched sheets. Here's how:

1. Make a sheet of paper and couch it.

2. Arrange the stems or sprigs on top.

3. Make another sheet of the same paper. Couch it on top of the first sheet with the stems or sprigs.

4. Press and peel back portions of the laminated sheets to reveal the shapes of the stems and sprigs.

Lavender Paper

Lavender paper makes a fragrant liner for shelves and drawers. You can use dried buds, dried leaves, or fresh leaves to make the paper.

INGREDIENTS

2 tablespoons (30 g) dried lavender buds or fresh lavender leaves

1 cup (???) prepared and strained recycled paper pulp

INSTRUCTIONS

1. Place the recycled paper pulp in the blender container. Add water until the container is about three-quarters full.

2. Blend for 30 seconds.

3. Remove the leaves from the fresh lavender stems and place them in the blender or add the dried lavender buds to the blender.

4. Pulse 2 to 3 seconds to distribute the leaves or buds.

5. Follow the steps in the Paper Making Process section to make your paper.

Lettuce Paper

The fibers of lettuce leaves give papers personality, texture, and interest, and the natural plant pigments from lettuce leaves can produce very subtle shades in papers. When boiled, the plant materials create a concentrated liquid that can be used to stain (ass color to) the pulp. Purchased cotton pulp will take the stain much better than recycled pulps. For a deeper tint, allow the liquid pulp to sit for 4 to 6 hours or overnight before using it to make paper sheets.

INGREDIENTS

1 cup (240 ml) chopped lettuce leaves

1 cup (240 ml) prepared and strained paper pulp

Acid-free additive

TOOLS

Large nonreactive pot and spoon

Large strainer

Stovetop or hot plate

INSTRUCTIONS

1. Put the lettuce leaf pieces in the pot and fill it with enough water to cover the plant materials. Bring to a boil.

2. Reduce the heat to a simmer and continue cooking for 1 hour, stirring after 30 minutes.

3. Drain and rinse the leaves, reserving the cooked liquid.

4. Add the paper pulp and acid-free additive to the blender. (Follow the package instructions regarding how much additive to use.) Add the reserved liquid to the blender until the container is three-quarters full.

5. Blend for 30 seconds.

6. Add the cooked leaves to the blender and pulse for 2 to 3 seconds.

7. Follow the steps in the Paper Making Process section to make your paper.

Birch Bark Paper

Loose bark from river birch trees makes gorgeous naturally textured paper sheets. You can use this recipe to make papers using any kind of thin tree bark. Thin bark will flatten and adhere to the wet sheets much better than thick bark, and thin bark will not add a lot of weight or thickness to the paper.

INGREDIENTS

½ cup (120 ml) river birch bark

1 cup (240 ml) prepared and strained recycled paper clip

Acid-free additive

INSTRUCTIONS

1. Place the recycled paper pulp in the blender container. Add water until the container is about three-quarters full.

2. Blend for 30 seconds.

3. Put the birch bark in the blender and pulse for 2 to 3 seconds.

4. Follow the steps in the Paper Making Process section to make your paper.

Cinnamon Paper

Mixing ground cinnamon with crushed cinnamon sticks makes a wonderfully fragrant, textured sheet. You can revive the scent of cinnamon papers with a few drops of cinnamon essential oil.

Continued ➡

PLANTS TO USE FOR PAPER MAKING

This list includes only a few of the dried and fresh plant materials that can be used to make papers. Almost any leaf or flower can be dried and added to your papers—the only limitations are your imagination and your willingness to learn about and experiment with processing plant fibers.

To retain most of the original qualities and colors of flowers, blooms, and leaves, press them and add them to the wet pulp or to the papers after they are dried. If you're adding fresh leaves to the pulp, they should be cooked to remove any impurities (thicker leaves should be cooked in an alkaline solution) and thoroughly rinsed. Dried materials will retain their color longer and will result in better archival quality papers; manufactured materials like fabric, recycled paper, coffees, and processed textiles will speed the deterioration of your papers. To avoid disappointment, consider how you will be using your papers before you make them.

Flowers
Baby's Breath
Bachelor Buttons
Carnations
Chrysanthemums
Cornflowers
Daffodils
Geraniums
Gladiolus
Hibiscus
Hollyhock
Iris
Larkspur
Lavender
Lilies
Marigolds
Pansy
Phlox
Queen Anne's Lace
Roses

Small Daisies
Statice
Strawflowers
Sunflowers
Wisteria

Leaves
Beech
Birch
Chestnut
Elm
Grapevine
Ivy
Kudzu
Maple
Oak
Willow

Leaves & Flowers
Hosta

Hydrangea
Crepe Myrtle

Grasses, Mosses & Other Greenery
Cedar
Ferns—All Varieties
Juniper
Lawn Grass
Mosses
Ornamental Grasses
Pine Needles
Seaweed Grass
Straw
Wheat

Vegetables & Herbs
Apples
Basil
Beets

Bell peppers
Carrot Tops and Roots
Chilies
Cinnamon
Cucumbers
Curry
Dill
Lettuce
Mint
Onions
Oranges
Oregano
Paprika
Parsley
Rosemary
Saffron
Thyme
Tomatoes
Tumeric
Zucchini

INGREDIENTS

3 thin cinnamon sticks

1 teaspoon (15 ml) ground cinnamon

1 cup (240 ml) prepared and strained recycled paper pulp

TOOLS

Blender

Small zipper-top plastic bag

Hammer

INSTRUCTIONS

1. Put the cinnamon sticks in the plastic bag. Pound them with a hammer to crush them.

2. Place the recycled paper pulp in the blender container. Add water until the container is about three-quarters full.

3. Blend for 30 seconds.

4. Put the crushed cinnamon pieces in the blender and pulse for 2 to 3 seconds.

5. Pour the pulp into the mold. Sprinkle the ground cinnamon on top of the wet pulp. Gently move the cinnamon pieces and ground cinnamon pieces and ground cinnamon around until they are evenly distributed.

6. Follow the steps in the Paper Making Process section to make your paper.

7. **Option:** Tie bundles of dried cinnamon sticks or other stems or twigs to the individual sheets with ribbons or twine.

Handmade Paper Projects

I created the projects in this section with the intention of inspiring you to think about using your handmade papers in different ways. Recipes for most of the papers I used, along with photos, are included in the Paper Making Recipes section. Here are some general tips for working with handmade papers.

- Play with tearing and layering your papers. Reposition them until you are happy with the results, then glue everything together.

- Almost all papers have a grain or direction in which they can be most easily folded or torn. The best way to determine the grain is to test it by gently attempting to fold it horizontally and vertically. Notice which is easier. That's how the grain runs.

- If you glue papers and other materials with PVA, they can be easily removed with a little water.

- To cover any unsightly spots in a piece of paper, simply layer another piece of paper on top of it or cover it with another leaf or flower petal.

- Sometimes the most beautiful pressed leaf or flower is not the most perfect one. This is also true for handmade papers. The advantage of working with handmade papers and botanicals is the natural art that is created when you allow the fibers to blend together to form one-of-a-kind pieces. The natural imperfections that sometimes appear in your papers can be used to enhance your finished designs.

- Personalize! When making gifts for friends and family members, find out what their favorite flowers and plants are. Use that information to concoct unique, one-of-a-kind gifts.

Cutting Your Papers

Use scissors, a rotary cutter with decorative blades, or a craft knife to cut your papers. Cut on a self-healing mat to protect your work surface.

Tearing Papers

You can also tear papers. The torn edges will not be perfectly straight; if the paper gets creased or wrinkled, don't worry—it will flatten when you glue it. An additional benefit of tearing is the whiff of wonderful fragrance some papers provide. Mint Paper, for example, releases scent each time you peel back a torn edge, and the scent remains on your fingers for several minutes.

Using a metal deckle edge ruler to quickly tear an uneven edge.

Step 1: To create an almost straight torn edge, first fold the paper where you want to tear it. Use a clean paintbrush to apply water along the fold. (A drop of water can also help separate the fibers if your paper is highly textured.)

Step 2: Hold the paper on either side of the fold with the thumbs and forefingers of both hands and tear toward your body. For best results, tear in small sections— about ½" at a time

Plantable Seeds Greeting Card

This plantable seed paper contains sunflower seeds. They were mixed with the pulp in the blender. This makes a great gift for a gardener friend. The paper can be planted in the spring just like regular seeds would be planted. Be sure to include the planting instructions inside the card.

SUPPLIES

Ingredients and Tools for Plantable Seed Paper (See the Paper Making Recipes section.)

Sunflower seeds with hulls

Writing paper, 8 x 6 inches (20.5 x 15 cm)

Glue

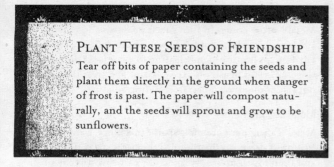

INSTRUCTIONS

MAKE THE PAPER

Make one 8½ x 11 inches (21.5 x 28 cm) piece of Plantable Seed Paper, using the recipe in the Paper Making Recipes section. Add the sunflower seeds to the blender and pulse before pouring the paper into the mold.

MAKE THE CARD

1. Tear the plantable seed paper to make a 9 x 6 inch (23 x 15 cm) piece.

2. Fold the piece in half to make a 4½ x 6-inch (11.5 x 15 cm) card.

3. Fold the writing paper in half to make an insert for the card.

4. On the left inside, write instructions for using the seed paper. On the right inside, write a greeting.

5. Slip the folded paper inside the card and attach to the crease of the card with dots of glue.

Tip—Make an instructional greeting entitled Plant These Seeds of Friendship on a piece of paper and slip it inside the card.

Include these instructions or print on the inside of the card.

Flower Saver Book

I like to make small books and fill the pages with my favorite pressed flowers to give as gifts. The cover of this one is handmade rose petal and leaves paper; I used pieces of lettuce leaf paper on the inside to hold pressed flowers. You can glue the pressed flowers to the paper with tiny dots of glue. I used red and green yarn fibers to hold the book together. You could substitute several folded pages of text-weight paper for the lettuce leaf paper to make a special journal or memory book.

SUPPLIES

1 piece rose petals and leaves paper, 8 x 6 inches (20.5 x 15 cm) (Use the recipe in the Paper Making Recipes section for Flower Petal Paper and use both dried rose petals and dried rose leaves.)

1 piece Lettuce Paper, 8" x 6" (See the Paper Making Recipes section for instructions.)

Photo and paper protectant spray

Red and green yarn or fibers

Awl

Scissors

Glue

INSTRUCTIONS

1. After making, pressing, and drying the handmade Rose Petals paper, spray the piece with photo and paper protectant. Allow to dry.

2. Fold the rose and leaves paper in half to make the front and back covers.

3. Tear the lettuce leaf paper in half to measure 4 x 6 inches (10 x 15 cm) so they fit inside the folded rose paper cover.

4. Place the lettuce lead pages inside the folded paper cover.

5. Use the awl to make two holes near the fold through all pieces of paper.

6. Thread the red and green yarn fibers through the holes and tie the ends in a loopy bow near the upper hole.

OTHER IDEAS FOR BINDING BOOKS

There are a lot of different ways to bind your books without making hard covers—just be sure that your materials are strong enough to hold the pages, and that they allow the pages to move easily without tearing.

- Use small strips of paper and glue to make tapes and attach them horizontally across the spine to hold the pages and covers together.

- Use a needle and strong thread or ribbons, raffia, leather laces, or fibers to tie or sew the pages to the covers.

- Make an accordion-style book by folding and gluing or sewing pages together.

- Stack the covers. Place the pages between the covers. Punch or drill holes through the covers and pages. (Copy shops can drill them for you.) Align the holes and hold the pages and covers together with posts and screws or nuts and bolts from the hardware store.

- Thread decorative wires with beads or items that relate to your theme through punched holes in the covers and pages.

Book Lovers Botanical Bookmarks

Dried lavender buds, oregano, and fresh rosemary make gorgeous bookmarks. These bookmarks will retain some of their herbal scent for a time. When the scents fade, refresh them with a few drops of essential oil.

Pictured left to right: Oregano Bookmark, Lavender Bookmark, Rosemary Bookmark.

Bookmarks can be easily made from scraps of paper left over from other projects. You'll find instructions in the Paper Making Recipes section for making Lavender Paper and Herb Paper. Use the Herb Paper recipe to make the oregano paper (using both buds and stems) and rosemary paper.

SUPPLIES

For each bookmark:

1 piece of handmade paper, at least 7 x 3 inches (18 x 7.5 cm)

Fibers, yarn, or twine in coordinating colors

Hole punch

INSTRUCTIONS

1. Carefully tear the handmade paper to make an irregular rectangular shape approximately 6 inches (15 cm) long and 2 inches (5 cm) wide.

2. Use a hole punch to make a hole in one end of the bookmark.

3. Thread fibers or twine through the hole and loop using a lark's head knot. (I used green and gold fibers with the rosemary paper, twine with the lavender paper, and violet and green fibers with the oregano paper.)

Birch Bark Paper Desk Accessories

To make the paper that covers this desk blotter and pencil cup project, I recycled some brown and orange papers to make the pulp, which looked dark brown in the blender. Birch bark and cedar needles were blended with the pulp to make these beautiful nature-inspired sheets. When dry, the sheets were several shades lighter than the wet pulp had been.

SUPPLIES

1 cup (240 ml) birch bark and other ingredients for 4 sheets Birch Bark Paper, 8½ x 11 inches (21.5 x 28 cm)

1 cup cedar needles

2 cork squares, 12 inches (30.5 cm)

Brown corrugated cardboard, 12 x 20 inches (30.5 x 51 cm)

Antiquing spray

Recycled soup can

Scissors

Ruler

Pencil

Glue

INSTRUCTIONS

MAKE THE PAPER

Following the instructions for Birch Bark Paper in the Paper Making Recipes section, mix and measure two separate batches of Birch Bark & Cedar Paper to make four sheets in all. Use ½ cup (120 ml) birch bark and ½ cup (120 ml) cedar for each batch.

Continued ➛

ASSEMBLE

1. Measure, mark, and cut two 12 x 4½ inches (30.5 x 11.5 cm) strips of cork from one of the cork squares. Place the two cut pieces on opposite sides of the other cork square. Glue the cork pieces to the corrugated cardboard.

2. Cut two 2¾-inch (7 cm) squares of cork to make the base for the soup can.

3. Take the cardboard and cork pad, the soup can, and the two small cork squares outside. Spray them with antiquing spray. Allow to dry.

4. Roll the soup can across one of the paper sheets and mark the length of paper needed to wrap around the can. Add ¼ inch (6 mm) for overlap and mark.

5. Add approximately 1 inch (2.5 cm) to the height of the can and mark this measurement on the paper.

6. Tear the marked paper piece. Wrap it around the can and glue the seam.

7. Glue the three remaining paper sheets to the top of the cork and cardboard blotter, overlapping them slightly.

8. Place the can on one cork square. Glue. Position the other cork square under the first as shown in the photo and glue.

Rose Petals Gift Box

When you give a gift in a box covered with handmade paper, there is no doubt that whatever is inside is special. And a gift in a box like this is really two gifts in one. I covered this little box with air-dried rose paper with embedded rosebuds and embellished it with red fibers and dried leaves and rosebuds.

SUPPLIES

Ingredients for making one sheet of Flower Petal Paper, 8½ x 11 inches (21.5 x 28 cm)

3 dried rosebuds and leaves

Cardboard box or papier mache box, 4 inches (10 cm) square

Red yarn

Scissors

Glue

Binder clips or clothespins

INSTRUCTIONS

MAKE THE PAPER

1. Make one sheet of Flower Petals Paper with dried rose petals and leaves.

2. After removing the wet sheet from the mold place two rosebuds on the paper.

3. Use your fingers to put some wet pulp on top of the rosebuds, covering the stem ends.

4. Couch the wet paper sheet and allow it to air dry.

COVER THE BOX

1. With the rosebuds centered on the box top, cut a piece of paper to cover the top of the box. Cover the box top, securing it with glue. Hold the paper in place with binder clips or clothes pins until the glue dries.

2. Cover the sides of the box with the remaining paper.

3. Glue the remaining dried rosebud to one side of the embedded rosebuds. Glue three dried leaves to surround the rosebud.

4. Put the gift in the box. Wrap the box with red yarn and tie them in a loose bow on top of the rosebuds.

—FROM *Handmade Paper from Naturals*

QUICK & CLEVER GIFT WRAPS

Nicole Steiman

Getting Started

If you love creating things, chances are you have most gift-wrapping supplies already at your fingertips, even though you may not be currently using the, to wrap gifts. Mixed media, scrapbooking, quilting, painting, and rubber-stamping supplies can all be used to create unique and clever packages for special occasions.

Gift wrapping is art that you give away, making the creation a celebration all by itself. Look through your office supplies, fabric, and wallpaper scraps, restaurant to-go bags, and even printed papers and charms. Before long you'll be coveting the plain, brown-handled bags at the store just as much as the purchases they contain. So gather your supplies and friends together to have a wrap party that will engage all of your creative juices.

Embellishments

Alcohol Ink

This type of ink adheres well to nonporous, slick surfaces. It is packaged in dropper bottles and can be applied directly on surfaces, applied with a felt applicator, or painted on with a brush.

Beads and Flat-backed Crystals

Almost anything can be decorated by adding beads. Adhere larger beads with strong-hold glue. Smaller beads and flat-backed crystals can be adhered quickly with extra tacky double-sided tape.

Brads

Brads are ideal for wrapping because they not only decorate but also attach and hold wrapping items together. Studs are similar to brads except that they have multiple prongs along the outer edge of the head, which are then pushed through the paper or fabric. Eyelets make interesting lace-up effects for bottles and cylinders, as well as decorated patterns.

Charms

There are a multitude of shaped charms for endless occasions, made of materials ranging from plastic to metal. Adhere charms with a hot-glue gun or clear-drying metal glue. Small flat-backed charms will even stick with extra tacky double-sided tape.

Foil

Metallic and colored foils add a shiny, raised dimension. Foil is a common supply at printer shops and also art supply stores. Adhere it shiny side up to projects using double-sided tape, foiling and glue pens, and even glue sticks.

Glitter

Glitter comes in various forms, from superfine to chunky, mica powders, and flakes. Glitter glue has adhesive already mixed with the glitter, which makes it easy to apply. It works particularly well for superfine lines and topcoats, and to create free-form shapes and borders.

Metal Leafing

Metal leafing comes in thin sheets or flakes and is generally found in silver, gold, copper, or variegated colors. For fast application, apply leafing to extra tacky double-sided tape and brush off excess flakes. For areas that are not flat enough for tape, use a leafing adhesive.

Metal Leafing Pens

Metal leafing pens are metal paint in a marker applicator. Just press down on the tip until the paint starts flowing, and then touch up your projects by coloring directly on the item.

Metal Sheets

Available in different materials, usually aluminum or copper, metals come in various gauges. Can be embossed, crimped, and even punched with craft punches to make charms. The higher the gauge, the thinner the metal. Use a gauge between 36 and 40 to crimp or emboss designs.

Ribbons

Ribbons come in endless combinations of colors and materials. Common types are satin, grosgrain, and wired and unwired organdy sheer. Generally, the more elaborate the wrapping, the simpler the bow, and the smaller the package, the smaller the ribbon width.

Stencils and Templates

Use ready-made stencils or create your own from heavy cardstock or stencil film. Letter and number oil board stencils are available from office supply stores and add an interesting graphic look.

Trims

In addition to ribbons there are countless other interesting trims that can be wrapped around a gift or glued to the center of a bow. Pom-pom fringe, strips of paper, and netting suggest a wide ribbon effect. In addition, bunches of flowers, sprays, seashells, hanging tassels, and feathers are just a few of the add-ons that make great toppers for gifts.

Techniques

Applying Alcohol Ink

Alcohol inks work best on glossy, nonporous surfaces, which allows the paint to float on the surface. This floating quality of the ink allows you to create color blending. For more floating, apply a blending solution before painting and also during the application for interesting effects. Inks can be dropped right out of the dropper bottles or sponged on with a felt applicator. The metallic paint of leafing pens acts as a resist to the inks, causing veining that resembles marbling. Applying alcohol inks is a quick way to create an elegant painted surface on a metal object, such as a tin flower can or mint tin. Just dab the color and leafing pen right onto the felt, and then quickly sponge onto the project surface.

Applying Foil

Foil provides metallic accents and is usually found on a roll or packaged in small sheets. Although commercial printers use hot press machines to create these shiny, raised accents, it is very easy and fun to do using basic tools. To apply random highlights of foil, simply swipe a glue stick around the edges or across the top of your paper and before the glue dries, place a sheet of foil, shiny side up, on top of it; rub firmly, and then lift the sheet. Because of the quick-drying nature of a glue stick, some parts of the foil will stick while others won't, creating a random effect that looks great, especially around edges of photos. If you want the foil to stick more thoroughly, use a foiling pen. Simply write a word, draw a picture, or accent a patterned paper. The glue will appear tinted blue when it first comes out. Let the glue dry until it is tacky and clear. Then press your foil down, shiny side up, and lift. Micro-fine glitters and leafing metals also adhere easily to foiling pens.

Setting Studs

Place paper or fabric right side up on top of a thick foam cushion. Place stud in desired location, push firmly through paper or fabric, and then lift out of the foam and turn material over to the back side. Using the flat edge of a bone folder, bend each prong toward the center of the stud. If you are setting a large number of studs, there are setters that make the process seamless. Simply follow the manufacturer's instructions.

Time-Saving Tip: Sealing Wax

Sealing wax is an elegant way to close an envelope flap or hold a ribbon or feather in place. Use real wax sticks that contain a little polymer for flexibility. This will ensure that the wax does not get too brittle and crack when mailing or being handled.

Stamping with Bleach

Creating your own patterned papers is easy by using premade stamp designs. Instead of inkpads, try making your own bleach pad by carefully pouring undiluted bleach onto a sponge set in a tray or on a plate. Stamp in the same manner as with an inkpad. After stamping, allow time for the bleach effect to appear. Make sure to dispose of your sponge afterward. For safer options, you can also purchase inkpads that mimic the effects of bleach or create a watermark effect.

Wrapping Neatly and Crisply

Anyone can wrap paper around something and tape it. Make your gift wrapping look more professional by cutting the appropriate amount of paper; extra paper creates a bulky, sloppy look. Cut enough paper to wrap around the width of the box, plus 2–4 inches (5–10 cm) more for the seam. For the ends of the box, cut paper long enough to equal the length of the box, plus one and a half times the box height. Use a measuring tape or marked string, or simply unroll the paper and cut using the package on top as a guide. Use double-sided tape under the edges that you secure rather than cellophane tape on top. Before taping down paper edges, fold them under to make a straight, crisp edge. When wrapping paper around a box, make the seam fall on the edge of the package or meet in the middle where you can cover it with ribbon. After wrapping, create crisp edges by running a thumb and forefinger along all the edges of the package, pinching them around the corners to create a tightly wrapped look.

Wrapping Ribbon Around a Gift

One common way to use ribbon on a present is to wrap it around all four sides, crossing underneath, and finally tying it in a shoelace bow on top. This is usually accomplished by flipping the box upside down and criss-crossing both ends of the ribbon, causing a section of twisted ribbon on the bottom of the gift. It's not a bad method, but who wouldn't want a flatter bottom? Following are a few refinements that will make your tied package look better and give it a less bulky bottom. **Note**—An added advantage to this technique is that you can leave the ribbon on the bolt, or figure out the needed length of ribbon by measuring around both sides of the box and adding either 24 inches (61 cm) for a shoelace bow or 8 inches (20.5 cm) for a simple knot.

When the instructions refer to the top of the box, it is the side you see when looking down from above.

Hold one end of ribbon on top center of the gift box with your thumb. Wrap remaining ribbon vertically around box back to top (Fig. 1).

Figure 1

Wrap longer ribbon length around shorter ribbon in a 90-degree angle and around the side, under box and back to top (Fig. 2).

Figure 2

Tuck long end of ribbon over and then under ribbon twist made in previous step (Fig. 3).

Knot ribbon ends and then tie in a shoelace bow, trim to desired length (Fig. 4).

Figure 3

Figure 4

Making Bows

There are many types of bows, but knowing just a few elegant ones will enable you to create the perfect embellishment for any gift, whether it's a box, bag, or bottle. **Note**—For many of the following instructions, you will need to use ribbon off a bolt rather than a specified length and then cut the ribbon once the bow is complete.

Shoelace Bow

The shoelace bow is the most common type of bow found on a gift and is named after the bow you tie on your shoe. Extra ribbons in various textures and colors can be tied onto the base of the bow to make it more decorative.

Wrap ribbon around the gift and tie a half-knot to secure, leaving a tail at least 10 inches (25.5 cm). From starting knot, form equal length loops with each ribbon end (Fig. 1).

Cross right loop over left loop, forming an X. Wrap top of right loop down over left loop, aiming for the hole in the bottom of the X (Fig. 2).

Figure 1 *Figure 2*

Figure 3 *Figure 4*

Thread right loop through hole (Fig. 3).

Pull loops tight, forming a bow; adjust as needed (Fig. 4). Trim tails to desired length.

Florist Bow

Florist bows have a variety of loops in graduated sizes. The loops are wired together and then spread apart to make a rounded shape with hanging tails. Bow-making devices are very helpful when making these types of bows because

---

Ribbon Bow Guidelines

As a general rule, the lighter or thinner the ribbon you use, the more loops your bow should have, usually 6–12 per side. And the heavier and wider the ribbon, the longer your loops should be, approximately 2–6 inches (5–15 cm).

Use this easy calculation to figure how much ribbon your bow will need. Amount of ribbon = 2 x (bow loop size) x (total amount of loops, both sides) + length of tails on each side. For example, a bow with twelve 3" loops will require 84 inches (214 cm) of ribbon (2 x 3 x 12 + 12 = 84). In other words, twelve 6 inch (15 cm) loops of ribbon, plus a 6 inch (15 cm) tail on each side. When at all possible, use ribbon off the bolt to allow for slight variations in the loop size.

---

they hold the loops together while you secure them with wire. Although more expensive, wired ribbon is also very useful to help the loops hold a more pronounced shape.

Note: Tying this bow takes some experience, so it's a good idea to practice making a few before creating one for your gift.

Pinch the ribbon and form a loop, leaving desired length of ribbon for one bow tail (Fig. 1). Make same-size loop in the opposite direction (Fig. 2).

Figure 1

Continue adding loops on each side, securing them under thumb and forefinger, decreasing loop lengths for each layer (Fig. 3).

Figure 2

Figure 3 *Figure 4*

Once you have desired number of loops, twist one last small loop around your thumb to make center loop (Fig. 4). Insert floral wire through center loop and twist tightly on bow back, securing all loops. Fluff out bow, starting with bottom two loops.

Pull loops tightly in opposite directions. Continue with remaining loops until you have desired bow shape (Fig. 5). Trim tails to desired length using an angled cut. To create a forked cut, fold end of ribbon in half lengthwise and cut at an angle toward folded edge.

Figure 5

Continued ➡

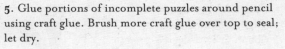
Birthday Baubles

MATERIALS

- Adhesives: dimensional glossy glue, double-sided tape
- Gift box
- Glass pebbles: ⅜-inch (1 cm) clear flat-backed
- Kraft paper
- Ribbon: 2-inch (5 cm) wired sheer light blue
- Scissors

INSTRUCTIONS

1. Wrap box in kraft paper, securing edges with double-sided tape.

2. Apply dot of dimensional glossy glue to center back of glass gem and press onto kraft paper. Repeat randomly across entire top of package. Wait a few minutes, and then turn to another side. Repeat for all remaining sides.

3. Wrap wired ribbon around package and tie in a shoelace bow. Shape wire as desired.

Time-saving Tip: Gluing on Porous Papers

This technique will not work well on glossy papers because the glue will have nothing porous to soak into. Although glass usually only adheres with super glue, the porous quality of kraft paper creates a nice bond that allows you to move to the next side almost as soon as you finish with the first.

Puzzle

MATERIALS

- Adhesives: ¼-inch (6 mm)-wide tacky tape, craft glue, glue stick, spray adhesive
- Craft knife
- Foam brush
- Gift box
- Papers: black kraft, corrugated cardboard
- Pencil
- Puzzle book
- Ribbon: ⅝-inch (1.5 cm) black grosgrain
- Ruler
- Scissors

INSTRUCTIONS

1. Cut length of corrugated cardboard long enough to wrap box. Cut piece of black kraft paper slightly smaller than cardboard so it doesn't extend past cardboard edges when folded. Apply spray adhesive to black kraft paper and lay cardboard on top with corrugated texture facing up. Let dry until tacky, about 10–15 minutes.

2. Wrap gift with layered paper, corrugated side facing out. Adhere sides with tacky tape.

3. Cut 2-inch (5 cm) square of cardboard to use as template. On corrugated box, trace around template with craft knife, creating random windows as desired. Be careful to only cut through cardboard layer. Remove cardboard layer to reveal black kraft paper underneath.

4. Cut out puzzles from puzzle book to fit in windows. Adhere using glue stick.

5. Glue portions of incomplete puzzles around pencil using craft glue. Brush more craft glue over top to seal; let dry.

6. Wrap ribbon around package and knot, leaving long tails for bow. Tie shoelace bow around pencil. Trim ribbon tails as desired.

Vintage Holiday

MATERIALS

- Adhesive: glue stick, hot-glue gun
- Brads: mini silver (3)
- Charms: silver pinwheels (3)
- Faux berries: small cluster
- Glitter glue: platinum
- Metal sheet: 5-inch (12.5 cm) square 38-gauge aluminum
- Paper: antique sheet music
- Piercing tool
- Punch: 1½-inch (4 cm) snowflake
- Ruler
- Trim: red pompom (8-inch [20.5 cm])
- Vintage image

INSTRUCTIONS

1. Tear piece of sheet music to 5½ x 8 inches (12.5 x 20.5 cm). Center and adhere to bag using glue stick.

2. Adhere vintage image to left side of sheet music with glue stick. Outline image with glitter glue; let dry.

3. Punch three snowflake shapes out of metal. Make hole in center of each shape with piercing tool.

4. Pierce three holes in a row along bottom of bag, spacing them evenly. Thread pinwheel charms and snowflakes onto brad prongs; attach brads to bag through punched holes.

5. Glue pompom trim along top edge of bag with hot-glue gun; glue sprig of berries to right side of sheet music.

Time-Saving Tip: Flattening Metal Charms

Punching shapes out of metal is a great way to make your own inexpensive metal charms. The punch usually pinches the edges of the cut design to finish off the edges nicely. To eliminate sharp edges, like the ones the snowflake creates, simply lay the charm flat and pound it with a rubber mallet to flatten it.

Sweetheart Candy

MATERIALS

- ¼-inch (6 mm)-wide tacky tape
- Candy; sweetheart necklaces (2)
- Eyelet setting tools
- Eyelets: ⅜-inch (1 cm) aluminum (4)
- Gift bag: 8 x 9½-inch (20.5 x 24 cm) glossy hot pink
- Ruler
- Scissors
- Sealer: clear protective spray
- Tissue paper: coordinating color (2–3 sheets)
- Wire: 20-gauge nickel or aluminum (48-inch [122 cm])
- Wire cutters

INSTRUCTIONS

1. Cut off bag handle using scissors. Insert eyelets into handle holes and set with eyelet setting tools.

2. Adhere candy to bag as desired using tacky tape. **Optional:** Seal candy before adhering to the bag by lightly spraying it with clear protective spray and letting it dry.

3. Cut two 24-inch (61 cm) lengths of wire for handles using wire cutters. On one side of bag, thread 4-inches (10 cm) of one wire length through one hole of bag from front to back. Bend wire back up and wrap it tightly around itself four times in a close spiral; trim any excess.

4. String candles from one necklace onto wire. Thread opposite end of wire into remaining hole and repeat wire wrapping. Bend handle to desired shape. Repeat on remaining bag handle. Insert gift and add tissue paper to cover.

Time-saving Tip: To Eat or Not to Eat

It's a good idea to apply a few coats of protective spray to preserve the candy if the gift will be exposed to humidity, heat, or rain. Be sure to warn the recipient that the candy is not to be eaten.

Sweet Treats

MATERIALS

- 1-¹⁄₁₆-inch (2.7 cm)-wide tacky tape
- Plastic file folder: frosted white
- Ponytail holder with acrylic beads: pink
- Ruler
- Scissors
- Tissue paper: dots, white

INSTRUCTIONS

1. Cut approximately 8 x 11 inches (21.5 x 28 cm) piece from plastic file folder after cutting off pockets, rings, and finished edges. Place a strip of tacky tape on one long edge and wrap into cylinder shape, overlapping opposite edge on top of tacky tape to secure. **Note:** The final cut size will vary, depending on how much of the folder must be cut in order to make a solid piece.

2. Wrap gift in tissue and place inside tube.

3. Wrap white tissue paper around cylinder several times, leaving approximately 3 inches (7.5 cm) extending past either end.

4. Cut dot tissue paper to wrap around cylinder once with 3 inches (7.5 cm) extending past either end. Wrap and secure with small piece of tacky tape.

5. Secure ends with pink acrylic ponytail holders, forming a wrapped candy shape.

Time-saving Tip: See-Through Surprise

Office dots, stickers and ribbons also make decorations for the tubes. Use lengths of decorative ribbons to cover the seam when joining the edges of the tube. After creating your tube, wrap it with clear cellophane instead of tissue to let the contents show through.

Paper Strips

MATERIALS

- Adhesives: craft glue, double-sided tape, quick-dry glue
- Beads: large (2)
- Paper strip: 1 x 12 inches (2.5 x 30.5 cm), 2 x 12 inches (5 x 30.5 cm) various black designs (12)
- Ribbon: ½-inch (1.3 cm)-wide black grosgrain (18 inches (45.5 cm)

INSTRUCTIONS

1. Adhere large bead to top of bottle with quick-dry glue.

2. Glue eleven paper strips to each other, allowing a 1-inch (2.5 cm) overlap with each new strip, to create 12-inch (30.5 cm) square piece of paper using craft glue.

3. Cover bottle on four sides and along bottom edge with double-sided tape.

4. Starting at backside, wrap paper square around bottle. Secure ends of paper with double-sided tape.

5. Tie ribbon into a bow around neck of bottle. Thread each ribbon end through a large bead. Knots ends of ribbon, if necessary.

Time-saving Tip: Keep Your Scraps

Paper is so fun to work with, and it's often difficult to let go of scraps of your favorite patterns. Keep in mind that leftover strips, squares, and other pieces can be placed together to make wrapping paper. Papers can also be adhered to a box with decoupage medium to make a permanent wrap.

Holiday Surprise

MATERIALS

- Adhesives: ¼-inch (6 mm)-wide tacky tape, glue stick
- Chipboard pieces: 1¾-inch square (4.5 cm) (2), 1¾ x 2¾ inch (4.5 x 7 cm) (1)
- Cord: gold (24 inch [61 cm])
- Embossing powder: gold
- Heat gun
- Inkpad: gold pigment
- Leafing pen: gold
- Marker: fine-point black
- Note card with envelope: 6½ x 4½ inches (16.5 x 11.5 cm)
- Paper: 4-inch (10 cm) square burgundy-and-gold marbled (2), 3¼ x 5-inches (8.5 x 12.5 cm) gold vellum
- Ribbon: ⅝-inch (1.5 cm)-wide gold-edged sheer
- Rubber stamp: snowflakes
- Scissors

INSTRUCTIONS

1. Create gift card sleeve using Sleeve Diagram and gold vellum (Fig. 1).

2. Apply glue stick to side flap. Fold opposite side over and attach to flap. Apply glue stick to bottom flap and fold up to close bottom of sleeve.

3. Wrap marbled paper around chipboard squares and adhere. Wrap gold cord around a wrapped square and tie in a shoelace bow. Repeat with remaining wrapped square.

4. Adhere vellum gift card sleeve to large chipboard piece. Tie shoelace bow using ribbon and adhere to card sleeve. Adhere sleeve and wrapped squares to card front using tacky tape.

5. Stamp snowflakes on note card using gold inkpad. Sprinkle with gold embossing powder and melt with heat gun. Color edges using gold leafing pen. Insert gift card into sleeve on card front and write message inside card.

Valentine CD Holder

MATERIALS

- Bone folder
- Cardstock: 12-inch (30.5 cm) square red kraft
- CD
- CD holder: cardboard
- Embossed foil borders: gold
- Foil: gold, red
- Foiling pen
- Glue stick
- Inkpad: black waterproof
- Paper: 12-inch (30.5 cm) square patterned
- Rubber stamp: 3½-inch (9 cm) heart
- Ruler
- Scissors

INSTRUCTIONS

1. Stamp heart on red cardstock with black inkpad; cut out. Apply foiling pen in swirled design on heart; let dry to become tacky and clear, about 15–20 minutes. Once dry, apply red foil shiny side up; press down and then peel off quickly, leaving foil accents on glued areas.

2. Carefully open CD holder where it is glued together on flaps and flatten. Adhere front of holder to back side of patterned paper with glue stick and trim excess paper. Adhere kraft cardstock to inside of holder and trim excess.

3. Retrace scored lines of holder with ruler and bone folder. Refold holder and glue flaps back together with glue stick.

4. Randomly swipe holder cover with glue stick. Immediately press gold foil on glue and lift off, leaving random foil designs; repeat as desired on front and back.

5. Using glue stick, apply gold-embossed foil borders to front cover, wrapping around to the inside. Adhere foiled heart to center of cover.

6. Rub black inkpad along top of inside edge.

7. Create card to match using remaining paper and cardstock; insert gift card into right side of holder. Insert personalized CD into sleeve on left side.

Coffee Bean Cup

MATERIALS

- Adhesives: ¼-inch (6 mm) tacky tape, glue stick
- Coffee beans (1 cup [340 g])
- Corrugated sleeve
- Foam cup with lid: 5¼-inch (13.5 cm)
- Inkpad: brown
- Marker: fine-point black
- Paper: coordinating colors and patterns (2)

Photo D

- Ribbon: ⅝-inh (1.5 cm)-wide black grosgrain (32-inches) (81.5 cm)
- Rubber stamp: coffee bean
- Ruler
- Scissors
- Shipping tag: 1⅜ x 1¾-inch (3.5 x 4.5 cm) kraft
- Tissue paper: 2½ x 9½-inch (6.5 x 29 cm) kraft circle

INSTRUCTIONS

1. Cut eight 1¼ x 5¼-inch (3 x 13.5 cm) strips of patterned papers. Glue strips vertically side by side at top of cup, overlapping strips to make it seem as if paper is tapered.

2. Adhere corrugated sleeve around middle of cup with tacky tape. Fold tissue paper in half lengthwise, wrap around center of slave and secure with glue.

3. Fill cup with coffee beans, insert gift card, and place lid on top. Wrap ribbon around cup and knot on top of lid.

4. Stamp shipping tag with coffee bean stamp and write message. Tie onto ribbon tail.

Time-saving Tip: Coffee Bean Surprise

Many coffee-houses will give you a cup full of beans at no charge when you purchase their gift cards. In addition, the cup sleeve can be turned inside out for an instant corrugated trim.

—FROM *Make It in Minutes: Quick & Clever Gift Wraps*

RECYCLED GIFT WRAP

Susan Wasinger

Wrapped Up

It's a wrap: We're making a list, checking it twice...then we're staying up past midnight begrudgingly wrapping gifts in sheets of overpriced flocked finery that we top with bows made in a sweatshop in China and tags that are as personal as an appointment reminder from the dentist. But all that's about to change. Check out the works of art that you can whip up with just a few humble materials and simple craft techniques, like the following: recycled newsprint, paper bags, manila envelopes that are crumpled so they resemble Florentine fabric, easy-to-do block printing, beautiful, colorful, eclectic wallpapers cut from discarded sample books, raffia, hemp, and jute string, an intriguing pastiche of baubles and beads, and old soda-pop caps.

Materials

Large sheets of paper to recycle: newspaper, paper bags, Tissue paper

Craft paints in various colors, including metallics

Cover-weight paper for tags and bows

Raffia, jute, or hemp string

Bottle caps

Continued ➡

You can use all kinds of things to make a print: a potato or apple can be cut into a simple shape to make a printing block. Even a rolled scroll of paper makes a print when the edge is dipped in paint.

Photo D

Tools

- Scissors
- Pinking shears
- Stapler
- Hole punch
- Paper plate for paint
- Drill to make holes in bottle caps

Crushed Paper

Transform paper that looks unfashionably utilitarian into something that has a handmade texture resembling crushed silk. Paper that would otherwise be too stiff to use as wrapping can be crumpled and crushed to make a soft paper that wraps beautifully and defies its roots. The secret is to ball up the paper first, then unroll it, then crumple it repeatedly until it crushes easily into a small ball. Unroll it, smooth it out, and it's ready to wrap.

What to recycle

- Newspaper or newsprint
- Plain white bond paper
- Brown paper bags
- Old sheet music
- Craft paper
- Maps
- Manila envelopes
- Last year's wrapping paper
- Wallpaper scraps
- Old books

Recycled Wallpaper Scraps

Wallpaper comes in a dizzying array of colors, patterns, and materials. Many papers are designed to look beautiful together—they share the same palette and are made for mixing and matching. This makes them ideal for decorating packages. You can use a wide swath of floral paper to wrap the package, then cut a thin band of striped paper to make a color-coordinated ribbon. Then cut out a paisley or a medallion to decorate the tag. Because wallpaper patterns change with each new season, wallpaper sample books are frequently tossed in the Dumpster, so they're free for the taking. Look for books full of more "papery" wallpaper, rather than the kind that's vinyl-coated and too thick or stiff to use for wrapping presents.

Where to find wallpaper samples

- Wallpaper and paint stores
- Interior decorators
- Some fabric shops

Baubles, Beads, and Tags

Use your imagination to top off a package: You can raid the junk drawer, the hardware aisle, the bead and button jar, and the recycling bin to find lots of beautiful baubles to decorate your gifts. For personalizing packages, keep a rubber stamp alphabet or letter stickers on hand. A fun trick: Recycle the postmarked stamp from mailed envelopes to make tags (see photo).

What to try

- Old game pieces
- Antique keys
- Seashells
- Large metal and glass beads
- Alphabet beads
- Pop bottle tops
- Brass washers
- Fancy brads
- Tags and stickers from the office supply store
- String
- Raffia

—From *Eco Craft*

CARD MAKING

Dawn Cusick & Megan Kirby, Editors

If you're a crafter looking for a new creative canvas, memory cards offer a fun way to explore the simple joy of the handcrafted gesture. With a multitude of possible materials and a few easy steps, you can honor cherished memories and create new ones with cards that will be treasured for years to come.

Paper

The most essential material for card making, paper now comes in an astonishingly wide range of weights, colors, patterns, and textures.

Glue

PVA (polyvinyl acetate) is the common white craft glue that dries clear and works well for almost any gluing job. Other options include glue sticks, spray adhesive, double-sided tape, and hot glue.

Craft Knife

Keep one of these at hand and replace the blades often to make a variety of precise, sharp cuts.

Cutting Mat

Protect your work surface with a purchased self-healing cutting mat. When in a bind, an ordinary kitchen cutting board will suffice.

Metal Ruler

A metal ruler provides necessary measuring guidelines while also serving as a straightedge for scoring and cutting.

Scissors

Besides the ordinary household scissors, there are also many paper edgers that can create interesting decorative effects—from a deckled edge to zigzags—on cards and collage materials.

Hole & Shaped Punches

Use a common hole punch or shaped craft punches to create paper shapes for collage or negative space in a larger piece of paper.

Bone Folder

This inexpensive tool is invaluable in creating crisp folds and a flat, even finish to glued papers.

Decorative Elements

Anything goes: junk jewelry, pressed flowers, hardware store finds, craft wire, fabric, eyelets, beads, buttons, photocopies, natural materials, ribbon, and so much more!

Basic Techniques

Gluing and Burnishing

Whether your glue of choice comes in a spray can, a stick, or a bottle, there is one method you should follow to glue materials to cards.

1. Lay the piece of paper on a scrap piece of paper, with the side that will be adhered facing up.

2. Brush, cover, or spray your adhesive on the entire paper surface, extending past the edges.

3. To seal the bond between the glued and dry surfaces (called burnishing), place a piece of scrap paper over the surface you have just glued, and press firmly along the entire area with a bone folder. The bone folder can alter the appearance of the paper it is burnishing, so the scrap paper provides a protective layer to keep you from damaging your card surface.

Note: Be sure to use a fresh sheet of paper each time you are gluing to prevent sticky residue from transferring onto your new paper.

Embellishing

The joy is in the details, especially when making cards. From decorative papers to photographs, fibers to three-dimensional objects, there is an infinite variety of embellishment materials waiting to be transformed into a mailable piece of artwork. Leftover scraps from other craft projects and even ordinary household items can find new life in the small canvas of a card. The only limit is your own imagination.

Making a Blank Card

While blank cards are widely available, you may wish to create your own blank card to suit your own particular needs.

1. Decide what size card you would like to create, and cut a piece of card stock that measures twice that size. For example, if you wish to create a 4- x 5-inch (10 x 12.5 cm) card, cut a piece of card stock measuring 8 x 5 inches (20 x 12.5 cm). If you are making a card to fit in a premade envelope, it will need to be approximately ⅛ to ⅜ inch (3 to 9 mm) smaller than the envelope.

2. Lightly mark the midpoint on the inside of the card paper. Line up a ruler along this midpoint. Using a bone folder, score along this line from one end to the other. This breaks the top layer of paper fibers, making it easier to create a good fold.

3. Fold the card in half along the scored midpoint. Run the edge of the bone folder across the fold, pressing firmly.

Note: You can add an interesting border to your card by cutting the front edge with a pair of decorative scissors or tear it along a deckle-edged ruler.

Setting Eyelets

Eyelets make beautiful additions to hand-crafted cards. See the Scrapbooking section for step-by-step instructions on setting eyelets.

Aging Materials with Tea and Coffee Dyes

Create an antiqued look by dyeing fabric or paper using a very strong brew of tea or coffee. Add a teaspoon of vinegar to the dye solution to keep your dyed items from fading.

Chamomile tea results in a yellow color, while many fruit teas can create shades of orange and red. Black teas such as oolong or pekoe vary from brown to beige. Coffee creates a rich amber to dark brown effect.

Dip the paper or fabric in the dye, and let it sit for 20 to 60 minutes, depending on the darkness you want to achieve. If the color is not dark enough, return it to the solution. You can also paint on the dye solution for a more controlled effect. If the dye runs into an area where you don't want it, use a cottonball or tissue to soak up excess.

Note: The tannic acid in tea is not archival and eventually (after 30 years or so) it will degrade your work, as all acids will do. Coffee dyes should not degrade work for 75 to 100 years.

Cutting Windows

Windowed cards are easy to make and let you create all sorts of interesting special effects.

1. To make a window, first measure and mark the area you'd like open on the front side of your card.

HANDLE WITH CARE:

Postal Tips

Now that you've spent your valuable time and creativity crafting a card, make sure that your card arrives at its destination safe and sound and in a timely manner. Handmade cards often use bulky, weighted materials and unconventional envelope sizes. Take the extra effort to protect your card. An extra layer of paper wrapped around the card before placing in an envelope can make all the difference. If you can, take your cards to the post office so that each item can be properly weighed and stamped as "fragile."

2. Open the card up (so there's no chance you'll cut through the back side), and cut out the window with a craft knife. If you are having trouble getting smooth, clean cuts, switch to a new blade.

Making Multilayered Cards

Multilayered cards are a great way to showcase specialty papers such as vellums. When layering, be sure to choose papers that are distinctly different in color and/or texture for maximum effect.

1. To make a multilayered card, first make multiple blank cards with the same dimensions. Pierce holes about an inch (2.5 cm) from the edges of the fold line at top and bottom.

2. Align the cards so their right sides face up, then thread an embroidery needle with 12 inches (30 cm) of ribbon (or yarn, colored wire, embroidery floss, etc.). Insert the threaded needle through hole at the top edge of the card on the inside and bring it up on the outside of the card. Unthread the needle, then go back to the inside of the card and rethread the needle. Bring it up through the hole closest to the bottom edge and out on the front side.

3. Turn the card over and tie the ribbon ends in a bow.

Projects

Colorful Crayon Card

Designer: Nicole Tuggle

Die-cut paper shapes are available in most craft stores, and offer an easy, inexpensive foundation for card-making creativity. This card can be made with any long, symmetrical die-cut shape. Simply write your message on the reverse side to surprise any young recipient.

MATERIALS AND TOOLS

3 large crayon-shaped paper die cuts, approximately 5 inches (12.5 cm) long

3 pages of primary colored card stock

2 pieces of white card stock, measuring 1 x 7 inches (2.5 x 17 cm)

Ruler

Bone folder

Scissors

Craft brush

Clear-drying craft glue

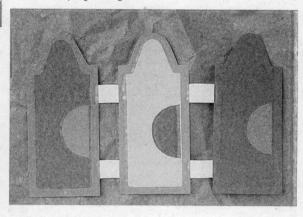

WHAT TO DO

1. Cut three half circles approximately 2 inches (5 cm) in diameter in three different colors. Glue one half circle at the right middle side of each crayon shape. Set aside to dry.

2. Brush a thin layer of glue along the entire back side of one of the crayon shapes. Press down onto a sheet of card stock in a different color. Burnish the surface to remove any wrinkles or air bubbles. With a pencil, lightly draw a line approximately ¼ inch (6 mm) around the entire crayon shape, following the contours. Cut along the pencil line. Repeat with other two crayon shapes.

3. Glue down the center of one of the white strips of card stock along the back of one of the crayon shapes, ½ inch (12 mm) from bottom. Glue the center of the other white strip ½ inch (1.3 cm) from the top.

4. Glue the two left strap ends to the back side of a second crayon shape, leaving ¾ inch (19 mm) of white paper between the two shapes. Glue the right two straps to the back side of the third crayon shape. Set aside to dry.

5. Using a bone folder, score the center point of each strap between each crayon shape. Fold along each score line. Fold again in the opposite direction so the card will fold upon itself with ease.

VARIATION

Glue smaller crayon-shaped die cuts onto a rectangular card to create a playful crayon-box effect.

Continued ➔

Eyelet Cards

Designer: Nicole Tuggle

Eyelets are one of the hottest trends in crafting. Available in a rainbow of colors and an ever-increasing variety of shapes and sizes, they serve as practical connective tools, add visual flair, and open a world of creative possibilities to the inventive card maker.

Thank-You Card

Take the time to show your gratitude with this simply elegant card. The use of the French word "Merci" adds a touch of worldly class.

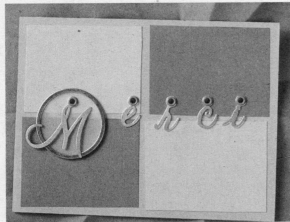

Materials and Tools

Light blue folded paper card, measuring 5½ x 4 inches (14 x 10 cm)

2 pieces of dark gray paper, measuring 1¾ x 2½ inches (4.5 x 6 cm)

2 pieces of light gray paper, measuring 1¾ x 2½ inches

5⅛-inch (13 cm) round blue eyelets

Circular metal-framed tag

Metal eyelet letters

Eyelet punch

Eyelet setting tool

Hammer

Clear-drying glue

Craft brush

Bone folder

Pencil

What to Do

1. Brush a thin layer of glue along the back side of one of the pieces of dark gray paper. Press down onto the top right corner of the card front, leaving approximately ⅛ inch (3 mm) of blank space along all sides. Glue one of the light gray pieces of paper onto the bottom right corner of the card. Repeat this step on the left side of the card with the other pieces of paper so that the dark piece is on the bottom left and the light on the top left. Be sure to leave ⅛ inch (3 mm) of blank space along all sides. Place a piece of scrap paper over the card surface, and burnish. Set aside to dry.

2. Select the letters needed for your chosen word. Place them on the dry card and play with layout options. Once you have decided how the letters will sit on the card, set all the letters aside.

3. Place the metal-framed tag on the exact spot on the card where it will appear. Mark the spot through the hole at the top with a pencil. Open the card so the back is safely out of the way of your punching surface, and place on a suitable surface. (If you do not have a punching mat, a small stack of magazines will do.) Punch a hole in the card directly over the pencil mark. Insert the eyelet into the hole of the first letter, through the hole of the circular tag, then through the paper surface of the card. Carefully turn the project

over, keeping the eyelet in place. To set the eyelet, position the setting tool into the back of the eyelet, then strike the setting tool with a hammer to flatten out the eyelet and secure it in place.

4. Repeat Step 3 for the remaining letters. Always be sure to open the card flat, leaving the back of the card out of the punching area.

Circular Frame Card

Eyelets are a great way to hold photos or other images in place. Here a photocopy of an old engraving takes center stage in this stunning study in blue.

Materials and Tools

Bright blue folded paper card, measuring 5 x 7 inches (12.5 x 18 cm)

Text paper (Try an old letter or page from an old book), measuring 3 x 4½ inches (7.5 x 11.5 cm)

Blue vellum, measuring 3¼ x 4¾ inches (8 x 12 cm)

4⅛-inch (11.5 cm) round blue eyelets

1⅛-inch (2.8 cm) round aluminum eyelet

Circular metal-framed tag

Photocopied image

Metal screen

Eyelet punch

Eyelet setting tool

Hammer

Clear-drying glue

Hot glue

Craft brush

Bone folder

Pencil

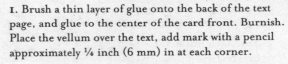

What to Do

1. Brush a thin layer of glue onto the back of the text page, and glue to the center of the card front. Burnish. Place the vellum over the text, add mark with a pencil approximately ¼ inch (6 mm) in at each corner.

2. Open the card so the back is safely out of the way and place it on a suitable surface. (If you do not have a punching mat, a small stack of magazines will do.) Holding the vellum in place over the text, punch a hole in the card directly over each pencil mark. Insert a blue eyelet into one of the holes, through the hole on the surface of the card. Carefully turn the project over, keeping the eyelet in place. To set the eyelet, position the setting tool into the back of the eyelet. Strike the setting tool with a hammer to flatten out the eyelet and secure it in place.

3. Repeat the above step with the remaining three corner eyelets. Always be sure to open the card flat, leaving the back of the card out of the punching area.

4. Place a dime-sized (1.5 cm) amount of hot glue on the center of the card. Press the metal screen down into the glue, taking care not to burn your fingers.

5. If you have a tag with a vellum face, brush a thin layer of glue onto the front surface of the photocopied image. Press the tag onto the surface of the image, cutting off any remaining paper from the metal frame with scissors. If you have a tag with a plain white face, brush glue along the back side of the photocopied image. Press the image onto the tag, and cut off any excess paper with scissors.

6. Pierce through the top hole of the tag again, then drop in the aluminum eyelet. Carefully turn over the tag onto a safe punching surface, position the setting tool into the back of the eyelet, and strike the tool with a hammer.

7. To finish, add a dime-sized (1.5 cm) amount of hot glue to the back of the tag, then press down lightly onto the metal screen.

Craft Punch Card with Ribbon Closure

Craft punches—available in a wide variety of fun shapes—serve as the centerpiece for this card. The clever ribbon closure demonstrates one of many practical functions for eyelets.

Materials and Tools

Light blue folded paper card, measuring 5½ x 4 inches (22 x 10 cm)

1 piece of dark gray paper, measuring 2½ x 4 inches (7.5 x 10 cm)

2 pieces of light blue paper, 1 inch (2.5 cm) square

Scrap of bright blue paper

Shaped craft punch

3⅛-inch (7.8 cm) round aluminum eyelets

2³⁄₁₆-inch (5.5 cm) square aluminum eyelets

Thin ribbon, measuring 12 inches (30 cm) long

Eyelet punch

Eyelet setting tool

Hammer

Clear-drying glue

Craft brush

Bone folder

Pencil

What to Do

1. Brush a thin layer of glue along the back side of the dark gray paper. Press down onto the center of the card front. Glue one of the light blue pieces of paper onto the top center point of the gray paper, leaving approximately ¼ inch (6 mm) of gray paper above the blue. Repeat this step with the second piece of blue paper, placing it at the bottom center point. Place a piece of scrap paper over the card surface and burnish, then set aside to dry.

2. Take the bright blue scrap paper and slip it inside the craft punch. Press down to punch out the paper shape. Repeat two more times. Glue one shape onto the center point of each gray square, and glue the third shape at the exact center point of the end. Set aside to dry.

3. Open the card so that the card back is safely out of the way of your punching surface. Place on a suitable surface. If you do not have a punching mat, a small stack of magazines will do. Using the eyelet punch, make three holes directly over the center point of each punched paper shape. Insert a round eyelet into one of the holes, through the hole on the surface of the card. Carefully turn the project over, keeping the eyelet in place. To set the eyelet, position the setting tool into the back of the eyelet. Strike the setting tool with a

hammer to flatten out the eyelet and secure it in place. Repeat with the other two holes.

4. Lightly mark the center point of the opening flap of the card with a pencil. Make sure this mark is at least ¼ inch (6 mm) in from the edge. Repeat Step 3, this time adding the slightly larger square eyelet. Repeat this entire step for the eyelet that will appear at the center point on the back flap of the card.

5. Thread the ribbon through each of the holes, and lightly tie in a bow. As the lucky recipient unties the card's bow to read your message, they will feel like they've received a gift!

Accordion Fold Cards
Designer: Nicole Tuggle

Here's a great card idea that takes advantage of today's growing array of colorful, patterned scrapbooking paper. There's so much room on this card that you could write an entire letter!

Hard-Covered Accordion Fold Card

The hard cover provides a sturdy canvas for added embellishment.

MATERIALS AND TOOLS

1 piece of solid colored scrapbooking paper, measuring 12 inches (30 cm) square

1 piece of patterned scrapbooking paper, measuring 12 inches (30 cm) square

2 pieces of binder's board or illustration board, measuring 3¼ x 4¼ inches (8 x 11.5 cm)

Ruler

Pencil

Bone folder

Craft brush

Clear-drying craft glue

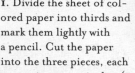

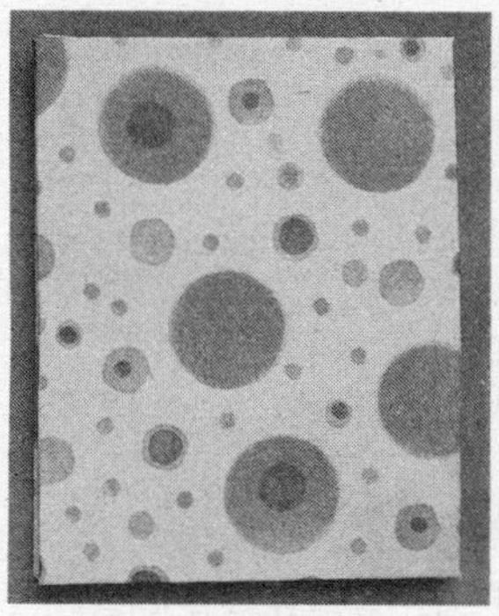

WHAT TO DO

1. Divide the sheet of colored paper into thirds and mark them lightly with a pencil. Cut the paper into the three pieces, each measuring 4 x 12 inches (10 x 30 cm). **Note:** You will use only one of these pieces for the card. Set aside the other two to make additional cards later or as scrap paper to make a collage embellishment for the cover.

2. Fold the colored piece of paper in half lengthwise. Take the flap and fold in half again toward the first fold. Turn the paper over and fold the other flap in half toward the first fold. You should now have an accordion fold measuring 3 x 4 inches (7.5 x 10 cm).

3. Place the patterned paper right side down on your work surface. Mark lightly with a pencil two rectangles measuring 4¼ x 5¼ inches (11.5 x 22 cm). Cut out each rectangle. Set the other paper scraps aside.

4. Take one of the board pieces and cover the entire surface with a thin layer of glue. Place face down on the back side of the patterned paper, leaving an even amount of blank paper along each edge of the board. Turn the board over and burnish the surface of the paper with a bone folder, eliminating any wrinkles or air bubbles.

5. Brush glue onto the side flaps and fold them over the board, smoothing the paper with fingers or bone folder. Dab a small amount of glue to the flaps at the top corners. Fold over each corner at a 45-degree angle. Be sure to angle the fold so the paper will not hang over the edges of the board. Repeat on the bottom corners.

6. Brush glue on the top and bottom flaps and fold them down onto the board. Take care to keep the angled corners tucked on the inside of the boards to prevent them from showing on the outside of the card.

7. Repeat Steps 4 through 6 for the other cover.

8. Brush a thin layer of glue onto the front flap of the accordion fold paper, taking care not to get glue on the other flaps. Press the glued flap down onto the center point of the uncovered side of one cover. Burnish with a bone folder.

9. Brush a thin layer of glue onto the back flap of the accordion fold paper. Press this last flap onto the center point of the uncovered side of the other cover. Burnish.

10. Press finished card between a couple heavy books to get a nice, flat finish.

Accordion Fold Journal

Use a much longer piece of paper to create a fun, snake-like accordion card that can double as a small gift journal.

MATERIALS AND TOOLS

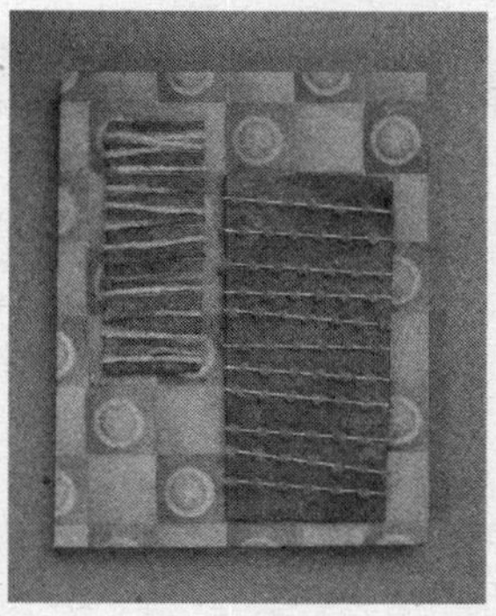

1 piece of white paper, measuring 5½ x 34 inches (14 x 86 cm)

2 pieces of patterned scrapbooking paper, 12 inches (30 cm) square

2 pieces of binder's board or illustration board, measuring 4¾ x 6 inches (12 x 15 cm)

2 pieces of binder's board, one measuring 1 by 3 inches (2.5 x 7.5 cm), the other 2 x 4¼ inches (5 x 11 cm)

Ruler

Pencil

Bone folder

Craft brush

Clear-drying craft glue

WHAT TO DO

1. Fold the white piece of paper in half lengthwise, then fold the flap in half again toward the first fold. Turn the paper over, and fold the other flap, in half toward the first fold. Repeat once more, until you have an accordion fold measuring 4½ x 5½ inches (12 x 14 cm).

2. Place one sheet of patterned paper right side down on your work surface. Mark lightly with a pencil a rectangle measuring 5¾ x 7 inches (14 x 18 cm). Cut out the rectangle. Repeat with second sheet of patterned paper. Set the other paper scraps aside.

3. Take one of the board pieces and cover the entire surface with a thin layer of glue. Place face down on the back side of the patterned paper, leaving an even amount of blank paper along each edge of the board. Turn the board over and burnish the surface of the paper with a bone folder, eliminating any wrinkles or air bubbles.

4. Brush glue onto the side flaps, and fold them over the board, smoothing the paper with fingers or bone folder. Dab a small amount of glue to the flaps at the top corners. Fold over each corner at a 45-degree angle. Be sure to angle the fold so the paper will not hang over the edges of the board. Repeat on the bottom corners.

5. Brush glue on the top and bottom flaps and fold them down onto the board. Take care to keep the angled corners tucked on the inside of the boards to prevent them from showing on the outside of the card.

6. Repeat Steps 3 through 5 for the other cover.

7. Brush a thin layer of glue onto the front flap of the accordion fold paper, taking care not to get glue on the other flaps. Press the glued flap down onto the center point of the uncovered side of one cover, then burnish with a bone folder.

8. Brush a thin layer of glue onto the back flap of the accordion fold paper. Press this last flap onto the center point of the uncovered side of the other cover. Burnish.

9. Press finished card between a couple heavy books to get a nice, flat finish.

10. Brush one side of the two smaller pieces of binder's board with glue and cover with decorative paper (a great use for scraps). Once dry, wrap a single strand of decorative fiber around the board, adhering the ends to the back side with a dab of hot glue. Glue the small pieces of decorated board onto the cover of the card wherever you want.

FIBER EMBELLISHMENTS

Many fabulous fibers—from threads and yarns to ribbons and cords—can add an eye-catching effect to your cards. Simply weave, twist, tie, or wrap fibers through the card surface or around other embellishments that can be added to the card surface. It couldn't be easier!

Romantic Layered Card
Designer: Nicole Tuggle

Offer this beautiful card as a touching gesture to a loved one. Keep your message on the innermost layer as a surprise, or add a touch of anticipation by writing a line on every page.

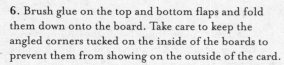

MATERIALS AND TOOLS

Sheet of burgundy card stock, 5½ x 8½ inches (14 x 22 cm)

Sheet of gray card stock, 5½ x 8½ inches

Sheet of botanical printed paper, 5½ x 8½ inches

24-inch (61 cm) length of thin organza ribbon

Pencil

Awl

Ruler

Bone folder

Cutting mat

WHAT TO DO

1. Fold each piece of paper in half to form a folded sheet measuring 4¼ x 5½ inches (12 x 14 cm). Hold the edges together with one hand and press down along the crease with a bone folder, taking care to match the corners exactly.

2. Stack the folded sheets together, one inside the next with the botanical paper on the outside, followed by the gray paper, and then the burgundy paper.

Continued ➡

3. Open the stack of paper, folded edge facing down. Measure I inch (2.5 cm) down from the top and bottom edge on the fold line and mark lightly with a pencil.

4. Holding all the layers together, carefully poke through each pencil mark with an awl. Be sure to go through all three sheets of paper.

5. Thread the ribbon through the holes, starting from the inside of the card. If you are using wide ribbon, you may need to poke the ribbon through the hole with the aid of the awl. Don't worry about fraying the edges of the ribbon, as the ends can be cut.

6. Tie the ribbon in a bow along the spine of the card.

PEEKABOO WINDOW VARIATION

Place the gray paper on the outside, botanical paper next, and burgundy paper on the inside. Follow the remaining steps above. Take the finished card, measure I inch (2.5 cm) in from each side, and mark an internal line with a pencil. Place the cover over a cutting mat, making sure the rest of the card is safely placed to the left. Using a craft knife and ruler, cut along the marked lines. Remove the cut rectangle to reveal a charming window through which the botanical paper can be seen.

—From *The Michaels Book of Arts & Crafts*

CREATIVE CHRISTMAS CARDS

Terry Taylor

Vintage Christmas Cards

Designed by: Skip Wade

A classic Christmas card doesn't have to spend the rest of its life in a drawer. Make a color copy to create a new card! A treasure from the past will someday become a treasure in the future.

WHAT YOU NEED

Vintage Christmas cards

Blank greeting cards

Craft knife

Spray adhesive

All-purpose glue

Glass seed beads or microbeads

WHAT YOU DO

1. Make a color photocopy of your chosen image from the vintage card. Measure the area to be shown on the blank card. With a straightedge and a craft knife, cut out window with these dimensions in the front of the card.

2. Trim the color copy to frame the chosen image with ¼ inch (6 mm) on all sides.

3. Spray the inside front of the card with spray adhesive. Center the image inside the window. Cut another blank card in half and spray one half with adhesive. Press the glued surfaces together with the color copy between.

4. Paint all-purpose glue on the areas of the color copy to receive colored beads (such as the poinsettias in the project photo) using a small paintbrush. Sprinkle the glued areas with seed beads. Once the glue has dried, shake off excess beads.

5. Paint all-purpose glue around the edges where the card meets the image. Sprinkle the glued area with seed beads and allow it to dry. Shake off the excess beads.

Cards of Christmas Past

Designed by: Terry Taylor

Everyone has a blurred, off-kilter, or overexposed photograph of a past Christmas that they lovingly treasure. Share that memory with family or friends in a one-of-a-kind card.

WHAT YOU NEED

Photograph

Spray adhesive or glue

Blank cards or cardstock

Sequins

Seed beads

Thread

WHAT YOU DO

1. Photocopy your photograph on a color copier or scan it into your computer and print out. Cut out your image and adhere it to the card.

2. Open up the card and place it flat on a work surface. Measure the diameter of your sequins. Use a needle to prick holes all around the edge of the photo, slightly less than a sequin's width apart.

3. Thread a needle and knot the end. Working from the back, bring the needle up through any pricked hole. Thread on a sequin, followed by a seed bead. Bring the needle back down through the hole and over to an adjacent hole. Keep working around the photo until you have completely covered the edge.

Santa's Tip: Don't have any bad or boring photographs? No problem! Search antique stores or online auctions for Christmas photographs. (Yes, people actually toss them out!)

Silver Snowflake Greetings

Designed by: Terry Taylor

Even if you live in Hawaii, snow and snowflakes are inextricably linked to the Christmas season. Now you can make and send holiday cards that evoke that same spirit. No two are exactly alike!

WHAT YOU NEED

Jar lid or other small circular object

Cards and matching envelopes

Silver embroidery floss

Snowflake beads or sequins

Seed beads

Tape

Craft glue

WHAT YOU DO

1. Trace the jar lid onto scrap paper. Cut it out and fold the circle in half. Fold the half circle into thirds. Unfold the circle and place it on a card. Mark the six evenly spaced points on the card. Open the card and pierce each mark with a needle.

2. Thread a needle with two 18-inch (45.7 cm) strands of silver floss. Thread the needle up through the back of the card. Pull the thread almost all the way through and then secure the end with tape. Pass the needle down into the opposite hole. Bring the needle back up through an adjacent hole and down through the opposite hole. Continue until you have three stitched lines.

3. Bring the needle up through an adjacent hole. String a snowflake and a seed bead. Bring the needle back down through the same hole, securing the beads. Work around the circle. Finish by taping the thread end to the card's back.

4. Hide the stitching on the back by cutting out a piece of matching cardstock or decorative paper slightly larger than your circle. Glue it in place.

Santa's Tip: These plastic snowflakes were purchased to be used as beads, but turned out to have no holes in them. No problem: anything can become a bead if you drill a hole in it!

—From *A Very Beaded Christmas*

MAKING HANDMADE BOOKS

Diane Flowers

General Instructions

Handmade papers make beautiful book covers, and handmade books make beautiful gifts. You will need handmade paper for the covers, text paper for the inside of the book, and a few basic tools.

A Book Maker's Toolbox

Awl, for punching holes

Scissors, for cutting lighter weight papers

Craft knife with extra blades, for cutting thicker papers

Thread (hemp, waxed linen, or any other strong thread or string that will not stretch), for binding

Large-eye needle, for sewing

PVA (polyvinyl acetate) glue. PVA glue is specially formulated to dry fast and is flexible enough to allow adjustments to be made without ruining your covers. It contains less water than craft glue and contains a preservative to prevent mold.

Pencil, for marking

Eraser, for erasing pencil marks

Metal ruler, to use as a guide for cutting or tearing papers, and for measuring

Cutting mat, to protect your work surface and aid in making straight cuts

Bone folder, for creasing

Brayer or roller tool, for smoothing

Metal binder clips in a variety of sizes

Paper press or boards and heavy book, bricks, etc., to keep the papers flat while the glue dries.

Waxed paper, to keep the covers and pages separated while the glue dries.

Thick cardboard, to cover your work surface when punching holes and cutting pages and covers

Following are general instructions that can be used to make a hardcover book of any size. Making a book is a four-step process. Here are some considerations for each step.

Step One: Choosing a Theme

- When making a gift, consider the recipient's favorite things, colors, animals, or fabrics.
- Consider how you will use the book or, if it is to be a gift, how the recipient will use it.

Step Two: Selecting Materials

- Use a smooth text-weight paper if the book is intended to be a journal. Thicker, textured papers don't work well for writing, but they are wonderful backgrounds for stories about nature and for attaching pressed flowers and leaves, notes, pictures, or postcards.
- For a hardcover book, you will need thick book board or thick poster board (it is stronger than regular cardboard) to use as a base for the cover. Plastic glass, metal, and wood also make good hardcovers.
- When you make your first book cover, practice with some scrap papers. After you understand how the process works, use your precious sheets of handmade papers.

Step Three: Designing the Cover and Pages

- Play with the materials and have fun with recycling and using new materials.
- You can cut sheets of paper for pages to size and stack them for binding or you can fold large sheets of paper to create pages. Folding a large sheet in half creates a folio (four pages). A quarto (eight pages) is created when you fold a sheet in half twice and trim the folds on one edge. An octavo (sixteen pages on eight paper pieces) is a page folded in half three times—folded twice and trimmed, then folded and trimmed again.

Step Four: Constructing the Book

- Be sure that the grain of the paper runs parallel to the spine. Sometimes with handmade paper, the sheets may not have an obvious grain. If you cannot determine the exact grain, then either way should work.
- If you put glue on one side of your paper, it could shrink unevenly as it dries. This can be avoided by putting glue on both sides or you can put it just on the corners—and use a paper press or heavy weights with boards to hold the book covers flat as they dry.

Making a Book, Step by Step

PROTECT PAPER

Because books might get a lot of use and be handled more than other handmade paper projects, I like to spray the handmade paper that I am using for the covers with Photo and Paper Protectant Spray. After making, pressing, and drying the handmade paper, spray the piece with photo and paper protectant. Allow to dry.

ASSEMBLE THE TEXT PAGES

1. Cut and/or fold your pages to the desired size.

2. Stack the sheets of your chosen paper so they are straight and aligned.

3. Use an awl to punch small holes along the spine edge, ⅛ inch (3 mm) away from the edge. Thread a needle with hemp or waxed linen thread. Stitch through the holes to join the pages. Tie a knot in the ends of the thread to secure and trim. You can also glue groups of folded pages together along the folds.

MAKE THE COVERS

1. Use a craft knife and metal ruler to cut the book board into two pieces to make the front and back covers. Cut the cover boards ½ inch (1.3 cm) wider and longer than the text page size.

2. Use your handmade paper to cover the boards for the back and front covers. You will need two pieces of handmade paper. The handmade paper needs to be ½ inch (1.3 cm) larger on all sides than the boards for the front and back covers.

3. Place the handmade paper piece for the front cover on the surface, wrong side up. Apply glue to the paper to within ½ inch (1.3 cm) of each edge. Position the cover board on the glue-coated paper, pressing it in place so it sticks. Flip it over. Use a brayer or roller tool to roll out any bubbles or creases, working from the center to the edges.

4. Turn over the covered board. Fold and trim the corners to miter them. Use the bone folder to crease the paper at the edges of the board.

5. Apply glue to the edges of the paper. Wrap the paper around the edges of the board, pulling it tight and securing it on the back of the board. Use the brayer or roller tool to smooth the folded edges and corners.

6. Repeat steps 2 through 5 to make the back cover.

MAKE & ATTACH THE SPINE

1. Measure the thickness of the stacked text pages. Measure the thickness of the two covers. This is the actual spine width. Add the two measurements plus 1½ inches (4 cm). This is the width of the spine piece for cutting.

2. Measure the length of the cover. Add 2 inches (5 cm). This is the length of the spine piece.

3. Use these spine width and spine length measurements to cut two pieces of handmade paper for the spine piece.

4. Place one of the spine pieces on your work surface. Position the covers side by side on top of the spine piece, leaving a gap between them equal to the width of the actual spine. Leave equal margins at top and bottom of spine piece. See Fig. 2 for how to position covers on spine piece. Lightly mark the placement of the boards. Remove the boards.

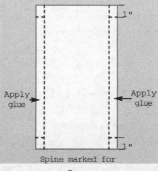

Figure 1

5. Put glue on the side sections of the spine, where you have marked the area for the cover placement. (See Fig. 1.) Reposition the board covers on the spine piece to attach them to the spine. (See Fig. 2.)

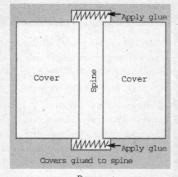

Figure 2

6. Put glue on the top and the bottom exposed portions of the paper spine piece. (See Fig. 2) Fold the margins to the inside over the top and bottom edges of the boards.

7. Trim 2½ inches (6.5 cm) off the length of the remaining spine piece. Apply glue to the wrong side of this piece. Position it to cover the inside of the other spine piece and the edges of the boards. The cover is complete.

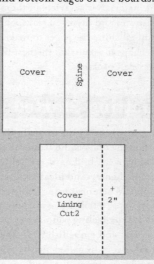

Figure 3

ASSEMBLE

1. Cut two pieces of handmade or decorative paper to line the insides of the covers. They should be ⅛ inch (3 mm) smaller on the three sides—top, bottom, and outside than each of the opened covers, with 2 inches (5 cm) added to the spine sides as flaps. (See Fig. 3) Fold the flaps to the inside. (The flaps will be attached to the first and last pages of the text section.)

2. Glue the lining pieces to the inside of the front and back covers, leaving the flaps loose and lining up the edges of both pieces at the spine. Use the brayer or roller tool to smooth the liner papers and remove any bubbles, rolling from the center to the outer edges.

3. Apply glue to the backside of the flaps. Attach them to the first and last pages of the text section. Press firmly to be sure they are adhered.

Continued ➡

4. Place pieces of waxed paper between the front and back covers and the first and last pages. Carefully close the book, making sure the first and last pages are securely glues to the liner flaps.

5. Place pieces of waxed paper on the outside of the front and back covers. Place the closed book in a paper press for 24 hours. If you do not have a paper press, place the waxed paper—wrapped book on a flat surface, such as a board. Put bricks, heavy books, or other weights on top. Leave in place for 24 hours.

Editor's Note: Although these instructions are for making books with handmade papers, commercially produced papers may also be used.

—From *Handmade Paper from Naturals*

MINI-BOOK MAKING

Roxi Phillips

Introduction

Everyone enjoys photo albums and scrapbooks, yet there is something charming about mini-books. They beg you to hold them in your hands, note every element, pull every tag, and read every word.

Mini-books come in all shapes, colors, and styles and provide a special place to gather thoughts and memories. They can evoke a feeling, document a special time, or provide a snapshot into the everyday happenings of life. In one of these little gems, even the simplest topic is given importance. After all, isn't it really the simple things in life that bring us the most pleasure?

In this section you will find a treasure trove of miniature albums created using basic techniques and a handful of materials in a variety of themes. They can be created in minutes and then you can spend as much time as you wish embellishing the pages to make them uniquely your own. Perhaps it's true that the best things in life really do come in small packages.

Getting Started

I think it is exciting to begin the creative process. Sometimes my ideas come from the most unusual places like a song lyric, billboard, or quote. Design compositions, color themes, and ideas are everywhere if your mind is open. When beginning a mini-book, consider the story you want to tell or the purpose the book will serve. Think about the feeling you want to portray and the colors, papers, and embellishments that will best accomplish that goal. Begin by gathering the materials, tools, photographs, memorabilia, and basic supplies. Familiarize yourself with the simple techniques and the list of tools contained in this section and you will be well on your way to creating amazing projects in very little time.

Embellishments

Ball Chains

Ball chains and fasteners have traditionally been used as lamp pulls and key chains but have found a new role as unique mini-book bindings. The chains and connectors can be purchased in an array of colors and lengths. Cut the chain between the linked balls using wire cutters or old scissors. Thread the chain through a hole in the book's spine and insert the last ball on the chain into the connector and pull into place, creating a loop.

Bookbinding Tape

Usually self-adhesive, bookbinding tape is available in a variety of colors and widths. It works well to reinforce bindings and to strengthen folds on paper and chipboard. Bookbinding tape also makes an interesting embellishment behind titles or as a background layer, and readily accepts ink to coordinate with other elements in a project.

Bookplates

Bookplates are label holders attached to a project with a brad on eithr side. A paper label is inserted into the top of the plate.

Brads

Brads come in many colors, sizes, and shapes and can be used to hold elements in place or as decoration on their own. They are simply pushed through paper using a small, pre-punched hole; the prongs are then spread open and flattened on the back to secure.

Buttons

Buttons can add a sense of whimsy or an elegant appeal. Adhere to projects with craft glue or glue dots or string several on wire or thread to create a dimensional accent.

Charms

There are charms for practically every theme imaginable. Dangle them from ribbons or fibers or adhere them with metal embellishments adhesive or glue dots.

Chipboard Cut Outs

Shapes of every sort, including alphabet letters, add an exciting dimension to a design. Cutouts can be painted, sanded, or covered with paper.

Craft Wire

This versatile product, available in a wide variety of colors and gauges, can be used to string beads, create spirals, or bind a mini-book. Adhere to projects with glue dots.

Die Cuts

Typically made of cardstock or paper, an enormous array is available to add the perfect touch to a paper craft project. Make-it-yourself die cuts, in a range of prices, are available as well.

Hardware

The aisles of a hardware store yield a variety of materials useful in creating paper projects, such as screen material, washers, paint chips, and fasteners. Most require metal embellishment adhesive or double-sided tape to support their weight.

Jewels and Sequins

Add glamour and sparkle to your pages with these little gems. Adhere to projects with craft glue or glue dots.

Office Supplies

Paper clips, safety pins, file tabs, shipping labels, and other office supplies are well suited for use in embellishing books.

Paper Flowers

Paper flowers add dimension and interest. Adhere using glue dots or craft glue. For an additional accent, punch a small hole in the middle of a flat flower and insert a decorative brad or an eyelet to mimic the center.

Photo Corners

Designed to hold a photo in place on a page, many photo corners are self-adhesive. They are available in many colors and sizes.

Ribbon

Use ribbon as embellishments to bind a book, knot onto tags, or adhere directly onto a page with glue dots or craft glue.

Rub-ons

These adhesive decals are applied to the surface of a project using a craft stick. Available in numerous colors, images, fonts, and styles, rub-ons are a wonderful way to add a decorative touch.

Slide Mounts

Originally used for photographic slides, these frames come in many sizes and materials such as plastic, paper, and metal. Use them to frame quotes, titles, memorabilia, or photos. Adhere with glue dots or double-sided tape.

Stapler and Staples

Decorative staples are used with a stapler designed specifically for their size. Regular staples can be colored with permanent markers.

Adhesives

  Adhesive dispenser

  Foam mounting dots

  Glue stick

  Craft glue

  Foam mounting tape

  Hot glue sticks

  Double-sided tape

  Glue dots

  Vellum tape

Additional Supplies

There are many everyday items that will help you craft and decorate miniature books. Some are as simple as a ruler, stapler, and pencils, while others are a bit less common. A bone folder, for example, is typically shaped like a letter opened and is essential in achieving a clean fold in paper and cardstock.

- Computer and printer
- Craft scissors
- Paper trimmer
- Cosmetic sponges
- Journaling pens
- Pencils
- Craft knife
- Metal-edge ruler
- Sandpaper

Tools

  Decorative-edge scissors

  Hole punch

  Needle-nose pliers

  Rubber stamps

  Eyelet-setting tools

    Setting mat

    Eyelets

    Craft hammer

    Eyelet setter

  Inkpad

  Paper punch

  Self-healing cutting mat

  Foam brushes

  Label maker

  Piercing tool

  Wire cutters

Techniques

Accordion Folding

Cut paper to desired size and then use a meal edge ruler to measure and mark equal increments on the top and bottom edges of the strip. Line the ruler up on each set of marks and draw a line with a scoring tool from top to bottom. You may need to go over the line a few times if you are working with thick cardstock or paper. Fold each scored line in the opposite direction as the previous scored line, like a fan. The folds that point down are referred to as valley folds and the folds that point up are mountain folds. Scoring boards, available on the market, easily make accurate scored lines.

Applying Rub-ons

Rub-ons come on a transfer sheet and often contain several images. Carefully cut out the chosen image. Position on the project and firmly rub the image with a craft stick or rub-on tool until it is completely transferred. Do not lift the backing paper off until you are sure you have a successful transfer. When rubbing images, avoid pushing too hard or it will cause cracks in the image.

Covering Chipboard and Mitering Corners

Apply a thin layer of craft glue to one side of the chipboard piece using a foam brush. Place chipboard, glue side down, onto a back side of decorative paper. Trim paper diagonally across all of the corners just outside of the chipboard piece. **Note**: The distance of the cut from the chipboard corners should be equal to the thickness of the chipboard. Fold and adhere paper onto the back side of the chipboard, allow to dry.

Heat Embossing

Stamp an image with embossing or pigment ink and then cover with embossing powder; tap off excess. Use a heat tool to melt the powder; allow to cool.

Inking

Simply tap a permanent inkpad around the edge of a paper or photograph for a distressed, framed effect. For a softer look, apply ink by patting a cosmetic sponge onto the inkpad and then dab it lightly onto the edges or surface of the elements.

Matting Photos

Cut a piece of coordinating cardstock or scrapbook paper ⅛"–¼ inches (3–6 mm) larger than the photo. Center and adhere it onto the back of the image with double-sided tape or an adhesive dispenser. For additional flair, trim the edges of the mat with decorative-edge scissors before adhering the photo.

Printing on Scrapbook Paper

To print on scrapbook paper, use 8½ x 11 inches (21.5 x 28 cm) pages or cut larger sheets down to that size and print as usual.

Rubber Stamping

For the best effect, pat the stamp on the inkpad several times. Press firmly onto the desired surface. Lift off carefully without smearing ink. **Note**: Dye ink typically dries quickly while pigment ink may take some time. To speed drying time, set pigment ink with a heat tool.

Setting Eyelets

To set an eyelet, punch a small hole in the paper with a piercing tool or hole punch where the eyelet is to be set. Insert eyelet through hole and position project face down on a craft mat. Using setting tool and hammer on a setting mat, flatten the eyelet's prongs and secure in place.

Note: Some eyelet setters don't require a hammer; simply follow the manufacturer's instructions.

Silhouetting Photographed Images

Carefully cut just outside the edge of desired image using sharp, pointed-tip scissors. Avoid cutting too close to the image, especially faces and hair. **Note**: This requires some practice, so cut out a photocopy of the image first.

Tearing Paper

Holding the edge of desired paper, with a hand on either side of the area to be torn, pull one hand towards yourself. To tear a straight line, paint a line of water to weaken the paper where you want it to tear. **Note**: This is especially effective with mulberry and natural fiber papers. Most paper has a grain and will tear better in one direction than the other.

Stab Binding

MATERIALS

- Book
- Pencil
- Craft scissors
- Ruler
- Heavy-duty hole punch
- Waxed thread

INSTRUCTIONS

1. Mark and punch two holes on binding of book ½ inch (1.3 cm) from edge and evenly spaced from top and bottom edges. **Note**: If you don't have a heavy-duty hole punch, take the book to a copy shop and have the holes drilled.

2. Cut waxed thread to equal approximately four times length of book spine; thread through needle.

3. Working on bottom hole, guide waxed thread through hole from front to back, leaving 4-inch (10 cm) tail in front (A).

4. Loop around bottom of binding and back through bottom hole (B).

5. From back, loop around left edge of binding and back down through bottom hole (C) and then up through top hole.

6. Repeat Steps 3–5 for top hole.

7. Tighten tails and knot on center front of book; trim as desired.

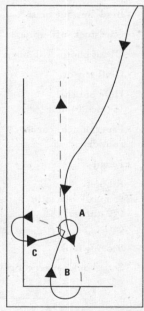

Projects

You Make Me Laugh

MATERIALS

- Acid-free adhesive dispenser
- Binder ring: 1½-inch (4 cm)
- Cardstock: navy blue (1), white (2)
- Chipboard
- Cosmetic sponges
- Craft scissors
- Hole punch: ¼-inch (6 mm)
- Inkpads: black, blue, coordinating colors (3)
- Ribbon scraps: coordinating colors (10–12)
- Rubber stamps: small alphabet
- Sanding block
- Scrapbook paper: double-sided coordinating colors and patterns
- Stickers: large letters, coordinating colors
- Tag: 1¼-inch (3 cm) metal-rimmed circle

INSTRUCTIONS

1. **To create covers**: Cut two 6 x 3-inch (15 x 7.5 cm) rectangles from chipboard. Trim two corners from one end to make tag shape. Holding tag horizontally with trimmed edge on left, punch ¼-inch (6 mm) hole ½ inch (1.3 cm) in from left side.

2. Cut two 6 x 3-inch (15 x 7.5 cm) rectangles from navy blue cardstock; adhere to one side of each chipboard piece.

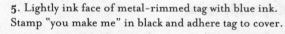

3. Cut two 6 x 3-inch (15 x 7.5 cm) rectangles from scrapbook paper; adhere to remaining sides of chipboard pieces. Sand away extra paper around edges using sanding block.

4. **To embellish cover**: Ink edges of strips of paper with coordinating inkpads and cosmetic sponges; adhere onto front cover.

5. Lightly ink face of metal-rimmed tag with blue ink. Stamp "you make me" in black and adhere tag to cover.

6. Stamp "a book of family quotes" in black at bottom of front cover. Spell "laugh" with colored letter stickers.

7. **To create pages**: Cut eight 6 x 3-inch (15 x 7.5 cm) pieces of white cardstock. Trim corners and punch holes in cardstock pieces using chipboard cover as template.

8. **To assemble book**: Layer covers, metal-rimmed tag, and pages on binder ring in desired order. Knot 4-inch (10 cm) lengths of ribbon on binder ring. Embellish pages as desired.

Time-saving Tip: Double-Takes

Use coordinating double-sided scrapbook papers to give pages an instant design that requires minimal time and embellishment,.

Four Steps to Success

MATERIALS

- Acid-free adhesives: double-sided tape, foam mounting tape, glue stick
- Cardstock: brown
- Cosmetic sponge
- Craft knife

Continued ➜

- Craft scissors
- Elastic hair band: black
- Hole punches: ¼-inch (6mm), 1¼ inches (3 cm) square
- Inkpad: brown
- Photo
- Rub-ons: words
- Scoring tool
- Scrapbook paper: coordinating (3)
- Stick: 6-inch (15 cm)

INSTRUCTIONS

1. To create cover: Cut 6 x 12-inch (15 x 30.5 cm) piece of coordinating scrapbook paper and two 6 x 12-inch (15 x 30.5 cm) pieces of cardstock. Score and fold paper and cardstock pieces in half; place cardstock pages inside paper cover.

2. Punch three squares on right side of paper, ¾ inch (2 cm) from edge. Outline squares with foam mounting tape on inside of cover. Place photo behind squares; adhere front cover panel to first cardstock page using double-sided tape. Tear edges of remaining three brown pages.

3. To create pages: Cut eight 6-inch (15 cm) squares of coordinating scrapbook papers; adhere one square each onto inside front and back covers. Tear one edge of each remaining square approximately ⅛ inch (3 mm) narrower than cardstock pages. Ink edges of torn squares with inkpad and cosmetic sponge; adhere to cardstock using double-sided tape. Embellish as desired.

4. To create binding: Punch two ¼-inch (6 mm) holes in covers and pages, ½ inch (1.3 cm) in from left edge at 1 inch (2.5 cm) and 5 inches (12.5 cm) from top. Thread elastic hair band through holes from back and loop over stick ends. Embellish cover as desired.

Key to My Heart

MATERIALS

- Acid-free adhesives: dispenser, double-sided tape, vellum tape
- Cardstock: antique gold metallic, cream
- Craft knife
- Craft scissors
- Embellishments: 2½-inch (6.5 cm) metal slide mount, skeleton key
- Embossing powder: gold
- Foam core board
- Heat tool
- Hole punch: ¼-inch (6 mm)
- Metal-edge ruler
- Paper punch: 1-inch (2.5 cm) square
- Pens: copper leafing, embossing
- Ribbon: 1½-inch (4 cm) antique gold satin (24 inches) (61 cm)

- Scrapbook paper, coordinating patterns
- Vellum: gold

INSTRUCTIONS

1. To create covers: Cut two 4 x 7-inch (10 x 18 cm) pieces of foam core board using craft knife and metal-edge ruler. Cut and adhere two 6 x 9-inch (6 x 23 cm) pieces of gold metallic cardstock and cover foam core boards, mitering corners onto back of board. Punch holes in each board, ¾ inch (2 cm) from side and ½ inch (1.3 cm) from top.

2. Cut 2-inch (5 cm) square of gold vellum. Draw heart on vellum with embossing pen. Sprinkle heart with gold embossing powder and heat with heat tool until powder is melted.

3. Paint metal slide mount using copper leafing pen; allow to dry. Mount vellum square under slide mount then onto front cover using double-sided tape.

4. To create pages: Cut eight 3¾ x 6½-inch (9.5 x 16.5 cm) pieces of cream cardstock. Print photos and journaling onto vellum and trim to fit pages. Mat journaling boxes using cream cardstock and vellum tape.

5. Punch ten 1-inch (2.5 cm) squares of textured gold paper. Cut each square diagonally, creating four triangles; adhere onto corners of photos and journaling boxes with adhesive dispenser.

6. To assemble book: Assemble pages in desired order. Punch ¼-inch (6 mm) holes in pages, using cover as a guide. Thread ribbon through all layers and tie in front.

Our First Year

MATERIALS

- Acid-free double-sided tape
- Brad: antique brass
- Cardstock: off-white
- CD of photos with blank label
- Craft scissors
- Hole punch: ⅛-inch (3 mm)
- Paper punch: corner rounder
- Pencil
- Ribbon: ¼-inch (6 mm)-wide satin (32-inches) (81.5 cm)
- Scoring tool
- Scrapbook paper: coordinating colors and patterns

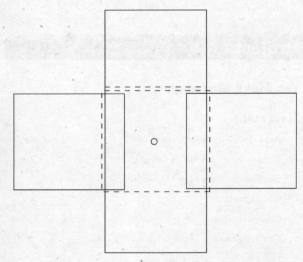

Flaps provide perfect spots to add photos as a preview for what you'll find on the CD. Embellish the CD label with computer-generated or handwritten journaling and rub-on flourishes.

INSTRUCTIONS

1. To create cover: Cut one 5 x 12-inch (12.5 x 30.5 cm) and two 5½ x 4⅞-inch (14 x 12.3 cm) pieces of cardstock. Score lines on large piece across short width 3⅞" from top, 4" from top, and 3" from bottom. On each smaller piece, score line across short width 1" from one edge. (See Diagram.)

2. Adhere flaps of shorter pieces to either side of middle section of large piece. **Note:** Project will resemble cross, with shortest flap at bottom. (See Diagram.) Score and fold all creases. Round all outside corners with paper punch.

3. Open project completely and mark center of middle section using CD as a template; punch hole. Insert brad through back of book and open prongs to hold CD.

4. Center and adhere ribbon just below hole on middle section. Embellish inside panels, CD, and cover as desired.

5. Fold side flaps in, bottom flap up, and top flap down. Tie ribbon to close book.

Time-saving Tip: Edge Options

Use a coordinating ink color to cover the cut edges of paper and photos. Using an ink pad directly on the paper's edges results in a sharp-looking edge, while inking with a cosmetic sponge creates a softer effect. You can even color the edges with a felt-tip pen.

Man's Best Friends

MATERIALS

- Acid-free adhesive dispenser
- Acrylic paint: light blue
- Copper post fasteners
- Cosmetic sponge
- Craft scissors
- Foam brush
- Hole punch: ¼-inch (6 mm)
- Inkpads: brown, light blue
- Rubber stamp: chicken wire background
- Scoring tool
- Scrapbook paper: striped
- Tags: 6¼ x 3⅛-inch (7.8 x 15 cm) white (11)
- Yarn: coordinating color

INSTRUCTIONS

1. To create pages: Lightly brush watered-down acrylic paint onto tags with foam brush; allow to dry. Stamp tags with chicken wire background stamp and light blue ink.

2. Cut eleven 3⅛ x 6-inch (7.8 x 15 cm) pieces of scrapbook paper. Fold each piece in half, matching short ends; center fold over flat end of tag and adhere with adhesive dispenser. Ink tag with brown inkpad and cosmetic sponge.

3. Score 1 inch (2.5 cm) from square end of tag; crease. Embellish tags as desired.

4. **To assemble book:** Punch holes in left edge of tags ½ inch (1.3 cm) from outside edge and ½ inch (1.3 cm) from top and bottom; insert copper post fasteners. Cut eleven 6-inch (15 cm) lengths of yarn and thread one through hole in each tag; knot.

Time-Saving Tip: Hole How-Tos

Save time by measuring and marking hole placement on the cover tag. You can then use the tag as a template for the remaining tags.

Girlfriends

MATERIALS

- Acid-free adhesives: bookbinding tape, double-sided tape, glue stick
- Chipboard
- Cosmetic sponges
- Craft scissors
- Inkpads: coordinating colors
- Ribbon: ⅝-inch (1.5 cm)-wide coordinating color (1 yard [91.5 cm])
- Scrapbook paper: coordinating colors and patterns (6)
- Stickers: quotes

INSTRUCTIONS

1. **To create accordion:** Cut six 4 x 6-inch (10 x 15 cm) pieces of chipboard and ten 6-inch (15 cm) strips of bookbinding tape. Lay panels side-by-side, long sides together, leaving ⅛-inch (3 mm) gap between each; adhere together using tape strips. Turn connected panels face down and adhere strips between panels on back side. Ink edges of all panels and tape strips using coordinating inkpads and cosmetic sponges.

2. **To create binding:** Cut two 18-inch (45.5 cm) lengths of ribbon. Center 3 inches (7.5 cm) of ribbon end vertically and adhere to outside of front panel using double-sided tape. Repeat with remaining ribbon and back panel.

3. Cut twelve 4 x 6-inch (10 x 15 cm) pieces of scrapbook paper; ink edges and adhere to each side of all panels using glue stick. Embellish panels as desired.

Time-saving Tip: Smoothing Out the Rough Spots

Use a sanding block or nail file to smooth edges of chipboard pieces. This is also a quick and easy method of distressing scrapbook paper.

Happy Birthday

MATERIALS

- Acid-free adhesive dispenser
- Craft scissors
- Photos
- Scrapbook paper: double-sided coordinating colors and patterns (4)
- Spiral binding system
- Sticker letters

INSTRUCTIONS

1. **To create pages and cover:** Cut seven 6" squares of double-sided scrapbook paper. Embellish one square with strips of coordinating scrapbook paper and sticker letters for cover.

2. Embellish pages as desired. Reserve last page for photo of birthday child with message.

3. Bind book using spiral binding system according to manufacturer's instructions. **Note:** If you don't have access to a spiral binding system, take the book to a copy shop to have the pages bound.

—From *Make It in Minutes: Mini-Books*

PAPER QUILLING

Alli Bartkowski

Introduction

Welcome to the amazing art of quilling, or paper filigree! It is definitely an art form that excites and impresses you from the very first quilled piece. At first glance, most people say, "What is it?" "How did you do that?" or "Is that really paper?" But once they try rolling and shaping their first quilled piece, their mood changes to excitement and they'll say, "Wow, I can't believe how simple it is!" and ask, "What else can I make with rolled paper strips?" Then before they realize it, they're hooked.

The art of quilling dates as far back as the 16th and 17th centuries when the French and Italian nuns and monks would decorate reliquaries, holy pictures, and frames with quilled pieces. The strips of paper were wrapped and rolled around a feather quill, hence the name "quilling." Silver and gold gilded-edge papers from books were trimmed off, rolled, and attached to their artwork to imitate the look of metal filigree. This clever technique was much more affordable, versatile, and easier to do than actual metalwork. It eventually spread to England where many "ladies of leisure" and proper young ladies would be taught this decorative and elegant paper art. Like needlework, they used their pastime to quill on tea caddies, jewelry boxes, screens, handbags, and furniture. It was brought to the American colonies were the art continued to be taught and placed on pictures, sconces, and wooden boxes.

Today, quilling complements very nicely with scrapbooking, card making, framing, and other well-made crafts because, as in any handmade treasure, it's done with patience, pride, and love. From my experience, a handmade quilled card always touches the heart of the recipient and a framed, quilled wedding invitation will be cherished by the bride and groom for a lifetime.

Perhaps the undeniable appeal for this art may be the fascination people have with paper. How often do you take a paper brochure, map, or ticket and roll it until it's beyond recognition? Then, there is the relaxing, or "calming of the nerves," effect when paper is worked between the fingers. It could also be the satisfied feeling and amazement when you see a finished quilled project that looks incredibly intricate to create when it actually was very simple to produce. Whatever the case, you will not be disappointed with the possibilities that this art presents to you. It's an art form that many past generations have enjoyed, treasured, and preserved. So, get ready to discover the amazing art of quilling and find your creative side.

Quilling Basics

Quilling originally started with a feather quill, strips of paper, and very creative hands. Some traditional quillers enjoy rolling their paper strips with their fingers and fringing papers by hand. However, most of today's quillers love time-saving and ergonomically designed tools to quickly and easily roll their papers. They also enjoy simple and creative designs that can be completed in one sitting, which is perfect for making scrapbook pages, gift tags, and homemade cards.

One of the best things about quilling is that it is inexpensive and very portable. The basic slotted and needle tools range from $3 to $5. Then you'll need strips of paper to help you get started. A useful and multifunctional tool is a circle template board. It's a great tool to help beginners and experts achieve uniform-size coils for symmetrical quilled designs, like snowflakes and flowers.

There are many other useful quilling tools and accessories designed to stretch your creativity. Some of them are not needed right away to learn the basics of quilling. But once you fall in love with this paper art and you have tried all of the techniques, you will find the other tools and accessories a wonderful addition to your quilling supply collection.

Supplies & Tools

For the most basic quilling project, you will need a few tools and paper strips to learn the fundamentals of quilling. Once you've tried it, you'll be pleasantly amazed how quick and simple it is to learn the basic quilled shapes and scrolls. This section in the book will describe in more detail how to use each of the tools and other supplies.

General Quilling Tools

Slotted tool is a tool for beginners because the slot at the tip helps with the start of rolling. It leaves a slightly larger center with a small fold at he center of the coil. It is easier to learn to quill with this tool. See page 00 on how to roll paper with the slotted tool.

Needle tool is the preferred tool by experienced quillers because it leaves a smaller center compared to the slotted tool. It takes a little more patience and practice to learn to roll the paper strip with the needle tool. The metal tip of the needle tool can also be used for scoring papers and piercing holes for a decorative look. See pages 00–00 on how to roll paper with the needle tool.

Fine-tipped tweezers make a great substitute for fingers. They are helpful for holding, gluing, positioning, and assembling quilled piece. They are almost essential when working with small pieces, especially with miniatures.

Quilling paper is readily available in various widths, weights, and colors.

Craft glue can have a big influence on the look of the finished quilled piece. Use a paper craft glue that dries clear, quickly, and rubs off easily from your fingers and tools. Note: A good test to see if a glue is too tacky for

Continued ➤

quilling is to place it on your finger and rub it between your fingers and thumbs. If it easily "balls up" and falls off your fingers, then it's good for quilling.

Sticky-notepad sheet is used for holding a puddle of glue.

Circle template board is used for creating consistent and perfectly proportioned quilled coils and shapes.

Ruler is used if your circle template board does not have a ruler on it.

Fine-tipped scissors are for hand-fringing, trimming, and cutting detailed shapes.

Straight pins are for making off-centered circles and shapes, husking, weaving, and assembling the quilled pieces together. Rustproof pins are recommended if using pins where it may come in contact with glue for a long period of time, such as a plug for the glue bottle.

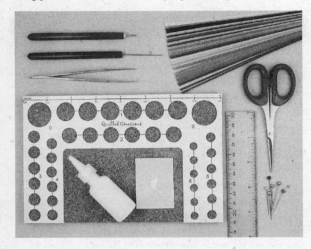

Quilling Papers

Quilling papers come in different widths and lengths. They can range from $1.40 to $5.00 per pack, depending on the number of strips and variety of colors in the pack.

Acid-free

As in scrapbooking and card making, you want your designs and cherished masterpieces to last for generations. It's best to choose and use quilling papers that are free of acid to help protect your photographs and artwork.

Types & Weights

Text-weight paper is the most common and the easiest type with which to quill. It creates beautiful small centers in the coils and it can be pinched easily into various shapes. Professional precision-cut quilling papers produce the best designs because of their clean-cut edges and uniform paper width. When all of the pieces are put together, the design will be even from one shape to the next. Strips of paper can be cut by hand, using scissors, with a small paper cutter, or with a paper shredder; however it may be difficult to keep the assembled pieces all the same height.

Vellums give an interesting translucent effect in your quilling artwork. It can be a little tricky to roll because of its smooth surface. It also will take the glue slightly longer to dry on vellums.

Cardstock can also be used to quill simple designs. It can be rolled by hand or with a tool, but it's more difficult because the fibers can split apart when rolling. Many experienced quillers do not recommend this paper weight because your quilling will not be as detailed and intricate since the coils are thicker and bulkier. The techniques and tools described in this book are designed for text-weight papers.

Widths

The majority of quilling is done with the ⅛-inch (3 mm) width paper. This width is the easiest to learn to roll and it works perfectly with scrapbooking and card making.

The wider widths, ¼-inch (6 mm) and ⅜-inch (9 mm), are useful for making fringed flowers, folded roses, and paper sculpting. The narrow width ¹⁄₁₆-inch (1.5 mm) is often used for miniatures or low-profile quilled designs. It isn't used that often, but a simple way to make ¹⁄₁₆-inch wide paper strips is to cut a ⅛-inch wide paper in half lengthwise.

Graduated & Dark-center Graduated Color

Graduated-color quilling papers offer a unique look to quilled designs. The graduated-color papers start as a solid color and gradually fade to white. The dark-centered graduated papers are the same as the graduated; but they start with white at one edge, fade to the solid color in the center, then gradually fade back to white. The subtle shift in the colors results in eye-catching dimensional shapes that really jump out against a dark background.

Metallic & Gilded Edge

Metallic quilling paper has a gold or silver finish on one side of the paper. It's also known as "quill trim." It should be rolled with the metallic finish showing on the outside. Gilded-edge papers are quilling papers with a metallic or pearlized finish on the edges of the paper strips. When it's rolled and shaped, the gilded edges bring out the beauty of the quilled coils. This effect also can be produced by applying watercolor metallic paints to the top of the quilled pieces.

Two-tone

Two-tone colored quilling papers offer another unique look to quilled designs. These papers are a solid color on one side and the other side is a lighter shade of that same color. As you quill with this paper, you will notice the two tones of the paper throughout each spiral. The beauty of this paper is brought out in the "husking" technique.

Other Tools Used For Quilling

After learning the simple basics in quilling, you will love these other tools and supplies that make quilling faster and easier to do.

Corkboard is used for quilling large patterns. Typically, larger patterns will have many small pieces that are held together by pins and glued together. **Note:** The board can be made with corkboard, foam-core board, or corrugated cardboard.

Waxed paper or transparent plastic bag is used to prevent glue from sticking to the pattern.

Grid or graph paper is used for husking, weaving, and other quilling techniques. Concentric circles and marked angles of 45 or 60 degrees are helpful for making symmetrical designs such as snowflakes.

Tracing paper is used for duplicating patterns and designs to protect the original design.

Fringer is used for fringing paper strips. It cuts and automatically advances wider-width paper strips. This tool is definitely a great time-saver and easy on the hands when making many fringed flowers.

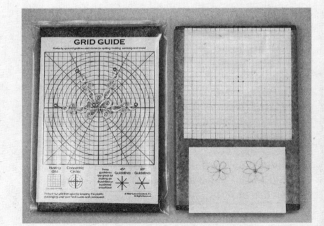

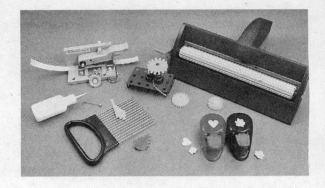

Crimper (large or small) is used for creating a zigzag look on the paper.

Paper punches are used for creating basic shapes. A punched flower or leaf complements nicely with quilling. The heart punch is a quick method for making flower petals.

Onion holder or **pick comb** is used for looping paper strips described in the combing technique to create interesting petals, leaves and wings.

Ultrafine-tipped glue bottle is used for quickly dispensing fine lines and drops of glue.

Other Supplies to Accent & Embellish Quilling

Fine-tipped pens & markers are used for writing, accenting, and embellishing projects.

Chalk palette & applicators are for creating a soft accent on projects.

Metallics, iridescent & watercolor paints are for accenting projects and the edges of quilled pieces.

Stamp & ink pad are for accenting and embellishing projects.

Beads, moveable eyes, rhinestones & sequins are for adding dimensional embellishments on projects.

Pearls, ribbons & trims are used for adding dimensional embellishments on projects.

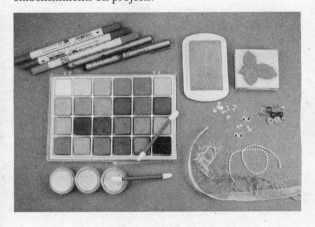

Card-Making & Scrapbooking Tools

It's extremely helpful to have some basic tools when card making and scrapbooking. Most quilling when card making and scrapbooking. Most quilling is done on keepsake items and cherished cards. So these tools will be useful when making projects in this book and for your future projects.

Paper trimmer is used for trimming paper and cardstock. Most paper trimmers have a cutting blade and a scoring blade. A 12-inch (30.5 cm) paper cutter is the recommended size since it will fit the popular size for scrapbook pages.

Tape runner or adhesive tabs are for dispensing small, precut, double-sided adhesive tabs that allow you to quickly mount paper together. This can be better than wet glues, which may wrinkle or leave "air bubbles" in the paper.

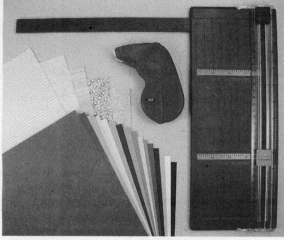

Photo D

Patterned papers are used as the background pages or to embellish a background page.

Cardstock is used for the background page.

Rolling Coils

To begin rolling paper, practice rolling with 8-inch (20.5 cm) paper strips.

Slotted Tool

1. Slide the end of the paper into the slot, from the top.

2. Twirl the tool in either direction. Use the tip of your finger to support the coil and your thumb to guide the paper while rolling.

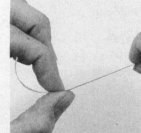

3. When you get to the end of the strip, remove the coil by pushing from behind, or underneath, the coil instead of pulling the coil off from its sides. **Note:** This prevents the center of the coil from being pulled out.

4. Place the coil in the circle template board or on a smooth table surface. Let the coil expand open.

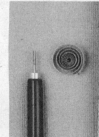

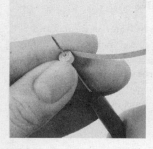
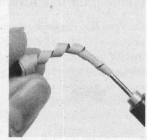

Needle Tool

1. Pull the paper between your forefinger nail and your thumb to curl the paper. **Notes:** It's a helpful technique to soften the paper and break the fibers in preparation for rolling.

You can also moisten the end slightly so that it sticks to the needle when you are ready to roll it.

2. Wrap the paper end around the needle tool.

3. Keep the needle tool stationary, then move your thumb and finger in opposite directions to get the roll started. Keep constant light pressure on the coil as you roll so that it does not unravel.

4. Slide the coil off the needle tool. Place it in the circle template board or on a smooth table surface. Let the coil expand open.

Rolling Techniques

Every quiller rolls their paper strips slightly differently. We all use different fingertip pressure and tension, creating a variety of coil sizes. Below are some useful tips and techniques to help fix any quilling quirks.

Pulled-out Centers

Instead of pulling, push the coil off the tool to avoid the centers from staying behind on the tool.

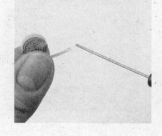

Pulled-out centers

Pop-ups

Try keeping the paper's edges even as you are rolling the paper strip. This pop-up quilling "quirk" will go away with practice.

Pop ups

Tight Twirler

If your coils aren't expanding, then try relaxing the winding tension, or fingertip pressure, on the roll. Sometimes holding the rolled paper in your hand for too long will prevent the coil from expanding.

Tight twirler

Uneven Coils

Using the slotted tool, apply firm, even tension, or fingertip pressure, on the paper strip while rotating the tool.

Using the needle tool, try to use constant fingertip pressure as you are rolling.

Uneven coils

Uneven Tight Circles

Use less tension, or fingertip pressure, as you roll so that the paper can shift slightly after rolling. Then after the paper's end is glued, place it on a hard surface and use the tool's handle to roll over the top edge, like rolling out a piecrust.

Uneven tight circles

Other Quilling Techniques

Tearing Paper Strips

Tearing the paper strip is a favorite technique among quillers because it leaves a feather end. When the paper's end is glued to the coil, the feathered tear is virtually seamless. Conversely, cutting the strip will leave a blunt end that is more visible.

Gluing a Coil

After the coil has been rolled and expanded open, glue the end to the coil, using the following method.

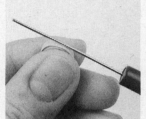

1. Place a puddle of glue on a sticky-notepad sheet.

2. Using the needle tool, place a dab of glue at the paper's end.

3. Use the needle tool to press the glues end flat against

the coil.

Using Patterns

For each project, patterns are provided to help show the actual size of the quilled piece or final design. Since everyone quills with slightly different fingertip pressure, line-drawings are a great reference to make your pieces to scale. The patterns in each project may include the individual quilled shape and/or the assembled finished project. If you would like to use the patterns as a guide, use the following instructions:

1. To protect the original patterns in this book, use a pencil to copy the pattern or patterns onto tracing paper.

2. Roll each piece as instructed. Place the quilled piece on the traced pattern to check the size and placement as shown in 2a.

Tip—It is easier to make all of the pieces first and then glue the pieces together or to your background.

Some of the projects will only show a half pattern as shown below. If the design is symmetrical, copy half of the project pattern, then flip it over and trace the remaining half to make the complete pattern.

If the pattern shows eccentric circles or shapes within the design as shown below, this indicates that the coil should be made into an off-centered circle.

Continued ➜

Gluing onto the Background

After quilling all of your pieces, use the following method to glue individual pieces or a small quilled assembly to the background.

1. Place a puddle of glue on a sticky-notepad sheet.

2. Using fine-tipped tweezers, pick up the quilled piece. Hold the piece by the outer coils to get a good grasp on the piece without changing its shape.

3. Dip the quilled piece into the puddle of glue. If there is too much glue on the strip, then tap the piece on the notepad sheet to remove any excess glue.

4. Place the glued piece on the background.

Storing Your Supplies & Tools

Quilling doesn't take up much space. It's a lightweight and portable craft that can be taken on long road trips or even on vacation. It's best to work on a flat and clean surface like a tabletop, or on a lap-desk if you like to work in front of the television.

Storing Supplies

Group papers together by colors or widths. Store the papers in a plastic container or shoe box for portability. It's an easy and quick way to take papers with you. Another method is to use a metal ring and the hang hole in the packaging to hook the papers together. The best way to keep the papers in good shape and in their original packaging is by making an opening in the bag. Pull out one strip at a time from the inside layer.

Embroidery floss boxes are very effective for separating finished quilled pieces. It's a great way to build up your supply of quilled pieces so they are readily available for use.

Storing Tools

Tools can be stored on your crafting table by pushing them into a Styrofoam block. It is a convenient holder to keep your tools from rolling away and within reach.

Framing Quilled Artwork

Shadowboxes are the best type of frame to display and protect your quilled artwork. These frames have a ½–1-inch (1.3–2.5 cm) space between the glass and the surface background of your quilled artwork. More stores are carrying shadowbox frames, since memento and keepsake frames are very popular. If you need a customized shadowbox frame or mat, a frame shop is a great resource for ideas and materials.

Another simple way to keep the glass away from your quilled artwork is to make "tight circle" paper spacers. See Tight Circle on page 25. First, choose the paper width based on how far away the glass should be away from the quilled artwork. Roll small tight circles with the paper strips, then glue them around the perimeter of the framed artwork, hidden behind the framework.

Preserving Quilled Artwork

Preserving your quilled artwork will ensure that it will last and give it some durability. Many quillers use an acrylic spray sealant to protect their work. Whatever the case may be, practice on a scrap quilled piece first to be certain it is the finish that you prefer.

The Basics

How do I make the basic quilled shapes?

Once the basic quilled shapes are learned, they can be joined together for an endless array of quilled designs. For example, there are many different ways to make quilled flowers with the basic shapes. The points on the shape can all be facing in toward the center or away from each other for different types of flowers.

Basic Shapes Techniques

Loose Circle

Roll the paper strip with the slotted or needle tool. Refer to Rolling Coils under "Quilling Basics." Remove from tool and let it expand on a flat surface or in the circle template board. Glue the end to the coil. Refer to Gluing a Coil. **Note:** Quilled shapes begin as loose circles, then they are pinched into different shapes.

Teardrop

Roll a loose circle. Pinch one side of the circle to form a point.

Marquise

Roll a loose circle. Pinch two points at the same time on opposite sides.

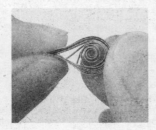
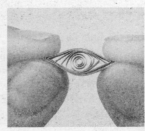

Triangle

Make a teardrop. Hold the point of the teardrop in one hand and with the other hand, press the rounded end inward to form three points.

Half Circle

Make a teardrop. Pinch a second point on the teardrop near the first point. **Note:** The distance between the two pinched points will determine the height of the half circle.

Square or Diamond

Make a marquise. Turn the marquise 90 degrees and pinch two more points on the opposite sides. **Note:** Each side should be the same length.

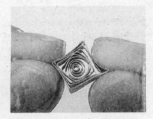

To form a diamond shape, press two opposing points close together toward the center.

Rectangle

Make a marquise. Turn the marquise slightly and pinch two more points on opposite sides. **Note:** There should be two short sides and two long sides.

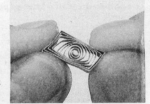

Hexagon

Make a rectangle. Turn the rectangle 90 degrees. Pinch two more points on the longer opposite sides.

Tight Circle

1. Roll a tight circle, using one of the following methods:

Method A:

- Using the slotted tool, place the paper end into the slot and twirl the tool to start rolling. Roll the paper, using steady tension as you twirl. Once you've rolled to the end, use the needle tool to place a dab of glue on loose end, press it against the tight circle. Push it off the tool.

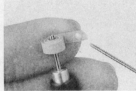

Method B:

- Using the needle tool, wrap the paper end around the needle and start rolling. Keep constant light pressure on the coil as you roll so that it does not unravel. Once you've rolled to the end, slip it off the needle tool and do not let it expand. Place a dab of glue on the loose end and press it against the tight circle.

2. To even out the edges, place the tight circle on a hard surface and use the handle of the tool to roll across the top of the edges.

Grape Roll

Roll a tight circle from a paper strip. Gently push the center of the tight circle out with your finger or the end of the tool to form a dome. To push the

center out evenly, slightly rotate the tight coil after each push. Place a thin layer of glue on the inner (or outer) surface to preserve the shape. Note: It may take up to a day for the piece to be "cured" and permanently keep its shape.

Tip—If you are making multiple grape rolls of the same size, then use a mold (e.g. wooden ball, marble, dome, etc.) to shape each piece.

Cone Roll

Roll a short paper strip into a tight circle, but off-set the paper's edge on a slight angle while rolling. Glue the end to the tight circle.

Curving Basic Shapes

Curving the basic quilled shape's point or side can give the piece more character and artistic detail.

Curving a shape can be done, using one of the following methods:

Method A:

- Using your fingernail, curve the point.

Method B:

- Using the quilling tool, curve the point.

Pinching the basic shapes will allow you to create endless shapes and designs, which is why so many crafters are fascinated by quilling. A helpful method to hide the seam of the paper on your roll is to pinch the point at that seam. Rounding sides inward is also a fun way to change the shape of your quilled piece. Paper is a very forgiving material. So reshape and repinch points whenever necessary to make the right shape.

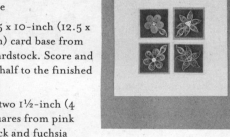

Flower Card

Here's How:

Finished size: 5 inches (12.5 cm) square

1. Cut 5 x 10-inch (12.5 x 25.5 cm) card base from white cardstock. Score and fold in half to the finished size.

2. Cut two 1½-inch (4 cm) squares from pink cardstock and fuchsia cardstock.

3. Cut four burgundy squares that are slightly smaller than the pink and fuchsia squares.

4. Center and mount the burgundy squares to the pink and fuchsia squares with adhesive tabs.

5. Quilling Instructions

For Teardrop Flower:

- Roll six 6-inch (15 cm) pink paper strips into teardrops. Glue the points together to form a six-petal flower. Roll a 4-inch (10 cm) white paper strip into a tight circle. Glue to the flower's center as shown in 5a.

5a

For Marquise Flower:

- Roll six 6-inch (15 cm) pink paper strips into marquises. Glue the points together to form a six-petal flower. Make three 2-inch (5 cm) white paper strips into tight circles. Glue to the flower's center as shown in 5b.

5b

For Curved Teardrop Flower:

- Roll five 6-inch (15 cm) pink paper strips into curved teardrops. Glue rounded portion of the teardrops together, forming a five-petal flower. Roll a 2-inch (5 cm) white paper strip into loose circle. Glue to flower's center as shown in 5c.

5c

For Grape-roll Flower:

- Roll five 16-inch (90.5 cm) fuchsia paper strips into grape rolls. Pinch a point on the wider portion of the roll to form a teardrop. Glue the points together to form a five-petal flower. Roll a 2-inch (5 cm) white paper strip into a cone roll. Glue to flower's center as shown in 5d.

5d

FOR LEAVES:

- Roll four 6-inch (15 cm) green paper strips into curved marquises. Glue a single green leaf to each flower.

6. Using the tweezers, pick up each flower and glue it to each square. Center and mount the squares with flowers to the card base with adhesive tabs.

Tip—To make uniform petals, use a circle template board.

How do I make off-centered or eccentric circles?

Off-centered or eccentric circles are made from basic loose circles. It is a great technique to add visual perspective to your large quilled circles. A helpful hint: when you are ready to glue it to the background, place the glued side face down so that it does not show in your final quilled artwork.

WHAT YOU NEED TO GET STARTED:

General Quilling Tools

⅛-inch (3 mm)-wide quilling papers: two shades of yellow

Adhesive tabs

Cardstock:

    black

    dark green

    moss green

Paper trimmer with cutting and scoring blades

Yellow patterned papers

OFF-CENTERED CIRCLE TECHNIQUE

1. Roll a strip of paper and place it in the circle template board. Let it expand and unroll into the size of the circle opening. Add a dab of glue behind the paper's end to form a loose circle.

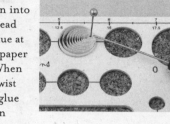

2. With a straight pin, pull the center off to the side and push the pin into the board. Then spread a small amount of glue at the top edges of the paper strip near the pin. When the glue has dried, twist to release any dried glue stuck to the pin, then remove the pin.

Tips—Use tweezers to arrange and even out your coils before gluing the off-centered center.

To make off-centered circles without a circle template board, use a corkboard and place pins around the loose circle to hold it in place, then use a pin to pull the center off to one side and pin it down into the board.

Sunshine Card

HERE'S HOW:

Finished size: 5½ x 4 inches (14 x 10 cm)

1. Cut a 5½ x 8-inch (14 x 20 cm) card base from the moss green cardstock. Score and fold in half to the finished size. Cut a 5¼ x 3¼-inch (13.5 x 8.5 cm) rectangle from the dark green cardstock and mount to the card base with adhesive tabs.

2. Cut a 2-inch (5 cm) square from the moss green cardstock. Cut a 1¾-inch (4.5 cm) square from black cardstock. Center and mount onto the moss green square with adhesive tabs.

3. Print on the yellow patterned paper, "You are my sunshine…" Trim around saying as desired. Center and mount onto black cardstock. Trim black cardstock as desired.

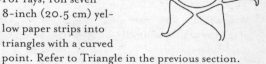

4. Quilling Instructions

  For Sun:

- For center, roll a 16" light yellow paper strip into off-centered circle as shown in 4a.

- For rays, roll seven 8-inch (20.5 cm) yellow paper strips into triangles with a curved point. Refer to Triangle in the previous section.

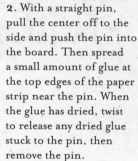

5. Place the sun with the glued side face down in the center of the black square. Arrange the rays around the sun.

Continued ➡

6. Using the tweezers, pick up each piece and glue it to the black square. Mount the square piece with the quilled sun and the "You are my sunshine…" piece to the dark green card base with adhesive tabs.

How do I make basic quilled scrolls?

Scrolls are made by rolling a strip of paper, but the end is not typically glued to the roll. This is a popular technique for making vines, borders, and alphabet letters. The other scroll techniques described in this section will show how to give your scrolls an artistic and whimsical look.

WHAT YOU NEED TO GET STARTED:

General Quilling Tools

⅛-inch (3 mm)-wide quilling papers:

    ivory

    moss green

    pink

5 x 7-inch (7.5 x 18 cm) shadowbox with black mat

Photograph

BASIC SCROLL TECHNIQUES

LOOSE SCROLL

Start rolling the paper strip at one end. Leave the other end loose or straight.

HEART SCROLL

Make a fold at the center of the paper strip, then roll each end inward toward the fold. Use a dab of glue to keep the heart scrolls closed.

"C" SCROLL

Roll both ends of the paper strip to the center.

"S" SCROLL

Roll one end of the paper strip to the center, then turn the strip and roll the other end to the center.

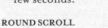

"V" SCROLL

Make a fold at the center of the paper strip and roll each end outward.

"Y" SCROLL

Make a fold at the center of the paper strip and roll each end outward. Place a dab of glue between the paper strips near the fold.

SPIRAL

Roll a spiral, using one of the following methods:

Method A:

- Using the slotted tool, roll the paper strip around the tool. While the coil is on the tool, gently pull the end away from the coil at an angle, unraveling the strip and creating a spiral.

Method B:

- Using the needle tool, place the end of the paper at an angle near the middle of the needle. Roll the paper around the needle so that the spiral rolls up toward the tip of the tool. **Note:** Spirals made with the needle tool will be smaller and tighter than the slotted tool.

Tip—After forming the spiral on the tool, tighten it by holding both ends of the spiral and stretching and retwisting it to the desired thickness.

OTHER SCROLL TECHNIQUES

The helpful scroll techniques described below are great for making alphabet letters and beautiful scrolled border designs.

OPEN SCROLL

This is a very simple technique to make the scroll larger with more space between the coils. First unravel part of the scroll, then gently reroll the scroll.

PINCHING A POINT

Place a small amount of glue at the fold. Pinch the fold closed and hold for a few seconds.

ROUND SCROLL

Pull one end of the paper strip along the needle tool to round or curl end to the desired shape.

ZIGZAG SCROLL

Make two opposing folds near the center of the paper strip. Make two more opposing folds to form the zigzag. Place glue between the folds and press the strips together. Roll the ends of the paper strip.

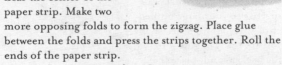

Scrolled Border Frame

HERE'S HOW:

1. Quilling Instructions

For Vine:

- Roll two 8-inch (20.5 cm) moss green paper strips into "S" scrolls. Using the open scroll technique, make the scrolls larger.

- Roll two 4-inch (10 cm) moss green paper strips into "C" scrolls. Using the open scroll technique, make the scrolls larger.

- Roll four 4-inch (10 cm) moss green paper strips into tight circles and four 2-inch (5 cm) moss green paper strips into tight circles. Refer to Tight Circle under "How do I make basic quilled shapes?"

For Heart:

- Roll two 6-inch (15 cm) pink paper strips into heart scrolls.

For Flower Buds:

- Roll four 6-inch (15 cm) ivory paper strips into half circles. Curve the points to make the shape of a flower bud.

For Leaves:

- Roll four 6-inch (15 cm) moss green paper strips into curved marquises. Refer to Marquise under "How do I make basic quilled shapes?"

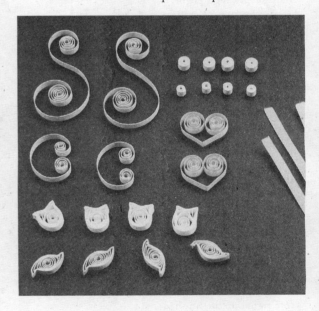

2. Make certain that you have all of the necessary quilled pieces.

3. Arrange the scrolls and quilled shapes on the black mat as shown in 3a. Using the tweezers, pick up each piece and glue onto the mat.

4. Mount the photograph to the mat and insert in the shadowbox.

SCROLL DESIGN VARIATIONS

Assemble, arrange, and position the scrolled pieces into any desired design. This is where you can use your imagination to play with the different scroll designs. When you finally have a design that fits the layout, use the tweezers to pick up each piece and glue into place on the mat.

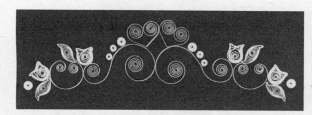

How do I use the husking technique?

The husking technique is simply taking quilling paper and wrapping it around pins. The diamond is a simple looping pattern. Once you see how simple the technique repeats, you can make just about any geometric shape. A fine-tipped glue bottle works great with this technique because you are constantly placing tiny drops of glue on the paper after each loop.

WHAT YOU NEED TO GET STARTED:

General Quilling Tools

⅛-inch (3 mm)-wide quilling papers:
    blue
    red
    white

Chalk palettes:
    blue
    red

Corkboard

Foam-tipped chalk applicator

Grid or graph paper (this project uses 5 squares per inch [2.5 cm])

Paper trimmer with cutting blade

Pencil

Printed verse or photograph

Small wooden frame

Straight pins (at least 5)

Waxed paper or clear plastic bag.

HUSKING TECHNIQUE

1. Using a pencil, trace a copy of the diamond pattern as shown in 1a. Place graph paper onto a corkboard protected by waxed paper or clear plastic bag to keep the glue from sticking to the pattern. **Note:** This pattern will also be used for the project.

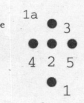

2. Make a small fold at one end of strip to aid in placement of the glue and the pin. Form a loop by placing a dab of glue between the fold as shown in 2a. Place a pin in the loop of the paper strip. Pin it down in Point #1 of the diamond pattern as shown in 1a.

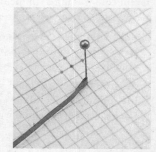

3. Place a pin in Point #2. Wrap the paper around that pin. Extend the paper down and around Pin #1. Glue the paper strip below Pin #1 to hold it in place. Repeat this around Pin #3 as shown in 3a.

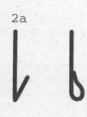 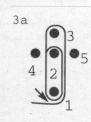

4. Place a pin in Point #4. Wrap the paper around Pin #4. Extend the paper down and around Pin #1. Glue between the paper strip below Pin #1 to hold it in place. Repeat around Pin #5 as shown in 4a.

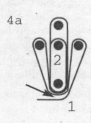 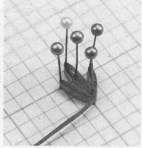

5. Wrap a collar around the outer pins. To help keep the shape of the husking pattern, place glue between the strips at each pin. Glue the strip below Pin #1 as shown in 5a. Trim off the excess paper.

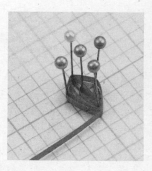

Tip—When husking, place one pin at a time into the husking pattern. Glue below Pin #1 after each wrap to hold the loops together.

To prevent the tip of your glue bottle from clogging, place the bottle upside-down with the tip in a damp sponge.

HUSKING PATTERN VARIATIONS

Create patterns with or without a grid. You can also wrap the collar around the pins without gluing it to the loops. This will make it easier to pinch the piece into different shapes.

Pattern variations

Patriotic Stars Frame

HERE'S HOW:

1. Apply blue and red chalk around edges of verse. Insert verse into the frame.

2. Quilling Instructions

  For Star:

  • Using a pencil, trace a diamond pattern onto graph paper. Use five 8-inch (20.5 cm) red paper strips to husk the diamond pieces.

Continued →

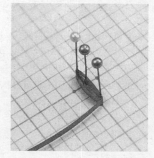

- Glue the five shorter points together to form the star as shown in 2a. Repeat to make a blue star and a white star.

3. Glue the three stars onto the wooden frame.

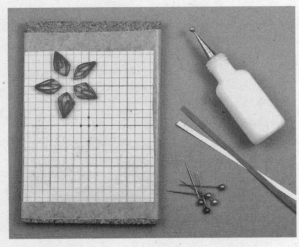

How do I use the alternate-side looping technique?

Alternate-side looping and wheatears looping is similar to husking, but the loops are made in your hands instead of with pins. The beauty of this method is the flexibility to make spectacular wing-like shapes and petals.

WHAT YOU NEED TO GET STARTED:

General Quilling Tools

⅛-inch (3 mm)-wide quilling papers:

  blue

  green

  light blue

  pumpkin or light brown

3-inch (7.5 cm)-diameter glass paperweight

Black cardstock

ALTERNATE-SIDE LOOPING WITH SINGLE PAPER STRIP TECHNIQUE

1. Make a 1-inch (2.5 cm) in height loop with a full-length paper strip. **Note:** This loop is called the "center loop."

2. Wrap the paper strip around the bottom of the loop, or "stem."

Step 1   *Step 2*

3. Form a slightly smaller loop on the right side of the center loop and fold the paper around stem.

4. Form another smaller loop on the left side of the center loop. Fold the paper around the stem.

Step 3   *Step 4*

5. Continue making loops with the paper strip, alternating sides.

6. Finally, wrap a collar around all of the loops and glue the end to the stem. **Note:** You can pinch a point to make a leaf shape.

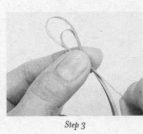

Step 6a   *Step 6b*

ALTERNATE-SIDE LOOPING WITH MULTIPLE PAPER STRIPS TECHNIQUE

To make each step easier to follow start with three different colors as noted in the instructions. **Note:** Excess length can be trimmed and reused for smaller pieces.

1. Layer and glue the ends of three full-length paper strips together in the following order: purple, yellow, and blue.

2. Form the "center loop" so that the purple is on the top, or outside. Hold the paper strips in your hand by the papers' edges, with the glued end out.

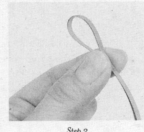

Step 1   *Step 2*

3. With the strips hanging below your hand, find and gently pull the inner blue paper strip down to create a smaller inner loop inside.

4. Gently pull the middle yellow paper strip down to create the middle loop.

Step 3   *Step 4*

5. Fold the three paper strips around the glued stem to form another, slightly smaller loop next to the center loop. Pull the purple paper strip down to create the smaller inner loop. Pull the yellow paper strip down to create the middle loop. Wrap all the paper strips around the stem. Form another loop on the other side.

6. Repeat this process, alternating sides, forming loops and pulling the paper strips to create the inner loops. Finally, wrap a collar with all three paper strips. Glue each paper strip to the stem. Trim off excess paper.

Step 5   *Step 6*

WHEATEAR LOOPING TECHNIQUE

1. Use a single paper strip and make a small loop at one end. Continue making loops that are slightly larger than the last, wrapping and pinching each loop at the stem.

2. Glue the stem layers together. Pinch and curve the top to make simple leaves and stems. **Note:** This technique can also be done with pins and a corkboard, as with the Husking Technique.

Butterfly Paperweight

HERE'S HOW:

1. Cut the black cardstock to fit the bottom of the paperweight.

2. Quilling Instructions

For Butterfly:

- For wings, use the technique for alternate-side looping with three paper strips and make a large wing with four loops from blue, light blue and green papers as shown in 2a. Pinch a point on the wing. Make a smaller wing with three loops and pinch a point on the wing.

- For body, roll an 8-inch (20.5 cm) light blue paper strip into a curved teardrop as shown in 2a.

- For butterfly's head, roll a 4-inch (10 cm) light blue paper strip into a loose circle as shown in 2a.

- For antenna, roll a 2-inch (5 cm) light blue paper strip into "V" scroll where both scrolls are in the same direction as shown in 2a.

For Leaf:

- Using the alternate-side looping with single paper strip technique, make two small leaves from green paper.

For Twig:

- Roll a 4-inch (10 cm) pumpkin or light brown paper strip paper into a spiral. Trim to a 2-inch (5 cm) length as shown in 2a.

3. Glue the wings and head to the body. Glue the antenna to the head.

4. Using tweezers, pick up and glue the butterfly, leaves, and twig onto the black cardstock.

5. Mount glass paperweight over the quilled pieces.

How do I boondoggle with quilling paper?

Boondoggle is a technique that is usually done with fibers or plastic strands. When I first tried the classic knot with quilling paper, I wasn't quite sure what to do with the results. But with some creativity, I found that you can create some exciting pieces.

WHAT YOU NEED TO GET STARTED:

General Quilling Tools

⅛-inch (3 mm)-wide quilling papers:

red

white

Silver embroidery thread

Boondoggling Technique

The easiest method of explaining boondoggling is by assigning quadrants and numbers to the paper strips.

1. Take two paper strips and glue to form a cross. **Note:** The photographs show different quadrants and numbered paper strips. This will show you where each paper strip will be placed.

Step 1

2. Fold Strip #1 into Quadrant A. Fold Strip #2 into Quadrant B. Fold Strip #3 into Quadrant C.

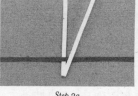

Step 2a

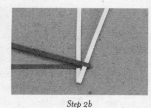

Step 2b

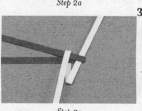

Step 2c

Step 3

3.

Fold Strip #4 over and under the white paper strips to Quadrant D.

4. Gently pull all of the paper strips tight to flatten and form a classic knot. Repeat Steps 2–4 to desired length.

Step 4

Candy Cane Ornament

Here's How:

1. Quilling Instructions

For Candy Cane:

• Boondoggle a full length of a red and a white paper strip. **Note:** When you need more paper, glue the new paper strips end-to-end as you go. Continue boondoggling until candy cane is the desired size as shown in 1a. Fold over and glue paper ends. Curve one end of boondoggle to form top.

2. Attach a thread to the candy cane for hanger.

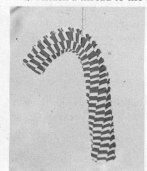
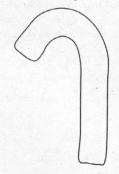

—From *Paper Quilling for the First Time*

DECOUPAGE

Dawn Cusick & Megan Kirby, Editor

You learned the skills you need for decoupage in kindergarten: cutting and pasting. Though the techniques are basic, you can create amazingly sophisticated and long-lasting decorative items and works of art with a few simple tools and your imagination.

Materials and Tools

Cutouts

Once you start looking for paper scraps and printed images to use in decoupage, you will quickly have a large supply. Keep a box or storage container handy and deposit any potential scraps. Use a photocopy machine or a scanner to enlarge or reduce images or to make color images black and white. The lighter-weight the paper, the better the results usually are.

Adhesives

A number of adhesives can be used in decoupage, including PVA (white) glue, wallpaper paste, wood glue, and spray adhesive. Which type you use depends on the cutout being applied and the surface you're applying it to. Often, PVA glue is a good choice.

Paint

Consider the object that will be painted when choosing paint for your project. Decorative painting and decoupage often go hand in hand, and the painting techniques you choose can be as complicated or as simple as you wish.

Paintbrushes

Available in a variety of sizes and widths, paintbrushes are very useful in applying glue, paint, and varnish. Use clean, high-quality brushes to minimize stray hairs or bristles to minimize stray hairs or bristles getting caught in paint or varnish.

Varnishes

Polyurethane varnishes work well on wood surfaces; in addition, varnishes are sold that create a colored, tinted, or crackled surface. Use the varnish that best suits the material that is being coated, and always read the manufacturer's instructions before using. Water-based varnishes will not affect the color of the piece, while oil-based varnished impart a yellowish color. PVA glue acts as a varnish as well.

Paper Sealer

Print fixative spray, shellac, and white French polish (sometimes called button polish) are a few of the paper sealers that prevent paper cutouts from discoloring. This step, while not always essential, also helps give structure and durability to flimsy or poor-quality papers.

Scissors/Craft Knife

Sometimes scissors work best to cut out decoupage scraps, while a craft knife is useful for cutting very straight lines or detail work. Make sure your craft knife has a very sharp blade and that you use a mat or piece of cardboard to protect the work surface. Small manicure or embroidery scissors (again, with a very sharp blade) are good tools for cutting out small pieces.

Basic Techniques

Preparing the Surface

A hard surface made of just about anything—metal, wood, ceramic, or paper, to name only a few—is suitable for

---

decoupage. As you become more experienced with this craft, you will find the process of applying cutouts to found objects (rescuing them, if you will) very pleasing.

1. Thoroughly clean the surface of the object to be decoupaged with a mild detergent and warm water, and allow to dry. If using a metal object, remove rust with steel wool, then wash surface with a solution of half vinegar and half water. Clean and sand wood surfaces and fill any holes with wood putty.

2. Prime or seal the object. Any porous object will need to be sealed with a sealant or varnish. Wood surfaces will need to be primed (for painting) or sealed (for projects in which you want the wood to show). Metal surfaces will need a primer coat; a coat of rust-proofing sealant is an optional step. Apply gesso, if desired.

3. Paint the object, if desired. Usually, several coats of paint are necessary. Sand lightly between coats. Lightly sand the surface of the object one last time with fine sandpaper so that cutouts will adhere more easily.

Preparing the Cutouts

Your decoupage project is only as interesting as the cutouts you choose. Wrapping paper, photocopies from books, magazine images, and even stickers and fabric scraps can result in terrific, one-of-a-kind decoupage designs.

1. Use scissors to cut the paper into manageable sizes, then use smaller scissors or a craft knife to cut out the shapes. To avoid white edges that may show in the final piece, cut at a slight angle.

2. Determine how the cutouts will be positioned on the surface of the object and arrange on the work surface. This is easy when using a flat surface, and more challenging with curved surfaces.

Applying the Cutouts & Finishing

Sometimes you will find that randomly applying cutouts is the most fun, although it always makes sense to put a little thought into the design before you begin to glue. An adhesive with a longer drying time will make it easier to rearrange cutouts as you work.

1. Apply adhesive. Spread glue with a paintbrush onto the base surface (not to the underside of the cutout). Spray adhesive should be sprayed directly on the cutout, using a

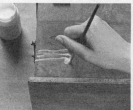

Continued →

piece of scrap paper underneath to protect the work surface.

2. Press the cutout down on the surface and rub firmly from the center to the outside with a clean, soft cloth. Try to remove any air bubbles as you apply pressure. Allow adhesive to dry, then wipe off any excess glue with a warm, wet cloth. (**Note:** Follow manufacturer's guidelines for glue drying times, as some glue dries very quickly and some very slowly.)

3. Apply varnish in thin, even strokes, according to manufacturer's instructions. Allow to dry thoroughly, then apply additional layers of varnish, if desired. Once varnish has dried, you can consider your decoupage project to be complete. Apply any additional finishes, such as antique wax or crackle finish, last.

Projects

Garden Decoupage Dinner Plate

Designer: Chris Rankin

Look at that stack of lovely paper napkins leftover from your garden tea party. Don't you wish you had a set of dishes in that pattern? Wish no more.

MATERIALS AND TOOLS

- Clear glass plate
- Paper towels or lint-free cloth
- Flat paintbrush, 1 inches (2.5 cm) wide
- Floral-printed paper dinner napkins
- Light-colored scrap paper
- White or cream-colored glass paint
- Scissors
- Decoupage medium, matte finish
- Clear aerosol varnish
- Glass cleaner
- Flat paintbrush, 2 inch (5 cm) wide

WHAT TO DO

1. Cut the flowers and other attractive images or text from the napkins. Experiment with their arrangement on the plate as you go to refine the layout you'll use and to determine how many cutout images you'll need.

2. Place the light-colored scrap paper on your work surface (You'll need a light background to work on so you can see how your design will look). Wipe your plate clean—front and back—with glass cleaner and a paper towel or lint-free cloth. Then place the plate on the scrap paper, face down.

3. Your napkin images may be several layers thick, but for maximum transparency, you'll just need the upper printed layer. Peel away the other layers just before you're ready to begin gluing the images in place.

4. Select an area on the back of the plate to begin decoupaging. Keep in mind that you're essentially working in reverse—the images at the forefront of the design should be applied first. (For the plate shown, for instance, the cluster of flowers at the center was applied first; then the text image was added "on top" of it.)

5. Using the 1-inch (2.5 cm)-wide paintbrush, apply a thin, even layer of decoupage medium over an area of the plate just slightly larger than the image you're about to place. Carefully position the napkin image with the image side facing the glue. Use your fingers to lightly press the napkin to the surface, creating a secure bond and smoothing out any wrinkles or bubbles. Apply another layer of decoupage medium over the back of the napkin, sealing it in place.

6. Repeat Step 5 until your design is complete, allowing the decoupage medium to dry between each paper application. If you find it difficult to work in reverse, lift the plate by its edges and turn it toward you to check the image placement.

7. After you've completed the collage, use the 2-inch (5 cm)-wide brush to apply a thin but even layer of white or cream-colored glass paint to entire to dry. Then, working in a well-ventilated area and following the manufacturer's instructions, spray the back of the plate with varnish. If you choose to apply additional coats of varnish, be sure to allow the previous coats to dry first.

Magnetic Decoupage

Designer: Martha Le Van

Finally, refrigerator magnets that are just as wonderful as the prized drawings and photographs they hold. Because they're made from clear glass and decoupage paper, you can create a set of magnets to fit a theme, match a room, or complement a personality. Go ahead—express yourself!

MATERIALS AND TOOLS

- Clear glass half-marbles
- Decoupage papers
- Decoupage medium, matte and gloss finish
- Flat paintbrush, 1 inch (2.5 cm) wide
- Fine-tip artist's paintbrush
- Glass cleaner
- Paper towels or a lint-free cloth
- Fixed-blade craft knife
- Sponge brush, 1 inch (2.5 cm) wide
- ¼-inch (6 mm) circular magnets

WHAT TO DO

1. Cut the selected images out of the decoupage paper with scissors, allowing a generous border on all sides. A square of decoupage paper that's 2 x 2 inches (5 x 5 cm) accommodates both large and small half-marbles. Make sure the picture or pattern you want to show through the half-marble is in the center of the square.

2. The quality of the half-marbles varies greatly, even within the same package, so discard those that are cracked, scratched, or have large bubbles in the glass. Clean the flat surface of one half-marble with glass cleaner and a paper towel or lint-free cloth.

3. Dip the flat brush into the matte decoupage medium and apply a thin, even coat to the flat surface of the half-marble. Place the marble on the center of one paper square. Lift the marble and paper off your work surface and squeeze them together to distribute the decoupage medium. Check the position of the image and make any small adjustments in the paper's placement, taking care not to cause wrinkles or tears. Let the glue dry completely. Repeat this process for all the marbles, letting them completely dry before proceeding to Step 4.

4. Use scissors to trim away the excess paper from the marble. Because they have a curved surface, it's easy to make a close cut that's slightly underneath the outer edge of the glass. With the fine-tip paintbrush, reglue any paper edges as needed. Allow this glue to dry.

5. With the sponge brush paint a thin topcoat of gloss-finish decoupage medium over the back of the paper. The glue acts as a varnish and gives the back of the magnets a nice finish. Allow the glue to completely dry.

6. Glue the magnets to the paper-backed glass with a few drops of epoxy, then hold them firmly together until the epoxy forms a tight bond.

Gift Wrap Chest

Designer: Martha Le Van

Don't just throw your gift-wrapping gear in the back of the closet—store it in style. Simple wood chests can be had for very little money, although you may well have a suitable piece in your attic or basement. Choose themed papers—wedding, birthday, Christmas, and so forth—to help create a visual organization system.

MATERIALS AND TOOLS

- Wooden chest with drawers
- Wood putty and putty knife (optional)
- Sandpaper
- Clean cloth
- Gloss latex paint
- Paintbrush
- Gift wrap
- Scissors
- Foam brush

Decoupage medium, matte or gloss finish

Cutting board

Craft knife

Acrylic craft paint (optional)

WHAT TO DO

1. Remove any drawer pulls on the chest. Following the putty manufacturer's instructions, fill any holes, splits, or knots with wood putty. Let the putty dry, then sand. (You will not need to fill the drawer pull holes, as they will be hidden.)

2. Sand the chest and the drawers, as needed, to smooth any rough surfaces, uneven edges, or seams. Wipe the surface of chest and drawers with a clean cloth.

3. Use a paintbrush to apply gloss latex paint in the color of your choice to the chest and the sides of the drawers. Paint as many coats as necessary to achieve the desired color saturation and gloss level, allowing paint to dry thoroughly between coats.

4. Determine which areas of the gift wrap you would like to use for the drawer front. Measure the dimensions of the drawer, then cut a section from the gift wrap to a size that is slightly larger than the size of the drawer. Repeat this step until you have a piece of gift wrap for each drawer.

5. Lightly dip the foam brush into the decoupage medium, then spread a very thin and even coat of medium over the entire surface of a drawer front.

6. Carefully position a piece of gift wrap so that it completely covers the drawer front. Use your fingers to carefully smooth the paper to remove any air bubbles. Set aside drawer to dry. Repeat Steps 5 and 6 until all the drawer fronts are covered.

7. Turn the drawers upside down on top of a cutting board and carefully trim the excess gift wrap with a very sharp craft knife.

8. Place the covered drawers back into the chest in a pleasing arrangement. If desired, use acrylic craft paints to cover any unfinished drawer edges.

—FROM *The Michaels Book of Arts & Crafts*

MORE DECOUPAGE PROJECTS

Nathalie Mornu

Design Ideas

Cutting-edge decoupage isn't about making bad imitations of traditional decoupage. Instead, it strives to use an old technique in a fresh way. This section showcases projects that reflect the philosophy of less is more. We asked our designers to be unpredictable and to create work with a restrained, appealing aesthetic; they rose to the occasion.

Mix Styles

Decoupeurs have always done it, so feel free to combine any images you like or find intriguing. Don't ever think you have to use an entire image; just include the interesting parts.

Choose a Focal Element

Rather than popping a bunch of images onto an object willy-nilly, select a central motif around which to focus the rest of the pieces. For example, the Nippon Box has an overall pattern of honeycombs surrounding the bird, which is the dominant component.

Leave Negative Space

Blank areas spotlight the cutouts in them....

Know When to Stop

Arrange and rearrange your cutouts before gluing them down. (If your surface is curved or vertical, reusable adhesives, like putties or waxes and low-rack, double-sided, or marking tape, will let you experiment with placement.) Try different combinations, adding and removing imagery until the composition feels right. Only then should you glue the different parts down.

Overlap Elements

Once the design satisfies you, photograph the arrangement or make a sketch of it to note the positioning of the various elements. Then remove the cutouts and glue on the bottom elements first, adding the successive layers while referring back to your drawing or snapshot.

The Projects

Wash Day

Designer: LuAnne Payne

The vintage-styled papers on these clothespins hark back to a time when people hung their laundry outside to dry.

PAPER

5 sheets of paper, each printed with a different pattern

OTHER MATERIALS

5 wooden clothespins

Decoupage medium

Fine-grit sandpaper

TOOLS

Pencil

Ruler

Craft knife

Brush or paint sponge

Scissors

WHAT YOU DO

1. Place a sheet of paper face down on the worktable. Put the flat side of a clothespin on the paper and trace around it with a pencil. Move the clothespin over an inch (2.5 cm), and trace around it a second time. Cut out both rectangles.

2. Apply a thin layer of decoupage medium to one face of the clothespin and firmly press one of the paper rectangles to it, holding the paper in place for a few seconds. Repeat on the other side of the clothespin. Trim any protruding edges with small scissors. Allow to dry.

3. Repeat steps 1 and 2 to decoupage the rest of the clothespins.

4. To give the clothespins a slightly worn appearance, lightly sand the wood alongside the edges of the paper. Apply a thin layer of decoupage medium to seal and protect your work.

Tips—You might use these clothespins to fasten to-do lists together or to clip opened bags of snacks closed so they remain fresh and crispy. If you glue a magnet to one face, you can place them on the refrigerator door to hang a child's drawing. Attach them upside-down to a base for displaying photographs.

Confetti

Designer: Terry Taylor

Let the kids join in on this project! All you need is colorful wrapping paper and a few paper punches...along with the willingness to surrender creative control.

PAPER

Colorful, striped wrapping paper

OTHER MATERIALS

2 child-sized wooden chairs

Sandpaper

Acrylic paint in two shades

Decoupage medium

Acrylic varnish

TOOLS

Brushes

Ruler

Craft knife

Decorative paper punches

WHAT YOU DO

1. If your chairs are finished, sand them before painting them. If you're using unfinished chairs, simply paint them as desired. (To avoid a lot of cleanup, you might not ask the kids to help with this task.) Allow the paint to dry.

2. Cut the paper into strips the width of your paper punches. Round up your helpers and have them punch out plenty of shapes. They may say they've punched out a bunch, but assure them you can never have too many.

Continued ➡

3. Have the kids adhere the punch-outs to the chairs using decoupage medium. (They'll undoubtedly tire of the novelty quickly, so be prepared to finish the project yourself!) Allow everything to dry.

4. Give the chairs one of more coats of varnish to protect the paper.

Tip—While this project features paper dots in three different sizes, you can find punches that create a variety of more exotic motifs—hearts, locomotives, leaves, and dogs, among others—in the scrapbooking section of craft retailers.

Hanging in Style

Designer: Nathalie Mornu

There's a certain type of woman who can never have too many shoes or handbags. This project celebrates her existence. Of course, draping anything but scarves or pants on these hangers will hide the designs.

PAPER

Napkins printed with purses and shoes

MATERIALS

Sandwich bag

2 wooden clothes hangers

Fine-grit sandpaper or 320-grit sanding sponge

Decoupage medium

TOOLS

Scissors

Brush

WHAT YOU DO

1. Cut out images of the pumps and purses, avoiding the ones printed on the textured edges. Gently separate the layers of napkin, keeping only the printed sheet. Store them in a sandwich bag because the slightest waft will cause them to flutter away.

2. Lightly sand the hangers.

3. Paint a very thin coat of decoupage medium to the hangers on the areas where you'd like to attach the handbag and shoe images. Place the images on the medium and lightly press down on them with your fingers. Allow them to dry.

4. Paint three coats of decoupage medium all over the hangers, allowing it to dry between applications.

Tip—Clamping the hangers in a table vise during the process of applying the cutouts freed up both hands to handle the delicate napkin paper.

Corinthian Shade

Designer: Colette George

The elegant print of this shade is both sophisticated and playful. The symmetrical arrangement of the pattern conjures images of Roman columns.

PAPER

2 large sheets of patterned wrapping paper

OTHER MATERIALS

Ceramic lamp with a drum shade

Quick-drying adhesive spray designed specifically for paper

White spray primer

Spray paint

TOOLS

Tape measure

Pencil

Ruler

Craft knife

Scissors

Clothespins or paper clips

WHAT YOU DO

1. Measure the height and circumference of the shade. Add 2 inches (5.1 cm) to the circumference measurement for the seam overlap, and 2 inches (5.1 cm) to the height. Draw a rectangle of these dimensions on the back of the paper, and cut it out.

2. Turn the top edge of the rectangle under 1 inch (2.5 cm). Do the same on the bottom edge.

3. To add more layers of visual interest, cut out sections of the remaining paper to decoupage onto the rectangle. Spray a very thin layer of adhesive onto the backs of the cutouts and glue them into place.

4. Wrap the paper around the shade. Use adhesive spray to affix it to the shade in a few discreet places, as well as along the entire seam of the overlapping edges. Hold the paper in place with clothespins or paper clips until it dries.

5. Spray the lamp base with white primer. After it has dried completely, spray the base in a color that coordinates with the patterned paper.

VARIATION

You can apply patterned paper directly to smooth shades, but some lamp shades have an uneven surface texture that requires you to cover them with a stiff paper, such as wallpaper liner, to which you can mount the patterned paper.

In this case, cut the liner paper to the dimensions as instructed in step 1, and for the patterned paper, add 4 inches (10.2 cm) to the circumference as well as to the height. Place the patterned paper face-down and center the liner paper over it. Mark the placement of the liner paper, remove it, and use adhesive spray to adhere it to the patterned paper. Fold the top and bottom allowances of the liner paper, creasing them neatly with a fingertip to avoid ripping the paper or having any of its color lift away.

Proceed from step 3; for step 4, center the covered liner along the height of the lamp shade.

Coleoptera Platter

Designer: Judy Carmichael

Natural beauty adorns this dish. Working on the underside of the glass makes the platter look seamless, creating an elegant impression.

PAPER

Striped paper

Paper printed with old-fashioned script for the background

OTHER MATERIALS

Image of an insect

5 insect-related words (see the Tip on page 00)

Glass plate, 5½ x 11¾ inches (14 x 29.8 cm)

Matte medium

Water-based varnish

Gold-colored permanent marker

TOOLS

Scissors

2 medium-size brushes

Craft knife

Paint scraper

Note: When decoupaging onto glass, always attach the images face-down to the underside of the object unless instructed otherwise.

WHAT YOU DO

1. Cut out the insect and the words. Cut four strips of the striped paper, each 5/16 inch (8 mm) wide and the length of the plate's sides.

2. Turn the plate upside down, eyeball where you wish to place the insect image, and paint matte medium onto that area. (It bears repeating: be sure to attach the paper face-down on the underside of the object.) Place the image on the matte medium. Working from the center of the image outward, press out any air bubbles and extra adhesive.

3. Determine where to place the words along the plate edges, paint matte medium onto those spots, and use the method described in step 2 to attach them. Allow them to dry, then attach the striped strips with more matte medium along all the edges, gluing them directly over the words. Allow the medium to dry.

4. Brush matte medium over the entire bottom of the plate and glue the background paper to it (see the Tip). Trim away any extra paper with a craft knife, and allow the plate to dry.

5. Apply four coats of varnish to the bottom of the plate. After the varnish dries, pick up just a wee bit of paint on the tip of a dry brush. Lightly graze the bottom of the plate with the brush to give it an antiqued appearance.

6. Use a paint scraper to remove dried matte medium and varnish from the plate's edge. Draw a line of gold along the edge of the plate with the marking pen.

Tip—To make it easier to fit the background paper over the plate's curves, the designer cut the background paper into horizontal strips. She applied a watercolor wash to each; it emphasizes the aged look of the paper, and also disguises the seams between the seven strips she used.

Nippon Box

Designer: Pamela Cowdery Franceschetto

This delicate box is in the Japanese *maki-e* style, which translates as "seed picture." It features an innovative technique that uses a home ink-jet printer to reproduce classical Japanese imagery onto sheets prepared with imitation metal leaf.

[insert PAP 10-6 and 10-7 (opt.)]

PAPER

Printer paper

Single-sided metallic origami paper

Japanese rice paper or washi paper

OTHER MATERIALS

Unfinished wooden box

Putty

Wet/dry sandpaper in 280, 320, and 400 grits

Gesso

Black acrylic paint

0000 steel wool

Water-based polyurethane varnish

Masking tape

Tinted metallic mica powders in bronze, deep gold, and light gold

Metallic gold acrylic paint

Water-based sizing

Imitation gold leaf in gold, copper, and silver

Transparent acrylic spray

Digital images of Japanese clip-art drawings

PVA glue

Mother-of-pearl sheet (see Tip under step 6)

Tracing paper

Acrylic wallpaper glue

Water

Paper towels

Micro-mesh polishing kit

Mild liquid dishwashing detergent

Furniture paste wax

Tools

Assorted brushes

Old toothbrush

Ink-jet printer

Pencil

Curved nail scissors

Files for artificial fingernails

Rubber roller

Cotton rag

Note: When creating a complex decoupage project such as this one, apply a coat of varnish after each step. It will preserve the work beneath it; if one of the steps turns out not to your liking, you just have to remove and complete that step, not the entire project.

What You Do

1. Fill any holes or imperfections in the box with putty. Allow it to harden, then sand the box, inside and out, until smooth.

Apply several coats of acrylic gesso to the exterior of the box, letting each coat dry completely. Sand, using 320-grit sandpaper moistened slightly to form a slurry as you work. Repeat as necessary until the surface of the box is absolutely smooth and without imperfections.

2. Apply several light coats of black paint, letting each coat dry completely. Sand the box lightly with dry 400-grit paper.

Apply a final coat of paint diluted with water. Let it dry, then lightly sand it with steel wool to create a smooth, matte finish.

Apply a coat of varnish to protect the surface.

3. Use masking tape to cover the areas of the box that you wish to remain black.

Add water to each of the mica powders; the mixture should have the consistency of whipping cream.

Create the speckled finish by using the toothbrush to lightly spatter each color onto the box, working from the darkest shade to the lightest.

Paint the edges of the lid with gold acrylic paint. Let it dry. Remove the masking tape, and apply a coat of varnish. Set the box aside.

4. Apply water-based sizing to sheets of printer paper. Following the manufacturer's instructions, after the sizing becomes tacky, apply the imitation leaf. Let the sheets dry overnight or longer.

Using a soft brush, gently brush away excess leaf. Apply several light coats of acrylic spray to protect the foil and prevent it from oxidizing. Allow the paper to dry for at least 24 hours.

5. Print the digital images directly onto the foil-prepared sheets. Wait a few minutes, then apply two or three light coats of acrylic spray. Allow to dry completely. Cut out the images and set them aside.

Tip—With most home ink-jet printers, the printed images must be sealed using either transparent acrylic spray or clear shellac to prevent the colors from running when gluing and varnishing. This is not necessary with heavy-duty laser printers or color photocopiers. When in doubt, immerse a printed cutout in water to test its colorfastness.

6. Glue the mother-of-pearl pieces to the sheets of metallic, origami paper—the color underneath the shell will determine the shade of its final appearance. Let the glue dry completely for one or two days.

Working from a print-out of your imagery, determine which parts of the design you wish to replace with mother-of-pearl. Using tracing paper, transfer these to the back of the mother-of-pearl. Carefully cut them out, using short snips of the nail scissors. File the edges smooth.

Tip—You might look for mother-of-pearl in sheet form through stores or catalogs that sell guitar-making supplies, fine woodworking materials, or items for jewelry making. You'll definitely find a large array of it online in gorgeous patterns and dyed in eye-popping colors; perform a search using the term "mother-of-pearl veneer."

7. Mix up an adhesive that's three parts glue, one part wallpaper glue, and one part water.

8. Compose the cutouts from step 5 on the box, mixing and matching the different metals to highlight the design elements. Cut away the details that you plan to replace with the mother-of-pearl.

Glue down a cutout, place a damp paper towel over it, and use a small rubber roller to press out air bubbles. Attach the rest of the cutouts in the same fashion, then glue the mother-of-pearl details into place. Allow to dry 24 to 48 hours.

Check for loose edges or air bubbles, then coat the entire object with white polymer glue. Allow it to dry completely.

9. Apply 20 coats of varnish, brushing each on in alternate directions. Follow the manufacturer's instructions for drying times between coats.

10. Sand the box, first using 280-grit paper dipped in water with a squirt of detergent. Use a regular, back-and-forth motion over small sections, repeating until the entire object has been sanded. Immediately repeat the process with 320-grit paper. Rinse the box and let it dry at least 24 hours.

11. Apply five more coats of varnish. Sand the box, employing the same procedure as in step 10 but using 400-grit paper. Rinse the box and let it dry.

Repeat this procedure until the box becomes perfectly smooth and you can no longer feel the thickness of the mother-of-pearl. Allow the box to dry completely.

12. Lightly rub the box with steel wool until it's no longer shiny. Polish the box using a micro-mash kit of graded polishing sponges dipped in soapy water. After polishing is complete, wash the box and let it dry.

13. Apply paste wax to the box with a wet rag. After it dries, buff it with a soft polishing cloth.

14. Finish the interior of the box by cutting the rice or washi paper to the size of each panel and gluing it into place.

—From *Cutting-Edge Decoupage*

PAPER WREATHS
Taylor Hagerty

Happy Birthday

Materials

½-inch (1.3 cm) circle punch

14-inch (35.5 cm) wicker wreath

Acrylic paint: blue, green, pink, purple, white, yellow

Birthday candles (about 24)

Cardstock: assorted scraps, pink, white

Chipboard scraps

Curling ribbon: blue, green, pink, white

Die-cut balloons (6)

Fine-point marker: black

Floral wire: white

Glue stick

Greeting card: small

Hot glue gun and glue sticks

Party horns (6)

Ruler

Scissors: craft, decorative-edge

Spray paint: white

Tissue paper: blue, pink, yellow

Wire cutters

Instructions

1. Spray paint wreath white; let dry. Arap with curling ribbon.

2. Cut two 3-inch (7.5 cm) chipboard circles. Arrange candles in an arch on chipboard, with about ½-inch (1.3 cm) of candle base on chipboard, hot glue in place. Glue additional circle to top of candle base to stabilize.

3. Hot glue chipboard circles/candles to lower back of wreath.

4. Paint die-cut balloons with acrylic paint; let dry. Attach to floral wire with hot glue. Arrange balloons so at least one is touching top of wreath and hot glue in place. Hot glue remaining balloons to each other for stability and twist wire together at base. Attach to back of candle base with hot glue.

Continued ➜

5. Cut eight 6-inch (15 cm) circles from tissue paper with decorative-edge scissors. Twist center of each circle to form flower shape. Attach an equal number to each side of wreath and one behind candle arch. Add party horn to each side and glue on additional candles using hot glue.

6. Curl two 10-inch (25.5 cm) lengths of each curling ribbon with scissors. Adhere to lower center of wreath with hot glue.

7. Punch circles from assorted scraps of cardstock and adhere randomly on 2 x 3-inch (5 x 7.5 cm) piece of white cardstock with glue stick. Draw black lines to suggest strings.

8. Cut 2½ x 3½-inch (6.5 x 9 cm) piece of pink cardstock, adhere card with circle shapes, and tuck into wreath.

Time-saving Tip: Maintaining Balance

In wreath making, as in life, balance and scale are very important. Choose embellishments with the scale of the wreath in mind. While you're making and decorating your project, occasionally step back and view your wreath from a distance to ensure the elements are distributed evenly.

Valentine's Day

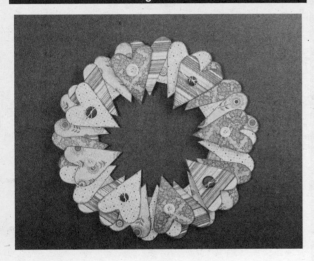

Materials

½–¾-inch (1.3–2 cm) buttons (8)

4½-inch (11.5 cm) cookie cutter: heart-shaped

Cardstock: coordinating prints (4)

Craft knife

Craft scissors

Double-sided tape

Embroidery floss: off-white

Foam core board

Foam dots

Inkpad: brown

Pencil

Ruler

Instructions

1. Draw 14-inch (35.5 cm) circle with 12-inch (30.5 cm) circle centered inside foam core to create wreath; cut out with craft knife.

2. Cut 24 hearts, six from each print of cardstock, using cookie cutter as template.

3. Edge hearts with brown ink by rubbing edges directly on inkpad. Position 16 hearts on surface of foam core wreath; adhere with double-sided tape.

4. Layer eight hearts by attaching with foam dots on top of others.

5. Tie embroidery floss through buttons with small bows on top; adhere to center of each heart in top layer with double-sided tape.

6. Cover any exposed foam core with scraps of cardstock left over from heart cutouts.

Time-saving Tip: Die Cut Your Hearts

To speed up this project, use a heart die-cut machine instead of hand tracing and cutting out the hearts.

Family Heirlooms

Materials

14-inch (35.5 cm) square foam wreath

Bookplate: large oval

Cardstock: black

Computer and printer (optional)

Cosmetic sponge

Craft glue

Craft scissors

Decorative paper: cream, vintage-themed

Dried flowers (5–6)

Family photos (10–12)

Fine-point marker: black or brown

Foam brush

Hot glue gun and glue sticks low-temp

Inkpad: brown

Keys: large skeleton (2)

Photo corners: black (4 per photo)

Raffia: natural

Instructions

1. Using craft glue and foam brush, cover wreath with torn pieces of vintage-themed decorative paper. Add antique look by lightly rubbing brown ink onto wreath's surface using cosmetic sponge.

2. Tie dried flowers and skeleton keys to lower side of square with raffia; reinforce with hot glue if necessary.

3. Computer print or hand-write family name on cream decorative paper to fit large bookplate. Mount to lower corner of wreath.

4. Mount photos on black cardstock, leaving about ⅛-inch (3 mm) border around photo. Place photo corners on all photos except ovals. Arrange and adhere photos to wreath with craft glue.

Gardener's Delight

Materials

⅛-inch (3 mm) hole punch

Adhesives: cellophane tape, glue dots

Craft scissors

Eyelet setting tools

Eyelets (2)

Inkpads: colors of your choice (3)

Millinery flower stem

Playing cards with decorative backs (6)

Ribbon: ½-inch (1.3 cm) black-and-cream checked

Rubber stamps: sea-themed (2)

Ruler

Seed packets (8)

Shipping tag

Instructions

1. Punch holes in upper right and upper left corners of seed packets. Attach eyelets in seed packet that will serve as centerpiece.

2. To determine length of ribbon to cut, measure from hole to hole of punched packets, then multiply by 3 and cut. Wrap piece of tape around end of ribbon and use to thread through punched holes as shown; thread last packet so it will dangle.

3. Center packets, then tie both ends of ribbon to form circle.

4. Using glue dots in upper right and upper left corners of back of playing cards, attach one between each of the seed packets. Add more glue dots if needed to further stabilize.

5. Using rubber stamps and inkpads, stamp design onto shipping tag, then slip ribbons through hole in tag until tag reaches knot in ribbon. Tie into simple bow.

6. Slip millinery stem through shipping tag hole and make loop out of stem to hang wreath.

—From *Make It in Minutes: Wreaths*

PAPER PARTY WARES

Bethany Lowe

Party Poppers

Holiday poppers originated in England as Christmas party favors filled with candles or prizes for each guest. When pulled to open, a loud popping sound was made and the guest received their prize. The vintage poppers could be used only once. These poppers are made as party favors that can be used again and again.

MATERIALS

Cardstock: white, 8½ x 10 inches (21.6 x 25.4 cm)

Craft wire: 24-gauge

Crepe paper: orange

Newspaper

PVC pipe: 1½ x 3¾ inches (3.8 x 9.5 cm) (4)

Ribbon

Rubber cement

TOOLS

Computer and printer or color copier

Craft scissors

Hot glue gun and glue sticks

Paintbrush: small

Ruler

INSTRUCTIONS

1. Cut four 6 x 10-inch (15.2 x 25.4 cm) rectangles from orange crepe paper. Brush rubber cement over the exterior of each PVC pipe piece and down into the ends of the pipe. Wrap a crepe paper rectangle around each pipe, and then tuck the ends of the paper inside the ends. Press firmly into place; let dry.

2. Cut sixteen 3 x 31-inch (7.6 x 78.7 cm) strips of orange crepe paper. Cut a ¼-inch (6 mm)- wide fringe on eight of the strips.

3. Gently roll one strip of the uncut crepe paper starting on the short end, pinching at the bottom. Roll one strip of fringe around the rolled uncut paper, pinching the bottom tightly. Wrap the piece with wire. Fluff the fringe. This will make one tassel end. Repeat for remaining seven ends.

4. Cut sixteen 4-inch (10.2 cm) circles from orange crepe paper. Tightly wad a small piece of newspaper into a ball about ¾ inch (1.9 cm) tall by the width of the PVC pipe. This will slip in and out of the ends of your pipe like a stopper. Place the wad of newspaper in the center of a double thickness of 4-inch (10.2 cm) circles. Bring the side of the circle around the newspaper. Pinch the opening closed so it will have a shape. Open this area, squirt hot glue liberally onto the packed newspaper, and set the tassel onto the hot glue. Bring the sides of the 4-inch (10.2 cm) circle around the tassel base and tie with craft wire. The ends should easily slip into the PVC pipe.

5. Copy the Checkerboard Paper and Party Popper images onto cardstock and cut them out. Using a small paintbrush, apply rubber cement onto each popper and adhere the paper and images. Fill as desired then tie the ends of the poppers with ribbon.

Checkerboard Paper

Party Popper images

Editor's Note: Your own decorative paper and art images can be substituted for the Checkerboard Paper and Party Popper images supplied here.

Tips & Tricks: PVC-Free Poppers

The party poppers can also be made using empty bathroom tissue cylinders. Just adjust the measurements of the crepe paper used to cover them.

Tassel Masks

These fun paper-and-glitter masks were inspired by 1920s-era Halloween-themed plumed hats. Created by my assistant designer, Wendy, the masks provide instant

costumes for party guests, or they can be used to decorate a pumpkin. The masks also make great centerpieces.

MATERIALS

Cardstock: white, 8½ x 10 inches (21.6 x 25.4 cm) (4)

Cellophane tape

Crepe paper: black, orange

Glitter: black

Poster board

Rubber cement

Stretch cord: gold (13 inches [33 cm])

TOOLS

Computer and printer or color copier

Craft knife

Craft scissors

Paintbrush: small

Piercing tool

INSTRUCTIONS

1. Copy the Cat and Pumpkin Mask and Nose templates and Cat and Pumpkin Mask Toppers templates onto cardstock; cut out.

2. Brush rubber cement onto the back of each shape and adhere the shapes to poster board; let dry. Trim around the shapes. Fold the nose sharply on the crease lines. Using the craft knife and cutting mat, make slits in the mask for the nose piece.

3. Brush rubber cement on the black mask and the features of the Mask Topper face. Sprinkle the wet rubber cement with black glitter; let dry.

4. Using a piercing tool, poke a small hole in both sides of the mask. Thread gold stretch cord through the holes and secure in place with a knot.

5. Slide the flaps of the nose piece through the slits and fold the nose back crisply to lock in place.

6. To make the tassel: Using desired color, cut two 4 x 36-inch (10.2 x 91.4 cm) crepe paper strips. To form the fringe, cut the ¼-inch (6 mm) strips along the 36-inch (91.4 cm) edge, leaving ½ inch (1.3 cm) uncut. Starting at the 4-inch (10.2 cm) edge, roll the crepe paper tightly, jelly-roll style. Wrap the uncut end with a piece of cellophane tape to keep the tassel tightly rolled. Fluff the tassel.

7. Brush rubber cement on the tapes area and adhere the tassel to the tip of the hat, or the ear.

Cat and Pumpkin Mask and Nose. Enlarge 200%.

Continued ➔

*Cat and Pumpkin
Mask Toppers.
Enlarge 275%.*

Crepe Paper Party Hats

None of us ever outgrow the pleasure of "dressing up," so give your guests a cap to don. These crepe paper party hats are recreations of 1930s German party hats. Crepe paper hats became generally popular beginning in 1912 when craft books that showed easy-to-make Halloween ideas for hats, costumes, and decorating were published. Since these hats were fragile and disposable, not many exist today, making them a favorite of collectors.

MATERIALS

Cardstock: white, 8½ x 11 inches (21.6 x 27.9 cm)

Cellophane tape

Crepe paper: black, cream, orange

Rubber cement

TOOLS

Computer and printer or color copier

Craft scissors

Paintbrush: small

Pencil

Ruler

INSTRUCTIONS

TO MAKE THE HAT BAND

1. Cut one strip of cardstock measuring 1 inch (2.5 cm) wide and the circumference of the head size you want the hat to fit. Add 1 inch (2.5 cm) to allow for overlap. **Note:** You may need to piece strips together to reach desired length.

2. Cut a strip of crepe paper on the bias (to keep it from stretching) of the color you wish for your hat band.

3. Using the paintbrush, spread rubber cement on one side of the cardstock strip and apply it to the crepe paper strip. Press firmly; let dry.

TO MAKE THE HAT BODY

1. Cut a piece of crepe paper as long as your hat band and 8½ inches (21.6 cm) tall.

2. Using the paintbrush, spread rubber cement on the back of the hat band. **Note:** Put rubber cement only on the top ½ inch (1.3 cm) of the strip.

3. Place a large sheet of crepe paper on the rubber cement and press gently; let dry. Using the paintbrush, spread rubber cement carefully on one end of the band and on one end of the crepe paper. Bring the two ends together, overlapping about 1 inch (2.5 cm). **Note:** We glued the band first and placed a paper clamp to hold the ends together.

4. Gently bring the edges of the crepe paper hat body together (this will form a cylinder shape); let dry.

Pumpkin, Cat, and Skeleton Crepe Paper Hat images. Enlarge 150%.

TO SHAPE THE HAT

1. Crease the sides of the hat. Do not pull the crepe paper. **Note:** The glued seam is the center front of the hat.

2. Fold the right corner to make a seam. Fold the left corner to make a seam, overlapping to form another ¼-inch (6 mm) seam. Adjust as needed to form a nice point on the tip of the hat. Glue the seam together with rubber cement.

TO EMBELLISH THE HAT

1. Cut one 4 x 18-inch (10.2 x 45.7 cm) strip of crepe paper. Cut a 3-inch (7.6 cm) fringe along the 18-inch (45.7 cm) side of the strip.

2. Fold the strip to make a tassel and wrap the tassel with cellophane tape. **Note:** Our tassel is 1½ inches (3.8 cm) wide at the top. The tassel needs to be flat as you will adhere an image to cover the tape.

3. Using the paintbrush, apply rubber cement to the base of the folded triangle on the top of the hat.

4. Copy the Cat, Pumpkin, and Skeleton Crepe Paper Hat images onto cardstock; cut out. Using the paintbrush, apply rubber cement to the back of each image and adhere to the cellophane tape on the tassel.

—FROM *Bethany Lowe's Folk Art Halloween*

STAMPING

Dawn Cusick & Megan Kirby, Editors

Watch out! Stamping is not only fun, it's addictive! Simple enough to beguile beginners, yet sophisticated enough to attract accomplished artists, this craft has seen an explosion in both popularity and new techniques. Learn the basics of stamping, and you'll soon be making your own unique impressions on paper, fabric, wood, polymer clay, ceramics—just about every surface in sight.

Materials and Tools

Manufactured Stamps

There are literally thousands of stamp images available. Stamps are usually made of rubber or foam mounted on a wood or plastic handle. You can also find stamps mounted onto rollers; these are good for adding borders to all sorts of surfaces, including walls.

Stamp Inks

Available wherever stamps are sold; see Stamp Inks for an explanation of the five principal types of ink.

Brayer

This tool is similar to a small paint roller, but is made of rubber. Use it to ink large stamps or to create colored backgrounds for stamping. Ink your brayer by rolling it on a large ink pad or by pouring paint or ink onto a sheet of glass and then rolling the brayer until it's coated.

Stamping Surfaces

You can stamp just about any object with a smooth surface: paper, wood, fabric, polymer clay, glass, ceramic, terra-cotta, leather, and even the walls of your home. Just be sure to choose the best ink for each project.

Stamp Cleaner

Many cleaners are widely available, but you can also use diluted window cleaner or nonalcohol baby wipes.

Embossing Powder

This powder is made of tiny plastic pellets that melt when heated to merge with the stamped ink and create a raised image. The powder can be clear, translucent, opaque, or glittery. Use colored powder with clear embossing ink and clear or translucent powder with colored pigment ink.

Embossing or Heat Gun

This easy-to-use tool blows extremely hot air out of its nozzle to melt embossing powder. You can use an alternative form of heat, such as an iron, electric element, hot place, or toaster. Hair dryers do not blow hot enough to melt embossing powders.

Materials to Enhance Stamping Projects

Add color to your stamped images with colored pencils, markers, watercolor paints and watercolor pencils.

Stamp Inks

The five principal types of ink used for stamping are described below. The type of ink that's best for your project will depend primarily on how porous that project's surface is.

Dye-based Inks

Translucent, water-based inks. These quick-drying inks are suitable for stamping on all papers, although the colors may bleed slightly on absorbent, uncoated papers. Dye-based inks are not fade-resistant and usually cannot be embossed.

Pigment Inks

Thick, opaque inks. These slow-drying inks are suitable for stamping on uncoated paper, coated paper if used with embossing powder, wood, polymer clay, and fabric.

Embossing Inks

Clear or slightly tinted inks that dry slowly so embossing powders will melt and fuse with their stamped image when heat is applied.

Fabric Inks

Water- or solvent-based inks that remain on fabric after laundering. Some must be set with heat.

Permanent Inks

Water- or solvent-based inks that can be used on paper, wood, glass, and fabric. Once it has dried, permanent ink won't run, so it's useful for stamping images you want to enhance with watercolor pencils or water-based markers or paints, or for projects that require a protective finish.

Basic Techniques

Basic Stamping

The basic technique of stamping isn't difficult once you get the hang of it. The hard part will be keeping yourself from compulsively stamping every surface in sight!

1. To start, make sure the material you're stamping is flat. Iron any wrinkles if you're working with fabric or wrinkled paper. If possible, use masking tape to hold the object you're stamping in place.

2. Lightly tap the stamp on the ink pad's top. Do not press the stamp into the pad or rub it across the pad's surface.

3. Test the stamp on scrap material (paper if you are using paper, wood if you'll be stamping wood, etc.) for too much or too little ink. Re-ink if the image is faint or spotty; blot the stamp on a paper towel if it's over-inked.

4. Hold the stamp firmly and press down on the paper or other material being stamped. Do not rock or move the stamp or the image will be blurred. You may need to stand to create more pressure when using an extra large stamp. Press each corner carefully to make sure the entire image is left behind.

5. Lift the stamp straight up, again being careful not to rock or move the stamp.

6. Clean the stamp as directed by the manufacturer after each stamping session.

Making a Stamp

You can make your own stamp from erasers, linoleum, wood, rubber, foam, or even fruits and vegetables. The basic steps are the same, whatever your material.

1. Draw or trace your design onto tracing paper. (Keep in mind that the image will be reversed when you stamp it, so numbers and letters must be reversed.) Trans-fer the design to your stamp surface by sandwiching a piece of carbon or graphite paper (treated side down) between the tracing paper and the surface, then retrace the lines. If you're using a cut fruit or vegetable, press a cookie cutter into its exposed surface instead of trying to draw on it to create a carving.

2. Insert the small V-shaped tip into the linoleum-carving knife and use it to carve a rough border around the image's lines. Remember, whatever part of the material you carve away will be

unprinted white space when you use the stamp. The raised (uncut) portions will be what prints. For smooth edges, make shallow cuts, not deep gouges. You should be able to see the upper edges of your blade above the material you are carving. Use a larger, U-shaped tip to carve away large areas of the design.

3. Use a craft knife to cut around the perimeter of the stamp's design. Ink the stamp and make a test print on paper to see if any rough edges need to be trimmed.

4. When you are happy with the image the stamp prints, you can use it as is or add a handle by gluing it to a piece of wood or doweling.

Tip—To get reversed numbers or letters for your handmade stamp, first write them normally on tracing paper. Retrace them with a dark marker. Set the tracing paper image-side down on your stamp surface and sandwich a piece of carbon or graphite paper (treated side down) between the tracing paper and the surface. Now use a pencil or pen to redraw the lines showing through to the back of the tracing paper and a reverse image will transfer to the stamp surface.

Projects

Rubber Stamped Gift Wrap

Designer: Chris Rankin

Create this gift wrap to show special love on Mother's Day—or on any occasion when you want to give a gift "with love." Look for compatible large floral and foliage stamps. The complementary use of metallic paint with a highlight of gold paper as a border, makes for a rich and inviting presentation.

CLEANING AND CARING FOR YOUR STAMPS

Clean your stamp after each use (and between colors). To do so, simply press your stamp onto a paper towel moistened with water and commercial stamp cleaner or diluted window cleaner until all the ink is removed. Nonalcohol baby wipes can be used instead, and the moisturizers in them will help condition the rubber. Some inks will stain your stamps. Don't worry: this stain won't affect the color of future stampings, as long as you clean your stamps well. Stamps will last for years if cared for properly. Never submerge mounted stamps in water, and always store stamps image-side down in a cool location where they'll be protected from sunlight.

MATERIALS AND TOOLS

Ivory wrapping paper

Acrylic paint in dusty purple and metallic gold

Paper plates and paper towels

Wedge sponges

Rubber stamps, one larger floral stamp, preferably with an engraved look; a smaller "engraved" foliage stamp; cursive script to spell "With Love"

Scissors

Cellophane tape

Glue

Paper in deep rose and metallic gold

Gold gift tag

Ribbon

WHAT TO DO

1. Lay the ivory gift wrap on a hard, flat surface.

2. Pour small amounts of the dusty purple and gold paint onto a paper plate.

3. Using one of the wedge sponges, pink up some purple paint and apply it to the large floral stamp using a patting motion. Stamp onto the wrapping paper and repeat to create an allover pattern. You may have to reapply the paint several times as you work. Allow the paint to dry and clean the stamp well.

4. Repeat the stamping process on the piece of deep rose paper using the metallic paint and the smaller foliage stamp.

5. Wrap the gift with the stamped ivory wrapping paper using cellophane tape and glue.

6. Tear a strip of the stamped deep rose paper to fit around the gift. Tear a strip from the gold paper that is slightly wider than the deep rose strip. Wrap both around the gift, placing the wider strip of gold paper under the deep rose strip. Using glue, adhere the edges.

7. Using the dusty purple paint, stamp "With Love" onto the gold gift tag.

8. Tie the ribbon and gold tag around the wrapped gift.

Continued ➜

Stamped Keepsake Box

Designer: Chris Rankin

Use your favorite stamps to create a collection of coordinated projects—from tags to greeting cards to gorgeous gift bags. If you need to impose a little organization on your creative chaos, store your gift-giving ensemble in a matching keepsake box—it's the project you get to make just for yourself!

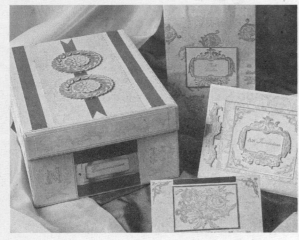

Materials and Tools

Shoebox

White contact paper

Scissors

Cream-colored cardstock

White craft glue

White paper

Large background stamp

Border stamp

Focal stamps (we used a bow and a wreath)

Gold ink pad

Gold satin ribbon

Craft knife

Double-sided poster tape

What to Do

1. Cover the shoebox and its top in white contact paper. Fold edges over on the inside and trim excess with scissors or a craft knife.

2. Cut a rectangle of cream-colored cardstock to cover each side of the box, including the top of the box and its sides. Each rectangle should be just slightly smaller than the side it will cover: Glue each rectangle in place, centering it over the side it's covering.

3. For the sides of the box bottom, cut two rectangles of white paper for the long sides and two rectangles of white paper for the short ends. The rectangles should be slightly smaller than the cardstock rectangles.

4. For the top of the box, cut one rectangle of white paper slightly smaller than the cardstock rectangle.

5. For the sides of the box top, cut two rectangles of white paper for the long sides and two rectangles for the ends. The rectangles should be slightly smaller than the cardstock rectangle.

6. Use the large background stamp to stamp all the rectangles for the sides of the bottom of the box and for the top of the box. Use the border stamp to stamp the narrow rectangles for the sides of the top of the box.

7. Before gluing each stamped paper rectangle to the cardstock, try positioning it over the cardstock rectangle. You may find that you want more of a cardstock border. Cut the stamped rectangles accordingly, then glue them in place over the cardstock rectangle.

8. Stamp three or four bow focal stamps. Cut them out and glue to three or four sides of the bottom of the box. Since one end of our box has a label holder, we used three bows.

9. Stamp and cut out six wreath focal stamps.

10. Use the craft knife to cut around the central motif of two of the wreath stamps. Set aside. Then use the craft knife to cut the borders from two of the wreath stamps. And set aside.

11. Position and glue the two uncut wreath stamps on the top of the box in positions of your choice.

12. Use your scissors to cut small pieces of the double-sided poster tape. Position and stick the tape around the borders of the two wreaths glued to the top of the box. Position the cut-out border over the tape and gently press to adhere. Do the same with the cut-out centers.

13. Decorate the box as you will with lengths of ribbon to highlight the placement of the stampings.

Scrapbook Pocket Page

Designer: Chris Rankin

Capture time in a scrapbook pocket page. You can keep memories safely and beautifully with this design. The pocket invites the reader to find the photo of the letter writer and recipient many years later—friends forever with fond memories of the lives they shared.

Materials and Tools

Burgundy paper

Small sea sponge

Acrylic paint in metallic gold and black

Paper plates

Pocket-watch rubber stamp

Black stamp pad

Black card stock

Embossing paste

Scissors

Sewing machine (optional)

Glue (optional)

Decorative silk leaf

What to Do

1. Place a small amount of the metallic gold paint on a paper plate. Dip the sea sponge in the paint, then dab it on the burgundy paper to create a sponge-painted, textured background. Allow to dry.

2. With the pocket-watch stamp and black ink pad, stamp the watch in an allover pattern on the burgundy and gold paper. Allow to dry.

3. Mix the embossing paste with the black paint, using the pocket watch stamp, gently stamp the black cardstock in an allover design and allow to dry.

4. To make the pocket, cut the burgundy paper slightly less than half the size of the black cardstock. Use a sewing machine to topstitch the pocket to the cardstock, allowing for a ¼-inch (6 mm) seam. If you don't have a sewing machine, you can handstitch the pocket, or you can glue the pocket in place.

5. Position the memorabilia in the pocket as desired and glue if necessary. Tuck the decorative leaf in place for the final touch.

Designer Tip

If you use markers instead of an ink pad, you can apply different colors to specific parts of the stamp's image. If the marker's ink dries too fast, hold the stamp's inked image close to your mouth and breathe on it several times—you should be able to get a few more stampings.

SCRAPBOOKING: AN INTRODUCTION

Dawn Cusick & Megan Kirby, Editors

Scrapbooking offers a world of creativity to anyone with memories and a wish to share them. Specialty papers, embellishments, stickers, die cuts, and cropping tools to suit every taste are widely available. Crafters once daunted by the tedious nature of photograph storage and display now try a new technique with every page.

Materials and Tools

Albums and Pages

Choose a large-format album to hold school memorabilia, or a petite one to present to a friend in honor of a special occasion. Sturdy, removable pages are especially helpful, as you may need to add to or move them from time to time.

Specialty Papers

Discover embossed, sueded, metallic, marbled, textured, and watercolor papers, just to list a few.

Vellum

Vellum adds dimension and texture to your scrapbooking pages. It comes in a rich array of patterns and colors, and can be used to create terrific impressions of snow, ice, clouds, glass and windows, water, smoke, rays of sunshine, rain, fire, and bubbles. You can also write on vellum in ink, chalk, or paint.

Miniatures

Nearly anything you want to express is available in miniature these days, from beach sandals to wedding gowns, lettering, baby themes, state symbols. If anything, you will want to edit your choices so as not to overcrowd your pages.

Hole Punches and Die Cuts

Use hole punches with heart, boat, or butterfly shapes to decorate paper edges and build a theme. Laser kits provide precision-cut images such as butterflies, barnyard animals, stars and moons, baby things, delicate flowers and grasses, musical instruments, and more.

Pockets

Memorabilia pockets can be used to attach locks of hair, pressed flowers, or a button from a favorite shirt.

Wire

Available fine or thick, colored or metallic, and easily manipulated with simple tools, wire is a dynamic element among photographs and as a connector for unusual elements.

Ornaments

Embellish pages with metal charms, foreign or special postage stamps, beads, chains, fabric blossoms and leaves, pearls, eyelets and brads, glitter, and even tinsel. Let your imagination roam over your most cherished belongings, and preserve or represent them in your scrapbook.

Adhesives

A variety of adhesives is available for scrapbookers. Look for brands specifically labeled as "acid free."

Collecting Memories

- Gather into a convenient place information about yourself, your family and its history, vacations (dates, place names, people and places visited), school records and events, and other important data. Ask family members if they have memories or, even better, photos or mementos to share. When you can, tape-record the stories of special people to be able to quote them in their own words. Determine ages of children depicted, if possible.

- Capture the feeling of a holiday meal together, or a great ski trip—even a summer spent at the pool—by picking up postcards, matchbooks, membership cards, and small souvenirs during the year. Group them in envelopes or shoe boxes, and store them with careful notations of date, place, and the people you want to remember.

- Don't you wish you knew what your ancestors thought and felt about significant events of their time? Keep a journal especially for recording reactions to what happens in the world. Where are you and who are you with when it happens? How does it affect you, physically, emotionally, spiritually? How did life change as a result? Keep clippings, e-mails, and notes on conversations you have about major events. Save quotations, contemporary lyrics, and headlines that say it best. You'll be grateful to have such a trove when you decide to make a statement about your experiences in your scrapbook.

- Once you are in the habit of collecting special objects and "memory triggers," you can relax and enjoy the fun of creating pages in your mind, before you attempt to record things permanently. Allow yourself the freedom to dream, and then practice on the page by moving things around until you achieve the look you want.

Basic Techniques

Creating Borders

Borders add style, color, and visual interest to your scrapbooking pages. Create them with purchased border templates, or create your own with your imagination.

1. To use a border template, place the template over a piece of background paper and trace the shape.

2. Cut out the shape with a craft knife. If you have difficulty getting a clean edge, change to a new blade. Gently remove the cut paper, then position it over your photo.

3. To create a custom border, choose a paper item such as a doily that has an interesting shape. Use a craft knife to cut out a picture "window."

4. Gently remove the cutout paper, then position your photo within the opening.

5. Fancify your borders with punches or decorative-edged scissors.

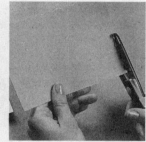

Layering Papers

The days of a single background paper are over, leading to virtually endless fun for the passionate scrapbooker.

To choose papers, take your photos to the craft store and play with color, pattern, and thickness. Handmade papers might be perfect. Or polka dots. Or a transparent vellum.

Cropping Photos

Let's be honest: Even our favorite photos often have unnecessary clutter in their backgrounds, and you definitely don't want clutter in your favorite scrapbooking pages.

1. To crop a photo, first measure and cut a ¼- to ½-inch (6 to 13 mm) border on the inside of a piece of paper. Now cut your narrow rectangle into two L shapes.

2. To determine precisely where to crop your photo, arrange your two L shapes in different places around the photo. When you're happy with the effect, lightly mark the new corners with a pencil.

Typography

Typography possibilities are virtually endless. Look for peel-'n'-stick or press type letters, or create your own on a computer or with magazine cutouts.

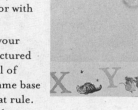

Remember when your first grade teacher lectured you about keeping all of your letters on the same base line? Well, forget that rule. Position your letters however they look nice on a page—scattered about, up and down, tipped at angles—whatever you like.

Tags

A proliferation of tag materials now lends dimension and storage capacity to a geometric shape on which to write, stamp, or otherwise decorate. Use tags for titles, quotations, photo frames, sticker blocks; tuck a blossom, ribbon, message, or 3-D trinket into a tiny envelope.

Adding Charms

Ceramic and metal charms add a special feel to scrapbooking pages, and they're easy to attach.

To attach a charm, first make two small holes in the paper with a hole piercer. Thread thin-gauge wire through the charm, then thread one end of the wire through each hole. Twist the wires on the back side of the paper until they hold the charm in place. Trim excess wire with wire cutters.

Setting Eyelets

Eyelets are one of the most exciting newcomers on the crafting scene. They make great decorative additions to scrapbooking pages and handmade cards, and they're also a pretty way to attach letters, paper cutouts, and charms.

1. Begin by lining your work surface with a layer of cardboard or an old magazine, then use the punch portion of the eyelet setting tool to make a hole where you want the eyelet to appear by hitting the back of the tool with a small hammer.

2. Push the eyelet through the hole so its front side is on the front side of your paper. If you plan to use the eyelet to attach something, place it through the hole first, then position the eyelet over it.

3. Turn the paper over so the front side faces downward. Match the eyelet setting tip to the size of your eyelet, then position it over the eyelet. Anchor the back of the eyelet in place by hitting the back end of the setting tool with a small hammer.

Continued →

While you're on holiday, save souvenirs such as hotel tabs, tickets to museums or shows, transit tokens, currency, maps, and so forth. Capture the flavor of the place by noting common colors and textures; pay attention to foliage, architecture, and other indications of regional character. Photocopy documents, or sections of them that you wish to include, and cut the copies apart. Designer: Dana Irwin

This carefully planned memory page opens from the center; it is shown closed at right and opened above. The page commemorates the separation and reunion of two young people—Dot and Bud—who courted and married during World War II. The designer constructed the page to emphasize the couple's interconnection. While the thoughts of each person are recorded in a different script, each side of the page opens to reveal photos of the other person, and the two background papers reverse on the inside—his becomes hers, and hers, his. Designer: Jeanne Jacobowski

This graphic page combines papers in bold colors and a quotation from a beloved author to celebrate a bold and beloved little girl. Designer: Jeanne Jacobowski

This birthday page combines corrugated paper, colored wire, and three bright feathers to celebrate two buddies turning 10 years old. Designer: Jeanne Jacobowski

"Best friends" are well worth celebrating, and this page records a friendship that lasted through childhood and into adulthood. Designed to mimic a bulletin board, the page's background consists of paper squares with a cork board pattern. Then charms, photos, trinkets, and an excellent report card are attached as randomly and playfully as they would be on a real bulletin board. Designer: Jeanne Jacobowski

This outstanding page uses pockets constructed of romantic floral paper to hold "grandmother's treasured memories"—beloved family photos and two love notes from her husband. The two outside pockets fold in for a three-dimensional effect. Tags identifying the mementos are attached with striped ribbon in subtle shades. Designer: Anna Griffin

Decorative papers enliven this treasured heritage photo. The designer used long strips of pink-flowered paper for a border of flattened bows around the edge of the page. She fringed the same paper to frame the photo and cut floral motifs from it as added decorations. Designer: Anna Griffin

—From *The Michaels Book of Arts & Crafts*

SCRAPBOOKING TIPS

Kerry Arquette & Andrea Zocchi

Shake Things Up

There are a million and one ways to construct any single scrapbook page layout. The eight variations shown here and on the next spread demonstrate how mixing things up and shifting them around results in unique page designs!

One

Go for the Extreme Image: Use an enlarged photo, one so big it gobbles up half of your layout! Your engaging photo subject will draw attention and the simple design will save you time.

Marla Kress

Two

Layer Your Images: Using multiple images on a page can cause some design headaches, but if you contain the support images within a corner of the focal image, it is as if you are designing with one photo.

Marla Kress

Three

Create Contrast in the Title: This impactful title creates energy because of its layered effect. Pick two contrasting letter styles (here the artist mixed large block letters with a fun script style) and two contrasting colors for a title that says, "Hey! Look at me!"

Four

Use Leading Lines: A background composed of strong lines helps guide the eye toward the photo. The horizontal strips of patterned paper add energy and color to the fun-filled scrapbook page.

Marla Kress

Five

Go Bold with Patterns: This pattern-blocked background is a paper quilt of fun and vibrance. Group photos and journaling. Mat them on dark cardstock to distinguish them from the bouncy background.

Marla Kress

Six

Simplify a Design: Try limiting yourself to only four or five products for a clean and uncluttered design.

Seven

Think Outside of the Title Block: Go ahead and get funky with that title. Run it on a curve, add shapes, mix up the fonts and letter cases. Don't limit yourself at all!

Eight

Stencil It In: Oversized letters make a definite impact on any layout. Have fun with stencils by combining them with patterns, personal handwriting or whimsical pen details.

Marla Kress

Finding Creative Inspiration

It's hiding in plain sight

It is said that mimicry is the most sincere form of flattery. In publishing, copying is associated with that wicked word *plagiarism* (not a good choice!), but inspiration and plagiarism are not synonymous. Being inspired by something = being excited and spurred on to make your own original, creative work. You may be inspired by colors, a shape, a technique, a phrase or some other element of a piece. Once inspired, you mold the element, mix it with other items, massage it and make it uniquely your own....

Around the House Inspiration

Your own home can provide wonderful ideas for scrapbook pages. Draw inspiration from your children, family members and their favorite pastimes. Toys, drawings, books, even a beloved stuffed animal can become the subject of a meaningful photograph and a great scrapbook page.

Finding Inspiration at the...Grocery Store

Fruit displays: Find wonderful color combinations among the fruits and vegetables of your grocery store.

Product aisle-by-aisle directory: This big, bullet-pointed list would translate well into a journaling concept.

Product packaging: Manufacturers pay graphic designers a lot of money to create packaging that attracts attention. Look for fun color combinations, bold and elegant fonts as well as page-layout inspiration.

Floral display: Again, a great place to find color combinations but also textures and ideas for embellishment groupings.

Receipts: This memorabilia helps create price-comparison pages (A loaf of bread used to cost __ and now it costs __). They also are fun embellishments for day-in-the-life pages.

Makeup aisle: Definitely the place to go when seeking complementary color combinations. Also, check out the applicators—they are great for adding chalk and other colorants to pages.

Continued ➡

Finding Inspiration in the…Classroom

Mini masterpieces: Illustrate your pages and create accents and page backgrounds with your children's artwork.

Crayons and finger paints: Whisk yourself back in time by decorating a page background with these fun supplies.

Gold star: Give yourself an A+ by using these coveted stickers on school-themed pages.

Tablet paper: Your little writer's wide-lined paper will make extra-spiffy journaling blocks.

Finding Inspiration in…Sports

Logos and emblems: Re-create with paper punches, stamps and pens to use as embellishments.

Awards: Show pride in your child's progress and achievement by using ribbon to mimic karate belts or the actual ribbons that have been awarded. Photograph trophies and plaques and include the images on your pages.

Inspirational quotes: Look online for appropriate sayings that can be used as page titles or journaling.

Found objects: Use shoelaces, trading cards, schedules, and more to decorate your pages.

Finding Inspiration in…Nature

Seed packets: These make great envelopes for journaling strips. Or trim them into blocks and use them to paper-piece a background.

Seeds: Create funky flower embellishments by gluing together interesting seeds to form petals and stems. Or encase them inside a shaker box.

Textures: Let Mother Nature's lovely patterns and textures inspire page designs.

Botanicals: Grass, tree bark, leaves, pressed flowers—all of these delicacies can be used as page accents.

Finding Inspiration at the…Fabric Store

Colorful fasteners: Embellish pages with buttons, buckles, brads, rivets, and snaps.

Zippers: Use them as borders between two portions of the page or open the zipper and mount journaling or mementos between the rows of teeth.

Fabric: Stretch fabric across chipboard or sturdy cardstock. Or quilt together pieces to form an unusual background.

Fiber: Knit or crochet photo mats or use fibers to create borders and embellishments.

Lace and rickrack: Weave lace and rickrack for mats and borders or lace it through eyelets and tie it in a bow.

Colorants: Use fabric dye to paint or rub color on paper page elements. Use fabric paint to change the color of cardstock or paper embellishing forms.

Appliqués: Seek out patches, rhinestones, and iron-ons to match your theme.

Techniques: Warm pages up with simple crisscross stitches or machine-stitch paper blocks together for a quilted look.

Finding Inspiration at the…Museum

Brush strokes: Identify the quality of the brush strokes in your favorite paints and mimic the texture. For example, allow a Monet painting to inspire a collage background created from mulberry paper.

Color combinations: Abstract art often relies heavily on color theory. Look for bold and subtle combinations to bring into your own artwork.

Light: How is light reflected in a painting? Look for interesting light angles to inspire new photographic adventures.

Line quality: Dramatic paintings and sculptures have a discernible line quality. Some are soft and understated while others are bold and hard. Study how the artists used line and shape.

Frames: Most of the paintings in a museum are framed. Get lost in the ornate details, distressed textures, and rich golds of the frames, and dream of re-creating the look for your pages.

Finding Inspiration at the…Import Store

Place mats: Create layout backgrounds from woven pieces of straw.

Paper lanterns: Cut lanterns and use the paper itself as a background for your layout.

Batik fabric: Crumple tissue, smooth it out, and then use a stamp pad to apply a batik-like pattern to the raised portions.

Buttons and beads: Embellish scrapbook pages with exotic beads.

Picture frames: Use lightweight frames to showcase photos on your scrapbook layouts.

Exotic art: Re-create painted or carved designs with stamps, freehand rendering, or punch art.

Scrapbooking On-the-Go

On your mark. Get set. Annnnnd you're off to Junior's soccer practice. Or perhaps you are heading out on a family vacation. No matter where you plan to end up, be sure to take along your scrapbooking supplies and make the most of your downtime.

Packing a Portable Scrapbooking Kit

You can't take it all with you, and, really, you don't need to. Plan ahead, and you'll have the tools and supplies you need to scrapbook on-the-go.

Create individual page kits: Sandwich photos between sheets of photo-safe paper, and slip them into a sturdy envelope. Use small plastic bags to protect stickers and other paper embellishments. Put papers into a folder to keep them from bending.

Build an on-the-go tool kit: A plastic container with a sturdy-seal top is the best option for transporting tools. Pack a good pair of straight-edged scissors, a corner rounder punch, a ruler, small paper cutter, and craft knife. Put a small variety of adhesives in zip-lock plastic bags. A small cutting board can also serve as a work surface.

Splurge on a portable ink-jet printer: To scrapbook on-the-go, purchase a mini printer (prints 4 x 6-inch [10 x 15 cm] prints) that can plug in to your car cigarette lighter. Also, keep spare camera batteries, film and/or media cards handy.

Create a Patterned Paper Background With Cardstock and…

Ink: Rub an ink pad over the bottom of a shoe, along the stitching of a ball or the treads of a tire and "stamp" cardstock.

Paint: Paint a nicely shaped leaf and press it against your cardstock. Repeat with varying colors and different shaped leaves.

Marbles: Place a piece of paper in the bottom of a box. Squirt several colors of paint onto the paper. Drop in marbles and gently roll them around.

Crayons: Tear two large pieces of waxed paper. Put broken pieces of crayons between them. Place several layers of old toweling on your ironing board. Set your "crayon sandwich" on the towels and cover with more toweling. Turn an old iron to medium heat and press against the waxed paper until the crayons are melted. Cool and use to scrapbook.

Stamps: Use a single design or a collection of different designs to create a patterned background.

Sketches or paint: If you are comfortable with your drawing skills, paint or sketch an original background that works with your page theme.

Children's art: Ask your child to finger-paint a special background using the colors of your page palette.

Veneer or Plexiglas: Scrapbook directly on a thin piece of wood veneer or Plexiglas. Experiment by placing some images beneath the glass and others on top.

I'm Outta Embellishments! What Should I Use?

Embellishments are an addiction for many scrapbookers. And who can blame us? Stickers, those easy-to-use pieces of eye candy, come in incredibly handy for decorating photo mats, lending a spark of color to a somewhat bland page, adding balance to a design and covering up uh-oh's (pen splotches). Fibers are so fluffy and nubby you can't wait to touch them! And beads, baubles and metallics are pure bling. So what do you do if there are no embellishments available? Read on.

Hot Hardware Art

When the house junk drawers offer no embellishment inspiration, head to the garage. Those jars of nails, screws, washers, nuts and bolts can be used to create titles and add metal magnetism to your pages. They are perfect on pages that call for rustic distressing and also for male-themed layouts.

Utility Drawer Finds

Open up any utility drawer and you're sure to find a treasure trove of things you have been meaning to give away or store away. Paperclips, rubber bands, trinkets and giveaways are jumbled up with really nifty things like old dog collars and tags. Collars that your puppy has outgrown, make great embellishments for a pet page.

It's All About the Bling

It is a rare woman whose jewelry box doesn't include unmatched pairs of earrings. We hold on to them because we are *absolutely sure* that someday the MIA piece will turn up. Nestled up against the solitary earring is a tangle of necklaces with missing links and broken clasps that we have every intention of getting fixed---someday. It's time to clear the clutter and use your mismatched pieces of jewelry to decorate your favorite scrapbook pages. This page proves how pulled together your layout looks with a little dressing up.

Katie Watson

Leftover This-and-That

Why, why, why do we insist on taking things like coasters home when we leave restaurants? And why do we insist on holding on to clothing tags when they have been cut off of new outfits? Maybe it is because a little voice in the very back of our brains says, "This could be useful someday." This page is proof. The smaller photo is mounted on a restaurant coaster, the fleur-de-lis is stamped on a clothing tag and the large decorative corner design is created using a chipboard frame as a stencil. All elements are painted to coordinate, which gives this page much to admire.

Debbie Hodge

Block Buster

If you aren't a hoarder by nature but love the idea of using "kept" objects on your scrapbook pages, get to know your local thrift stores. For almost nothing, you can pick up used clothing from which you can snip cool buttons, embroidered elements, leather straps, buckles, zippers, and other embellishments.

Bubbly Bathtub Toys

Do you remember how good it felt to bite on something that was firm but slightly squishy and feel that pressure against your gums? (Experts swear that we can't remember anything prior to about the age of 3 or 4, so how can it be that so many of you are nodding along with me?) Well, this little cutie won't forget the sensation because her mom has captured the moment in a wonderful photo. The layouts title is created with bath alphabet letters similar to those she's munching.

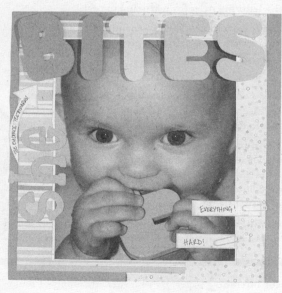

Miranda Ferski

I Found It in the…

Family room: Coasters, long matchsticks, photocopied illustrations from old books, magazines to use for collage

Bedroom: Old scarves to quilt together, forgotten-about belts, silk flowers, decorative purse snap, feathers from a boa, linens in need of repurposing

Bathroom: Bobby pins and other hair clips, sponges for adding texture, makeup such as lipstick and eyeliners, gauze for light fabric-y texture, towels, bath toys

Kitchen: Wine corks, bottle caps, coffee beans, seeds, dried beans, fruits and veggies, napkins

Label Art

Wrappers from products can be colorful and fun to use on pages. This layout, featuring a budding artist, is appropriately embellished with crayon wrappers. They supply just the right touch on a theme-driven layout.

Jodi Heinen

Homemade Stickers

Patterned paper can be the perfect option when you simply do not have the stickers you need to complete a page. Select patterns that work well with your background paper. Carefully cut out individual patterned paper elements. Combine them for major impact.

Sticker Substitutes

Consider using these other items to replace stickers on your scrapbook page.

- Large decorative button
- Embroidered patch
- Punched and layered decorative shapes
- Cunningly cut pieces of fabric
- Broken piece of decorative pottery
- Small decorative tiles
- Colorized stamped image cut to shape

Digital-Download Images

Many Web sites offer free clip art you can download. Print the images and cut them out. Use your colored pens (or your child's colored crayons or pencils) to decorate the pieces before adhering them to your scrapbook page. Or, browse the Web until you find a colorful image that suits your needs (say, a photo of a field of flowers). Print the image and carefully cut out the flowers you most admire. Adhere them to your page in place of the elusive stickers you swore up and down you had.

"Simple" Is *Not* a Dirty Word (Just scrapbook)

The elegant arch of a country bridge; a whistled familiar melody; a single pearl—simple but stunning. Many of the best scrapbook pages find beauty in simplicity. They rely on clean lines, balance and the strength of the photos for impact.

Because scrapbook supplies are so much fun, it is easy to feel compelled to use as many of the colorful, sparkly, shiny embellishments as possible on every layout. Not such a great habit (time-consuming and expensive). If Overembellishments R You, reconsider. Designing a classy scrapbook page is much like designing the perfect outfit: A simple black dress and a good strand of pearls = classy. A loud patterned frock and loads of jewelry = tacky.

When to Say "Enough!"

How do you know when it is time to *stop* adding elements to a scrapbook page? Ask yourself the following:

- Is the page balanced or does it "weigh" heavier in one corner? What can you remove or spread out to help lighten the load?
- Are the color choices effective or are there too many, preventing accent colors from popping off the page?
- Are the title and journaling emphasized, or do they seem to get lost among the chaos?
- Does the page rely on the title, photos, and journaling to convey the story or the embellishments (Hint: it should be the former!)?
- Is the sheer variety of embellishments stealing the show from the one embellishment that should not, under any circumstances, be overlooked?

Block Buster

When designing a simple and elegant page, dress it in subtle colors (cardstock and supporting patterned papers). Use clean white type. Allow the photo to provide the layout with all the accent color necessary.

Streamline Your Scrapbooking

Eight logical steps to creating multiple pages at once

Cramming. Remember that doomed feeling the night before finals when you had not studied for that impending essay test? Scrapbooking should never resurrect that anxiety-laden, coffee-fueled, hair-pulling, sanity-snapping feeling. Instead, be smart about your scrapbooking by looking at it as a task-driven activity. Become an assembly-line scrapbooker who groups tasks for better productivity.

Step 1: Get Organized!

Begin by deciding whether to sort photos by theme or chronologically. Take a weekend to sort your photos. Then, maintain your system with every new batch of pictures you take. If you use a film camera, organize and label your photos as soon as they are developed. If you take digital photos, download the images, delete rotten shots, name the keepers, and create duplicate files for any photos that you wish to crop and edit.

Organize papers, embellishments, pens, and colorants by theme and color. Store often-used supplies within easy reach of your work surface.

Continued ➡

Step 2: Choose Photos

Select your favorite photos relating to the topic you plan to scrapbook. Determine the themes of the pages you will be working on and designate potential photos for each layout. For example, if you are scrapbooking Junior's birthday, divide the photos in to separate piles featuring guests, presents, and birthday games. Decide which photos will be focal images and which are to be cropped or enlarged.

Step 3: Write Journaling

Many scrapbookers save the journaling for last, but journaling early in the process helps you determine the voice and mood of your page. This makes the selection of a page design and appropriate products much easier. Allow your photos to help determine the energy and emotion you hope to capture with your artwork. Writing journaling for multiple pages at the same time ensures a consistent voice. Once journaling is completed you will have a much better idea of the amount of space to dedicate to text on your layout. Concept a title for each layout.

Step 4: Choose Papers

Select two or three solid colors of cardstock for page backgrounds, mats and other small accents such as photo corners. Next, choose two to three patterned papers to match. Don't feel that your paper palettes have to match the colors within your photos. Photos can always be manipulated to black-and-white if you have set your heart on using a particular series of papers.

Step 5: Find Accents

Select similar accents for all the pages that you are scrapbooking within your series. Try to use accents you already own. Alter them with inks, paint, sanding, rub-ons, etc. to make them better suit your layout concept. Never underestimate the power of simple geometrics. Paper circles, squares and rectangles can be used in their native form or be spiffed up with decorative-edged scissors, glitter glue, or clear gloss medium. Use only enough accents to emphasize your design.

Step 6: Design

Grab a freshly sharpened pencil, some paper, and a ruler and start sketchin'. Look to magazine layouts and ads for inspiration. Can you adopt an idea for your own page? If so, think of three variations on that idea to use on your following pages.

When designing a layout, think in terms of individual page elements: photos, journaling, title and accents. Decide which element will be the focal point. Designate a place of honor for it in your page design. Arrange the rest of the elements around the focal point so that the eye moves easily across the page.

Step 7: Finalize Photos & Journaling

Now that you have a solid design plan, go back to the photos and journaling. Are you still comfortable with your earlier photo selections or do you wish to modify them? Does your layout sketch accommodate the length of your journaling? If not, perhaps you'll want to incorporate a flip-up photo. You can hide portions of your journaling underneath it. After you make these decisions, crop your photos and create your page title.

Step 8: Assemble the Pages

Collect necessary adhesives (photo sticks and tape runners for photos and journaling; glue dots for dimensional accents; foam adhesive to secure items you plan to pop off of your background); pull out your sewing machine or needle and thread for stitched elements; collect hinges or bookbinding tape if you plan to create flip-ups or fold-outs. Tape your sketches to the wall in front of your work surface and begin assembling your layouts. Mount the photos and then the journaling block. Add the title and finish with the accents.

Instant Scrapbook Pages Using Kits

Ever since Betty Crocker introduced America to her fantastically simple and fantastically tasty cake mixes, we have counted on prepackaged products to make our lives easier. With the right combination of ingredients and some instruction, it is possible to make a perfect cake every time. With prepackaged scrapbooking kits it is possible to make perfect scrapbook pages that take the cake every time! Add some special touches to make it your own.

Digital Downloads

When dropping by your local scrapbook or craft store is impossible, let your fingers do the walking by logging on to one or more than 100 digital scrapbook sites. There, you can purchase digital papers, embellishments, and journaling treatments. Simply purchase, download, and create your own digital designs or print the supplies on photo-quality paper, cut out, and go nuts!

Make the Digital Distinctive

Go from drag-and-drop to pizzazz and pop!

Change the size: Some of your digital accents can be enlarged or reduced. Play with the size scale for maximum effect.

Change the color: Some digital elements will benefit from color shifts. That pink digital chipboard alphabet for example, can be turned blue with little effort.

Apply filters: See if applying a digital special effect from your image-editing software will add a little spunk to your layout.

Make it personal: Add your own touch by scanning and including a piece of memorabilia or a hand-written note.

Change your printing paper: Print your digital page on a different kind of paper. Experiment with transparent and translucent materials.

Block Busters

Take a few minutes to concept your scrapbook page before you order a kit. Kits vary dramatically. All contain papers, but some may include die cuts, stickers, embellishments, templates, fibers, ribbons, vellum, or overlays. Make sure you know what you are getting with your purchase. Shop around for the best buy. There are so many kits on the market, you should never drop your money on a kit unless your jaw has dropped first.

D Is for Devilishly Easy!

With a scrapbook kit, creating a page is as easy as putting down the money and putting in the time. Many kits are sold with layout suggestions and templates. They most often include papers and an assortment of embellishments.

Make It Your Own

Time saved matching product can be spent getting creative.

Distress it: Take those pristine new papers and dirty them up with brown or black stamping ink. Crumple that paper. Tear those edges. Sand, sand, sand!

Add glitter: Oooh! Who doesn't love sparkle and shine? A little glitter glue will go a long way.

Paint it: Want that shabby chic look? Add a bit of paint to the edges of your page.

Get dimensional: Pull out the foam adhesive and start making things pop off the page.

Emboss it: Add a bit of the "Wow" factor with a shiny embossed stamp.

Timesaving Titles

Titles may be the last element you add to your scrapbook page, but they are one of the most important. Keep titles creatively simple by using products at your immediate disposal. Taking a quick gander through your supply stash is much more efficient than taking a trip to the store (and cheaper, too!). When you find suitable letter accents and fonts, think of simple ways to dress them up.

Computer Fonts and Stickers

A simple mix of a script font and playful letter stickers creates a title with sass and ease. Reverse-print the font onto your desired paper and carefully trim with a craft knife. (Hint: The bigger and blockier the font, the easier it is to cut out.) Adhere the letters to your page and add stickers.

Die Cuts and Chipboard

Who wants to use a boring die-cut letter when all sorts of new lettering accents exist? You do! Mix older products with new ones for fresh looks.

Rub-ons and Letter Beads

Oh, fun! Rub-ons are all the rage and are available in gazillions of styles! Letter beads are perfect for adding a whimsical touch.

Letter Stamps and Lettering Template

Reacquaint yourself with your lettering templates—they transform your handwriting into the funkiest of fonts. Mix with oversized letter stamps for a look that demands attention.

Tips for Tempting Titles

These tricks will have you creating titles that bellow.

Mix cases: Throw convention out the window and mix capital and lowercase letters for spunk.

Turn letters backward or upside down: A letter that faces the wrong way will bring the right smile to your reader's face.

Stack two treatments of the same title: Double your pleasure with this title trick. Be sure to pick two distinctive lettering styles for maximum impact.

Use foam adhesive for dimension: How high can it go? You decide. Allow letters to tower atop each other.

Use images instead of letters: An "eye" for an "I," and a "u" for a "you." Get it? Good!

Mix media: We've already told you this a few times—mixing media, such as chipboard and stamps or stamps and die cuts or die cuts and chipboard is definitely a good thing.

Consider placement: Titles don't always have to be placed at the top of a page. Nor do titles need to follow a straight line. Experiment by running them along the page bottom or along a diagonal and in curving lines or off-kilter designs.

Highlight letters within a word: Throw a frame around a special letter or print it in a different font, color, etc.

For interesting paper, try your local art supply or stationery store, but don't overlook the recycling bin for possibilities. Just make sure the paper is thick enough so that it doesn't become transparent when glued.

Never-fail Templates

Use these terrific layout templates when you need a fresh idea for a scrapbook layout. You may wish to reproduce a template exactly, or modify it to better showcase your elements. The templates range from symmetrical (#3) to less structured (#8).

1.

2.

3.

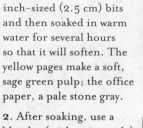
4.

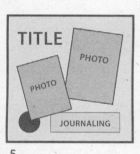
5.

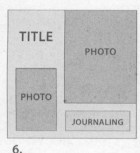
6.

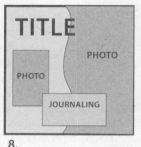
7.

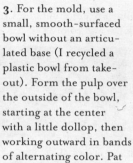
8.

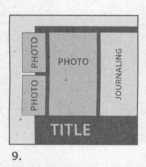
9.

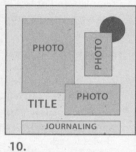
10.

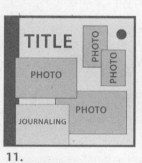
11.

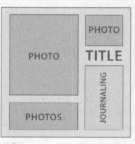
12.

Great Topics for Family Scrapbook Pages

Looking for inspiration for your scrapbook themes? Here you go!

- A day in the life
- Your religion
- Values and ethics
- Lessons learned
- Traditions
- Common grounds
- Physical characteristics
- The home
- Things my (parent/child/grandparent/etc.) taught me
- Family sayings
- How I'm like my (parent/grandparent/sibling/etc.)
- Growing independence
- Favorite pastimes
- School
- Family tree
- How to handle adversity
- The good, the bad, the ugly
- Holiday retrospective
- Then and now, with present immediate family as well as ancestors (fashion, traits, homes, occupations, cars)

—From *Scrapbooking for the Time Impaired*

RECYCLED PAPER CRAFTS

Susan Wasinger

Bowled Over

Materials

Yellow pages to recycle

Used office paper

Water

Tools

Smooth plastic bowls to use as molds

Mixing container

Blender or blender stick

Strainer

Knife or spatula

Sculptural Pulp

Here's a recipe for successful paper recycling: just add water. A short soak and a quick twirl in the blender turns recycled yellow pages

and office paper into the wonderfully workable material used to make these cunning little bowls. The process is simple child's play, but a little imagination and a graphic eye can transform common trash into uncommon treasure.

Make It

1. The paper is torn into inch-sized (2.5 cm) bits and then soaked in warm water for several hours so that it will soften. The yellow pages make a soft, sage green pulp; the office paper, a pale stone gray.

2. After soaking, use a blender (stick or jar-style) to whir the watery slurry into a smooth pulp with the consistency of a thick smoothie. Press the pulp through a strainer to squeeze out excess water until it's workable like clay.

3. For the mold, use a small, smooth-surfaced bowl without an articulated base (I recycled a plastic bowl from takeout). Form the pulp over the outside of the bowl, starting at the center with a little dollop, then working outward in bands of alternating color. Pat the pulp in place first with your hands then slap it with the flat blade of the knife or spatula. This smoothes the surface, eliminates air bubbles, and works the separate bands into one continuous surface.

4. Let the pulp dry overnight. It must be completely dry, or it will be hard to remove from the mold. Use the knife edge to carefully loosen the dried bowl, then gently pop it off the mold.

Drawer Dividers

Materials

Plastic to-go containers

Newspaper—find black-and-white pages for best results

Colored tissue paper (recycle it from store packaging or last year's birthday party)

White craft glue

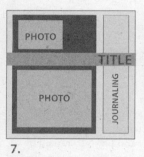

Tools

Craft scissors

Small paintbrush

Mixing container and stirring stick

Open Up a Clamshell to New Possibilities

It might be cherry tomatoes or maybe that piece of quiche-to-go from the deli, but if you're taking it home, it's likely you're taking home a plastic or polystyrene clamshell, too. Don't add the container to the landfill; recycle it into a perky little container to make a delectable drawer divider or delicious addition to your drab desktop. These dividers whip up in a jiffy and keep your junk drawer looking spiffy.

Continued ➜

Make It

1. Cut the clamshell apart where the lid meets the base. Trim around the rim of the clamshell, making sure you cut off the flanged edge at the top. This will give the container straight sides and ensure that the final papier-mâché piece has neat, smooth, rigid sides.

2. Tear the newspaper into strips that are about 1 inch (2.5 cm) wide. You can tear the strips into workable lengths as you go, depending on the size of your container and the part of it you're covering.

3. Mix one part white craft glue with three parts water in a container that's big enough to allow you to comfortably dip the paper strips. A recycled quart-sized (946 ml) yogurt container works well. The glue mixture should look like whole milk in terms of thickness and color.

4. Dip a strip of paper in the glue mixture, making sure you saturate it completely. Squeegee the strip between your fingers to squeeze off any excess glue. Drape the strip across the clamshell and smooth it into place. Cover the entire clamshell with strips going in one direction, then cover it again in strips running the other way. Make sure to press the strips down firmly, making contact with the entire surface of the clamshell, and squeezing out any air bubbles.

5. & 6. To cover the corners, use 2 x 5-inch (5.1 x 12.7 cm) strips of newspaper. Dip one of the strips into the mixture, then center the piece on one of the corners and tear the ends vertically into two narrower strips. Fold these narrow strips over one another to form a smoothly contoured corner. Use this technique for strips on the outside corners as well as the interior corners. To ensure that the end product is sturdy, the container should be covered with at least three layers of newspaper strips. Let the container dry.

7. With a small brush paint the interior of the container with the glue mixture. Tear colored tissue paper into pieces (about the size of tortilla chips), leaving one straight edge on each piece. Position the paper's straight edge along the top edge of the container and gently press it into place. Paint over the tissue-paper piece with the glue mixture, making sure you smooth out air pockets. Layer on tissue-paper pieces until the interior surface is completely covered. Let the container dry completely.

Can Be Beautiful

Materials

Decorative papers

Fiberboard food containers

White craft glue

Cork lids or coasters

Wine corks

Wood screws

Oversized, black rubber washers (optional)

Tools

Scissors

Small paintbrush

In the Can

Stow away kitchen stuff like tea bags and dry pasta—maybe even your secret cash stash—with these natty little canisters. They're uptown enough for the top shelf, but they have humble beginnings as packaging for oatmeal, raisins, and sea salt. Specialty bookmaking papers, wrapping paper, origami paper, old maps, and playbills can all be mixed and matched to make surprisingly elegant, super-simple storage.

Make It

1. Try your local art supply or stationery store for interesting papers. Make sure the paper is thick enough so that it doesn't become transparent when glued.

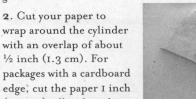

2. Cut your paper to wrap around the cylinder with an overlap of about ½ inch (1.3 cm). For packages with a cardboard edge, cut the paper 1 inch (2.5 cm) taller than the height of the cylinder so the paper can be folded over the top. For those with metal edges, cut the paper to fit between the metal rims at the top and bottom of the container. Brush the wrong side of the paper with diluted white glue or paste. Then position the paper so that it's even with the bottom edge and press it around the cylinder, smoothing out wrinkles as you go. Burnish the paper firmly with the heel of your hand.

3. Clip the overhanging paper so that it's perpendicular to the canister edge to make folding tabs. If necessary, brush the tabs with a little extra glue before folding them down into the canister.

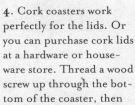

4. Cork coasters work perfectly for the lids. Or you can purchase cork lids at a hardware or houseware store. Thread a wood screw up through the bottom of the coaster, then wind a wine cork onto the screw until it's finger-tight. You can use the optional, oversized black rubber washers for a decorative finish.

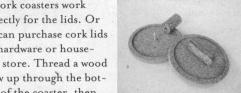

Magazine Shapes

The diamonds are made just like the spheres, but you start with 2- to 3-inch (5 to 7 cm) squares in order to make them. Both the fold and the staple are done on the diagonal.]

Materials

old magazines, catalogs, brochures or calendars

thread or wire for hanging

Tools

circle cutter or scissors

stapler

needle or hole punch

Make It

1. Cut 2-inch (7.6 cm) circles out of pages using a circle cutter. You can also use a glass or lid as a template and draw a line for cutting along with scissors.

2. Stack 20 to 30 circles together. Fold the top one in half, then unfold. That fold line will tell you where to position your staple. One staple in the middle should pin all the circles together.

3. Unfold the stapled stack, fanning each sheaf of paper as you go until you have a symmetrical sphere. Poke a hole with a needle through all the layers at the top of the stack and hang with a thread or wire.

Sewing & Stitching

BRAIDED RUGS

Norma J. Sturges & Elizabeth J. Sturges

Introduction

Braiding rugs is an American tradition that, as with many crafts, developed out of a need and developed into an art.

It was kept alive in the 20th century to enrich homes with a timeless quality, compatible with decor of many styles.

A braided rug is a satisfying, personal, artistic expression, and may well turn out to become an heirloom, passed on from generation to generation. Above all, a braided rug is an object of beauty, with the unmistakable warmth, richness of texture, and depth of color that only pure wool, braided with care, can deliver.

Technically, a braided rug is three *strands* of wool, with their edges turned in, joined by repeatedly pulling the right *tube* to center position and then the left—just the way you braid hair. The *continuous braid* is then *laced*, or sewn, together.

In the early days of braiding, old clothing was used to make rugs. Today, any type of fabric or fiber can be used, but the strength of wool makes it the best choice for a long-wearing rug.

Wool coats with torn pockets or faded colors can be rejuvenated; colors come back to life after seams are opened and the coat is washed in the washing machine. Recycled in this way, the old wool faces a longer life than if it had remained a coat.

However, today's rug braiders usually don't have the time to take apart clothing. Fortunately, there are sources available for purchasing new, reasonably priced wool. The equipment needed is minimal: a clamp, lacing thread and needle, and probably Braid-Aids (used to fold in the edges of the wool strands)....

The Braided Rug Book represents my desire to share braiding with a wide audience. The rugs and patterns you'll find here will allow you to create beautiful rugs for your home and family. All of the patterns come with complete instructions and can be executed in your choice of colors. Other rugs are presented in different sizes with individual color plans. For the adventurous, there are even hexagon, strip, three-circle, scalloped, watermelon, and multi-strand rugs.

When you braid a rug by hand for a special place or person, you take part in the long tradition of making functional, one-of-a-kind works of art. The welcome rug (braided, of course) has been rolled out for you. I invite you to enter the world of braiding and find out how simple and satisfying this time-honored craft can be.

Planning Your Rug

The first thing you need to identify is the meaning behind the rug. Is it for a cozy nursery, family country kitchen, reading nook, first impression in the entryway, or is it a gift? You then interpret the desired image into decisions about size, color, and style.

Those decisions are primarily based on where you're going to put the rug. Is it a hard-use area like in front of the kitchen sink, under the table, or in an entryway? If so, you need to be sure to use sturdy wool of medium to dark colors so that your rug will wear well and resist soil. If your goal is to create a rug for a light traffic area such as a bedroom, you can use pastels and white wool.

Do you want the rug to dominate the space or blend in? Use strong colors if you want it to be a focal point; solid colors tend to look brighter. If you want it to blend into the room, use subtle colors, gradual shading, and many strands of blender colors—grays, browns, camel, beige, and tweeds in every row. Blenders tend to soften the look of the rug. If you're not sure where the rug is going to be placed, just braid in colors you like or colors you wear and you will find a place for it.

My students usually make what I call "decorator rugs." They bring beautiful swatches of upholstery fabric, drapery material, or wallpaper to match to the wool. This shows us what their color needs are.

Planning the Size of Your Rug

The second reason for knowing where you plan on putting the rug is so you can measure the area and braid an appropriate size rug. The eventual size of the rug is governed by the length of your center row.

Continued ➜

How do you get the right size if you are making an oval rug? The rule is *measure your space, subtract the width from the length, and add one inch (2.5 cm) for every foot (30.5 cm)*.

Here's an example: The space is 4 feet wide and 5 feet long (1.2 x 1.5 m). Subtract: 5 minus 4 = 1 foot plus 1 inch. The center braid needs to be 13 inches (33.5 cm) long. You calculate every size oval rug this same way. Here's a second example: You want a 9-by-12-foot (2.8 x 3.7 m) rug. Subtract: 12 minus 9 = 3 feet (92.5 cm) plus 3 inches (8 cm). The center braid needs to be 3 feet (92.5 cm), 3 inches (8 cm) long, or 39 inches (100 cm).

Planning the size of a circle rug is even easier. You start by braiding six *twice overs* and continue braiding until the rug is the right size.

I recommend starting small so you can get your technique under control. The 2-by-3-foot (62 x 92.5 cm) oval rug is specifically designed for beginners.

Planning the Type of Rug

Beginner Level Rugs

Beginners should keep their color plans simple; don't use a great many color changes, unless you are making a hit-or-miss rug. This is so you will concentrate on your braiding and lacing. First make a flat, well-shaped rug and then get more creative on your next rug.

The easiest type of rug to make is to braid any one wool plaid in pleasing colors and use the wool for all three strands. This works well for a chair seat but may be a bit monotonous for a whole rug.

Hit-or-miss rugs are also easy. There are several types:

1. Add any color wool at any time.
2. Select wools that are predominantly shades of one color.
3. Carry one color in one strand throughout the rug. Use a second color for the second strand throughout the rug and randomly vary the color in the third strand.
4. Another easy plan is almost the same as the one above. Continue with one color per strand for two of your strands and vary the third. The difference is that instead of randomly changing the color in your third strand, you always change the color on the shoulder (as per oval directions). Coordinate your colors.

To avoid having obvious color changes, you should change only one color at a time and change the color on the shoulder (see oval rug directions)....

For the Advanced Braider

As an advanced braider, any number of color changes are fine. If you want to change all three colors at the same time, you need to utilize the *butting* technique. In order to butt, you need to rattail your *continuous braid*, and then start a new braid that you butt or join together.

One basic color rule: Don't place your darkest rows in the center or the rug will appear to have a hole in the center. Start your center with medium or light rows. If you start with medium-colored wools, you can shade lighter or darker. To shade lighter, take out your darkest wool strip and add a lighter strip. To shade darker, take out your lightest shade of wool and add a darker strip. Thereafter, alternate between the dark and the light bands.

I usually finish my rugs with a few rows of fairly dark wool. This frames the rug. If you like, though, you can end with medium or light rows; this tends to make your rug flow into the room.

In my early days of rug braiding, I made monochromatic rugs. Monochromatic rugs always create a peaceful, blended look, and they are easy to design. One of our bedrooms was blue, so I made a predominantly blue and gray rug. In the gold bedroom, I used many shades of gold, camel, beige, and rust. Two of my three early rugs have survived 30-something years of wear in "hard use"

bedrooms. In our bedroom, we had green, blue, and gold wallpaper, so I became more adventurous and combined all three colors.

Students tend to make rugs that duplicate their teacher's "look." I try to encourage individuality and creativity, but this usually takes the experience of making a few rugs. It has always seemed harder to me to mix a lot of colors.

There are many good-looking rugs in magazines and books that you can use for inspiration. If you like the rug, you can figure out approximately the color choices necessary to get the same look. Many times beginners can't translate their ideas into a color plan without a model to go by. The joy of braiding is in creating individual rugs. You need to enjoy the colors you are working with and the style you have chosen. It is only through trial and error that you will be able to judge what works for you.

Wool Talk

Wool truly is the premium clothing fiber of all time, unmatched by today's man-made fibers.

Rug braiders have recognized wool's great qualities since the first braided rugs were made. Woolen rugs are soil resistant; vacuuming is all they usually need. They last almost a lifetime even in a hard-use area. My 2-x-3-foot (62 x 92.5 cm) rug in front of the door from the garage is holding up better than the wall-to-wall carpet it sits on. My front hall braided rug has stood proudly for over ten years in that demanding place.

Wool is water repellent. When I wash wool in the washing machine, I have to push it down with a long wooden spoon to get it to absorb the water. Rug braiders also appreciate the fact that wool dyes beautifully, is flame resistant, and has great bulk.

Here are answers to the most commonly asked questions I hear about wool.

What is the best weight rug wool?

I recommend wool that is easiest to braid and wears the longest. One test is to fold the edges of a 1-1/2-inch-wide (4 cm) strip into the center and then fold the edges together again: does the strip make a nice, well-rounded tube?

Braiders often buy wool by the pound. Wool that weighs between 1 pound (454 grams) and 1-3/4 pounds (794 grams) per yard is preferable. If you don't have a scale handy, the best wool includes medium-weight skirt material. Wool blends are fine as long as the weight is good.

Why is the weight of the wool important?

Lightweight wool produces a rug with tweaks and folds in it. This results in an unattractive rug and one that is not totally reversible. You have to cut/rip lightweight wool into 2- or 3-inch-wide (5 or 7.5 cm) strips; this means extra folding which is more time consuming; it also doesn't wear as well.

On the other hand, heavy, stiff, or flat wool, like military uniforms, Melton cloth, heavy bonded wool, and heavy blankets, is generally hard to work with. It doesn't fold easily, is hard on the hands, and makes a larger braid. Men's worsted suiting is too lightweight and flat. Loosely woven tweeds need to be cut, won't wear well, and get caught in the Braid-Aids.

Why shouldn't I recycle old wool clothes?

If you are a beginner braider, resist the temptation to use every piece of wool you have. I know that our grandmothers did this, but I believe our tastes in decorating are not the same. Many rug books extol the virtues of using any old wool garment you own or see in thrift stores, but I have only had a couple of students interested in making rugs from used clothing.

My students have found that it takes longer to make a rug when they have to take apart the garment. Moreover, it takes a lot of practice to successfully work with the dif-

fering weights of wool recycled from a cashmere coat or plaid skirt.

I suggest that you start with wool that is easy to work with—60-inch-wide (152.4 cm), clean, new, ready to use wool. You then measure 1-½ inches (4 cm), snip, and rip from selvage to selvage to get a 60-inch-long (152.4 cm) strip ready to braid. This is a big time saver. Coat-weight wool usually has a fuzzy and a flat side, I almost always use the flat side, but this is just a personal choice. Using the fuzzy side makes the braid look larger. Helen Howard Feeley who wrote the 1957 classic, *The Complete Book of Rug Braiding*, preferred the fuzzy side.

Gauging the weight of wool is often hard for beginners. The solution is to braid practice strips. This will help you recognize when your braid is getting larger or smaller. As you get more proficient in your braiding, you can work comfortably with varying weights of wool by varying the width of your strip.

Should I precut or prerip the wool?

No. I know it is a temptation. It looks neat to have it all ready to braid. But every time you change colors and sew on a new piece of wool, the added strip has to make the same width braid. If all of your strips are precut, you don't have this option and this might limit your color choices.

What is a good width braid?

Measure from the top dent to the bottom of the loop. My braids are usually ⅞ inches (2.2 cm) wide. A few people braid ¾ inch (2 cm) to produce a small braid. Years ago, many rug makers braided a larger braid—up to 2 inches (5.5 cm) wide. It just depends on the look you want; it is a personal choice. The wider your braid, the more wool you use. With a wide braid, you have a heavier, thicker rug, and it braids up faster.

Some people think the larger braid looks more "country." Perhaps they do go well in rustic homes or ranches. I like "country" but I also have always made the smaller braid.

How much wool will you need?

A good rule of thumb is ⅔ pounds per square foot of rug; a 2-by-3-foot rug is 6 square feet times ⅔ = about 4 pounds of wool. The metric version of this formula is the area of the rug in square meters x 3.2 = the approximate weight of wool in kilos....

What if I really want to recycle old wool?

Here are some tips if you can't resist taking wool clothing apart. I rip every seam, but I cut out the collar and hard-to-rip parts. These parts are usually too small to use anyway. After the garment is completely apart, I wash the pieces in the washing machine with cold water on the wool setting, using a little detergent made for washing wool. Then, I hang the pieces to dry. If hems and seams need ironing, use the wool setting and a pressing cloth. If your wool is lightweight or flat and needs to be made bulkier, try hot water and dry it in the dryer. Be careful of tweeds; wash them more gently (shorter cycle) or they will fray.

Be very selective in the clothing you take apart; for example, I never buy a bonded wool garment. Before you buy the garment or take apart your mother's old coat, ask yourself: Does it have a lot of seams? Is there a sewn-in belt? These things will shorten your strips and you will have a lot of waste.

I had two 1960s pleated skirts that looked almost the same; they weren't. One had three pieces including the skirt band and 11 ounces of usable wool. The other had 10 pieces, totaling 9 ounces of wool, and of course, a lot of wasted time and wool.

What other fabrics can I braid with?

People always ask about braiding with cotton. The technique is the same except you rip your strips wider. Making cotton rugs is not a satisfying craft for me. Cotton makes a firm, hard braid that is full of creases and tweaks;

you are always battling the loose threads. Quilted cotton works okay; your bulk is sewn in. If you want to use cotton, I recommend that you crochet a rug.

Any fabric that has the same bulk or body as wool can be braided. One student was allergic to wool and made a good, colorful rug out of velour. Another student, Judith Felsburg, made a terrific rug out of denim to match her son's bedroom.

I started this chapter by saying that wool lasts almost forever....

I don't mean to discourage you from braiding old wool. It is fun using some wool you can identify as belonging to a family member or friend. Once I was told that my "Old Sparhawk" rug was lost in shipping. My response was, "Oh no, my father's bathrobe and son's Valley Forge pants are in it!" Recycled wool does present certain technical and design challenges, and you may want to make a first rug using new wool.

Sometimes when I am demonstrating, people are surprised that one or several of the strands I am using came from coats I have taken apart. This appeals to people, especially when I demonstrate at historic places. They like the fact that we are still doing rugs the way they were done in the "olden" days.

Getting Started

You are now ready to start braiding. Rug braiding, like many crafts, is accomplished by using a number of specialized and general tools. If you are new to braiding, I recommend that you acquire the following items on the list below. You'll see that compared to other crafts, braiding requires very few gadgets. If you own a basic sewing machine and can use a needle and thread, you are off to a great start!

Basic Equipment

Table to attach a braiding clamp to and to lace on

Sewing machine to attach strips

Braiding clamp

Vari-Folder Braid-Aids (optional)

Braidkin (lacing needle)

6-ply linen lacing thread (or)

Braided cotton splicing thread (or)

Beeswax nylon thread

1-¼-inch (3.2 cm) T-pins or plastic-headed pins

6-inch (15.2 cm) metal ruler

Sharp dressmaker scissors

6 #2 safety pins

Sewing needles and matching thread

Medium-size tapestry needle, #18 or #19

Needle-nose pliers or hemostat

Loose-fitting glove with fingertips cut off for wearing on lacing hand (optional)

Rug braiding stand (optional)

General Rules for Easy Braiding

There are a few general rules to follow that really do make it easier to braid well.

First of all, find a comfortable place to braid. You will need to work at a large table. Sit in a comfortable chair and make sure you have good lighting.

Attach a clamp to the table or use a floor stand. A clamp does a good job of holding your braid while you work. Set up your sewing machine close to your work table. Although wool strips can be attached by hand, I find it quicker and the stitches tighter when I use a sewing machine. Last, but by no means least, always lace on a table or other flat surface.

Preparing Wool Strips

Prepare strips only when you are ready for them. Wool weight varies so much that it's important to have the flexibility of varying the width.

Rip the wool whenever possible. When ripping strips, use a metal ruler. Measure each strip carefully, cut a couple of inches and rip the rest. Check the width to make sure the wool is ripping straight. Tweeds sometimes need to be cut. When cutting, measure all along the wool to keep the width uniform.

When ripping or cutting wool, go from selvage to selvage or the length of the piece, whichever produces the longest strip.

My instructions say to cut or rip your strips 1-¾ inches (4 cm) wide. This is for the best weight wool, coat weight. No two pieces of wool are the came. When you're starting a rug or changing colors, try one strip and check the look of the braid. The braid needs to remain the same width.

If you have only lighter weight wool, your strips should be anywhere from 1-¾ inches (4.4 cm) to 2-½ inches (6.4 cm) wide. Lightweight wool (like skirt weight) tends to tweak. This means there are wrinkles in your braid. If possible, use only one strand of lightweight wool along with two strands of good weight wool at a time.

If you are a beginner, try to find the best weight wool so that the edges fold in easily. Advanced braiders can braid all types and weights of material.

My braids are approximately ⅞ inches (2.2 cm) wide, measuring from the dent on one side to the hump opposite it.

Basic Techniques

Instead of reading through a basic techniques section in advance of the projects, you will learn all the techniques you need as you braid a complete rug.

We'll start with the oval rug, by far the most popular braided rug shape. This is a small rug—a good beginner size. We'll meander slowly and carefully through this project, stopping often to learn in detail how to execute all the elements that go into braiding a rug.

The fourth project—the strip rug—is an advanced project, with still fewer directions. You can always refer to the earlier project to review basic techniques if needed.

Before you begin the projects, read the glossary so that you will recognize the braiding terms. Also, read the project instructions at least twice, and try to visualize and reason through all the steps. That way, you'll be familiar with the road we're going to take.

GLOSSARY

Banana-shaped—A rug that isn't straight; both ends curve in one direction.

Band—Several rows of braid using the same color combinations.

Barbells—An oval rug with ends that bulge, the result of skipping on the straight sides before the curve should begin or after the curve should end.

Braid—Three tubes braided together.

Buckling—Not enough slaps. This is quite common for beginners. It forces the center of the rug up and the edges up (into a hat shape). The only remedy is to take out the lacing until the rug is flat. Make sure you slap more often when relacing.

Butting—Method of joining the beginning of a row to the end so that it forms a complete circle. This gives the rug a finished look. Usually used for the last two rows. Can be used for all or part of a rug.

Continuous braid—The way almost all rugs are made. Keep braiding, forming a spiral. You braid, lace, change colors, add new strips, and braid again to make the rug larger and larger.

Fold—The side of the tube that has the raw edges turned in towards the center.

Hit-or-miss rug—Braided with small strands of wool of various colors randomly scattered throughout the rug.

Lacing—Method of attaching the new braid to the body of the rug.

Lacing needles—Needles designed for lacing braided rugs. There is a variety available. Braid-Aid has a lacer that is easy to use because it has a flat, curved design. Rounded, tipped tapestry needles are also good.

Lacing thread—Such as three-ply Irish linen for lacing small items. This would be good for a mat or a chair pad. A rug calls for a heavier lacing thread, such as six-ply Irish linen.

Loop—One of the three tubes after it has been braided.

Multi-strand braid—Using more than three strands or tubes braided together.

Plaiting—The dominant braiding method used many years ago, and still being used today. It is a flat, folded braid. It produces a fold on the back side, and the side of the braid is straight.

Pulled loop—After braiding twice overs, the single loop on the opposite side is pulled tightly, therefore called a pulled loop.

Rattailing or tapering—Method of ending a continuous braided rug.

Reverse e—One method of lacing the first row; named because the thread forms an e in reverse.

Row—Three loops braided and laced to a rug.

Scallops—Too many slaps make the rug raise up and down. To resolve, don't skip at all on the next row. This will usually flatten it out.

Shoulder—The beginning and end of the curve.

Skip—When lacing on the curved end of- the rug (or all around a circle rug), you have to routinely skip one loop on the row you are attaching in order to make a flat, wellshaped rug.

Strand or strip—One length of wool ready to braid.

Tstart—The method used to begin the rug.

Tweaks—Dents/folds in your tube. Tweaks usually occur when braiding with lightweight wool.

Tube—A strip of wool after the edges have been turned in.

Twice overs—Braiding twice from one side then once from the other side.

V—Formed by braiding twice overs in both the top and bottom of heart-shaped rug.

Weight—The number of pounds of wool per yard. Medium-weight wool is 16 ounces per pound. I recommend that you try to use approximately the same weight wool throughout the rug.

Working braid—The braid you are attaching to the rug.

Continued ➡

Cat Rug Braiding Stand with Storage Box

Original design by Bill Lucas and Richard Beauvais–Niki, modified by Karen Kafka

What You Need

One 1-inch-thick (2.5 cm) piece of lumber (I used pine), 8 inches (20.3 cm) wide x 4 feet (1.22 m) long

Scrap of fiberboard, ¼ inch (6 mm) thick

Scrap of plywood, ¾ inch (1.9 mm) thick

Wood glue

Wood filler (optional)

Sandpaper, coarse and fine-grit

Paint, stain, or clear polyurethane

Paintbrush

2 carriage bolts, ¼ x 2 inches (6 mm x 5.1 cm) with washers and nuts

One ¼-inch (6 mm) butterfly or wing nut

One ¼-inch (6 mm) x 3-inch-long (7.6 cm) spring

2 decorative hinges

Latch for box top

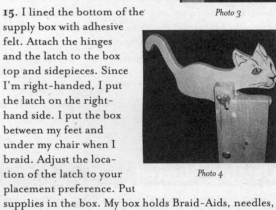

What You Do

1. Rip a 4-inch-wide (10.2 cm) board 4 feet (1.22 m) long.

2. Crosscut from the 4-inch-wide length of board:

Two 15-inch (38.1 cm) pieces for box sides or sidepieces

One 9-inch (22.9 cm) piece for box top

One 4-inch (10.2 cm) piece for box front

One 2-⅝-inch (6.7 cm) piece for box back

3. Crosscut from the remaining piece of board:

One 15-inch (38.1 cm) piece for the crossbar

4. Rip that remaining board length to a 3-inch-wide (7.6 cm) board. Crosscut one 30-inch piece (76.2 cm) for the staff.

5. From the ¼-inch-thick (6 mm) fiberboard, cut a piece 3 x 7-½ inches (7.6 x 19.1 cm) long for box bottom. Cut after dados to check for fit. It should extend ¼ inch (6 mm) beyond sidepieces to insert into box-front dado.

6. Enlarge the template of the cat to 3 x 6 inches (7.6 x 15.2 cm); that's 125%. Trace the pattern onto a piece of ¾-inch (1.9 cm) wood or plywood and cut out.

7. Make dados in left and right box sidepieces, box front and box back piece. Make notches in box sidepieces as shown in diagrams below.

8. Cut a 2-inch-wide (5.1 cm) x 1-inch-high (2.5 cm) notch at the top of the 30-inch (76.2 cm) staff (photo 3). Fill areas as needed with wood filler. Sand all pieces smooth. Check fit of all pieces before final assembly. The staff should fit snugly into the vertical dados of sidepieces.

- The box bottom should slide into the horizontal sidepiece dados.
- The crossbar should fit the notches on the sidepieces.
- The box should sit evenly on a level surface (photo 2).

Photo 2

9. Assemble box with glue, screws, and nails, or pegs. Secure the crossbar to the box.

I like to decorate the cat with a face and the box with a design.

10. Paint, stain, or polyurethane all wood pieces.

11. Drill a ¼-inch (6 mm) hole about 1 inch (2.5 cm) from the tip of the cat's leg or whale's lip for one end of the spring, or hold spring in place with a screw. Drill a ¼-inch (6 mm) hole 1 inch (2.5 cm) down and ⅝ inch (1.6 cm) in on post or extension on top of staff, and measure down 4-¾ inches on the same side of the staff, and drill a ¼-inch (6 mm) hole for bolt.

12. Attach spring. I put the washer, nut, spring, and nut on the bottom hole to hold the spring away from the wood (photos 3 and 4).

13. Line up upper ledge of cat's leg or whale's lip with the 2-inch (5.1 cm) ledge of notch made in staff. Drill a ¼-inch (6 mm) hole through cat or whale for bolt and wing nut (photo 4).

14. When the wing nut is loosened and the tail is pushed down, the braid releases and can be moved; when the tail is released, the spring creates tension on the braid, is held in place by the tightened wing nut, and secures the braid for braiding. (Note: Place the tail on the left side for right-handed persons; tail on the right side for left-handed persons. Photo shows tail for right-handed person.) The spring will be on the side of the staff away from the braider.

Photo 3

15. I lined the bottom of the supply box with adhesive felt. Attach the hinges and the latch to the box top and sidepieces. Since I'm right-handed, I put the latch on the right-hand side. I put the box between my feet and under my chair when I braid. Adjust the location of the latch to your placement preference. Put

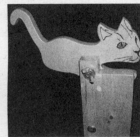

Photo 4

supplies in the box. My box holds Braid-Aids, needles, pins, thread, tape measure, hemostats, etc. I also made a tapestry bag that carries the stand, the rug, and pieces of rug wool to those wonderful rug-braiding activities.

Portable Rug Braiding Stand

Designed and made by Karen Kafka

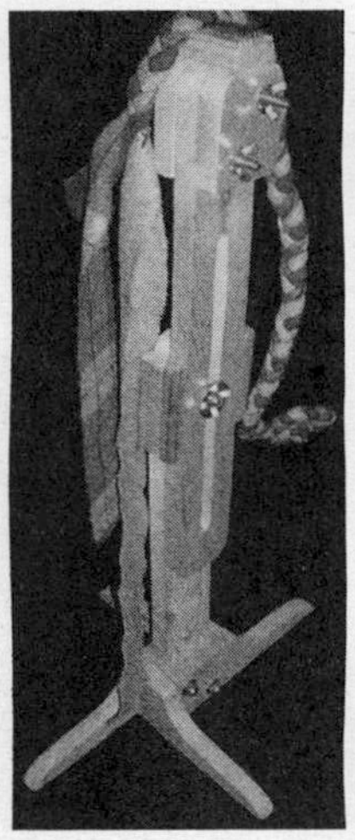

Take your portable rug stand with you to all those wonderful rug-braiding retreats around the country. It's only 18 inches long and 10 inches wide (45.7 x 25.5 cm) and weighs a mere 3 pounds (1.6 kg), even with the hardware, and even less than that if the wood is secured with screws or pegs.

What You Need

Pieces of wood:

Two 1 x 2-½ x 17-½ inches (2.5 x 6.4 x 44.5 cm) long for staff

Two 1 x 2-½ x 3 inches (2.5 x 6.4 x 7.66 cm) long for top

Two ¾ x 1-½ x 3 inches (1.9 x 3.8 x 7.6 cm) long for side stabilizers (pre-drill when nailing to prevent splitting)

Wood for top, if making the interchangeable units (photo 5).

Two 1 x 2-⅝ x 6-¾ inches (2.5 x 6.7 x 17.1 cm) long for base

Two 1 x 2-⅝ x 8-¾ inches (2.5 x 6.7 x 22.2 cm) long for base (base designed by Ken Kafka; I cut a nice curving shape.)

Wood glue, wood filler, coarse and fine-grit sandpaper

Paint, stain, or clear polyurethane finish and paintbrush

Two carriage bolts, ¼ x 2-½ inches (6 mm x 6.4 cm) long for staff with washers and nuts (I like wing nuts.)

One heavy-duty ¼ x 1-¼-inch-diameter (6 mm x 5.1 cm) washer

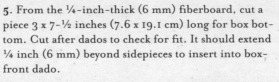

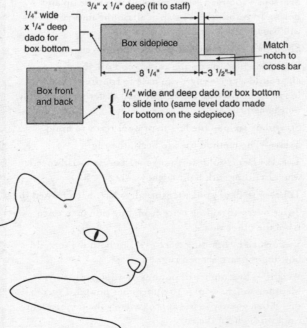

¾" x ¼" deep (fit to staff)

¼" wide x ¼" deep dado for box bottom

Box sidepiece

Match notch to cross bar

8 ¼"   3 ½"

Box front and back

¼" wide and deep dado for box bottom to slide into (same level dado made for bottom on the sidepiece)

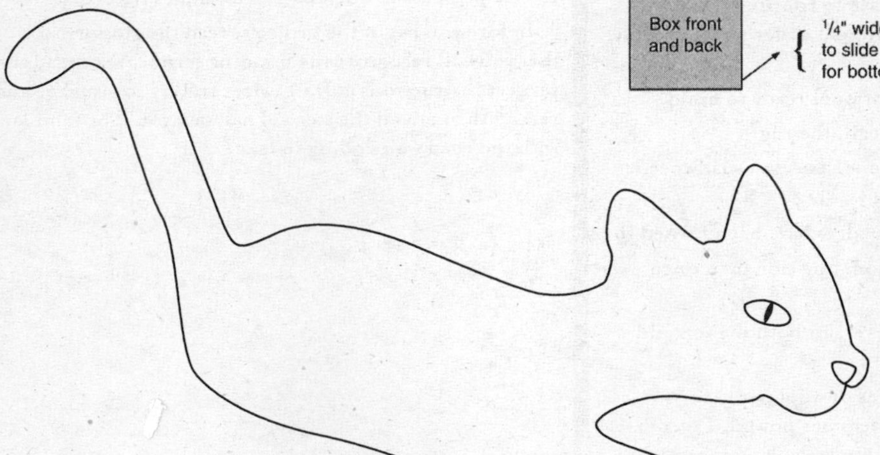

Original cat design by Karen Kafka. Enlarge pattern 125% for actual size

What You Do

1. Sand all pieces of wood smooth.

2. On one of the 17-½-inch-long (44.5 cm) pieces, make a ⅜-inch-wide (9.5 cm) mortis, starting 1-¾ inch (4.4 cm) from the end and ending 4-½ inches (11.4 cm) from the other end. The mortis allows the stand's height to adjust to 30 inches (76.2 cm) (photo 2).

Photo 2

3. On the other 17-½-inch-long (44.5 cm) piece, measure 2 inches (5.1 cm) from the end and drill a ¼-inch (6 mm) hole to insert the 2-inch (5.1 cm) carriage bolt through the hole. Secure the ¾ x 1-½-inch (1.9 x 3.8 cm) side stabilizers to the staff, centered to the drilled ¼-inch (6 mm) hole, or use two bolts 2 (5.1 cm) inches apart (photo 3).

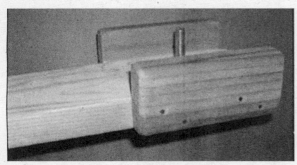

Photo 3

4. Assemble the base to fit the staff (photo 4). The longer boards go toward and away from you. The shorter boards are pointing out to the side. The assembled base can be one unit or bolted with the staff sandwiched between the base units.

5. If you just want one kind of unit, secure the top pieces or drill ¼-inch (6 mm) holes through the two 1 x 2-½ x 3-inch (2.5 x 6.4 x 7.6 cm) top pieces and the end of the mortised piece for unit interchanges between a three-stand unit and a multi-stand unit. Rug hookers have a metal strip to hold the rug; works well for braids. I stapled the metal hooking strip to the piece of wood crossing the top (photo 5).

Photo 4

Photo 5

6. Wood-fill areas as needed, finish sanding, and paint, stain or polyurethane to finish.

The Oval Braided Rug

The oval rug is one of the easiest to make. It is the most popular shape, probably because it fits a great many areas. My "Country Spring Oval" is 2 by 3 feet (61.5 x 92.5 cm), a good size for the beginner braider.

Calculating the Length of the First Row

To figure out the length of the first row, subtract the 2-foot width (61.5 cm) from the 3-foot (92.5 cm) length. This gives you 1 foot (31 cm). Add 1 inch (2 cm): the center braid is 13 inches (33 cm) long.

This is a standard design, going from medium shades in the center to darker bands, then some light, and ending with the darkest bands. Beginners may not want to include as many colors. Yellow, purple, and green could be eliminated and the look would be almost the same. This would leave six colors, a good number for the novice braider. Light gray could be substituted for white, making the rug more soil resistant.

How to Count Rows

Basic to braiding is knowing how to count rows. Here's how it's done:

The first 13 inches (33 cm)—or the distance to the twice overs—is Row 1. Row 2 is all the way around the center row. Row 3 and the following rows are a complete circuit of the rug.

Materials

The "Country Spring Oval" uses about 4-½ pounds (2.1 kilos) of wool, or 4 yards (3.7 m). Review the equipment listed under "Getting Started." Make sure you have matching sewing thread.

Country Spring Oval

Rows 1-3	White	Med. Blue	Lt. Blue
Row 4	Dusty Rose	Med. Blue	Lt. Blue
Rows 5 & 6	Dusty Rose	Med. Blue	Blue Gray
Row 7	Dusty Rose	Med. Purple	Blue Gray
Row 8	Dusty Rose	Med. Purple	White
Row 9	Lt. Pink	Med. Purple	White
Row 10	Lt. Pink	Lt. Yellow	White
Row 11	Lt. Pink	Lt. Blue	White
Row 12	Med. Blue	Lt. Blue	White
Row 13	Med. Blue	Lt. Blue	Med. Green
Row 14	Med. Blue	Blue Gray	Med. Green
Row 15	Med. Blue	Dusty Rose	Dusty Rose
Row 16	Dusty Rose	Dusty Rose	Dusty Rose

Illustrations

Figure 1 diagrams all the key elements of the oval rug. You will refer to this illustration a number of times as you follow the instructions. In all the illustrations, black, white, and gray indicate different colors of wool.

T-start

All braided rugs begin with a *T-start*.

1. Cut or rip one strand each of your chosen colors 1-½ inches (4 cm) wide. If the selvage is bulky, cut it off.

2. Put the right side of one strip facing up.

Tip: Some wool looks alike on both sides. Other wool has a flat side, which I call the right side, and a fuzzy

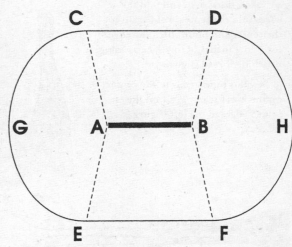

Figure 1: A — "T" Beginning, B — 2-Twice overs, C — D and E — F — No skip areas, D — F and E — C — Skipping Areas, B to F — Color change area, F — Rattail area, G — Butt here for 1st butted row, H — Butt here on last row

side, called the wrong side. Other braiders like to use the fuzzy side as the right side. Whichever you choose, be consistent. Always sew the right sides of the wool together.

3. Put the right side of a second strip at right angles on the end of the first strip (right side down). In other words, place the right sides together (figure 2).

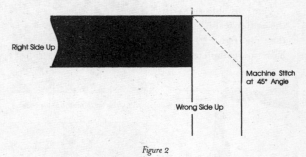

Figure 2

4. Machine stitch from the top left corner to the side, using matching thread (figure 2). Trim close to the stitching, leaving approximately ⅛ inch (.5 cm) as shown in figure 3.

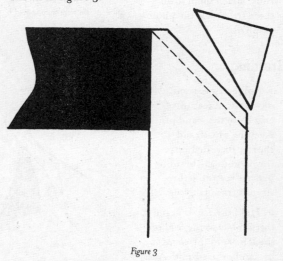

Figure 3

5. Working on the wrong side of the combined strips, turn in ¼ inch (1 cm) on both sides of the diagonal seam for 2 to 3 inches (5 to 7.5 cm); pin to hold. Overcast both the top and bottom, using matching sewing thread (figure 4). The stitches should not show on the right side.

Figure 4

Continued ➡

4. Take a third strip and fold the edges into the center. Fold again to the center and blind stitch the edge for 2 to 3 inches (5 to 7.5 cm), using matching thread (figure 5).

5. Sew this tube firmly to the center on the lower seam. Position the folded edges to the left (figure 6).

Figure 5

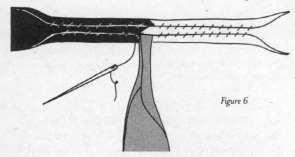

Figure 6

6. Fold the top half of the combined strips over the bottom half and blind stitch 2 to 3 inches (5 to 7.5 cm) on both sides of the center seam, enclosing the tube (figure 7). You have now completed the *T*.

Attaching the third strip to the center

Braid-Aids in place on completed T

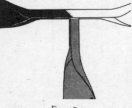

Figure 7

7. If you are using Braid-Aids, attach them to all three strips (see the photograph).

Braiding

1. Roll up one strand of wool to 2 feet (61.5 cm) from the *T* and pin. Keeping one strand shorter or rolled up throughout the braiding process keeps the three strands from tangling.

2. Hold the *T* so that the third tube has the fold on the left. Fold the edges in by hand or use Braid-Aids to fold.

Figure 8

3. Pull the right tube *over* the center tube and hold (figure 8). *Always keep the folds on the left.*

4. Now pull the left tube *over* the middle to the center and twist so the fold is on the left (figure 9). Hold with your left hand.

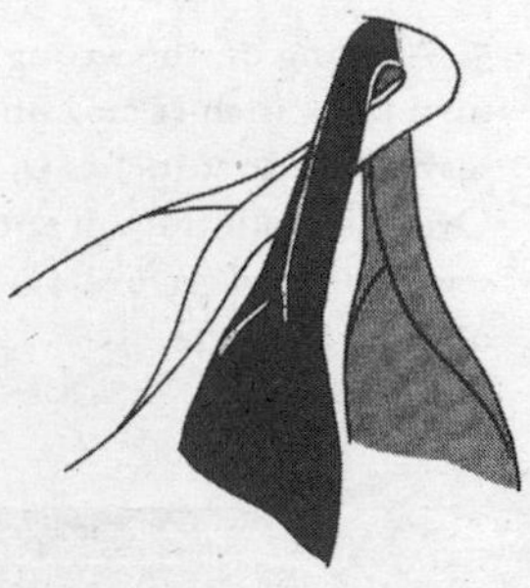

Figure 9

5. Continue braiding. Fold the edges in, take from the right, put the tube in the center and hold with the right hand. Now fold the edges in on the strand on the left, pull tightly to the

center, and hold with the left hand. Make sure your folds are on the left. Check the other side of the braid to make sure that the folds aren't showing.

6. Put a large safety pin through the loops to hold the braid together when you stop.

7. Braid for 2 inches (5 cm) and put the braid into the clamp. Always keep some tension on your clamp. Pull as you're braiding (see photographs).

8. Braid for 13 inches (33 cm), and then braid two *twice overs*.

  a. Take a tube on the right and braid (figure 10a).

  b. Take the next tube from the *right*, braid and hold (figure 10b).

  c. Braid the tube from the left and pull *tightly* (figure 10c).

  d. Repeat a, b, and c once more (figure 11). This is the only time a corner is braided in.

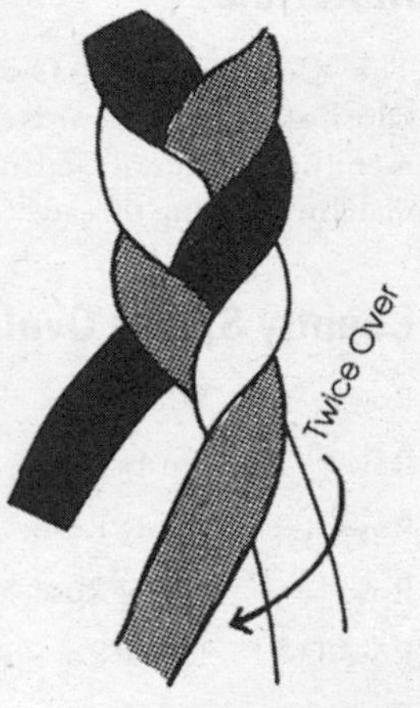

9. Braid about 36 inches (92.5 cm). When you attach your strips, place the right sides together as per figure 2 and trim as in figure 3.

Tip: You may want to take your braid out now and practice until you have an even, tight braid.

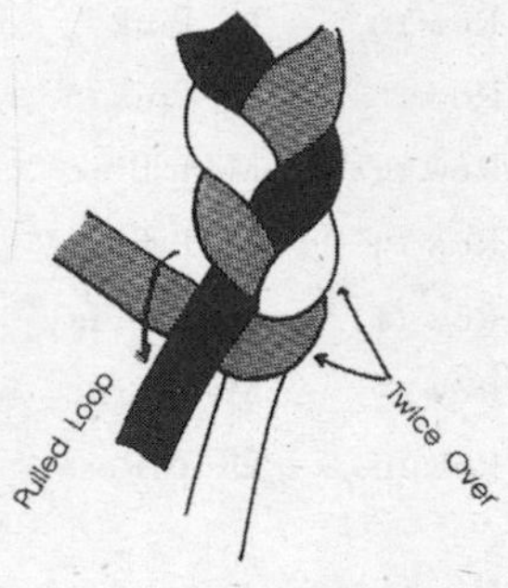

Lacing

1. Now we're ready to *lace* or sew the braid together. Take about 5 feet (152.4 cm) of lacing thread. Thread it into the *tapestry* needle and knot.

Tip: Keep the right side of the rug up; this is the side that is up when you are braiding.

2. Position the *T* away from you and to your left (figure 11).

Figure 10a

Twice Over

Figure 10b

Pulled Loop *Twice Over*

Figure 10c

1st twice over

1st Pulled Loop

2nd Pulled Loop *2nd twice over*

Figure 11

3. Insert the needle through the wool into the second *pulled loop*. After braiding twice overs, the single loop on the opposite side is pulled tightly, therefore called a pulled loop. This attaches the thread firmly and hides the knot (figure 12).

1st Pulled Loop

2nd Pulled Loop

Figure 12

4. The lacing technique for the first 13 inches (33 cm)—the first row—is different from the rest of the rug. The reason is that the braid in these first inches (until the *T* is reached) goes in the opposite direction from the braid in the next 13 inches (33 cm).

There are two methods of lacing this first 13 inches (33 cm).

Method #1:

Insert the tapestry needle as mentioned above and shown in figure 12. Sew each loop, alternating the sides on the fold side of the braid (figure 13). Pull the lacing thread rightly after each stitch. Continue until you reach the *T*.

This method is easy to do. The stitches are hidden, it is sewn tightly, and the loops are alternating as in the rest of the rug.

Figure 13

Method #2:

Method #2 is called a *reverse* e because the stitches look like an "e" going backward (figure 18). This method has been the accepted way for many years.

  a. Insert the tapestry needle as in figure 12. Now switch to the *lacing needle* (the Braidkin).

  b. Insert the lacing needle through the space between the next loop to the left (figure 14).

  c. Cross to the upper braid, insert the needle into the opposite loop going from the left to the right. Use the lacing needle to hide the thread and pull (figure 15).

  d. Cross back down to the lower braid, lace in the loop already laced, going toward the left (figure 16).

  e. Lace in the loop to its left (for the first time). Hide the thread and pull (figure 17). For example: Go from 1 to 2, then up to 3 (going from left to right), back to 4 again and then to 5 (figure 18).

Figure 14

Figure 15

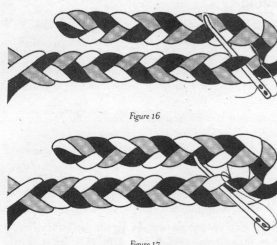

Figure 16

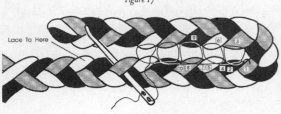

Figure 17

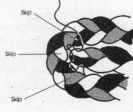

Figure 18

This method is harder to learn. If you're using three strands of solid-colored wool, it is a bit hard to hide your stitches. It also leaves a line down the center because your stitches aren't woven together, as in the rest of the rug.

It is a good idea to learn both methods as both have advantages.

The directions from here on are the same for both methods.

5. Lace until you reach the *T*.

6. Switch to the tapestry needle. Insert it through the bottom of the *T*, halfway from the bottom to the top. Take a ¼-inch (1 cm) stitch. Skip one loop on the braid you are attaching the lace the next loop. Pull the thread. Turn your rug as you are going around the *T*.

7. Take a ¼-inch (1 cm) stitch at the end of the *T* and skip the next loop on the row you are attaching; lace the next loop (figure 19).

8. Take one more stitch on the other side of the *T*, skip a loop on the row you're attaching (working braid), then lace the next loop. The *T* is now laced.

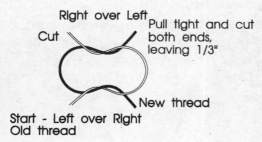

Figure 19

9. Return the thread to the lacing needle.

10. The following is the technique to be used for the rest of the rug.

   a. Lace only in one direction—toward your *left*.

   b. Lace through the loop to the left of the *T*, going from right to left; pull the thread.

   c. Lace the next loop in the braid you are attaching. Cross up to the body of rug and lace going from right to left. Hide the lacing thread and pull, *holding both braids flat as you pull* (figure 20).

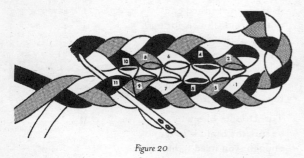

Figure 20

d. Continue lacing in this manner until you reach the curved end. Never skip on the straight side of the rug. Lace in every loop.

e. Skip four times on this second curve (skip every other loop). Skip only on the outside braid—never on the body of the rug.

11. Continue braiding and lacing until three rows are completed.

Tip: To attach a new piece of lacing thread, use a square knot: Left over right and around; then right over left and around. Pull tightly (figure 21). Always hide the knot. Push it into the folds with the lacing needle and check the back of the rug to make sure it's completely hidden.

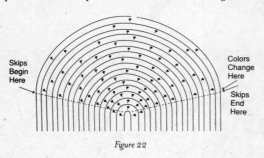

Figure 21

General Rules for Lacing and Skipping

It's a good practice to braid a row and then lace it. This is the time to decide if you want to change a color. Here are some general rules for mastering lacing.

- Four to six skips (increases) on the curve normally will keep it flat. Space your skips evenly around the curve.

- Skip about the same number of times on both ends of the row.

- If the rug scallops, there are too many skips. If it cups up, there are not enough.

- Establish a routine; for example, lace three loops (on the braid you are attaching) and skip one loop all around the curve. The key is to skip evenly and alternate your skips. As the rug gets bigger, the skips get farther apart. Figure 22 diagrams the approximate placement of skips and shows where to change colors.

Figure 22

- It is impossible to make a hard-and-fast rule regarding how many skips and how often. If you have changed the width of your braid, skip less if it is wider; skip more if it is narrower.

Lacing and Skipping on the Oval Rug

- When lacing on the curved ends, always lace the loop on the braid you are attaching; then lace the next loop on the body of the rug. Hold flat and pull. Evaluate whether to skip the next loop on the row you are attaching. If the lacing thread is ahead of the next loop on the row you are attaching (working braid), skip it and lace the next loop. Now lace the top loop on the body of the rug (figure 23).

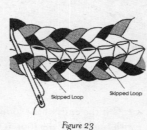

Figure 23

- Starting on the third row, put a T-pin in every skipped loop. Keep them in place for approximately five rows.

- Avoid skipping in the same place. If you place a pin where you skip, it will mark the place where you skipped in the previous rows.

- Mark the *T* and the twice overs with a large straight pin on A and B (figure 1). This will help you know when it is time to start thinking about starting or ending your skips.

Not ready to skip   *Time to skip*

- Start skipping when the ends of the rug start forming the curve. Early or late skips will make barbells or bulges where it should be straight.

- Check the straight sides of your rug every row for these first two to four rows, line the side up with the edge of the table and mold the rug into a straight line. Your rug will be pliable now. If it is banana-shaped now, you won't be able to correct this later.

Tip: The photographs below show regular lacing. Notice how I laced the plaid in the photograph on the left, pulling the braid open. This enables the thread to line up in the space between the loops so that the lacing thread can be hidden. The other photograph shows lacing the top loop. Hold the braids together and pull tightly to hide the lacing thread with the needle.

Lacing the braid you are attaching   *Lacing the top loop*

Changing Colors

When you change colors, you want to avoid being obvious, you want tour new color to make its appearance in a subtle fashion. To change colors successfully, follow these steps:

1. Change to a new color on the opposite end of the *T* (figure 1 and figure 22).

2. Complete 3 rows (or the number of rows you would like before making a color change.)

3. Braid beyond the curve.

4. Hold a ruler along the straight side of the rug or put the rug along the side of a table.

5. The outside loop to the right of the edge is the loop to remove.

6. Put a T-pin *above* and *below* the preceding loop in the loop to be removed (figure 24).

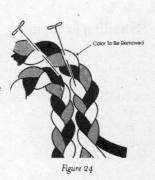

Figure 24

Continued ➡

7. Unbraid 2 inches (5 cm) beyond the T-pins and cut between them at a 45-degree angle (figure 25).

8. Sew the strip of new color to the unbraided strip you just cut; sew along the cut line. Rebraid the three strands. The seam you just sewed should be under the preceding loop; the new color will be on the right side of the braid.

Cut On 45° Angle Between "T" Pins

Figure 25

Cutting between the T-pins

Placement of new color

New color sewn in

Braiding with new color

Sewn edge concealed by braid

New color appears in braid

9. Continue braiding, lacing, and changing colors as per the color chart until you've completed 14 rows or the number of rows you need to almost finish the rug.

10. Change only one color at a time to blend colors well.

Tip: Some braiders hide their seam when attaching a new strip. This is done by having the seam fall under the loop as shown in figures 24 and 25. I recommend hiding the seam if you're using solid colors. If your rug is tweedy, or when you use more neutral or darker colors, the seams don't show anyway. I have never found that these seams wear quickly. Tight, sewing machine stitches hold up well. If you are attaching strips by hand, it may be better to hide the seam.

Rattailing or Tapering

Rattailing or tapering is a method of ending a continuous braid. Many braiders end their rugs this way. I use rattailing at the point in the rug where I want the continuous braid to end; then I butt to finish the rug.

1. Refer to figures 1 and 26 for areas to rattail. Put a T-pin in the braid

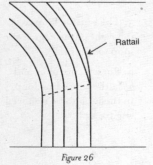

Rattail

Figure 26

where the curve ends. This is where the braid should end.

2. Cut off the braid 1 inch (2.5 cm) below this pin and unbraid 8 inches (20.5 cm).

3. To taper, cut all three strands so that they measure ⅝ inch (1.6 cm) on the ends; cut up both sides for 6–8 inches, gradually widening your cut until the wool is a normal width (photo).

4. Rebraid the rattail as far as you can, still folding the edges in. When the rattail gets so narrow that the edges can no longer be folded by hand, blind stitch the remaining edges. These ends should be small as you can make them. Braid all but the final inch (2.5 cm) and pin to hold.

5. Lace to the last inch (2.5 cm).

Strand cut to ⅝ inch (1.6cm) on ends

Lacing the rattail to the last inch

6. Using needle-nose pliers, weave the most obvious color strand into its matching color in the rug, if possible. Pull through one loop onto the body of the rug (figure 28). Twist the remaining two loops around each other and weave the next most obvious color through the next loop in the rug. Weave the final loop in the same color loop in the rug. If this doesn't look smooth or is too obvious, try again. Sometimes you can do better using a different combination.

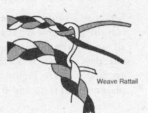

Weave Rattail

Figure 27   *Figure 28*

First strand ready to pull in   *Pulling in first strand*

Pulling in second strand   *Pulling in third strand*

7. Cut the ends of the loops (on the back of rug) even with the side of the loop it was pulled through. Take a needle and matching thread and sew to secure these ends. This completes your continuous braid.

Butting

Butting is a method of forming one complete row by weaving the two ends of a braid together to form a necklace; then you lace the necklace around the rug. All loose ends are carefully concealed. Butting seamlessly frames, and thereby finishes, the rug. I always end my rugs with one or two butted rows.

Butting is also the best technique for radically changing colors without showing a color change.

In addition, butting protects the rattail from coming unraveled. And it is a wonderful way to add rows to large rugs and thereby avoid having to carry the whole rug to the sewing machine every time you need to add strands of wool to your continuous braid.

The last point I need to make here is that butting is the most challenging aspect of making a braided rug. In my classes, this is the technique students need the most help with. An easy way to visualize butting is to think of it as joining two ends of braid together by leaving same-colored loops through each other. Once you get the hang of it, you'll be able to butt with the best of them.

If you are butting the whole rug, or any part of it, use the following directions.

Butting—Row 15 (or your next-to-the-last row)

1. Fold in the edges of all three strands. Pin each strand with a #2 (large) safety pin (figure 29).

2. Place the folds to the left and put all three tubes into your clamp. The large pins will hold the tubes in the clamp.

Figure 29

3. Braid a few inches (5 or 6 cm) and put a fourth pin across all the loops (figure 29).

4. Braid until you have a length of braid long enough to go around the rug once.

Three tubes secured in clamp

5. Place the ends to be butted on a curve (figure 1). Remember to place the braid clockwise (in the same direction as the rest of the rug), with the top of your braid up.

6. Leave 5–6 inches (13–15 cm) of lacing thread and start lacing 4 inches (10 cm) from the beginning of the braid.

Length of braid ready to butt

7. Lace all around the rug, leaving 4 inches (10 cm) unlaced on the end.

8. Braid enough so that you can overlap the two ends of your braid by 3–4 inches (7.5–10 cm).

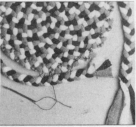

9. Place the pinned end of the braid (the beginning) on top of the other end. Match the same colors: for example, place white on top of white, gray on top of gray (figure 30).

Beginning of lacing butted rug

Tip: Double-check to be sure the braid is long enough; you need to have enough braid to lace the final 8 inches (20.5 cm) to the rug without stretching the braid.

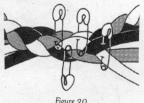

Figure 30

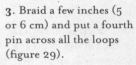
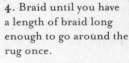

10. Pin two matching loops together on the fold side (inside); for example, pin white to white, and gray to gray. Pin the third loops (between these two) together on the outside (figure 30).

Beginning of row pinned over end of row

Matching colors pinned together

11. Take out any pins left on the ends and unbraid to the pinned loops. Cut the ends of the braid so that approximately 2 inches (5 cm) remain on each end of the braid.

12. You will start to butt with the ends of one loop of each color free on the fold side. Both loops will be free on the outside (figure 31).

Tip: Hold onto the butting area firmly with your left hand; don't let go. Do all of your pinning, etc., with your right hand.

13. Work with the outside loops. Cross the top loop over the bottom loop and pull out all the fullness. Make sure the edges are folded in. Unpin and repin along the side of the braid (figure 32).

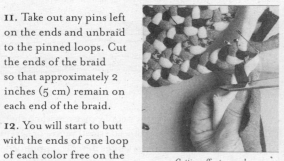

Cutting off extra wool

Figure 31

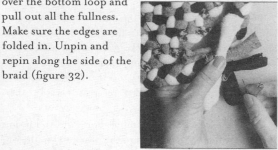

Removing pins; hold firmly in left hand

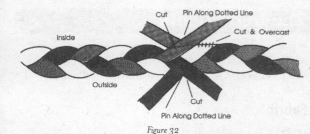

Figure 32

14. Next work on the loop to the right on the fold side. Insert the lacing needle in front of the back loop and pull the end up and out; it will be crossed behind its matching loop. Pull to tighten. Unpin and repin along the edge of the braid.

Repinning along edge

Pulling inside loop through and crossing over

Pinning lengthwise

15. Using the lacing needle, insert it in front of the front loop on the left. Pull the end out; it will cross in front of the matching loop. Pull out all the fullness. Unpin and repin along the edge of the braid. You have now woven your two ends together.

Pulling last loop through

Crossing over and pinning lengthwise

16. Unpin the outside loops and cut both the front and back loops even with the edge of the braid (figure 32). Hold the cut edges together. Overcast firmly with matching thread.

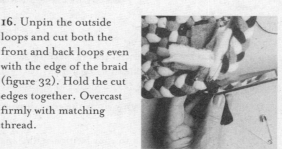

Cutting outside loop even with edge of rug

Sewing edges together even with side of rug

Outside edge, sewn

17. Repeat for the top loops. Cut the loops on the right even with the edge of the braid and overcast. Then cut the loops on the left even with the braid and overcast. The sewn edges should fall between the rows so the stitching doesn't show.

18. Lace the final 8 inches (20.5 cm) of braid to the rug. Weave the lacing thread through the loops until you come back to where you started to lace and tie.

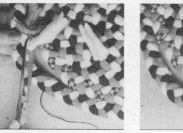

Cutting next loop even with edge

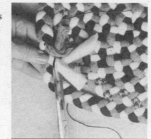

Cutting second loop even with edge

All loops cut and sewn

Butting—Last Row

The instructions for the last row are a bit different—all your butting seams are on the fold side (inside). Repeat steps 1–9. Then continue with steps 19-28.

19. Pin all three loops on the inside, with one pin on the outside, just to hold (figure 33).

20. Unbraid to the pinned loops. Take out any pins left on the ends. Cut the end of the braid so that only about 2 inches (5 cm) remains on the end of the braid.

21. You will be starting to butt with only two strands in the final place (up), one on the left, and one on the right (figure 34). Hold firmly and remove the outside pin.

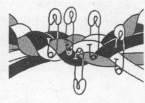

Figure 33

Pinning matching colors

Extra braid cut off

22. Insert the lacing needle into the front of the middle loop and pull the end up and out. Insert the needle into the front of the rear middle loop. Pull the loop up and out. Cross the front over the back, pull out any fullness, making sure the edges are turned in. Unpin and repin evenly with the side of the braid.

23. Work on the loop to the left. Insert the needle into the front loop, pull it out, cross over the back loop, pull out the fullness, and pin. Unpin and repin evenly with the side of the braid (figure 35).

24. Unpin the right loop. Pull the inside loop out of the braid, *slip your finger in where the loop came out, and insert the outside loop in the hole, pulling it toward the fold side.* Pull the fullness out, fold the edges in, cross over the back loop, and pin (figure 35). The last row is now woven together.

Figure 34

Third loop after first and second loops are pulled through and pinned

Figure 35

Putting fingers through braid where loop came out

Inserting outside loop through hole

Crossing over and pinning even with inside edge

Continued ➡

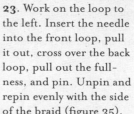
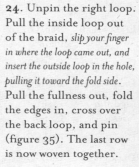

25. Unpin the loops to the right, cut evenly along the edge, and overcast firmly with matching thread.

26. Repeat with the middle and left side loops. All of the seams should fall between the rows so the joined ends don't show (figure 36).

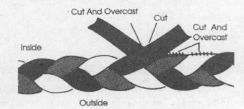

Figure 36

27. Lace the final 8 inches (20.5 cm) to the rug.

28. Weave the ends of the lacing thread through the loops until they meet, and tie.

Congratulations! You have just completed your oval braided rug. I'm sure you now have your own stories about this "first rug" to share with friends and family.

The Strip Braided Rug

Simply braiding straight rows with the traditional three-strand braid creates the strip rug. Each of the rows must be the same width, and your lacing even, or your rug will pull out of shape.

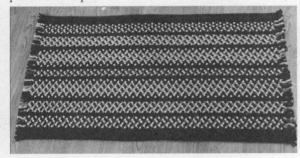

Materials

"Forest Green Strip" is a rectangle 26 x 49 inches (66 x 124.5 cm). You will need about 6 pounds (2.7 kg) of wool. Review the list of equipment you'll need under "Getting Started." Make sure you have matching sewing thread as well as clear nylon thread for stitching across the ends.

Forest Green Strip Rug

COLOR PLAN

26" x 49" (66 x 124.5 cm)

Color Plan

Row 1	Dark green	Light green	Red/Green Plaid
Row 2	Dark Green	Dark Green	Dark Green
Row 3	Dark Green	Dark Green	Light Green
Rows 4–6	Dark Green	Medium Green	Light Green
Row 7	Dark Green	Dark Green	Light Green
Row 8	Dark Green	Dark Green	Dark Green
Rows 9–11	Dark Green	Medium Green	Light Green
Row 12	Dark Green	Dark Green	Dark Green
Rows 13–15	Dark Green	Light Green	Red/Green Plaid
Rows 16–18	Dark Green	Dark Green	Dark Green

Starting the Row

1. Start each row by folding the edges in, then folding together again, as in a regular braid, and pin to hold (figure 29), under "Butting-Row 15," of the oval rug instructions.

2. Put the three strands into a clamp. The pins will hold the braid in place. (See photo under figure 29.) Put a fourth pin across the braid to keep it from unbraiding.

3. Braid to the length you want your finished rug to be.

4. Lace the center two rows together.

5. As you braid more rows, add them on one side of the center, then on the other side of the center.

6. It is important to lace in every loop. Never skip on a strip rug.

7. I lace on a rotary cutting mat. This way I can make sure that the sides of the rug are straight.

8. Leave at least 4 inches (10 cm) of lacing thread on both ends of each row.

9. After adding your desired number of rows, it's time to finish off the ends.

10. Use the lines on the cutting mat to determine where the ends need to be sewn.

Mark both ends with masking tape. Note: I then took my rug to a woman who has an industrial sewing machine, and she sewed the ends. I recommend using a clear, 100% nylon thread so the stitching is as invisible as possible.

11. Cut the excess braid evenly along the edge, leaving some for the fringe.

12. Put the lacing thread into your lacing needle, and lace back into the body of your rug for a few loops, and cut it off. This, plus the machine sewing, should make a sturdy end.

13. Another method of finishing a strip rug is to machine stitch, as in step 10, then cut the excess close to the stitching, and sew on a binding.

Creating a Pattern

A strip rug is a great rug to work in a pattern. Here's one possibility:

Row 2	3 strands of dark green
Row 3	2 strands of dark green and 1 light green
Row 4	1 strand of dark green, 1 light green, and 1 medium green.

By lacing the dark green on row four between the two dark greens on row three, you create a pattern (figure 37).

Figure 37

Finished rug detail

—FROM *The Braided Rug Book*

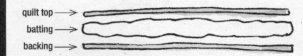

QUILTING BASICS

Linda Kopp

La Quilt Sandwich

There's really nothing mysterious about the quilting process, especially when you break it down into parts (see figure 1). Think of your quilt as a sandwich (mmmm…) made of the quilt top, the batting, and the backing.

quilt top ⟶
batting ⟶
backing ⟶

Figure 1

The quilt top is what most people envision when they think "quilt." Whether it's pieced (small pieces or scraps of fabric sewn together into a larger design), appliquéd (fabric shapes stitched onto the quilt top fabric), or embroidered (shapes, designs, and even text created using various decorative stitches), the quilt top is the most visual part of the quilt design. Consequently, you'll want to spend the most time and creativity on your quilt top, especially if you plan on showing off your creation, which we highly encourage.

Batting is the layer of fabric stuffing that ensures your quilt is warm and cozy. There are a variety of batting materials out there to choose from, each with different qualities as well as levels of thickness (we'll talk more about batting later).

The backing is essentially the underside of the quilt. Although largely outshined by the quilt top (alack and alas), you can make your backing as plain or as decorative as you like. You can use a complementary fabric to those featured on the quilt top, sew together larger blocks of fabric for a little bit of interest, or create a whole other design for a reversible quilt…the choice is yours.

When you're ready to assemble your quilt, you'll simply stack these layers one on top of the other and quilt—or stitch—them together. Bada-boom, bada-bing!

The Ingredients

If you need an excuse to do a tiny bit of shopping, look no further. You'll need to gather a few assorted materials and tools before you sit down to make your masterpiece.

Fabric

If you spent more time at a fabric store than cleaning your house last month, you're in good company. Picking out fabrics is super fun, and it's an easy way to put your creative stamp on a project. Whether paisley prints, snappy stripes, or hand-dyed solids are your poison (and you don't have to pick just one), the options are endless. And they don't stop at the fabric store; try using thrift

PLEASANTLY PLUMP QUARTERS

Okay, they're called fat quarters and, thank you very much, they're just the right size. Sold individually at fabric stores and mildly addictive, fat quarters are handy when you need just a little bit of many different fabrics. They measure 18 by 22 inches (45.7 x 55.9 cm), meaning they're essentially a quarter yard cut in half.

store finds—such as curtains, sheets, or pillowcases—or family "heirlooms" (untossable concert or vacation T-shirts, much-loved childhood bedsheets, and the like).

If you're new to sewing, it might be a good idea to stick to simple cotton since it's easier to work with and less likely to pucker. Steer toward midweight cottons over thinner cottons: midweight will hold up much better over time. If you've fallen hard for a particular fabric, go ahead and buy a little extra since sometimes accidents do happen. In most cases, you'll need to prewash your fabric to avoid any later color bleeding or shrinkage snafus.

Batting

Although essentially utilitarian in nature, batting is the "meat" or "veggie burger" if you prefer) of your quilting sandwich. Low-loft batting, or thinner batting, is a great choice for a quilt with a lot of detail. This thickness is perfect for your sewing machine and most climates. High-loft batting—thicker stuff like that in a comforter—will be warmer and puffier. However, in all that lofty luxury, you might lose some of the quilt's definition, especially any hand-stitched elements.

Besides thickness, batting is available in a variety of materials from cotton to blends to polyester. Since your quilt is likely for a wee one, you might want to pick batting that's hypoallergenic and/or organic. You should also think about how the quilt will eventually be washed: polyester and polyester blends can usually survive a gentle machine wash and tumble dry, while cotton batting cannot. For the most flexibility, pick a batting that is fairly stable and strongly woven, meaning it won't move, shift, or bunch with use.

You can buy batting at most fabric stores. It's available in a variety of widths right off the bolt, like fabric, or in precut sizes, including an ultra-handy crib size that measures 45 x 60 inches (114.3 x 152.4 cm). In general, follow the pattern instructions for the type of quantity of batting to purchase. Keep in mind that your batting will need to be a few inches longer and wider than your quilt top, so shop accordingly. If you can't find batting that's exactly as wide or as long as your edges, don't sweat it. Using a simple zigzag stitch along the edges, you can easily join pieces of batting to make the size you need.

Thread

In most cases, your average all-purpose thread, usually a cotton-polyester blend, will do just fine. Many of the quilts in this book call for quilting thread, which is slightly finer and stronger than all-purpose thread. If you want your quilting stitches to blend in with the background, pick a color that matches your main fabrics or you might even try a clear nylon thread. If, however, the quilting stitches are an important design element, make them stand out by selecting thread of bold, contrasting color.

Scissors or Rotary Cutting System

You won't get very far in quilting without a fabulous pair of scissors, and it's best to have a pair dedicated just for

this purpose (no Fido-hair-trimming or cardboard-fort-making allowed). To make life easier, you might also think about investing in a rotary cutting system, perfect for cutting strips and blocks of fabric often used in quilting. The system includes a rotary cutter (think pizza cutter, but avoid the temptation!), a measured and grid-lined mat, and a clear, thick plastic ruler with grid lines and measurements. All you do is line up your fabric on the grid, place the ruler where you'd like to cut, and roll the cutter along the ruler's edge. The cutter can easily slice through a couple of layers of folded or stacked fabrics, cutting your time in half and, in some instances, making your cuts more accurate.

Sewing Machine, Etc.

A definitive benefit of the modern age, a sewing machine is a must if you want to complete your quilt quickly, especially since the arrival of your quilt's intended recipient can be a little hard to predict. Any standard sewing machine will suffice for most of the projects in this book, but machines with special stitching capabilities (like satin, zigzag, or blanket stitches) can help you fake those hand-stitched details like a pro.

Needles for Hand Sewing

Try as you might, you'll probably have to do a teensy amount of hand stitching before your quilt is ready for battle. Have a few all-purpose sewing needles (a.k.a. sharps) on hand for times when precision work is needed.

Quilting Frame

Nothing brings to mind quilting days of yore like ye olde quilting frame. While certainly not necessary, a frame is handy for making sure your quilt top, batting, and backing are flat before you start stitching the layers together. If you're handy with a saw and hammer, it's easy to find free instructions to make a quilting frame online, at a local fabric shop, or in back issues of quilting magazines at the library. For flattening small areas, an embroidery hoop will work nicely, especially the kind with a screw that tightens the outer loop.

Other Supplies

You probably already own the rest of the supplies you'll need to create the projects in this book: a collection of safety or curved basting pins (pins with a bend in the poker arm for reaching through thick quilt layers), appliqué pins (often with a flower-shaped head), quilting pins, a ruler, a fabric marker (either chalk or water-soluble ink), a tape measure, and an iron and ironing board.

Appliqué and Embroidery Supplies & Tools

If you're planning on doing any amount of appliqué or embroidery on your quilts, you'll need a few extra supplies and tools. All you really need for either technique is fabric, a needle, and thread, but a few additional items will make your life much easier.

While hand appliqué is certainly a noble pursuit, do yourself a favor and get some fusible web. Cheap and easy to use, fusible web is attached to the back side of the fabric before the appliqué design is cut out, essentially creating an iron-on appliqué shape. Although an unlikely ally, freezer paper deserves a definite spot in your supply closet, making those tiny appliqué seam allowances a breeze to master.

For embroidery designs, you'll need to gather the usual suspects: embroidery needles (a standard embroidery needle is fine for most materials), embroidery floss or perle cotton, and an embroidery hoop. Having graphite paper and a pencil on hand can make planning and transferring embroidery designs a snap.

Getting Started

Sure, you're excited, but you've still got a few more steps before the quilting extravaganza can commence. A little planning and prep work can help you make the most of your fabric, your time, and this book. Once this work is done, it's time to get the show on the road...

Cutting

Before you do anything else, make sure you wash your fabrics first, using the same settings that will be used when laundering the finished quilt. If your fabric gets super wrinkly in the wash, give it a quick pressing before you continue working. Then, and only then, should you begin cutting (seriously, we have spies).

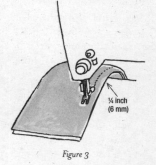

Figure 2

Whether you're using a ruler or templates to cut your fabric, you'll need to add about ¼ inch (6 mm) to each edge to accommodate the seam allowance (see figure 2), unless the instructions tell you not to or your appliqué shapes will not be turned under (in which case you can cut right next to the template). The instructions for each project tell you what you should do, so don't worry. You can cut all your pieces before you start or cut them along the way as needed; it's best to keep your pieces organized and even labeled if you're working with a complicated pattern.

Putting Things Together

You've embraced the sandwich concept, you've prepped and cut your fabrics, and you've got a master plan. You, my friend, are ready for action.

Sewing

Pheww...finally, on to the sewing! For all sewing tasks, you'll need to be mindful of the seam allowance—the distance between the seam and the cut edge of the fabric. Most of these sewing specific tasks involve the same process: pinning fabric pieces together with right sides facing, stitching along one edge, and then ironing the seams open or to one side. The position of the seam allowances, whether together on one side of the seam or pressed open, is important because the seam allowances do add bulk and stability. Most of the project instructions will tell you what to do. When this guidance isn't included, you can do what seems right for your quilt. The rules change a bit when it comes to appliqué and embroidery, but the basic sewing principles and tools are essentially the same.

The seam allowances will be listed in each project, although ¼ inch (6 mm) is pretty standard. If you're using a sewing machine, use the measurement lines on the throat plate as a guide while you feed the fabric along, as shown in figure 3. But don't worry: no rocket science is necessary!

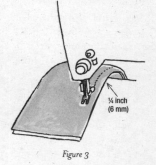

¼ inch (6 mm)

Figure 3

Piecing

While some quilts only involve appliqué or embroidery (in which the design elements are added directly on top of the quilt top), others involve some amount of piecing, a process used in most traditional quilts. During the piecing process, individual fabric pieces (hence the name) of the quilt top are sewn together into small units. The small units are then sewn together into larger units that

Continued →

QUILTING TOOL KIT

- Scissors and a rotary cutting system
- Needles for hand sewing
- Safety or basting pins
- Fabric chalk, marker, or pencil
- Iron and ironing board
- Sewing machine (optional)
- Appliqué (or other straight) pins
- Tape measure

are then sewn together again (depending on the quilt) to create the overall quilt design.

If you have an abundance of free time on your hands, or don't have access to a sewing machine, piecing by hand can be quite a satisfying endeavor, and some people find hand stitching to be relaxing. For the rest of us, a sewing machine is best, and, with a few shortcuts, the piecing process will fly by. Either way, the steps are quite simple.

1. Lay two pieces of fabric together with right sides facing.

2. Pin the pieces together along the edge where they will be joined.

3. Either by hand or using a machine, straight stitch along the side, about ¼ inch (6 mm) in from the raw edge of the fabric (figure 4).

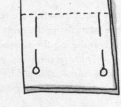

Figure 4

4. Lay the pieces out flat, and, using an iron, press the seams to one side (so they lie under a darker fabric, if possible) or open depending on the pattern instructions (figure 5).

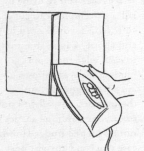

Figure 5

Cutting Corners

Chain Gang

Got a whole stack of piecing to do? Feed them through your sewing machine one right after another with just a little space between them. In the end, you'll have a length of pieces that you can cut apart and use individually.

Attaching a Border

Many quilts use borders to accentuate or frame the central design. Like piecing, you'll attach a border using the ¼-inch (6 mm) seam allowance and then iron the seams to one side. The steps are fairly similar for adding sashing—strips of fabric that run like a grid between individual quilt units—except that you'll be attaching fabric to both sides of the strip.

1. Following your pattern instructions, cut fabric strips in the correct dimensions for each border of the quilt.

2. Working on a short side of the quilt, pin the border strip to the quilt top with right sides together.

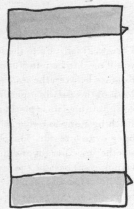

Figure 6

3. Stitch along the edge, using a ¼-inch (6 mm) seam allowance. Press the seam out toward the border (figure 6).

4. Repeat steps 2 and 3 for the quilt's other short side, then for the two long sides (figure 7).

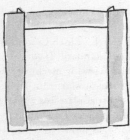

Figure 7

Appliqué

Maybe it's that fancy accent mark, but something about "appliqué" sounds a little intimidating. In reality, it couldn't be more basic: the term refers to a process in which a decorative shape is cut from one fabric and stitched on top of another fabric. Once you've cut out your fabric shape (using a pattern or your own design),

you'll pin or fuse the shape onto the quilt top and then attach it by machine or hand sewing using decorative stitches. Voilà!

Fusing Fabric

If fusible web isn't already your best friend, it will be soon. There are a number of types on the market, but the paper-backed kind is the best choice for quilting. Basically, fusible web keeps your appliqué shapes from moving while you stitch them in place. And it's super easy to use.

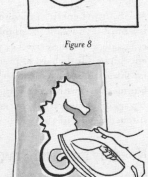

Figure 8

1. Trace the appliqué shape onto the paper backing, keeping in mind that the shape will need to be in reverse of the actual pattern (figure 8).

2. Cut out the tracing and, following the manufacturer's instructions, iron it onto the wrong side of the fabric with the paper side up (figure 9).

3. Using the tracing as a guide, cut out the appliqué shape (figure 10).

Figure 9

4. Peel off the paper backing (figure 11), place the appliqué on the quilt top, and iron it in place. Stitch around the edges of the shape following the pattern instructions.

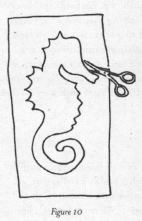

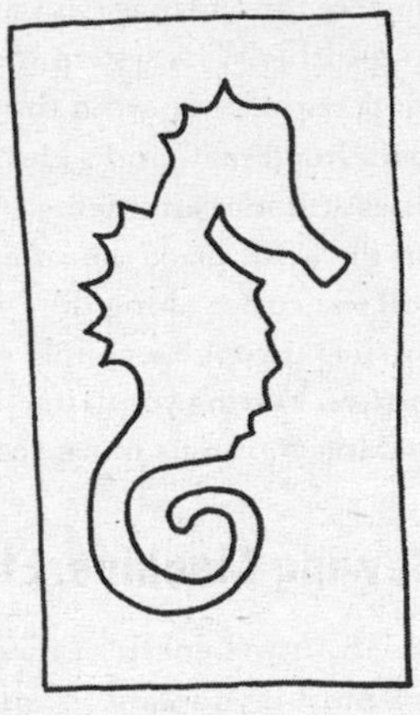

Figure 10   *Figure 11*

Turning the Edges

Many... appliquéd quilts... leave the appliqué edges raw for a lovely, if slightly imperfect, finish that frays gently with time and use. Others feature turned-under edges for a clean, professional look. You can spend your days pressing under those tiny seam allowances with a hot iron, and likely scorch the bejeezus out of your fingertips, or you can use freezer paper (see below). Some folks skip the pressing altogether and use the appliqué stitch, which turns under the seam allowance and stitches the shape in place at the same time.

Cutting Corners

Freezer Pleaser

As it turns out, plastic-coated freezer paper is great for avoiding freezer burn and iron burns. This handy kitchen product can help you turn under appliqué seam-allowance edges before you stitch your shape onto the quilt top. First, trace the appliqué shape onto the dull side of the freezer paper. Cut out the tracing, iron it onto the wrong side of the fabric with the shiny side down (it'll stick to the fabric), and then cut the fabric using the tracing as a guide, adding enough for a seam allowance around the edges. Use spray starch on the seam allowance,

clip along the curves, press the edges over onto the freezer paper, and remove the freezer paper. Presto, chango, your appliqué is ready to go.

Sewing the Edges

Once you've secured your appliqué in place—using fusible web or pins—you'll need to finish the edges with a little bit of stitching (see the Stitch Glossary). You can hand stitch the stitches indicated in the pattern instructions (we salute you) or just imitate them with your sewing machine; sadly, you won't be able to bluff them all.

If you're planning on leaving the edges raw, use a straight, running, or backstitch to topstitch along the sides of the shape about ¼ inch (6 mm) in from the edge. To avoid fraying, try a thicker stitch, like machine zigzag or satin stitch or hand-worked blanket stitch, around the outside of the shape to cover the raw edge of the fabric.

If you want to turn the appliqué edges under, you'll need to use the freezer paper method or the appliqué stitch, and you'll likely have to work by hand. To make sure your background fabric stays flat, try securing both your appliqué shape and the background fabric in an embroidery hoop.

Cutting Corners

AppliQuilting

Made-up words are the best, aren't they?...For this process, you'll stack all the quilt layers together (appliqué shape, quilt top, batting, and—depending on the instructions—backing) before you begin to attach the appliqué. The stitching that you do to attach the appliqué to the quilt top will also quilt the layers together in one simple step. You can use embroidery stitches in a similar manner, creating your design on the quilt top and quilting all of the layers together at the same time.

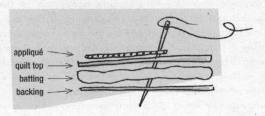

Embroidery

Since you can't use beads or buttons to embellish your quilt, given obvious choking hazards, embroidery is a great way to add safe texture and creative interest to your quilt. Compared to appliqué stitching, embroidery stitches are much more decorative in nature. In this process, you're not attaching fabric to fabric; you're simply making decorative stitches through a layer of fabric.

Transferring Embroidery Patterns

Before you get to the stitching, you'll need to do some prep work to transfer the embroidery pattern to your piece of fabric. For light fabrics that you can see through, simply lay the fabric over the design and trace it with a sharp pencil or fabric marker. For darker fabrics, you can transfer the design by using a light box, fabric transfer paper, or drawing the design freehand with a water-soluble fabric marker.

Creating the Stitches

There are whole books dedicated to the subject of embroidery stitches, but our handy Stitch Glossary lists all the stitches you'll need for the project in the next section, "Baby Quilt Projects". Thicker than standard sewing thread, embroidery floss or perle cotton are the best choices for this type of needlework, especially if you want all that hard-earned handwork to show up against a background (and trust us, you do!). Refer to the pattern instructions to see how many strands to use; some may ask you to split the embroidery floss down to two or three strands. To make sure your fabric doesn't pucker as you work, you might want to use an embroidery hoop.

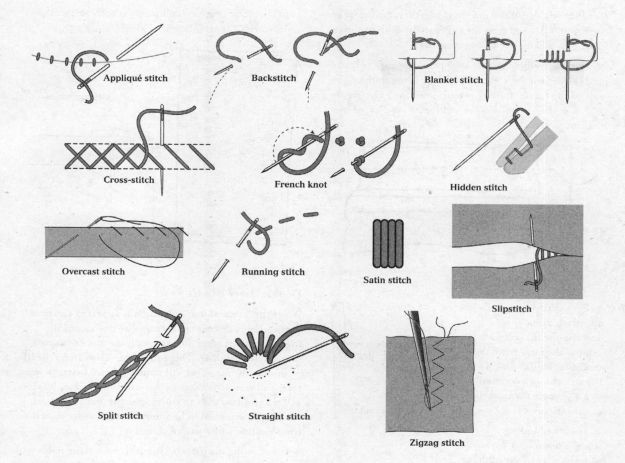

Appliqué stitch · **Backstitch** · **Blanket stitch**

Cross-stitch · **French knot** · **Hidden stitch**

Overcast stitch · **Running stitch** · **Satin stitch** · **Slipstitch**

Split stitch · **Straight stitch** · **Zigzag stitch**

Stitch Glossary

Many of the stitches used in appliqué can be used for embroidery, and vice versa. There are a few stitches—like the French knot—that have to be done by hand, but you'll be able to use a sewing machine for many of these.

Basting

Finished your lovingly crafted quilt top? Check. Got your batting and backing? Check. Now, for the moment of truth: putting it all together into one deliciously cozy quilt sandwich. Before you start sewing your layers together, you'll need to stack and baste the quilt top, batting, and backing to make sure they stay flat during the quilting process.

First, iron your layers so they're smooth and free of wrinkles. Lay them out on a flat surface in the following order, with each layer centered on top of the previous one: put your backing, right side down, on the bottom followed by the batting and then your quilt top, with the right side up (figure 12). Starting in the center of the quilt and working out, pin, or baste the layers together with safety or quilting pins spaced about 6 inches (15.2 cm) apart (figure 13). When you've pinned your way around the quilt, take a quick look at the quilt top and the backing to make sure all the layers are smooth and flat.

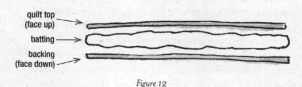

quilt top (face up)
batting
backing (face down)

Figure 12

Note: If you're finishing the edges using the quick-turn method (when you stitch your layers together while inside out and then flip them right side out instead of binding the edges), you'll need to stack your layers in a different order before you baste them. Take a look at "Quick Turning a Quilt" for more information.

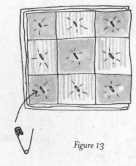

Figure 13

Quilting

This part of the assembly process is what makes a quilt a quilt. Once your quilt top, batting, and backing have been stacked and basted, your next step is to stitch through the quilt sandwich to connect all the layers and secure the batting in the middle. Sometimes quilt stitching (merely called quilting by those in the know) can be as simple as a grid of straight lines. Other times, the quilt stitching itself is a design element.

As with many other steps in quilt making, quilting can be done by hand or machine, and each method has its own benefits. Whether you're working by machine or by hand, start by planning your stitch pattern. If you're doing something really complicated, you might consider drawing out the pattern on your quilt top with chalk or a water-soluble fabric marker. You have several options when it comes to quilting patterns, and the projects in this book use a wide array of styles.

Straight-stitch Quilting

Workable by hand and especially by machine (our favorite), straight-stitch quilting is probably the most basic type; it's the same type of stitch you used in piecing the quilt and other standard sewing tasks. If you're straight stitching by hand (also called a running stitch), keep your stitches short and even. For a clean finish, pull your knots through so they are hidden in the batting. On your machine, you might need to loosen the needle tension and lengthen the stitch to accommodate the thick layers. Since it can sometimes be difficult to handle all those thick layers, especially if your quilt sandwich has lots of, er…condiments, rolling up the edges can help you access the whole quilt in sections (figure 14).

Figure 13

Using a straight stitch, you have some further options. Stitch in the ditch is a process that involves stitching along the seam lines of the quilt top's pieced sections, hiding your quilting stitches in the piecing seams.

You can also use the straight stitch to outline various design elements—such as appliqué or pieced shapes—to accentuate those lovingly crafted details.

For a classic geometric finish, straight stitch parallel lines across the quilt top using a handy quilt bar attachment or make a statement by creating decorative shapes, like circles or swirls, to oppose the straight lines of the quilt top.

Feeling extra creative and ambitious? Try creating shapes to go along with the theme of your quilt…

Free-Motion Quilting

A perfect approach for independent types, free-motion quilting means you have complete control of the quilting stitch pattern, giving your project oodles of texture and even more handsome appeal (if that's possible). For free-motion quilting on the machine, a darning foot—which has a circular opening for the needle to pass through—can help. You'll also need to disengage the automatic feed mechanism (called feed dogs in some machine manuals); in this method, you control the movement of the fabric, and thus the shape of the stitch, by using two hands to spread the fabric out flat under the needle (figure 15). Guide the fabric to create any shape you like: free-form clouds, teensy circles, or winding doodles.

Figure 15

Tying

Here's a technique that speaks to the shortcut lover in us all, and it's okay to love shortcuts. Instead of stitching across the quilt, tying involves connecting the quilt layers with a few stitches placed in a grid and tied, with the knots on the top of the quilt. You can use embroidery floss, perle cotton, or yarn for this process, depending on the look you're going for. The end result has a charming, folksy feel that is undeniably handmade.

1. Use a ruler and chalk to mark a grid on your basted quilt top—you'll place your stitches where the lines intersect—or place the ties randomly, as long as they're a suitable distance apart. Check your batting for spacing suggestions, but 2 to 6 inches (5 to 15.2 cm) apart should be enough.

2. Thread a sharp hand-sewing needle with yarn (or whatever material you're using).

3. Stitch straight down through the quilt layers and then back up, making sure the layers don't shift as you work.

4. Tie the yarn tails in a knot—a square knot works well (figure 16)—and then trim them to ¾ to 1 inch (1.9 to 2.5 cm) long. Repeat steps 3 and 4 for each tie.

Figure 16

Cutting Corners

Tying the Knots

If you're creating a lot of ties on your quilt top, use a single long piece of floss to create the stitches in a row instead of stitching each tie individually. Create a stitch at each intersection across the row, leaving extra floss between each stitch. Then cut the floss at the midpoint between each stitch and use the tails to tie knots at each point.

Finishing Up

By this point in the process, you've probably got something that actually looks like a quilt (bravo!). But no premature flaunting: you've got a few more steps before your project is ready for its big debut.

Continued ➔

Binding

There's no clear way to fit this step into our nifty sandwich metaphor—darn it—but the results might lead to an exotic culinary invention. In quilting, it's a little less exciting; binding refers to the process of covering the edges of the quilt with a strip of either single- or double-layered fabric so you no longer see the individual quilt layers. When you've finished the binding, your work is done...although you'll need to follow up with a requisite amount of gloating. That process is easy: show your creation off to anyone who'll look!

Making Your Own Binding

You can buy premade binding at the fabric store—although your color and width options might be limited—or you can make your own, in which case you'll have plenty of fabrics and widths to choose from. Some designers make a separate length of binding for each edge, although the majority make one very long length of binding and attach it around all of the edges in one fell swoop. The instructions will tell you to cut your binding strips either lengthwise, crossgrain, or on the bias—diagonally across the length of the fabric (figure 17). Bias-cut binding strips have a little more stretch to them, but they do require more fabric.

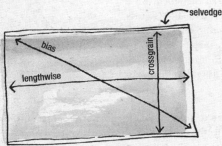

Figure 17

1. To figure out how long your strip will need to be, add the lengths of the top, bottom, left, and right edges of the quilt, plus a few inches extra.

2. Once you've calculated the length you need, cut your strips following the recommended width in the pattern instructions.

3. To connect the strips together, you have two options. For the first method, pin and stitch the short ends together, with right sides facing, until you have one long strip, then press the seams open (figure 18).

For the second method, pin the short ends together at a right angle, with right sides facing, and stitch diagonally across the corner (figure 19). Trim the seam allowance and press the seams open.

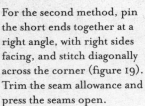

Figure 18

Single Binding with Mitered Corners

The project instructions will tell you whether to use single-fold or double-fold binding, but feel free to pick the method that works best for you. If you're like the majority of quilters, you'll probably make one strip of binding that's long enough to wrap around the entire quilt. When you reach a corner on the quilt, you need a special way to wrap the binding so that it looks neat and lies flat. In these steps, we'll cover mitered corners—which create a clean diagonal pleat in the binding at each corner—but butted corners might be even easier if you're new to working with binding.

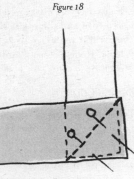

Figure 19

1. Once you've quilted the layers together, lay the quilt completely flat and trim the edges so the quilt top, batting, and backing are all the same size.

2. Starting midway on one edge or near a corner, pin and then stitch the right side of the batting to the right side of the fabric, folding over the starting edge (figure 20). Use the seam allowance width that's indicated in the instructions.

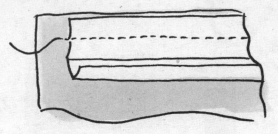

Figure 20

3. Stop stitching as you approach the corner, and clip the threads to remove the quilt from the machine. Fold the binding straight up over itself so a 45° angle forms at the corner (figure 21).

4. Fold the binding straight down so it's even with the edge of the quilt, and then continue pinning and stitching the binding in place (figure 22). Continue working your way around the quilt, using the same process for the rest of the corners.

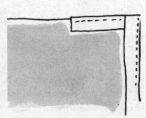

Figure 21

5. As you near your starting point, stitch your binding strip over the folded-over starting edge of the binding strip. There's no need to fold back the raw edge at the very end of the binding strip—it'll soon be hidden.

6. Fold the binding strip over the edges—but not too tightly—to the back of the quilt. Turn under the raw edge just enough to cover the seam that you just stitched. (This edge will already be folded to the wrong side if you're using purchased binding, and you already have a folded edge if you're using double-fold binding.) Place the prepared edge just barely over the seam line that attached the binding, and pin it down along each edge. Create diagonal folds at each corner and then pin the corners in place.

7. Use a slipstitch by hand or stitch in the ditch—working from the top of the quilt—using your machine to attach the binding to the back of the quilt (figure 23).

Figure 22

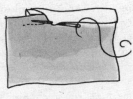

Figure 23

Butted Corners

Maybe butted corners aren't quite as clean and neat as mitered corners, but those quilt corners are probably going to end up covered... anyway, right?

1. Working one edge at a time (instead of a continuous strip), pin and then stitch binding along the two short edges on the right side of the quilt.

2. Fold the binding to the back, tuck under the raw edge if the binding is single fold, and then stitch it down on the back using the slipstitch or stitching in the ditch of the seam you just created (figure 24).

3. Measure and then cut the length you'll need for the long edges of the quilt, adding a little extra to each end, and attach binding to the edges as you did with the short edges.

4. Turn under the extra binding at each end and use a slipstitch to secure the ends closed (figure 25).

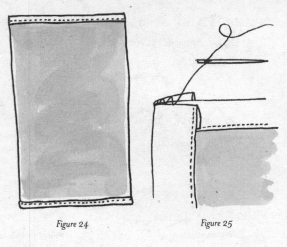

Figure 24   *Figure 25*

Double-layer Binding

While this method may only initially appeal to certain overachievers among us (ahem, we're not mentioning names), the steps are essentially the same as using a single-layer binding. This process can also extend the life of your quilt; the edges will stand up much better to wear, tear, and teething. Projects that use double-layer binding will tell you how wide to cut your strips, but in general, your strips will need to be about six times wider than the final binding width you're planning.

1. Following the pattern instructions, cut the strips and then sew them together.

2. Fold the binding strip in half lengthwise with wrong sides together and then pin it to the right side of the quilt top, lining up the raw edges (figure 26).

3. Stitch the binding in place using the recommended seam allowance, mitering the corners (although you can also use this technique with buttet corners) as you work around the quilt.

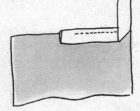

Figure 26

4. Fold the binding to the back of the quilt, and then pin and stitch it in place. Since the fabric has been folded in half, you don't have to worry about turning under any raw edges (figure 27).

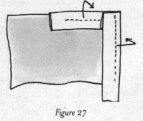

Figure 27

Cutting Corners

In a Bind

If you're feeling plucky, you could try binding both sides of the quilt at the same time. To do this, press under the seam allowance on both sides of your binding strip. Fold the strip over the edges of the quilt, and then pin and topstitch along the edge, making sure you stitch through all the layers, stopping a few inches (cm) short of where you started attaching the binding. Fold under the loose end of the binding strip, and pin it over your starting point. Continue stitching to the end of your binding strip and then a little beyond that, just to be safe.

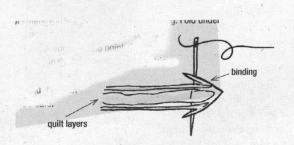

Quick Turning a Quilt

Okay, the secret's out on this super handy quilting shortcut. This process allows you to skip binding altogether, and you're left with edges that are clean, if not quite as crisp as bound edges. This technique works particularly well if you plan on tying your quilt.

1. Stack your quilt by placing the batting on the bottom followed by the backing, with right side up, and the quilt top, centered with the right side down (figure 28).

2. Pin the layers together along the edges, placing a few pins in the middle of the quilt to keep the layers smooth.

3. Stitch almost all the way around the outside edge of the quilt, using a ½-inch (1.3 cm) seam allowance. Leave about 10 inches (25.4 cm) unstitched; you'll use this opening to turn the quilt through (figure 29). If your quilt is especially large or thick, you may need a bigger opening.

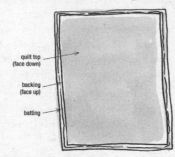

quilt top (face down)

backing (face up)

batting

Figure 28

10 inches (25.4 cm)

Figure 29

4. Trim along the edges so all three layers are the same size, and cut across the corners to decrease bulk. Turn the quilt right side out and hand stitch the opening closed (figure 20).

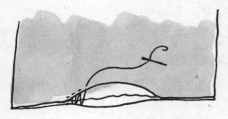

Figure 30

5. Baste the quilt using pins, and then quilt, or tie, the layers.

Hanging

Creating a quilt wall hanging—an art quilt of sorts—opens up a whole other world of design possibilities.

If your quilt has heavy interfacing or backing, add buttons and a simple strand of elastic to create a hanger.

If your quilt is a little longer, consider adding a sleeve for a dowel rod. Cut a strip of fabric that's about 4 inches (10.2 cm) wide and almost as long as your quilt's width. Turn and stitch under the short raw edges, and then pin and stitch the long edges together with right sides facing (figure 31). Turn the sleeve right side out and place it seam side down on the backing. Pin and hand stitch the sleeve in place along the top and bottom edges (figure 32). The sleeve will accommodate most dowel rods, or slide ribbon through the sleeve for an easy transition to a superhero cape.

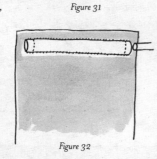

Figure 31

Figure 32

—From *Quilts, Baby!*

BABY QUILT PROJECTS

Linda Kopp

Rock-a-Bye, Baby!

When you think of a baby quilt, what comes to mind: happy little rainbows, dancing cherubs, smiling clowns—all rendered in pastels? Perhaps plump cavorting puppies and simpering kittens with a ghastly eye-to-face ratio? Or heaven forbid, the dreaded licensed cartoon character? Frankly, we think all of those are kind of scary, especially the clowns. And we feel the baby in your life deserves something cooler...way cooler....

A little iffy with the sewing machine? Baby quilts make the perfect starter projects for new quilters, but they're also the ideal mini-canvas for seasoned pros who want to add oodles of detail to their creations. If you're new to quilting or just need a refresher on some of the techniques, you'll find in depth instructions in the previous "Quilting Basics" section, in many cases accompanied with step-by-step illustrations.

We realize quilting is a methodical, time-honored tradition, but we also recognize that not everyone has vast amounts of leisure time. So we challenged the designers to come up with knock-your-socks-off quilts that could be made pretty much in a weekend. That being said, many of the quilts feature clever, bold designs, and shortcuts, snippets, and tidbits that will help speed you on your way and make the most of your time. Variation ideas provide the perfect inspiration for customizing the designs to your tastes (we mean baby's tastes, of course) or for creating a quilt design that's all your own imagining.

A handmade quilt is the perfect gift for a baby. It's personal and will be used and cherished long after most other gifts are outgrown. There's really nothing quite like being wrapped up in or tucked beneath a handmade quilt, especially when that quilt is über chic!

Planning

The designs in this section are meant to supply inspiration. You can use the designs as they are presented, make small adjustments to suit your taste, or use one of these quilts as a springboard for your own imaginative design. Whatever your approach may be, it's best to plan it out well in advance. Use a notepad to jot down a list of things that you'll have to go to the fabric store for, to scribble out yardage calculations or adjustments (yuck!), and to draw the design for your next quilt when inspiration strikes (probably soon!).

Sizing Things Up

Unless they're intended to be art quilts or wall hangings, most of the quilts measure between 36 x 48 inches (91.4 x 121.9 cm) and 48 x 60 inches (121.9 x 152.4 cm) to fit the standard crib size, which is 28 inches (71.1 cm) wide by 52 inches (132.1 cm) long. A rectangle seems like the most obvious choice, but you can make your quilt any size or shape. A larger quilt might make sense if the babushka is a little older, whereas a smaller quilt might be better if you're using it as a throw or for traveling purposes, where it will no doubt (hint, hint) have a larger pool of potential admirers. Any of the quilts in this book can be made larger or smaller; just enlarge the templates and measurements as you see fit.

Using Quilting Charts and Templates

Along with the absolutely splendid designs... you'll find a number of highly useful cutting charts and whole quilt templates. Cutting charts are just that: charts that tell you how big or small to cut your various fabrics. You'll find them right with the quilt instructions along with the whole quilt templates—which serve as patterns for cutting your fabric.

To use the whole quilt templates and the appliqué and embroidery patterns, enlarge what you need on a photocopier. Then for whole quilt templates or appliqué patterns, cut out the paper piece (or pieces) and trace the shapes onto fabric with a fabric marker, or pin the template (right side up) to the fabric (also right side up) to use as a guide while you cut. For embroidery patterns, transfer the design lines to your fabric for easy, follow-the-lines stitching.

Life Savers

A bedsheet or printed fabric that features a colorful repeating pattern, such as the circles on the purchased duvet cover used in this project, is an ideal starting point for a quilt top. Just cut around the motif to make a square, and use that as the center of each block. You can even substitute or add circles or motifs from other fabrics.

Fabric

All fabric is cotton: 44 inches (111.8 cm) wide

Quilt Top

Bedsheet, duvet cover, or yardage printed with a repeating motif in a variety of sizes

¼ yard (0.2 m) each of 27 different fabrics, 70 to 80% solids and 20 to 30 % prints, for the pieced strips: 8 blues, 8 greens, 4 oranges, 2 pinks, 3 reds, and 2 yellows

Backing

1½ yards (1.4 m) of a coordinating yellow-and-white print

Binding

¼ yard (0.2 m) of a coordinating blue print

Notions & Such

Quilting Tool Kit (see "Quilting Basics")

Tracing paper or clear template material

Low-loft cotton batting

All-purpose cotton-wrapped white sewing thread

White machine-quilting thread

Continued →

Finished Size

36 x 45 inches (91.4 x 114.3 cm)

Instructions

All of the seam allowances are ¼ inch (6 mm) wide.

Get Scrappy

1. Cut the bedsheet, duvet cover, or yardage into 20 squares that are all centered around a circle for other motif). Include a border beyond the motif of at least ¼ inch (6 mm) for a seam allowance (see figure 1). Pck motifs of different dimensions so that you have center squares in several sizes. Malka used circles with diameters of 2, 3½, 4, and 6¼ inches (5, 8.9, 10.2, and 15.9 cm).

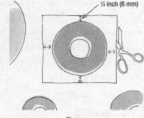

¼ inch (6 mm)

Figure 1

2. Cut 12-inch-long (30.5 cm) strips freehand from the 27 lengths of fabric you chose for piecing. Let the width of these strips range from 1 to 5 inches (2.5 to 12.7 cm) wide.

Building Blocks

3. Sew a lengthwise edge of a fabric strip to an edge of a center square with right sides together. Use the white sewing thread for all of the piecing and for joining the blocks together in later steps. Press the seam allowances to one side, and trim off the excess length of the strip beyond the seam line. Sew a second strip perpendicular to the first strip, and also trim it off at the end of the seam.

4. Add two more strips, one at a time, to complete the square.

5. Continue adding strips until you have a block that measures 9½ inches (24.1 cm) square. You don't need to measure the block, but if you'd like reassurance, cut a 9½-inch (24.1 cm) square from the tracing paper or template material, and lay it on top of the block to check the size. If the block is too large, use the tracing paper as a pattern piece: shift the block around underneath this pattern piece until you like the composition of your block, and then trim off the excess fabric so that the block is the same size as the paper. Make 19 more blocks.

Sew It Up

6. Refer to the whole quilt illustration (see figure 2) throughout the rest of these instructions. Join four blocks to make an 18½-inch (47 cm) square. As you assemble the blocks, press the seam allowances together and toward one side. If your four-patch is too small, add a strip of fabric along the edge that comes up short. If it's too big, use a ruler and rotary cutter to trim it to size.

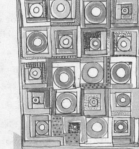

Figure 2

7. Assemble more blocks. When you have an eight-patch, it needs to measure 18½ x 36½-inches (47 x 92.7 cm). Your 16-block piece should be 36⅞ inches (92.7 cm) square. Make a row with the last blocks, and join it to the 16-patch to finish the top.

8. Stack and baste the quilt layers together.

9. Switch to the white quilting thread, and quilt a spiral pattern inside a colored circle in the center of a 9½-inch (24.1 cm) block. Quilt the outside edge of the same circle, and then stitch the surrounding strips in concentric lines spaced ¼ inch (6 mm) apart. Quilt each circle block independently, always starting in the center of the circle.

It's a Wrap

10. Bind the quilt with your desired method. Malka started with 1½-inch-wide (3.8 cm) strips to make a single-fold binding using ¼-inch (6 mm) seam allowances and mitered corners.

Intersection

Laura Ducommun

Asymmetrical lines and offset fabric strips combine to create a simple, yet striking design. Perfect angles aren't important in this quilt. Let the simple pieced strips set the pattern and then follow the seams outward.

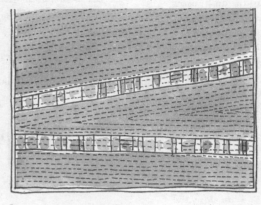

FABRIC

All fabric is cotton, 44 inches (111.8 cm) wide.

QUILT TOP

2 yards (1.8 m) of pink fabric

10 to 15 fat quarters or fabric pieces at least 3 inches (7.6 cm) wide: pink, purple, and red, plus a few blues, browns, and multicolored prints

BACKING

2 yards (1.8 m) of a large print

BINDING

⅜ yard (0.4 m) of red-and-white print

NOTIONS & SUCH

Quilting Tool Kit (see "Quilting Basics")

Low-loft batting

Water-soluble fabric pen or fabric chalk pencil

All-purpose cotton-wrapped white sewing thread

White cotton quilting thread

FINISHED SIZE

42 x 50 inches (106.7 x 127 cm)

INSTRUCTIONS

All of the seam allowances are ¼ inch (6 mm) wide.

Get Scrappy

1. Refer to the whole quilt template (see figure 1) throughout these instructions. Cut the fat quarters or fabric scraps to different lengths and at least 3 inches (7.6 cm) wide. You can work with smaller pieces: simply sew them together to create the size you want.

Figure 1

2. Sew the pieces together by chaining them through your sewing machine. Keep the fabric order random. Continue joining the pieces until you have two long strips. Trim the edges so that both are 2½ x 45 inches (6.4 x 114.3 cm).

3. Cut the top fabric so it's 42 x 50 inches (106.7 x 127 cm). Now cut it into three pieces with diagonal lines. Don't worry if the angles aren't exactly as shown in figure 1.

Sew It Up

4. Sew the multi-fabric strips between the three large pieces. The strips will make the top larger, so again trim it to 42 x 50 inches (106.7 x 127 cm).

5. Stack and baste the quilt layers together.

6. Draw the first quilt line on the pink fabric above the top pieced strip. Use the water-soluble fabric pen, and follow the angle of the seam line. Continue drawing parallel lines ¾ inch (1.9 cm) apart all the way to the top of the quilt. Do the same on the bottom of the quilt. In the middle area (between the two multi-fabric strips), draw the lines parallel to both seam lines, and work your way in so that the lines meet somewhere in the middle to create angled points (see figure 2).

7. Quilt the layers together using the white quilting thread. Don't worry about each line being perfectly straight or exactly ¾ inch (1.9 cm) apart. Follow your drawn lines, and have fun.

Figure 2

It's a Wrap

8. Bind your quilt with your desired method. Laura cut a 2-inch-wide (5 cm) strip and used the double-fold binding technique with mitered corners.

Monkey Business

Laurraine Yuyama

The monkey tummy, eye, and nose patch appliqués are sewn on after the quilt has been assembled in a process dubbed appliquilting. The stitching you do to attach the shapes to the quilt top will also quilt the layers together in one simple step.

SNIPPET
Embrace the opportunity to cut fabric like you would draw a freehand line. You'll be amazed by how well you can cut a straight line without a ruler, using only a rotary cutter and self-healing mat.

Monkey: 8¾ inches (22.2 cm) tall

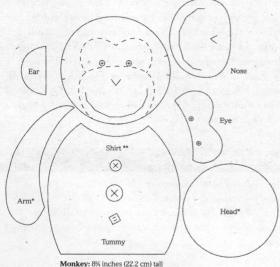

Fabric

All of the fabric is 44 inches (111.8 cm) wide

Quilt Top

10½ x 12-inch (26.7 x 30.5 cm) pieces of 9 cotton prints for the monkey blocks

3½ x 12-inch (8.9 x 30.5 cm) pieces of 6 cotton prints for the short sashes

⅛ yard (0.1 m) of 6 cotton prints for the inner borders

½ yard (0.5 m) of 4 cotton prints for the outer borders and sashes

Appliqués

6 x 12-inch (15.2 x 30.5 cm) pieces of 8 cotton prints for the shirts

½ yard (0.5 m) of brown corduroy for the monkeys

½ yard (0.5 m) of cream cotton print for the ears, faces, and tummies

Backing

2⅜ yards (2.1 m) of brown striped fabric

Notions & Such

Quilting Tool Kit (see "Quilting Basics")

Appliqué and quilting patterns

Pattern transfer materials and tools

Felt scraps: black for the eyes and a variety of colors for 24 buttons

Single-hole paper punch

Pinking shears (optional)

Chopstick or knitting needle

Embroidery needle

High-loft polyester batting

All-purpose cotton-wrapped sewing thread: dark brown, tan, and colors matched to the felt and shirts

Skein each of embroidery floss*: black, brown, and light gray

*Use six strands when embroidering.

Finished Size

49 x 54 inches (124.5 x 137.2 cm) after washing

Border Cutting Chart

Name of piece	Quantity to cut	Size
Outer border	(2)	55" x 7½" (139.7 x 19 cm)
		7½" x 46½" (19 x 118.1 cm)
Inner border	(2)	37½" x 2¾" (95.3 x 7 cm)
		2¾" x 46½" (7 x 118.1 cm)
Sash	(6)	3½" x 12" (8.9 x 30.5 cm)
		37½" x 3½" (95.3 x 8.9 cm)

Appliqué Cutting Chart

Name of piece	Fabric	Quantity to cut
Shirt	8 prints	(16)
	Brown corduroy	(1)
Arm	Brown corduroy	(9)
		Flip and cut (9) more
Head	Brown corduroy	(9)
Ear	Brown corduroy	(18)
	Cream print	(18)
Tummy patch	Cream print	(2)
Nose patch	Cream print	(18)
Eye patch	Cream print	(18)
Eye	Black felt	(18)

Instructions

All of the seam allowances are ¼ inch (6 mm) wide unless otherwise noted.

Get Scrappy

1. Refer to the whole quilt template (see figure 1) throughout these instructions. Cut all of the pieces according to the border cutting chart. Some strips are longer than the fabric yardage, so sew together shorter pieces to create the longer borders.

Figure 1

Way to Appliqué!

2. Enlarge the appliqué patterns, and cut the fabric shapes as listed in the appliqué cutting chart. As you cut the shapes from corduroy, rotate the templates so that the fabric's surface texture travels in different directions. Use the hole punch to cut the eyes.

3. Arrange the pieces for the eye patch, nose patch, and shirt in matched pairs. Match each corduroy ear with a cream-colored one. Sew the pairs together wrong side out, leaving open the tops and bottoms of the shirts and the bottoms of the eye patches and ears. Cut a slit in one side of each nose and tummy patch (see figure 2). Using the chopstick or knitting needle, turn the pieces right side out. Press them.

Figure 2

4. Machine-embroider the nose and mouth on every nose appliqué, using thin, narrow satin stitches and the dark brown thread.

5. Attach the felt eyes to the eye patches with a horizontal straight stitch using the black embroidery floss and a vertical stitch with the light gray embroidery floss.

Building Blocks

6. Pin a monkey head, shirt, and arms on each block, tilting the heads in different directions. One block, which will be the center of the quilt, will feature a shirtless monkey. Use the corduroy body instead, and follow the same procedure for attaching the appliqués.

7. Lift a shirt away from the arms on one of the blocks. Sew along the outer edges of the arms using brown thread and dense, wide satin stitches. Fold in both sides of an ear so that the cream-colored print peeks out from the interior (see figure 3). Fold another ear, and pin both under the head at different angles. Replace the shirt with the top edge tucked under the head. Sew around the head with the same stitch and thread. Sew the appliqués to the rest of the blocks.

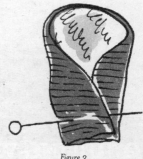

Figure 3

8. Cut 24 felt buttons in a variety of shapes. Tack three to each shirt with the brown embroidery floss. Sew around the edge of each button with straight stitches and matching thread.

9. Piece three monkey blocks, side by side, with a short sash between each one. Make two more rows of monkey blocks and short sashes. Sew the rows together with a longer sash between each one.

Continued ➔

293
Craft Wisdom & Know-How

10. Sew the shorter inner border strips to the top and bottom. Next, add a longer inner border to each side. Sew the shorter outer borders to the sides. Finally, add the longer outer borders to the top and bottom.

11. Cut and sew the backing to a suitable shape and size.

12. Following the quick-turn method, place the backing face up on top of the batting and center the quilt top facedown on top. Pin and sew around the edge using a ½-inch (1.3 cm) seam allowance and leaving a 10-inch (25.4 cm) opening at the bottom. Cut off the excess batting and backing, and trim across the corners. Turn the quilt right side out. Use the chopstick to punch out the corners, and hand sew the opening closed with appliqué stitches.

Sew It Up

13. Baste the layers together, and machine quilt along all of the seam lines using the tan thread in the needle and brown thread in the bobbin.

14. Set the sewing machine for blanket stitches, and sew down the sides of the shirts using a different color thread for each one. Switch to dark brown thread and straight stitches, and sew closely around the outside edges of the arms and the heads.

15. Pin the tummy, eye, and nose patches to the monkeys, tilting the faces to match the angle of the ears. Sew around them with tan thread and machine blanket stitches. Don't sew over the felt eyes.

16. Enlarge the quilting templates, and make paper templates. Trace the shapes on the quilt top: bananas on one outer border, circles on another, numbers on a third, and flowers on the fourth. Quilt the shapes with matching thread.

Inspire Me!

If monkeys just don't do it for you, use the same design idea to create a quilt chock full-o-bunnies.

QUILTING WITH WOOL

Nathalie Mornu

Why Wool?

Ready to take your quilting to the next level? It's time to throw wool fabrics into the mix. They've got texture, color, sophistication. Chameleon-like, raw wool can be turned into all types of cloth—and whether they're heavy or lightweight, smooth or textured, soft or stiff, these fabrics always look rich, crisp, and appealing.

You might not immediately think to quilt with wool, but it's clear why this warm, fuzzy material is an emerging trend with quilters, sewers, and crafters. Its extra weight makes any project especially cozy; wools come in great patterns and solids in lustrous, divine hues; you can sew them to cottons, silks, and other fabrics without

a bit of fuss; and, oh, their tactile appeal! Just imagine the contrast of a fuzzy boiled wool quilt bound with cool satin, or a smooth wool suiting embellished with nubby wool appliqués…

Wool has been the fiber of choice of countless cultures for thousands of years. You sensible types can already sing its praises: entirely renewable and natural, water-repellent, wrinkle- and fade-resistant, warm in cold temperatures and cool in warm weather. (Some wools are even machine washable!) So flip through these pages to admire all the great quilted projects you can make. Now pick one, gather some wool, and take your quilting up a notch. You'll wonder why you didn't start quilting with wool sooner.

Wool Fabrics

The first step in making wool fabrics involves gathering fleece from sheep or lambs, or from Angora rabbits, alpaca, camels, and other animals, too. Though you can feel free to shear your favorite sheep, it's far simpler to gather your wool fabrics from a fabric store….

For the projects in this section, you don't have to start with a big piece of fabric; you can make quilt block units from scraps of repurposed fabric. You can even recycle old sweaters, jackets, blankets, scarves, and just about anything else in your "I-dunno-what-to-do-with-this-but-it's-too-cool-to-throw-away" stash. Whether you purchase or repurpose your fabric, make note of the care requirements on the end of the fabric bolt or the care labels on the garments.

There are two basic types of wool fabrics, both suitable choices for quilt making. Woolens are made from loosely spun short fibers, so they tend to be soft with a fuzzy texture and have little or no sheen. Worsteds have a smoother surface because they're made of longer fibers that are combed and straightened before spinning. They often have gloss or shine to their surfaces, and are lighter weight than woolens. The following is a list of suggested wool fabrics, but also consider taking apart an old wool coat or cut up a blanket to repurpose the yardage.

Boiled wool is a soft, compact, knit wool that's been shrunk and felted. It's a favorite coat and jacket fabric and very suited to quilt making.

Bouclé has loops or curls on one or both sides. It can be light- or heavyweight and soft or crisp. It's very versatile and often used in dresses, suits, and jackets.

Camel's hair is a wool-like hair fiber from—duh—the camel. It's soft and lustrous and ranges in color from light tan to dark brown.

Cashmere is a very soft fiber that comes from the hair of the Kashmir goat. Cut up an old cashmere sweater and make yourself a luxurious little head pillow.

Crepe is similar to suiting, but with a matte, crinkled surface that's usually created by weaving hard-twist yarns.

Double-cloth is reversible, so that each side might differ (or not) in weave, color, yarn, and pattern. Some double cloth can actually be cut apart into two separate layers.

Fashion fabrics include the woolens and worsted wools that are available in a wide array of weights, weaves, and patterns. Some popular fashion fabrics that quilt beautifully include **challis**, which has a printed or woven pattern; **gabardine**, which has a high sheen; **tartan**, that highly recognizable plaid fabric; and **jersey**, a knit wool fabric. Other popular and perfectly suitable wool fabrics include **herringbone** (a chevron pattern), glen plaid (a small, even check design), **houndstooth** (a four-pointed star check pattern), and **jacquard** (which includes any number of highly complex woven patterns).

Felt is not a woven fabric; instead, it's a mat of fibers bonded together through the application of heat, moisture, and pressure. It comes in many different weights and colors. Wool felt has a more substantial feel to it than the cheap synthetic felts you'll find in craft stores.

If you have an old sweater or a piece of knitted wool

that isn't quite dense or strong enough to use as a fabric, you can turn it into felt by compressing the fibers. It's as easy as tossing it into a washing machine. You've probably already felted a wool sweater by accident, in which case you know what to do! (But in case you want instructions on felting, see "Getting Started").

Flannel is a soft, often lightweight fabric that's been napped to create a fuzzy surface on one or both sides. Flannel is perfect for baby quilts and other lightweight blankets.

Melton is a dense fabric with a short **nap** (which gives a fabric different shades from different angles). It's not glossy, but it's very durable and is often used to make coats, jackets, and blankets.

Merino is one of the softest wools, although it's not as soft as cashmere.

Mohair is made with the long-lustrous fibers of the Angora goat. It's very strong and somewhat spongy and is often blended with other wools to make jackets and scarves.

Overdyed wool is any wool that's been dyed with several different colors of dye (from the same family), one at a time, for a subtle saturation of deep, rich colors. It's gorgeous…

Recycled or repurposed wools are those that you take from an existing garment or existing item…. You can obtain substantial pieces of fabric when you cut apart an old coat or an oversized sweater. Just cut the items along the seams and throw the strips of seams away. If the wool ravels, run a zigzag stitch along the cut edges. Use the cut-apart item just as you would fabric yardage.

Suiting refers to a variety of worsted wools that are used to make suits. They're medium- to heavyweight with a smooth surface and are easy to work with. Suiting is a fairly generic term that includes many weaves, textures, and fibers. The most common suiting has a gray base color with different color striped patterns; however, you'll also find other base colors, such as brown and black.

Tweed is a medium- to heavyweight woolen with a textured hand and mottled color due to the combination of different color yarns. It's typically used to make suits and coats. **Donegal tweed** is known for its thick slubs of colored yarns. **Harris tweed**, on the other hand, has a very soft feel.

Drawn and Quartered

Typically, if you purchase a ¼ yard (22.8 cm) of fabric, you'll get a piece 9 inches (23 cm) long by the width of the fabric, which isn't always wide enough for quilt shapes. So some quilt shops precut 1 yard (91.4 cm) of fabric into four fat quarters, which they sell individually. Each measures half the width and length of the yard, approximately 18 x 22 inches (45.5 x 56 cm). Quilt shops often bundle complementary colors and prints into fat quarter collections.

Getting Started

Whether you're making an entire quilt or a smaller quilted novelty, the techniques will be similar. Not every technique is used in every project, but the following techniques provide a basic understanding of the quilting craft.

Prep Work

Before cutting, prepare your fabrics, trims, and batting. If you're using cotton backing or other cotton fabrics, machine wash and dry them, and press to remove wrinkles. If you're using silk or satin, dry-clean or hand wash them in cold water with mild detergent. It's also a good idea to hand wash trims in cold water with mild soap to preshrink them and remove excess dyes. If you're using batting, note the manufacturer's recommendations

because some batting should be washed and dried before it is used.

Wool, on the other hand, should be hand washed in cold water and mild detergent, or machine washed in the delicate cycle. Press the wool by setting the iron to the wool setting and fill the reservoir with distilled water. Wool requires more steam than heat. Press with an up and down motion (instead of the gliding motion of ironing) to avoid stretching or distorting the fabric shape. The iron can cause surface shine, so use a press cloth between the iron and the fabric. If you inadvertently cause fabric shine from the iron, avoid a press mess by sponging the fabric surface with a clean cloth and white vinegar. Rinse out the vinegar.

Upcycled Fabric

Press the garment, blanket, or whatever you're cutting apart to remove wrinkles that might distort the shape and size of the cut pieces. If you're "harvesting" fabric from a garment, cut away seams, zippers, buttons, and labels with scissors. Rough-cut the largest possible piece of smooth fabric and press it again. Establish a clean, straight edge to measure from by aligning the cut edges with a straight line on a gridded mat or ruler. Mark and cut along the straight line.

Felting Wool

Think of felting wool as tangling the fibers into a dense mat. This couldn't be simpler. Just toss your 100 percent wool sweater or fabric into the washing machine with a clean pair of jeans and mild laundry detergent. Set the appliance for a hot wash cycle and cold rinse cycle. The hot water, soap, and agitation do the job. The longer the cycles, the more the fibers felt together, so check the wool periodically. Remove it when it has felted enough, or keep it in the washer to felt it even more (you can even run it through the wash multiple times). Then, partially or completely dry the wool in the dryer—it stops felting once you remove it from either the washer or the dryer. If it's still damp, lie it flat on a towel to finish drying. Notice how you've completely changed the hand of the fabric: it's thicker and stiffer.

Cleaning and Storing Wool

Clean the projects the same way you prewashed the fabrics before you started sewing. Because you're likely to store wool blankets and clothing during the summer months, make sure they're clean before putting them away. Body oils and even the tiniest food stains attract insects, especially moths, and those moths will eat holes in your wool.

Store wool items in airtight plastic bags or bins with tight-fitting lids. It's better to fold them than to hang them, but you might want to wrap or fold them in white tissue paper to prevent wrinkling. If you're concerned about pests, add cedar chips (instead of strong smelling mothballs). They're a natural insect repellent. Avoid putting the chips directly on the fabric; instead, hang them in small, loosely woven fabric bags (muslin works well). Store the bags or bins away from direct sunlight and temperature extremes.

Projects

Project One

Designer: Lisa Macchia

Protect your laptop in a lumberjack-plaid case decorated with a cute timber-inspired appliqué. Slide it out, and you're ready to log on.

Gather

1 yard (90 cm) of wool fabric

1 yard (90 cm) of muslin

1 yard (90 cm) of batting

2 inches (5.1 cm) of black elastic, ¼ inch (6 mm) wide

White thread

Small piece of brown felt, for the appliqué

1 button with 2-inch (5.1 cm) diameter

Basic Sewing Kit

Seam allowance ½ inch (1.3 cm) unless otherwise noted

Make

1. Cut two rectangles of wool, two of muslin, and two of batting, all 2 to 3 inches (5.1 to 7.6 cm) wider and longer than the size of your laptop. Mark the top and bottom edges of the wool fabrics with a disappearing ink fabric marker.

2. To make the back, hand baste the batting to the wrong side of the muslin along the top edge. Pin the wool fabric and muslin with right sides together along the top edge.

3. Measure and mark the center of the top edge. Fold the black elastic into a loop and sandwich it between the wool and the muslin at the marking so the loop extends toward the center of the cover. Sew across the top edge, through all the layers, with a zigzag stitch. Turn the fabrics right side out and press the seam so it rests slightly toward what will be the inside of the cover, as shown in figure 1.

Figure 1

4. To make the front, repeat steps 2 and 3 with the remaining pieces, omitting the elastic.

Quilt and Embellish

1. Hand baste the layers together along the sides and bottom of both the front and the back pieces.

2. With the wool side up, mark diagonal lines for quilting about ¾ inch (1.9 cm) apart, with a disappearing ink fabric marker, on both pieces. Straight stitch over the markings with white (or contrast) thread to quilt the layers.

3. Copy the appliqué template and use it to cut the appliqué out of brown felt. Pin the appliqué in the center of the front cover piece and edgestitch it in place with a straight stitch. Using white thread, add straight and zigzag lines of stitching to create the textured effect of knots and wood grain (figure 2).

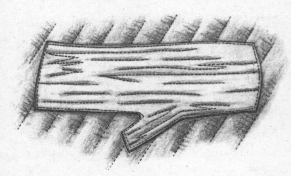

Figure 2

Assemble

1. With right sides together, pin the front and back around the sides and bottom. Check that your laptop fits inside. If the cover is too big, trim the pieces to fit.

2. Use a zigzag stitch to sew around the bottom and sides, leaving the top open. Trim away any excess fabric and threads.

3. Turn the cover right side out. Double-check the fit of the laptop inside. Hand sew the button onto the front of the cover opposite the elastic loop.

Appliqué template; enlarge 200%

Project Two

Designer: Joan K. Morris

Who says a container has to be rigid? The panels of this soft box feature flower shapes cut from luxe silk; they're emphasized with outline quilting.

Continued ➡

GATHER

½ yard (45.7 cm) of brown tweed

½ yard (45.7 cm) of pink mohair

⅛ yard (11.4 cm) of jacquard-embellished wool knit

Scrap of orange silk dupioni

1 yard (90 cm) of felt interfacing

Invisible thread

1 yard (90 cm) of upholstery batting

Kit for making 4 covered buttons, ¾ inch (1.9 cm) in diameter

Basic Sewing Kit

Spray basting adhesive

Seam allowance 5/8 inch (1.6 cm) unless otherwise noted

MAKE

1. Cut five 9-inch (22.9 cm) squares each from the tweed, the mohair, and the felt interfacing. Cut five 8-inch (20.3 cm) squares from the upholstery batting.

2. Using the templates, cut four flower shapes from the mohair and four circles from the wool knit.

3. Following the manufacturer's instructions, use the spray adhesive to attach a flower in the center of each of four tweed squares. With invisible thread in the needle on your sewing machine and colored thread in the bobbin, zigzag around the edge of the flowers to attach them to the tweed. Position a circle of wool knit in the center of each flower with spray adhesive and zigzag to hold them in place.

4. To make the sides and bottom of the box, create five sandwiches, starting with the felt interfacing on the bottom. Place a piece of batting over each piece of interfacing and then a tweed square (one square doesn't have a flower; it will serve as the bottom of the box) over the batting. Pin the layers together, and then machine baste ½ inch (1.3 cm) from the edges of all five sandwiches.

5. Pin the mohair squares to the sandwiches with the right sides of the tweed and mohair together. Stitch 5/8 inch (1.6 cm) from the edge around all sides, leaving a 5-inch (12.7 cm) opening for turning. Clip the corners and turn the pieces right side out. Press the seams flat, folding the edges of the opening to the inside. Topstitch around the perimeter of each piece, ½ inch (1.3 cm) from the edge, being sure to stitch the opening closed.

6. To quilt the four sides, zigzag again around the edge of each flower, as well as the flower center, with invisible thread in the needle and colored thread in the bobbin. Straight stitch concentrically out from the flower edge, in ¼-inch (6 mm) increments, until the entire tweed background is quilted (figure 1).

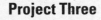

Figure 1

7. On the remaining sandwich (the bottom of the box), straight stitch concentrically around the square in ¼-inch (6 mm) increments, working from the perimeter to the center (figure 2).

Figure 2

8. Align the four sides with the bottom, so the edges abut. Using the widest possible zigzag stitch, sew the sides to the bottom (figure 3).

Figure 3

9. Fold up the sides of the box so they meet and hand stitch the inside edges together.

10. Following the manufacturer's instructions, cover the buttons in dupioni silk. Stitch them to the centers of the flowers, hiding the knots under the buttons so they don't show inside the box.

Templates; enlarge 400%

Project Three

Designer: Belinda Andresson

Punctuate the elegance of an understated cushion with a few lines of vivid sashiko-inspired stitching, using a heavy, matte thread.

GATHER

¼ yard (22.9 cm) each of four gray wools, for the front

¼ yard (22.9 cm) of printed cotton, for the front

Muslin, 13½ x 21½ inches (34.3 x 54.6 cm)

2 pieces of back fabric, each 13½ x 13 inches (34.3 x 33 cm)

1 skein of perle cotton (size 8) or embroidery floss (color to match printed fabric)

12-inch (30.5 cm) zipper

Pillow form, 13 x 20 inches (33 x 50.8 cm)

Basic Sewing Kit

Zipper presser foot

Chopstick

Seam allowance ¼ inch (6 mm) unless otherwise noted

MAKE

1. Use a rotary cutter to cut five panels for the front pillow cover to the following measurements:

2 pieces, 15 x 4 inches (38.1 x 10.2 cm)

2 pieces, 15 x 4½ inches (38.1 x 11.4 cm)

1 piece, 15 x 5 inches (38.1 x 12.7 cm)

2. Lay the five front panels out in any order. Press the muslin; it will serve as the foundation fabric.

3. Starting from the left, place the first panel right side up on the muslin so the left-hand edges of the muslin and fabric panel align. Stitch the panel to the muslin along the outer edge, backstitching at both ends (figure 1).

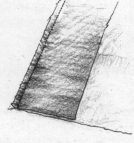

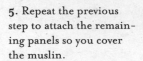

4. Working from left to right, position the second panel, with right sides together and right edges aligned, on top of the first panel. Stitch through all the layers, including the muslin (figure 2). Press the layers flat, and then press the second panel to the right.

Figure 1

5. Repeat the previous step to attach the remaining panels so you cover the muslin.

6. Trim the wool, if necessary, to the same size as the muslin. Machine stitch the front pillow cover and muslin together around the perimeter, ¼ inch (6 mm) from the edges.

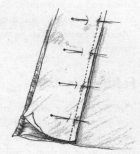

Figure 2

7. Using a running stitch and perle cotton or three strands of embroidery floss, hand quilt the middle three panels, stitching ¼ inch (6 mm) to the left of the seam.

8. Pin the two pillow back pieces with right sides together along the 12-inch (33 cm) edges. Install the zipper in the seam using a zipper presser foot and following the instructions for a lapped zipper.

9. With the right sides together, pin the pillow back cover to the pillow front cover with the raw edges aligned. Don't be alarmed if you have excess fabric on the sides; simply pin the pieces together and trim away any extra fabric.

10. Open the zipper. Using a ½-inch (1.3 cm) seam allowance, stitch around the perimeter of the pillow cover.

11. Serge or zigzag the raw edges. Turn the pillow cover right side out. Use a chopstick or similar tool to push the corners out. Press the cover flat and insert the pillow form. Close the zipper.

Project Four

Designer: Tamara Erbacher

Warm-hued wool + luxurious cotton prints = heirloom quilt

Installing a Lapped Zipper

A lapped zipper has a lip of fabric that covers the zipper so the teeth are completely hidden away from sight. Install a zipper presser foot on your machine.

1. Pin the two pieces with right sides together using a seam allowance 1½ inches (3.8 cm) wide.

2. Stitch the pieces together for ½ to 1 inch (1.3 to 2.5 cm), depending on the length of the zipper and the length of the opening; backstitch. Switch to a basting stitch and continue across the seam until you are ½ to 1 inch (1.3 to 2.5 cm) from the edge. Switch the sewing machine back to a regular stitch length and finish stitching the rest of the seam (figure 3).

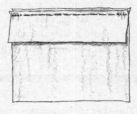

Figure 3

3. Press the seam open. Fold one of the seam allowances ¼ inch (6 mm) from the seam and press. With the zipper right side up, pin the folded seam allowance onto the zipper tape (figure 4).

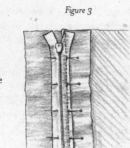

Figure 4

4. Install the zipper presser foot on the machine and stitch along the folded piece of fabric ⅛ inch (3 mm) from the zipper teeth.

5. Turn the piece over so the wrong side faces up, and fold it along the seam so the seam allowance that isn't yet attached to the zipper extends out. Sew the other side of the zipper to the seam allowance (figure 5).

Figure 5

6. Turn the piece over to the right side and mark a line ¾ inch (1.9 cm) to the right of the seam and across the ends of the zipper. Stitch along the marking, through all the layers, including the zipper tape (figure 6).

Figure 6

7. Starting in the center, use the seam ripper to open only the basting stitches. Open the zipper.

pin through the seam intersection points perpendicular to the seam you're sewing. If some of these points don't meet accurately, stretch the fabric to avoid forming tucks.

Assemble

1. Make the quilt sandwich as described in "Stacking the Layers." Use basting pins to pin the quilt sandwich together, from the center out toward all the corners, keeping the pins about 3 inches (7.6 cm) apart.

2. Attach the walking presser foot to your machine, and, using the edge of the presser foot as a guide, machine stitch on each side of all of the vertical joining seams, starting in the center of the quilt and working toward each side (figure 4).

3. Trim away any excess batting. Use a ruler and rotary cutter to trim the edges of the quilt straight.

4. Press the binding fabric and cut six strips across the width of the fabric, each 2½ inches (6.4 cm) wide. Piece the strips together to make one continuous binding strip, and then press the binding strip to make single-fold binding.

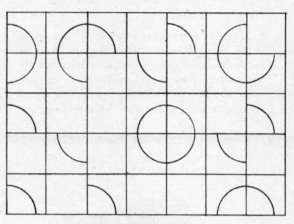

Figure 4

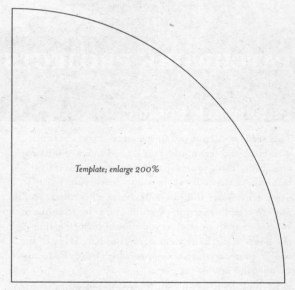

Template; enlarge 200%

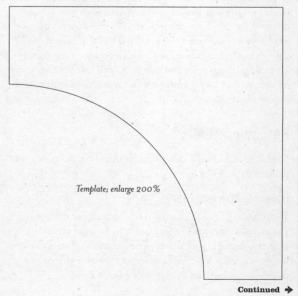

Template; enlarge 200%

Gather

21 different fabrics, cotton prints and solid-colored wools.

1¾ yards (1.6 m) of 40-inch (101.6 cm) wide fabric for the backing

15 inches (38.1 cm) of 45-inch (114.3 cm) wide fabric for the binding

Batting, 55 x 60 inches (139.7 x 152.4 cm)

Basic Sewing Kit

Template plastic

Craft knife

Quilt-basting pins

Walking presser foot

Masking tape

Finished Measurements

40 x 56 inches (101.6 x 142.2 cm)

Seam allowance ¼ inch (6 mm) unless otherwise noted

Make

Cut

1. Trace the templates onto the template plastic and cut them out with a craft knife.

2. Cut the fabrics, following the chart on the facing page. Use a rotary cutter to cut the squares, but cut any curves with scissors.

3. Arrange the pieces as shown in figure 1.

Piece

1. To piece the squares, follow the schematic and work with one square at a time. Fold the corresponding outer circle and the inner circle in half and then in half again and pin or press mark the folds. This provides equidistant marks for matching the two pieces (see figure 2).

Figure 2

2. With right sides together and the inner circle on top, pin the outer circle and inner circle together, matching the markings (figure 3). Use a lot of pins—more pins are better than fewer when it comes to piecing curves. Sew slowly, being careful to maintain the ¼-inch (6 mm) seam allowance. Press the seams open, and then press the front.

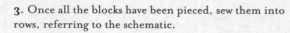

Figure 3

3. Once all the blocks have been pieced, sew them into rows, referring to the schematic.

4. Complete the quilt top by sewing the rows together. To align the squares as accurately as possible, place a

Continued ➡

5. To attach the binding strip to the quilt, refer to continuous binding. Be sure to use the walking presser foot and a scant ⅜-inch (1 cm) seam allowance.

6. Hand stitch the binding to the back of the quilt using a slipstitch.

Editor's Note: For details on making a continuous binding strip and a single-fold binding, see "Quilting Basics" earlier in this chapter.

—From *Quilt It with Wool*

STACKING THE LAYERS

If you're working on a multilayer quilted project, you'll need to assemble the layers before you stitch them together.

1. Once you've completed the design or the front of the project, trim the backing and batting to the same size as the front.

2. Place the three layers together: quilt top, then batting, and finally backing fabric, with the right sides of the quilt top and backing facing out. This is the quilt sandwich.

3. Pin the layers together with safety pins, starting in the center of the quilt. Place the pins about 4 inches (10.2 cm) apart so the layers don't shift. If you prefer, you can hand baste the layers together, again starting from the center and working toward the sides, but pin and smooth the layers first.

PATCHWORK PROJECTS

Patchwork Basics

This section will put you in the know about the tools, materials, and techniques you'll need to make the projects. Even if you're an experienced sewer, you'll find tidbits here that will enable you to create your patchwork items faster and easier. If you're a beginner, you'll want to read this section carefully and refer to it often. Whether expert or novice, you should start by gathering the items in the Basic Patchwork Tool Kit. Many of the tools and materials in it can probably already be found among your sewing supplies.

Beyond the basic kit, you'll learn here about the other tools and the wonderful range of materials you'll use, depending on which projects strike your fancy. Just as you probably have most of the essential tools on hand, you'll find that a quick rummage through your sewing materials (and perhaps your junk drawer) will uncover all sorts of scraps, odds, and ends you can transform into prized pieces of patchwork.

Patchwork Tools

In this section, we'll run through the essential items that make up the tool kit.

Rotary Cutter and Mat

If you're a longtime patchworker or quilter, the rotary cutter has something in common with things like cell phones, e-mail, and late afternoon double lattes. You know you must have functioned somehow before they came along, but you're not sure exactly how.

MAKING THE CUT

When cutting, use a mat and ruler and hold the rotary cutter at a 45° angle, with the blade set firmly against the ruler's edge. Keep even pressure on the cutter, and always cut away from yourself. When not in use, use the safety latch and follow the manufacturer's instructions when it's time to replace the blades.

Together with a transparent ruler or straightedge and a self-healing cutting mat, the rotary cutter makes short work of cutting fabric pieces—lots of them—to just the right size. If you've never used a rotary cutter, try one at your local fabric store. In general, the larger the rotary blade, the easier it is to cut fabric. A mid-size cutter will do the job for the projects...

Measuring Tape and Transparent Ruler

For measuring out larger pieces of fabric to cut, a measuring tape is all you need. A transparent quilting ruler holds down several jobs without breaking a sweat: You can use one to measure and mark precise distances, determine a perpendicular line to your fabric's edge, and guide a rotary cutter straight and sure.

Sharp Sewing Scissors

Even if you have a rotary cutter to cut pieces to size, good-quality sewing scissors are still an essential part of your sewing kit. You'll need two pairs. For basic cuts, a pair of 7- or 8-inch (17.8 or 20.3 cm) dressmaker's bent-handled shears will do the job. The design of the handle allow the fabric to lay flat as you cut. To cut tight curves and do other detail work like trimming seams, a pair of fine-tipped, 4- or 5-inch (10.2 oe 12.7 cm) sewing scissors is the way to go.

Craft Scissors

Just as sewing scissors are meant for fabric and thread, craft scissors are perfect for paper. You'll need a pair of them to cut out the templates in several patchwork projects. Find a pair that feels comfortable in your hand. A short to moderate length is best for making fine cuts on curves and corners.

Fabric-Marking Pen or Pencil and Tailor's Chalk

You'll want to use a water-soluble fabric marker for marking lines for cutting, embroidering, and sewing. The ink should vanish with plain water, but test your pen on a scrap piece of fabric first, as the dyes in some fabrics can make the ink hard to remove. Besides fabric-marking

BASIC PATCHWORK TOOL KIT

- Rotary cutter and mat
- Measuring tape
- Transparent ruler
- Sharp sewing scissors (for fabric)
- Sharp fine-tipped scissors (for detailed work)
- Craft scissors (for paper)
- Fabric-marking pen or pencil and tailor's chalk
- Straight pins
- Hand-sewing needles
- Scrap paper (for patterns)
- Sewing machine
- Sewing machine needles
- Seam ripper
- Iron

pens, a variety of fabric chalks—both traditional and new-fangled—are available.

Straight Pins

Any basic dressmaker's pins will work for holding fabric pieces in place when sewing. Longer ones with plastic or glass heads are easier to handle, and easier on your fingertips. They're also easier to spot and remove as you stitch your way past them.

Hand-Sewing Needles

A variety pack of needles should include all the types you need for the projects. You'll want to use a finer needle for lightweight fabrics and a thicker, longer needle for the thicker fabrics. Regular woven fabrics and silks do best with the sharp pointed needles known—unsurprisingly—as "sharps." Round-tipped needles, or "ball-points," are better for knit materials, as the rounded point pushes between the fibers without piercing them, which can cause a run or pull.

Some projects ask specifically for an embroidery needle. This type has a longer eye to make it easier to thread several strands of embroidery floss at once. You can use embroidery needles for detailing and for regular hand stitching as well.

Seam Ripper

Everybody makes mistakes at least once in a while, so this handy tool is essential. It easily removes incorrect stitches without anyone being the wiser.

DON'T DO THE TWIST

Tired of licking and twisting thread ends trying to get them—steady now!—through a needle's eye? Instead, just use that handy helper known as a needle threader. Pull its wire loop through the needle, insert the thread, pull back, and you're ready to sew.

Sewing Machine

To make the many seams patchwork requires, a sewing machine is impossible to beat for speed and efficiency. If you're sewing thicker fabrics, be sure to use longer stitches and to reduce the pressure on the presser foot to allow the fabric to glide through the machine. For raw edges, a zigzag stitch keeps the fabric from fraying.

Sewing Machine Needles

Always keep extra sewing machine needles on hand. Just as sharp scissors make cutting fabrics a piece of cake; it's easier to sew with sharp needles. It's a good idea to use a new needle at the beginning of each sewing project. That way you won't be using a dull needle in the middle of it.

Iron

Beyond its everyday job of getting out wrinkles, an iron can take on a number of tasks in the patchwork process. You can use it to apply interfacings and appliqués, and to press seams open.

Optional Tools

Some of the following tools will make an occasional cameo appearance in the projects..., while others will be frequent supporting stars for the everyday tools above.

Pinking Shears

Pinking shears have a serrated edge and leave a zigzag pattern that can help limit fraying. You can also use them to make decorative cuts and edges.

Glue and Adhesives

Besides just thread, the projects you'll find ahead use a variety of methods to connect pieces of fabric together.

PRETTY IN PINKING

Hold your pinking shears straight when cutting fabric and close the blades completely to make a full cut. If a fabric is too delicate for pinking, place it on top of a sturdier fabric and pink through both layers.

These include such items as spray adhesive, white glue, glue sticks, and hot glue with a glue gun. The right one to use depends on the amount of strength, durability, and quickness of setting the project requires.

Assorted Other Tools

As you browse through the "What You Need" lists in the projects, a variety of other tools will pop up. These include:

- A craft knife, sometimes used to cut out templates
- An embroidery hoop, to hold fabric taut as you detail it
- A knitting needle or chopstick, to push out corners
- A funnel, to neatly add stuffing material
- A staple gun, to attach material to a frame

Many of these tools are probably already somewhere around your house. A few tools employed in the projects are a little more specialized—for example, a loop turner, which is a slender metal rod you use to turn bias tubing inside out.

Patchwork Materials

Because patchwork can employ pieces of fabric in just about any size, shape, or pattern, you almost certainly already have some materials on hand. It's just a question of seeing what fabrics you need to add to your selection, and which specialized materials—like batting or interfacing—require a trip to the fabric store.

Fabric Varieties

Natural fabrics are usually your best bet. Cotton in particular is always a safe choice and is used in many of the projects in this book. Here's a brief description of the fabrics you'll encounter in the projects:

Cotton

Cotton is durable, easy to sew, and has a soft, natural feel. Luckily for your patchwork combinations, it comes in an endless array of colors and prints. Cotton is more likely to shrink than many other fabrics, so prewashing it is a must.

Canvas

Canvas is a heavy-duty fabric used for sails, tents, and backpacks. It's a great choice for making sturdier patchwork projects. In the United States, canvas is graded by weight (ounces per square yard) and by number. The numbers run in reverse of the weight, so number 10 canvas is lighter than number 4.

Linen

Linen is lustrous, strong, and durable. Like cotton, you can find it in an assortment of wonderful colors and prints. Also like cotton, linen is prone to wrinkling, so it's best to press your fabric both before and after sewing to have a smooth surface.

Silk

Sturdy is all well and good, but how about adding a little luxury to your projects? Silk offers a refined touch and a lustrous look. Choose a medium-weight silk that can stand up to some wear and tear, and be sure to use a sharp, new needle when sewing. Silk also ravels or frays easily, so seams should be finished.

Felt

As materials go, felt is pretty much foolproof. It's non-woven, soft, doesn't ravel, and has no right side or wrong side to worry about. Traditionally felt is made from wool, though the felt you see in craft stores is usually synthetic.

Wool

Speaking of wool: this classic fabric can be fuzzy or smooth, and fleecy or ribbed. It's soft, durable, and very absorbent.

CHARMING QUARTERS

Two terms to know before heading to the fabric store: Charm squares are squares of fabric cut to predetermined sizes, with 5 inches (12.7 cm) square a common size. A fat quarter is a half-yard of fabric that has been cut in half so that each piece measures approximately 18 x 21 inches (45.7 x 53.3 cm).

Selecting Colors and Patterns

In choosing your types of fabrics, you consider qualities like workability and durability (yawn!). When it comes to picking colors, however, the most essential quality is fun. Another thing to keep in mind with colors, though, is how well they work together in your patchwork composition.

Values, also known as tones, refer to the lightness or darkness of a color, not its particular hue. When combining colors, you can choose between medium or darker tones or lighter, more pastel values. Whether you seek to match all the values in a piece or create dramatic juxtapositions is up to you.

Besides the colors themselves, you need to choose from among solids, stripes and patterns. Just be sure you're aware of what effect the mixture of colors and patterns you choose produces. No one piece should visually stand out from all the others—unless you decide you want it to!

Thread

Bargain thread is no bargain. Your best bet is to buy a quality polyester thread for your machine and hand sewing to create strong seams that will remain that way. A good-quality all-cotton thread can also work well with the woven, natural fabrics (like cotton, for example) used in most of the projects in this book.

Embroidery Floss

Embroidery floss is a decorative thread that comes in six loosely twisted strands. You can buy it in cotton, silk, rayon, or other fibers and in every color of the rainbow. You'll use an embroidery needle to sew decorative stitches with it.

STAND BACK, LOOK CLOSE

When combining different fabrics and colors, make sure of your choices before you sew them all together—you really don't want to be using that seam ripper. Place your different fabrics in position, and take a few steps back to see how the colors and contrasting patterns look together. One trick sometimes used by painters is to squint at your composition to see if anything leaps out visually.

COMPLEMENTARY GETS COMPLIMENTS

Choose a thread in a complementary color with your fabrics. A thread that is slightly darker than the fabric is less likely to stand out. For a quilting pattern, you may want a more contrasting thread to make the decorative element apparent, or just to announce, "Hey, look at all the sewing I did!"

Layering and Stuffing Materials

Unlike in quilts, where a middle layer is to be expected, not all patchwork projects require a filling between the outside layers of fabric. When they do, a common choice is cotton batting. It's durable, easy to work with, and available in different thicknesses. Felt is another option, depending on the thickness and feel you're looking for.

Some patchwork projects, like pillows, require stuffing. Polyester fiberfill is a good choice that keeps its shape well. Grade one variety is soft, resilient, and non-allergenic; it's easily available at craft and sewing stores.

Interfacing

You can add support and structure to your projects with interfacing. The type used most often in the projects here is fusible interfacing, which means that you apply it by using the heat and pressure of an iron. Paper-back fusible web is a material that bonds on both sides when set with heat. It's useful for making appliqués.

Piping

Piping is that round edging often used in furniture upholstery. It makes a great accent for pillows, pincushions, potholders, and even some things that don't begin with the letter P. To make your own piping, buy the inner cord at a fabric store, wrap it in a bias strip that matches or contrasts your piece, and stitch close to the cording. You can also buy ready-made piping.

Rickrack and Ribbons

Rickrack is a great material for easily adding curvy detail and creative edging to your patchwork. And, as every crafter (and gift wrapper) knows, you can never have too much ribbon. Think outside the spool and try different varieties of ribbon such as velvet and grosgrain.

Beads and Buttons

Talk about unlimited options for decorating your patchwork! Just walk into any bead or fabric store and see how many choices you have. Buttons can be sewn on as is, or you can purchase specially made blanks for buttons and cover them with a fabric of your choice.

Patchwork Techniques

Tools and materials at the ready, it's almost time for the (sewing) pedal to hit the metal. First, though, here are some techniques and tips you'll need to know to make the patchwork creations that follow.

Cutting Out Patchwork Pieces

Before cutting up your patchwork components, prepare your fabrics. Wash your fabrics before starting on a project. This is especially important for fabrics that may shrink significantly, like cotton, or that have colors that might bleed (ruining that careful color combination you've just created). Press the fabric while it is still damp to remove any creases.

You can then measure your pieces with a measuring tape or ruler, and cut them with sewing scissors. Or—and this really pays off when you have many pieces to cut—you can cut them with a rotary cutter, self-healing cutting mat, and see-through fabric ruler as follows:

1. If the fabric has an uneven edge, straighten it by placing the ruler about ½ inch (1.3 cm) over the edge, making sure the ruler is at right angles to the straight grain of the fabric.

2. Place the rotary cutter against the ruler at the place on the fabric nearest you. Holding the cutter at a 45-degree angle—and pressing down on the ruler with your other hand—wheel the cutter away from you along the ruler's edge.

3. Once you have a straightened edge, you can cut the pieces you need individually. To do it most efficiently, cut strips to the width you need, place several on top of one another, and cut them together. Depending on the

Continued →

fabric weight, about four to six pieces can be cut at once. If you have to force the cutter to cut through the layers, try using fewer pieces at a time.

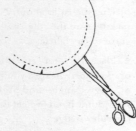

Machine Stitching

Before we begin to make patchwork, let's discuss some sewing basics. When using a sewing machine, make sure the sewing tension is set properly for the fabric you are using. Test a scrap of fabric (never in short supply when patchworking) before getting to work on the real thing. Then follow these basic steps:

1. Pin the fabric pieces to each other with straight pins placed at right angles to the seam. Right sides should be together and edges properly aligned.

2. Machine stitch to the correct seam allowance, removing pins as you go.

3. To stitch around a corner, keep the needle down at the corner point and pivot the fabric.

4. When machine stitching, be sure to let the machine do the work of pulling the fabric along.

Clipping Corners and Curves

When you sew a piece inside out, the material in the seam allowance can bunch together when turned right side out. Luckily, getting rid of all that bulk and preventing the dreaded bunchiness is just a few snips away.

For fabric on a corner, before you turn the material right side out, clip straight across the seam allowance, halfway between the stitching and the corner of the fabric (figure 1).

For fabric on a curve, snip about two-thirds of the way into the seam allowance in several places (figure 2). This will allow the fabric to overlap slightly where it was snipped. The result is a smoother curve and seam on the right side.

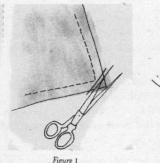

Figure 1   Figure 2

Basic Piecing

Patchwork consists of pieces of fabric that are stitched together. They can be very symmetrical and stitched together to make even squares or rows, or they can be stitched in a more free-form manner.

When sewing rows of fabric squares together, pin the first two squares together, right sides facing, then stitch along the edge using the desired seam allowance. Add more squares in the same way. When your row is complete, pin and sew the rows together. Press seam allowances as you go to ensure more accurate piecing.

Strip Piecing

One common (and easy) method for piecing fabric together is called strip piecing. You can use this technique to combine a number of rectangular strips into one larger piece. Just follow these steps:

1. Place your strips right sides up in the position they will be in the final piece. Put a needle through the left piece with the point sticking straight up (figure 1). This will be your "guide pin."

Figure 1

2. Stitch the left piece (the one with the guide pin) to the one next to it, right sides together and the two near edges aligned. Turn the stitched piece to the right side (figure 2).

Figure 2

3. Continue stitching pieces together (second to third, and so on) until the larger piece is complete. To check that you are stitching the correct edges together, just put your piece back down with the guide pin on the left and pointing up before you pick up the next strip to be attached. Finish by pressing open all the seams at once.

Foundation Piecing

Another way of assembling smaller pieces into a larger whole is called foundation piecing. This technique involves sewing fabric pieces onto a foundation of fabric (often muslin or lightweight cotton) or paper. A simple example of this method follows:

1. Place your foundation flat on your working surface. Lay down the first piece you're sewing onto it, with right side up and with its outer left edge flush with the edge of the foundation (figure 1). Working consistently left to right helps to avoid confusion. Stitch the first piece to the foundation along its outer edge.

Figure 1

2. Position the second piece on top of the first, with right sides together and right edges aligned (figure 2). Stitch through all layers (the two pieces and the foundation) along this right-hand edge with

Figure 2

a ¼-inch (6 mm) seam allowance. Press the seam flat, and then press the second piece to the right.

3. Add your third piece just as you did the second piece in step 2. Repeat until all pieces are stitched to the foundation. To finish the piece, trim the top and bottom edges and machine baste along the perimeter.

Quilting

Quilting is the process of sandwiching batting between two layers of fabric and stitching through all the layers to create a decorative, textured effect. Some projects in this book are quilted, and this can be easily done on any sewing machine.

Whenever you are quilting, you need to make sure the layers are all held in the proper position. You can add basting stitches (long running stitches). Begin in the middle and smooth out all the layers as much as you can. Another way to hold the layers together as you work is to use temporary spray fabric adhesive.

The quilting stitches themselves can be made by hand or by a machine. You usually quilt in straight lines or curved patterns, For those who always refused to color inside the lines with their crayons, a more advanced technique known as free-motion quilting allows you to use stitches to create more random or elaborate designs.

Hand Stitches

We've talked a lot about machine stitching, as that's very likely to be your main method for sewing patchwork. But even the most dedicated sewing-machine-head will need to make some stitches by hand. Here are those you may need to know for the projects in this book.

Appliqué Stitch

To camouflage the stitching holding on an appliqué, poke the needle through the base fabric and up through the appliqué, right next to the fold of the turned-under edge of the fabric. Bring the needle back down into the base fabric just a wee bit away. Repeat, as shown in figure 1.

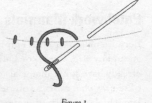

Figure 1

Backstitch

The backstitch is a basic hand-stitching method for creating a seam (figure 2). It's good for holding seams under pressure or to outline shapes or text.

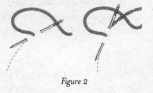

Figure 2

Basting Stitch

Basting is a way to temporarily secure two edges of fabric where a seam will go. The basting stitch is the same as a running stitch (figure 5). You just make it with very long stitches you can remove more easily once the permanent stitch is in place.

Blanket Stitch

The blanket stitch is a decorative and functional technique you can use to accentuate an edge or attach a cut shape to a layer of fabric (figure 3).

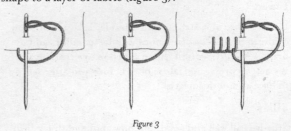

Figure 3

Chain Stitch

The chain stitch, or "Lazy Daisy stitch," can be worked in a circle to form a flower (figure 4).

Figure 4

Running Stitch

You create this stitch by weaving the needle through the fabric at evenly spaced intervals (figure 5).

Figure 5

Slipstitch

The slipstitch is also a good stitch for closing up seams. Slip the needle through one end of the open seam to anchor the thread, then take a small stitch through the fold and pull the needle through. In the other piece of fabric, insert the needle directly opposite the stitch you just made, and take a stitch through the fold. Keep going until you're done (figure 6).

Figure 6

Whipstitch

The whipstitch (also called an overcast stitch) is used to bind edges to prevent raveling. Sew the stitches over the edge of the fabric (figure 7).

Figure 7

Projects

Home Sweet Home Coasters

Designer: Wendy Aracich

Protect your coffee table in style with these down-home coasters. Made from felt and fabric remnants, these coasters can be pieced together in a flash.

WHAT YOU NEED

Basic Patchwork Tool Kit

Remnants of three coordinating fabrics

Thread

¼ yard (22.9 cm) wool felt

Utility knife

Embroidery floss

Embroidery needle

SEAM ALLOWANCE

¼ inch (6 mm)

WHAT YOU DO

1. Cut 3½ x 1-inch (8.9 x 2.3 cm) rectangular strips from the coordinating fabrics for a total of 64 strips. Cut eight 4¾ x 4¾-inch (12 x 12 cm) squares of felt.

2. Arrange strips vertically (longer sides together) into eight rows of eight rectangular strips. Join strips one row at a time, starting by pinning the right edge of the first strip to the left edge of the second strip, with right sides together. Next, pin the right edge of the second strip to the left edge of the third strip. Repeat until all strips in a row are pinned. Set aside, and repeat with the remaining rows.

3. Machine stitch along the pinned edges. Press seams open.

4. Pair stitched rows, and stitch the bottom of the top row to the top of the bottom row. Repeat with remaining rows to make a total of four pairs. Machine stitch along pinned edges. Press seams open.

5. On the wrong side of four pieces of left, center the template and trace with the pencil. Using the rotary cutter or a utility knife, cut out shapes carefully along the traced lines, and take care not to cut through the area outside of the traced line.

6. Pin patchwork, right side up, to the underside of the cut felt. Adjust the placement of the felt to compose your patchwork within the house shape. Don't worry if the patchwork extends beyond the sides of the coasters.

7. With the embroidery floss, sew a running stitch around the perimeter of the house shapes, ¼ inch (0.6 cm) from the edge, and take care to catch the patchwork with the stitches. Turn the coaster over, and carefully trim the patchwork about ½ inch (1.3 cm) outside the stitches.

8. Pin the coaster back to the front, wrong sides together. Machine stitch around the perimeter. Repeat with the remaining coasters.

Home Sweet Home Coasters template; enlarge 200%

Outside the Box

Designer: Aimee Ray

Think outside the box with these soft storage containers. They're perfect for stashing sewing supplies, bathroom essentials, and anything else that needs a little home.

WHAT YOU NEED

Basic Patchwork Tool Kit

Several patterned fabrics of different colors

Colored embroidery floss

SEAM ALLOWANCE

¼ inch (6 mm)

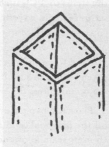

WHAT YOU DO

1. Cut 2-inch (5.1 cm) squares from the fabrics. You will need six squares for each rectangle and four for each square. Sew the 2-inch (5.1 cm) squares together using ¼-inch (6 mm) seams to form larger squares or rectangles for the sides. All measurements in the project include seam allowances.

2. For the horizontal box, cut two 3¼ x 4½-inch (8.3 x 11.4 cm) patchwork rectangles, two 3¼-inch (8.3 cm) patchwork squares for the sides, two 3¼-inch (8.3 cm) fabric squares, and four fabric rectangles for the lining and bottoms.

3. For the vertical box, cut four 3¼ x 4½-inch (8.3 x 11.4 cm) patchwork rectangles for the sides, four fabric rectangles for the lining, and two 3¼-inch (8.3 cm) fabric squares for the bottoms.

4. For each box, sew the four patchwork pieces together at the sides with a ¼-inch (6 mm) seam to form the box shape, using either a fabric square or a rectangle for the bottom. Sew together the remaining fabric pieces to make another box the same size and shape for the lining. Leave half of one side open at the bottom of the lining.

5. Turn the patchwork piece right side out and the lining inside out. Fit the patchwork piece inside the lining, and line up the top edges. Pin them together, and sew around the edge (figure 1).

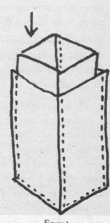

Figure 1

Continued ➡

6. Turn the piece right side out through the open hole in the lining, and then sew the hole closed. Push the lining down inside the outer box. Press the corners and top edge of the box.

7. With the embroidery floss, stitch a decorative line of embroidery—such as the blanket stitch, chain stitch, and running stitch—along the top edge of each box.

Hanger with Care

Designer: Valerie Shrader

Special clothes deserve special treatment, and this patchwork design will pamper your best threads. For intimate apparel and garments with straps, the button detailing acts as a clever non-slip device.

What You Need

Basic Patchwork Tool Kit

Fabric for patchwork, ⅛ yard (11.4 cm) of 6 different prints

Coordinating sewing thread

Wire hanger

Fabric for back, ¼ yard (22.9 cm) of a solid color

Coordinating decorative, variegated rayon thread

2 half-ball covered buttons, 7/16 (1.1 cm) in diameter

Seam Allowance

¼ inch (6 mm)

What You Do

1. Cut seven 3 x 9-inch (7.6 x 22.9 cm) strips of fabric with the rotary cutter. If desired, trim a couple of the strips to 2 x 9 inches (5.1 x 22.9 cm). Lay out the strips (each in a vertical position) from left to right on your work surface in the order you'd like in the final piece. Start with the left piece and use the strip-piecing method to assemble the strips together. The final pieced block should be at least 9 x 16 inches (22.9 x 40.6 cm). Press the seams to one side.

2. Place the hanger on the patchwork so the strips flow on the diagonal, and trace around it, adding a ¼-inch (6 mm) seam allowance. Cut out the cover. Using the patchwork piece as a guide, cut an identical backing piece from the solid fabric.

3. With the decorative thread, topstitch along one side of each seam of the patchwork.

4. With the right sides together, pin the back to the front, and leave most of the bottom open. Stitch, beginning and ending on the bottom, 1 inch (2.5 cm) around the corner. Leave a 1-inch (2.5 cm) opening at the top through which to slide the hanger neck. Notch the curves (figure 1).

Figure 1

5. Turn and press the open edges under. Slide the hanger into the cover, beginning with the neck, and slipstitch the bottom closed. To make it easier to stitch, pull the edges together under the hanger bottom and pin.

6. If desired, add the covered buttons to prevent delicate straps from sliding off the hanger. Place buttons at the upper edge.

Yoga to Go

Designer: Valerie Shrader

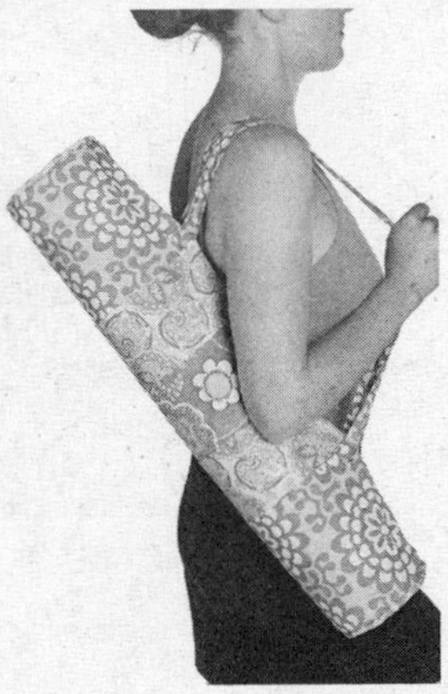

Here's a way to make your fabric scraps really stretch. With straps long enough to fling over one shoulder and a zippered top to keep your mat securely snug, you'll be practicing the Downright Diva pose in no time.

What You Need

Basic Patchwork Took Kit

Main fabric, ½ yard (45.7 cm)

At least 3 complementary fabrics, ¼ yard (22.9 cm) each

Matching thread

24-inch (61 cm) separating zipper in a complementary color

Zipper foot

¼-inch (6 mm) cord for piping, 1 yard (91.4 cm)

Seam Allowance

Varies

What You Do

1. Cut the following: of the main fabric, two pieces each 8 x 16¾ inches (20.3 x 42.5 cm) and two circular ends 6 inches (15.2 cm) in diameter.

2. On the circular ends, mark the four spots 90° apart that are the "corners" of the circle.

3. Cut six pieces of complementary fabric (you also can include the main fabric used in this project) that are each about 7 inches (17.8 cm) square. Stack the fabrics, and cut them freehand into about four asymmetrical slices. Create a patchwork rectangle by using one strip from each section. Using a ¼-inch (6 mm) seam allowance, stitch the strips together, and press the seams to one side. Make at least three pieced rectangles. Trim each of the rectangles to 5 x 5 inches (12.7 x 12.7 cm). These will be placed in a staggered fashion on the carrier.

4. Cut panels in which to inset the patchwork. Each consists of three pieces, including the patchwork inset. Each finished panel should measure 5 x 16¾ inches (12.7 x 42.5 cm). Cut a strip from each of three different fabrics that is 5 x 13¾ inches (12.7 x 35 cm). Then cut each strip into two pieces with the following measurements:

- First strip: 5 x 2½ inches (12.7 x 6.4 cm) and 5 x 11¼ inches (12.7 x 28.6 cm)
- Second strip: 5 x 3½ inches (12.7 x 8.9 cm) and 5 x 10¼ inches (12.7 x 26 cm)
- Third strip: 5 x 4½ inches (12.7 x 11.4 cm) and 5 x 9¼ inches (12.7 x 23.5 cm).

5. Sew one patchwork panel between each piece from each strip, using a ½-inch (1.3 cm) seam. Stitch the panels to one another with ½-inch (1.3 cm) seam. For added durability, finish the seams, or use a serger to stitch them together.

6. Using the 8 x 16¾-inch (20.3 x 42.5 cm) pieces you cut in step 1, stitch them at either end of the patchwork

panel, using a ½-inch (1.3 cm) seam. Trim the piece so it's 16¾ x 26 inches (42.5 x 66 cm).

7. To install the separating zipper, press under ½ inch (1.3 cm) on the long raw edges of the panel. Pin the zipper in place, and center it between the long edges. Separate the zipper, and baste each side in place by hand. Then install the zipper with the zipper foot. Note that you won't stitch a seam at either end of the zipper as with a conventional installation. Be sure to backstitch at the end of each line of stitching.

8. Make bias piping strips about 18 inches (45.7 cm) long for the ends of the carrier. (You'll discard the excess.) Baste each strip in place using a piping or zipper foot. Mark the "corners" of the carrier as you did with the ends in step 2.

9. Turn the carrier inside out, and unzip the zipper partially. With right sides together, pin the circular ends to the body of the carrier, matching the "corner" marks. Clip the carrier body as necessary. Stitch using the piping or zipper foot.

10. For the end flaps that underlie each end of the zipper, choose one of the fabrics, and cut two 2 x 6-inch (5.1 x 15.2 cm) pieces. Cut each piece in half so you have four 2 x 3-inch (5.1 x 7.6 cm) pieces. With right sides together, sew the sets of two pieces to one another, and leave one end free. Turn and press.

11. With the carrier inside out, place a flap at each end of the zipper and center it, with the raw edges even with the raw edges of the carrier. The finished end of the flap faces the opposite end of the zipper. Stitch in place on the existing ½-inch (1.3 cm) seam line.

12. To make the straps, create two patchwork strips, each 3 x 30 inches (7.6 x 76.2 cm). Fold each strip in half lengthwise with right sides facing. Stitch in a ½-inch (1.3 cm) seam, and leave one end free. Turn and trim away the seam on the short end so you can press the strap flat, and place the seam in the middle of the strap. Press under the short raw ends ¼ inch (6 mm), and topstitch along both sides.

13. With the carrier right side out, unzip the zipper completely. Pin one strap to the front of the carrier, and place the ends 1½ inches (3.8 cm) below the zipper and directly beside the patchwork inset. Stitch in place, and reinforce with a second line of stitching. Repeat to sew the remaining strip to the front; then stitch both straps in place at a corresponding spot at the back of the carrier.

Mint Julep Hat

Designer: Valerie Shrader

The Kentucky Derby is known as the "most exciting two minutes in sports," but even off the track, you'll look too fabulous in this patchwork hat. From a garden party to a beach vacation, this hat's the winning ticket.

What You Need

Basic Patchwork Tool Kit

Pattern for wide-brimmed hat

Fabric for hat, probably at least 1 yard (91.4 cm), based on pattern

Fabric for patchwork insets, ¼ yard (22.9 cm) of 5 different prints

Coordinating thread

Notions, such as an interfacing and fusible web, based on pattern

SEAM ALLOWANCE

¼ inch (6 mm)

WHAT YOU DO

1. Following the layout from your pattern, cut out the fabric for the hat. Set aside.

2. To create the patchwork insets, begin by cutting six 7 x 9-inch (17.8 x 22.9 cm) pieces from the fabrics. Include a piece from the hat fabric.

3. Stack the six pieces of fabric with the right sides facing up. Cutting freehand, use the rotary cutter to slice the stack into six or seven sections, and make gentle curves as desired (figure 1).

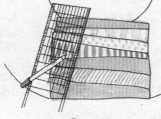

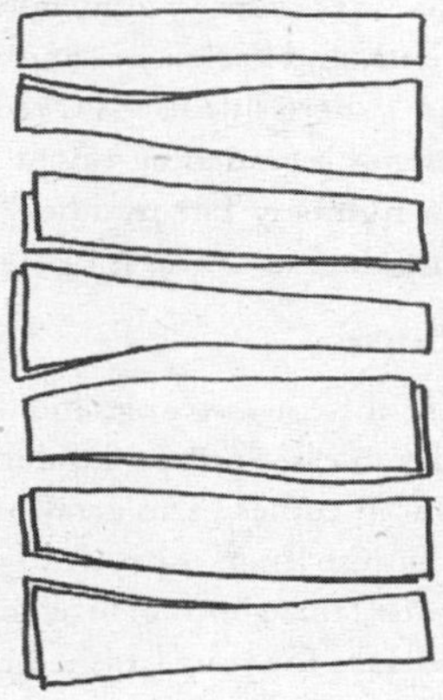

Figure 1

4. Create a patchwork rectangle by using one strip from each section. Using a ¼-inch (0.6 cm) seam allowance, stitch the strips together, and press the seams to one side. Make about four pieced rectangles, depending on your hat pattern.

5. To insert the patchwork, you'll cut a corresponding piece or pieces from the brim, and stitch the patchwork inset in its place. To begin, place one rectangle on the fabric piece you cut for the brim.

6. With the brim pattern piece as a guide, mark and then trim the patchwork rectangle to fit the curves of the brim (figure 2). Remember to include a ¼-inch (6 mm) seam allowance on each side. Trim as many rectangles as desired.

7. Place a trimmed patchwork piece on the fabric piece you cut for the brim, and mark its desired location. Don't forget to factor in the side-seam allowances you'll use

Figure 2

to stitch the patchwork inset to the brim piece. Before you cut, be sure to include an extra ¼ inch (0.6 cm) on both pieces.

8. Trim the shape of the inset away from the brim where marked. With right sides together, stitch the patchwork inset into the brim piece, using a ¼-inch (6 mm) seam allowance. Grade the seam, and closely trim the inset. Check the accuracy of your inset by comparing the brim to the paper pattern piece if necessary.

9. Repeat steps 6 through 8 to insert the patchwork into the crown of the hat and along the brim as desired.

10. Follow the instructions in your pattern to construct the hat. If the pattern calls for a bias binding, as in this project, include strips from the patchwork fabrics as well.

MAKING IT ACROSS

You may need to stitch two of the rectangles together to span the brim. If so, use a ¼-inch (0.6 cm) seam. In this project, the patchwork rectangles were trimmed so they were wide at the bottom.

Belt it Out

Designer: Erin Harris

Do you want to get the belt? Well, then stop what you're doing and make one! With groovy cotton prints and an adjustable loop, you'll be amazed how fun these are to make—and wear.

WHAT YOU NEED

Basic Patchwork Tool Kit

Small amounts of 8 to 12 different cotton prints, each at least 2 x 4 inches (5.1 x 10.2 cm)

Thread

¼ yard (22.9 cm) of 45-inch (1.14 m) wide heavy fusible interfacing

2 D-rings, each 1½ inches (3.8 cm)

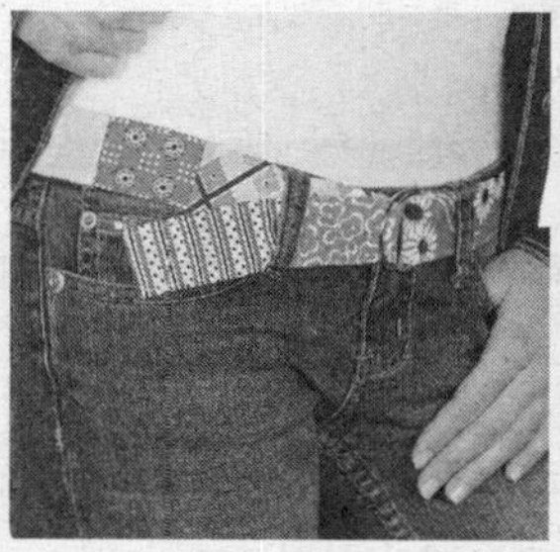

SEAM ALLOWANCE

Varies

WHAT YOU DO

1. Take your belt measurement around your waist or hips, and add 6 inches (15.2 cm) to the number to get what we'll call measurement Y. That gives you about a 5-inch (12.7 cm) overlap when you pass the belt through the D-rings.

2. With the rotary cutter and ruler, cut your fabric into 4-inch (10.2 cm) strips of various widths with no piece narrower than 2 inches (5.1 cm).

3. Lay out your fabric as you choose. Starting from the left, sew your strips right sides together along the 4-inch (10.2 cm) side using a ¼-inch (6 mm) seam allowance. Keep piecing left to right until your strip is equal in length to your measurement Y. Press all seams open.

4. Cut a piece of the interfacing into a strip that is 3 inches (7.5 cm) high and 1 inch (2.5 cm) shorter than your measurement Y from step 1. With the wrong side of the belt facing up, center the interfacing on the belt, fusible side down, and leave a ½-inch (1.3 cm) border on all sides.

5. Iron the interfacing onto your belt following the manufacturer's instructions. Fold in both short ends of the belt ½ inch (1.3 cm), and press in place. Fold the top and bottom of the belt down ½ inch (1.3 cm), and press in place.

6. Fold the belt in half and press. Pin in place. Starting at one end, sew your belt together by topstitching ⅛ inch (3 mm) from the open edge. At the corners, keep your needle in the down position, and pivot 90°. Continue until you have topstitched all four sides of the belt.

7. Insert an inch (2.5 cm) of the belt through the D-rings, and fold it over. Topstitch two parallel lines about ¼ inch (6 mm) apart to secure the D-rings. Backstitch at both ends of both lines to make sure the belt won't come apart.

—FROM *Pretty Little Patchwork*

POTHOLDERS

We made them in camp, we tossed them in drawers, and we've even singed a few over the years—talk about trial by fire. But now they're back. Out of the drawers and out in the open. Potholders.

You probably never imagined you'd spend time thinking about potholders. All things domestic once seemed so dreary, and hot pads—well, they're just plain ordinary. Think again. We're not talking about those homely store-bought squares that take the fun out of functional. The potholders in this book are pretty and practical, but they're really miniature canvases for experimenting with yummy fabrics and cool-looking textile techniques....

Bring these cool projects from the craft room into the kitchen, and you'll be ready to handle just about anything. Best of all, since potholders are small, they take no time at all to whip up. You can start a project after lunch and have it ready to show off by supper. After that, plates won't get dished up near the stove. No, no, no—these projects are so cute, you'll want to serve a steaming casserole at the dinner table, putting it down with a flourish and placing your new potholder beside it, just so.

And do yourself a favor—toss those ratty old singed potholders in the trash.

Potholder Basics

In this section, you'll get the background on the tools, materials, and techniques you need to make the projects.... For some this will be a quick refresher, but for others it's everything you need to know to "be in the sew," and you'll want to refer to these pages often. Either way, you should start by assembling your Basic Potholder Tool Kit. Most projects call for these items so, novice or not, you'll want to have them at hand.

Chances are, you already have many of the supplies listed, so dig through your desk drawers and crafts closets before hitting the stores. As you rummage, consider uses for your craft cache. Making potholders is the perfect opportunity to get creative with your scrap fabrics and odds and ends.

Potholder Tools

Sharp Sewing Scissors

Sharp, quality scissors are an absolute necessity and the centerpiece of any sewing kit. Never use sewing scissors on paper as this will dull the blades quickly and make them useless on fabric.

Some projects may call for fine-tipped sewing scissors for cutting tight curves, detailed work, and fraying elements. These should also stay far, far away from paper, so don't leave them lying around in the kitchen drawer.

Craft Scissors

Craft scissors are ideal for paper, and you'll need some to cut out the pattern pieces from your project templates. Find a pair that feels good in your hand, with a comfortable grip and moderate length so you can make expert cuts on curves and corners.

Pinking Shears

Pinking shears have a serrated edge and leave a zigzag pattern that can help limit fraying. They can also be used for decorative cuts and edges....

Continued ➡

Hand-Sewing Needles

A variety pack of needles should include everything you need for the projects in this book. Choose a finer needle for lightweight fabrics and a thicker, longer needle for thicker fabrics. Regular woven fabrics and silks do best with sharp pointed needles, and for some projects you'll need an embroidery needle for detailing.

Needle Threader

Can't get those renegade threads through your needle? Use this little tool. Put the wire loop through the needle, insert the thread, pull back, and voilà! Sew simple.

Seam Ripper

Think of the seam ripper as your true friend. We all make mistakes sometimes—stitch happens—but this friend won't judge or tell on you. It can steer you out of tight situations where scissors aren't able to tread and help you get back on track.

Sewing Machine

If you're the sort who prefers snail mail to e-mail and walking over driving, then you may take great pleasure in sewing these projects by hand, but for efficiency and speed a sewing machine can't be beat. For thicker fabrics, remember to use longer stitches and to reduce the pressure on the presser foot to allow the fabric to glide through the machine. For raw edges, use a zigzag stitch to keep the fabric from fraying.

Sewing Machine Needles

Because it's easier to sew with sharp needles, be sure to keep extras on hand in case the one in your machine gets dull mid-project.

Rotary Cutter

If you've never used a rotary cutter before, visit your local fabric shop and try some on for size. Generally, the larger the rotary blade, the easier it is to slice through fabric. A good midsize cutter should do the trick and will work well for all the projects in this book.

Iron

For most, an iron is only good for getting wrinkled out of clothing, but to the clever crafter it's much, much more. Use it to apply iron transfers and appliqués and to press seams for patchwork and piecing projects.

Embroidery Hoops

Hoops keep the fabric taut while you embroider, so it's much easier to do the stitching. They come in different sizes, but you won't need anything large for embellishing potholders.

> ## SMALL FRY
>
> For detailed work where your fingers need to get close to the iron, consider a mini iron.
>
> Not only will this little helper get into tight spaces with ease, but it won't burn your digits when making bias tape or turning seam allowances under. You can find these small wonders in any craft store or fabric shop.

> ## ON YOUR MARK
>
> Completely remove any fabric pen marks with water before laundering or ironing to avoid brownish-looking marks that may set permanently.

> ## PRACTICE SAFE CRAFT
>
> If you want your potholders to be fetching and functional, you'll need to practice safe craft. That means choosing materials that won't catch on fire or melt when exposed to high temperatures. If in doubt, leave it out. Synthetic fabrics and embellishments like trims or dangling beads might not be the best choice for a potholder you want to use in extreme heat. Use common sense for each project, and take care to use enough insulation to protect yourself. It never hurts to err on the side of safety.
>
> Always keep potholders away from hot burners and open flames. The only thing we want to ignite is your enthusiasm for creating these marvelous little works of art.

Water-Soluble Fabric Marker

For several projects you'll want to use a water-soluble fabric marker for embroidering, designing, and sewing. The ink will show up where you need it to, and should vanish with just plain water. But be careful—sometimes certain dyes in a material can make the marks difficult to remove, so always test your pen first on a scrap piece of fabric.

Potholder Materials

Thread

Buy a quality polyester thread for your machine and hand sewing to create strong seams that will hold up over time. Unless otherwise noted, use thread that matches the fabric for your potholder project.

Floss

Embroidery floss is a decorative thread that comes in six loosely twisted strands. It's available in cotton, silk, rayon, or other fibers and comes in every color of the rainbow. Although it can be time-consuming (depending on the scope of the project), an embroidered element will transform your potholder from simple to simply spectacular and is well worth the effort.

Fabric

Steer clear of synthetic fabrics. They burn more easily, and you don't want to get caught in a major meltdown. Cotton is always a safe choice and is used in most of the projects in this book. But don't limit yourself to fabric by the yard: tea towels and napkins are great choices, too, and have pre-finished seams so they're easy to use. Here's a brief description of the fabrics you'll encounter in the projects:

Cotton

Cotton is an obvious choice for crafts because it's durable, easy to sew, and comes in an endless array of colors and prints. With ample fillers, medium-weight cotton should work fine for most projects.

Heavy Canvas

Canvas is a heavy-duty fabric used for making sails, tents, and backpacks, and it's a great choice for potholders, where sturdiness is required. In the United States, canvas is graded by weight (ounces per square yard) and by number. The numbers run in reverse of the weight, so number 10 canvas is lighter than number 4.

Linen

It's lustrous, strong, and durable (even stronger wet than dry in case your potholders take a dunk in the sink), and it comes in an array of wonderful colors and prints. Because linen is prone to wrinkling, it's best to press your fabric both before and after sewing to have a smooth surface for your finished potholder.

Fat Quarters

A fat quarter is a half-yard of fabric that has been cut in half so that each piece measures approximately 18 x 21 inches (45.7 x 53.3 cm). You've likely seen bundles of them in the quilting aisle of any fabric store. Size-wise, fat quarters are perfectly suited for potholders.

Silk

Who says silk doesn't belong in the kitchen? Silk adds a refined touch to even the most basic potholder. Choose a medium-weight silk that can stand up to some wear and tear, and use a sharp new needle when sewing. Silk also tends to ravel or fray easily, so seams should be finished....

Corduroy

Corduroy is essentially a rigid form of velvet composed of tufted cords. Many projects... call for corduroy because it's durable, inexpensive, and pleasing to the touch. When pressing seams in corduroy, use a thick towel on your ironing board and keep the iron temperature on the lower side, especially if your corduroy is a stretch blend.

Insulating Materials

Most projects call for cotton batting, which is a safe, durable choice. As an insulator, cotton batting provides dense, even layering, and prevents heat build-up. It also won't melt from high heat, making it the natural choice for potholders.

Another good insulating option is the silver material you see on the cover of ironing boards, which is available by the yard at your local fabric store. It's usually made from 100% polyester that's been treated with a nonstick coating. Slip a layer on the inside of your project along with some batting, and you'll be ready to handle (almost) anything.

Needle-punched insulated lining also works well with cotton batting to reflect heat or cold back to the source. It consists of hollow polyester fibers needle-punched through a heat-reflective surface. It's important to note, however, that these materials are heat-resistant, not heatproof.

For other insulating materials, fleece and felt make good choices. Just remember that you may need to use more than one layer to make your potholder functional. The same is true for terry cloth. For extra protection, pair with a layer of batting for added insulation.

Iron-On Interfacing

You don't want your culinary experiments to flop, and your potholders or hot pads shouldn't flop either. Add support and structure to your project with iron-on interfacing. It's incredibly easy to use, but take caution: you won't want to use it on velvet or corduroy, as the iron will crush the nap. For these delicate fabrics, you'll want to sew on some non-woven interfacing instead.

> ## BASIC POTHOLDER TOOL KIT
>
> - Sharp sewing scissors (for fabric)
> - Sharp fine-tipped scissors (for detailed work)
> - Craft scissors (for paper)
> - Measuring tape
> - Ruler
> - Straight pins
> - Hand-sewing needles
> - Thread
> - Insulating material
> - Scrap paper (for patterns)
> - Pencil with an eraser
> - Iron
> - Sewing machine
> - Water-soluble fabric marker

Potholder Embellishments

Getting Loopy

With potholders this beautiful, you'll want to display them where they can be fully appreciated. Adding a hanging tab or loop to your potholder will help ensure it doesn't get stuck in a drawer somewhere. Depending on the project, you may opt to stitch your tab to the front or the back of the potholder, or to baste it in between the front and back layers. Here are some materials you can use to make hanging tabs in a flash:

Rickrack

Not only does rickrack add fanciful detail and creative edging to your potholder, but it makes a useful tab.

Ribbon

As any true crafter knows, you can never have too much ribbon. Put some of yours to good use with a pretty loop to complement your potholder.

Jewelry Clasps

Jewelry clasps such as round toggles add a touch of shine and sophistication to your project. They're also available in different shapes and sizes, so you can get exactly what you're looking for.

Bias Tape

You can easily turn the tail of the bias tape into a hanging loop. For instructions on how to make your own bias tape, turn to "Basic Techniques."

Donut Beads

Stone, wood, shell, and metal varieties make striking tabs and don't cost much. Surf the Web or visit your local bead shop for these round little gems.

ATTRACTION ACTION

If you're short on hooks, you can always sew small, powerful magnets into your potholders and stick them to the magnetic surfaces in your kitchen.

Basic Techniques

Clipping Curves and Corners

When you sew a potholder inside out, all of the material in the seam allowance can bunch together when turned right side out. Getting rid of all that bulk doesn't have to pose a problem, however.

For fabric on a corner, before you turn the potholder right side out, clip straight across the seam allowance, halfway between the stitching across the seam allowance, halfway between the stitching and the corner of the fabric (figure 1).

For fabric on a curve, snip about two-thirds of the way into the seam allowance in several places (figure 2). This allows the fabric to overlap slightly where it was snipped and results in a smoother curve and seam on the right side.

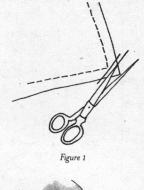

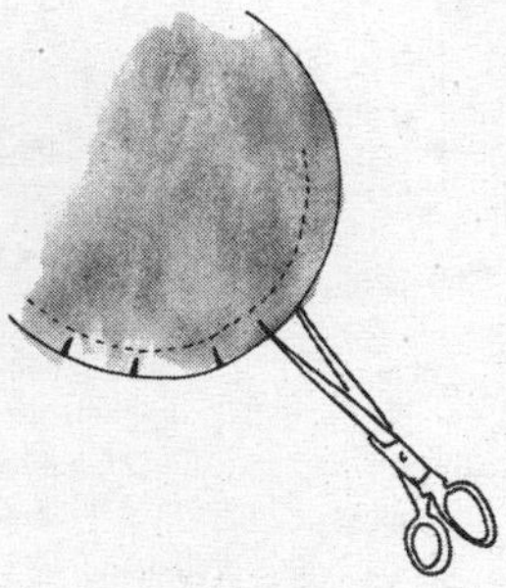

Figure 1

Figure 2

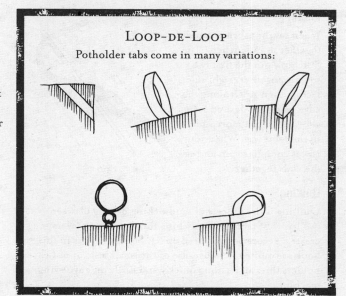

LOOP-DE-LOOP

Potholder tabs come in many variations:

How to Sew Rickrack in Seams

Add a splash of fun to pockets or to the edges of your potholder by sewing rickrack into the seam....

1. Position the rickrack on the right side of a piece of fabric so it is centered over the seam allowance. Pin the rickrack to hold it in place. Baste along the center of the rickrack (figure 3).

2. Stitch the two pieces of fabric with right sides together. When you turn them right side out, the rickrack will be sandwiched between, with only half of it showing.

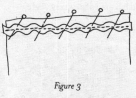

Figure 3

In a Bind

Attaching bias tape (which is also known as "bias binding") might seem tricky at first, but if you follow these instructions you'll never get caught in a bind.

1. Measure the circumference of the potholder, add 5 inches (12.7 cm) and cut this length of binding strip. If you don't purchase double-fold bias tape, fold the strip in half and iron it. Pin the raw edge of the binding to the raw edge of the potholder. Stitch around the edge in the crease (see figure 4). Stop stitching 3 inches (7.6 cm) from the starting point. Clip the loose end so that 1 inch (2.5 cm) of tape overlaps the part that's stitched down.

2. Turn the bias tape to the other side, folding the long edge under, and pin in place. Slipstitch by hard to make an invisible seam (see figure 5), stopping 2 inches (5.1 cm) from the starting point. Alternatively, you can machine sew right along the edge of the tape, so the stitching hardly shows and catches the binding on the back (see figure 6).

3. To tidy up the ends, lap them by folding the loose tail under ½ inch (1.3 cm), as shown in figure 7. Finish stitching the binding down.

How to Make Your Own Bias Tape

Purchased bias tape is like a TV dinner—cheap and convenient, but ultimately pretty boring. For the perfect decorative finish, make your own bias tape. It only takes a few minutes and will make your potholder really pop.

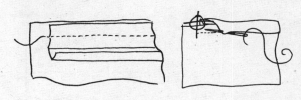

Figure 4   *Figure 5*

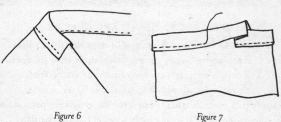

Figure 6   *Figure 7*

1. Cut strips four times as wide as your desired tape at lines running 45° to the selvage (see figure 8). You need enough strips that, stitched together, will cover the circumference of the potholder plus some extra.

2. Place one strip over the other at a right angle with the right sides together. Stitch diagonally from one corner to the next of the overlapping squares (see figure 9).

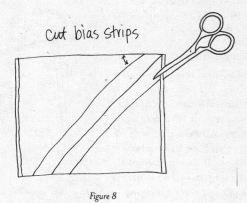

cut bias strips

Figure 8

3. Cut off the corners of each seam, leaving a ¼-inch (0.6 cm) seam allowance (see figure 10). Open up the seams, and press the allowances flat. Fold the strip in half lengthwise right side out and press. Open the strip, and press the raw edges into the center. Now you have single-fold bias tape (see figure 11).

4. To make double-fold bias tape, fold again in the center and press, as shown in figure 12.

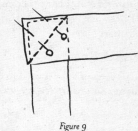

Figure 9

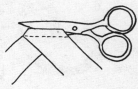

Figure 10

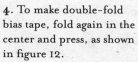

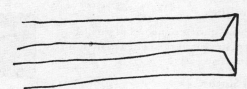

Figure 11

Figure 12

Hand Stitches

A few of the potholders in this book call for hand sewing in specific instances to mask the thread. If you don't mind seeing the stitching, however, go ahead and use your machine instead....

Continued ➡

Hidden Stitch

Use the hidden stitch (figure 17) to close the openings you've left in seams to turn the potholders right side out.

Editor's Note: For descriptions of and directions for other hand stitches, see "Patchwork Projects" earlier in this chapter.

Embroidery

If you're new to embroidery, the following illustrations should help you master it in no time. Once you get the hang of it, you'll be hard-pressed to put it down. (Seriously, it's addictive.) Embroidering can be very relaxing, plus you can squeeze it in here and there. (Commercial breaks are a good time to get your stitch on!) Each stitch has its own unique function, and the overall look will transform your potholder into a refined little work of art....

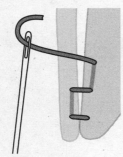

Figure 17

Editor's Note: For other embroidery stitches, see "Patchwork Projects" and "Quilting Basics" earlier in this chapter.

French Knot

This elegant knot is used to create decorative embellishment and texture (figure 22).

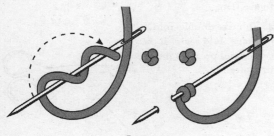

Figure 22

Satin Stitch

The satin stitch is composed of parallel rows of straight stitches, often to fill in an outline (figure 24).

Seed Stitch

Use this stitch to fill in an outline with texture or color, like in Handle with Flair. Create it by randomly making small straight stitches, all the same length and facing in the same direction, surrounded by empty space (figure 25).

Figure 24

Split Stitch

Make a first stitch. For the second stitch, bring the needle up through the middle of the first stitch, splitting it. Then follow the line, with the needle coming up through the working thread and splitting it (figure 26).

Figure 25

Piecing

When sewing fabric squares together as in Kitchen Stitchin', pin the first two squares together, right sides facing, then stitch along the edge using the desired seam allowance. Add more squares in the same way. When your row is complete, pin and sew the rows together.

Figure 26

Quilting

Quilting is the process of sandwiching batting between two layers of fabric and stitching through all the layers to create a decorative, textured effect. Some projects in this book are quilted, and because of the small scale of potholders this can be done quickly and easily on any sewing machine....

Projects

Dot's Diner

Designer: Wendi Gratz

Who doesn't love polka dots? Even better, you can slip your hand in the secret pocket and hold a steaming hot dish in safe, sassy style.

WHAT YOU NEED

Basic Potholder Tool Kit

¼ yard (22.9 cm) of fabric

⅛ yard (11.4 cm) of fabric for bias tape

¼ yard (22.9 cm) of cotton batting

inches (20.3 cm) of rickrack ½ inch (1.3 cm) wide

SEAM ALLOWANCE

¼ inch (0.6 cm)

WHAT YOU DO

1. Copy the templates. Cut two pieces of fabric from each of batting using the larger pattern piece, which serves as the front and back of the potholder.

2. Pin the rickrack to the front of one of the pockets (the smaller fabric pieces), ½ inch (1.3 cm) from the edge of the straight side and stitch.

3. Pin the pocket pieces right sides together. Sew on the stitching line created in step 2 with the rickrack embedded between. Open the seam and press. The rickrack should peek up from the seam.

4. Put the front piece face down on your work surface. Place the batting over it and then the back piece, face up. Finally, put the pocket on top, matching all the curved edges. Pin the layers together.

5. Make a strip of bias tape 2¼ inches (5.7 cm) wide and 40 inches (101.6 cm) long. Fold it in half the long way and press.

6. Starting from the square corner, pin the bias tape along the edge of the potholder with the raw edges together. Stitch slowly around the curves to ease the fabric in, and when you get back to the corner where you started, stop the machine, and leave the potholder where it is. Turn under the binding at the beginning to the back of the potholder, and continue stitching about 4 inches (10.2 cm) past the edge of the potholder. Remove the potholder from the sewing machine.

7. Turn the binding to the back of the potholder. Hand stitch the folded edge of the binding to the back of the potholder. Stitch the extra tail of binding to itself so the raw edges are enclosed. Turn the tail into a hanging loop, and stitch the end securely to the potholder.

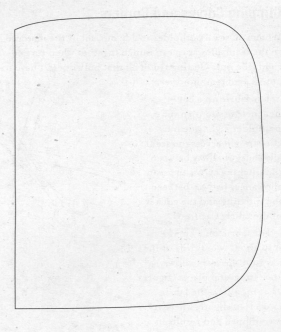

"Dot's Diner" templates; enlarge 400%

Kitchen Stitchin'

Designer: Betsy Couzins

You'll never forget to pick up the milk again—not with this nine-patch hot pas that elevates kitchen staples with simple embroidery.

WHAT YOU NEED

Basic Potholder Tool Kit

Fat quarters of all-cotton fabric in 3 prints

Embroidery floss

Tapestry needle

Embroidery hoop

Rotary cutter

Self-healing cutting mat

Low-loft quilt batting

Extra-wide, double-fold bias tape

"Kitchen Stitchin'" templates; enlarge 200%

SEAM ALLOWANCE

¼ inch (0.6 cm)

WHAT YOU DO

1. Transfer the embroidery template onto one of the fabrics, leaving plenty of room around each design. Using the split stitch, embroider each motif.

2. Iron the embroidered fabric. Draw four squares with sides 3¼ inches (8.3 cm) long around the motifs, centering the designs within them. Cut them out. Iron the two other fabrics, and cut out five more blocks with sides 3¼ inches (8.3 cm) long. Lay out the blocks in a checkerboard design.

3. Placing the right sides together, sew the squares of the top row. Press the seams to the side. Repeat for the two other rows. Again with right sides together, sew the top row to the middle row. In the same way, sew the middle row to the bottom row.

4. Cut a back 8½ inches (21.6 cm) square from one of the fabrics. Cut a piece of batting 8½ inches (21.6 cm) square. Place the backing fabric right-side down on the work surface. Place the batting on top of it. Put the nine-patch on top of the batting, right side up, and pin all three layers together.

5. Cut four strips of bias tape about 9½ inches (24.1 cm) long, and bind each edge.

Handle with Flair

Designer: Nathalie Mornu

Slip these covers on the handles of your pots, and you'll get instant cred for keeping it cool. Make one or more in complementary colors, and hand embroider for added oomph.

WHAT YOU NEED

Basic Potholder Tool Kit

12 x 12 inches (30.5 x 30.5 cm) of main fabric

8 x 5 inches (20.3 x 12.7 cm) of backing fabric

⅓ yard (30.5 cm) of fabric for making bias tape

8-inch (20.3 cm) embroidery hoop

Embroidery needle

1 skein of embroidery floss

¼ yard (22.9 cm) of insulating material

WHAT YOU DO

1. Enlarge and cut out the template. Pin the template to the main fabric along the grain, and trace around it with the water-soluble pen. Remove the template.

2. Inside the traced line, lightly draw the design you wish to embroider onto the potholder. (Pressing heavily will cause the ink to wick across the fabric, resulting in a line that's not crisp.) Center the design in the embroidery hoop. With three strands of floss in the needle, embroider the entire design with seeding stitches.

3. Leaving the fabric in the hoop, follow the manufacturer's instructions to cause the ink marks to disappear. Iron the embroidered design.

4. Cut along the traced line of the template. Place the template along the grain of the backing fabric, trace it, and cut it out. Zigzag along the top edges of both pieces to prevent the fabric from fraying. Turn both pieces under along the fold line and press.

5. Cut two templates out of the insulating material, and trim away at the fold lines of each. Tuck one piece of insulating material into the fold of the main fabric, matching the lower, curved sides. Keep the insulation in place by hand stitching along the top edge of the main fabric, sewing through all three layers, ⅛ inch (0.3 cm) from the edge of the fold. Repeat with the backing.

6. Cut a strip of bias tape 1 inch (2.5 cm) wide and 18 inches (45.7 cm) long, as explained under "How To Make Your Own Bias Tape." Pin it to the main fabric, working from the center of the curve toward either end. Turn under both ends of the bias tape then stitch. Press the seam from the front.

7. Stack the main fabric over the backing, with the insulated pieces facing each other and matching all edges. Pin to keep them in place, and hand sew through all the layers, stitching just on the outside of the seam holding the bias tape on. Flip the bias tape to the back side, and slipstitch it down.

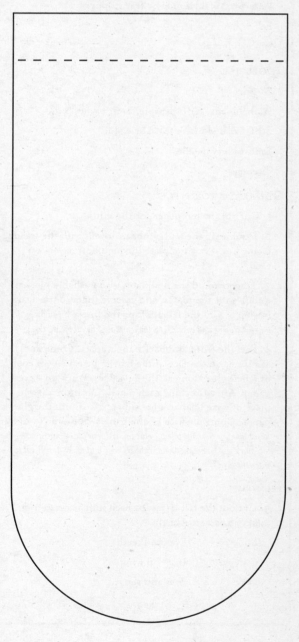

"Handle with Flair" template; enlarge 200%

Continued ➜

Woodland Friends Wash Mitts
Suzie Millions

Bucky

Foxy

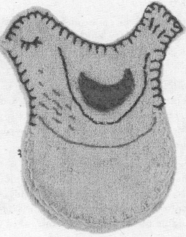
Chirpy

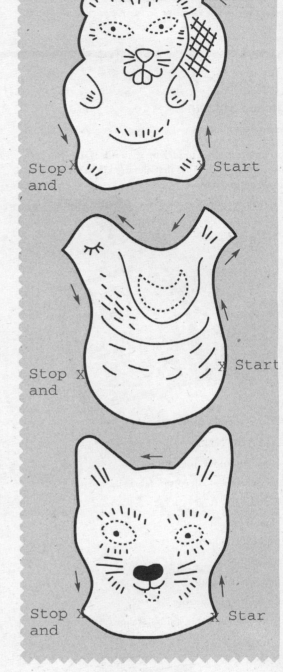

Templates. Copy on tracing paper at 230% to make 6" mitts

MATERIALS

Templates copied on tracing paper

Washcloths and/or towels in three colors

Straight pins

Waxed paper

Waterproof fabric glue or fray stopper

Felt

Embroidery floss

TOOLS

Scissors

Washable marker (washable, as in washes out)

Stiff-bristled brush for fabric glue

Embroidery needle

Tweezers

GET READY TO STITCH

1. Cut out the templates for the mitts.

2. Double up the washcloths or towels with the inside facing out. Pin a template through both layers on each.

3. Trace around the templates with washable marker. Remove the templates, and reserve them to use again in step 8. Cut the fabric along the lines. *If you prefer to skip the tracing and cut around the templates, by all means do.*

4. Peel the front and back panels apart. One panel at a time, on the face of the fabric, brush a thin coat of fabric glue along all the cut edges. Work on waxed paper. After finishing each panel, put it on a fresh piece of waxed paper, glue side up. Toss out the gluey paper. Continue with all the panels. Set aside to dry. *Resist the urge to really pile the glue on; it doesn't take much. Using too much will give you an odd, rubbery edge and make it difficult to stitch through.*

FELT TRIMS

5. Cut out the felt trims for each mitt (*indicated with dotted lines on the templates*):

Bucky:	Eyes and teeth
Chirpy:	Inset on wing
Foxy:	Eyes and tongue

6. Brush fabric glue on the back of the felt trims, and stick them in place on the front panel of each mitt.

STITCH THE DETAILS

Be sure the edges are dry before continuing.

7. Blanket stitch around the felt trims.

8. Pin the template to the face of the front panel of each mitt and embroider the details on each, stitching through the tracing paper.

9. When you're done stitching, remove the pins from the template, and remove the paper. Use tweezers to remove any stubborn bits of paper that cling to the stitches, being careful not to pull any of the stitches or the loops in the terrycloth.

STITCH THE PANELS TOGETHER

Stitch the sides and top of the front panel to the back, leaving the bottom of the mitt open for wet, soapy hands.

10. Pin the front panels to the backs, placing the pins to avoid the outer edges, where the mitts will be stitched together.

11. Begin at the start point indicated on the template. Blanket-stitch around the right side, over the top, then down the left side, joining the front panel to the back as you stitch. Stop when you reach the *Stop-and-Drop* point on the left side (indicated on the template).

STITCH THE BOTTOM EDGE

12. When you reach the *Stop-and-Drop*, drop the back panel and continue blanket stitching on the bottom edge of the front panel until you reach the starting point.

13. When you reach the starting point, tack a couple of stitches to reinforce that end of the opening. Then blanket-stitch back across the bottom of the back panel, until you reach the *Stop-and-Drop* point again. Tack a couple of stitches to reinforce that end of the opening. Knot off the thread, clip it, and you're done.

14. Get out the bubbles and run the bath.

—FROM *The Complete Book of Retro Crafts*

Nifty Fifties

Designer: Autum Hall

Think June Cleaver with far more sass! This charming potholder and oven mitt set mixes '50s-style fabrics with cute, contemporary flair.

WHAT YOU NEED

Basic Potholder Tool Kit

Up to ¼ yard (22.9 cm) each of cotton fabric scraps in red and aqua or any combination

¼ yard (22.9 cm) natural-colored linen fabric

¼ yard (22.9 cm) fleece

12 x 20 inch (30.5 x 50.8 cm) piece of heavy canvas in a light color

4-inch (10.2 cm) square of red gingham

Rotary cutter

Cutting mat

White thread

Black embroidery floss

Embroidery needle

Seam ripper

Chopstick

Aqua button

Fusible tape (optional)

WHAT YOU DO

FOR THE POTHOLDER

1. Referring to the chart below, cut the fabric pieces.

2. Referring to figure 1 for placement, stitch pieces 1, 2, and 3 together sequentially. Press each seam open and then to the side with a ¼-inch (6 mm) seam allowance. Stitch this strip to piece 4, and set aside.

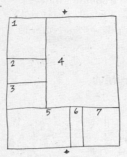 

Figure 1

Retro kitchen print	Piece #1: 4-inch (10.2 cm) square
	Piece #5: 4 x 5-inch (10.2 x 12.7 cm) rectangle
Red and white print	Piece #2: 4 x 2-inch (10.2 x 5.1 cm)
	Strap: 2 x 4 inches (5.1 x 10.2 cm)
Solid aqua	Pieces #3 and #6: each 4 x 2 inches (10.2 x 5.1 cm)
Blue and green floral	Piece #7: 4-inch (10.2 cm) square
Linen	Piece #4: 6½-inch (16.5 cm) square
	Back: 10-inch (25.4 cm) square
Red gingham	Yo-yo: circle 4 inches (10.2 cm) in diameter
Fleece	2 pieces, 10 x 10 inches (25.4 x 25.4 cm)

3. Stitch pieces 5, 6, and 7 together sequentially. After pressing each seam open and to one side, stitch this strip to the block made in step 2.

4. Copy the teapot design. Transfer it to the lower right-hand corner of the linen square using a temporary-ink marking pen or pencil. Embroider it, using a backstitch for the outline of the teapot and steam. Satin stitch the heart.

5. Place the potholder top on top of the two layers of fleece. Use straight pins to hold it in place for machine quilting. With a long, straight machine stitch, topstitch close to the seam line on one side of each seam. Trim excess fleece from the edges, and square up if necessary.

6. To make the hanging tab from the 2 x 4-inch (5.1 x 10.2 cm) piece of fabric, fold the scrap in half the long way and press it. Then open and fold each long side in

to the center and press. Fold in half to enclose the raw edges, and stitch down the open side. Fold in half, and pin in place at the upper right corner, about ½ inch (1.3 cm) in from the right edge.

7. Place the 10-inch (25.4 cm) linen square over the potholder top, right sides together. Pin in place around all four sides. Sew around all sides, and leave a place on one side for turning right side out 3 to 4 inches (7.6 to 10.2 cm).

8. Clip the corners, and turn right side out through the opening. Push out the corners with the chopstick. Press neatly, and pin the opening closed. Secure it with a hidden stitch.

FOR THE MITT

Cut the fabric:

8 to 10 fabric scraps, 2 to 4 inches (5.1 to 10.2 cm) long x 4 inches (10.2 cm) wide

8 to 10 fabric scraps, various widths x 3 inches (7.6 cm) long for binding strip

Strip of red gingham, 2 x 20 inches (5.1 x 50.8 cm)

Strip for hang tab, 2 x 4 inches (5.1 x 10.2 cm)

Rectangle from linen, 6½ x 20 inches (16.5 x 50.8 cm)

Rectangle from fleece, 12 x 20 inches (30.5 x 50.8 cm)

Rectangle from canvas, 12 x 20 inches (30.5 x 50.8 cm)

2. Sew enough of the fabric strips together to make a piece about 20 inches (50.8 cm) long. Press seams to one side. Attach this patchwork strip to the gingham along one long side, and on the other long side attach the linen.

3. To make the binding, sew strips together to create a patchwork piece 3 x 15 inches (7.6 x 38.1 cm). Press.

Teapot design, "Nifty Fifties"; full scale

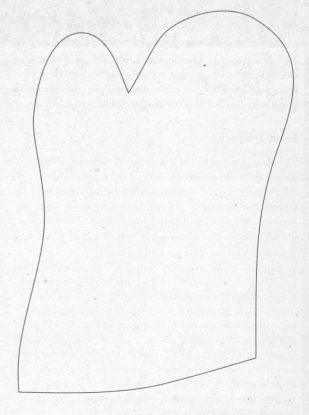

"Nifty Fifties" ove mitt template; enlarge 300%

Continued ➡

the seams to one side, and fold it in half the long way, wrong sides together. Set aside. Make the hang tab. Set aside.

4. To prepare the patchwork for quilting, make a sandwich with the canvas on bottom, fleece in the center, and patchwork on top, right side up.

5. Machine-quilt with a long machine stitch in a random pattern. Fold the quilted fabric in half, right sides together, and be sure the seam between the linen and patchwork matches up. Cut out the oven mitt shape using the pattern. Stitch up the thumb side only to the top of the thumb. Open up, and pin the binding to the right side of the mitt along the bottom edge, raw edges together.

6. Stitch the binding to the mitt with a ⅜-inch (1 cm) seam allowance. Fold the binding around to the back and press. Pin in place to secure for stitching.

7. Stitch in place by stitching in the ditch, or stitching from the front side right at the seam line so the stitching is nearly invisible. Pin the hang tab in place on the open side near the bottom. Be sure to pin it so the raw edge of the tab is even with the raw edge of the mitt. Turn the right sides together, and finish stitching around the mitt.

8. Trim the seams, and clip to the seam line at the V between the thumb and hand section. Turn right side out, using the chopstick if needed to push the thumb out.

—From *Pretty Little Potholders*

THINGS TO KNOW BEFORE YOU SEW: SEWING MACHINES & SUPPLIES

Valerie Van Arsdale Shrader
Susan McBride, Illustrator

Meet the Sewing Machine

The next step is to develop a meaningful relationship with your sewing machine, since it's the tool that will free you from skirt envy. Give it a friendly little pat and let's get to know it better…. I love my sewing machine! I really do.

How It Works

This fantastic invention creates a lockstitch when the thread from the needle (on top of the machine) and the thread from the bobbin (inside the machine) loop together in the fabric. This happens a gazillion times per minute when you sew. (Aren't you glad you don't have to do it by hand? I sure am.) That's the long, the short, and the zigzag of it.

Although machines share common characteristics, they vary by manufacturer. When I keep referring you to your own machine's manual, I'm not trying to ignore your needs; it's because there are some important yet subtle differences between machines that might confuse you. For instance, the thread on my machine disappears inside for part of its journey—yours might not. My bobbin winds on the front of the machine—yours might be on top. I have a pressure foot dial, but you might have a lever. Despite that rambling disclaimer, let's have a go at some general information anyway.

… [A] typical machine has a spool (or spools) for the thread; controls for stitch width, stitch length, thread tension, and presser foot pressure (say that three times fast); a handwheel; a take-up lever; tension disks; a presser foot lever; thread guides; a bobbin winder; a needle; a presser foot; feed dogs; a needle plate; and a bobbin. All of these things furiously work together to create the little lockstitch….

A Sewing Machine Overview

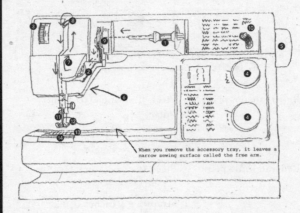

When you remove the accessory tray, it leaves a narrow sewing surface called the free arm.

1. The spool holds the thread.
2. This dial adjusts the thread tension; turn it in tiny increments.
3. Adjust the pressure of the presser foot with this dial.
4. These dials adjust stitch selection, including width and length.
5. The handwheel revolves when you sew, and you can turn it by hand for precision work.
6. The presser foot lever (hiding in the back) lifts the presser foot and engages the tension disks. Remember to put it in the down position when you sew! But lift the presser foot when you thread your machine.
7. The tension disks, tucked inside the machine, regulate the movement of the thread.
8. The take-up lever carries the thread while the machine is sewing, pulling the exact amount it needs for each stitch. If this lever isn't threaded properly, an unsightly gob of thread will appear on your fabric.
9. The thread guides move the thread through the machine in an orderly fashion.
10. The bobbin winder winds the thread on the bobbin. (It's not named very creatively, is it?)
11. The needle pierces the fabric and creates a stitch when it's looped together with the thread from the bobbin. Use the right size needle for your fabric, and use a new needle for each project.
12. The presser foot keeps the fabric snug against the feed dogs, the little serrated thingies that move the fabric as you sew.
13. The needle plate is the metal surface through which the needle grabs the bobbin thread. It has handy guidelines for seam allowances.
14. The bobbin is wound with thread and lives inside the machine. The looping of the thread from the spool with the thread from the bobbin forms the basic lockstitch.

Most modern machines have a detachable accessory tray that's part of the sewing surface; when it's removed, a narrow sewing surface called a free arm remains. The free arm lets you stitch around narrow openings like sleeves.

In case you could have possibly forgotten (!), your sewing machine manual is the best source of information for your particular model. It will have detailed information about threading the machine; winding the bobbin; adjusting stitch width and length; and selecting any specialty stitches. Read through the manual thoroughly before you begin to make your skirt and practice stitch-

ing to familiarize yourself with the operation of your machine. It will be fun!

Use the Right Needle

There's no great mystery to choosing the proper needle for your sewing project. The three major types are sharps, for use on finely woven fabrics; ballpoints, for knits; and universal points, for all-purpose sewing on both knits and woven fabrics. Needles come in different sizes, with the smaller numbers for use on lightweight fabrics and the larger numbers for heavyweight material. They are marked in both European (60, 70, etc.) and American (10, 12, and so on) sizes; which number comes first depends on the manufacturer. A universal point in the medium range (70/10 or 80/12, for instance) will suit most… fabric…. For the easy way out, try this: when you buy your fabric, smile brightly at the clerk and ask for a recommendation.

Use the Right Presser Foot

The presser foot is the gismo that keeps the fabric secure against the feed dogs; the feed dogs are the gismos that move the fabric along as you sew. There are lots of specialized presser feet designed to perform specific tasks, but we keep it simple in this book by only using two: a general presser foot that allows both straight and zigzag stitching, and the zipper foot, which lets you stitch close to the zipper when you're installing it. That handy manual of yours will instruct you on changing the presser feet.

Got Sewing Machine?

…If you don't have a sewing machine, here are a few things to consider when buying or borrowing one.

· You don't have to spend a ton of money to get a perfectly good entry-level sewing machine. But you really should go to a dealer and test-drive before you buy. Sew over different thicknesses of fabric, thread it yourself, wind the bobbin, check out the stitch selection, make a buttonhole—dealers expect and welcome this level of scrutiny from their customers. Many dealers offer an introductory class after you've purchased a machine.

· If you buy a used machine, insist on that test-drive, too. Stitching can look dreadfully wonky when there's actually not much wrong (maybe just a tension adjustment on the bobbin), but then again, maybe that poor machine has been abused. Have a reputable dealer inspect it before you plunk down your hard-earned cash. Make sure that you have a complete operating manual, too.

· If you borrow a machine, please don't make the mistake of hauling a dusty machine out of someone's attic and thinking it will sew beautifully. Maybe it will, but probably it won't; sewing machines need to be tuned up regularly, just like cars. They work awfully hard, and they accumulate lots of dust from fabric and thread. (This dust migrated into the screwiest places, too.) Get a proper introduction from the machine's owner (do a lot of the same things I suggest when you're shopping for a machine) and have the owner point out its important features. Don't forget to borrow that manual, also. (As if!)

Gather the Tools and Supplies

In addition to the sewing machine, you need to gather up a few other tools and materials before you begin your first skirt. All of these items are readily available at any fabric shop.

Scissors. If you invest in only one quality item, I suggest a good pair of 7- or 8-inch dressmaker's bent-handled shears. The design of bent-handled shears allows the fabric to remain flat, so it doesn't shift while you're cutting. A pair of sewing scissors, say 4 to 5 inches long, is perfect for other cutting tasks, such as trimming seams. Buy the

best scissors you can afford, because they'll be your friend forever. I still use my grandmother's sewing scissors, which are at least 30 (if not 40) years old.

Though you should use dressmaker's shears to cut out your project, a pair of pinking shears is handy to finish seams. And they're cute, too.

Seam Ripper. Change is inevitable, and so are mistakes. Use a seam ripper to remove stitches that displease you.

Measuring Tools. If the only measuring tool you had were a tape measure, you could certainly make a sewing project. But a couple of other gadgets will be useful, too: a clear ruler helps while cutting out fabric, and a sewing gauge is a nifty little tool that has a slider for marking lengths. I find that I rely on my sewing gauge quite often—for marking hems, placing trim, and all types of petite measuring tasks.

Pins & Needles. Basic dressmaker's pins will be fine for your early… projects. Later in, you may want to add thin silk pins or long quilter's pins (with adorable colorful heads) to your stash of sewing supplies.

You'll do very little hand sewing for the projects in the next two sections of this chapter. An assortment of sharps (all-purpose sewing needles) is fine.

Pincushion. Store all of your pins and needles in a pincushion. You can get the ubiquitous tomato or the groovy felt orb, or perhaps try a magnetic pincushion. Lately I've come to favor the magnetic variety because they can grab the pins that have misbehaved and escaped to the floor.

Thread. All-purpose thread, which is cotton-wrapped polyester, is fine. As your adventure in sewing continues, you may eventually want to use all-cotton thread (great for woven, natural fiber fabrics) or perhaps all-polyester thread (good for fiber blends and knits). When you're choosing a thread color, either match it to the fabric or choose a shade that's slightly darker.

Bodkin. Sounds like something from Tolkien, doesn't it? Actually, a bodkin is an ingenious tool used to thread elastic through casing…. (For the thrifty, a big safety pin is a good alternative to using a bodkin; just pin it to the end of the elastic and feed it through the casing.)

Marking Tools. Your pattern pieces will have some markings (circles, center points, darts, and the like) that need

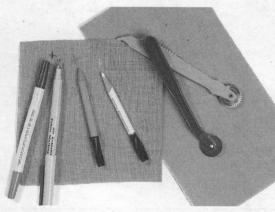

Marking tools

to be transferred to the fabric. There are several different ways you can accomplish this: with tailor's chalk or chalk pencil, with water-soluble or air-soluble (i.e., disappearing) fabric pens, or with tracing paper and a tracing wheel. You should always test your marking supplies on a scrap of fabric before you begin your sewing project.

Iron. You can't make a project without an iron; pressing is very important to set seams and to the success of your final product. Note that we're not talking about ironing, which is sliding your iron across the fabric. We're talking about pressing. Pressing is moving the iron across the fabric in increments by pressing it up and down. Press open each seam before it's overlapped or crossed by another seam. Remember—up and down, not side to side. Ironing can distort the grain of your fabric.

—From *Sew Cool, Sew Simple: Stylish Skirts*

SEWING CURTAINS
Valerie Van Arsdale Shrader

Guide to Making Fabulous Curtains

There's a curtain to fit every window, of course, whether you've got modern sliding windows or funky sash windows. Your first decision will be the kind of window treatment you want, so let's consider the variables: Do you want to provide privacy? Allow some light filtration, but screen out a boring view? Provide some spark in a drab room? Supply additional insulation? Keep in mind that your window treatments should match the character of your room, yet provide an opportunity to express your personal style. While you're thinking about those questions, here's some information about window treatments.

Pick a Type

At its most basic, a curtain is a piece of fabric that's hemmed on all four sides and hung with clips. There's a difference between *curtains* and *draperies*; while curtains are generally unlined, draperies are lined with an additional layer of fabric, and sometimes have a third layer of interlining fabric. Most of the projects in this book, you'll be delighted to hear, can be defined as curtains. This simple shape can be transformed by way of adding headers, tabs, ties, embellishments—once you understand the basics, you can apply your creativity to the form. Let's look at some common types.

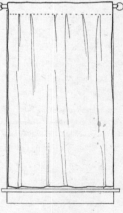

Rod pocket

Rod Pocket. This basic curtain hangs from the rod by way of a casing, also called a rod pocket. Using a perky fabric for this simple curtain can add a spark to the room, and no one will have to know how easy it is to make. (We certainly won't tell!)

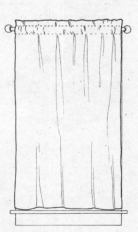

Rod pocket with header

Coupled with a distinctive curtain rod, this window treatment is a good choice for a quick room makeover.

Rod Pocket with Header. To take the basic curtain one step further, add one more line of stitching to create a decorative header above the rod. A header will add another few inches of curtain to your room, offering you the opportunity to enjoy your fabric a bit more.

Valance. The valance is a short little curtain that hangs at the top of a window. It can soften the bare window frame, while not screening out light or a fabulous view.

Café. The opposite of the valance, this is a short little curtain that covers only the bottom half of the window. It allows light in, but also provides some privacy. This curtain is easily hung with a tension rod, which makes installation a breeze.

Tab Top. As an alternative to a casing, you can add tabs at the top of your curtain. And a variation on this style would be to use ties, rather than tabs. Either of these methods can be used if you want a more casual look.

Shade. A shade can cover all or part of a window, depending on your needs, and takes relatively little fabric to make. Although technically not a curtain, we think any book on window treatments ought to have one or two super-easy shades—don't you?

Drapery. In this section, we have a set of draperies that are lined and involve some more sophisticated construction than our curtains. But fear not—we'll teach you all the skills you need to make these stylish window treatments. When you're looking for an uptown look, consider making some draperies.

Valance

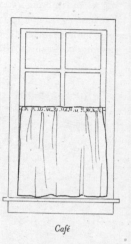

Café

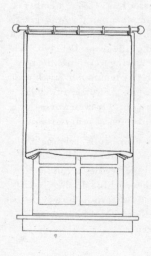

TabTop and Tie Top

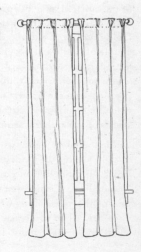

Continued ➜

More Things To Know Before You Sew: Stitching Seams

Valerie Van Arsdale Shrader

Stitch a Seam

To avoid boggling your mind, we've kept the sewing fairly simple in "Sewing Curtains" and "Stylish Skirts," using only basic techniques. There are three stitches: the straight stitch, the basting stitch, and the zigzag. The straight stitch is the foundation of your curtain, you can also do the straight stitch in reverse to anchor the beginning of your seams or to provide reinforcement at certain points, such as the end of a line of trim. (Consult our friend the manual for reverse stitching.) The basting stitch is simple a straight stitch set to a longer length. Use basting stitches to hold layers together temporarily or to gather fabric. Zigzag stitches are used to finish the raw edges of seams, or for just plain fun.

Our three stitches

When you're practicing, use a contrasting thread so you can easily see what's happening. Also, use two pieces of fabric for the best results; sewing machines are designed to join two layers of fabric, so the top and bobbin stitches meet in the middle. Refer to You Know What for the proper way to thread your machine, wind the bobbin, and accurately set the stitch length. A setting of 10–12 stitches per inch is average for the type of sewing we're doing.

To sew a seam, align the fabric edges and pin them together with the pins perpendicular, with the heads near the edge. Line up the fabric to the ½-inch (1.3 cm) guideline on your sewing machine's needle plate; ½-inch (1.3 cm) seam allowances are standard in home décor sewing. Place the fabric underneath the needle just a tiny bit (oh, ¼ inch [6mm]) away from the end of the fabric. Lower the presser foot. (Do remember to do this because gnarly things happen if you forget.) Hold the bobbin and top threads while you backstitch a couple of stitches to the end of the seam. Let go of the threads and stitch forward, pausing to remove the pins as you go. Don't, don't, don't be tempted to stitch over the pins—you can break a needle, or worse, ruin your machine's timing by hitting a pin. Or even worse, have shards of metal flying around you and your curtain.

Guide the fabric lightly with your hands, keeping it straight against the guideline on your needle plate. Watch the guideline and not the needle—it can be hypnotizing. (Really!) Let the machine do the work of pulling the fabric along (that's what those busy little feed dogs do). When you reach the end of the seam, backstitch for a few stitches to secure.

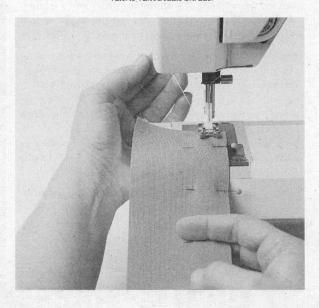

Congratulations—you've just stitched your first seam. Go get a latte.

Balance the Tension

After your coffee (and maybe a snack too), take a moment to admire your first seam. Look at both sides of the fabric; the stitches should look nearly identical on each side, being locked between the two pieces of fabric. If they don't look identical, you may need to adjust the thread tension on your machine. Each thread (top and bobbin) has its own tension. You may need to make adjustments to the tension according to the type of fabric you're using to make your curtain. Every time you sew with a new fabric, you should check the tension first.

The examples at the right show correct tension; top tension that's too tight; and top tension that's too loose. When the top tension is too tight, it yanks the poor bobbin thread up to the right side of the fabric; the opposite happens when the top tension is too loose. Following the instructions in (guess what?) your manual, make small adjustments at a time and do test seams until you're happy with the tension setting.

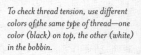

To check thread tension, use different colors of the same type of thread—one color (black) on top, the other (white) in the bobbin.

This example shows top tension that's too loose

Here, the top tension is too tight.

The example above shows correct tension.

Pivot

When you're sewing, you occasionally have to change direction—just like driving. When you need to do an about-face, you do so like this: stop with the needle in the fabric. Raise your presser foot and turn the fabric. Lower your presser foot and have at it!

2-7a

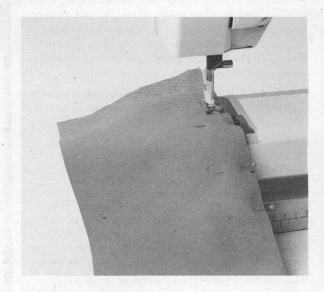

Guide the Fabric

Sometimes you don't need a complete change of direction, just some friendly guidance. Use a gentle pull of the fabric to keep the fabric aligned on your needle plate.

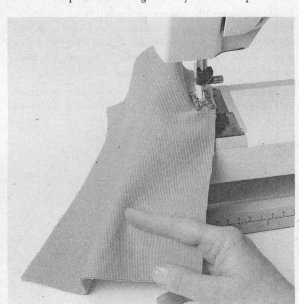

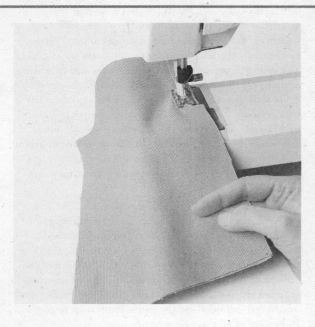

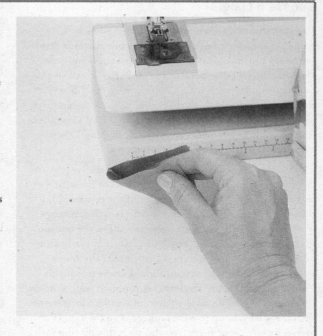

Curved seams demand a little extra attention. If you have any curved seams, you'll need to notch the curves every inch or so to allow the seams to lie flat. Cut notches in the seam allowance to eliminate fullness, using just the tips of the scissors, or use your pinking shears for quickie notching.

Finish the Seams

Conventional sewing wisdom says that all exposed seams should be finished in some manner, to prevent raveling and increase the longevity of your project. Sounds like good advice to me. Because of the construction of many of our projects, most of our raw edges are covered (unless we left them on display on purpose). So we have very few seams that require finishing. But here are a few simple methods we used every once in a while.

Zigzag. If you want to finish the seams before you sew, sew a line of zigzag stitching into the seam allowance, as close to the cut edge as you can. This is a good choice for fabrics that tend to ravel easily. After stitching the seam, press it open. If you're using a lightweight fabric, you might find that it's a little tricky to stitch into the single thickness without the fabric puckering, so use one of the methods that follow instead.

Double-Stitched. The double-stitched seam is good for extra stability. After the seam has been sewn, stitch a parallel line of stitching in the seam allowance, then trim away close to the second line of stitching. Press to one side. (You could do a second line of stitching in a frisky little zigzag, too.)

Pinked. This is a good choice for tightly woven fabrics. After stitching the seam, trim with pinking shears. Press open to finish.

French Seam. This is an enclosed seam that's perfect for sheer fabrics. Begin by stitching the wrong sides together in a ¼-inch (6 mm) seam. Trim the seam to within a millimeter of its life (that is, very short) and turn the fabric inside out so the right sides are together. Now, stitch together in a ¼-inch (6 mm) seam, encasing the raw edge. You've created a traditional-looking seam on the outside and a neat fold on the inside. You can use this method on straight seams only.

—From *Fun & Fabulous Curtains to Sew*

Trim Seams and Clip Curves

When you sew, you occasionally need to trim a seam, especially if you're using bulky fabric. Our project instructions will tell you when to do this. Generally, you trim a seam to reduce bulk in the finished project. Simply use your shears to trim away the seam allowance to about ¼ inch (6 mm).

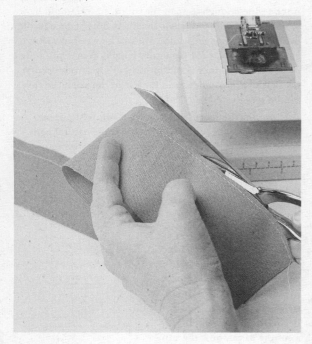

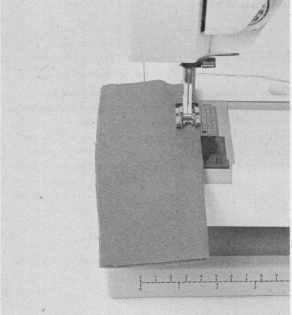

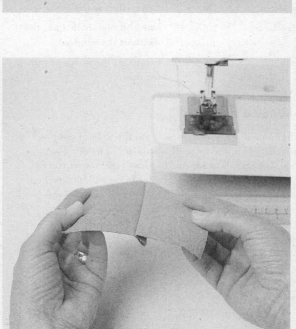

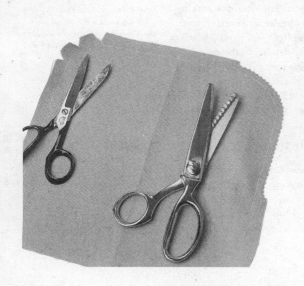

Continued →

Choose a Length

Just as there are different categories of window treatments, there are also reasons to make your curtains different lengths, the most important of which is your own aesthetic. Some other reasons are practical—if you've got a radiator underneath your window, you probably don't want your curtains so long they cover up your heat source or become a fire hazard. Generally, you'll find that more formal window treatments are often floor-length, while more casual styles are usually shorter.

There are some general guidelines for curtain lengths. We just discussed valances (on the upper part of the window) and café curtains (on the lower part of the window), but note there are three other lengths. Sill length can range from about ½ inch (1.3 cm) above the sill to the bottom of the framework; apron length can fall from the bottom of the framework to 6 inches (15 cm) below the framework; and full-length curtains should drape to roughly ½ inch (1.3 cm) above the floor. If you want your window treatments to puddle on the floor, make them longer than floor length, up to a foot longer if you'd like. (Pet lovers, beware: your furry friends may enjoy playing with your ultra-long curtains.)

Choose a Width

Just as there are general notions for the length of a curtain, there are similar ideas about curtain width. This refers to how full the curtain will be. Recommendations vary slightly, so we'll offer you a range of options.

Tailored curtains are the same width as the window, standard curtains are from one and one-half to two times the width of the window; and full curtains are two to three times the width of the window. The figures are also somewhat dependent on the fabric you choose; a sheer fabric can be gathered to a greater degree than heavy linen can, for example. To simplify matters (which is what we're all about, remember), we used the formulas you see in the box when we made our projects. You'll see the fullness icons that refer to these formulas (1X, 1.5X, 2X) again in the instructions that accompany our lovely curtains.

When we discuss measuring, you'll also see a helpful illustration about length and width.

Tailored	1X	same width as the window
Standard	1.5X	one and one-half times the width of the window
Full	2X	two times the width of the window

Choose a Heading

After you've got a basic idea about the style of your curtain, you should decide what kind of heading you want. The terms header or heading refer to the top of the curtain, the area of the curtain that will be attached to the curtain rod or pole. These terms can also refer specifically to the decorative fabric that extends above the casing (figure 1), and you'll probably find the terms used interchangeably. (In other words, the curtain experts disagree on the definitions.)

For our purposes, tabs, ties, pleats, casings, etc., will all be considered types of headings. A heading can be as plain as a simple rod pocket

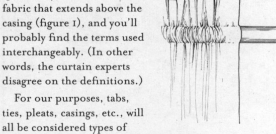

Figure 1: A decorative header

casing, or as elaborate as a series of triple pleats. The latter are created rather simply by using special tapes that create all sorts of lovely effects, as you'll see below. If your taste tends to the classic or formal, you may want to investigate these products. But if your taste tends to the funky, headings can also be embellished with ribbon or fringe,

because the header is the perfect canvas on which to play. We'll learn to make the basic types of headings when we Learn to Sew! (I can't wait!)

Buy Your Hardware

For the greatest accuracy, it helps to have the hardware in place when you measure for your window treatment project. (We'll learn how to measure under "Measuring.") We've used fairly straightforward rods for most of our projects, again with simplicity and ease in mind. It makes sense to have the hardware before you begin to make your curtains for several other reasons, too. The diameter of the rod itself is important if you're making curtains with a rod pocket and/or header, because that will affect the length of your curtains—as well as how they fit the road. We'll talk about this some more under "Calculating").

There are decorative considerations as well. Even though the selection of hardware is huge, maybe it's not as huge as you thought. What I'm trying to say is this: Don't assume the perfect hardware will be there after you've already invested time and money in your window treatments. If the color and style of the hardware is vitally important to your overall vision, buy it first so it becomes part of the planning process for your curtain projects. While you can extrapolate and say, "Well, I know I'll put the rod 2 inches above the window," it's really best to mount it first.

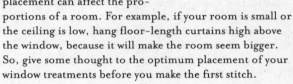

We're not interior designers around here, but here's an interesting idea about the placement of your window treatments. A well-conceived placement can affect the proportions of a room. For example, if your room is small or the ceiling is low, hang floor-length curtains high above the window, because it will make the room seem bigger. So, give some thought to the optimum placement of your window treatments before you make the first stitch.

Choose Your Fabric

Even the most outrageously easy-to-make curtain can look extraordinary when you choose the right fabric.

A little general background first. Fabrics can be woven or knit, and are made of fibers of various origins. Since you're interested in sewing, you probably already have a basic knowledge of the different types of fabric and what they're made from: the natural fibers, such as cotton, linen, wool, and silk; and the synthetic fibers, like polyester, acrylic, and nylon. (Isn't chemistry wonderful?) Rayon straddles these two categories, as it's synthesized from wood pulp; it's man-made, yet from a natural source. Other synthetic fabrics are made from sources such as petroleum products, and many fabrics are blends of natural and synthetic fibers.

Each bolt of fabric in the store will be labeled with its fiber content, its width, its price, and occasionally its laundering requirements. Now, the mention of the word "launder" brings up another important question about your curtains—every now and then, they're going to need to be cleaned. This factor directly relates to the kind of fabric that would be most appropriate for your window treatments, and it also relates to the all-important pocketbook. Most silks, you probably know, need to be professionally cleaned. So, do you want to be able to wash the curtains yourself, or are you willing to pay to have them dry-cleaned? Be sure to ask about laundering the fabric before you buy it, so you understand how you must care for your curtains after you've made them. Washable fabrics need to be preshrunk before being sewn, which simply means laundering them according to the manufacturer's recommendations before you start to sew. (Don't worry; we're going to go through the whole process step-by-step....)

If a fabric is woven, its weave gives it specific characteristics. Satin, velvet, twill, and so on describe the structure of the fabric and not its fiber content. Velvet can be made from silk, cotton, or polyester, for example. The only types of fabric that should be avoided in making curtains are those that are very stiff, because they won't drape well. For a happy sewing experience, consider using cotton fabric for your first project because it handles and washes well, it's durable, and it's easy to sew. Cotton is also relatively inexpensive, and this is not an unimportant consideration: depending on the style of window treatment you choose, you could need many (perhaps *many*) yards of fabric.

When you're shopping, you've got two choices. You can look in a shop that specializes in dressmaking goods, or you can visit a store that offers decorator fabrics for home décor applications. There are wonderful fabrics to be had at each type of shop. Dressmaking fabrics (also called fashion fabrics) are usually folded lengthwise and wrapped around a cardboard bolt. Decorator fabrics are usually left unfolded—so the entire width is on display—and rolled in all their glory onto a tube.

A major difference between the two types of fabric is the width, most dressmaking fabrics are 44 or 45 inches (111.8 or 114.3 cm) wide, while decorator fabrics are 54 or even 60 inches (137 or 152.4 cm) wide. This extra width could be significant, as a few more inches of width could prevent you from having to buy lots of additional fabric. For example, if you're dressing a very wide window, and you want a full curtain, dressmaking fabric may not be wide enough to span the width, so you would have to stitch two widths of fabric together. Since fabric is sold by the length, not the width, you still have to buy enough additional yardage for the entire length, even if you only need a few extra inches of width (figure 2). And, decorator fabrics are also designed for use in the home, so they can be very durable.

Consider the fabric's weight when you're shopping. A lightweight, sheer fabric will allow some natural light while camouflaging a less-than-perfect view, while a heavyweight fabric will help insulate and block out light, providing more privacy, if that's what you're after. (And let's face it, some of us do want more privacy.) It's a good idea to get swatches of the fabrics that interest you and take them home so you can hold them up to the window you're going to decorate. This is helpful for a couple of reasons: the sunlight may have an effect on the fabric, perhaps making it appear more sheer, and the light will probably affect the density of the color, too. You may consider buying just enough fabric (¼ yard or 22.9 cm) to practice sewing with it, too, to be sure you and the fabric are compatible.

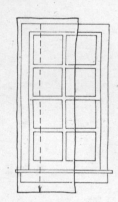

Figure 2. In most cases the length of fabric will flow down the window in one continuous piece. You may occasionally add additional width (indicated by the dashed line) for a wide window treatment.

Design Your Window Treatment

Now that we've talked about form and function, let's get down to the nitty-gritty and plan your window treatment. Then, we'll figure out your yardage requirements so you can buy fabric, and then we start sewing! The fun will soon begin. Here's a little list of things to think about.

Style

Length

Fullness

Heading

Fabric

Okay. You've got a couple of windows that desperately

need some excitement. Your style is casual, with some bohemian elements tossed in for drama. You're a beginning sewer, so how about a simple pair of rod-pocket curtains? This decision covers both the style and the heading, too. A cool fabric, maybe an interesting print, will add just the touch your room needs.

So, how about the length? Floor-length curtains are probably a bit formal for you. And sill length will leave some of the window framework exposed, and it's not what you might call beautiful. Let's consider apron length, which will cover the window frame. Perfect.

Next, we'll consider the fullness. You probably want a little romance, so your lovely fabric can billow about with the spring breeze. Let's decide on a standard width, which is one and one-half times the width of the window. The fabric will cover your window with some extra fullness to spare.

As to the heading, we're going to keep it simple for this first project, so we already picked a simple rod pocket, or casing, for the header. So our final decision becomes the fabric. After a delightful afternoon of browsing fabric stores, we decided on a lovely cotton print, with paisley and flower motifs. Our swatch looked fabulous when we displayed in on our window, with the light illuminating the print. We loved it! So now we figure out how much fabric to buy. Please put your thinking caps on for a few minutes while we talk yardage.

Calculating Yardage Requirements

Now that you've decided what kind of window treatment you want, it's time to buy your fabric. To purchase the proper amount of fabric for your windows, you have to do some measuring and some figuring. (Yes, this means a little math. But it's not hard. Trust me.) The yardage you'll need will depend upon several factors, including the finished length of the curtain, the fullness of your curtain, and the width of the curtain rod.

Measuring

As we mentioned earlier, it's best to have the rod in place before you measure, because you've got to factor in its placement when you plan your curtains. There are no real rules for placing the rods (and if there were, we wouldn't care, would we?) Current wisdom suggests that the brackets should be mounted about 2 to 4 inches (5 to 10 cm) above the window frame and from 2 to 4 inches (5 to 10 cm) on either side. Feel free to use your best judgment, however, and install the rods where you think they'll look best.

If possible, use a locking metal tape measure for the greatest accuracy. Measure from the rod to the desired length, or drop, of your curtain; if you're planning to attach your curtains with clips, hang a clip onto the rod and measure from the bottom of the clip, not the rod. If you're making floor-length curtains, you may want to measure at several spots along the width of the window, as the window may not be completely plumb, or your floor may not be exactly level. For the width, measure the rod from bracket to bracket, not the window, unless you plan to mount your curtains inside the window frame. And if you're dressing more than one window in a room, measure each window, even if you think they're all the same size.

Figure 3 details the areas to measure. Next, we'll figure out some yardage so you can see how it's done.

Calculating

We're going to use the same rod-pocket curtain we planned under "Design Your Window Treatment" as an example in this little exercise. Let's figure the length first, as it's quite straightforward.

1. We measured from the top of the rod to our desired finished length, which is the bottom of the sill (55 inches [140 cm]).

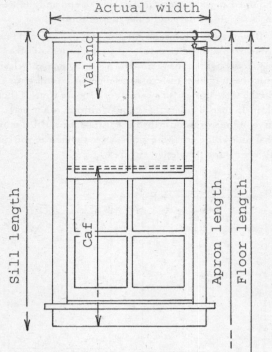

Figure 3. Here are the areas to measure, including some common curtain lengths. You should measure for the length from the top of the rod (unless your curtain will hang from drapery clips), and measure the width between the finials, from bracket to bracket. Variations in length are indicated by dashes at the ends of the lines.

2. Now, to the finished length, we added an allowance for the rod pocket (3 inches [7.5 cm]).
3. Next, we added an allowance for the hem (6 inches [15 cm]).
4. We totaled these figures for our cut length (64 inches [162.5 cm]).
5. Because we plan to have a rod pocket header, e need to allow for the diameter of the rod, which will cause our curtain to be a little shorter. This is called the take-up allowance. If your hem length is critical (for instance, if you want to have your curtains hit just at the edge of the sill, as we did), you'll need to factor in the take-up distance. Add the diameter of the rod (⅝ inches [1.5 cm], in our case) to your length (so our total is 64⅝ inches [164 cm]). If your hem length can vary a little, you don't have to worry about the take-up distance….
6. Next, we measured the width from bracket to bracket (53 inches [134.5]).
7. We divided this figure by the number of panels we want, which is two (53÷2 = 26½ inches [67.5 cm]).
8. We decided to use the standard fullness (1.5X) for this project, so we multiplied the standard fullness by the actual width of each panel (1½ x 26½ inches = 39¾ inches [4 x 67.5 cm]), and rounded up to the next whole number (40 inches [101.5 cm]).
9. We then added on the additional allowances for the side hems, 4 inches (10 cm) on each side of each panel. So we added 8 inches (20.5 cm) to the width of each panel to reach our cut width for each panel (40 + 8 = 48 inches [122 cm]).
10. To calculate our yardage, we need the total width for our curtain, so we'll multiply by 2, since we have two panels (48 x 2 = 96 inches [144 cm])….
11. We divided our total cut width (96 inches [144 cm]) by the width of our fabric (96÷54 = 1⅘ widths).
12. We rounded up the figure from step 11 to 2 widths. (Always round up, people, because you can't buy less than a full width of fabric.)
13. Finally, we multiplied the number of widths we needed (2) by the length we needed (64⅝ inches [164 cm]) to figure our total fabric requirement (2 x 64⅝ = 129¼ inches [328 cm]).
14. To figure yardage, we divided 129¼ inches by 36 (a bit over 3½ yards [320 cm]). To be on the safe side,

we rounded up to have a little extra fabric, so we purchased 4 yards [366 cm] of cotton.

15. From our 4 yards, we'll cut two panels that are each 48 inches wide (122 cm) (from step 9) x 64⅝ inches long (164 cm) (from step 5).

Use the chart below to calculate your fabric needs. If you're putting a very full curtain on a super-wide window, you'll need to stitch widths of fabric together. If so, add an extra inch of fabric in step 9 for each seam you need.

FABRIC CALCULATOR

_____	1. Finished length
+ _____	2. Header
+ _____	3. Lower hem
_____	4. Cut length per panel
+ _____	5. Take-up allowance (if applicable)
_____	Total cut length
_____	6. Width of curtain (bracket to bracket)
÷ _____	7. Number of panels
_____	Width per panel
× _____	8. Desired fullness
_____	Total fullness per panel
+ _____	9. Side hems
_____	Cut width per panel
× _____	10. Number of panels
_____	Total cut width
÷ _____	11. Fabric width
_____	12. Total widths needed (round up)
× _____	13. Total cut length
_____	Total fabric needed
÷ _____	14. Inches per yard
_____	Total yardage needed
_____	15. Dimension of each cut panel

Learn to Sew!

In all honesty, a curtain is just about the easiest sewing project you can imagine. We're going to cut the fabric; mark the pieces, if we need to; and stitch it up. That's it! Sewing is really a lot like the process of cooking: you choose a recipe (the curtain style); buy the ingredients (fabric and notions); do the washing and chopping (preparing and cutting out the fabric); then add the ingredients to one another according to the recipe (sew by following the project instructions). See—easy as pie. Or, if you'd rather—a piece of cake….

Continued →

Prepare the Fabric

You have to know a little more about fabric to understand the importance of the proper layout and subsequent cutting of your window treatment, so bear with me a moment. When we discussed fabric earlier, we talked about prewashing. Now, prewashing actually means *shrinking*, as many washable fabrics will do just that when laundered. Generally, the looser the weave, the more shrinkage is likely to occur. Washing also removes sizing or finishes that may affect the quality of your stitches. Check the label on the bolt of cloth for the laundering recommendations, and launder the fabric the same way you plan to launder your curtain. Please don't neglect this very important step, because you'll be totally bummed to wash your curtain for the first time and then find that it's become too small for its window! After you've laundered your fabric, press it to remove any wrinkles. (Remember: press, not iron.)

Align the Grain

Your fabric must be correctly aligned before you cut out the curtain pieces, and here's why. (We'll get to the how in just a few minutes.) Woven fabric is made of lengthwise and crosswise threads. In a perfect world, the crosswise threads are perpendicular to the lengthwise threads. The direction of these threads is called the *grain*.

Your curtain pieces must follow the proper direction of the grain, or they won't hang properly. Most garment pieces follow the lengthwise (or straight) grain, because the lengthwise threads are designed to be stronger to withstand the tension of the weaving process. Curtains almost always have to be cut along this lengthwise grain because the width is finite (45 inches [114.5 cm], 54 inches [137 cm], etc), while the length is not. Generally, you don't see curtains with seams bisecting the length, as you want a continuous flow of fabric along the drop.

You should also know about *bias*; the bias flows along the diagonal between the lengthwise and crosswise threads. This is the direction in which woven fabric has the most stretch. While we won't cut any fabric along the bias, file this fact away because it helps you understand why it's so important to cut the fabric properly—your curtain may stretch out of shape if it's not cut along the lengthwise grain.

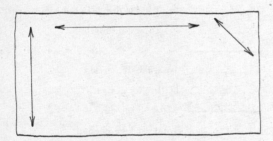

Here's how the grain flows in a length of fabric.

When making almost anything else except a window treatment, you would fold the fabric before you cut out the pieces. But with a curtain, you're generally using the entire width for one panel, so you should place the entire piece, unfolded, on a flat surface. Smooth out the fabric so it's flat. To align the grain, you'll square the fabric edges, working from the finished border on the length of the fabric, which is the selvage. This border differs in appearance from fabric to fabric, but you'll be able to recognize it.

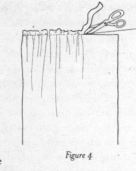

Figure 4

There are several ways to square the edges. One is to clip into the selvage and pull out a crosswise thread across the entire width of the fabric. Then, trim the edge evenly along this visible line, as you see in figure 4. After you've trimmed away the excess fabric, the cut end and the selvages should be perpendicular to one another.

If your fabric seems too thick to pull out a thread (and some decorator fabrics are), here are a couple of other ways to straighten the grain. Use a cutting mat and clear ruler to straighten the crosswise edges or, as in figure 5, do the same thing with a carpenter's square (one of those shiny L-shaped rulers that your significant other may have in the workshop). If you're using fabric with a motif that follows the crosswise grain across the fabric, you can also cut along this design (figure 6).

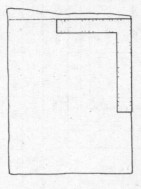 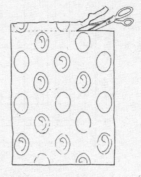

Figure 5 · *Figure 6*

Cut Out the Curtain Pieces

Since you're all smart enough to make your own window treatments, you've probably figured out that you need a lot of space to cut out your curtain panels. And you'd be absolutely correct. A large table, or a nice clean floor, will do nicely if you're thrifty; if you'd like to invest in your sewing future, buy an extra-large cutting mat.

After squaring the fabric, use your measurements to cut each panel, marking the dimensions with a fabric pen, pencil, or chalk. (If your fabric is wider than your panel will be, you may need

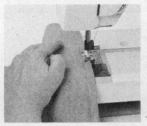 

Cutting the fabric to the proper length

to cut away some of the width, too. If your finished panel needs to be wider than your fabric, remember to add an inch to the finished width for each seam). Follow your markings as you cut, using shears or a rotary cutter. Mark the top of each panel. Trim away the selvages.

Remember when we talked about the grain of the fabric? One of our projects (Stylish Swag) has pieces that need to be aligned with the straight grain of the fabric when you cut them out. On the pattern pieces you'll see a line with arrows at either end; place the pieces on the fabric, with the line following the lengthwise grain. Measure from each arrow until they're the same distance from the selvage; keep tweaking until they're equidistant and the line is parallel with the selvage. Pin in place and cut.

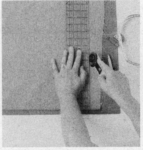

Aligning with the straight grain

Start to Sew

In the following section, we'll talk about the basic techniques that we've used in our curtain projects. Don't try to remember everything at once, but read it through so you have a general understanding of the process. Later, in the Make a Curtain! Section, you'll see how the techniques work in context when you make your own curtain. We've presented them here with contrasting stitching so you can easily see what happens during each step. Furthermore, we've used fabric that's similar to what we used for many of our curtains (cotton), so you can see

real-world examples of how these fabrics behave when they're sewn. This isn't computer-enhanced sewing we're doing here.

And you may notice real-world sewing in your projects, too—fabrics fray when they're handled and some techniques put more stress on the fabric, so you'll probably see a thread or two. So tidy up when you're done, trimming all loose threads.

Editor's Note: For directions on stitching seams, see "More Things to Know Before You Sew: Stitching Seams."

Right Sides Together

You'll almost always sew the pieces of your curtain with the right sides together (facing each other). This is the most basic fact you need to remember about sewing in general. If your fabric doesn't have easily recognizable right and wrong sides, you'll have to decide which is which. Then be sure to mark each piece.

Make a Narrow Hem

Several of the curtains have edges that are finished with narrow hems. It's just like it sounds: a skinny little hem that's stitched in place on the machine. Typically they're made like this: Stitch ½ inch (1.3 cm) or so from the raw edge and press up along this line of stitching. Tuck under the raw edge to meet the stitching, forming a nice fold. Press and stitch in place along the fold.

Now, there's also a very narrow hem, which is great for sheer or lightweight fabrics. To make a very narrow hem, machine-stitch ⅜ inch (1 cm) from the raw edge. Turn under on the line of stitching and stitch close to fold. Trim the fabric close to the stitching line. Turn under ⅛ inch (3 mm), encasing the raw edge. Stitch the hem in place. Press.

Make a Double Hem

Most simple curtains... are hemmed at the sides and the bottom. Standard practice is to use a *double hem* (also known as a double-fold hem). Double hems provide stability and add weight to the edges of your window treatments.

You can probably guess what a double hem is: two equalized folds that are stitched down. The most accurate way to do this is to first fold the complete depth of the hem, let's say 4 inches (10 cm). Press the fold. Now, turn under the raw edge to meet the pressed fold, which leaves a 2-inch (5 cm) hem. Press again, and stitch in place. The fold we just described would be referred to as a 2-inch (5 cm) double hem.

Add a Heading

As we talked about before, there are many ways to construct the top of your curtain. If you were planning just a basic curtain—a rectangle hemmed on all four sides—you could simply hang it with clip rings and be done with it. But you might want more from your curtain—and you shall have it!

Rod Pocket. This easy heading, also called a casing, or maybe even a channel, is formed by a couple of simple folds. Turn under 2½ to 5 inches (6.5 to 12.5 cm) (depending on the diameter of your curtain rod) and press. Turn under ½ inch (1.3 cm) on the raw edge and press. Pin and stitch in place.

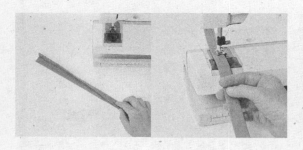

Rod Pocket with Header. This header is made from extra fabric that forms a flourish at the top of the curtain. To construct it, you'll add one more row of stitching between the top of the curtain and the rod, forming an inner casing, so you must factor in the extra fabric. Add twice the depth of the header to the amount you allow for the casing. (For instance, if you allowed 4 inches (10 cm) for your casing and wanted a 2-inch (5 cm) header, you would add another 4 inches (10 cm) for the header, allowing 8 inches for the header and casing combined.) For the best fit, your lines of stitching should snugly encase the rod.

Tabs. This heading style really suits casual curtains, yet can be used for sophisticated silk or linen curtains, too. Tabs offer a great opportunity to show off a decorative curtain rod, as much of it will be visible through the tabs.

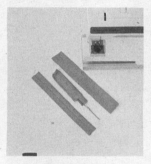 

Tabs can be as narrow as an inch, or as wide as several inches, depending upon your preference. To determine the length of your tabs, wrap a scrap of fabric around your curtain rod and mark your desired size. Add an inch for seam allowances and double your desired width, again adding an inch for seam allowances. Cut as many tabs as needed; they should be spaced from 6 to 8 inches (15 to 20.5 cm) along the top of your curtain.

To make the tab, you'll place the right sides together and fold the piece in half along its length. Stitch in a ½-inch (1.3 cm) seam. Turn the tab right side out and place the seam in the center of the back of the tab. Press.

Tabs are usually basted to the window treatment and stitched in place between the curtain and a facing, an extra piece of fabric that's cut to the width of the curtain. Look to the individual project instructions for specifics on adding tabs.

Ties. There are a couple of ways you can make ties for your curtains. The easiest tie is created like so: cut a piece of fabric to the length you want the tie. Fold it in half lengthwise and press; turn each raw edge into the center and press again. Stitch. Knot the ends. Stitch to the curtain according to the project instructions.

Making a skinny tube tie is slightly more involved, but not much. Here are two methods. For the first, stitch a length of fabric together with the right sides facing and—presto!—turn it inside out. Because these ties are narrow, you'll need some way to turn them inside out. There are several gadgets you can buy to turn tubes, or you can just attach a safety pin to one end and thread the pin back through the tube, pulling it right side out.

For the second method, fold the fabric with right sides together and stitch along the length, pivot, and stitch across the end. Use an object like a pencil to push against the seam on the end, turning the tube inside out.

Grommets and Header Tapes. You'll also see a couple of projects… that employ these nifty things to make curtain headings. Although we give some general advice in the project section, we're going to cop out and ask that you follow the manufacturer's instructions when you use these products, because each company's stuff is a little bit different. Ask for assistance at your fabric shop if you need some guidance about these items.

Clip Rings. If you use clip rings, all you have to do to the heading of your curtain is finish it with a double hem and you're ready to hang. A link ring is a variation of a clip ring; it has two interlocking rings instead of a clip. Often, these will be sewn into place.

Miter the Edges

Occasionally, you'll hem all the way around a curtain, and you'll want to have some tidy corners. A mitered corner is one that's been folded to eliminate bulk and, well, just look good, too. This technique works when you're hemming an equal length on each side.

Photo 1 *Photo 2*

Photo 3 *Photo 4*

Press under your desired hem on each edge. Open out the folds. (If you've got a double hem, unfold one fold only.) Fold the corner diagonally at the spot where the two fold lines intersect; the previous fold lines should align (photo 1). Press across the corner fold. To check what you're doing, fold again along the original hemline. Your edges should meet in a perfect little angle. Unfold once more and trim away the excess corner (go ahead, do it!), leaving about ½ inch (1.3 cm) of fabric (photo 2). Fold back into the mitered edge (photo 3). Stitch in place (photo 4), slipstitching the mitered edges together if desired.

Add a Facing

A facing is a piece of fabric used to finish an edge. In our projects, facings are used to finish he heading of a curtain. They're usually cut to the length of the piece being finished and are several inches wide. We used a facing when we stitched on the tabs on, remember?

Add a Ruffle

Ruffles add a little bit of whimsy to anything. You can use ruffles to decorate the edge or hem of a curtain, and you can also use them as a simple decorative element. A ruffle is simply a long strip of fabric that is gathered to fit your curtain. A single ruffle is gathered along one long edge, while a double ruffle is gathered in the middle, between its two long edges. (In a fancy magazine, you may also see a double ruffle referred to as a *ruche*.)

To make a single ruffle, make a narrow hem along one long edge. Gather the ruffle by making two rows of basting stitches along the remaining long edge; don't trim the thread ends. Pull the threads to gather the ruffles to the approximate length needed. Pin in place and adjust the gathers for balance. To make a double ruffle, follow the same procedure as just described, but finish both long edges and make the rows of basting stitches down the center of the fabric.…

Stitch by Hand

You need only a few basic hand stitches to make the curtains in this section. Begin all hand stitches with a knot in the thread.

One stitch you're likely to use is the hemstitch. A hemstitch is begun with the needle inserted into the fold of the fabric. Work from right to left as you pick up just a thread or two in the fabric and then insert the needle into the edge of the fold above the first stitch; the needle should be perpendicular to the fold. Repeat, making stitches every ¼ inch (6 mm) or so.

Another stitch you may use is the slipstitch, a fairly invisible little stitch. A slipstitch is used between two folded edges, to secure a mitered edge, for instance. From the wrong side, insert the needle into the fold of the fabric and pull the thread. Work from right to left as you pick up just a thread or two in one fold and then insert the needle into the fold opposite the first stitch. Repeat, making stitches every ¼ inch (6 mm) or so.

There are several other hand stitches you may find useful. The tack is simply a straight stitch used to join layers of fabric. You can repeat them in place, or make a series of straight stitches. Use a series of tacks to sew on a curtain ring, for example. The backstitch is a stitch worked from left to right, with each stitch ending at the edge of the previous stitch. It's a sturdy stitch because the thread overlaps on the back side of the fabric.

Finish a line of hand stitching in one of two ways. Make a series of small backstitches repeated several times in place. You can also make a quick knot. Make a wee stitch on top of your last stitch on the wrong side of your fabric,

Continued ➤

forming a small loop. Pull the needle through the loop until a second loop forms. Pull the needle through the second loop tightly to form a knot.

Check the Fit

Does this seem like a silly idea? On the contrary, fitting your window treatments before you hem the bottom is probably a good idea, at least until you feel confident with your measuring and sewing skills. If you need to tweak the hem allowance, it's easier to do it *before* you've stitched the hem than after! However, if you've measured carefully, cut out carefully, and stitched carefully, your window treatment should fit.

Fix a Mistake

The trick to making curtains successfully is all in the measurement, as most of the sewing is fairly straightforward. However, we all make mistakes, even the most experienced seamstresses (especially when our caffeine level is low). There's not much that can't be repaired by simply ripping out all the stitches and trying again. When you're using a seam ripper to remove stitches, be careful not to tear the fabric by ripping too enthusiastically. I know how much fun it can be (she says sarcastically).

If you're having a weak moment and feel unsure about something you've just stitched, chill a second and make sure it's correct before you do any trimming or clipping.

Embellish Your Curtain

Sometimes a window treatment needs a little TLC to make it extra special. The expanse of a curtain panel is the perfect canvas to decorate, and the embellishments you add offer you another opportunity to express your style. Here are a few ways that we've adorned our window treatments.

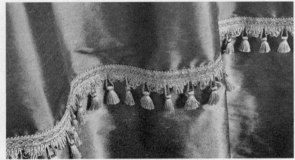

Photo 1

An obvious choice is to add decorative trim to make your curtain more beautiful. We merely stitched this luxurious trim onto the front of the curtain as a finishing touch (photo 1). You can use decorative stitching when you're sewing, too. Experiment with the placement and pin the trim or fabric in place before you begin, if necessary. And have some fun with trim, too, as we did in the valance project (photo 2).

Photo 2

Finally, you just can't write a book about curtains without including a ruffle or two. We have some ruffles in our café curtain (photo 3) that offer a modern deconstructed twist; these ruffles have raw edges.

Photo 3

Anatomy of a Curtain

It's so easy to make a curtain. Who knew?

1. Measure your window and add allowances for side and bottom hems. Cut out your panels to match your measurements.

2. Make double hems on the sides and the bottom.

3. To make a rod pocket casing, press under several inches at the top and turn under ½ inch (5 cm) on the raw edge.

4. Pin and stitch the casing in place.

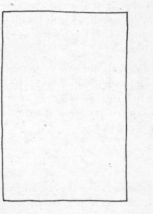
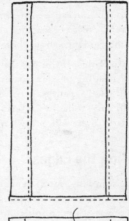
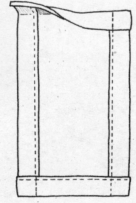
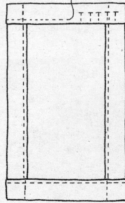

Projects

Key

Each of our projects is rated according to ease of construction. (Please note that I didn't say difficulty of construction.) Here's how we've organized them.

● Absolute Beginner
Suitable for the first-time sewer.

Basic skills you'll use:

Right sides together

Double hem

Add a header

Making tabs

● ● Easy Beginner
Suitable for the new sewer who understands the basics and is ready for more fun.

New skills you'll use:

Trim seams and clip curves

Make a French seam

Make a very narrow hem

Add grommets

Add a ruffle

● ● ● Experienced Beginner
Suitable for the sewer who's mastered the basics and is ready to redecorate the neighborhood.

New skills you'll use:

Use heading tape

Add a facing

● Simple Print Curtains

Can the easiest thing you could possibly make also be the most beautiful? You be the judge.

What You Need

Basic curtain-making tools and supplies

Fabric to fit your window (we used 6 yards [5.5 mm] of lightweight cotton)

Matching thread

Curtain Specs

Window #4

Width 1.5X

2 panels

How You Make It

1. Measure your window, include the appropriate allowances for hems and heading, and calculate your yardage according to the instructions. We added the following allowances to each panel: to the width, 8 inches (20.5 cm) for the side hems; and to the length, 6 inches for the lower hem, and 3 inches (7.5 cm) for the rod-pocket casing. Since the length of this curtain is critical, hitting just at the bottom of the sill, we factored in an additional ⅝ inch (1.5 cm) for the take-up allowance. Cut out two panels based on your measurements.

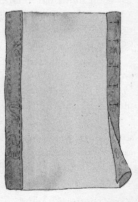

Figure 1

2. Make a 2-inch (5 cm) double hem at each side, folding under 4 inches (10 cm) and pressing, then folding the raw edge in to meet the fold. Press, pin, and stitch (figure 1).

3. Create the casing at the top of each panel. Press under 3 inches (7.5 cm) , and then turn under ½ inch (1.3 cm) on the raw edge. Press (figure 2). Pin in place and stitch (figure 3).

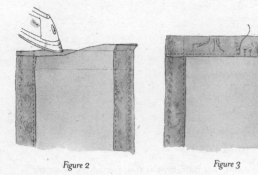

Figure 2   *Figure 3*

4. Make a 3-inch (7.5 cm) double hem at the bottom of each panel, using the same method you used in step 2.

• • Easy Shade

When you want to dress a window and enjoy your view, too, consider this gauzy window treatment.

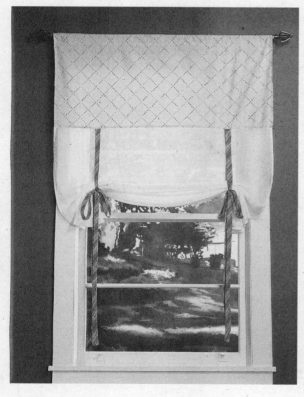

WHAT YOU NEED

Basic curtain-making tools and supplies

Fabric to fit your window (we used ¾ yard (68.5 cm) of linen/cotton blend, 1½ yards (137 cm) of sheer fabric, and ¼ yard (23 cm) of striped linen/cotton blend for the ties)

Matching thread

CURTAIN SPECS

Window #1

Width 1X

1 panel

TIP

FYI, our shade is almost floor length, so we have plenty of the sheer fabric t gather up in the ties.

HOW YOU MAKE IT

1. Measure your windows, include the appropriate allowances for hems and headings, and calculate your yardage. We added the following allowances to the shade: to the width, 2 inches (5 cm) for the side hems; determine the proportion of the panels to one another (the linen panel should be from one-third to one-fourth the length of your window) and to these dimensions, add 3⅝ inches (9 cm) to the linen panel for the header and the seam allowance, and 3⅝ inches (9 cm) to the sheer panel for the bottom hem and the seam allowance.

Cut out the linen panel and the sheer panel based on your measurements. We also cut four ties that were each 1½ x 55 inches (4 x 140 cm); you'll add two ties to the front of the shade and two ties to the back of the shade.

2. To make the ties for the back, fold under ¼ inch (6 mm) on each short end and press. Fold under ¼ inch (6 mm) on each long edge and press (figure 1), and then fold the fabric in half lengthwise. Press and pin. Topstitch along the edges. Make the ties for the front as those for the back, but turn under ¼ inch (6 mm) on one short end only, leaving the other end with raw edges.

Figure 1

3. Stitch the linen panel to the sheer panel with a ⅝-inch (1.5 cm) French seam. Begin by stitching the wrong sides together in a ¼-inch (6 mm) seam. Trim the seam and turn the fabric inside out so the right sides are together. Before you finish the French seam, you'll attach the ties.

4. Mark the location of the ties; our ties are about 8 inches (20.5 cm) from the side edges. Place the front ties between the panels, with the ends with the raw edges butting up to the seam (figure 2). Stitch together in a ⅜-inch seam, encasing the raw edges of the seams and the ends of ties. Press the seam toward the linen panel.

Figure 2

5. Make ½-inch (1.3 cm) double hems at each side of the shade, folding under 1 inch (2.5 cm) and pressing, then folding the raw edge in to meet the fold. Press, pin, and stitch.

6. Hem the bottom of the curtain by pressing under 3 inches (7.5 cm), and then turning under ½ inch (1.3 cm) on the raw edge. Press. Pin in place and stitch.

7. Add the remaining ties to the back of the shade, matching their placement to those on the front. Pin the ties in place (figure 3) and baste. Topstitch the French seam to the linen panel, sewing the ties in place at the same time. Remove the basting stitches.

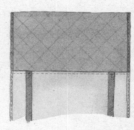

Figure 3

8. Create the casing at the top. Press under 3 inches (7.5 cm), and then turn under ½ inch (1.3 cm) on the raw edge. Press. Pin in place and stitch (figure 4).

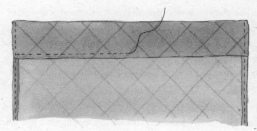

Figure 4

9. After hanging the shade, gather and tie as desired.

• • Café Curtain

The raw edges on these ruffles lend contemporary flair to a traditional window treatment. The charm lies in mixing and matching fabrics.

WHAT YOU NEED

Basic curtain-making tools and supplies

Fabric to fit your window (we used ¾ yard (68.5 cm) of lightweight cotton for the curtain, ½ yard (45.5 cm) for the large bottom ruffle, and ¼ yard (23 cm) for the small ruffles)

Matching thread

Café clip rings

Tension rod

CURTAIN SPECS

Window #2

Width 1X

1 panel

HOW YOU MAKE IT

1. Since you can adjust a tension rod to hand anywhere in a window, you don't have to do any complicated calculations for this curtain. Measure from the top to the bottom of your window, and divide this figure in half. This will be the length of your curtain (minus the bottom ruffle); round that number to the nearest ⅛ yard (11.5 cm) and purchase that amount of fabric (27 inches = ¾ yard (68.5 cm), for example) and use it as is—no additional cutting is necessary.

TIP

In the interest of full disclosure, we admit that this curtain is a just a teeny bit wider than 1X since we used the entire width of the fabric without any additional cutting. Thus, this design can accommodate windows that are less wide—but not wider—than the fabric itself. For example, our fabric was 44 inches (111.8 cm) wide, and our window was 36 inches wide, so we have some gentle gathers in our café curtain.

Continued ➡

For the large bottom ruffles, cut enough 6-inch-wide (15 cm) strips to equal 3 and one-half times the width of your finished curtain. For the smaller ruffles, cut enough 2-inch-wide (5 cm) strips to make two strips that are each 2 and one-half times the width of your finished curtain.

2. Make 1-inch (2.5 cm) double hems at the top and the sides of the curtain, mitering the edges. Fold under 2 inches (5 cm) and press, then fold the raw edge in to meet the fold. Press the double hem in place. To miter, undo the second fold and fold the corner diagonally at the spot where the two fold lines intersect; the previous fold lines and the seam should align (figure 1). Press the corner. Trim away the excess fabric, leaving about ½ inch (1.3 cm). Fold back into the mitered edge. Press, pin, and stitch the hems.

Figure 1

3. Using the fabric for the bottom ruffle, make a long strip to the length suggested in step 1. You'll need to sew several pieces together to reach the appropriate length; press all the seams open. Make ¼-inch (6 mm) double hems along both of the short edges, folding under ½ inch (1.3 cm) and pressing, then folding the raw edge in to meet the fold. Make two rows of basting stitches along one of the long edges, stitching the second row ¼ inch (6 mm) away from the first. Leave the thread ends long. Pull the threads gently and evenly gather the strip until it matches the width of the curtain (figure 2).

Figure 2

4. Place the curtain right side up and mark a line 1 inch (2.5 cm) away from the edge. Place the upper edge of the ruffle along the marked line (figure 3) and pin. Topstitch ¼ inch (6 mm) from the upper edge of the ruffle, then remove the basting stitches.

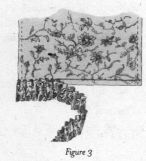

Figure 3

5. Using the fabric for the small ruffles, make two strips that each equal the length suggested in step 1; you'll have to sew several pieces together to reach the appropriate length. Press the seams open. Sew two rows of basting stitches along the center of each strip, then gather the fabric evenly until each matches the width of the curtain (figure 4).

Figure 4

6. Place the curtain right side up and mark a line 1½ inches (4 cm) from the top edge of the ruffle attached in step 4. With the right side up, pin one of the small ruffles to the curtain, placing its lower edge along the marked line. Stitch along the center of the ruffle. Carefully remove the basting stitches.

Figure 5

7. Mark a line 2½ inches (6.5 cm) from the top edge of the curtain. Place the remaining ruffle along this line (figure 5) and stitch as in step 6. Attach the café clip rings to the upper edge and hang as desired.

••• Stylish Swag

Although this swag has a traditional shape, its dangling bobbles give it a playful feel. And guess what? It's reversible.

WHAT YOU NEED

Basic curtain-making tools and supplies

Fabric and trim to fit your window (we used 1 yard each of medium-weight cotton in two coordinating patterns—fabrics A and B, 2 yards (1.8 m) of wide ultra-lightweight fusible web, 2½ yards (2.3 m) of ⅜-inch ribbon, and 2½ yards (2.3 m) of bobble fringe)

Matching thread

Adhesive tape

Templates

CURTAIN SPECS

Window #4

Width 1X

1 panel

HOW YOU MAKE IT

1. Although this pattern was designed for a window that's 49 inches (124.5 cm) wide, you can easily make it fit your window by altering pattern piece 1.

Determine how much narrower (or wider) you want the swag, and divide that figure in half. You'll revise the pattern from the centerline, either making it shorter (for a narrower curtain) or making it longer (for a wider curtain). For example, let's say you want to make a curtain that's 39 inches wide (99 cm). That's 10 inches (25.5 cm) narrower than our pattern; half of 10 inches is 5 inches (12.5 cm) away into the existing pattern piece. Trim the pattern piece along the new

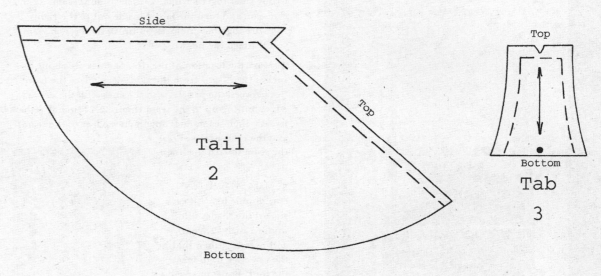

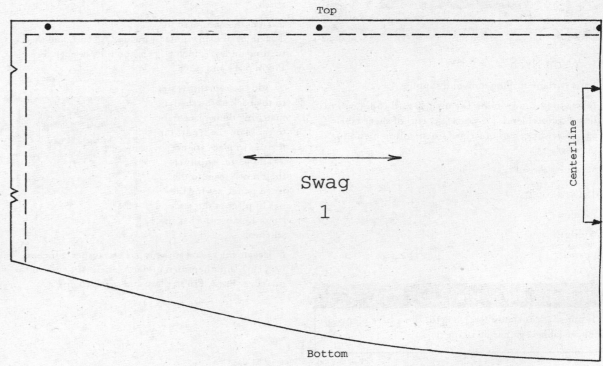

"Stylish Swag" templates; enlarge 500%

centerline. Adjust the center dot so it's equidistant between the dots at either end.

To widen the swag, tape a big sheet of paper onto the centerline. Determine how much wider than 49 inches (124.5 cm) you want the swag. Divide that figure in half, and mark a new centerline on the extra sheet that extends that distance from the pattern piece. It should be parallel to the existing centerline. Extend the gentle curve at the bottom of the swag so it crosses the revised centerline. Adjust the center dot as indicated above.

If you need to alter the pattern, check your accuracy—before cutting your fabric—after you've taped both halves of the paper pattern together in step 3. Measure the pattern piece and compare it to your window measurement.

2. Measure your windows, and calculate your yardage...Using the templates, enlarge the pattern pieces as directed and cut them out. Mark the dots and cut the notches.

3. Make a photocopy of pattern piece 1, cut it out, flip it, and tape it to the original, matching the centerlines. When using a directional fabric—one with a print that has an obvious top and bottom—be sure to place the pattern pieces with the upper edge facing toward the top of the fabric. Using fabric A, cut out one of pattern piece 1, cut two of pattern piece 2 (one with the pattern piece face up, and the other with the pattern piece face down, to make a left side and a right side), and cut 10 of pattern piece 3. Repeat, using fabric B. For the fusible web, cut one piece of pattern piece 1, and two of pattern piece 2.

4. Using fabric A, pin and sew pattern pieces 2 (the tails) to either side of pattern piece 1 (the swag), placing the right sides together and matching the notches. Press the seams open. Repeat with fabric B, making an identical piece from the coordinating fabric.

5. Repeat step 4 with the fusible web, but don't press the seams. (Using heat will not only activate the fusible web too soon, but it will ruin your iron and ironing board by covering them in melted glue. Yuck.) Pin the fusible web piece to the wrong side of fabric A (figure 1), matching all the edges, and stitch completely around the exterior, ¼ inch (6 mm) from the edge. Again, don't press!

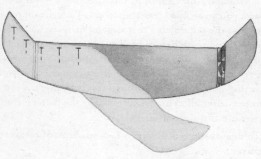

Figure 1

6. Begin making the tabs by pinning together one pattern piece 3 from fabric A and one pattern piece 3 from fabric B, right sides facing and matching the notches. Stitch along the notched edges. Press the seams open (figure 2).

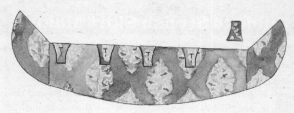

Figure 2

7. With right sides together, place one of the pieces made in the previous step atop another, matching the fabrics (figure 3). Stitch along both curves. Use the remaining pieces to make a total of five tabs. Notch the seams and press them open. Turn right side out and press.

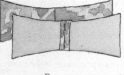

Figure 3

8. Attach the tabs as desired, displaying either the identical fabric, the contrasting fabric, or a combination of the two. (The tab floating above figure 4 shows how the contrasting fabric will look.) To display the contrasting fabric, pin the right side of a tab made of fabric A to the right side of the swag cut from fabric B, matching circles and raw edges. Baste ¼ inch (6 mm) from the raw edges. Repeat with the remaining tabs.

9. Fold each tab in half, matching circles and raw edges; pin and baste (figure 4 again).

Figure 4

10. Put the swags cut from fabrics A and B together, right sides facing. Pin the top edges, including the tails, together. Stitch along the top edge of the swag and the tails. Notch the seam allowance where the swag and the tails are stitched together. Use a *cold* iron to press open the seam.

11. Matching the edges, pin both sides of the curtain together around the whole exterior, smoothing away any wrinkles as you proceed (figure 5). Carefully iron the entire surface to fuse the fabrics together (finally!), following the manufacturer's instructions. Trim the edges even, if necessary.

Figure 5

12. Pin the ribbon to the bottom edge of one side of the swag, tucking both raw ends under. Stitch. Whipstitch the bobble fringe to the other side of the swag (figure 6).

Figure 6

• • • Elegant Silk Draperies

When you're ready for a sophisticated look, consider these drapes. Pleating tape makes the decorative heading quick and easy.

What You Need

Basic curtain-making tools and supplies

Fabric, trim, and accessories to fit your window (we used 4 yards (3.65 m) of blue silk for the top panels, 2 yards (1.8 m) of green silk for the bottom panels, 6 yards of lining fabric, 3 yards (2.75 m) of tassel fringe, and 4 yards (3.65 m) of pleating tape)

Thread to match each color of silk

Clear nylon thread

Tape hooks

Link rings

Curtain Specs

Window #3

Width 1.5X

2 panels

How You Make It

1. Measure your windows, include the appropriate allowances for hems and heading, and calculate your yardage and the instructions with your pleating tape. (See *Why?*) We added the following allowances to each panel: to the width, 3 inches (7.5 cm) for the side hems; determine the proportion of the panels to one another (our bottom piece is roughly one-quarter the length to the top piece), and to these dimensions, add 8½ inches (21.5 cm) to the top panel for the heading and a seam allowance, and add 8½ inches (21.5 cm) to the bottom panel for the hem and a seam allowance. Purchase the same amount of lining fabric as curtain fabric.

Cut out pieces for two panels based on your measurements. For the lining, see the instructions in step 3.

2. With right sides together, stitch the top and bottom pieces of each panel. Press the seam open. Cut a piece of fringe to the width of the panel. On the right side of the panel, pin it over the seam. Machine stitch the fringe in place along each edge (figure 1).

Figure 1

3. For the lining, measure the panels you made in step 2, and subtract 4 inches (10 cm) from the width and 3 inches (7.5 cm) from the length. Cut two lining panels to this measurement.

4. Place each lining and curtain right sides together, aligning the top edge and one side edge. Pin and stitch the side seam. Now, pin and stitch the other side edge (figure 2). You'll have more of the curtain material than the lining material, by design. Turn right side out. Press the

Figure 2

Continued ➔

long edges, leaving a 1-inch (2.5 cm) overlap of the fabric on the wrong side.

5. Make a 4-inch (10 cm) double hem at the top edge of each panel; fold under 8 inches (20.5 cm) and press, then fold the raw edge in to meet the fold. Press, pin, and stitch. Cut the pleating tape to the width of your curtain, adding an extra inch or two on each side. Follow the manufacturer's instructions to apply the pleating tape; with the type we used, we centered the tape and stitched along both edges, following stitching lines printed on the pleating tape. There are strings along the edges that pull the tape into pleats, so be careful not to stitch over the pull strings (figure 3).

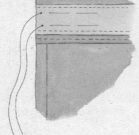

Figure 3

6. At one end of the pleating tape, tie a double knot in each string (figure 4). Pull the strings simultaneously from the other end. Keep pulling and creating the folds as you go until you have all the pleats in place, making sure the area between the folds stays flat. When you're satisfied with the pleats, knot each string. Repeat on the other panel.

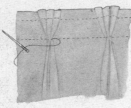

Figure 4

7. On the right side, make a small tack at the base of each pleat (figure 5).

8. Place the tape hooks at each pleat (figure 6). The kind we used are inserted through the back of the tape and flipped around to secure.

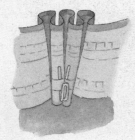

Figure 5   Figure 6

9. Make a 4-inch (10 cm) double hem at the bottom, using the same method you used in step 5, stitching the curtain over the lining.

11. Rather than place these drapes on a sliding track, we used simple link rings to attach them to the curtain rod.

—From *Fun & Fabulous Curtains to Sew*

STYLISH SKIRTS

Valerie Van Arsdale Shrader

Guide to Stylish Skirt Making

When you're afflicted by skirt envy, what happens? You're attracted to the style, of course, so the skirt's appearance has to please you. When you touch the fabric, you can't wait to put it on. These two elements, the design and the fabric, are the key to making a skirt you'll love. Deciding which comes first—the fabric or the pattern—depends on your mind-set.... [L]et's start with the pattern, the actual design you'll use to make your first skirt.

If you're new to sewing (remember, you've got to learn how if you want to make a skirt), it helps to understand the information in a pattern and how the kind of skirt you want to make will be affected by your fabric choice.

Pick a Pattern

...Patterns (and all that stuff inside) sometimes seem intimidating, but actually the pattern is the key to the skirt of your dreams. Let's talk about patterns in general terms now; we'll find out how to actually use them when we Learn to Sew!

Fabric shops offer a variety of catalogs from the major pattern companies. Each company issues a new catalog seasonally, just as designers continually produce new collections, so you can be sure to find current designs as well as classic silhouettes. The pattern catalogs are like Fashion Week in a book! When you visit your local fabric shop, look through the skirt sections of the various catalogs for all the possibilities. When you find a style that appeals to you, read through the information about the skirt. Generally, you'll find out how much fabric you need, what type of fabric is recommended for that style, and which other notions (zippers, buttons, etc.) you'll need to make the skirt. Most patterns offer variations on the basic design, sometimes as many as six in one envelope. (More for your money!) The variations are usually labeled with letters (View A, Skirt B, etc.).

Outside the Pattern Envelope

Now, after you find an irresistible design in the catalog, study the pattern envelope itself for even more information. Practically every pattern used in this book was labeled "Easy" or "Fast" or something similar. Until you've gained some skills and confidence (which won't be long), stick to patterns that are similarly labeled. Refer to the illustration on the opposite page as we talk about what you'll learn from the pattern envelope.

Style, Fit, and Construction Details. It may say something like, "Loose-fitting pull-on skirt in two lengths and bias skirt in three lengths," or "A-line, below mid-knee length skirt has asymmetrical hemline and side zipper." This listing gives you specific information about the style of the skirt and its construction.

You should also know about ease. Patterns include varying amounts of wearing ease and design ease. Wearing ease is the additional sizing included in your skirt so you can move in it, while design ease is added to achieve a particular silhouette. The terms you see on your pattern envelope, such as "loose-fitting" or "fitted," refer to design ease. The amount of ease you prefer is personal, so if you like things close-fitting, don't buy a pattern for a loose-fitting garment.

Notions. Patterns list all the additional items that you need to finish the project, such as "1 yard (91.5 cm) of ½-inch (1.3 cm) elastic" of "7-inch (18 cm) zipper, 3 yards (2.75 m) of ¾-inch-wide (2 cm) ribbon trim."

Fabric Suggestions. Most companies list a range of fabrics that will be suitable for the skirt designs, including things like "silks and silk types, cotton and cotton blends, and lightweight denim." We'll spend more time talking about fabric in just a few minutes, but the important thing to understand now is that you'll have lots of appropriate fabric choices for each design.

Fabric Requirements. You'll find out how much fabric you need to make your chosen skirt.

Finished Measurements. The extend of this information varies among pattern companies, but generally you'll find the hip measurements, length, and width of the finished skirt. Note that the hip measurements will differ from actual body measurements because they include ease, as we just discussed.

Inside the Pattern Envelope

The envelope contains the pattern pieces themselves, printed on tissue paper, and the instructions for the skirt. Don't be overwhelmed by the information inside, because it's all presented in small digestible bits. We should be thankful that the pattern companies have figured out how to give us so much useful stuff in such a tidy package.

Pattern Pieces. Modern patterns generally contain more than one size, and all the pieces for the skirt will be printed on one or more large sheets of tissue paper. When you've identified your size and the style you want to make (Skirt B, let's say), refer to the instruction sheet for a key to tell you which pieces you need to use.

Instructions. You'll find cutting layouts, which illustrate how to place the pattern pieces on the fabric and cut them out. You'll also have sewing directions, which give you step-by-step instructions on making your skirt. There are also come general sewing tips to supplement the instructions; we're going to cover all this basic information here, too. Read over the instructions completely before you begin making your skirt so you understand the sequence of its construction. *Please.*

Which Size?

You probably won't admit it, but I bet this is the real reason you've avoided learning to sew. Pattern companies don't use the same sizing that apparel manufacturers use. Take a deep breath before I tell you that you may need to buy a pattern that's two, three, or possibly four sizes larger than what you'd buy in ready-to-wear. I hear you moaning now, but think through this logically, it's just a number, after all. The system of sizing the pattern companies use is simply different.

To demonstrate this, here's a comparison of measurements:

	Major Pattern Company	Major Apparel Company
Bust	32½ (82.5 cm)	32½ (82.5 cm)
Waist	25 (63.5 cm)	25 (63.5 cm)
Hip	34½ (87.5 cm)	35 (89 cm)
U.S. Size	10	U.S. 2

Amazing, isn't it? This, my dear, is a practice called *vanity sizing*: the garment industry cuts its clothing generously while putting a teeny little size on the tag. Neither be fooled nor disappointed by this trickery.

To make sure your skirt fits, measure yourself accurately according to the illustration. Buy the size that most closely matches your hip measurement. Measure your hips approximately nine inches below your waist or at the spot where your hips are the widest. Now, forget about the garment industry—you're making your own skirts now.

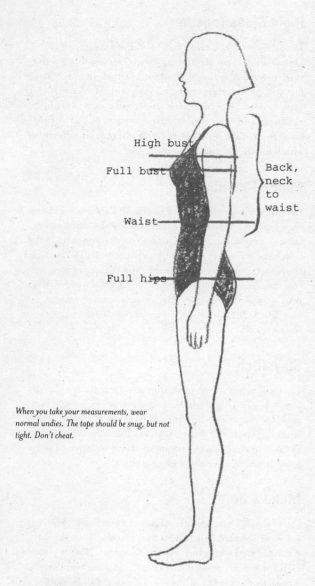

When you take your measurements, wear normal undies. The tape should be snug, but not tight. Don't cheat.

Choose Your Fabric

Okay, you've found a pattern for a great skirt. You love it! Now the search for fabric begins. This is the exciting part of making a skirt, because your project starts to breathe when you can feel the fabric. Imagine that you're in Paris and you could have any skirt you wanted; making your own skirt is absolutely no different, because you can have anything you want. Spend some quality time looking for fabric. If you don't like the color, or the print, or the drape of the fabric, you won't like the skirt. Remember that your pattern envelope will offer you a variety of fabrics that are suitable for your skirt, so be sure to choose one of the types that's suggested.

Fabric Basics

...Fabrics are made of fibers of various origins. Since you're into clothes, you probably already have a basic knowledge of the different types of fabric and what they are made from: the natural fibers, such as cotton, linen, wool, and silk; and the synthetic fibers, like polyester, acrylic, and nylon. (Thank you, chemists!) Rayon straddles these two categories, as it's synthesized from wood pulp; it's manmade, yet from a natural source.

Other synthetic fabrics are made from sources such as petroleum products, and many fabrics are blends of natural and synthetic fibers.

The weave of the fabric gives it certain characteristics. Satin, velvet, twill, and so on all describe the structure of the fabric, and not its fiber content. Velvet can be made from silk, cotton, or polyester, for example. But when you're learning to make a skirt, the properties of the fabric (drape, texture, weight, etc.) are just as important as the fiber content. As long as it hands the way it's supposed to, you have some flexibility as to what you can use. These are the parameters the pattern companies use when they suggest a range of fabrics for a specific design. Isn't that thoughtful of them? I think so.

Will It Work?

So how do you know whether your fabric will drape properly? Well, you can tell a lot from fabric by touching and manipulating it before you buy it. (Don't worry. The folks in the fabric stores are used to people fondling fabric.) In all seriousness, you really must feel the material, as you'll be working with it and wearing it—is it smooth? Thin or heavy? Stiff or soft? Unfold a length of fabric from the bolt and observe how it hangs. If you want a skirt with a little flounce that drapes just so, you need a lightweight fabric; if you want a crisp silhouette, a medium-weight linen might be just perfect.

Each bolt of fabric will be labeled with its fiber content, its width, its price, and occasionally its laundering requirements. Be sure to ask about laundering the fabric before you buy it, so you understand how to care for your skirt after you've made it. Washable fabrics need to be preshrunk before being sewn, which simply means laundering them according to the manufacturer's recommendations before you start.

For a first skirt, I suggest a medium-weight cotton, because it handles well, it's durable, it's easy to sew, and it washes well. Most of the skirt projects in this book are made from cotton, linen, rayon, or blends of those fibers. (All of these are woven fabrics; there are no knits used in *Stylish Skirts*.) While slinky charmeuse or flimsy chiffon might be beautiful, they're a little more difficult to handle than the fabrics listed above and thus not well suited for a first skirt project. (Now, a second or third project? That's a different story.)

Simply put, don't use a fabric that feels slippery for your first skirt, because it's likely to scoot around when you cut it or sew with it, and you're likely to get discouraged. A common mistake that beginners make is choosing a luscious fabric that requires some experience to properly handle. Believe me when I tell you that there are beautiful cottons available that will make your first skirt a happy experience.

Learn to Sew!

Without further ado, or even a drumroll, let's begin to make a skirt. If the process of sewing has intimidated you before, maybe you ought to think about it as you would the process of cooking. You choose a recipe (the pattern); buy the ingredients (fabric and notions); do the washing and chopping (preparing and cutting out the fabric); and then add the ingredients to one another according to the recipe (sew by following the pattern instructions.) See— easy as pie. Or, if you'd rather—a piece of cake!

Prepare the Fabric

You have to know a little more about fabric to understand the importance of the proper layout and subsequent cutting of your skirt, so bear with me a moment. When we discussed fabric earlier, we talked about prewashing. Now, prewashing actually means *shrinking*, as many washable fabrics will do just that when laundered. Generally, the looser the weave, the more shrinkage is likely to occur. Washing also removes sizing or finishes that may affect your stitches. Check the label on the bolt of cloth for the laundering recommendations, and launder the fabric the same way you plan to launder the skirt. Please don't neglect this very important step, because you'll be totally bummed to wash your skirt for the first time and then find that it's way too small for you. After you've laundered your fabric, press it to remove any wrinkles.

Align the Grain

Your fabric must be correctly aligned before you cut out the skirt pieces, and here's why. (We'll get to the how in just a few minutes.) Woven fabric is made of lengthwise and crosswise threads. In a perfect world, the crosswise threads are perpendicular to the lengthwise threads. The direction of these threads is called the grain. Your

pattern pieces must follow the proper direction of the grain so your skirt hangs correctly. Most garment pieces follow the lengthwise (or straight) grain, because the lengthwise threads are designed to be stronger to withstand the tension of the weaving process. Some of the skirts in this book are cut along the bias; the bias flows along the diagonal between the lengthwise and crosswise threads. Garments cut on the bias have wonderful drape and cling to the body because this is the direction in which fabric has the most stretch.

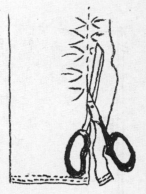

Straighten the fabric ends, as shown here.

The finished border on the length of the fabric is the selvage. This border differs in appearance from fabric to fabric. Most cutting layouts will have you fold the fabric lengthwise with the selvages aligned; smooth out the fabric so it's flat. If you can't get the wrinkles out and the fabric won't lie flat, you may need to straighten the crosswise edges and try again. Why? Sometimes the length of the fabric wasn't perfectly cut along a crosswise thread. If you're starting to get that creepy home ec feeling, chill; this is easier than it sounds, I promise. To find a crosswise thread, clip into the selvage and pull out a crosswise thread across the entire width of the fabric. Then, trim the edge even along this visible line, as you see so easily done below. Fold the fabric again, aligning the crosswise ends and the selvages; the ends and the selvages should be perpendicular to one another. Now that you're educated about fabric preparation, you're ready for the next step.

Prepare the Pattern Pieces

Grab your pattern and take out the pattern tissue and the instruction sheet. Look for your skirt letter (let's say Skirt B), and you'll find a listing of all the pieces you need for Skirt B. Cut the pieces you need from the large sheets of tissue; be sure to cut out the proper sizes. If you're using a multi-size pattern, which you probably are, you might want to highlight your cutting line. To remove the wrinkles from the pattern pieces after you've cut them from the large pieces of tissue, press each piece with a dry iron set on low heat.

Let's look at the pattern pieces themselves for a moment. Some pieces will be cut on the fold, which will be indicated by a pair of arrows pointing to the edge of the pattern. These are very easy to place correctly. Other pieces will be cut on the straight grain, indicated by a straight line with arrows on either end. These arrows must be parallel to the selvage so the fabric piece is cut on the straight grain. You ensure this by measuring from each end of the arrow and adjusting until each end is the same distance from the selvage. Some pieces, such as facings, are often cut out from both fabric and interfacing, and this too will be indicated on the pattern piece. (A facing gets very lonely if you forget to cut its interfacing, so take note.)

Fold the Fabric

Find the cutting layout for Skirt B according to your size and your fabric width. Place your fabric on a flat surface and align it properly as discussed...following the directions in your patterns' cutting layout. Sewing gurus disagree on whether to fold the right side of your fabric (the face) to the inside or outside; sometimes you need to be able to see the pattern on the fabric, so the face should be on the outside. However, it's probably most convenient to fold the right side to the inside for a couple of reasons. First, it's easy to mark with the wrong sides outside, and second, the right sides need to be facing when you sew anyway. Before you start to pin the pieces to the fabric, place them all on the fabric to make sure you understand the layout.

Continued ➨

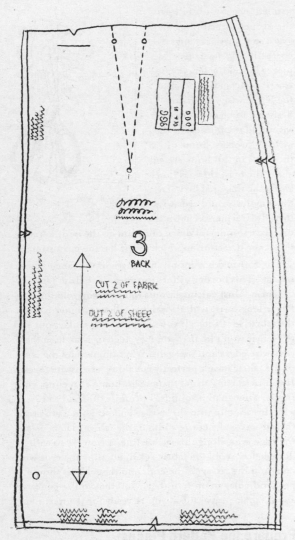

And here's a typical skirt back. It has a couple of features that need to be marked, the dart and the circle. The arrow indicates it will be cut on the straight grain. All the notches should be cut, as you'll need to match them when you make the skirt.

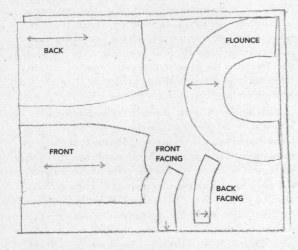

Here's a typical cutting layout. This is similar to the one we used for the Flirty Flounce skirt. The pieces that have arrows at the edge are cut on the fold, and those with straight arrows are cut on the lengthwise (straight) grain. Remember to cut the correct number of each piece.

Pin in Place

Keep fiddling around with the pieces until the measurements agree and your piece follows the straight grain. Pin the grain-line arrows and the foldline arrows in place first and then pin the edges of each piece, with the pins on a diagonal facing into the corners. Finally, pin around the edge of each piece. The sewing gurus also give some differing advice about pinning, but most suggest placing all the pins perpendicular to the cut edge. To begin, how about pinning them the way that's most comfortable for you? Pin all the pieces in place before you cut the first one and refer to your layout to be sure you've placed each of the pieces for your skirt.

Cut Out the Skirt

Keep the fabric flat as you work, holding the pattern piece in place with your free hand as you cut. The notches you see are important markers for you when you're making your skirt; these help you properly match the various pieces when you're stitching them together. While you can cut them outward, I've found that it can be tricky to keep the fabric flat while you navigate the scissors around them, so I zip right through the notches and cut them inward after I've cut the piece out. This method saves a little time, too. Be mindful that there are single, double, and even triple notches, so cut them as such. You'll match single notches to single notches, double notches to double notches, and so on.

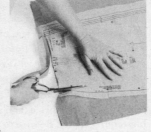

Lightly hold the fabric in place as you cut, keeping it as flat as you can.

Mark the Fabric

Your pattern pieces may have marks such as circles, darts, or pleats that need to be transferred to the wrong side of the fabric. The simplest way to do this is to use dressmaker's tracing paper and a tracing wheel. Usually, you can mark both pieces at the same time, unless the fabric is textured or heavyweight. Remove as few pins as possible to allow you to access the area you need to mark. Place the colored side of the paper to the wrong side of the fabric and trace over the markings with the wheel. If you're transferring straight lines, a ruler can be useful in accurately tracing the lines and keeping the pattern tissue in the proper position.

There are many tools to mark fabric. If you need to transfer only a dot, you can mark it with a fabric marking pen or chalk pencil. Be sure to test the markers you use on a scrap of fabric to be certain you can remove the marks is necessary. Because you may sometimes have to mark a placement line on the right side of the fabric, it's important to test your markers.

Start to Sew

...In the following section, we'll talk about the basic techniques that we've used in our skirts. Don't try to remember everything at once, but read it through so you have a general understanding of the process. Later, in the Make a Skirt! section, you'll see how the techniques work in context when you make your skirt. We've presented them here with contrasting stitching so you can easily see what happens during each step. Furthermore, we've used fabric that's similar (in some cases identical) to what we used for our skirts (linen, and a linen/rayon blend), so you can see real-world examples of how these fabrics behave when they're sewn. This isn't airbrushed sewing we're doing here.

And you may notice real-world sewing in the Make a Skirt! section, too—fabrics fray when they're handled and some techniques (like gathering) put more stress on the fabric, so you'll probably see a thread or two. You'll see them on your own skirts, too. Since you're learning, you shouldn't be overly stressed out about what the inside of your garment looks like, but do tidy up your skirt when you're done, trimming all the loose threads. This isn't work now—it's fun and you're just beginning. So plug in the machine, turn on the lights, and let's sew. If you need a refresher course when you're making your skirt, you can always flip back to these illustrated techniques.

Editor's Note: For directions on stitching seams, see "More Things to Know Before You Sew: Stitching Seams."

Right Sides Together

Despite what I just said (don't you hate that?), you'll almost always sew the pieces of your skirt with the right sides together (facing each other). This is the most basic fact you need to remember about garment sewing if your seams are to be hidden away inside your skirt. If your fabric doesn't have easily recognizable right and wrong sides, be sure to mark each piece so you can quickly determine which is which, 'cause it's important.

Match Notches

Remember when we cut the notches? Patterns include a series of notches to insure that you sew the right pieces (and the right sides of the pieces) to one another. If the notches don't seem to line up as the pattern instructions show, you may have one piece facing the wrong way, or you may be trying to pin the wrong edge of a piece. The notches should match exactly. Studying your pattern carefully will help you understand the proper orientation of the pieces.

Staystitch

This will generally be your first step in making a skirt. *Staystitching* is simply a line of stitching sewn ½ inch (1.3 cm) into the seam allowance to stabilize the piece. Staystitching is usually done on pieces that have curves, such as the waistline of a skirt. Staystitching is designed to be permanent (unlike most boyfriends).

Make a Dart

Darts shape a skirt so it conforms to your body, so darts are your friends. Stitching a dart often follows the staystitching step when you're making a skirt. If your pattern calls for a dart, mark it carefully. You'll see that there's a peak in the center of the dart; fold the fabric at the peak and match any markings. Pin in place and stitch, beginning at the wide end of the dart. When you get to the narrow end of the dart, take a few stitches at the fold, but don't backstitch. Backstitching prevents the dart from lying flat. Instead, cut the threads long enough to tie into a knot to secure the end of the dart. Your pattern will tell you which direction to press the dart; it's usually toward the center.

Install a Zipper

Skirts with elasticized waists are wonderful, because they're comfy and easy to make. But eventually—perhaps even this afternoon—you'll want to make a fitted skirt. Of course you've got to get into (and out of) said fitted skirt, so you need to learn to install a zipper. A zipper is a wonderful device, so let's figure it out.

There are several ways to put in a zipper, but the standard for skirts is the lapped zipper. We may as well learn this method because it's not the least bit hard. Our version calls for a zipper that's a couple of inches longer than the pattern asks for. This technique eliminates some fumbling around with the zipper pull during installation as well as the need for a hook and eye closure. (If you've never fumbled around with a zipper pull, you're lucky; if you have, you know exactly what I'm talking about.) Be sure to buy a zipper with nylon coils (not metal) because you have to trim off the excess and stitch right over it, too.

You install a zipper in a seam that is partially sewn. Most patterns will have you stitch to a notch or a marked circle. Let's pretend that we've done that, too.

1. After stitching the seam to the appropriate spot, backstitch for a few stitches to anchor it. On the right opening edge, press under the seam allowance to ½ inch (1.3 cm). Press under the left opening edge to the seamline, ⅝ inch (1.5 cm).

2. Place the closed zipper under the right edge, placing the zipper stop at the notch or the marked spot. Have the zipper teeth close to the pressed edge of the fabric. Pin the zipper in place at the end of the zipper tape. Put the zipper foot on your sewing machine and baste this side of the zipper in place (photo 1); it doesn't have to be close to the zipper teeth just yet. Change the stitch length to a normal setting and adjust your zipper foot so you can stitch close to the fabric edge and the zipper teeth (photo 2).

3. Lap the left opening edge over the right (photo 3) and baste in place, as in step 2.

4. Reduce the stitch length and adjust your zipper foot to stitch the left side of the zipper in place; you won't need to stitch quite as close to the pressed edge on this side. Begin at the seam and stitch across the lapped end. Pivot the fabric by stopping with the needle in the fabric, lifting the presser foot, and turning to stitch up the right side (photo 4). Remember to put the presser foot back down after you pivot!

Photo 1

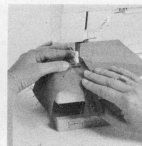
Photo 2

Photo 3

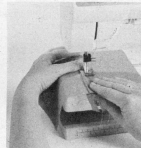
Photo 4

5. Remove the basting stitches (photo 5). Your zipper's just about finished (photo 6).

6. Lower the zipper pull and trim off the excess zipper (photo 7). The raw end of the zipper tape will be encased in the facing or waistband of your skirt.

Photo 5

Photo 6

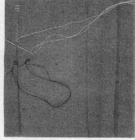
Photo 7

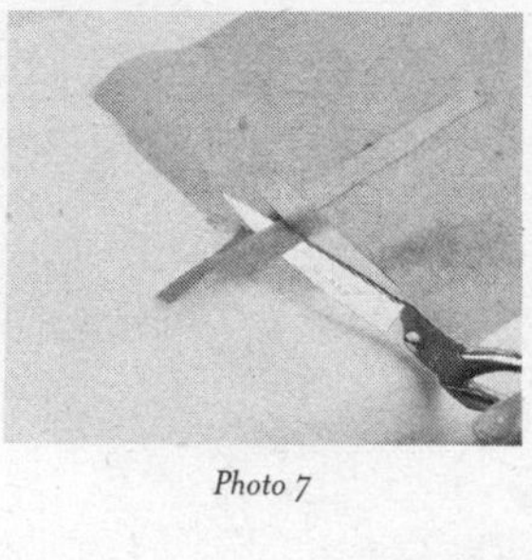

Understitch the Facings

Understitching is used on facings to make them behave and stay out of sight on the inside of a garment. After the seam has been trimmed and clipped, press the seam allowance toward the facing. From the right side, stitch close to the seamline through all layers of the facing. After understitching, turn the facing to the inside.

Ease to Fit

Sometimes, to insure the proper fit or drape, you'll sew one piece to another that's ever-so-slightly longer. This is called easestitching, created by gently gathering a portion of the longer piece.

Easestitching is done with a row of basting stitches that are pulled to fit, with the fullness distributed in the seam allowance and not visible in the skirt.

You can also ease the fullness of a hem.

Make a Narrow Hem

Most of the skirts in this section are finished with narrow hems. It's just like it sounds: a skinny little hem that's stitched in place on the machine. Typically they're made like this: Stitch ⅜ inch (1 cm) from the lower edge of the skirt and press up along this line of stitching. Tuck under the raw edge to meet the stitching, forming a nice fold. Press and stitch in place along the fold.

Stitch by Hand

You only need a few basic hand stitches to complete these skirts. A basic *hemstitch* can multitask to secure facings at the zipper as well as to hem your skirt. A *tack* will hold facings to seam allowances.

Begin with a knot in your thread; make a simple loop in the end and pull the needle through. Sometimes a second knot is necessary to keep the thread from pulling through the fabric. A hemstitch is begun with the needle inserted into the fold of the fabric. Work from right to left as you pick up just a thread or two in the skirt and then insert the needle into the edge of the fold above the first stitch. Repeat, making stitches every ¼ inch (6 mm) or so.

Finish a line of hand stitching in one of two ways. Make a series of *backstitches* (a small stitch made from left to right and repeated several times in place). You can also make a quick knot. Make a wee stitch on top of your last stitch on the wrong side of your fabric, forming a small loop. Pull the needle through the second loop tightly to form a knot.

A *tack* is simply a straight stitch used to join layers of fabric; you can repeat them in place or make a series of straight stitches. You'll use them in your skirts to anchor facings to seam allowances. Make sure your tacks don't go through the skirt itself, just the facings and seam allowances.

Hemstitches in white thread; tacks in black thread.

Check the Fit

Try on the skirt after each major step, such as when the side seams are sewn and the waistband added. Don't wait until the skirt has been completed, because it will take a lot of sweat and even more tears to unmake it if you need to tweak the fit. Remember that it's better to err on the side of being too big than too small when you're deciding on a size. If you need to make the skirt smaller, do so in teeny increments, such as ⅛ inch (3 mm). Exhibit A: If you're taking in the side seams, this seemingly tiny measurement translates into ¼ inch (6 mm) on each side of the skirt and ½ inch (1.3 cm) for the entire skirt.

If you're stressed about fit, use the traditional couture approach of making a muslin. A muslin is a sample garment that's made of inexpensive material (i.e., cotton muslin) for the purpose of testing fit. The sample garment need only have the major pieces stitched together, with no seam finishes or completed details. A perk with making a muslin is that you can practice sewing before you begin your actual skirt. Then you're tweaking the muslin, and not your precious fabric. With a muslin, you'll be confident your skirt will fit after you've invested time and money in it.

Fix a Mistake

The best way to fix a mistake is to avoid it in the first place (excuse me if I'm beginning to sound like your mother). But o course, we all make them, even the most experienced seamstresses. There's not much that can't be repaired by simply ripping out all the stitches and trying again. When you're using a seam ripper to remove stitches, be careful not to tear the fabric by ripping too enthusiastically. I know how much fun it can be (!).

If you're having a weak moment and feel unsure about something you've just stitched, chill a second and make sure it's correct before you trim the seam allowances or clip the curves.

Embellish Your Skirt

Most of the skirts you love are likely to have some sort of embellishment—lovely ribbon, funky rickrack, or whatever suits your fancy. Several of our stylish skirts are so decorated, and you can choose to include these embellishments as you wish. (But why wouldn't you? It's easy.) Even if your pattern doesn't call for trim or a decorative technique, you can still include them if you want. Here's the scoop on adding accoutrements to the skirts in this book.

If your skirt is constructed in panels, you can decorate each seam with trim. Center the trim atop the seam, and pin it in place if you'd like. Adding the trim gives you another opportunity to be creative—will you use a complementary thread, or choose a contrasting one for pizzazz?

You can sew it in place with a simple straight stitch along both edges of the trim (photo 1), add a decorative stitch down the center (photo 2), or even layer trims to add a personal touch. When you're actually stitching on the trim, sew at a medium speed so you can easily guide the trim.

Pinning the trim in place makes a lot of sense if you don't have a seam to follow, or if you have several pieces of trim to coordinate, or if you're just picky. To decorate one of our skirts, rickrack was added around the yoke after being pinned in place first (photo 3). If you pin the trim to your skirt, remove the pins as you come to them. (Remember, no stitching over the pins!)

You can add trim before you finish the skirt, or after. If you add trim before the skirt is complete, the raw ends of the trim are usually hidden inside a facing or turned under to the hem, for example. If you add trim after the skirt is finished, you'll need to hide the raw ends of the trim, if you care about that kind of thing. When you cut the trim, remember to add an extra ½ inch (1.3 cm) or so for tidying the ends, folding under one end to cover the other (photo 4). If you want a deconstructed look, simply add the trim without turning under the ends. What the heck.

Continued ➜

Another easy way you can enliven your skirt is to use contrasting fabrics. We used this trick to add fabric "ribbons" and a bright band for visual interest (photo 5).

The fabrics we used had the same print, but were in a different colorway. When you're shopping for multiple fabrics to use in a project, be sure to take a swatch along with you. If your pattern calls for ribbon, keep in mind that you can use fabric to make your own custom trim.

Exposed seams add depth and dimension to a garment. Remember, we gave you one method for making them, which depended on washing the skirt to make the edges bloom. But you can also make cool frayed edges in other easy ways, too. Here's a simple method that works without the washing step: after you stitch the seam (with the wrong sides together, of course, so it shows on the outside), use a toothbrush to fluff the raw edges....

Photo 1

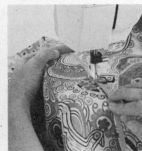
Photo 2

Photo 3

Photo 4

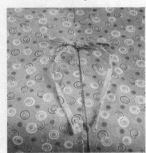
Photo 5

Anatomy of a Skirt

Here's a quick visual recap of the skirt-making process. Could it be any easier?

1. Staystitch the edges and make the darts in the front.
2. Staystitch the back sections, stitch them together partway, and add the zipper.
3. Stitch the facing sections together and sew it to the waistline.
4. Stitch the flounce sections together, make a narrow hem in the flounce, and stitch to the skirt.

Presto! Your very own handmade skirt. Wear proudly.

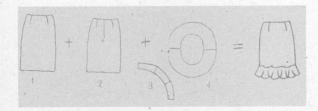

Projects

Each of our projects is rated according to ease of construction. (Please note that I didn't say difficulty of construction.) Here's how we've organized them.

Key

• Absolute Beginner
Suitable for the first-time sewer.

Basic Skills You'll Use:

Matching notches

Narrow hem

Right sides together

• • Easy Beginner
Suitable for the new sewer who understands the basics and is ready to install a zipper.

New Skills You'll Use:

Install a zipper

Seam finishes

Hand stitches

Staystitching

Trim seams and clip curves

Understitching

• • • Experienced Beginner
Suitable for the sewer who's mastered the zipper and is ready to sew at warp speed.

New Skills You'll Use:

Easing to fit

French seams

• Polka Dot Perfection

Whip up a new look with a simple pattern, a fabulous fabric, and a little attitude.

WHAT YOU NEED

Pattern for a bias-cut, pull-on skirt

Fabric and notions per the pattern envelope (we used cotton fabric, contrasting thread, and ½-inch (1.3 cm) elastic)

Basic skirt-making tools and materials

Bodkin

HOW YOU MAKE IT

1. Cut out and mark the skirt according to your pattern's instructions. Remember to finish the seam allowances of your skirt, using the method of your choice.

2. Stitch the skirt front and back sections together at the side seams, right sides together, matching the notches (photo 1).

Photo 1

3. In the next step, you're going to make a casing for the elasticized waist. First, to save yourself the frustration of getting the elastic stuck in the seam allowances when you insert it in the casing, begin by basting the upper 3 or 4 inches (7.5 or 10 cm) of the side seam allowances to the skirt (a peek of this step appears in photo 2.

4. Make the casing by pressing 1 inch (2.5 cm) of the upper edge of the skirt to the inside. Press under ¼ inch (6 mm) on the raw edge. Stitch close to the lower edge of the casing, leaving an opening to insert the elastic (photo 2). Note the line of basting stitches from step 3, visible at the seam.

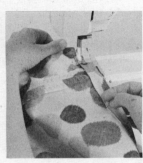
Photo 2

5. Cut a piece of elastic to fit your waist, plus 1 inch (2.5 cm). Pin the free end of the elastic to the skirt so it doesn't disappear inside the casing and insert the other end of the elastic through the casing using a bodkin (photos 3 and 4). Overlap the ends and pin them together so you can try on the skirt. Adjust the elastic to fit if necessary.

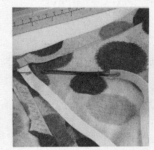
Photo 3

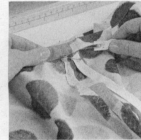
Photo 4

6. Stitch the ends of elastic together securely (photo 5) and stitch the opening closed. Distribute the fullness evenly through the waist. Remove the basting stitches at the seam allowances. (If you want, you can secure the elastic in place by stitching through the casing at each side seam.)

7. Let the skirt hang overnight. Try it on and mark the desired length. If necessary, trim the depth of the hem evenly, allowing ⅜ inch (1 cm) for a narrow hem. Stitch ⅜ inch (1 cm) from the lower edge of the skirt. Press up the hem along this line of stitching, then tuck under the raw edge to meet the line of stitching. Press. Stitch the hem in place (photo 6).

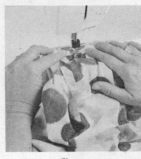
Photo 5

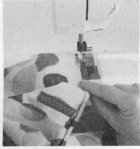
Photo 6

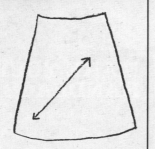
• • Flirty Flounce

No wardrobe is complete unless it contains a skirt with a playful flounce; make yours in just a few hours.

What You Need

Pattern for a straight skirt with a zipper and a flounce

Fabric and notions per the pattern envelope (we used cotton fabric and matching thread)—*remember to buy a longer zipper*

Basic skirt-making tools and materials

How You Make It

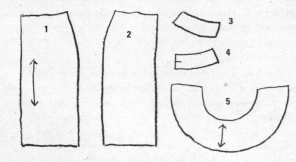

Pattern schematic, "Flirty Flounce": 1. Back, 2. Front, 3. Back Facing, 4. Front Facing, 5. Front and Back Flounce.

1. Cut out and mark the skirt according to your pattern's instructions. Remember to finish the seam allowances of your skirt, using the method of your choice.

2. Staystitch the upper edge of the front ½ inch (1.3 cm) from the cut edge; be sure to stitch in the direction your pattern indicates. Make the darts in the front (photo 1); press them toward the center of the skirt.

3. Staystitch the upper edges of the back pieces ½ inch (1.3 cm) from the cut edge; be sure to stitch in the proper direction.

4. Make the darts in the back and press them toward the center of the skirt. Stitch the center back seam from the notch to the lower edge, right sides together, matching the notches (photo 2). Backstitch at the notch to reinforce the seam.

Photo 1   *Photo 2*

5. To install the zipper in the back, turn in ½ inch (1.3 cm) on the right opening edge; press. Turn in the left opening edge along the seamline and press. Place the closed zipper under the right opening edge, placing the zipper stop at the notch and the zipper teeth close to the pressed edge. Pin the end of the zipper tape to the skirt. Using a zipper foot, baste the zipper to the skirt and then stitch close to the edge (photo 3). Lap the left opening edge over the right opening edge, matching seamlines. Baste and then stitch in place, pivoting below the notch. Trim the excess length from the zipper.

6. Stitch the front to the back at the side seams, right sides together, matching the notches.

7. Now you'll add a facing to the waistline. Apply fusible interfacing to the facing sections following the manufacturer's directions. Stitch the side seams of the facing sections, right sides together. Finish the long unnotched edge by stitching ¼ inch (6 mm) from the edge, turn under along the stitching, press, and stitch.

8. With the right sides together, pin the facing to the skirt, matching the centers, the notches, and the side seams (photo 4). (The facing extends ½ inch (1.3 cm) beyond the right opening edge and ⅝ inch (1.5 cm) beyond the left opening edge.) Baste in place. Stitch along the seamline. Trim the seam and clip the curves.

 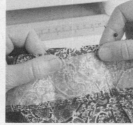

Photo 3   *Photo 4*

9. To understitch the facing, press it away from the skirt, pressing the seam toward the facing. With the facing side up, stitch close to the seam through the facing and the seam allowances.

10. Turn the facing to the inside, turning under and hemstitching the edges to the zipper tape; press (photo 5). To keep the facing in place, tack it to the seam allowances.

11. Stitch the front and back flounce sections together at the side seams, right sides together. Stitch along the seamline on the notched edge of the flounce so you can clip to this line of stitching in step 13.

Photo 5

12. Make a narrow hem at the lower edge of flounce: Stitch ⅜ inch (1 cm) from the lower edge. Press up the hem along this line of stitching, then tuck under the raw edge to meet the line of stitching. Press. Stitch the hem in place.

13. Clip the notched edge of the flounce to the line of stitching, being careful not to clip through the stitching. With the right sides together, pin the flounce to the lower edge of the skirt, matching first the side seams, then the centers, and lastly the notches (photo 6). Stitch. Press the seam toward the skirt, pressing the flounce out.

Photo 6

• • Gloriously Gathered

This billowy skirt features playful fabric with yards and yards of pretty trim.

What You Need

Pattern for a skirt with a zipper and multiple ruffles

Fabric and notions per the pattern envelope (we used cotton fabric, matching thread, 1-inch (2.5 cm) vintage trim, and ¼-inch (6 mm) twill tape)—*remember to buy a longer zipper*

Basic skirt-making tools and materials

How You Make It

1. Cut out and mark the skirt according to your pattern's instructions; we marked three placement lines on the yoke for the trim, one of which is below the zipper. Remember to finish the seam allowances of your skirt, using the method of your choice, and be sure to transfer all of the markings. There's lots of sewing in this skirt, but none of it is difficult. Promise.

2. Staystitch the upper edge of the yoke front ½ inch (1.3 cm) from the cut edge; be sure to stitch in the direction your pattern indicates. Make the darts in the front and press them toward the center of the skirt.

Continued ➡

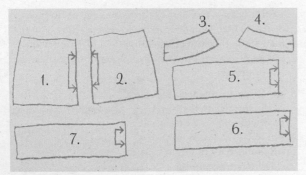

Pattern schematic, "Gloriously Gathered": 1. Yoke Front, 2. Yoke Back, 3. Front Facing, 4. Back Facing, 5. Upper Ruffle, 6. Middle Ruffle, 7. Lower Ruffle

3. Staystitch the upper edge of the yoke back ½ inch (1.3 cm) from the cut edge; be sure to stitch in the direction your pattern indicates. Make the darts in the back and press them toward the center of the skirt.

4. Stitch the yoke front to the yoke back at the side seams, right sides together, leaving the left side open above the notch. Backstitch at the notch to secure the seam….

5. Cut a piece of trim to the width of the yoke at each placement line, adding ¾ inch (2 cm) to the longest piece that will fall below the zipper. (The pieces will vary in length since the yoke is narrower at the top.) Pin the two shorter pieces of trim to their corresponding placement lines, having the ends even with the open edges on the left side. Pin the longest piece along its placement line below the zipper, turning under the excess to cover the raw end at the side seam. Stitch the trim in place along both edges.

6. Stitch the notched ends of the upper ruffle sections together, right sides facing; these are the side seams. Gather the upper edge by making two parallel rows of basting stitches within the seam allowance, leaving the thread ends to gather gently (photo 1); you'll adjust the gathers to fit when you stitch the sections together.

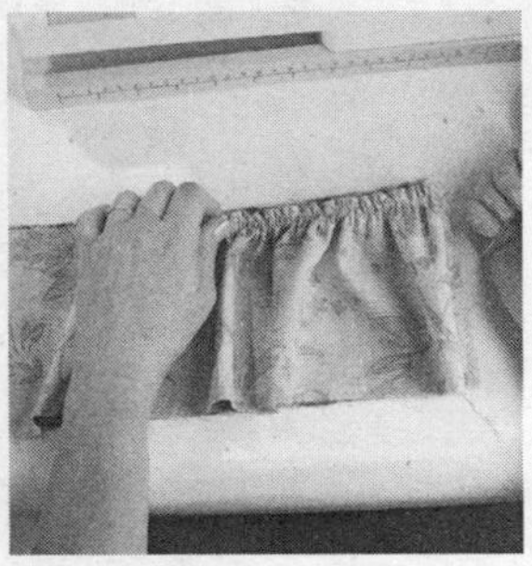

7. Stitch the notched ends of the middle ruffle sections together and gather the upper edge, as in step 6.

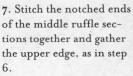

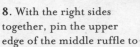

Photo 1

8. With the right sides together, pin the upper edge of the middle ruffle to the lower edge of the upper ruffle, placing one seam at the center back of the upper ruffle and the remaining seams at the marked dots on the front of the upper ruffle. Pull up the gathering stitches to fit, distributing the fullness evenly. Baste. When you're working with lots of fabric, it helps to arrange it carefully at the machine before you begin to sew. Stitch; as you accumulate a lot of fabric in front, gently rotate it under the free arm of the machine. Press the seam up. This is how your skirt will look after this step (photo 2).

9. Stitch the notched ends of the lower ruffle sections together and gather the upper edge, as in step 6. Make a narrow hem at the lower edge of this section: Stitch ⅜ inch (1 cm) from the lower edge. Press up the hem along this lien of stitching, then tuck under the raw edge to meet the line of stitching. Press. Stitch the hem in place.

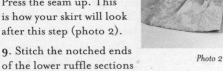

Photo 2

10. Fold the lower ruffle in half at one seam and place a pin opposite the seam; the pin will mark the center front and the seam will be the center back. Fold the

ruffle in half again and place pins at these folds (you've folded it into quarters now). These pins will mark the side edges. (If you'd like, use a marking tool to mark these four spots.)

11. With the right sides together, pin the upper edge of the lower ruffle to the lower edge of the middle ruffle, placing the seam at the center back and placing the pins (or the marks) at the center front and the side edges of the middle ruffle. Pull up the gathering stitches to fit, distributing the fullness evenly. Baste. Stitch and press the seam up.

12. With the right sides together, pin the upper edge of the ruffle to the lower edge of the yoke, matching the centers and the side seams. Pull up the gathering stitches to fit, distributing the fullness evenly. Baste. Stitch (photo 3) and press the seam toward the yoke.

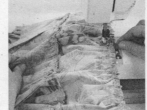

Photo 3

13. Measure and cut pieces of trim to the width of each seam on the skirt, plus ¾ inch (2 cm). Place the appropriate piece of trim along the yoke seam and pin in place, turning under and lapping one end at the left side seam (photos 4 and 5). Stitch both edges of trim in place. Repeat to add trim to each remaining seam.

14. To install the zipper on the left side, turn in ½ inch (1.3 cm) on the back opening edge; press. Turn

Photo 4

Photo 5

in the front opening edge along the seamline and press. Place the closed zipper under the back opening edge, placing the zipper stop at the notch and the zipper teeth close to the pressed edge. Pin the end of the zipper tape to the skirt. Using a zipper foot, baste the zipper to the skirt and then stitch close to the edge. Lap the front opening edge over he back opening edge, matching seamlines. Baste and then stitch in place, pivoting below the notch. Trim the excess length from the zipper.

15. Now you'll add a facing to the waistline. Apply fusible interfacing to the facing sections following the manufacturer's directions. Stitch the right side seam of the facing sections, right sides together. Finish the long unnotched edge by stitching ¼ inch (6 mm) from the edge; turn under along the stitching, press, and stitch.

16. With right sides together, pin the facing to the skirt, matching the centers and the right side seams. (The facing extends ½ inch (1.3 cm) beyond the back opening edge and ⅝ inch (1.5 cm) beyond the front opening edge.) Baste in place. To prevent stretching, baste a length of twill tape along the seamline. Stitch along the seamline. Trim the seam and clip the curves. (Don't clip the tape.)

17. To understitch the facing, press it away from the skirt, pressing the seam toward the facing. With the facing side up, stitch close to the seam through the facing and the seam allowances.

18. Turn the facing to the inside, turning under and hemstitching the edges to the zipper tape; press. To keep the facing in place, tack it to the seam allowances.

—From *Sew Cool, Sew Simple: Stylish Skirts*

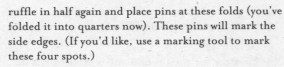

MAKE YOUR OWN HANDBAGS

Valerie Van Arsdale Shrader

Design Your Bag

Here's where I always start—choosing an absolutely amazing material that will be the foundation for my handbag. When I find it, I know it with absolute certainty. It almost calls my name. You've got to be excited about how your bag will look and feel to conjure up the creative magic to make it, so plan to spend some time picking out the materials and embellishments that you'll use. After we talk about material, you need to know a little something about constructing a bag, including some basic techniques as well as some amusing options, and of course we'll chat about the ever-so-important adornments that complete your bag. I'll toss in a bit about the tools and materials that make for happy sewing and we're ready to reach handbag nirvana—the projects. Center yourself and let's get going.

Choose Your Fabric

The sky's almost the limit with fabric. In some ways, it's difficult to give advice about fabric because you're an independent gal who knows her own mind. Love natural fibers? Use cotton or silk. Don't mind a little polyester? Then maybe you'll want to use a vintage 1970s necktie fabric. Think about the qualities you adore in fabric and keep those in mind while you're looking. You should be sure it's exactly what you want *and* need.

Here's how to start thinking about fabric. Consider how you'll be using your handbag. Is it an evening bag that may hold only a credit card or a roll of mints? Then a slinky charmeuse will do. Or is it a bag for everyday that needs to be durable enough to withstand the rigors of real life, like riding the subway? Maybe a rugged upholstery fabric is the best choice. Each type of material has special attributes—and maybe a few tiny limitations, too.

Although the intended use of your bag will likely dictate the proper material for its construction, its design will give you an indication of how structured the bag should be. If you choose a tote design, then it doesn't need to be stiff. (It will stand up on its own after you load it with stuff!) But if your design calls for more structure, then you'll want to add interfacing or even rigid lining materials such as crinoline or buckram to make your bag really stand its ground. Remember that the lining of your bag might be on display every now and then, so give ample consideration to it, too.

But hey, don't feel hemmed in by conformity (a little sewing pun there); handbags are being made of wire mesh, papier-mâché, rubber, even recycled plastic bags! Even so, let's take a look at more traditional materials now. The spells you can cast with fabric alone are remarkable. Learning just a little about the properties of various materials will help you choose the right ones for your handbag. Fabrics are composed of fibers, and that seems a logical place to start, doesn't it? So here's some information about fibers and the fabrics that are made from them.

Cotton

What's not to love about cotton? It's washable, breathable, and comes in a mind-boggling array of weights and textures. Its ease in sewing makes it a perfect choice for a first handbag—or a second or third, as a matter of fact. Cotton's strengths are its durability, its density, and its ability to drape well. You're probably aware of its limitations—it tends to shrink and wrinkles fairly easily. Be sure to prewash cotton fabric before you sew. I mean it.

Linen

With its lustrous fibers from the flax plant, linen so impressed the Egyptians that they swaddles their mummies in it. Linen is more expensive than cotton, but offers many of cotton's advantages: it comes in a myriad of weights, from handkerchief to suiting; is strong and durable (even stronger when wet than dry, just in case you and your bag get caught out in the rain); and dyes beautifully. As wonderful as it is, linen wrinkles like crazy and loses its characteristic crispness when laundered (so you really don't want to get caught in the rain with your linen purse). But these are less important considerations for a bag than a garment, because after all, you won't be wearing it, will you?

Hemp

Hemp is certainly hip (you know what it's made from) and relatively new on the apparel scene. It's three times stronger than cotton and takes dye very readily. It's not as soft as other natural fibers, though it does soften with each washing and is extremely durable. You'll most often find it in its natural color (which is natural, interestingly enough), which makes it perfect for surface design such as simple dyeing, stenciling, or stamping.

Silk

While linen is lustrous, silk is just plain luxurious. It can be delicate and diaphanous (that would be sheer) or crisp and textured. Because it's just so luscious, silk is an obvious choice for a special handbag, whether tuck-under-your-arm-and-go-to-the-theater formal or sling-over-your-shoulder-and-take-to-the-club kitschy. Yes, silk is expensive, but you don't need much fabric for a handbag. Silk doesn't soil readily and resists wrinkling, but it is damaged by serious light exposure and can be affected by perspiration or body oils. Even though silk seems delicate, it's actually quite durable and strong.

Wool

While you don't often see handbags made of wool, there's no reason not to consider it if your muse commands. (Who knows? She might.) Wool comes in many weights, from soft challis to heavy cashmere coating. It can be fuzzy or smooth, fleecy or ribbed. Wool is soft and durable, but is very absorbent. Like silk, wool has a fair complexion and doesn't like prolonged exposure to sunlight. By the way, it's a myth that moths eat wool—it's the moth larvae that feed on wool. A woolen article (like your hip new bag) should be thoroughly cleaned before being stored, as stains and perspiration are attractive to the adult moths that are looking for a cozy little place to lay their eggs.

Felt

Felt, a nonwoven fabric, is wonderful because it doesn't ravel, so you don't have to finish the edges. (Say hurray if you're a lazy sewer!) It has a nice soft feel and a minimal hassle factor—a combination made in heaven. Traditionally made from wool, felt is now made from synthetic fibers, too.

Synthetics

Speaking of synthetics, there are zillions of varieties, including fabrics blended from both natural and synthetic fibers. The first synthetic fiber was rayon, which is formulated from cellulose (wood or cotton fiber). Rayon (viscose to you Brits) is somewhat of a changeling; it imitates cotton, silk, or linen. It's an economical choice, but tends to ravel a lot. A toss in the dryer will eliminate its body and probably shrink it.

Polyester, acrylic, and vinyl are also synthetic fibers. Back in the 1970s, when everything was polyester, you could wear a pantsuit for a year with no wrinkling. But it would have smelled pretty funky, because polyester is not particularly breathable. Nowadays, when you're looking for fabric for a handbag, you're likely to find synthetic fibers in materials such as metallics, faux furs, or faux suedes. Modern synthetics rival rayon in the ability to imitate natural fibers. The wearability and hand (how it feels) of synthetics have improved greatly over the years. They are often an economical choice, too.

So What About…

Satin and velvet and yummy fabrics like that? Well, both satin and velvet refer to the weave and texture of the fabric, not the fiber content. So satin can be made from silk or polyester or clever rayon (there it goes, changing again), but each of these fibers would be woven in a standard technique that produces satin's characteristic sheen and smoothness. Same thing with taffeta, charmeuse, and velvet, just to name a few. Velvet's plush, to-die-for pile can be created from cotton, silk, or synthetic fibers—it's the weave that's the key. And as you can imagine, synthetic velvet will be just the teeniest bit more affordable than velvet woven from silk.

And How About…

Home décor fabrics make awfully cool handbags, as you'll see. And you can spend hours in one store comparing colors and textures, feeling each fabric to decide if you're ready to commit or not. (I'm going to call these *decorator fabrics* because it sounds so fancy.) Sometimes even the folks who work in the stores can't tell you the exact fiber content of these materials, especially if you're shopping at an outlet; it's some sort of conspiracy perpetrated by the fabric manufacturers. But all you have to do is touch the material to know whether you like its hand or not.

There are splendid weaves in decorator fabrics that are similar to garment fabrics in that they can be produced from many different fibers. Damask, jacquard, tapestry, twill, brocade, and chenille are all fabrics you might meet in the home décor section. You probably know these: chenille has the characteristic pile you want to sink into, while brocade has embossed designs that seem to float on the surface. Jacquards are handy for purse making, because it's like getting two fabrics in one: the wrong side of the fabric is the reverse of the right side in both pattern and color. Pretty nifty.

Fabrics intended for draperies are generally lighter in weight than traditional upholstery fabrics and are sometimes marked in the selvedge as to fiber content (if you've just *got* to know). Companion fabrics are often available in complementary colorways, too, which can be helpful if you'd like to combine fabrics in your handbag design.

Upholstery fabrics are heavier and way durable, although some materials may be too dense to manipulate while sewing a small bag. To increase their longevity for their intended purpose, some have backings that make them a bit stiff and a little obstinate when introduced to the presser foot on your sewing machine. That said, be sure to take a look at the dazzling variety of decorator fabrics. There are beautiful materials to be had—great prints, wonderful textures, even some with knock-your-socks-off embroidery and appliqué as well as novelty shirred and crinkled fabrics. And they're usually 54 inches (137 cm) wide, so you can get a lot of purse (or purses) per yard. One more advantage to decorator fabrics is that they tend to be pretreated for stain resistance. Yippee! No worries about a sudden rainstorm or a spilled latte.

Fabric and Pattern

There are a few things to keep in mind about your fabric's motifs. If the pattern repeats are large, you may not be able to capture the essence of the fabric's design on the small canvas of a bag. On the other hand, you may like just the suggestion of the motif on the face of your bag. If you're choosing stripes and you want to match them, you may need extra fabric. Keep the scale of your bag in mind while you're shopping for fabric (or digging through your stash, as the case may be).

Other Materials

Okay, enough about fabric. How about other interesting things you can use to make bags?

Leather and Suede

It's hard to argue the durability of leather and suede (suede being the finished, skin side of leather). Garment-weight leather and suede can be sewn easily with just a few considerations. First, use small binder clips, rather than pins, to secure the pieces for sewing. Be sure to use a needle designed for leather; these needles have unique beveled points. Use a nonstick presser foot and finger press the seams open, …then tap them with a mallet. Glue or stitch seam allowances open. Here's the good news—these materials don't ravel, so you don't have to finish the edges. Do I hear another hurray from the lazy folks?

Alternative Materials

At its heart, a purse is a pretty simple concept: it needs to hold things. So just about any material you can use to make a container will make a purse. Rubber carpet padding, wire mesh, faux grass turf, wicker, polymer clay, fabricated metal, recycled tin cans…go for it, honey….

Lining Your Bag

To line, or not to line? It's really not a question for me; bags last longer and usually look better if they're lined. A lining keeps the inside of your purse tidy, especially if you add a few pockets. Because there are no exposed seams or little pieces of thread to get caught on your rings or intertwined with your keys, linings just make your purse happier. And you're happy when your purse is happy. You can dig away, merrily excavating to find the receipt for your new shoes and not cause undue wear and tear because the lining will protect your purse. You're in charge of the shoes.

Choose Your Lining Material

Generally speaking, you'll want a material that's a little lighter in weight than the fabric you're using to make the bag. This decision is a personal choice. Do you want a contrasting lining, or one that minds its own business in the background? The lining material you choose ought to be as durable as the bag itself because you want the two to live happily ever after. Your fabric and your lining should have compatible laundering requirements.

When you shop for lining, be sure to take a swatch of your fabric so you can truly compare the color, weight, and texture. Don't trust your memory to gauge the color of the fabric you've got on the shelf at home. Word to the wise.

Select the Interfacing

Yes, you'll likely want to add interfacing, too. There are a billion weights of interfacing, both fusible and sew-in types, to suit every bag. Usually, the more structured the bag, the heavier you'll want your interfacing to be. Buckram (the stiff stuff that keeps the bill of your trucker hat in shape) is very rigid; crinoline, as in the old petticoats, also provides a lot of body. Hair canvas is the traditional interfacing used in tailoring and has some flexibility. (Yes, it's actually made with hair. From a goat.)

The fine folk at your fabric store will surely be friendly if you're feeling squirrelly about the selection. Tell them what kind of fabric you're using and a little about the design of your bag and they can help you decide which one is best. It's important you tell them what kind of fabric you're using, because fusible interfacings aren't suitable for all fabrics; follow the manufacturer's instructions when using it. Having the proper interfacing is an important part of creating a handbag that looks the way you want it to, so do consider your choice carefully.

Continued →

Handbag Basics

Let's get down to the nitty-gritty. What kind of sewing skills do you need to have to make a bag? Just the most basic, really; if you've put in a zipper and lined anything, you understand the fundamentals. Generally, you can make a bag in a day (depending on your caffeine intake), so it's not a long drawn-out project like getting your significant other to put the dishes in the dishwasher within a 24-hour time period. Still working on that myself.

There are a number of techniques that are used repeatedly throughout the book to construct these chichi handbags. And the really great thing is that you can choose the details you want and add them to your own bag…In the bag patterns and the project instructions, you'll see constant references to this "Handbag Basics" section. I know we've been having a lot of fun so far, but now you need to concentrate for a few minutes.

Standard Techniques

A bag can have only one pattern piece, like The Clutch (guess what it looks like?). Most of the designs have just three: a bag piece (from which you'll cut both the front and the back of the bag), a bottom piece (square or round perhaps), and straps (or handles). Very simple. Here are some common construction methods that will transform these pieces into your new handbag. Since I've convinced you that you must line your bag, let's start there.

Add a Lining

Basically, you construct the lining with the same pattern pieces that you use to make the bag. There are two methods of lining used in the bag patterns. The first, Lining A, used in …The Tuck… is stitched in place with your sewing machine. Lining B is whipstitched to a zipper by hand.

Lining A

1. First, stitch the front and back bag lining pieces together, right sides facing. Then add the bottom lining piece, again with right sides together, *but leave a 5-inch (12.5 cm) section open in the bottom* (figure 1). Don't forget the little bit in italics or you'll be sorry. Trim the seams and press them open. Leave the lining wrong side out.

2. With right sides together, slip the lining over the bag and align the top edges. Pin them together, making sure the handles are between the fabric and the lining and not caught in the seam allowance. Match the side seams. Stitch (figure 2), then trim the seam and clip the curves.

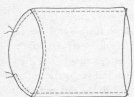

Figure 1   *Figure 2*

3. Turn the bag right side out through the 5-inch (12.5 cm) opening in the bottom of the lining (figure 3). That's why you shouldn't forget that little bit in italics in step 1! Stitch the opening closed by hand or machine. Push the lining into the bag and press the top

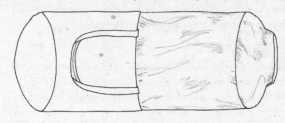

Figure 3

edge. Topstitch if you want to.

Lining B

In The Clutch… [a bag] with zipper closures, the lining is stitched to the zipper tape by hand.

1. Take the lining pieces and construct them as you do the bag, with right sides together, but leave the top edge open (where the zipper is on the handbag). Stitch in from the edge for 1 inch (2.5 cm) (figure 4); clip any curves.

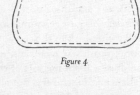

Figure 4

2. Turn the seam allowance under on the open portion of the lining and press. Leave the lining wrong side out (figure 5). Place it inside the bag, matching the seams. Whipstitch the pressed edge of the lining to the zipper tape, hiding the stitches as much as possible.

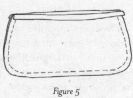

Figure 5

So while we're talking about zippers, let's learn how to…

Install a Zipper

This technique works very well for zippers in handbags. It's used in the basic patterns for The Clutch. Here's the best part—it's *muy* easy too. Only two steps.

1. Place the appropriate fabric pieces right sides together and pin them in place along the edge where you'll install the zipper. From each edge, stitch for 1 inch (2.5 cm), leaving the middle open (figure 6).

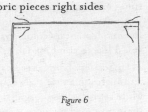

Figure 6

2. Press the seam open, turning under the raw edges in the middle. Place the zipper under the pressed edges and pin in place (figure 7). Use your zipper foot and begin stitching at the top of the zipper and continue down one side until you reach the end of the zipper

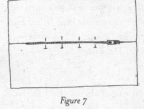

Figure 7

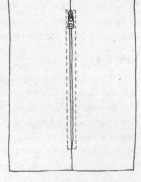

Figure 8

and continue down one side until you reach the end of the zipper. Lift the zipper foot, leaving the needle in the down position, and pivot the fabric. Lower the zipper foot and stitch across the bottom of the zipper. Pivot again, stitch back up the other side of the zipper, pivot, and stitch across the top (figure 8). Check to make sure the zipper runs freely.

Add a Strap

If it's long, it's a strap; if it's shorter, it's a handle, but the method is the same to make your own from fabric. Here are several variations. Ask your bag which one it wants.

Strap A

1. To make the straps, first apply fusible interfacing to the wrong sides of each piece. Fold one strap piece in half lengthwise, right sides together. Stitch the length of the strap, pivot at the corner, and stitch across one end (figure 9). Repeat for the second strap. Turn the straps inside out through the open end.

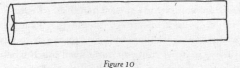

Figure 9

1. Now that you've turned the straps, trim the seam from the short ends so each strap has two open ends with raw edges. Press both pieces flat with seam in the center (figure 10).

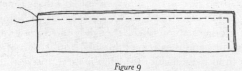

Figure 10

2. Pin the straps to the bag as desired, right sides together. You'll be looking at the seam in the strap if you've got it right. Be sure the straps are situated as shown (figure 11).

3. If you use fairly heavy or stiff fabric, which you certainly might for a handbag, don't, don't, *don't* try to make long straps or handles by turning them inside out. It makes for a very unhappy afternoon of sewing, because they're very difficult to turn. Use the more agreeable technique that follows.

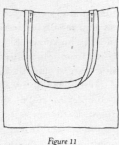

Figure 11

Strap B

An easy way to make a strap is to simply fold the edges in, fold in half, and stitch. This works well for skinny little straps or little skinny loops….

1. To make the straps, fold the pieces in half lengthwise, wrong sides together, and press. Fold the two raw edges into the pressed crease in the center and press again (figure 12).

2. Roll the strap in half again, lengthwise, and stitch as close to the edge as you can (figure 13). *Très facile.*

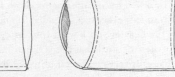

Figure 12

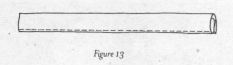

Figure 13

Strap C

An alternate method is to insert cording into the strap.... Instead of being sewn into the seam around the top of the handbag, these straps are sewn onto the outside of the bag.

1. To make the straps, take the pieces of fabric you've cut and fold them together lengthwise, right sides together. Before you sew, adjust the width to the seam so the cord has just enough room to slide into the strip after you've stitched the seam. Stitch across one short end, pivot, and stitch down the long side. Turn the strap right side out. Now that you've turned the strap, trim the seam from the short end so you have two open ends, just as in Strap A.

2. Cut the cord into two pieces; each piece of cord should be 3 or 4 inches (7.5 or 10 cm) shorter than the length of the strap. To get the cord into the strap, use this not-very-technical-yet-highly-efficient method: Tape one end of the cord to the end of the chopstick, and scoot the chopstick through the strap. Once the cord is through, liberate the chopstick (figure 14). There are other ways to feed the cord through; attach it to a safety pin, for example.

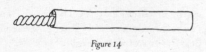

Figure 14

3. Center the cord inside each strap; there should be excess fabric on each end. Press this fabric flat and fold the end under about ¼ inch (6 mm).

4. Decide where you want to place the straps on the body of the bag—remember the ½-inch (1.3 cm) seam allowance along the top of the bag. Pin in place on your handbag and stitch as shown (figure 15).

See, these things are easy. Now, here are some ways you can customize your bag to suit your lifestyle.

Figure 15

Optional Techniques

Maybe you're the organized type who needs everything in its place. If so, you'll probably want to add some pockets to your purse. Perhaps you want to add some grommets or a flap to keep your handbag closed. Here are some ideas for the little options that really make life worth living.

Make a Pocket

There are two types of patch pockets used in this book, lined and (guess what?) unlined? There's also a third, a slash pocket, when you seriously want to stash things away.

Lined Pocket

Easy, easy, easy. Cut the pocket piece twice as long as you want the finished pocket to be, plus the seam allowances. Fold the pocket in half, right sides facing, and stitch around the edges, leaving an opening in the bottom to turn the pocket (figure 16). Pull the pocket through to the right side, press, and slipstitch the opening. Add to your handbag where you want a pocket.

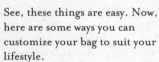

Figure 16

You can also use two pieces of fabric cut to the same measurements to make a lined pocket; maybe you want the inside of your pocket to be of contrasting material, for example.

Make it just as described in "Make a Pocket." This construction would be fun when you want to have a contrasting pocket visible on the outside of the handbag and not hidden away in the lining.

Unlined Pocket

Just as easy, easy, easy. Cut a piece of fabric to the desired size of your pocket, plus seam allowances on the side and an extra inch at the top. Make a narrow hem along the top edge and fold it over to the outside at the 1-inch (2.5 cm) mark. Stitch along the edges of the fold following the seamline (figure 17). Turn the top to the inside and turn under the sides and bottom. Press. Then stitch it to your purse or your lining.

Figure 17

Slash Pocket

This is like a welted pocket without the darn welts (but with a zipper). Cut a piece of fabric that is 1 inch (2.5 cm) wider than you want the pocket and 1 inch (2.5 cm) longer than twice the pocket's length. Mark with a line the place on the right side of the fabric where you want the opening of the pocket (this is the slash). Center the pocket piece along this line. Stitch a narrow rectangle around the line. Then, carefully cut along the slash line and clip to the corners (figure 18). Turn the pocket piece through the slash to the wrong side of the fabric. Press.

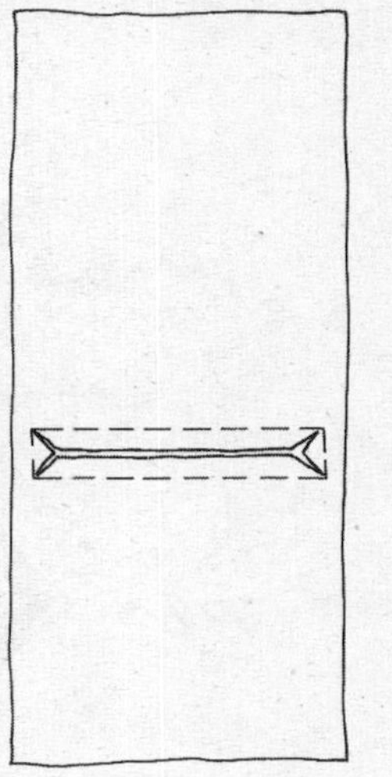

Add a zipper in the slash exactly as described under "Install a Zipper." (You'll probably have to shorten a zipper to fit into a handbag-sized pocket.) After you've installed the zipper, fold the pocket, right sides together, and stitch together the raw edges (figure 19). These nifty pockets work equally well on the outside of a purse or in the lining.

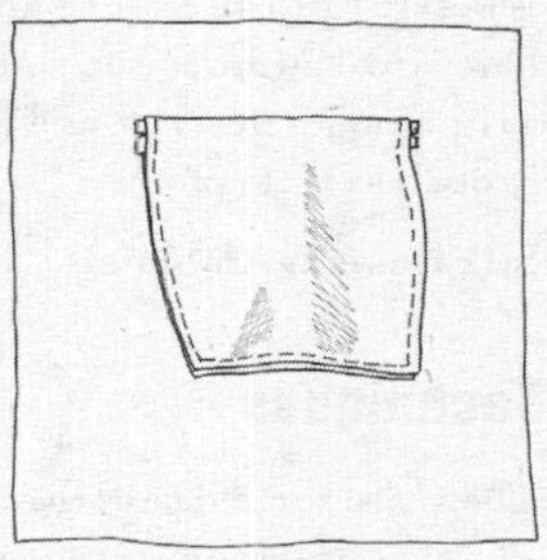

Okay, we've added a detail for the orderly folks. How about one for the insecure among us?

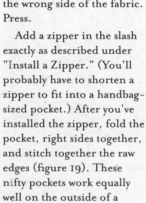

Figure 18

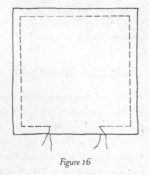

Figure 19

Add a Flap

A flap is a quick and easy addition to your bag, whether it's for work (to add a closure such as a magnetic clasp) or for play (it just sits there and looks cool).

Actually, you make a flap in virtually the same way you do the Lined Pocket (either version, come to think of it). The slight difference is that you stitch only the side seams and leave the bottom completely open to turn the flap. You add the flap to the bag before you line it, aligning the raw edges of the flap with the top of the bag (figure 20). So while we're at it...

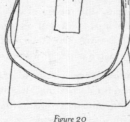

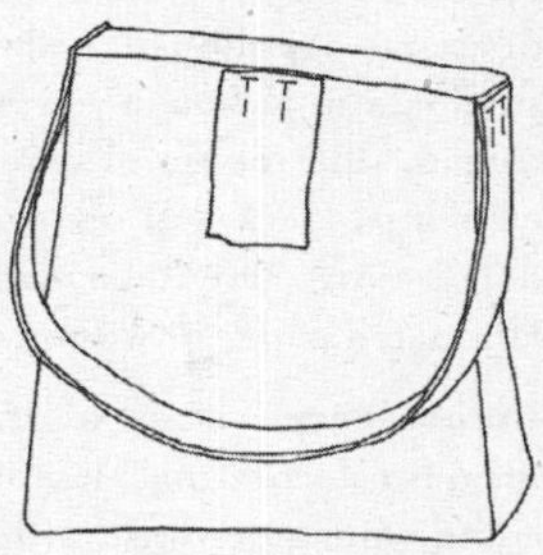

Figure 20

Keep It Closed

In addition to the faithful zipper (you can't question its loyalty), there are also magnetic clasps, buttons, snaps, frogs (loop fasteners made of fabric or cord), and ties. Options abound for keeping your purse closed. When you're planning a handbag, think through the construction process to decide when you need to add a clasp or a buttonhole. You don't want to stitch your flap in place before working that buttonhole or adding that clasp. Another word to the wise.

Add Piping or Cording

Piping or cording (one's just skinnier than the other) is a detail that can add a lot of definition to your handbag. You can buy purchased piping or make your own. In either case, it should be pinned and basted along the seamline of your bag with your zipper foot before you line or face the piece that the piping will decorate (figure 21). Stitch the seam with your zipper foot, too.

Make your own piping by first cutting bias strips from the stretchy diagonal grain of your fabric (figure 22). Then encase the cording in the bias strips, stitching close to the cording with the zipper foot (figure 23). Then, just add the piping to your bag as instructed above.

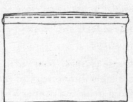

Figure 21

Figure 22

Figure 23

Create Fabric Panels

Maybe, just for the heck of it, you want to create panels in your bag. Simply divide your pattern into pieces as you wish (figure 24); a copy machine is helpful in this process so you can duplicate your original pattern for use with each project. *Remember to add a seam allowance to each new piece you make.* Stitch the panels together before you construct the bag.

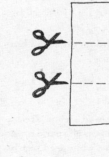

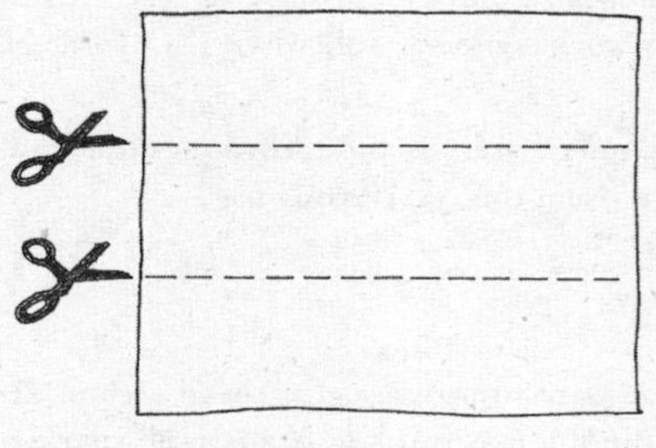

Figure 24

Add Grommets or Eyelets

A grommet is just a big eyelet, you know. Follow the manufacturer's instructions to install these wondrous gizmos that allow you to attach things to or dangle things from your handbag. You'll need several layers of fabric between the halves of the grommet so it will install and function properly, just as the instruction sheet will tell you. Believe it.

Add Handbag Accessories

There are some accessories that have been developed specifically for purses and you just might want to incorporate some of these items into your happenin' handbag. If you have a well-stocked craft store in your neighborhood, it will probably have a section for handbag crafting where you can examine many of these things. Surf the Net for suppliers, too.

Continued ➜

Handles. Although the basic pattern instructions for *Hip Handbags* tell you how to make your own straps from fabric, you can certainly add purchased handles to perfect the look you're after. You'll be amazed at the variety of handles available, in every size, shape, and color of the rainbow. There are beaded handles and handles you can decorate with beads. There's purse chain. There are acrylic and bamboo handles. And on and on. Depending on the design of the handles, they can be added in a variety of ways: inserted through a fabric casing, attached by a thin fabric loop, or secured with purse hooks. Read about these thingamajigs next.

Hooks. Attach straps or handles or whatever you want with some specialized hooks. Some have bars that screw in, while others swivel; some are quite lovely, actually. Most of these hooks are manufactures in various colors of metal, such as nickel or bronze....

Clasps. Magnetic purse clasps work fantastically and are very easy to install. There are more sophisticated clasps available, too, that close and lock.

Purse feet. Yes, you can get little studs for the bottom of your bag.

Purse frames. There is an astonishing array of frames available with which you can build your bag in any style, from prim and proper Victorian to get-outta-my-face polished metal. None of the patterns in this book are designed to use frames, but they may interest you at some point during your lengthy handbag-making career.

Beautify Your Bag

Now for the pretty stuff. In addition to the embellishment techniques you'll see in the handmade handbag projects, there are also 15 examples of how you can adorn a plain bag and turn it into something quite spectacular.... You can, of course, incorporate any of these ideas into your handmade bag. In fact, please *do*.

Many of these kinds of embellishments should be done to your bag pieces before you construct the handbag, particularly if you're doing something like embroidery where you want to conceal the stitching under the lining of your bag.

It makes sense to hide your work for a number of reasons, the most sensible (I guess we should be sensible every now and then) being the lack of threads or knots that snag and pull every time you reach inside your purse. Your work is more stable when it's protected by the lining.

Here are some materials and techniques that you can use to create visual interest in your bag.

Materials

Beads. If you want some extra glitz, bead accents are perfect. While you may think of beads as all sparkle, wood or bone beads can add ethnic accents, while seed pearls are quite elegant and sophisticated. Many beads can be stitched on with regular sharps and thread, but you may have to use a beading needle and nylon beading thread depending on how teeny your beads are.

Buttons. They're not all work and no play, you know. Though they will keep your bag closed quite contentedly, let buttons have a little fun as a decorative accent. Look for retro buttons, antique mother-of-pearl buttons, or even art-to-wear buttons made by enamellists or silversmiths. Use just one great button, or a grouping.

Stitch on beads for some flash.

Trims. Shop for trim—cording, piping, ribbon, fringe, lace, braid, tassels—in both the garment and decorator sections of the fabric store. You can make your own fabric trim with a bias tape maker, and boy is it fun. There are some spectacular trims available, embroidered and beaded by hand, that may be more expensive than the fabric you'll buy! But a little funky lime-green rickrack may be just the thing for *your* bag.

Novelty yarns. If you have a good knitting shop nearby, pay it a visit. The over-the-top popularity of knitting has led to some dynamite materials on the market, from cotton cord to variegated silk.

Sequins. For true dazzle, add a sequin (or a couple hundred). And they're not just tiny and round anymore—they're square, oblong, bursting with color, and *big*. Shop for specialty sequins on the Internet.

Tulle. Tulle is not just for tutus. If you want sheer drama, add some tulle as a top layer on your bag, or make trim from lengths of it. Tulle's cousin, netting, has a larger weave.

Eyelets and grommets. Like buttons, grommets and eyelets can be very functional, but they like to have fun too. They can be totally decorative—make a swirl of eyelets or a swoosh of grommets—and installing them is very easy. The pliers are particularly simple to use; just practice a time or two to get the right amount of pressure.

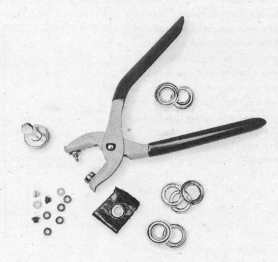
Add eyelets or grommets in the blink of an eye.

Jewelry. Just like Romeo and Juliet, handbags and jewelry have a real attraction to one another. Add a bracelet as a wrist strap, a necklace as a fashionable handle, or an old brooch as focal piece.

Silk flowers. Absolutely. No more needs to be said.

Techniques

There are some decorative techniques you can use to adorn your handbags too—some that you create with your sewing machine.

Appliqué. The art of applying material to the surface of fabric is used frequently in this book. Because it's ideal, of course. Appliquéd embellishments don't have to be stitched on, although you can really play with sewing thread, silk ribbon, or embroidery floss to add decorative elements. Heck, just use some glue if you want. And your details don't have to be made from fabric—how about laminated paper or wire mesh?

Embroidery. The art of ornamental needlework is also ideal for decorating a handbag. Did you know that you could embroider with raffia? Or silk ribbon? Experiment with various media; have a selection of needles with large eyes on hand. Computerized sewing machines also embroider (and if you have one, I'm jealous). This is not your grandmother's embroidery, dear,....

Appliqué doesn't have to be stitched; these playful elements are glued in place.

Couching. Couching feels like something between appliqué and embroidery, though technically it is an embroidery technique. Couching is creating a motif with decorative yarn or thread on your handbag, securing the decorative elements in place with a series of small stitches.

These stitches can be as laid-back or as in-your-face as you want. You can also couch by machine, using a zigzag stitch and the wizardry of invisible thread. Or don't—use regular thread if you'd rather the zigzag stitching be visible.

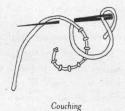
Couching

Snazzy sewing machines have special presser feet that allow you to couch with decorative stitches, even adding strings of pearls. Or so I've been told.

Quilting. Here's the first of several effects you can create at your sewing machine. Simple machine quilting can add dimension to your handbag, not to mention a little fluffiness, too. It's fun to follow the lines of stitching on your fabric's design motifs as you quilt. Simply place a layer of batting between your fabric piece and a piece of thin cotton backing fabric (quilters call this *making a sandwich*), pin carefully, and then stitch in place as desired on your machine. Use a complementary or contrasting thread, depending on how zany you're feeling.

Ruffles and pleats. These construction details add style. A simple ruffle is just gathered and stitched into place. Finish the edges of the ruffle if you want...or don't. No rules here. Pleats can really emphasize the glory of your fabric because you get to marvel at it in abundance. Simply make folds in your fabric and stitch them down when you're sewing the seam.

Topstitching and edgestitching. While topstitching can be functional, helping to hold a lining in place, it's also decorative. Technically speaking, topstitching is a line of stitching done on the right side of the fabric, parallel to an edge or a seam. Edgestitching is topstitching done just at the finished edge, about as close as you can get to it. Topstitching with a contrasting thread creates visual pizzazz.

Prepare to Sew

Okay, the fun is just about to start. But first, let's review the tools and materials you'll need. And let's talk about sewing for *just* a minute. Then on to the hip projects!

Tools and Materials

To make handmade bags, you need a sewing machine, of course, and all of the tools and materials that any sewer has on hand—pins, needles, thread, marking tools, scissors, pinking shears, tape measures, and the like. For either handmade or embellished purchased bags, you'll likely want a wide array of decorative treatments such as beads, sequins, and novelty trims.

Sewing machine. To make the handbags, you don't need a special machine or attachments; about all the machine needs to do is stitch forward, reverse, and zigzag. Well, you might make a few buttonholes, too, come to think of it. Make sure you haven't lost your zipper foot, because you may need that. Before you begin sewing in earnest, check the thread tension using a piece of the fabric you'll be using for your bag.

Of course, you can't sew without good, sharp needles on your machine. Have a range of sizes available and remember to change them often. Every time you hit a pin, you'll need a new needle. Doggone it.

Thread. Gotta have it. Match it to your fabric or choose a color that contrasts if that's the look you're after. Cotton-wrapped polyester should work just fine for your handbags. Invisible thread—nylon monofilament—is wonderful for attaching adornments, because it's so very invisible, of course. You can also use it in your sewing machine if you want to.

Pins and needles. This is how you feel when you're ready to cut out your first bag. Kidding. Regular dressmaker's pins are essential to piece your bag together; the newer and sharper, the better. Silk pins—longer and thinner than dressmaker's pins—should be used on light- to medium-weight fabrics.

You'll probably find an assortment of craft needles helpful, depending on the kind of embellishment you're inspired to create. A variety of embroidery needles will probably do the trick. For hand sewing with regular thread, have several sizes of sharps on hand.

Marking tools. You won't be doing much marking for these patterns, but you will probably use a water-soluble marking pen or dressmaker's pencil at some point. Check the disappearability (no, it's probably not a real word) of the marking pens on a scrap of your fabric. I beg you.

Turning tools. There are some little tools that can really help when you're making a handbag, and one of them is a pointer and creaser, also called a point turner. The tip of this wood or plastic tool pokes out the angles of any piece that needs it, such as the corner of a square flap. When you're shopping, you may find this tool in the quilting section.

You may also want a bodkin or a loop turner to turn a bias strip or strap inside out. My loop turner and I are not on very good terms, but maybe you have a better relationship with yours.

Measuring tools. I've found that I use my hem gauge an awful lot in making handbags because of the scale of the projects. Have a tape measure and a ruler on hand, too.

Bias tape maker. A wonderful gadget that lets you make your own bias tape.

Seam ripper. Oh boy. I hope you use yours less than I use mine. It's such an indispensable tool that I have three, in varying sizes—mishap, mistake, and disaster.

Fabric scissors. A good sharp pair of dressmaker's shears is a necessity; maybe you'll want some pinking shears, too. Embroidery scissors are nice to have for more detailed work.

Clean newsprint or similar paper. To make your patterns from the grids included in this book, you need some thin paper. While there are some fairly long pieces used in the book (I think the largest is about 31 inches (78.5 cm) long), you can always tape smaller pieces of paper together. An art supply store is a good place to look for pattern-making paper.

Pencils and markers. Have a few around for making and marking the patterns.

Craft scissors. Do not use your fabric scissors on paper. *Verboten!* Use these instead.

Iron and ironing board. Keep the iron plugged in. While it's sometimes difficult to press after every step while handbag sewing, so the best you can. Important: Test every fabric with the iron before you use it on your

actual handbag, especially if you've got a remnant and you're unsure of its fiber content. Some fabrics develop a shine when pressed.

If you really get into making handbags, there are some specialized pressing aids that tailors use that will help you reach into the tight spaces and curved areas of a handbag. Pressing hams, pressing mitts, and seam rolls will make it easier to press your bag.

Decorative materials. Well, I'm going to leave this up to you (and your ever-present muse). The materials used as embellishments in this book include embroidery floss, fabric swatches, raffia, tulle, shells, jewelry, feathers, beads, trim, buttons, sequins, rickrack, ribbon, artificial flowers, decorative papers, wire…celebrate the possibilities.

Sewing 101

I'd feel better if we can review some basic sewing terms so we're all on the same page (literally!). Somewhere along the way to handbag nirvana, you'll undoubtedly be instructed to do some of these things.

Baste. Use a line of long stitches to hold pieces in place temporarily.

Clip. Snip into the seam allowance; you definitely want to clip the inward curves of your bag.

Face. Finish a raw edge or a handbag piece with a facing.

Finger press. Some sturdy upholstery fabrics don't press well due to weight or fiber content. And really, sometimes it's difficult to press a handbag because of its inherent design. Finger pressing is useful here: use your fingers to apply pressure to open a seam or push a lining flat.

Hem. In this book, this term usually means finish the edges, as in those of a pocket, by narrowly turning under the raw edges; pressing; turning the edge under again; pressing; and then stitching.

Notch. Cut a notch into the seam allowance; you definitely want to notch the outward curves of your bag.

Pivot. To turn the fabric in another direction while you sew. Lift the presser foot, leaving the needle in the down position, and pivot the fabric. Depending on your fabric choice, it may be helpful to clip the corner of one of the pieces to make the turn easier. Then lower the presser foot and continue.

Press. Did you know there is a difference between pressing and ironing? When you press, you don't move the iron across the fabric—that's ironing. To press means just that—pressing the iron against the fabric. Generally, you should press each seam after you stitch it.

Seam allowance. The amount of fabric between the cut edge and the seamline. In this section, it's *always* ½ inch (1.3 cm).

Seamline. The seamline is the stitching line.

Topstitch. Decorative (or functional) stitching on the right side of your handbag.

Trim. Trimming seams is usually a good idea to eliminate bulk. You can also grade the seam allowances, which is to trim one layer shorter than the other.

Turn. In this book, you'll need to turn lots of straps through to the right side. Depending on the material, this can be easy (silk) or not so easy (upholstery fabric). The straps in these projects usually have a seam that you can push against to turn the strap inside out. You can use the pushing or pulling tool that seems to work for you—a bodkin, a loop turner, a chopstick, whatever.

Whipstitch. These are tiny hand stitches you'll use to attach linings; technically speaking, the stitches appear slanted.

Making Your Pattern

Instead of including actual patterns in this book, we've provided templates on a grid so you can make your own patterns at home, reducing or enlarging them to your heart's content. The scale we've used is 1 square equals 2 inches (5 cm). Simply create your own grid to these measurements and draw in the pattern pieces. Our patterns *include*, I repeat *include*, the ½-inch (1.3 cm) seam allowance, so you don't have to make additional adjustments. After you've drawn the pieces on paper, using the grid system, cut them out with a pair of craft scissors.

If you want the bag smaller, reduce the size of the squares, but keep the proportions (the number of squares in each piece) the same. Want it bigger? Make the squares larger, again keeping the proportions of the pieces the same. (If math is not your thing, here's how you can cheat: Make your pattern pieces the size we've used in the

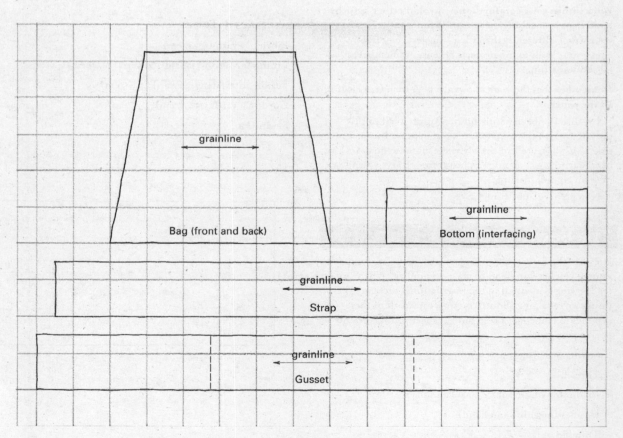

A template like this is provided for all the basic patterns. Make your pattern pieces from these grids; one square equals 2 inches.

Continued ➔

book. Trim off the seam allowances. Then, fiddle with the pattern pieces at a copy machine, *reducing or enlarging each pattern piece the same percentage until you've reached the size you want.* Remember to add the ½-inch (1.3 cm) seam allowance to the pieces after you've sized them.)

Read Me! (Please.)

You know when you're installing new software on your computer, there's always that annoying file that screams READ ME? Well, there's one in this book, too. I'm sorry; I know you're ready to sew, but here are some last-minute reminders that will make your hip handbag experience a happy one.

Ask the good folks at your fabric or crafts store for advice if you're unfamiliar with the properties of the fabric that interests you. Tell them what you're doing, and ask if they have any advice about sewing with the fabric you've chosen. Same applies for interfacings, too.

Prewash all your fabrics that can be washed.

Press the fabric before you cut out the pieces for your handbag.

Cut all the pieces on the lengthwise grain if possible; crosswise is okay, too, if the amount of your fabric is limited. If you make your own piping, those pieces should be cut on the bias.

Test dressmaker's pencils or marking pens on a scrap of your fabric.

Check the tension on your machine by using a swatch of your fabric. Make sure you have the needle size right; the needle ought to be good and sharp, too.

Make a practice "mistake." Some materials don't leave you any room for error, for if you stitch a seam and then have to rip it out, the needle holes remain. Bummer. Leather, suede, and novelty nonwoven fabrics (like vinyl) fall into this category. Before you sew, it's a good idea to do a test seam on a scrap and then try to remove it to see how your fabric responds to the oops factor.

Test all your new techniques on a scrap piece of your fabric before you commit to incorporating it into your handbag. I'm talking about things like installing grommets and magnetic clasps as well as decorative techniques such as embroidery or quilting. Just maybe it won't turn out as you hoped, so check it out first. Please.

Work within your comfort zone—if you'd rather baste by hand than by machine, have at it. If you'd rather make your straps differently than what I suggest, feel free. Apply your skills to the projects because, remember, it's all about the fun.

Remember that the seam allowance is ½ inch (1.3 cm) for all the patterns.

I realize I've been a little bit of a know-it-all in this part of the book. Why? Well, it's not because I'm so smart—it's because I've already made all these mistakes I've been warning you about. I'm just trying to save you a lot of seam rippin', darling.

Now go have some fun!

The Sewing Kit

Here are the basic tools and materials that we're going to assume you have on hand to make a handbag. When you see "Sewing Kit" listed in the instructions, these are the things we're talking about. You won't need all of these supplies to embellish a bag, but I suspect you'll certainly need a pair of scissors.

Sewing machine

Thread

Nylon thread, invisible (clear) and dark

Needles (machine and hand)

Thimble

Pins

Pincushion

Marking tools—water-soluble pens or dressmaker's pencils

Turning tools—point turner, bodkin, loop turner

Measuring tools—tape measure, hem gauge, ruler

Seam sipper

Scissors—embroidery scissors and shears

Craft scissors

Clean newsprint or similar paper for making patterns

Pencils and markers

Iron and ironing board

The Patterns & Projects

Pattern: The Messenger

Over the shoulder and off you go. Put on The Messenger, give it an adoring pat, and feel secure that it's right by your side.

MATERIALS & TOOLS

Fabric, ½ yard (45.5 cm)

Lining (or second fabric), ½ yard (45.5 cm)

Fusible interfacing, ½ yard (45.5 cm)

Cord, 1¼ yards (114.5 cm)

Sewing kit

PIECES TO CUT

Bag—1 of fabric, 1 of lining (or second fabric), and 1 of interfacing

Remember to use ½-inch (1.3 cm) seam allowances.

Handbag Basics

HOW YOU MAKE IT

1. Apply the interfacing to the wrong side of the fabric piece.

2. Measure 9 inches (23 cm) down from one end of the bag, marking at each side. Pin one end of the cord to each side at the marks, making sure the raw edges are even (figure 2). Pin the fabric piece to the lining, right sides together, with the cord between the two layers and not caught in the seam allowances. Stitch around the bag, leaving a 4-inch (10 cm) section open in the end away from the cord.

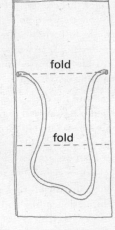

Figure 2

3. Turn the bag right side out through the opening and press. Stitch the opening by hand or machine. Fold the bottom up to the cord and press.

4. Stitch the sides in place by hand or machine, sewing very close to the edge.

Cool Alternative

This bag can be completely reversible if you desire, so choose a hip fabric for the lining, too.

Hot Tip

You can vary where you place the cord and the fold depending on how long you want the flap to be.

The Marie Antoinette

This bag is opulent and extravagant just like its namesake, yet far more gracious.

HIP INDEX

Totally Elegant

BAG PATTERN

The Messenger

SPECIAL TOOLS OR MATERIALS

Upholstery trim, ¼ yard (23 cm)

Cording, ¾ yard (68.5 cm)

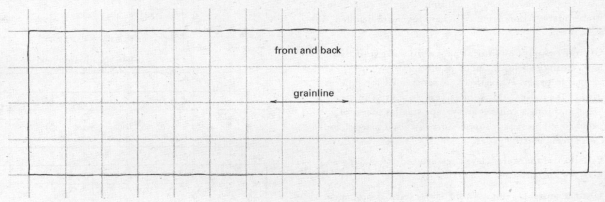

front and back

grainline

Figure 1

Handmade by Allison Chandler Smith

FABRIC

Decorator brocade; brocade lining

HOW IT'S DIFFERENT

This bag is a scaled-down version of The Messenger, the bag pattern piece reduced to about 9 x 22 inches. Leave the flap end open when you stitch the fabric and lining together.

HOW IT'S SPECIAL

Fold under the raw edges of the flap; sandwich the trim between the two layers. Baste in place by hand. Fold the bottom edge as desired, but don't stitch the sides just yet. Now, decide how long you want the strap, remembering to figure in the length of the sides of the bag, and cut the cording. Sandwich the flange of the cording between the two folded layers of fabric. Stitch the sides and use a small pair of scissors to remove the exposed flange along the handle.

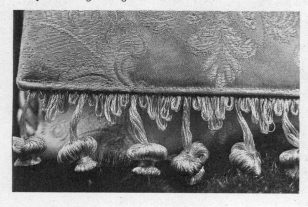

The Clutch

This bag will never leave you, for it likes to be held close. It's just big enough to hold life's essentials—keys, cash, and lipstick.

MATERIALS & TOOLS

Fabric, ¼ yard (23 cm)

Lining, ¼ yard (23 cm)

2 pieces of felt, 9 x 12 inches (23 x 30.5 cm)

Zipper, 9 inches (23 cm)

Sewing kit

PIECES TO CUT

Bag—2 of fabric, 2 of lining, 2 of felt (for interfacing)

Remember to use ½-inch (1.3 cm) seam allowances.

Handbag Basics

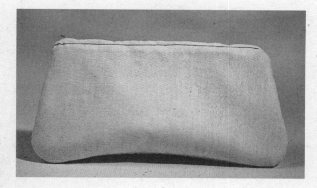

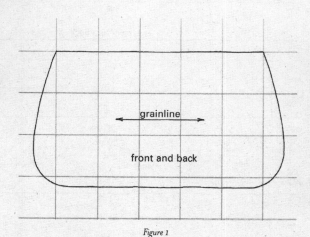

Figure 1

HOW YOU MAKE IT

1. Place the fabric pieces right sides together and pin in place along the top edge. You'll be inserting a zipper as in the Handbag Basics, but stitch ½ inch (1.3 cm) from each end instead of 1 inch (2.5 cm).

2. Press the seam open, turning the raw edges under. Place the zipper under the pressed edges and pin in place. With a zipper foot, begin stitching at the top of the zipper and continue down one side until you reach the bottom. Lift the zipper foot, leaving the needle in the down position, and pivot the fabric. Lower the zipper foot and stitch across the bottom. Pivot again, stitch back up the other side of the zipper, pivot, and stitch across the top. Make sure the zipper runs freely.

3. To give your bag some nice squeezable support, add the felt interfacing to the wrong side of the bag pieces. Trim ½ inch (1.3 cm) off the top of each of the felt pieces that cut out so the top edges of the felt pieces fall just at the edge of the zipper. Whipstitch the top of the felt to the edge of the zipper tape. Baste the sides and bottom of the felt to the inside of the bag, stitching as close as possible to the edge (figure 2).

Figure 2

4. Open the zipper about 1 inch (2.5 cm). (If you've decided to add a strap, now is the time to pin it in place at the corner [or corners], the raw edges even with the raw edges of the side seams of the bag. Be sure the strap is between the layers and be careful not to catch it in the seams as you sew). Take the handbag, place the right sides together, and pin in place. Stitch all the way around the sides and bottom of the bag (figure 3). Trim the seams and clip the corners. Fully open the zipper and turn the bag right side out.

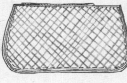

Figure 3

5. Take the lining pieces and place them right sides together, pin in place. Stitch around the sides and bottom but leave the top edge open, stitching in only ½ inch (1.3 cm) from each edge. Clip the curves. (This is Lining B in the Handbag Basics.)

6. Turn under the seam allowance on the open portion of the lining and press. Leave the lining wrong side out. Place it inside the bag, matching the edges. Whipstitch the pressed edge of the lining to the zipper tape, hiding the stitches as much as possible.

The Summer Day

Oh, picnics and sunshine. The Summer Day is totally reversible and totally fun.

Handmade by Allison Chandler Smith

HIP INDEX

Somewhere in Between

BAG PATTERN

The Clutch

SPECIAL TOOLS OR MATERIALS

Fusible interfacing, ¼ yard (23 cm)

FABRIC

Decorator cotton; decorator sateen lining

HOW IT'S DIFFERENT

Choose two complementary fabrics to use for this clutch; since it's reversible, either fabric could be the lining or the exterior, to suit your whim. To make it easy, let's call one the fabric (the exterior) and one the lining (inside). Cut out three clutch pieces from both the fabric and the lining (six in all), and three clutch pieces from fusible interfacing. Apply the interfacing to the wrong side of all three pieces cut from the fabric.

Make the front flap by sewing one piece of the fabric to one piece of the lining, right sides together, leaving the top edge open. Turn and press. With right sides together, sew the remaining two lining pieces together, leaving the top edge open. Turn and press. Repeat to make the body of the clutch from the remaining two fabric pieces. Turn and press.

Okay, now concentrate. To assemble the clutch, stack all three sewn pieces together like so: on the bottom, the body of the clutch, back facing up; in the middle, the flap of the clutch with the lining side facing up; and on top, the lining of the clutch. Pin together the three pieces along the top, leaving the bottommost layer of fabric and the topmost layer of fabric free. Stitch through the pinned layers only, as shown in figure 1. Push the lining into the bag and press flat. Turn the raw edges under and whipstitch the lining to the front of the bag.

Figure 1

Continued ➡

Cool Alternative

If you were feeling a little less like summer and more like spring, you could reverse this bag to display the fabric used in the inside. Clever, huh?

Pattern: The Tuck

The tidy Tuck fits just under your arm or hugs your side; it loves you! And you'll love it, too, through thick and thin.

MATERIALS & TOOLS

Fabric, ½ yard (45.5 cm)

Lining, ½ yard (45.5 cm)

Buckram, ¼ yard (23 cm)

Fusible interfacing, ½ yard (45.5 cm)

Sewing kit

PIECES TO CUT

Bag—2 of fabric, 2 of lining, 2 of interfacing

Strap—2 of fabric, 1 of interfacing (optional)

Gusset—1 of fabric, 1 of lining, 1 of interfacing

Bottom—1 of buckram

Remember to use ½-inch (1.3 cm) seam allowances.

Handbag Basics

HOW YOU MAKE IT

1. Mark the dashed lines on the gusset (this is the bottom of the bag). Trim the seam allowances from the buckram and place it in the center of the gusset between the marked lines. Apply the interfacing to the gusset, sandwiching the buckram between the fabric and the interfacing. Apply the interfacing to the wrong sides of the fabric bag pieces.

2. Pin one of the fabric bag pieces to the gusset, right sides together (figure 2). Stitch in place, starting at the top, and continue to within ½ inch (1.3 cm) of the corner; pivot and stitch to the next corner. (It may be helpful to clip the corner of the gusset to make the turn easier.) Pivot and stitch to the top. Stitch the gusset to the remaining bag piece.

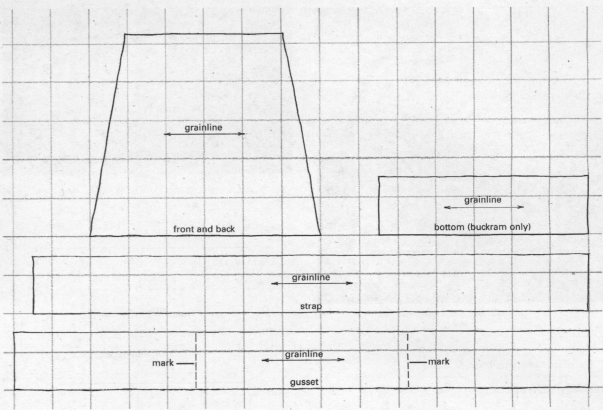

Figure 1

3. Trim the corners. Press the seams open and turn the bag right side out.

4. Make the strap using a slight variation of Strap A in Handbag Basics. Place the strap pieces right sides together and pin. (For extra strength, add interfacing to one of the strap pieces.) Stitch the two long sides together, leaving the ends open; because this strap is fairly wide, it's easy to turn inside out through one of the ends. Turn and press.

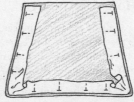

Figure 2

5. Pin one end of the strap to the gusset, right sides together, and stitch in place. Making sure the strap is not twisted, pin and stitch the other end of the strap to the gusset on the other side of the bag.

6. Make the lining as in step 2, leaving a 5-inch (12.5 cm) opening in one of the bottom seams. Press the seams open. (Look at Lining A in the Handbag Basics if you want to take a peek at the illustrations for this method.) Leave the lining wrong side out.

7. Place the lining over the bag, so the right sides of the bag and the lining are together. Be sure the strap is situated properly between the bag and the lining. Pin the raw edges of the lining and the bag together, matching the side seams. Stitch all the way around the top. Trim the seams and clip the curves.

8. Turn the bag right side out through the 5-inch (12.5 cm) hole in the bottom of the lining. Stitch the opening closed by hand or machine. Push the lining into the bag and press the top edge. Topstitch if desired.

Hot Tip

If you want a really stiff bag, use buckram (½ yard (45.5 cm)) instead of fusible interfacing. Then you can omit the buckram insert in the gusset.

The Cosmos

This bag comes from a candy-coated universe where everyone is in the pink, and you will be too when you're carrying this cosmic confection.

Handmade by Nathalie Mornu

HIP INDEX

Absolutely Funky

BAG PATTERN

The Tuck

SPECIAL TOOLS AND MATERIALS

Buckram, ½ yard (45.5 cm)

FABRIC

Felt

HOW IT'S DIFFERENT

You won't be adding the strap to this variation of The Tuck. Instead, cut a space into the bag pieces for the handle. Divide the gusset into two pieces, one for the sides and one for the bottom; remember to add the seam allowance to the new pieces. Since The Cosmos is lined with felt, cut out four bag pieces, four side pieces, and two bottom pieces.

From the buckram, cut one front, one back, two side pieces, and one bottom piece. Trim away an additional ⅜ inch (1 cm) from all the buckram edges, including those around the handle areas. Now the buckram won't peek through after the bag is stitched.

For each piece, sandwich the buckram between the two layers of felt and pin together. Cut out felt circles in a variety of sizes. Arrange as desired and pin. Topstitch in place. Then topstitch around the handles. The sides with appliqués on them will be the exterior of the purse. Assemble the pieces with wrong sides facing and pin, beginning with the sides. Stitch with the seams on the outside. Then sew the bottom to the bag. Topstitch along the top of the bag and trim any seams if desired.

How It's Special

Appliqué is an easy way to add some life to the surface of your handbag. These felt appliqués are easily stitched on by machine.

Helpful Hint for Happy Sewing #1

Because felt doesn't ravel, you don't have to finish the raw edges and you can leave the seams exposed.

Helpful Hint for Happy Sewing #2

Adding the cosmic appliqués after you've assembled the felt "sandwich" helps keep the pieces together. But you might find it a little easier to put the appliqués on before you assemble the sandwiches, as you'll be working with fewer layers of felt.

—From *Hip Handbags*

FELTING
Katheryn Tidwell Bieber

Basics

Felting 101

What is felting, anyway? Technically speaking, felting occurs when you combine animal fibers (wool, fur, or hair) with moisture, heat, and agitation. Hot soapy water makes it easy for the fibers to slip around and become entangled. Agitation increases the fiber contact, and when the wool fibers have become so entangled that there is no more room for them to move, they form a firm, felted fabric that can be cut with scissors without unraveling.

Felting is actually a very old technique. Textile manufacturers of the Middle Ages felted (the technical term is *fulled*) fabric by scouring it in hot water with a cleaning agent, beating it or walking over it, then rinsing it in cool water. Today, many crafters knit extra large items and then felt them by agitating them in hot water by hand or in a washing machine. The fast-felting method this book will teach you saves both time and effort because you simply felt pre-made sweaters in a washing machine, cut them up, and then stitch together the felted fabric to create all kinds of new items.

What Is Fast Felting?

It begins with shrinking a pre-made sweater or other knit item on purpose, using soap and agitation to cause the fibers to interlock and become a felted fabric. You can then cut and sew this fabric like you would any other.

What You'll Need

The supplies list for fast felting is fairly short and simple. Chances are good you already have many of the needed items.

Here are the essentials for felting:

- Wool sweater or other knit item
- Zippered lingerie bag or pillow protector
- Wool wash or mild dishwashing soap
- Washing machine
- Clothes dryer (optional)

Once you felt your pieces, you'll cut them apart, and—following the patterns provided—stitch the fabric to create the projects in this book. For this part of the process, the following supplies will come in handy:

- Chalk marker
- Measuring tape
- Scissors
- Hand-quilting thread and all-purpose thread
- Cotton darning or milliner's needle
- Tapestry needle
- Lining fabrics
- Sewing machine
- Iron
- Pins and pin-back fasteners
- Plastic canvas

As you gain experience and move beyond the basics, you may want to consider the following items for embellishing your projects to make them unique:

- Beads, bells, crystals, and other embellishments
- Buttons
- Embroidery floss
- Ribbons and yarn
- Vintage jewelry

Finding the Right Sweater

Since one of the joys of fast felting is saving time, I recommend using pre-knit wool sweaters (you can use scarves, too). Large and extra-large sweaters yield the most material, but keep your eye out for children's sweaters, too. They often come in delightful colors and are great for flowers and other projects. Another key element of my approach to fast felting is to keep it inexpensive. I do this by relying on castoffs and thrift store finds. Once you catch "fast felting fever" you will begin to find great sweaters everywhere.

When selecting a sweater to felt, start with one that's much larger than you want the final piece of fabric to be. Although most sweaters shrink up by about one-third, remaining about two-thirds of their original size, every sweater felts differently depending on the wool, how it was knit, and whether or not it was pretreated. It's possible that a loosely knit sweater that goes to your knees could end up toddler size. Also, don't let color deter you from a great find—light colors can be changed by dyeing them,… and you can often use a less-than-favorite color of felt as

---

No Moths Allowed

I have noticed from time to time that along with wool sweaters, I seem to have attracted a few moths. A good way to keep that from happening is to felt your sweaters soon after bringing them into your house. I also have learned that, in addition to cedar, lavender flowers do a good job of repelling moths too. I keep lavender flower sachets and bundles of dried flowers around my craft area. It keeps the moths away and I get to enjoy the aromatherapy!

an accent or in hidden parts of a project. Try using the material as a flower or leaf embellishment or as the soles on a pair of slippers.

If you are concerned that you may not have enough sweater fabric to complete a desired project, now is the time to be creative. Find another sweater or child's sweater in a complementary or contrasting color. Use a different color for slipper soles, purse handles, stripes, or mitten cuffs. Think of the little challenges that pop up along the way as opportunities, and you'll make fun discoveries, as quilters do when they "make do."

Some items are pretreated to prevent shrinkage. If this turns out to be the case with a sweater you've selected, don't despair—there are plenty of other ways you can use it. Cut it as desired, finish the seams with a zigzag stitch if you're worried about unraveling, and use it with a lining. Or make embellishments, such as the Rolled Victorian Roses.

Sweater Shopping Checklist

Not all items knitted of the same type of yarn will shrink and felt exactly the same way, but you can improve your chances of getting what you want by following a few simple guidelines:

- Select items that are 85 to 100 percent wool or other animal fiber for optimal shrinking and felting.
- When in doubt, look for sweaters with "dry-clean only" on their tags.
- Start with items that are significantly larger than you intend the felted piece of fabric to be.
- Select several sweaters in complementary colors, as though making a quilt. This will ensure that you have plenty of felted fabric for a project.
- Look beyond the design of a sweater and consider its potential as a flower, leaf, or background color.
- Be flexible—if a sweater doesn't felt the way you want, save it for a different project.

The Fast Felting Process

The washer and dryer are a felter's power tools, saving you the time and effort that hang-felting requires. For best results, shrink one or two like-colored sweaters at a time in a single load, because some colors may bleed onto others. Since the felting process can generate a lot of lint, place your sweaters in a zippered lingerie bag or pillow protector to protect your washer from excessive

Continued ➔

lint buildup. Although you may use your normal laundry detergent for the felting process, I've found that it can cause bleeding and other harsh effects. I prefer to use either a small amount of mild dishwashing soap or detergent specially formulated for woolens (sometimes called wool wash).

As you work, keep in mind that felting is not an exact science. Some yarns felt faster and shrink more than others. Typically, loosely woven wool sweaters tend to shrink up tight and thick while finer, more tightly knit sweaters may not felt as densely and may require more agitation time in the washer.

- Loosely knit 100% wool shrinks and felts tightly.
- Loose open stitch tightens and fills in.
- Designs and patterns become softly muted after felting.
- Angora shrinks and felts moderately, still retaining its soft drape.
- Acrylic knits do not felt or shrink.

Fast felting takes from 20 minutes to an hour and a half, depending on how felted you want your sweater fabric. You may need to reset the agitation cycle on your washer as many as three or four times. Because it's best to check the progress of your fabric, a top-loading washing machine is ideal. A front-loading model requires you to run complete cycles and doesn't allow you to reset only the agitation cycle.

1. Place your sweater in a zippered lingerie bag or pillow protector.

2. Set your washer to the lowest water level and the longest cycle (mine is 12 minutes), and select the hot wash/cold rinse option. Add about 1 tablespoon of mild dishwashing soap or wool wash and start the washing cycle. I set my kitchen timer for 10 minutes.

3. Near the end of the agitation cycle, check the progress. The more the fabric is felted, the denser it is and the harder it feels. If the sweater isn't sufficiently felted, reset the washing machine for another agitation cycle. You can let it run the full cycle and then reset your machine; it will just take longer.

4. Once the sweater is rinsed and the cycle is finished, remove the felted sweater from the washer. If more shrinkage is desired, machine-dry it; otherwise, hang to dry. Occasionally when drying a sweater in the dryer, you may get some folds or creases; if so, simply steam them out with your steam iron set on wool.

Note for Knitters

If you want to knit items from scratch and then felt them, great! Just keep in mind that with fast felting, items can shrink as much as 50 percent or more, so be prepared to knit an item that is much larger than the final size of the project.

Off with the Buttons

When you fast felt sweaters with buttons and want to take advantage of the buttoned area, remove the buttons first. After felting, sew the buttons back on to align with the buttonholes so there won't be any gaps or bulges from uneven shrinking.

Cutting Fast Felt

You'll find patterns for the projects in the back of the book. To use a pattern, adjust it to the desired size by using the enlarge/reduce function on a photocopied or by using the gridded background to enlarge it by hand. Copy the pattern, cut it out, then lay the paper shapes on your felted fabric and pin them into place with straight pins. Seam allowances are included in all the patterns unless otherwise noted. Place the patterns to make the most efficient use of your felted fabric, or place them as directed in the project instructions, Some of the project instructions will tell you or show in illustrations exactly where to cut pattern pieces for best use of fabric, or to include ribbing material needed for the project. Others will tell you to cut sleeves off or cut ribbing off.

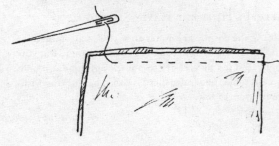

When you're sure you have fabric for all the pieces of your pattern, cut out the fabric using good-quality, sharp scissors—the kid our moms hid from us as kids so we wouldn't cut up paper, clay, and pipe cleaners with them! Don't be afraid—if you don't cut, you'll never make that fabulous purse!

Cut your felted sweater apart at the seams, and spread the pieces out so you can see how much fabric you have to work with.

A Note about Boiled Wool Sweaters

In my quest for sweaters, I often come across those that some people call "boiled wool." These are basically sweaters made from wool that is felted and then stitched into the final garment. Although you can shrink these further for a very thick felt, they are wonderful to use as is.

Sewing

If you can sew on a button, you have all the sewing skills you need for the projects in this section. You don't even need to have a sewing machine, although it can certainly be a great time-saver, and I use a sewing machine whenever possible.

There are a few things that will make your sewing go more smoothly. First, keep in mind that because felt is very thick, you'll usually need a larger-than-normal stitch length for best results—usually between ⅛" (3 cm) and ¼" (6 mm) long if you're hand-stitching. Select a needle that is long enough to travel easily through the thick felt. I like to use a milliner's needle or a cotton darner. Both are long and thin and have large, easy-to-thread eyes. Unless otherwise indicated, sew your seams ¼" from the edge of the felted fabric (this is the seam allowance).

It's important to match the color of your thread to your project for all parts that will show, such as a purse handle or the hem of a hat. Use cotton or a cotton-poly blend thread for most of the sewing in this book. For flowers, slippers, purses, and gathering, I prefer hand-quilting thread because it's nice and sturdy. This type of thread is a bit more expensive, but it is very strong. You don't need to have a lot of colors for flowers because the stitches don't show when they're in place; I simply use beige thread on light flowers and black on dark ones.

Sewing by Machine

If you're using a sewing machine, select a longer-than-normal stitch length or, if you want the stitches seam to have a little give, choose a short zigzag stitch. Be sure to brush away the lint from the bobbin case and other areas of your machine often; lint buildup can clog the works.

Sewing by Hand

There are a few stitches that I regularly use to complete fast felted projects. Each offers different advantages, so select which stitch to use according to the situation.

Hand running stitch. Use this for sewing ¼" (6 mm) seams. Make the stitches as small and close together as possible (figure 1). If the item will get a lot of use, you may want to stitch once, then go back again in the opposite direction to make two lines of stitches.

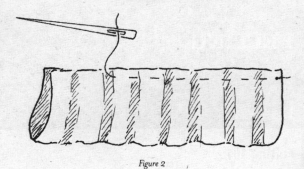

Figure 1

Hand-gathering stitch. Use a hand-gathering stitch (figure 2) when you will need to pull fabric into gathers. It is simply a longer version of the running stitch.

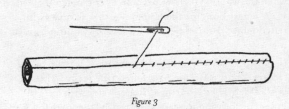

Figure 2

Whipstitch. Use this stitch when you need strength, when attaching a purse handle, for example. Insert the needle in one area and bring it out in another, as close as needed to hold two fabric pieces together (figure 3).

Figure 3

Blanket stitch. When the stitches will show, I often use a blanket stitch for its decorative look (figure 4).

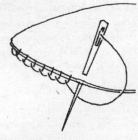

Figure 4

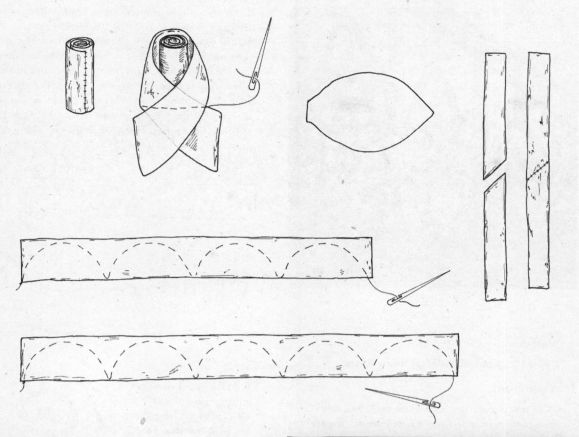

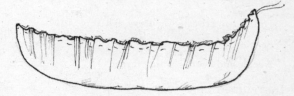

Figure 2

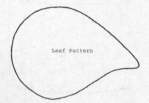

2. Hold one end of the folded strip and roll it into a spiral to create the rose (figure 3). Stitch securely at the bottom. Make three roses.

3. Cut three leaves from the green felted squares, using the pattern. Arrange three roses together with three leaves behind them and stitch them together. Stitch the 2" (5 cm) green circle to the back of the flower and attach a pin-back fastener. Trim excess fabric from the green circle, if desired.

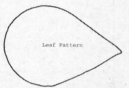

Figure 3

Leaf Pattern   Leaf Pattern

Figure 5

Tack stitch. Although this term can mean various things to different people, I define it as creating several stitches on the same spot for strength and permanence (figure 5).

Piecing Felted Strips

There may be times when you need to piece shorter strips of felted fabric together to make one long strip for a purse handle or scarf. A good trick is to cut and piece the fabric on the diagonal. Butt the cut edges together and use small whipstitches to secure them together. When you roll it to make the handle, it will be less bulky at the seam.

Lining Fabrics

Some projects in this book are lined for added comfort and beauty. To keep my fast felted projects economical, I look no further than my scrap bag for material to use as linings. The red silk in the Basket of Roses Purse came from scraps left over from my daughter's prom dress, and the purple satin lining the slippers had been part of an old pirate costume. Be as creative in your search for lining fabrics as you are in your quest for sweaters to felt.

Projects

Rolled Victorian Roses

Rolled roses are easy to make and are a great way to use softer, fluffier felted sweaters and sweater scraps. Make them in clusters and use them to accent a jacket, sweater, purse, or hat. Or use one as a unique bow on a gift-wrapped package. These roses can also be made from those gorgeous silk and cotton sweaters in delicious, irresistible colors that I find in thrift stores. They don't felt, but they are perfect for creating these fabulous flowers.

MATERIALS

Three 2" x 10" (5 x 25.5 cm) strips of violet felted sweater

Three 2½" (6.5 cm) squares of green felted sweater

One 2" (5 cm)-diameter circle of green felted sweater

Needle and hand-quilting thread

Scissors

Pin-back fastener

INSTRUCTIONS

I. Fold each 2" x 10" (5 x 25.5 cm) strip of felted sweater fabric in half lengthwise. Run a hand-gathering stitch around three sides of the strip, curving around the corners (figure 1). Pull the thread slightly at each end to gather the fabric, and then knot to secure it (figure 2).

Figure 1

Change the Look

Use a matching thread color and take stitches along the folded edges of the petals of a finished flower at intervals of ½" to 1" (1.3 to 2.5 cm). Pull on the stitches to draw the edges down, creating a scalloped, more vintage look to the rose.

The Ten-Minute Baby Hat

When a sweater doesn't felt as tightly as you'd hoped, turn a negative into a positive by creating an extra-soft baby hat. Even better, this design can be created in as few as 10 minutes. Just imagine how many you and your friends could make in an afternoon! Donate a batch of them to a community shelter, and you'll feel the warmth of a job well done.

11-16

Continued ➡

MATERIALS

Ivory angora sweater or sleeve, felted

Scissors

Needle and hand-quilting thread

INSTRUCTIONS

1. If using a sleeve, cut an 8" x 9" (20.5 x 23 cm) tube—a 9" (23 cm) length of sleeve that is 8" (20.5 cm) wide (figure 1). This will create a tube that is 16" (41 cm) around. If using the body of the sweater, cut a 9" x 16" (23 x 40.5 cm) rectangle of the sweater, with the 16" (16 cm) length along the ribbing edge. Fold it in half and sew along the 9" (23 cm) side.

2. Roll up the end of the tube twice to make a 1½" (4 cm) brim. Tack the brim in place with small stitches (figure 2).

3. Turn the hat wrong side out and run a hand-gathering stitch ½" (1.3 cm) from the top edge with hand-quilting thread (figure 3). Pull the stitches tightly and knot to secure. Turn the hat right side out (figure 4).

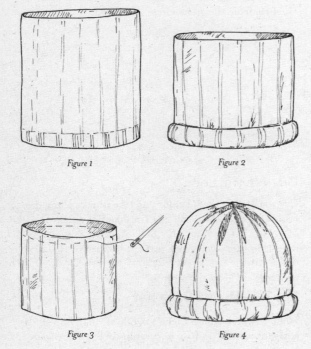

Figure 1   Figure 2

Figure 3   Figure 4

MAKE THE MOST OF A SWEATER

You can use many different parts of a sweater to make the Ten-Minute Baby Hat. Make hats from the sleeve, cowl neck, or bottom front and back ribbed edge of soft felted or unfelted sweaters. You can also use the main body of the sleeve or sweater without ribbing; simply zigzag the bottom raw edge, roll it up twice, and tack it in place at the sides.

Basket of Roses Purse

Argyle sweaters are some of my favorites to work with. I love the combination of soft flowers with the graphic design. The roses on this project are perfect for using those bright colored silk, cotton, or acrylic sweaters that don't shrink or felt like wool. I lined these purses with leftover fabric from my daughter's prom dress. The instructions are written for a bold black and white purse with red roses, but you can create a much softer look by substituting a light gray and pink argyle sweater and pink roses.

MATERIALS

Argyle sweater, felted

Red sweater, felted

Scraps of two green felted sweaters

Scissors

Sewing machine (optional)

Needle and thread

Pins

Plastic canvas

⅓ yard (30.5 cm) silk or other lining fabric.

INSTRUCTIONS

1. Cut one purse front, one purse back, and one purse bottom from the argyle felted sweater (figure 1), enlarging the pattern to the size of your choice. Cut two 1½" x 14" (4 x 35.5 cm) strips from the felted sleeve for the purse handles (figure 2).

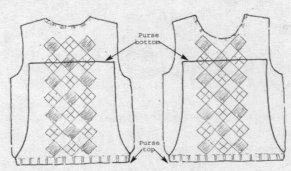

Purse bottom

Purse top

Figure 1

2. With right sides together, stitch the purse front and back at the sides by machine or by hand. Turn the top edge of the purse down 1" (2.5 cm) to the inside and hand-stitch. Pin the purse bottom to the purse, right sides together, and stitch.

3. Cut a piece of plastic canvas the size of the purse bottom (minus the seam allowance) and hand-stitch it to the inside bottom of the purse for support. Turn the purse right side out.

4. Tightly roll each handle strip lengthwise and hand-stitch along one long edge (figure 3). Whipstitch the handles in place on the inside-front and inside back edges of the purse.

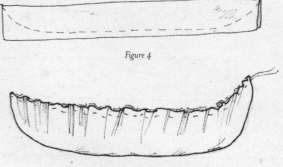

1½"   1½"

Handl   Handl

Figure 2

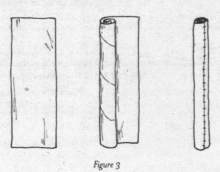

Figure 3

5. Cut two pieces of lining fabric using the purse pattern and one piece of lining fabric using the pattern for the purse bottom. With right sides together, stitch the lining pieces together at the sides. Pin the purse bottom to the sides, right sides together, and stitch in place. Clip the curved seams, if needed. Turn the top edge of the lining down ½" (1.3 cm) and pin in place. Insert the lining into the purse, having the right side out inside the purse. Hand-stitch in place along the top edge.

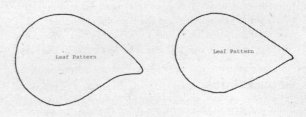

Figure 4

Figure 5

6. Make rolled roses by cutting three 3" x 17" (7.5 x 43 cm) strips from the red felted sweater. Fold each strip of fabric in half lengthwise and run a hand-gathering stitch along the three open sides of the fabric strip (figure 4). Pull the thread slightly and secure it with a knot (figure 5). Roll the strips up into a rose and stitch to secure (figure 6). Stitch three roses to the front of the purse. See Rolled Victorian Roses for additional details, if needed.

Figure 6

7. Cut ten green leaves from the green felted scraps, using the leaf patterns. Tuck and arrange the leaves behind the roses and stitch in place.

Leaf Pattern   Leaf Pattern

Warm Fuzzy Hat and Mittens

My daughter, Skylar, learned to make "warm fuzzy" pompoms at school and often leaves one as a calling card after performing a kindness. She taught me how to make them and I just had to top a hat with one to pass on warm fuzzy feelings.

Hat

MATERIALS

Rose sweater, felted

Striped sweater, felted

One 2½" x 22" (6.5 x 56 cm) strip of ivory felted sweater ribbing

Scissors

Needle and hand-quilting thread

Pins

Wool yarn

6. To make the pompom, spread apart your fingers. Wrap yarn around three fingers at least 50 times (figure 2). Tie the lengths of yarn in the center with another piece of yarn (figure 3). Cut the loops open on each end and fluss (figure 4). Stitch the warm fuzzy pompom to the top of the hat.

Figure 2

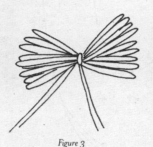

Figure 3

Figure 4

3. Thread a tapestry needle with worsted-weight yarn. Sew with a blanket stitch around the edge of the wrist, making each stitch ¼" (6 mm) apart.

4. To create the wristband, cast 24 stitches of knitting worsted yarn onto the knitting needles. Knit 56 rows in garter stitch, creating 28 ridges. Compare the knitting to the mitten to see if you need more rows to match the distance around. Knit two to four more rows as needed and cast off. Hand-stitch the short ends together with the yarn.

5. Stitch the knitted wristband to the bottom of the mitten, by stitching through the blanket stitches.

6. Repeat steps 4 and 5 to make the second wristband and complete the other mitten.

Lined Slippers

These lined slippers make toasty toes on cooler days. For a nice tough, sew some vintage silver buttons to the top center of each slipper. For the pink slippers, I used a cable-patterned felted sweater and omitted the buttons.

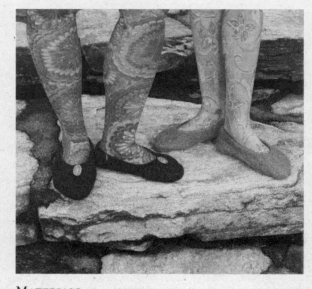

CUTTING

From the rose felted sweater, cut:

Two 9" x 11" (23 x 28 cm) rectangles

From the striped felted sweater, cut:

Two earflaps from the sleeve (pattern on page 117)

Two 2½" x 14" (6.5 x 35.5 cm) strips

INSTRUCTIONS

1. With right sides together, sew the two 9" x 11" (23 x 28 cm) rose felted pieces together along the 9" (23 cm) sides.

2. Pin the ribbing to the bottom edge of the hat, pinning the right side of the ribbing to the wrong side of the hat so that the ribbing will hide the seam when the edge of the hat is flipped up (figure 1). Sew the seam. With right sides together, stitch the side seams of the hat, including the ribbing. Trim the seam, if desired, and turn right side out.

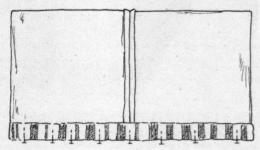

Figure 1

3. Hand-stitch the earflaps in place on either side of the hat. Try the hat on first to determine the best placement of the flaps. If desired, line the flaps with a layer of felted wool before stitching them to the hat: layer the flap and lining right sides together, stitch around the curved sides, and turn them inside out.

4. To make the hat straps, roll each of the two 2½" x 14" (6.5 x 35.5 cm) strips of striped felted fabric along the long edge and whipstitch along the outside raw edge. Leave one end slightly unrolled. Stitch the unrolled end of the tie to the bottom center of an earflap. Repeat to complete the second earflap.

5. Run a hand-gathering stitch 1½" (4 cm) down from the top edge of the hat. Pull the stitches tightly and knot to secure.

Mittens

MATERIALS

Striped sweater, felted

Scissors

Needle and hand-quilting thread

Large tapestry needle

Knitting worsted yarn (approximately 2 ounces [56 g])

U.S. size 8 (U.K. size 6, or 5 mm) knitting needles

INSTRUCTIONS

1. Refer to Making Mittens to create your pattern. Do not extend the mitten pattern beyond your wrist for this project.

2. Lay the patterns on top of the sweater. Cut out two right-hand and two left-hand mittens without cuffs. Lay each mitten with right sides together and hand-stitch around the mitten, leaving the wrist area open.

MAKING MITTENS

Creat a custom mitten pattern by drawing around the left or right hand on paper, adding 1" (2.5 cm) to the top of the fingers, and rounding the sides as shown. Draw a second line ¼" (6 mm) beyond the first outline for the seam allowance. Cut out the mitten pattern, trace it in reverse for the other hand, and cut out the second pattern. To cut out mittens, lay the patterns on a felted sweater, aligning the bottom of the pattern with the ribbed edge of the sweater. Be sure to match any pattern and align stripes on the sweater, if necessary. Pin and cut out two left-hand mittens and two right-hand mittens, one layer at a time.

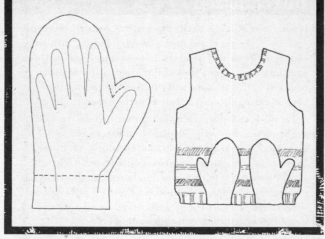

MATERIALS

Medium to large felted sweater

Scissors

⅜ yard (34.5 cm) satin lining fabric

Needle and hand-quilting thread

Pins

2 vintage buttons (optional)

INSTRUCTIONS

1. Make patterns by tracing the slipper sole and slipper top patterns.

2. Cut out two soled from the felted sweater, two soles from satin lining fabric, two slipper tops from felted fabric, and two slipper tops from lining fabric. Flip the right slipper top pattern over to cut the left slipper top.

Note: *I can usually cut one slipper top from the sweater front and one from the back. I cut one sole from each sleeve.*

3. Lay each slipper sole section onto a lining sole section, right sides together, and stitch around the outside edge, leaving a 3" (7.5 cm) opening to turn right side out (figure 1). Clip curves and turn right side out. Stitch the opening closed. Press.

4. Lay each slipper top section onto a lining section and stitch right sides together, leaving one center back edge open for turning. Stitch around the other center back seam. Clip the curves, turn right side out, and press. Turn the raw edges from the remaining center back seam under ¼" (6 mm) to the inside and whipstitch this opening closed.

Continued ➜

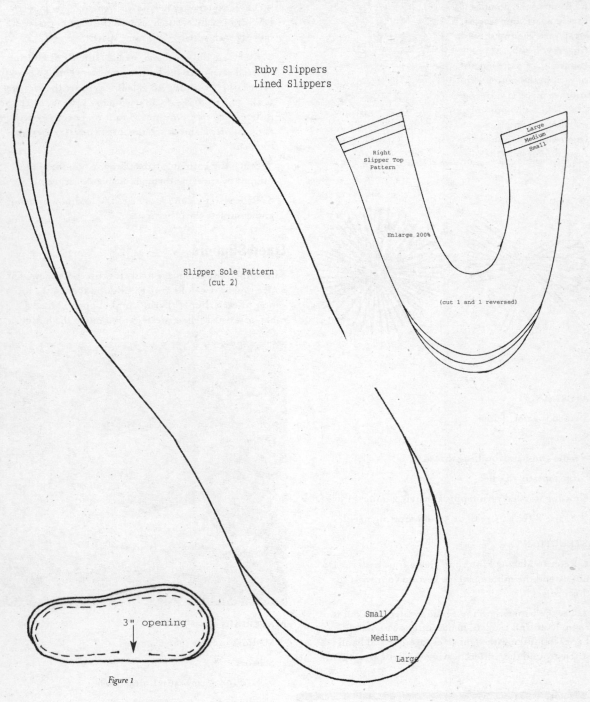

Ruby Slippers
Lined Slippers

Right
Slipper Top
Pattern

Large
Medium
Small

Enlarge 200%

(cut 1 and 1 reversed)

Slipper Sole Pattern
(cut 2)

Small

Medium

Large

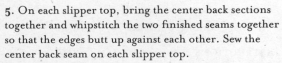

3" opening

Figure 1

5. On each slipper top, bring the center back sections together and whipstitch the two finished seams together so that the edges butt up against each other. Sew the center back seam on each slipper top.

5. Lay the slipper top on the slipper side, right sides together, and pin in place, matching center fronts and center backs. Use plenty of pins, one every ¾" (2 cm) or so. Whipstitch the slipper tops to the slipper bottoms around the outside edge using hand-quilting thread. As you stitch the top to the bottom, this seam will become nearly invisible.

6. Embellish with vintage buttons, if desired.

Use Your Scraps

Slipper lining can be made form almost any satiny or soft material—an old dress, a discarded cotton bedspread, even the satin pirate pants your child wore in the school play.

—From *Felt It! Stitch It! Fabulous!*

NEEDLE FELTING

Terry Taylor & Candie Cooper

Introduction

If your idea of felt is limited to brightly colored sheets on craft store shelves or perhaps a laundry disaster involving your favorite pair of hand-knit wool socks, let us broaden your horizons. Take a look at the imaginative creations featured in this section, and you'll soon discover the beauty, versatility, and artistic appeal of needle felting.

People have been making felt for centuries. Typically, the process involves two elements—moisture and agitation. (Remember the mishap in the washing machine?) In more modern times, a process called needle felting— also known as dry felting—was developed commercially for making felt yardage. (That's where those brightly colored sheets begin.) This process uses barbed needles instead of water and agitation to entangle wool fibers.

Stop the Draft
Susan Wasinger

Draft Evader

Even the tightest, best-built house has places where cold air can sneak in. Under the door is a favorite spot and an easy one to fix. This colorful, hip, easy-to-make draft blocker looks nice doing its job, then folds in half and hangs so it's out-of-the-way but always-at-the-ready.

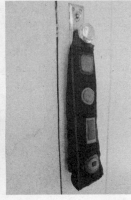

Made of easy-to-sew 100-percent wool felt, this draft blocker takes just minutes to make. It sports modern, graphic shapes of contrasting felt in four different colors on a black background. To make this piece, I used a pleasing and simple visual rhythm of shapes within larger shapes. But you can be creative and invent your own.

Over the years, fiber artists and crafters have experimented with the needle-felting process to produce a wide range of modern, innovative items....

The basics section covers everything you need to know to get started. It contains information on materials and tools, as well as a rundown of the basic felting techniques you should be familiar with to create these fabulous projects. The basics section will also get you acquainted with varieties of wool and how it becomes felt. Making a sheet of felt is easy, and once you get the hang of it, you'll be ready to tackle all of the fun ideas included here.

Whether you're an experienced felter looking for fresh ideas or someone who's just getting started with the craft, you've come to the right place. So pick out a project, gather your tools and materials, and get ready to felt with a needle!

Needle Felting Basics

Materials

Wool—which comes from sheep—is essential to making felt. Different breeds of sheep produce different types of fiber. Some kinds are extremely coarse, while others are extremely fine. It takes many steps to get wool from a sheep into the consumer's hands. Shorn wool, called fleece, must be picked through to remove bits of dirt and straw. Once this process is complete, the fleece is washed in hot water to rid it of dirt and oil. The fleece is then laid out to dry. At this point, the wool is pretty much the same as it was when still on the sheep, except that now it's clean. The curly or straight pieces of wool car called locks.

After it dries, the wool is put through a carding machine. The carding machine—also known as a carder—combs out the fibers. It transforms the curly locks of wool into either a sheet called a batt or a long, continuous strand called roving. You can make felt from either form of carded wool.

As you begin working with felt, you'll discover that certain fibers work better with wet felting, while others are better suited to needle or dry felting. The felting process hinges on the wool's fiber properties. Each fiber has little microscopic scales that open and close. In traditional wet felting, soap and hot water prompt the opening of the scales: with agitation, pressure, and dish soap (for lubrication and pH factors), the wool's fibers get tangled around each other to create felt.

During the dry-felting process, special felting needles penetrate the wool repeatedly. During this penetration, the barbs on the felting needles latch onto the fibers in the wool, tangling and drawing them together to make felt.

You don't have to choose one form of felting over the other—you can combine wet-felting and dry-felting (also called needle felting) techniques in different and innovative ways to create a variety of fabulous projects.

Wools for Felting

Try experimenting with different types of wool, so that you can familiarize yourself with all of the unique qualities the material can have. Through fiber stores and websites, you can purchase wools of all kinds and colors, from natural shades to bright hues, from super-soft to coarse.

You can also dye wool yourself to produce unique colors. Interesting novelty fibers like metallic strands or recycled denim scraps can also be blended into your wools. Ultimately, the type of wool you use will depend on the project you're making. One type of wool may be better suited for one project than another. Before purchasing a large quantity of wool, consult with the owner of your local fiber shop or with a fellow felter for a second opinion about your project. Below are some general suggestions about the kinds of wools that work best with needle and wet felting.

Needle Felting Wool

In general, medium to coarse wools work best for needle felting, but all wool can be felted with a needle. Check out the list on this page for information regarding different sheep breeds and uses for their wool. You'll also find specific wools included in the materials lists of the projects in this book.

Wet Felting Wool

Finer wools such as Merino work well for wet felting. Merino creates a soft, smooth felt that can also be great for needle felting. Gotland is also conducive to wet felting and makes a very soft felt. For a truly unique surface, try felting mohair locks together—this will produce a soft yet curly, shiny surface. You can experiment with other kinds of wool by wet felting a small test sheet to see whether you like the finished appearance.

Bases for Needle Felting

Polystyrene Foam

A polystyrene foam shape can provide a sturdy core for needle felting wool…. Use the white porous foam and pre-made foam shapes from the floral section of your local craft store. You can also buy blocks of foam and cut out your own shapes with a serrated knife. Stay away from green florist's foam, because it's too soft and creates a fine dust that will contaminate your wool. If you cut your own shapes, be sure to remove all the bits of foam before felting. Use a hair dryer to blow off the dust and excess pieces.

Fabrics

Wool yardage in tweed, cashmere, houndstooth, and jersey knit can be purchased from your fabric store and used for needle felting. Some fabrics can be felted as they are on the bolt, while others may need to be fulled in the washing machine first. If you aren't sure you like a certain fabric, test a small piece of the material to see whether the finished look appeals to you. If not, remedies such as a different felting needle, a different type of wool, wet felting, or ironing may do the trick.

Wool isn't the only base fabric you can use for needle felting. Cottons, denim, and acrylic craft felt work well in needle-felting projects because of their tight weave. It never hurts to experiment with a swatch of fabric. Check the clearance racks at the fabric store for unusual fabrics, such as knit yardage or printed corduroy to embellish with your felting needle and wool.

Purchased Felt Shapes

If you're familiar with felting, you probably already know that you can create your own felt balls using wool, a little soap, and water. But you can also find felt balls in fiber and craft stores or online. The balls come in a variety of colors, and you can decorate them with needle-felted designs or stitching. Felt bracelets, flowers, hearts, and loops are also available and can be used as fun additions to your designs.

Embellishing Materials

Surfaces can be embellished as plainly or as intricately as you like. Fiber and craft stores are full of interesting materials that you can add to your felted surfaces. For example, you can embellish a project by needle felting novelty yarns and wool into the piece, or use other techniques such as hand-stitching with beads and sequins.

The possibilities are infinite, and you can produce some gorgeous textures. My favorite embellishing materials are listed below.

Embroidery threads, including metallic, satin, and cotton, can be used for decorative stitching on felt surfaces. You can also cut the skeins into confetti-like pieces and sprinkle them onto a pile of wool before wet felting.

Wool and novelty yarns can transform the look of a project. Try needle felting eyelash yarn into felt sheets, balls, or foam forms for a distinctive surface.

Metallic or iridescent fiber strands blended with wool roving or batt will add sparkle to your creations.

Recycled silk yarn (from Nepal) can be shredded and wet felted into place or needle felted for an alternate texture.

Raw fibers such as wool, angora, cotton, and locks can be blended into wool by wet felting or needle felting.

Fabrics or acrylic craft felt cut into small pieces can be appliquéd onto felt surfaces or needle felted.

Silk hankies—try pulling one apart, cobweb-fashion, and laying it over a pile of wool that's ready to be wet or needle felted.

Seed beads and sequins will add a bit of sparkle and pizzazz to any felted surface. These materials come in a range of colors, shapes, and sizes, and can be used one at a time, in multiples, or stacked on top of each other. Seed beads are generally classified by numbers ranging from 15/0 to 1/0—the larger the number, the smaller the bead size.

Needle Felting Tools

Felting Needles

Warning: *These needles are extremely sharp. Use caution when needle felting, and keep the needles away from children at all times.*

Just as painters use several different types of brushes as they work, needle felters use a variety of needles. The basic felting needle is a 1½- to 4-inch long (9 to 10 cm) piece of steel wire with a triangular or star-shaped shaft. The shaft has a sharp point and hard-to-see barbs along all the sides. Felting needle sizes are indicated numerically. Different shapes and sizes allow for versatility—some needles are better for certain jobs than others. With practice and experimentation, you'll easily be able to figure out which size works best for a specific task, and which wool types the needles should be paired with. Here's a list of felting needles and their suggested uses:

Single Needles

A 36-gauge triangular felting needle is good for beginning work such as needle felting wool to a precut shape, working with coarse wool, and general sculpting.

A 38-gauge triangular felting needle is a great multitask needle. From the start of a piece to the finishing stages, this is an all-around handy needle.

A 38-gauge star-blade needle is also very versatile in that you can use it to attach yarn or wool to a finished piece or to work the wool in the beginning stages. The difference between this needle and the 38-gauge triangular felting needle is that there are four barbed sides instead of three, which allows you to needle felt the fibers a bit faster.

Continued →

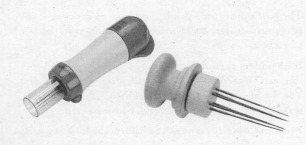

A 40-gauge triangular felting needle is very fine compared to the first three needles. Because of its small size, this needle is perfect for detailing and embellishing work. It can smooth out a surface if there are pockmarks. It's also handy for adding yarns, silks, and other materials.

Other Types of Felting Needles

Felting needles with special rubberized ends for easy and comfortable gripping can be found on the Internet or in fiber supply shops. These needles cost a bit more than regular felting needles, but they're handy—especially if you're needle felting for long periods—because they provide a better grip.

Multi-needle holders that can accommodate three or more needles at a time are also available. Because they let you cover a lot of space in a short time, multi-needle tools are wonderful for working on pieces with large surface areas, such as a two-dimensional wall piece or a hat. These holders can accommodate needles of all gauges. You can easily change needles, as well.

Needle-Felting Machines

A needle-felting machine works in much the same way as a multi-needle holder, except that the machine does all the work. The machine contains several felting needles. The needles push the fibers into the base fabric, and you control the fabric feed. You can needle felt much more quickly with a machine. It's a wonderful tool for embellishing pre-made garments and household items with novelty yarns, wool scraps, threads, roving, or fabrics.

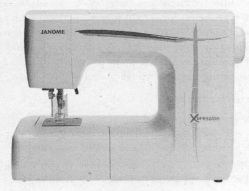

Needle-felting machine

Work Surfaces for Needle Felting

Before you get started on a project, set up your workspace. A table covered with one of the following materials is ideal for needle felting.

Upholstery Foam

High-density foam about 2 inches (5.1 cm) thick makes a great surface for needle felting. The foam will support the piece you're working on and keep the needles from breaking. Inexpensive upholstery foam scraps or chair pads are available at fabric supply stores. Foam forms made especially for needle felting hats and purses are also available, although you can easily saw or carve the foam into a special shape with a serrated knife to suit specific project needs. Keep in mind that the foam will get brittle with use and need to be replaced. To remove stray fibers from the foam, use a sticky lint brush.

You may decide to needle felt purposefully into a piece of upholstery foam or polystyrene foam. Instead of pulling your wool away from the foam, you'll be pushing it down into the pores of the foam with the felting needle. The foam thus becomes a permanent work surface that will end up as a decoration.

Brush Block

The brush block is a new type of needle-felting work surface. A brush block looks a lot like a large scrub brush. It has a base that sits on the work surface and stiff bristles that point upward. The bristles are dense enough to provide adequate support for your wool and tall enough to keep needles from making contact with the base and breaking. You can remove loose fibers from the bristles with a comb.

Upholstery foam and brush block

Other Tools

Scissors

Fabric scissors are useful for cutting out felt pieces and wool fabric. Small, sharp scissors come in handy for snipping threads.

Needles

When working with fibers, it's good to have a variety of needles on hand. A straight upholstery or tapestry needle is key when stringing felted pieces, because the eye of the needle is big enough to accommodate the wire. A basic sewing needle for embellishing wool surfaces with embroidery or seed beads is also useful.

Felting Techniques

Although this section focuses on the magic of needle felting, we've also included some basic information on wet felting so that you'll have another creative option when working with wool. The technique you choose will depend on the look you want for the finished piece. Needle felting and wet felting are related, but they're very different. To get a feel for each technique, try experimenting with small pieces of fabric. The most important thing to remember is that there are no strict rules here. Have fun and let your imagination take over!

Preparing Wool for Felting

Splitting Wool Roving

Roving is wool that's been washed and then carded (meaning that the fibers have been cleaned, separated, and straightened) into long, ropelike lengths or rolls. To pull off a length of wool and split it, you must first divide the roving up widthwise. Place your hand 8 or more inches (20 cm) from the end of the roving, and pull a length of wool from the roll with your other hand. Then split that piece lengthwise into smaller, thinner segments. These small pieces are called slivers.

Blending Different Colors of Wool Together

Small amounts of two different colors of wool can easily be blended by hand. When felted, the swirling colors of fiber create a beautiful effect….

To blend two different colors of wool, start by tearing off two 6-inch (15.2 cm) lengths of wool of each color, and then lay one piece on top of the other. Grab the pieces by each end and pull them apart. Next, lay these two pieces on top of each other and repeat the process until you're happy with the overall blend.

Needle Felting

One of the great benefits of needle felting is that you have more control over the fiber than you do when wet felting…. If you make a mistake while needle felting, you can simply erase it by pulling the piece of wool off and starting again.

When punching into wool with a felting needle, the bottom ¾-inch (1.9 cm) barbed section of the needle does the work. As you punch in and out of the wool, the barbs latch onto the fibers, repeatedly picking them up and then dropping them. Sometimes you'll punch deeply into the wool with the needle. Other times, you'll use just the tip of the needle to penetrate the surface. It all depends on the type of project you're making. Felting needles will also change with the type of task you're completing—some needles are good for general sculpting, while others are good for detail work. For more information on felting needles, check out the Tools section.

As you needle felt, insert the needle into the wool, and then bring the needle back up and out of the same hole it went into initially. Always move the needle in a straight up-and-down motion. The needle in your hand moves just the way it would on a sewing machine—in and out, up and down. As you progress, resist the temptation to use the felting needle to pull the wool over to a certain spot. This can lead to a broken needle.

Working in Two Dimensions

Needle Felting a Flat Sheet of Wool. To make a flat sheet of felt by needle felting, start by tearing off six to eight small, even-length tufts of wool. Position two pieces of wool side by side on your work surface so that the edges of each piece just barely overlap one another.

Lay two more pieces on top, in the same fashion, but position these pieces so that they're perpendicular to the first layer. The next layer should be laid out perpendicular to the second layer. Take care when laying out the wool that there are no holes or thin spots. Fill in any thin areas with a small, wispy tuft of wool. The number of layers determines the thickness of the finished wool sheet. Start with three of four layers—you can always add more layers later.

Next, poke the layers of wool with your felting needle in a straight up-and-down fashion. A multi-needle felting tool can come in handy here, as it will speed up your felting time considerably. Gently pull the piece off the work surface from time to time to prevent it from getting too deeply enmeshed in the foam or bristles (see Work Surfaces for Needle Felting). Loose edges of wool can be folded over and felted into the piece. You can needle felt both sides of the sheet as well. If you decide your piece of felt is too thin, simply add a couple of extra layers as you did when you initially laid out your wool and continue needle felting.

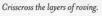

Crisscross the layers of roving. *A multi-needle tool speeds the felting process*

Needle Felting into a Base Fabric Shape. Another fun way to needle felt is to cut a shape out of a good base fabric and needle felt wool onto it. The base fabric serves as a template or a guide, making it easy to create a specific shape as you work. Simply place the fabric shape face up on top of your work surface, and lay out tufts of wool that roughly fit

into the shape. Then poke the wool into the shape, making sure it's covered evenly. Continue building up a thick layer of wool. You can also add a thin layer on the back side to cover the base fabric. If the sides don't look round enough, tack some wool on the front and bring the opposite end around to the back, and felt it in….

Needle-Punch or Felting Machine. If you have used a multi-needle tool to attach layers to a base fabric, then you can pretty much imagine the possibilities of what a needle-punch machine can do. Base fabric and fiber of all sorts along with this machine can create ultra-rich textures for wearables or home décor. As mentioned in the Materials section, felt, denim, and cottons work well as base fabrics. Position your fibers, be they roving, yarns, scraps of wool, or anything else, on top of the base fabric. If you choose to pin your fibers in place, take care not to run over the pins with the felting needles. Put your piece into place below the needles and use the pedal to control the needle action and your hands to control the fabric feed.

Working in Three Dimensions

Believe it or not, fluffy wool can actually be sculpted into a solid, three-dimensional object. You can needle felt the wool by itself or felt it into polystyrene or upholstery foam core shapes. Using only wool, your objects can be super-dense or light and airy—it all depends on the amount of poking you do with your needle. Try using less expensive wool for your core shape, then covering it with dyed wool. For example, you could build a doll using neutral-colored wool, and then add clothing by needle felting dyed wool onto the body.

A good way to approach three-dimensional needle felting is to break your design into parts. Let's go back to the doll example. You would have to needle felt each body part—torso, head, legs, and arms—separately. Since these parts can easily be translated into simple forms like tubes, spheres, and ovals, the task isn't as difficult as it might sound. Try to keep your shapes on the fluffy side rather than stiff and dense, which will make it easier to connect the parts. Once the pieces are joined, you can needle felt the assemblage further, as a whole.

Tear off a piece of roving and roll it into the desired shape—a tube, for instance, or an oval. Work on a non-skid surface like upholstery foam, so you can keep the center snug and tight. For sphere shapes, such as a bead or a head, try tying a knot at one end of the roving and then wrapping the wool around the knot. Don't let go of the rolled piece because it can easily unwind. Use a felting needle to tack the piece in place as you roll. If you're happy with the dimensions of the shape and have too much wool, simply

Roving rolled into a tubular shape

pull the excess away with your spare hand while holding on to the core piece. Don't use scissors to remove the extra wool—a bluntly cut edge won't blend into the rest of the piece as nicely as a torn edge well.

Once you've finished rolling, poke the shape with the felting needle in different directions. You'll find that the wool will move in the direction you poke it, so if a piece is too tall or too long, poke it with the felting needle to draw it in. Take care not to poke the felting needle in so deeply that it comes out the other side of the piece. If you feel the piece is too small, don't worry—you can always wrap more wool around it and continue needle felting.

Many needle-felted shapes can be connected to each other with a felting needle. Start with the biggest shape and connect the smaller pieces to it. Position the small piece where you want it, then poke through the two pieces, angling the felting needle in different directions to make a secure connection. If, after needle felting, you don't like the placement, simply pull the two pieces apart, reposition them, and start again. A small tuft of wool can

be wrapped around the joint area and felted to conceal the connection. Depending on your design, a wispy area of wool can be intentionally left on the piece. This wispy section can then be spread across an area of the base and needle felted into place. For finer details, such as fingers or cheeks, fold and roll some small tufts of wool, then needle felt them into place.

Covering a Polystyrene Foam Shape

You can needle felt wool into a piece of polystyrene or upholstery foam…. Polystyrene foam is sturdy, while upholstery foam is soft. You can create your own foam is soft. You can create your own foam shapes by blocking out your design on the foam with a permanent marker, then using a serrated knife to carefully carve out the piece.

Wool in roving or batt form can be used to cover the shape. Roving is easiest to use because it can be wound in one continuous piece around the shape. Put a piece of cardboard underneath your foam shape before you begin working, because the needles may leave marks on your tabletop. Find your starting point on the foam, then place the end of your roving there. If you're working with a wool batt, lay it over the area you want to cover. Depending on the size of your piece, you can use a single or a multi-needle tool on the foam. Many pokes with the needle will produce a tight, smooth surface, while fewer pokes will produce a fluffier surface. You can add as many layers of wool as you wish. Novelty yarns and fibers can be needle felted into the core, too. For added sparkle, try stringing beads and sequins onto straight pins and gluing them in place.

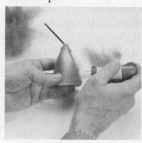 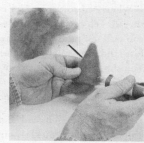

Embellishing

Adding Designs to a Flat Sheet of Felt

You can add imagery very easily to sheets of felt. The designs can be as simple as a coloring book page or as complex as an impressionistic painting. You can needle felt roving and other fibers to a sheet of felt with a single needle or multi-needle tool. This is where different gauges of felting needles come into play, because certain needles will respond better to the task and to the fiber than others will.

You can split or twist the wool roving to create skinny, detailed lines, or use the roving as it is to create thick lines and blocks of color. Fewer pokes with the needle will produce a raised surface. It's worth mentioning that there is no "right" or "wrong" side to a needle-felted sheet. You may like the appearance of one side better than the other.

You can adhere pieces cut from other felt sheets and fabrics to your sheet by placing the piece on top and needle felt it to the base. (Note: Always needle felt on your special work surface, so that the needles have a soft place to land.) Decorated sheets such as these can then be wet felted for a laminated effect….

Use a single needle tool to tack a felt shape into place

Using a multi-needle will speed up the needle felting process

Needle Felting into a Base Fabric

Some of the projects… embellish premade objects with needle felting. Also, you don't have to limit yourself to working on wool or felt; your base fabrics can be cotton and denim. You can embellish these base fabrics easily with wool, novelty fibers, or even cut fabric. No threads or sewing needles are required. Just lay your pieces on top of the base fabric and punch through the two layers with your felting needle. The fibers from the two pieces will become entangled, making a bond. If you experiment, you'll find that some fabrics work better than others with this technique. The use of a needle-felting machine or multi-needle tool can make the process go faster, depending on the complexity of the design….

Pattern and Stencil Options

For a specific shape, try using a cookie cutter as a stencil. You can find cookie cutters of all shapes and sizes in kitchen supply stores or in the polymer clay section of most craft stores.

Simply lay the cookie cutter on your work surface or base fabric. Fill the inside of the cookie cutter with a thin, even layer of wool. Poke your felting needle into the wool next to the wall of the cookie cutter and continue around the perimeter of the shape to secure the outline. Fold any loose edges in toward the center of the shape and needle felt them into place.

Next, work the middle of the design with the felting needle. At this point, you can add more wool and needle felt as you did before, making the design puff up from the surface. You can also try filling the cookie cutter with yarns, silks, or a new color of wool and needle felting the material into the shape.

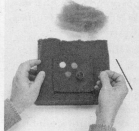 

Start with a small amount of wool

Remove the cutter to neaten the edge of your shape.

Wet Felting

A little bit of knowledge about wet felting is very useful so that you can combine the technique with needle felting. Agitation, some soapy water, and wool are all that you need to wet felt. If you've ever accidentally washed a wool sweater, you're probably aware of the shrinkage that can result. When washed in hot water, wool can draw up in size anywhere from 33 to 45 percent, depending on the type of fiber. When laying out your wool, remember that it will be half its original size after it's felted.

TROUBLESHOOTING TIPS

When you make a mistake: It's possible to erase mistakes by backtracking—just grab the tail of the wool that's connected to the piece, pull the wool off, and start again. You can also fix problems by adding more wool.

Pockmarks: Those small holes left by the felting needle in the surface of your material are known as pockmarks; 36-gauge needles are notorious for leaving trails of these tiny holes. Sometimes the combination of fiber and needle can lead to problems, so it never hurts to experiment with these elements.

To get rid of pockmarks, try working over the piece with a fine needle, such as a 40-gauge needle. Skimming the surface of the piece with this needle can clear up the holes. Wet felting the piece will also remove pockmarks.

Continued ➜

Making a Sheet of Felt

Tear a 10-inch (25.4 cm) length of wool roving from the ball and split the length in half. Then tear off small, even-length tufts of wool from the two halves and lay them side by side in the same direction on a rubber mat, making sure that the edges just barely overlap one another.

Lay a second layer of wool on top of the first layer, perpendicular to it. The third layer should then be laid out perpendicular to the second one, and so on. Make sure there are no holes in the piece as you work (if you can still see the rubber mat, do a little more layering). Three or four even layers of wool are usually sufficient to make a standard sheet of felt. As you practice making these sheets, you'll learn what works for you, and how thick you want your felt to be.

Note the size of your wool before you begin wet felting. Later, when you're checking to see whether the piece is fully felted, the size will serve as an indicator—the piece should be roughly half its original size after felting.

Start the wet-felting process by drizzling some warm soapy water over the layers of wool. Then add a few drops of dish soap. Make sure your hands are wet and soapy as you pat the wool's surface, pushing out bubbles and checking to see that the wool is totally saturated. Soak up any standing water with a sponge. Make small, circular motions with your hands, taking care not to disturb the layers. This step may take several minutes, so be patient. A layer of bubble wrap, bubble side down, is also good to use for rubbing.

Once the fibers feel like they are strong enough to be moved, turn the piece over and rotate it 90°. You can add more pressure as the piece shrinks and strengthens, but make sure the piece remains slippery and wet. Otherwise, the wool may start to pill or make "fuzzies" on its surface. Avoid felting the wool in standing water.

The next step in the process is called *fulling*. Fulling is intense agitation. To achieve this, roll up your piece like a scroll, then roll it back and forth on the rubber mat. Next, dunk the piece in hot soapy water and lay it out flat on the mat. Then roll up the piece like a scroll in the opposite direction, and roll it back and forth again on the mat. Repeat this process for all four sides.

You'll know when a piece is fully felted by checking the size and checking to see whether there are any loose layers. Do this by trying to pull the sides of the sheet apart—you shouldn't be able to. Continue felting until there are no loose layers, and you have a strong piece of felt. There are no hard and fast rules that say you must wet felt to this point, however. Loosely felted pieces can also be used for needle felting, and you can always wet felt the pieces further, if you like.

Once you've finished wet felting, rinse the piece in cool water and let it dry.

Wet Felting Needle-Felted Objects

You can easily wet felt a piece that has been needle felted, but keep in mind that doing so will change the surface appearance and size of the piece. Wet felting will also tighten the fibers considerably, causing the piece to shrink. Two-dimensional pieces can be wet felted by simply laying the piece on a rubber mat and saturating it with warm soapy water. You can then use Bubble Wrap as an agitator.

Fulling Woven or Knit Wool Yardage

A few of the projects in this book involve needle felting into a fulled knit bag, wool suit, or sweater. You can easily turn woven or knit wool fabric into felt—just let your washing machine do the work!

Diagram A   *Diagram B*

To full the wool yardage, set your washing machine for a small load, on hot. Then add a bit of laundry soap (maybe one-quarter of what you would normally use) and the wool fabric, shut the lid, and let the machine do its thing.

When the washer is finished, you can check to make sure the wool is completely fulled by making a small cut with scissors to see whether the threads unravel. If the threads are still loose, wash the wool again. When the fabric has completely fulled, you can dry it in the dryer on low. And lastly, don't forget to clean the lint trap!

Surface Embellishments

There are endless possibilities and combinations for decorating felt surfaces. Fabrics, threads, sequins, novelty fibers, and beads are just the tip of the iceberg when it comes to embellishments. Once you begin felting, you can concoct your own unique ideas. Here are a few to help you get started.

Using Embroidery Stitches

Embroidery stitches can be used to add fantastic details to your felted work. Simple stitches can produce fun surfaces, while more elaborate stitches can be used to create a sophisticated look. Try using different types of threads, such as pearl cotton or metallic threads. Strands of embroidery floss can also be used—try dividing up a strand. Check out embroidery stitch encyclopedias for interesting stitches. Practice the stitch on a scrap of fabric before applying it to the actual piece. You don't want to have to rip out stitches and risk damaging the felt surface.

When embroidering, try not to tug on the needle and thread. Felt pieces sometimes have a porous surface. If you pull too hard on the thread, small stitches can get lost, and long stitches can be reduced to short stitches. You should pull just hard enough on the needle and thread so that the stitches sit on top of the felt. The stitches should be neither too loose nor too tight.

Anchoring the Thread. Before you begin sewing and embellishing on your felt surface, you must first anchor the thread. One way to anchor your thread is by tying a knot at the end of the thread and bringing your needle through to the front so the knot catches on the back of the fabric. Another way is to thread the needle with the desired thread and secure it to the felt surface by making two forward stitches and one backstitch.

If you're embellishing a felt sheet, you can easily anchor your thread to the back side of the fabric. Anchoring thread to a felt ball is a little trickier, but with careful planning, you can find a discreet spot and possibly cover it with a bead or stitch later if it shows.

Here are a few simple stitches to get you started:

Straight Stitches. You can use a straight stitch in multiple ways. To make a straight stitch, tie a knot in the thread and pass it up through the back of the fabric where you want the stitch to begin. Then pass it down through the top of the fabric where you want the stitch to end and then back up where you want the next stitch to begin.

A running stitch is another form of straight stitch, but it produces a dashed line. To make a running stitch, bring the thread over and then under, then back over, and so forth. You can also make asterisks and Xs with a straight stitch.

Chain Stitch. To make a basic chain stitch, tie a knot and pass the thread up through the back of the fabric. Make a loose stitch in the fabric, beginning and ending close to the same point. Leave the thread loose on the top so that it makes a loop. Make the loop as long as you want your chain. Holding the loop with your finger, pass the thread

back up through the fabric at point A (see diagram A) and pull the thread until the loop tightens, but not so tight that it pulls the fabric. Repeat the stitch for each link in the chain, keeping each link the same length. At the end of the chain, take a small stitch to hold the last loop in place (see diagram B).

Lazy Daisy Stitch. The lazy daisy stitch is similar to the basic chain except the stitch remains separate instead of being connected to the other stitches. This stitch is often used for making patterns that look like flower petals (see diagram C).

Diagram C

Diagram D

To make a lazy daisy stitch, repeat the steps for making a chain stitch, but do not make the second loop. Instead, make one straight stitch over what would be the wide end of the petal. Then poke the needle through to the place where you want the next petal to start (see diagram D).

French Knot. A French knot is a small, knotted stitch that resembles a seed bead. French knots can add a great deal of texture to a felt surface depending on how closely they're spaced.

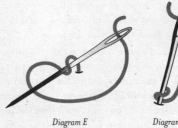

To make a French knot, anchor the thread on the surface. Holding the needle in one hand, use your other hand to wrap the thread around the needle two or three times. Then position the tip of the needle next to the place where the thread came up and pull the wrapped thread to remove all the gaps. Poke the needle down through the fabric and don't let go of the wrapped thread end until you've pulled the needle through and removed all the slack, creating a secure stitch. See diagrams E and F.

Diagram E   *Diagram F*

Whipstitch. A whipstitch can be used to stitch a small felt piece to a larger felt piece. It can also serve as a decorative edge on a piece of fabric (see diagram G).

To make a whipstitch, anchor the thread on the back of the small felt piece and bring the needle up through the front of the piece. Then poke the needle back down through the middle of the large felt piece and up through the small piece, just down from where the last stitch started. This creates a little gap between the stitches. Repeat this stitch around the border of the small piece, and then anchor the thread on the back again.

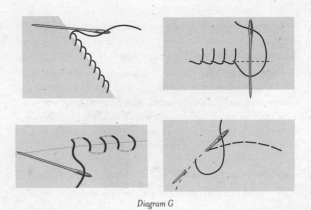

Diagram G

Seed Beads and Sequins

Before you begin working with beads and sequins, make sure the needle you plan to use fits through the holes in these materials. Thread one bead over the needle and onto the thread, and then insert the needle close to the place where you started. Angle the needle so that it comes up close to where you want to place your next bead. String one sequin followed by a seed bead, and then thread the needle back through the hole in the sequin so that the seed bead holds the sequin in place. Anchor the thread as you did when you started, and trim the end.

Appliqué

You can stitch other fabric pieces onto felt surfaces using a straight stitch. Stitch on small circles of wool or cotton print with an outline or by making small, hidden stitches and turning the edges of the fabric under.

Yarns

All kinds of yarn can be needle felted into wool pieces for added embellishment. Novelty yarns make for some very interesting textures.

Simply place the end of the yarn in the spot where your design starts and begin needle felting. A finer needle—a 38- or 40-gauge—is useful for securing the yarns in place. If you want to speed up the process after you've secured the yarns in place, use a multi-needle tool. Some yarns look very different once they've been needle felted into place, so experiment on a scrap piece of felt before committing to your real project. You will also find that some materials take a little more effort to work in than others.

Securing yarn in place with a single needle   *Securing yarn in place with a multi-needle tool.*

Projects

Bubble Pillows

If you're looking for a quick way to update your living room, these cushions are a cool solution. Make them in black and white, or use colorful fibers that coordinate with your home furnishings.

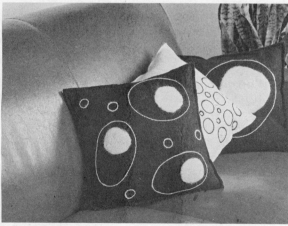

Lindsay Obermeyer, designer

SKILL LEVEL

Beginner

FELTING METHOD USED

Dry Felting

FINISHED MEASUREMENTS

15 x 15 inches (38.1 x 38.1 cm)

WHAT YOU NEED

Marking chalk or pen

Ruler or yardstick

100% wool handmade felt in black, 16 x 24 inches (40.6 x 61 cm)

100% wool Spanish felt in black, 18 x 18 inches (45.7 x 45.7 cm)

Scissors

Wool roving in natural, 48 inches (121.9 cm)

Upholstery foam, 16 x 16 x 3 inches (or larger) (40.6 x 40.6 x 7.6 cm)

40-gauge felting needle

38-gauge star felting needle

Pins

1 skein of 100% wool yarn in cream or natural

Sewing machine

Polyester pillow batting

Black thread (cotton-wrapped polyester)

WHAT YOU DO

1. Using the marking chalk and ruler to guide you, measure a 15½-inch (39.4 cm) square from the handmade felt and a 15-inch (38.1 cm) square from the Spanish felt.

2. Cut a 5-inch (12.7 cm) piece of the roving, and then split it in half. Roll one half into a loose ball and lay the second half over the ball.

3. Lay the handmade felt on the upholstery foam and position the mass of roving approximately 2½ to 3 inches (6.4 to 7.6 cm) from the upper left corner of the handmade felt.

4. Begin needle felting with the 40-gauge needle. Work along the edge of the mass, tucking in edges as you go. Remember to occasionally rotate the black felt square to prevent it from sticking to the foam.

5. Once you've firmly tacked down the edges, continue with the center. When it's fairly matted, switch to the 38-gauge star needle. Continue until the circle is dense and firmly attached. If there is a spot with black peeking through, add more roving to the surface and needle felt it into place.

6. Repeat steps 2 through 5 to create a second circle in the upper right corner and a third circle in the lower middle portion of the square. The three dots form a triangle.

7. Pin down the beginning of the yarn ½ inch (1.3 cm) from the top of the upper left circle. Continue pinning down the yarn in a rough egg shape, with the narrower edge close to the circle and the wider portion facing downward (see detail photo). Cut the yarn, leaving a ½-inch (1.3 cm) tail.

8. Using the 40-gauge needle, begin loosely needle felting the yarn around the entire circumference. If the shape looks smooth and curvilinear, continue to felt until the yarn is firmly attached.

9. Switch to the 38-gauge star needle and continue felting. Felt down the tail of the yarn, overlapping the beginning. Remove the pins.

10. Repeat steps 7 through 9 for the upper right circle and the lower circle. For the lower circle, pin down the wider portion of the egg shape on an angle for the right instead of facing downward.

11. Repeat steps 7 through 9 to make five 1-inch-diameter (2.5 cm) circles sprinkled across the pillow's surface.

12. Place the handmade felt right side down, and then center the Spanish felt square, right side up, on top of it. Pin the two surfaces together with the black

thread, leaving a 3-inch (7.6 cm) gap for the stuffing. Machine- or hand-sew together the two pieces, leaving the gap. Remove the pins.

13. Stuff the pillow with the batting, being certain to push it into the corners. Pin the gap and sew it closed. Then carefully trim the handmade felt to the edge of the Spanish felt.

This project was completed with:

A Child's Dream Come True 100% wool handmade felt in black

A Child's Dream Come True 100% wool Spanish felt in black

Wistyria 100% wool roving in Natural (#100)

Cascade 220 100% highland wool yarn in Cream/Natural (#8010)

Stained Glass Pincushion

Too nice to tuck away in your sewing basket, this pincushion is as pretty as it is useful. Make it with the yarns you see here or customize the design with your favorite shades.

Sandie O'Neill, designer

SKILL LEVEL

Beginner

FELTING METHOD USED

Dry Felting

FINISHED MEASUREMENTS

About 4 inches (10.2 cm) in diameter

WHAT YOU NEED

50 grams of 100% wool roving in light green

36-gauge triangular felting needle

Upholstery foam

10 grams of 100% wool roving in lilac, purple, medium green, dark green, and black

Small amount (about 1 gram) of 100% wool roving in bright yellow

38-gauge star felting needle

40-gauge triangular felting needle

Pincushion base, such as a candlestick

Multipurpose adhesive

WHAT YOU DO

1. Tear off about 11¾ inches (30 cm) of the light green roving and roll it into a ball, making sure the surface is smooth. Then use the 36-gauge triangular felting needle to needle felt the surface of the ball, using the upholstery foam as your work surface. Jab the ball two or three times, roll it evenly, and then jab it again. Rolling the ball in all directions helps it keep a round shape.

Continued →

2. Once the ball holds its shape, wrap a bit more of the light green roving around it and needle felt the surface again. If you wrap the roving tightly, it should felt quickly. Continue adding roving and needle felting until only about 2 inches (5.1 cm) of roving remain. Put this aside in case you need it later to fix a problem. You should now have a large, squishy ball.

3. Using the 36-gauge needle, needle felt in a circular area on one side of the ball to create a flattened area that can serve as a base. Turn the piece over and needle felt across the top surface, maintaining a dome shape as you work. Work all across the surfaces—if you work in one area, you'll create another flat spot. Continue felting until you have a dome shape that feels firm.

4. To make the petals and leaves of the pansy (see detail photo), tear off small tufts of the roving in lilac, purple, and both shades of green. Only use what you need.

Wind the tufts into flat, coiled disc shapes—you can poke them a few times with a felting needle to help them keep their coil shape—and set them aside. Using the project photo as a guide, attach a purple coil/petal to the green ball shape with the 36-gauge needle. Punch the whole surface of the petal to secure it to the green ball. If the petal is too small, tear off another sliver of roving and felt it to the perimeter of the petal to make it bigger.

. After you've roughly attached the first petal, continue by attaching more petals in the same manner. If you need to remove a piece, just tug it gently off the work. Then you can move it or replace it with a new color. Once you've added all the petals, start adding the two-tone green leaves. Use the same technique you used with the petals. Finish by needle felting a small circular tuft of bright yellow roving into the center of the flower.

6. Tear off several pieces of the purple roving. Refer to the project photo to needle felt it onto the work to form a curved line around the base. Next, cover the bottom with the same color and needle felt that into place.

7. Tear off long, fine strips of the black roving. Twist the pieces between your fingers and your palms, so that you have very thin strips. Using the project photo as a guide, lay the strips around the edges of the petal/leaf designs, and use the 36-gauge needle to needle felt it. Then use the 38-gauge needle to work over the lines very carefully, needle felting along the edges so that you produce a crisp, clear line. You should also work over the rest of the pincushion periodically to ensure that you're needle felting it to the same consistency all around and that the lines don't sink into the pincushion.

8. To produce a more three-dimensional piece, use the 38-gauge needle to needle felt evenly over the background surface of the pincushion. This will cause the background to recede and make the pansy look raised.

9. With the 40-gauge needle, work over the whole surface, using shallow stabs. This will smooth out the surface, eliminate any fuzziness, and make the needle holes less apparent.

10. Find a suitable base for your pincushion—candleholders make terrific stands—and glue your pincushion to the base using a multipurpose adhesive.

Oooh la la Berets

With these chic chapeaux in your winter wardrobe, you'll welcome chilly weather. Use wool roving in bold neutrals or soft pastels to needle felt the floral motif.

Patricia Spark, designer

SKILL LEVEL

Advanced Beginner to Intermediate

FELTING METHODS USED

Beret One: Dry Felting and Wet Felting

Beret Two: Dry Felting

FINISHED MEASUREMENTS

Medium Beret (about an 11-inch [27.9 cm] diameter)

WHAT YOU NEED

Merino wool top roving, 1 ounce of each color listed below:

Beret One: buff, peach, vanilla, and turquoise green

Beret Two: pewter, white, dark chocolate, and mocha

Colander, pot with lid, and stove (for preparing the roving)

Newspaper

Flower motif

2 commercially made knit-felt berets

Pencil

Upholstery foam pad, 4 x 6 x 1½ inches (10.2 x 15.2 x 3.8 cm)

Two 40-gauge triangular felting needles

WHAT YOU DO

Note: If you use roving as it comes from the manufacturer, you can have problems. To return its normal curly crimp, steam the fiber (see steps 1 and 2).

Beret One

1. Coil the top roving into a colander suspended over a pot of boiling water on the stove. Place newspaper between the lid of the pot and the fiber. The newspaper absorbs the condensation from the lid and doesn't let any drip down onto the fiber. Cover and steam the fiber for about 15 minutes, until it has plumped up and the crimp has returned.

2. Remove the fiber from the colander and let the steam dissipate. After a few minutes, the fiber will have cooled down enough to use.

3. Transfer the drawing of the flower motif to the beret. See the detail photo for placement. I used a sharp pencil and drew the motif freehand on the beret, but you could use some other transfer method.

4. Lay the beret open on the foam pad. Break up the roving for the center of the flower into ½- to ⅝-inch (1.3 to 1.6 cm) pieces. Start with the inside shapes and then work your way to the outside shapes. Lay the roving on the shape you're filling so it extends beyond the edge a little. Crisscross the pieces for better coverage.

5. Needle felt around the outside of the shape with the 40-gauge triangular needles. Don't push the needles all the way down to the hilt, which can push the majority of the fiber out the back of the beret. You can get enough tangled attachments by just using a few of the needle's barbs.

6. After you've needle felted the outline, fold the extended fiber into the center and needle felt it down, from the border toward the center of the shape. If needed, add more fiber to get better coverage. Break it into small pieces so it's not too bulky.

7. Continue to follow the color pattern and fill in the rest of the shapes.

8. Turn the piece over and needle felt a little from the back side.

9. Turn the beret back to the front side and use just the ends of both needles to punch the surface of the felt to tighten it up. The needle tip has one barb in it; if you hole two needles together in your hand and gently jab with just the tips, you'll tighten the felt surface without causing the colored fiber to push out the back of the beret.

10. You can wet felt the finished product. If you wish. (Se e Wet Felting) I decided to wet felt Beret One as an experiment, but the beret shrank a little and became less flexible. Whether to wet felt or not is a decision you should make carefully.

This project was completed with:

Ashland Bay Brand top roving

"Ooh la la Beret" template. Enlarge as desired

Beret Two

Marbles and Swirls Jewelry Pouch

Just what you need to stash your favorite accessories. Marble beads and needle-felted swirls accent the front of this soft pouch, while ribbon serves as a casing for the satin drawstring—details that make this a bag to treasure.

SKILL LEVEL

Beginner

FELTING METHOD USED

Dry Felting

FINISHED MEASUREMENTS

6 x 9 inches (15.2 x 22.9 cm)

WHAT YOU NEED

2 pieces of wool or wool-blend felt, each 6 x 9 inches (15.2 x 22.9 cm)

Upholstery foam

Swirl design (below)

2 yards (1.8 m) of wool yarn in black

36-gauge felting needle

12 inches (30.5 cm) of satin-faced ribbon, ⅞ inch (2.2 cm) wide

Sewing machine

Carpet thread to match wool felt

Sewing needle

25 to 40 marble design beads

Dressmaker's pins

1 yard (91.4 cm) of satin rattail or twist cord, cut in half crosswise

"Marble and Swirls Jewelry Pouch" template. Enlarge as desired.

WHAT YOU DO

1. Place one 6 x 9-inch (15.2 x 22.9 cm) piece of felt on the upholstery foam. Using the swirl design as a guide, needle felt swirls of the black wool yarn into the felt with the 36-gauge needle. Anchor the tail of yarn at the center of each swirl and work your way outward. This felt piece will serve as the front of the bag.

2. Cut the ribbon into two 6-inch pieces to be casings for the bag's drawstring. To form the casings, fold each ribbon end under ¼ inch (6 mm) and machine-stitch the folds in place. Then lay the ribbons ½ inch (1.3 cm) from the top of the bag's front and back, wrong sides together, and stitch along the side edges of the ribbon.

3. Using the carpet thread and sewing needle, hand-stitch one marble bead to the center of each needle-felted swirl on the front of the bag.

4. Place the front and back of the bag together, wrong sides facing in. Pin them together along the edges. Using a ¼-inch (6 mm) seam allowance, stitch just below the ribbon casings, stopping just before the casings on the opposite side.

5. Pull the rattail cords through the casings and knot the ends. Secure them by hand-stitching a bead to each cord end. A few stitches will do the trick.

6. Hand-stitch the remaining beads evenly across the top and bottom edges of the front of the bag.

Polka Dot Pets

Too cute to resist. Sturdy yet soft, these cuddly critters are the perfect companions for any child—or child at heart.

SKILL LEVEL

Beginner/Intermediate

FELTING METHODS USED

Dry Felting and Machine Felting

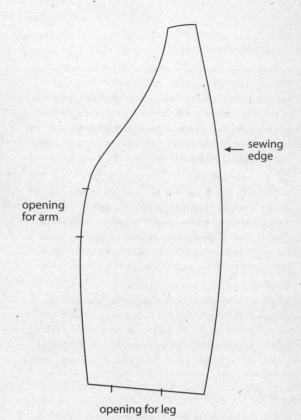

L.K. Ludwig, designer

FINISHED MEASUREMENTS

20 inches (50.8 cm)

WHAT YOU NEED

2 wool sweaters (one for each pet), in suitable solid colors

Washing machine and dryer

Dog and cat patterns

Paper and pencil

Scissors

Wool roving in accent color(s)

Upholstery foam or needle-felting mat

38-gauge multi-needle felting tool and mat

Thread to match the sweater

Sewing needle

4 safety eyes (2 for the dog and 2 for the cat)

Polyester fiberfill

Straight pins

Seam ripper

Embroidery thread in a dark color and needle

Plastic cat whiskers

Small piece of felt in accent color (for dog nose)

Unsharpened pencil

"Polka Dot Pets" ½ cat head. Enlarge as desired.

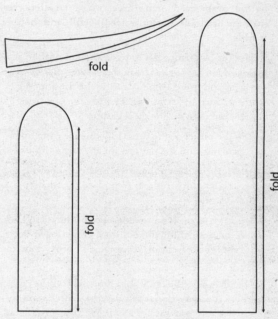

"Polka Dot Pets" torso. Enlarge as desired.

opening for arm

sewing edge

opening for leg

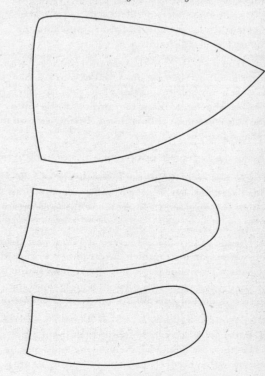

fold

fold

fold

"Polka Dot Pets" arms, legs, and tail. Enlarge as desired.

"Polka Dot Pets" dog ears and ¼ head. Enlarge as desired.

Continued ➡

What You Do

TO MAKE THE PATTERN PIECES

1. Full the wool sweaters in the washing machine (see Fulling Woven or Knit Wool Yardage). Then use the pattern pieces to trace and cut out the heads and torsos of the dog and the cat from the sweaters. Remember when cutting two or more pieces off the same pattern piece to reverse the pattern for the second piece. If you're cutting both pieces at the same time, reverse the fabric.

2. To make the spots, tear off four equal-size tufts of the wool roving. Lay one tuft on the upholstery foam, then lay another tuft on top of it, positioned perpendicular tool to needle felt the layers together, tucking the edges in as you go so that they make a dot shape. Make as many spots as you like, then set them aside.

3. Use the pattern pieces to assemble one side of each head and one side of each torso, placing the pieces on the foam, right side facing upward, one at a time. Then arrange the polka dots and use the felting tool to needle felt the polka dots to the torso pieces. Don't worry if a good bit of wool fiber pokes through the reverse side.

TO ASSEMBLE THE POLKA-DOT CAT

1. Use the matching thread and the sewing needle to sew the pieces of the cat's head together, leaving the bottom of the head open. Insert two of the safety eyes, stuff the head with the polyester fiberfill, and then set it aside.

2. Use the pattern pieces to trace and cut out the arms, legs, and tail for the cat from the sweater pieces. Sew the arms and legs together, leaving the tops open for stuffing. Stuff the arms and legs, sew the openings closed, and then set the pieces aside.

3. Sew the pieces of the torso together, leaving openings as marked on the pattern for the arms and legs.

4. Insert the legs into the torso, secure them with the pins, and hand stitch them into place. Do the same with the arms.

5. Stuff the torso, then sew the neck of the torso closed. Insert the neck of the torso into the opening at the bottom of the cat's head, secure it with pins, then hand stitch it into place.

6. Decide where the tail would look best on the cat, then use the seam ripper to open the center seam in the spot where you want to add the tail. Insert the tail and stitch the seam closed.

7. Use the embroidery needle and thread to make a satin stitch for the nose and a chain stitch for the mouth (see detail photo).

10. Trim the plastic cat whiskers until you're left with just a handful. Then use one point of your scissors to poke a tiny hole in one side of the cat's face where whiskers should be. Insert four or five whiskers into the hole and stitch the hole closed. Do the same on the other side of the cat's face.

TO ASSEMBLE THE POLKA-DOT DOG

1. Use the needle and thread to sew the sides of the dog's head together, leaving openings where the ears will be (see diagram A). Insert two of the safety eyes and then set the piece aside.

2. Use the pattern pieces to create the floppy ears from the sweater pieces. Topstitch the ear pieces, wrong sides together. Then slide the end of one of the ears into the slit in the dog's head and stitch it in place. Stuff the head with the polyester fiberfill, then insert the second ear, hand-sew it into place, and sew the head shut.

3. Position the piece of contrasting felt in the place where the nose should be, then use the multi-needle felting tool to needle felt around it, shaking it into a nose and attaching it securely.

4. Use the pattern pieces to create out the arms, legs, and tail for the dog from the sweater pieces. Sew the pieces of the arms and legs together, leaving the tops open for stuffing. Stuff the arms and legs, sew the openings closed, and then set the pieces aside.

5. Sew the pieces of the torso together, leaving openings as marked on the pattern for the arms, legs, and neck. Then insert the legs, secure them with the pins, and hand stitch them in place. Do the same with the arms.

6. Stuff the torso, then insert an unsharpened pencil into the neck, making sure the pencil protrudes 2 to 3 inches (5.1 to 7.6 cm) from the neck. Sew the neck closed.

7. Cut an opening into the back of the head (see diagram A again). Then insert the neck of the torso (the pencil) into the head. Pin the neck into place, and sew the opening closed.

8. Decide where the tail would look best on the dog, then use the seam ripper to open the center seam in the spot where you want to add the tail. Insert the tail and stitch the seam closed.

—From *Designer Needle Felting*

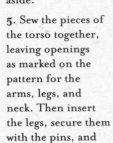

leave open for ears

side view of head opening for ears

back of head

cut opening to insert neck of torso

Diagram A

EMBROIDERY FOR BEGINNERS

Aimee Ray

Embroider Your World

Embroidery is one of the easiest crafts you can learn. If you're just starting out, there's no need for a huge commitment to buying a bunch of new supplies. The tools are simple and inexpensive; all you really need to get started are a needle, embroidery floss, and some fabric. Learning the basic techniques is simple for someone of any age or experience level. (Thanks to my mom and grandma, I first picked up a needle and thread at about the age of five.)

"Doodle-stitching" is the type of simple embroidery you'll learn in this section. It is also called freeform, or freestyle embroidery. That means there are no rules. You won't have to carefully count your stitches or decipher strange codes. Just thread your needle and start stitching. You'll find lots of whimsical, doodle-style line designs you can use for your embroidery projects, or try your hand at doodling your own. Simply follow a line art design that you've transferred onto your fabric, picking out stitches and colors a you go. You're free to just have fun and be creative!

Embroidery is extremely versatile. You'll find lots of ways to use it in other craft projects or to create a work of art by itself. It can be as simple as a one-stitch decorative edging on a skirt or a tablecloth, or as complex as a full-color picture that you plan to frame and hang on a wall. You can pick and choose your favorite colors and stitches, use an entire pattern or just a small section of it, or combine different elements to custom-design a pattern for your specific project.

Once you learn the basics, you'll also find embroidery to be very relaxing. There's something meditative about filling in a design stitch by stitch and watching it gradually take shape.

Embroidery projects are great to work on while watching a movie on the couch, during long car or plane rides, or just as a way to unwind—wherever you are. Embroidery projects are very portable. Not a lot of preparation is required to get started once you have transferred your pattern to the fabric. Your embroidery also is easily set aside and picked up again whenever you have time to work on it. Whether your day allows you a few free hours, or 10 minutes here and there, you can literally put away your project in mid-stitch and pick it up again later if you need to, right where you left off.

This section will show you, step-by-step, the basic skills you need to start embroidering doodle-stitch style. You'll find lots of fun patterns and project ideas as well. I hope they'll inspire you to pick up a needle and thread and embroider your world.

Embroidery Essentials

Embroidery isn't complicated, but knowing a bit about the tools and materials will make your stitching a lot more fun. In this section, you'll learn what to look for and how best to use the items you buy. After you've gathered these essentials and picked your first project, see Getting Started for more help. Soon, you'll be turning out great embroidery pieces.

Materials and Tools

You need to track down a few basic items before you can start embroidering. The materials and tools are relatively inexpensive, and chances are good that you probably have some of them already on hand. If not, you can find them at your local craft store, and they won't empty your piggy bank.

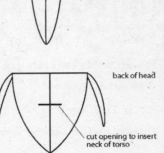

MATERIALS AND TOOLS CHECKLIST

Here's a list of supplies you'll need for almost every project in this section, plus a few extra items that are nice to have on hand.

- 6-inch (15.2 cm)-diameter embroidery hoop
- Embroidery and hand-sewing needles
- Embroidery floss
- Fabric stabilizer
- Fine-lead pencil
- Iron
- Nonpermanent fabric marking pen
- Ruler
- Scissors
- Straight pins
- Thimble, leather or rubber
- Tracing and transfer tools
- Tweezers

Fabrics

The most common fabrics used for embroidery are quilter's cotton, linen made for handwork, and Aida cloth (a heavy fabric with a large weave). However, almost any fabric is suitable for embroidery. Delicate materials such as chiffon and silk may require an extra bit of care while stretching on a hoop so the weave won't distort or stretch. Also make sure that the stitching isn't so dense that it weighs down—or is visually unbalanced by—a lightweight fabric.

Fine fabrics and stretchy fabrics like cotton T-shirts usually behave better if you apply a removable fabric stabilizer before you start stitching.

Heavier fabrics such as felt or denim are easy to work with. They don't pucker and may not need to be placed in a hoop (called hooping).

Craft felt is a sturdy fabric. It can handle hand- and machine-stitching and generally won't pucker when embroidered. You don't need to use a hoop with craft felt.

If you're just starting to embroider and need some fabric, take a look at your wardrobe or linen closet. You never know what might inspire you to add a touch of thread to it.

Embroidery Floss

Although you can embroider with just about any thread, the most common is embroidery floss. Each long strand is sold in a small bundle, or skein, and available in any color you can think of. Every color has a number designation, which is printed on the wrapper. Manufacturers, distributors, and stitchers all use the numbers, rather than the names, to identify colors. Some colors are very similar. When you're starting a project, it's a good idea to jot down the numbers you're using in case you need to get more later.

Every floss manufacturer has its own unique set of color numbers. To avoid confusion, the materials and supplies list (What You Need) call for floss by color name. At the end of every project, you'll find a list of the floss brand, color, and color names that were used for the sample shown in the accompanying photo.

If you want to stitch your version of a project with the same colors, but only have access to a different brand of floss, there's an easy solution: Just use the color descriptions in the project's What You Need list as your guide. Or, you can look up the product name and color number on a color conversion chart to find the equivalent number that's available from another company. Almost all specialty shops have a conversion chart to help customers; some retailers sell them, and you can find several free on the Internet by typing "embroidery floss conversion chart" into an Internet search engine.

A length of floss is made up of six smaller strands, or plies, that are twisted together. You can use all of them to stitch a thick line, or divide them up and use two, three, or four plies for a thinner line on fine details. The designs in this book are meant to be embroidered with all six plies, unless indicated otherwise. However, if you're embroidering a design at a reduced size, you may want to decrease the number of plies.

There are a variety of specialty threads, such as linen, metallic, silk, and wool, which are also fun to try.

Needles

A good embroidery needle is medium sized, with a sharp point and a long opening, or eye, at one end, which makes threading your floss through it much easier. It's a good idea to have a small-eye needle on hand as well, for sewing fabric by hand with a single ply of floss or sewing thread. Buy a packet with several sizes and types of needles to ensure that you have on hand, whatever size you want to use.

Embroidery Hoops

An embroidery hoop is a two-piece frame. Plastic hoops are sturdier than wood and last a long time. Hoops come in many sizes. A 6-inch (15.2 cm) diameter hoop is good for almost any project; small designs will fit inside the circle and, for larger designs, you can move the hoop around as needed.

Scissors

Keep a pair of small sharp sewing scissors on hand while embroidering. You need them to cut lengths of floss and snip off any leftover floss when you're finished stitching.

Tools for Transferring

To transfer a design—and sometimes a pattern—from this book or from another source to your fabric, start by copying it onto tracing paper...or by making a photocopy.

The next stop is getting the design or pattern onto the fabric. Depending on the fabric and density of the completed stitching, you might be able to trace the lines with a lead pencil or chalk. Otherwise, you can draw on your fabric using a nonpermanent fabric marking pen or pencil that's specially made for this purpose. (The instructions advise when a lead pencil or chalk is suitable.) Nonpermanent fabric marking pens come in several varieties. Some make marks that wash away with water, and others have marks that simply fade over time. If you choose a fabric pen that has disappearing, or air-soluble, ink, be sure it's not for a project that you'll be working on for several days. Your tracing may fade before you're finished.

Dressmaker's carbon paper can be purchased at most craft stores. It comes in several light and dark colors, to suit dark or light fabrics.

Iron-on transfer pencils allow you to trace the design onto tracing paper, and then iron it onto your fabric.

Marks from some transfer tools become permanent when ironed. Test, test, test on a scrap of the project fabric!

Other Useful Tools

Pins and a small pincushion are always good to have around when doing sewing projects.

If you have trouble threading your needle, a needle threader makes the job quick and easy.

You'll be glad to have a thimble on your finger when pushing the needle through tough fabrics like denim or canvas. A leather or rubber thimble will protect your fingers and also help you get a good grip on the needle. Place the thimble on the index or second finger of your dominant hand—whichever one you use to push a needle through any fabric. You also might want to place another thimble on your opposite hand to protect the finger that receives the needle underneath your work.

The more embroidery projects you do, the more floss you'll accumulate. You might find it useful to organize the strands by wrapping each color on a plastic or cardboard holder; write the color number on the holder; and then store them together in a box. Special boxes are sold to contain these, but you can use an ordinary, clear plastic fishing tackle box.

Finally, although the real purpose of pinking shears is to keep fabric edges from fraying, their toothed blades can create decorative edges on appliqué shapes.

Getting Started

Beginning your embroidery project is wonderfully simple. All you need to do is transfer the design, hoop it, thread the needle with embroidery floss, and start stitching. For more tips—and information on a few simple techniques—read on.

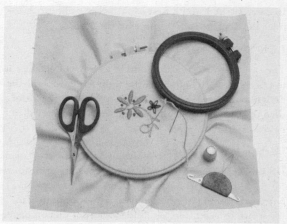

Grab your hoop, a needle, some floss, and a design...these items, plus a few basic tips will get you on your way.

Choosing a Design

In this section you'll find lots of unique designs for you to use for your embroidery projects. You can stitch up these designs according to the project instructions, or mix and match them to create your own compositions.

Using a photocopier, you can even reduce or enlarge these designs so that each one perfectly fits your project. Some of the designs in this book are the right size for the patterns and dimensions in the instructions. When a design (or a pattern) has to be enlarged, there's a note to this effect. You'll see it when you trace or photocopy the book page.

But don't stop here! Almost anything can be used as an embroidery design. An image with strong outlines and simple details works best. Look at clip art books or Web sites, coloring books or, of course, draw your own. You have an artist inside you, whether you know it or not. Does your drawing ability limit itself to the doodles you make while talking on the phone? Guess what? Those simple little pictures and shapes can become great embroidery designs, as shown in the photo above. Draw large, or enlarge your little doodles on a photocopier. Cut them up and arrange the doodles into an interesting composition. Try overlapping different shapes or adding a decorative border. Words also make great designs. Use your own handwriting, or type them up using your favorite font and use the printout as your design. Transfer your completely original design to fabric, just like you would any other.

Transferring a Design

In order to transfer an embroidery design or pattern to your fabric, you can use one of the methods explained here. In a few projects, a specific method is suggested because it's most successful for the featured fabric. You can use any method you like when none is suggested.

Whatever method you choose, it's important to first preshrink the fabric by washing and drying it the same way that you'll care for the finished piece. Then you should press the fabric because it needs to be wrinkle-free before it's hooped. Since marks from some transfer tools become permanent when ironed, it's best to press your fabric before transferring a design to it.

If you're feeling particularly adventurous, doodle directly on your fabric with a fabric pen or regular lead pencil...or don't use a design at all. Just grab a favorite color of floss and start stitching. Add more designs, shapes, or pictures as you go, and you'll end up with a truly unique work of art.

Continued ➜

In every method, you'll first want to either photocopy or trace the designs from the pages of this book.

Light Method

The easiest way to get a design onto a light-color fabric is to trace it, using a light box or a sunny window. Tape the design to the light source, place your fabric over it, and then trace the design with a regular lead pencil or fabric pen.

Carbon Paper Method

Dressmaker's carbon paper in a contrasting color is ideal for dark- or light-color fabric. Spread your fabric on a hard surface and position the design on top, both with the front, or right side, up. Slide a sheet of carbon paper between the layers, transfer side down. Pin or tape the fabric and design together so they don't move while you work, and then trace over the design with a ballpoint pen, pencil, or other blunt tool, like a knitting needle or chopstick. Press hard. The chalky marks from transfer paper sometimes fade as you work. If you notice the design is wearing off, go over the lines with a fabric pen or white chalk.

Transfer Pencil Method

A third way to transfer your design to fabric is to use an iron-on transfer that you make with a special pencil. First, trace the design onto tracing paper using a pencil or fine-tip marker that'll give you dark lines. Flip the paper over and trace your lines again, on the opposite side, with the transfer pencil. Now tape the paper, transfer side down, on the fabric. Press it with a hot iron to transfer the design to the fabric.

Adding Fabric Stabilizer

Stretchy, flimsy, and loose-weave fabrics are much easier to embroider if you first apply a fabric stabilizer to the back. A stabilizer keeps fabric from stretching while you work to help make a smooth finished product.

There are many stabilizers, usually identified by the way that they're applied: sprays; liquids; adhesive sheets (press-on or iron-on); and a type that's hooped with the fabric and secured so it as you stitch (sew-on). Stabilizers also are classified by the removal method: tear away, water soluble, or heat soluble (heated with an iron until it crumbles). Some stabilizers are designed to remain on the back of the work. In almost all categories, there are thick and thin versions that are sold as fabric or plastic-like sheets, strips, or rolls. With so many options, you're sure to find a stabilizer that's suitable for your fabric, techniques, and personal preferences.

Whenever a project sample made for Doodle-Stitching needed a stabilizer, a self-adhesive product was used. Look for a thinner, press-on stabilizer intended for machine embroidery because it's easier to stitch through.

To apply the stabilizer, cut a piece slightly larger than the entire design. Iron the fabric to remove wrinkles and then apply the stabilizer to the back of the fabric, or wrong side, according to the instructions on the package.

After embroidering the entire design, you can remove the stabilizer. To remove tear-away stabilizer, carefully pull the paper off the fabric. Rip the stabilizer into smaller pieces, if necessary, to avoid tugging at your stitches. Use tweezers to remove bits of paper caught under the stitches....

Preparing the Fabric and Floss

Even if you back your fabric with a stabilizer, you still should use a hoop. Only firm fabrics, such as denim and felt, don't need to be hooped.

To make your fabric taut, spread it over the smaller inside hoop and fit the larger (outside) one over the top with your fabric in between. Tighten the little screw that's on the outer hoop and gently pull on all the edges of the fabric until you have a taut surface (figure 1).

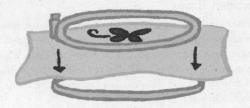

Figure 1

The edges of the stabilizer can be caught in the hoop. Next, thread the needle. Start with a length of floss 12 to 18 inches (30.5 to 45.7 cm) long.

Getting all six plies of a strand of embroidery floss through the needle's eye can be a challenge. It may help to slightly dampen your finger and twist the end to a point, or squeeze the floss ends flat between your thumb and forefinger. Slide the needle's eye onto the floss (instead of pushing the floss through the eye). If all else fails, use a needle threader; it'll save you a lot of headaches.

After you've inserted an end of the floss through the needle, knot the longer end. Wrap the floss end around your finger, roll it off, and tighten it (figure 2).

Figure 2

Stitching the Design

You can complete all of the colors and stitch types in a section of the design before moving on. Or, you can work a single color throughout the design, then switch to a new color and work it in the same manner.

Starting at the back of the fabric, pull the needle and floss through until the knot catches. The floss will likely twist up after a while. To correct this problem, hold up the hoop and let the needle and floss hang straight down loose, so that the strand can untwist. Be careful, and don't lose your needle!

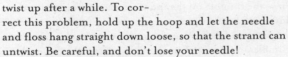

Figure 3

When you're down to a 2- or 3-inch (5.1 or 7.6 cm) length of floss on the needle, pull the strand through to the back of the fabric. Pass the needle under a stitch, bring the needle back through the floss loop, and tighten (figure 3). Snip off the loose end near the knot.

Finishing Your Work

You may want to hand-wash the finished piece in cool water with a mild detergent. Gentle laundering removes any unseen oil and dirt that accumulated during handling and any marks from the transfer pencil. Squeeze out the excess water by rolling the work in a towel. Spread your project flat to dry. When it's dry or just slightly damp, place it face-down on a clean terrycloth towel and iron out any wrinkles from the back. Pressing from the back prevents the iron from crushing the embroidery stitches.

Stitch Library

It's time to play! Now that you've gathered your supplies and learned the basic process that's involved in embroidering a motif, you're ready to start stitching.

Embroidery stitches are easy to learn. By mixing and matching a few simple stitches, you can create almost any look that you can dream up. Don't be afraid to experiment. As you embroider more and more, you'll discover techniques best suited to your style. Soon you'll be designing your own projects.

Outline Stitches

Outline Stitches are the base of almost any design. You'll use these to "draw" on the fabric, following the lines of the design, or design lines. On their own, outline stitches can be combined to create a graphic image that's full of lush detail.... Whenever you make outline stitches, it's most important that the fabric you're working on is taut. These stitches are the foundation of your design, so it's important to start with quality work.

Outline Stitches can be used to trace lines, or arranged in rows for an interesting pattern.

Straight Stitch

Pull the needle and floss to the front of the fabric at A (figure 4). Move the needle forward along the design line, and then return to the back of the fabric at B. The distance from A to B can be as long or short as desired.

Figure 4   *Figure 5*

Several Straight Stitches in a row are called *Running Stitches*. They can be worked on a straight or curved design line. Usually, the individual stitches are the same length, and the distance between each stitch is the same.

You can scatter small Straight Stitches for a random pattern, which are called *Seed Stitches* (figure 5). You can make Seed Stitches as long or as short as desired.

A Straight Stitch is as basic as embroidery gets.

Split Stitch

On the front of the fabric, make a small stitch that's twice as long as the desired finished stitch, from A to B (figure 6). Bring the needle up through the center of the stitch, at C, to split the floss in half. Make another long stitch on the surface, and then split it, to continue the line of stitching.

Figure 6

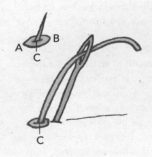

The Split Stitch is great for nice, thick outlines, plus it's easy and quick to make.

Back Stitch

Start with a small stitch in the opposite direction, from A to B (figure 7). Still underneath the fabric, start a "forward" stitch that's twice as long as the first. Bring the needle to the front of the fabric at C. To make each new Back Stitch, once again start by working backward on the surface, inserting the needle at the end of the previous stitch, at A.

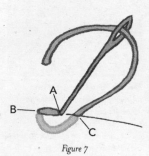

Figure 7

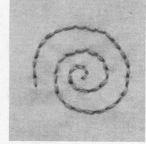

Used alone, the Back Stitch is an attractive design element. It can also give a design a clean outline

Stem Stitch

Make a stitch, from A to B (figure 8). Leave the floss a little loose. Pull the needle through to the front at the midpoint and just to one side of the previous stitch, at C. Pull the floss tight. Continue this process to make a length of Stem Stitches along the design line.

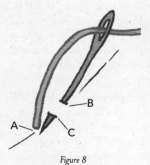

Figure 8

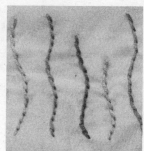

The Stem Stitch works well for curves, which makes it ideal for representing a flower stem.

Chain Stitch

Pull the needle and flow to the front of the fabric at A. Insert the needle and floss back into the fabric at A (figure 9). Pull the floss to the back of the fabric until you have a loop about ⅛ inch to ¼ inch (3 to 6 mm) long. This loop is secured at the same time you start a new one, as follows: Bring the needle and floss to the front of the fabric near the top of—and inside of—the previous loop at B (figure 10). Pull the needle and floss to the underside, still at B, until the new loop is the same length as the previous one (figure 11). Continue making additional loops in the same manner. To secure the last loop in a line of Chain Stitches, bring the needle to the front of the fabric as if you're starting a new loop. Make a tiny stitch over the end of the loop.

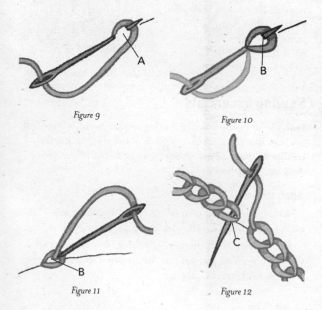

Figure 9

Figure 10

Figure 11

Figure 12

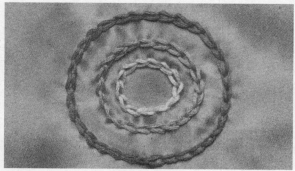

The Chain Stitch is fine for outlining shapes, but it's a little thicker than a Split Stitch and works better for decorative borders.

Ending a Chain-Stitched circle is slightly different. Work Chain Stitches, as described above, around the circle until you're one stitch shy of the first loop. Pull the needle and floss to the front of the fabric as if you're going to make a new loop. Slide the needle underneath the start of the first stitch, at C, and then insert it back into the fabric at the end of—and inside—the last finished loop (figure 12).

Decorative Stitches

Your creativity is best expressed by decorative stitches. While there's a specific way to make each one, you get to decide the length and angle that determine the personality. A blanket stitch, for example, can be sharp and modern, or you can make each stitch looser—for a more romantic effect. As you make the designs in this book, let your style shine through. Some of the described stitches are meant to be worked in a continuous line, while others are made independent of each other.

Practice all of your Decorative Stitches on a single piece of fabric and you'll have a work of art when you're finished.

Blanket Stitch

Starting on the design line, make a loose diagonal stitch away from the line, from A to B (figure 13). Bring the needle up to the front of the fabric on the design line at C (if working at an edge, you won't stitch over the edge). Catch the first stitch under the needle tip and pull the floss tight to the design line (or fabric edge). Make a new diagonal stitch, on the opposite side of the design line, to start the process again.

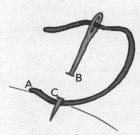

Figure 13

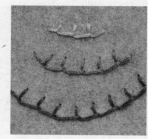

The Blanket Stitch is great as a border or an edging.

Scallop Stitch

Make a loose stitch on the design line, from A to B (figure 14). Finger-press the stitch flat to one side of the line, so the center of the top is the desired depth of

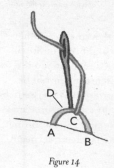

Figure 14

Scallop Stitches have long been favored for borders, but stacking them in rows is a less common treatment.

the finished scallop. Bring the needle to the front of the fabric at the center of the previous stitch, at C. Insert the needle on the outside of the loop to hold the top of the scallop in place, at D.

Threaded Running Stitch

Make a line of small, close Running Stitches (figure 15). End this floss. Start a second floss strand, in another color, at the same spot as the first line of stitches, at A (figure 16). Working only on the front—without stitching through the fabric—insert the needle under the first Running Stitch, then through the second Running Stitch. Continue weaving the second color back and forth under the Running Stitches until the end of the line. End this floss. Weave additional lengths of floss through the straight stitching—on top of the fabric—in any manner, if desired.

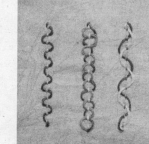

Color 2

Color 1

Figure 15

Figure 16

The Threaded Running Stitch has a unique look—especially when worked in several colors and with more than a single line of weaving on the surface.

Cross Stitch

Start with a small diagonal Straight Stitch, from A to B (figure 17). Make a second stitch from C to D. Rows look neater when the lines for each cross (X) overlap in the same direction. Connected Cross Stitches become Herringbone Stitches, as shown in the lowest row of the photo.

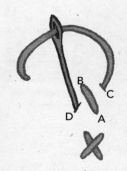

Figure 17

Herringbone Stitch

Decide the height of the finished stitch. Draw a parallel line this distance from the design line. Starting on the design line, make a loose diagonal stitch to the next line, from A to B (figure 18). Make a short horizontal stitch on the back of the fabric by bringing the needle to the front at C. For the downward diagonal stroke, insert the needle on the design line, at D.

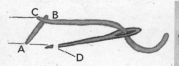

Figure 18

Made much the same way, the finished appearance of a line of Herringbone Stitches takes on a different effect than multiple Cross Stitches.

Continued →

For a line of Herringbone Stitches, as shown in the photo at left, top, for each stitch, bring the needle to the front of the fabric slightly to the left of the last position, and make a new diagonal stitch between the design and parallel lines.

French Knot Stitch

Bring the needle and floss to the front of the fabric at A (figure 19). Wrap the floss around the base of the needle in the direction shown. Place the needle back into the fabric close to the previous position, at B (figure 20). Pull the floss tight and close to the fabric as you pull the needle through to the back of the fabric.

Figure 19   *Figure 20*

Most of the French knots used in this book's designs are made by wrapping the floss around the needle once. A label on the design will tell you if more than one wrap is needed.

The French Knot is a nice accent stitch for making tiny dots. You also can use it to fill an entire area with an interesting texture.

Lazy Daisy Stitch

Make a small loop by pulling the needle and floss to the front of the fabric at A, and then returning to the back of the fabric at A (figure 21). Finger-press the loop flat. Anchor the top of the loop to the fabric with a small stitch, from B to C. A Lazy Daisy Stitch can be a single petal, as explained above. For a daisy, make additional loops, always starting in the center, at A.

The Lazy Daisy Stitch is used to make flower petals or leaves. Use Satin Stitches or French Knots to define the flower centers.

Figure 21

Star Stitches

Start a Cross Stitch Star by making a Cross Stitch. Now make a Straight Stitch on top, from A to B (figure 21).

Start an Eight-Point Star by making a Cross Stitch Star. Now make one more Straight Stitch on top, from C to D (figure 22).

Start a Center Point Star with a Straight Stitch that begins at the center, at A, and goes in any direction, to B (figure 23). Again bring the needle out at A, this time going down in a different position, at C. Make as many stitches as desired, all the same length, beginning at A, and ending in a previously unstitched spot.

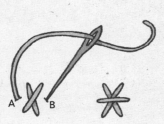

Figure 22   *Figure 23*

Figure 24

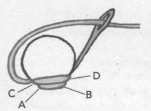

Stars can be stitched in several different ways. French Knots are scattered as accents.

Feather Stitch

Starting on the design line, make a loose diagonal stitch away from the line, from A to B (figure 25). Beside B, bring the needle to the front of the fabric on the design line, at C. As you pull the needle through at C, catch the previous diagonal stitch under the tip of the needle. Make another diagonal stitch in the opposite direction, to D (figure 26).

For a line of feather stitching, bring every loose diagonal stitch back to the design line by catching it under the needle tip, and alternating the direction of the diagonal stitches.

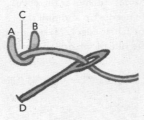
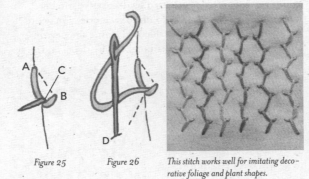

Figure 25   *Figure 26*   *This stitch works well for imitating decorative foliage and plant shapes.*

Fly Stitch

Make a loose horizontal stitch, from A to B (figure 27). Finger-press the stitch flat to one side. Bring the needle to the front of the fabric at the center of the previous stitch, at C. Make a second, longer, stitch perpendicular to the first by inserting the needle at D, thus trapping the center of the previous stitch.

Figure 27

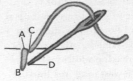

Like the Feather Stitch, the Fly Stitch is unique and makes good foliage. Use a different stitch for the flower heads.

Fill Stitches

The Satin Stitch and the Long and Short Stitch are two of the more common ways to fill spaces. You also can use Straight Stitches, French Knots, or Cross Stitches to fill larger areas of your embroidery with interesting textures.

Satin Stitch

Make a Straight Stitch from one design line to another, from A to B (figure 28). Make a second Straight Stitch close to the first, again going from a design line to the opposite one, from C to D. The stitches might not be the same length, but it's more important that every stitch starts and ends on opposing design lines. Continue making additional stitches in the same manner, positioning each one close to the next so that the fabric underneath isn't visible.

Solid areas of color are eye-catching in embroidery pieces.

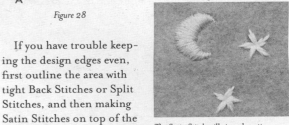

Figure 28   *Figure 29*

If you have trouble keeping the design edges even, first outline the area with tight Back Stitches or Split Stitches, and then making Satin Stitches on top of the Outline Stitches (figure 29).

The Satin Stitch will give a beautiful, smooth finish to solid areas of your design. It's best to use the Satin Stitch only for small spaces. Since the stitches are long and sit on top of the fabric, they can sometimes get snagged.

Long and Short Stitch

The name Long and Short Stitch is misleading, because only the first row has different stitch lengths.

Start Row 1 with a long stitch, beginning on the design line and extending into the area you want to fill, from A to B (figure 30). Don't try to make the stitch reach the opposite design line. Bring the needle and floss to the front of the fabric at the design line, beside the previous stitch, at C. Go down at D, so the new stitch is parallel to the first but only half as long. Make another long stitch, then a short one, and so on to the end of the row. Don't work the first row around a curve. Instead, start a second row, as explained below, so every row is straight.

In all of the following rows, the stitches are all one length. Start the second row by making a stitch above the last one of the first row, from E to F (figure 31). The next stitch is the same length, worked above the second last stitch of row 1, from G to H. The row 2 stitches appear to be different heights because they're stacked above a long or short stitch. In the same manner, continue stacking new, same-length stitches on top of the ones below, adding more rows as needed to fill the space.

You can create a blend between light and dark colors by stitching a few rows in a light color, and then the next few in a darker shade, and so on. Don't worry too much about keeping the length of your stitches exactly uniform and, as you fill in your shape, you'll probably need

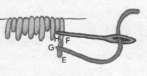

Figure 30   *Figure 31*

to add an extra stitch here and there to fill in spaces as needed. Just try to keep all your stitches going in the same direction, and you'll have an evenly filled area when you're finished.

The Long and Short Stitch is used to cover large areas with a solid or blended field of color.

Sewing Essentials

Don't worry—the projects in this section involve very little sewing. But you do need to learn some very simple techniques so that you can showcase your beautiful embroidery on a finished project.

Appliqué

Stitching a piece of contrasting colored or patterned fabric onto a fabric surface adds more depth to embroidery.

Felt is great for appliqués. It's thick, easy to cut, and doesn't fray. You just cut out the finished shape, and sew it to the background fabric.

When using cotton or other fabric, you can cut the appliqué edges with pinking shears to give them a decorative look and reduce fraying.

Felt and pinked appliqués are attached to the background fabric with outline or decorative embroidery stitches, appliqué stitches (figure 32), or hidden stitches.

One of the more traditional ways to make an appliqué yields a clean, folded edge. Start by drawing a shape on the appliqué fabric. Now cut it out ¼ inch (6 mm) beyond the outer lines of the shape. Press the ¼-inch (6 mm) seam allowance to the back of the appliqué shape. You can attach this shape to the background with appliqué stitches (figure 32).

Appliqué Stitch

Place the appliqué on the background fabric. Pull a knotted length of floss or sewing thread from the underside of the background fabric to the front at A, which is very near—and through—the edge of the appliqué (figure 32). Still on the front of the work, insert the needle through only the background fabric at B, to make a tiny stitch perpendicular to the edge of the appliqué. Don't pull the needle through to the back of the fabric.

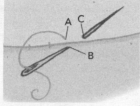

Figure 32

Instead, start the next stitch by inserting the needle tip at C. Continue making even-length, equally spaced stitches around the perimeter of the appliqué.

Embroidering with Beads

There's no end to the number of effects that are possible by adding beads to embroidery.

The process isn't tricky as long as you use a needle that's suitable for the bead. The size of the holes in different beads will vary, so check that your embroidery needle can be pulled through the hole. If it can't, pick up a package of beading needles. These are long skinny needles with tiny eyes. Available in a range of sizes, they're designed to pass through the hole of even the tiniest bead.

After threading the needle with matching sewing thread or one or more plies of embroidery floss, again pass the needle through a bead to make sure that the floss isn't too thick for the hole. If it is, switch to a same-size bead with a larger hole, or get slightly larger beads.

Pony beads are large enough for you to pull yarn through, and they're usually plastic. You don't need a special needle to thread these. Seed beads are glass or plastic. Your local craft shop might sell these tiny beads in several sizes, all of which are small enough to sit on the tip of a slightly long fingernail. Pick whatever seed bead size you like, because any will look great worked into the designs in this book.

Beads can be stitched to fabric one at a time, using a Straight Stitch or a Back Stitch. With the needle and floss on the front of the fabric, just slide the bead onto the needle, snug it up against the fabric, and complete the stitch in the usual manner.

Double Hem

Your projects will look neat and professional with this hem. You just fold under the fabric edge twice, and then stitch it in place. Every project that calls for a double hem will tell you the desired finished width.

Here's the process for making a ½-inch (1.3 cm) double hem:

Along the cut, or raw, fabric edge, fold ½ inch (1.3 cm) to the underside. Press the fold. You now have a flattened fold at the edge. Turn this under, to the back of the fabric, so that the

Figure 33

new fold is ½-inch (1.3 cm) wide (figure 33). Sew a line of Straight Stitches along the top of the innermost fold, through all of the fabric layers.

Hidden Stitch

This is an invisible stitch used to close holes in pillows or toy animals after they're stuffed.

Use sewing thread that's the same color as the fabric. You'll be working from the outside, or right side, of the piece. Fold under the excess fabric (the seam allowances) along each side of the opening. Butt the folded edges together.

Thread a needle with matching sewing thread with a knot at the end. From the back of the fabric, insert the needle through one of the folded edges so the knot is trapped in the fold and the thread is on the outside of the fabric at a folded edge, at A (figure 34).

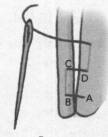

Figure 34

Pull the needle and thread through the folded edge at B, directly across from A. Slide along the inside of the fold and pull the needle to the outside at C. This traps the stitch inside the fold. Insert the needle through the opposite fold, at D, which is directly across from C.

Tug on the thread to pull the two sides of the fabric together. Continue sewing back and forth, trapping the stitches inside the folded edges. Keep your stitches small and close together and you'll barely see them when you're finished. End the thread with a tiny knot buried in the underside of one of the folds.

Topstitch

Topstitching is worked after fabric pieces are sewn together, and the project is turned right side out. You work by hand or by machine.

Just sew a line of small Straight Stitches. Keep the stitches close together, evenly spaced, and all the same length. The stitches are usually placed close to—and parallel with—an edge, but they can be made anywhere.

Whip Stitch

This is a great way to add a decorative touch while joining pieces of fabric along matched edges. You can use it to sew together two edges by stitching loosely and then opening the pieces flat when the seam is complete.

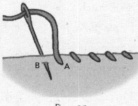

Figure 35

For extra punch, use contrasting floss rather than sewing thread.

Starting at the back—or between two pieces of fabric—bring your needle and floss through to the front at A (figure 35). Bring the needle over both layers, at the edge. From the outside of the bottom fabric layer, insert the needle through both fabrics, at B. Continue stitching along the matched edges, making every diagonal stitch the same length and the same distance apart.

Projects

There are hundreds of ways to stitch embroidery into your daily life. As you start to embroider, you'll find more and more ways to use your work and surround yourself with unique, personalized items that express your creativity. Here are some fun and easy projects to get you started.

Songbird Wristlet

Keep music at your fingertips with this wristlet made for an MP3 player.

WHAT YOU NEED

Singing Bird design and Songbird Wristlet pattern

9 x 12 inches (22.9 x 30.5 cm) aqua or light blue fabric

Embroidery floss, 1 skein of black*

Sewing thread to match fabric

8 inches (20.3 cm) of black ribbon, ½ inch (1.3 cm) wide

½-inch (1.3 cm) circle of hook-and-loop tape

*The author used DMC embroidery floss in color 310.

STITCHES

Lazy Daisy Stitch

Satin Stitch

Stem Stitch

Straight Stitch

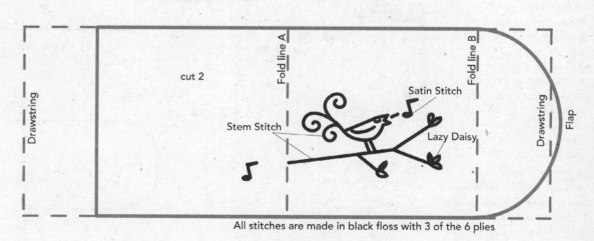

All stitches are made in black floss with 3 of the 6 plies

Singing Bird design and Songbird Wristlet pattern. Enlarge 200%

Continued ➜

¾ x 2½ x 4 inches (1.9 x 6.4 x 10.2 cm)

INSTRUCTIONS

Note: The following instructions make a holder with a flap top. To create a drawstring holder, before cutting the fabric alter the Songbird Wristlet pattern. Follow steps 1 to 3. Continue with step 4, making a ½ inch (1.3 cm) opening at each corner, along the long edges and starting ¾ inch (1.9 cm) from the end. Turn the piece right side out. Don't sew the openings shut at any point. Topstitch along both short ends and again 1 inch (2.5 cm) from the top edge. Continue with steps 7 to 10, ignoring the ribbon references. Draw the ribbon through the openings and sew the ends together.

1. Fold the fabric in half. Trace the Songbird Wristlet pattern onto the top layer of the fabric. Mark the pattern fold lines.

2. Cut the pattern shape from both layers of fabric. Set aside one of the fabric pieces for use in a later step, as the lining.

3. Copy the Singing Bird design to the front of the remaining fabric shape. Embroider it, using three plies of floss for all of the stitching.

4. Place the front of the lining against the front of the embroidered pieces. Match all of the cut edges. Join the fabric pieces by sewing around the perimeter ¼ inch (6 mm) from all of the edges, leaving a 2-inch (5.1 cm) opening along one edge (figure 1).

5. Turn the joined pieces right side out. Sew the opening closed with the Hidden Stitch. Press the seams flat.

6. The rounded end will be the flap that covers the top opening of the finished Topstitch along the opposite short end (figure 2).

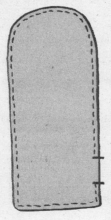 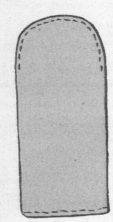

Figure 1   *Figure 2*

7. Fold the short end of the joined piece along fold line A, with the embroidered design on the inside and the lining on the outside. Match the short end to fold line B.

8. Bring together the ends of the ribbon to make a loop. Tuck the ribbon inside the folded wristlet, just below fold line B. Let the ribbon ends extend beyond the edges at one side. Sew the layers together along each side, catching the ribbon ends in the stitching at the top of one side (figure 3).

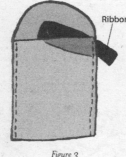

Ribbon

Figure 3

9. With the lining still on the outside, pull the front away from the back at one bottom corner to make a triangle that has the bottom seam on one side and the side seam on the

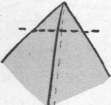

Figure 4

opposite side of the same corner. Pinch this corner flat. Sew a line straight across it, ¼ inch (6 mm) from the point (figure 4). Stitch the remaining bottom corner the same way.

10. Turn the pouch right side out. For the closure, sew or press the hook-and-loop tape to the center of the flap and a corresponding position on the front.

Tag-Along ID Holder

Finding your bag at the airport will be a snap.

WHAT YOU NEED

Growing design and Casing pattern piece

Interior pattern piece

9 x 12 inches (22.9 x 30.5 cm) of orange craft felt

Embroidery floss, 1 skein each of coral, light coral, green, and light green*

½ inch (1.3 cm) button

The author used DMC embroidery floss in colors 352, 353, 471, and 472.

STITCHES

Feather Stitch

Fly Stitch

French Knot

Satin Stitch

Whip Stitch

3¾ x 2½ inches (9.5 x 6.4 cm), excluding the strap

INSTRUCTIONS

Note: You might want to try embroidering without transferring the design to the felt. Just keep in mind that the space nearest the end line will be covered with the strap and button when the finished piece is closed.

1. Transfer the Casing and Interior pattern pieces lines and the design to the felt.

2. Cut each fabric shape from the felt. Cut out the windows as indicated and cut slits for the buttonhole.

3. Embroider the design. You don't need to use a hoop with craft felt.

4. Line up the interior felt piece on the wrong side of the casing and pin it in place. Using the Whip Stitch and a single strand of embroidery floss, join the two shapes around the edge of the strap and the window (figure 1). You can tuck your knots between the two layers of felt to hide them. Leaving the end knotted of the floss with a ½ inch (1.3 cm)-long tail will make this easier.

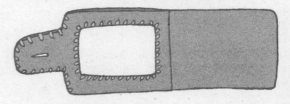

Figure 1

5. Fold the casing along the marked line, with the interior felt shape inside. To join the layers, Whip-stitch along the remaining raw edges (figure 2). Don't stitch the straight, outer edge of the interior shape, which is aligned with the fold line of the casing.

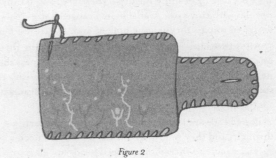

Figure 2

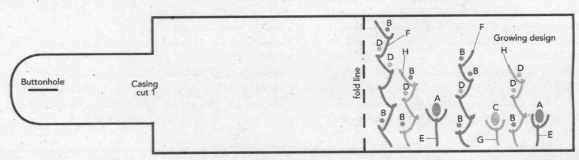

Growing design and Casing pattern piece. Enlarge 153%. Key: A—coral Satin Stitch, B—coral French Knot, C—light coral Satin Stitch, D—light coral French Knot, E—green Fly Stitch, F—green Feather Stitch, G—light green Fly Stitch, H—light green Feather Stitch

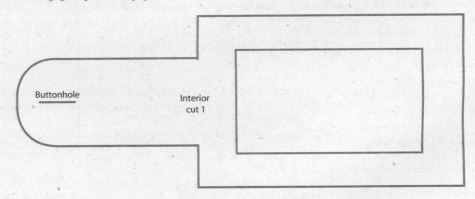

Interior pattern piece. Enlarge 121%.

6. Join the layers at the buttonhole by sewing around the edges of the slit with Whip Stitches, keeping the stitches very close together.

7. Sew the button to the embroidered side of the holder, centered ¾ inch (1.9 cm) in from the edge (figure 3).

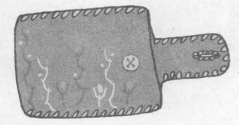

Figure 3

Mod Napkins

The dinner table will be fashionably outfitted with these retro embroidered napkins.

WHAT YOU NEED

Circles and Dots design

20-inch square (50.8 cm) linen napkins

Embroidery floss, 1 skein each of aqua and red*

The author used DMC embroidery floss in colors 321 and 598.

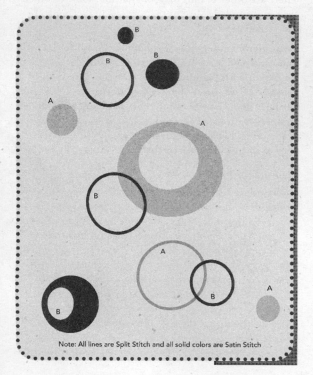

Note: All lines are Split Stitch and all solid colors are Satin Stitch

Circles and Dots design. Key: A-aqua, B-red. Enlarge 135%

STITCHES

Satin Stitch

Split Stitch

INSTRUCTIONS

Note: You can make a different version of this pattern by flipping it around and switching which shapes are red and aqua.

1. Transfer the Circles and Dots design to a corner of each napkin.

2. Embroider the design.

Mine All Mine Towel

Give your towel a dazzling personality.

WHAT YOU NEED

Mine design

Bath towel with a smooth surface (low nap), at least 20 inches (50.8 cm) wide

White carbon paper

Nonpermanent white fabric marking pen

Embroidery floss, 2 skeins of light purple and 1 skein of metallic silver*

The author used DMC embroidery floss in colors 3743 and Light Effects (Jewel) E168.

STITCHES

Center Point Star Stitch

Satin Stitch

Straight Stitch

13-74

INSTRUCTIONS

Note: Metallic thread will make your design extra sparkly. It can be difficult to work with, however, so it's better to use it only for accents, such as the stars in this design.

1. Using white carbon paper, transfer the Mine design to one end of the towel, centering it in the border area 1 to 2 inches (2.5 to 5.1 cm) from the edge. You may find transferring the design onto a fluffy towel challenging. Be sure to work on a hard surface and don't worry if your carbon paper tears. After you get the basic shapes onto the towel, trace over the transferred marks with the fabric pen.

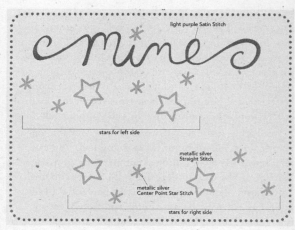

light purple Satin Stitch

stars for left side

metallic silver Straight Stitch

metallic silver Center Point Star Stitch

stars for right side

Mine design

2. Embroider the design. Notice how the direction of the lines of Satin Stitches change as the lines curve and become thicker and thinner. You want your stitching to do the same as you work along the lines. You may want to stitch over the lines twice to make them stand out against the long fibers of the terry cloth.

—From *Doodle-Stitching*

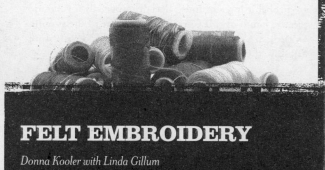

FELT EMBROIDERY

Donna Kooler with Linda Gillum

Introduction

Felted fabric is versatile, useful, and great fun to work with. You can cut it, shape it, and poke it with needles, as well as paint it, glue it, and stitch it. The bold colors of this smooth surface perfectly complement embroidery work, allowing the yarn, or thread to really pop....

In the Basics section, you'll learn about all the materials and techniques you need to make the finished designs. You'll learn how to cut the felt in the provided patterns, layer the pieces in complementary colors, and embroider them with fanciful swirls, beautiful borders, and decorative stitches. Embroidery and felt go together so well because felt has no grain: It's easy to embroider intricate designs in any shape, without worrying about how the fabric will react.

The projects will inspire you to experiment, and with so many possibilities, you'll never lack for ideas.

Every day is a very good day to indulge in making this wonderful traditional art and craft with modern flair. So select a project, pick up a needle, and discover that wherever you go around the wide world, felt, embroidery, and your own creative fancy go together beautifully.

Basics

Materials

To complete the projects,... you'll need supplies. First and foremost on the list is felt fabric, but on the following pages, you'll find descriptions of all the basic materials and supplies.

Continued ➡

Felt Fabric

Felt is made from loose webs of natural or synthetic fibers that are locked together by the combination of moisture, heat, and repeated pressure to create a wonderful fabric for clothing as well as art and craft projects. With no raw edges, felt doesn't ravel, which makes it ideal for many craft projects. You can use three types of felt for the projects…: wool felt, wool/rayon felt, and synthetic felt.

Wool felt is made from natural fibers. Available in many colors, it has a beautiful look and feel. You can purchase it locally or online as cut pieces or as yardage. Yardage widths vary, so note the width before you buy. Wool/rayon blend felt resembles 100 percent wool felt, but is less expensive because of the addition of rayon fibers. Projects made with wool or wool/rayon felt should be dry-cleaned.

Synthetic felt is made from 100 percent acrylic fiber and comes in many colors. Very reasonably priced, it is available in local craft and fabric stores as well as online. Like the other types of felt, you can buy it as cut pieces or as yardage, usually 72 inches (182.9 cm) wide. While you can hand- and machine-wash it, you should lay it flat to dry.

Other Materials

You'll need just a few other things to make the wonderful creations in this section, although most of these materials are probably in your house already, especially if you enjoy creative handwork. If you don't have some of the supplies on the list, a quick trip to your neighborhood craft store will solve the problem.

- Wool embroidery yarn (e.g., Paternayan yarn)
- Embroidery floss (e.g., DMC floss)
- Measuring tape or ruler
- Pencil
- Freezer paper
- Tracing paper
- Straight pins
- Large sewing scissors
- Small embroidery scissors
- Water-erasable marking pen
- Sewing thread in colors to match your felt
- Sewing and tapestry needles
- Nap riser brush
- Polyester fiberfill
- Rotary cutter, clear ruler, and cutting mat (optional)
- Sewing machine (optional)
- Fabric glue

Basic Techniques

Got your supplies on hand? You'll also need to know some basic (as in simple and easy-to-learn) techniques to make the projects you'll find in this book. The following sections begin with general techniques for cutting felt and working with patterns, and then move on to step-by-step instructions for constructing bags, pillows, purses,… and more.

Using a Rotary Cutter

Cut straight lines through fabrics quickly and easily with a rotary cutter, a self-healing mat, and a clear plastic ruler. Often, these tools are sold as a set. Review the instructions included in the package. Here are a few things to remember when working with a rotary cutter:

- The blade is very sharp, so be sure to engage the safety guard when the cutter is not in use, even if you lay it down for just a minute! Also, keep the cutter out of the reach of children and pets.

- Make sure the blade is sharp and free of fabric bits. If the cutter isn't working properly, check that the nut holding the blade is not too tight or too loose.

- Lay your fabric on the self-healing mat and line up the clear ruler with the lines on the mat. Press firmly on the ruler with your non-dominant hand, taking care that your fingers are not too close to the cutting edge. Hold the rotary cutter with your dominant hand and stand so that your head is directly over the blade and you can see the cutting line. Position the blade next to the ruler, but lean the top slightly away from the ruler. Always cut away from your body by pressing and rolling the blade along the edge of the ruler. Peel away the cut fabric and continue with your next cut.

- You can stack fabric layers to cut multiple pieces at one time, but make sure the layers are not too thick or the cutter might bunch the fabric or cut inaccurately.

Making Pattern Pieces

You can choose from a variety of ways to make pattern pieces:

- If you're making a simple shape, trace the pattern onto tracing paper. Pin the tracing paper onto the felt and cut out the shape. Leave the pattern pinned to the felt until you're ready to use it.

- Freezer paper also makes easy-to-use pattern pieces. Trace the shape onto the smooth side of the freezer paper and cut loosely around the tracing. Place the shiny or waxy side of the paper on the felt and press it lightly with an iron. The freezer paper will stick to the felt and make the shape easy to cut.

- For patterns with embroidery designs, transfer the pattern and the embroidery design at the same time, using the transfer method described below.

Transferring Designs

Trace the design onto tracing paper. Poke small holes in the paper about ⅛ inch (3 mm) apart along the design lines. Gently dab inside each hole with a water-erasable marking pen to leave a mark through the tracing paper onto the felt. Remove the tracing paper and if the design is hard to read, connect the dots with the marking pen.

Constructing a Basic Pillow

1. After completing the embroidery on the pillow top, pin the top and bottom, with right sides together. Sew the front to the back using the recommended seam allowance and a thread that matches the color of the pillow top. Leave a 5-inch (12.7 cm) opening for turning along the bottom edge. If you are stitching by hand, use a backstitch.

2. Turn the pillow right side out. Stuff it with polyester fiberfill to the desired fullness. Pin and hand-stitch the opening closed.

Constructing a Purse

1. Cut one strap of each color to 60 x 1½ inches (152.4 x 3.8 cm). Sew the end of each strap together using a ¼-inch (6 mm) seam to form a complete circle.

Figure 1

2. Place the straps wrong sides together, matching the seams. Pin them in place (figure 1).

3. Stitch the edges together using a ¼-inch (6 mm) seam.

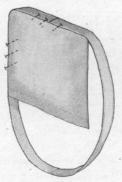

Figure 2

4. Pin the embellished front onto the contrasting piece of felt. Sew along the top using a ½-inch (1.3 cm) seam. Repeat for the back piece.

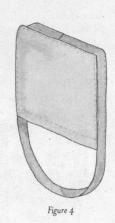

Figure 3   Figure 4

5. Position the seam on the strap at the center of the purse's bottom edge (figure 2). Pin the strap to the purse front piece.

6. Stitch the purse front to the strap using a ¼-inch (6 mm) seam (figure 3). Then pin the strap to the purse back piece.

7. Stitch the purse back to the strap using a ¼-inch (6 mm) seam (figure 4).

Basic Embroidery

Here is everything you need to know about hand embroidery.

Embroidery Threads

The projects… use either crewel wool or cotton-embroidery floss. For some projects, you may choose to use either thread. We've provided colors and numbers for both Paternayan Persian wool yarn and DMC embroidery floss. If we've listed only one or the other, it's because that thread suits the design better. When you have a choice, the first thread listed is the thread we used for the project, the one shown in the photo.

When substituting threads, adapt the strands as follows:

1 strand wool = 6 strands floss

2 strands wool = 12 strands floss

Crewel wool gives embroidery a lush, rich look. It shows more texture than floss and is good for larger projects because it covers an area quickly. It comes in a beautiful array of colors and can be purchased at local stores or online. Paternayan wool is sold as three strands, which can be separated as indicated in the project instructions. It is sold in small skeins of 8 yards (7.3 m) and in larger hanks with the amount varying depending on the source. There are other brands of wool available, some of which are two-stranded. Most of the projects in this book use one strand of wool.

Cotton embroidery floss is a popular thread for embroidery, and rightly so. It's inexpensive, washable, and easy for beginners to handle. Plus, it comes in hundreds of colors. The two most popular manufacturers, DMC and Anchor, offer the greatest number of colors, while other companies specialize in unique threads, such as hand-dyed colors. Floss is sold in six-stranded skeins. Most designs in this book use six strands of floss.

Embroidery Tools

Embroidery needles are the most essential tools in embroidery. Poorly made needles have small imperfections, so buy the highest quality you can afford to ensure yourself a pleasurable stitching experience. The size of the needle is important. A needle that's too small might damage the thread because the thread won't slide easily through the eye. A needle that's too large might leave holes in the fabric and produce sloppy stitches. Buy a package of embroidery needles with several different sizes and slide the thread through the eye of a few different ones to find the right size. Keep in mind that the larger the needle number size, the smaller the eye of the needle.

Crewel needles are basic to embroidery. These average-length needles have long-oval eyes and sharp points for piercing fabric. Use crewel needles for all the designs in this book. A size 22 needle is a good size for most threads.

A thimble protects your middle fingertips as you stitch. It's a personal choice; some stitchers wouldn't stitch without one, while others find them distracting. Practice with a thimble to see if you like it and don't give up right away. It takes time to get used to it.

A thread organizer keeps your embroidery threads clean and untangled. The simplest solution is a set of labeled, plastic resealable bags. If you do a lot of stitching, invest in a large sectioned box designed just for stitchers.

Stretcher bars or hoops are frequently used in traditional embroidery to keep fabric taut during stitching. In this book, all the projects are stitched on felt, which might stretch when it is pulled, so stretcher bars and hoops are not used. Instead, hold the felt in your hands during embroidery.

Embroidery scissors are small and sharp. Keep them separate from your other scissors and only use them for embroidery so they stay clean and sharp. Keep them in a sheath to protect the points (and your hands!).

Embroidery Techniques

Here are the basic techniques you'll need to understand to embroider.

Separating floss or wool strands, also known as "plying," is often the first step. It separated and prepares the number of strands you need to stitch each area. Separating the strands before stitching helps them fluff out to cover the fabric better. Even if you intent to stitch with the remaining strands on your length of floss, separate and recombine them nevertheless.

To straighten the strands, locate a loose, cut end of a skein of six-stranded floss or three-stranded wool and cut a length not longer than 18 inches (45.7 cm). Hold the thread at one end and "fan out" the individual strands; select one strand and pull it out. Repeat with the remaining strands and straighten each one after each separation. Place the strands together and thread them through the needle.

Threading the needle is another vital skill. Pinch the floss ends together tightly between your thumb and forefinger (or thumb and middle finger) with fingernails touching, allowing the warmth of your fingers to press the floss ends as flat as possible. Roll your fingers back to expose the ends, and insert them into the needle's eye.

Securing the thread is necessary to begin and end a section of stitching. The debate among stitchers is whether to knot or not. Pro-knotters suggest that if the design features raised effects, why not knot? Anti-knotters believe that embroidery should look as flat as possible, and consider knots undesirable. Feel free to decide for yourself.

Eliminating the starting knots will ensure a clean look. Use an in-line waste knot when you begin a new thread. Plan the direction you'll be stitching, make a knot, and insert it (from the top of the fabric) along that same path, but further ahead of the first stitch. Stitch over the thread and clip the knot off just before you reach it. Sometimes using a knot is virtually unavoidable, such as when a French, Colonial, or Bullion Knot is isolated from other stitches. Try this nearly inconspicuous knot that appears as a tiny stitch on the right side of the fabric.

1. On the back of the fabric, pick up two (or so) fabric threads with the threaded needle to make the first stitch, leaving ¼-inch (6 mm) thread tail.

2. Take a backstitch at the same spot, but at a right angle to the first stitch.

3. Take another backstitch at the same spot in the same direction as the second stitch.

Begin and end individual threads as neatly as possible, as some projects show the back of your stitching. Do not carry threads from one area to another unless the distance if ⅛ inch (3 mm) or less. Even if the back of your project will be concealed by the finishing treatment, it's a good idea to minimize carrying threads between areas, especially if you are using a light-colored fabric.

Correcting mistakes is inevitable. As you stitch, you are bound to make stitches that you want to correct. You may have executed the stitch sequence incorrectly or simply produced a stitch that looks less than lovely.

In the first case, it's a good idea to pull out the offending stitches and re-stitch. In the second case, use your best judgment, keeping in mind that embroidery is a hand-done art form that is not intended to look as "perfect" as machine-done work.

If the stitches in question are few and you are still using the same thread, simply remove the needle and, working on the back of the fabric, gently pull the thread back through the fabric as far as you need to, then re-thread the needle and continue stitching. However, if you need to remove more than a few stitches, you will stress the thread and possibly ruin its appearance by pulling it through the fabric so many times. In this case, it's best to discard that particular thread and re-stitch with a new thread.

Ending the thread is the final step. To end a thread, turn your work over and weave the thread in and out of completed stitches of the same color. If the stitches are long and loose on the back (as with satin stitches), take one or two backstitches into the backs of the stitches (not into the fabric) to secure the thread. Avoid weaving a dark-colored thread through the back of light-colored areas.

Embroidery Stitches

You don't have to memorize these stitches because as you do more embroidery, they will become more and more familiar to you. Until then, refer to the instructive illustrations....

- Backstitch
- Blanket Stitch
- Chain Stitch
- Feather Stitch
- Fishbone Stitch
- Fly Stitch
- French Knot
- Herringbone Stitch
- Lazy Daisy
- Long and Short Stitch
- Outline Stitch
- Palestrina Stitch
- Running Stitch
- Satin Stitch
- Slipstitch
- Straight Stitch
- Whipped Spider Stitch
- Whipped Stem Stitch
- Whipstitch
- Woven Picot

Feather Stitch

A decorative line stitch, this works well on straight or curved lines. Work from the top to the bottom.

Feather stitch

Fishbone

Each time the needle returns to center, insert it slightly to the left or right of the central guideline.

Fishbone

Outline Stitch

Work from left to right, keeping the stitches the same size.

Outline stitch

Palestrina

A series of intricate knots that when finished create a line with a beaded look.

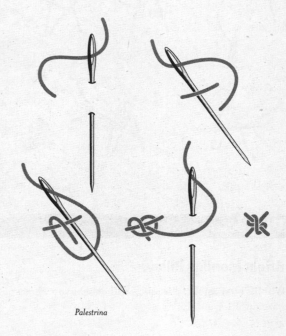

Palestrina

Whipped Backstitch

Stitch all backstitches. Then weave a whipping thread at one end over and under the backstitches without piercing the fabric.

Whipped Backstitch

Whipped Spider Stitch

A series of backstitches around a series of straight stitches, it resembles a wheel.

Continued ➔

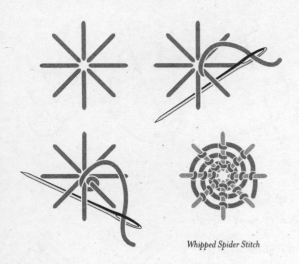

Whipped Spider Stitch

Whipped Stem Stitch

Complete evenly spaced Stem stitches. Then wrap it with a whipping thread without piercing the fabric.

Whipped Stem Stitch

Woven Picot

Make a loop on top of the fabric. Use a pin to hold the loop in place and weave the thread over and under the loop without piercing the fabric.

Woven Picot

Projects

Bright Morning Pillow

With its bold colors, this pillow will delight you when you wake up. Rise and shine!

What You Need

FELT

Yellow, 18 x 22 inches (45.7 x 55.9 cm)

Medium Blue, 16 x18 inches (40.6 x 45.7 cm)

Orange, 6 x 6 inches (15.2 x 15.2 cm)

Dark blue, 10 x 10 inches (25.4 x 25.4 cm)

Medium pink, 4 x 4 inches (10.2 x 10.2 cm)

DECORATIVE THREAD

Paternayan yarn or DMC embroidery floss

PATERNAYAN YARN

Pink (#962), 1 yard (91.4 cm)

Yellow (#770), 6 yards (5.5 m)

Green (#699), 1½ yards (1.4 m)

Blue (#552), ¾ yard (68.6 cm)

DMC EMBROIDERY FLOSS

Pink (#961), 1 yard (91.4 cm)

Yellow (#972), 6 yards (5.5 m)

Green (#700), 1½ yards (1.4 m)

Blue (#322), ¾ yard (68.6 cm)

Other Supplies

Straight pins

Sewing needle

Sewing thread, invisible or matching felt colors

Basting spray (optional)

Sewing machine

Polyester fiberfill

What You Do

1. Cut the yellow felt to 16 x 18 inches (40.6 x 45.7 cm), the same size as the piece of medium blue felt.

2. Transfer the patterns onto the felt, referring to the project photo for the correct colors. Cut them out.

3. Pin the orange shape A onto the yellow square. Pin the yellow square onto the dark blue felt. See the project photo for placement.

4. Pin the orange shape B onto the dark blue felt the slipstitch it in place with orange sewing thread.

5. Pin the finished dark blue felt piece onto the medium blue pillow top and slipstitch it in place with dark blue sewing thread.

6. Stitch the petal according to the project photo. Pin the flower to the pillow top at the opening in the border marking; slipstitch it in place with pink sewing thread.

7. Mark where the flower stem will go on the pillow top, using the project photo for guidance. Stitch it down according to the stitch instructions on the project photo.

8. Refer to the stitch instructions in the project photo for the border.

9. Pin the wrong side of the medium blue pillow top to the yellow pillow back and mark a stitching line 1 inch (2.5 cm) from all the sides. See Constructing a Basic Pillow for finishing instructions.

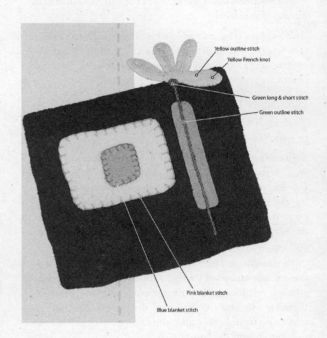

Yellow outline stitch
Yellow French knot
Green long & short stitch
Green outline stitch
Pink blanket stitch
Blue blanket stitch

Bright Morning Pillow patterns. Enlarge to desired size.

Rainbow Band Bracelet

This bright bangle will show off your stitching and dazzle your friends.

What You Need

FELT

Fuchsia, 12 x 4 inches (30.5 x 10.2 cm)

DECORATIVE THREAD

DMC embroidery floss, 1 yard (91.4 cm) each

    Yellow Orange (#742)

    Orange (#970)

    Green (#704)

    Purple (#208)

    Turquoise (#996)

    Light Fuchsia (#3609)

OTHER SUPPLIES

Strip of 14-count plastic canvas, 12 x 1¼ inches (30.5 x 3.2 cm), or a piece of Buckram, 12 x 3¾ inches (30.5 x 9.5 cm)

Sewing needle

Sewing thread, invisible or matching felt

Straight Pins

What You Do

1. Measure your wrist and add 4 to 5 inches (10.2 to 12.7 cm) so the bracelet will slip over your hand. Cut the piece of 14-count plastic canvas or Buckram to this length. If you are using plastic canvas, overlap the short ends by 1 inch (2.5 cm) and stitch them firmly closed using floss or strong thread. If you're using Buckram, fold it in thirds lengthwise to provide more stiffness before overlapping and stitching. This piece should be able to slip over your hand. Set the piece aside.

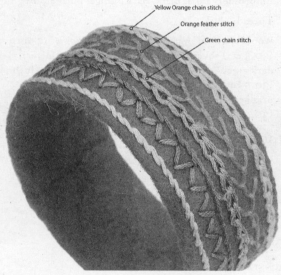

Yellow Orange chain stitch
Orange feather stitch
Green chain stitch

14–16

Purple outline stitch
Turquoise straight stitch in a zigzag pattern
Light Fuchsia outline stitch

2. Cut the fuchsia felt 2½ inches (6.4 cm) wide by the length of the bracelet from step 1, plus ¼ inch (6 mm).

3. Copy the stitching lines onto the felt using the project photo as a reference.

4. Refer to the stitch instructions on the project photo.

5. Center the embroidered felt, wrong side down, over the plastic bracelet and turn under one short end ⅛ inch (3 mm). Position the folded felt edge away from the overlapped plastic or Buckram ends to minimize bulk and slipstitch it to the bracelet with matching sewing thread.

6. Bring the other short end around to the folded, stitched-down edge. Fold this end under so that the felt is taut and slipstitch it down right next to the first folded edge.

7. Wrap the sides to the inside of the bracelet. Make sure the felt is taut; trim it if necessary to smooth the right side. Pin it down and ladder stitch the edges together with matching sewing thread.

Starry Night Headband

Out for a night on the town? Make the rounds while these flashy stars orbit your head.

What You Need

FELT

Red, 4 x 23 (10.2 x 58.4 cm)

Black, 4 x 23 inches (10.2 x 58.4 cm)

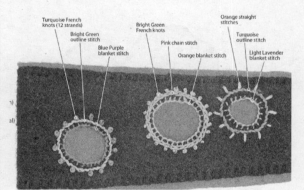

Turquoise French knots (12 strands)
Bright Green outline stitch
Blue Purple blanket stitch
Bright Green French knots
Pink chain stitch
Orange blanket stitch
Orange straight stitches
Turquoise outline stitch
Light Lavender blanket stitch

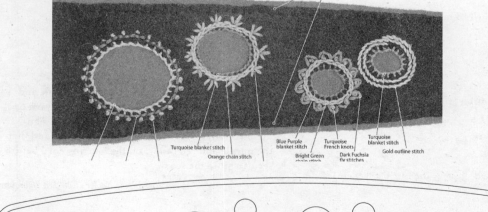

Turquoise blanket stitch
Orange chain stitch
Bright Green chain stitch
Blue Purple blanket stitch
Dark Fuchsia fly stitches
Turquoise French knots
Turquoise blanket stitch
Gold outline stitch

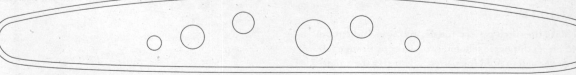

Starry Night Headband pattern. Enlarge to desired size.

DECORATIVE THREAD

DMC embroidery floss, one skein each

    Turquoise (#3844)

    Light Lavender (#210)

    Orange (#970)

    Pink (#602)

    Dark Fuchsia (#3804)

    Bright Green (#907)

    Gold (#728)

    Blue Purple (#3746)

    Black (#310)

OTHER SUPPLIES

Small, sharp scissors

Black elastic, 3 x 1 inch (7.6 x 2.5 cm)

Basting spray

Sewing needle and thread (optional)

Sewing machine (optional)

What You Do

1. Transfer the headband pattern, use the outside line for the red felt and the inside line for the black felt. Cut them out. Copy the stitch designs from the project photo onto the black felt. The circles do not have to be in the same exact locations. Carefully cut out the circles along the markings.

2. Add stitching around the circles as instructed in the following steps, but don't stitch the blanket stitches until you've joined the two headband pieces. Refer to the stitch instructions in the project photos.

3. Start with the starburst design at the right end of the first project photo and follow the stitches for the first three circles.

4. Flip around the headband and continue from left to right with the last four circles, as shown above. Then center the embroidered black felt piece over the red piece and blanket stitch them together. Blanket stitch inside each circle to attach the two pieces.

5. Using an embroidery needle or a sewing machine, attach one end of the elastic to one end of the headband. Try the headband on and pin the elastic to the opposite end to make it fit comfortably. Take the headband off and sew the elastic in place either by hand or by machine.

Continued ➡

Floral Whimsy Purse

Sparkling sequins surround a delightful flower to brighten your day. A tassel adds to the fun.

WHAT YOU NEED

FELT

Purple, ¾ yard (68.6 cm)

Orange, ¾ yard (68.6 cm)

DECORATIVE THREAD

Paternayan yarn or DMC embroidery floss

Paternayan yarn

Yellow (#772), 1 yard (81.4 cm)

Light Orange (#814), 4 yards (3.7 m)

Black (#220), 1 yard (91.4 cm)

Green (#669), 1 yard (91.4 cm)

Red (#97), 1 yard (91.4 cm)

DMC embroidery floss

Yellow (#743), 1 yard (91.4 cm)

Light Orange (#742), 4 yards (3.7 m)

Black (#310), 1 yard (91.4 cm)

Green (#701), 1 yard (91.4 cm)

Red (#817), 1 yard (91.4 cm)

BEADS AND JEWELS

5 red flat-backed jewels, 4–5 mm

Pink flat-backed jewel, 7–8 mm

Package of multicolor flower sequins

Large green bead

Purple pony bead, ¼ inch (6 mm)

Red pony bead, ¼ inch (6 mm)

OTHER SUPPLIES

Fabric glue

Sewing machine

Sewing thread in invisible, purple, and orange, or matching bead colors

Straight pins

Sewing needle

Lightweight cardboard, 3 x 3¼ inch (7.6 x 8.3 cm)

WHAT YOU DO

1. Make the stitch pattern the desired size, and cut out two pieces of purple felt and two pieces or orange felt large enough to hold the pattern. Transfer the stitch pattern to one piece of the purple felt.

2. Stitch the design according to the project photo.

Floral Whimsy Purse pattern. Enlarge to desired size.

3. Refer to Constructing a Purse under "Basic Techniques" for detailed instructions for cutting, assembling, and finishing the purse. Use matching color floss and thread. Add the beads and sequins as shown in the project photo.

Flower sequin and gold bead

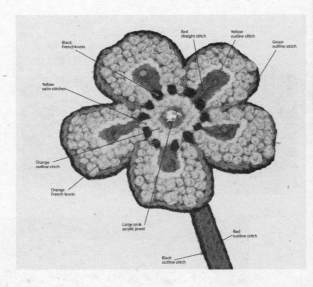

Black French knots

Yellow satin stitches

Red straight stitch

Yellow outline stitch

Green outline stitch

Orange outline stitch

Orange French knots

Large pink acrylic jewel

Red outline stitch

Black outline stitch

4. Make a 3¼-inch (8.3 cm) tassel with Purple and Orange yarn or floss for the tassel and Black yarn or floss as the hanging cord and to attach the tassel to the purse strap. Thread the green bead first, and then the purple and red beads, on the hanging cord before securing it to the strap.

—*From Donna Kooler's Kool Felt Embroidery*

EMBROIDERED HALLOWEEN PROJECTS

Bethany Lowe

Trick-or-Treat Table Runner

Halloween is the perfect time to add a touch of whimsy to your home. This table runner features a scaredy cat and petrified pumpkin. Made from wool in a layered style and appliquéd using a blanket stitch, this runner is similar to penny rugs that were made in the United States during the Civil War. The layering technique adds color and dimension to any project. Remember that wool runners are for decorative use and not recommended for areas where food is served or eaten. They are dry clean only.

MATERIALS

Chenille needle: size 20

Embroidery floss: black, dark orange, purple, soft gold

Thread: black

Wool: black—1½ yards (1.37 meters); brown—12-inch (30.5 cm) square; dark gold—½ yard (0.46 meter); dark green—½ yard (0.46 meter); dark red—12-inch (30.5 cm) square; gold—12-inch (30.5 cm) square; orange—12-inch (30.5 cm) square; purple—12-inch (30.5 cm) square; white—12-inch (30.5 cm) square

TOOLS

Computer and printer or color copier

Ruler

Scissors: craft, embroidery

Sewing machine

INSTRUCTIONS

RUNNER

1. From black wool, cut one 12¾ x 37-inch (32.4 x 94 cm) piece, one 12¾-inch (32.4 cm) square, and one 8½ x 13-inch (21.6 x 33 cm) piece. From dark green wool, cut two 3 x 13-inch (7.6 x 33 cm) pieces.

2. Starting at the seam on the top side of the runner, sew the green strips to the smallest black rectangle with ¼-inch (6 mm) seams. Sew the black squares on each end with a ½-inch (1.3 cm) seam. Do not attach the back panel.

SQUARE EMBELLISHMENTS

1. Using the Large and Small Square templates, cut six large squares from purple wool and six small squares from gold wool.

2. Using three strands of black embroidery floss, sew the small gold squares on top of the large purple squares with a blanket stitch.

3. Using three strands of soft gold embroidery floss, appliqué the purple squares to the background in two rows of three with the top row along the seam, joining the end pieces to the middle piece with a blanket stitch.

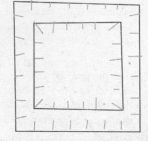

Large and Small Square. Enlarge 125%.

CAT EMBELLISHMENTS

1. Using the Cat Background template, cut one shape from dark green wool. Using the Cat Face template, cut one shape from black wool.

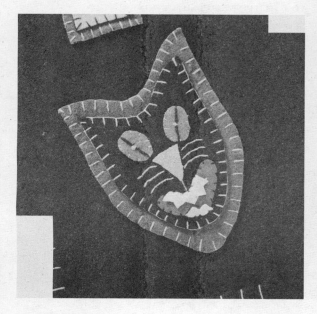

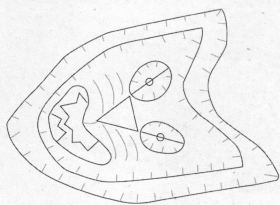

Cat Background, Car Face, Cat Eyes, Cat Nose, Cat Mouth. Enlarge 175%. Gray lines denote stitching pattern.

2. Using the Cat Eyes template, cut two shapes from dark gold wool. Using the Cat Nose template, cut one shape from gold wool. Using the Cat Mouth template, cut one mouth shape from dark red wool and one of each teeth shape from white wool.

3. Center the black cat face over the green cat background. Using three strands of soft gold embroidery floss, sew the pieces together with a blanket stitch.

4. Position the mouth and sew to the face with a backstitch using three strands of black embroidery floss.

5. Position the eyes and nose on the face and sew on with an appliqué stitch using three strands of soft gold embroidery floss. Add a French knot in the center of each eye.

6. Using three strands of soft gold embroidery floss, sew the finished cat face to the runner with a blanket stitch.

7. Using three strands of soft gold embroidery stitch. Using three strands of black embroidery floss, form the lines through the eyes with a couching stitch.

8. Repeat steps 1–7 for the cat on the opposite end of the runner.

PUMPKIN EMBELLISHMENTS

1. Using the Pumpkin template, cut one shape from orange wool. Using the Pumpkin Eyes template, cut two large shapes from white wool and two small shapes from brown wool.

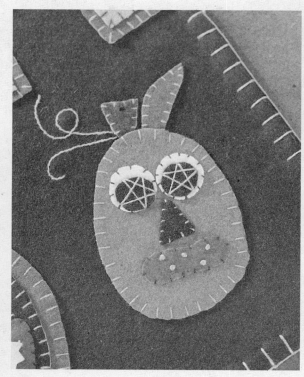

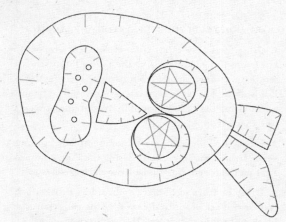

Pumpkin, Pumpkin Eyes, Pumpkin Nose, Pumpkin Stem, Pumpkin Leaf. Enlarge 175%.

2. Using the Pumpkin Nose template, cut one shape from black wool. Using the Pumpkin Mouth template, cut one shape from dark red wool.

3. Using the Pumpkin Stem template, cut one shape from brown wool. Using the Pumpkin Leaf template, cut one shape from dark green wool.

4. Using three strands of black embroidery floss, add white eye shapes to the pumpkin with appliqué stitching. Using three strands of soft gold embroidery floss, sew the brown eye shapes to the white eye shapes with stitches in the shape of a star.

5. Using three strands of soft gold embroidery floss, sew the nose on the pumpkin with appliqué stitching. Using three strands of black embroidery floss, sew the mouth on the pumpkin with appliqué stitching. Using three strands of soft gold embroidery floss, add French knots to the mouth.

6. Position the pumpkin, stem, and leaf on the runner and sew on using three strands of soft gold embroidery floss and blanket stitching. Using two strands of soft gold embroidery floss, stitch the pumpkin vine with running stitches.

7. Repeat steps 1–6 for the pumpkin on the opposite side of the runner.

BAT EMBELLISHMENTS

1. Using the Bat Background template, cut one shape from gold wool. Using the Bat Body template, cut one shape from black wool.

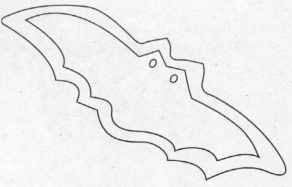

Bat Background, Bat Body. Enlarge 125%. Gray lines denote stitching pattern.

2. Using three strands of soft gold embroidery floss, sew the bat background to the runner with appliqué stitching.

3. Using black embroidery floss, sew the bat body to the bat background using appliqué stitching.

4. Using two strands of soft gold embroidery floss, sew the eyes to the bat face.

5. Repeat steps 1–4 for the bats on the opposite side of the runner.

CANDY CORN EMBELLISHMENTS

1. Using the Candy Corn Base template, cut five shapes from gold wool. Using the Candy Corn Tip template, cut five shapes from white wool.

2. Layer the white shapes on the gold shapes and sew to the runner using three strands of soft gold embroidery floss with appliqué stitching. Using three strands of dark orange embroidery floss, embellish each layered shape with satin stitching around the center of the shapes.

Candy Corn Base, Candy Corn Tip. Enlarge 125%.

3. Using three strands of purple embroidery floss, create the vine with running stitches. Add French knots using dark orange and gold embroidery floss.

4. Repeat steps 1–3 for the candy corn on the opposite side of the runner.

Continued ➡

TO FINISH THE RUNNER

1. Place the right side of the front and back runner pieces together and machine stitch with ¼-inch (6 mm) seam. Make sure to leave an open area to turn the piece right side out.

2. Turn the runner right side out and blanket stitch around the edges using six strands of soft gold embroidery floss.

Crazy Quilt Pumpkin Pillow

Beautiful embroidery and hand stitching make this pillow a true piece of history. It features a log cabin block border and embroidery techniques that have evolved over time. The combination of deep fall foliage colors lends richness and charm. Spider webs and spiders are two of the most-often-used symbols appearing on early Victorian needlework quilts or pillows. Today, they provide an ideal Halloween background.

MATERIALS

Beads: large black (4); small black iridescent (11); small white pearl (approximately 130)

Chenille needle: size 20

Embroidery floss: black, burnt orange, dark red, ecru, gold, light green

Graphite paper

Polyester fiberfill

Thread: black

Wool: black—6½-inch (16.5 cm) square; 12-inch (30.5 cm) square; plus 3-inch (7.6 cm) square for spider; dark green—2½ x 13½-inch (6.4 x 34.3 cm) piece plus small piece for leaf; gold—2 x 8-inch (5.1 x 20.3 cm) piece; light green—2½ x 9½-inch (6.4 x 24.2 cm) piece plus small piece for stem; orange—2 x 6½-inch (5.1 x 16.5 cm) piece plus small piece for pumpkin; orange-and-black plaid—2 x 9½-inch (5.1 x 24.2 cm) piece; purple—2½ x 11½-inch (6.4 x 29.2 cm) piece; purple-and-black plaid—2½ x 11½-inch (6.4 x 29.2 cm) piece; red—small scrap; rust—2 x 8-inch (5.1 x 20.3 cm) piece plus small piece for eyes; white—3-inch (7.6 cm) square

TOOLS

Computer and printer or color copier

Ruler

Scissors: craft, embroidery

Sewing machine

INSTRUCTIONS

TO FORM THE QUILT SQUARE PILLOW TOP

1. Machine stitch a ¼-inch (6 mm) seam attaching the strips in the following order, beginning with the left side of the black square: orange, rust, gold, orange-and-black plaid, light green, purple-and-black plaid, purple, and dark green. **Note**: You will be progressing in a clockwise fashion.

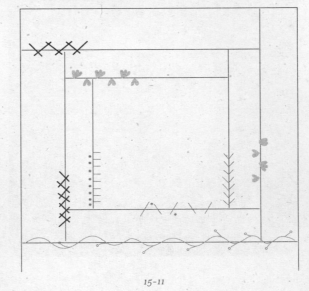

15-11

TO MAKE AND ATTACH THE PUMPKIN TO THE PILLOW TOP

1. Using the Pillow Pumpkin template, cut one pumpkin from orange wool. Using the Pillow Pumpkin Eyes template, cut two shapes from rust wool. Using the Pillow Pumpkin Nose template, cut one shape from red wool. Using the Pillow Pumpkin Teeth template, cut one shape from white wool.

2. Using the Pillow Pumpkin Stem template, cut one shape from light green wool. Using the Pillow Pumpkin Leaf template, cut one shape from dark green wool.

3. Using one strand of black embroidery floss, attach two large black beads to the eyes. Using two strands of black embroidery floss, sew the eyes and nose to the pumpkin face with a backstitch.

4. Using two strands of dark red embroidery floss, stitch the teeth on the white mouth with a backstitch. Using two strands of ecru embroidery floss, appliqué the mouth to the pumpkin with a backstitch.

5. Using the project photograph for reference, position the pumpkin on the pillow top. Using two strands of black embroidery floss, appliqué the pumpkin to the pillow top with a blanket stitch. **Note**: The stitches shown are ¼ inch (6 mm) long.

6. Using two strands of light green embroidery floss, stitch the vein on the leaf with a backstitch then appliqué the leaf to the pillow top using a backstitch.

7. Using two strands of black embroidery floss, appliqué the light green stem to the top of the pumpkin with a backstitch.

TO STITCH VINES AROUND PUMPKIN

1. Using two strands of light green embroidery floss, sew the vines with a backstitch. Using gold embroidery floss, add French knots to the vines.

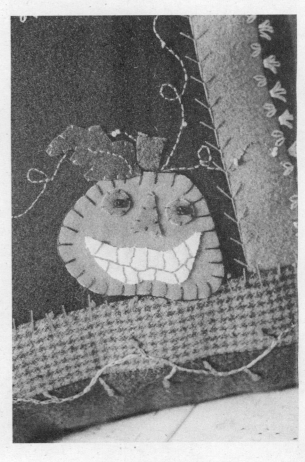

Pillow Pumpkin, Pillow Pumpkin Eyes, Pillow Pumpkin Nose, Pillow Pumpkin Teeth, Pillow Pumpkin Stem, Pillow Pumpkin Leaf. Enlarge 125%. Gray lines denote stitching pattern.

TO SEW BORDER STITCHES

1. Using three strands of burnt orange embroidery floss, sew a fern stitch on the border of the black center square and rust wool.

2. Using three strands of gold embroidery floss, sew a lazy daisy stitch in loops of two and three along the borders of the rust and black wool and gold and purple wool. **Note**: The stitches shown are ¼ inch (6 mm) long with the center three stitches slightly longer.

3. Using four strands of light green embroidery floss, sew a chain stitch along the bottom of the pillow top to create a vine. Using two strands of dark red embroidery floss, add French knots to the ends of the light green vine.

4. Using two strands of dark red embroidery floss, straight stitch along the top of the bottom border and the left side of the black center square. Randomly add 40–45 long and short stitches and 40–45 French knots.

5. Using three strands of black embroidery floss, add a herringbone stitch on the right side border of the light green strip and the bottom border of the black-and-purple plaid strip. **Note**: The stitches shown are ½ inch (1.3 cm) long.

TO MAKE AND ATTACH SPIDER WEB AND SPIDER

1. Using the Pillow Spider Web template and graphite paper, trace the design onto the pillow. Using one strand of ecru embroidery floss, sew the web design using a chain stitch. Add the small white pearl beads along the web.

2. Using the Pillow Spider Body template, cut the spider from black wool. Using one stand of black embroidery floss, sew the small black iridescent beads in a cluster on the spider's back, then sew two large black beads on the head for eyes.

3. Position the spider as shown. Using two strands of black embroidery floss, appliqué the spider onto the web with a backstitch. Using two strands of black embroidery floss, chain stitch eight legs onto the spider.

15-14

Pillow spider web

TO FORM THE PILLOW

1. Place the right sides of the pillow top and the 12-inch (30.5 cm) black wool square together and machine stitch using a ¼-inch (6 mm) seam. Leave an opening at the bottom of the pillow for turning and stuffing.

2. Turn right side out and stuff the pillow with polyester fiberfill. Hand sew the opening closed with black thread.

Pillow spider body

Door Hangers

Adorn your doorknobs or add these little pillows to a Halloween vignette on a shelf or side table. You can also fill them with potpourri for a touch of fall fragrance. Their harvest moon and window light will case a ghostly spell on all who enter.

Frightfully Fun Feline

MATERIALS

Beads: small amber (2); small white (1)

Embroidery floss: black, ecru

Polyester fiberfill

Ribbon: black-and-white polka dot 12 inches (30.5 cm)

Thread: black

Wool: black—7 x 9-inch (17.8 x 22.9 cm) pieces (2) plus 6-inch (15.2 cm) square; gold—4½ x 6¼-inch (11.4 x 15.8 cm) piece; white—5 x 7-inch (12.7 x 17.8 cm) piece

TOOLS

Computer and printer or color copier

Needles: chenille size 20, sewing

Ruler

Scissors: craft, embroidery

Sewing machine

INSTRUCTIONS

TO MAKE THE FRIGHTFULLY FUN FELINE DOOR HANGER

1. Using the Moon template, cut one shape from gold wool. Using the Cat template, cut one shape from black wool. Using the Fence template, cut one shape from white wool.

2. Using three strands of ecru embroidery floss, sew the moon to 7 x 9-inch (17.8 x 22.9 cm) piece of black wool. **Note**: This is the pillow top. Our stitches are ¼ inch (6 mm) long. The moon is 1¼ inches (3.2 cm) from the top and is centered on its sides.

3. Using two strands of black embroidery floss, sew the cat to the moon with blanket stitching, making sure to center the cat on the moon. Sew on amber beads for the eyes and a white bead for the nose. Using two strands of ecru embroidery floss, chain stitch three whiskers on each side of the cat's face.

4. Position the fence on the pillow top overlapping the moon and cat's paws. (The bottom edge of the fence is 1¼ inches (3.2 cm) from the edge of the pillow.) Using two strands of black embroidery floss, sew the fence to the pillow top using blanket stitching.

Continued ➡

365

Craft Wisdom & Know-How

Moon, Cat, and Fence. Enlarge 125%.

TO FINISH THE FRIGHTFULLY FUN FELINE DOOR HANGER

1. Place the right sides of two 7 x 9-inch (17.8 x 22.9 cm) pieces of black wool together and machine stitch together with a ¼-inch (6 mm) seam. Leave an opening at the bottom for turning and stuffing.

2. Turn right side out and stuff the pillow with polyester fiberfill. Hand sew the opening closed with black thread.

3. Using six strands of ecru thread, blanket stitch the edges of the pillow. Our blanket stitch is 3/8 inch (9 mm) long.

4. Cut two 6-inch (15.2 cm) pieces of ribbon. Stitch one piece on each top corner of the pillow. Tie the ribbons together at the top to form a bow.

Ghoulish Ghost

MATERIALS

Embroidery floss: black, ecru

Polyester fiberfill

Ribbon: black-and-white polka dot (12 inches [30.5 cm])

Thread: black

Wool: black—7 x 9-inch (17.8 x 22.9 cm) pieces (2) plus 6-inch (15.2 cm) square; gold—6 x 8-inch (15.2 x 20.3 cm) piece; white—4-inch (10.2 cm) square

TOOLS

Computer and printer or color copier

Needles: chenille size 20, sewing

Ruler

Scissors: craft, embroidery

Sewing machine

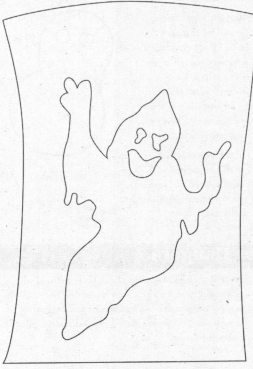

Window and Ghost. Enlarge 125%.

INSTRUCTIONS

TO MAKE THE GHOULISH GHOST DOOR HANGER

1. Using the Window template, cut one shape from gold wool.

2. Cut one ¾ x 1¼-inch (1.9 x 3.2 cm) piece of black wool.

3. Cut two ¼ x 4½-inch (6mm x 11.4 cm) strips and two ¼ x 6½-inch (6 mm x 16.5 cm) strips from black wool.

4. Using the Ghost template, cut one shape from white wool, and then cut out the mouth and eyes. Attach ¾ x 1¼-inch (1.9 x 3.2 cm) piece of black wool behind the open mouth and eyes of the ghost by overhand stitching around each opening using one strand of ecru embroidery floss.

5. Using two strands of black embroidery floss, stitch the black strips to the window shape using an overhand stitch.

6. Using three strands of ecru embroidery floss, stitch the window to one 7 x 9-inch (17.8 x 22.9 cm) pieces of black wool with blanket stitching. Note: Our blanket stitches are ¼ inch (6 mm) wide.

7. Using two strands of ecru embroidery floss, sew the ghost to the window with blanket stitching.

TO FINISH THE GHOULISH GHOST DOOR HANGER

1. Place the right sides of two 7 x 9-inch (17.8 x 22.9 cm) pieces of black wool together and machine stitch with a ¼-inch (6 mm) seam. Leave an opening at the bottom for turning and stuffing.

2. Cut two 6-inch (15.2 cm) pieces of ribbon. Stitch one piece on each top corner of the pillow. Tie the ribbons together at the top to form a bow.

3. Turn right side out and stuff the pillow with polyester fiberfill. Hand sew the opening closed with black thread.

4. Using six strands of ecru embroidery floss, blanket stitch around the edges of the pillow. Note: Our blanket stitches are ⅜ inch (9 mm) wide.

—FROM *Bethany Lowe's Folk Art Halloween*

Wood-working

WOODWORKING BASICS FOR BEGINNERS AND YOUNG WOODWORKERS

Kevin McGuire

Supplies & Tools

You don't need a shed that's stocked floor to ceiling with wood or a workshop full of the most expensive tools. Just start small and buy the supplies, tools, and wood you need for a single project.

Lumber

Lumber is the term used to describe wood—usually lots of it. But even if you're buying just one foot-long board for a project, it's called lumber. You can find lumber at your local lumberyard or home-improvement store. Standard lumber (the most commonly used boards) is sorted by type, grade, and size.

The grain of the wood (the thin, wavy lines that run along it) flows along the faces and edges of the board, and stops at the ends. Knowing the terms for these parts will help you understand how a project fits together.

TYPES OF LUMBER

There are two basic types of wood, softwoods and hardwoods. Pine, spruce, and fir trees are common sources of softwoods. Softwoods are light-colored, lightweight, and fairly strong. It's easy to hammer a nail into a softwood board. One drawback of softwoods is that sometimes they don't have a pretty grain. So they're best to use for projects that you want to paint.

Poplar and oak trees are common sources of hardwoods. Hardwoods are generally heavier and more durable than softwoods. They can cost more, too. Because hardwoods tend to have a pretty grain, use them for projects that you want to finish with a stain or varnish. If a project will look or work best using hardwood, the instructions will say so.

GRADES OF LUMBER

Lumber's grade refers to how the board looks. So the grade of your lumber depends on how many knots and

other defects it has. (A knot is the place where a tree's limp entered the trunk of the tree.) The grade can also affect how easy it is to work with the wood—it's hard to hammer or drill into a knot! Unfortunately, better grades cost more. Just buy the best grade you can afford. Clear grade is the best. Select grade is in the middle. (Each board will have one good side and one so-so side). Common grade has the most knots and defects.

LUMBER SIZE

The wood of the lumber is sorted, named, and sold by its nominal size. Nominal means "in name only." The wood is a slightly different size than its name suggests. The nominal sizes were used many years ago, when the common lumber sizes were thicker and wider. The projects in this book list the nominal size in the Shopping Lists because that's how lumber is sold. For example, if the project tells you to get a 2 x 4, you'll get a board that actually 1½ inches (3.8 cm) high and 3½ inches (8.9 cm) wide.

PLYWOOD, DOWELS, LATTICE, AND MORE

Occasionally you'll use wood that comes in a different form, such as plywood, which is made from wood slices glued together to form a flat sheet. Plywood is inexpensive yet very strong. You'll use it for large projects. Like board lumber, it comes in different grades and sizes. The lumberyard will cut plywood to the size you need, so you don't have to wrestle with a huge sheet. (They may charge you a small fee for this service.)

There are a few other special forms of lumber you'll use for these projects: dowels (round poles); lattice (thin strips); craft lumber (small sanded pieces); and balsa

THE PARTS OF A BOARD

Woodworkers refer to three different parts of a board: edges, faces, and ends. The edges are the two narrow sides that run the length of the board. The faces are the board's two wide, flat surfaces. And the two ends are located—where else?—at the opposite ends of the board.

edge

face

end

Continued ➤

wood (lightweight, very breakable). You can choose the diameter, thickness, and/or length you want. Lumberyards, home-improvement stores, and some craft stores sell these items.

Other Supplies

The supplies listed here will get you off to a great start. You'll add more supplies as you make more projects. When you choose a project to make, remember to check its Shopping and Tools lists. You may need to add to the list before you begin the project.

- Finishing nails: 1¼ inch (3.2 cm) (3d), 1½ inch (3.8 cm) (4d), and 2 inch (5 cm) (6d)
- Common nails: 2½ inch (6.4 cm) (8d) and 3¼ inch (8.3 cm) (12d)
- Brads: No 17 x ¾ inch (1.9 cm) and No. 17 x ½ inch (1.3 cm)
- Phillips flathead wood screws: sizes 6, 8, and 10
- Sandpaper: 180-grit and 100-grit
- Wood glue (yellow carpenter's glue)
- Latex primer
- Latex satin or semigloss enamel paint
- Oil-based sanding sealer
- Oil-based stain and varnish
- Mineral spirits
- Paintbrushes: 2-inches (5 cm) flat, 1-inch (2.5 cm) flat, and a selection of smaller detail brushes
- Clean, lint-free rags, newspapers, and paper towels
- Sticks for stirring
- Safety glasses
- Paper dust masks

Tools

Good tools can be expensive, so add tools when you can afford them and when your project requires them. Eventually, you'll have all these tools. (Of course, if someone in your home already has some, save money by sharing tools until you get your own.) You'll find more information about each of these tools in the next section.

- Pencil
- Tape measure, 8 or 12 feet (2.4 or 3.6 cm) long
- Pocket square
- 2 clamps, 6-inch (15.2 cm) Claw hammer, 14- or 16-ounce (414 or 473 ml)
- Handsaw*, total length 20 inches (50.8 cm) or less
- Screwdriver, No. 2 Phillips
- Coping saw (with a selection of replacement blades)
- Rasp (half-round) fitted with a handle
- Electric ⅜-inch (.95 cm) drill, and a selection of bits
- Electric jigsaw with a selection of blades
- #12 Extension cord, 25Ð length

*You can use a crosscut handsaw or a ryoba saw instead.

SCRAPS

What is scrap wood, exactly? Every time you cut a piece of lumber to the size it needs to be, you have a leftover piece of wood. This is scrap wood—save it! Put the scraps in a scrap bin. Use them to build other projects and to protect your workbench when you drill and finish your project.

Workshop Safety

Building safely is the only way to go. Why? Because all the fun disappears when someone gets hurt. Think of your tools as friends who treat you just as well as you treat them. Give them the respect they deserve, and they'll do wonderful things for you.

Here are four things to keep in mind while working with wood:

Take Your Time: Don't rush to slap a project together. There's no hurry. When you go too fast, you're more likely to make mistakes. Or worse—injure yourself!

Take Breaks: Try to limit how long you work on a project at any one time. When you start feeling tired or are having trouble concentrating, the best thing to do is walk away for a while, get some fresh air, and relax. When you're ready to start work again, you'll feel much better, and you'll do much better work.

Pay Attention to Your Work: Pay close attention while you work. If you find that your attention is drifting, put everything away and call it a day....

COMMONSENSE SAFETY

A safe workshop area will help you build your best projects. Whether you set up your shop indoors or out, get some help arranging it so that you have enough room to move boards around and enough light to see your work clearly. Your workbench should be about 30 inches (76.2 cm) high, sturdy, and large enough to support the tools and lumber that you're using.

Pick up any scrap wood off the floor so you don't trip on it, and never leave a board that has sharp nails in it lying on the floor—even for a moment.

If you have long hair, tie it up or wear a cap so that it won't catch in your tools. Like long hair, loose clothing can also catch on sharp tool edges. Roll up your sleeves, and hang your scarf on a peg before you begin.

Flying nails and wood splinters can hurt your eyes, so wear a pair of safety glasses whenever you pick up a hammer or use power equipment. Keep the glasses clean and store them carefully to prevent scratching.

Oil-based stains and varnishes, mineral spirits, and turpentine give off poisonous and flammable fumes, so when the weather's good, do your finishing work outdoors. When you need to work indoors, keep the windows open and turn on a strong fan to provide plenty of fresh air. And no matter where you work, stay away from any source of heat or open flame.

A paper dust-mask will help keep sawdust out of your lungs. Get several when you buy your supplies so you'll have an extra for your adult assistant. Make sure the mask fits snugly over your mouth and nose. The mask may feel uncomfortable at first, but you must wear it whenever you're sanding. Replace the mask when you can see dirt from the sawdust on it.

Of course, every builder expects a small splinter or scrape now and then, so keep a first-aid kit in your shop.

And remember: you can build safely by taking your time, paying attention to your work, and asking for help when you need it.

Techniques

Making your layouts, sawing, drilling, hammering, and sanding—these are the basic skills you'll need to become an expert woodworker. If you already know how to do some of these things, think of this as a refresher.

This section has complete explanations of all the basic woodworking techniques. There are lots of step-by-step photographs to make it easy for you to learn—or relearn—the skills. Read this chapter before you start your first project. Later, when you're working on a project, you can always turn back to these pages to remind you how to use the techniques.

Cutting

Before you make that first cut, there's lots to do, including squaring, measuring, and marking, or using a pattern or illustration to lay out the piece. You may need to clamp the piece. After you make the cut, there will be times when you'll need to transfer layout marks or patterns onto your project pieces. (These marks will help you build the project.) Each of these steps is explained in this section.

SQUARING

To square a piece of lumber is to make sure the end of the board is perfectly straight. This is the first step you'll take in every woodworking project. Without a square end, you can't get an accurate measurement, and that means your project pieces won't fit together.

A square is a tool you use to check square. ("Square" is both an action and a thing.) A square is L-shaped and has two parts, a handle and a metal blade. These parts are at a right angle (which is square) to one another. The square's shape is important, because its main job is to help you check and make right angles. The blade is marked with inches and fractions of inches, like a tape measure.

CHECKING A BOARD'S END FOR SQUARE

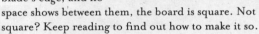

1. Hold the side of the square's handle tightly against one edge of the board and hook the metal blade over the board's end.

2. If the board's end lines up exactly with the blade's edge, and no space shows between them, the board is square. Not square? Keep reading to find out how to make it so.

SQUARING A CROOKED BOARD

1. Press the edge of the square's handle tightly against the edge of the board. Lay the metal blade flat across the board's face, at least 1 inch (2.5 cm) from the crooked end.

2. Use a pencil to draw a line along the blade's edge, from one edge of the board to the other. Saw along this line to remove the crooked end.

SQUARING ACROSS A WIDE BOARD

Sometimes you'll need to square across a board that's wider than your square.

1. Square across the board as far as you can with your square and pencil.

2. Flip the square to the board's other edge and line up the blade's edge with the line you've just marked. Use your pencil to complete the line.

3. If there's still a gap between the lines you made, use a straight piece of wood. Line it up between the squared lines you've made. Use your pencil to mark the line.

MEASURING AND MARKING

How will you know where to cut the lumber to make your project pieces? Don't guess! Just measure and mark. You'll need a tape measure, a pencil, and a square. These are your layout tools.

MEASURING

Use your tape measure to measure the required distance from the end or edge of the board. (Where you measure from depends on whether you are cutting the board to a certain length or to a certain width. In these how-to photos, we measured to create an 8-inch-long (20.3 cm) piece.)

1. Slip the tape's hook over the board's end or edge. You'll notice that the hook is a little loose. Don't worry; it should be.

2. Pull the case so the tape extends along or across the board. Make sure the tape is straight—if it's at an angle your measurement will be off.

3. Find the length you need on the tape measure and use your pencil to mark that spot on the board.

4. Line up the arm of the square with the spot you marked, just as you did when squaring a crooked board. Use a pencil to draw a line along the blade's edge, from one edge of the board to the other.

Using Patterns

With some projects, especially ones with curving lines, you'll use a pattern to transfer the shape of the piece onto the board. You'll need to either trace the pattern or photocopy it (and sometimes enlarge it).

TRACING PATTERNS

1. Set the pattern flat on your work surface, and put a piece of tracing paper on top of it. You'll see the pattern through the tracing paper. Tape the tracing paper in place. Lightly trace the pattern.

2. With scissors, carefully cut out the pattern on the tracing paper.

3. With your wood flat on your workbench, hold or tape the cut-out pattern to the wood's face. Trace carefully around it with your pencil.

Using an Illustration

For some projects, you'll need to make marks on the project pieces to show where the center is, or places where you'll drill holes for dowels or screws. These are referred to as layout marks. Use your tape measure and pencil to transfer the layout marks shown in the project's illustration onto your pieces. See the section on drilling for help with the drilling part.

Cutting and Labeling Pieces

Now you're ready to clamp, cut, and label the pieces you need for your project. You'll use a handsaw for cutting lumber to length and making rip cuts. You'll use a coping saw to cut curves or make inside cuts. All these techniques are explained in this section.

Clamping

A clamp acts like an extra pair of hands that makes sure your board stays put on the workbench when you saw it. The miter box and bench hook you build on page 428 and page 442 can be used in place of clamps in some instances. Read about how and when to use them on those pages. (When you drill holes in pieces you've cut out, you'll need to clamp the piece to the workbench, as well.)

USING YOUR CLAMP

1. Lay the board on the workbench, with the line you want to cut hanging over the edge of the workbench by about 2 inches (5 cm). If you're right-handed, clamp the board so the line you want to cut will hang over the right edge of the workbench. If you're a lefty, switch the board to the workbench's left edge.

Tip

Put a small, flat piece of scrap wood between your project pieces and the clamps. This will keep the clamps from denting the project's surface.

1. Now put the clamp in place, with one of the grippers on the board and the other on the workbench. Make sure it won't get in the way of your saw.

2. Turn the clamp's handle clockwise (to the right as you're looking at it). This will tighten the clamp and hold the piece firmly in place.

3. If you're using more than one clamp, position them both loosely (so they hang on) and then slowly tighten them. Tighten one clamp a little bit, and then tighten the other.

4. Make sure the clamp is tightened securely. Now you're ready to cut. Readjust your clamp and your work piece whenever necessary as you continue with your project.

Handsaw

The saw you'll need is called a crosscut handsaw. It cuts straight lines both across the grain (called crosscutting) and in the same direction as the grain (called ripping). You can get either a Japanese ryoba saw that cuts on the pull stroke, or a crosscut panel saw with teeth that cut on the push stroke. Use whichever kind you prefer. Get a wooden-handled saw that's 20 inches (50.8 cm) long or less. It'll be easier to use. Don't buy a ripsaw; it isn't designed to cut across the grain of the board.

MAKING A CROSSCUT

After you've marked a cut line on the board, and it's clamped firmly to the workbench, you're ready to use your saw.

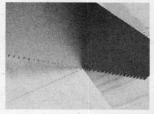

1. Place the blade on the saw on the waste side of the cut line. (The waste side of the board is the side that isn't part of the project piece.) The saw is going to remove about 1/16 inch (1.6 mm) of the wood as it cuts, so it will change the length of the board if you make your cut right on the line.

2. Set the thumb of your free hand lightly against the saw blade's side, just above the teeth.

3. Pull the saw lightly back and forth, being careful to keep the saw's teeth away from your thumb. The saw will make a little groove in the wood, called a kerf.

4. Move your free hand away from the saw. Put it on the board, well away from the saw's teeth. Line up your eyes, your sawing arm, and shoulder behind the blade. This position puts the power of your upper body behind the saw and will make sawing easier. Plant both feet a little apart and continue to saw.

5. As you saw back and forth, tilt the point of the saw at a 45-degree angle to the floor. Keep the blade straight up and down. (Imagine a square lining up the side of the saw with the face of the board.) Don't let it lean to the left or right. The blade will follow the cut line. Cut slowly and steadily, and take a break whenever you need one.

6. If the saw begins to wander from the cut line, guide it back by gently twisting the saw's handle very lightly as you make your cut. Keep your eyes on the marked line and your sawing straight and true! Have a helper carefully support the wood that hangs over the edge of your workbench so that it doesn't tear off as you finish your saw cut.

7. Label the piece you just cut out. (This will help you figure out which piece goes where when you build your project.)

MAKING A RIP CUT

Ripping a board is a lot like crosscutting, except that it's easier for your saw to wobble off the line you marked. The projects in this book only require that you rip very short distances, so you can use your handsaw.

1. Clamp your board in place. The marked line should hang over the edge of your workbench.

Tip

Always mark and saw along a pencil line that's straight and square. You'll like the results.

1. Line up the blade with the mark and make a kerf in the end of the board, as you did when crosscutting.

2. Carefully cut along the line you marked, using the same techniques you used with crosscutting. Make sure the blade cuts straight along the line.

Coping Saw

This strange-looking saw is used to cut curved lines, circles, and inside boards. The blade rotates so you can cut in any direction. That's why this saw cuts oddly shaped lines and in places no other saw can reach. The saw's teeth point back toward the handle and it cuts as you pull the blade. A little pin at each end of the blade is tightly held to the frame's ends with two pin holders, creating tension. The tension allows the thin blade to cut through wood. If the handle is loosened, it won't cut cor-

SHOP TALK
Never use a saw with teeth that are bent, broken, or dulled. If the handle is loosely attached to the blade, don't use the saw. Nothing is more aggravating (and dangerous!) than working with a beaten-up handsaw. Keep your handsaw in good shape by storing it so that its teeth don't bump against other metal tools. A local "sharp shop" can sharpen the teeth when they're dull.

Continued ➤

369

Craft Wisdom & Know-How

rectly because the tension disappears and the blade flops around. Practice on scrap wood to get the hang of using this tool.

CUTTING CURVES

Sometimes it's easier to use your coping saw when the board is clamped straight up and down. Do whatever feels most comfortable.

1. Grip the saw's handle with one hand. Set the blade on the edge of the wood, even with the line that you've marked, and gently push and pull the blade across the wood. (You don't have to make a kerf with this saw.) Keep a little pressure on the blade, but don't press too hard. This will bend or break the blade. Remember, the saw cuts on the pull stroke; use just enough pressure to keep the blade in place on the push stroke.

2. Watch the marked line and turn the handle slightly so that the handle slightly so that the blade follows that line. Don't turn the saw's blade too tightly to follow a curve, or the blade may bend or break. You'll get a feel for how tight your turns can be after you've made a few cuts.

3. Keep the blade of your saw aimed in the direction you want to cut, and you won't go wrong.

4. If the frame bangs against the outside of the wood, you can't continue sawing. Turn both pin holders, turning the frame away from the wood. Then keep sawing. Do this as often as you need.

5. When you're done cutting out the piece, label it with the pencil.

REPLACING THE BLADE

When the coping saw's blade breaks, you'll need to replace it. This can be tricky. Four hands are better than two, so ask for some adult help.

1. Look at how the two pin holders grip each end of the blade. Loosen the handle by turning it until you can remove the blade.

2. Insert a new blade onto the two pin holders, turning the teeth back toward the handle.

3. Tighten the handle so that the blade is held tightly in the frame.

INSIDE CUTS WITH A COPING SAW

1. Start by boring a hole at least ¼ inch (.5 cm) wide just inside of the shape you want to cut out.

2. Remove the blade from your coping saw, slip the blade through the hole, and tighten the blade back into the saw frame. Now cut out the shape.

Building Your Project

Now that all the pieces are cut, you're ready to assemble the project. You'll nail or screw (and sometimes glue) the pieces together. The places where pieces are fastened are called joints. Each project has an illustration that shows how all the pieces fit together. Refer to it often as you build your project.

MAKING JOINTS

The projects in this book only use two types of joints: face joints and right-angle joints. A face joint is made of two boards fastened face to face. This point is very strong. Right-angle joints are two boards fastened together at a 90-degree angle. This joint is weak on its own, but when you put several right-angle joints together (as you do with a box), your project will be strong.

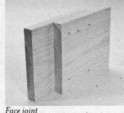

Face joint

Fasten together these joints with nails or screws. Glue helps to strengthen the joints, especially if they're going to hold weight. Each project will tell you exactly how to fasten the joints.

Right-angle joint

MAKING JOINTS FIT

No matter how carefully you cut, sometimes the pieces of your project won't fit together perfectly. One board might be a tiny bit too long, or the cut might not be straight. A rasp can scrape a little wood from the end of a piece to make it fit. (Unfortunately, if the piece is too short, you'll have to measure and cut a new piece.)

USING YOUR RASP

A half-round rasp has a flat side to use on flat surfaces, and a curved side to use on the inside of curved saw cuts.

1. Clamp the piece securely to your bench.

2. Hold the rasp's handle in one hand, and place the teeth where you want to remove wood. Keeping the rasp flat, push it across the wood. It may be helpful to put a little pressure on the steel with the fingers of your other hand. (You'll hold the rasp in the same position when you're shaping curved lines.)

3. A rasp only cuts away the wood as it's moving forward, so pick it up to bring it back to the starting position. Push it forward again, lift it up, move it back, and push it forward.

4. Test the fit of the piece. When it fits, you're done.

FASTENING WITH GLUE

Wood glue (sometimes called carpenter's yellow glue) can help hold pieces of wood together when you need a really strong joint. After you glue a joint, always fasten it with nails or screws. The trick to gluing is to use the right amount of glue—enough to make the pieces stick together, but not too much! When glue drips or squeezes out from the project you're building, you've used too much. Wipe it up quickly with a damp paper towel or rag. If the drips have already started to dry, you can peel them up with your fingernails. If they're really dry, ask your adult assistant to help you get rid of them.

GLUING A FACE JOINT

If you want to glue the faces of two boards together, do this.

1. Run several thin lines of glue along the boards' matching faces.

2. Set the boards together. Drive nails or screws into them.

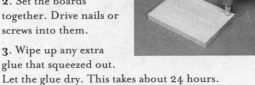

3. Wipe up any extra glue that squeezed out. Let the glue dry. This takes about 24 hours.

GLUING A RIGHT ANGLE JOINT

When you glue an end or an edge of one board to another board, do it like this:

1. Run a thin line of glue along the center of the edge.

2. Set the boards together. Drive in nails or screws.

3. Wipe up any extra glue that squeezed out. Let the glue dry. This takes about 24 hours.

FASTENING WITH NAILS

You can use nails to fasten joints. They come in many types and sizes. The three types you'll need for the projects in this book are common nails, finishing nails, and brads. The project instructions will tell you what type and length of nail you'll need for each project.

Using the right length of nail is particularly important. You want the nail to be long enough to go through the first board and into the second, but not so long that it comes out the other side. Look at the photo below. The nail on the left is too long for the boards. The nail on the right is the perfect length. The only tricky thing about nails is that their length is measured two different ways: in inches and in "pennies." I 2-inch-long (5 cm) nail is also called a 6d nail. (The "d" stands for penny.") Nail boxes list both measurements. The project instructions measure nails in inches rather than pennies. But here's a handy chart just in case.

Penny	Inches
3d	1¼" (3.2 cm)
4d	1½" (4 cm)
6d	2" (5 cm)
8d	2½" (6.4 cm)
10d	3" (7.6 cm)
12d	3¼" (8.3 cm)
16d	3½" (8.9 cm)

Left: *A finishing nail is thinner and has a small head. Use it to hammer into thin pieces of wood and when you want a neater-looking project.* **Middle:** *A common nail has a wide head. Use it to nail together thick pieces of wood, such as two 1½ x 3½-inch boards.* **Right:** *A brad is like a tiny finishing nail. Use it to nail together really thin pieces of wood.*

USING YOUR HAMMER

There are two different parts to the head of the hammer. The flattened, circular end is for pounding nails. (You can also use it to tap on a piece of wood so it lines up with another board.) The steel claw is for pulling out nails that are bent in the wrong place.

Caution: Sometimes a nail will fly in the air when you hit it with your hammer, so always wear your safety glasses. Hammering well takes a little practice, but you'll get plenty of it as you build your projects.

HAMMERING NAILS

Practice hammering with common nails and scrap wood. (The bigger head makes the nails easier to hit.) Always wear your safety glasses.

1. Grip the hammer handle with the hand you write with. The farther from the head you hold the handle,

the more power you'll have (but the less control). Grip the handle wherever it feels best to you.

2. Turn the steel face of the hammer down and away from you. Line up the handle with your elbow. Hold the nail in between the index finger and thumb of your other hand. Set the nail's point where you want it to enter the wood. Make sure you're holding the nail straight up and down. (Tilting the nail will make it bend or go out the side of the board when you pound it.)

3. To start the nail, tap its head several times with the hammer until the point of the nail sticks into the wood. Move your other hand away from the nail. Use it to steady the board.

4. Keep your eye on the nail's head as you swing the hammer down onto it, and hit the nail sharply. If the nail doesn't sink into the board a bit, hit it harder. Swing your hammer from the elbow and arm to use the power of your whole upper body, not just your wrist. Swing carefully and steadily.

5. When the nail is almost all the way in, start hitting it very lightly until the head is flat on the wood's surface. Try not to dent the wood with the hammer.

Tip

Don't try to hammer a nail through a knot in the wood—you'll just bend the nail! Be careful not to put a nail too close to the edge or end of a board. It will split the wood.

PULLING A BENT NAIL

Sometimes a nail bends before it's driven all the way in, the tip pops out the side of the board, or it goes in the wrong place. If this happens, pull the nail back out.

1. Grip the nail with the V-shaped slot of the hammer claw. Place the steel top of the hammer flat on the wood next to the nail, with the hammer straight up and down.

2. Use one hand to hold the board still. With the other hand, pull the handle down toward the board and away from the nail until the nail comes out.

3. If you're having a hard time, slip a piece of scrap wood between the board and the top of the hammer's head.

4. Start the nail in a new spot and try it again.

Tip

When you're trying to hammer a nail really close to the end of the board, this trick will help you avoid splitting the wood: Turn a nail upside down and dull the sharp point a little bit with a light whack or two from your hammer. Then turn the nail right-side up, position it, and pound it in. The nail will drive straight and won't split the end of the board! The nail's dulled point crushes straight through the wood's grain instead of following the grain and going at an angle. This is one case where sharper isn't always better.

CHECKING FOR A RIGHT ANGLE

After you've nailed a right-angle joint, use your square to make sure it's at a 90-degree angle.

1. Fit the square into the inside corner where the two boards meet. Press the handle against one board, and check to see whether the edge of the blade is tight against the other board.

2. If your square won't fit inside the corner of your project, hold the square tightly against the outside corner instead and check that the pieces are square.

3. If there's a space between the blade and the board, you'll need to adjust the assembled boards a bit so the joint is square. Use your hammer to tap lightly on one of the boards in the direction it needs to go. Check the joint for square again.

FASTENING WITH SCREWS

A screw fastens joints like a nail, but goes in a little differently. The threads grip the wood tightly, so it's a little more secure than a nail. The first thing you'll need to do is use the electric drill to bore a pilot hole. This will help keep your screw from splitting the wood. Then you'll use your screwdriver to drive the screw into the joint.

There are many types, thicknesses, and lengths of screws. The projects in this book use flathead Phillips screws. They're the easiest kind of screw to put in, and the head fits flat against the wood. The Phillips screw has two slots that cross to make an X shape on its head.

Screws are sized by their thickness (No. 6, No. 8, No. 10, and so on; the smaller the number, the smaller the screw), and by their length. For these projects, the Shopping List will tell you which screws you'll need.

USING AN ELECTRIC DRILL

The electric drill is the only power tool you'll use regularly when making these projects. The drill bores holes in the wood. Have someone help until you feel completely comfortable with this tool. The drill has a trigger, which turns it on and off. (Some drills drill at different speeds, depending on how hard you press the trigger.)

The chuck is a circular sleeve that holds the bit. The bit is a small metal piece that goes into the wood. Bits come in different sizes: the larger the bit, the larger the hole will be. The drill also has a button that reverses the direction the bit spins. You'll use this button to the back the drill out of the hole after you finish drilling.

CHUCKING A BIT

When you put a bit into your drill it's called chucking.

1. Grip the drill with one hand and rotate the chuck with your other hand until the jaws open. (Rotate the chuck in both directions to see how the jaws work.)

2. Slip the end of the bit without the spiral grooves into the jaws. It should go in about ½ inch (1.5 cm).

3. Rotate the chuck in the opposite direction to tighten the jaws onto the end of the bit. Make sure the chuck is completely tightened.

Tip

Some drills have a chuck key, a small tool used to loosen and tighten the chuck. Insert the key into a hole in the chuck. Twisting the key will loosen and tighten the chuck.

DIMPLING THE PILOT HOLE

1. Before you drill a hole, dimple the mark for your drill's bit. This will help keep the bit from slipping around on the board.

2. Set the tip of a large nail on the mark where the hole goes. Tap the nail lightly once or twice with your hammer.

3. Remove the nail. There's your dimple!

DRILLING THE PILOT HOLE

Now you're ready to drill.

1. Put on your safety glasses.

2. Set the dimpled board flat on your workbench.

3. Slip a piece of scrap wood beneath the board, and then clamp the "sandwich" to your workbench. The scrap wood will keep you from drilling holes into your workbench.

Tip

If your bit slips in the chuck as you drill a hole, stop and tighten the chuck securely.

4. Set the tip of the bit in the dimpled layout. Hold the drill straight up and down.

5. Squeeze the drill's trigger to begin drilling. Apply pressure straight down to drive the bit into the wood.

6. Stop drilling when the bit pops through the bottom of the board.

You'll feel this happen as the bit enters the second board, or comes out the other side if the board is hanging over the edge of the workbench.

7. Reverse the drill direction to back the bit out.

FLAGGING A BIT

Sometimes you want to drill a hole that doesn't go all the way through the board. Use a piece of tape to show you when to stop drilling.

1. Lay your bit on your workbench.

2. Use your measuring tape to measure the depth of the hole on the length of the bit, starting from the tip.

3. Wrap the end of a piece of masking tape around the bit, so the edge of the tape is at the depth you want to drill. Let the other end of the tape stick out like a flag.

4. Chuck the bit into your drill, dimple the hole, and drill it. Stop drilling when the edge of the flag touches the face of the board. Reverse the drill to back the bit out.

SCREWDRIVERS

Screwdrivers are used to drive screws into wood. There are two different types of screwdrivers. Each has a different tip. The flattened tip of a standard screwdriver is used to drive slotted-head screws. The X-shaped tip of a Phillips screwdriver fits into the X on the head of a Phillips screw. Since the projects in this book use Phillips screws, make sure you get a Phillips screwdriver. Screwdriver tips come in different sizes. Get a No. 2 tip. It's medium-sized and will work well with all the screws you'll use in the projects.

HOW TO DRIVE A SCREW

After you've bored the pilot hole, you're ready to drive the screw.

1. Set the screw's point into the pilot hole. Then set the screwdriver's tip into the X-shaped slot on the head of the screw.

Continued →

2. Turn the screwdriver clockwise, using the power in your shoulder to drive in the screw. Keep the screwdriver's tip centered in the head of the screw so that it won't slip out.

To back the screw out, turn the screwdriver counterclockwise.

Finishing Touches

You didn't think you were done, did you? There's one last, very important step: finishing! This makes your projects look and feel great, and protects them so they'll last a long time. First you'll sand the project. Then you'll paint, varnish, or stain it. Each finish gives wood a different appearance, but the main job of finish is to protect the wood and seal out dirt and dampness.

When the weather's good, finish your project outdoors. If you have to work indoors, be sure that there's plenty of fresh air in your workshop, and stay far away from any sources of heat or open flame.

SANDING

Sanding smoothes out any rough spots on your project and prepares the wood surface for finishing. Because sanding creates a lot of floating sawdust, always wear a paper dust-mask to help keep it out of your lungs.

There are many kinds of sandpaper, but for this book's projects, you'll use 100- and 180-grit garnet sandpaper. Sandpaper grit gets smaller in size as the grit number increases, so 100-grit is rougher than 180-grit. You'll use the 100-grit sandpaper to take off the rough spots. Then you'll use the 180-grit sandpaper to smooth everything out. (You can substitute another kind of sandpaper if you can't find garnet, but get both grit sizes.)

Sanding sponges are soft rubbery blocks coated with sandpaper grit. You can use one of these if you like. They're great for sanding curving edges made with your coping saw and your rasp.

Your rasp is perfect for sanding inside holes, around curves, and other places the sandpaper won't reach easily. It's also great for taking off the teeth marks your saw left on the ends of boards.

Tip

If you're sanding a large, flat surface, wrap the sandpaper around a small block of scrap wood so it fits in your palm.

HOW TO SAND YOUR PROJECT

Your goal is to get rid of all the rough spots and sharp edges. Always wear your paper dust mask when sanding.

1. Fold the 100-grit sandpaper in quarters. Unfold it and then tear along the creases to get smaller pieces.

2. Hold a piece of sandpaper and rub the grit across the wood. Whenever you can, rub in the same direction as the wood grain. This gives a smoother surface than rubbing across the grain.

3. Sand the edges, ends, corners, and faces of every piece of your project.

4. Wipe the sawdust off and run your fingers over every part of your project, checking for rough spots. Look at it closely under a good light. If you see or feel any rough spots, sand them smooth.

5. Wipe the sawdust off, then repeat steps 1 through 4 with the 180-grit sandpaper. This will make the surface extra smooth.

PAINTS, VARNISHES, AND STAINS

To make your projects look their best and to help them last as long as possible, apply a finish. There are several finishes to choose from: paint, varnish, and stain. The type of finish you choose depends on how you want your project to look. This final step seals the wood, protecting it from dirt and moisture.

Once you put finish on your project, it will last a long time. Each of the projects in this book recommends a way to finish it.

Buy the best paintbrushes you can afford and take good care of them by cleaning the brushes immediately after using them. Inexpensive brushes leave behind a trail of sticky hairs.

CHOOSING PAINT

Get paint in any color you want. Use semigloss or flat, latex enamel paint. Latex enamel paint is water-based, which means it cleans up with warm water. Semigloss (sometimes called satin) paint is sort of shiny. Flat paint isn't shiny at all. High-gloss paint shows every little imperfection on your projects, and who wants that?

If you plan to use your project outdoors, look for the word exterior on the paint can's label. If your project is going to stay indoors, choose an interior paint instead. Before you paint, prime the wood. Primer seals the wood and raises the grain. It makes a nice surface for the paint to stick to.

Tip

Applying primer and paint to every surface of your project is easier than it sounds. First, prime the top and sides. Let the primer dry. Then flip the project so it rests on its top. Prime the bottom. Use the same technique to apply paint.

PRIMING

Before you grab your paintbrushes, wipe every speck of sawdust and dirt from your workbench and your project with a damp rag. If dust sticks to the finish, it will ruin the smooth surface.

1. Cover your workbench with newspapers. Set your project on top of a few pieces of scrap wood so that it isn't touching the newspaper. (If it's touching, the newspaper will stick to your project when the primer dries.)

2. Put some clean rags and a bucket of water nearby to clean up spills and wipe off your hands.

3. Open the can of primer. Stir it with a clean piece of scrap wood.

4. Dip the tip of your brush into the primer, wiping off extra paint on the side of the paint can. (If you put too much primer on your brush, it will drip.) Brush it on to the project. Brush with the grain, covering the project with an even coat. Let the primer dry.

5. Sand the project again with the 180-grit sandpaper. (The primer soaks into the wood and raises the grain, making the surface rough, so don't skip this step!)

APPLYING PAINT

After you've primed and sanded your project, it's time to paint it.

1. Lay out newspaper and scrap wood on your workbench, just as you did to prime the project.

2. Put some clean rags and a bucket of water nearby for cleaning up spills and wiping off your hands.

3. Open the can of paint. Stir it up with a piece of clean scrap wood.

4. Dip the tip of your brush into the paint. If you put too much paint on your brush, it will drip. Brush it onto the project. Brush with the grain, covering the project with an even coat of paint.

5. Let the paint dry. Then repeat step 4 to add another coat of paint. Always use at least two coats of paint.

Tip

If you're painting multiple colors, start with the lightest shade. Let the paint dry before painting the next color.

CHOOSING STAIN AND VARNISH

Stain and varnish are finishes that let the grain of the wood show through. Look for water-based kinds—they're easier to clean up and a lot less toxic. When you use either of these products, read the can carefully for any additional instructions.

APPLYING STAIN

Stain makes the wood a slightly different color.

1. To see what your stain will look like before you apply it to your project, brush some on a scrap of the same wood as you used for the project. The more coats of stain you put on, the darker the wood will become, so go easy until you're sure how much to use!

2. Paint the stain on your project. (You don't need to prime or seal the wood first. The stain soaks in.)

3. Sand everything with 180-grit sandpaper when the stain is dry.

4. Apply two coats of varnish to seal the project.

APPLYING VARNISH

Semigloss or satin varnish gives your wood a nice glow.

1. After you've finished sanding the project, apply a coat of sanding sealer. Then follow the instructions for priming.

2. When the sanding sealer is dry, add two coats of varnish. (Follow the instructions for painting.)

Tip

Never store your paintbrushes standing on their bristles. The weight of the handle will bend the bristles. Lay them on a shelf or other flat surface.

CLEANING YOUR BRUSHES

Your paintbrushes will last a long time if you clean them well immediately after you use them.

1. Dip the paintbrush in warm water. Squeeze the bristles.

2. Gently run your fingernails along the bristles of the brush. Don't bend the bristles in ways they don't want to go.

3. Repeat steps 1 and 2 until all the finish is removed. Change the water whenever you need to.

4. Set the paintbrush on its side to dry.

You're Finished!

Ready to try out your new skills? Start building a few tools for your workshop.

—FROM *The All-New Woodworking for Kids*

WOODWORKING SURFACES

Andy Rae

One tool that stands above all else as the primary holding and supporting device for any woodworking endeavor is a workbench. If you're just beginning to acquire tools, there's no better place to start than with a quality bench.

A good workbench should be solid and heavy, free from racking (cocking side to side or front to back), have a variety of built-in clamping or gripping devices, and possess a dead-flat top. The heavier the bench, the better. A weighty bench absorbs the pushing, pulling, prying, and pounding that goes hand in hand with our tools, and transmits this energy to the floor—not into the work or back to the tool. Solid, heavy parts resist racking, and a flat top surface allows you to use your bench as a reference plate for activities where flatness counts, such as hand-planing or cutting joints.

Although these days you can buy a decent workbench, most woodworkers prefer to build their own, saving money in the bargain. There are many great workbench designs that have been published in books and magazines; check your local library. Good wood choices for benches are hard maple and beech, both dense and heavy woods that are relatively stable. You can pack up most of the necessary bench hardware at a hardware store; specialty hardware such as vise screws and handles are available from woodworking stores and catalogs. In addition to a thick top and stout legs, the key to a solid bench is in the lower rails: make these thick and wide enough, and your bench won't rack.

My favorite bench is a traditional European-style joiner's bench, as shown in the photo. At roughly 2 feet (70 cm) wide by 7 feet (213 cm) long, it's plenty big enough for all my handwork. Don't overlook the height of your bench—it's a key factor in using your tools effectively. Too high, and you'll have a hard time pushing or pulling a tool, such as when face planning. Too low, and

Faithful and dependable. *The author's European-style maple workbench has a massive, flat top and a stout undercarriage that resists racking.*

you won't be able to see the action without stooping over your work, an important consideration when it comes to joinery work. The right height gives you maximum control over your tools, and lets you work for hours at the bench without fatigue.

The optimum height of a bench is a personal matter, yet it's always a compromise. I've settled on a bench height of 36 inches (91 cm) for my work. It's low enough for comfortable hand planning, yet high enough for laying out and cutting joints without getting a sore back. But don't take my word for it; adjust the height of your bench to suit your

Fig. 2: Calculating Workbench

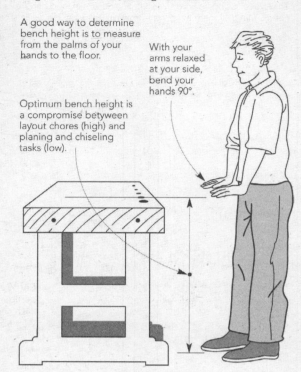

A good way to determine bench height is to measure from the palms of your hands to the floor.

With your arms relaxed at your side, bend your hands 90°.

Optimum bench height is a compromise betyween layout chores (high) and planing and chiseling tasks (low).

own particular needs and your physical stature. Try working at various heights on other people's benches, or set up temporary surfaces to get a feel for a height that's best for you. One good rule of thumb for determining bench height is to stand with your arms resting by your sides and your hands bent at 90 degrees, then measure from your palms to the floor, as shown in figure 2.

Sawhorses shouldn't be overlooked as convenient tools for supporting and holding work. With a sheet of plywood on top, a pair of sawhorses can quickly become a useful workstation or staging platform. You can pick up sturdy sawhorses at home centers, or you can build your own at a height that suits your work. For example, low horses (18 inches (45.7 cm) or so—I call 'em "ponies") are great for assembly tasks on the floor or purchased high on a table, while higher horses (34 inches [86.3 cm] or higher) are well suited for joinery and layout chores.

The traditional carpenter's sawhorse incorporates compound-angled legs, which flare outward for stability. This kind of sawhorse is very stable, but can be tedious to build because of its complex joinery. And I've seen many a carpenter's horse wobble like crazy after a couple of week's hard work when the joints start to loosen. I prefer trestle-style sawhorses for their superior strength, as shown in the photo.

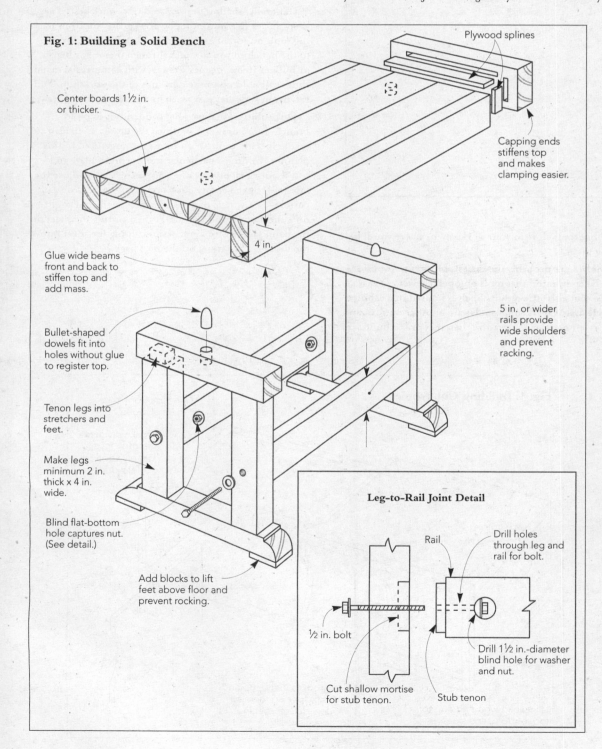

Fig. 1: Building a Solid Bench

Plywood splines

Center boards 1½ in. or thicker.

Capping ends stiffens top and makes clamping easier.

4 in.

Glue wide beams front and back to stiffen top and add mass.

5 in. or wider rails provide wide shoulders and prevent racking.

Bullet-shaped dowels fit into holes without glue to register top.

Tenon legs into stretchers and feet.

Make legs minimum 2 in. thick x 4 in. wide.

Blind flat-bottom hole captures nut. (See detail.)

Add blocks to lift feet above floor and prevent rocking.

Leg-to-Rail Joint Detail

Rail

Drill holes through leg and rail for bolt.

½ in. bolt

Drill 1½ in.-diameter blind hole for washer and nut.

Cut shallow mortise for stub tenon.

Stub tenon

Horse work. *Trestle-style sawhorses are lightweight, yet stable and strong, and can be made in any height you choose. The trestle design allows you to nest horses together, making it easy to carry two in one hand and store them out of the way.*

If you build your own horses, be sure to use a strong hardwood. Species such as maple, oak, cherry, or mahogany are all suitable choices. Avoid softwoods. They don't have the necessary beam strength to safely carry heavy loads. (See fig. 3.)

—From *Choosing & Using Hand Tools*

Continued ➜

Fig. 3: Trestle-Style Sawhorse

This svelte sawhorse is lightweight, knocks down, and handles a big load. Build the height and length to suit your needs. Make all the main parts from ¾ in. thick by 3 in. wide stock, except for the feet, which are 1 in. thick.

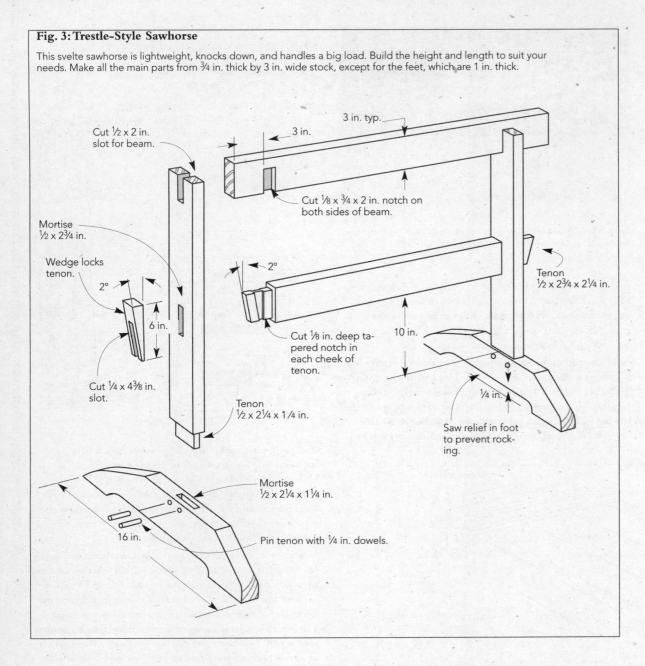

Cut ½ x 2 in. slot for beam.

3 in. typ.

3 in.

Cut ⅛ x ¾ x 2 in. notch on both sides of beam.

Mortise ½ x 2¾ in.

Wedge locks tenon.

2°

2°

6 in.

Tenon ½ x 2¾ x 2¼ in.

Cut ¼ x 4⅜ in. slot.

Cut ⅛ in. deep tapered notch in each cheek of tenon.

10 in.

¼ in.

Saw relief in foot to prevent rocking.

Tenon ½ x 2¼ x 1/4 in.

Mortise ½ x 2¼ x 1¼ in.

16 in.

Pin tenon with ¼ in. dowels.

Pegged in order. Pegboard and metal hooks are a snap to put on a wall, and will hold a wide variety of tools or your entire spokeshave collection.

Hanging racks can come in many forms. Most of us are familiar with pegboard, a sheet of thin hardboard with a series of small holes perforating its surface. Metal wires fit into the holes and hold tools. Use ¼-inch-thick (.6 cm) pegboard, not the thinner version, so that wires stay put and the panel stays flat when loaded with tools.

More elaborate hanging systems include custom-fitted racks and narrow shelves for specific tools. Planes and other bulky tools can be housed on ledges. Horizontal dividers and wooden hooks attached to a box-type door are another option. The dividers fit into dry dovetail sockets in the door frame, allowing you to install a new divider as your tool collection grows or changes.

Drawers are my perennial favorites for storing tools, especially for small gear. Drawers are easy to access, keep your tools clean, and can be efficiently organized with the use of dividers, as shown in figure 2 on the next page.

Generally, shallow drawers and trays work best. They keep clutter to a minimum by preventing you from stacking tools on top of each other, and they can be brought to the bench so you can pick through them. For bigger or bulkier items, deeper drawers with commercial metal slides will hold up to the demands of the workshop. Full-extension slides let you reach to the very back of a drawer.

One solution that pays big dividends is to build French-fitted drawers, in which the drawer is divided to cradle specific tools. With your tools organized in this manner, finding a particular tool is child's play, and you'll notice right away when a specific tool is in use (or missing!) by the empty pocket or slot it leaves. You can custom-fit any type of drawer by first laying out your tools on a sheet of plywood or MDF, then cutting the sheet on the band saw or with a jigsaw, and gluing the sheet into the drawer. (See fig. 3 on the next page.)

STORING TOOLS

Andy Rae

If you can't find it, you probably won't use it. That's ample motivation for finding creative storage solutions for your hand tools. Other reasons include protecting your tools from mishandling, dirt, grime, and—the worst culprit of all—moisture, which promotes oxidation and rust. Kept in a clean area, a properly stored hand tool should be easy to get to, and it should be just as easy for you to notice when it's missing. After all, what good is a tool if you can't find it easily? Luckily, several strategies fill the bill.

Shelves, hanging racks, drawers, and toolboxes are all likely candidates for harboring your tools. But before you commit tools to specific spaces, first gather them into functional groups, such as all your saws, and your entire hand plane collection. Then try to find an appropriate space where your tool grouping can reside. This will organize your collection, making it easier to find specific tools without hunting all over your shop. Equally important is to store all those tools close to your workbench, where you'll be using them.

Shelves are probably the easiest solution to tool storage. Keep in mind that tools on open shelves are easy to see, but also attract dust. Shelves housed in a cabinet stay cleaner. Open cubby-holes are another option, and they're even easier to organize than they are to build. (See fig. 1.)

Easy to see. *Arranging tools on shelves housed in a cabinet keeps them clean and makes them easy to grab*

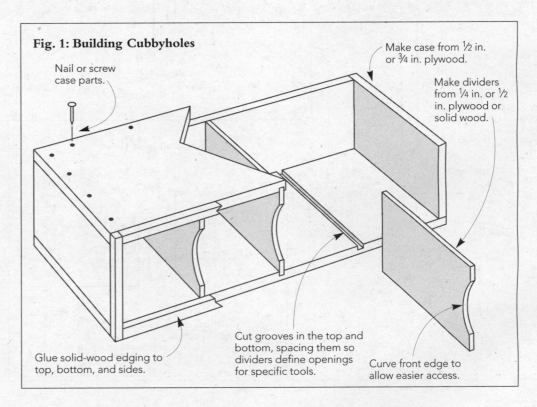

Fig. 1: Building Cubbyholes

Nail or screw case parts.

Make case from ½ in. or ¾ in. plywood.

Make dividers from ¼ in. or ½ in. plywood or solid wood.

Glue solid-wood edging to top, bottom, and sides.

Cut grooves in the top and bottom, spacing them so dividers define openings for specific tools.

Curve front edge to allow easier access.

Fig. 2: Dividing a Drawer

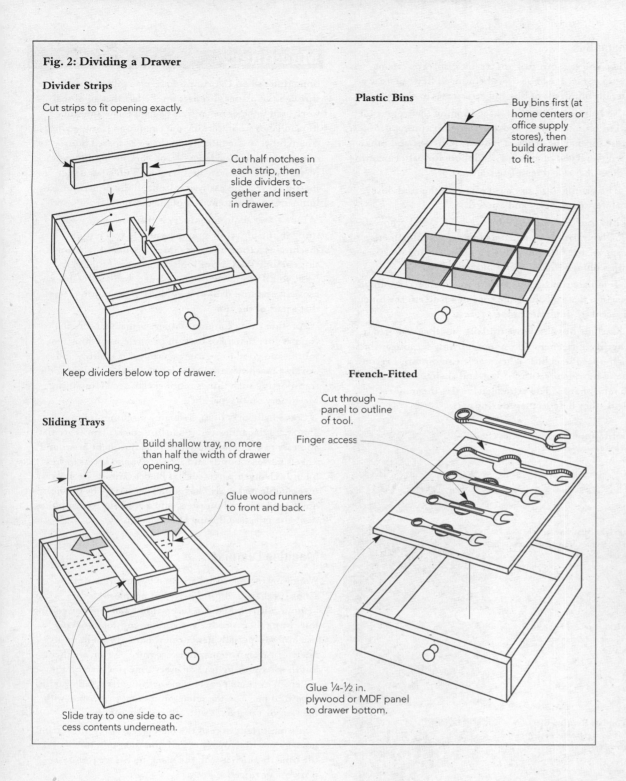

Divider Strips

Cut strips to fit opening exactly.

Cut half notches in each strip, then slide dividers together and insert in drawer.

Keep dividers below top of drawer.

Plastic Bins

Buy bins first (at home centers or office supply stores), then build drawer to fit.

Sliding Trays

Build shallow tray, no more than half the width of drawer opening.

Glue wood runners to front and back.

Slide tray to one side to access contents underneath.

French-Fitted

Cut through panel to outline of tool.

Finger access

Glue ¼-½ in. plywood or MDF panel to drawer bottom.

Fig. 3 French-Fitted Drawer

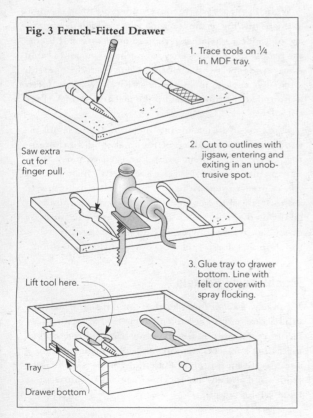

1. Trace tools on ¼ in. MDF tray.

2. Cut to outlines with jigsaw, entering and exiting in an unobtrusive spot.

Saw extra cut for finger pull.

3. Glue tray to drawer bottom. Line with felt or cover with spray flocking.

Lift tool here.

Tray

Drawer bottom

Toolboxes and cabinets date back to the earliest woodworkers, and are the ultimate tool-storing devices. Toolboxes can employ all of the storage ideas already mentioned, keeping your hand tools in one convenient spot. Besides, making your own toolbox is a long-standing tradition among woodworkers, and you'll be left with something you'll be proud to call your own. The sky is the limit when it comes to toolbox design, and there are many good books and articles on the subject to help you get started.

A portable toolbox, or tote, can hold lots of small tools in an organized manner, and allows you to take them with you. If you take the time to build a showcase box, it can be your calling card to potential customers. Larger collections require bigger boxes. A traditional six-board tool chest fits the bill, and was a common sight in eighteenth-century shops. Fitted with lift-out drawers and trays, a

Fitted files and wrenches. *Organizing your tools into custom pockets inside a drawer, called French-fitting, makes them easy to get to.*

chest will hold lots of tools yet lets you sort through the contents easily. And a hinged lid keeps out dirt and dust.

Tool cabinets can be built in (attached to walls or floors) or freestanding, and can range from base units with worktops to large, tall cases that store the bulk of your tools. A low cabinet, similar to kitchen cabinets-type construction, stores tools very efficiently with its pull-out drawers and trays. It also provides a heavy-duty work-surface.

More elaborate tall cases with drawers and hinged doors can hold a surprising number of tools. My own tool cabinet has every square inch maximized for tool storage, keeping my most-used tools visible and immediately accessible.

Tools at a glance. *Favorite tools in the author's freestanding tool cabinet are stored in plain sight on the doors, perched atop narrow ledges, and inside cubbyholes. A bank of narrow drawers holds small tools and accessories. Less frequently used tools are stored below behind doors.*

—From *Choosing & Using Hand Tools*

TOOLS

Marilyn McEwen

What you need—and when and how to get it.

Like many woodworkers, I enjoy the process of finding and procuring tools. But the process can be both confusing and even a little addictive considering the huge variety of tools and the growing number of supply sources—catalogs, retail stores, the Internet, and the like. How does anyone sort through this maze and know what to buy? Putting a few things in perspective might help.

Let's start by dividing tools into four main categories: small handheld power tools, machinery, hand tools, and clamping devices. At every stage of woodworking, you'll be using tools from each of the categories. A small shop will have fewer, simpler, and more generalized tools; a larger shop will have these tools, too, but they'll be larger and more powerful, and will often be specialized to optimize their use for specific functions....

Handheld Power Tools

This vast category of tools contains everything from drills and sanders to biscuit joiners and circular saws. Look at a catalog and you'll be astonished at the variety of what's available. Some of these tools are essentials—the first things a beginning woodworker should buy. Others are nice to have because they save time, while some are so job specific you might never need one.

Here's a list of the handheld tools I consider an essential foundation for doing good work.

Drills

A battery-powered drill/driver is sufficient for most shops. I recommend getting one that's at least 14 volts and capable of handling a ½" (1.5 cm) bit—with an extra battery included. You'll use it for boring holes and driving screws. If you're drilling a lot of holes (especially large diameter holes), a corded electric drill is useful.

Continued ➡

Since you'll be using your drill a lot, you want one with good balance, one that feels right in your hands. Each brand and model is unique, so this is one tool you should get your hands on before you buy.

Jigsaw

You can make straight cuts with a jigsaw, but they're best at cutting curves. You'll use it to cut curves in solid wood or plywood (in lieu of a band saw) and for rough cutting lumber. And even if you do have a band saw, occasionally you'll need a jigsaw to make a cut that the band saw just can't handle.

Circular Saw

Widely used in the construction trades, woodworkers tend to limit their circular saw use to cutting down sheets of plywood that are too large or unwieldy to put on the table saw, and for crosscutting lumber to rough length.

Biscuit Joiner

A biscuit joiner allows you to make a special kind of joint, called (surprise) a biscuit joint. The biscuit is a football-shaped wafer made of pressed wood. It's glued into special slots that are cut into the mating edges of the boards with a tool called a biscuit joiner. The biscuit spans the joint, making it significantly stronger.

Routers and Router Tables

The router is one of the most versatile tools in the shop. Fitted with the right bit, it can flatten, profile, or cut a complex joint. (See Router Bits in next column.) You'll want both a fixed base router and one with a plunge base. A plunge base is a fairly complex spring-loaded affair that lets you raise and lower the bit while the router is running, giving you better control over the depth and location of certain types of cuts. They're important for many joinery operations such as mortising and making stopped cuts.

A 1½ horsepower motor is the minimum I suggest. You can buy one router motor with both a fixed and a plunge base, or you can buy two different routers. If you go that route, I recommend getting a plunge router with more horsepower.

Put your router into a router table, and it's even more versatile. Used with the right jigs and fences, the router can make complicated joints, moldings, and decorative profiles. It's easy to get overwhelmed by the sheer number of router table designs out there. I wouldn't bother with any that didn't have aluminum tables at least ¼" (.6 cm) thick. They stay flat and aren't as bulky and difficult to deal with as wood composite tables. Sold as a set, they usually come with a fence and insert accessories.

The router is perhaps the most versatile tool in the shop. Fitted with the right bit, it can be used to profile an edge, cut joints, make inlay, or produce identical parts from a template—among other things.

Router Bits

When you see your first router-bit display or catalog, try not to panic! It can be overwhelming at first—there are literally hundreds of bits and accessories to choose from.

To help sort things out, keep in mind that router bits fall into three basic categories: those for cutting profiles; those for making grooves, rabbets, mortises, and other joinery-related operations; and those for pattern cutting (sometimes called template routing).

The profile bits I use most often are the roundover, chamfer, cove, ogee, and astragal.

Bits used for joinery, rabbets, dadoes, and grooves are usually straight bits and come in a variety of diameters from ⅛" to 1" (3 mm to 2.5 cm). For cutting mortises with a plunge router, spiral bits work best.

Template routing bits feature tip-or shank-mounted bearings that roll along the edge of a pattern; the bit cuts an accurate duplicate in the process.

Carbide bits cost more initially, but they're worth it. They'll cut cleaner and without burning far longer than high-speed steel bits. Whenever it's an option, I recommend buying bits with ½" (1.5 cm) shanks rather than ¼" (6 mm) shanks. The extra metal makes them more rigid—they'll deflect less during cuts.

Profile Bits: *a chamfering bit on the left and a roundover on the right*

Straight Bits: *A rabbeting bit with several bearings can cut a wide variety of widths and depths.*

Spiral Bits: *A spiral bit works best for removing material in most plunge-cut situations.*

Template Routing Bit: *This template routing bit with a shank-mounted bearing will follow the plywood template to cut the edge of solid wood below so that it's exactly flush with the template.*

Finish Sanders

Most of the time, a random orbit sander is the tool of choice for finish sanding. It's aggressive enough to save time, but not so aggressive that it leaves unsightly scratches. Just about the only time you shouldn't use a random orbit sander is when the edge of the disk might tough an adjoining surface. If it does, it'll probably abrade a nice little notch. When this is a possibility, use an oscillating sander. Either square or rectangular, they're designed to hold quarter- or half-sheets of standard sandpaper in such a way that they can go up to an adjoining surface without marring it.

A random orbital sander offers just the right combination of aggressive material removal and smooth finish. Shown here is a 5" pneumatic sander, powered by compressed air delivered through the yellow hose. An electric-powered random orbit sander works just as well.

Machinery

Sometimes when I'm runnisanderng a pile of boards through the planer, I reflect on the fact that all of that work used to be done entirely by hand. The amount of human labor woodworking once required is stupefying. Thankfully, in the modern world we're spared hours of repetitive physical labor—woodworking machines are plentiful and relatively inexpensive. With a few basic machines, you can easily crank out all the dimensioned lumber you need to make unique creations from wood.

One thing about machinery is that you must always thing in the plural. It's not practical to buy just one machine at a time; there are interdependent relationships among the various tools' functions. At the very least, you'll require a jointer, planer, band saw, table saw, crosscut saw, and drill press. Add to these as you please; that's part of the fun.

Another thing about machinery is that you get what you pay for. Beware of bargain pricing—something that sounds too good to be true probably is. Quality woodworking machines are heavy and accurate; building and transporting such things is not cheap (see Maintaining Machinery on this page).

Some hallmarks of high-quality machines follow: Tables are flat and without hairline cracks; fences are flat and easy to calibrate and position; adjustment levers and wheels move smoothly and accurately; and access to frequently changed parts (such as blades, knives, etc.) is easy. A reputable maker also has good tech service by phone, quick turn-around on parts, and a gracious return policy if all else fails (see Buying Used Machinery).

Machine Learning

Woodworking machines are used by hundreds of thousands (perhaps millions, even) of people each day without mishap. Manufacturers don't want anyone getting hurt using their products, so by design, woodworking machines (especially newer ones) have a lot of built-in safety features. You may not recognize or even see them, but they're working for you every time you turn on the switch. Why some people remove things like blade guards is beyond me. Use the safety equipment that comes with the saw, or upgrade it with aftermarket versions.

It's important to read the manual and fully understand how the machine operates and how to keep it tuned. Take the time to practice with the machine before you start work on a project.

While in theory you're more vulnerable to an accident at the beginning of the learning curve, a high percentage of accidents befall experienced operators. For them, the problem is complacency, or perhaps you could call it overconfidence. Most accidents occur when the operator knowingly engages in an unsafe activity but simply doesn't want to take the time to set up the machine to make the cut safely.

Don't take on a machining operation if you're not in good mental, physical, and emotional condition. Brain fog is a serious problem around heavy machinery. Fast-moving blades will not forgive a moment's inattention. If you're preoccupied with a problem; feel angry or upset; are suffering with a cold or the flu (especially if you're taking medicine—even over-the-counter medications); or are behind on your sleep, find something else to do in the shop that doesn't require your undivided attention.

Machines on Wheels

If you have a small shop, keep in mind that any machine can become mobile, even a big table saw. Most manufacturers sell custom-fitted mobile bases for the tools in their line, and several companies sell generic bases in sizes that fit most tools. I sometimes make my own bases from wood and add big locking casters that I purchase from catalog suppliers.

Maintaining Machinery

Well maintained machines work better and are safer to use. It's that simple. Here are some things to keep in mind:

Switches and power cords. Worn cords and switches cause erratic on/off behavior. Keep them clean and in good working order.

Motors and fans. Sawdust is quite abrasive and will shorten a motor's life. Use a compressor and/or vacuum cleaner to keep these areas clean.

Tables. Dirty or rusty tables increase friction. Remove rust with fine sandpaper, steel wool, plastic scrubbing pads, or any number of proprietary products made for the purpose. Use paint thinner to remove any sticky residue. When the table is clean, apply a few coats of household paste wax to protect it from moisture (and incidentally to make it more slippery).

Foreign objects. Don't use your machines as extra horizontal space for storing tools or other items. Though they seem substantial, heavy woodworking machines are surprisingly delicate. A heavy object stored even for a short while on the edge of a table saw or jointer table can cause misalignment. A small item inadvertently left on the table could contact a spinning blade on start-up and cause all kinds of problems to the tool and the surrounding area.

Drinks. Whether it's your morning cup of coffee, a can of soda, or a bottle of water, don't put it on the machinery, where it could spill or leave a ring of rust.

Buying Used Machinery

People often ask me about buying used or reconditioned machines. It's tempting, especially when the deals are for older American-made machines, which are considered desirable. But I usually find it too difficult to trust the stories behind old machines. It takes a discerning eye to see how a machine may have been mishandled. You may end up with less than you bargained for, and face a complicated process to get the machine properly adjusted. I don't recommend buying used or reconditioned unless tinkering with machinery is something you like to do almost as much as woodworking.

Table Saw

A proper woodworking shop simply can't operate without a table saw. It's amazing just how many tasks this saw can perform, from cutting intricate joinery to ripping lumber and cutting plywood. Perhaps no other tool is as important or as critical for doing good work. For that reason, you want to invest in the best table saw you can afford.

With table saws, the more horsepower the better. An under-powered saw will bog down when cutting 8/4 lumber. If the motor gets too hot, it'll shut itself down completely, forcing you to wait until it cools enough to resume your work. Don't bother with less than a 1½ hp motor, the size found in a typical contractor's saw. A three horsepower cabinet saw is infinitely better in terms of power and accuracy, but the price is considerably more.

The table saw fence is almost as important as the motor. A good fence system slides smoothly and locks securely. It should also be easy to calibrate, since a misaligned fence can cause dangerous kickbacks. Several companies offer aftermarket fence systems, and some are significant improvements over the original fences.

TABLE SAW ACCESSORIES FOR SAFETY

Most table saw accidents occur when the wood binds between the fence and the back edge of the blade. If the wood can't travel past the blade to complete the cut, there's a good chance the blade (turning at more than 100 MPH) will pick up the workpiece and hurl it back at you with surprising force.

This should never happen when crosscutting because you always use a miter gauge or a similar device for this operation. Without one, it's simply not possible to hold a piece of wood steady enough to eliminate any possibil-

ity of twisting it slightly at the end of the cut and causing it to bind. New table saws come with miter gauges. (Given their critical safety importance, it would seem that manufacturers have a moral if not legal obligation to provide them.) But you should look into aftermarket miter gauges, crosscut sleds, and sliding tables. They offer significant improvements in accuracy and ease of use.

You can make ripping safer by using a hold-down device that keeps your hands well away from the blade at all times. With it, you can let go of the material if need be and walk around to the back to pull the piece through (this works especially well with plywood).

Band Saw

Though many people think them less important than table saws, in my book, band saws are right up there. You need one for cutting curves and making quick cuts safely (if not terribly accurately). More importantly, you need one capable of heavy-duty use in milling rough lumber to dimension. You can't use a table saw on rough lumber—in many cases the band saw is your only means to prepare a board for the jointer.

Band saws are sized according to the distance between the blade and saw frame (which dimension also happens to be the diameter of the wheel). A 14" (35.6 cm) saw is just about the minimum size suitable for serious work; bigger is better. A larger saw is more powerful for ripping and resawing, and the larger throat distance lets you work with wider panels. I have two band saws: an 18" (45.7 cm) saw set up for ripping and resawing, and a 14" (35.6 cm) saw that I keep for finer work. If I had to choose only one band saw, I'd pick the bigger one. In the long run, it's more versatile.

BAND SAW BLADES

Saw performance has a lot to do with choosing the right blade for the job. Dull blades or those with too many teeth for the job cut slowly, requiring you to push the wood quite forcefully to achieve a cut. The blade overheats, ruining its temper and burning the wood. Eventually the blade breaks from the stress.

For cutting curves and all-around duty, I keep a ¼"-wide (.6 cm) blade on my 14" (35.6 cm) band saw. I use a skip tooth blade with 4 TPI (teeth per inch). It's capable of making tight cuts and is aggressive enough for slicing through thick pieces of wood. I like bimetal blades—they cost a bit more than regular steel blades, but they stay sharp much longer.

Larger saws can handle wider blades, so I keep a 1"-wide (2.5 cm) blade on my 18" (45.7 cm) saw. It, too, is a bimetal blade, with the 4 TPI stick-tooth pattern.

Jointer

Think of the jointer as the foundation machine—the one that creates the initial flat and straight reference surfaces

from which all other work derives. The width of your jointer determines the width of the widest board you can mill. A 6" (15.3 cm) jointer is a good place to start, but a wider jointer lets you work with wider boards. Unfortunately, the price jump between a 6" (15.3 cm) jointer and an 8" (20.3 cm) jointer is significant. Just get the widest jointer you can afford.

Planer

The planer runs more than any other piece of machinery in the shop. It is by far the hardest working machine and possibly the loudest, creating a whining roar as it shaves a board down to finished thickness (see Get a Thickness Sander ASAP, below).

In recent years, a number of small, affordable portable planers have come on the market, and they work very well. They can handle boards up to 12" wide (conveniently twice the width that a 6" (15.3 cm) jointer can handle), and work fine in a nonproduction situation. Stepping up the next size planer, about 15" (38 cm) wide, more than doubles the price and weight. As with most machines, the extra weight is a good thing—it increases stability and helps the machine run more smoothly with fewer vibrations. The 15" (38 cm) planer is, in the long run, a better investment.

GET A THICKNESS SANDER ASAP

A planer does a great job of removing material quickly but has its limitations. Some woods (notably maple) are nearly impossible to plane without literally tearing small chunks out of the surface, and the more figured the wood, the more likely it is to tear out. Nor do planers work well on really thin pieces.

A thickness sander picks up where the planer leaves off. Instead of using knives to chip away material, it uses a sandpaper-covered drum to sand the surface smooth. Fitted with a coarse abrasive, it quickly gets to the bottom of tear-out and other defects. You can thickness boards to less than ⅛" (3 mm), and you can thickness sand some pieces that would be too small to run through the planer safely. Switch to a finer abrasive (150 or 180 grit), and the machine leaves a remarkably smooth surface. You'll still need to do a final hand sanding prior to applying a finish, but a thickness sander can save countless hours of orbital sanding.

I suggest you make getting a thickness sander a priority, no matter how small your shop.

You can do your thickness sanding any time after planning, but do it before cutting to final length. An improperly adjusted sander can snipe the end of a board just as easily as a planer can. Keep in mind that the entire sanding process, from 80 grit through 180 grit, removes about 1/16" (1.6 mm) of material. You'll have to factor that into your milling process so you don't end up with boards that are nice and smooth, but too thin.

Drill Press

Handheld drills are great, but when you need accuracy and/or power, you need a drill press. It's the only way you can make sure the hole you're drilling is exactly 90° to the surface, or exactly 32" (81.3 cm) if that's what you need. Fitted with a fence and stops, this machine can drill holes in exactly the same location in multiple workpieces. It's capable of turning much larger bits than a hand drill, and by changing the drive belt configuration, you can control the rpm—a handy feature that makes certain operations (like drilling metals) easier. Turn a sanding drum instead of a drill bit, and you have a great means of shaping contours and curves.

I suggest you get a floor-mounted drill press. Bench-top models have limited power and capacity; a floor model is far more convenient to use and offers more drilling options. I wouldn't consider buying any drill press that didn't have rack and pinion adjustment for the table height.

Continued →

Sliding Compound Miter Saw

The ability to get accurate, square crosscuts is critical to any project. Without it, things start on the wrong foot and get cumulatively worse as the project progresses. The sliding compound miter saw, originally developed as a job-site tool for trim carpenters, is designed for one thing: making smooth accurate crosscuts.

This saw can crosscut an end perfectly square to the edge or miter the ends at a wide range of angles. It can also cut a bevel on an end (a bevel is a cut made at an angle other than 90° to the face). Since you can set it up to do both of these at once, it's called a compound miter saw. The word "sliding" refers to the fact that the blade slides back and forth on rails to crosscut wide boards.

I suggest you get a 12" (30.5 cm) sliding compound miter saw. It can cut boards up to 12" (30.5 cm) wide or 6" (15.3 cm) thick. It's more expensive than a 10" (25.4 cm) saw, but you'll be glad you have the extra capacity. Treat it like a stationary tool, and bolt it to a bench, and build an accurate fence with a stop system for repetitive cuts.

Radial arm saws once filled the crosscut niche in many shops, but various idiosyncrasies, notably their tendency to wander out of square, render them inferior to modern sliding compound miter saws. I do keep a radial arm saw in my shop, but I use it only for rough crosscutting, a job for which it is well suited, given its powerful motor. If you have the space, I think it's worth having a radial arm saw for this task alone.

Stationary Belt/Disc Sander

Not to be confused with portable belt sanders (though some of the functions are the same), belt/disc sanding machines are extremely useful for many tasks, from fine-tuning a joint or shaping parts to sanding joints flush (such as dovetails or stile-to-rail connections on cabinet doors). Both bench and floor models are available, with disc sizes ranging from 6" to 12" (15.3 to 30.5 cm). It's well worth owning one of these handy machines, no matter what size you can afford.

A belt/disc sander is invaluable for all kinds of smoothing and shaping jobs. Here the author uses the belt portion to smooth the head of a mallet. The sanding disc shows in the left foreground.

Dust Collection

Machines make dust and chips. A lot of dust and chips. Dome of it goes on the floor, some of it goes in the air, and pretty much all of it's a problem. Machines simply can't operate well if chips and debris accumulate around the blades and motors. Nor is the shop environment healthy or safe with piles of chips on the floor and dust floating around.

Get some kind of dust collection system for gathering dust and chips at the source. Your machines will operate better, your cleanup will be faster, and you'll protect your respiratory system from harmful wood dust.

There are many good dust collectors on the market. Designs vary somewhat, but all rely on an impeller fan and a fairly large motor to pull waste into a collection bag or canister. A two-stage filter exhausts cleaner air, but even a simple one-bag system is capable of capturing particles as small as one micron.

For a one-woman shop, a dust collection system with a one-horsepower motor system is adequate. If you plan on running more than one machine at a time, get the next larger size. Don't be tempted to use your dust collector as a vacuum cleaner. Sucking up small objects like screws or small chunks of wood does serious damage to the impeller blades and shortens the life of the machine.

For general cleanup duty, get a heavy-duty shop vacuum. It's designed to handle the kinds of stuff you'll clean up in the shop—gritty particles, chunks of wood and metal, and all kinds of chips and dust. When I buy a shop vacuum, I focus on the quality of the hose and how it's attached to the machine, as well as to the accessories (cleaning brushes, extension tubes, etc.). These are often irritatingly underdesigned.

Finally, invest in an air filtration unit and hang it high on the ceiling where the fine dust lingers. Though many people consider it an optional piece of equipment, I consider it an important part of healthy woodworking. The very fine dust that dust collectors and vacuum cleaners miss can lodge in the nasal linings and lungs, increasing your susceptibility to allergies and respiratory infections. Keep in mind that long-term exposure to wood dust at very high concentrations (the kind of exposure that full-time workers in heavy industrial environments experience) has been deemed carcinogenic.

At the minimum, run the air filter whenever you run a machine, engage in a dusty activity like sanding, and sweeping, or cleanup. Studies have shown that it takes fine dust a few hours to settle, so keep the unit running for two or three hours after you complete the dust-generating activity.

Hand Tools

This category comprises a wide variety of different tools, such as planes, saws, chisels, marking tools, and measuring devices—all of which are operated by body power and finesse.

When getting started, you don't need hundreds of hand tools—just a few good-quality ones. As your skill level increases, you'll discover and appreciate a never-ending array of useful tools to add to your collection. Since this category is so vast, my goal is to help you narrow down the selection and focus on the tools you'll use most, not the ones that will end up just sitting on a shelf.

As a rule, hand tools are your most delicate tools, so store them with care. Left strewn on a bench top, tools get pushed around. They can collide and nick each other, roll off the bench, or get bumped to the floor. A tool won't always survive a crash to the floor. If it hits just right, it can be damaged beyond repair.

Find places for each of your hand tools so they can sit or hang in safety in convenient drawers, tool boxes, or cabinets. Protect blades with leather or any suitable material that is convenient to take on or off—old socks work well.

I have slots on some of my workbenches to hold chisels. You can also use magnetic bars. Just find a place where the tools you're currently using are safely out of the way yet readily accessible—and where they won't damage the workplace.

Hand Planes

I use both Japanese hand planes and the more familiar planes of the European tradition (often called Western planes when differentiating them from the Asian varieties). Modern Western planes typically have metal bodies and work on the push stroke. Japanese plane bodies are made of wood and are designed to cut as you pull the plane toward you.

Western planes are easier to adjust and understand, so I suggest you learn to use them first. Once you understand the principles of planning and sharpening, you'll be in a better position to deal with the Japanese plane's rather finicky tune-up operations and the difficulty of correctly fitting the plane body to the cutting iron. To make the transition a little easier, I suggest taking a class or a few private lessons from someone who understands Japanese tools.

Western planes have a curious nomenclature, which can be somewhat confusing to beginners and professionals alike. The common bench plane, used for edge and

surface planning, comes in various sizes, with names like smooth, jack, and jointer.

A smooth plane is about 9" (22.9 cm) long. It's used for final smoothing of a board that's already flat. A jack plane is around 15" (38 cm) long and is an all-purpose plane—a jack of all trades, so to speak. A jointer plane is something like 22" (55.9 cm) long and is used for getting surfaces truly flat so joints fit perfectly.

You'll also need a block plane for working end grain and a shoulder plane for joinery.

I don't have an extensive collection of hand planes. I seem to meet all my planning needs with three bench planes (smooth, jack, and jointer); two block planes (one made of metal and one made of wood); and two Japanese planes (similar in size to a jack plane and block plane).

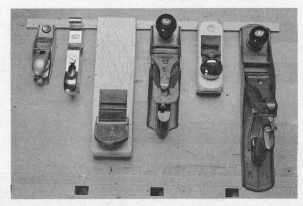

From left to right: *Bronze block plane, shoulder plane, Japanese plane, smooth plane, wooden block plane, jack plane. Resting the front of a plane on a slip of wood keeps the blade off the bench and prevents damage to the cutting edge.*

BUYING PLANES

If you've shopped around for Western planes, you know that the price for the same size plane can vary widely. The difference lies in the quality of materials and manufacture. An inexpensive plane can work as well as a very expensive one, but it's more likely that cutting corners to lower the price will result in some performance problems. A quality plane has a truly flat sole, good machine work in the body, and a good blade.

Many people look for good deals on planes at flea markets and antique shops, but in my experience, such places rarely have planes that are worth the bother. To get them up and running often requires a trip to a machine shop for flattening, a new blade, and a replacement handle. Unless the plane is of vintage character, I'd rather spend that money on something new.

Chisels

Start your woodworking practice with a couple of sets of butt chisels. They're the tools you'll reach for first. Buy a medium-priced set of four or six chisels to use in rough jobs like cleaning up glue, and a more expensive set for finer tasks. Stay away from low-end chisels; they're probably made from inferior steel. They won't sharpen properly, won't hold an edge, and are prone to break.

My Japanese butt chisels are by far my favorites, and I reach for them when doing any fine joinery or paring work, especially when making dovetails. Japanese chisels are made by laminating a layer of hard steel around an inner core of softer steel. The hard outer layer sharpens to a keen edge, but it's also somewhat brittle. It takes a little extra finesse to sharpen and use a quality Japanese chisel, so I recommend you gain some basic chisel experience before buying a set.

Explore catalogs and become familiar with the many types of chisels available. Someday you'll run into a problem that a specialty chisel can solve. Two specialty chisels you'll need sooner rather than later are a dogleg chisel and a mortising chisel or two. The dogleg lets you get down into the bottoms of mortises, grooves, and dadoes to fine-tune a fit. Mortising chisels are made for heavy pounding; they're heftier than ordinary chisels and have a steeper cutting angle.

It is better, in my opinion, to strike chisels with wooden mallets. This is true even for Japanese chisels, which are said to be designed for striking with special metal hammers. I think a wooden mallet is more pleasant to use and easier to control. Never use a carpenter's claw hammer for striking a woodworking chisel.

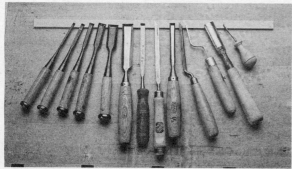

You'll need a variety of chisels and chisel-like tools to build the projects in this book. From left: a set of five Japanese chisels, a wooden-handled bench chisel, a plastic-handled chisel, a skew chisel (good for cleaning out dovetails), another bench chisel, two dog-legged chisels for cleaning out the bottoms of dadoes and grooves, and two gouges for carving.

Sharpening Supplies

Sharpening is an integral part of woodworking and is something you need to master as soon as possible. It's a simple process, but the details are important; the details can make it seem more complicated than it really is.

With only a few good waterstones and a simple holding jig, achieving a good, sharp edge on plane and chisel blades is well within your grasp. In fact, the ability to sharpen is tantamount to reaching a higher level of woodworking skill.

Using stones to sharpen and refine an edge is called honing and involves five stones ranging in grit from 220 to 6000. You probably won't use all five stones every time you hone an edge. Use only as coarse a grit as necessary. For instance, removing a small nick and an edge can be a lot of work, so you want to start with a coarse 220-grit stone to remove material as quickly as possible. On the other hand, touching up an edge that's in pretty good shape might require only a few passes on a 6000-grit stone. With practice you will learn to intuit what is required; it's not really all that complicated.

Rather than trying to hold the blade at the correct angle, I suggest you get a jig to hold the blade at a consistent angle during honing. There are a number of jigs on the market, and in this case the more expensive ones aren't necessarily better.

If your blade gets a bad nick, using a grinder can save a lot of time. A coarse wheel removes a lot of metal in a hurry, but keep a light touch—it's easy to overheat the blade and ruin its temper.

I suggest a slow-speed grinder to reduce the likelihood of overheating, and I prefer ones with a wheel that turns in a water bath. I get such great results with my waterbath grinder that I now look forward to grinding.

Japanese Saws

Once I started using Japanese saws, my Western saws became wall ornaments. Their pull-stroke design, razor-

Japanese saws. *From top: kataba ripping saw, kataba crosscut, ryoba saw with rip and crosscut edges, ryoba azebiki saw with rip and crosscut edges.*

sharp teeth, and thin blades make cutting wood by hand almost effortless. These saws are well suited for women because they don't require nearly as much muscle power as push saws—making it possible to focus on precision rather than endurance.

Be patient with your first saws; they take a little getting used to. The steel in Japanese saws is very hard and brittle, so you must take care not to bend or stress the blade beyond its capacity. It's all in the stance and grip. When you're holding the saw properly, sawing is easy.

There are many different types of Japanese saws, but for general woodworking you only need to concern yourself with two basic styles: ryoba and kataba. Ryoba saws have two different cutting edges, one with teeth set for ripping and one for crosscutting. Kataba saws have only one cutting edge. Within these styles, you'll find all kinds of saws with varying shapes, lengths, and tooth styles—each intended for a specialized task.

To start out, a general purpose ryoba saw will serve well for ripping, crosscutting, dovetailing, cutting angles, and cutting tenons. I like saws with replaceable blades because I don't have to bother resharpening them.

Another handy saw, the azebiki, is useful for starting cuts in the middle of material, making stopped cuts, cutting grooves, and even creating end rabbets. The kugihiki is fine toothed and has no set to the teeth. It's excellent for flush cutting protruding dowels and the like without scratching the surface. Finally, there's a hefty saw called anahiki, which is used for rough crosscutting and is so effective that it's often more convenient than taking lumber over to the radial arm saw, or finding and plugging in a circular saw.

Shaping Tools

In woodworking, we frequently wander off the straight and narrow—situations where we want curves and edges that aren't perpendicular. Then we must rely on hand tools to help shape things up. Woodworkers who incorporate extensively shaped parts in their furniture often have arsenals of tools, both hand and power, to accomplish their tasks. Sculptural woodworking is a labor-intensive proposition. But adding texture and form with a few curves, some low relief areas, and profiles is easily accomplished with just a few simple hand tools.

RASPS AND FILES

Files are made for working both wood and metal, but they're not interchangeable. Metalworking files are much less coarse and don't work very well on wood. Wood files are best for finish-shaping work. Rasps look like files, but the tooth pattern cuts more aggressively. I like patternmaker's rasps, which have relatively fine, sharp teeth and cut wood quickly and cleanly. Rasps that aren't flat are called rifflers, and they're useful for smaller detail work.

Files and rasps are usually sold without handles, and you can use them that way. You'll find it a lot more comfortable if you also purchase the special wooden file handles made to fit the ends of these tools. Keep your rasps and files free of dust and debris. Use a file card to scrub the teeth clean, and store these tools carefully so the teeth aren't dulled by contact with other metal objects.

SPOKESHAVES

You don't need a fancy designer spokeshave; just get a run-of-the-mill, metal-bodied version and learn to use it. A spokeshave works best on outside curves and profiles, but it will take some practice to get the feel of using it. You've go to hold it at just the right angle to cut properly. Chatter is the big problem with spokeshaves, and you can reduce that problem somewhat by replacing the blade with a thicker one. You'll need to enlarge the blade opening slightly, but that's easily accomplished with a metal worker's file.

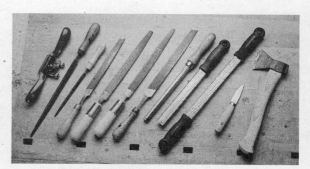

Shaping tools, from left: spokeshave, large triangular file, small triangular file, fine wood file, coarse patternmaker's rasp, fine patternmaker's rasp, metal file, round garter-style rasp, medium-sized grater-style rasp, large two-handed grater-style rasp, carving knife, and small axe.

Measuring, Marking, and Layout Tools

Accurate measuring and marking is a critical part of woodworking. At first, you're likely to find the whole measuring/marking/accuracy thing a little daunting. You may have a few mind blocks surrounding fractions, measuring, or just dealing with numbers in general.

Most adults are a little rusty with fractions. They're not things most people use on a daily basis, and as with a foreign language, fluency is quickly lost without practice. In woodworking we're normally concerned with fractions $^1/_{16}$" and larger; get out a tape measure or ruler and reacquaint yourself what these measurements mean: $^1/_{16}$", $^1/_8$", $^3/_{16}$", $^1/_4$", $^5/_{16}$", $^3/_8$", $^7/_{16}$", $^1/_2$", $^9/_{16}$", $^5/_8$", $^{11}/_{16}$", $^3/_4$", $^{13}/_{16}$", $^7/_8$", and $^{15}/_{16}$". For easy addition and subtraction, it helps to memorize the decimal equivalents of the more common fractions ($^1/_8$" = .125", $^1/_2$" = .5", and so on). Until it comes easily, keep a fraction/decimal conversion chart handy.

At this point, you might need some reassuring. Don't worry, your woodworking needn't be bogged down with numbers. They're just a way to convey information. If the increments are too small to see, such as 32nds or 64ths, I dispense with them all together and figure out another way to solve the problem.

MEASURING DEVICES

Perhaps the most basic of all woodworking measuring devices is the tape measure. You probably have a few lying around, but if they're old and hard to read, get a new one. You don't need a 25' (7.6 m) tape if you're building furniture. You rarely need the length, and it's awkward to hold and too bulky to keep in a tool apron. A 16' (4.9 m) tape is perfect.

A few metal rules will be helpful in the shop. I always have a 6" (15.2 cm) rule in my tool apron for quick access, and a 24" (61 cm) rule nearby. I prefer rules marked in increments of $^1/_{16}$" and $^1/_{32}$" on one side and 1 mm and 0.5 mm on the other. The metric system is handy on occasion.

Though many people associate it with metalworking, I find a dial caliper very handy around a woodworking shop. It's an easy way to measure the thickness of wood as it comes out of the planer, and to measure the insides of mortises and the outside of tenons, and it serves as a depth gauge as well. Woodworking calipers don't need to be as precise or as expensive as machinist's calipers. Look for a pair made for woodworking, with a dial graduated in fractions of an inch. My favorite caliper gives readings in three units: fractions of an inch, decimal inches, and millimeters.

SQUARES

Possibly no other tool in the shop is more often used and relied upon than the combination square. Don't scrimp here. A cheap square simply won't cut the mustard. I recommend both a 6" and a 12" (15.2 and 30.5 cm) square. You need the larger one frequently, but the smaller one fits in your work apron pocket and will be your constant companion.

Marking perfectly square lines on both the face and edge of a board can be difficult with a square, so I suggest purchasing a set of saddle squares to make this job much

Continued ➔

easier. Saddle squares have a lot of surface area, so you don't have to balance the square with one hand while you mark with the other. A set of saddle squares should include a 90° saddle square and two others to mark standard dovetail angles.

PENCILS AND KNIVES

Elementary as it may seem, the right pencil is important for accurate woodworking. More often than not, students arrive in my classes with those big, square carpentry pencils meant for marking 2 x 4s for house construction. They're worthless for fine work. A crisp narrow line is what you need—a line you can cut to with a fine-toothed Japanese saw.

You might think a mechanical pencil would be ideal, but the lead breaks almost immediately on wood. The best thing is a common No. 2 pencil. Keep it nice and sharp (I use an electric pencil sharpener). It leaves a line that's dark enough to see, fine enough to cut to, and soft enough not to dent the wood under any lines you may need to erase later.

Sometimes even a pencil line is too wide. When you're cutting dovetails (or tenons), being off by a pencil width is too much. In those situations, mark with a knife line. It leaves a tiny kerf that you can find by feel to start the saw cut, or pare to with a chisel. Any woodworking marking knife is fine for this job, as are surgical knives.

MARKING GAUGE

A marking gauge is a way to make a long knife cut without a ruler. You adjust the gauge against the edge of the wood so the knife is positioned just where you want it. Rather than an old-fashioned kind that uses an actual knife, I prefer the kind that uses a wheel. They make very clean and distinct lines.

Take care to store this tool in a box or protective cover, as a nick in the wheel will render it useless. Wheels can also come loose from stems; tighten them periodically so you won't have wobbly marks.

TOOLS FOR ANGLES

If you're only dealing with 90° or 45° situations, a combination square will serve you well. But for other angles, you'll need to enlist a few more tools.

A sliding bevel gauge with an adjustable arm lets you measure and transfer angles from layout to workpiece to machine, as necessary. You don't need a fancy one—this is one case where an inexpensive home-center tool will work fine.

A drafting protractor will come in handy from time to time, as will a 6' (1.8 m) steel engineer's protractor. From time to time, you'll need a larger 10" (25.4 cm) adjustable protractor. These are usually clear plastic and have two arms that you lock at the appropriate angle with a knurled knob.

Clamps

You can't do woodworking without clamps. Integral parts of everyday life in the shop, they're used for gluing pieces together and as holding devices. Woodworkers often lament that they never have enough clamps.

For gluing up wide surfaces such as tabletops, you will need pipe of bar clamps. Pipe clamp fixtures come as a set (head and tail piece) that grip any length of ¾" (1.9 cm) (or ½" [1.3 cm] for lighter-duty applications) black pipe from a home or plumbing-supply store. Bar clamps are purchased as complete units, and it's a good idea to have a variety of sizes on hand. I keep my eyes open for catalog specials, and buy four or six clamps whenever I see a good deal. Plan to have a few light-duty bar clamps as well—they're available in lengths as short as 4" (10.2 cm) and have a deeper reach than typical bar clamps. Again, a variety of sizes will be useful.

Definitely have at least several C-clamps and a few deep-reach clamps in your shop. Some spring clamps are handy for light-duty work—since you can set them with one hand, they can make life a lot easier. Occasionally you need a strap to clamp around an object. For that I use web straps wth ratcheting buckles sold as automotive tie-downs.

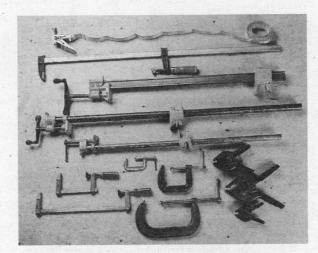

Clamps, from top: strap clamp, long light-duty bar clamps, heavy bar clamp, heavy-duty pipe clamp, light-duty pipe clamp, light-duty bar clamps, C-clamps, and spring clamps.

Workbenches

You may not think of workbenches as tools, but in reality they are perhaps the most important tools in the shop—without them we could achieve very little. If you have the room, I recommend more than one bench.

Your first purchase should probably be a traditional European-style bench. Equipped with thick tops, often of maple or beech, and a sturdy base, these hefty benches provide a solid foundation from which to work. Typically mounted with a different type of vise on each end, they offer a variety of ways to secure your work. You can purchase plans and build your own bench, or you can buy one ready-made.

Your second bench should be a large multipurpose table, where gluing, sanding, and other messy tasks can take place. An easy way to create such a table is to build a frame 48" (122 cm) wide and 96" (244 cm) long from 1½"-thick (4 cm) poplar, then glue and screw a sheet of ½" (1.3 cm) plywood to both sides of the frame. To create a solid base for the tabletop and some additional storage space as well, construct three cabinets out of ¾" (1.9 cm) shop-grade plywood.

Let the top overhang the cabinets by about 3" (7.6 cm) all around so you can easily clamp things down to the edges. Bolt a vise or two to this bench, if you like.

A folding workbench with a built-in vise (readily available at hardware stores and home centers) is right there when you need it. These small but sturdy benches are easily moved about the shop or folded down for storage or transport. For more stability, I add a shelf down low to hold a toolbox filled with heavy, little-used tools.

Finally, consider having a bench that is low enough to sit on, thus utilizing body weight as yet another way to hold parts while working on them.

Safety Equipment

Safety may not be the most stimulating subject in woodworking, but given the somewhat hazardous nature of working with sharp tools and flying bits of wood, it's an integral part of learning how to be in a wood shop.

Protecting your eyes and ears is fairly simple. Safety glasses or goggles are readily available and inexpensive. What you end up with is largely a matter of personal preference. The trick is to make sure you wear the devices every time a hazard is present. Don't let yourself get away with inventing any excuse for why you don't need to bother this one time.

Even though you have a dust collector and air filters working for you, don't rule out wearing a dust protection mask, especially when you're using a router or other tools that defy dust collection. A dust mask is not the same as a respirator. A dust mask is a fairly simple item, which protects against particles in the air. A respirator is designed to filter harmful chemicals from the air. The two are not interchangeable.

Wearing eye-, ear-, and respiratory-protection gear all at the same time can be problematic, especially if you wear eyeglasses. Many respirators fog up your glasses, and earmuff-type hearing protectors squeeze your glasses tightly against the temples. I've had a lot of success with an air helmet. Powered by a battery/filter pack worn at the waist, it pumps clean air into a face shield/helmet apparatus, thus protecting lungs and eyes at the same time.

Gloves can spare you from the most common woodworking injuries—splinters. I've come to prefer rubber-coated gardening gloves for milling tasks. Since gloves can make some tasks difficult (I won't wear them when using the drill press, for example), keep some tweezers, a needle, and a magnifying glass at the ready.

Keep a first-aid kit in the shop, and make sure it includes eyewash. Have an emergency plan ready in case of a more serious injury.

Have a couple of fire extinguishers (more if your shop is large). Locate them near the exits, and keep one in the middle of the room as well. Use those rated ABC, and get the rechargeable type with the metal head. Check them regularly to make sure they're fully charged and ready to go. Fire multiplies in intensity very quickly, extinguisher or not. Act fast, and don't hesitate to call the fire department sooner rather than later.

—FROM *Woodworking 101 for Women*

FUNDAMENTAL WOODWORKING TECHNIQUES

This section offers you an array of techniques and methods commonly used to build furniture—concepts that can be used repeatedly throughout your woodworking practice. Though there is often more than one way to accomplish the same task, I offer these particular techniques based upon ease, safety, and suitability for the novice to intermediate woodworker in a small shop situation. These are techniques I use on a frequent basis in my own shop as well. As you grow with your practice, you may wish to extrapolate from this information and try variations or entirely different methods. The woodworking book of rules is somewhat malleable, inviting change, experimentation, and adaptation.

This section covers the fundamental techniques required to build the projects. I have arranged the information based upon the techniques themselves rather than explaining them via each individual project. In woodworking, there are "ties that bind," whether you're building a box, cabinet, table, or chair. A groove is a groove, a dovetail a dovetail—the size or layout may vary, but the technique to produce it remains the same. In some instances, I offer both machine and hand-tool techniques.

Practice on scrap wood until you become comfortable with the various techniques. It's often easier to learn using softwoods, where resistance between tool and wood is lessened. Of all the techniques used in this book, dovetailing will probably require the most concentrated amount of effort and practice.

Moving Your Axis: Woodworking and the Body

While having a huge set of muscles may provide some advantages to a woodworker, it's certainly not a prerequisite for success. Enthusiasm, willingness, and curiosity are attributes that are more important. Woodworking is more about problem solving than anything else, and body strength is only part of the equation.

Keep in mind that when you first begin using many of the techniques here (hand planing is s good example), you'll discover your muscles are not up to the task. You might feel as if the wood is working you, not vice versa. Keep working, and your muscles will rapidly strengthen. Practice your skills, and before long, you'll reach what I call the fluidity stage, where your body, the wood, and the tools are all working in harmony.

Woodworking is a give and take activity. You can't force the tools or materials to do something just because you want it to happen. Nor can you force yourself to work beyond your (current) physical limitations or level of skill. When things don't work out the way you want, and your frustration level rises, take a step back. Reassess. Working wood is not about strength and control. It's about innovation and information.

Difficulties and mistakes are not things to be overcome and defeated. Most mistakes in the shop are merely the result of inadequate information or experience, and not an indication that the woodworker is inadequate to the job. Make this your mantra: "Mistakes are just information." Repeat it often.

Woodworking does involve a degree of hard work; much of the process is moving things around. If you decide to build a large, solid wood entertainment center, be prepared for hard physical labor from the get go. But information and innovation come into play here, too. You can design the center with your physical limitations in mind. Create the structure from three smaller units, each of which you can manage on your own. Once the units are on site, you can assemble them into the monolithic unit you had in mind from the start.

I suggest you work your way up to larger projects, building your physical and mental muscles in the process. Start with small, easily managed projects and build upon your mistakes (and success, though that's often more difficult). In time, you'll be able to handle the entertainment center in every sense of the word.

Milling Lumber Four-Square

The journey from rough boards to refined parts is a logical sequence of steps, a well-worn path you must follow if you intend to mill parts that are flat and square. Parts that aren't flat and square cause problems at every step of your project—you can't make accurate measurements, machine identical cuts, or assemble close fitting joints. It's vital that you start your projects with every board milled four-square, even those that will be sawn or shaped into curves.

When a board is four-square, every surface is flat and every corner is square. It's flat along both its length and width. The two faces are parallel, and the edges are perpendicular to the faces. The ends are parallel to one another and perpendicular to both the sides and the faces (see fig. 1).

Exposing fresh surfaces by milling can cause a board to shrink or swell, depending on its moisture content and the ambient humidity. Ripping can release tensions developed as the tree grew toward the sun, possibly causing the boards to twist or bow. If you don't consider these things and plan your milling accordingly, your four-square lumber can twist out of shape in a matter of hours.

The key to preventing such a disaster is to run through the milling process twice. The first time, make the pieces larger in all dimensions than you need. Then let them sit in your shop for at least a few days. The oversize boards will acclimate to the humidity in your shop, moving and chang-

ing as they must. Then mill them again, going through each step, assuming the lumber is no longer four-square.

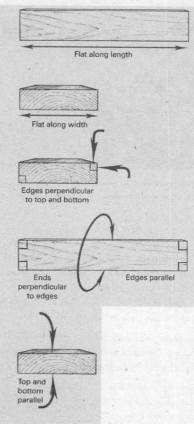

WHAT IS FOUR-SQUARE?

Flat along length

Flat along width

Edges perpendicular to top and bottom

Ends perpendicular to edges

Edges parallel

Top and bottom parallel

Figure 1

Preliminary Dimensioning

The first step in milling is conceptual—deciding what parts of the project each board will yield. Take a close look at all the boards and note any problems, such as troublesome knots, hairline cracks, end checks, wild grain, and severe cup or twist. It takes practice to develop a sense about wood—there's a fine line between "defects" that might be called character and ones that mean trouble. Think about the visually important areas of the project and lay out those parts on the best-looking boards.

The first step in any project is deciding how to lay out the pieces on your lumber. Mark rough lengths and widths with a grease pencil. Use a dark color for light woods and a light pencil for dark ones.

Break down your lumber into manageable lengths with a circular saw. The author often does this outdoors, before the lumber even goes into the shop.

As you lay out all the pieces, leave plenty of room all around—at least an inch if possible. I use a grease pencil to mark out the pieces (dark pencils for light-colored woods, light ones for dark woods). Their bold lines are much easier to see.

Cut to Rough Length

Short boards are easier to deal with, so cut them down early in the process. In fact, I sometimes crosscut long boards outside, before I even get them into the shop. I use a circular saw, but you can also use a hand saw. Either way, support the wood in a few places so it won't buckle and bind the saw. If I need to rough cut the wood to shorter lengths once it's indoors, I use a radial arm saw.

Cut your boards at least 1" (2.5 cm) longer than you need, and 2" (5 cm) if you're going to laminate them or glue them into a wider panel.

Straighten One Edge

The simplest way to get a straight edge is to run it over the jointer. Make as many passes as necessary.

If the board is too crooked to joint, draw the line first and then use the band saw to cut to the line (don't use a fence; cut freehand). Then use the jointer to get the edge truly straight.

Don't be tempted to use the table saw for this. Safe operation of that tool requires a straight edge to run against the fence, and you don't yet have one.

Run the workpiece through the jointer facedown to establish an initial flat, straight surface. To get a straight edge, run the piece through the jointer again, this time with the face side against the fence.

Rip to Rough Width

Ripping can release pent-up energy within the wood, sometimes causing it to bow and twist immediately after sawing. If you're using a table saw, this can result in a dangerous kickback. That's why I prefer to use the band saw (with fence this time) for rough ripping. Make your wood about ¼" (6 mm) wider than your final dimension.

Resaw to Rough Thickness

If your project calls for boards that are significantly thinner than what you can get at the lumberyard, you can slice it up by resawing. Generally, if you need to plane off more than ⅜" (9.5 mm) to arrive at the desired thickness, consider resawing. If I need ⅝" (1.6 cm) lumber from 4/4 stock, I'd plane it down. If I needed ½" (1.3 cm) or less, I'd resaw. It takes less time than planning, and it would reduce the wear and tear on the planer knives (always a consideration because changing the knives is an involved process).

1. Resaw the stock on the band saw to about ⅛" (3 mm) thicker than the desired rough thickness.

2. Run the boards through the planer, taking them down to the desired rough thickness.

Though it's possible to resaw on the table saw, I prefer the hand saw. With its thinner blade, you waste less material cutting the kerf. Table saws make a smoother cut (you may be able to forego the planer), but they make a much wider kerf, and the maximum blade height limits you to narrow boards (typically about 3½" [8.9 cm] wide). You can resaw wider boards on the table saw, but you still need to use a band saw. The usual process is to run a groove down both edges of the workpiece on the table saw, and then use the kerfs to guide your resawing on the band saw. You'll still have to run the pieces through the planer to remove the saw marks.

In any event, you can't use the table saw on rough lumber. The surface that goes against the fence on a table saw must always be jointed flat and straight, or you run a considerable risk or kickback.

Final Dimensioning

Woodworking mistakes are cumulative, so any errors you make during milling will lay the foundation for further

Continued ➔

complications later on. Monitor the process, checking for square at each step, and making corrections before it's too late.

JOINT FACE AND EDGE

1. Run one face of the board over the jointer as many times as necessary until the tool takes a full-length, full-width cut.

2. Put that face against the fence and flatten the adjacent edge.

PLANE TO THICKNESS

When milling parts to thickness, the actual final thickness is not as important as consistency. All the boards need to be exactly the same thickness, and it usually doesn't matter if it's a tiny bit more or less than specified.

It's hard to get the exact same thickness setting in a planer twice in a row, so run all the parts through the planer at a given setting, then lower the head and run them all through again. Continue until you reach the desired thickness.

1. Lay the jointed face down on the planer table, set the planer, and take a fine cut off the top. The first couple of cuts will only remove the high spots.

2. Plane the top surface until you get a full-width cut on the top. Then plane the faces alternately as you work toward the desired thickness. This equalizes tension in the wood.

RIP TO WIDTH

1. Set the table saw fence for the final width.

2. Run the jointed edge against the fence and rip to final width.

CROSSCUT TO FINAL LENGTH

1. Square up one end by crosscutting on a miter saw.

2. Use this square end as the origin, and carefully mark the final length.

3. Cut to final length.

When cutting multiple parts, assure consistency by clamping a block of wood to the fence (usually to the left of the saw), positioning it so that when the squared end is pushed against it, the saw automatically cuts the correct length.

Biscuit Joinery

A biscuit is nothing more than a football-shaped wafer of pressed wood set into semicircular slots on either side of a joint (see fig. 2). When saturated with glue, the wafer expands, locking the wood in a joint that's easy to make and incredibly strong.

Biscuit joinery can solve any number of woodworking problems, but in this book, we mainly use these joints for alignment when gluing up wide panels from two or more narrower boards, for attaching solid wood edging or frames to exposed plywood edges, and for corner joints in frame and panel construction. While the football wafers come in several sizes, all of this book's biscuit joinery uses moderately sized #20 biscuits.

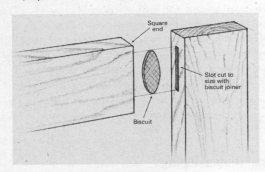

Laying Out and Cutting the Slots

1. Position the pieces on the bench in their final configuration.

To cut a slot, just align the mark on the indexing fence with the mark on the workpiece. Press the fence firmly downward to cut the biscuit slot parallel to the face.

2. Draw a pencil line across the joint at a 90° angle. This line represents the centerline of the biscuit slot. If you're working on a corner joint, the centerline of the biscuit slot should be in the middle of the end grain piece. When joining edges, it doesn't matter where the slots go. Just make sure you locate them so a later step won't expose the pressed wood biscuit.

3. Label each piece so you know exactly what it is because once you cut the slots, the pieces will only go together the way they were when you first marked the slots.

4. Adjust the biscuit fence to position the slot relative to the workpiece's face. The slots should be in the approximate middle of the material. Move the fence up or down, testing the cut in a piece of scrap until the slot is in the correct location.

5. Line up the reference mark on the biscuit joiner's fence with the mark on your workpiece. Then just press the trigger and push the cutter into the work. Small side-to-side misalignments don't matter since the biscuit is a little smaller than the slots. You can adjust the alignment a bit during glue-up, at least until the glue causes the biscuits to swell and lock the joint closed.

A simple plywood jig holds the work steady, even under the inward pressure of the cut.

6. While position is not crucial, the orientation of the slot is. It's essential to hold the machine steady so the slot is parallel to the top of the workpiece. Otherwise, the biscuits won't slip into their slots when the pieces are joined. This is much easier when the workpiece doesn't move around. Clamp the piece to the bench or make a simple fixture such as the one shown in the photo.

Biscuits and Edge-Gluing Wide Panels

Most lumber from commercial suppliers ranges in width from about 5" to 12" (12.7 to 30.5 cm). Occasionally you can find wider boards, but these days it's difficult to find boards even 12" (30.5 cm) wide. When your plans call for a wide surface such as a tabletop (or even a shelf), you'll have to create it by

Position the boards in a panel to minimize the glue line. Try to match the color tone of adjoining boards, and do your best to align the boards so the grain appears to swirl across the joint.

edge joining two or more pieces of lumber to create a panel. There are two keys to success in this operation: Mating edges that are perfectly straight and square, and keeping the panel flat during clamp-up.

A long edge-to-edge glue joint is quite strong but is also slippery and prone to shifting under clamping pressure. Biscuits are an excellent way to keep the boards properly aligned and under control while applying clamps and cauls. Here's how to put together a strong, flat panel with the aid of biscuits.

1. Start the process with your boards milled to the desired thickness. Lay them out as a panel, and arrange them so the grain patterns seem to flow across the joints. If adjoining boards have very different color or grain patterns, the eye is drawn to the joint (see photo).

2. Draw a large triangle across the surface so you can reposition the boards in correct order during the glue-up (see the photo). Additionally, mark the face of each board with "in" and the back with "out" for quick, positive identification later.

Preserve your layout by drawing a large triangle across the panel. Reassemble the boards incorrectly, and the triangle won't come out right.

3. To get good joints, it's important that the edges be straight and square to the face. Make sure your jointer fence sits at 90° (see the photo). Get into the habit of periodically checking it, and calibrate it as necessary.

Square edges are the foundations of successful joinery. When milling lumber four-square, assume nothing—frequently check that your jointer continues to cut square.

4. Having good joints on the edges of the boards is so important that even after setting the fence, you should work as though the fence is not perfect. Account for any minor discrepancies by running each edge over the jointer, alternating the face in or out to the fence, so mating edges will end up with complementary angles.

5. Once you've achieved straight edges, lay the boards back in order. Mark for biscuits and cut the slots as described above.

6. Make a test run of your glue-up, without setting any biscuits or applying glue. This alerts you to any problems and ensures that all the necessary materials are at hand. Follow steps 10 to 13 below, omitting the glue and biscuits. Then repeat from step 7, as written.

7. While applying glue, it is helpful to hold the first board in a bench vise. Use a roller to apply glue to the edges, and a bottle with a special biscuit tip for getting glue into the slots. Similarly, apply glue to the mating edge of the next board.

Applying glue with a roller assures even coverage. It's also neater.

A special biscuiting glue tip spreads glue down in the slots. A glue-starved biscuit joint isn't very strong.

8. Tap biscuits into the slots on the board in the vise only.

Biscuits swell quickly; add them just before closing the joint.

9. Assemble the joint, tapping it closed with a wooden mallet.

Lightly tap the joint to close it. Don't clean up the squeezed-out glue—you'll only spread it around. Wait until it's dry.

10. Lift the entire piece onto awaiting clamps. Draw the boards together with light clamping pressure, then clamp 2 x 4s (or any wood of similar dimensions) across the ends of the panel to hold the surface flat, as shown in the photo above. Known as cauls, these boards distribute the clamping pressure as well as protect the surface of the panel from being damaged by the clamps. A little paste wax on the cauls keeps them from sticking to the panel.

11. Crank each panel clamp tight, and then tighten down the C-clamps on the cauls.

12. Check for flatness and adjust the clamps as necessary.

13. Don't clean up any glue squeeze out—it only smears the adhesive into the grain. Wait until the glue is dry, and then remove it with a scraper.

14. Leave the panel under pressure for at least an hour.

Good clamping technique helps keep wide panels flat. Position the long bar clamps so at least two span the top surface of the panel, and clamp stiff cauls on the end.

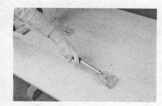

After the glue cures (about an hour at room temperature), remove it with a paint scraper.

Double Biscuit Joints

For additional strength, you can cut two biscuit slots per joint (see the photo below). Proper procedure is important here. Test your setup on scrap wood exactly the same thickness as your workpiece. It may take a few cycles of trial and error to get the right setup.

A double biscuit joint is stronger than one joined with a single biscuit.

1. Always work from the same side of the material (top or bottom). From the start, label everything clearly to avoid confusion.

2. Cut the first slot in the lower third of the thickness, about 7/16" (1.1 cm) down from the top for 3/4" (1.9 cm) material. The exact position is not crucial—but don't cut the slots too close together or too close to the edge.

3. Slip a spacer under the fence (on top of the workpiece) for the second cut. For 3/4" (1.9 cm) material, a 3/16" (4 mm) spacer works well.

Biscuits for Frame and Panel

Traditional frame and panel is an attractive method of construction, and it's also an excellent system for dealing with wood movement. The narrow frames bear the structural load, while a thin, lightweight panel keeps the dust out. The panel floats in a groove cut in the edges of the frame, allowing it to shrink and swell with changes in humidity.

These days, panels are often made of plywood, which doesn't leave much seasonal movement. Rather than dealing with those grooves, we can simplify the construction by simply biscuiting the panel to the frame.

Most of the time, the joints are made with the face of the panel set back about 1/4" (6 mm) from the edge of the frame (see fig. 3). Occasionally a design calls for the face of the frame and the panel to be flush, with no setback. Getting the desired outcome depends on the thicknesses of the materials used, as well as following the proper sequence when cutting biscuits.

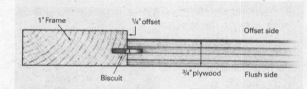

Let's say your frame is 1"-thick (2.5 cm) solid wood fitted with a 3/4" (1.9 cm) plywood panel. If you lay out the assembly face up on the bench, you'll be able to see the offset on the top. The natural tendency is to mark for the slots on the top surface, then use that top surface as a reference for the biscuit joiner fence. If you do it this way, when you assemble the panel the frame and panel will be flush on the top surface, with the offset in the back—exactly what you don't want.

Following is the proper sequence for building biscuited frames and panels:

1. Cut the panels to final length and rough width, do all surface prep, and apply the final finish.

2. Leave the rails and stiles a little long, and put some finish on what will be the offset. It's easier to do now rather than later, especially if the frames and panels have different finishes. It's important to keep finish off any gluing surfaces.

3. Lay out the rails and panels and mark the biscuit locations. Remember, the offset surface goes face down on the bench. Typically, this is the outside or front face of the frame and panel.

4. Cut the slots with the biscuit cutter fence on the surface that's supposed to be flush (that is, the non-offset surface—typically the back).

5. Apply glue to the rails, the mating edge of the panel, and the biscuit slots.

6. Tap the biscuits into the rails, and attach the panel. Do both rails on each panel, and clamp in place. You may need cauls across the ends to keep the assembly flat. Let dry for an hour.

7. When the glue is dry, remove the panel from the clamps, and clean off any excess glue from the setback with a sharp chisel.

8. Use a Japanese saw or miter saw to cut off most but not all of the rail overhangs on one side. Don't bother to get them flush—that comes later.

9. Run that side against the table saw fence, and cut the rails flush with the plywood of the other edge.

10. Run this edge against the fence, and cut the panel to final width.

11. Lay the panel on the bench with the rough length stiles in position.

12. Mark the locations of the biscuits that will attach the stiles to both the panel and the rails.

13. Apply glue and biscuits and clamp the assembly together. Use cauls as necessary to keep the assembly flat.

14. Remove the assembly from the clamps, cut off the overhangs, and sand flush with a stationary belt sander or a random orbit sander.

Keep the panel flat with sturdy cauls clamped from rail to rail.

Cut one edge of the overhanging rails so they are almost (but not quite) flush with one edge of the panel. Use a handsaw or miter saw so they end up like the top edge here.

Place the cut edge against the fence and rip a small amount off the panel, leaving a flush edge. Then place that edge against the fence and rip to final width.

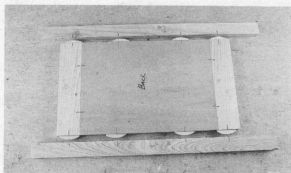

With the panel at final width, biscuit the rough length stiles in place. Trim the excess flush after the glue dries.

Continued ➡

Efficient hand planing is not something most people can do without practice. It takes a while to get used to the movement and find your rhythm. It's a little like learning how to ride a bicycle—it's hard to do until you've done it. Then you never forget.

The biggest problem with learning how to use hand planes is that no amount of practice or technique can overcome a dull or poorly adjusted hand plane. I remember struggling with hand planes until a knowledgeable woodworker friend led me through the process. With an experienced guide, it took less than an hour for me to make the breakthrough. A sharp blade is half the battle. If you're just learning how to hand plane, I suggest you start with sharpening. Next, learn to adjust the blade for a good, clean cut.

1. Hold the plane close to your chest, with its front handle up, and sight down the sole.

2. Extend the blade by turning the depth-adjustment screw counterclockwise until you can see it above the sole.

3. Adjust the skew with the lever located just behind the blade assembly. Turn it side to side until the blade is parallel to the sole, with no skew at all.

4. Retract the blade until it's just barely visible above the sole. At some point, you may realize it's skewed again. Adjust as necessary.

5. Make a test cut. If the blade is retracted too far to make shavings, lower it with less than a quarter turn of the depth-adjustment screw.

6. Keep your cuts light and your shavings thin. Light cuts create a smoother surface with less effort.

Another key factor in planning success is holding your work. Proper planning uses your whole upper body, not just your arms. If the workpiece is too high, it's impossible to get your strength behind the plane. I like to work with the piece at waist height. When I'm working with small pieces, it's usually easiest to lock them in the bench vise of my traditional European workbench. This method puts wider pieces well above my waist, so I clamp them to my low workbench.

Using Japanese Saws

Japanese saws are thin and delicate. They cut on the pull stroke and are sensitive to your alignment. If you're perfectly positioned, with saw, hand, wrist, and arm in one straight line, sawing is effortless. If you're not aligned, the saw will bend, bind, and drift off the mark. Hand sawing to a line is a skill that requires practice to get and keep. I suggest making many practice cuts in softwoods as a way of gaining intrinsic knowledge of the tool (and yourself).

Cutting Joints

Japanese saws cut well when the handle is tilted downward slightly, rather than with the edge parallel to the floor.

1. Use a square to mark your cut lines on both sides of the material.

2. Stand directly in front of the material and grip the saw with your dominant hand. Make sure your hand, wrist, and arm are aligned with the handle.

3. Angle the saw slightly, rather than cutting parallel to the surface. Check your cut lines on both sides of the board frequently as you saw.

Crosscutting

1. Lay out cut lines with a square on the face of the material.

2. Place the workpiece on a low surface and kneel on it to hold it down.

3. Keep your alignment and hold the saw at a slight angle.

Keep the work low when crosscutting, and use your knee as a hold down.

Ripping

1. Lay out your cut lines with a square or marking gauge. Lightly pencil in the knife cut so you can see it.

2. Angle the workpiece in a vise or on the low workbench. Alternatively, put the work on the bench and climb on top to hold it.

3. Keep your alignment and hold the saw at a slight angle to the work.

Ripping requires less effort when the work is held at an angle (here on the tilted top of the low workbench), and the saw is held approximately parallel to the floor.

Edge Treatments

Softening the Arris

Though it's a perfectly modern word, most people don't know what an arris is until they take up woodworking. It's the sharp edge or ridge at the point where two surfaces meet—the edge of the tabletop or the cutting edge of a chisel. In furniture making, we treat every arris to make the piece softer to the touch (you can actually cut yourself on a crisp hardwood edge) and to give a more elegant, refined appearance.

A light shaving planed off the corner of an edge softens the arris.

1. Take a very light shaving right off the arris with a block plane.

2. To prevent tear-out at the corners, change the planing direction at each end so you're always planning into the long grain from the end grain.

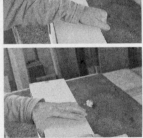

To avoid tear-out at the ends, plane inward from each corner.

3. Light softening can also be done with sandpaper, but be sure to use a block or pad with a flat surface. The arris is very sharp, and sanding without a block is a splinter hazard.

When softening an arris by hand sanding, always use a block or pad so the sanding surface is flat.

Chamfers

A strongly beveled arris is called a chamfer. While you can cut chamfers by eye, they'll be more consistent and look better if you take the time to lay them out and plane to a line.

Layout lines make it easier to hand plane consistent chamfers. The angle on the side gives a visual clue for how to tilt the plane when starting.

1. Rest the combination square with its base on the edge to be chamfered. Draw lines on either side of this edge to set the limits of the chamfer. It's helpful to connect the lines on the side. This gives you a visual clue for the angle at which you should hold the plane.

Use a block plane for chamfers on end grain and a bench plane on long or side grain.

2. Plane the end grain with a block plane. If you're chamfering long grain, use a bench plane. Depending on the species of wood, you may need to plane towards the middle from each end to prevent tear-out.

On big projects, I sometimes use a handheld router with a 45° or 30° chamfer bit. It's faster and makes chamfers that are more consistent.

Edge Profiles with the Router

While chamfers are simple and elegant, some projects want a more complex edge treatment. In the old days, every woodworker had a collection of specialized planes to do this, but we have routers. Any woodworking catalog lists an inspiring collection of edge profile bits that can be used singly or in combination.

The router-made combination of 3/8" roundover on the top edge and a 30" chamfer on the bottom is an easy and attractive edge treatment.

One combination I like to use on a table or cabinet top is a ⅜" (9.5 cm) roundover bit on the top edge, and a 30" (76.2 cm) chamfer on the bottom edge. Whenever possible, I use a handheld router and profile the edge after assembly.

Whenever possible, profile the edges after assembly with a hand-held router and your choice of bearing bit.

Narrower pieces (2" [5 cm] wide or less) make it hard to stabilize the router for handheld operations. Think ahead—it may be easier to profile the parts on the router table before assembly.

Making an Edge Appear Thinner

Rather than calling attention to an edge, you sometimes want to minimize it. This is common on tables, where a long chamfer on the underside makes the edge appear thinner and more elegant (see fig. 4).

Use a hand plane to cut the long, wide chamfer on straight edges. For curves, you'll need to use a spokeshave.

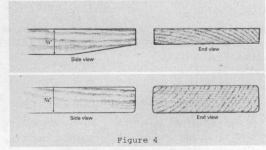

MAKING AN EDGE APPEAR THINNER

Side view — End view

Side view — End view

Figure 4

Mortise and Tenon Joints

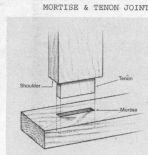

MORTISE & TENON JOINT

The mortise and tenon joint is one of the strongest joints in woodworking. It's best for connecting things at right angles, such as aprons to table legs or door rails to door stiles. Sturdy, stable, and good looking, the joint has a number of variations to its credit.

The basic joint consists of a square or rectangular socket cut into one piece of wood—the mortise. The end of the mating piece is trimmed into a tenon with a close fit for the socket (see above). The shoulders on the tenon prevent the joint from racking into a parallelogram, and cover any of the mortise's imperfections.

Long the gold standard for strength and beauty, mortise and tenon joints can be time-consuming to construct. Careful layout and fitting is crucial—a sloppy mortise and tenon is simply not a strong joint.

The Open Mortise

Over the years, woodworkers have devised a variety of ways to make square holes. I typically use a plunge router or a drill press, but the easiest way to make mortises is to plan ahead and use the sandwich method for open mortises.

In this case, two halves make a hole. Rather than trying to cut a square hole in the middle of a board, glue up the necessary thickness from two narrower boards and cut half of the mortise out of each board before assembly. These cuts can be accomplished with a number of methods, using both hand and power tools.

Create an open mortise by laminating two grooved pieces. In this case, two halves make a hole.

1. Clamp the laminates in position and clearly mark the mortises on each piece. Careful layout is important here, and so is labeling the parts so you can keep track of mating pieces.

2. Using the drill press, bore ¼" (6 mm) alignment holes near the ends of the piece. Later, you'll insert dowels into the holes to keep the mortises aligned during glue-up.

Alignment is crucial when creating open mortises. Clamp the pieces together in perfect alignment, and then bore two holes near the ends of the pieces. To return to this perfection during glue-up, slip wooden pins into the holes. Trim them flush after the glue dries.

3. Remove the clamps and cut the half mortises using either a table saw, a band saw, or by hand.

TABLE SAW METHOD

A good dado blade capable of cutting a clean, flat bottom makes short work of open mortises. It's essentially the same process as cutting a dado.

If you don't have the right dado blade, you can use a regular blade. Use your miter gauge to make the shoulder cuts, and then make a number of passes between the shoulder and the ends. With the intermediate cuts, it's easy to pop out the waste with a sharp chisel. A router with a ½"-wide

After cutting the groove on the table saw, clean up the bottom of the cut with a router and a wide straight bit, keeping the bit away from the shoulders. Clean up the corners with a chisel.

(1.3 cm) straight bit quickly removes final waste from the bottom while leaving it perfectly flat. Keep the router about ¹⁄₁₆" (1.6 mm) away from the sides and clean up the corners with a chisel.

BAND SAW METHOD

You can also remove most of the wood with a band saw. It'll take a couple of cuts to get close to the line. Cut just shy of the bottom and use a router with a straight bit to get it just right.

Cutting an open mortise with a band saw is a multistep process. Cut the shoulder lines first, then cut from near the left edge toward the right, angling down to the depth line gradually. Saw along the line right up to the right shoulder line. Flip the piece over and saw from roughly the middle back to the other shoulder, right on the line. You'll need to clean up the bottom of the open, mortise with a shoulder plane or router.

HAND TOOL METHOD

Cut the shoulders with a Japanese azabiki saw. Make a number of intermediate cuts between the shoulders and pop out the waste with a chisel. Clean up the bottom of the cut with a router and a straight bit, or a shoulder plane if there's room. Check that the mortise halves align before glue-up.

Lay out the shoulders and cut to the line with a Japanese azebiki saw. Cut a few lines between the shoulders, taking care not to cut too deep.

1. Once the mortises are cut, apply the glue, and sandwich the pieces together. Put the ¼" (6 mm) dowels in each alignment hole to keep the pieces from sliding around.

2. Clamp up the pieces.

3. When the glue is dry, use a sharp chisel to flush-up any minor misalignment. You'll cut the tenon to fit, so this is not a problem.

The waste pops out with a light blow to the chisel. (This is an angled mortise.)

Standard Mortises

DRILL PRESS METHOD

When half mortises are not possible or desirable, you can use a drill press and chisel to make a mortise. The drill press removes most of the waste, and then you use the chisel to square up the ends and clean up the sides.

1. Lay out the mortise with a wheel-type marking gauge. Mark the centerline and determine the depth of cut.

2. Use a drill bit with a diameter about ⅛" (3 mm) less than the width of the mortise.

3. Drill a series of holes along the centerline. If this is a through mortise, drill down from both sides of the piece to prevent tear-out.

4. Use a sharp chisel to finalize the mortise borders. Orient it with the bevel side to the mortise.

5. Chop out the waste to the line, using a mortising chisel.

Remove the waste on the drill press, using a bit that is smaller than the finished mortise.

Use a mortise chisel to chop out the waste.

Plunge Router Method

A plunge router and the right jig make mortising almost easy. The jig defines the sides of the cut; gradually plunging the router more deeply handles the depth (see figs. 6 and 7). The jig takes a little time to make, but it's readily adaptable to other projects, so you'll use it again and again.

Figure 6: Plunge Router Mortising Jig, side view

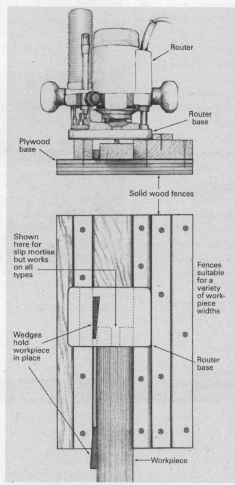

Router

Router base

Plywood base

Solid wood fences

Shown here for slip mortise but works on all types

Fences suitable for a variety of workpiece widths

Router base

Wedges hold workpiece in place

Workpiece

A portable workbench with a vise makes a good "jig" for plunge routing mortises. Hold the workpiece in the vise, and clamp a straight-edged board to the bench top as a fence.

Continued ➜

If you want to forego the jig-making for now, a portable workbench with a vise works well. Clamp the fence into the vise as shown in the photo.

Because of the bit radius, the corners of a router-made mortise are always rounded; you'll need to square up the mortise corners with a chisel.

The Tenon

Always cut the tenon to fit the mortise. It should just slide in with a bit of friction. You need to leave the room for the glue. The ideal fit requires no force to put together but is not loose.

1. Use a combination square to find the centerline on the tenon piece, and mark it.

2. Hold the tenon over the mortise, with its centerline aligned with the centerline of the mortise.

3. Mark the sides of the mortise on the tenon piece.

4. Using a sliding square, lay out all the sides of the tenon.

5. Set the height of your table saw blade to match the width of the tenon shoulders, and use a miter gauge and stop block to cut the shoulders all around. If the shoulder is not long, you can use a dado blade to cut the shoulders and length in one step.

Lay out the tenon on all sides of the workpiece.

6. Move to the band saw to cut the tenon thickness. Use a fence to keep the sides parallel. Err on the side of too thick; you can easily trim the tenon with a block plane and/or a shoulder plane.

7. Check the fit. A good fit is snug but doesn't require excessive force to drive home. If the tenon is too tight, use a shoulder plane to take a thin shaving from each side of the tenon. If it's too loose, glue a shim of paper (business cards work well) or veneer to the tenon.

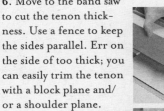

Saw the tenons on the band saw (use the fence), and clean up and fit the tenon with a block plane and a shoulder plane.

Dadoes, Rabbets, and Grooves

Though many people use the words interchangeably, properly speaking, a groove runs in the same direction as the grain, while a dado goes across the grain. You'll find dadoes and grooves in a variety of woodworking situations. They're often cut as part of a joint but can also be used for decorative purposes. Simple though they may seem, careful cutting and fitting is crucial for both appearance and structural integrity.

A groove runs the length of a workpiece; a dado runs across the width.

You can think of a rabbet as a groove right on an edge, or put it another way, it's a shoulder. Rabbets are typically used at corner joints for simple boxes and drawers (see fig. 8). While not as strong as a dovetail, the joint is adequate when reinforced with dowels or screws. Rabbets are often cut around the back edge of a cabinet to hide the end grain on the back panel.

Figure 8: Exploded View, Rabbet Joint,

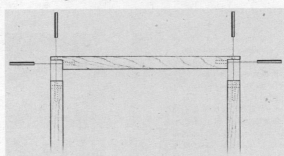

A rabbet is a shoulder along an edge. It can be cut lengthwise or across the end of a board.

A rabbeted corner joint is not as strong as a dovetail, but it's much easier to make. When reinforced with dowels or screws, it's adequate for light- to medium-duty applications.

Full-length Dadoes and Grooves

The table saw is the easiest and fastest method to cut dadoes and grooves, and is best used for cuts that go from one edge of the material to the other. If you need a stopped cut, use a router or router table instead.

When cutting grooves, set things up so the part you're removing is closest to the fence. If you're removing much material, you'll get better results with less effort and more safety if you take two or more passes to do it.

Always use a miter gauge when cutting dadoes, using the fence as a stop or point of reference. It's perfectly safe to use the fence as a stop when cutting in this manner, but never use the table saw fence as a stop when you're crosscutting all the way through a piece of material.

You can cut narrow grooves and dadoes with a standard table saw blade, but for anything wider, you'll want to use a dado blade.

To cut a full-length groove or dado on the router table, you use essentially the same method as you do on the table saw. Set up so the material to be cut is nearest the fence, and use hold downs.

Stopped Dadoes and Grooves

A cut that doesn't go full length and that starts or ends away from an edge is called a stopped cut. A quick way to make small stopped cuts (less than ¼" [6 mm] deep) is with the router table and fence.

1. Mark the workpiece with the location of the stopped cut.

2. Put the workpiece on the table and determine where the cut will begin and end. Make marks on the fence to indicate where to start and stop feeding the material.

3. Set the blade height to match the desired depth of cut.

4. With the blade turning, just lower the material onto the blade while holding it firmly against the fence.

5. Run it against the fence for the middle portion of the cut.

6. Lift the workpiece up and off the bit when reaching the marks that indicate the end of the cut.

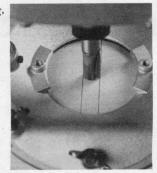

After laying out the stopped cut, position the plunge router with the bit centered over the dado.

It's best to make deeper stopped cuts with a plunge router guided by a fence clamped to the workpiece.

1. Lay out the dado (or groove), clearly marking the stopped ends.

2. With the router unplugged, locate the router bit directly over the dado, and make a mark at the outside of the base.

3. Use a square to extend this line the full length of the stopped cut. This is where you should clamp the fence.

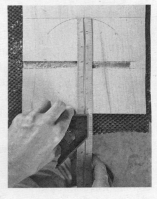
Mark the outside edge of the router base to locate the fence.

4. Holding the router firmly against the fence, make the plunge, and rout until you get to the stopped end. Then raise the router.

5. Make the cut in two or more passes, lowering the bit about ⅛" (3 mm) with each pass.

Use a square to extend the fence line parallel to the edge.

Hold the router against the fence, and plunge to start the cut. Raise the router when you reach the stopped end.

Grooves and Splines on Miters

A groove and spline joint is similar to a biscuit joint, except it spans the joint with one long solid wood spline rather than several small biscuits. It was a common joint before biscuits became popular. These days, I use it mostly for strengthening big mitered joints.

1. Tilt the table saw blade to 45° to cut a bevel along one edge of the workpiece. This is a table saw situation that produces a lot of heat and friction during the cut. You can make things a lot easier by making the cut in two passes.

A rectangular hardwood spline slips in the grooves on the two angled faces of the splined miter. The spline spans the joint, significantly strengthening it.

Though the face is angled, cut the groove with the dado blade at 90°

2. Raise the blade only enough to cut above halfway through the material, and run the workpiece through the saw.

3. Raise the blade to cut all the way through and complete the angle on the second pass.

4. Install a ¼" (6 mm) dado blade in the table saw. Set it at 90° and raise the blade to cut a ¼"-deep (6 mm) groove.

5. Put the miter face down on the table and guide the material along the fence for the cut. This is a safe and easy operation. You may need to attach an auxiliary fence to the table saw to facilitate a smooth operation.

Rabbets

You can make rabbets in any number of ways, but the easiest is with a router and a rabbeting bit. Since the bit has a bearing, there's no need for a fence or any complicated setup.

For long rabbets in four-square milled wood, nothing beats the efficiency of the table saw and a dado blade. Always work so you're removing material from the side against the face—it's safer and gives you more control.

If you're cutting a narrow rabbet, attach a sacrificial wooden auxiliary fence to your existing table saw fence. Rather than trying to get the exact dado width, it's easier to just let the blade chew into the sacrificial fence.

When cutting narrow rabbets on the table saw, save your fence by attaching a sacrificial wooden fence.

Dadoes, Rabbets, and Grooves By Hand

Cutting dadoes and end rabbets by hand is amazingly simple and fun to do.

1. Lay out both sides of the cut with a marking gauge. If you're making dadoes and grooves, you'll lay out the two sides of the groove. If you're making a rabbet, mark the width on the face of the board and the depth on the side.

2. Use an azebiki saw, with a jig if desired, to cut on the lines.

3. If you're making a groove, remove the waste between the kerfs with an offset chisel. Check the depth frequently.

Use an azebiki saw and a shop-made fence to guide it when cutting the shoulder line.

Remove the waste between the shoulders with an offset chisel. Check the depth often.

Run a shoulder plane against the jig fence and plane the rabbet. Alternatively, remove the bulk of the waste with the azebiki saw and clean up the cuts with the plane.

4. If you're making a rabbet, you can sometimes skip the sawing and just run your shoulder plane against the jig.

Half Laps

When two pieces of wood form an X (or a +, or something similar), we join them at the intersection with a half-lap joint. As the name suggests, half of each part is removed at the overlap (see fig. 9). Though made of two pieces of wood, the resulting joint is the same thickness as a single piece.

Figure 9: Exploded View, Half-Lap Joint,

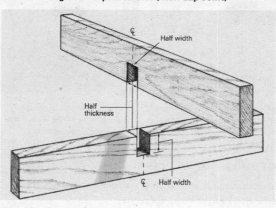

Lay out and mark the intersection point (usually the centerline) on one edge of both pieces.

2. Determine the measurement of half the thickness of the pieces.

3. On each piece, measure half the thickness outward from the intersection point toward both ends. This establishes the shoulders.

4. Square this line downward from the edge.

5. Set a sliding square at half the width of the pieces and use it to mark the depth of cut on both pieces.

6. Set a dado blade in the table saw to equal the thickness of the material, or alternately make multiple cuts with a regular blade and remove the waste with a chisel.

7. Raise the saw blade to the depth of the cut mark. Use a miter gauge and make a few test cuts on scrap to get the setup perfect. The fit should be snug and the top and bottom surfaces flush.

8. Cut the shoulder lines.

9. I often reinforce half laps with a screw right in the middle of the joint.

Dovetails by Hand

You don't need dozens of tools to cut successful dovetails, but you do need the right tools. Over the years, I've settled on these: A wheel-type marking gauge; a dovetail gauge (you could use a sliding bevel instead); a marking knife; a set of saddle squares that includes a dovetail saddle; sharp chisels; a mallet; and a general purpose ryoba saw. I don't recommend using saws with extremely fine teeth, even though they are sold as dovetail saws. The finer the teeth, the more strokes it takes to complete the cut. And more strokes means more opportunity to wander off the cut line. Since most of the saw cuts you make in dovetails are rip cuts, what you really want is a not-too-coarse rip blade, such as the blade on a ryoba saw.

Visual Aids

The spatial relationships between the two boards that make up a dovetail joint can be confusing (see fig. 10). Don't worry if you don't get it—most woodworkers struggle with the concept at first. It's helpful to make a full-size drawing on wood and boldly mark the material to be removed (see fig. 11). This gives you something to hold in your hands so you can get a better sense of what's going on in three dimensions. Keep this visual aid handy when you cut your first joints—the most common dovetail mistake is to remove exactly the material you want to keep.

Follow steps 1 through 4 in the next section to lay out your sample board. When you cut the joint, you'll create the tails by removing the material around them. In this exercise, use a black marker and blot out the area to be removed.

DOVETAIL JOINT

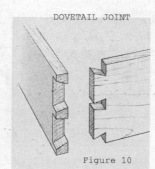
Figure 10

LAYOUT FOR VISUAL AID EXERCISE

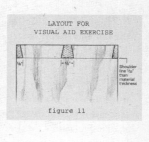
figure 11

Use a black marker to color the negative space around the tails. This is what you'll remove when you cut the joint.

LAY OUT AND CUT THE TAILS

Throughout any dovetail project, it is important to keep the parts oriented. Always mark what will be the inside of the box. Think of each tail/pin combination as a matched set, and keep these numbered.

1. Set your marking gauge for approximately ¹⁄₃₂" (.75 mm) larger than the thickness of the boards. This will ensure that the completed joints stand proud of the surface. Later, you'll sand them flush.

2. Mark the shoulder lines all the way around both ends of all your pieces. From here on, you'll fit one set of pins and tails at a time.

Mark the shoulder line on all four sides of the board. For the visual aid, you need to mark only one end of each board. When you're making dovetails, use the same setting to mark both ends of each board.

3. Draw the tails on the face of one board, using a sharp pencil and a dovetail gauge or a sliding bevel set at 12" (30.5 cm).

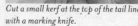

You can mark the tails with a dovetail gauge as shown, or use a sliding bevel set to 12". Draw them from the end of the board down to the shoulder line.

4. To mark the saw cut, first cut a small kerf in the end grain of the board with a marking knife. Place the tip of your pencil in the kerf and slide the saddle square up to it. This positions the saddle square correctly for marking the end of the board.

5. Mark the waste with a bold X.

Cut a small kerf at the top of the tail line with a marking knife.

Place your pencil in the kerf and slide a saddle square up to it. Draw the line across the end of the board.

Continued →

387

Craft Wisdom & Know-How

6. Hold the piece on the edge of a low workbench, with the tail end slightly overhanging.

7. Using the rip edge of a ryoba, begin cutting at the top corner, gradually working the saw across and down with each stroke. Strive to split the line—that is, cut away about half of its thickness, but do not obliterate the line. You need to leave the line as a point of reference. Later, you may need to trim down to the line with a chisel, but that usually does more harm than good. It's better to split the line with the saw rather than trying to refine it with a chisel.

Rather than holding the tall board in a vise for sawing, let it hang over the edge of a low workbench. Cut the tails with the rip edge of a ryoba.

CHOP THE WASTE

The tails are created by the negative space around them. You'll use a chisel and mallet to chop away the waste. A crisp shoulder line is critical to the final appearance of the joint, so take care. Make sure you're chopping against a solid surface.

1. Place the tip of the chisel in the shoulder line, with the bevel toward the end of the board. Angle the chisel backward slightly to undercut the line.

2. Chisel and mallet work in tandem; tap down from the top, then in from the end.

3. Don't try to remove too much material at once. Work down halfway through the material, then flip the piece over and work down from the other side. The undercutting will leave a slight hollow in the middle of the board.

4. Remove the waste at the outer corners by crosscutting with the ryoba.

To remove the waste, first place the tip of the chisel in the shoulder line. Use the mallet to make a light cut, then cut inward from the end, removing a small chip.

Remove the waste at the outermost corners by crosscutting, then ripping with the ryoba.

MARK THE PINS

Use the completed tails as a template to mark the pin board.

1. Hold the pin board in a vise.

2. Position the tail board across the end of the pin board, taking care to align the edges.

3. Mark the pins from the tails.

4. Before you lose track of their positions, mark bold X's on the ends of the pin board, on the surface that was covered by the tails in step 3.

This is the material that must be removed to accom-

Hold the pin board in a vise and position the tail board over it.

Mark the pins from the tails.

modate the tails; it's the negative space that creates the pins. The X marks the waste.

5. Remove the pin board from the vise and use a saddle square to continue the marks around the face of the board. Mark both sides of the board.

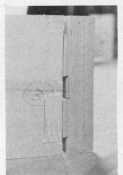

The X's show the material to be removed from the pin board to accommodate the tails.

Use a saddle square to continue the pin lines down the fence of the board. These lines are perpendicular to the end.

CUT AND CHOP THE PINS

Check the layout against your visual aid to make sure you've marked the waste correctly.

1. Split the line to cut the pins with the ryoba. Hold the piece on the edge of the bench and squat down to hold the saw at the correct angle.

2. Chop the pin waste using the same undercutting technique used for the tails.

When cutting the pins, squat down to hold the saw at the correct angle.

Chop the pin waste down and then in, undercutting slightly to hold a crisp shoulder line.

TEST THE FIT

Dovetails go together in only one way. Don't worry if it takes you a while to figure out exactly how they mate. The joints should slide together with a little friction. You should have to push but not pound. Forcing the pins into the tails can split the board like a wedge. Ultimately, you'll glue the joints, so you need to leave a little room for the glue.

The joints will probably need a little fine-tuning. Remember that the pins were cut to match the tails—if you need to remove any material, it should be from the pin board, not the tail board.

A finished set of dovetails goes together only one way. The joint should be tight enough to slip together with a light mallet tap. Forcing the joint closed can split the wood.

GLUING UP A DOVETAILED BOX

You can't just clamp up the corners of a dovetailed box—because the joints stand a little proud of the surface, they can prevent the clamps from working. You'll need to make cauls with cutouts so the clamping pressure is properly applied.

1. Cut four cauls on the band saw from ¾" (1.9 cm) scrap material.

2. Lay a sheet of plastic on the bench and lay out the parts in order, with the inside faces up. Sequence is important, so be sure to run through the assembly process once without glue. Orient the pieces so assembling the joint can be done with a light downward pressure.

3. Spread glue into the joints with a small acid brush.

4. Slide the pieces together, tapping lightly with a mallet to seat the joint.

5. When the box is assembled, position the cauls and clamps.

6. Before tightening the clamps fully, check for square.

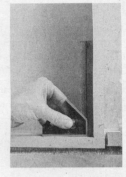

Clamping a box requires two bar clamps and four cauls.

To clamp up a dovetail box, you'll need cauls that make way for the proud ends of the pins. Without them, you can't properly apply the clamping pressure to the tails.

Check for square before tightening the clamps.

FINAL SMOOTHING

To get the protruding pins and tails flush with the surface of the box, use an orbital sander and 100-grit paper. If you have a stationary belt sander, use it instead.

Dealing with Curves

Drawing Curves

The hardest part of working with curves is drawing them. The first step is easy—lay out the beginning and end points, as well as one or two points in between. Then you bend a flexible batten through the points and draw the curve.

The key to this operation is a batten made of a material that's flexible enough to sweep through the curve yet stiff enough to prevent localized bumps or hollows. For smaller curves, a metal ruler fits the bill nicely. For longer curves, use a 2"-wide (5 cm) strip of ¼" (6 mm) plywood on edge. Hold the ends in place and bend the middle up to the intermediary points. This is at least a three-handed job, so if you're alone, use clamps or light weights to hold the batten in place while drawing.

Template Routing Curves

Whenever you need two or more parts with identical curves, the easiest and most accurate way to make them is to use a shop-made template with a router and a flush trim bearing bit. The template sits atop the workpiece, and the bearing runs against the template edge. Because the bearing diameter matches the bit diameter, the bit trims the workpiece beneath exactly flush with the template.

As the bearing runs along the template, the bit reproduces the curve in the wood below.

Use ½" or ¾" (1.3 or 1.9 cm) plywood for your templates, and take special care to lay out and cut smooth curves. The flush trim bit cuts exact copies of the pattern, flaws and all. My preferred flush trim uses a shank mounted bearing on a ½" (1.3 cm) shank, with a ½" (1.3 cm) cutter diameter and a 2" (5 cm) cutting length.

1. Start by laying out your curve on the template material.

2. Cut the curve on the band saw, leaving the line as a reference point. Refine the template, but trim down to the line with files, a spokeshave, and/or any helpful sanding devices at your disposal.

3. Use the template to draw the outline of the curve on each workpiece.

4. Cut away most of the waste with the band saw or jig saw. There's no need to cut any closer to the line than about ⅛" (3 mm); the router will take care of the rest.

5. Use clamps, hot-melt glue, or double-sided carpet tape to secure the template to the workpiece.

6. Secure the workpiece/template to your bench and adjust the bit height so the bearing is against the template. Rout from left to right.

Circle Inlays with a Plunge Router

Inlay is an easy way to embellish furniture. Though wood is the most common inlay material, you can use almost anything—stones, glass, metal, plastic, even jewels.

To do the inlay as described here, you need a router inlay kit consisting of a guide collar, a bushing that fits over the guide collar, and a ⅛" (3 mm) spiral down-cut carbide bit. There's a precise relationship between these pieces that makes it easy to use the same template to cut the recess for the inlay and the inlay itself without a lot of math. All you do is make the template larger than the finished inlay by a set amount, and cut the recess with the bushing in place. Remove the bushing and use the same setup to cut perfectly fitting inlay.

Create the Template

1. Draw a large + on the ¼" (6 mm) plywood template. The center point marks the center of the circle, and you'll need those lines to position the template on the workpiece. Make sure your template is large enough so the clamps that hold it down are well out of the way when routing.

2. The circle in the template must be ⅜" (9.5 mm) larger than the inlay circle. This is to accommodate the guide collar and the bushing. When positioned against the oversize template, they'll cut in the correct location.

3. Set the cutting arm on a circle cutter to the template diameter and cut the circle with the drill press.

Cut the circle into the template with an adjustable circle cutter chucked in the drill press. Note the marked lines that extend beyond the circle. These help position the template on the work.

Cut the Recess

1. Clamp the template on the workpiece and set up the inlay kit in the router.

2. The guide collar and bushing run against the template, positioning the router before plunging. You'll have to run some tests on scrap to get the bit set at the right cutting depth (slightly less than ⅛" [3 mm]).

3. Plunge the router and run it around inside the template, then move to the middle of the template and remove all the material in the recess.

Rout the recess with the bushing in place.

Create the Inlay

1. Resaw the inlay material to about ⅛" (3 mm) thick.

2. Stick the template to the inlay material with double-sided tape. Put the band-sawn side up, and be sure some tape is on the part you'll cut out so the inlay can't shift at the end of the cut.

3. Remove the bushing from the guide collar.

4. For this final cut, it's very important to keep the guide collar firmly against the template. Stick to the perimeter and don't wander into the middle. When the cut is complete, don't raise the bit. Just turn off the router and remain motionless until it stops.

5. The result should be a perfect circle ⅜" (9.5 mm) smaller in diameter than the template, but exactly the rise of the recess.

Install the Inlay

1. Glue the inlay to the recess, with the smooth side down. Use hand pressure, clamps, or a vise, if necessary.

2. Sand the top surface smooth.

Installing Butt Hinges

Learning how to deal with hinges is an integral part of woodworking. Over the years, I've used many types of hinges, but for fine cabinetry, my favorite is the old-fashioned butt hinge. Typically, butt hinges are used for inset door applications, where the door hangs within the frame, as contrasted to the overlay door frames commonly used on kitchen cabinets.

When it comes to hardware, especially hinges, adhere to one important rule: Don't buy cheap products! Poor-quality hinges are more difficult to install because the manufacturing isn't precise or consistent, and in the long run, they simply don't hold up under use. Don't expect to find furniture-quality butt hinges in home centers, and be wary of woodworking supply catalogs that sell, but don't specialize in, hardware.

Butt hinges are sized according to their fully opened width and length. The projects in this book use 1 ⅜" x 2 ½" (3.5 x 6.4 cm) brass hinges. These come in bright brass or with an antiqued patina, which I prefer. You have a choice of loose pins or fixed. Loose pins slip out of the hinge barrel, allowing the two halves to separate, which makes them much easier to install.

Whether used on a jewelry box or a heavy front door, a properly installed butt hinge is mortised into the door and the frame, flush with the surrounding surfaces. Both small and large mortises require the use of a few hand tools and a router or laminate trimmer and a ⅛" (3 mm) bit. Careful layout and correct orientation of the hinge to both frame and door are necessary for successful results.

1. Locate the hinges. Hold each hinge in place and carefully mark its perimeter.

2. With a knife and sliding square, carefully mark the edges of the mortise.

3. Remove the waste with a router or laminate trimmer, staying away from the lines you have marked. Fine-tune the shoulders with a sharp ½" (1.3 cm) chisel. Work incrementally, taking out only small pieces at a time. Use a light touch—chisels can easily cause wood to split. Check the mortise for fit often, and sneak up on it.

4. Once the mortise is cut, position the hinge in the mortise and use the proper diameter self-centering bit to bore the screw holes.

5. Fasten the hinges after the final finish is applied to the project. Use a small amount of paste wax to lubricate the screws and the pins.

Hold the hinge in place and trace its outline on the workpiece.

Mark the edges of the mortise with a knife. The tip of the chisel will slip into the kerf, making it easy to cut clean edges.

Remove the waste with a router or laminate trimmer, keeping well away from the shoulders. Trim back to the line with a sharp chisel.

Bore the hinge screw holes with a self-centering bit.

With a bit of wax on their tips, screws are easier to drive. While you're at it, put a little wax on the hinge pins to keep them swinging freely.

Low Relief with a Spokeshave

Low relief may sound like a gastric remedy—something we might need by chapter's end. Humor aside (but never far away), let me tell you how I spell relief: s-p-o-k-e-s-h-a-v-e.

I first learned about this amazing (and inexpensive) tool early on in my career, at a chair-making class. Ironically, I have made very few chairs since then, but the spokeshave has become a favorite tool of mine. I often use it for light shaping tasks and creating subtle contours.

The spokeshave is a free-form tool guided by eye, hand, and intuition. Learning to use it is a process of unfolding, deciding where to begin and end each cut as things take shape. The workpiece must be firmly held by clamps or a vise, and the blade must be very sharp and adjusted for light cuts. Set correctly, the blade should sweep over the material as it cuts—not grab.

The spokeshave can be used by pulling or pushing. For working across the grain, you'll have more control when you push. Working long grain usually goes better when pulling, but it can go either way.

When using the spokeshave, push down on your index fingers, applying pressure to the front area just over the blade. This gives you a good sense of contact with the material so you can make small adjustments in the pressure and angle to make clean shavings.

Creating the low-relief contour requires only a couple of marks to show how far from the end the relief extends, and how deep to cut. There's no need to draw the curves.

Work from both edges toward the center of the relief to avoid tearing out an edge. Work your way down to the lines, using your hands and eyes to blend the cuts. Light sanding is acceptable to finish, but I don't fuss much over the tool marks—they're part of the character.

Hold the spokeshave so you can push down with your index fingers and feel the cut.

Continued ➜

Surface Prep for Finishing

A fine smooth finish adds beauty and value to a piece, but that shining surface can alsl magnify its flaws. Undulating surfaces, scratch marks, and dust can make an otherwise fine piece of work look less than ordinary. It's been said that 90 percent of achieving a fine finish is in the surface prep. If you prepare the surface properly, even a thick coat of paint looks good.

Good surface prep involves a lot of steps, and if you want the best results, you must complete each one in order. It's not a difficult process, but it is time-consuming and often rather dull. Your goal is to create surfaces that are flat (or sweetly curved), smooth, and clean.

Sand for Flatness

1. Remove machine marks and other high spots, using 100-grit sandpaper. If hand sanding, use a block or pad to create a truly flat sanding surface and sand with the grain.
2. If you're using a random orbital sander, keep the machine moving randomly over the surface. Staying in one place too long creates a low spot.
3. Take care not to round the edges.
4. Be careful when sanding end grain. It scratches very easily, and those scratches are hard to see. But once the finish goes on, they'll be all too visible.

Step Through the Grits for Smoothness

Smoothing any surface is a matter of replacing coarse scratches with finer ones. This is most easily done by increasing the grit in small steps. It doesn't take long for 150-grit sandpaper to remove enough wood to get below the depth of 120-grit scratches. It takes considerably longer to sand away 120-grit marks with 220-grit paper.

1. Clean the surface with a brush, compressed air, or a vacuum cleaner to remove dust and grit.
2. Sand with 120-grit paper until the surface is smooth. Typically, this takes about half the time it took to flatten. Take care with the edges.
3. Clean the surface again. Leaving any 120-grit dust or abrasive will nullify the effects of finer grit.
4. Sand with 150-grit paper, and clean the surface. Repeat with 180 and then 220 grit.
5. Clean the surface with a vacuum or compressed air.

Raise the Grain

These next steps are very important, albeit a little strange. If you omit them before applying finish, the wood soaks up the first-coat and raises the grain. It ends up needlessly rough, requiring you to send it smooth, thus removing most of the finish you just applied. Raise the grain before applying any finish and save time.

1. Take a fairly damp cloth and wipe down the entire surface.
2. Allow it to dry (this usually takes only a few minutes).
3. Sand with 220-grit paper.
4. Wipe down the surface once more, allow it to dry, and sand it again with 220-grit.
5. If you wish to do some final sanding by hand, use 400-grit black wet/dry paper to leave a nice surface.

Final Cleaning

Thoroughly vacuum the piece to remove all dust. While you're at it, vacuum the bench top and as much of the surrounding area as you care to clean. If the area is dusty, your every movement during finishing can churn up dust. Dust in the air can settle on the finish, making it appear as rough as if it hadn't been cleaned.

—From *Woodworking 101 for Women*

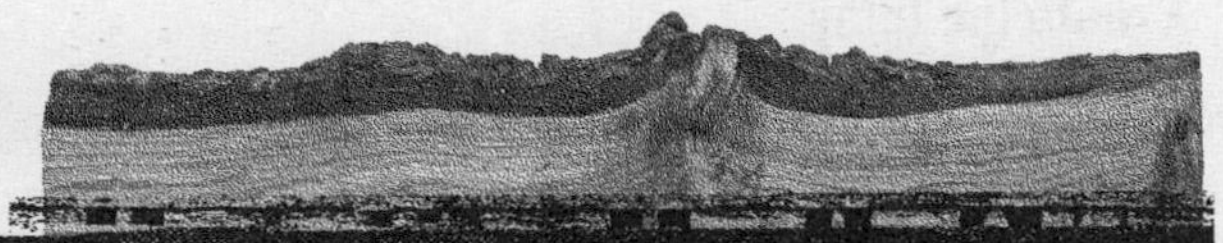

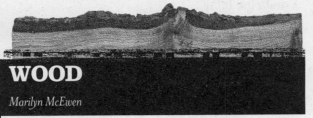

WOOD

Marilyn McEwen

Choose wisely, and start your projects right. Think of trees as gigantic conduits for water, every cell working to provide the necessary fluid and nutrients to sustain these marvelous living organisms. The cells are saturated with water, and the moisture content of a newly felled tree is something like 80 percent (the actual percentage varies by species). At the mill, the green logs are rough sawn into boards and placed in a kiln for rying.

The kiln environment is carefully controlled to drive the moisture from the wood, but not completely. The boards come out of the kiln with an 8 percent moisture content, and slightly smaller dimensions because wood cells shrink as they dry.

If the board could maintain that 8 percent moisture content, it would stay exactly the same size and shape that it was when it came out of the kiln, but the moisture content changes, and the board undergoes some dimensional changes.

The moisture content—and therefore the dimensions—of a board are directly related to the humidity level of the air around it. The higher the humidity, the higher the moisture content of the wood. As the moisture content increases, the cells reabsorb some of the water they lose in drying, and swell. The converse is also true. As humidity decreases, so does moisture content. The board shrinks.

The shrinking or swelling occurs tangent to the growth rings—in a typical board that means across its width. Exactly how a board's dimensions change depends on how the grain runs, which in turn depends on the board's position in the log before sawing (see fig. 1).

Figure 1

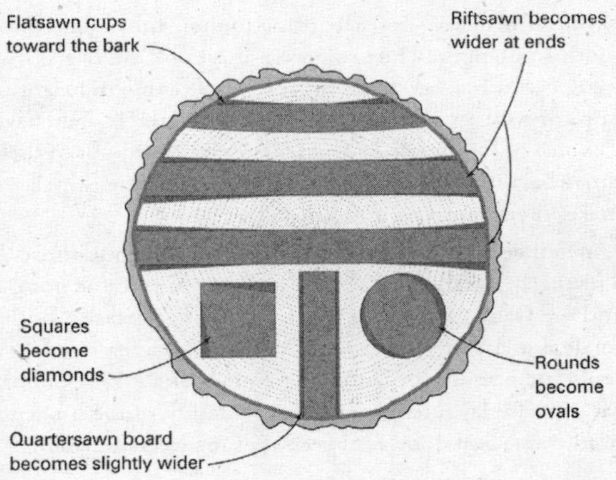

Flatsawn cups toward the bark
Riftsawn becomes wider at ends
Squares become diamonds
Rounds become ovals
Quartersawn board becomes slightly wider

Wood shrinks and swells roughly tangent to the growth rings. Exactly how this affects dimensional changes depends on the board's location relative to the center of the tree from which it came.

Rough sawn boards left outdoors (and properly stacked) will eventually dry to around 15 percent moisture content. It takes about one year of air drying per inch of thickness to reach this level. Without that drying-out period in the kiln, air-dried lumber can be unruly and unpredictable. Don't expect it keep on the straight and narrow. It seems hell-bent on thwarting any plans you might have for it, and sometimes contorts into unbelievable forms.

This is what happened with the big hickory mantel. It was air dried outdoors in high humidity, and its moisture content was at least 15 percent. Since it was so thick, the moisture content was probably even higher in the middle of the board. Once installed indoors, where humidity levels are considerably lower, the wood rapidly lost moisture, causing it to crack and twist.

When building furniture, use only kiln-dried lumber. Its 8 percent moisture content is comparable with indoor humidity levels and its big shrinking days are over. It will remain fairly stable, but be prepared for the occasional minor binge during times of extreme humidity. An unusually long rainy spell can cause swelling, and a very cold, dry winter will cause some shrinkage.

Designing and Building for Changes

Knowing that your wood will change with the seasons makes it possible for you to design and build your furniture so it can gracefully accept those changes.

Take for instance the top of the Table for Two. It's 27 ½" (70 cm) wide. Interpolating from figure 2, you can expect a total of about ⅜" (9.5 cm) of change in width with changes in humidity (indoors only). When you fasten the top to the aprons, you must allow for that movement, or the top will pull itself apart. There are many ways to fasten a tabletop, but the easiest is to drill oversize pilot holes for the screws and put washers under the screw heads (see fig. 3).

I rarely do any kind of calculations. In the summer, my shop is very humid. If I'm hanging doors on a cabinet, I know to leave only a 1/16" (1.6 mm) gap between them. That way, when winter rolls around and the cabinet is in a heated space, the doors will shrink slightly, leaving a visually pleasant amount of space.

Reputable lumber dealers typically sell only kiln-dried lumber—if you want air-dried wood, you'll have to search a bit to find a supplier. Rarely will you encounter improperly dried wood, so it isn't necessary to arrive at the yard with any suspicions. However, improper storage can increase moisture content. Kiln-dried lumber stacked outside in the weather is functionally the same as air-dried lumber.

If you do have any doubts or curiosity about the moisture content, there's usually a moisture meter floating around the yard somewhere. Son't hesitate to ask someone for verification if something feels fishy.

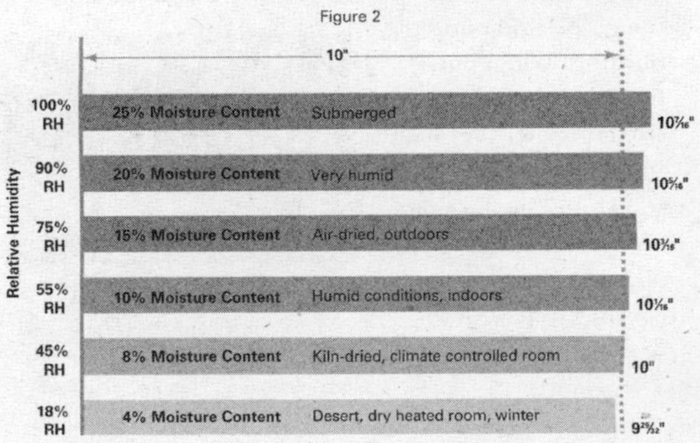

Figure 2
10"
Relative Humidity
100% RH
25% Moisture Content
Submerged
10 7/16"
90% RH
20% Moisture Content
Very humid
10 5/16"
75% RH
15% Moisture Content
Air-dried, outdoors
10 3/16"
55% RH
10% Moisture Content
Humid conditions, indoors
10 1/16"
45% RH
8% Moisture Content
Kiln-dried, climate controlled room
10"
18% RH
4% Moisture Content
Desert, dry heated room, winter
9 29/32"

Wood changes dimension with changes in local humidity. This chart shows how a board ripped to 10" wide at 8 percent moisture content will vary in size depending on the humidity. This is a generalization; each species of wood is affected to a different degree.

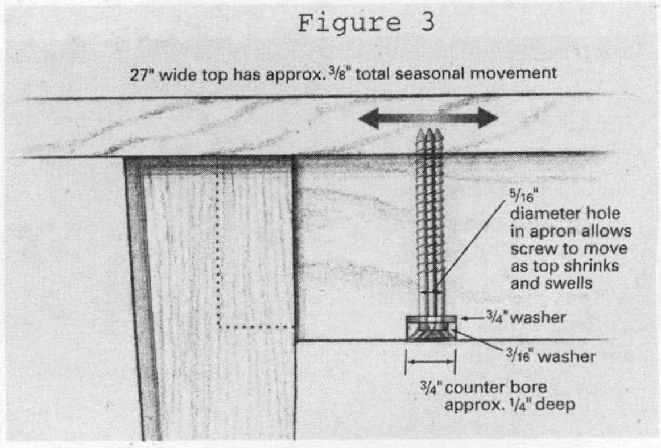

Figure 3
27" wide top has approx. 3/8" total seasonal movement
5/16" diameter hole in apron allows screw to move as top shrinks and swells
3/4" washer
3/16" washer
3/4" counter bore approx. 1/4" deep

Design for changes in dimension. When fastening a top to a table, you must allow room for the top to shrink and swell.

The Plywood Question

Substituting plywood for solid wood can also help prevent a problematic wood/water situation. Plywood is made by gluing up several thin layers of wood under high pressure, and it undergoes virtually no dimensional changes, no matter what the humidity is. Building with plywood can make things a lot easier—you don't have to worry about making complex joints that can withstand dimensional changes.

Another advantage of plywood is that it's sold in 4' x 8' (1.2 x 2.4 m) sheets. Rather than going through the rather involved process of jointing and edge gluing narrow boards to achieve wide panels, all you have to do with plywood is cut the sheet to whatever dimensions you want. You will need to cover the unsightly substrate that shows at the cut edges, an added step that becomes part of the process of working with plywood. Everything has a trade-off.

Plywood has a reputation for cheapness (with all its unsavory connotations), but quality plywood is an excellent material for building furniture. I use it mainly for built-ins like kitchen cabinets and bookcases. I sometimes use it for building drawers, and I use it extensively for cabinet backs and drawer bottoms....

Choosing Hardwoods

Lumber for making furniture is typically purchased from hardwood suppliers (as opposed to home centers or builders' suppliers, though these may carry a limited selection of locally popular hardwoods). Stock varies from region to region and even from dealer to dealer, but most small yards carry a standard variety of domestic hardwoods. In most places, you can get red oak, white oak, hard and soft maple, hickory, cherry, walnut, poplar, birch, and ash. There's a growing market in fancy domestics selected for exceptional grain patterns, with names like curly, strong, flame, and bird's eye, and many yards will have at least a limited selection of such boards.

Most hardwood dealers will have some mahogany and other common imported woods like Brazilian cherry, rosewood, wenge, or teak. For anything rarer, you'll need to find a company that specializes in exotics.

If you need softwoods for your furniture projects, check with your hardwood dealer first. Unlike what you'd find at the builders' supplier, a hardwood yard will sell softwoods that are clear-grained, and properly stored and dried.

Buying hardwood lumber is a little different from purchasing softwood lumber from a builders' supplier or home-improvement store. Builders want standardized lumber dimensioned to industry standards for thickness, width, and length. These are the familiar 2 x 4s, 1 x 6s, and 2 x 12s used in home construction and sold by the linear foot. Since builders aren't too concerned with moisture content, this lumber is usually dried to about 15 percent moisture content and stored outdoors with little or no protection from the elements.

Hardwoods are sawn to get the best boards of a given thickness from a log—not necessarily the most boards. As a result, the boards vary in width and length. They also vary a bit in thickness.

Understanding Boards

When you specify the thickness of a rough sawn board, you talk about quarters of an inch. In this lingo, a rough sawn board about 1" (2.5 cm) thick is referred to as "four quarter," written as 4/4. When the board was sawn from the log, the sawyer made it a bit more than 1" (2.5 cm) thick to account for shrinkage during drying. The board is probably a little more than 1" thick along most of its length, but since it's rough sawn on both sides, there's a strong possibility that could be less than 1" thick in places.

It's a time-honored convention that a 4/4 rough sawn board yields a flattened and planed board that's ¾" (1.9 cm) thick. Sometimes you can get as much as ⅞" (2.2 cm), but don't count on it. Similarly, a 5/4 board yields 1" (2.5 cm). Most yards also sell 8/4 lumber, and 10/4, 12/4, or even 16/4 boards in some species.

Because every hardwood board is a little different in length and width, you pay for hardwoods not by the linear foot, but by volume. Oddly enough, the unit of volume is called a board foot.

You're not expected to tally your lumber purchase, but understanding board feet and how they work makes it easier to evaluate the boards you have to choose from. I've made up a stick that serves as a simple board-foot calculator. This way I can at least estimate the cost of each board, which helps me evaluate its suitability for the project.

The lumber industry has a baffling system that grades boards according to their quality. If you're buying a boxcar of lumber sight unseen, this is important, but for a one-woman shop, it's almost a non-issue. If it comes up, you want FAS grade, which stands for firsts and seconds. The industry specification for this says such lumber must be at least 5½" (14 cm) wide and 8" (20.3 cm) long and that it can have a few troublesome defects. You could also get the grade called Select & Better, but you'll pay a premium for it. If you're milling the lumber yourself, you can easily deal with the few defects in FAS and save some money. The grade called No. 2 Common & Better costs less, but the specification allows for up to one-third of each board to contain defects that make it hardly worth your time. With so much waste, it may end up costing you more.

MOISTURE METERS

Just in case you are wondering, and I hope you are, moisture meters measure the electrical conductivity of the wood. A small electrical impulse travels easily through cells filled with water, which the meter shows as higher moisture content. Drier wood doesn't conduct electricity as well, giving a lower reading. Though useful, a moisture meter is not an essential tool. I use mine only rarely.

Choosing Plywood

Plywood is sold in 4' x 8' (1.2 x 2.4 m) sheets (or sometimes the metric equivalent thereof). The most commonly available thicknesses are ¼", ½", and ¾" (.6 cm, 1.3 cm, and 1.9 cm).

For utilitarian projects or jigs, I use what's called shop-grade plywood. The veneers on the front and back are decent looking (usually birch), but the interior plys of shop-grade plywood can have knots or voids, which weaken the material.

For quality work, specify veneer-core plywood (they'll call it VC at the yard) and stick with A1 or A2 grade. The letter A refers to the quality of the front veneer, and A grade looks good enough to coat with clear finished (lower grade B or C faces are only suitable for painting; higher grade AA faces use veneers chosen and matched for exceptional grain patterns). The numbers refer to the quality of the veneer on the back face. Back grade 1 has no major defects, but it's not as good-looking as an A face.

Most hardwood dealers offer these higher grades of plywood with a variety of species for the outer veneers. Birch, oak, maple, luaun (similar in appearance to mahogany), walnut, and cherry are usually easy to find, and virtually any species of wood is available as a special order.

All Dressed Up and No Place to Go

...One of the things I remember most vividly about my early woodworking days was becoming enamored with fancy, highly figured woods. It developed into a little obsession and became a habit that was had to support financially. Worst of all, every time things didn't go according to plan, it was as though Mr. Fancy Wood kept telling me I was not worthy. He seemed to sneer, "You've ruined my outfit with those sloppy joints!"

I remember being intrigued with an exotic wood called purpleheart (it really is purple, dense, and as hard as can be). I got the bright idea of making a dovetail box as a gift. Chopping out those dovetails was a nightmare; they didn't come out as well as I had envisioned. And as if that weren't bad enough, some months later I discovered that my beautiful purpleheart had oxidized to a dull brown.

It took some time, but I finally learned that beautiful woods can't save you from poor design or lack of technique. I came to prefer a plain but skillfully crafted piece to a poorly executed, ill-conceived piece constructed out of fancy woods.

Learn from my experience and make it easy on yourself. Start with relatively inexpensive Plain Jane woods like poplar, basswood, and soft maple. They're easy to work using both machines and hand tools, and they're excellent for chopping out joints, especially dovetails. With these woods, a mistake doesn't seem so catastrophic. Plain Jane just seems to say, "I'm not a fancy dresser. It's the overall effect that matters. This is no big deal. Let's get over it and move forward."

Ignore the lure of Mr. Fancy Wood and listen to Plain Jane for a while, eventually broadening the circle of conversation to include cherry, walnut, oak, and maple. Listen and you'll understand that each wood speaks a little differently. Learning the nuances is part of the fun. You'll hear how the conversation flows between them and how their looks can complement one another and enhance your design.

Eventually, you'll be ready to understand what Mr. Fancy and his fashionable friends are talking about. But get familiar with them slowly; start using them as accents to the outfit. If you really want to get all dressed up, make sure you have a place to go!

Let's Go Shopping

You've done your homework; it's time to enter "Lumber World." I hope you encounter competent people who appreciate your business, but don't take it personally if the reception doesn't feel too warm. Just put on your lizard skin and get right down to business.

Before you negotiate with the natives, make up a shopping list that states the number of boards you need of a given thickness, width, and length. Don't get intimidated if the people there start slinging arcane lingo. Just explain that you need boards that will finish to a certain thickness and width and length, and they'll help you get the right wood. It never works out that they have exactly what's on your list—usually the boards are wider or narrower or longer or something else that your list doesn't account for. You'll have to think on the fly, but always err on the side of extra wood. Nothing is more frustrating than running out of wood in the middle of a project.

Lumberyards are busy places. Stacks of wood levitate by forklift, and trucks arrive to load and unload materials; be watchful of all that's going on around you and assume that those drivers are not aware of your presence. Customers and yard hands are sifting through stacks and bins of lumber, pulling out boards for scrutiny. Watch out for things strewn about the floor like metal banding, reject boards, and maybe even an occasional blob of tobacco spit.

Continued →

The more familiar lingo of 2 x 4s describes the construction-grade lumber used to build houses. If you've ever built anything with this kind of lumber, you know that a 2 x 4 is not 2" thick and 4" wide. It's actually 1½" (3.8 cm)thick and 3½" (8 cm) wide. When you talk about a 2 x 4, you're talking about nominal dimensions, not actual dimensions. A 2 x 4 was probably 2" x 4" when it went into the kiln, but after drying it was milled straight and flat, and the corners were heavily rounded to reduce splintering. It ends up smaller. To figure the actual dimension, just subtract ½" from the nominal dimension. This works fine until you get to boards with a nominal dimension of 8" or wider. Then the actual dimension is ¾" narrower.

FUN WITH BOARD FEET

One board foot is the volume of wood in a board that's 1" (2.5 cm) thick, 12" (30.5 cm) wide, and 12" (30.5 cm) long. Multiply those three together, and you get the volume of said board—144 cubic inches. But we're not talking about cubic inches, we're talking about board feet. And to get that unit, you must divide the volume in cubic inches by 144. To calculate the cost of a board, just multiply the price per board foot by the number of board feet.

Here's the math:

Board Feet = (Thickness x Width x Length) (in inches, not feet)/144

Here's how it works in the yard. You're looking at a 4/4 board that's 6" (15.2 cm) wide and 10' (25.4 cm) long.

Board Feet = (Thickness x Width x Length)/144= (1 x 6 x (10 x 12))/144 = (6 x 120)/144 = 720/144 = 5.06 bf

It works the same for thicker boards. This time let's assume we have an 8/4 board that's 6" (15.2 cm) wide by 10' (25.4 cm) long.

Board Feet = (2 x 6 x (10 x 12))/144 = (12 x 120)/144 = 1440/144 = 10 bf

Some companies plane lumber or make moldings on site, so there could be a giant machine roaring incessantly in the background. Bring some earplugs.

You'll need to go through stacks of lumber to select your boards, so bring a tape measure, your board-foot stick, and some gloves to prevent splinters. The best kind are the rubber-coated ones sold in the garden department. They fit better than leather gloves and have a lot of gripping power.

First, look for obvious defects. I start by sighting the board from end to end. You want to avoid boards that appear twisted or greatly curved. Check both sides of a board for defects such as cracks or knots, and pay close attention to any area of the board that has stains. Stains are usually the result of water damage from improper storage somewhere along the line. Stains often go deep into the wood itself, so planning may not completely remove them.

Most of the boards in a pile are flatsawn or riftsawn. Flatsawn boards show the growth rings as arcs on the ends of the boards (see fig. 1). They have the familiar cathedral grain on the face and a straight run of grain on the edges. Riftsawn boards' end grain shows the growth rings running diagonally. The grain appears fairly straight. These boards are more stable than flatsawn wood but less stable than quartersawn boards, in which the growth rings appear on the end grain as vertical lines. If you find a

couple of random quartersawn boards in the pile, grab them; they're the most dimensionally stable and beautiful. Most of the time, quartersawn boards are segregated into another pile, and you'll pay a premium for them.

If the boards you purchase are 10' (3 m) or longer, you can have the yard cut them to shorter lengths that are easier to transport and unload. Most places do this at no extra charge, even for sheets of plywood. This is no time to get fussy or indecisive. I usually just ask that they cut the boards in half, and I rarely ask them to make more than one cut per board. Think of this as a convenience only; don't assume the cut is in any way accurate, especially on plywood.

After you get the lumber back to your shop, it's a good idea to let it acclimate to the environment before you start to work, giving it a few days to reach moisture equilibrium with your shop's humidity level. Don't ever lay your lumber directly on the shop floor for any reason, where it could pick up grit or even extra moisture. I usually stack my newly purchased lumber against the wall, with air space between the boards.

Stack your lumber against the wall where air can circulate around the sides.

CARRY A BOARD-FOOT STICK

Lumbermen don't like customers using their expensive board-foot rules, and I've spent too much time standing around lumberyards waiting for someone to tally up my lumber to see if I've pulled more than I need from the rack. I finally got smart and made my own easy-to-read board-foot stick.

It's a combination width ruler and board-foot chart on a piece of plywood. Along the top edge, I've measured out widths from 4" to 14" (10.2 to 35.6 cm), in 2" (5 cm) increments. The second row (labeled "8" in the photo below) shows the number of board feet in an 8' board at each width. The third row shows the board feet in a 10' (2.4 to 3 m) board, and the fourth tallies a 12-footer. For 8/4 lumber, I just double the readings. There's a similar table for 5/4 lumber on the other side.

I used a waterproof marker and made the numbers big enough so I can see them without my glasses. Now I can easily keep a running board-foot total as I select boards. The yard guys think it's kind of geeky, but I think it's great.

A shop-made board-foot stick is a quick way to figure out how many board feet are in a prospective purchase. It roughly measures width, and tells you the board feet in a given length.

A good finish serves three purposes: It helps to slow the moisture exchange between the wood and the air around it, thereby reducing the amount of shrinking and swelling; it protects the surface from wear and tear, and it improves the appearance of the wood. What constitutes an improvement is a matter of opinion.

Each project has different finishing requirements depending on what it's made from, and how and where it will be used. In my shop, planning any project includes a sanding and finishing strategy—often decided before the cutting begins. There are many things to consider, including sequence—contrary to what you might think, finishes often need to be applied before parts are assembled.

Sanding and finishing are inextricably linked; how well you sand is a determining factor in how well your finish will look at the end (see Surface Prep for Finishing on p. 00).

There are hundreds of different brands of finishing products, which can make things a bit confusing. I try to stick with those that are durable, easy to use, and relatively low in toxicity.

Take the time to read the labels on any finishes you use and follow the manufacturer's directions and warning. Thin with the specified solvent. Store used solvents in appropriate cans and don't mix solvent types together. Consult your local government about safe disposal of old finishes and solvents. Never pour used finishes into a septic or sewer system, or even into the ground.

Oil-Resin Finishes

This family consists of Danish oil, varnish, polyurethane, linseed oil, tung oil, and the like. The two solvents for all of these are paint thinner (mineral spirits) or turpentine, which is quite pungent.

Danish oil is perhaps the most common type of finish, and the easiest to use. However, it is somewhat messy and smelly. When the weather is warm enough, I like to apply it outside. Despite the old-world, hand-rubbed mystique surrounding this type of finish, there's no big mystery. All Danish oils are the same—a mixture of linseed or tung oil, alkyd resin, and mineral spirits.

Apply it by flooding the surface with a foam brush, let it penetrate for 30 minutes or so (directions may vary slightly among brands), flood again, let dry 45 minutes or so, and wipe off the excess. Wiping off—that's where the hand-rubbed part comes in. Buy a Danish oil brand that is locally available to avoid shipping costs. Sometimes there are extra shipping charges associated with solvent finishes.

Danish oil is excellent for enhancing the natural tone and grain of woods such as oak, cherry, and walnut. But I think its slightly yellow cast isn't attractive on a light wood such as hard maple.

Because of its somewhat flat appearance, I think of Danish oil as a way of initially enhancing and sealing the wood. After at least 78 hours of drying time, you can apply other finishes on top for more pizzazz and protection. For items that don't generally receive a lot of wear, such as a table base, paste wax may be all that's required. For a bit more substance, polyurethane gel finish will improve appearance and protection. For tabletops, especially dining tables, I like to go the extra mile with three coats of water-based polyurethane. If you're applying water-based finish over oil, make sure the oil finish has had at least a week to cure.

I don't bother with straight linseed oil; it doesn't harden on its own. Nor do I mess with tung oil. I dislike the smell, long drying time, and short shelf life.

Of late, I have enjoyed great success with gel varnishes. Application couldn't be easier—just wipe on three or four coats with a soft cotton cloth. Shelf life is an issue with these finishes, as well, so I use an oxygen blocker when storing them.

Brushed on varnish finishes, if done well, require a little more work than most other finishes. The results certainly justify the effort. A successful varnish finish has excellent durability and visual appeal. I like this finish for wide surfaces such as tabletops and headboards.

For your first efforts, it's best to start small; save the 8' (2.4 m) dining tabletop for another day. You'll need to apply at least three or four coats (with 24 hours drying time between them), sanding lightly with 220-grit paper between coats. Cleanliness is important with a high-gloss, slow drying finish. Work in an environment that's as free of dust as possible, and use lint-free rags for best results.

There are only a few companies producing high-quality, furniture-appropriate varnishes. You can pretty much rule out home-store-variety polyurethane and spar varnishes, which tend to be too soft and flexible. A good varnish has less oil and more resins, making it harder and more brittle—much better for achieving good results.

I don't have much use for straight polyurethane or spar varnish finishes; these are too soft and flexible for furniture. They're great for exterior doors and the like, where temperature and moisture extremes require a flexible finish. However, I use them as a base for what I call "3-2-1 Oil." This traditional recipe is similar to Danish oil but is thicker and easier to build up to a greater sheen. Mix three parts paint thinner, two parts polyurethane varnish, and one part linseed oil. Flood the piece with oil using a foam brush; wait until it becomes slightly tacky, then wipe it off. Let it dry overnight and repeat the process two more times. After a few days of drying time, you can buff and/or wax the surface with 0000 steel wool.

Shellac

I am very fond of shellac. I use it most often on cabinet panels, drawer interiors, and small projects. It takes only about 30 minutes for one coat to dry, so you can build a beautiful three- or four-coat finish in no time flat. A coat of paste wax at the end adds a nice touch.

Shellac comes in two forms; premixed in a can or as flakes that you dissolve as needed in the appropriate amount of denatured alcohol. I used to buy the flakes but have lately switched to premixed. Overall, the results are about the same, but without the mixing hassle and shelf-life problems associated with flakes. Flakes do have the advantage of a few more color selections, whereas canned shellac is available in only amber or clear.

Shellac is best applied with a high-quality brush that's made for shellac application only. Since shellac dries so quickly, I don't always clean the brush between coats—I put it in a tightly sealed plastic bag. For final cleaning, change the alcohol at least three times or until it's clear. Store the contaminated alcohol in a metal can for later disposal.

Water-Based Polyurethane

These clear finishes are relatively new to the finishing scene and seem to be improving all the time. They give off very little odor when drying, are easy to apply, and are durable enough to protect tabletops. I like to use them on maple, where I want the grain to show through without the yellowing effect of oil-based finishes.

Most of the time I use a foam brush to apply water-based poly, and sometimes a high-quality synthetic brush. Its low odor/toxicity level is a real plus, and cleanup couldn't be easier—just use a little soap and water.

Lacquer

I mention this finish in the hope that you will avoid it, especially if you have any chemical sensitivity issues. This highly flammable and toxic finish is frequently used in the furniture-making industry. However beautiful the finish and excellent its spraying characteristics, small shops are generally not equipped to use this finish in a safe manner. An explosion-proof fan is necessary to evacuate fumes, and you'll need a respirator that provides

a continual supply of fresh air. Some local air quality and fire regulations simply do not permit its use. Ironically, lacquer finishes are readily available.

Adding Color

Afraid of color I am not, nor am I a "purist" when it comes to wood. Au naturel can be beautiful, but it's often desirable to create more balanced tones on wood that is swirling with sapwood and heartwood variations, such as walnut. And sometimes it's nice to add a dash of color here or there.

Rarely do I use ready-mixed stains; their appearance is too generic. I don't ever seem to find the exact tones I want. The stains all look murky and generic to me, like those on pieces of factory-built furniture. Instead, I find aniline dyes to be an excellent way to alter the color of wood without obscuring the grain. These easy-to-use products are mixed with water and applied with a foam brush. You can get a subtle range of color and tone by mixing various colors before application or by applying each color in turn. Aniline dyes come in a variety of colors and are amazingly colorfast.

Seal in the color with a few coats of shellac, and apply a final coat of water-based polyurethane. If you're using an oil-based varnish, you can skip the shellac.

An array of color awaits you at the local art store—artist's oils or acrylic paints in a tube work perfectly well on wood. Though this may seem elementary, use like with like—don't mix oil with water. Use oil-based paints with Danish oil as a medium to flow on the color, and apply it with a soft cotton cloth. Acrylic can be used to tint water-based poly finish. Don't be afraid to experiment; that's how you will find the answers.

Just for fun, I once applied an earthy orange artist's oil paint to an unfinished pine tabletop. Using oil as a medium, I simply flowed the color on with a cloth. Then I applied a coat of black over the orange, using cheap brushes to create streaks and graining effects. The result was an unusual and exotic-looking table. Without fail, visitors to my shop are intrigued and ask what species that wild looking wood is.

Using milk paint is yet another way to add color to your work, but it's not subtle. Milk paint has a thick, solid, flat appearance. The off-the-shelf colors tend to be in the primary zone, but they can be mixed to create variations. Pitch black is excellent for ebonizing parts. If you want some sheen, apply three coats of gel varnish.

Sometimes I am not in the mood for the fuss of mixing milk paint for ebonizing. Then I head straight for the local drug store and pick up some black leather shoe dye. I apply two coats with the foam applicator on the bottle or with a foam brush, sanding lightly between each coat. Three coats of water-based poly provide protection and shine.

—From *Woodworking 101 for Women*

EASY WOODWORKING PROJECTS FOR KIDS

Kevin McGuire

Look-Inside Birdhouse

The top of this birdhouse lifts off. That makes it easy to clean out the nesting materials after the baby birds have flown away.

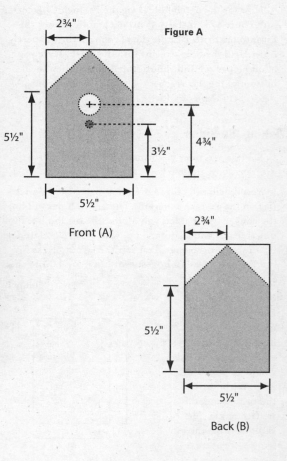

Estimated Time:

4 hours

Shopping List

- 1 x 6 x 36" (2.5 x 15.2 x 91.4 cm) softwood
- 1 x 8 x 12" (2.5 x 20.3 x 30.5 cm) softwood
- ⅜" x 12" (.95 x 30.5 cm) dowel
- 1¼" (3.2 cm) finishing nails
- 100-grit and 180-grit sandpaper
- Latex primer and paints
- 3' (.9 m) length of #200 twist chain (a ¼" [.6 cm] rope could be used instead)
- Wire (optional)

Tools

- Layout tools
- Handsaw
- Clamps
- Drill with ⅜" (.95 cm) and 1¼" (3.2 cm) bits*
- Rasp
- Miter box
- 1" (2.5 cm) paintbrush

This birdhouse's doorway is the perfect size for a house wren or a downy woodpecker. Before you begin this project, visit your library. Find out what birds live in your area, and what size doorway they prefer. Then use a different bit size to drill the doorway if local birds prefer a larger or smaller door.

Starting with the Front

1. Lay out and cut the front (A) and back (B) from the 1 x 6 board. Use the diagram on page 394 as a guide.

Figure A

2¾"

5½"

5½"

4¾"

3½"

Front (A)

2¾"

5½"

5½"

Back (B)

Continued ➔

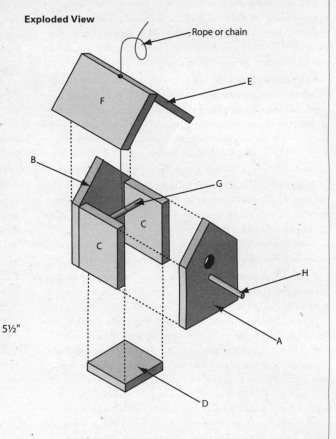

Exploded View

Rope or chain

F — E

B — G

C

C

H

A

D

Cut List, Look-Inside Birdhouse

Code	Part	Number	Size	Material
A	Front	1	¾" x 5½" x 8¼" (2 x 14 x 21 cm)	Softwood
B	Back	1	¾" x 5½" x 8¼" (2 x 14 x 21 cm)	Softwood
C	Side	2	¾" x 5½" x 8¼" (2 x 14 x 21 cm)	Softwood
D	Bottom	1	¾" x 4" x 4" (2 x 10 x 10 cm)	Softwood
E	Short roof	1	¾" x 7¼" x 5" (2 x 18.5 x 12.7 cm)	Softwood
F	Long roof	1	¾" x 7¼" x 5¾" (2 x 18.5 x 14.5 cm)	Softwood
G	Hanger	1	⅜" x 4½" (1 x 11.5 cm)	Dowel
H	Perch	1	⅜" x 3½" (1 x 9 cm)	Dowel

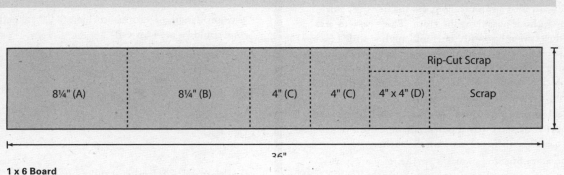

| 8¼" (A) | 8¼" (B) | 4" (C) | 4" (C) | 4" x 4" (D) | Scrap |

Rip-Cut Scrap

5½"

36"

1 x 6 Board

2. Use Figure A to help you lay out the front (A) and back (B). On the front piece, be sure to mark the center points for where the 1½-inch (4 cm) doorway and ⅜-inch (.95 cm) perch should go.

3. Use your saw to cut along the outside lines of the front (A) and back (B). Label both pieces and set the back aside.

4. Time to start drilling! Place the front (A) piece face up on your workbench with some scrap wood between the piece and the workbench. Then clamp the wood to the bench. Dimple the hole layout for the doorway. Chuck the 1½-inch (4 cm) bit into your drill. Have your adult helper assist you with this step: carefully bore straight through the mark for the doorway.

5. Now for the perch hole. Flag the ⅜-inch (.95 cm) bit to bore a ⅜-inch (.95 cm) deep hole. Chuck the bit into the drill. Dimple the bore mark for the perch hole. Drill the hole straight into the mark. Have your adult helper remind you to stop drilling when the bottom of the flag reaches the surface of the front (A) piece. Set the piece aside.

Making the Sides

6. Cut the two sides (C) from the 1 x 6 board. Use the diagram above to help you.

7. You'll drill two more boreholes, using the ⅜-inch flag on the ⅜-inch bit again. These boreholes will hold the hanger (G) that lets you mount the birdhouse. Find one side (C) and set it face-up, with scrap wood under it, on your workbench. Transfer the layout marks for the ⅜-inch (.95 cm) hole shown in Figure B onto the face.

8. Clamp the wood. Dimple the hole layout. Drill the hole. Have your adult helper remind you to stop drilling when the bottom of the flag reaches the surface of the side (C) piece. Set the

Figure B

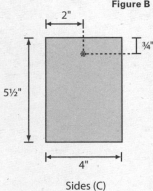

2"

¾"

5½"

4"

Sides (C)

drilled piece aside. Repeat this step to bore a hole in the other side piece.

Making It Fit

Figure C

9. The bottom (D) piece needs to be a square. To cut it to the correct width, you'll need to rip the remainder of your 1 x 6 board. Measure 4 inches from one edge of the board in two places. Mark that line and cut the piece. Discard the scrap wood (that's

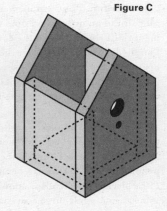

the piece measuring 1½ inches [4 cm] wide). Now cut the 4-inch (10.2 cm) wide board so that it is 4 inches long. Label the piece and set it aside.

10. Before you start nailing, it's important to make sure that all the pieces of your birdhouse fit together. Lay the bottom (D) face up. Place the front (A), back (B), and sides (C) around the bottom. Overlap their edges as shown in Figure C. Do they fit? Great! If not, use the rasp to shave off a bit of wood on the boards that don't fit. Set all the pieces aside except for the bottom and one side.

Attaching the Sides

11. Line up the 4-inch (10.2 cm) edge of the side (C) with the bottom (D). Make sure the hole for the hanger (G) on your side piece is facing inside. Have your adult helper hold the pieces together tightly. Hammer two nails through the side into the edge of the bottom. Space the nails about 2½ inches (6.4 cm) apart.

12. Use your miter box to cut the hanger (G) and the perch (H). Label the pieces and set the perch aside.

13. Stick the hanger (G) into the hole in the side (C) you just nailed to the bottom (D). Line up the second side, sandwiching the hanger (G) between the two sides so that it fits into both holes. Line up the bottom edge of the second side with the edge of the bottom. Pound two nails through the side into the edge of the bottom.

Attaching the Front and Back

14. Lay the assembly on its side, so that it makes a C when you look at it from above. Line up the front (A) so that it overlaps the edges of the bottom (D) and sides (C). Make sure the borehole you drilled for the perch (H) is facing up. Have your adult helper hold the front (A) in place while you drive six nails through it into the sides and bottom. Space the nails 1½ inches (3.8 cm) apart.

15. Flip the assembly and repeat step 14 to attach the back (B).

16. Put a few drops of glue on the end of the perch (H) and then set it firmly in the hole in the front (A).

Adding the Roof

17. Next, you'll cut out the short (E) and long (F) roof pieces from your 1 x 8 board.

18. To make the roof, ask your adult assistant to stand the short roof (E) on its end. Line up the end of the long roof (F) so that it overlaps the end of the short roof (see Figure D). Have your adult helper hold both boards in place while you drive two nails through the long roof into the end of the short roof. Space the nails about 3 inches (7.6 cm) apart.

Figure D

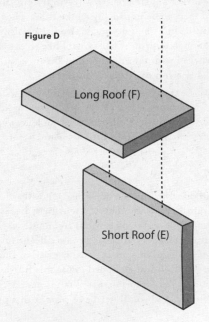

Long Roof (F)

Short Roof (E)

19. The chain will go through the roof of the bird-house. To make a hole for the chain, flip the roof and rest its peak on top of a piece of scrap wood. With your adult assistant holding the roof in place, mark a hole in the center on the joint, about 3⅝ inches (9.2 cm) from each end.

20. Drill a ⅜-inch (.95 cm) hole through your mark on the roof. Hold the drill straight up and down so the bit comes out the peak of the roof.

Finishing Touches

21. Sand the birdhouse. Use a rasp a smooth out the entry hole. You don't want the birds to get splinters! Wipe off the sawdust and make sure everything is smooth.

22. Prime and paint the birdhouse. There are cow spots on the birdhouse in the photo on this page. To do this to your birdhouse, cover the primer with white paint, let it dry, and then add the black spots.

23. Thread the chain through the hole in the roof. You can use a piece of wire to fasten the chain to the hanger (G). Hang up your birdhouse outside and wait for your feathered visitors to move in!

Bird Buffet

This project will provide a feast for your feathered friends.

Estimated Time:

6 hours

Shopping List

- 1 x 8 softwood, at least 10" (25.4 cm) long
- 1 x 10 softwood, at least 12" (30.5 cm) long
- ¾" x 1½" x 12" (1.9 x 4 x 91.4 cm) craft lumber
- ½" x 1½" x 36" (1.3 x 4 x 91.44 cm) craft lumber
- 17-gauge x 1" (2.5 cm) brads
- 1½" (3.8 cm) finishing nails
- (2) 3/16" x 3" (.5 x 7.6 cm) screw hooks
- #200 twist chain, at least 4' (1.2 m) long
- 100-grit and 180-grit sandpaper
- Latex paint and primer
- Bird seed

Tools

Cutting out the Pieces

- Layout tools
- Clamps
- Handsaw
- Miter box
- Hammer
- Drill with 3/16" (.5 cm) bit
- Screwdriver
- 1" (2.5 cm) paintbrush

Lay out, cut, and label the bottom (A) piece from the 1 x 8 board. Set it aside.

2. On the 1 x 10 board, lay out and cut the roof (B) to length. Label it and set it aside.

3. Measure and mark the length of both posts (C) on the ¾ x 1½-inch (1.9 x 4 cm) board. Clamp the board and cut out the pieces. Label them and set them aside.

4. Now for the sides. Lay the ½ x 1½-inch (1.3 x 4 cm) board on your workbench. Lay out both long sides (D).

Code	Part	Number	Size	Material
		Cut List, Bird Buffet		
A	Bottom	1	¾" x 7¼" x 10" (2 x 18.5 x 25.5 cm)	Softwood
B	Roof	1	¾" x 9¼" x 12" (2 x 23.5 x 30.5 cm)	Softwood
C	Post	2	¾" x 1½" x 5" (2 x 3.8 x 12.7 cm)	Softwood
D	Long side	2	½" x 1½" x 10" (1.3 x 3.8 x 25.5 cm)	Softwood
E	Short side	2	½" x 1½" x 6¼" (1.3 x 3.8 x 16 cm)	Softwood

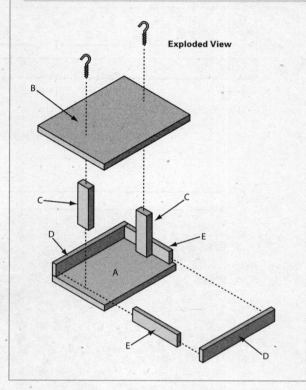

Exploded View

Clamp the board and cut out the pieces. Label them and set them aside.

5. Using the same board, lay out and cut the short sides (E). Don't forget to label them.

6. You'll start building your Bird Buffet by nailing together the long sides (D) and the short sides (E) to form a box. Ask your adult helper to stand a short side on end. Lay the face of one long side on top of it, making an L shape. Hammer two brads through the face of the long side and into the end of the short side. Space the brads about ½ inch (1.3 cm) apart (see Figure A). Set the L-shaped piece aside.

7. Repeat step 6 to put together the other long (D) and short sides (E).

8. Now you'll nail the two L-shaped pieces together to make a box. Set the first L-shaped piece on its long side, with the short side (E) sticking up. Put the second L-shaped piece on top, so they form a box with the second long side (D) overlapping the short side. With your adult assistant holding the pieces together, hammer two brads through the face of the long side and into the end of the short side. Space the brads about ½ inch (1.3 cm) apart.

9. Flip the box and nail the last joint together with two brads as you did in step 8.

Attaching the Bottom

10. To add the bottom (A) to the box, rest the box on the edges of the long (D) and short (E) sides. Set the bottom on the box, lining up its edges with the sides.

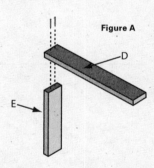

Figure A

11. Hammer several nails through the bottom (A) and into the edges of the sides. The nails should be about ¼ inch (.64 cm) from the edge and about 3 inches apart.

Adding the Posts

12. Now you'll attach the posts (C) to the box. To mark where they will go, flip the box so that it rests on its bottom (A). On one short side (E), draw two diagonal lines on its face from opposite corners. They'll intersect in the center of the face.

13. Repeat step 12 to mark the center of the opposite short side (E).

14. Set the first post (C) face up on the workbench. Measure the mark the center of the post (¾ inch [1.9 cm] from each edge) near the end.

15. Set your square on the end of the post (C), and mark a line lengthwise (from end to end) through the center of the post.

16. Repeat steps 14 and 15 to mark the other post (C).

17. Have your adult assistant help you attach the posts (C) to the box. Set the first post inside the box, lining up its centerline with the mark you made in the center of the short side (E). Make sure the end of the post is flat against the bottom (A).

18. With your adult assistant holding the post in place, hammer a brad through the face of the short side (E) and into the face of the post (C). Is the post at a right angle to the bottom? Use your square to check. If it's not, wiggle it or tap on it gently with your hammer until it is. Then hammer another brad through the side and into the post.

19. Repeat steps 17 and 18 to attach the other post to the other side of the box.

Adding the Roof

20. Now you're ready to add the roof (B). Lay the roof face up. Measure and mark the center point of the short edges on both ends. Use your square to connect the center points so that a line runs through the center of the roof from end to end.

21. Set the box on your workbench. Put the roof on top of the posts (C). Line up the centerline on the roof (B) with the centerline on the posts.

22. Measure how far the ends of the road (B) overhang the posts (C). Is it the same distance? Great! If not, adjust the position until the same amount of roof overhangs each post.

23. While your adult assistant holds everything together, hammer two nails through the roof (B) and into the end of the first post (C). These nails should go into opposite corners of the post.

24. Repeat step 23 to attach the roof (B) to the other post (C).

25. To hang the Bird Buffet, you'll need to put two screw hooks in the roof (B). (Both ends of the chain will attach to the hooks.) The screw hooks need to go through the roof into the center of the posts (C). Use your layout tools and Figure B to mark the roof where the center of each post is.

Continued ➡

26. Dimple the marks you made in step 25. Flag a ³/₁₆-inch (.5 cm) bit to bore a ¼-inch (.64 cm) hole. Chuck the bit into your drill and bore a hole through each mark, stopping when the bottom of the flag touches the wood.

27. Insert a screw hook into one of the pilot holes and twist it clockwise with your fingers to drive the screw into the wood. If it's too hard to turn, put the end of your screwdriver through the hook and twist it.

28. Repeat step 27 to put the other screw hook in the roof (B).

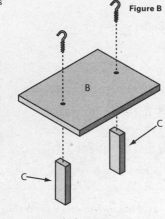

Figure B

Finishing Touches

29. Sand the Bird Buffet. Wipe off the sawdust.

30. Prime and paint the Bird Buffet.

31. Decide where you want to hang it. Thread one end of the chain through a screw hook. Do the same on the other side.

32. Hang the Bird Buffet. Fill it with birdseed and keep an eye out for your first customers!

Quintuple Bike Stand

You don't have to wrestle with a tangled pile of bikes any-more. Five rides fit in this easy-to-build rack.

ESTIMATED TIME:

8 hours

Shopping List

- (3) 2 x 4 x 6' (70 x 122 x 183 cm) softwood
- (2) 2 x 2 x 8' (70 x 70 x 244 cm) softwood
- ¾" x 24" x 48" (1.9 x 61 x 122 cm) plywood
- 3¼" (8.3 cm) galvanized nails
- 2½" (6.4 cm) galvanized nails
- 100-grit and 180-grit sandpaper
- Exterior-grade wood sealer

Tools

- Layout tools
- Handsaw
- Miter box
- Clamps
- Hammer
- Drill with ⅛" (3 mm) bit
- 2" (5 cm) paintbrush

Cutting the Braces, Stiles, and Stretchers

1. Lay out and cut the braces (B) and stiles (C) to length from the three 2 x 4 boards. Label the pieces and set them aside.

Code	Part	Number	Size	Material
			Cut List, Quintuple Bike Stand	
A	Side wall	2	¾" x 24" x 24" (2 x 61 x 61 cm)	Plywood
B	Brace	2	1½" x 3½" x 21" (3.8 x 9 x 53.4 cm)	Softwood
C	Stile	6	1½" x 3½" x 26½" (3.8 x 9 x 67.3 cm)	Softwood
D	Stretcher	4	1½" x 1½" x 38½" (3.8 x 3.8 x 98 cm)	Softwood

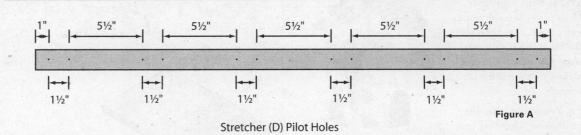

Stretcher (D) Pilot Holes

Figure A

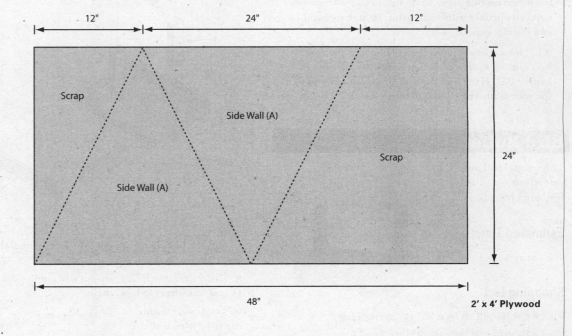

2' x 4' Plywood

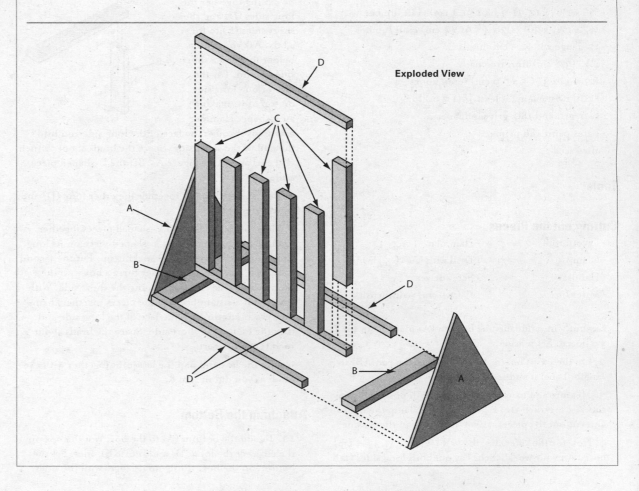

Exploded View

2. From the two 2 x 2 boards, lay out the lengths for the stretchers (D). Use the miter box to crosscut the pieces. Don't forget to label them.

3. Only two of the four stretchers (D) will have pilot holes for nails. Transfer the 12 pilot-hole marks in Figure A onto each of the two stretchers.

4. Clamp one of the marked stretchers (D) to your workbench so a pilot hole hangs over the edge. Dimple the hole layouts. Chuck the 1/8-inch (3 mm) bit into your drill. Then have your adult assistant help you with this step: Carefully bore straight through one mark. Adjust the piece and repeat to drill all of the pilot holes.

5. Repeat step 4 to drill all of the pilot holes in the second stretcher (D) piece. Set both pieces aside.

6. Because the pieces you're working with are so large, you may need to do the next few steps on the floor. First, you'll attach the stiles (C) to two of the stretchers (D) to make the middle part of the bike stand. The stretchers you'll use for the next few steps are the two with pilot holes.

7. Lay the first stretcher (D) face up. Set the first stile (C) face up with its end touching the bottom edge of the stretcher at one end. The two pieces will form a corner. While your adult assistant holds the pieces together, hammer two 3¼-inch (8.3 cm) nails through the pilot holes in the edge of the stretcher and into the end of the stile.

8. Repeat steps 6 and 7 to line up and nail a second stile (C) to the other end of the stretcher (D), forming a corner at the opposite end.

9. Lay the second stretcher (D) against the bottoms of the stiles (C). Hammer two 3¼-inch (8.3 cm) nails through the pilot holes in the stretcher and into the ends of the stiles. You've just made a rectangle.

10. Attach the four remaining stiles (C) between the stretchers (D), spacing them equally between the attached stiles. The stiles should be about 3½ inches (8.9 cm) apart. Set the middle part of your bike stand aside.

Building the Ends

11. Measure and mark the two side walls (A) on the plywood. (Use the diagram as your guide to draw the two triangles.)

12. Clamp the plywood to your workbench and cut out the pieces. Label the side walls (A).

13. Now you'll attach the braces (B) to the side walls (A) of the bike stand. Lay the first brace on its edge. Have your adult helper hold the first side wall on top of the brace. Line up the 24-inch (61 cm) side of the triangle with the face of the brace. Center the brace between the corners of the side wall. The side wall should overhang the ends of the brace by 1½ inches (4 cm) on either side. Hammer a row of 2½-inch (6.4 cm) nails through the face of the side wall and into the edge of the brace. Space the nails about 2 inches (5 cm) apart.

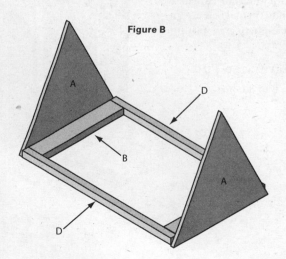

Figure B

14. Repeat step 13 to attach the other brace (B) to the other side wall (A).

15. Now you'll attach the stretchers (D) that don't have any holes drilled in them to the side walls (A). Stand the side walls on the floor (the braces will balance them). Line up the side walls so the braces (B) are on the inside, facing each other. Lay the two stretchers on the floor between the side walls (see Figure B). The ends of each stretcher should connect the side walls at the outside corner, forming a rectangle. One edge of each stretcher will be pressed against a brace.

16. With your adult helper holding the parts together, hammer two 2½-inch (6.4 cm) nails through a side wall (A) into the stretcher (D).

17. Repeat step 16 on the other three corners of the side walls (A), nailing both of the stretchers (D) in place.

18. The last step is to attach the middle part of the bike stand to the side walls (A). Have your adult assistant hold the middle part between the side walls. The bottom should rest on top of the braces (B). Use your layout tools to make sure the stand is centered between the side walls and is straight up and down.

19. With your adult helper holding the pieces tightly together, drive a row of 2½-inch (6.4 cm) nails through the first side wall and into the edge of the stile. The nails should be spaced about 6 inches (15.2 cm) apart. Repeat this step to attach the other end.

Finishing Touches

20. Sand all the parts of the bike stand. Wipe off the sawdust.

21. Seal your project with two coats of clear exterior-grade wood sealer, letting each coat dry completely.

22. Your bike stand will last for many years if you keep it in a sheltered place such as under a carport or in your garage. Now get rolling!

Favorite Things Shelf

Display your keepsakes in this easy, multi-shelf unit. Lay or hang it on any side for just the right fit and look.

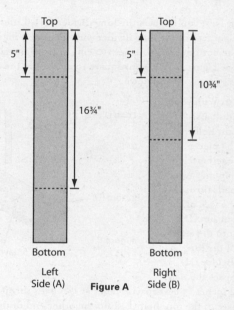

ESTIMATED TIME:

6 to 8 hours

Shopping List

- (2) 1 x 4 x 6' (2.5 x 10 x 183 cm) hardwood*
- 1¼" (3.2 cm) finishing nails
- 100-grit and 180-grit sandpaper
- Latex stain and polyurethane varnish
- 4½" x 3" (9.75 x 7.5 cm) flat corner braces with screws**

If you want to stain your display shelf like this one, use a hardwood like oak. If you'd rather paint your project, use a softwood.

**Use these special pieces of hardware to make your display shelf sturdier. Ask for help finding them at the lumberyard or hardware store.*

Tools

· Layout tools	· Cotton rags
· Handsaw	· 1" (2.5 cm) paintbrush
· Hammer	· Drill with 1/16" (1.6 mm) bit
· Rasp	· Screwdriver

Cutting the Pieces

1. Lay out and cut all of the pieces. Use the two diagrams of the 1 x 4 boards to help you. Be sure to square both ends of each piece; all of the pieces need to fit together perfectly to create this shelf. And label those pieces—there are a lot of them!

Building the Box

2. You'll start by transferring the layout lines in Figure A to the left side (A), right side (B), top (C), and bottom (D). On the sides, be sure to label the "top" and "bottom" ends. On the top and bottom, label the "left" and "right" sides.

3. Now it's time to make a simple box. Ask your adult assistant to stand the left side (A) on end so the bottom is touching the floor. Lay the left side of the top (C) on the end of the side, lining up the edges. Hammer two finishing nails through the face of the top into the end of the left side. Put the nails about 2 inches (5 cm) apart. Now you have an L shape.

4. Repeat step 3 to attach the right side (B) to the right end of the bottom (D), making another L-shaped piece.

5. To finish making the box, fit the L-shaped pieces together, matching the corners of the sides (A & B), top (C), and bottom (D). Ask your adult assistant to hold the pieces while you hammer two nails through the face of the top and into the end of the right side (B). Space the nails about 2 inches (5 cm) apart.

6. Flip the box so it rests on the top (C), and then repeat step 5 to nail the bottom (D) to the left side (B).

Top — Top

5" — 5"

16¾" — 10¾"

Bottom — Bottom

Left Side (A) — **Figure A** — Right Side (B)

Inserting the Shelves

7. The shelves and the dividers go in next. Rest the box on the edges of the sides (A & B), top (C), and bottom (D). Use the exploded view to help you set the shelves and dividers in the box. Do the pieces fit? Great! If a piece is too long, use your rasp to remove wood until it fits or cut another piece a bit shorter. If a piece is too short, cut a new piece and try it again.

8. First you'll attach the top shelf (E). Align the top face of the top shelf with the top layout marks on the left (A) and right (B) sides (5 inches [10 cm] below the top). See Figure B. While your adult assistant holds the pieces in place, hammer two nails through the face of one side and into the end of the top shelf. Space the nails about 2 inches (5 cm) apart. Hammer two nails through the face of the other side and into the other end of the top shelf.

Continued ➡

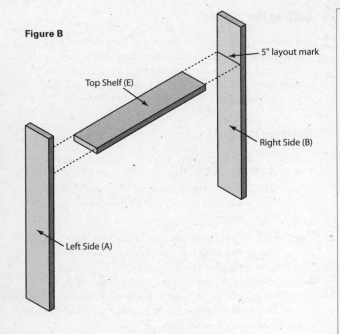

Figure B

Top Shelf (E)

5" layout mark

Right Side (B)

Left Side (A)

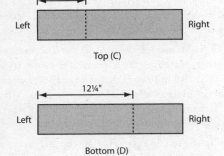

5¾"

Left Right

Top (C)

12¼"

Left Right

Bottom (D)

Cut List, Favorite Things Shelf

Code	Part	Number	Size	Material
A	Left side	1	¾" x 3½" x 22½" (2 x 9 x 57 cm)	Hardwood
B	Right side	1	¾" x 3½" x 22½" (2 x 9 x 57 cm)	Hardwood
C	Top	1	¾" x 3½" x 18" (2 x 9 x 45.7 cm)	Hardwood
D	Bottom	1	¾" x 3½" x 18" (2 x 9 x 45.7 cm)	Hardwood
E	Top shelf	1	¾" x 3½" x 16½" (2 x 9 x 42 cm)	Hardwood
F	Short shelf	1	¾" x 3½" x 5" (2 x 9 x 12.7 cm)	Hardwood
G	Bottom shelf	1	¾" x 3½" x 10¾" (2 x 9 x 27.3 cm)	Hardwood
H	Long divider	1	¾" x 3½" x 16¾" (2 x 9 x 42.5 cm)	Hardwood
I	Short divider	1	¾" x 3½" x 5" (2 x 9 x 12.7 cm)	Hardwood

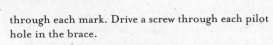

| 22½" (A) | 22½" (B) | 16½" (E) | 5" (F) | Scrap |

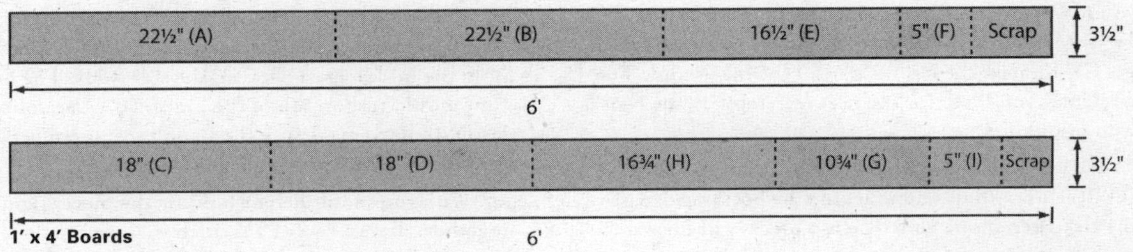

3½"

6'

| 18" (C) | 18" (D) | 16¾" (H) | 10¾" (G) | 5" (I) | Scrap |

3½"

1' x 4' Boards   6'

9. Next you'll attach the long divider (H). Line up the right face of the long divider with the layout mark on the bottom (D), 5 inches (10 cm) in from the right. See Figure C. Use your square to make sure the divider is straight up and down.

10. With your adult assistant holding the pieces together, hammer two nails through the face of the bottom (D) into the end of the long divider (H). Space the nails 2 inches (5 cm) apart. Hammer two nails through the face of the top shelf (E) into the other end of the long divider.

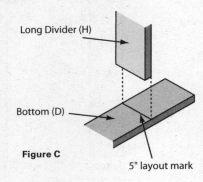

Long Divider (H)

Bottom (D)

Figure C

5" layout mark

11. Now you can put in the bottom shelf (G). Line up the top face of the bottom shelf with the remaining layout mark on the left side (A). This should place the shelf 5 inches (10 cm) above the bottom (D). Make sure the joint between the side and the shelf is square.

12. With your adult assistant holding the pieces together, hammer two nails through the face of the left side (A) into the end of the bottom shelf (G). Space the nails 2 inches (5 cm) apart. Hammer two nails through the face of the long divider (H) into the other end of the bottom shelf.

13. Now for the short pieces. Start with the short shelf (F). Line up the top face of the shelf with the top layout mark on the right side (B). Make sure the joint is square.

14. With your adult assistant holding the pieces together, hammer two nails through the face of the right side (B) into the end of the short shelf (F). Space the nails 2 inches (5 cm) apart. Hammer two nails through the face of the long divider (H) into the other end of the short shelf.

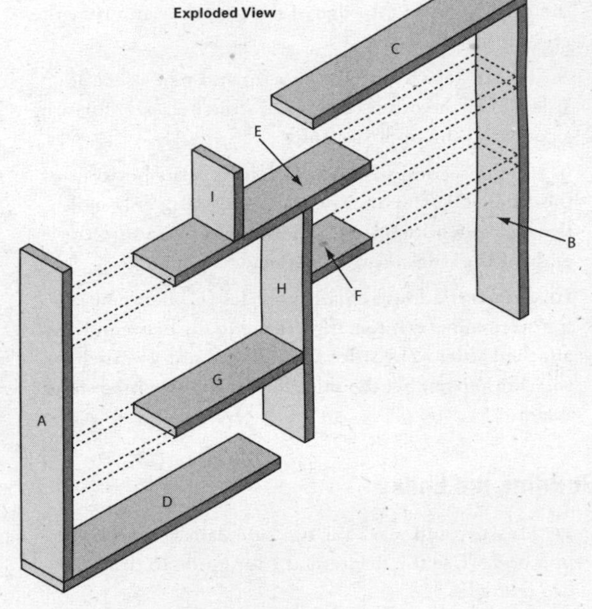

15. It's time to put in the last piece! Line up the left face of the short divider (I) with the layout mark on the top (C), 5¾ (14.6 cm) inches from the left side (A). Make sure the joint is square.

16. With your adult assistant holding the pieces together, hammer two nails through the face of the top (C) into the end of the short divider (I). Space the nails 2 inches (5 cm) apart. Hammer two nails through the face of the top shelf (E) into the other end of the short divider.

Tip

Nailing pieces together when you don't have quite enough room to swing your hammer can be tricky! To make this easier, hold the nail at a slight angle. (Not so much that it will pop through the face of the pieces you're nailing into though!) Then you can swing your hammer at an angle to hit the nail, which gives you a little more room.

Exploded View

Sanding and Varnishing

17. Sand all parts of the Favorite Things Shelf. Wipe off the sawdust.

18. To stain the shelf unit, use a clean cotton rag to wipe stain onto all of its parts. Don't apply the stain so thickly that it gets drippy or puddles up on the project. Let the stain dry completely.

19. Paint two coats of varnish onto the Favorite Things Shelf, letting the first coat dry before applying the second. This will seal the wood.

Adding the Corner Braces

20. Lay the shelf unit face-down on top of newspaper or cloth. Line up a corner brace on the edge of a corner where the left side (A) joins the top (C). Center the brace on the corner. Use your pencil to mark where the screws will go through the bracket into the edge of the side and top.

21. Flag a ¹/₁₆-inch (1.6 mm) bit to drill a ½-inch (1.3 cm) deep pilot. Dimple each mark. Chuck the bit into your drill. With your adult assistant holding the shelf unit firmly, drill a pilot hole

through each mark. Drive a screw through each pilot hole in the brace.

22. Repeat steps 20 and 21 to put a corner brace in each corner of the shelf unit. Now put your favorite things on it!

Round and Round Media Tower

Fill this multilevel storage unit with your favorite CDs and DVDs. Then just give it a spin to grab what you want.

ESTIMATED TIME:

6 to 8 hours

Shopping List

- 1 x 10 softwood, at least 3' (91 cm) long
- 2 x 4 softwood, at least 4" (122 cm) long
- 1 x 4 x 6' (183 cm) softwood
- 1" x 20" (2.5 x 50.8 cm) softwood dowel
- 1½" finishing nails
- No. 8 x 2" screws
- 100-grit and 180-grit sandpaper
- Latex primer and paints

Tools

- Layout tools
- Handsaw
- Miter box
- Clamps
- Hammer
- Drill with 1¼" (3.2 cm) and ⅛" (3.1 mm) bits
- Wood glue
- Screwdriver
- Rasp
- 1" (2.5 cm) paintbrush

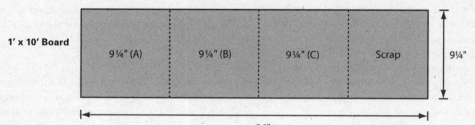

Cut List, Round and Round Media Tower

Code	Part	Number	Size	Material
A	Top	1	¾" x 9¼" x 9¼" (2 x 23.5 x 23.5)	Softwood
B	Bottom	1	¾" x 9¼" x 9¼" (2 x 23.5 x 23.5)	Softwood
C	Base	1	¾" x 9¼" x 9¼" (2 x 23.5 x 23.5)	Softwood
D	Collar	1	1½" x 3½" x 3½" (3.8 x 9 x 9 cm)	Softwood
E	Side	4	¾" x 3½" x 16" (2 x 9 x 40.6 cm)	Softwood
F	Center post	1	1" x 19½" (2.5 x 49.5 cm)	Dowel

1' x 10' Board — 9¼" (A) | 9¼" (B) | 9¼" (C) | Scrap — 9¼"

Cutting All the Parts

1. Using the diagram of the 1 x 10 board as your guide, lay out and cut the top (A), bottom (B), and base (C). Label the pieces and set them aside.

2. Lay out and cut the collar (D) to length from the 2 x 4. Label the piece and set it aside.

3. Now for the sides (E). Lay out and cut the four sides from the 1 x 4. Label the pieces and set them aside.

4. Lay out the center post (F). Use your miter box and handsaw to cut the dowel to length. Label it and set it aside.

Drilling the Parts

5. First you need to lay out where you want the bore holes. Place the top (A) face-up on your workbench. Mark a diagonal line between each of the two corners, so that you have an X crisscrossing the face. The center of the X is where you'll drill the hole for the center post (F). Set the piece aside. Repeat this step for the bottom (B), base (C), and collar (D).

6. Place a piece of scrap wood between the bottom (B) and the workbench. Then clamp the wood. Dimple the hole layout in the center of the piece. Chuck the 1¼-inch (3.2 cm) bit into your doll. Carefully drill straight through the mark. Set the drilled piece aside. Repeat this step for the collar (D).

7. Flag the 1¼-inch (3.2 cm) drill bit to bore a ½-inch (1.3 cm) deep hole. Then clamp the top (A), with scrap wood beneath it, to the workbench. Dimple the hole layout. Drill straight into the mark. Stop when the bottom of the flag reaches the surface of the piece. Set the piece aside. Repeat this step for the base (C).

8. Now you'll drill a pilot hole in the bottom of the base (C) so a screw can be inserted into the center post (F). Flip the base so that the borehole is face down. Draw diagonal lines from the corners to find the center (see step 5).

9. Clamp the base (C) and some scrap wood to the workbench. Dimple the hole layout. Chuck the ⅛-inch (8.1 mm) bit into your drill, and bore a hole through the center mark and the borehole on the other side.

Assembling the Base

10. Flip the base (C) so that the larger borehole is now face up. Run a line of glue around the borehole, making a circle of glue. Set the collar (D) on top of the base, lining up the boreholes in both pieces. Press them together.

11. Hammer four finishing nails through the collar (D) and into the base (C). Set each nail about ½ inch (1.3 cm) from each corner of the collar.

12. Put a few drops of glue on the end of the center post (F) and set it in the borehole.

13. Ask your adult helper to hold the assembly upside down so that it's resting on the end of the center post (F). Drive a screw through the pilot hole in the base (C) and into the end of the center post. This will help hold the dowel in place. You may need a hand with driving the screw. Set the base assembly aside.

Building the Cage

14. Next you'll attach the top (A) and bottom (B) to the sides (E) to build the CD/DVD cage. Start with the top and one side. Ask your adult helper to stand the side on end. Set the top on the side, lining it up with one corner (see Figure A).

15. Make sure the face and edge of the side are aligned with the corner and edge of the top. Hammer two nails through the top and into the end of the side. Space the nails about 1½ inches (3.8 cm) apart.

16. Repeat step 14 to attach the other three sides (E) to the top (A). Each side will line up with one corner of the top. See Figure A.

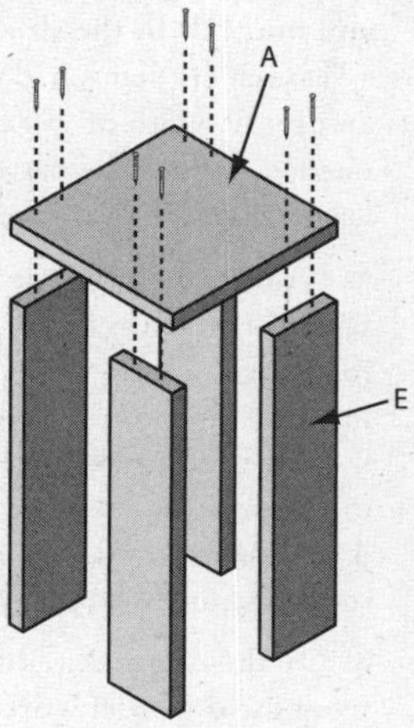

17. Time to attach the bottom (B). Flip the assembly so that it rests on the top (A), with the sides (E) sticking up. Set the bottom on the ends of the sides, lining up the corners. While your adult assistant holds everything in place, hammer two nails through the bottom and into each side. Space the nails about 1½ inches (3.8 cm) apart. (You'll hammer eight nails total.)

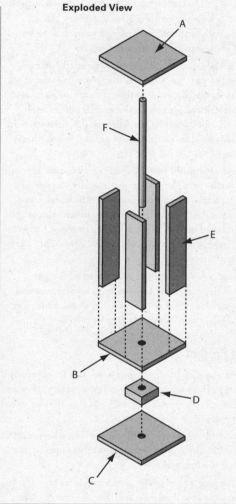

Figure A

18. Slide the case over the dowel. Does it spin easily? Great! If it doesn't, use your rasp to make the holes in the top (A) and bottom (B) a little larger.

Finishing Touches

19. Sand the Media Tower. Wipe off the sawdust. Prime and paint the project.

20. After it dries, go ahead and fill it with your favorite music and movies.

—From *The All New Woodworking for Kids*

Exploded View

Continued ➔

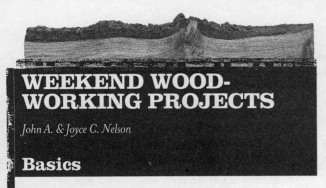

Using the Drawings for Each Project

With each project there is at least a two-view drawing provided. One is almost always called the front view, and the other is either the side view or the top view. The front view is always the most important view and the place you should start in studying the drawings. At times a section view is used to further illustrate some particular feature of the project. The section view is sometimes a partial view that illustrates only a portion of the project, such as a particular molding detail or way of joining parts.

Most of the projects also have an exploded view, which fully illustrates how the project goes together. Make sure that you fully understand how the project is to be assembled before you begin any work on it.

There is a Materials List of supplies needed for each project, and the part numbers in the lists correspond to the numbers in the illustrated views that accompany each project. This will enable you to see exactly where each part is located and how it fits together with other parts in the design. Note: all measurements are in inches unless otherwise noted.

Multiple parts should be made exactly the same size and shape. Every now and then a project requires a pair of parts—that is, a right-hand piece and a left-hand piece. In such a case, take care not to make duplicate pieces, but rather a left-hand and right-hand pair. In most projects requiring a pair, this is noted, but for any multiple parts double-check if in doubt.

Throughout, when practical, I numbered all the parts of a project in the order that I would suggest you make and assemble them. You might want to make and assemble your project some other way, but this is what worked best for me.

Making a Project

After you thoroughly study the project, start by carefully making each individual part. Take care to make each piece exactly to the correct size and exactly square—that is, each cut at 90° to the face, as required.

Sand each individual piece, but take care to keep all the edges sharp. Do not round the edges at this time; some will be rounded after assembly.

After all the pieces have been made with great care, dry-fit the pieces—that is, cautiously put together the entire project to check for correct fit throughout before final assembly. If anything needs refitting, this is the time to correct it.

When the pieces all fit correctly, glue and/or nail the project together, again taking care that all fits are tight and square. Sand the project all over; it is at this time that edges can be rounded, if necessary. The project is then ready for finishing.

Enlarging a Pattern or Design

Many of the drawings are reduced relative to the actual size of the parts so that all of the information can be presented on the page. In some projects the patterns for irregular parts or irregular portions of parts must be enlarged to full size. A grid of squares is drawn over these parts, and the original size of the grid is noted on the drawing.

There are four ways a design or shape of the irregular part or parts can be enlarged to full size.

Method One

One of the simplest and least expensive ways is to use a photocopy machine with an enlarging/reducing fea-

ture. Simply put the book page on the machine, choose the enlargement mode you need (usually expressed as a percentage of the original), and make a copy. In a few cases, you may have to make another copy of the enlargement copy in order to get the required size. Once in awhile you will not be able to get the exact size required, but the result will be close enough for most work, perhaps requiring a little touching up, at most.

Method Two

A very quick and extremely accurate method is to ask a local commercial printer to make a P.M.T. (photomechanical transfer) of the area needed to be enlarged or reduced. This is a photographic method that yields an exact size without any difficulty. This method will cost a little money, depending on the size of the final P.M.T., but if your time is valuable, it might be worth it.

Method Three

Another simple, quick method is to use a drawing tool called the pantograph. It is an inexpensive tool that is very simple to use for enlarging or reducing to almost any required size. If you do a lot of enlarging or reducing, the cost of this tool may be well worth the price.

Method Four

Most authors assume woodworkers will use the grid and dot-to-dot method. It is very simple; you do not have to be an artist to use the method. It can be used to enlarge or reduce to any size or scale and requires just eight simple steps.

1. Note what size the full-size grid should be. This is usually indicated on the drawing near the grid. Most of the grids used with the project drawings must be redrawn so that each square is ½ inch or 1 inch (1.3 or 2.5 cm) per side.

2. Calculate the overall required width and height. If it is not given, simply count the squares across and down and multiply by the size of each square. For example, a ½-inch (1.3 cm) grid with 15 squares across requires an overall width of 7½ inches (19 cm). The paper size needed to draw the pattern full size should be a little larger than the overall size of the part.

3. It will be helpful but not necessary, if you have a few basic drafting tools. Tools suggested are: A drafting board, a scale (ruler), a T-square, a 45° triangle, masking tape, and a sheet of paper a little larger than the required overall size of the pattern. Tape the paper to the drafting board or other surface, and carefully draw the required grid on the paper, using the drafting tools or whatever tools you have.

4. On the original, reduced drawing in the book, start from the upper left corner and add letters across the top of the grid from left to right, A through whatever letter it takes to get to the other side of the grid. From the same starting point, add numbers down, from 1 to whatever number it takes to get to the bottom of the grid.

5. On your full-size grid, add letters and numbers in exactly the same way you did on the original.

6. On the original reduced drawing, draw dots along the pattern outline wherever it crosses the grid.

7. On your full-size grid, locate and draw the same dots on the grid. It is helpful to locate each dot by using the letters across the top and the numbers along the side. For example, a dot at B-6 can easily be found on the new, full-size grid by coming down from line B and over on line 6.

8. All that is left to do is to connect the dots. Note: you do not have to be exact; all you have to do is sketch a line between the dots using your eye to approximate the shape of the original, reduced drawing.

Transferring the Pattern from Paper to Wood

Tape the full-size pattern to the wood with carbon paper in between for transferring the pattern, and use a pen to trace over the pattern. If you are going to copy the pattern many times, make a template instead. Simply transfer

the pattern onto a sheet of heavy cardboard or ⅛-inch thick hardboard or plywood and cut out the pattern. This template can then be used over and over by simply tracing around the template to lay out the pattern for each copy.

If the pattern is symmetrical—that is, exactly the same size and shape on both sides of an imaginary line—make only a half-pattern and trace it twice, once on each side of the midline. This will ensure the perfect symmetry of the finished part.

For small patterns—8½ inches x 11 inches (21.5 x 27.9 cm) or smaller at full size—make a photocopy of the full-size pattern using any copy machine. Tape the copy, printed side down, and using a hot flatiron or hot wood-burning set, heat the back side of the copy. The pattern will transfer from the paper directly to the wood. This method is very good for very small or complicated patterns.

Another method for small patterns—8½ inches x 11 inches (21.5 x 27.9 cm) or smaller at full size—is to make a photocopy of the pattern, and, using rubber cement or spray-mount adhesive, lightly glue the copy directly to the wood. Cut out the piece with the copy glued directly to the wood. Simply peel the copy away from the wood after you cut out the piece. Then sand all over.

Selecting Material for Your Project

As lumber will probably be the most expensive material you will purchase for each project, it is a good idea that you have some basic knowledge about lumber so that you can make wise choices and save a little money here and there on your purchases.

All lumber is divided into two kinds, hardwood and softwood. Hardwoods are deciduous trees, trees that flower and lose their leaves seasonally; softwoods are the coniferous trees, which are cone-bearing and usually evergreen. In actuality, a few hardwoods are softer than some softwoods—but on the whole, hardwoods are harder, closer grained, much more durable, tougher to work, and take a stain beautifully. Hardwood typically costs more than softwood, but it is well worth it.

All wood contains pores—open spaces that serve as water-conducting vessels—that are more noticeable in some kind of wood than in others. Woods such as oak and mahogany have pores that are very noticeable and probably should be filled, for the best-finished appearance. Maple and birch are what are called close-grained woods, which provide a beautiful, smooth finish.

The grain of wood is the result of each year's growth of new cells. Around the tree's circumference each year, annular growth forms a new and hard fibrous layer called a ring. Growth in most trees is seasonal but somewhat regular so that these rings are evenly spaced. In other trees this annular growth is not very regular, thus creating uneven spacing and thickness. The pattern formed by the rings when the tree is cut into lumber is what we see as the grain pattern.

The softwoods I used for most of the projects are pine, spruce, and fir. Pine was the favorite since it is the easiest to work, especially for simple accessories such as those found in this book. The hardwoods I used most were maple, walnut, oak, cherry, poplar, and birch.

Always buy dried lumber, as green lumber will shrink, twist, and warp while drying. Purchase the best lumber you can find for these projects since none of them require a great deal of material. Your work will go more easily, and the finished project will be so much better for the superior-quality wood. The actual cost difference between an inexpensive piece of wood and the best you can find will be quite small since the overall cost of any of these projects is very low to begin with.

A few projects call for wide boards. I believe the projects would look best if you could find the correct width. The correct width also adds to the authenticity. If this is not possible, glue narrower boards together by edge joining them to produce the necessary width. Try to match grain patterns with great care so that each joint will not be so noticeable. Even though I prefer the look of the single, wide board, I should point out that a glued joint is as strong as a single piece of wood and probably will not warp.

Lumber is sold by the board foot. A board foot is a piece of wood that is I foot wide, I inch thick, and I foot long. A piece of wood 4 inches wide (⅓ foot), I inch thick, and I2 feet long contains 4 board feet of wood. The formula is: width in feet x thickness in inches x length in feet = board feet (in the example, ⅓ x I x I2 = 4 board feet).

In the Materials Lists, the dimensions given of the wood needed for each project are listed in inches, first thickness, then width, and then length. For example: Body—½ x 6½—14 long.

Finding Board Feet Using a Factor

Using the table below to find the appropriate factor, we can easily calculate that a board I inch thick, 5 inches wide, and I2 feet long can be converted to board feet by multiplying I2 (linear length) times 0.417 (factor) to give 5.004 board feet of lumber. (The term linear length refers to the actual length of any board as it is measured.)

Dressed lumber comes in actual sizes other than the nominal size would indicate because of the finishing process. For example, a I x 6 measures about ¾ inch by 5⅝ inches in actual size. The chart below indicates what some of the actual sizes may be. Note: today, the actual width may vary—in some areas a I x 6 might be 5½ inches wide rather than 5⅝ inches wide. Check around in your area before buying wood.

Rough Size	Finished Size
I x 2	¾ x I⅝ (2 x 4.I cm)
I x 3	¾ x 2⅝ (2 x 6.7 cm)
I x 4	¾ x 3⅝ (2 x 9.2 cm)
I x 5	¾ x 4⅝ (2 x II.7 cm)
I x 6	¾ x 5⅝ (2 x I4.3 cm)
I x 8	¾ x 7⅝ (2 x I9.4 cm)
I x I0	¾ x 9½ (2 x 24.I cm)
I x I2	¾ x II½ (2 x 29.2 cm)

Hardware for Your Project

The extra money spent on hardware of high quality versus that saved on low-cost hardware is—as noted in purchasing lumber—a very small difference since the overall cost of your project is already quite low. Don't forget, the hardware is usually what is most visible, so the little extra spent will be well worth the increased look of quality for many years to come.

Board Feet Using Linear Length

½" Thick Board		I" Thick Board	
Width	Factor	Width	Factor
2	.083	2	.167
3	.125	3	.250
4	.166	4	.333
5	.209	5	.417
6	.250	6	.500
8	.333	8	.666

Kinds of Joints

The projects require four kinds of joints—and, for the most part, only three. These basic joints are the butt joint, the rabbet joint, the dado joint and, in a few instances, the dovetail joint. These can be made by hand without power tools. If you do have power tools, use them; early crafters would have used them if they had had them.

Most of the simpler projects use the butt joint. This is the simplest of all joints and, as its name implies, is simply two boards that are butted up against each other and joined together, perhaps with glue and nails or screws. The major disadvantage of the butt joint is that there is less surface area available for gluing or nailing than for other joints. Nails sometimes back out of the joint over time, which also makes an opening at the joint. A rabbet joint is an L-shaped cutout made along the edge or end of one board to overlap the edge or end of the mating board. This joint can also be nailed and/or glued together. Because rabbet joints are often cut into side pieces, the nails—put in from the sides—may be hidden somewhat from view. Dado joints are similar to rabbet joints, except that the cut is made leaving wood shoulders on both sides. A drawer side is an excellent example of the use of both a dado joint and a rabbet joint. The most difficult joint is the dovetail joint, but with a little thought and careful layout, they can be easily made. Dovetail joints are made by interlocking ends of boards that have had notches cut into them.

Gluing

Glue was not in general use until after I750. Therefore, most of the antique projects featured in this book probably were simply nailed together. If by chance they were glued together, they were probably glued together with hot animal, or hide, glue.

Wood glues are either hot or cold glue, depending on whether or not heat is used to prepare them. Hot glue is made from animal parts and is very strong and quick-setting. Until very recently, old-fashioned hide glue was considered the only true, satisfactory kind of glue to use in cabinetmaking. Recent developments in new and better cold glues have made this generalization debatable. Cold glues are all derived from synthetic material of one kind or another. They vary in durability and strength. For the simpler projects cold glue is, by far, the easiest to use, and I recommend its use. In using cold glue, always follow the instructions given on the label.

When gluing, always take care to clean all excess glue from around the joint. This is a must if you are going to stain the project. The excess glue will not take the stain and will appear white. I find that by waiting for I0 to I5 minutes, just until the glue is almost set. I can carefully remove most of it with a sharp wood chisel. Do not wipe off the excessive glue with a wet cloth as the water will weaken the glue joint and possibly spread glue irretrievably into the pore space, staining the wood.

For the few projects that are a little difficult to hold together properly while gluing, the new hot-glue guns can be very helpful. Hot-glue guns use solid glue sticks that are inserted, heated to their melting point, and then liquid glue is pushed through the tip while very hot. This kind of glue dries very quickly and sets in about I0 seconds without clamping. Take care if you use this kind of glue as it is difficult to get good tight-fitting joints every time. The glue sets up so quickly that you have to work very fast. This kind of glue is good to use for special applications but not for everything; the slower-drying cold glue is still better to use for most of the projects.

Finishing

Once you have completed assembling your project, you are then ready to apply a finish. This is an important part and should not be rushed. Remember, this is the part that will make the biggest impression for many years to come. No matter how good the wood and hardware you use, regardless of how good the joints are, a poor finish will ruin your project. If it takes eight hours to make the project, plan on eight hours to finish it correctly.

Preparing

I. All joints should be checked for tight fits. If necessary, apply water putty to all joints, and allow ample time for drying. Apply water putty to fill those nail heads also.

2. Sand the project all over in the direction of the wood grain. If sanding is done by hand, use a sanding block, and be careful to keep all corners still sharp. Use I00-grit sandpaper. Resand all over, using a I80-grit sandpaper, and, if necessary, sand once more with 250-grit sandpaper. Take care not to round edges at this time.

3. If you do want any of the edges rounded, use the I80-grit sandpaper, and later the 250-grit sandpaper, specifically to round the edges.

4. A copy of an antique that looks new seems somehow to be a direct contradiction. Distressing—making the piece look old—can be done in many ways. Using a piece of coral stone about 3 inches in diameter, or a similar object, roll the stone across the various surfaces. Don't be afraid to add a few random scratches here and there, especially on the bottom or back, where an object would have been worn the most. Carefully study the object, and try to imagine how it would have been used through the years. Using a rasp, judiciously round the edges where you think wear would have occurred. Resand the entire project and the newly worn edges with I80-grit paper.

5. Clean all surfaces with a damp rag to remove all dust.

Fillers

A paste filler should be used for porous wood such as oak, ash, or mahogany. Purchase paste filler that is slightly darker than the color of your wood as the new wood you used will turn darker with age. Before using paste filler, thin it with turpentine so it can be applied with a brush. Use a stiff brush, and brush with the grain in order to fill the pores. Wipe off with a piece of burlap across the grain after I5 or 20 minutes, taking care to leave filler in the pores. Apply a second coat if necessary; let it dry for 24 hours.

Staining

There are two major kinds of stain: water-based stain and oil-base stain. Water stains are commonly purchased in powder form and mixed as needed by dissolving the powder in hot water. Premixed water-base stains have recently become available. Water stain has a tendency to raise the grain of the wood, so that after it dries, the surface should be lightly sanded with fine sandpaper. Oil stain is made from pigments ground in linseed oil and does not raise the grain.

I. Test the stain color on a scrap piece of the same kind of lumber you are using to make certain it will be the color you wish.

2. Wipe or brush on the stain as quickly and as evenly as possible to avoid overlapping streaks. If a darker finish is desired, apply more than one coat of stain. Try not to apply too much stain on the end grain. Allow to dry in a dust-free area for at least 24 hours.

Finishes

Shellac is a hard, easy-to-apply finish and dries in a few hours. For best results, thin slightly with alcohol and apply an extra coat or two. Several coats of thin shellac are much better than one or two thick coats. Sand lightly with extra-fine sandpaper between coats, but be sure to rub the entire surface with a dampened cloth. Strive for a smooth, satin finish—not a high-gloss finish coat—for an antique effect.

Varnish is easy to brush on and dries to a smooth, hard finish within 24 hours. It makes an excellent finish that is transparent and will give a deep-finish look to your project. Be sure to apply varnish in a completely dust-free area. Apply one or two coats directly from the can with long, even strokes. Rub between each coat, and after the last coat, with 0000 steel wool.

Oil finishes are especially easy to use for projects such as those in this book. Oil finish is easy to apply, long-lasting, never needs resanding, and actually improves wood permanently. Apply a heavy wet coat uniformly to all surfaces, and let set for 20 or 30 minutes. Wipe completely dry until you have a pleasing finish.

Painted Projects

Use a high-quality paint, either oil- or water-base. Today, the trend is towards water-base paint. Prime your project, and lightly sand after it dries. Apply two light coats of paint rather than one thick coat. We like to add some water to thin water-base paint since we feel that water-base paint tends to be a little thick. On all projects for children, and for all toys, always be sure to use a non-toxic paint.

Note: for a very satisfying feel to the finish and professional touch to your project, apply a topcoat of paste wax as the final step.

Achieving an Aged Look

Follow the five steps outlined for preparing your project as described under Finishing. Then follow these steps to distress your project.

Continued →

3. Seal the wood with a light coat of shellac with 50% alcohol. After the shellac is dry, rub lightly with 0000 steel wool. Wipe clean.

4. Apply an even coat of oil-base paint, taking care to use an antique color paint. Let dry for 48 hours. Do not paint the backs or bottoms—these were seldom painted on the original pieces.

5. Sand with 120-grit sandpaper all the rounded edges you prepared for wear marks in step 4 of Preparing. Remember, if these edges were worn, the paint surely would have been removed also. Sand away paint from all sharp edges and corners since edges and corners would wear through the years.

6. Lightly sand all over to remove any paint gloss, using 180-grit sandpaper. Wipe clean.

7. Wipe on a wash coat of oil-base black paint with a cloth directly from the can. Take care to get the black paint in all corners, and in all distress marks and scratches. Don't forget the unpainted back and bottoms. Wipe all paint off immediately before it dries, but leave black paint in all corners, joints, scratches, and distress marks. If you apply too much, wipe off using a cloth with turpentine on it. Let dry for 24 hours. Apply a light coat of paste wax.

Alternative One

For a really aged look, apply two coats of paint, each a totally different color (for example, first coat, a powder blue; second coat, antique brick red). Allow 24 hours between coats. After the second coat has dried for 48 hours or more, follow steps 3 and 4 above, but sand the topcoat off so that the first color shows through here and there at worn areas. Finish up with step 5 as outlined above. This is especially good on projects such as footstools or large painted wall boxes.

Alternative Two

If you want your painted project to have a crackled finish, follow these additional steps. After step 1, page 00, apply a coat of liquid hide glue over the intended painted surfaces. Let dry four to 12 hours. Then paint on a coat of gesso (a form of base paint in use since the sixteenth century). Paint lightly and do not go over any strokes. In 10 to 15 seconds, the gesso will start to crackle. Let dry for 24 hours in a very dry area. After 24 hours or more, continue on to step 2. (It would be a good idea to experiment on scrap wood before applying any of this to your finished project. Some crafters combine step 2 with the crackling by mixing their paint with the gesso, two parts gesso to one part paint.)

Visits to museums, antique shops, and flea markets will help you develop an eye for exactly what an original antique looks like. This will give you an excellent idea of how antiques have been worn through the years. With this firsthand experience, you will have a much clearer idea of what kind of finish you are after, so that your careful reproduction will realistically look hundreds of years old.

Hardware

Some of the projects in this book require special hardware—special parts such as hangers, hooks, clock quartz movements, hands, bezels, wheels, axles, hinges, latches, etc. If you are going to do any woodworking at all you should acquaint yourself with the various companies that specialize in handling these special items. You should write for as many woodworking supply and clock component catalogs as possible, in order to have a large choice of parts. This also gives you the opportunity to compare prices and to save a little money.

Before starting any project it is a good idea to obtain the parts ahead of time, in order to modify your projects to fit the parts, if necessary.

To get a good selection of catalogs, go to a local library and check out a woodworking magazine or two, to find companies to contact for catalogs. You also could check for hardware on the Internet.

Toaster Tongs

If you're like most folks, you start off the day in frustration. You can't get the darn toast out of the toaster! Once you make this simple, handy kitchen implement you'll be ready to face each morning—at least after a cup of coffee.

1. Select the wood. There are several ways to make a pair of toaster tongs. My approach is to start with a piece of oversized stock—¾ inch thick x 1⅛ inches wide x 9 inches long (19 x 28.5 x 228 mm)—and then work it down to the finished dimensions. Use a hardwood such as maple or cherry.

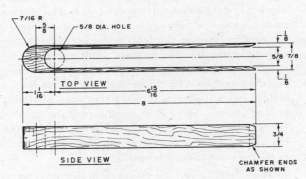

TOP VIEW

SIDE VIEW

CHAMFER ENDS AS SHOWN

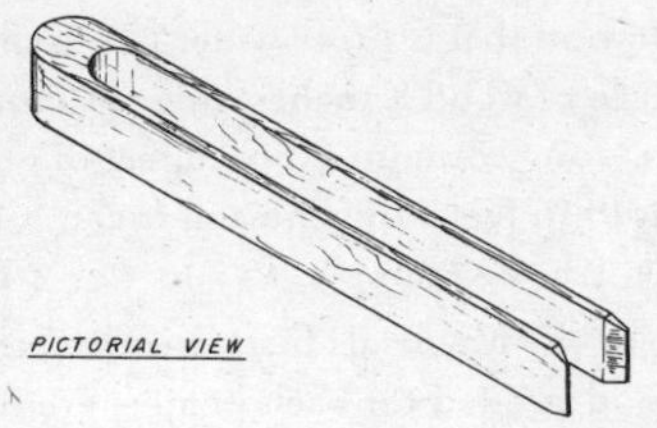

PICTORIAL VIEW

2. Lay out the tongs. Draw a line down the center of the wide side of the stick. At a point on the line roughly 1½ inches from one end, mark the center of a ⅝ inch (15.9 mm)-diameter hole and draw the hole. To lay out the insides of the legs, draw two lines: each one is tangent to the hole and parallel to the sides of the stock, as shown.

3. To lay out the outside of the tongs, locate a second point on the center line, ⅝ inch (15.9 mm) above the center of the hole. Swing a ⁷⁄₁₆-inch (11 mm) arc from that point, as shown in the top view. Extend a line from the bottom of the arc to lay out the outside of the legs. If you've measured correctly, the outside lines are ⅛ inch (3 mm) from the inside lines.

4. Cut out the tongs. Drill out the hole and cut along the layout lines with a band saw. Saw just outside the lines and sand down to the final leg thickness of ⅛ inch, taking care to make the legs as nearly identical as possible.

5. Finish the tongs. Either leave the wood unfinished, or apply a coat of vegetable oil or salad-bowl finish.

Classic Cutting Board

Cutting boards come in all shapes and sizes. There are pigs, chickens, turkeys, and even rabbits as cutting boards. This design is a simple rectangle with a round handle. Most any kind of hardwood and most any thickness of wood can be used. I used 1-inch-thick (24.4 mm) ash for the one pictured. As cutting boards are very popular, keep your full-size pattern. You'll probably be making more than one cutting board, especially after everyone sees the first one.

1. Carefully lay out the full-size pattern on a piece of cardboard about 12 x 22 inches (30.5 x 55.8 cm) in size. Cut out the full-size pattern, and transfer the shape to the wood. If you have to glue up material to get the full 11-inch-wide (27.9 cm) board, be sure to use waterproof glue.

2. Carefully cut out the cutting board, and sand all edges and surfaces. Using a ⅜-inch-radius (9.5 mm) router bit with a ball-bearing follower, rout the top and bottom edges, and then resand all over.

3. Be sure to use a finish that is nontoxic, such as one labeled as saladbowl finish.

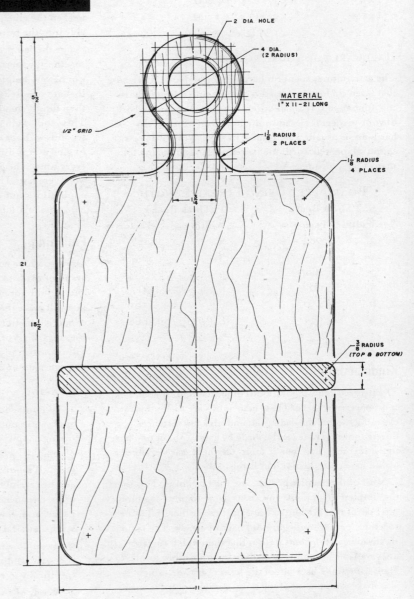

2 DIA HOLE

4 DIA. (2 RADIUS)

MATERIAL 1" X 11 – 21 LONG

1½ RADIUS 2 PLACES

1⅛ RADIUS 4 PLACES

½" GRID

5½

1¼

21

15½

⅜ RADIUS (TOP & BOTTOM)

11

In/Out Mail Basket

To add a little class and color to your desk, replace your plastic in/out basket with this good-looking substitute for the standard office supply.

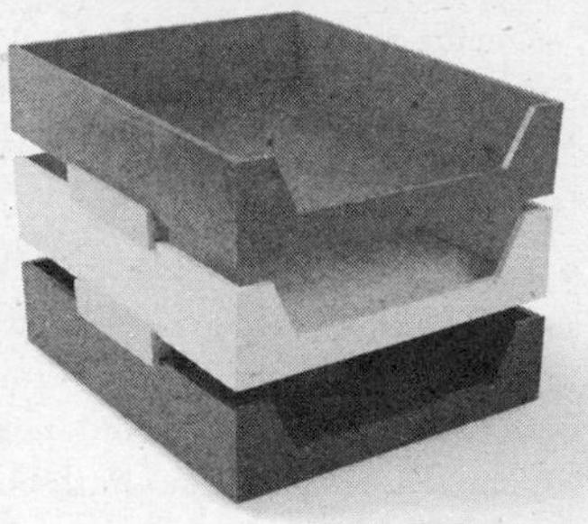

Materials List

No.	Name	Size	Req'd.
1	Front/back	¼ x 2½ - 10 Long (6.35 x 63.5 x 254 mm)	1 ea.
2	Side	¼ x 2½ - 11¾ Long (6.35 x 63.5 x 298 mm)	2
3	Bottom	¼ x 9-¹¹⁄₁₆ – 11¾ Long (6.35 x 246 x 298 mm)	1
4	Spacer	⅝ x 1⅛ – 4 Long (15.8 x 28.5 x 101 mm)	as req'd.

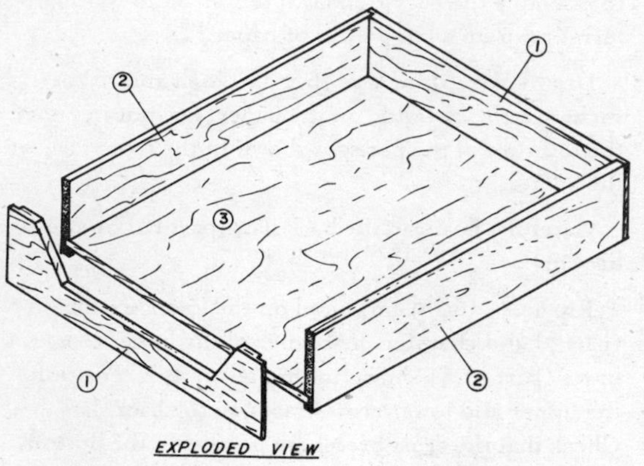
EXPLODED VIEW

1. Select the stock and cut the parts. Any hardwood will do, but oak and ash strike me as appropriate for an office. I chose ash for the basket in the photo. The entire piece is made from ¼-inch (6.35 mm) stock.

Decide how many units the basket will have. The Materials List gives the number of parts required to make one unit. With a couple of simple spacers, you can stack two units on top of each other; four spacers will let you stack three units, as shown here.

Cut all pieces to the sizes listed in the Materials List. Lay out the notch in the front (part 1) and cut it out on a band saw or jigsaw. If you are making more than one basket, tape the fronts together in a pile and cut out all the notches at once. Sand the edges of the notches while the fronts are still together.

2. Rabbet the front and back to accept the sides (part 2). Cut a groove for the bottom in the front, back, and sides, as shown in the side view.

3. Cut a piece of ⅝-inch (15.8 mm) stock for the spacers (part 4), making it about an inch longer than the combined lengths of the individual spacers you'll need. Rout or cut grooves along both the top and bottom edges of this piece, as shown in the spacer detail. Cut the piece into the individual 4-inch-long (101 mm) spacers.

4. Assemble the basket. Dry-fit the parts. Trim as necessary and glue up the parts, keeping everything square. Do not glue the bottom (part 3) in place, so that it can expand and contract with the weather. Sand the basket and spacers.

5. Finish the basket. The basket in the photo has a coat of light stain and two coats of varnish, but the distinctive grains of ash and oak look equally good without stain.

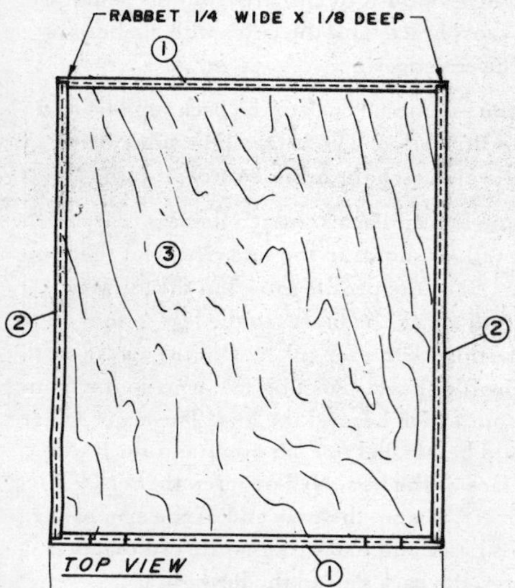
RABBET 1/4 WIDE X 1/8 DEEP
TOP VIEW

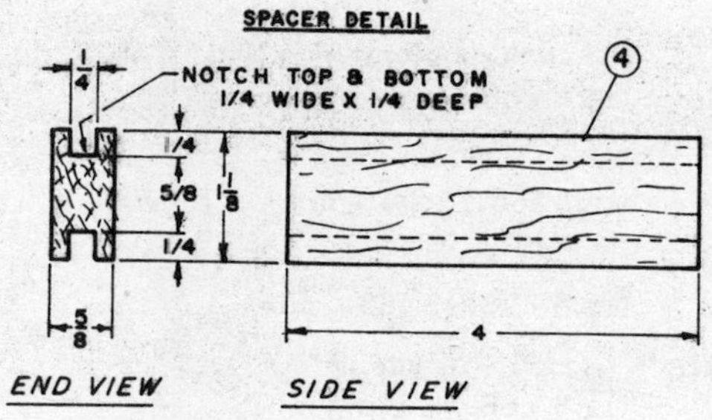
SPACER DETAIL
NOTCH TOP & BOTTOM 1/4 WIDE X 1/4 DEEP
END VIEW
SIDE VIEW

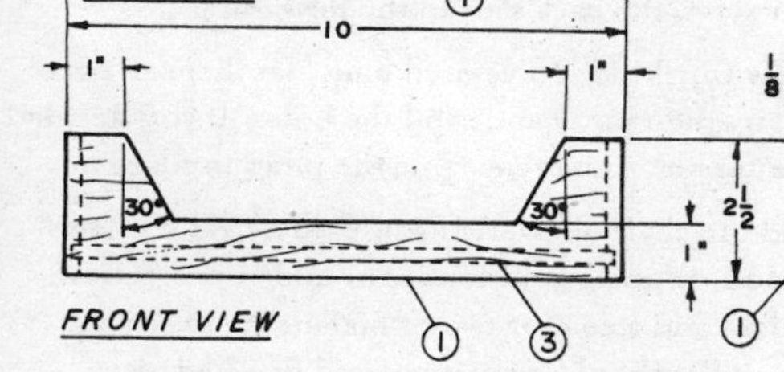
FRONT VIEW

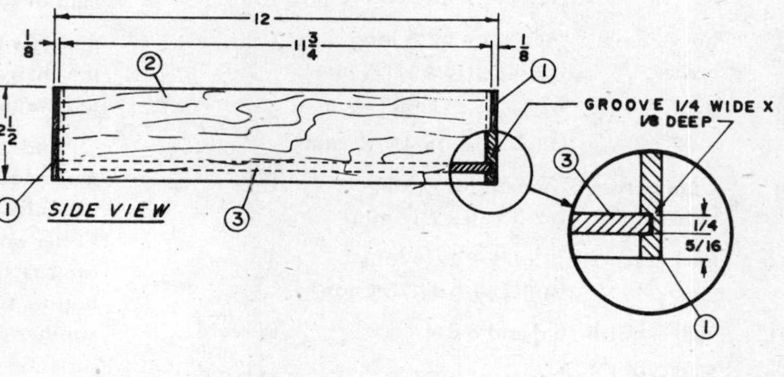
GROOVE 1/4 WIDE X 1/8 DEEP
SIDE VIEW

Full-Size & Child's Adirondack Chair

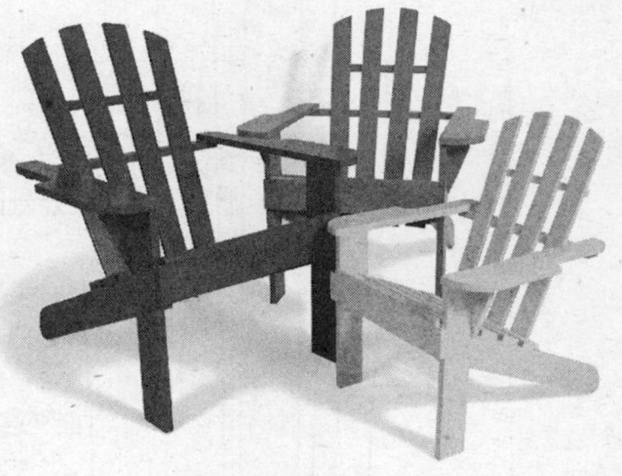

The design for the original Adirondack chair is credited to H. C. Bunnel. He received a patent for his straight, boxy version in 1905. The chair was named for the region in upstate New York where it was designed and first used.

Over the years, Bunnel's design has been modified by others to make it more accommodating to the body. Backs have been rounded, and the seats contoured. But the chairs you see here stay quite close to the early chairs. They are exact copies of one made by my grandfather around 1918, when he was living in the Adirondacks. As a very young woodworker, I copied one of my grandfather's rotted chairs in 1949. You can see that the design is unpretentious—no frills, no curved back or seat. And yet it is quite comfortable. The chair is roomy enough for you to prop yourself on a pillow or two. You can lay a book or a drink on the wide arms. On becoming a grandfather myself, I made a child's version, scaled down about a quarter. Either it or the full-size chair can be made with these plans and instructions. The Materials List gives two sets of overall dimensions. Note that even the thickness of the stock has been reduces for the child's chair—⁹⁄₁₆ inch (14 mm), rather than ¾ inch (19 mm).

The chair can be put together with either brass-plated flathead screws or water-proof glue and finishing nails. You may want to countersink the screws ³⁄₁₆ inch (4.7 mm) or so and cover them with plugs cut from dowels; nails should be set and puttied.

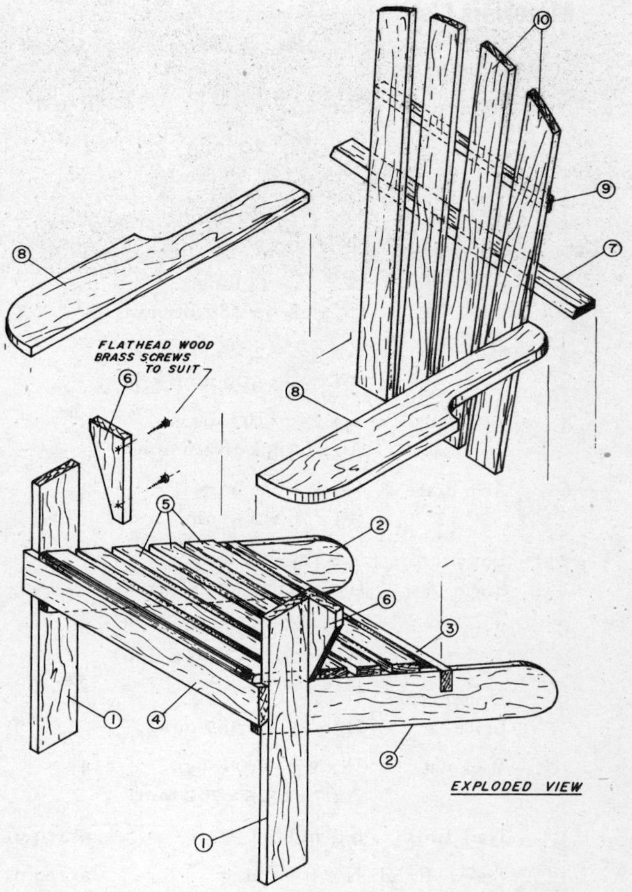
FLATHEAD WOOD BRASS SCREWS TO SUIT
EXPLODED VIEW

Continued ➔

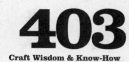

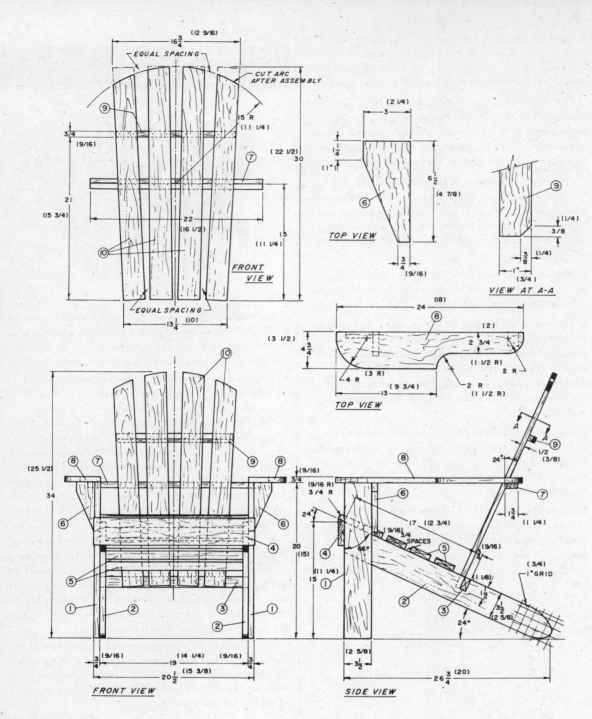

Materials List

ADULT'S CHAIR

No.	Name	Size	Req'd.
1	Front leg	¾ x 3½ - 20 long (19 x 90 x 508 mm)	2
2	Seat rail	¾ x 3½ - 30½ long (19 x 90 x 774.7 mm)	2
3	Back support	¾ x 1½ - 19 long (19 x 28.5 x 482.66 mm)	1
4	Front brace	¾ x 3½ - 20½ long (19 x 90 x 508 mm)	1
5	Seat slat	¾ x 2½ - 19 long (19 x 63.5 x 482.6 mm)	5
6	Arm brace	¾ x 3 - 6½ long (19 x 76 x 165 mm)	2
7	Lower cross brace	¾ x 1¾ - 22 long (19 x 44.5 x 559 mm)	1
8	Arm	¾ x 4¾ - 24 long (19 x 120.6 x 609.6 mm)	2
9	Upper cross brace	¾ x 1 - 15¼ long (19 x 25.4 x 387 mm)	1
10	Back slat	½ x 2½ - 30 long (12.7 x 63.5 x 762 mm)	4
11	Nail-finish	6 d and 8 d	as req'd.
12	Screw—fl. hd.	No. 6 – 1 long No. 8 – 1½ long	as req'd.

CHILD'S CHAIR

No.	Name	Size	Req'd.
1	Front leg	9/16 x 2⅝ — 15 long (12.8 x 66.7 x 381 mm)	2
2	Seat rail	9/16 x 2⅝ - 22½ long (12.8 x 66.7 x 571.5 mm)	2
3	Back support	9/16 x 1⅛ — 14¼ long (12.8 x 28.6 x 368.3 mm)	1
4	Front brace	9/16 x2⅝ — 15⅜ long (12.8 x 66.7 x 390.5 mm)	1
5	Seat slat	9/16 x 1⅞ long (12.8 x 47.6 mm)	5
6	Arm brace	9/16 x 2¼ - 4⅞ long (12.8 x 57.2 x 128.8 mm)	2
7	Lower cross brace	9/16 x 1¼ - 22½ long (12.8 x 31.8 x 571.5 mm)	1
8	Arm	9/16 x 3½ - 18 long (12.8 x 88.9 x 457.2 mm)	2
9	Upper cross brace	9/16 x ¾ - 11½ long (12.8 x 19 x 292 mm)	1
10	Back seat	⅜ x 1⅞ — 22½ long (9.5 x 47.6 x 571.5 mm)	4
11	Nail - finish	6 d and 8 d	as req'd.
12	Nail - fl. hd.	No. 6 – 1 long No. 8 – 1½ long	as req'd.

1. Select the stock and cut the parts. In New England, knot-free pine or spruce are common choices for making lawn furniture. If primed and kept painted, the wood should last 20 years or more. Woods especially suited for outdoor furniture include Honduran mahogany, oak, redwood, and teak.

Decide which chair model you are going to make. Cut the parts to the thickness and width given in the Materials List, but leave pieces with curved or angled ends an inch or so long.

2. Make the seat. An Adirondack chair begins with the seat. You can save time when cutting details in the seat rail and other paired parts by joining the pieces temporarily with double-sided tape. Lay out the details on one board, and then cut both boards at once.

Cut a notch in each seat rail (part 2) to accept the back support (part 3). Round-over one end of the seat rail, following the pattern given and cut the other end at a 66° angle, as shown. Cut the seat rail to the proper length in the process.

After you've cut the seat rails to the proper profile, nail or screw the slats (part 5) to them. Attach the back support. Rip a 24" (60.9 cm) bevel on one edge of the front brace (part 4) and nail or screw it in place.

Round-over the front slat, as shown, with a router and the appropriately sized round-over bit.

3. Make the back subassembly. I found that the best way to assemble the back is to lay it out on a full-size pattern drawn on a large sheet of paper.

Draw a box 30 inches (76.2 cm) high and 16¾ inches (42.5 cm) wide on the paper. Lay out in pencil the location of the parts, as shown in the front view of the back.

Carefully position the back slats (part 10) on the drawing.

Rip a 24" (60.9 cm) bevel on the lower cross base (part 7) and chamfer the corner of the upper cross brace (part 9), as shown in the view at A-A. Position the upper and lower cross braces on the back slats. Check that the cross braces are parallel to the bottom of the box and then attach the slats to them with screws or nails and glue.

To lay out the cut for the curved top of the back, draw a 15-inch-radius (38 cm) arc from the center of the upper cross brace. Cut the curve with a saber saw and sand the cut edges.

Clamp the assembled back to the back support and glue or nail it in place. The back will be somewhat flimsy until you attach the arms, so treat it with respect.

4. Attach the legs and arms. Attach the legs (part 1) to the seat rail, as shown in the side view. Cut the arm braces (part 6) to the profile shown in the top view of part 6, and attach the braces to the legs so the top surfaces are flush with each other. Cut the arms (part 8) to the profile shown. Position the arms so the front extends about 1 inch beyond the legs. The arms' inner edges should be parallel to each other and flush with the inner face of the legs. Nail or screw them to the leg and arm brace. Clamp the back end of the arm to the upper cross brace and nail or screw the two together. Nail or screw the back slats to the lower brace.

5. Apply finish. If you've used nails, set them all over the chair, then putty and sand the holes. If you decided to countersink the screws, glue the plugs in place now.

Sand the chair all over. If you used a weather-resistant wood, your work is done. For added protection, you might add a coat or two of marine spar varnish. Other woods should be primed and finished with two coats of exterior paint. Don't forget to cover the bottom surfaces of the legs. You can expect to apply another coat of paint every two or three years.

Eight-Sided Jewelry Box

This box makes an excellent gift. In addition to jewelry, it can be used for anything from a clock case to a music box.

As with other projects in this book, I made a lid that matches the box perfectly by first making a completely sealed box. Then I cut the box open to form the lid. Unlike most other projects, this box has a dust lip: a lip on the box fits inside a rabbet in the lid.

A friend of mine, Jerry Ernce, showed me how to cut the lip and rabbet in the process of cutting the box apart. I call it the Jerry joint in his honor and now use this lid on nearly all the boxes I make.

Before jumping into this project, take the time to study how the box fits together and how the Jerry joint is made.

Materials List

No. Req'd.	Name	Size	
1	Side	½ x 4¾ - 2⅝ long (12.7 x 120.6 x 66.7 mm)	8
2	Top/bottom	¼ x 6 — 6 long (6.35 x 152 x 152 mm)	1 ea.
3	Hinged catch		1
4	Hinge		1
5	Rubber foot	½ long (12.7 mm)	4

1. Select the wood and cut the board for the sides. I suggest using a hardwood. If you choose to make it out of an undistinguished wood, you can make it resemble rosewood with the directions at the end of the project. I used bird's-eye maple in this version.

Begin the box by cutting a ½-inch-thick board 4¾ inches wide and at least 24 inches long. In step 2, you will cut the eight sides (part 1) from this board.

Cutting the Jerry joint involves cutting a groove on what will be the inside of the box before assembly. Later, an adjoining groove on the outside will create the dust lip. For now, cut a groove ¼ inch wide and ³⁄₁₆ inch deep on the inside, as shown in figure 1.

2. Cut the sides. Set the blade of a table saw at 22½". Cut some sample joints to make sure the pieces will come together in an octagon without leaving gaps at the joints. Adjust as necessary and then cut the 24-inch-long piece into the eight sides, each exactly 2⅝ inches long, as shown in figure 2. Dry-fit the eight sides to make sure they come together as they should.

Glue the octagon with the help of masking tape. Here's how: put a long strip of tape on the bench, sticky side up. Place the outside face of one side on the tape with the top edge parallel to the tape. Put an adjoining side on the tape next to the first side. The toes of the miters—the long narrow edge that you will see from the outside of the assembled box—must touch along their entire lengths. Position the sides so that the grooves are in line with each other. Continue the process, side by side, until you've taped all eight pieces to form a long line.

Put glue in the miters, fold the pieces together to form an octagon, and clamp with a band clamp or heavy rubber band.

3. Cut the top and bottom. Cut the octagonal top and bottom (part 2) slightly oversized. Sand the edges flush

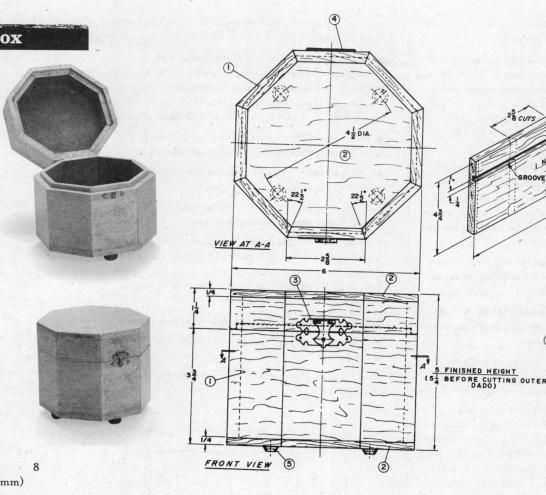

VIEW AT A-A

FRONT VIEW

FIG. 1

FIG. 2

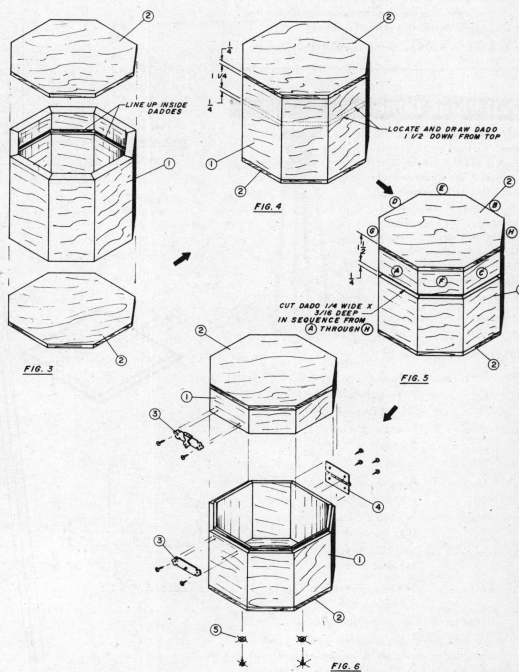

LINE UP INSIDE DADOES

FIG. 3

FIG. 4

LOCATE AND DRAW DADO 1 1/2 DOWN FROM TOP

CUT DADO 1/4 WIDE X 3/16 DEEP IN SEQUENCE FROM A THROUGH H

FIG. 5

FIG. 6

Continued ➡

with the box after you've assembled it. Glue the top and bottom to the box, as shown in figure 3.

4. Measure for the lid cut. The sealed box should now look as shown in the drawing for figure 4. When the glue has dried, sand the top and bottom edges flush with the sides. Draw a line around the box, 1½ inches down from the top surface and parallel to it. This will be the top of a groove that separates the lid from the box.

5. Cut the lid. To free the lid, cut a groove along the line, ¼ inch wide and ³⁄₁₆ inch deep, as shown in figure 5. It should meet the inside groove to form a lipped lid. Follow a sequence of cuts as indicated by the letters A through H. If the lid fits too tightly, sand the lower of the two lips.

6. Attach the hardware. Temporarily add the hardware (parts 3, 4, and 5), as shown in the drawing for figure 6. Remove it to apply the finish.

7. Apply finish. Varnish the piece if you like the look of the wood as is. Or, use one of the following methods to suggest the appearance of rosewood.

Apply two coats of oil-based orange or red paint, sanding between coats. Next apply two coats of varnish or shellac, rubbing with steel wool between coats.

Or, dilute oil-base, black paint with paint thinner until it is the consistency of milk. You will make a design in a coat of wet black paint with a goose or turkey feather, but first dip the feather in thinner and run your thumb over the edge from tip to base in order to separate the individual hairs. Apply a coat of black paint to the box; then, drag the thinner-dampened feather over it to suggest the swirling grain of rosewood.

8. When the finish has dried, reinstall the hardware.

Tall Plant Table

Here is an old-style plant stand. I remember my grandmother had one just like it in her parlor. It's simple to build and will make an interesting stand for your plants. A biscuit joiner was used in making my copy, but ¼-inch-diameter dowels would work just as well. Your friends and plants will love this stand.

Materials List

No.	Name	Size	Req'd.
1	Leg	1 x 1 – 42½ long (25.4 x 25.4 – 1079 mm)	4
2	Skirt	¾ x 5¾ – 4¾ long (19 x 146 – 121 mm)	4
3	Biscuit	to suit	8
4	Shelf	¾ x 9½ – 9½ long (19 x 241 – 241 mm)	1
5	Block	¾ x ¾ – 2½ long (19 x 19 – 63.5 mm)	2
6	Screw- fl. hd.	No. 8 – 1-³⁄₈ long (35 mm)	6
7	Top	¾ x 10 – 10 long (19 x 254 – 254 mm)	1

1. Cut all pieces to size. Sand all over.

2. Cut the bottom taper of the legs (part 1) 3 inches (76 mm) up, as shown, on the two inside surfaces only. Cut two slots with the biscuit joiner on the two inside

surfaces as shown in the drawing of the exploded view. Sand all over.

3. Lay out the skirt (part 2). Cut two slots with the biscuit joiner to match the legs. Using a ½-inch-radius (13 mm) cove cutter with a ball-bearing follower, make a cut on the lower inside edge of the skirt to give a thin appearance, as shown in the view at B-B. Sand all over.

4. Following the given dimensions, cut a notch in all four corners of the shelf (part 4). Sand all over.

5. Using a router with a ³⁄₈-inch-radius (9.5 mm) round cutter, make up the top (part 7).

6. Glue the skirts (part 2) to the legs (part 1) and clamp. Check that everything is square.

7. Slide the shelf (part 4) up into place. The top surface should be about 14¾ inches (375 mm) above the floor. If everything is okay, glue it in place. (You might want to drill and nail it in place if you plan to have heavy plants on the shelves.)

8. Add the two blocks (part 5) with the screws (part 6).

9. Screw the top (part 7) to the blocks (part 5). Do not glue in place.

10. This is another project that could be either stained or painted.

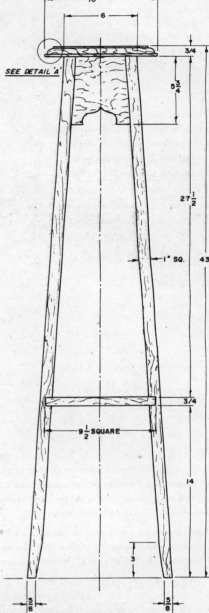

DETAIL 'A'

SEE DETAIL 'A'

FRONT VIEW

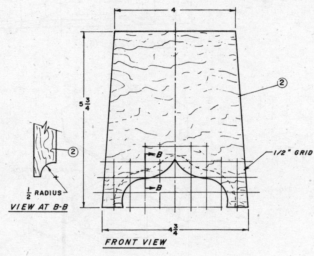

VIEW AT B-B

FRONT VIEW

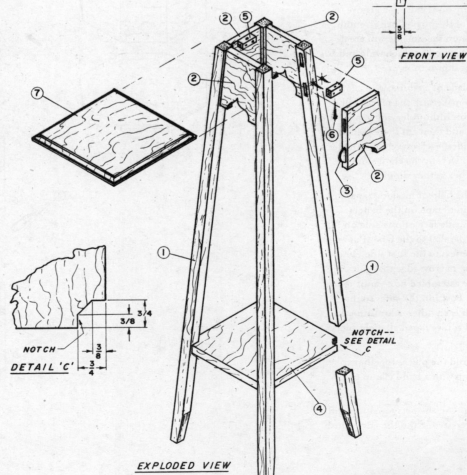

DETAIL 'C'

NOTCH-- SEE DETAIL C

EXPLODED VIEW

Child's Bench

This bench is a scaled down version of a sleigh bench that was used for an extra seat in a horse-drawn open sleigh years ago. These slightly decorated sleigh benches were especially popular in Pennsylvania.

Today this smaller version makes an excellent bench for a child's room. This project can be made of either soft or hard wood as its design produces a very sturdy construction.

Materials List

No.	Name	Size	Req'd.
1	End	¾ x 7½ - 12 long (19 x 190–304.8 mm)	2
2	Support	¾ x 1½ - 5¾ long (19 x 38–146 mm)	2
3	Seat	¾ x 7½ - 12 long (19 x 190–304.8 mm)	1
4	Skirt	¾ x 1½ - 12 long (19 x 38–304.8 mm)	2
5	Screw- fl. hd.	No. 8 – 1¼ long (37.15 mm)	6
6	Finish nail	6 d	14

1. Cut all the pieces to overall size, and sand all edges. Lay out the patterns for the ends and skirt. Transfer the patterns to the wood, and cut them out.

2. Using a router bit with a ⅛-inch-(6.35 mm) radius cove-cutter and ball-bearing follower, rout the top edge of the ends, the arched leg sections, and the seat, as shown in the drawings.

3. Locate and attach the seat supports to the ends. Glue and screw these in place. Note: the supports should be ¾ inch in from each side. Glue the skirt pieces and seat to the ends. Check that everything is square.

4. Finish to match the room in which you will put this bench, if possible.

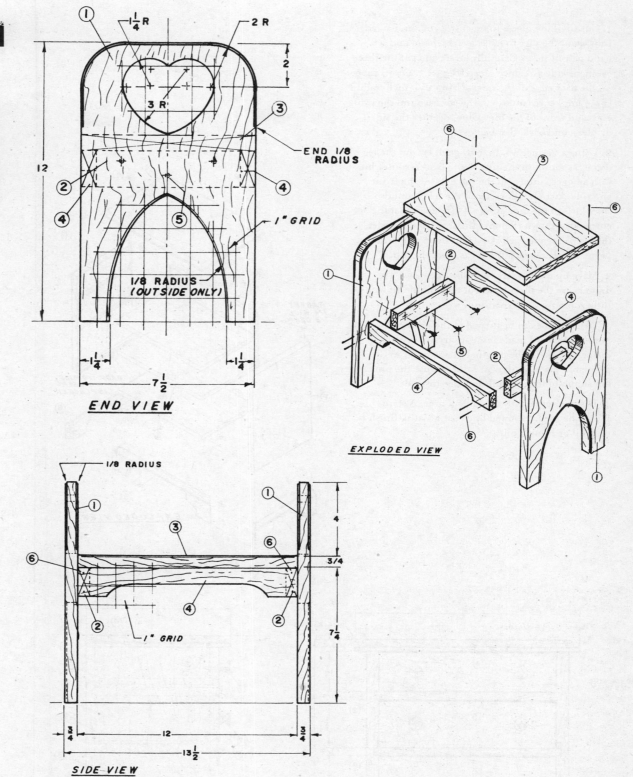

END VIEW

EXPLODED VIEW

SIDE VIEW

Child's Small Chest of Drawers

The original chest of drawers from which this project is drawn was made expressly for Master Joseph Warren of Boston, Massachusetts, in 1745. He used the chest of drawers as his toy chest. Incidentally, Warren later became a doctor and eventually lost his life at the battle of Bunker Hill in 1775, at the age of 34. Today, this small chest of drawers can be used as a jewelry box or even as a child's toy chest—just as the original chest was.

Materials List

No.	Name	Size	Req'd.
1	Side	⅜ x 4-⅛ - 5¾ long (9.5 x 104.–146 mm)	2
2	Divider	¼ x 3-⅜ - 5¾ long (6.35 x 85.7–146 mm)	3
3	Back	¼ x 5½ - 5¾ long (6.35 x 139.7–146 mm)	1
4	Top	⅜ x 4½ - 7 long (9.5 x 114.3–177.8 mm)	1
5	Skirt-front	⅜ x 1¼ - 4½ long (9.5 x 31.75–114.3 mm)	1
6	Skirt-side	⅜ x 1¼ -4½ long (9.5 x 31.75–114.3 mm)	2
7	Front	⅜ x 1¼ - 5½ long (9.5 x 31.75–139.7 mm)	1
8	Side	¼ x 1¼ - 3⅝ long (6.35 x 31.75–92 mm)	2
9	Back	¼ x 1¼ - 5¼ long (6.35 x 31.75–133.4 mm)	1
10	Bottom	¼ x 3½ - 5½ long (6.35 x 88.9–139.7 mm)	3
11	Front	⅜ x 1½ - 5½ long (9.5 x 38–139.7 mm)	1
12	Side	¼ x 1½ -3⅝ long (6.35 x 38–92 mm)	2
13	Back	¼ x 1½ - 5¼ long (6.35 x 38–133.4 mm)	1
14	Front	⅜ x 2⅛ - 3⅝ long (9.5 x 54–92 mm)	1
15	Side	¼ x 2⅛ - 3⅝ long (6.35 x 54–92 mm)	2
16	Back	¼ x 2⅛ - 5¼ long (6.35 x 54–133.4 mm)	1
17	Pull	⅜ dia. – ¹³⁄₁₆ long (9.5–20.6 mm)	6
18	Pin	⅜ long (9.5 mm)	6

Continued ➡

1. Cut all of the pieces to exact size and sand all edges. Important: be sure to make a right-hand and left-hand pair of sides. Carefully locate and cut the three ¼-inch-wide x ⅛-inch-deep (6.35 x 3.2 mm) rabbet on the back edge of the sides. Using a ¼-inch-radius (6.35 mm) cove cutter, cut the cove around the two ends and front of the top. Glue together the sides, dividers, and back. Sand all over.

2. Using a ¼-inch (6.35 mm) grid, lay out the leg detail, as shown in the side view. Using a router bit with an ogee cutter, cut the top edge of the front and side skirt. Temporarily fit the front and two side skirts to the case using a 45° miter cut at the corners, as shown. Remove the skirts and transfer the leg pattern to each skirt. Cut them out, and permanently reattach the skirts. Add the top.

3. Make up the drawers to fit the openings. The drawers are the flush type, but they should fit with a little room for any expansion.

The six pulls can be turned to the ⅜-inch (9.5 mm) diameter. I made mine up from ⅜-inch-diameter dowel. The original drawer pulls were pinned in place, as shown; I did not use the pins, but simply glued the pulls in place instead.

4. Distress very lightly; resand all over. A stain should be used, followed by a coat of satin-finish tung oil or Danish oil.

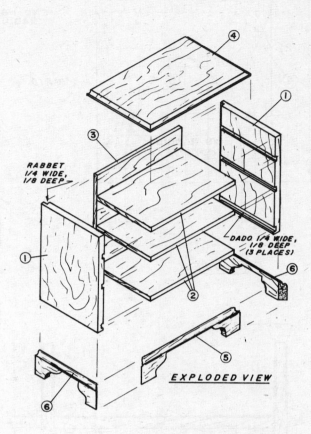

RABBET
1/4 WIDE,
1/8 DEEP

DADO 1/4 WIDE,
1/8 DEEP
(3 PLACES)

EXPLODED VIEW

Folk Weather Vanes

Weather vanes are as popular today as they were a hundred years ago. Both of these patterns are taken directly from antique weather vanes. You can distress these if you want yours to look old. Weather vanes have been used for centuries, perhaps even millennia. The rooster is an old symbol used to identify places of worship. The arrow points into the wind and stays aligned as the wind changes. The cock weather vane on church steeples signified how easily faith could be swayed.

These weather vanes also make great wall hangings.

1. Lay out either or both patterns on a ½-inch (12.7 mm) grid.

2. Transfer the pattern(s) to the wood and cut out.

3. Paint to suit. I prefer sanding the edges slightly and staining over the paint to get an old look.

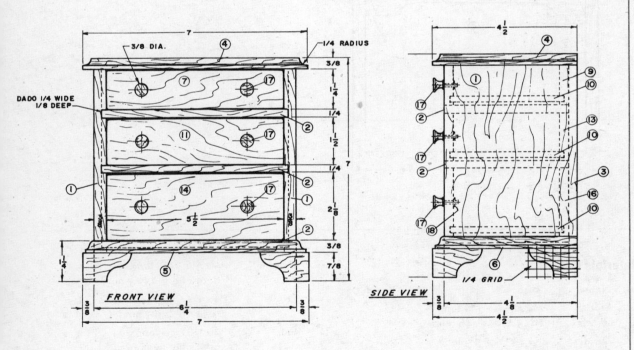

3/8 DIA.

1/4 RADIUS

DADO 1/4 WIDE
1/8 DEEP

FRONT VIEW

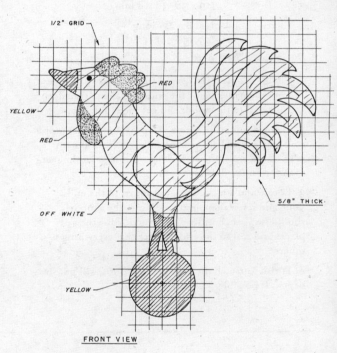

SIDE VIEW

1/4 GRID

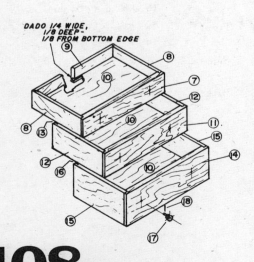

DADO 1/4 WIDE,
1/8 DEEP-
1/8 FROM BOTTOM EDGE

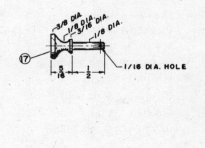

3/8 DIA.
1/8 DIA.
3/16 DIA.
1/8 DIA.

1/16 DIA. HOLE

1/2" GRID

RED

YELLOW

RED

OFF WHITE

5/8" THICK

YELLOW

FRONT VIEW

5/8" THICK

RED

YELLOW

1/2" GRID

ANTIQUE WHITE

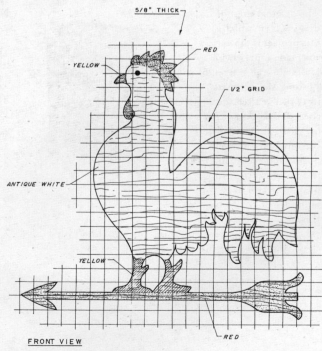

YELLOW

RED

FRONT VIEW

Small Wheelbarrow Planters With Boy & Girl Figures

This is the kind of project that was very popular in the early 1940s. Today they are collectibles. As a kid, I can remember most everyone made small projects such as these and displayed them proudly around the house. I found the originals of these two particular workers at a flea market and would guess that they are from this period. My newly purchased collectibles were in bad shape, but enough was left to create a pattern and redraw the plans. They are brightly colored and will add a lot to your plants. You can make one or the other, or both, if you choose.

Materials List

No.	Name	Size	Req'd.
1	Body (either)	⅝ x 4 – 8 long (15.9 x 101.6–203 mm)	1
2	Arm	¼ x 2-⅛ x 3½ long (6.35 x 54–90 mm)	2
3	Bottom	¾ x 2 – 2¹¹⁄₁₆ long (19 x 50.8–68 mm)	1
4	Front	¼ x 2 – 3¹¹⁄₁₆ long (6.35 x 50.8–93.6 mm)	1
5	Side	¼ x 3 – 3¾ long (6.35 x 76–95 mm)	2
6	Handle	¼ x ⅝ – 6⅜ long (6.35 x 15.9–162 mm)	2
7	Leg	¼ x ⅝ – 3⅛ long (6.35 x 15.9–79 mm)	2
8	Wheel	½ – 2 square (12.7 – 50.8 mm)	1
9	Brad	½ long (12.7 mm)	8
10	Pin (wheel)	⅛ dia. – 1⅛ long (3.2 – 28.5 mm)	1

1. Lay out all the parts full size on a sheet of heavy paper or cardboard. Be sure to note the location of all holes. Transfer the pattern and hole locations to the wood. Cut out all the pieces according to the plans. Don't forget to make a saw kerf to divide the legs of the figures.

2. To make the wheelbarrow, glue the bottom and front together; then attach the two sides. Sand all over when the glue sets. Make up the left and right-hand handles. Make up the wheel and attach the two handles with the wheel temporarily attached. Add the two legs, and the wheelbarrow is done, ready for painting.

3. To make the figures, simply attach the arms to the body. To get the exact position of the arms, temporarily attach the hands to the wheelbarrow. Check that the wheelbarrow and feet are resting flush on the surface. Note: You will have to trim the handles of the wheelbarrow and the hands slightly to get the proper fit. The originals had the arms set at a slight angle.

4. Separate the wheel and hands from the wheelbarrow, and prime all of the parts. Using fast-drying latex paint, paint the features similar to what is shown in the plans. Use your imagination as you wish.

The colors called off in the plans are the colors used on the originals I purchased, but any color combination can be used. Permanently reattach the wheel and hands to the wheelbarrow. Make sure the feet rest squarely on the surface before the glue sets.

Add a small plant, and you're back in the forties.

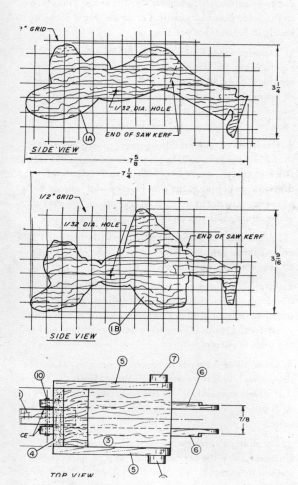

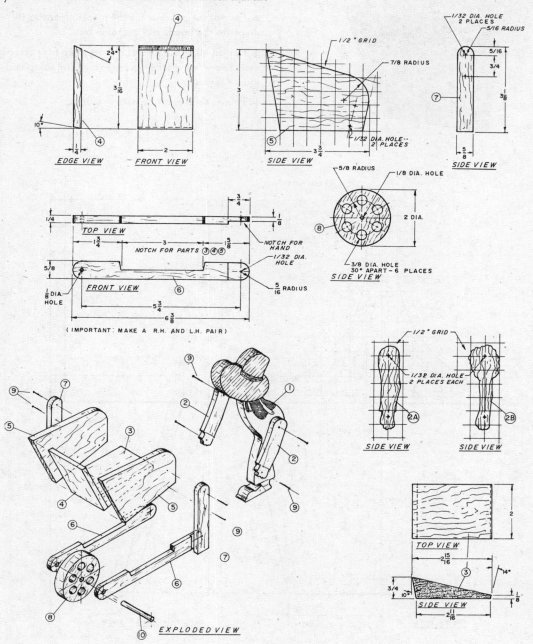

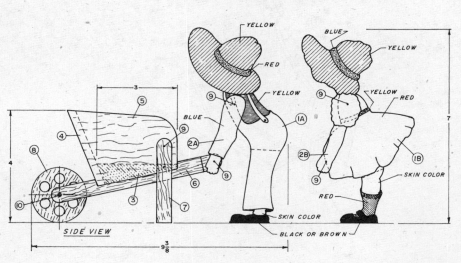

Continued ➜

Salt Box

This is a scaled-down version of a somewhat larger salt box. The original was painted a dark, blackish-green color.

Materials List

No.	Name	Size	Req'd.
1	Back	½ x 9 – 13 long (12.7 x 228 – 330 mm)	1
2	Side	½ x 4 – 6-5/16 long (12.7 x 102 – 160 mm)	2
3	Front	½ x 9 – 6¾ long (12.7 x 228 – 330 mm)	1
4	Bottom	½ x 2 – 5-⅜ long (12.7 x 50.8 – 136.5 mm)	1
5	Nail – sq. cut/finish	1¼ long (square cut) (32 mm)	15

1. Cut material to overall size. Sand all over.

2. Lay out the patterns for the pieces. Transfer the shapes to the wood, and cut them out.

3. Dry-fit all of the pieces. If everything fits correctly, nail the pieces together. Keep everything sharp and square as you go.

4. Prime; then paint or stain to suit.

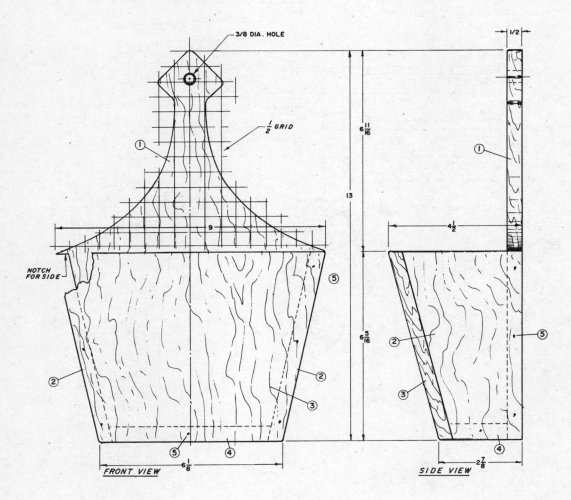

FRONT VIEW   SIDE VIEW

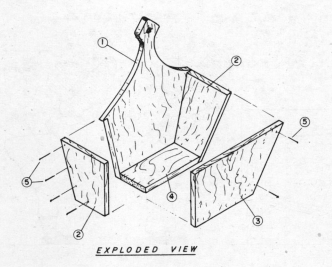

EXPLODED VIEW

Cricket Footstool

Footstools were very popular in years gone by. They were found in just about every early Colonial American home. Originally they were called crickets, although I don't know why. Footstools came in all shapes and sizes. Formal footstools, such as this one, were made of a fine hardware and usually stained. More country footstools were very plain, made of a soft wood, and usually painted. However, I found an interesting combined treatment in many footstools from Vermont that had stained tops with painted legs and rails.

Materials List

No.	Name	Size	Req'd.
1	Top	½ x 6½ – 15 long (12.7 x 165 – 381 mm)	1
2	Rail	½ x 2¼ - 13⅞ long (12.7 x 57 – 352 mm)	2
3	Leg	⅝ x 4⅞ – 6⅛ long (16 x 124 – 156 mm)	2
4	Nail – sq. cut/finish	1 long (25.4 mm)	18

1. Study the plans carefully. Note how each part is to be shaped. As you study the plans, try to visualize how you will make each part and how the project will be assembled. Note which parts you will put together first, second, and so on, exactly how you will put it together.

2. The matching rails (part 2) are irregular in shape and will have to be laid out on a 1-inch (25.4 mm) grid to make a full-size pattern. Lay out the grid on heavy paper or cardboard, and transfer the shape of the piece to the grid, point by point. A compass would come in handy to lay out this pattern.

3. Transfer the full-size pattern to the wood, and carefully cut out the pieces. Check all dimensions for accuracy. Sand all over with fine-grit paper, keeping all edges sharp. I recommend that you tack or tape the two rails together when cutting out and sanding so that your rails will be a perfectly matching pair.

4. Carefully cut the remaining parts to size according to the Materials List. Take care to cut all parts to exact size and exactly square (90°). Stop and recheck all dimensions before going on. The top and bottom ends of the legs (part 3) are cut at 15°, as shown. Be sure to make one right-hand and one left-hand leg.

Lightly sand all surfaces and edges with medium sandpaper to remove all tool marks. Take care to keep all edges square and sharp.

5. After all of the pieces have been carefully made, dry-fit the parts, that is, put the complete project together without glue or nails to check for accuracy and good-fitting joints. If anything needs refitting, now is the time to correct it.

6. Once all of the parts fit together correctly, assemble the project, keeping everything square as you go. Check that all fits are tight. If you used a hardwood, be sure to drill pilot holes for the nails so that the wood will not split.

7. Finish to suit, following the general finishing instructions in the introduction. This project can be stained or painted.

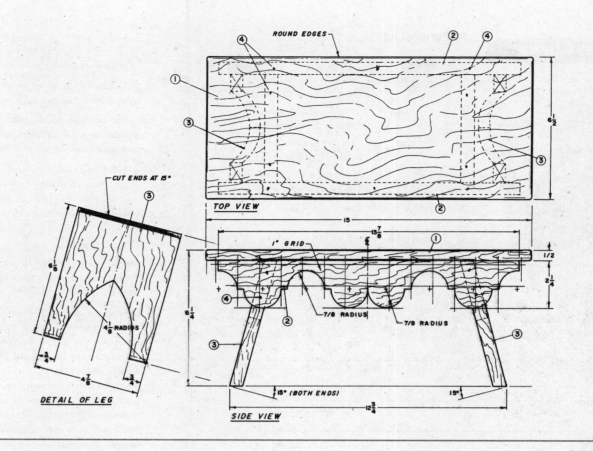

TOP VIEW

ROUND EDGES

DETAIL OF LEG

CUT ENDS AT 15°

4⅛ RADIUS

SIDE VIEW

1" GRID

7/8 RADIUS 7/8 RADIUS

15° (BOTH ENDS) 15°

Colonial Wall Shelf

This Colonial shelf uses a cyma curve—a curve that turns back on itself—at the top and bottom. It has graceful lines. In laying out the sides, locate the compass swing points, set the compass at the given radius, and draw the outer shape.

Materials List

No.	Name	Size	Req'd.
1	Side	⅜ x 5¹/₁₆ – 18 Long	2
2	Shelf, Lower	⅜ x 4⅞ – 29¼ Long	1
3	Shelf, Upper	⅜ x 2¹³/₁₆ – 29¼ Long	1
4	Brace, Lower	⅜ x 2 – 29¼ Long	1
5	Brace, Upper	⅜ x 1½ – 29¼ Long	1

1. Lay out the shape of part 1. Transfer the pattern to the wood, and cut out the piece. It is a good idea to tape or tack the two sides together when cutting and sanding so that both sides will be exactly the same size and shape. Sand all edges.

2. Cut the two shelves and brace to size. Make the ⅛-inch-radius (3 mm) bead in the braces (parts 4 and 5).

3. (Optional.) Cut the plate groove, if you wish, approximately ¼ – ⅜ inch wide (6.4 – 9.5 mm), and about ⅛ inch (3 mm) deep.

4. Glue and nail the shelf together. Check that it is square.

5. This project is usually stained, but it could be painted to blend into any room setting.

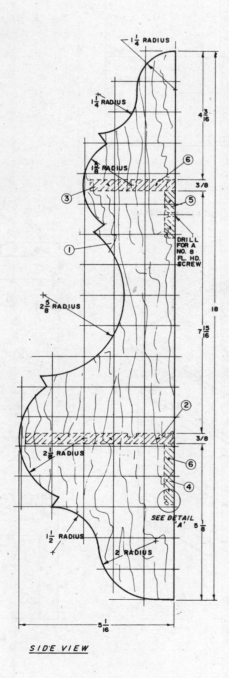

SIDE VIEW

1¼ RADIUS

DRILL FOR A NO. 8 FL. HD. SCREW

2⅝ RADIUS

SEE DETAIL 'A'

1½ RADIUS 2 RADIUS

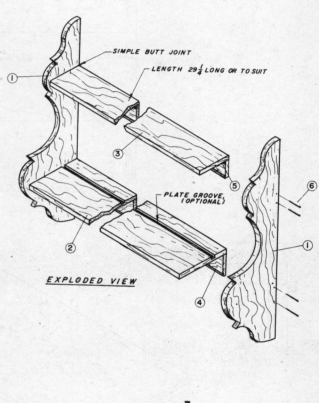

SIMPLE BUTT JOINT

LENGTH 29¼ LONG OR TO SUIT

PLATE GROOVE, (OPTIONAL)

EXPLODED VIEW

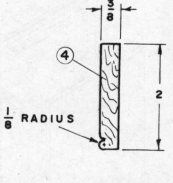

⅛ RADIUS

DETAIL 'A'

Continued ➜

Small Child's Blanket Chest

Six-board blanket chests were one of the things the Pilgrims brought to this country from Europe. They were, in effect, their luggage. These wonderful chests came in all shapes and sizes. Most simple ones were painted. Today, if and when we can find an original, it usually has two or three coats of paint on it. Note the wonderful snipe hinges. A very similar snipe can be made from four large cotter pins.

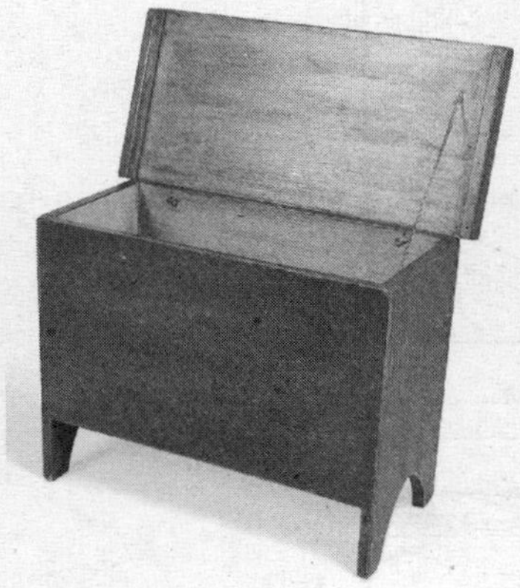

Materials List

No.	Name	Size	Req'd.
1	End board	¾ x 11 – 17¼ long (19 x 279 – 438 mm)	2
2	Front/back	¾ x 13 – 22 long board (19 x 330 – 559 mm)	2
3	Bottom	¾ x 9½ – 20½ long board (19 x 241 – 521 mm)	1
4	Lid	¾ x 11½ – 22⅝ long (19 x 292 – 575 mm)	1
5	Batten board	¾ x 1 – 11¼ long (19 x 25.4 – 286 mm)	2
6	Snipe hinge	cotter pin – 1¾ long (44.5 mm)	2 pr.
7	Square-cut nail	8 d	42

1. Cut all pieces to overall size. If you want a real old look, hand-plane the front and back surfaces slightly to get a wavy effect.

2. Glue and clamp wood for the 13 inch-wide (330 mm)front and back boards (part 2).

3. Lay out and cut the ends (part 1), following the given dimensions. Don't forget to make a notch for the front and back boards.

4. Glue and nail the two ends (part 1) to the front/back (part 2) and bottom (part 3). Check that everything is square. Don't try to hide the nails; most original six-board chests were somewhat crude, and the nails did show.

5. Nail, but do not glue, the batten board (part 5) to the lid (part 4). This allows for expansion of the lid. Place them about 1/16 inch (1.5 mm) away from the sides of the chest.

6. Using a drill, drill holes at about 45° as shown in the drawing at View at A-A. Assemble two cotter pins, and place them into the holes, one into the lid and the other into the back board. Temporarily drive them in a little deeper than you think you need, and then with a pair of needle-nose pliers, loop the tips of the cotter pins around and down into the wood. Hammer them down into the wood. This will make a slightly loose fit, but it will look very original. If you don't like snipe hinges, a regular pair of brass butt hinges can be used.

7. Sand all over. Since you want this to look old, round edges where you feel wear would have occurred.

8. Paint or stain to suit. As we like an old-looking blanket chest, we distressed ours and painted it two different colors, one on top of the other. Sand down through the top-coat here and there to show the first color. If you really want it to look old, use a crackle coat, and a top-coat of a black wash.

—From *The Big Book of Weekend Woodworking*

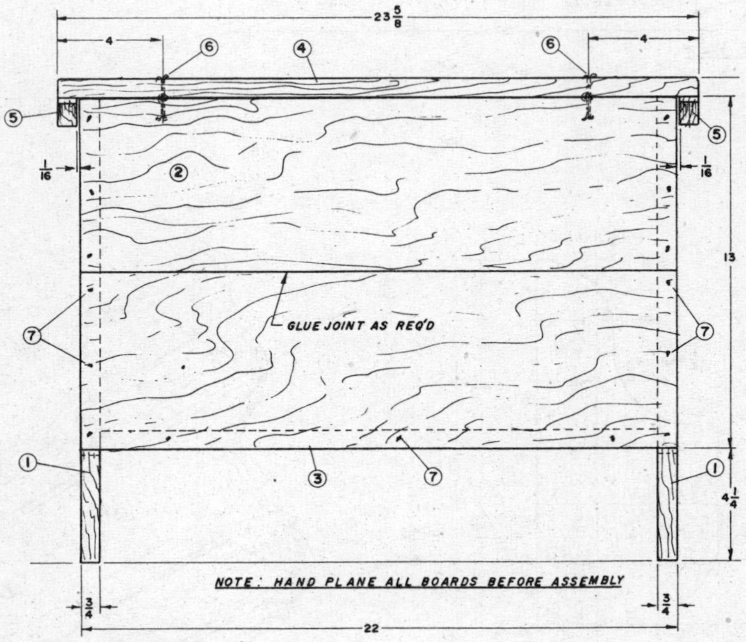
23 5/8
GLUE JOINT AS REQ'D
NOTE: HAND PLANE ALL BOARDS BEFORE ASSEMBLY
22

FRONT VIEW

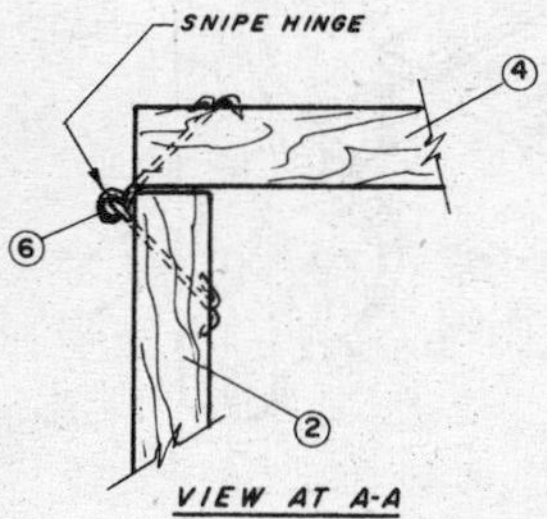
SNIPE HINGE

VIEW AT A-A

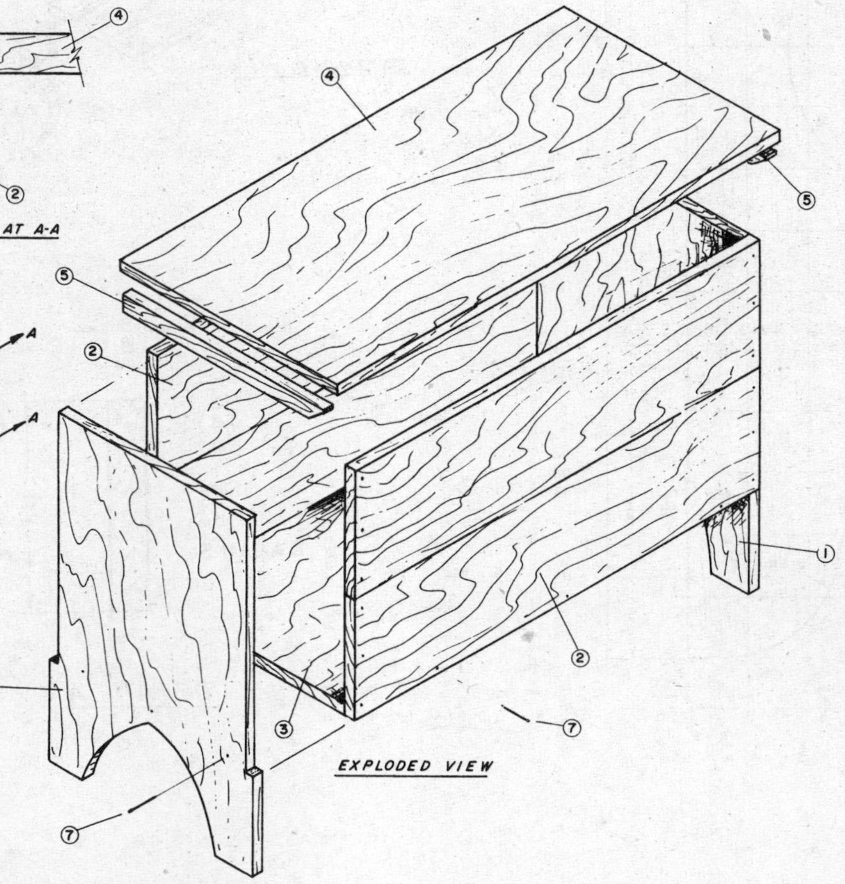

EXPLODED VIEW

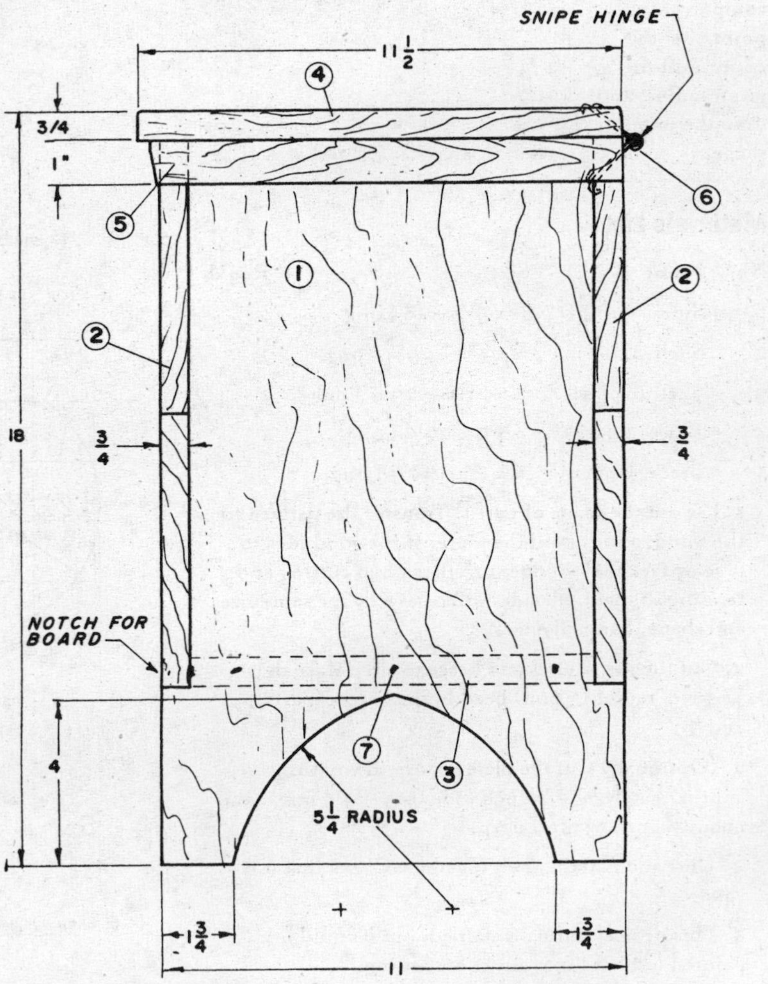
SNIPE HINGE
11 1/2
3/4
1"
18
NOTCH FOR BOARD
5 1/4 RADIUS
11

SIDE VIEW

WOODEN TOY PROJECTS

John A. and Joyce C. Nelson

Piggy Bank

Having raised pigs in northern Vermont years ago, I really appreciate them. They are very smart, fun to have around, and, believe it or not, a very clean animal. This is a pig that you can take to the bank. Perhaps, if you're lucky, this project will instill thrift in your little ones.

You can paint it any color you like—I especially like a pink pig. Don't forget to add a new penny for luck!

Materials List

No.	Name	Size	Req'd.
1	Body/legs	¾ x 5½ – 6¾ long (19 x 140 – 95 mm)	2
2	Center	½ x 4¾ – 7¼ long (13 x 120.5 – 184 mm)	2
3	Center/slot	¼ x 4¾ – 7¼ long (6.5 x 120.5 – 184 mm)	1
4	Ear	⅛ x 1¾ – 2½ long (3 x 44.5 – 63.5 mm)	2
5	Plug	¾ dia. (19 mm)	1
6	Eye (oval)	⅝ size (16 mm)	2

1. Cut all parts to overall size, and sand the top and bottom surfaces.

Lay out the pieces on a 1-inch grid. Note: there are five pieces that make up the body; two ¾ inch (19 mm) thick, two ½ inch thick, and one ¼ inch (6.5 mm) thick. Don't forget to lay out the interior cut for the center pieces (parts 2 and 3).

Transfer the patterns to the wood.

2. Cut out the center areas of the three center pieces (parts 2 and 3). Cut the tail in part 3 only.

Line up all pieces except the center piece (part 3) and cut away the wood where the tail would be. (Tail is only on center piece.)

Line up the three center pieces (parts 2 and 3) and cut away the wood where the legs would be.

Line up all of the pieces and glue them together.

3. Make the rest of the outer body cutout starting and ending in the tail section. (Don't forget to leave the tail on the center section and the legs on the two outer pieces.)

4. Drill ¼-inch-diameter (6.5 mm) holes in the tail and nose.

Drill a ¾-inch-diameter (19.5 mm) hole up from the bottom for the plug.

Sand all over and round all edges slightly. (I used a ⅛-inch-radius router bit with a ball-bearing follower.)

5. Cut out and add the ears (part 4) as shown.

6. The eyes can either be painted on, or you can use ⅝-inch-diameter jiggling eyes that glue on. If small children might get their hands on this piggy bank, only use non-toxic paint for the eyes.

Add a plug, either a purchased rubber plug or one you make yourself.

Paint to suit.

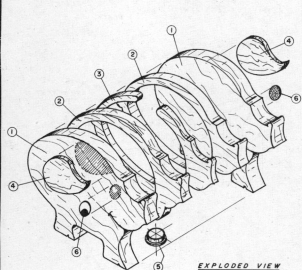

EXPLODED VIEW

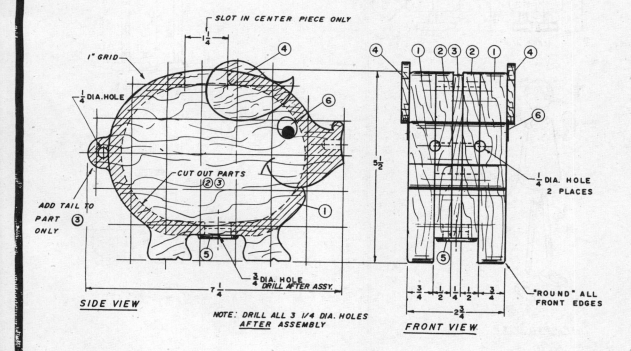

SLOT IN CENTER PIECE ONLY

1" GRID

¼ DIA. HOLE

CUT OUT PARTS ②③

ADD TAIL TO PART ③ ONLY

¾ DIA. HOLE DRILL AFTER ASSY.

SIDE VIEW

5½

¼ DIA. HOLE 2 PLACES

"ROUND" ALL FRONT EDGES

FRONT VIEW

NOTE: DRILL ALL 3 ¼ DIA. HOLES AFTER ASSEMBLY

Doll Chair

Here's a replica of a small chair I saw hanging on a wall outside an antique shop in New Hope, Pennsylvania. I especially liked the dovetail joint holding the sides together. The original was painted and very weathered. I'm not sure how the original chair was used, but this one will make a great doll's chair.

Don't worry about making the dovetail joints; they are really quite easy to make. If you've never cut a dovetail joint before, this is just the project to practice on.

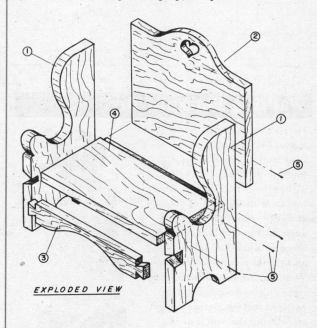

EXPLODED VIEW

Materials List

No.	Name	Size	Req'd.
1	Side	¾ x 5⅜ – 10½ long (19 x 136.5 – 266 mm)	2
2	Back	¾ x 9¼ – 8 long (19 x 235 – 203 mm)	1
3	Brace	¾ x 1⅝ – 10¾ long (19 x 42 – 273 mm)	1
4	Seat	¾ x 5½ – 9¼ long (19 x 140 – 235 mm)	1
5	Nail – finish	6 d	14

1. Study the plans carefully. Note how each part is to be shaped. As you study the plans, try to visualize how you will make each part.

The two sides, back, and brace (parts 1, 2, and 3) are irregular in shape and will have to be laid out on ½-inch grids to make full-size patterns. Lay out the grids on heavy paper or cardboard, and transfer the shape of each piece to the appropriate grid, point by point.

2. Carefully cut all of the parts to overall size according to the Materials List. Take care to cut all parts to exact size and exactly square (90°). Stop and recheck all dimensions before going on.

3. Lightly sand all surfaces and edges with medium sandpaper to remove any burrs and all tool marks. Take care to keep all edges square and sharp at this time.

4. Transfer the full-size patterns to the wood, and cut out. Check all dimensions for accuracy. Resand all over with fine grit sandpaper, still keeping all edges sharp. It is a good idea to make the two sides (part 1) while they

Continued ➔

are either tacked or taped together so that you have a pair of exactly matching sides.

5. Carefully lay out and cut out the tail and pin of the dovetails in the side and brace pieces (parts 1 and 3).

6. After all of the pieces have been carefully made, dry-fit all of the parts; that is, put the complete project together without glue or nails to check for accuracy and good-fitting joints. If anything needs refitting, now is the time to correct it. Once all of the parts fit together correctly, assemble the project starting with the two sides and brace. Then, fit the other parts to these pieces. Keep everything square as you go. Check that all fits are tight.

7. Finish to suit, following the general finishing instructions given in "Weekend Woodworking Projects." on page 401.

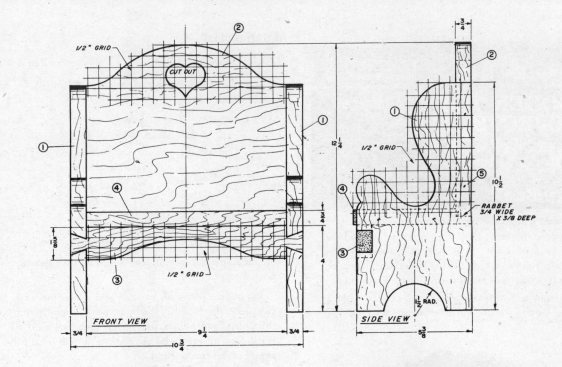

Walking Penguin Toy

Here's a toy that walks, yet it has no batteries or motors. It's a copy of a now-antique toy enjoyed by children in an earlier time. Years ago, walking toys came in all kinds of shapes and sizes—even four-legged animals. We found the penguin this one is based on in an antique shop in St. Johnsbury, Vermont. To make it work, you need only a smooth, slightly inclined surface. Before you get started, not that you'll need a lathe to make this toy.

Materials List

No.	Name	Size	Req'd.
1	Head	1¼ dia. x 1¼ long (32 x 32 mm)	1
2	Body	1¾ dia. x 2¾ long (44.5 x 70 mm)	1
3	Beak	¼ dia. x 1¼ long (6.5 x 32 mm)	1
4	Leg	¼ dia. x 3¹⁄₁₆ long (6.5 x 78 mm)	2
5	Foot	¼ x ⅝ – 1¼ long (6.5 x 16 – 32 mm)	2
6	Flipper	¹⁄₁₆ x 1 – 2 long (leather) (1.5 x 25 – 51 mm)	2
7	Tail (leather)	¹⁄₁₆ x 1 – 1⅛ long (1.5 x 25 – 28.5 mm)	1
8	Spacer	³⁄₁₆ dia. x ³⁄₁₆ long (5 x 5 mm)	1
9	Pin	¹⁄₁₆ dia. x 1⅜ long (1.5 x 35 mm)	1

1. Turn the body in a lathe exactly as shown. Be sure to hollow out the interior. Locate and drill the ¹⁄₁₆-inch-diameter (1.5 mm) hole, ⁷⁄₁₆ of an inch (11 mm) down from the top as shown. Carefully make the ¹⁄₁₆-inch-wide (1.5 mm) saw kerf for the tail at a 45° angle as shown.

2. Turn the head on a lathe. Check that the ⅞-inch-diameter (22 mm) neck fits tightly into the body. Drill a ¼-inch-diameter (6.4 mm) hole ½ inch (13 mm) deep at 10° as shown for the beak. Make up a beak and glue it to the head.

3. Cut the two legs from a ¼-inch-diameter (6.4 mm) dowel, and carefully locate and drill a ¹⁄₁₆-inch-diameter

(1.5 mm) hole at 4" (102 mm), as shown. Make up the feet and glue them to the legs. Important: be sure they are 90° to the ¹⁄₁₆-inch-(1.5 mm) diameter hole. Check the 2⅞-inch (73 mm) radius from the hole to the bottom of the feet—this is crucial for the toy to walk.

4. Assemble the legs and feet to the body with ¹⁄₁₆-inch-diameter (1.5 mm) stiff wire and a small spacer piece between legs; a small piece of tubing or a large bead will do. There should be a tight fit between the wire and body, but a loose fit between the wire and legs; the legs must swing freely.

5. Paint the body, head, and legs white and black, to suit, using a nontoxic paint. Carefully cut the wings and tail from a piece of ¹⁄₁₆-inch-thick (1.5 mm) black leather or plastic (leather was used on the original). Attach the wings and tail, and your penguin is ready to walk. Place it at the top of a smooth, slightly inclined surface and watch him walk.

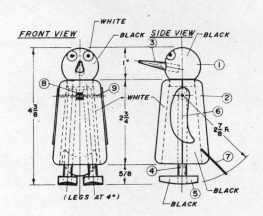

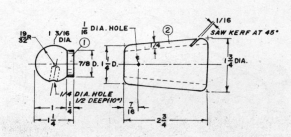

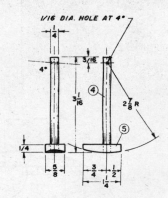

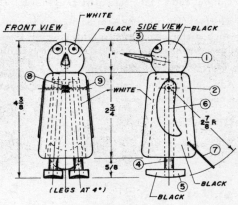

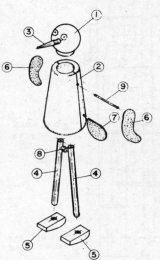

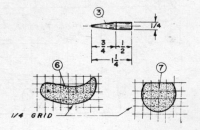

Monkey Business Balancing Trick

This is a take-off on the old pipe-shaped belt trick. I simply made the old trick into a monkey. To use the balancing monkey, center and balance a regular belt in the tail, as shown. Balance the monkey on your finger or the edge of a table at point A.

1. Transfer the monkey pattern to a piece of high-grade ¼-inch to 5/16 inch-thick (6.5 to 8 mm) plywood. (Marine or aircraft plywood is best.)

2. Carefully cut out, as shown. Sand all over.

3. Paint to suit, and apply three or four coats of varnish to help strengthen the wood.

¼" PLYWOOD

5 5/8

BELT

FRONT VIEW

4 1/8

Stegosaurus Puzzle

Dinosaurs are really big with kids. Our grandchildren have all kinds of dinosaur toys in all shapes, colors, and sizes. This is a simple puzzle that the very young will enjoy.

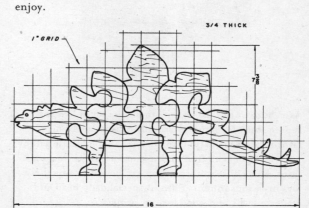

3/4 THICK

1" GRID

7 7/8

SIDE VIEW

16

1. On a 1-inch grid (25 mm), lay out the pattern. Transfer the pattern to the wood.

2. Cut the outside surfaces first, and slightly sand all edges. Sand along the bottom of the feet so that the assembled puzzle will stand up.

3. Paint to suit. Redraw the inner pieces.

4. Cut the inner pieces, as shown. If you stray slightly from the pattern, don't worry, no one will ever know.

5. Touch up all paint, as necessary.

Toy Blocks

If you tend to make an incorrect cut now and then and waste a little wood, as I do, you can recycle these leftovers by turning them into children's blocks. You don't have to reproduce the exact shapes shown here, of course. I offer these as examples.

To make it a little easier for kids to fit the blocks together, restrict yourself to a few overall widths and heights.

1. Cut out the block shapes, following the shapes in the drawings. They are in increments of a full inch. As illustrated, they're all ¾ inch (19 mm) thick, but again that's up to you.

2. Sand the blocks lightly, rounding the corners somewhat and removing splinters.

3. Finish the blocks with a coat of salad-bowl finish or a nontoxic paint. For the safety of younger children who might gnaw on blocks, don't use leftover paints that may contain toxic chemicals.

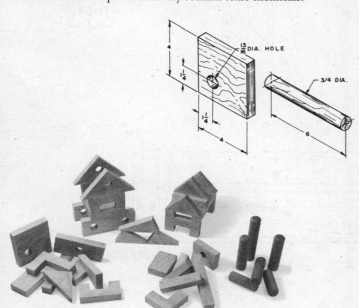

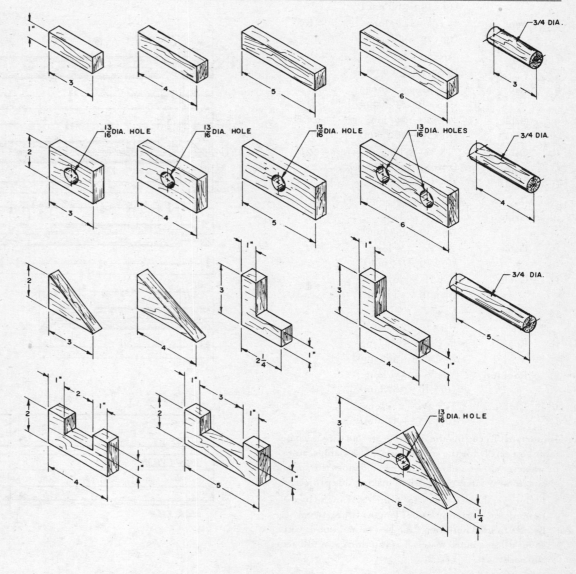

Log Cabin

As a child, one of my favorite toys was a set of logs that kept me busy for hours. Naturally, this is one of my favorite projects. I also think this is a very educational toy, since it teaches children to think and use their imaginations. Many different structures can be built using these logs in various combinations. A special dado head and router bit will be needed for this project.

Materials List

No.	Name	Size	Req'd.
1	Locking pin	¾ x ¾ – 1½ long (19 x 19 – 38 mm)	96
2	Wall	¾ x ¾ – 3½ long (19 x 19 – 90 mm)	48
3	Wall	¾ x ¾ – 9 long (19 x 19 – 228.5 mm)	6
4	Wall	¾ x ¾ – 9 long (19 x 19 – 228.5 mm)	8
5	Wall	¾ x ¾ – 14½ long (19 x 19 – 368 mm)	4
6	Wall	¾ x ¾ – 14½ long (19 x 19 – 368 mm)	6
7	Wall	⅜ x ¾ – 14½ long (9.5 x 19 – 368 mm)	2
8	Wall	⅜ x ¾ – 14½ long (9.5 x 19 – 368 mm)	2
9	Gable	¾ x ¾ – 10¼ long (19 x 19 – 260 mm)	2
10	Gable	¾ x ¾ – 9 long (19 x 19 – 228.5 mm)	2
11	Gable	¾ x ¾ – 7½ long (19 x 19 – 190 mm)	2
12	Gable	¾ x ¾ – 6 long (19 x 19 – 152 mm)	2
13	Gable	¾ x ¾ – 4½ long (19 x 19 – 114 mm)	2
14	Gable	¾ x ¾ – 3 long (19 x 19 – 76 mm)	2
15	Gable	¾ x ¾ – 1½ long (19 x 19 – 38 mm)	2
16	Roof	¼ x 1⅜ – 15¼ long (6.5 x 35 – 387 mm)	20
17	Roof top	⅝ x ⅝ – 15¼ long (16 x 16 – 387 mm)	2
18	Chimney	¾ x 2¼ – 2¼ long (6.5 x 57 – 57 mm)	2

Important: In cutting the dadoes, extreme care must be taken, especially for the smaller parts. Use clamps, stops, or whatever else you have in cutting all dadoes. Be sure, as always, to wear safety glasses when making this project.

1. Cut overall sizes exactly to ¾ inch x ¾ inch (19 x 19 mm) and 5-foot or 6-foot lengths (13 or 15 cm). Be sure to use knot-free, straight-grained wood. Cut about twice as much material as you think you will actually need.

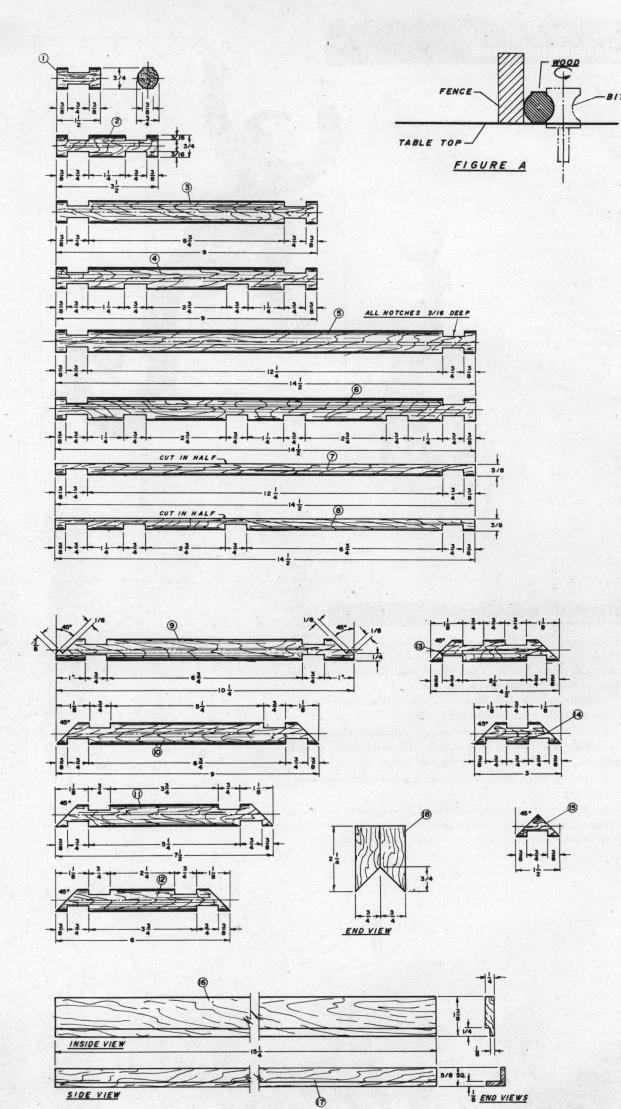

2. Set up the router to make the curved cuts, and run all the stock through at the same time at the same setting, as shown in figure A.

Note: multiple parts must be exactly the same size and shape; therefore, use whatever stops or jigs you have at your disposal.

3. Square one end.

4. Locate and cut ¾-inch-wide dadoes exactly ³/₁₆ inch deep, (19 x 19 mm) as shown.

5. Cut to specified length, again using stops to ensure uniformly.

Note: all dadoes are made before each piece is cut to final length in order to give you something to hold on to while making the dado cuts. Again, take extreme care; these cuts could be dangerous.

6. Sand all over, removing any sharp edges.

7. Roofing material (parts 16 and 17) and chimney (part 18) should be made as shown.

8. I recommend that you stain all the logs with a light walnut stain. Because there are so many pieces, you might want to consider just dipping them in a can of stain.

9. Paint roof material green or any color of your choice, and the chimney red.

Checkers Game

Believe it or not, the game of Chinese checkers was not invented many years ago in Sweden. Today, it's still a popular game.

1. On heavy paper, lay out the grid for the location of the holes. The sheet should be about 16 inches (40.5 cm) square or so. It would be helpful if you have a drafting board, T-square, and a 30°/60° triangle.

2. Refer to the drawings for each step to locate the holes. Draw horizontal and vertical lines through the middle of the paper. At the center, draw a circle using a 6¹⁵/₁₆-inch (17.5 cm) radius. Divide the circle into three equal parts. Make a triangle with 12-inch (30.5 cm) sides. Make another triangle (upside down) with 12-inch sides. Divide each leg of both triangles into 1-inch spaces (2.5 cm). Draw parallel lines from point to point as shown. Where the points cross is the exact center point for each hole.

3. Tape or glue your pattern to a piece of wood that is approximately 16-inches square (40.5 cm). Be sure it cannot move. Using a prick punch, ice pick, or similar tool, prick punch the centers of all 121 holes.

4. Remove the pattern and locate the center hole. From this point, swing a 7¾-inch (19.5 cm) radius for the outside edge. Cut and sand the outer edge.

5. Using a ¼-inch-radius (6.5 mm) cove cutter with a ball-bearing follower, make the cove cut around the upper, outer edge, as shown. Sand all over.

6. Using a drill press and a ½-inch-diameter (13 mm) drill with a ³/₁₆-inch-deep setting, drill the 121 holes.

7. Sand all over with fine-grit sandpaper. Apply a high-gloss coat of varnish. Optional: glue a piece of felt cloth to the bottom surface and trim along its edge. Use marbles or pegs for pieces.

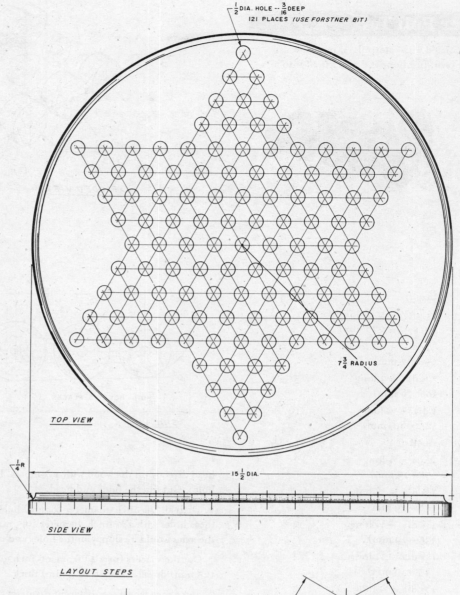

½ DIA. HOLE – ³/₁₆ DEEP
121 PLACES (USE FORSTNER BIT)

7¾ RADIUS

TOP VIEW

¼ R

15½ DIA.

SIDE VIEW

LAYOUT STEPS

6 15/16 R

FIG. 1

60°   60°   60°

FIG. 2

60°   60°   60°

FIG. 3

FIG. 4

FIG. 5

FIG. 6

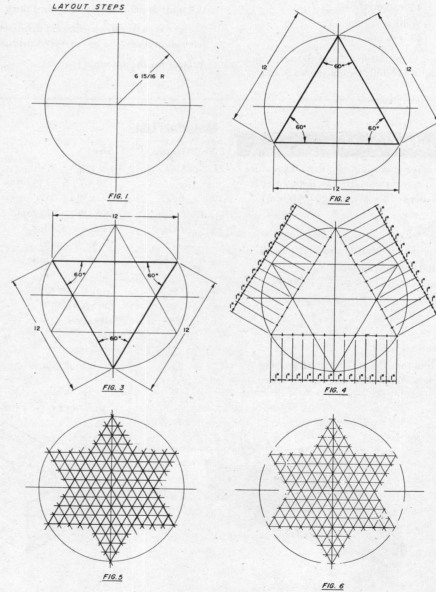

Continued ➔

Caterpillar Pull Toy

Children are fascinated with caterpillars; now they can have one of their own. Just hope it doesn't turn into a butterfly!

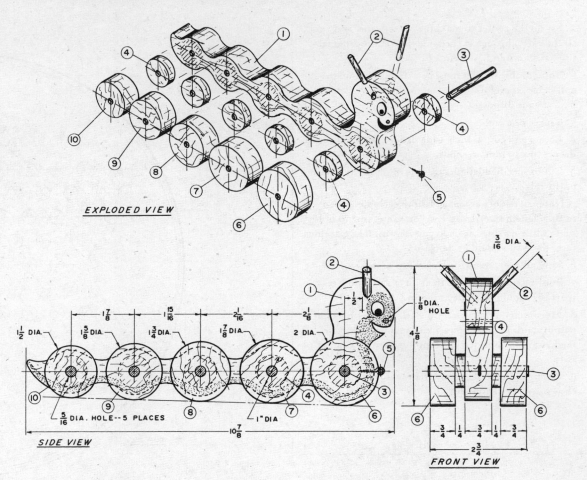

EXPLODED VIEW

Materials List

No.	Name	Size	Req'd.
1	Body	¾ x 3¾ – 10⅞ long (19 x 95 – 276 mm)	1
2	Antenna	3/16 dia. – 1¼ long (5 – 32 mm)	2
3	Axle	5/16 dia. – 3 long (8 – 76 mm)	5
4	Spacer	1 dia. – ¼ long (25 – 6.5 mm)	10
5	Screw – eye	small	1
6	Wheel 1	2 dia – ¾ long (51 – 19 mm)	2
7	Wheel 2	1⅞ dia. – ¾ long (48 – 19 mm)	2
8	Wheel 3	1¾ dia. – ¾ long (35 – 19 mm)	2
9	Wheel 4	1⅝ dia. – ¾ long (45 – 19 mm)	2
10	Wheel 5	1½ dia. – ¾ long (38 – 19 mm)	2

SIDE VIEW

FRONT VIEW

1. Cut out all pieces to overall size. Sand all over. Using the given dimensions, carefully lay out the body and head directly on the wood with a compass. Locate all holes. Cut out the body and head.

2. Drill all 5/16-inch-diameter (8 mm) holes. I drilled these holes with a ⅜-inch diameter (9.5 mm) so that the axles would be sloppy in the holes and not bind.

Cut the spacers (part 4) from a 1-inch-diameter (25 mm) dowel, ¼-inch (6.5 mm) thick.

Since each wheel is a different diameter, each of the five pairs will have to be cut out individually.

3. Drill for the antennas (part 2).

Glue the spacers (part 4) onto the body (part 1). You might have to re-drill the 5 holes.

Drill a ⅛-inch-diameter (3 mm) hole for the nose.

4. Temporarily assemble all of the pieces. Check that everything fits correctly.

5. Disassemble and paint. Use your imagination; a caterpillar is typically green and yellow, but this one is painted green and orange. Assemble after painting, and add the eye screw (part 5) and string.

Crayon Tractor-Trailer

This toy truck is great for your budding artist. It provides a handy place to hold crayons when they're not in use. It can be made from a piece of 2 x 4-inch (38 x 90 mm) wood.

1. Cut pieces to overall size.

4. Carefully lay out the cab (part 1) and box (part 2).

3. Drill all required holes, as shown.

4. The wheels (part 4) can be cut from a 1½-inch-diameter dowel (½ inch wide) or you can purchase 1½-inch-diameter wheels.

5. Dry-fit all pieces.

6. Paint to suit, and assemble.

7. Glue the wheels to the axles. Let them turn freely inside the cab or box. Add a set of crayons, and the tractor-trailer is ready for the artist.

Materials List

No.	Name	Size	Req'd.
1	Cab	1½ x 3⅛ – 5¼ long (38 x 79.5 – 133 mm)	1
2	Box	1½ x 3½ – 10¾ long (38 x 90 – 273 mm)	1
3	Axle	¼ dia. – 2¾ long (6.5 – 70 mm)	4
4	Wheel	1½ dia. – ½ long (38 – 13 mm)	8
5	Peg	⅜ dia. – 2¼ long (9.5 – 57 mm)	1
6	Crayon set	all colors	24

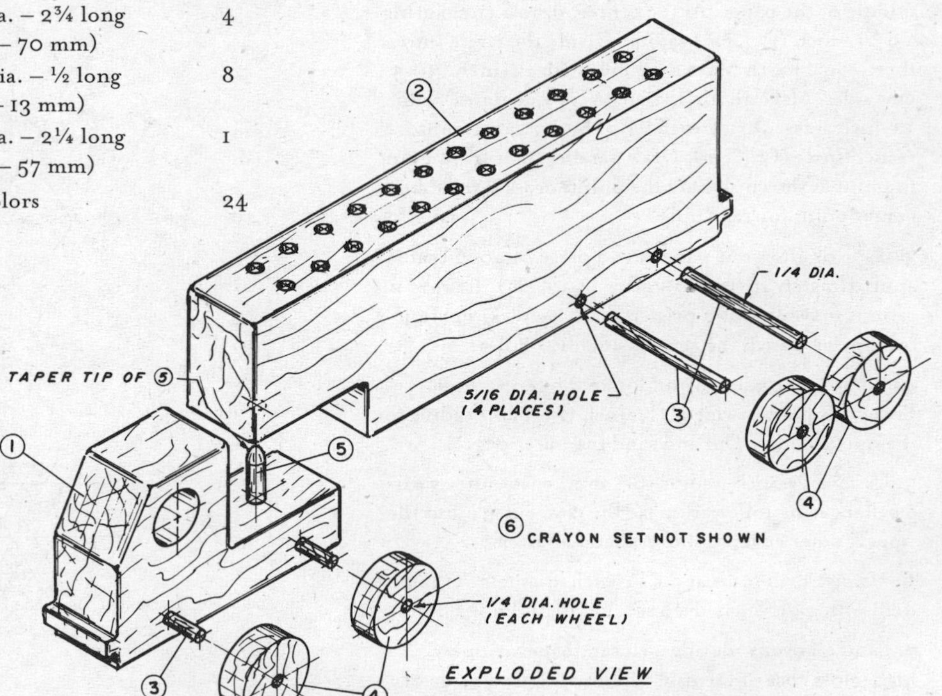

EXPLODED VIEW

Train with Passengers

One of the most popular toys ever is the toy train. I tried to come up with a simple train that could be made up of all those scrap pieces of wood you usually burn or throw away. I chose modern round magnets and tacks to hook the train cars together. This project can be left natural or painted.

Materials List

No.	Name	Size	Req'd.
1	Base	½ x 1¾ – 3-⅞ long (13 x 44.5 – 98.5 mm)	1
2	Base	½ x 1¾ – 2¾ long (13 x 44.5 – 70 mm)	1
3	Base	½ x 1¾ – 3¼ long (13 x 44.5 – 82.55 mm)	2
4	Base	½ x 1¾ – 4½ long (13 x 44.5 – 114 mm)	1
5	Wheel	1 dia. – 3/16 long (25 x 5 mm)	20
6	Tack		28
7	Magnet	½ dia. (13 mm)	8
8	Cab	¾ x 1½ – 1⅞ long (19 x 38 – 47.5 mm)	2
9	Boiler	1¼ dia. – 1½ long (32 – 38 mm)	1
10	Chimney	⅜ dia. – 1⅛ long (9.5 – 28.5 mm)	1
11	Light	¾ dia. – ½ long (19 – 13 mm)	1
12	Roof	¼ x 1¾ – 2 long (6.5 – 45 mm)	1
13	Plug	¾ dia. – 7/16 long (19 – 11 mm)	6
14	Guide	cut from 6d nail	1
15	Side	¼ x 1½ – 2¼ long (6.5 x 38 – 57 mm)	2
16	Front	¼ x 1½ – 1 long (6.5 x 38 – 25 mm)	1
17	Support	5/16 dia. – 2⅛ long (8 – 54 mm)	2
18	Cargo	1¼ dia. – ½ long (32 – 13 mm)	6
19	Cab	¾ x 1-⅞ – 4 long (19 x 47.5 – 101.5 mm)	2
20	Roof	¼ x 1¾ – 4½ long (6.5 x 44.5 – 114 mm)	1
21	Cab	¾ x 1-⅞ – 2¾ long (19 x 47.5 – 70 mm)	2
22	Roof	¼ x 1¾ – 3¼ long (6.5 x 44.5 – 82.5 mm)	1
23	Lookout	½ x ¾ – 1¼ long (13 x 19 – 32 mm)	1
24	Roof	¼ x 1 – 1¾ long (6.5 x 25 – 44.5 mm)	1
25	Chimney	3/16 dia. – ¾ long (5 – 19 mm)	1
26	Passenger	11/16 dia. – 1¾ long (14.5 – 44.5 mm)	6

1. Cut all pieces to overall size. Glue up required pieces as necessary. Drill all holes according to the sizes given. Dry-fit all pieces.

2. Glue up each car (refer to the exploded view). Don't forget to add the passengers.

3. The wheels can be cut from a 1-inch-diameter (25 mm) dowel (3/16 inch [5 mm] thick) or you can purchase 1-inch wheels. Add wheels to cars last.

4. Paint cars to suit or leave them natural. Add the magnets. Don't forget to orient the magnets north to south so that the cars will attach correctly.

5. Paint and add wheels; check that they turn freely.

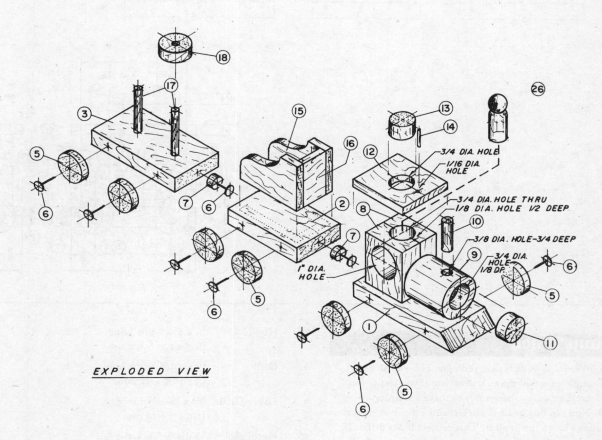

EXPLODED VIEW

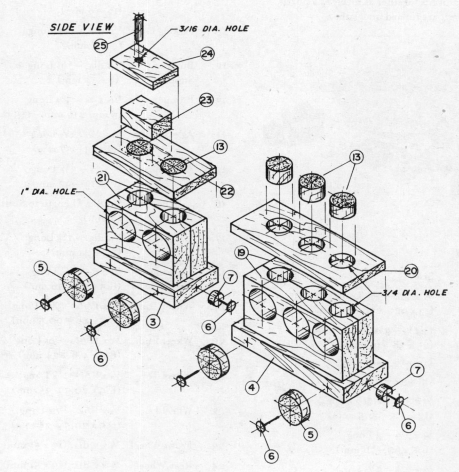

SIDE VIEW

Continued ➡

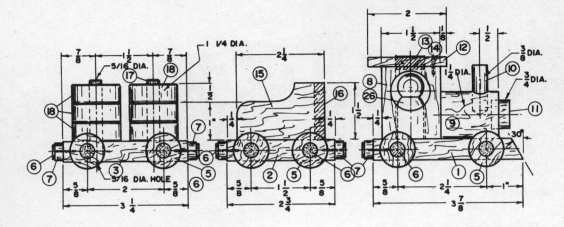

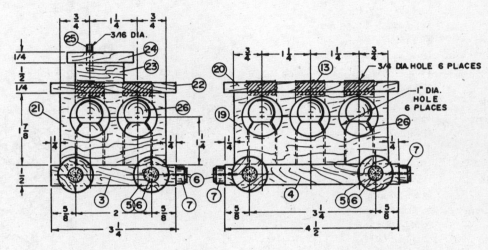

Dump Truck

This toy truck is built for rugged play. I based the design on a couple of actual dump trucks, but if you want, you can omit the dump subassembly to make a simpler utility truck. You can buy treaded wheels, and I think their realism adds a lot to the project. This project looks difficult at first glance, but it fits together as nicely as a puzzle. Note that four parts are turned on a lathe.

Materials List

No.	Name	Size	Req'd
1.	Base	½ x 3⅝ – 9⅜ Long (13 x 92 – 238 mm)	1
2.	Seat	1 x 1½ – 3⅝ Long (25 x 38 – 92 mm)	1
3.	Back	½ x 3⅝ – 3¼ Long (13 x 92 – 82.5 mm)	1
4.	Front	½ x 3⅝ – 2⅝ Long (13 x 92 – 66.5 mm)	1
5.	Side	¼ x 2¼ – 3 Long (6.5 x 92 – 76 mm)	2
6.	Top	¼ x 2¼ – 4⅛ Long (6.5 x 92 – 105 mm)	1
7.	Hood	¼ x 4⅛ – 2¼ Long (6.5 x 105 – 92 mm)	1
8.	Grill	⅛ x 4 1/8 – 2¼ Long (3 x 105 – 92 mm)	1
9.	Lower Grill	1/16 x ⅛ – ¾ Long (1.5 x 3 – 19 mm)	8
10.	Headlight	⅝ dia. – 5/16 Long (16 – 8 mm)	2
11.	Parking Light	3/16 dia. – 3/16 Long (5 – 5 mm)	4
12.	Bumper Support	5/16 dia. – 9/16 Long (8 – 14 mm)	2
13.	Bumper	3/16 x ⅝ – 5⅝ Long (5 mm x 16 mm – 143 mm)	1
14.	Axle Support	½ x ½ – 2¼ Long (13 x 13 – 57 mm)	2
15.	Axle Support	½ x ½ – 3⅝ Long (13 x 13 – 92 mm)	1
16.	Axle Peg	5/16 dia. (Length to Suit) (8 mm)	6
17.	Gas Tank	1/16 dia. – 1⅝ Long (1.5 – 41 mm)	2
18.	Housing	¼ x 1 – 4 9/16 Long (6.5 x 25 – 116 mm)	2
19.	Wheel Top	¼ x 1 13/16 – 3 9/16 Long (6.5 x 46 – 90.5 mm)	2
20.	Wheel End	¼ x 1 13/16 – 15/16 Long (6.5 x 4.6 – 24 mm)	4
21.	Wheel Top	¼ x 13/16 – 1⅜ Long (6.5 x 20.5 – 35 mm)	2
22.	Wheel End	¼ x 13/16 – 15/16 Long (6.5 x 20.5 – 24 mm)	4
23.	Front Wheel	¾ x 2 dia. (19 x 51 mm)	2
24.	Rear Wheel	¾ x 2 dia. (19 x 51 mm)	8
25.	Muffler	11/16 dia – 4 ¾ Long (17.5 – 120.5 mm)	2
26.	Muffler Support	3/16 dia. – ¾ long (5 – 19 mm)	4
27.	Dump Base	¼ x 5 – 5 9/16 Long (6.5 x 127 – 141 mm)	1
28.	Dump Side	¼ x 3 ¾ – 6¾ Long (6.5 x 95 – 171.5 mm)	2
29.	Dump Front	¼ x 3⅞ – 5⅞ Long (6.5 x 98.5 – 149 mm)	1
30.	Dump Board	¼ x 3 – 5¼ Long (6.5 x 76 – 133 mm)	1
31.	Top Board	5/16 x ½ – 5⅞ Long (8 x 13 – 149 mm)	1
32.	Dump Support	¾ x 1 ¾ – 5 9/16 Long (19 x 44.5 – 141 mm)	1
33.	Pin	¼ dia. – 2¼ dia (6.5 mm – 57 mm)	1

1. Select the stock and cut the parts. Order the axle pegs and wheels (parts 16 and 23). Use any hardwood for this one. I made the truck shown here out of ash.

Cut the parts to the sizes given in the Materials List. To save yourself the trouble of cutting tight radii in the corners of the cab front (part 4) and sides (part 5), lay out and drill the ¼-inch-diameter (6.5 mm) holes before cutting out the parts.

2. Lay out the parts and cut them to shape. Use the measurements in the drawing to lay out the various parts. Drill all holes before cutting the parts to their final shapes so that the parts will be easier to hold.

If you're building the dump subassembly, drill the ¼-inch-diameter (6.5 mm) hole in the dump support (part 32), and use this hole as a guide for drilling the ¼-inch-diameter (6.5 mm) holes in the wheel housing (part 18).

As you cut out the parts, dry-fit them so that you can catch any errors at the earliest possible stage.

3. Turn the gas tanks and mufflers. Turn the gas tanks (part 17) and mufflers (part 25) on a lathe. If you don't have a lathe, substitute dowels: make the gas tanks from two 1⅝-inch lengths of 1 inch-diameter dowel; make

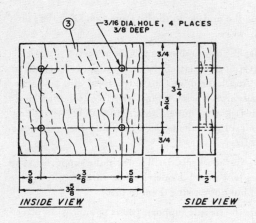

3/16 DIA. HOLE, 4 PLACES
3/8 DEEP

INSIDE VIEW   SIDE VIEW

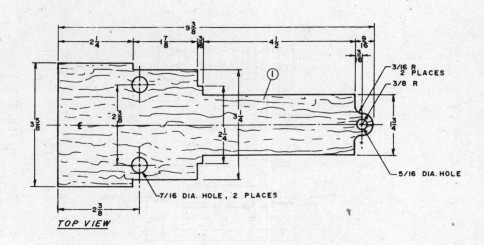

3/16 R
2 PLACES
3/8 R

5/16 DIA. HOLE

7/16 DIA. HOLE, 2 PLACES

TOP VIEW

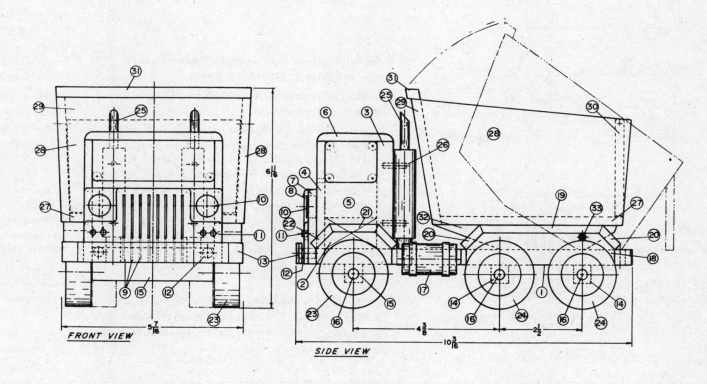

FRONT VIEW   SIDE VIEW

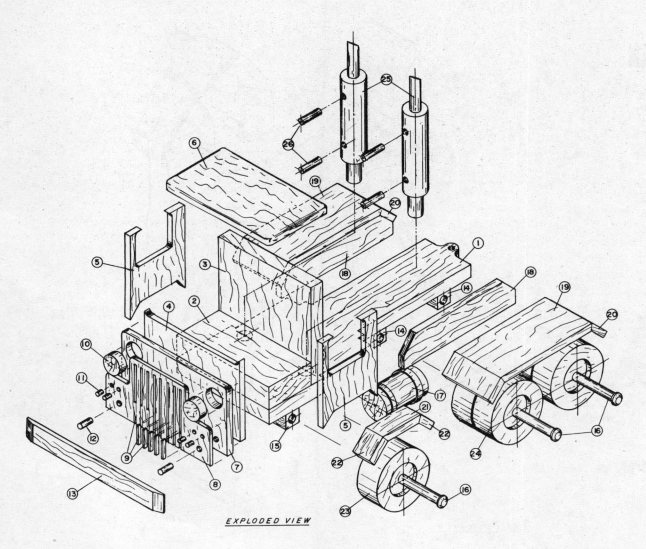

EXPLODED VIEW

Continued →

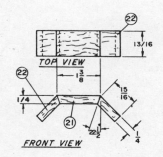

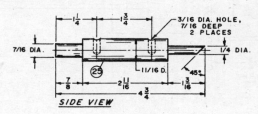

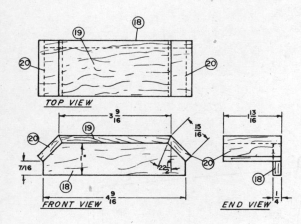

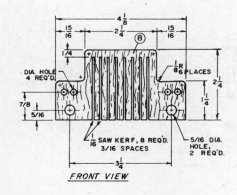

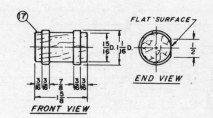

the mufflers from three dowels with diameters of ⅞, ¹¹⁄₁₆, and ¼ inches (22, 17.5, 6.5 mm).

4. Make subassemblies. Assemble the truck in a series of smaller subassemblies.

First, make two rear wheel wells from parts 18, 19, and 20. Make front fender assemblies from parts 21 and 22. Make the grill subassembly from parts 7, 8, 9, 10, and 11. Make the cab from parts 2, 3, 4, 5, and 6 and dry-fit the cab to the base (part 1). Trim the base if necessary. Glue the cab to the base and then glue the grill subassembly to it.

Cut the bumper (part 13). Drill holes in it for the bumper support (part 12). Glue one end of the bumper support in the bumper and the other end in the grill. Glue it in place.

Glue the rear wheel wells to the base. Fit the front fenders to the cab. You may have to notch the front fenders slightly to fit over the hood. Glue the fenders in place.

Glue the muffler to the base and cab. Glue the gas tank in place.

Make the dump subassembly from parts 27, 28, 29, and 31, but don't attach the dump support (part 32) to it yet. Attach the dump board (part 30) with 4d finishing nails or ¾-inch (19 mm) lengths of ¹⁄₁₆-inch-diameter (1.5 mm) dowel. Be sure to drill before nailing to avoid splitting the wood. Check that the dump board moves freely.

5. Dry-fit the wheels. Drill holes in the supports to suit the peg length and diameter. Make sure the wheels turn freely, but do not glue them in place.

Glue the six axle supports (parts 14 and 15) in place, as shown in the side view of the assembled truck. The given distances between the axle centers are only an approximate guide. Center the wheels within the wheel wells, as shown in this view.

6. Add the dump subassembly. If you don't care to have an operable dumping bed, simply glue the bed to the base. Otherwise, proceed as follows:

Enlarge the ¼-inch-diameter (6.5 mm) hole in the dump support with a ⁹⁄₁₂-inch (19 mm) drill bit. Attach the dump support to the truck by putting the pin (part 33) through the hole in one of the wheel wells, into the hole in the dump support, and out through the second wheel well.

Glue the dump to the dump support, positioning it so it will not hit any parts as it moves. Make sure that the dump subassembly looks centered when seen from the top, both sides, and the rear. Use large rubber bands to hold everything together until the glue sets.

7. Apply finish. The truck can be left unfinished, protected with clear varnish, or painted. Glue the axle pegs in place.

Country Rocking Horse, c.1935

I made a rocking horse for each of our grandchildren, and I think it was by far the most popular toy I ever made them, at least until they outgrew it. It always fascinated me that they knew instinctively exactly how to ride the horse. This one is a copy of one I bought at a flea market in southern New Hampshire. It was painted yellow with red and black edges.

Note: This is a very simple project except for fitting the legs to the seat. Refer to View at A-A, page 423. This is a cross section of the final assembly. Note that the ½-inch diameter holes must be drilled at an angle of 70°, as shown. Fit the top section of the legs (part 2) to the seat (part 1).

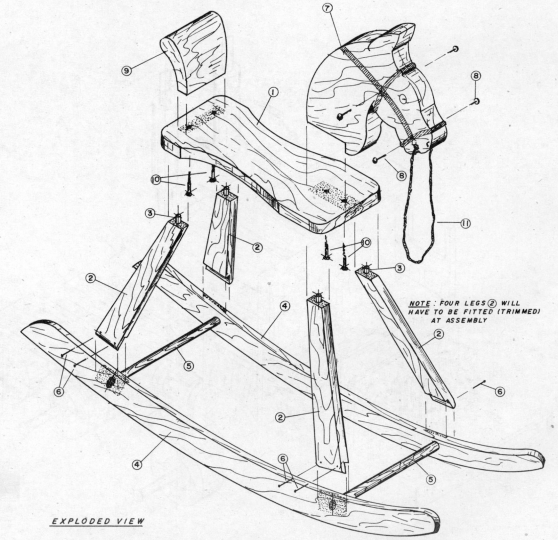

EXPLODED VIEW

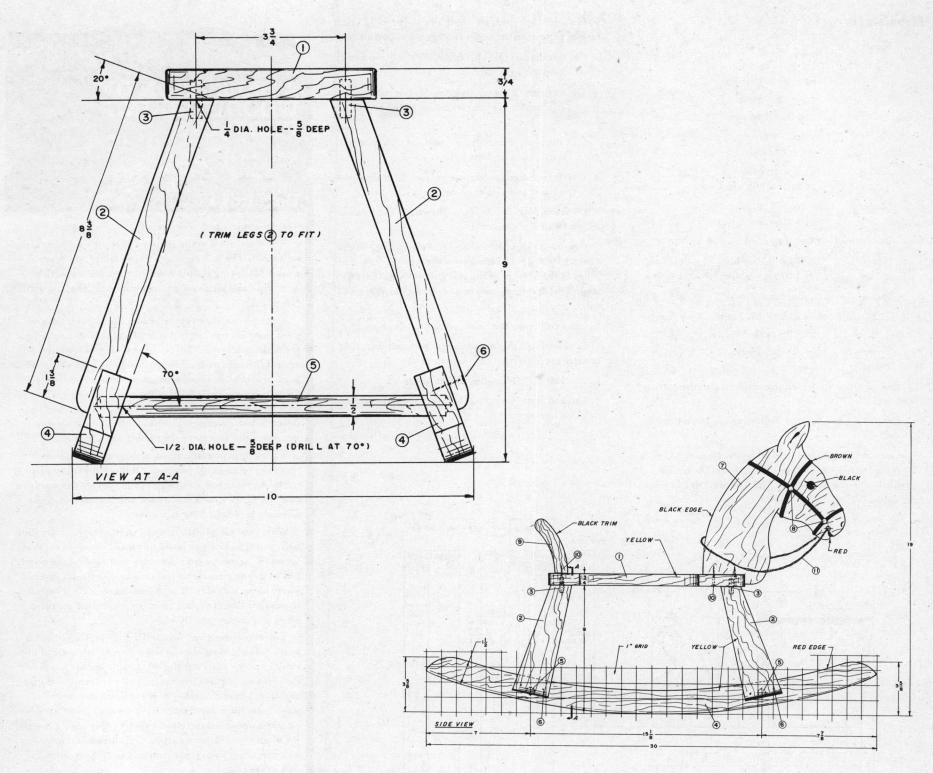

VIEW AT A-A

SIDE VIEW

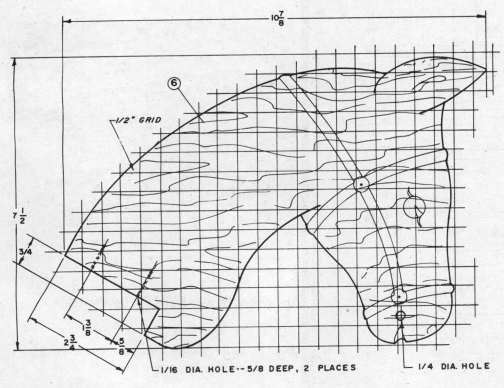

SIDE VIEW

Continued →

Materials List

No.	Name	Size	Req'd.
1	Seat	¾ x 5¼ – 12¾ long (19 x 133 – 324 mm)	1
2	Leg	¾ x 2⅜ – 8⅝ long (19 x 60 – 219 mm)	4
3	Pin	¼ dia. – 1 long (6.5 x 25 mm)	2
4	Rocker	¾ x 4 – 30 long (19 x 101 – 762 mm)	2
5	Spacer	½ dia. – 8½ long (13 – 216 mm)	2
6	Brad	1 long, (25 mm)	12
7	Head	1¼ x 7½ – 10⅞ long (32 x 190.5 – 276 mm)	1
8	Tack	⅜ dia. head	4
9	Tail	2⅛ x 3½ – 3¾ long (54 x 90 – 95 mm)	1
10	Screw – fl.	No. 8 – 2 long hd.	4
11	Twine	to suit	1

1. Cut all pieces to overall size according to the cutting list.

Lay out the seat (part 1), following the given dimensions.

Cut out the seat, and drill all holes. Important: note that the four ¼-inch-diameter (6.5 mm) holes are drilled from the bottom, ⅝ inch (16 mm) deep. Sand all over.

2. On a ½-inch grid, lay out the head (part 7). Transfer the pattern to the wood and cut out. Sand all over.

Cut out the tail (part 9), following the given dimensions. Sand all over.

3. On a 1-inch (25 mm) grid, lay out the rockers (part 4). Transfer the pattern to one of the two rocker pieces.

Tack the two pieces together, and cut out. Sand all over. Be sure to round the bottom edge.

4. Carefully cut out the four legs (part 2) as shown. (See the front and side views for details.)

Locate and drill all holes, as shown. In the legs (part 2), add dowel pins (part 3).

Dry-fit the legs (part 2) and spacers (part 5) to the rockers (part 4). Use the ¼-inch-diameter (6.5 mm) holes in the bottom of the seat and the pins (part 3) as a guide in dry-fitting the pieces. If necessary, trim to suit.

5. Glue and screw the head and tail to the seat.

Glue and nail the legs to the rockers and seat. Add the spacers (part 5) at the same time.

6. Sand all over, rounding all sharp edges.

7. Paint to suit. Note the colors that were used on the original horse.

—From *The Big Book of Weekend Woodworking*

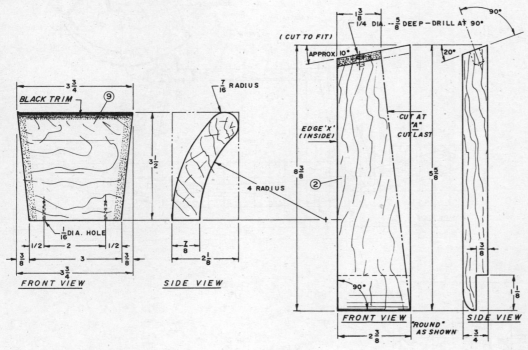

FRONT VIEW · SIDE VIEW · FRONT VIEW · SIDE VIEW

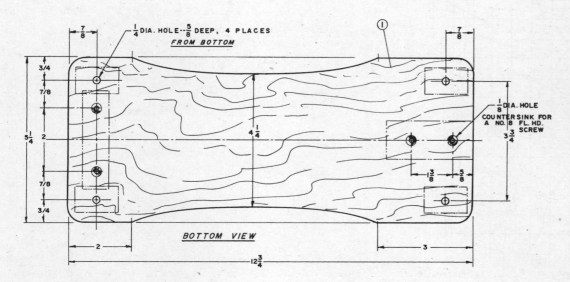

BOTTOM VIEW

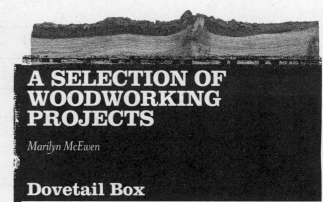

A SELECTION OF WOODWORKING PROJECTS

Marilyn McEwen

Dovetail Box

Tease the mind and tame the saw.

Woodworkers love the virtuous dovetail—it is a wonder to behold. The joint is both an eye pleaser and brain teaser. Mastering it adds visual interest and strength to your work and challenges your brain to think along a different path.

Some people are so apprehensive about this ingenious joint that they head right out and buy the latest router jig for making dovetails. There are a number of arguments against this approach. Using a dovetail jig is no walk in the park. It creates an enormous amount of dust and noise, and setting up the jig for the first time is not easy. Plus, with their seamless perfection and symmetry, router-jig dovetails lack character. I think hand-cut dovetails add intrinsic value to a piece—imperfections and all.

With a little practice, hand-cut dovetails don't take that long to make. At first, your mind will want to play tricks—so make several practice joints before you start this project. Once you've made a set, you'll understand why woodworkers hold it in such esteem.

With a couple of well-fitting practice joints under your belt, you'll be ready to build this small basswood toolbox. Granted, basswood isn't the most exciting-looking wood, but its demure character seems to help you relax and not worry about mistakes. It is an excellent wood for learning handwork, and is slightly aromatic—a pleasant surprise when you remove the lid.

This box is designed for carrying tools. The inner tray keeps delicate tools out of the bottom of the box and provides a resting place for the lid. Simple leather handles make it easy to grasp the box, as well as to remove the lid and tray. I have a number of these boxes in a variety of sizes. I use them for transporting my tools when I teach or take a woodworking class. I always experience a sense of joy when my tools arrive safely, and these boxes provide a welcome sense of organization and familiarity when I'm in a strange land.

Handle your box with care, but don't pamper it. This is a working box, made all the more interesting by the marks of time.

Overview: How to Build the Dovetail Box

BUILD THE MAIN BOX

Build the main box using simple hand-cut dovetails and a plywood bottom set in stopped grooves.

FIT THE TRAY AND TOP IT OFF

The tray is simply a smaller, lower box that fits neatly inside the main box. It's built in the same way as the main box, but of lighter, more delicate materials.

DETAILS, DETAILS

There are no fancy latches or hinges on this box. The chamfered lid simply slips inside the box and sits atop the tray. Finish with shellac and wax.

Step by Step: Building the Dovetail Box

BUILD THE MAIN BOX

CUT THE DOVETAILS

1. Start by making the dovetails following the steps outlined in "Fundamental Woodworking Techniques" page 387.

2. Note that the dovetail layout for the main box uses half tails on the side pieces, while the layout of the tray uses half pins on the end pieces (see the Dovetail Layouts).

3. Since you're building a box rather than sample joints, be careful about labeling all your parts. Cut all the joints and refine the fit, but don't glue it up. Once the joints mate, you can proceed.

LAY OUT AND CUT THE BOTTOM GROOVE

4. Lay out the groove for the plywood bottom on the inside face of the sides and ends. Note that the groove is full length on the sides, but stopped on the ends. If the groove extended the length of the end pieces, it would show as a notch in the lower pin.

5. Rout ¼" x ¼" grooves (6.5 x 6.5 mm) (full length and stopped) using a router mounted in a table.

FIT THE PLYWOOD BOTTOM

6. Dry fit the box and bottom to check the fit of the bottom. Make sure there's plenty of room for the glue. It's common to misjudge this fit, only to find during the clamping that the joints won't draw closed because the bottom is too big.

FINISH THE INSIDE

7. I like to use clear shellac on the insides of the box. Because it dries quickly, you can apply three coats in an hour. Shellac looks nice, but it also makes cleaning up the glue easier. If any glue seeps out during assembly, just let it dry. The glue won't stick to the shellac, and it pops off easily with a chisel. If you prefer not use any finish, I suggest you wipe a thin coat of paste wax along the shoulder line. Whether you use shellac or wax, keep it off the pins and tails so it doesn't interfere with the bond.

GLUE UP AND SMOOTH THE BOX

8. Remember to make a test run with the clamps before applying glue; make sure the bottom fits properly.

9. Apply the glue. After it has dried, clean off the excess and sand down the protruding tails and pins with an orbital sander and 100-grit paper (or a stationary belt sander if you have one).

Cut List and Supplies for Dovetail Box					
Number of Parts	Description	Dimensions in Inches			Comments
		Thickness	Width	Length	
Solid wood (basswood or other softwood					
2	Sides	⅝ (16 mm)	5 (12.7 cm)	15 (38 cm)	
2	Ends	⅝ (16 mm)	5 (12.7 cm)	8 (20.3 cm)	
2	Tray sides	½ (13 mm)	2 ⅜ (16 cm)	13 ½ (34.3 cm)	
2	Tray ends	½ (13 mm)	2 ⅛ (5.5 cm)	6 ½ (16.5 cm)	
2	Lid	½ (13 mm)	6 ⅝ (16.8 cm)	13 ¾ (40 cm)	Glue up from narrower pieces if necessary
Plywood					
1	Box bottom	¼ (6.5 mm)	7 ⅛ (18 cm)	14 ¼ (37 cm)	
1	Tray bottom	⅛ (3 mm)	5 ¾ (14.5 cm)	13 (33 cm)	Use plywood or hardboard, and cover with decorative paper if desired
4	Tray posts	¼ (6.5 mm)	¼ (6.5 mm)	2 ¼ (5.7 cm)	
Other materials & supplies					
	Leather	1/16 (1.5 mm)	1 (25 mm)		Cut to length as needed for handles
	Brass screws				For attaching handles, use #4 or #5, ⅜" long

FIT THE TRAY AND TOP IT OFF

1. The tray is just another, smaller box. Size it for an easy fit inside. Dovetail the corners and cut the grooves for the bottom. It's easier to cut these smaller grooves with a plunge router and fence. For an even nicer appearance, you can add decorative paper to the bottom.

A tray is simply a more delicate box that fits inside the main box.

2. Sand, and if you're finishing the inside of the tray, do so before assembly. The tray doesn't require much clamping pressure, so you don't need bar clamps or cauls.

MAKE WAY FOR THE TRAY

3. A fast and simple way to create a tray support is to glue four small posts (¼" x ¼") into each corner of the box. Cut the posts to length with a handsaw. Apply the glue and simply press the posts into place. You don't need clamps; the suction from the glue is strong enough to hold them.

TRAY HANDLES

4. Without handles, the only way to remove the tray is to tip the box upside down. Attach the handles to the inside upper edge. I use leather, tacked or screwed in place, but you could make wooden pulls instead.

5. If you have material that's wide enough, the lid can be one piece, but you can also edge-glue two pieces together. There are no fancy latches or hinges; the lid simply rests on top of the tray. Don't get too fussy with the fit—you want easy access to your tools.

The chamfered lid merely sits on top of the tray.

6. Once the lid fits, plane a 45° chamfer around it (see p. 00). Take care to avoid tear-out during this process.

DETAILS, DETAILS

1. Lightly soften all the edges with a plane or sandpaper.

2. Apply finish to the outsides of the box and tray, and to both sides of the lid. Apply a thin coat of paste wax over all.

3. Fasten a handle to the lid.

Continued ➡

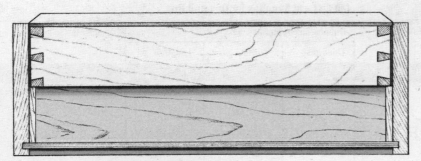

CUTAWAY FRONT VIEW

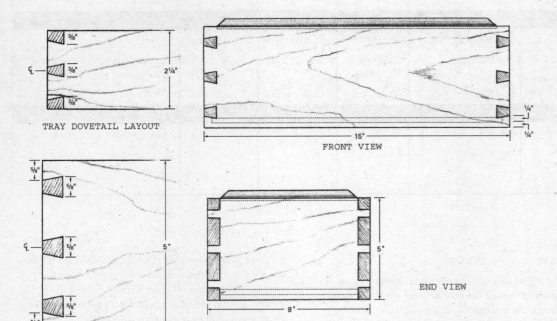

3/8"
3/8"
⌀
3/8"
2¼"

TRAY DOVETAIL LAYOUT

5/8"
5/8"
⌀
5/8"
5"
5/8"

BOX DOVETAIL LAYOUT

¼"
¼"
15"

FRONT VIEW

5"
8"

END VIEW

Furniture From a Box

Simple elements combine to make the whole.

When I was a child, I didn't play much with dolls, but building blocks captured my imagination. The fascination continued during my college years, and I was still at it—building furniture in my dorm room out of rubber blocks and cheap planks. The furniture was easy to reconfigure into a variety of coffee tables, seats, bookcases, and storage units, and quick to deconstruct when it was time to depart for life's next adventure.

Many moons later, as a woodworker, I updated the idea, using wooden boxes for blocks, nice hardwood planks, and few additional elements for stability and visual interest. I used different construction methods for the boxes, but finally settled on dovetail joinery. Taking the extra time to hand cut dovetails adds character and strength to a piece, and is an excellent way to increase its intrinsic value.

The linear design lends itself to experimentation, and it's fun to find ways to transform the boxy, basic look into something elegant. In this case, I used my trusty spokeshave to cut a gentle relief curve into the bottom of each end of the top. From a distance, the slight curve offers relief to the eye and adds an exotic Asian flavor. Laminated feet stabilize the piece and provide

As simple as cinder blocks and planks, but far more elegant, this bench features a mahogany top, hard maple boxes, and ebonized poplar feet.

another opportunity to move away from straight lines.

Though this project makes an elegant bench or table, you can reconfigure the dimension and stack the elements to make a bookcase. Simply build a few more boxes, and

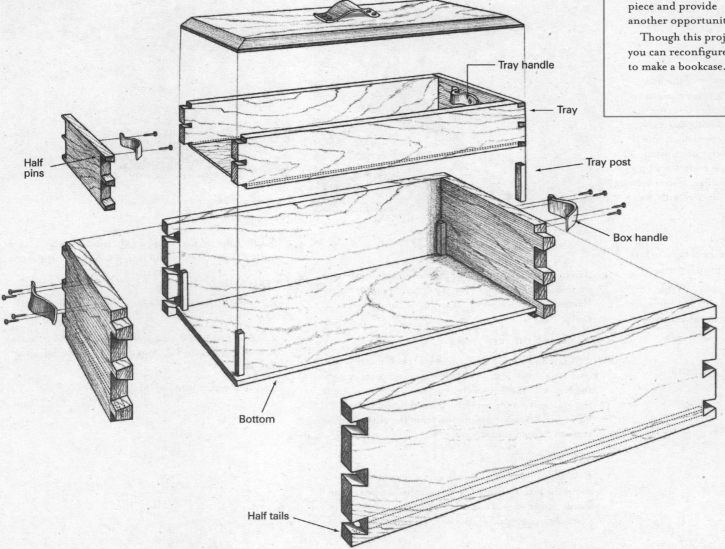

Tray handle

Tray

Tray post

Half pins

Box handle

Bottom

Half tails

EXPLODED VIEW

Cut List & Supplies for Furniture from a Box Box

Number of Parts	Description	Dimensions in Inches			Comments
		Thickness	Width	Length	
Solid wood					
2	Top (mahogany)	1½ (38 mm)	6 (15.2 cm)	52 (1.3 m)	Glue up into one 12"-wide panel; cut to finished length of 48". Some species of wood are easy to find in 12"+ widths; use them if available and skip the glue-up.
4	Box sides (maple)	¾ (19 mm)	4½ (11.4 cm)	12 (30.5 cm)	
4	Box ends (maple)	¾ (19 mm)	4½ (11.4 cm)	8¾ (22.3 cm)	
2	Cross piece (mahogany)	¾ (19 mm)	3⅜ (8.5 cm)	9¾ (24.8 cm)	
6	Foot laminates (poplar)	1⅝ (41 mm)	2¾ (7 cm)	12 (30.5 cm)	Laminate and mill to make two feet, each 2⅝" x 11⅜"
Other materials & supplies					
	2" drywall screws				For attaching top and feet
16	⅜" washers				Under the heads of the drywall screws

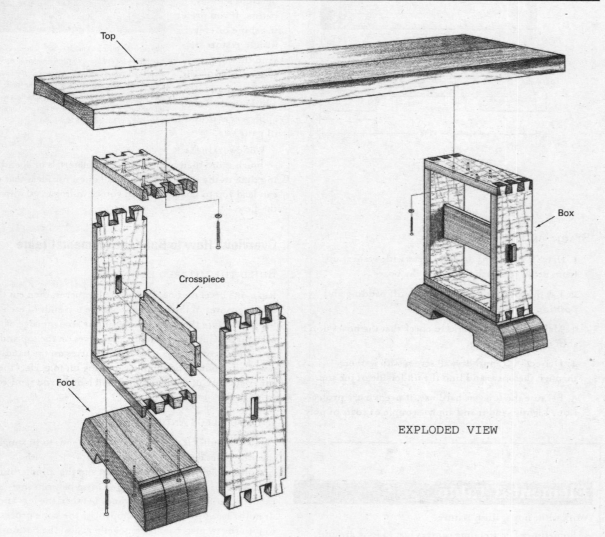

Top

Crosspiece

Foot

Box

EXPLODED VIEW

bolt them together with carriage bolts for strength and easy disassembly.

It takes me back to the simplicity of my first furniture creations. Life changes, but some things never do.

Overview: How to Build Furniture from a Box

BUILD THE TOP

The top is just a 12"-wide panel—use a single plank if you can get one wide enough, or glue up a panel from narrower boards. Cut a low relief curve in the underside of the ends, using a spokeshave.

BUILD THE BOXES

Two boxes hold up the top. Hand-cut dovetails look great for the box joinery, but a rabbeted joint works as well.

Before assembling the box, cut and fit the crosspiece. It's mortised into the sides of the box. Shape the curve on the lower edge of the crosspiece. Once all the joinery fits, glue up the boxes with the crosspieces in place.

BUILD THE FEET

Laminate the foot blanks from three layers of 1¾" wood. Square up the blanks and then cut the curves on the band saw. Refine and smooth the curves and countersink and bore the screw holes for fastening to the boxes. Stain or ebonize the feet at this point if so desired.

STACK 'EM UP

Attach the feet to the boxes, then attach the boxes to the top.

Step by Step: Building Furniture from a Box

BUILD THE TOP

GLUE UP THE PANEL

1. If you're not using a single wide board for the top, glue up a 12"-wide panel from narrower boards. Use biscuits, as described in "Fundamental Woodworking Techniques."

2. Cut the top to final length and width.

SHAPE THE TOP

3. Cut a small relief area on the underside of each end of the top, as shown in the illustrations. See "Fundamental Woodworking Techniques" page 381 for details on using a spokeshave.

4. Refine the surfaces with hand and orbital sanding. Since these areas are below eye level, you needn't go crazy with the sanding.

SURFACE PREP

5. Spend some time sanding the visible surface of the top.

6. Pay careful attention to the end grain and edges.

7. Work your way up to 220 grit.

BUILD THE BOXES

CUT THE BOX JOINERY

1. Cut the box joinery. Dovetailed boxes look impressive. However, if you want to paint or stain the boxes, I suggest building them with no visible joinery. Painted dovetails just don't look good.

MORTISE THE BOX SIDES

2. Once the structural joinery on the boxes is complete, you need to cut mortises in the box sides to accept the crosspiece. Lay out the mortises as shown in the illustrations.

3. Cut the mortises with a drill press or plunger router and jig.

COUNTERSINK THE BOX TOPS

4. Bore and countersink screw holes on the underside of the box tops. Make the shank holes oversize to allow for seasonal movement.

TENON THE CROSSPIECE

5. Temporarily assemble the box, clamping it so the corners are tight and square.

6. Measure the inside dimensions of the box to determine the location of the tenon shoulders. Note that the ends of the crosspiece protrude beyond the box sides by ½" (13 mm).

7. Cut the tenons as described in "Fundamental Woodworker's Techniques" page 381.

8. Test fit the crosspieces.

9. Remove the crosspieces, and use sandpaper on a block to hand sand a bevel on the protruding ends of the tenon. Keep these edges crisp—no rounding over.

SHAPE THE CROSSPIECE

10. Lay out the curve on each crosspiece.

11. Cut the curve on the band saw.

12. Smooth the curve with a 3"-diameter (76 mm) sanding drum mounted in the drill press. Alternatively, smooth it by hand with a spokeshave, files, scrapers, and sandpaper.

SURFACE PREP

13. Final sand the crosspieces and the inside surfaces of the boxes up to 220 grit.

ASSEMBLE THE BOXES

14. Glue up and clamp the boxes.

Continued ➡

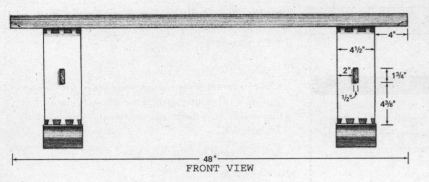

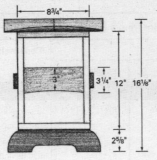

FRONT VIEW

END VIEW

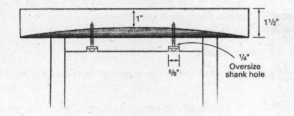

1½"

¼"
Oversize
shank hole

5/8"

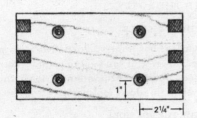

1"

2¼"

TOP FASTENING DETAIL

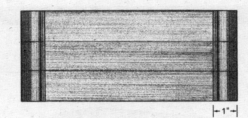

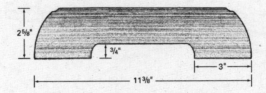

2⅝"

¾"

3"

11⅜"

FOOT DETAIL

Although this table isn't made to withstand direct exposure to the outdoors, its rugged materials and a couple of coats of paint make it perfect for use under a porch roof. The top is a concrete stepping-stone with a little spray paint on it, and the spindles are copper tubing. The splined mitered legs are made of white oak and painted with milk paint.

15. Sand the outside of the box so the joints are flush and smooth.

16. Finish sand up to 220 grit, softening all the edges.

Build the feet

GLUE UP THE LAMINATES

1. Each foot is built up from three thinner laminates. You can glue up and clamp both feet (two sets of three laminates each) at the same time.

2. Apply enough clamps to provide even pressure all around the block.

3. Allow at least two hours for the glue to dry.

SHAPE THE FEET

4. Remove all the dried glue with a paint scraper.

5. Run one face of each lamination through the jointer to establish a flat reference surface.

6. Mill the feet four-square to their final dimensions.

7. Lay out the curves on the foot blocks.

8. To cut the outside curves, start on the band saw and saw up to where the profile terminates, then slowly back out of the curve. To complete the cut, use a miter gauge on the table saw to create a crisp shoulder line.

9. To cut the curve on the bottom of the foot, make one continuous cut on the band saw.

10. Refine and smooth the curves by hand and orbital sanding. For the radius on the bottom of the feet, wrap sandpaper around a 1" (25 mm) dowel.

11. Sand up to 220 grit.

12. Countersink and counterbore as you did to attach the top.

STAIN THE FEET

13. If you want to stain or ebonize the feet, do so now.

14. Flood the top and boxes with oil and let them dry thoroughly before handling.

Stack 'em Up

1. Drive 2" (51 mm) drywall screws with washers up from below to attach the feet to the boxes.

2. Lay the top face down on some soft padding and position the boxes.

3. Make a couple of marks to check that the boxes don't shift during fastening.

4. Drive 2" (51 mm) drywall screws with washers through the boxes and into the underside of the top.

5. Because the top gets hard use, it needs extra protection. Lightly sand it and apply a couple of coats of poly.

Elemental Table

Work with, not against, nature.

Sometimes I go to home centers just to look around, but it's not what you think. I am not there for retail therapy, unlike so many others. I visit the home center with the sole intention of seeing something different. I comb the aisles, surf the displays, and let the waves take me where they will. This is apparently unusual because puzzled clerks keep cycling back to me, asking, "May I help you find something?" "No thanks," I reply. "It has to find me."

Inspiration recently found me in the garden center of my local home store. A concrete stepping-stone stopped me in my path. Thunderstruck, I gazed at it, whispering, "All it needs is a little embellishment with spray paint, and there it is: an instant weatherproof tabletop!" I found myself headed to the plumbing aisle as if propelled by a strong sea current, then to the paint department for copper metallic spray paint. I sailed on, first to the local lumberyard for some wood, and then back to my shop, where I was soon building the first Elemental Table.

The stepping-stone set the tone for the design. Only rugged materials would complement it, so I chose white oak for the table base and legs. I built bold but slightly curved mitered legs, painting them with pitch black milk paint for contrast. Paint is always a good finish for wooden furniture that needs to stand up to the elements. It's tougher and more durable than any clear finish, and it does a better job of locking moisture out of the wood.

Instead of building wooden aprons, I joined the legs with spindles cut from copper tubing pressed into holes drilled in the legs. Copper tubing is light and easy to cut with an inexpensive wheel-type tubing cutter. Over time, the copper loses that bright surface and develops a lovely patina. If you prefer the shine or ever wish to restore it, sand the copper tube with 400-grit sandpaper and use a little steel wool to apply a coat or two of paste wax.

Woodworking is so much more than buying tools and materials or spending time in the shop. It's an eternal quest for ideas that can lead you to many places—if you're willing to go with the flow.

Overview: How to Build the Elemental Table

BUILD THE MITERED LEGS

Rip a 45° bevel on one edge of the leg pieces, then cut the spline grooves in the bevel. Rabbet the top ends of each leg piece. Bore the spindle holes in the straight edge of each piece. Cut a template for the curves on the top and inside edges of the legs, and cut the curves on the band saw. Use a router and template-cutting bit to perfect the inner curve. Cut the legs to finished length, and sand and paint them.

JOIN THE LEGS AND ADD THE TOP

Cut the spindles to length and sand the ends to fit snugly into the holes drilled in the legs. Join two legs with spindles; no gluing is involved—just slip the spindles into the holes. Use a plywood clamping form between the rabbet shoulders to set the distance between the legs and draw the legs together with clamps. Use the same process to join the two leg assemblies together. Seal the bottoms of the legs and install three gliders on each leg.

Run a line of construction adhesive around the shoulders and press the top in place.

Step by Step: Building the Elemental Table

BUILD THE MITERED LEGS

CUT THE SPLINED MITER AND RABBET THE TOPS

1. Cut the splined miters in the leg pieces.

2. Lay out the rabbet on the top end of one leg piece (see the Leg Corner Detail).

3. Set up the table saw with a dado blade and cut the rabbet in each leg piece.

BORE FOR SPINDLES

4. Lay out the spindle locations on the inner surface of one leg, measuring down from the shoulder (see the

Leg Detail). Use this as a pattern to lay out the hole locations on the other leg pieces.

5. Bore ⅝"-diameter x ¾"-deep holes (16 x 19 mm) on the drill press.

SHAPE THE LEGS

6. On a piece of ¼" (6.4 mm) plywood, lay out the inner edge curve of the leg (see the Leg Curve Detail). Use the method described in "Fundamental Wood-working Techniques" on page 381.

7. Use a flexible metal ruler to draw the curve on the top of the template.

8. Cut the template on the band saw, and refine the curve with a sanding drum, files, and/or a hand sander.

9. Use the template to draw the top and inner curves on all the leg pieces.

10. Cut the curves on the band saw, being sure to leave the line for reference. Save the offcuts to use later as cauls.

11. Use a template-cutting bit and a router running against the template to refine the long curve on the inner edge of the leg.

12. Shape the top curve with a sander. A stationary belt sander is best, but if you don't have one, you can use a random orbit sander. Don't spend too much time on this—you can't get the curve perfect until the two leg pieces are glued up.

SURFACE PREP

13. Finish sand the inside surfaces up to 150 grit.

14. Apply a thin coat of paste wax along the insides of the miter edges, but keep the wax off the gluing surfaces.

CUT THE SPLINES

15. Resaw the spline material on the band saw. Cut it approximately in half.

16. Plane the splines to final thickness, frequently checking for a snug fit in the groove.

ASSEMBLE THE LEGS

Gluing the legs requires a lot of clamps and is a somewhat awkward process. I suggest enlisting a friend to help. Make a practice run before the glue flows.

17. Lay two clamps on the floor, with the offcut cauls in place.

18. Spread a thin layer of waterproof glue on each mitered surface. Run a thin bead in the grooves.

19. Insert the spline in one piece, then press the two miters together.

20. Place the leg in the clamps. Use the offcuts as cauls on the curved edge, and thin scraps of plywood on the miters.

21. Check that the shoulders align. They must be perfectly flush at the joint.

22. Stand the leg on end and add more clamps in opposing directions.

PREFINISH

23. Perfect the top curve.

24. Final sand the outside surfaces with a random orbit sander, working your way up to 220 grit.

25. Cut the legs to final length, measuring downward from the rabbets.

26. Mix up the milk paint as directed by the manufacturer. Brush two coats on all surfaces of the legs, lightly hand sanding with 400-grit paper between coats.

27. Seal the milk paint with three coats of gel varnish. Lighty hand sand with 400-grit paper between coats.

JOIN THE LEGS AND ADD THE TOP

TWO LEGS WITH SPINDLES

1. Hold the copper tubing lightly in a metal vise—its thin walls are easy to collapse.

Number of Parts	Description	Dimensions in Inches			Comments
		Thickness	Width	Length	
Solid wood (white oak)					
8	Leg pieces	1 ⅜ (35 mm)	4 ½ (11.5mm)	24 (61 cm)	Cut to finished length of 23½" (60 cm) after rabbeting shoulders
4	Spline material	¼ (6.5 mm)	1 (25 mm)	24 (61 cm)	
Plywood					
2	Clamping forms for tops of legs	¾ (19 mm)	2 (51 mm)	16 1/16 (41 cm)	Any scrap material is fine, even plywood.
1	Clamping form for bottom of legs	¾ (19 mm)	14 ¼ (36 cm)	14 ¼ (36.2 cm)	Any scrap material is fine, even plywood.
Other materials & supplies					
12	Spindles	⅝ (16mm)	10 ¼ (26 cm)		Use ½"- (1.3 cm) diameter M-type copper tubing.
1	Concrete stepping-stone	1 ½ (38 mm)	16 (40.5 cm)	16 (40.5 cm)	
1 tube	Construction adhesive				
12	Nylon gliders				Use three small gliders per foot.
1 tube	Clear silicone caulk				
	Waterproof glue				

Cut List & Supplies for the Elemental Table

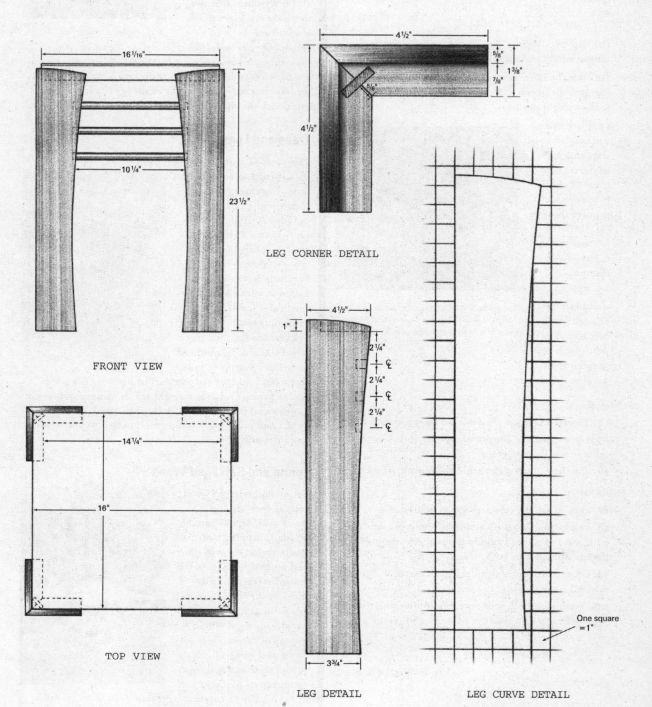

FRONT VIEW

TOP VIEW

LEG CORNER DETAIL

LEG DETAIL

LEG CURVE DETAIL

One square = 1"

Continued →

2. Cut the copper to length with a plumber's tubing cutter—an inexpensive home-center item.

3. Test the spindles' fit in the ⅝" (16 mm) holes previously drilled in the legs. They must fit tightly enough to hold the table in its assembled position until the top goes on. Sand the ends of the spindles lightly to get the desired fit.

4. Lay a leg on a protective mat spread upon the bench. Tap the three spindles in place with a rubber mallet. Don't hit the tubing directly, or you may dent it. Hold a wood block atop the tubing and strike it.

5. If the spindles fit well, you needn't glue them to the legs. Brush a little oil finish in each hole to help the tubing slip in. If the fit is too loose to hold the table together, you can use glue. Omit the oil and put a little epoxy in the holes. Before the glue cures, make sure the top fits between the shoulders.

6. Tap the other leg onto the ends of the spindles. You needn't seat the spindles in the ends of the holes—just get them started.

7. Place the 16¹⁄₁₆" (41 cm) plywood clamping forms in the rabbets that will later hold the top.

8. Use clamps to draw the legs together. The clamping form establishes the correct distance between the legs, assuring proper alignment.

9. Repeat with the other two legs and the remaining spindles.

FOUR LEGS WITH SPINDLES

10. Slip spindles into the remaining holes in the two subassemblies and join the four legs together.

11. Place the 14¼"-square (35.7 cm) plywood clamping form on the bench and move the leg/spindle assembly to the upright position.

12. Place one of the long plywood clamping forms in the rabbets to establish the proper position for this new leg. Draw the two assemblies together with clamps.

13. The spindles should fit tightly enough for the base to hold its position for the remaining steps. Remove the clamps.

The spindles fit snugly in their holes, but they don't really hold the table together. The structural integrity comes from the construction adhesive that joins the top and the legs.

GLIDERS

14. Turn the base upside down on the protective mat.

15. Lightly coat the bottom of each leg with silicone caulk to seal the end grain.

16. Tap three small gliders into the bottom of each leg.

GLUE THE TOP IN PLACE

17. Spray paint the concrete top as desired.

18. Load a tube of construction adhesive in a caulking gun, and apply a thin film to the rabbeted shoulders at the top of each leg.

19. Squeeze out an additional little blob of caulk in the mitered corners.

20. Set the top in the adhesive, and push down with all your weight to compress the adhesive and set the joint.

21. Check for adhesive squeeze-out. If you find any, remove it with mineral spirits.

—FROM *Woodworking 101 for Women*

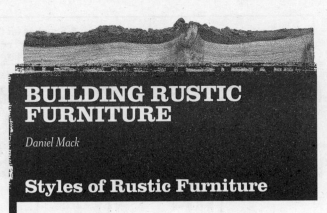

BUILDING RUSTIC FURNITURE

Daniel Mack

Styles of Rustic Furniture

Stick or Twig

Stick or twig furniture is made from young trees and branches, connected in a manner that echoes their natural form. Despite its fragile appearance, stick furniture is sturdy enough for everyday use, if the pieces are cut fresh and then allowed to dry thoroughly. The wood can be used as is or peeled. This rustic style is spontaneous and interactive. Because there are few plans to follow and very little or no reshaping required, stick

Philip Crandon, Andrea Franz

furniture is a good style for beginners. Whether the joints are nailed together, fastened with dowels, or glued with mortise and tenon joints, the challenge lies in selecting wood with the right proportions.

Trees and Logs

Tree or log furniture is stick furniture on a grand scale. Logs are good for constructing beds or outdoor seating. They're also used to build rustic gazebos, pergolas, and arbors. Although log furniture lacks the detail found in stick and twig furniture, it can be made with roots and burls, which will give the finished piece visual interest. For indoor furniture, lodgepole pine, aspen, and juniper are popular; white cedar is a good choice because it has low weight for its volume and is easy to work and finish. For outdoor work, black locust, white cedar, and redwood hold up well if peeled to minimize bug infestation.

Found and Salvaged Wood

Found and salvaged wood, such as chestnut logs, fence rails, and discarded wooden shipping materials (pallets), has become more and more the object of the rustic maker's imagination. By the time the rustic gets hold of it, the wood has already experienced a history of use—aside from being part of a tree. Many rustics reclaim wood from various parts of old houses or barns. Cheek cuts and irregular wood from sawmills are also good for combining with fresh-cut wood. Driftwood is coveted because of its naturally finished surfaces.

Any wood left long enough in the hostile environment of oceans, lakes, or rivers will begin to lose hard edges and revert toward its original form.

Bentwood

Bentwood, a popular rustic style that involves careful planning, is created by bending and nailing long, straight, and thin branches or tree suckers around a sturdily built frame. Patience is required to shape the fresh wands of wood into graceful curves and other patterns. Builders of bentwood furniture can be found throughout the United States, wherever there are supple, fast-growing woods, such as willow, alder, or cottonwood.

Split Work, Mosaic, and Swiss Work

These three names denote the style in which full or half-rounded branches are nailed or glued over a wooden frame. This careful, often painstaking work, creates volume and intricacy, delicacy and geometry. A lavish visual variety can be created by using a variety of woods or different forms of the same species.

Bark Appliqué

Bark appliqué is a technique in which birch or cedar bark is appliquéd on top of existing casework. Many times, the edges of the surface are finished with Swiss work which functions to keep the bark from curling. Bark work is rarely used on chairs, but more commonly on cupboards, tables, desks, clocks, and picture frames. The bark for this rustic furniture is harvested twice a year in areas where durable white-paper birch, golden birch, and fire cherry are found.

Root and Burl Work

This rustic style creates furniture using intricate, dense root systems of trees and shrubs. The roots of mountain laurel, rhododendron, and juniper are traditional favorites for this type of rustic building. These materials are often found in the form of driftwood or discarded wood on land being cleared for development. Aesthetic and technical skills are required to successfully combine the gangly roots with other wood to make an appealing piece of furniture.

Burls, the wartlike knobs sometimes found on tree trunks and limbs, are natural growths formed by trees to protect or heal themselves. They are cherished for their unusual grain pattern and are often used in veneers. Some rustic builders split the burls and polish the grain face for use as a tabletop. Others use them as a design element in stick or log furniture.

Materials, Techniques, and Tools

This section discusses the finding, choosing, cutting, storing, and drying of materials; the various methods of joining the materials together; the tools available for accomplishing this joinery; and different ways of finishing the wood. Because rustic work has more to do with looking and dreaming than with measuring and planning, the information in this section has a somewhat circular and interlacing shape to it. I start out talking about materials, but can't help discussing something relevant about cutting. Or, when I finally say all I have to about tools, some of it may already sound familiar because of what I described about techniques.

This section mirrors how I make rustic furniture. The way in which I think about materials is related to where I can find them and how I need to cut them; how I choose to join the pieces to make, let's say, a chair, is an extension of the tools I like to use and what the wood looks like. Eventually I will deliver you to an intended destination, and you'll know what you need in order to make a table or a chair with the materials and tools of your choosing. But getting there may have some unexpected detours, recurring switchbacks, and, I hope, a few pleasant surprises.

Materials

It's very likely that if you purchased this book you already have some of the pieces of the Weekend Rustic puzzle. You probably have wood squirreled away from a trip to the beach or the woods. You may have some tools you like working with. Maybe you sketched out an idea or clipped a photo from a magazine that shows one of your dream rustic projects. These are all anchor points for working with this book. Nonetheless, I'll go through all the various ingredients. If you have them, great; if you need some reminders, here they are.

Materials are the most distinguishing characteristic of rustic work. You, the Rustic, hunt for wood—not lumber—and leave it in the shapes and textures pretty much as you found it; you just change its lengths and the way it relates to other similar pieces of wood.

ANY NATURAL FORM MATERIAL WILL DO. ANY NATURAL FORM MATERIAL WILL DO…AGAIN?

You can make something from anything. So find a farmer with an overgrown field. Talk to your local Parks or Highway Department. Attend a Planning or Zoning Board meeting and meet developers. Call the local Extension Service and inquire about getting a cutting permit. Ask your neighbors what they're planning to turn or prune. Look in the back of this book for the names of materials suppliers. So now you've solved your access to the materials. That's the easy part.

WHAT DO YOU WANT TO DO WITH THE MATERIALS?

It's likely that you have some thoughts about just what materials you think are most desirable. Preparing, sizing, and storing the materials are more difficult issues. If you like that Peeled Wood look, you're in for a lot of quiet time—you, the knife, and the branches. If you want to do mortise and tenon work (peg-in-hole joinery), you'll have to dry at least some of your wood pretty well before you use it. That means time…near the furnace, in a kiln, in a dry area somewhere. If you'd like to do something NOW, then go to get a saw, a hammer and nails and you can work with wood so fresh it's still cool.

My point here is that Materials is a prism of the way you like to do things. It's a reflection of your particular ingenuity at finding something unusual, exercising your imagination, developing stamina, being resourceful at finding storage, deciding whether to wait to work the wood dry or actively tangle yourself up in a project right now.

The area of Materials will be approached differently by every single person. That simple word "materials" hides many different gremlins waiting to challenge each of us. They appear to any such things as:

"You'll never find the right saplings to do this.

The saplings you get will have bugs and rot and you'll poison everybody.

Dan Mack has already used all the best saplings.

You might get arrested.

You will hurt yourself.

This is a waste of time and everybody will laugh at you.

You're just going to clutter up the house, the yard, the garage, and…

There are better way to spend your time."

My own gremlins usually play to my fear of a fatal, long-standing hidden flaw in my plans:

"Oh sure, the materials look right, but just wait until you start to work with them or just wait until you bring the finished chair indoors, then you'll see. Fool!"

Gremlins are a fact of life, and must be recognized as such and worked with. Make a little gremlin chair or shrine. Every time you hear the gremlin voice coming in to demolish you and your project, put a few wood chips at the chair or shrine…or a bent nail or a drop of glue. Gremlins fall quiet for a while when they are recognized. But they do not go away.

DRYING YOUR WOOD

The key thing to remember is that you want to delay the process of the tree returning itself to the earth. The natural cycle for a tree is to appear, leaf out, produce seeds, go dormant—and then repeat this for its entire life cycle (which is usually longer than a human life). When the tree has exhausted itself or been attacked by too many bugs, bacteria, whatever—it dies and its cells slowly decay with the help of water, oxygen, and microorganisms.

This thumbnail science lesson is interesting because by being rustic we insinuate ourselves into the very processes of life and afterlife. We jump right in with those trees and start to boogie—influencing, altering, elaborating what they do until the trees crumble to dust.

To put this another way, if you want your weekend rustic project to last, you have to interrupt the natural processes of wood decay. You have to dry the wood, either before or after you build with it, and keep the wood out of contact with the microorganisms that will help it decay

SELECTING YOUR MATERIALS

Even if you have access to a hundred acres, chances are you'll be limited to a few, maybe a half dozen, species of wood that are in the sizes you either want or can manage.

I suggest first seeing what is available to you. Then think, dream, and doodle with this specific wood in mind and see what happens. If it's a fast-growing pliant wood, such as willow, alder, or certain shrubs, you might think bentwood work—nails and hammers and curves. If the wood is small saplings, such as maple, hickory, or beech, you might think tables, ladders, bookcases, or a chair. Squint and see what your other eye sees when it imagines that tree disguised as something in your house.

Be guided, too, by what you need. What does your spouse need? What about the kids? Your mother?

Your approach to materials depends on the rest of your life. No two people see the trees, the woods, the materials, in the same way. In fact, no two people see a 2x4 in the same way.

A FEW TIPS, WARNINGS, AND GUIDELINES ABOUT CUTTING MATERIALS

YOU ONLY NEED A FEW THINGS:

Bow saw or folding camp saw

Tape measure

Clippers

Rope and bailing twine

Sharp knife

Drinking water and fruit

First-aid kit

DO THE CLEAN UP IN THE WOODS.

There is a certain drama to hauling a full tree out of the woods. But it will have to be trimmed up somewhere and cleaned up. Do it in the woods. Clip off leaves and small branches. I always size the wood in the woods as small as I dare. Usually, I cut and bundle wood in four- or five-foot lengths right in the woods. It's easier to move and move again and again. (And the shorter the length, the faster it dries.) With one-inch stock for rungs, I cut it in 24-inch lengths.

PACE YOURSELF.

Remember, for every tree you cut there is about another half an hour of clipping, sizing, moving, bundling, loading. You have to drive home, unload, and store the cut wood in a dry airy place. The cutting is the easy part. I often don't get all the materials I need on the first trip or even the second. Remember, "rustic" is as much about altered ways and times of working as it is about odd furniture.

DEEP FOREST TREES ARE GOOD.

They have had to survive in close, fierce proximity with their cousins. This has made them strong and dense with tight growth rings. This means you can get a lot of strength from a seemingly small diameter tree.

TWISTED IS NOT ALWAYS BETTER.

One of the first delights of rustic work is finding odd trees: big open ulcers, burls, vine twists, knot-like curves…Wow! But watch out…I still own most of the ones I cut in the early 1980s. Some are so unusual, they defy furniture. Some are just unusual enough that they call too much attention to themselves in a piece of furniture. Instead of "My, what a nice chair," all you hear is "What a twisted piece of wood!" It's nice to have a few pieces—they keep you humble.

GO FOR THE NORMAL PIECES.

The special quality to rustic work is the silk purse from the sow's ear…over and over; "Oh my, something so beautiful from materials so common!" Your job as a Rustic Warrior is to transform the plain into the special, the regular into the charmed—to illuminate the magic tucked into the regular. So the materials you want are the simple little trees. And then you invest your time and your sense of proportion in the making of some object you or part of your clan wants.

IT HELPS TO SEE WHAT YOU HAVE.

Unless you are blessed with a remarkable memory, you have to be able to see what wood you have. Look at pictures of how other rustics keep their wood. Last year I thought plastic garbage pails would do it. Then I tried plywood bins, then 2x4 racks, then metal shelves tipped back. I'm heading into year 20 of the always-less-than-

Continued →

perfect storage solution du jour. Really, my all-time favorite is to just lean everything against the wall!

SOMETIMES YOU DON'T NEED MORE MATERIALS.

Once in a while I just build from what I already own…no trip to the woods…just say no to the Woods. And if I'm lucky, I get a little, tiny corner of space returned to me for some other use.

IF YOU LIKE THE LOOK OF PEELED WOOD, BE PATIENT.

You have to cut the trees just after they put out leaves if you want to peel off the bark. There are about six weeks when it is very easy to peel the bark off in long strips; after that it's inch by inch, and it looks all knicked up.

Techniques

There is a collection of techniques used to handle wood in a rustic manner. None of these is very unusual, and all have been adapted from other forms of woodworking and craft. They fall into several overlapping categories, covering cutting, collecting, storing, constructing, and finishing.

CUTTING

Integral to this topic are two questions: Where can I get wood? What's the best time of year to cut?

CUT-YOUR-OWN WOOD

It's best to cut trees in the winter when the sap is down and the trees are least swollen. This means that when the cut pieces finally dry, there is less water to let off and less chance of the bark drying in a different way from the wood itself or blistering off. In addition, winter cutting minimizes the chances of active bugs and microorganisms.

However, life is not always fair, and it may not be possible to cut in the winter. I have cut every month of the year due to deadline, opportunity, wind storm, or some other contingency. Sometimes the wood has blistered as it has dried; other times it's been fine. This is all part of the magic of rustic; so don't let this "winter-cut" wisdom keep you from building.

I cut with a small folding saw. I have used bow saws and chain saws. All of these tools get the work done—some slower, some faster. Faster is not necessarily better. With the slowness of the bow saw comes some heat—and time to think about each cut and about where these wonderful pieces of tree might end up. A chain saw can deafen us to such thoughts. It usually demands attention like a two year old. It needs gas, oil, sharpening, coaxing, and it whines too much. It outrages us when it refuses to work. Our thoughts about the trees get lost.

The process of making a piece of rustic furniture literally starts in the woods: which tree, what diameter, and into what lengths is the tree to be cut for moving and storage. Decisions made then and there really shape the chair in a way no one piece of lumber can shape a piece of cabinetry.

FIND-YOUR-OWN WOOD

Road crews are always trimming, tree services are always servicing, neighbors are always pruning, developers are always "clearing," town dumps always have brush piles. I will pay one dollar to anyone who can't find—within two miles of where he lives—wood to build with. I was able to find wood even when I lived in Manhattan! If you try to claim the one dollar prize, and I come to your town and find wood, you have to pay me two dollars!

BUY-YOUR-OWN WOOD

In the last few years, several small mom-and-pop businesses have appeared that will sell you small amounts of kiln-dried saplings. In addition, you can call a local sawmill and ask about loggers who might cut you some smaller materials.

BUT WHICH WOODS ARE THE BEST?

The best wood for rustic work is arbor availabilis. Before you go to the tree guide, that means any wood you can get your hands on. Available Wood is very good wood because it lets you start making rustic furniture right away. Rustic work is local work, regionally inspired work. Get local woods and work with them. Soon you will become the local expert, not on which "woods are best," but on what all the different local woods are "best for." Remember, "rustic" is an attitude, not just a technical aptitude. This attitude is fundamentally different from the prevailing attitude of what constitutes "best," "efficient," or "productive." Rustic has much more to do with discovery, adventure, a lull, intuition, a hunch.

PEELED WOOD

You can peel wood all year long, but for most of the year, the bark comes off in tiny little chunks that look like anchovies, and the wood itself ends up looking like a leftover at a beaver buffet. Easy peeling happens with a butter knife and comes off in very long, slurpy strips. To achieve that creamy smooth, no-tool-marks look, there is definitely a best time of year to peel wood. That's when the tree has just leafed out, and the juices are up and going, and before the heat of the summer thunks in. Where I live in lower New York state that time ranges between late May and mid-July. In Maine one summer, I was still peeling maple in August. Again, just keep trying. You'll find out to the day when it's "best" for you. I have been weaving seats this season with the long peelings from hickory that I stripped in June and early July.

I have used a pressure washer both at home and at the local car wash to remove the bark from trees. It makes for an odd afternoon. Some rustic makers wash the hand-peeled wood to get the dirt and sugars off the surface, and then they seal the ends with a wax or urethane. I do not. I just use the natural staining as part of the "look."

DRYING TECHNIQUES

Dry wood is better than wet wood; it doesn't shrink, move, or check. Saplings, one to two inches in diameter, dry in a warm airy place in about two to four months. They are dry when they clack when you knock them together. The shorter you size the wood, the faster it dries.

There are several approaches available for drying wood. You can let wood sit in a dry, well-ventilated location; that might dry the wood in six months to two years. You can buy a kiln or build a kiln and dry a 4 x 4 x 15-foot (1.2 x 1.2 x 4.5 m) load in a month. There are dehumidification kilns available for under $2,000. Many of the woodworking and boatbuilding magazines have featured articles about how to make your own. I have never used a kiln, but other rustics do. A kiln is good insurance against bugs hiding out in your wood, and a kiln is a good place to store wood for a while.

You can buy dry wood from suppliers. You can choose a form of construction that doesn't really depend on dry wood.

WHAT ABOUT BUGS?

There is a good chance that wood that has spent time on the forest floor or in your friend's woodpile has been visited by insects, fungus, and mildew. Look at the wood carefully before you decide to collect it for rustic work. If bugs are living in the wood, you may be bringing home more than the rungs for a chair.

The most damaging insects are the three kinds of wood-boring beetles—lyctids, anobids, and bostrichids. They are attracted to the starch in sapwood and are hard to discourage. To persuade beetles to relocate, I've injected turpentine into their holes, and I've heated the wood with a heat gun or heat lamp until the beetles leave. The best approach is to leave behind any wood that has obvious holes made by insects. When you get home, if you discover any wood with stowaway beetles, throw it out.

Insects are less likely to inhabit driftwood, but you may find mildew and fungus on this type of wood; try stabilizing the wood with heat.

STORAGE

You can never be rich enough or have enough space to store sticks. That's a venerable truth. So make sure that whatever space you do have is dry and airy. That probably rules out a place behind the garage under a tarp, and it probably rules out the basement in the summer. It probably does make you think of the rafters in the garage, and maybe of building a rope-like scaffolding in your living room.

Wherever you store the wood, try to cut your wood into manageable lengths (48 inches [61 cm] or less). You will be appalled at how many times you have to move the same bundles of wood until you actually get to use them. And the shorter the lengths, the faster the wood dries.

RUSTIC JOINERY

RUSTIC WORKSHOP 101: JOINERY TECHNIQUES

(Brief summary): First you think and then you think some more. Then you cut. You mark. You drill. You whittle. You fit the pieces together. Then you look some more. Finally you tweak and glue.

That really is the whole picture. What varies is how you choose to join the pieces. There are several methods, ranging from a hammer and nail to the more challenging, but still fairly simple, mortise and tenon.

Before I review these traditional techniques, I would like to offer some alternatives. If rustic work is seen as a branch of woodworking, then the dominant woodworking tools and techniques would seem to be most sensible. But if you are making something rustic, which actually refers to life outside the dominant traditions—something "other"—then there is a world of techniques all competing for the attention of the Weekend Rustic.

For example, rustic fencing uses several forms of joinery techniques that can be applied to other forms of rustic work. The combination of pressure, weaving, and interlacing of branch material is a very effective and simple form of joinery. Sometimes, when you find a beautiful rustic stump or a piece of driftwood or a few beach stones, the most ancient form of joinery, gravity, works best. Simply put the objects down and watch how they stay there. Walls and split rail fences are made this way.

There are other techniques even more fanciful. I have seen pieces of small rustic chairs joined with yarn, hot wax, hot glue, and Velcro. If you are a rustic inventor and not just a rustic drone, then there are no weird joints, just weird people. These rustic makers are experimenting with the conventional sense of time; they are not impressed with making something that seems immortal. They are joining a sense of humor and play and a message of the fleetingness of life into their work.

CONVENTIONAL CONSTRUCTION WITH NAILS AND SCREWS

Mechanical techniques and devices are fine for getting two pieces of wood to stay together for a long while. All you need to do is position the pieces of tree where you want them, and put a nail into that spot, or a screw or lag screw, or a bolt. You can also use a wooden peg or dowel. It helps to predrill the top piece of wood with a bit that is slightly larger than the screw or nail, the head of the screw or nail squeezes the first piece of wood tightly against the second. These joints are usually face joints where one piece of wood overlaps and crosses another. The appeal of this method is the quickness and relative simplicity of the tools and skills involved. The main drawback is the appearance of all those cut ends of wood blinking out from the finished piece. Another drawback is that you have to add diagonal pieces to prevent racking, pivoting, or hinging—the professional terms for wiggling.

Nails are the fastest and crudest form of this type of joinery. Nails go into the wood and resist coming out, so you probably only have one chance to decide which way you like things put together. Laura Spector puts her nails in with a heavy-duty, air-driven nailer. Andy Gardner uses a hammer.

("I see you used nails," says the Gremlin to the Rustic. "Yeah, so what!" says the Rustic.) I use mechanical joints for certain table designs and I think they are appropriate. The appearance of very small-headed trim screws has helped make the evidence of the mechanical joint less evident. But even if these nails or screws are very evident, there is an honesty in building and using ordinary supplies that is important in rustic work.

Author [Daniel Mack] using an electric drill to drive screws.

THE RUSTIC PRINCIPLE OF REVERSIBILITY

Mechanical joints—screws, bolts, braces, and brackets, but not nails—move the job right along and can often be reversed or changed if the results need changing. Remember, rustic work is interactive design: one never really knows how a project is going to turn out until it's done.

Other mechanical joints include rope for lashing, and wire for lacing and sewing. In this application, the rustic is again not thinking like a woodworker, but as a sailor, seamstress, tailor, cook, cobbler, farmer, tinker. We all have old tradespeople buried in our DNA. There are "old ways" just waiting to be invited to the Rustic Workshop.

MORTISE AND TENON JOINERY

The prevailing construction technique in rustic work is the mortise and tenon—that's the old peg-in-the-hole, time-honored approach. The joinery is strong and makes the piece look like "real" furniture. It also takes a while to do. Put very simply, for most rustic work, a round peg is made on the end of one tree part, and this part fits snugly and deeply into an identically sized hole in the outer tree part. Make sure to use very dry wood for your tenon (or peg). If a wet tenon shrinks as it does in the hole, the joint may wobble.

WAYS OF MAKING HOLES

The simplest way to make a hole is to use an electric drill with a sharp bit that puts the hole right where you want it. This means that the tip of the bit has to bite into the knurly, round face of the tree part and cut an accurate hole. For this job there are several different bits you can use.

Brad point bits have one sharp little toothy tang that keeps the bit from drifting. Sometimes these bits, also referred to as Bullet Bits or Irwin Bits, are available in hardware stores.

Spade bits are big flat bits with a long fang to keep themselves in place. I like these bits, but they are very hungry for wood and will eat right through a small piece of wood. So use them on big wood, over 1¼ inches in diameter. Under that diameter, use brad point bits. These bits are good for rustic work requiring holes from ⅝ inch to 1½ inches in diameter.

Big bits and extra long bits are available in some hardware stores, as well as in building-supply centers and plumbing and electrical-supply outlets. These may be needed for making 2-inch diameter holes for beds and big benches; the long bits may be needed for lamps or other unusual projects.

These bits fit in any of the electric drills on the market. I have a few different drills and prefer the cordless ones if I have enough extra batteries available.

FINISHES FOR BARK

Finishing a rustic piece with a 1:1 mixture of boiled linseed oil and turpentine or mineral spirits changes the color of the wood. A finish of this type keeps the energy of the piece going: it's unexpected; the wood still looks like a tree and feels so smooth. This recipe works well for all types of wood with bark, except cherry and birch, which don't absorb liquids very well.

Here's what you do:

Saw or grind any branch scars or rough bark areas that are too sharp or abrasive.

Fine sand these areas only with a finer paper until you get them as smooth as desired.

With a fine paper (220 or 150) or a sanding sponge, wipe down the rest of the piece, emphasizing areas of possible wear with a little extra sanding. Don't dig in too much. The purpose is to clean off dirt, small burrs, and open the surface of the bark so the oil mixture can be absorbed easily.

Put on neoprene gloves and wipe the mixture onto the wood.

After a day or two repeat the oil application and let the wood dry thoroughly.

Wipe down the wood with a cloth.

Apply a wax with 0000 steel wool; then buff.

TAKE YOUR CHOICE: HAND AND POWER TOOLS FOR CUTTING TENONS

There are several ways to cut tenons or pegs for rustic furniture. There are many hand tools available that the casual maker can learn to use pretty quickly. There are a few ways to make these tenons with power tools, as well.

HAND TOOLS

A selection of hand tools for cutting tenons, left to right: Hatchet, pocket knife, brace operated hollow-auger and spoke pointer, and the Veritas tenon cutter

This is a quick and crude way to get a stick shaped down to fit in a hole.

Whittling gives you much more control... and calluses. Sometimes people start with the hatchet and finish up with the knife.

This recent tool, the Veritas tenon cutter, is really just a knife blade mounted in a solid wood block. When properly adjusted, it can quickly cut an accurate tenon.

POWER TOOLS

Several power tools for cutting tenons, clockwise from upper left: 18v cordless drill, heads for a stationary industrial tenon machine, Veritas tenon cutters, hole saws, spur cutters.

Veritas tenon cutter for a drill. This cutter tapers the wood as it cuts and often a pre-tapering is not needed. It puts a curved shoulder on the tenon which is very obvious. There is a level built in to help keep the tenon straight on the wood.

Spur cutters fit only a ½" drill or a drill press, leaving a collar to be trimmed off. To start, the wood has to be tapered with a grinder, rasp, or spoke pointer.

WAYS OF MAKING TENONS

The better the fit, the stronger the joint. So there is quite a bit of care required to make a good tenon.

Whittling is a time-honored method: it's just very careful hatchet work. You use a sharp knife to whittle an almost perfect cylinder on the end of the stick. This needs to be done so well that the pieces actually squeak when you fit them together. If you succeed, you will feel proud and amazed, and then you will spend the next 20 minutes looking at the blisters on your right hand! I spent the first three years of building staring at these blisters which quickly turned into calluses.

Rasping is a folk approach to tenon-making. Here, a piece of wood, held in a vise, is filed away with a rasp of shirform tool, and made to fit the hole. People who don't like knives and don't want to use electric cutters are "raspers." It works.

ANTIQUE TOOLS

There is a pair of tools, the spoke pointer and the hollow auger, that used to be the Fred Astaire and Ginger Rogers of rustic work—lovely, traditional, the reference for all else. They were brace-operated. They are now somewhat difficult to find. If you find them, they will have to be adjusted and the small blades sharpened frequently. But they work. The spoke pointer, like a big pencil sharpener, tapers the wood to a point small enough to fit into the hollow auger, which is a two-edged cutter that makes perfect tenons of various diameters.

Veritas tenon cutters have revolutionized the rustic world. Sculptor and arts teacher, Paul Ruhlmann, saw the antique hollow auger and spoke pointer at a workshop I taught in the early 1990s. He saw how fussy the old tools were—and they are hard to find. But he also observed what a great job the cutters did. So he developed two different types. One fits into a brace and works quietly; the other fits into a ⅜-inch electric drill and sounds like a piglet. They both cut accurate, handsome pegs. And they are affordable.

Selection of tenon making tools and their product, left to right: pocket knife for whittling; Veritas tenon cutter for brace; spur cutter for drill.

Hole saws, spur-headed tenon cutters, and lathes can all be used to make tenons. I suggest that a new weekend rustic builder use a knife, or the Veritas cutters, or invent some personal way to accomplish this task.

Another way to make a mortise and tenon joint is to use a traditional woodworking blind-dowel joint. For rustic work, you will need to put a hole in both tree parts to be joined; then you insert and glue a length of purchased dowel between the two members.

Continued ➡

DESIGN TECHNIQUES (OR) WHAT SHOULD I MAKE?

One very workable approach to get you started is to find a nice chair, table, or bookcase, and copy it using sticks for parts. Don't worry—no intellectual property lawyers will come after you. And you will be amazed at how the sticks will change even the simplest design of a table, bench, or chair. There is an easy design approach described in the Panel Section, and great-looking rustic work throughout the book to inspire you.

CONSTRUCTION TECHNIQUES: WHAT GLUE DO YOU USE?

After you've made the holes and squeaked the near-perfect tenons into them, you must take it all apart and glue it. You must. Carefully wipe regular yellow carpenter's glue on all faces of the wood and then fit the pieces back together. I often mark each piece and its position with chalk so it ends up looking like it first did. It's very important that you clamp or strap the glued pieces together for the first four to six hours after you glue them. Most carpenter's glues set under pressure. Bar clamps and vise clamps are okay, but web clamps or strap clamps are best for conforming to the usually odd shapes of rustic work. There are several new glues on the market that set chemically, but I haven't used them.

FINISHING: WHAT DO YOU DO AFTER IT'S DONE?

After the frame is assembled, there is still a task ahead to get the piece "finished" so it looks like more than a bunch of tree parts glued together. This finishing is a process of softening and aging the look of the piece. Some rustic woods resist finishing. Golden birch is "finished" almost as soon as you have decided to use it; so is cherry and white birch—although all of these can handle a coat of tung oil varnish to make them look a little less "new."

For maple, hickory, and beech, I sand with 220-grit paper and then apply several costs of boiled linseed oil, cut with mineral spirits (50/50). Then I wax over that and buff.

Staining rustic work is something I do only when asked. Sometimes the client wants a very consistent color in the finished piece. In that case, I lightly sand the bark, stain the piece with a walnut stain, finish with a linseed oil and mineral spirit mix, and then wax and buff.

With peeled woods, I apply an oil-base urethane, followed by a clear butcher's wax applied with 0000 steel wool; then I buff.

To preserve driftwood's weathered look, but to make it feel smooth, I lightly sand it with a 220-grit paper to remove the dirt and burrs. Then, just to harden the surface, I apply a coat of acrylic urethane, diluted with water 50/50. Lastly, I wax over that using 0000 steel wool. Then I buff the wood.

OTHER WAYS TO FINISH WOOD

An oil finish makes the wood look like old leather. Basically, the finish I like best is one that makes the wood look old. Here are two other techniques I have been using in the last few years for finishing and aging raw wood.

White vinegar, when applied with steel wool, reacts with certain woods to turn them a darker color—from a silver toning on maple to jet black on cedar. I'm still experimenting with the number of applications, the use of the sun, and various woods. But on this fresh red cedar, I was able to speed up the aging process so that the wood looked the way out cedar would if left outside for a year or so. This gave the newly finished piece a consistency of tone.

Lye, usually a tablespoon to a quart of warm water, wiped on cherry wood, darkens and deepens the color to what it would be after years of exposure to the light.

For both of these treatments, I wear neoprene gloves and safety goggles, and I try to work outside the shop. Then I apply a polyurethane or oil finish, over the raw wood treatment, and finish with a wax applied with 0000 steel wool.

Please notice that these treatments give an inconsistent result; that is, there are darker parts and lighter parts. This is not a negative for me: the effect reflects the subtle inconsistencies of all rustic materials. I prefer the inconsistency. There is a homemade quality to them or to the way I do them that I like. Stains from cans are so predictable and dull compared to the vibrancy of some of these old-time finishing techniques. Remember, they work on raw, unfinished wood.

SEATING TECHNIQUES

Seating is the last frontier of rustic work. Everybody's sense of what's "right" is a bit different. I won't attempt to convince you that my current attraction to the upholstered seat is more or less "correct." There are several ways to work.

The wooden rustic seat is very traditional. Planks of wood are screwed or nailed or pegged onto the frame. These pieces might be small, full-round branches, splits of a small log that are band sawed or sanded and grinded out, or worked on a shaving horse with a drawknife. A wooden seat of this type keeps the country-tree-rustic feel of the chair frame going.

Woven seats are often the most comfortable. Various materials are interwoven onto the chair frame. Shaker types have been popular and are available, with instructions, from a variety of places. But first, I suggest you go to a local upholstery shop to look for belting or cording or even materials that can be folded into strips and woven. Craft-supply stores carry a wide variety of natural and manufactured materials suitable for weaving. Large building-supply stores carry a variety of ropes, strings, and other materials that can be crafted into use as seating. Approach these places with the same sense of adventure you bring to the woods. Directions for the weaving can be found at craft shops.

Upholstered seats are my favorite. With these, I cut a piece of ⅝-inch (16 mm) plywood to fit the seat frame of the chair. I drill four holes in the center area of the seat board to let air in and out. Then I take the board to my local upholsterer with a fabric I have selected, and have it professionally covered as a tight seat, or a seat with welting, or any of the options offered. Then I screw the finished seat into the frame from beneath, through a hole I have predrilled, so that the screw head is countersunk.

I tried upholstery myself and quickly learned that my rustic upholstery looks cheesy. Other rustics, like Michelle Ellsworth seem to have a greater talent for doing this themselves.

Insider Tips from a Rustic Maker

West Coast builder Gordon Grabe sent along a few of his time-tested methods of working with natural wood.

VINEGAR AND IRON WOOD STAIN

I use a mixture of vinegar and steel wool to forcibly age the ends of branches and bare wood.

The Formula:

   1 gallon of vinegar
   2 washed pads of steel wool.

Stuff the steel wool pads down the neck of a jug and cover the jug opening with cloth, securing with a string or rubber band around the neck. Important Note: Do not seal jug with a screw cap; a chemical reaction is taking place and the jug will explode!

This formula works best with woods containing tannic acid. Most hardwoods and softwoods, such as pine, have tannic acid. One of the exceptions is oleander, which contains oxalic acid; this acid will actually bleach out the effects of the vinegar and iron natural wood stain. This is true for citric acid or fabric bleach, as well. A solution of water and potassium permanganate or a solution of water and baking soda also reacts with tannic acid, each giving a different color of stains.

I apply the vinegar/iron stain with a brush. The stain will darken with age; the concentration of the solution and the moisture in the air cause the wood to darken. Making tests with different concentrations over a period of a month or so will give you a good gauge as to what the properties of your formula should be. Tip: Low concentrations are the best way to start. I've been surprised as to how long-acting and powerful this stain is. Suggestion: Try 1 cup of water to 1 tablespoon of a one-week-old vinegar and steel wool solution. You may want to strain the steel wool out of the jug and label the jug, using it to mix from as you need it.

These chemicals have been used for centuries and are discussed in a lot of books on woodworking, but their application in the rustic craft is not much talked about. There seems to be a gap in old traditional woodworking techniques and the rustic furniture techniques. It seems like there has been little communication between the two woodworking traditions.

PEELING WOOD

Be careful using pressure washers to peel bark; they'll blow the bark away on old dried branches, and, on new branches, they can blow right gown to the wood and beyond, if you're not careful.

The "no pressure wash" that I use the most is to soak branches in water, alternating with periods of drying, over a period of two months. I have a creek out back, and, when it's running, I soak a tied bundle of branches. It's just like making your own driftwood.

CURING BRANCHES

If you put wax on the ends of your cut branches, it will prevent them from cracking and splitting.

FINISHES

For bare wood indoor furniture I use a paste wax only. If I leave the bark on, I use a clear, waterborne, satin polyurethane varnish. Varnishing bark toughens the loose parts of the bark. For outdoor furniture I use varnish, linseed oil, and turpentine mixed equal parts.

ORNAMENTALS

I have made furniture using mulberry, oleander, Japanese plum, Hollywood juniper, persimmon, twisted willow, eucalyptus, rose cane, English walnut, and fig. We have a moderate climate out here in California where just about anything grows. I find that using ornamentals adds more choices to the rustic furniture maker's palette. One of my favorite pieces is a rose cane basket with a fig branch handle. It's for carrying roses in from the garden!

Tools

Four rustic tools you already have: the Body, the Eye, Time, and the Hand.

Normal woodworking tools are made for handling lumber, a distant cousin—the American Cheese—of trees. These tools are meant to make things straight and flat. There is almost nothing like that in the woods. The woods are bumpy, curved, sinuous, and arching. The Woods reflect perfectly the crooked ways of life. It's difficult, sometimes unpleasant, to be reminded of this, so it's tempting to dismiss the woods and the Rustic Furniture which reflects it, as unrefined, clumsy, and oafish.

Rustic woodworking offers a doorway into another world of making where you must discover and confront your own sense of design and proportion and invoke the beautiful in your own way. It's an opportunity for a meandering, impromptu encounter where all of several choices might work.

The key tool is the Body. It provides the essential frame of reference—the viewpoint on the world and the physical connection to gesture, the human animation through which we convey unspoken messages to our fellows. Our body and the bodies of others are a rich grammar of emotion and action. The gesture of the arm, the foot, the extended hand, the arched back, the tilted head, the open chest...body language is a fundamental part of all furniture and especially rustic furniture. When these gestures are discovered and selected from the trees, they become doubly powerful as the message of furniture because, along with the gesture intended by the furniture maker, is the residual shape, texture, and history of the tree itself.

The Eye estimates. It admires, sizes up, approves, squints, winces at the rights and wrongs of making work from trees; I believe we all have an aesthetic sense. It may not be highly practiced, but in every course I teach, the people who claim they have "no eye" for this work are the ones who become very choosy about branches of the right diameter, curve, or texture. With a little encouragement, their personal sense of beauty starts to emerge, and they begin to feel a special kind of authorship for their work.

Rustic woodworking requires an altered sense of Time. The rustic worker is linked to the rhythms of the seasons for cutting and drying wood, to the mysteries of various tree blights and insect attacks, and to the creative rhythm of making something without a pre-set design. Rustic woodworking is responsive woodworking: responsive to the seasons, the idiosyncrasies of individual trees, and the murkiness of the creative process. The moods of the maker are affected by time. I try to think about what's going on, what time of day it is...is this a good time to keep working? I try to pay attention to the less than loud voices that are always informing me about what's going on. Intuition and patience are a few of the key attitudes required in good making. All of this makes for less than a production-line schedule. It's hard to predict when certain rustic projects will get finished. In that way, rustic woodworking seems a bit out of control and gets talked about as a folk art or native furniture.

The Hand is the Proto-tool. It has strength and near-infinite motions to grasp, turn, angle, pose, position, twist, grab, and discard. Units of measurement are hand-based: the inch, a pinch, a handful, two fingers. Remember, hands are not perfect; they are different sizes. Fingers have been cut, sliced, and healed oddly; fingers curl and stiffen. Strength comes and goes.

OTHER TOOLS—EXTENSIONS OF THE HAND

There are only really three kinds of invented tools needed for rustic work; they are all extensions of your hands. There is now a very rich selection of tools available, with great attention paid to balance, ergonomics, beauty, and even the fact that people other than 200-pound loggers might wan to use a tool. You need:

1. Cutting and shaping tools, used for getting the wood into the sizes and forms you can use;

2. Drilling tools, for making the holes for pegs, tenons or nails and screws;

3. Assembly tools, for getting and keeping the work together.

CUTTING TOOLS

Not surprisingly, these include saws. I like the folding camping and pruning saws; they fit into your back pocket, and the blades have fast-cut double-set teeth. The new Fiskars model has a very comfortable black handle and a good blade locking system. Both the Coghlan's and Coleman folding camping saw work well also. These saws can also be used in the shop for bench work, but I like a bigger saw. The Jack Pro or the Stanley Shortcut are both short enough and rigid enough for good bench trimming.

I use several power saws. I have several chain saws—a few gas-powered ones (which I haven't used in years) for the woods, and a few of the smallest electric ones I can find, usually with a 10-inch bar. This one is very helpful for roughing various projects in and just outside the shop; it's small enough to still be an extension of my body, and it doesn't spit out all the exhaust of the gas models.

I have used a 10-inch miter saw or chop saw for the last ten years as my primary shop saw. I now use a 12-inch DeWalt; it's comfortable and reliable, and the fence is big enough to wedge odd-shaped sticks against it.

I have a circular saw and a newer 18-volt battery operated one that handles a lot of the simpler flat cutting jobs.

I have never owned a table saw, but I did have a 12-inch radial arm saw in one shop for about seven years. It was more than I needed and had the habit of dominating me every few eeeks by spitting a stick through the window. I abandoned it when I left that shop.

I keep a few Japanese dozuki saws near my worktable, but the blades are generally too thin for the quirks of rustic work.

OTHER CUTTING TOOLS

Clippers are very important to me. I have several different kinds, and more, if you add loppers into the category. Clippers, loppers let me cut up to 1-inch (25 mm) stock with just the squeeze of a hand. The kinds I use are rachet operated.

SANDING-GRINDING

I consider sanding tools a variation of cutting tools: they remove stock.

The key took here is a sander-grinder—not the disc that goes on the electric drill—but a tool of its own. It's faster than a drill-sanding attachment, and really lets me shape and sculpt the ends of sticks. Plus, it softens knots, branch scars, and swells.

I have lots of different sanders: belt sanders, palm sanders, random orbital sanders...they all get used sometimes. But I also like the palm-size sanding sponges that come with different grits on opposite sides. These sponges let you respond gently to the contours of rustic work in a way a power sanding device cannot.

DRILLING TOOLS

I use an old Craftsman drill press from 1962 that I bought at a yard sale. It's simple and friendly. And I like the way it looks back at me; it has a nice face.

I must have a dozen other drills: old ¼-inch (6.5 mm) chrome-bodied ones from the '50s and '60s, as well as a good assortment of ones with cords and ones that are battery operated. It's essential to own a ½-inch (13 mm) drill; this means the opening on the chuck is big enough to take an attachment, such as a drill bit, which has a ½-inch (13 mm) diameter shank. This kind of drill is very powerful boring into green and dry wood, and will throw you around if you're not holding on very tight. Some come with an additional side handle. I may have three or four drills ready on any one building project. Each will have a different drill bit or screwdriver head or chamfering bit.

HOLDING TOOLS

I can still count all 10 of my fingers, thank you. That is due, in part, to how I hold tools.

There are several methods for holding tools. For example, when I use the drill press, I usually use V-blocks to hold stock. Sometimes I use a drill-press vise. Sometimes I use spring clamps or vise clamps to hold something together while I drill. I'll use pipe clamps to really pull a panel together, and I'm always using strap clamps or webclamps in my chairmaking. I have a few dollies around the shop to hold and move boxes. There are a few bench-mounted vises; the Workmate table is a good holding tool. I'm always grabbing for the vise grips, channel pliers, or needle-nose pliers.

TIPS ABOUT TOOLS AND STICKS

It's an unhappy relationship...what can I say? The toolmakers think flat and square when they design tools. Nature doesn't think—it's all this way and that...fluid-curvy. That's what we rustics are drawn to. So there has to be some extra thought given to using tools, especially power tools with natural forms.

WORK DOWN.

Get a worktable that you can rest your elbows on comfortably. This will allow you to have more control over the work and the tools. Work with your arm as close in to your body as possible. You'll have more coordination and be able to use all your strength. This is especially important for women; the right height worktable will give you maximum control on the tools and the work. You have the best chance to make work rather than tire yourself fighting the table. Try working at different height tables to see what I mean. I have three different height worktables for different kinds of projects, and I still find myself on my knees on the floor a lot.

STING THE WOOD.

Again, most tools are made for addressing flat lumber. For the round, erratically round, surfaces of rustic work, you need tools which bite in or sting the wood where you want to. The Speedbore bits have a long toothy tang and there are a lot of brad-pointed bits around—drill bits with a small sharp tooth in the center to keep the bit in place so it doesn't wander or jump.

DRESS FOR THE JOB.

I now wear gloves as much as possible: thin, tight leather "ranch-hand" gloves for handling material, latex gloves for some finishing, and neoprene gloves for work with bleach, lye, and other finishes.

I try to keep my shirttails tucked in...there are a lot of hungry spinning devices around.

KEEP THE AIR CLEAN.

I have a three-part air filter in my 5400-cubic-foot shop, and recently I put in an air ionizer and ozonator. When I have to sand in the shop. I hook a vacuum up to a sanding tray.

Continued →

Tool List

A list of the tools and supplies I used in my shop last year.

Cutting

De Walt 18v cordless
DeWalt 12v cordless
Drill press
Extra batteries
Makita 7.2v cordless

½-inch (13 mm) Porter cable corded
Chargers
Makita corded

Drills

Folding handsaw
DeWalt 12-inch (30.5 mm) miter saw
Fiskars loppers
Surform rasps
Shortcut or jacksaw

Pruning clippers
Hitachi corded circular saw
Circular DeWalt 18v cordless
Knives/chisels
Electric chain saw

Drill Bits

Full set brad point
Short/extra long bits

Large bits 1½" (38 mm)
Speedbore bits

Tenon Cutting

Lee Valley tenon cutters
Hole saws

Spoke pointer

Electric

Extension cord
Webar

Halogen clamp light
3-prong to 2-prong adaptor

Holding

Workmate table
Needle nose pliers
Tension clamps
Vise grips
Quick Grip clamps
Web clamps

C-clamps
Channel pliers
Vises
Pipe clamps
Folding sawhorses
V-blocks

Other Tools

Hammer
Sawhorses
Tape measure
Hachet/adze
Rubber mallet

Grinder discs
Random orbital sander/paper
Sander/grinder

Supplies

Trim head screws
String/rope
Sandpaper
Polyurethane glue
Duct tape
Tarps
Pens/pencils
Level
Extra heads #1 and #2
Finishing nails
Sanding sponges
Epoxy
Masking tape
Flashlight

Chalk
Chalk line
Decking screws
Linseed oil
Carpenter's glue
Tacks/brads
Rags
Broom
Extra driver heads
Framing square
Pliers
Allen wrenches
Vacuum cleaner
Compass

Safety

Work gloves
Finger tape
Adhesive bandages

Dust mask
Peroxide
Safety glasses

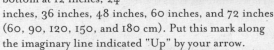

Projects

Building Approaches to Projects

In this section I start by explaining and illustrating the primary way I build rustic furniture by making simple ladders or panels and joining them together. For some of you this will be the "aha" you've been wanting. You'll see several kinds of furniture you can make with a simple ladder construction.

Secondly, I explain and illustrate how I make one particular form of furniture: a table. I show different construction approaches, some of which will be more appealing to you than others.

Thirdly, like a good magician, I disappear...or seem to. I invited eight weekend rustics to demonstrate how they make things. This gives you a chance to see other ways of thinking and working with natural-form materials. On the way, I offer a number of asides that reflect my experience as a rustic builder and as a maker of things. For instance, I have a particular admiration of joinery using only gravity.

I would suggest reading through the three sections first. Then you can decide in what way you want to make projects and where to start. All the ways are fine.

MAKING PANELS

One orderly way to create rustic furniture is to make panels. I take four, five, six, or more pieces of wood and combine them into frames, ladders, or panels; then I join them to form chairs, beds, tables, bookcases, room dividers, arbors, fences, gates, stools, etc. When you make panels, you are reducing and simplifying the number of pieces of wood you are working with—combining several pieces to make one panel. At the end, you have one piece of furniture. This approach has served me well in my 20 years of building.

The panel can be made by attaching the wood pieces with nails, screws, glue, rope, or rawhide. Some of these methods work better than others with particular materials and designs. Experiment to see what works best for what you are trying to make.

Making a Seven-Foot Ladder

The ladder form is the basis of the panel. It's made with two vertical upright posts and several horizontal rungs or stretchers, and, if you like, a diagonal or two.

WHAT YOU NEED

2 straight posts of 2- to 2½-inch (50–64 cm) saplings, each about 84 inches (213 cm) long

6 rungs of 2-inch (5 cm) saplings, each about 18 inches (46 cm) long

measuring tape

cutting tools

black marker

vise and vise clamps
chalk
tenon-cutting tools
drill with ¾-inch (2 cm) spade bit or brad bit in a drill press
rubber mallet
hammer
finishing nails

WHAT YOU DO

1. Cut the posts square on the bottoms.

2. Hold the posts together so they line up; then mark arrows on the bottoms to help you remember the lined-up position.

3. Lay out your posts so they will stay straight and in place. You can accomplish this with a vise and vise clamps.

4. Use chalk to mark each post from the bottom at 12 inches, 24 inches, 36 inches, 48 inches, 60 inches, and 72 inches (60, 90, 120, 150, and 180 cm). Put this mark along the imaginary line indicated "Up" by your arrow.

5. Drill a ¾-inch (2 cm) hole about 1 inch into each of the posts at the indicated marks. You can do this with a spade bit in a drill or a brad bit in a drill press.

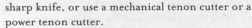

6. Prepare tenons on the ends of each of your rungs. Make sure the tenons are 1-inch (25 mm) cylinders. You can whittle the tenons with a sharp knife, or use a mechanical tenon cutter or a power tenon cutter.

7. Assemble the ladder by fitting all the rungs into one post and then into the other. You may have to twist each rung until you find the best way to fit them all together.

8. Use a rubber mallet to get a secure fit.

9. Put a small finishing nail through the face of the ladder, into the tenon.

10. If the ladder racks or wiggles, you may want to add one or two 45-degree diagonal braces to steady it. Use scraps of 1-inch saplings for this purpose.

Basic Bookcase

Here's some advice on building a bookcase using two tall ladders. The finished bookcase shown here is about 36 inches wide, 48 inches tall, and 12 inches deep (90 x 120 x 60 cm). Once you've built this one, you'll have your own ideas about variations to make it taller, wider, or narrower, perhaps with deeper shelves or more decoration.

WHAT YOU NEED

For the two ladders

4 posts of 2-inch saplings, each 60 inches (150 cm) tall

4 rungs of 1-inch saplings, each 13 inches (33 cm) long

For the two stretchers

2 pieces cut from 1-inch saplings, each 36 inches (90 cm) long

measuring tape

cutting tools

Surform rasp

tenon-cutting tool

drill and assorted bits

rubber mallet

screwdriver

decking screws

WHAT YOU DO

Building the Ladders and Frame

1. Make the two ladders, following the instructions [for "Making a Seven-Foot Ladder"].

2. Now make the four stretchers.

3. Put ¾-inch (19 mm) tenons, 1 inch (25 mm) deep, on each end.

4. Drill holes into the face of each ladder post, measured up from the bottom at 11 inches and 47 inches (28 and 119 cm).

5. Assemble the bookcase frame by putting all the rungs into one ladder, then fit the other on in place. Twist the stretchers until there is a snug fit and the frame sits squarely on the floor. Because of the variations in natural forms, you may choose to replace one or two of the 36-inch (60 cm) long stretchers with shorter or longer ones.

6. After this basic frame is acceptable, knock it apart; then glue the tenons into the mortises or cross nail each joint with a finishing nail.

Adding Shelves

This bookcase was designed for regular 1 x 12 lumber from your local building-supply outlet. You can choose pine or hardwoods or the composite shelving sold by many of these stores.

7. Measure the distance from the outside edges of the ladders that make up the sides of your bookcase. If you made it as I suggested, that distance should be about 36 inches (60 cm).

8. Now cut your shelving about 2 inches (51 mm) longer than that measurement.

9. Measure the distance between the posts of your ladder; that might be about 11 inches (28 cm). Your store-bought shelves are about 11½ inches, which means you'll have to take a little notch out of each corner of your 36-inch-long (60 cm) shelves to make them fit and look fitted. There are several ways to do this, using a handsaw, jigsaw, or Surform rasp.

10. Put your shelves in place and straighten up the bookcase, making sure it's not leaning too much in any one direction. If you're happy with what you see, fix the shelves in place with screws from the bottom side or the top side. You should predrill the wood first.

11. How does the bookcase look? Done? Congratulations!

12. Not quite done? Does it wiggle? Add a few curved braces. Does it look too square? Cut the front posts down to 1 inch above the shelf. Does it look too bare? Add a few decorative pieces on the back, front, or sides. Does it look too new? You can sand the edges of the boards, or you can sand the saplings a bit and put some linseed oil on the wood. If you want, you can paint the shelves. Does it still wiggle? You can brace the bookcase right to the wall when you find the perfect place for it.

Four-Panel Room Screen

This is one way to build a room screen or divider using a basic panel construction. The one shown here measures about 48 inches wide, 84 inches tall, and 12 inches deep. Depending on the materials you collect, yours might have only three panels, be wider or shorter, or have more or less embellishment.

WHAT YOU NEED

For the four ladders

8 posts of 2-inch (51 mm) saplings, each 84 inches (213 cm) tall

16 rungs of 1-inch (25 mm) saplings, each 22 inches (59 cm) long

measuring tape

cutting tools

tenon-cutting tool

drill and assorted bits

150-grit sandpaper or sanding sponge

mixture of 50/50 boiled linseed oil and mineral spirits

4 pairs of rawhide boot laces, 36 inches (60 cm) long

materials for decorating the screen

WHAT YOU DO

Building the Ladders

1. Follow the instructions for "Making a Seven-Foot Ladder", but omit the rungs at 36 and 48 inches (60 and 120 cm).

2. Do you like the gray color of the wood? If so, skip ahead to step 5.

3. Do the ladders look too rough? If so, lightly sand the ladders with a 150-grit sandpaper or sanding sponge; then rub on a mixture of 50/50 boiled linseed oil and mineral spirits to darken the wood.

4. Do you want the wood to be lighter? Add water to white latex paint to get a 50/50 mix, and rub it on with a soft rag. Let the paint dry. Then lightly sand the wood and oil it as described in step 3.

Assembling the Screen

5. Lay a pair of ladders next to each other on the floor, about an inch apart.

6. Tie the pair together loosely with rawhide laces, just above the top rung and again just above the bottom rung. Repeat this procedure with the next pair of ladders. Last, join both pairs together, as shown in the photograph below.

7. Stand the screen up and admire your work so far.

8. You have built a room divider with a hole in the middle of every panel. What do you want to do with it now? Here are a few suggestions: You can staple on sheets of translucent Japanese paper to create an oriental affect. Fabric tied to the panels in strategic places could look beautiful. You can weave leather over and under the rungs. How about gluing or nailing on delicate twigs and sprigs of berries? You can string beads or seashells onto string and tie them to the screen. These are just a few possibilities.

PANEL CHAIRS

A good way to sneak up on the challenges of chair-making is to make a panel chair. A chair made from two panels can serve as a model for deciding what you like and want to change about the next chair.

First, construct a ladder that is 45 inches (114 cm) tall. Position the first rung 7 inches up from the floor, the next at 15 inches, the next at 20 inches, and the last at 40 inches (38, 51, and 101 cm). Use rungs that are 16 inches (40 cm) long. This modified ladder will give you the rung positioning for the seat and back supports of a chair. You may want to vary these numbers somewhat when you build other chairs of this type.

For the front, make a small panel measuring 24 inches tall, with the first rung positioned at 7 inches and the second at 15 inches (61, 18, and 101 cm). Again, use rungs that are 16 inches long. Many chairs are trapezoids, with the front measuring up to four inches wider than the

Continued ➡

back. This front rung could be 20 inches long, if necessary.

Join the two panels with 16-inch long rungs, attached 9 inches and 16 inches from the floor (41, 23, and 40 cm).

The front legs have been left long enough to accept arms. If you don't want arms, saw them off after the chair has been glued together and has dried. To complete the chair, take a look at the discussions of finishing and seating.

Panel Benches

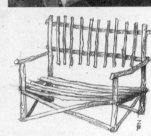

This panel bench is a very simple design in which the top rung is also the back support. This bench doesn't have any twiggy designs in it and can be made from any kinds of wood. The seat is rough cut wood, screwed into the front and back panels to create a rigid form.

This particular panel bench is 36 inches high and 48 inches wide (90, 120 cm). The top rail in the back is positioned 27 inches from the floor and the next ones down are at 14 inches and 7 inches (68, 35, and 38 cm). The front panel has just one rung, positioned 15 inches (38 cm) from the floor. The side rungs are at 9 inches and 21 inches (23 and 53 cm). I do not glue these pieces together. I clamp them and put a screw through the joints.

A panel bench is a very good way to learn to make a rustic bed. Just imagine the side rungs stretched out about 6 feet (1.8 m): there, a bed! For a twin-size bed, use rungs 38 inches wide; for a full size, use rungs 54 inches wide; for queen size, use rungs 60 inches; for king size, use rungs 76 inches wide (and beefy) (96, 137, 152, and 193 cm). For side rails, the twin and full use 80-inch-long rungs, and the queen- and king-size beds use 84-inch-long rungs (203 and 213 cm).

Tables

The tables I am describing here are merely ways of seducing you into becoming a Maker. After your first success, you will have this object, this little defenseless table that you made. It will need a home, a place. It will begin to generate stories around itself—stories of you, of making—and stories are what hold life together. It may not be The Greatest Story Ever Told...but how many of them can there be?

In this section of the book you will find three different approaches to making tables. You will no doubt discover many more of your own.

How big are tables? As big as you want!

Tables are somewhat more standard than chairs, although they should cooperate with the needs of the user and the surrounding furniture. Key decisions for dining tables involve the distance to set back the legs from the ends and sides to give stability yet allow for easy sitting on the ends and sides. Each person should have 24 inches of tabletop and the apron should be 24 inches from the floor (61 cm). Another variable is the finished height from the floor; this varies from 29 to 31 inches (74 to 79 cm). Often rustic tables include roots and twisted branches that eat up available space and diminish the utility of the table.

DINING TABLES

Sample size and seating capacity

Rectangular tables

L" x W"	Seating
120 x 48 (305 x 122 cm)	1–12 people
108 x 48 (274 x 122 cm)	8–10 people
84 x 42 (213 x 107 cm)	8 people
72 x 36 (103 x 91 cm)	6 people
60 x 30 (152 x 76 cm)	4 people

Square tables

L" x W"	Seating
60 x 60 (152 x 152 cm)	8–12 people
54 x 54 (137 x 137 cm)	6–8 people
48 x 48 (122 x 122 cm)	6–8 people
42 x 42 (107 x 107 cm)	4 people
36 x 36 (91 x 91 cm)	4 people

Round tables

Diameter	Seating
60" round (152 cm)	7–8 people
48" round (122 cm)	5–6 people
42" round (107 cm)	4–5 people

Other Tables

	Height	Length	Width
Coffee	14–18" (35–46 cm)	min. 24" (61 cm)	min. 20" (51 cm)
Sofa Table	26–31" (66–79 cm)	min. 60" (152 cm)	12–18" (30–46 cm)
Side Table	19–21" (48–53 cm)	24" (61 cm)	8" (20 cm)
Nightstand	21–27" (53–69 cm)	min. 12" (30 cm)	min. 12" (30 cm)
Desk	29–30" (73–76 cm)	min. 54" (137 cm)	min. 24" (61 cm)

BASIC PLANT STAND

This is a simple plant stand or side table measuring 12 inches square on top and 21 inches (30, 53 cm) tall. To make it, you can use any type of flat top. You might have an old breadboard, cabinet door, piece of marble or Formica. Everybody has flat things hidden somewhere. Tables from early in this century were made from parts of orange crates. These would make an excellent tabletop. Be resourceful. Potential tabletops are everywhere.

WHAT YOU NEED

Tabletop measuring 12 x 12 inches (30 x 30 cm)*

4 saplings, at least 2 inches in diameter, and about 20 inches long (5, 51 cm)

tape measure

drill with ⅝- or 1-inch bit (16 or 25 mm)

tenon-cutting tools

rubber mallet

wood glue

hammer

finishing nails

pencil

handsaw or rasp

This tabletop is a 2 x 12-inch piece of pine from a lumberyard.

WHAT YOU DO

1. Drill holes in the top. Depending on your sense of design and the size of your table, either a ⅝-inch hole or a 1-inch hole will work. The holes can go straight into the wood or at an angle. I sometimes use a drill press, but a hand-held drill is just fine, too.

2. Cut tenons on one end of each of the four legs. The tenons can be made in any of the ways described in the Techniques section.

3. Glue and/or nail the legs into the top.

4. After you've put the legs in, the table may still wiggle. You can use diagonals or angled cross pieces to steady up the table.

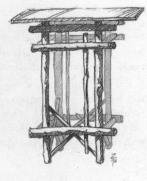

5. Now, even though the table is stable, it may not stand quite straight because one of the legs may be a little long. Is there never any end to these rustic surprises? Hang the long legs over the edge of the worktable, and mark with a pencil how much of it hangs off. Cut off that little wedge or coin size piece with a handsaw, or if it's really small, use a rasp to take it off.

Simple Panel Table

Sometimes I approach a table as if it's a chair with a flat top. This means I can use the panel method of building discussed earlier. I have made this table by connecting two panels or ladders, similar to the bookcase. What you have

to watch for is the leg and kick room needed for a table, which means that sometimes the stretchers are in the center of the piece. Susan Nagel built this table in a day.

WHAT YOU NEED

4 legs cut from 4-inch saplings, each about 18 inches long (10, 46 cm)

8 pieces for the stretchers, each about 4 inches wide and 24 inches long (10, 61 cm)

1 x 12 finished planed oak boards, ½ inch thick (13 mm)

4–6 battens, pieces of 1 x 3-inch (76 mm) wood

tape measure

cutting tools

tenon-cutting tools

rubber lammet

circular saw or jigsaw

drill with assorted bits

carpenter's glue

pipe clamps, bar clamps or web-strap clamps

sander-grinder, rasp, or sandpaper

hammer

nails

screwdriver

screws

sandpaper

linseed oil

mineral spirits

wood stain or polyurethane

paintbrush

WHAT YOU DO

1. The frame is made using the panel method described in "Making a Seven-Foot Ladder." Once you have test-fitted the panel, glue up the frame. Carpenter's glue needs to set under pressure, so it's good to clamp your frames together. Some people make a tourniquet-like clamp from rope or rubber tubing.

2. With a circular saw or jigsaw, trim the oak boards so they fit the size and shape of your base. You may want to round the edges with a sander-grinder, rasp, or just sandpaper to help the wood look more rustic.

3. Attach the two oak boards to one another using battens screwed on from the bottom side. Using battens for this purpose replicates the design used in old barn doors, where several small pieces of wood running perpendicular to others hold everything together. The battens can be screwed in or nailed on. Usually the boards are held tightly together with clamps while the battens are being put on.

4. Screw on the top through oversized holes on the stretchers.

5. Lightly sand the frame and the legs. Then apply the mixture of 50/50 linseed oil and mineral spirits.

6. If you like, add your own embellishments such as moldings, slices of pinecone, small mosaics of twig, bark appliqué, etc.

Bentwood Armchair
Designer/Builder: Andrew Gardner

WHAT YOU NEED

For the chair frame

2 front legs: 2 x 16 inches (5 x 41 cm)

2 back legs: 2 x 32 inches (5 x 81 cm)

8 pieces 1½ x 24 to 26 inches (4 x 61 x 66 cm)

3 Y-shaped pieces: 1½ x 24 to 26 inches, 15 inches from base to fork (4 x 61 x 66 cm, 38 cm)

2 pieces 1½ x 26 to 28 inches (4 x 61 x 66 cm)

1 piece ¾ x 26 inches (2 x 66 cm)

2 pieces 1¼ x 48 inches (3 x 122 cm)

14 reasonably straight pieces, 4 to 5 feet long, 1 inch at base (1.2 – 1.5 m, 25 mm)

7 reasonably straight pieces, 6 to 7 feet long, 1 inch at base (1.8 – 2.1 m, 25 mm)

20 straight pieces, 4 to 5 feet long, ½ inch at base (1.2 – 1.5 m, 25 mm)

18- or 21-inch bow saw (46 or 53 cm)

anvil-style hand pruner/cutters

small Stanley Surform rasp

16-ounce carpenter's hammer (453.5 g)

nail set (or drift punch)

spring clamps (optional)

hacksaw

flat bastard file

drill and assorted bits

tape measure

nails: 8d, 10d, 12d twisted, galvanized decking or patio nails; 1 and 1⅝-inch annular ribbed shank panel or hardboard nails

WHAT YOU DO

Building the Basic Frame

1. The first step is to collect the willow, or "swamp willow," which can be found along most rivers and streams. This bush type plant is incredibly strong for its weight, quite flexible even when seasoned, and doesn't split when nailed. Also, once the willow has aged, insects will not move in. Each piece must be reasonably straight. Willow is a renewable resource that thrives with cutting.

2. Join the front and back legs with two horizontal pieces, 1½ x 24 to 26 inches (4 x 61 x 66 cm) (figure 1). The one on top should be Y-shaped, with the Y towards the back. The front end should be about 1½ inches (4 cm) below the top of the front leg. The bottom piece should be about 5 inches from the floor. Use two nails at each point of contact, excluding the lower branch of the Y.

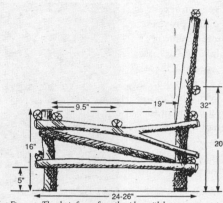

Figure 1. The chair frame from the side—with key measurements

3. Make sure the seat drops slightly from front to rear—1 to 2 inches (25–51 mm) at the most. Notice, also how the back slopes away from the front—again no more than about 2 inches.

4. Make a mirror copy of this first side.

5. Join the two sides together in front with two horizontal pieces of the same size. The top support should rest on top of the Y pieces. Secure the back in the same manner as the sides, with a Y piece on top and a straight 24- to 26-inch (61 to 66 cm) piece on the bottom.

6. To make the frame rigid, nail a diagonal brace from front to rear on both sides of the chair (figure 2). Start by nailing these to the outside top of the front legs. Then straighten the chair to give it the symmetric shape you desire. Now you can nail each diagonal brace to the bottom inside of the back legs. Again, use two nails at each point of contact.

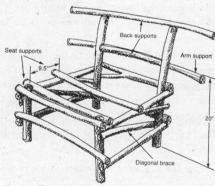

Figure 2. The completed frame

7. Nail the second branch of the Y pieces to the back legs (figure 2).

8. Place another 1½ x 24- to 26-inch (4 x 61 x 66 cm) piece directly behind the front legs, on top of the Y pieces. Secure with two nails at each contact point as before.

Continued ➡

9. Nail another piece of the same size in the same manner, halfway between the front and back legs.

10. Cut a piece to fit securely between the back legs. Nail it in between the legs, 20 inches (51 cm) off the floor. This is called the back spreader.

11. Immediately behind the back spreader, secure one of the 48-inch (122 cm) pieces for an arm support.

12. Secure the other 48-inch piece on top of the back legs.

13. Set all the nails, and cut off the exposed nail ends.

14. Trim off any excess wood and bevel all cut ends with the Surform.

15. Now sit on the frame. Is it sturdy? Your seat should fall slightly behind the middle bar and your shoulders probably will touch the top of the back support.

Creating the Arms

The arms are built cane by cane so that any stress placed on the frame is uniformly spread across the chair. Because these branches are a bit more delicate than those in the frame, you may want to predrill nail holes as you go (in case you're not sure where each randomly placed cane will wind up).

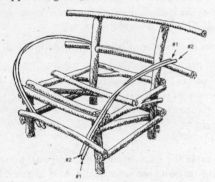

1. Flex each cane to limber it up a bit before starting.

2. Maneuver the first cane from the inside lower front up to the top of the arm support (figure 3).

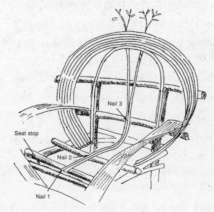

Figure 3. Showing the position of the first and second arm canes

3. Nail this first piece, using long panel nails, in three places: on top of the arm support, in front of the seat stop, and behind the lower horizontal support. Leave the nail heads exposed so you can remove them later, if necessary.

4. Position the second cane next to the first at the bottom front support; place the other end next to the first on the arm support. Make sure the canes are touching along their entire length (see figure 3).

5. Beginning with the second cane, nail each to the frame and to its neighbor, using both long and short panel nails.

6. When the last arm cane is in place, drive in and set the nails.

Wrapping the Back of the Chair

When placing subsequent canes, alternate which side you started the base of the cane.

1. Hook the first cane under the arm and over the top of the frame. Bend the cane so that the other end can be placed under the opposite arm (see figure 4).

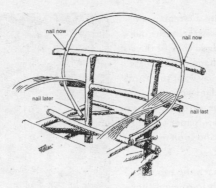

Figure 4. Showing the position of the first back cane

2. Nail the cane only to the top horizontal piece on the back of each side.

3. Add the other canes in the same manner, nailing each new cane to the top of the previous ones at 6- to 8-inch intervals.

4. Once all the back canes are in place, the ends can be trimmed uniformly and spread out at equal intervals from the back leg to the center seat support. Nail each one into place. Also nail the canes where they come into firm contact with the arms.

5. Sit down in the chair and see how rigid it has become.

Constructing the Seat

1. Measure and mark the center point on the seat support between the front legs. Repeat this process with the center seat support and the back support.

2. Cut a piece ¾ inch (19 mm) in diameter, slightly shorter than the top front frame piece.

3. Place this piece on top of the front seat support against the top of the leg. Nail it into position about every 3 inches with nails at opposing angles (see figure 5). This "seat stop" conceals the front ends of the seat canes and helps to keep them from rising up when you sit in the chair.

4. Next, select a uniform seat cane and flex it a bit. Place the leaf end up behind the back and lay it along one side of the center line (see figure 5). Nail it first in front and then in the middle.

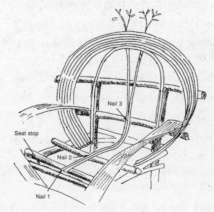

Figure 5. Showing the position of the first two seat canes

5. Press the cane down slightly just before it curves up the back, and nail it to the lower back support.

6. Place the second cane next to the first and repeat the nailing process.

7. Place the third cane slightly more than 1 inch from the first and nail it as you did the first two.

8. Place the fourth cane next to the second, etc. The seat canes can be paired at intervals throughout or interspersed with single canes.

9. Once you have finished securing the seat canes, spread them out in a fashion that suits you, and nail them to the upper back support.

10. Drive in any unsecured nails, set them, and trim up the back.

11. On the back side, nail the top of the seat canes three times each to different back canes at opposing angles.

12. Sit down, rest, and enjoy your handiwork!

Turning Your Chair into a Rocker

A rocker is built the same way as the chair except that the legs are two inches shorter. Pattern the runner, or rocker, after one you know rocks well for you. Yellow pine stair tread is a good wood to use, and is available at most larger lumberyards.

1. Trace the pattern on the wood, and free-cut with a saber saw.

2. Dress the edges and stain the wood with three coats of oil stain.

3. Place the runner on the outside of the legs, with only the pointed end extending beyond the front leg. Draw a line on the led where the runner meets.

4. Turn the chair upside down and place a straight board on its edge, from front to back leg down the middle. This ensures the alignment of the runner.

5. Draw a line on each leg bottom along this line, dividing the leg in half. Extend these lines along the legs, beyond the side mark for the runner.

6. Carefully sawing, cut from the side runner marks to the halfway marks. Then either chisel or saw down to the saw cut.

7. Lay the rocker in place and check for fit, adjusting as needed with a chisel.

8. When the rocker and legs fit reasonably well, clamp them in place and drill a ¼-inch (6.5 mm) hole through the middle of each leg and rocker where they join.

9. Connect your rockers to your chair with ¼ x 2½-inch (6.5 x 63.5 mm) round head or carriage bolts with hex nuts and washers on both sides.

10. Sit down and rock your cares away!

—From *Rustic Furniture Workshop*

WOODCARVING

John Hillyer

Tools

The first question most beginning carvers ask is, "What tools do I need to get started?" You really only need a few tools when you start carving, and instead of buying a complete carving set, purchase tools as you need them. Usually, when you buy a set you don't save any money, plus, you end up with some tools you rarely use. Buy the best quality you can afford; good, pre-sharpened, high-carbon steel tools will save you money in the long run.

Purchasing tools by catalog or over the Internet can be difficult since you can't feel the tool to see if it's a good fit for you and your project. There are woodcarving stores that provide tools, books, blanks, and other carving supplies.

Knives

You'll need a good knife—one that feels good in your hand. There are three types to choose from: a folding blade (pocket knife), a fixed-blade (bench knife), or an interchangeable blade knife. I prefer a fixed-blade knife primarily because it's safer. There are also many blade shapes and styles in a variety of steels. Select a high-carbon steel blade with a hardness of RC 55 to 60. It will hold its edge longer than a stainless steel blade or low-carbon steel blade. For general carving, roughing out, and shaping I prefer a blade about $5/32$ inch (4 mm) thick and $1\frac{1}{2}$ to 2 inches (3.8 to 5.1 cm) long. A smaller narrower blade is better for detail work. A Kolrosing knife has a small blade and is used to incise.

Some carvers prefer the interchangeable blade knife because it uses disposable blades, eliminating the need to resharpen the blade when it loses its edge. Another good feature is that this knife handle can be used with some small gouges as well.

Gouges

Gouges come in a variety of widths and sweeps (curvatures). The sweep is denoted by a number. The flatter the curvature, the lower the number. Thus a #3 gouge is almost flat compared to a #11 U-shaped veiner. Obviously, a #10 or #11 gouge will make a deeper cut and remove more wood than a #4 gouge. On the other hand, the #3 gouge will give you a smoother finishing cut. The V-tool, or #12 gouge, is available in a number of different angles, from 24° to 90°. The most common angles are 60° to 70°.

Clockwise from the top: an interchangeable knife, a curved knife, two fixed-blade knives, and disposable blades and gouges for the interchangeable knife

Standard gouges for use with a mallet

Choose gouges with handles that don't easily roll when laid on your work surface. (You'll spend less time repairing damaged cutting edges due to the tools rolling off the table.)

Keep in mind the size and type of carving you want to do when selecting your gouges. For handheld work, palm gouges are more convenient than standard gouges. Microgouges are needed for miniature work. Sculptures and large carvings, as well as relief carvings, require standard gouges with heavier handles to withstand pounding with a mallet.

Figure 1: Gouges and Their Cutting Lines: A & B Veiners; C. Deep Sweep; D. Fishtail; E. Straight; F. Spoon; G. Long Bend; H. V-tool; I. Firmer; J. Skew

Saws

Woodcarvers use a number of saws depending on the task, though a coping saw is probably the most common one used. It uses replaceable high-carbon steel blades, fitted in a steel frame with a handle. It can be used to cut narrow curves, though it requires a degree of patience to keep the blade from breaking or bending. You can also use it with a fret board to cut out your designs. Another useful saw is the backsaw, which can be used to help cut out waste wood.

Coping saw

Specialty Cutting Tools

These tools are not necessary for the projects in this book, but they may come in handy for some specific tasks.

A draw knife is used to remove bark or for fast rough removal of wood, as in shaping long pieces for furniture. A scorp is a type of knife with a curved, circular blade that's ideal for scooping out bowls, spoons, or masks.

Abrasive Tools

Files and rasps remove waste wood quickly and smoothly. They come in coarse, medium, and fine filing cuts. Flat, half round, and round shapes are available—always use them with handles. Rifflers are double-ended files or rasps that come in a wide variety of shapes. Use them for getting into tight corners and hard-to-reach places to remove small slivers of wood. Sanding sticks that use small sanding belts also help get into the tight spots to smooth out small, rough areas. A flexible sander is excellent for curved surfaces. Drum sanders for use in drill presses and hand drills, as well as sanding stars and flapper sanders, are a big help in finish sanding. Sanding mediums come in a wide variety of grits and materials to meet any need. I prefer cloth-backed abrasives or open abrasives. I also use flexible plastic pads for final smoothing. Use sandpaper only after you've finished carving—the loosened particles of abrasive become lodged in the wood and will quickly dull your tools.

Sanding tools

Power Tools

If and when you begin to make your own blanks (the roughed out design) in quantities, a bandsaw is indispensable. The large selection of blades allows you to make difficult cuts with ease, far surpassing anything you can do with a coping saw and a fret board. A jigsaw can do inside cuts, but is limited in the thickness of stock it can handle. Belt, disc, and flapper sanders are helpful in the finishing operations as well as for removing bark. Many carvers use rotary tools with a wide variety of bits to carve details, such as feathers. There are handheld grinders, flexible shaft units, and small high-speed (35,000 rpm) micro-motor carvers. There are also at least four reciprocating power gouge carvers available today that make it possible for carvers with arthritic hands and "tennis elbows" to continue to carve.

Holding Devices

If you use a vise to clamp your carving, use one that has jaws that won't mark your carving (or fasten a waste block to your work before putting it in the vise). I have often used a $\frac{1}{4}$-inch (6 mm) lag screw with a washer and a wing nut to fasten my carving to the bench. You may want to use a carver's glove of coated steel wire to protect your non-carving hand while holding your piece. I have a longtime carving friend who wears a heavy leather apron to protect himself when he carves against his chest. When finishing or painting your pieces you may want to use an awl or painting stick screwed into the bottom of your project.

FRET BOARD

To help support your wood as you cut out your blank with a coping saw, I suggest you make a fret board, which is a simple board that supports the wood while you saw it. Simply clamp it to your bench or table, and hold your coping saw vertically in the "V" as you cut out your blank. See figure 2 for the fret board dimensions.

A fret board on top of a bench hook

Continued ➜

BENCH HOOK

If you plan on doing any relief or in-the-round carving, then I also suggest you create this simple bench hook (see figure 3). The cleat underneath holds the hook in place, while the corner created by the two cleats on the top keeps your carving or blank from sliding away from you as you carve. Clamp the bench hook to your work surface.

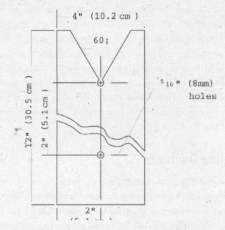

Figure 2: Fretboard dimensions: Use a ½ x 4 x 12 (1.3 x 10.2 x 30.5 cm) piece of board

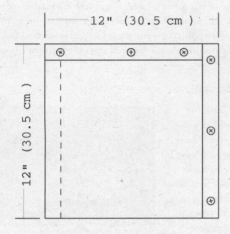

This is the top view of the bench hook. You'll need one piece of ¾ x 12 x 12-inch (1.9 cm x 30.5 x 30.5 cm) plywood for the bench hook. You'll also need two pieces of 1 x 1 x 12-inch (2.5 x 2.5 x 30.5 cm) lumber, and one piece of 1 x 1 x 11-inch (2.5 x 2.5 x 30.5 cm) lumber for the three crosspieces. Attach the crosspieces as indicated with glue and screws.

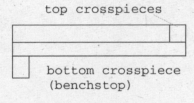

Figure 4: Side view of bench hook

Miscellaneous Tools

Electronic woodburning tools can be used to texture, color, and sign your work. If you're using power tools, you'll need dust masks and dust collectors. You'll also need artist tools and brushes when finishing a carving with paint or lacquer. I also suggest using tracing paper and graphite paper for transferring your designs to the wood. A good light source that's color corrected with a magnifying device is great for the eyes when doing fine detail work.

Tool Care

Periodically, you should inspect your tools, wiping them off with an oily rag to guard against rust. Store your tools in individual compartments or in a cloth roll to protect them and reduce your time spent resharpening them.

SHARPENING TOOLS

Always keep your tools sharp, and stop carving every so often to hone them to keep a keen edge. Every carver I know has developed his own system for sharpening; each has found a procedure that works for him, and that's what counts. Some use oil stones, water stones, or man-made stones, and some power sharpen.

The first step is to whet the blade, using a medium-to fine-grit abrasive, such as a diamond hone or emery paper. Push the edge into the hone until you develop a burr or wire edge on the blade. Then turn the blade over and develop the burr on the other side. The next step, using a finer grit, is called honing, and it removes the edge burr and surface roughness produced in the whetting stage. Your final step is to polish the blade and edge to a mirror finish with a polishing compound to further reduce the surface friction between the blade and the wood.

How do you tell if your blade is sharp? Check the sharpness by making a cut across the grain of a piece of scrap wood. If you get a shiny, smooth cut, then the blade's sharp. If the grain tears out, or if the surface is rough or grooved, then you know that you need to hone the edge some more.

SUGGESTED TOOLS

As a minimum, you should have the following tools and materials for the carving projects in this book.

CARVING TOOLS

Knife (fixed-blade is recommended)

Four straight gouges (palm gouges will do fine)

#3 sweep gouge, ½ inch (1.3 cm) wide

#7 sweep gouge, ½ inch (1.3 cm) wide

#11 sweep (veiner) gouge, ¼ inch (6 mm) wide

#12 sweep (V-parting) gouge, ¼ inch (6 mm) wide

DRAWING SUPPLIES AND PATTERN-MAKING MATERIALS

Use of a photocopying machine

Coping saw

Fret board

Drawing supplies

Pencil

Ruler

Compass/dividers

Tracing paper

Graphite paper

SANDING TOOLS AND MATERIALS

Sandpaper (150 to 400 grit)

Cloth-backed abrasives

Open-abrasive screens

Flexible plastic abrasive pads (gray and white)

HOLDING DEVICES

(at least one of the following)

Bench hook (see page 443)

C-clamp

Vise

Lag screw

Rubber pad to carve on (router pad)

FINISHING MATERIALS

Tack cloth

Wood glue

Penetrating and/or surface finishes, as desired

SAFETY EQUIPMENT

Bandages

Carving glove

Finger guards

The natural beauty and unique qualities of wood allow a carver to transform it with patience and care into a vision of beauty and warmth. You can buy wood, blanks or rough outs for carving from craft and hobby stores or over the Internet. Woodcarving catalogs are also a good source. Of course, you can also make your own blanks. But before purchasing or finding your wood, there are some major factors to consider.

Moisture Content

Freshly cut green wood is easier to carve than the same wood after it has been seasoned or kiln-dried. Green wood is also more susceptible to cracking and splitting as it dries out, unless you take steps to control the drying or relieve the internal stresses. You'll have fewer of these problems using kin-dried wood for your projects.

Weight or Density

While the moisture content does contribute to the weight in freshly cut green wood, you'll find, in general, that heavier, denser woods are more difficult to carve than lighter woods. In my experience, it usually takes me two to three times longer to carve the same project in walnut as it does to carve it in basswood or sugar pine.

Condition of the Wood

The grain, knots, and other defects, as well as inclusions in "found" wood, can result in serious problems. Nails, barbed wire, bullets, and sand inclusions can damage your tools. A heavy or twisted grain may cause your tools to follow it instead of going where you want them to go, particularly when you're carving against the grain. The key is to always look over your wood closely to avoid difficulties in carving.

Kinds of Wood

There are softwoods, hardwoods, and imported woods to choose from. The availability and cost are important factors to consider. In general, hardwoods are more difficult to carve than softwoods. Wood with a wild grain is harder to carve, but it often produces beautiful, smooth, stylized carvings. A close-grained wood is better when you need fine details. In my opinion, the following woods are the most easily carved in each category:

Imported woods

Lime (linden)

Mahogany (Honduran)

Spanish cedar

Softwoods

White pine

Sugar pine

Ponderosa pine

Hardwoods

Basswood (linden)

Butternut

Buckeye

The fun comes in finding just the right wood for your project, or finding a piece that speaks to you. Several years ago, one of my students had an old pine board with four knots in it. She carved a beautiful relief carving of two owls sitting on a branch. She used the knots as the eyes of the owls. She enjoyed every minute she spent carving her serendipitous piece.

In the event you can't find wood the right size for your project, you can always resort to gluing thinner boards together. You may want to use this technique to build strength into your blank by orienting the grain in a particular direction for a specific area of your carving. In some cases, this will also reduce the amount of waste wood that needs to be removed. The joints are no problem for a painted project. By using different colored woods and carving away the layers, you can obtain other interesting effects.

Finally, if you're new to carving, start with basswood or sugar pine until you acquire some experience. Both woods are relatively easy to carve and hold carved details well.

Patterns and Blanks

Once you've chosen your wood, the next step is to transfer the pattern or template to the wood. Always begin by marking the horizontal and vertical centerlines on the pattern and the wood. Next, carefully align the two sets of centerlines to check the fit of the pattern to the wood (1). You may want to adjust your location to avoid defects in the wood or to take advantage of the grain, color, or imperfections in the wood.

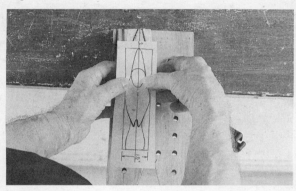

Photo 1

Transferring the Pattern

You can use any of the following methods to transfer the pattern to the wood (2):

- Glue your patterns directly to the wood with rubber cement.
- Tape one edge of your pattern to the wood and place a sheet of graphite paper under your pattern (don't use carbon paper). Then trace the pattern using a colored pencil so that you can be sure you have transferred the complete design.
- Chalk or graphite the back side of your pattern, and rub the front side with a stylus to mark the wood.
- By ironing a photocopy of the pattern onto the wood, you'll obtain a reverse image of your design.
- Scan actual completed carvings on your computer scanner, and use the printed scan as the pattern.

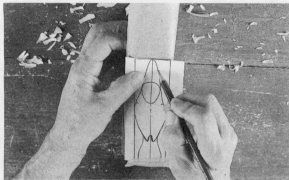

Photo 2

For in-the-round carvings, align the centerlines and transfer both the side profile view and the front or top view to the wood. I usually use graphite paper for this purpose.

For relief carvings, you need only a single view. It's helpful in relief carving to use a graph system on both your pattern and on the wood so that you can re-establish the design after you've carved away the various levels.

Cutting the Outline (Creating the Blank)

Use the fret board clamped to your work surface to support the wood to help you cut a square edge with a coping saw. Or better yet, use a jigsaw or bandsaw to cut out your blank. Always be sure your wood is square before you start. It's usually best to cut out your side profile first and tape or use rubber cement to reattach the waste wood you've cut off (3). This gives you a square surface for your next cuts. Then cut out the top or front profile. Now mark the centerlines on all four sides of the cutout blank. You're now ready to start carving.

Photo 3

Carving Techniques

All the projects in this book can be classified as either in-the-round or relief. In-the-round carving consists of creating a three-dimensional piece, while relief carving is two dimensional. And though both kinds of carving involve different techniques and tools, you'll follow the same four basic steps or phases for both.

During the outlining phase you begin by using the design pattern to cut out your blank or outline your design (if doing relief carving). During the shaping phase, you're removing waste wood to arrive at the basic design shape. During the detailing phase, you use smaller, defined cuts to bring out the details one by one until you're satisfied with the overall appearance. Finally, during the finishing phase, you can leave your project as it is, or decide on the many different kinds of finishes noted under "Finishing."

In-the-Round Carving

My years of teaching woodcarving have taught me that the best way to learn is by doing. So in order to describe the techniques needed for the in-the-round carving projects in this book, I'll first show you the basic cuts you need to master, and then launch you right into a project that you can't possibly mess up. This learning project is called Ur Bird, and the best thing about this bird is that no two are alike, and there's no right or wrong way to carve it. If you make a mistake or have a problem, don't hesitate to change the design. Have fun, relax, and enjoy this project. You'll not only develop the technical skills needed for the rest of the projects, but also learn the limitations of your tools and materials.

The Cuts to Know

When working on three-dimensional pieces, you'll usually use your knife to make the cuts that gradually shape your design. There are five types of cuts used.

- The stop cut is probably the most important carving cut of all. It severs the grain so the next cut will slice into it and not damage the design.

Stop cut

- The slicing cut is a straight pushing cut that slices across the wood fibers, usually removing long curls of wood. Used in combination with the stop cut, you can safely rough out the basic shape.

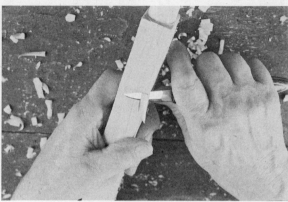

Slicing cut

- With the paring cut, the blade is pulled towards the thumb of the hand holding the knife, while the thumb steadies the woods. Be sure to keep your thumb out of the way or protect it with a thumb guard, tape, or glove.

Paring cut

- The levering cut is useful in tight areas where close control is required. With the cutting edge facing away from you, use the thumb of the other hand as a fulcrum point on the back of the blade and pivot the knife into the wood by pulling back on the knife handle. You can really nibble the waste wood away with this cut.

Continued →

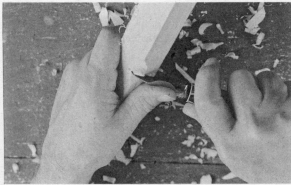

Levering cut

• The rolling and slicing cut is used in curved areas where you need to scoop out the waste wood. As it scoops and rolls in the curve, the blade of the knife also slices across the fibers, producing a smooth surface.

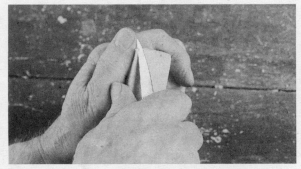

Rolling and Slicing cut

Cutting Tips

• A lot of cutting is done with the tip of your knife. When you're making tight curves, stand your knife up and use the tip to reduce the amount of drag. Use the tip when you're starting a hole or in detailing. At times, a rocking or sawing action with your knife will be useful.

• Carving with the grain is always easier than carving against or across the grain. With experience, you'll learn by feel when you're carving against the grain. When an experienced carver feels this happening, he'll automatically turn his wood 180° so that he's carving with the grain.

• Another important cut is an undercut. This is used to cast a shadow that produces depth in your carving. It is particularly useful in relief carving. It's an angled stop cut. Your slicing cut that removes the waste wood ends up under the edge of the design.

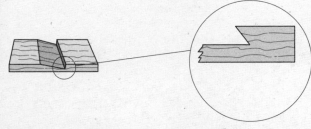

The normal view shows how the slicing cut ends at a stop cut. The exploded view shows what an undercut looks like.

UR Bird

Now that you've got the basic cuts down, it's time to carve! Use basswood or white pine for this project. Examine your wood carefully for flaws, and check the grain direction. Make sure the grain runs lengthwise to the bird. Check the list to make sure you have the tools you need.

The Outlining Phase

See "Transferring the Pattern" for instructions on marking your centerlines and transferring the pattern to the wood.

Undercutting

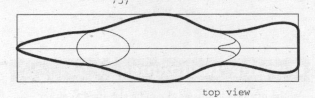

top view

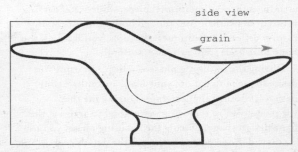

side view

grain

UR Bird pattern. Enlarge 200 percent to use.

Once you've cut out the basic design, you now have the blank.

The Shaping Phase

As you carve, try not to carve away the centerlines, which you'll use to help you carve symmetrically so you don't end up with a lopsided bird. If you carve the centerline away, redraw it right away. Try to carve out equal amounts of waste wood on either side of the centerlines.

The first cut you make is a stop cut across the tail at the end of the wing (4). Carve away the waste wood on the top of the tail with a slicing cut (5). Because the tail is thin, use light slicing cuts; and in order to maintain strength, taper the tail to the outer edges, keeping the full thickness along the centerline. The thin edge tricks the eye into thinking the tail is thin. The slicing cut can fool you. As you push the blade through the wood, you must also move it to one side so that it slices the fibers.

Photo 4

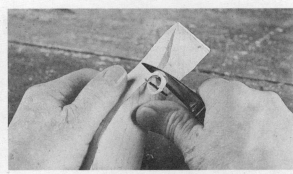

Photo 5

Now use this same slicing cut to round over the rest of the blank. Take care to use fairly long, light strokes to begin with. Woodcarver Rick Butz has a saying: "Three small cuts are better than one big cut." So take it easy until you've learned when to make a heavy cut. You'll also find it necessary to use the other basic cuts as you develop the form.

Mark a circle on the top of the bird's head to help as you round off this area using paring cuts (6). A bird's neck tapers from the head to the body, and there's no distinct necking in, so don't remove too much wood in this area. Now use a series of paring or slicing cuts to taper the beak. Check the grain direction and carefully carve the shape you want. You'll probably find it necessary to use the levering or push cut during this rounding and shaping phase. Work all around your blank and continue to develop the overall shape (7).

Photo 6

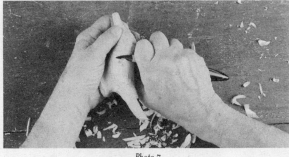

Photo 7

Now look at the base. What shape do you want to create? Square, oval, round? Mark the bottom outline to guide your next cuts. This curved area from the body to the base is a difficult area to carve (you're carving across the surface grain in a tight area), requiring the use of the rolling and slicing cut. As you make your cut, roll the blade in a scooping action, and try not to force your blade straight through the wood. This will result in a tear out of the grain. Try to make it slice across the grain at the same time you roll it (8). This will result in a smooth surface rather than a rough area of pulled-out fibers.

Photo 8

The Detailing Phase

Having developed the basic shape you want, you can now begin to detail your bird. Use a pencil to establish the wing lines and the eye positions. Use a narrow strip of paper folded in half to make sure the eyes are level. Align the fold with your top centerline, with the strip draping over both sides. Mark the eye position on one side through the paper, and remove the paper strip. Fold it in half as before, now mark through the paper so that the eye position is the same distance from the fold (9). Align the fold with the centerline again, and mark the eye position on the other side of the bird. The same technique can be used to draw in the wing lines.

Photo 9

Stop cut along the wing line from the breast to the tail (10). Don't cut too deeply. Now undercut from below into the stop cut. Reshape the area under the wing. You may also want to carve some feathers in the wing and in the tail (11). Use an eye tool, nail set, or awl to form the eyes (12).

Photo 10

Photo 11

Photo 12

The Finishing Phase

Use the information under "Sanding and Finishing" to finish your bird, or leave it as it is. You can do as little or as much as you want in the way of detailing, but remember that simple is usually better than too much. Don't forget to sign and date your masterpiece.

Relief Carving

There are basically four types of relief carving. The simplest is incised carving, which is a lot like engraving. Usually the relief carving you see is low relief and is relatively shallow. When more than half the thickness of the wood is removed, it's called high relief or deep-relief carving. Reverse relief is where the design is carved into the background. Butter or cookie molds are carved this way. Half round and pierced carvings are usually considered versions of relief carvings. When first trying relief carving, select relatively simple designs. Avoid intricate shapes and heavy undercutting.

The value of shadows and the effect of lighting is very important in bringing out the beauty of the design. From time to time as you're carving, step back and hold up your carving to check the effect of light and shadows. To create the illusion of depth, you must follow the rules of perspective. Objects in the background must be smaller in size. All lines that are parallel will eventually narrow to a vanishing point. Check drawing books for a more complete explanation of these principles of perspective.

Relief Carving: Four Stages

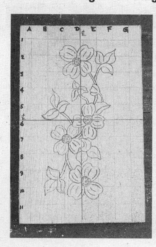

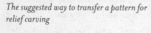

The suggested way to transfer a pattern for relief carving

A relief-carved piece during the outlining phase (notice the rounded corners—try to avoid square corners)

Using Gouges

Though you can use a knife for many steps, gouges will often make life easier for you. When using a gouge, hold its handle in your right hand (if you're right-handed), with your thumb pointing toward the cutting edge. Your left hand should grasp the blade with the thumb pointing toward the handle. Push with your right hand, or use a mallet to make your cut. Your left hand guides the tool or holds back to control the cut. You can also use the palm of the right hand to push the gouge. Stand erect and avoid stooping over to reduce overtiring and/or a backache. When using a mallet, snap your wrist and let the mallet do the work.

A similar carving with a rounded outline during the shaping phase

Sanding and Finishing

When you lay down your knife and gouges, thinking that you're done, you'll find that you're actually only halfway through. Now the sanding and finishing stage starts.

Take a good look at your carving. Hold it up to the light. How does the light affect its overall appearance? Do the shadows enhance the design? What shading or color do you want to use? Is the surface texture right? Do you want the "as carved" look, or do you think a sleek, smooth overall appearance would be better? What type of finish do you need to protect and seal the wood satisfactorily? However you answer these questions, the important thing to remember is that a poor finish or bad color combination can ruin even the best carving.

Sanding

If you want a really smooth finish, sanding is vital. I like to use an open abrasive rather than fiber-backed abrasives, because they do not load up, and I can vary the width of the abrasive in a flexible holder to suit the carving. Experiment with different abrasives until you find the ones that work best for you.

A completed carving with a more natural-looking border

Most abrasive sheets are graded from coarse to very fine. The coarse abrasives (60 to 100 grit) can be used to actually remove as much wood as you could using a knife. Some carvers use them for roughing out to get the basic shape. Use 120- to 180-grit abrasives for initial smoothing and 200- to 600-grit abrasives for final smoothing.

SANDING YOUR CARVING

Most of your sanding should be done with the grain. Always keep moving your abrasive so you don't cause grooves or flat spots in the wood. Don't push too hard; let the abrasive do the work. Be aware that you can actually burn the wood with a power sander. Also, breathing in too much wood dust can be dangerous, so use a dust collector or wear a face mask.

Establishing the border outline with a gouge

Use a sponge or spray to moisten (don't soak) the wood with water or a 50/50 solution of water and alcohol to raise the wood grain. When the wood dries, sand off the fuzz with a 320- to 400-grit abrasive or a plastic abrasive pad. This will lessen the amount of fuzz when you apply a sanding sealer.

Let your carving set for 24 hours or longer and then sand it again. Any changes in the humidity will also raise the fuzz. By waiting and sanding a second time you'll get a smoother finish. A sanding sealer will also raise the grain, requiring additional sanding for that really smooth finish.

Finishing

The purpose of a finish is to protect the wood, and selection of a finish is a matter of choice. Any finish will change

Continued ➤

the color of the wood to some degree, so experiment on a scrap of wood first. Or, better yet, prepare different wood samples with different finishes as a reference.

SURFACE FILM FINISHES

Surface film finishes penetrate the wood surface only slightly, with each coat building upon the previous one. Among them are varnish, shellac, lacquer, clear plastic, and polyurethane finishes. Some of these products have a nitrocellulose base and are highly flammable and toxic. Even mineral-base finishes are unpleasant to use without good ventilation. All finishes can be brushed, sprayed, or dipped on. You can also use a sanding sealer, which has a filler in it that fills the pores and grain, to produce a level base for a final finish.

APPLYING SURFACE FILM FINISHES

Regardless of the resin type or kind of solvent, a beautiful, smooth finish can be obtained by following the manufacturer's directions. Good adhesion of the sealer coat (first coat) is important, and the higher the humidity, the more difficult it is to apply. Several thin coats are better than one heavy coat, and it's critical that each coat is completely dry before the next coat is applied. The first coat raises the grain. After this coat is completely dry, sand it back. Use a tack cloth to remove sanding dust, and apply the second coat. When cured, sand it back again, and apply the final coat. You can easily rub through the finish, so go easy and use very fine abrasives, or you may have to start over again to get the final finish the way you want it.

An old reliable finish is beeswax. Use a double boiler and melt the beeswax, then add boiled linseed oil (about half and half). Use a soft cloth and rub it in by hand. This gives your carving a protective coating that can be renewed easily anytime.

When applying a lacquer finish, I often make my carving of a size so that I can dip it directly in the can and get a heavier coat. A rule of thumb is that one dip coat is equal to two or three brush coats, and one brush coat is the equivalent of two or three spray coats.

PENETRATING FINISHES

Among the penetrating oil finishes are tung, linseed, and Danish oils. Danish oils are a mixture of oil and varnish. Both tung oil and linseed oil come raw and boiled (refined). Use the boiled varieties (or you'll be waiting an eternity for the raw oil finish to dry), and rub them in by hand. Apply as many coats as you like—the more coats, the more protection.

APPLYING PENETRATING FINISHES

With oil finishes, your wood must be clean, sanded or scraped, and wiped clean with a tack cloth. Then flood the surface with oil and rub off the excess. Wipe off the oil completely to obtain a hand-rubbed look. How long

you let it dry depends on the humidity, though usually 24 hours is enough. Watch for bleed back—excess oil that seeps out of the wood. The pores of the wood are usually sealed after two coats. The important thing to remember with oil finishes is that you're applying thin coats. Be patient; the subsequent coats will produce the finish and protection you want. The buildup of coats will last for years, though leaving too much oil on the wood surface or re-coating before the previous coat is dry can cause problems.

Caution: Dispose of your oily rags carefully, and let them dry outdoors. They can burst into flames under the right conditions. Keep them in a covered metal container until you dispose of them.

Mounts and Bases

Your finishing touch should be a base, frame, or mount that complements your carving. The base can easily make or break your carving's appearance. It should always provide a stable, secure mounting; think of the base as the bottom of a triangle. It may be an integral part of your carving, or it may be a simple frame around a relief carving. It should not overpower your carving. For a realistic animal or bird carving, select your habitat, twigs, rocks, leaves, etc., carefully. A finished walnut or mahogany base can be purchased from one of the carving supply houses.

You can use simple wooden blocks of varying size and color grouped appropriately to unite individual carvings. A simple shelf with a spotlight will really show off your carving. Experiment first with different arrangements before you select your final mounting for your masterpiece.

Safety

Most accidents can be prevented with a little common sense. We all assume nothing bad is going to happen, but accidents usually occur when we're tired or when we hurry. Here are some safety tips to consider before starting:

- Have bandages and a first-aid kit close at hand. Direct pressure with a gauze pad is the best immediate treatment for cuts.
- Maintain good working conditions. Have a place for everything and keep everything in its place. Provide good light and ventilation.
- Wear protective equipment, such as gloves, finger guards, dust masks, and goggles, when appropriate.
- Use properly grounded electrical equipment.
- Clamp or securely fasten your work, or hold your carving so you avoid carving toward your body.
- Check which way the grain runs, and carve with the grain as much as possible.
- Keep your tools sharp.
- Remember, three small cuts are better than one large cut that can slip and either damage your project or your body.
- Don't wear loose clothing around rotating power equipment.
- Keep flammable liquids and oil-soaked rags properly stored. Airborne fumes and wood dust can be explosive and are usually toxic.
- Molds and fungi reside in some wood and are released into the air when sanded. Respiratory ailments are common in the woodworking industry. Redwood dust, for example, can cause an acute illness that resembles pneumonia. Some exotic woods will produce skin irritations and glandular swelling. Many skin irritations are caused by contact with adhesives and solvents. Epoxies can cause blistering and scaling.
- Relax and enjoy your carving experience. Practice patience and it will pay off in the quality of your projects.

Projects

Trout Key Chain

Here's a great gift for that fisherman in your life who's so hard to buy for. You could also carve several trout and create a miniature mobile.

 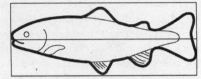

Enlarge 200 percent to use

YOU WILL NEED

- Cedar, walnut, or teak, ½ x 1½ x 4 inches (1.3 x 3.8 x 10.2 cm)
- Fixed-blade carving knife
- Cloth-backed abrasive, sandpaper, or open abrasive (180 to 220 grit)
- Desired finish
- Brass screw eye (small)
- Drill
- Brass key chain and split ring

1. Transfer the patterns to a squared piece of wood, and cut your blank. The grain of the wood should run the length of the fish. Make a saw cut for the mouth. Carefully consider the grain and develop a long "S" curve to portray a swimming action before carving. Mark the position of the side fins so you don't carve them off while shaping the fish. Use a combination of long slicing cuts and paring cuts with your knife to develop the "S" shape of the body.

2. Using the template as a guide, locate and draw the gills and side fins. Stop cut the gills and undercut to make them stand out more.

3. Stop cut and undercut the side fins that you drew in step 2.

4. With the knife, develop the shape of the head with levered or paring cuts.

5. Carve a curve into the tail with a paring cut. Make it wavy but not too thin.

6. Carve the wood out from between the two lower pelvic fins. Remember, this is a key chain, so don't make your edges too thin and fragile. Sand the trout smooth with 180- to 220-grit abrasive. Finish as desired. This trout was given three coats of spray lacquer. Install the small brass screw eye in the mouth. To avoid splitting, you may want to drill a pilot hole first. Use the brass chain with a split ring for the keys.

Inscribed Plate

A simple incised pattern or chip carving on a basswood plate makes a wonderful wall hanging. Basswood plates of different shapes and sizes are readily available at most carving suppliers, but cherry or walnut plates will probably need to be specially ordered or turned on a lathe for you. You can create incised patterns for almost any object, producing handcrafted items such as stools, tables, plaques, lamp bases, etc.

You Will Need

8-inch (20.3 cm) basswood plate or turned plate
Bench hook, clamped to work surface
Fixed-blade carving knife
V-tool gouge, ¼ inch (6 mm) wide (optional)
Cloth-backed abrasive, sandpaper, or open abrasive (220 or 320 grit)
Mineral, walnut, or vegetable oil (optional)
Desired finish

1. Transfer the pattern to the plate. Make sure you align the leaves in the pattern with the grain to minimize cross-grain cuts. Place the plate in the clamped bench hook, and use the knife to carve your cross-grain cuts first. Use the tip of your knife to go around tight corners. Try to visualize where the tip of your knife is going next. For good control, it's important to grip the knife close to the blade and to keep your thumb and knuckles of the carving hand in contact with the wood as you carve.

Enlarge 200 percent to use

2. When outlining with the knife, make sure you don't cut too deeply. About ¹⁄₁₆ inch (2 mm) is deep enough. Each line of the design will be cut twice by the knife. The first knife cut is a stop cut, followed by a sloping cut to form the V-groove. Turn your wood as you carve.

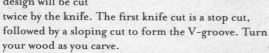

3. Some carvers prefer to use a V-tool to incise their design, since they only have to make one cut instead of the two they have to make with the knife. Using the V-tool is very much like engraving, and a light touch is needed. Start with your cross-grain cuts first.

4. Continue carving with the V-tool, and use care in the tight corners. Once you're finished carving (either with the knife or V-tool), erase all pencil and carbon marks. Sand very lightly with 220- or 320-grit abrasive in order to maintain the crispness of your cuts. Finish as desired. This project was finished with three coats of spray lacquer. An alternate finish that provides color is done by staining or painting your plate first and then carving through to expose the clear wood. A mineral, walnut, or vegetable oil finish should be used if you intend to use your plate with food.

Stretching Cat

The stretching cat on a block started out as just a cat that sat on the edge of a shelf. Unfortunately, vibrations from an 18-wheeler or a rambunctious child are usually enough to cause the cat to move off the shelf and fall to the floor, where it may end up with a broken tail or paw. As a result, I mounted the cat on a block, and now it stays put.

top view

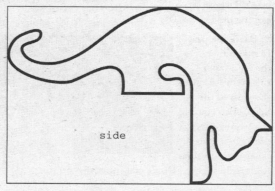

side

Enlarge 200 percent to use

Continued ➔

YOU WILL NEED

Basswood, walnut, cherry, or wood of your choice, 1½ x 3½ x 5¼ inches (3.8 x 8.9 x 13.3 cm)

Fixed-blade carving knife

Backsaw

Flexible sander

Riffler file

Cloth-backed abrasive, sandpaper, or open abrasive (150 to 320 grit)

Desired finish

Wood glue or double-sided adhesive tape

Wood block, 2 x 2 x 3 inches (5.1 x 5.1 x 7.6 cm)

1. Transfer the pattern to a squared piece of wood, and cut your blank. The grain of the wood should run the length of the tail. You may want to leave a little extra stock on the tail for sturdiness during the initial carving. Using the knife, carve between the ears and develop the shape of the head. As you carve the head, point the ears slightly. Keep the top of the nose flat. Use a rolling cut to form the eye sockets about halfway from the tip of the nose to the ears.

2. Use the knife to round over the body from the centerline. Work all over, and don't concentrate on any one spot too long. Try to leave your centerlines until you're ready to sand. Don't remove the wood between the legs at this stage or carve too much off the tail.

3. Carve the tail using paring and slicing cuts. Make sure to give the tail some curvature for action. Don't make it too thin.

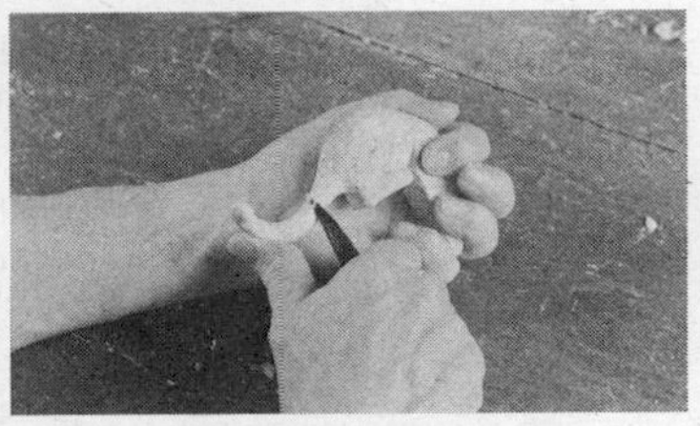

4. Saw a slit between the legs with the backsaw, and mark the outline of the bottom of the paws as a guide for how much to take off when carving the legs.

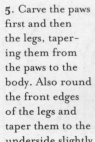

5. Carve the paws first and then the legs, tapering them from the paws to the body. Also round the front edges of the legs and taper them to the underside slightly. Don't make the legs too thin.

6. Little or no detailing is required in a stylized carving, since the beauty comes from the slick smooth shape. Using the flexible sander will make getting a smooth, curved surface easier. Use the riffler file or a strip of abrasive (150 grit) to smooth between the legs. Smooth out the knife cuts using 180-grit abrasive strips. When you're satisfied with the overall shape and smoothness, go back over the whole cat again with 220-grit abrasive, removing any 180-grit marks. You may have to repeat the procedure with 320-grit abrasive to get the final smoothness you want. Finish as desired. Use either glue or double-sided tape to attach the cat to its block.

Roly-Poly Santa

There are countless carved versions of Santa available from all over the world. This guy's a great fall weekend project—when the chill of winter keeps you indoors and the smell of white pine wood chips fills the air. So, pick up your knife and a block of wood, relax, and fall under Santa's spell.

YOU WILL NEED

White pine or basswood, 1½ x 1½ x 4 inches (3.8 x 3.8 x 10.2 cm) or a large basswood goose egg

Fixed-blade carving knife

70° V-tool gouge, ¼ inch (6 mm) wide

#3 gouge, ¼ inch (6 mm) wide

side   front view

Enlarge 200 percent to use

1. Transfer the patterns to a squared piece of wood, and cut your blank. The grain of the wood should run the vertical length of the piece. Mark the ear positions so you won't carve them away when you're shaping the carving. With the knife, round over the corner edges and develop the rounded egg shape with a flat bottom. Sketch the basic positions of the hat with the ball on the end. Use care not to cut the ball off in the shaping phase.

2. Sketch the fur trim on his jacket. Locate his arms and mittens. With the knife, stop cut the collar and the fur trim at the bottom of the jacket, as well as the cuffs. Stop cut the arms and mittens. Use the knife to round over the arms, cuffs, and mittens.

3. With the knife, use paring cuts to carve the trim and ball of the hat. This area is cross-grain, so use care, and don't apply too much pressure or pry with the knife.

4. The face is always a challenge. Every carver does it just a little differently, and once you have more experience, you'll develop your own method. Draw a horizontal line across the face area about ⅜ inch (1 cm) below the bottom of the cap, and stop cut along the line about ⅛ inch (3 mm) deep. Draw another line about ⅜ to ½ inch (1 cm to 1.3 cm) below the first line. This is the tip of the nose. Using a slicing cut, form the slope of the nose up to your first stop cut at the bridge of the nose.

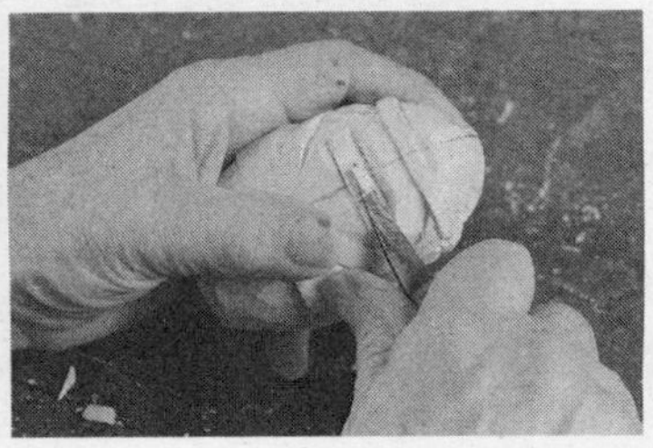

5. Mark vertical lines to designate the sides of the nose. Remove the areas on either side of the nose by slicing up to the stop cut at the brow line. You may have to deepen the brow line stop cut on both sides of the nose as well. This creates the area for the eyes.

6. Draw the shape of the eyes. Check the eye locations. Are they the same size and on the same level? Use the tip of your knife to stop cut the upper and lower eyelids in an oval shape. Use your knife to remove a narrow slit for the pupils.

7. Shape the beard and mustache area as one mass. You can carve the mustache separately if you like. Form the mouth by carving a deep triangular chip on the centerline.

8. Use the knife or V-tool to texture the beard and mustache. Also texture the rest of the hair, and round over the cheeks and nose. Using the tip of your knife, round the corners of the ears and

gouge out a small hole in the center. Use the #3 gouge to texture the cuffs and the fur trim on the jacket. You can sand for a smoother surface, but I like this Santa with an "as carved" surface along with a natural finish. If you want to paint your Santa, use thinned acrylic washes, and build up the coats until you have the color intensity you like.

Paperweight

This dogwood relief paperweight is in the form of a classic design called a roundel, which is an architectural carving in a flat, round ornamental style, similar to ones used during the Gothic period in England.

You Will Need

Butternut, cherry, walnut, or other hardwood, ¾ x 3 inches (1.9 x 7.6 cm) in diameter

Bench hook, clamped to work surface

Fixed-blade carving knife

60° V-tool gouge, ¼ inch (6 mm) wide

Assorted carving gouges (#3, #5, #7, #8, #11)

Riffler files

Desired finish

Large, 2-inch-diameter (5.1 cm) washer

Glue

Felt

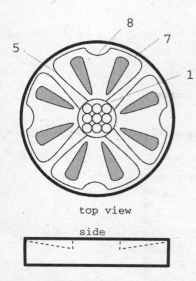

top view

side

Enlarge 200 percent to use. Numbers correspond to the gouge you should use in the areas indicated.

1. Transfer the patterns to the wood, and cut your blank. Place the blank in the bench hook, and use the knife or V-tool to outline the center circle and the petals with a series of stop cuts.

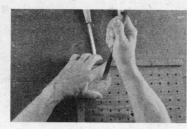

2. In relief carving, you should select your gouges to fit the shapes of the design (petals). This produces a sharp, clean outline. Use the gouges as noted on the template, and switch gouges to carve each of the different elements of the outline.

3. Using the #7 gouge, cut into the stop cut you made on the center circle. You're only removing about ⅛ inch (3 mm), so don't over cut. Slope your gouge away from the center so you don't undercut the circle and chance chipping it out completely. Continue using the #5 and #7 gouges to stop cut the outline of the petals. Remember to make your cross-grain cuts first.

4. Use the #7 and #8 gouges to remove the wood around the center, and taper the petals about ³⁄₁₆ inch (5 mm) into the stop cut around the center. Slope the stop cuts away from the petals. Be careful not to use too much pressure at the outer edges; the cross-grain can break out very easily. Don't pry; make clean slicing cuts.

5. Use the knife and small micro-gouges to lower the background between the petals and around the flower out to the outer edge. Don't undercut the petals at this stage. To carve the berries, cross-hatch the center circle at right angles with the V-tool and round over the corners with the knife. Now use the knife and gouges to undercut the petals lightly, and create shadows for depth. Sand the background to a smooth finish. You may need to use a riffler file to get into the small areas between the petals to remove all the fuzz.

6. Finish as desired. Antiquing the paperweight will give it an old look. Follow manufacturer's directions, or use a dark stain, rubbing off the excess to produce highlights. Hollow out the underside of the paperweight with a gouge or the knife, and glue the washer in place. Then cut out the felt and glue it to the bottom, covering the washer.

Spirit Face Hiking Staff

Hikers use staffs to maneuver rough terrain and ford streams. Hiking staffs come in all kinds of materials these days; however, a carved hiking staff commands special recognition on the trail. At home, they become conversation pieces and even family heirlooms.

You Will Need

Sourwood, maple, dogwood, birch, or spruce sapling, 1¼ inches (3.2 cm) in diameter and 5 feet (1.5 m) long

#3 gouge, 1½ inches (3.8 cm) wide

#11 veiner gouge, ¼ inch (6 mm) wide

Fixed-blade carving knife

Nail set

V-tool gouge, ¼ inch (6 mm) wide

Woodburning tool (optional)

Drill, with ¼-inch (6 mm) bit

Rubber or metal tip

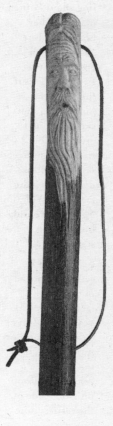

front   side

Enlarge 200 percent to use

Continued →

1. Find a piece of wood that'll work for your staff. If your wood is freshly cut, it'll be easier to carve than older air-dried wood. Be sure it's fairly straight. Clean off the bark from the top 12 inches (30.5 cm) of your staff with the #3 gouge. You don't need to remove all the bark. Mark a centerline and trace the patterns onto the wood. Then mark a horizontal line for the brow line about ¾ inch (1.9 cm) below the top of the staff. Mark another horizontal line about ¾ inch (1.9 cm) below the first line. This is the tip of the nose. Then, cut two horizontal grooves about ¼ inch (6 mm) deep on the two lines drawn across the face area. With the #3 gouge, round over the top of the staff.

2. With the #11 veiner, create an outline of the facial area. Mark two vertical lines either side of the nose. Then, with the veiner, remove the wood on either side of the vertical nose lines.

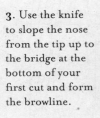

3. Use the knife to slope the nose from the tip up to the bridge at the bottom of your first cut and form the browline.

4. Make a stop cut at the tip of the nose, and notch back to remove the wood under the cheekbones, forming the top of the mustache.

5. Sketch the lower edge of the mustache, and stop cut it about ¼ inch (6 mm) deep. Round over the mustache, sloping it back into the upper edge of the mustache.

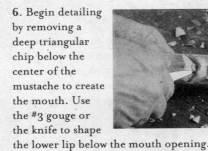

6. Begin detailing by removing a deep triangular chip below the center of the mustache to create the mouth. Use the #3 gouge or the knife to shape the lower lip below the mouth opening.

7. Round over the nose with the knife, and form the nose wings. Don't undercut the nostrils. Form the nostrils and flair them slightly. Pare down the cheek areas and smooth the lower cheekline. Round the forehead above the eyebrows back to the facial outline. Use the veiner to create the crease between the eyebrows above the nose.

8. Use the #11 gouge to round the eye sockets. Start at the centerline of each eye, and form the corners about ⅛ inch (3 mm) deeper. Sketch in your eyes. Be sure they're level and of equal size. Stop cut the upper and lower eyelids. Use the tip of the knife to remove a triangular chip in the corners. If you want him to look to the side, take a larger chip out of one side, and the eye will look to the other side. Round over the pupil, and add a circle using a nail set to form the pupil.

9. Use the V-tool to form the hair part. Just try to create the overall waves and flow lines of the hair out from the part and over and down the top of the staff. These first cuts should be fairly deep, about ¼ inch (6 mm). Now sketch in the mustache and beard flow lines. With the basic shape of the hair created, use the knife, V-tool, or woodburning tool to create the individual hair lines. Remember, hair is not straight, so keep your tool moving in graceful curves. Drill a ¼-inch (6 mm) hole through the hair area for a carrying loop. Finish the staff as desired. Add a rubber or metal tip to the bottom of the staff.

—From *Woodcarving*

Bibliography

For more information on any of the subjects in Crafting Wisdom & Know-How—and even more great projects—check out any of the books excerpted for each chapter. All books are published by Lark Crafts, a division of Sterling Publishing Co., Inc., unless otherwise noted.

Beadwork

Aimone, Katherine Duncan. *Beading With Charms: Beautiful Jewelry, Simple Techniques.* 2007.

Aimone, Katherine Duncan, and Jean Campbell. *Beading With Crystals: Beautiful Jewelry, Simple Techniques.* 2007.

Campbell, Jean (ed.). *Beading With Pearls: Beautiful Jewelry, Simple Techniques.* 2008.

Cusick, Dawn, and Megan Kirby (eds). *The Michaels Book of Arts & Crafts.* 2003.

Deis, Cynthia. *Beading With Filligree: Beautiful Jewelry, Simple Techniques.* 2008.

MacCarthy, Valérie. *Beading With Gemstones: Beautiful Jewelry, Simple Techniques.* 2007.

Mornu, Nathalie, and Suzanne J. E. Tourtillott. *Contemporary Bead & Wire Jewelry.* 2010.

Stevens-Heebner, Marty, and Christine Calla. *Beading Vintage-Style Jewelry: Easy Projects with Elegant Heirloom Appeal.* New York and Ogden, UT: Lark/Chapelle, 2007.

Taylor, Terry. *A Very Beaded Christmas: 46 Projects That Glitter, Twinkle & Shine.* 2009.

Wells, Carol Wilcox. *The Art & Elegance of Beadweaving: New Jewelry Designs with Classic Stitches.* 2002.

Candle Making and Decorating

Coney, Norma. *The Complete Candlemaker: Techniques, Projects, Inspirations.* 1997.

Cusick, Dawn, and Megan Kirby (eds). *The Michaels Book of Arts & Crafts.* 2003.

Ittner, Rebecca. *Candlemaking the Natural Way: 31 Projects Made With Soy, Palm & Beeswax.* 2010.

Miller, Marchianne. *Fantastic Gel Candles: 35 Fun & Creative Projects.* 2002.

Clay Craft

Cusick, Dawn, and Megan Kirby (eds). *The Michaels Book of Arts & Crafts.* 2003.

Dean, Irene Semanchuk. *Kids' Crafts—Polymer Clay: 30 Terrific Projects to Roll, Mold & Squish.* 2003.

————. *Polymer Clay: 20 Weekend Projects Using New & Exciting Techniques.* 2000.

Diffendaffer, Grant. *Polymer Clay Beads: Techniques, Projects, Inspiration.* 2007.

Lowe, Bethany. *Bethany Lowe's Folk Art Halloween.* 2008.

Steiman, Nicole. *Make It in Minutes: Quick & Clever Gift Wraps.* 2007.

Floral Crafts

Cusick, Dawn, and Megan Kirby (eds). *The Michaels Book of Arts & Crafts.* 2003.

Hagerty, Taylor. *Make It in Minutes: Wreaths.* 2008.

Thompson, Melody. *Make It in Minutes: Faux Flower Arrangements.* 2007.

Glass Crafts

Cusick, Dawn, and Megan Kirby (eds). *The Michaels Book of Arts & Crafts.* 2003.

Millions, Suzie. *The Complete Book of Retro Crafts: Collecting, Displaying & Making Crafts of the Past.* 2008.

Stevenson, Christine Kellmann. *Creative Stained Glass: Modern Designs & Simple Techniques.* 2007.

Wasinger, Susan. *Eco Craft: Recycle, Recraft, Restyle.* 2009.

Knitting and Crochet

Carron, Cathy. *Hip Knit Hats: 40 Fabulous Designs.* 2005.

————. *Knitting Sweaters From the Top Down: Fabulous Seamless Patterns to Suit Your Style.* 2007.

Davis, Jane. *Crochet: Fantastic Jewelry, Hats, Purses, Pillows & More (Lark Kids' Crafts).* 2005.

————. *Knitting with Beads: 30 Beautiful Sweaters, Scarves, Hats & Gloves.* 2003.

Emborsky, Drew. *The Crochet Dude's Designs for Guys: 30 Projects Men Will Love.* 2008.

Kopp, Linda. *Cool Crocheted Hats: 40 Contemporary Designs.* 2006.

Mornu, Nathalie. *Knit & Wrap: 25 Caplets, Cowls & Collars.* 2010.

Schapper, Linda P. *300 Classic Blocks for Crochet Projects.* Revised edition. 2008.

————. *The Complete Book of Crochet Border Designs: Hundreds of Classic & Original Patterns.* Revised edition. 2007.

————. *The Complete Book of Crochet Stitch Designs: 500 Classic & Original Patterns.* Revised edition. 2007.

Schreier, Iris. *Lacy Little Knits: Cling, Soft & a Little Risqué.* 2007.

Schreier, Iris, and Laurie J. Kimmelstiel. *Exquisite Little Knits: Knitting with Luxurious Specialty Yarns.* 2004.

Taylor, Terry. *The New Crochet: 40 Wonderful Wearables.* 2007.

Tourtillott, Suzanne J. E. *Expectant Little Knits: Chic Designs for Moms to Be.* 2007.

Mosaics

Germond, Suzan. *Found Art Mosaics.* 2007.

Hepburn, Alison. *Beginner's Guide to Mosaics.* 2005.

Jacobsen, Reham Aarti. *Mosaics for the First Time.* 2005.

Sheerin, Connie. *Backyard Mosaics.* 2002.

————. *Mosaics in an Afternoon.* 2000.

Paper Crafts

Arquette, Kerry, and Andrea Zocchi. *Scrapbooking for the Time Impaired: Advice and Inspiration for the Too-Busy Scrapper.* 2007.

Bartkowski, Alli. *Paper Quilling for the First Time.* 2006.

Cusick, Dawn, and Megan Kirby (eds). *The Michaels Book of Arts & Crafts.* 2003.

Evertson, Sandra. *Fanciful Paper Flowers: Creative Techniques for Crafting an Enchanted Garden.* 2007.

Flowers, Diane. *Handmade Paper from Naturals.* 2009.

Lowe, Bethany. *Bethany Lowe's Folk Art Halloween.* 2008.

Mornu, Nathalie. *Cutting-Edge Decoupage: 30 Easy Projects for Super-Cool Results.* 2007.

Phillips, Roxi. *Make It in Minutes: Mini-Books.* 2007.

Continued ➡

Steiman, Nicole. *Make It in Minutes: Quick & Clever Gift Wraps*. 2007.

Taylor, Terry. *A Very Beaded Christmas: 46 Projects That Glitter, Twinkle & Shine*. 2009.

Wasinger, Susan. *Eco Craft: Recycle, Recraft, Restyle*. 2009.

Sewing and Stitching

Bieber, Katheryn Tidwell. *Felt It! Stitch It! Fabulous!: Over 30 New Uses for Old Sweaters*. 2009.

Kooler, Donna, with Linda Gillum. *Donna Kooler's Felt Embroidery*. 2009.

Kopp, Linda. *Quilts, Baby!: 20 Cuddly Designs to Piece, Patch & Embroider*. 2009.

Lowe, Bethany. *Bethany Lowe's Folk Art Halloween*. 2008.

Millions, Suzie. *The Complete Book of Retro Crafts: Collecting, Displaying & Making Crafts of the Past*. 2008.

Mornu, Nathalie. *Quilt It With Wool: Projects Stitched on Tartans, Tweeds & Other Toasty Fabrics*. 2010.

Pretty Little Patchwork. 2008.

Pretty Little Potholders. 2008.

Ray, Aimee. *Doodle-Stitching: Fresh & Fun Embroidery for Beginners*. 2007.

Schrader, Valerie Van Arsdale. *Fun & Fabulous Curtains to Sew: 15 Easy Designs for the Complete Beginner*. 2006.

———. *Hip Handbags: Creating & Embellishing 40 Great-Looking Bags*. 2005.

———. *Sew Cool, Sew Simple: Stylish Skirts*. 2006.

Sturges, Norma M., and Elizabeth J. Sturges. *The Braided Rug Book: Creating Your Own American Folk Art*. 2006.

Taylor, Terry, and Candie Cooper. *Designer Needle Felting: Contemporary Styles, Easy Techniques*. 2007.

Wasinger, Susan. *Eco Craft: Recycle, Recraft, Restyle*. 2009.

Woodworking and Furniture Making

Hillyer, John. *Woodcarving: 20 Great Projects for Beginners & Weekend Carvers*. 2002.

MacEwen, Marilyn. *Woodworking 101 for Women: How to Speak the Language, Buy the Tools & Build Fabulous Furniture from Start to Finish*. 2006.

Mack, Daniel. *Rustic Furniture Workshop*. 2000.

McGuire, Kevin. *The All-New Woodworking for Kids*. 2008.

Nelson, John A. and Joyce C. *The Big Book of Weekend Woodworking: 150 Easy Projects*. 2005.

Rae, Andy. *Choosing & Using Hand Tools*. 2002.

Illustrators & Photographers

Beadwork

Bead and Wire Basics, Key to Wire Gauges, and Contemporary Bead-Jewelry Projects, Beaded Christmas Décor, Lark's Head Knot: Orrin Lundgren, illustrator; Stewart O'Shields, photographer

Beading Vintage-Style Jewelry: Orrin Lundgren, illustrator; Keith Wright, photographer

Beading With Charms, Beading With Crystals, Crimping, Beading With Gemstones, Identifying Gemstones [opt.], Beading With Pearls: Bonnie Brooks, J'aime Allene, illustrators; Stewart O'Shields, photographer

Beading With Filigree: J'aime Allene, illustrator; Stewart O'Shields, photographer

Beadweaving: Carol Wilcox Wells, illustrations; Evan Bracken, photographer

Home Beading: Steve Mann, Evan Bracken, photographers

Candle Making and Decorating

Basic Candlemaking, Beeswax Candles, Palm Wax Candles, Soy Wax Candles, Upcycled Natural Candles: Mark Tanner, photographer

Paraffin Candlemaking: Richard Babb, photographer

Gel Candlemaking: Even Bracken, photographer

Decorating Candles: Steve Mann, Evan Bracken, photographers

Clay Craft

Working With Polymer Clay, Polymer Clay Projects, Bread Dough: Steve Mann, Evan Bracken, photographers

Getting to Know Your Polymer Clay, More Polymer Clay Projects: Evan Bracken, photographer

Kids' Polymer Clay Projects: Orrin Lundgren, illustrator; Sandra Stambaugh, photographer

Halloween Party Picks, Play Clay Box: Zachary Williams, photographer

Textured Polymer Clay Beads: Orrin Lundgren, illustrator; Stewart O'Shields, photographer

Floral Crafts

Faux Flower Arrangements, Floral Home Accessories, Making Wreaths With Faux Flowers, Fruits & Greens: Zachary Williams, photographer

Silk Flowers, Dried Flowers, Sachets & Potpourris: Steve Mann, Evan Bracken, photographers

Glass Crafts

Painting Glass, Etching Glass: Steve Mann, Evan Bracken, photographers

Painted Recycled Glass Projects: Susan Wasinger, photographer

Retro Glass Crafts: Jennifer Jessee, Lance Wille, Susie Millions, illustrators; Steve Mann, photographer

Stained Glass: Orrin Lundgren, illustrator; Keith Wright, photographer

Knitting and Crochet

Basic Knitting Techniques; Knitted Caplets, Cowls, and Collars: [source book: Knit & Wrap, Nathalie Mornu]

More Basic Knitting Techniques, Knitting Materials and Tools, Knitted Clothes for Moms-to-Be: Stewart O'Shields, photographer

Knitted Lace: Patterns and Projects; Cool Crocheted Hats: Orrin Lundgren, illustrator; John Widman, photographer

Knitting With Specialty Yarns: Dana Irwin, Suzanne J. E. Tourtillott, photographers

Knitting With Beads: Wright Creative Photography & Design, Susan Stambaugh, photographers

Hip Knit Hats: Susan Stambaugh, Sean Moser, www.keithwright.com, photographers

Knitting Socks: Orrin Lundgren, illustrator; Lynne Harty, photographer

Sweater Rug: Susan Wasinger

Crochet: Getting Started; Crocheted Womenswear; Not Your Granny's Halter Top; Jammin' Jeans: Orrin Lundgren, illustrator; Stewart O'Shields, photographer

Basic Crochet Stitches: Orrin Lundgren, illustrator; Steve Mann, photographer

Crocheted Menswear, Convertible Cover: Orrin Lundgren, Karen Manthey, illustrators; Stewart O'Shields, photographer

Crochet Projects for Kids; Shirt Edging: August Hoerr, illustrator; Susan Stambaugh, photographer

Joining Crochet Blocks; Joining Crocheted Borders to Fabric: Orrin Lundgren, Karen Manthey, illustrators; Steve Mann, photographer

Mosaics

Mosaic Basics: Dianne Miller, PrePress Xpress, graphics; Greg Wright, photographer

Mosaics with Pressed Flowers Under Glass, Mosaic Projects for Your Garden: Dianne Miller, Kate Turpin, graphics; Pat Molnar, photographer

Mosaic Technique: Indirect Method, Found Art Mosaic Projects: Dianne Miller, Kate Turpin, graphics; Thomas McConnell Photographer, photographer

Special Mosaic Techniques: Kim Taylor, illustrator; Kevin Dilley for Hazen Photography, photographer

Paper Crafts

Handmade Paper, Making Handmade Books: Karen Turpin, graphics; Jerry Mucklow, Joel Tressler, photographers

Quick & Clever Gift Wraps, Mini-Book Making, Paper Wreaths, Paper Party Wares: Zachary Williams, Williams Visual, photographer

Recycled Gift Wrap, Recycled Paper Crafts: Susan Wasinger, photographer

Card Making, Decoupage, Stamping, Scrapbooking: An Introduction: Steve Mann, Evan Bracken, photographers

Creative Christmas Cards: Orrin Lundgren, illustrator; Stewart O'Shields, photographer

Paper Quilling: Alli Bartkowski, Don Cole, Zac Williams (Chapelle, Ltd.), photographers

More Decoupage Projects: Travis Medford, illustrator; Steve Mann, photographer

Paper Flowers: Thomas McConnell, photographer

Sewing and Stitchwork

Braided Rugs: Caroline Cleveland, Orrin Lundgren, illustrators; Michael Drejza, photographer

Quilting Basics, Baby Quilt Projects: Susan McBride, Orrin Lundgren, illustrators; Keith Wright, photographer

Quilting With Wool: Olivier Rollin, illustrator; Sandra Stambaugh, photographer

Patchwork Projects: Susan McBride, illustrator; Stewart O'Shields, photographer

Potholders: Susan McBride, Orrin Lundgren, illustrators; Stewart O'Shields, photographer

Woodland Friends Wash Mitts: Jennifer Jessee, Lance Wille, Susie Millions, illustrators; Steve Mann, photographer

Continued →

Things to Know Before You Sew: Sewing Machines & Supplies; More Things to Know Before You Sew: Stitching Seams; Sewing Curtains; Stylish Skirts: Susan McBride, illustrator; Stewart O'Shields, photographer

Make Your Own Handbags: Bernadette Wolf, illustrator; Keith Wright, photographer

Felting: Bernadette Wolf, illustrator; Stewart O'Shields, photographer

Needle Felting: Orrin Lundgren, illustrator; Stewart O'Shields, photographer

Embroidery for Beginners: Aimee Ray, illustrator; Keith Wright, photographer

Felt Embroidery: Bernie Wolf, Orrin Lundgren, illustrators; Stewart O'Shields, photographer

Embroidered Halloween Projects: Zachary Williams, photographer

Woodworking and Furniture Making

Woodworking Basics for Beginners and Young Woodworkers, Easy Woodworking Projects for Kids: Steve Mann, photographer

Woodworking Surfaces, Storing Tools, 20 Everyday Aids to Woodworking: Orrin Lundgren, illustrator; Evan Bracken, lead photographer; Andy Rae and Simon Cronley, how-to photography

Tools, Fundamental Woodworking Techniques, Wood, A Selection of Woodworking Projects: Melanie Powell, illustrator; Keith Wright, photographer

Weekend Woodworking Projects, Wooden Toy Projects: Evan Bracken, Steve Mann, Deborah Porter-Hayes, photographers

Building Rustic Furniture: Jennifer Zelman, illustrator; Jonathan Wallen, photographer; Bob Barrett, Ron Cedar, Bobby Hansson, David Horton, Daniel Mack, Rita Nicholas, SRC, and Nick Zungoli, additional photographer

Woodcarving: Orrin Lundgren, illustrator; Sandra Stambaugh, photographer

Index

Continued ➔

Continued →

H

Hacky Sack, 202
Hagerty, Taylor, 94, 263
Hahn, Angela, 134
Half double crochet stitch, 181
Half laps, 387
Hall, Autumn, 309
Halloween, 77; embroidered projects, 362–366
Halstead, Don, 197, 199
Halters, 190, 203
Hammered texture glass, 110
Hammers, 9, 114; using, 370–371
Hand tools, 378–380
Handbags, 328–337; basics, 330–332; embellishments, 332; fabric selection, 328–329; fasteners, 331–332; flaps, 331; interfacing, 329; linings, 329, 330; patterns, 333–337; pockets, 331; projects, 334–337; sewing, 332–333; straps, 330–331
Handle with Flair, 307
Hanger with Care, 302
Hanging in Style, 262
Hangings, 365–366
Happy Birthday, 251, 263
Hardware, 401, 402
Hardwoods, 442, 442; choosing, 391; exotic, 391
Hats, 340; knit, 165–171; men's, 194; party, 266; quilted, 302
Head Banned, 192
Headbands, 361
Healing stones, 29
Hearts & Flowers Gazing Ball, 219
Heels, 172
Hematite, 22
Hems, 316, 325, 355
Hepburn, Allison, 214
Herbs, 98
Herringbone stitch, 40–41, 126, 353, 359
Hettmansperger, Mary, 19
Hidden stitch, 355
Hiking staff carving, 449–450
Hillyer, John, 441
Hinges, butt, 389
Hipster sash belts, 185
Hirata, Vel, 19
Holiday crafts, 85–86
Holiday Surprise, 241
Home accessories, floral, 97–100
Home Sweet home Coasters, 301
Horn, Carole, 41
Houndstooth Lidcap, 199
House, Gina, 174
Huber, Robyn, 218, 220
Hulka, Donna, 204
Husking technique for quilling, 257
Hydrangea wreaths, 96

I

I-cords, 127, 138
Impulse, 129
In/out mail boxes, 403
Inc 1 stitch, 124
Inlays, 389
Iridescent glass, 110
Iris, 89
Ittner, Rebecca, 45, 49, 50, 52, 53

J

Jacobsen, Reham Aarti, 220
Jade, 22
Jammin' Jeans, 204
Japanese saws, 379; using, 384

Jars, masking tape pleather, 105
Jasper, 22
Jeans, 204
Jerseys, men's, 195
Jesse cap, 167
Jewelry box, eight–sided, 405–406
Jewelry, 225; vintage–style, 13–15
Jigs, 9; making, 21
Jigsaw, 376
Jock Block Hat & Scarf, 194–195
Joinery, biscuit, 376, 382–384; rustic, 432
Jointer, 377
Joints, 370; mortise and tenon, 385–386; types, 401
Jump rings, 9, 10, 13

K

Kafka, Karen, 280
Kapoor, Kalpna, 199
Kelley, Robyn, 187
Kellmann Stevenson, Christine, 110
Key chains, 446
Key to My Heart, 250
Kimmelstiel, Laurie J., 143, 145, 146
Kinsler, Gwen Blakley, 203
Kirby, Megan, 69, 72, 83, 91, 92, 98, 101, 108, 109, 259, 266
Kitchen gloves, 309
Kitchen Stitchin', 307
Knit hats, 165–171; pattern abbreviations, 166; patterns, 167; yarn and gauge, 167
Knit socks, 171–178
Knit stitch, 123
Knitted cast on, 138
Knitting in–the–round, 165–167
Knitting needles, 127; conversion chart, 128
Knitting, 10, 123–180; abbreviations, 127, 131, 132, 174; basic techniques, 123–127; materials, 127–128, ; tools, 127–128
Knitwear, stitching beads to, 148; washing, 148, 174
Knives, 441
Knobs, molded, 72
Knots, 35
Knotting, 25
Kooler, Donna, 357
Kopp, Linda, 128, 171, 197, 286, 291
Kotz, Melissa, 50
Kraft paper, 112
Kreuger, Debbie, 73
Kringle cap, 170
Kyanite, 22

L

Label art, 273
Labradorite, 22
Lace, 125, 151
Lace, knitted, 135–143; abbreviations, 136; basics, 135; measuring, 137; reading, 137; stitch patterns, 135–138; techniques used 138; terms, 136; tools, 137
Lacey Rainbow scarf, 188
Lacquer, 393
Ladders, rustic, 436
Laher, Mami, 12
Lamp shades, 225–226
Lapis lazuli, 23
Laptop case, 295
Larsen, Linda, 17
Lasso, 32
Lattice, 367
Lavell, Brenda, 130
Lavender wreaths, 97
Layered Pillar, 50
Lazy daisy stitch, 354, 359

Le Von, Martha, 260
Leading for glass, 101, 110, 117, 122
Leafing, metal, 238; pens, 238
Lee, Katherine, 187, 188
Letter stamps, 274
Library Mosaic Bookends, 213
Life Savers, 291
Light box, 114
Light switch plates, 73, 75
Light, Diana, 32, 103, 104
Lights, 222
Lined Slippers, 341
Links, 9–10; jig–formed, 10
Lisbon, 26
Locker mirror, 77
Log cabin, 416
Long and short stitch, 354, 359
Long stitch, 135
Longtail (Double) Cast–on, 123
Loop links, twisted, 29
Loops, 9–10
Loops, earring, 30
Loose cast off method, 138
Lots of Little Squares, 67
Lowe, Bethany, 77, 265, 362
Lucas, Bill, 280
Lucky necklace, 12–13
Lumber, 367; milling, 381–382; shopping for, 391
Lunn, Linda, 131
Lupo, Sandra, 20
Luxurious Hooded Cowl, 198
Luxury fibers, caring for, 138

M

MacCarthy, Valerie, 28
Macchia, Lisa, 295
Machinery, woodworking, 376–378; buying used, 377; maintaining, 377; wheeled, 376
Mack, Daniel, 430
Magazine Shapes, 276
Magnet, kite, 74
Magnetic Decoupage, 260
Malachite, 23
Man's Best Friends, 250
Mandrels, 9, 79
Marbles and Swirls Jewelry Pouch, 349
Marbles, 208
Marie Antoinette bag, 334
Marks, Ruthie, 190
Masking for glass crafts, 102
Masking Tape Pleather Jar, 105
Masks, 265
Maternity knit clothes, 131–135
Matthews, Dot, 198
Mattress stitch, 125
May, Donna, 189
McBride, Susan, 310
McCall, Mary, 177
McEwen, Marilyn, 375, 390, 424
McGuire, Kevin, 367, 393
McNutt, Marilyn, 17
Measuring, marking, and layout tools, 379
Media tower, 398–399
Meinhardt, Nan C., 43
Memories, collecting, 269
Mermaid's Tail Evening Bag, 146
Mesh use to make a mosaic, 222
Messenger bag, 334
Microwave drying chart for handmade paper, 233
Mile Long Scarf, 187
Miller, Marchianne, 63
Miller, Marty, 185, 189, 198
Milling lumber, 381–382

Continued →